THE OLIVER WENDELL HOLMES DEVISE
HISTORY OF THE SUPREME COURT
OF THE UNITED STATES

General Editor: PAUL A. FREUND

THE

Oliver Wendell Holmes

DEVISE

HISTORY OF
THE SUPREME COURT
OF THE UNITED STATES

VOLUME V

THE OLIVER WENDELL HOLMES DEVISE

History of the
SUPREME COURT
of the United States

VOLUME V

The
Taney Period
1836-64

By Carl B. Swisher

NEW YORK
Macmillan Publishing Co., Inc.

Collier-Macmillan Publishers
LONDON

Macmillan Publishing Co., Inc.

866 Third Avenue, New York, N.Y. 10022

Collier-Macmillan Canada Ltd.

Library of Congress Cataloging in Publication Data

Swisher, Carl Brent, 1897–1968.
  The Taney period, 1836–64.

(History of the Supreme Court of the United States, v. 5)
  1. United States. Supreme Court—History.
I. Title.
KF8742.A45H55 vol. 5   347'.73'26   72–93318
ISBN 0–02–541380–5

FIRST PRINTING 1974

PRINTED IN THE UNITED STATES OF AMERICA

Contents

Illustrations

ix

Illustrations

Foreword

FOR THOSE who have participated in administering the Oliver Wendell Holmes Devise as well as for legal scholars everywhere, the publication of another volume in the Holmes Devise *History of the Supreme Court of the United States* series is an important milestone. The current work—*The Taney Period, 1836–64* by the late Carl B. Swisher—is Volume V in the series and is the third to be published out of the twelve proposed.

Congress in 1955 enacted legislation to establish the Oliver Wendell Holmes Devise Fund and the Permanent Committee for the Oliver Wendell Holmes Devise (Public Law 84–246). In effect, this act determined that preparation and publication of a definitive history of the Supreme Court would be the most appropriate use to make of the funds bequeathed to the United States by the late Justice Holmes.

The first two volumes in the series were published in 1971—Volume I, *Antecedents and Beginnings to 1801*, by the late Julius Goebel, Jr., and Volume VI, *Reconstruction and Reunion, 1864–1888, Part One*, by Charles Fairman. Now the third, Mr. Swisher's analysis of the court during the years between the death of Chief Justice Marshall and the end of the Civil War, adds another tier to the monument erected to Justice Holmes.

The author of the present volume, Carl B. Swisher, was Thomas P. Stran Professor of Political Science at Johns Hopkins University, a former president of the American Political Science Association, and the author of a number of works on American constitutional history. Mr. Swisher, who retired from Johns Hopkins in 1967, had completed the manuscript for this volume before his death in 1968. Paul A. Freund, editor-in-chief of the Holmes Devise *History* series, has been responsible both for the final editing and for shepherding the work through the press.

Achievement of the aims of Public Law 84–246 has been shared by Mr. Freund, by the other legal scholars and historians selected to write the different segments of the *History of the Supreme Court of the United States*—of whom Mr. Swisher was one—and by the members of the Permanent Committee for the Oliver Wendell Holmes Devise. In accordance with the provisions of the act, thirteen public members (listed below) have been appointed by the President of the United States and have served for varying lengths of time since the Committee's inception. As Chairman *ex officio* I want to express my gratitude to the editor-in-chief, to the authors, and to the Committee members for their dedication and support.

L. Quincy Mumford
LIBRARIAN OF CONGRESS

PERMANENT COMMITTEE FOR
THE OLIVER WENDELL HOLMES DEVISE

(TERMS OF EIGHT YEARS EXCEPT FOR INITIAL APPOINTMENTS)

Charles T. McCormick	1956–58	(two-year term)
Edward S. Corwin	1956–60	(four-year term)
George L. Haskins	1956–58	(six-year term, but resigned 10/7/58)
Virgil M. Hancher	1956–64	
Frederick D. G. Ribble	1958–66	
Ethan A. H. Shepley	1959–67	
Nicholas Kelley	7/8/60–7/22/60	
Jefferson B. Fordham	1961–69	
Harry H. Ransom	1964–72	
Herbert Wechsler	1966–74	
Robert G. McCloskey	1967–69	
J. A. C. Grant	1970–78	
Alfred H. Kelly	1970–78	

Editor's Foreword

WHEN JOHN MARSHALL neared the end of his Chief Justiceship, he was deeply apprehensive of the future, fearful that the principles which he and his colleagues had moulded from the Constitution would be abandoned and betrayed. When, in turn, Roger Brooke Taney approached the close of his thirty-year term as Chief Justice, he despaired of the survival of the constitutional government which he had labored to preserve as he understood it. Taney's fears were by no means unfounded. In December 1860, an eminent fellow-Marylander, arguing before Taney's court in Washington could declare without excessive rhetoric that "This may be the last time that the Court will sit in a peaceful judgment on a Constitution acknowledged and obeyed by all."

Marshall's apprehensions, on the other hand, were surely exaggerated. It could not be expected that even the Great Chief Justice could contain the tensions and complexities of a growing and diverse country within simple and absolute doctrinal formulas. To continue the broad reading of the obligation of contract guarantee would have fettered the regulatory powers of government and the encouragement of economic competition; to apply literally the dictum that the power of Congress over commerce among the states is exclusive would have needlessly and single-mindedly sacrificed the interests of local welfare to the pressures toward a common market. What was needed was the practical and philosophical wisdom of a Lord Acton: "When you perceive a truth, look for the balancing truth."

This outlook, in the staple business of the Court, characterized the decisions, if not always the opinions, of the Taney period. Viewed against the background of the Marshall court their thrust was not upheaval but complementarity. Property was not subordinated; rather, it was seen that two kinds of property interests were generally in conflict: those already secured and those reflecting new and competing enterprise.

The contest was not so much over the vindication of property rights as over the conflict between the security of acquisitions and the security of transactions. The Taney Court's more tolerant view of public fostering of new competitive enterprise helped to make possible the advances in modes of transportation and the growth of an aggressive capitalism. Similarly in the field of federal versus state power over commerce, it was seen that many forms of local regulation, in the interest of health or safety or financial integrity, were not incompatible with the needs of a common market. Difficulties of a conceptual sort plagued the Court and fragmented it: must local regulation be justified not as a regulation of "commerce," but as an exercise of the "police power," or could the effect on commerce be frankly acknowledged and the measures justified under a concurrent power of the states to regulate, to some extent, commerce itself?

Beyond these conceptual difficulties lurked the unexorcised, intractable spectre of slavery in the Federal Union. Questions under the commerce power were potentially questions affecting slavery, fugitive slaves, and the covert foreign slave trade. Issues of state and federal power are vexing at best; when they are determined with an eye deflected to this overarching darkness, in terms of a judge's estimate of their implications and the intensity of his emotional involvement, it is no wonder that problems of federalism were not treated with the magisterial touch of a Marshall. Slavery brought its moral and intellectual ironies as well: courts and juries in the South resisting the enforcement of the laws against the slave trade, and in the North resisting the enforcement of the Fugitive Slave Law. For Supreme Court Justices sitting on circuit these challenges created painful confrontations with the populace.

The system of circuit duties is in fact a principal key to an understanding of the Court in the Taney period, and it is treated in rich detail in this volume. In the first place, the circuit-riding system severely conditioned the appointments to the Supreme Court. Since each Justice was required to sit with district judges in an assigned circuit to constitute the two-member circuit court, it was the practice to fill a Supreme Court vacancy from the bar or bench of the circuit served by the former Justice. A limited number of Senators thus had an interest in the appointment. In a period when party loyalties and animosities ran high, parochialism was added to partisanship in the selection of members of the highest Court. It is the less surprising, consequently, that political proclivities characterized many of the Justices after ascending the bench. Moreover, since the greater part of the year was spent on circuit duties, and since communication was slow, relations among the Justices, as well as between them and the Clerk and the Reporter, were often clouded by misunderstandings. The situation was not helped by the loose practice of revising an opinion after it had been announced but before publication.

Furthermore, circuit-riding contributed greatly to the beginning of a persistent problem for the Court, that of an excessive case load. Suggestions began to be advanced for an independent tier of courts of appeal, and a germinal beginning was made when an independent federal circuit judgeship was created for California in order to handle the immense litigation over land titles arising as a result of the gold rush. Such are the unpredictable ways of history.

The often intricate story of the Court at Washington and on individual circuit duty has been woven by Professor Swisher into a rich and comprehensible pattern. This he has done by drawing skilfully on records in the lower courts, on official and private correspondence and diaries, on contemporary newspaper accounts and journalistic commentary, as well as on legislative and executive documents.

The present volume is, sadly, a posthumous work. Fortunately the manuscript had been completed by Professor Swisher before his death. The volume will stand as his ultimate monument, the testament of a deep-ploughing scholar who was graced with an endearing humility.

Paul A. Freund

The Taney Period
1836-64

CHAPTER I

The Background of the Taney Court

I N THE HISTORY OF COURTS as of other institutions, transitions tend to come gradually. Accepted points of demarcation are apt to have been somewhat arbitrarily chosen. Although division of the history of the Supreme Court of the United States according to the terms of the Chief Justices provides a convenient mode of treatment, the separation of each period from its predecessor may be much less definite than it at first appears. As for the beginning of the Taney period, not even the date can be precisely stated. It is possible to choose the day in March, 1836, when the Senate confirmed President Andrew Jackson's nomination of Roger B. Taney for the office of Chief Justice; or the day later in the same month when in Baltimore Taney took the oath of office; or the day in the ensuing April when he began in Baltimore the circuit duties which at that time were required of all members of the Supreme Court; or the day in August when he went to Washington to perform prescribed duties at a vestigial August term of the Supreme Court; or, finally, the day in January, 1837, when he first presided over the Court which he was to head through a series of eventful years until his death in August, 1864.

Whatever the date selected to mark the beginning, telling the story of the Taney Court requires not merely an account of events beyond that point but some reference also to background items. Important was the body of tradition built up by the Court from the time of its establishment by George Washington and the first Congress. Important was the body of decisions, particularly of the third of a century ending with the death of Chief Justice Marshall in 1835, by which the work of the Taney Court was inevitably conditioned. Looming as a conditioning factor of a different kind was the Administration of Andrew Jackson, begun in 1829 and carrying through until shortly after the adjournment of the first term of the Taney Court, which brought vast changes in institutions and institutional behavior in which the Supreme Court was involved. Important also for a picture of the Taney Court in operation is some portrayal of Washington as the national capital during that period, and of the physical and atmospheric setting in which the Court performed its manifold tasks.

Concerning the background history of the Supreme Court, it is to be remembered that during its first decade, a decade partly of unsure beginnings, the Court had established itself firmly as a court of law and had refused to create a confused image of itself or to dilute its judicial performance by giving official advice either to the President or to Congress. The Taney Court, like the Court in succeeding periods, was to be the beneficiary of this initial strategy. Early in the Marshall period, furthermore, the Court had established in the face of political hostility the practice of inquiring into the constitutionality of Acts of Congress which it was called upon to enforce. Although not until 1857 did the Court for the second time exercise the power of striking down an Act of Congress found to be unconstitutional, it kept alive through the intervening years the practice of inquiry. At the beginning of the Taney period the practice was so thoroughly entrenched as to be relatively free from serious challenge. Thus the Court, which had limited its sphere to strictly judicial operations, had also established its authority as final interpreter of the Constitution in cases brought before it.

In a wide range of decisions, furthermore, the Marshall Court had defended broad exercise of the delegated powers of the federal government, asserted the doctrine of implied powers, and subordinated the states to the authority of the federal Constitution. It gave protection to property, and particularly to property in land, by enforcing against the states the superior authority of federal treaties and of constitutional provisions such as that forbidding impairment of the obligation of contracts. It included in the category of protected contracts those made by states as well as those made merely by private parties. It defined as contracts the grants made in charters of private corporations, affording federal protection which paved the way for development of so-called private enterprise in corporate form. Under the Commerce Clause it limited the power of states to regulate, and by implication confirmed broad regulatory powers in the federal government. In competition with state judiciaries, it asserted and exercised the right of the Supreme Court to review cases appealed from the highest state courts in which interpretations of federal law were involved.

Finally—or perhaps from a backward point of view it might be better to say initially—Chief Justice Marshall, at the beginning of his term, had led the Court to abandon the practice of its first decade whereby seriatim opinions had been handed down in important cases and to resort to an opinion of the Court in each case, written often, though not always, by the Chief Justice himself. The change had given the Court the appearance of the unanimity of an institution, almost of an organism, as against the earlier impression of a mere aggregation of judges making little attempt to achieve unanimity or synthesis.

The pattern of unanimity, it is true, was never completely established, and it crumbled somewhat during the later years of the Marshall period, with the Chief Justice himself on one important occasion writing a dissenting opinion on a constitutional question. Among his colleagues, dissenting and concurring opinions appeared with increasing frequency. Yet the ideal of unanimity, of institutional rather than individual spokesmanship, had become well entrenched in spite of some diversity of actual behavior. In this respect as in many others, the Taney period, for all its uniqueness, would evidence, to a high degree, continuation of the traditions and practices of the Marshall regime.

Yet it is also true that, for all its continuity with the past, the Taney period was to confront new problems and bring new approaches to their solution. For their comprehension it is necessary to look not merely at the Court and its personnel but also at the rapidly changing country as a whole. In a sense the American Revolution, proclaimed in 1776 and validated by war and by the Treaty of 1783, was still under way. The Revolution had broken the grip of monarchy, but it had by no means obliterated aristocratic tendencies in the former British colonies. There was still a broad assumption that the country was to be governed by the "best people," with quality measured partly by heritage and partly by the ability to acquire and hold property. The early Federalists had no illusion that the voice of the masses was the voice of Deity. Even the Jeffersonians, for all their paternalism and dislike of tyranny, had no illusion that one man was as good as another—in fact, as distinguished from theory.

Yet the leveling movement which had begun with the Revolution continued decade by decade, through the country and particularly on the frontier. The stream of population moved across the mountains into the West where a man's worth was measured far more by his current achievements than by his heritage, and where opportunity to earn a reputation and to acquire property was so widespread and diverse that class differentiation virtually disappeared. New states were formed without property qualifications for voting—which had its impact on federal elections, since under the Constitution the qualifications for voting for members of Congress in each state were those adopted for choosing the most numerous branch of the state legislature. Voting sentiments

3

became more and more those of the undifferentiated masses, and the selection of candidates as well as campaign methods was adjusted accordingly.

With the admission of Missouri into the Union in 1821, the total number of states became twenty-four. The member states reached from Maine to Georgia and from Georgia westward to include Louisiana. Other than Louisiana, the only state west of the Mississippi was Missouri, although by the middle 1830s Arkansas was making a bid for statehood. The northwestern tier of states consisted of Ohio, Indiana, and Illinois, while still further northward Michigan was also seeking admission. In spite, however, of the expansion westward to the Mississippi and beyond, the weight of federal power and of benefits remained with the East. It is significant that at the death of Chief Justice Marshall only one of the seven Supreme Court Justices had a Western circuit. Justice McLean was assigned to the circuit which included Ohio, Kentucky, and Tennessee. Six Western and Southern states lay outside the seven circuits and had only such circuit services as could be provided by the district judges, of whom there was one in each of these six states.

More important than Circuit Court services from the point of view of national evolution was the fact that until 1829 all Presidents of the United States had come from east of the Appalachians. Virginia had provided three of them, with two terms each, and Massachusetts had provided two, each of whom had a single term. It is true that Andrew Jackson of Tennessee, the military hero of the Battle of New Orleans, had been a close contender in the election of 1824, as had Henry Clay of Kentucky, but when the decision was passed to the House of Representatives the choice fell upon John Quincy Adams of Massachusetts, the son of an earlier President from the same state, and a member of the hierarchy of advancement to the presidency in that he had served as Secretary of State. But in 1828 Jackson won over Adams at the polls, and for the first time, in 1829, a Western man became President.

Both symbolically and in reality, the election of Jackson marked a kind of revolution in the United States. The center of power had shifted, both regionally and in terms also of the kinds of people who would determine dominant sentiments within the government. Awareness of the depth of the change was revealed in the lamentations of the ousted elements, which resembled those of the Federalists at the election of Jefferson in 1801 and somewhat also those of the South at the election of Lincoln in 1860. From now on the West was to play its rightful part in the government of the Union, and the Jackson regime was to be the regime of the common man. The change in emphasis with the coming of Jacksonian democracy is not to be obscured by the fact that the great body of experienced political talent was still to be found in the East, was to be employed in the federal government, and was to become part of a new political aristocracy which sheltered under the leadership of Old Hickory and under the label of democracy.

No more than any other period in history does the Jackson period have a simple explanation. It was filled with crosscurrents and inconsistencies, and it is hard at any moment in the period to tell what manifestations are dominant and what merely represent spasmodic upsurges. Diversity and conflict can be illustrated, indeed, from the performance of Jackson himself. He regarded himself as the people's President and talked much about the soundness of popular judgment and the political wisdom of relying on it. He took a stand against favoritism in government based on wealth or class, accepted the theory of his supporting politicians that one man was as good as another and as valuable as another in government employment, and at least allowed the development of what came to be called "the spoils system." With the Westerner's distrust of strong government in Washington dominated by Easterners, he took a states' rights position with respect to federal financing of internal improvements—a position taken also by a South fearful of the federal government save as federal financing might aid projects particularly helpful to the South. For multiple reasons he challenged and defeated the banking interests that had brought a linkage between the federal government and a concentration of banking control in the Bank of the United States.

Yet Jackson is to be classified with the strong Presidents of the United States rather than with the weak. He met the threat of nullification in South Carolina with such despatch and firmness as to win the approval of even such usually harsh critics as Daniel Webster. In preventing the recharter of the Bank of the United States he defeated the most powerful concentration of interests in the country, and won approval and brought about his own reelection amid the struggle. His swift political moves kept his political enemies in Congress and elsewhere in confusion and, with notable exceptions in his own state, he ended his two terms with such political strength as to be able to name his successor. He exercised in the Presidency the vigor and firmness and sometimes the ruthlessness of a general on the battlefield. Outstanding among the innumerable characterizations of the man was the following, written at the time of Jackson's death in 1845, by John Catron of Tennessee, who in 1837 became a member of the Supreme Court on Jackson's nomination and who maintained friendship with Jackson over a long period of years:

> One thing may be safely said of Genl. Jackson—That he has written his name higher on the temple of fame than any man since Washington, of those belonging to History in this country: And what is more remarkable in him than any American is, that he maintained his power

5

from Seventy, to *Eighty*, when he had nothing to give. This he did by the force of will and courage, backing his thorough out-and-out honesty of purpose. In this lay his strength always. His intuitive faculties were quick and strong—his *instincts* capitally good. The way in which a thing should be done struck him plainly—and he adopted the plan. If it was not the best, it would still answer the purpose, if well executed: Then to the execution he brought a hardy industry, and a sleepless vigilance few could equal. But this was not the best quality he brought to the task. He cared not a rush for anything behind—he looked ahead. His awful *will*, stood alone, and was made the will of all he commanded; and command it would and did. If he had fallen from the clouds into a city on fire, he would have been at the head of the extinguishing hose in an hour, and would have blown up a palace to stop the fire with as little misgiving as another would have torn down a board shed. In a moment he would have willed it proper—and in ten minutes the thing would have been done. Those who had never worked before, who had hardly courage to cry, would have rushed to the execution, and applied the match. Hence it is that timid men, and feeble women, have rushed to onslaught when he gave the command— fierce, fearless, and unwavering, for the first time. Hence it is that for fifty years he has been followed, first by all the timid who then knew him—and afterwards by the broad land, as a matchless man— as one they were ready to follow wherever he led—who with them, never was wrong—and who could sweep over all opposers abroad or at home, terrible and clear as a prairie fire, leaving hardly a smoke of the ruin behind.[1]

From the point of view of the history of the Supreme Court, and apart from the judicial appointments he made—which will be discussed elsewhere—the important factor is not so much the particular activities and policies Jackson espoused. It is rather the seminal stirring that he brought to a country already in ferment, already at the forefront of tremendous change. A timid President, or even a courageous President who believed in caution, might conceivably have gotten through the 1830s by temporizing and conciliating measures. He could have permitted the construction of such internal improvements as Congress saw fit to finance, letting others worry about undue centralization of power. He could have permitted renewal of the charter of the Bank of the United States, recognizing the theoretical soundness of centralized banking and credit control and ignoring the growing political power of the banking establishment. He might conceivably have been able to persuade Congress to reduce tariffs resented by the South and perhaps have persuaded John C. Calhoun to stay his hand with respect to nullification, without vigorous assertion of Presidential authority. Had he come from

---

[1] John Catron to James Buchanan, June 11, 1845.

one of the Eastern states, he might have slowed somewhat the flow of power toward the West—or rather the dispersal of power which included the West in some considerable degree along with the East and the South.

But in any event, changes were coming, whatever the circumstances and whatever the personalities involved. Readjustments were in the offing in the relations between the federal government and the states, between the states and private economic interests, within the realm of money and banking, and between the North and the South on issues of race relations. These changes would have their effect on the operation of judicial institutions and on the developing pattern of American law. It was conceivable that another John Marshall, alive to the issues of his times, might channel the course of American constitutional development and keep the Supreme Court depersonalized save as it was personalized in his own name, but on the whole the maintenance of the approximate unanimity of the Marshall period seemed highly improbable. Beyond that, for all his own willingness to take command and to wield the lash of authority, it was to be doubted whether President Jackson would, intentionally at least, select for the Chief Justiceship a man likely to exert such sweeping influence.

In the 1830s the Supreme Court met in Washington, D.C., as it does today, but it was a very different Washington from the present city, and the conditions of meeting were vastly different. In the later years of the Marshall period the city was a sprawling collection of villages of some 20,000 persons or more, scattered over an area that resembled a geographical outline map, from which timber had only recently been cleared, with the Capitol and the President's House—(not yet customarily called the White House) standing out as landmarks amid the clutter of usually small and unattractive buildings. Modern pavement was unknown. It was only during this period that Congress provided for the macadamizing of the broad and dismal and always muddy or dusty Pennsylvania Avenue running between the Capitol and the President's House.[2] Other streets were almost without improvements. Sewer facilities were primitive or nonexistent. Open ditches connected with running streams throughout the terrain of the city, and wagons on regular tour collected "night-soil" from the central area. A principal stream was Tiber Creek, renamed "Goose Creek" by provincials who knew or cared nothing about Rome's historic river and preferred names more characteristic of America. During the 1830s it flowed southwestward to pass beneath a culvert under Pennsylvania Avenue near Second Street,

---

[2] Many books have been written on the founding and history of the capital city. Much of the significant material is assembled in W. B. Bryan, *A History of the National Capital*.

where playing boys sailed their handmade boats and sometimes, in spite of problems of sanitation, dared go swimming "in the raw." The stream wound onward toward the Potomac, whose tidewaters backed up far into the city, over a portion of the relocated Tiber, which became a canal for local transportation. During the early years, springs throughout the city provided an abundant water supply. During the 1830s extensive use was made of pumps at street corners, where neighbors met neighbors and drew water without concern as to possible pollution from open sewers or other sources. At night the city lay in utter darkness save for lights from windows or open doors or from lanterns carried by pedestrians or lamps of moving carriages.

Fanny Kemble, the noted English-born actress of the day who was married to Pierce Butler of Pennsylvania, and who played in Washington early in 1833, commented on the strange appearance of the fledgling capital city, remarking that "Washington altogether struck me as a rambling, red-brick image of futurity, where nothing *is*, but all things *are to be*."[3] A Washington newspaper carried an item by another foreign observer to the effect that:

> Everybody knows that Washington has a Capital; but the mistortune is that the Capital wants a city. There it stands, reminding you of a general without an army, only surrounded and followed by a parcel of ragged dirty boys; for such is the appearance of the dirty straggling, ill built houses which lie at the foot of it.[4]

Life in Washington had the unevenness of life in a summer or winter resort. During the summer only the executive branch of the government was in extensive operation there, and the President and department heads and employees got away as much as possible from the sweltering city. But around the first Monday in each December members of Congress came pouring in for their annual session. Along with them came lobbyists, reporters, entertainers, and service people of all kinds. It was not until the second Monday in January that members of the Supreme Court assembled for their annual sessions in the crowded city. As of the middle 1830s, it was seldom that either judges or legislators brought their families with them. The stability of social life depended therefore on the members of the executive branch and the relatively few permanent residents who had high social status. For a few weeks each year, therefore, hotels, inns, taverns, and boardinghouses did rushing business. A historian of the city found in the directory for 1834

---

[3] "Extracts from the *Journal of Frances Anne Butler*," *St. Louis Commercial Bulletin*, May 20, 1835.

[4] The item is noted as "Extracts from Captain Marryat, Written by an English Observer of the American Scene," *Washington National Intelligencer*, Aug. 8, 1839.

reference to thirty-four taverns where alcoholic beverages were dispensed at retail, and thirteen hotels, most of them on or near Pennsylvania Avenue.[5] Gadsby's, one of the most popular, was located on Pennsylvania at Four-and-a-Half Street. Fanny Kemble, harsh in her criticism of the "untidy hovels above" the Capitol and "the scattered, unfinished, red-brick town below," said of Gadsby's that it was "an inn like a little town, with more wooden galleries, flights of steps, passages, door-ways, exits and entrances, than any building I ever saw."[6]

The transient character of the city was indicated by the listing of seventy-three boardinghouses, mostly kept, it was said, by widowed ladies. Some of these places were specially designated as "Congress boardinghouses," to indicate the constituency desired. There were also "oyster houses," emphasizing the specialty of the region.[7]

A Northampton paper noted in 1837 that Washington was the most expensive place to live anywhere in the country. The people who kept boardinghouses and worked for strangers during the sessions of Congress expected to make in a few weeks money enough to support them throughout the year. Board and room at Gadsby's cost two dollars a day, with the additional cost of fifty cents for a fire in the room. With incidental expenses for laundry and the aid of servants, the cost ran to about twenty dollars a week. This was regarded as extortionate.[8]

More reasonable were the costs of local transportation. An omnibus line operated from Georgetown down Pennsylvania Avenue with fares at twelve and a half cents. Hacks roved the central streets in large numbers. It was said that "Oftentimes, fifty are seen on Pennsylvania Avenue, and for 25 cents any man can play the aristocrat for half an hour, with elegant coach and livery." The rates were low because they were fixed by the government. When the drivers could evade the law, however, they charged unmercifully, demanding two or three dollars for carrying a passenger forty rods to an evening party.[9]

During the Congressional season parties were numerous and social life was intense and exciting, infused as it was with the pressures and issues of politics. Of the Washington atmosphere a correspondent wrote in 1836:

> The atmosphere of this city is perpetually filled with all sorts of idle and absurd rumors, as empty and as giddy as the wind clouds in a northern sky. Some of these rumors are mere gossip. Others are conjectures converted after two or three transmissions from one hand to

[5] S. C. Busey, *Pictures of the City of Washington in the Past*, 200.
[6] *Journal by Frances Anne Butler*, II, 85–86.
[7] Busey, *Pictures of the City of Washington in the Past*, 200.
[8] *Northampton Courier*, quoted in *Delaware State Journal*, Mar. 17, 1837.
[9] *Ibid.*

another into certainties. Others, again, are mere tricks, political devices, things set afloat for the purpose of feeling the public pulse, or acting upon the minds of particular individuals.[10]

Transportation into and out of Washington was both by water and by land. Construction of the "Long Bridge" across the Potomac from Washington, much to the disgruntlement of ferry operators and property owners in Georgetown, had long since given a land connection with Alexandria, but the advantages and conveniences of steamboat travel were such that Chief Justice Marshall and other visitors from the South preferred to come in by water. When Justice Duvall came from Maryland, however, as presumably other Justices did from the Northeast, he traveled by stagecoach. Of her trip over this line in 1833 Fanny Kemble wrote: "As for the road, we had been assured it was exceedingly good; but mercy on us! I can't think of it without aching."[11] The Justices riding circuit traveled over similar roads for hundreds of miles each year.

On the Baltimore line, however, better things were in sight. From Relay House a few miles outside Baltimore, a spur line of the Baltimore and Ohio Railroad was being built in the direction of Washington. So eager were passengers for transportation "in the cars" rather than by stagecoach that coach lines arranged to meet trains along the way at the various stages of the trip, for transportation the rest of the way to Washington. It was on August 24, 1835, that a train, carrying a load of dignitaries from Baltimore, first came puffing all the way into Washington to an improvised station at Pennsylvania Avenue and Second Street. The passengers were soon disillusioned, though, since the trains operated only from station to station and would not deliver them and their baggage to hotels and homes, and so for a time stage line service was resumed, only later to be permanently replaced by the iron horse.[12] In spite of depressions and wars and the resistance of competitors, railroad construction throughout the United States was to continue rapidly throughout the Taney period.

Although the Capitol building in which the Supreme Court began a new term on the second Monday in each January was the outstanding building in all Washington, it was by no means the huge structure that it is today—or that it became, indeed, before the end of the Taney period. Nonexistent were the two end wings now occupied respectively

---

[10] *Boston Daily Advertiser*, Mar. 1, 1836.

[11] *Journal by Frances Anne Butler*, II, 84–85.

[12] For one of the many sources see

Oliver W. Holmes, "Stagecoach Days in the District of Columbia," *Records of the Columbia Historical Society*, 50:1, 1952.

by the Senate and the House of Representatives, and the central dome, in harmony with the rest of the structure as it then stood, was lower and smaller than the one that now meets the horizon. In that smaller building the Senate, a little less than half its present number, met in the north wing, and the House of Representatives, rapidly growing with the increase of population, met in the south wing. A large section on the main floor was occupied by the Library of Congress. The Supreme Court met in a cellarlike room on the ground floor directly below the Senate chamber—the chamber to which the Supreme Court was to move in 1860 when the Senate had vacated it to occupy the new north wing. Critics of the Court's cellar home may be suspected of exaggerating its deficiencies for the sake of emphasis, yet there is so much agreement among them that they cannot be dismissed. In 1859 a writer for the *New York Daily Tribune* wielded his colorful pen in portraying the Court's habitation:

> Ten to one, that, in ascending the successive flights of steps that lead first to the esplanade, and thence wearily up, up, up to the rotunda, you lost your way, omitted one flight and found yourself unexpectedly groping about in a dark, damp, low, subterranean apartment, whose undefined dimensions melt away in distant shadows with here and there clusters of pillars of no classical style of architecture; in one corner a mountain of ashes and coal cinders; in another, a heap of dusty boxes, covered with dust, and piled up to the ceiling; on this side a mass of moldy barrels, strewed around in confusion, and whether empty or filled no one knows; and away off yonder, a furnace all aglow, and throwing a lurid streak across this mysterious cavern, and suggesting thoughts of Milton's "lower deep."
>
> You start back at first; but lured by the light of the furnace, you venture still further into this artificial cave. On reaching its center, you stumble against one of the beams of a strong frame-work of recently-erected timbers, starting from the floor in a thicket of pillars, and going up to the ceiling, evidently for the purpose of supporting the structure above, and giving you a most uncomfortable feeling that there is danger of being crushed to atoms in this grim catacomb.[13]

All this was a description prior to entrance to the courtroom itself. It can be said in answer to the criticism only that on some points there were different and less critical opinions. William Allen Butler, a member of the bar, spoke of the pillars as having grace and beauty. He noted that each column consisted of rows of corn stalks, one surmounting the other, with full-grown ears forming the capitals. He admitted that this adaptation from the classical Corinthian pattern might seem barbaric

---

[13] *New York Daily Tribune*, Mar. 26, 1859.

from the artistic point of view, but he found it pleasing as an association of the highest forms of ancient art with a common product of our western continent.[14] The newspaper writer might have taken this admirable intention into account, just as he might have explained in part the accumulation of boxes and supporting timbers in light of the fact that at that time that portion of the building was being redone and the Senate chamber overhead was being prepared for occupancy by the Supreme Court. Nevertheless a note of abiding authenticity remains in the *Tribune* writer's continued account:

> You discover a narrow passage, lighted with a dim lamp. You enter and, crowding between two walls of old deal boxes, see a distant glass door. As you approach, it seems to be guarded by a personage with a visage just dark enough to correspond with the general gloom around him. On a nearer view, you perceive that he is one of those hybrid bipeds who have no rights that a white man is bound to respect. Before you have time to knock him down for stopping up the way, he profoundly inclines his head, gently swings the door, and, descending two or three steps, you are ushered into a queer room of small dimensions, shaped over head like a quarter section of a pumpkin shell, the upper and broader rim crowning three windows, and the lower and narrower coming down garret-like to the floor; the windows being of ground glass, and the light trickling through them into the apartment. That which most arrests your attention is a long pew, just in front of these windows, slightly elevated above the floor, along which are ranged in a straight line nine ancient persons, clad in black-silk gowns. . . . A man stands in the pit, in front of them, shaking a roll of manuscript convulsively in the face of the central figure of the group . . . and blazing away at the whole nine like Mose at a fire. Half a dozen persons are lounging on chairs, or idling about the room. . . .[15]

We know from other writings, as for example those of Harriet Martineau,[16] that this account was authentic, not merely as to formal description but also as to atmosphere. The room was indeed in the shape of a half-circle, with the elevated Bench along the diameter line; the only windows were back of the Justices, so that counsel and spectators had to face into the light when looking toward the bench, with consequent difficulty in seeing the Justices' expressions. We know that the courtroom sometimes became stifling hot, especially when overcrowded with spectators during the argument of important cases or when distinguished counsel appeared before the Court, and that the Justices

---

[14] William Butler, *A Retrospect of Forty Years, 1825–1865,* 49.
[15] *New York Daily Tribune,* Mar. 26, 1859.
[16] See Harriet Martineau, *Retrospect of Western Travel,* I, 164–65.

and others regarded the dampness of the quarters as detrimental to health. We know that the supporting pillars stood annoyingly in the way of spectators. Yet we also know that there was a kind of beauty in the rounded ceiling which molded down toward the floor at the rear of the room. There was something striking about the figure of Justice beneath the rounded ceiling above the Bench, chiseled by the hand of Carlo Franzoni, who at the instance of Thomas Jefferson had also modeled and executed the corn pillars of which the journalist and the devotees of pure classical art so vigorously disapproved.[17] It is further to be remembered that if the courtroom seemed inaccessible and forbidding, the public as well as those responsible for legal business found their way to it when the occasion beckoned.

Apart from the courtroom itself, the quarters allocated to the highest court in the land were much constricted. As reported to the Comptroller of the Treasury by the Clerk of the Court, the suite of rooms included "The Court room (so called), the Court's office, anteroom, Attorney General's room, and Marshal's room."[18] The room listed in the name of the Attorney General, who as yet had no department of his own, was allocated to him to facilitate the argument of government cases for which he was responsible. The Marshal of the Court (in the person of the Marshal of the District of Columbia, with duties to perform also for the courts of the District) attended the sessions of the Supreme Court during the brief annual terms. The room listed as the Court's office was presumably occupied by the Clerk of the Court, who, during the 1830s and for many years thereafter, was William Thomas Carroll. The Clerk was the permanent officer of the Court in Washington, taking care of correspondence, the arrangement of the docket, the collection of fees, the location of rooms for the Justices on their annual visits to Washington, and other matters. No separate room seems to have been allocated to the Reporter, who as compiler and publisher of the opinions of the Court had no reason for being in Washington other than during the terms of the Court, and sometimes not even then. While that office was held by Richard Peters he did much of the work of preparing the annual volume at his home in Philadelphia.

In these limited quarters there was no room for the kind of dignified procession that in later courtrooms has marked the beginnings of daily sessions. Here, during the absence of the Justices, their black robes hung on pegs on the side wall just inside the door. On entering

---

[17] Elizabeth B. Johnston, "The Seal of the Columbia Historical Society," *Records of the Columbia Historical Society*, 6:220, 1903.

[18] William Thomas Carroll to George Wolf, Aug. 23, 1837, Clerk's Files.

the room, each Justice, perhaps with the aid of an attendant, took down and put on his robe, in full view of the assembled lawyers and other spectators, and at the appointed time made his way with his colleagues to the bench.[19]

In his statement in 1837 the Clerk made no mention of library space for the Supreme Court, for the reason that at this time the law library was under the jurisdiction of and housed with the Library of Congress, then located on the main floor of the Capitol. True, Congress in 1832 had directed the Librarian of Congress to segregate the law books in the library in a place easily accessible to the Supreme Court, making at the same time an appropriation of five thousand dollars for the purchase of law books under the direction of the Chief Justice.[20] Although repeated appropriations for law books were made thereafter, it was not until 1843 that a room was fitted out in the basement near the courtroom and the law books moved there for the primary use of the Court.[21] In addition, for many years during the Taney period, Congress made appropriations for a conference or consultation room "up town" in the area where the Justices rented rooms, and a supplemental library was maintained there. In 1860, when the Supreme Court was moved upstairs to what had hitherto been the chamber of the Senate, the basement library was moved to the room formerly occupied by the Court itself.

---

[19] Butler, *A Retrospect of Forty Years, 1825–1865*, 49–50.

[20] 4 Stat. 579.

[21] Edward G. Hudon, "The Library Facilities of the Supreme Court of the United States: A Historical Study," *U. Det. L.J.*, 34:181, 195, 1956. See also David C. Mearns, "The Story Up to Now," *Annual Report of the Librarian of Congress for the Fiscal Year Ending June 30, 1946*, 52.

CHAPTER II

The Taney Appointment

ALTHOUGH TECHNICALLY the story of the appointment of Roger B. Taney to succeed John Marshall as Chief Justice begins with President Jackson's submission of his nomination, on December 28, 1835, the significance of the appointment can be fully understood only in the light of much earlier happenings. It is necessary to go back to his service as Secretary of the Treasury and his part in the political and constitutional struggle with the Bank of the United States, to his preceding service as Attorney General, to his practice as a successful lawyer, still further back to his alignment with the friends of Andrew Jackson in the Presidential campaign of 1824, and, indeed, to his background as a product of a long line of planter ancestors in a tidewater county in southern Maryland.

The son of Michael and Monica Brooke Taney, Roger Taney was born March 17, 1777, in the midst of the American Revolution.[1] In early life he was saturated with the thinking of the planter aristocracy of the region and with the politics of the Federalist Party. He was educated at Dickinson College in Pennsylvania. Since his elder brother was chosen to inherit the family estate, Roger Taney was trained for a career at the bar and in politics. He read law in the office of Judge Jeremiah Townley Chase, of the Maryland General Court at Annapolis, and was admitted to practice in 1799. He served in the legislature of his home county for the term of 1799–1800. It was at this time that the Federalist Party went down to defeat before the forces of Thomas Jefferson.

For greater opportunities at the bar and a new start in politics,

---

[1] For general works on Taney's life and career see Charles W. Smith, Jr., *Roger B. Taney: Jacksonian Jurist*; Bernard C. Steiner, *Life of Roger Brooke Taney*; Carl Brent Swisher, *Roger B. Taney*; and Samuel Tyler, *Memoir of Roger Brooke Taney, LL.D.*

Taney moved to Frederick, Maryland, where he lived until he moved to Baltimore in 1823. There he married Anne Key, the sister of Francis Scott Key, later of "Star Spangled Banner" fame, and there were born six daughters, and a son who died in infancy. He was a Catholic and his wife a Protestant. He won distinction at the bar and continued as a leader in the Federalist Party of the state. The party split during the War of 1812. Taney went with the minority faction, which resisted the efforts of the majority and the more wealthy and powerful elements in the party to bring to an end the war which interfered with their prosperity. The Taney faction, nicknamed "Coodies,"[2] of which Taney was "King Coody," demanded loyalty to the national cause, and hailed the victory won by Andrew Jackson at the Battle of New Orleans. After the war this faction gained dominance, and before the general dissolution of the party Taney won election to the state senate in 1816 for a five-year term. There his major legislative interest seems to have been in coping with evils resulting from bad banking and unsound currency and in protecting the rights of Negroes, whether freemen or slaves.

On moving to Baltimore in 1823, Taney entered into the civic life of his new home and at the same time greatly expanded his professional activities. In Baltimore he practiced before the local courts and before the federal Circuit and District Courts there. He had a lucrative and important practice before the Maryland Court of Appeals at Annapolis. On occasion he had cases at the county seats of various Maryland counties. In 1825 he began to travel to Washington for appearances before the Supreme Court, making his debut there in two admiralty cases.[3] A year later, in a case involving the Bank of the United States, the "Monster" which Taney was later to help Jackson to defeat, he appeared against the Bank along with Daniel Webster[4]— who was later to be one of the Bank's most powerful defenders and one of Taney's harshest critics. Perhaps his most notable Supreme Court case was *Brown v. Maryland*,[5] in which the Court rejected his plea on behalf of the state and announced the famous "original package" doctrine as a device for determining the line to be drawn in foreign commerce cases between state and federal power. A clue as to Taney's standing with the Court is to be found in a letter of Justice Story's about a forthcoming argument in which he remarked that "Webster, Wirt, Taney, (a man of fine talents, whom you have not probably heard of,) and Emmet, are

---

[2] The nickname was derived from the character Abimilech Coody, created by Gulian C. Verplanck of New York in connection with political strife with De Witt Clinton. For discussion see Swisher, *Roger B. Taney*, 60–61.

[3] Manro v. Almeida, 10 Wheat. 473 (1825) and *The Gran Para*, 10 Wheat. 497 (1825).

[4] Etting v. Bank of the United States, 11 Wheat. 59 (1826).

[5] 12 Wheat. 419 (1827).

the combatants, and a bevy of ladies are the promised and brilliant distributors of the prizes."[6]

Taney had nothing of the imposing presence or the magnificent organ tones of Webster. Chronically ill throughout most of his life, so that a few days spent in arguing cases or later as a judge would send him to bed exhausted, he imparted no such sense of physical well-being and camaraderie as came from his frequent competitor, William Wirt. He was tall and flat-chested, with broad, stooping shoulders. His features were irregular, his teeth discolored with tobacco, his gums visible when he smiled. His black clothes seemed never quite to fit him, and his prominently veined hands rendered no service in revealing gesture. His voice was flat and hollow.

And yet, it was said, when he spoke his audience never thought of his appearance. Avoiding all the devices of conventional oratory, he talked simply and directly to judge or jury as the situation might require. Grounded to bedrock in the facts and law of his cases, he laid materials bare—in terms, of course, of the interests of his clients—and created the impression of absolute clarity in his presentation. An observer remarked that "There was an air of so much sincerity in all he said that it was next to impossible to believe he could be wrong."[7] Taney's capacity for capitalizing on lack of adornment in delivery in an era of great orators and his ability to give a sense of deep conviction was a sharp challenge to his opponents. Both to William Pinckney[8] and to William Wirt[9] is attributed the comment that it was possible to answer his argument and to cope with his logic, but that nothing was so much to be dreaded as his "apostolic simplicity." This trait, it is true, could be regarded by an enemy—as it came to be by Daniel Webster—as "cunning and jesuitical."[10]

In 1827 Taney was appointed attorney general of Maryland, a position more of honor than of professional responsibility. Delegating most of the state work to subordinates, he held the position until he became Attorney General of the United States in 1831. This was the most active and lucrative period of his private practice, a practice limited to Maryland and the District of Columbia but one nevertheless of high repute.

In spite of the collapse of the Federalist Party, Taney remained deeply interested in state and national politics. In 1824, when the party

[6] *Life and Letters of Joseph Story*, William W. Story, ed., I, 493.

[7] John E. Semmes, *John H. B. Latrobe and His Times*, 203.

[8] *Ibid.*

[9] "Roger Brooke Taney," *Southern Literary Messenger*, 4:349, 1838.

[10] Daniel Webster to Jeremiah Mason, Feb. 3, 1837, from a copy as sent by William D. Mitchell to Chief Justice Harlan F. Stone, filed with Harlan F. Stone to William D. Mitchell, Jan. 9, 1945, Mitchell Papers.

of Jefferson split in many directions over the selection of a President, Taney aligned himself with the cause of Andrew Jackson. Then, in preparation for the campaign of 1828, he became a leader in organizing the forces of the Jackson party in Maryland. He did not immediately share in the spoils of office. It was James M. Berrien of Georgia who initially replaced William Wirt as Attorney General. For a variety of political reasons Jackson reorganized his cabinet during the summer of 1831, and appointed Taney Attorney General. Taney accepted a recess appointment, serving also for a time as acting Secretary of War, and was confirmed as Attorney General in December, 1831.

Anticipating no extensive duties as law officer of the federal government, Taney accepted the office expecting to continue to supplement his income from private practice as his predecessors had done, and he did continue that practice until he became Secretary of the Treasury in 1833. The Attorney General received four thousand dollars from the government, by contrast with the Secretaries of State, Treasury, War, and Navy, who as the heads of departments as well as Cabinet members received six thousand dollars. Peter V. Daniel—in 1841 to become a member of the Supreme Court—declined appointment as Attorney General in 1833 in Taney's place allegedly because of the difficult character of the office and the low compensation. He called it the most troublesome office in the government: "With the duties of a Cabinet Minister, with the liability of being called on for instructions by every Bureau, with the necessity of encountering not one or two, but every one in succession of the ablest counsel in the nation, each separately and deliberately prepared on every varied department of jurisprudence foreign & domestic, the office of the Attorney General is decidedly the most onerous in the government. The salary of that officer ought to be ten thousand dollars in just proportion to the salaries of the heads of other Departments."[11]

It is impossible to tell to what extent Daniel got his impressions of the duties of the office of Attorney General from Taney. As for the argument of cases before the Supreme Court, Taney's total for two annual terms ran to about twenty. There was indeed great diversity in the cases, but some were presented on briefs without argument and in some of them opposing counsel did not appear. Few of them are regarded today as even historically important, but the occasional involvement of vast interests is illustrated by a case having to do with Spanish land grants in Florida, in which Taney had William Wirt associated with him and opposing counsel included Daniel Webster and former Attorney General Berrien.[12] However great the pressure may have been during

---

[11] P. V. Daniel to John Y. Mason, July 19, 1845, Polk Papers.

[12] United States v. Arredondo, 6 Pet. 691 (1832).

the two or more months of each session, it did not prevent Taney from continuing his practice in Annapolis.

Although the scope of his administrative duties was light—a clerk and a messenger made up the staff of his office—he had multiple duties beyond those of argument of cases. Particularly important was the drafting of official opinions on legal matters for the President and the heads of the departments. His first official opinion, for example, was addressed to the Secretary of the Treasury on the interpretation of a recently enacted statute giving relief to insolvent persons who owed debts to the United States.[13] Taney's opinion[14] displeased James Buchanan and Daniel Webster, who had had much to do with enactment of the statute. "With the most unfeigned respect for the opinions of the Attorney General," wrote Webster, "I cannot persuade myself to think that he has taken the right view of the provisions of the act. If he has done so, we are very clumsy law-makers."[15] It is of interest that at this early stage of his career as a federal officer Taney was in disagreement with "the Godlike Daniel," with whom in succeeding years he was to clash again and again in battles in which Webster ceased even to pretend respect for Taney's opinions.

The great body of official opinions, of course, dealt with matters of transient importance. In two fields, however, that of the rights of Negroes and that of the status of the Bank of the United States, Taney became involved in constitutional issues which were to play a part in his judicial task in later years. With respect to Negroes he took a position to their original degraded status in the United States very similar to that taken a quarter of a century later in the Dred Scott case. At this time his opinion remained unpublished and attracted little or no public attention.

It was with respect to the Bank of the United States that he came completely out in the open—in a controversy which likewise will require treatment in connection with the work of the Supreme Court.[16] The Bank had been chartered in 1816 for a twenty-year period, with the federal government as a minority stockholder and a major depositor. It did much to restore financial order after the War of 1812, and it

---

[13] 4 Stat. 467.

[14] 2 Ops. Att'y Gen. 451 (1831).

[15] Benjamin R. Curtis, *Life of Daniel Webster* I, 406. By amendment Congress clarified the statute a year later: 4 Stat. 595. For important items in the mass of literature on the subject see R. C. H. Catterall, *The Second Bank of the United States*; Thomas P. Govan, *Nicholas Biddle, Nationalist and Public Banker, 1786–*

1844; and Bray Hammond, *Banks and Politics in America from the Revolution to the Civil War.* For Taney's own account see Swisher, ed., "Roger B. Taney's 'Bank War Manuscript,'" *Maryland Historical Magazine*, 53: 103–30, 215–37, 1958, hereafter cited as Bank War Manuscript.

[16] See Chapter V, "The Realm of Finance."

demonstrated the fact that with careful management it could restrain the financial excesses of multiple banks chartered by the states under inadequate regulatory laws. State banking interests resented what they regarded as arbitrary interference by an essentially private institution which had the backing of the federal government. The proper drawing of the line between economic statesmanship and the arbitrary exercise of financial power was often a matter of opinion, and to many it was clear that even if the Bank of the United States had not hitherto greatly abused its powers, it was in a position to do so if the interests and the egotism of its management so decreed. While the need for some central control of banking and currency was at least dimly recognized by many, there were also many intelligent and statesmanlike people whose thinking had not gone much beyond reliance on gold and silver as circulatory mediums, with locally chartered banks to make loans and provide bank notes for strictly local circulation. Taney himself had been interested in local banks both in Frederick and in Baltimore, and he seems to have thought of these institutions as the safer means of meeting such currency needs as could not be met by the exchange of specie. Such also seems to have been the position of Andrew Jackson, although for some considerable time it was not official.

Aware that its charter must be renewed by 1836 if it was to continue in business, and fearful of the politicians of the Jackson regime, the Bank interests, around which were grouped the leading Whig and anti-Jackson politicians, sought to force a renewal of the charter as early as 1832, with the threat that the power of the Bank would be used to defeat the reelection of Jackson if he dared oppose it. Congress passed the bill. Other members of the Jackson Cabinet were hesitant or were opposed to a veto on the merits, but Taney advised a veto, and when Jackson took action he called Taney in to play a major part in drafting the veto message. The message became a campaign document and the object of Whig denunciation throughout the campaign, even as the Bank of the United States used its power over credit to attempt the overthrow of Jackson and the election of Henry Clay to the Presidency.

Jackson was reelected. He began his second term determined to insure the dissolution of the Bank with the expiration of its current charter. To curb its economic and political power and prevent any chance of charter renewal, with Taney's advice and support he determined immediately to weaken the enemy by ceasing to use it as a federal depository. The Secretary of the Treasury, William J. Duane, refused to make the change. On September 23, 1833, Jackson peremptorily removed him and appointed Taney in his place.

The period between that date and Taney's rejection by the Senate

II: *The Taney Appointment*

on June 24, 1834, was the most dramatic period in Taney's life.[17] In the face of all the financial pressure that the Bank of the United States could create and all the political pressure that Jackson's political enemies could mount, Taney selected a group of state banks in the principal regions of the country to act as federal depositories and cut off the flow of federal funds to the Bank of the United States. For all the embarrassments that were placed in his way, Taney operated with great smoothness and made reports possessing the sharp clarity and the illusion of simple truth that marked his strength before judicial forums. In exasperation Jackson's enemies denounced Taney as the pliant instrument of the President, one who lacked integrity and allowed himself to be used as a replacement for a man whose own integrity had prevented him from taking action against the Bank of the United States.

In his official position Taney could make no effective reply to such accusations. He remained in office, indeed, only because Jackson, shrewdly appraising the situation, refrained from sending his name to the Senate for confirmation until the session was near its end. Then, without additional debate, the Senate promptly rejected the nomination, and Taney was out of office. After the end of the session, Webster, at a public dinner at Salem, Massachusetts, again denounced Taney as a pliant instrument of the President. This time Taney, who hitherto had taken the advice of Martin Van Buren to refrain from replying to political attacks, wrote to Van Buren that it was due to himself and to the public to put Webster in his true position. He did so at Elkton, Maryland, on September 4, 1834, at one of a series of public gatherings assembled in his honor after his rejection. Here Taney again told the story of the bank war and the part he had played in it. He alluded to a fact which was to become notorious—that many friends of the Bank of the United States in Congress were the beneficiaries of loans from it. Accusing Webster of distorting the record, he continued:

Neither my habits nor my principles lead me to bandy terms of reproach with Mr. Webster or any one else. But it is well known that he has found the bank a profitable client, and I submit to the public whether the facts I have stated do not furnish grounds for believing that he has become its "pliant instrument," and is prepared, on all occasions, to do its bidding, whenever and wherever it may choose to require him. In the situation in which he has placed himself before the public, it would far better become him to vindicate himself from imputations to which he stands justly liable, than to assail others.[18]

---

[17] For discussion see Swisher, *Roger B. Taney*, 235–305.

[18] *Niles' Weekly Register*, 47:107, 1834.

It was undoubtedly true that Taney was deeply devoted and loyal to Jackson, and that also, in his own right, he was truly convinced that the Bank of the United States was a menace to the nation. Webster, on the other hand, was undoubtedly a firm believer in the value of the Bank of the United States, even while he served it as counsel and was the beneficiary of loans from it. It is questionable whether at this stage the accusations of either man carried conviction to persons who were not convinced already, and it would probably have been better for both if the exchange had not taken place. Certain it was that Taney further antagonized a powerful Senator at a time when confirmation of his Supreme Court appointment would be sought.

At this time the Fourth Judicial Circuit of the United States consisted of Maryland and Delaware. Since 1811 this circuit had been represented on the Supreme Court by Gabriel Duvall of Maryland, who at the beginning of the Jackson Administration was almost eighty years of age—he had been born in 1752—and who had long been almost completely deaf. A prominent aspirant for the succession was Louis McLane, who was appointed Secretary of the Treasury at the time of Taney's appointment as Attorney General. Martin Van Buren, who had great influence with Jackson in the matter of appointments, agreed to use it in behalf of McLane, who was fearful of the rivalry of Taney.[19] In his account of the bank war, Taney made no mention of the rivalry for the Supreme Court position but did tell at length of his struggle with McLane over the issue of rechartering the Bank of the United States, noting that "Mr. McLane was an ambitious man; loved power, and aspired to the Presidency which he confidently expected to reach."[20] McLane lost out in the bank struggle, was transferred to the Department of State before the issue of removal of deposits arose, and then left the Cabinet altogether.

In the meantime Taney, through his leadership in the bank struggle, had become the favorite of both Jackson and Van Buren, while Duvall, for all his deafness, had continued to occupy his judicial position. At about the time that Taney was exchanging charges with Webster about pliant instruments, the news began to spread that Justice Duvall was about to resign.[21] It is said that his hesitancy was due to his opposition to Jackson and his policies and the fear of an improper selection of a successor—possibly with McLane in mind. William Thomas Carroll, Clerk of the Supreme Court, in some way learned that

[19] John C. Fitzpatrick, ed., "The Autobiography of Martin Van Buren," *Annual Report of the American Historical Association for the Year 1918,* 2:577–79, 1920.

[20] Bank War Manuscript, 24.

[21] *Richmond Enquirer,* Oct. 28, 1834.

II: *The Taney Appointment*

Jackson hoped to appoint Taney and gave the information to Duvall,[22] who in January, 1835, resigned in the expectation that Taney would replace him. Jackson immediately sent Taney's name to the Senate.

Taney's friends, and others who knew of him as an able lawyer and a courteous gentleman of high integrity, were of course pleased with the nomination. Among the latter was Chief Justice Marshall, who, although having a peculiar dislike for Jackson, sent a confidential note to Benjamin Watkins Leigh, Whig Senator from Virginia, saying, "If you have not made up your mind on the nomination of Mr. Taney, I have received some information in his favor which I would wish to communicate."[23] But not even the support of the great Chief Justice could hold back the onslaught of the Bank and Whig forces, even though the opposition was waged covertly and by subterfuge rather than in the open.

From the time of the nomination in mid-January, 1835, until the session of the Senate adjourned *sine die* on March 3, Washington was afloat with rumors about the prospects of confirmation. Visiting Washington near the end of January, Reverdy Johnson, a prominent Baltimore lawyer and a man close to Taney even though of different political affiliation, reported that Taney's friends predicted confirmation but he himself was doubtful. The efforts to defeat Taney were untiring: "All kinds of stories are told by his out of door opponents, and many of them will remain uncontradicted. As far as I have been able to do so I have contradicted them but many I have no doubt are told that I shall not hear of."[24] A Richmond paper reported that the opposition prints were vehemently urging the Senate to carry out their proscription principle against Mr. Taney.[25] In the Maryland legislature, which was anti-Jackson in sentiment, a resolution was introduced in the lower house declaring that the nomination ought to be confirmed; the majority turned the resolution into adverse propaganda by ordering it expunged from the record.[26] A Boston newspaper hoped the Senate would not only "apply the veto to the pretensions of this man," but would also pass a decided resolution not to confirm any man who was not "perfectly sound in regard to the fundamental principles of the Constitution as expounded by Daniel Webster."[27]

The Whig-Bank forces in the Senate worked with careful strategy

---

[22] Tyler, *Memoir of Roger Brooke Taney*, 239–40.

[23] *Ibid.*, 240.

[24] Reverdy Johnson to David M. Perine, date probably Jan. 29 or 30, 1835, Perine Papers.

[25] *Richmond Enquirer*, Jan. 27, 1835.

[26] *Baltimore Republican*, Feb. 8, 1838. *Journal of the Proceedings of the House of Delegates, Dec. Sess., 1834*, 213, 223–24.

[27] *Boston Columbian Sentinel*, reprinted *Washington* (semi-weekly) *Globe*, Feb. 11, 1835.

23

to defeat the nomination, knowing that the decision might be close. In confidence Webster disclosed his plan on January 30 to Warren Dutton, who was waiting in Massachusetts to come to Washington for the argument of an important case if the vacancy was filled before the expiration of the term of the Supreme Court:

> I have in contemplation a movement, which will, if successful, supersede his nomination. It is, to unite Delaware and Maryland to the third circuit, and fill the vacant seat by an appointment in *the West*. Five Judges will do very well for the Atlantic States.[28]

On the same day John Sergeant, a prominent Philadelphia lawyer and friend of Nicholas Biddle, who was then in Washington arguing cases for the Bank, replied to an inquiry from Biddle by giving the same information, saying that he supposed it was a secret, "and as such I commit it to you."[29] Two days later Webster wrote to Jeremiah Mason about the same strategy, saying, "If we could get rid of Mr. Taney, on this ground, well and good; if not, it will be a close vote."[30]

Taney's political enemies had fixed upon sound strategy. Six Western and Southern states were without the benefit of service from United States Circuit Courts save as circuit jurisdiction was conferred upon district judges. They included Indiana, Illinois, Missouri, Alabama, Mississippi, and Louisiana. Each of these states felt that it was denied its rightful equality of position in the Union in not having membership in a circuit attended by a Supreme Court Justice. The matter was partly one of regional prestige. It involved suspicion that a Supreme Court consisting of six Easterners and one Westerner was not likely to do justice to the West. As for the substitute arrangement of conferring Circuit Court jurisdiction on district judges, although some of those judges were highly competent, others, appointed for regional political reasons, were not. Furthermore, if a district judge sat alone in a Circuit Court case it might be difficult to get a review in the Supreme Court, but when a Supreme Court Justice and a district judge sat together in Circuit Court, legal questions might be taken to the Supreme Court on certificate of division of opinion between the two judges.

For many years the Western states had been pressing for revision of the circuits to give them Supreme Court representation,[31] with service

---

[28] Daniel Webster to Warren Dutton, Jan. 30, 1835, Webster Papers (Dartmouth).

[29] John Sergeant to Nicholas Biddle, Jan. 30, 1835, Biddle Papers.

[30] *Writings and Speeches of Daniel Webster*, J. W. McIntyre, ed., XVI, 252.

[31] For discussion see Curtis Nettels, "The Mississippi Valley and the Federal Judiciary," 1807–37, *Mississippi Valley Historical Review*, 12:202, 1925.

on circuit. The debates always brought up the broader question whether Supreme Court Justices should be relieved of circuit duty to enable them to concentrate on Supreme Court work, and always there came the reply that the Justices needed to work in the states to have adequate familiarity with the law which they would be concerned with in Washington. Congressmen were concerned also lest members of the Supreme Court grow lax in the performance of their duties if relieved of circuit responsibilities, and possibly become too subordinate to the executive. Many of the Eastern spokesmen were horrified at the argument that the Supreme Court should be a regionally representative body, contending that its true constituency was the law and not regions of people and that appointments should be made from among the ablest jurists—with some implication that such jurists were likely to be found in the East.

Prior to 1835 the realignment of judicial circuits had come closest to fruition in 1826, but it had been defeated by a political maneuver on the part of Martin Van Buren to deny the Adams Administration the right to make a new appointment.[32] President Jackson, as a Westerner peculiarly concerned about the rights of the West, asked again and again for a revision of the circuit system, but hitherto without avail. In his most recent plea, on December 1, 1834, he had observed that the laws for the federal judiciary "leave one-fourth of the States without circuit courts."[33] Now Jackson was having his statesmanlike proposal used as a weapon in the bank war to defeat a nomination on which he had set his heart. The spokesman for this maneuver was Senator Theodore Frelinghuysen of New Jersey. He was an able lawyer and an ardent Whig and friend of the Bank of the United States.[34] He began formal action by offering a resolution that the Senate Committee on the Judiciary inquire into the expediency of annexing the Fourth Circuit to the Third Circuit in order to extend the circuit system to all the states. It was the Fourth Circuit that was now vacant. The Third Circuit was represented by Justice Henry Baldwin of Pennsylvania, who had himself been in favor of renewal of the charter of the national bank.[35] Frelinghuysen had already ascertained that Justice Baldwin would willingly cooperate by extending his circuit duties to Maryland and Delaware. He proposed the creation of a new circuit in the West to include Louisiana, Mississippi, Illinois, and Missouri. He had learned that Justice McLean, who at the very least had not been among the enemies of the Bank of the United States, would willingly add Indiana to his circuit of Ohio, Kentucky, and Tennessee. Evidently without consulting Justice Wayne,

---

[32] *Ibid.*, 222–23.
[33] J. D. Richardson, *A Compilation of the Messages and Papers of the Presidents*, III, 117.

[34] For Taney's comment on Frelinghuysen's part in the bank war see Bank War Manuscript, 116.
[35] *Ibid.*, 234–35.

a recent Jackson appointee who was loyal to the President in the bank war, he proposed adding Alabama to his circuit of South Carolina and Georgia.[36]

In his proposal Senator Frelinghuysen of course made no mention of the Taney nomination or of his feelings about the nominee. Since the Fourth Circuit was the smallest of the seven then in existence and was closest to Washington, and since Delaware offered little federal judicial business, as did also New Jersey, which was linked with Pennsylvania in the Third Circuit, the merger seemed to make sense as a device for providing circuit coverage for all the states. However, although nobody seems to have tried to make a case against the assumption of more work by Justice Baldwin if he wanted it, the fact remained that Pennsylvania was developing rapidly as an industrial and commercial state, with consequent increase in legal business. As for the Fourth Circuit, a Maryland Congressman dug out of judiciary committee records for 1833 the fact that although the Circuit Court had sat in Delaware only six days, it had sat in Maryland eighty-four days.[37] The Whig Senators from Maryland, however, did no fighting for the rights of their state.

Western Senators knew full well that this unwonted generosity from Eastern politicians had its selfish base but they were in no position to oppose it, however much they might want to support the President. They therefore protested at having plans made for the West without consultation and criticized the proposed circuit arrangement. Thomas Hart Benton of Missouri, an ardent Jackson supporter, scoffed at a Western circuit stretching from New Orleans to Lake Michigan. He thought operation of a circuit of such dimensions must await aerial navigation or that Southern trips would have to be made by attaching a car to periodic flights of wild geese.[38] The Westerners pressed their case in the face of reminders as to the navigability of the Mississippi, and in order to proceed with defeat of the Taney nomination, the Jackson enemies agreed to a bill providing for still another circuit in the West, cutting in half the new one originally proposed. As amended, the bill passed the Senate by a vote of thirty-one to five.[39]

In the meantime the House of Representatives, without direct power over appointments, was likewise concerned with the judiciary. Early in January, before Justice Duvall's resignation had been announced, Thomas L. Hamer, a Jacksonian Democrat from Ohio, offered a resolution instructing the Judiciary Committee to inquire into the

---

[36] For statement of Frelinghuysen's initial position see *Cong. Deb.*, 23rd Cong., 2nd Sess. 287–88 (1835).
[37] *Ibid.*, 1646.

[38] *Ibid.*, 585.
[39] See statement of Senator John M. Clayton, *Cong Deb.*, 24th Cong., 1st Sess. 59 (1836).

expediency of a constitutional amendment limiting all federal judges to a fixed term of years rather than to life tenure. The resolution was at first rejected by a narrow margin,[40] and then reconsidered and passed, likewise by a narrow margin. In explaining his support of the resolution, Benjamin Hardin of Kentucky urged that there should be some age at which a judge should be compelled to quit the bench. He noted that two members of the Supreme Court were now upwards of eighty years of age, and that one of these, because of deafness, had not for ten years *heard* a legal argument.[41] The deaf judge was, of course, Duvall. Although his name was not mentioned in the published debates, the other octogenarian—actually not to reach the designated age until nine months later—was Chief Justice Marshall. Duvall resigned and no action was taken under the resolution.

The House Judiciary Committee, to which had been referred the portion of the President's message dealing with the judiciary, was also working on a bill for the revision of the judicial circuits. Nominally because there was not time enough left in the session to deal with the subject, but perhaps in part because the bill would embarrass the President in connection with the Taney nomination, the House bill was dropped.[42] On February 25, however, in a term that was to end on March 3, the House received the bill passed by the Senate. The Democrats attempted to fight off consideration, realizing that the same local interests that had joined to support the bill in the Senate might bring about its passage in the House. Here, for the first time in the published record, a direct allusion is made to the political purpose of the bill. Richard B. Carmichael of Maryland, a friend of Taney's, said of the bill that "whilst it professes to sink a district, its effect is to despatch a judge. Its effect is to relieve the Senate of a responsibility imposed upon them by the constitution. . . . I must earnestly resist any proceeding, however presented, the manifest tendency of which is to impose upon this House a share of the responsibility devolved by the constitution upon the Senate of the United States; which will require of this House to dispose of executive nominations. And more especially, when the obvious effect of it is to affect injuriously the interests of Maryland, and to crush one of her most valued citizens."[43]

The bill was considered during the last hours of the session of March 3, amended, and finally put aside without passage. This continued consideration, however, gave the Senate an excuse for inaction on Taney's nomination and for final action of indefinite postponement, an action taken on Webster's motion and carried by a vote of twenty-

---

[40] *Cong. Deb.*, 23rd Cong., 2nd Sess. 943 (1835).
[41] *Ibid.*, 965.

[42] *Ibid.*, 1303–05.
[43] *Ibid.*, 1498.

four to twenty-one.[44] Since the session of Congress then came to an end, the nomination was as dead as if it had been rejected outright. The action, of course, did not restore Justice Duvall to his former position, and Circuit Court business in Maryland and Delaware was to remain undone save as it could be handled by the United States district judges. The six Western states not yet allocated to judicial circuits remained without the benefit of attendance by a Supreme Court Justice.

The prospect for the Democrats was less gloomy than it would otherwise have been because when Congress sat again, in December, 1835, the Senate would have a larger percentage of friends of the Administration, and the session would not have to come to an end at a designated date as had the one now ended on March 3. There would be more friends and more time for maneuvering, for arrangement of strategy.

Another important change was in the offing. On March 2 Justice Story wrote to a friend to say that although Chief Justice Marshall still possessed his intellectual powers in very high vigor, his physical strength was manifestly on the decline. He thought it obvious that after a year or two Marshall would resign because of the pressing infirmities of age.[45] On May 20 Story wrote in similar vein to Richard Peters, Reporter of the Supreme Court, whose home was in Philadelphia, adding, "I pray God that he may long live to bless his country; but I confess that I have many fears whether he can be long with us."[46] While holding court on circuit, Story learned from Peters that Marshall had come to Philadelphia to see a physician there and that his condition was bad indeed; Peters suggested that Story visit him there. On June 19 Story replied that in view of the imminence of Marshall's death such an interview would be too painful to justify itself and that he lacked the courage to face it.[47] It was on July 6, attended only by Justice Baldwin among his Supreme Court colleagues, that Chief Justice Marshall died.

The passing of the great Chief Justice brought a sense of tragedy far and wide throughout the nation. Those mourning most deeply were, of course, the believers in a higher degree of centralization of government than that advocated by Jackson, the people who as political partisans were Whigs, and the friends of the Bank of the United States. One of Nicholas Biddle's correspondents in New York reported, "The account of the death of the Chief Justice has cast a gloom on this community. A few do not show it, but they are few. It is a sore loss, the most so of any one since the death of Washington."[48] Another correspondent and

[44] S. Jour., 23rd Cong., 2nd Sess. 484 (1835).
[45] Life and Letters of Joseph Story, II, 193.
[46] Ibid., 194.
[47] Ibid., 199–200.
[48] R. Lenox to Nicholas Biddle, July 8, 1835, Biddle Papers.

an admirer of the Bank from Kentucky warned of dire days ahead, saying that Biddle was in imminent peril.

> The Supreme Court consists of Story McLean Baldwin Thompson Wayne & two blanks. Who will fill these blanks? *Partizans.* Party politicians. Those only who will shout morning, noon, & night, 'Great is Genl Jackson & great is _____ his Prophet.'
>
> Which of the present five can be relied on to do his duty *fearlessly & fully?*
>
> Genl J. says the Bk is unconstitutional. Mr. Van Buren echos the opinion and old Tecumseh follows suit. Will the Judges—*his* officers, dare to decide otherwise by & bye?[49]

John Quincy Adams, building a career for himself in the House of Representatives after his embittering defeat in seeking a second Presidential term, had praise for Marshall, the great Constitution builder who had been appointed by his father and who had "cemented the Union which the crafty and quixotic democracy of Jefferson had a perpetual tendency to dissolve,"[50] but he had no hope for the future of the Supreme Court. Jackson had already appointed three Justices. He had not yet made one good appointment. "His Chief Justice will be no better than the rest."[51] Justice Story refused to conjecture as to the new appointment. He wrote to Richard Peters that the new man would follow one who could not be equaled and that the public would see the difference. He added that "lest there should be some idle conjecture elsewhere, I have never for a moment imagined that I should be thought of. So that I am equally beyond hope or anxiety."[52] He wrote in similar fashion to Justice McLean, adding that he had always regarded the duties as peculiarly trying and difficult, and in the possession of an ordinary man, very apt to disgrace him. "I take it for granted that all of us who are on the Bench are deemed *hors du combat.*"[53]

As the death of John Marshall led to widespread discussion of his career, so the prospect of filling the office of Chief Justice brought widespread newspaper discussion all over the country.[54] The Whigs and nationalists, for all their knowledge of the ways of politics, their recollection of their warfare against the Jackson administration, and the reports of Jackson's sneering comments on the "school of Story and Kent,"[55] seemed unable to believe that their own sentiments would not be re-

---

[49] Leslie Combs to Nicholas Biddle, July 27, 1835, Biddle Papers.

[50] *Memoirs of John Quincy Adams,* Charles Francis Adams, ed., IX, 243.

[51] *Ibid.,* 244.

[52] *Life and Letters of Joseph Story,* II, 202.

[53] *Ibid.,* 208.

[54] For quotations and summaries of newspaper comments see Charles Warren, The *Supreme Court in United States History,* II, 1–18.

[55] *Life and Letters of Joseph Story,* II, 208.

flected in the appointment. Their candidates included Justice Story, who clearly would have welcomed such an appointment, even from Andrew Jackson, and who had been Marshall's own choice;[56] Daniel Webster, who, however much he might have liked the honor would not have liked the low income, and who in 1840 said that there never was a time when he would have taken the office;[57] Justice McLean, a Jackson appointee who was drifting more and more into the Whig camp and who no doubt would have liked the office even though his highest aspiration was the Presidency; and Horace Binney, a prominent Philadelphia lawyer.

The Democratic list of candidates was headed by Taney, but there were many others. These included Philip P. Barbour, a states' rights Virginian, who had had long service in Congress, had been president of the Virginia constitutional convention of 1829–1830, and was now a federal district judge in Virginia; Edward Livingston of Louisiana and New York, who had been for a time Jackson's Secretary of State; Henry St. George Tucker, president of the Virginia Court of Appeals; William Gaston, chief justice of the North Carolina Supreme Court; Thomas Hart Benton of Missouri, a loyal and effective Jackson man in the United States Senate; and Louis McLane of Delaware, who, as already indicated, had long been a rival of Taney for the Associate Justiceship representing the Fourth Circuit.

Whig leaders hoped to preserve the status quo as far as the Supreme Court was concerned, with its restrictions on the powers of the states and its broad nationalist doctrines. The democratic position, stated many times in many ways, was well expressed in a paragraph in the *Richmond Enquirer* declaring opposition to the appointment of Webster:

> For our parts, we do not hesitate to say that we should be against Mr. Webster, because of his ultra Federalist principles. These are too much in unison with the decisions of the Supreme Court itself, to command the support of the Republican party. The Court has done more to change the character of that instrument, and to shape as it were a new Constitution for us, than all the other departments of the Government put together.[58]

The Whig opposition to Taney was based on his commitment to Jacksonian democracy and on his alleged subservience to Jackson in the President's struggle with the Bank of the United States. For example, Philip Hone, a prominent New Yorker, admitted that Taney was a

---

[56] *Ibid.*, 210.
[57] *Writings and Speeches of Daniel Webster*, XVIII, 96.

[58] *Richmond Enquirer*, July 24, 1855.

lawyer of high repute but contended that his act of subserviency would "damn him to everlasting fame." He added sourly that since no one but a person having this kind of qualification could be appointed it was fortunate that the ermine had not fallen on even less worthy shoulders.[59] While some Whig opposition to Taney was based on the fact that he was a Catholic, it was noted that some of the opponents were willing to accept another Catholic, Judge Gaston of North Carolina, who had different political sentiments.[60]

A skillful but anonymous writer for a Maine newspaper set forth Taney's qualifications, continuing from a discussion of the bank war:

> The same controversy developed Mr. Taney's views as a "sound constitutional lawyer"; and they are such as should alone guide the actions of that important, yet to an alarming extent, irresponsible and delicate department of the government—a disposition to maintain the Federal Government in all its constitutional vigor within its appropriate sphere—always mindful of its specific and limited powers, of the rights reserved to the people and the States, and of that hearty sympathy which should be felt by every officer, with every steady movement of public opinion. To the bench of the Supreme Court, Mr. Taney would carry an industry equal to every duty—a comprehensive and vigorous mind—an ample knowledge of the constitutional and common law—the result of an unremitted application to study, and of a laborious, long, and successful practice at the bar, both in the State and Federal Courts—a deportment simple yet dignified, and a moral character without stain.[61]

The fear of the Democrats about Taney, insofar as they had any fear, was that his earlier Federalist affiliation might be revivified on the Court and leave them with a judiciary less changed than they hoped.[62]

The death of Chief Justice Marshall meant that the business of the Fifth Circuit, consisting of Virginia and North Carolina, as well as that of the Fourth Circuit, must go unattended until a new appointment had been made. For a number of positions in the executive branch of the government which fell vacant during the recess of Congress, including that of Secretary of the Treasury when Taney was appointed to that office, President Jackson made recess appointments, submitting the nominations to the Senate some time after it assembled. In July, 1835, it was widely rumored that Jackson had given Taney a recess appointment as Chief Justice. An anonymous writer calling himself "Causidi-

---

[59] *Diary of Philip Hone*, Alan Nevins, ed., I, 164.

[60] *Richmond Enquirer*, Aug. 14, 1835.

[61] *Portland Eastern Argus*, Nov. 19, 1835.

[62] See for example *Richmond Enquirer*, Nov. 27, 1835; *Portland Eastern Argus*, Aug. 5, 1835.

cus" wrote to the *National Intelligencer*, the influential Whig newspaper in Washington which, according to Taney, was virtually owned by the Bank of the United States,[63] to say that the rumor surely could not be correct. There could be no Justice of the Supreme Court who did not hold his office during good behavior. If Taney were given a recess appointment he would serve not during good behavior but at the will of the Senate, which might refuse its consent, or at the will of the President, who might alter his mind before the next session of the Senate and appoint another. The writer did not believe that Taney would take upon himself the duties of the office prior to confirmation by the Senate.

The *National Intelligencer* apparently accepted this position as its own—as a basis for opposition to an immediate appointment. The Democratic *Richmond Enquirer*, however, reprinted the "Causidicus" letter and took issue with it, quoting Article II, Section 2, of the Constitution to the effect that "The President shall have power to fill up all vacancies that may happen during the recess of the Senate, by granting commissions which shall expire at the end of their next session." The appointment, the *Enquirer* admitted, would be a qualified appointment, but qualified in harmony with the provision of the Constitution. The constitutional practice set up for the federal government was like that of a number of states. In these states, including Virginia, the executive had been accustomed to making recess appointments when judicial positions needed to be filled at once, thereafter submitting the names to the legislature.[64] It is not probable that Jackson stayed his hand because of constitutional qualms. He may have thought that a recess appointment would be bad politics from the point of view of ultimate confirmation, or, with vacancies in two adjacent circuits, he may have thought this an auspicious time to get circuit changes made before filling both Supreme Court positions. It is barely possible that he permitted the situation to ride with mere rumors of Taney's appointment until the opposition had wasted ahead of time the mass of its explosive power. In any event, there was much less public discussion when Congress assembled in

[63] Bank War Manuscript, 220.

[64] *Richmond Enquirer*, July 21, 1835, p. 3, col. 4. The *Enquirer* was in error in assuming that there was a uniform practice in this field with respect to the appointment of Supreme Court Justices. It listed Thomas Johnson, Brockholst Livingston, Gabriel Duvall, and Joseph Story as Justices who had been appointed in November, and therefore presumably in recess of the Senate. The record shows, however, that the Senate was in session at the time of the nomination of all these except Justice Livingston, and his nomination antedated the meeting of the Senate by twenty days. The *Enquirer* was right in saying that John Rutledge had been appointed Chief Justice on July 1, 1795, for Senate action the following December, but this illustration carried an ill omen since the Senate rejected the nomination.

December than there had been the preceding July and August. We go not to the public press but to private correspondence to find as of December 1 on the part of John Quincy Adams a denunciation of the democracy which had kept the Presidency almost exclusively in the South, and a prediction that "the next Chief Justice will be not only a southern slaveholder but a convert from the ranks of federalism to rank democracy and a man of exceedingly doubtful moral principle."[65]

In his annual message to Congress on December 7, 1835, Jackson again called attention to the defects in the federal judicial system, whereby the states derived unequal benefits, and asked Congress to "extend to all the States that equality in respect to the benefits of the laws of the Union which can only be secured by the uniformity and efficiency of the judicial system."[66]

Jackson waited four weeks before submitting a nomination for either vacancy, evidently hoping that Congress might act quickly on the rearrangement of circuits. On December 23 Webster wrote to his wife that no Chief Justice had yet been nominated but that it was expected Mr. Taney would be the man.[67] Finally, on December 28, Jackson decided to wait no longer and submitted two names—Taney to succeed Marshall as Chief Justice and Philip P. Barbour to succeed Duvall as Associate Justice. The nominations were referred to the Senate Judiciary Committee. They were reported out on January 5, 1836, with the recommendation that they lie on the table, presumably to await action on the rearrangement of circuits. On January 6 the Senate passed a bill similar to that passed at the preceding session except that instead of merging the Fourth Circuit with the Third it merged it with the Fifth. The bill was passed with but one dissenting vote[68] and had the support of all the Senators from the states immediately involved. If the bill became law, the Senate would have before it two Supreme Court nominations from the same circuit. While there was no legal requirement that a Justice should reside in the circuit which he served, such residence was regarded as eminently desirable and as if it ought to be mandatory. Taney and Barbour therefore came to be looked upon as rivals. The *Richmond Enquirer*, for example, assumed that if the bill were passed, a new Chief Justice would have to be nominated, the implication being that the consolidated circuit would go to Barbour.[69]

---

[65] "John Quincy Adams to Alexander H. Everett, Dec. 1, 1835," *American Historical Review*, 9:347, 1906.

[66] Richardson, *A Compilation of the Messages and Papers of the Presidents*, III, 177.

[67] *Writings and Speeches of Daniel Webster*, XVI, 263.

[68] *Cong Deb.*, 24th Cong., 1st Sess. 65 (1835).

[69] *Richmond Enquirer*, Jan. 19, 1836.

It may well be that defeating Taney in this fashion was involved in the strategy of Whigs who voted so nearly unanimously for the redistricting bill.

Although still fighting to defeat efforts to place Taney on the Supreme Court and to keep the Court staffed and operating in the Marshall tradition, the Whig-Bank faction was more pessimistic than it had been a year earlier when the great Chief Justice was still at the helm. On January 10, 1836, Webster wrote to his daughter-in-law that Judge Story had arrived in Washington, in good health but bad spirits: "He thinks the Supreme Court is gone and I think so too; and almost everything is gone, or seems rapidly going."[70] The House of Representatives, entangled in multiple rivalries over the rearrangement of the judicial circuits, took no action on the redistricting bill. This time, however, Jackson and Taney had enough friends in the Senate and enough time to prevent repetition of the stratagem of holding the nominations until the end of the session and then voting indefinite postponement. When Taney's Baltimore friends offered a petition in behalf of his confirmation, it was presented not by one of the two Whig Senators from Maryland, both of whom were opposed to confirmation, but by John M. Clayton of Delaware. Webster countered by removing the injunction of secrecy from the action to postpone Taney's nomination at the preceding term, evidently to stir strife among Democrats by showing that some who had pledged themselves not to vote against Taney had resorted to the subterfuge of agreeing to postponement.[71]

In the meantime Taney was engaged in preparing an argument to be made before the Maryland legislature to demonstrate that Maryland should pay for damage done by a mob to property in Baltimore. The victims were Reverdy Johnson, John Glenn, and others who had been connected with the now defunct Bank of Maryland in which members of the mob had lost their savings. Taney had taken the case not merely for the fees involved but because he felt under obligation to Reverdy Johnson who had rendered him important service in the bank war period. The case dragged on longer than was expected, and it began to appear that confirmation of the nomination might take Taney off the case. Evidently feeling that confirmation was assured, Taney wrote to Vice President Martin Van Buren indicating his willingness that Senate action be postponed until he had made his argument, lest it be suspected that he had pressed for early confirmation because of threats made against him for handling the case.[72]

---

[70] Daniel Webster to Caroline Webster, Jan. 10, 1836, Webster Papers (N.H.H.S.).

[71] S. Jour., 24th Cong., 1st Sess. 505 (1836).

[72] Taney to Martin Van Buren, Mar. 7, 1836, Van Buren Papers. See also Taney to Van Buren, Mar. 8, 1836, Van Buren Papers.

Taney wrote similar letters to his son-in-law, J. Mason Campbell,[73] and to his brother-in-law, Francis Scott Key. Key, who sometimes operated with more good intentions than skill, consulted Senator Clayton and wrote to other Senators asking for postponement of action. As soon as he heard of this Taney sensed the use that might be made of it by his political enemies, who could claim that he was playing with a judicial nomination while he argued a case that was deeply involved in politics. In great distress he again wrote to Van Buren, who had unmeasured skill in behind-the-scenes maneuvers, saying that he had already demonstrated good faith to his friends in Baltimore and that "I have no desire that my nomination should be postponed an hour on account of my engagements at Annapolis, and I do most anxiously desire not to be surrendered by my friends to the mercies of my adversaries."[74]

The Taney nomination was involved in intricate political maneuvering, even before it was initially made, as in connection with the selection of a United States Senator from Connecticut who might be expected to support Taney and other Jackson nominees for various offices.[75] It came up for discussion in connection with the involvement of state banks as well as the Bank of the United States in elections and in the making of appointments.[76] It stood in the background as Congress dealt with pressures to renew the charter of the Bank of the United States, with distribution to the states of surplus revenue in the federal treasury, with the reception of petitions on the subject of slavery, and other topics. Party lines were sharply drawn, as was noted by John M. Niles, the new Senator from Connecticut, when nearly all the Whig Senators left the floor as he began a speech—"they could not have shown more haste if a mad dog had leaped in among them."[77]

On March 15, the date of Taney's anxious letter to Van Buren, Senator Niles wrote to Gideon Welles, editor of the *Hartford Times*, that the first great struggle in the Senate had ended in a great victory. A preliminary struggle had taken place at a party caucus the preceding evening, when an attempt had been made to line up Democratic Senators in support of confirmation of the two Supreme Court nominations. Senators from Southwestern states were opposed to confirming the Barbour nomination because of fear that by doing so they would dis-

---

[73] Taney to J. Mason Campbell, Mar. 4, 1836, Gratz Collection, and Mar. 8, 1836, Etting Collection, Historical Society of Pennsylvania.

[74] R. B. Taney to Martin Van Buren, Mar. 15, 1838, Van Buren Papers.

[75] William H. Ellis to Gideon Welles, Dec. 10, 1835, Welles Papers.

[76] William H. Ellis to Gideon Welles, Dec. 31, 1835, *ibid.*

[77] John M. Niles to Gideon Welles, Feb. 19, 1836, *ibid.*

courage action on the bill to rearrange the judicial circuits which was still pending in the House of Representatives. Senator William C. Rives of Virginia, however, fought for the Barbour nomination on the ground that failure to act now would endanger elections in Virginia where Whigs had claimed that the nomination had not been made in good faith but was "only a sham." Agreement of the caucus to support Barbour was won by Rives' promise to do all in his power to bring about completion of the enactment of the judiciary bill.[78]

Earlier in the day on which the caucus was held, March 14, Democratic Senators had tried to get the Senate to go into executive session to deal with the pending nominations. The Whigs had defeated the move because of the absence of the Maryland Senators, both of them Whigs, allegedly because of illness. The Democrats won only what they believed to be a firm agreement to take up executive business on the following day. On March 15, however, as events were explained by Senator Niles, the Whigs, with the support of two interested Midwestern Democrats, won a vote to take up Henry Clay's land bill instead of the matter of the nominations. Thereupon the Maryland Senators returned to the floor, assuming that the matter was settled for the day.

However, Thomas Ewing of Ohio, on that day the principal spokesman for the land bill, was unable to maintain the debate, and the Whigs moved adjournment. The motion failed, and a motion was then carried to go into executive session.[79] The Maryland Senators again disappeared from the floor, and Taney's nomination as Chief Justice was confirmed, by a vote of twenty-nine to fifteen.[80] Barbour's nomination was then taken up. Webster moved postponement of consideration until the House had acted on the judiciary bill, but his motion failed and Barbour was approved by a vote of thirty to eleven.[81] Both the Fourth and the Fifth Circuits once again had representatives on the Supreme Court and Justices to hold Circuit Courts within their borders.

Pro-Jackson newspapers gloried in the victory. Letters of congratulation poured in upon the new Justices. On March 17 Taney wrote to Jackson to express his gratitude for placement in the only station in government he had ever wished to attain. He would rather owe the honor to Jackson than to any other man in the world. "I have been confirmed by the strength of my own friends, and go into office not by the leave, but in spite of the opposition of the men who have so long and so perseveringly sought to destroy me, and I am glad to feel that I do not owe my confirmation to any forbearance on their part." He

---

[78] John M. Niles to Gideon Welles, Mar. 15, 1836, *ibid.*
[79] *Ibid.*

[80] *S. Jour.*, 24th Cong., 1st Sess. 584 (1838).
[81] *Ibid.*, 585.

looked forward to administering the oath of the Presidential office to Van Buren, who had once been rejected by the same Senate that a year earlier had rejected him:

> And it is a still further gratification, to see, that if providence spares our lives, it will be the lot of one of the rejected of the panic Senate, as the highest judicial officer of the country to administer in your presence and in the view of the whole nation, the oath of office to another rejected of the same Senate, when he enters into the first office in the world, and to which it is now obvious that an enlightened and virtuous people are determined to elect him. The Spectacle will be a lesson; which neither the people nor politicians should ever forget.[82]

Very quickly, however, Taney began to feel the dignity and to sense the high standards of his new office. He wrote to an old friend in Frederick that his political battles were over, "and I must devote myself to the calm but high duties of the station with which I am honored."[83] He responded to Edward Livingston's congratulations on victory "over corrupt influence and party malignity"[84] by gloating over the fact that the so-called statesmen in the Senate had managed to elevate to high office those whom they most hated, but he also added that all this was now past. "I must hasten to forget it and as I look to the high duties of the station to which I am called, I feel sensibly the heavy responsibility which rests upon me."[85]

Whig newspapers and Whig politicians continued to denounce what they regarded as appointment of a servile individual unworthy of the high office. For some reason Senator John Davis of Massachusetts had voted for confirmation. He was of course soundly denounced by some of his conservative fellows. Webster excused Davis' vote on the ground that the Whig majority had been lost anyway so that there was no point in further opposition, and that Davis may have thought that defeat of Taney's nomination would bring an even worse appointment.[86] Charles Sumner, writing to the Reporter of the Supreme Court to ask a favor in behalf of his friend and former law teacher, Justice Story, who he thought should have been elevated to the Chief Justiceship, viewed a dismal prospect in the Taney appointment: "How he will hold the great scales which Marshall bore aloft remains to be seen! Perhaps upon him,

---

[82] Taney to Jackson, Mar. 17, 1836, *Correspondence of Andrew Jackson*, John S. Bassett, ed., V, 390.

[83] Taney to William M. Beall, Mar. 23, 1836, letter in the possession of Mrs. L. R. Lee, Washington, D.C.

[84] Livingston to Taney, Mar. 17, 1836, manuscript at Princeton University.

[85] Taney to Livingston, Mar. 24, 1836, Livingston Papers.

[86] Webster to John Davis, *Writings and Speeches of Daniel Webster*, XVI, 274.

who entirely deserved the place and was neglected, the duties will in the main fall."[87]

President Jackson, quite undisturbed and probably amused by Whig criticism, officially allocated the new Chief Justice to the Fourth Circuit. On March 28 Elias Glenn, United States district judge for Maryland, and the several officers of the court in Baltimore, waited on Taney at his home and escorted him to the courtroom, where before a crowd of friends and members of the bar he took the oath of office as Chief Justice of the Supreme Court of the United States and presiding justice of the Fourth Circuit.[88] On April 8 the Circuit Court commenced its regular session with Taney presiding. On August 1, 1836, he performed his first duty specifically as a member of the Supreme Court by appearing in Washington to assume his functions at a vestigial August term of that Court which had previously been allocated to the representative of the Fourth Circuit. From the minutes of the Court it appears that Justice Duvall had long since ceased to put in an appearance during the August term, leaving it to the Clerk of the Court to record the continuation of cases. Taney, however, appeared to bring about the recording of the appointments of himself and Justice Barbour, who in the meantime had taken the oath of office and begun his work on the Fifth Circuit. Although Barbour's term of service was destined to be short, Taney had now begun a judicial career which was to last more than twenty-eight years.

---

[87] Charles Sumner to Richard Peters, Nov. 23, 1836, in Vol. 2 of the bound volumes of the *Correspondence of Richard Peters*, deposited in the Cadwalader Collection, Historical Society of Pennsylvania.

[88] *Niles' Weekly Register*, 50:73.

CHAPTER III

Personnel of the Taney Court

AS OF 1836, or as of January, 1837, when all of them first assembled as a group, the personnel of the Taney Court in addition to the Chief Justice himself included Joseph Story of Massachusetts, appointed in 1811 by James Madison; Smith Thompson of New York, appointed in 1823 by James Monroe; and four appointees of Andrew Jackson, including John McLean of Ohio, appointed in 1829; Henry Baldwin of Pennsylvania, appointed in 1830; James M. Wayne of Georgia, appointed in 1835; and Philip P. Barbour of Virginia, whose nomination was presented along with Taney's and confirmed at the same time, on March 15, 1836. This Court had all the diversity characteristic of Justices appointed at different times, from different parts of the country, by different Presidents. The diversity was there even as to the five Jackson appointees, no two of whom could be said greatly to resemble each other. The panorama of differences reveals itself in biographical sketches of the initial members of the Taney Court, John Catron of Tennessee and John McKinley of Alabama, whose appointments in 1837 were to raise the membership of the Court to nine, and of Peter V. Daniel of Virginia, who replaced Justice Barbour upon the latter's death in 1841.

In many respects the outstanding member of the Taney Court at this time was Joseph Story. He was by twelve years the eldest of the Justices in point of service on the Court, although, born on September 18, 1779, he was eleven years younger than Justice Thompson. More than any other member of the Taney period, he embodied the Court under John Marshall, and he was Marshall's choice for his successor.[1]

---

[1] *Life and Letters of Joseph Story*, William W. Story, ed., II, 210.

An unsympathetic member of the Supreme Court of Georgia said of Story after his death:

> As to Judge Story, he is understood to have distinguished himself, somewhat, as a *Republican* partisan, before the war of 1812, in Massachusetts, where Republicans were rather scarce. Being a young lawyer of some promise, and about the only lawyer of that party, there, of much note, he was selected, by Mr. Madison, for the bench of the Supreme Court of the United States. But once on the bench, he forsook his party and became the humble interpreter of Marshall—the Dumont to Bentham. He made it his business to illustrate and to embody the political doctrines of his chief. And this he did, in what he styles his "Commentaries on the Constitution." This is a work of as rank a partisan character, on one side, as the Virginia and Kentucky Resolutions, and Mr. Madison's Report of 1798 and 1799, are on the other.[2]

Whatever the regional and partisan bias involved in this statement, it is true that through his published writings, and particularly through his *Commentaries on the Constitution*, Story did a great deal to entrench in the thought of the country the Marshall approach to the Constitution. Beyond that, he became during his thirty-four years on the Supreme Court deeply learned in many legal subjects other than public law and a prolific author of commentaries. The *Commentaries on the Constitution* appeared in 1833. On other subjects first editions appeared on bailments in 1832; on conflict of laws in 1834; on equity jurisprudence in 1836; on equity pleading in 1838; on the law of agency in 1839; on the law of partnership in 1841; on bills of exchange in 1843; and on promissory notes in 1845, the year of his death. Most of these works went through large numbers of editions and were extensively used at least until the latter part of the nineteenth century. To these works are to be added law review articles, encyclopedia articles, and miscellaneous writings and speeches in great variety.

In a letter written in 1841 Chancellor Kent said of Story's writings:

> I think all the treatises of my friend Story are, upon the whole, the most finished and perfect of their kind, to be met with in any language, foreign or domestic, and, for learning, industry, and talent, he is the most extraordinary jurist of the age.[3]

Many decades later Harold Laski expressed to Justice Oliver Wendell Holmes, Jr., some doubts about the quality of Story's work. He thought

---

[2] Padelford, Fay & Co. v. Mayor . . . of Savannah, 14 Ga. 438, 512 (1854).

[3] Quoted in a review of Story's *Commentaries on the Law of Partnership*, in *American Jurist*, 26:500, 1842.

Story a good summarizer but could see no traces of an original mind.[4]
Holmes thought such a judgment a denial of credit due:

> Grant, if you like, that he was rather a *vulgaristateur*, he was one on a
> great scale—did much to make the law accessible and intelligible and in
> short voluminous. Volume is usually in inverse ratio to intensity, but
> is itself a gift like the others.[5]

And again:

> As for Story, let me add . . . that I don't mind his writing being
> diffuse and thin—as I think I wrote that a three volume novel ought
> to be. The conclusion may be, don't write three volume novels, and
> certainly I have no ambition to write like Story.[6]

While among contemporary American critics all of Story's works
were received with the highest praise—apart from his writings in public
law, as illustrated above—even in his own country it was suggested
that "while all the works of Judge Story have been useful to the profession, it might have been better for his own reputation if they had
been fewer, and written with more care and deliberation."[7] The sug-

---

[4] *Holmes-Laski Letters*, Mark De-
Wolfe Howe, ed., I, 493, 639.

[5] *Ibid.*, 644–45.

[6] *Ibid.*, 652.

[7] "Death of Mr. Justice Story," *Law
Rep.*, 8:243, 1845.
It is to be noted that because of
Justice Story's stature with the legal
profession and with learned men generally the mere mention of his name
carried great weight. To attack effectively positions taken by him it was
therefore necessary to do so with
great force. An example of such an
attack was provided during the Civil
War by Isaac F. Redfield, who for a
quarter of a century had served on
the Supreme Court of Vermont, as
chief justice during the last eight
years of that period, and who, apart
from his judicial opinions, wrote extensively on legal subjects. Judge Redfield, characterizing himself as a
states' rights advocate, was here discussing Justice Story's argument that
the Declaration of Independence
emanated from the people and not
from the several states:
But Mr. Justice Story was not infallible; and although one of the
ablest lawyers that America has
produced, he was not a practical
statesman, nor a careful and
thorough student of public and
international law; except in his
own department of admiralty and
prize law. In common with most
other ambitious men he was,
sometimes, apparently more so-
licitous of acquiring reputation in
those departments outside his profession, than with its legitimate
and proper range. He consequently committed some errors
in his works not strictly of a professional character, where his
opinions are not received, upon
this side of the Atlantic, with the
same confidence as in some few
other of his works. His commentaries, therefore, upon the
American Constitution, while embracing a wide range of historical
research, are not always couched
in that precise and accurate
phraseology which he would have
used, if he had been more familiar with all the possible applications of his propositions.
"On Secession and State Rights," *L.
Mag. & L. Rev.* (London), 16:81,
85–86, 1863.

gestion, in short, was that some of his works were merely great repositories of law rather than well-arranged treatises. But admittedly even works of mere compilation were important in those times when good law libraries and good index systems did not yet exist.

Various of the commentaries were well received and highly praised abroad as well as at home. An English critic, however, was displeased with the study of equity pleading, lamenting so much reliance on English cases and so little presentation of "fresh lights thrown by American judges upon our equitable doctrines."[8] By contrast, Roscoe Pound in 1914 characterized Story's writings on equity as his most important service,[9] for by this work he made possible in the United States a better understanding of a system that had never been popular in a Puritan environment. If Story revealed to English readers very little in the way of American contributions to equity, the explanation may well lie in the fact that no great contribution had been made.

In an evaluation of Story's contribution we are not to be misled by the fact that during his last ten years—the decade which followed the death of Chief Justice Marshall—much of his correspondence and even some of his Supreme Court opinions ring out with lamentations at the passing of the old order and at evidence of the fact that life in the United States would never be the same again. It was also for him a period of great positive achievement. Pursuant to the requirement attached to the Dane Professorship of Law at the Harvard Law School that he publish his lectures, he brought out sets of commentaries synthesizing many of the holdings and much of the philosophy of the Marshall Court. Serving for a salary of one thousand dollars a year, he prepared, delivered, and published his lectures, and presided at moot courts, all the while spreading the gospel of federalism by his combined efforts. It is to be remembered also that although he wrote no large number of Supreme Court opinions during that last decade, he continued to write opinions in large numbers in cases decided on his New England circuit, cases collected in twelve volumes which have become part of the grist of American law.

For a man preoccupied with the writing of legal treatises, Story had an amazingly wide range of contacts with men and activities outside the judicial field. Usually acting through personal friends, he gave advice on public matters both state and federal. For use in Congress he drafted bills having to do with the exercise of judicial power, with

---

[8] From a review in the London *Law Magazine* for May, 1839, quoted in *American Jurist*, 22:233, 1839.

[9] Roscoe Pound, "The Place of Judge Story in the Making of American Law," *Am. L. Rev.*, 44:676, 694, 1914.

bankruptcy, with crimes, with taxation, and with admiralty jurisdiction. He was a staunch partisan, adhering to the Whig Party and to the group supporting the Bank of the United States. Within the Whig Party his closest contact was probably Daniel Webster, of his own state. He could give enthusiastic support to Henry Clay of Kentucky, but he had little use for William Henry Harrison of Indiana, who at times was used by the Whigs to make their appeal to the Westerner and the common man. To his friends Story spoke and wrote again and again of his despair of the survival of our institutions, since it seemed to be necessary for politicians to pander to the undisciplined emotions and the lowest interests of the people. An excerpt from a letter to Justice McLean, written in 1844, provides one of many examples:

> I utterly despair of a Republican government. My heart sickens at the profligacy of public men, the low state of public morals, and the utter indifference of the people to all elevated virtue and even self respect. They are not only the willing victims but the devotees of Demagogues. I had a letter a few days ago from Chancellor Kent, in which he utters language of entire despondency. Is not the *theory* of our government a whole failure?[10]

Lord Morpeth, a visiting Englishman, wrote in his diary in 1841 of a dinner given by Justice Story at which he and his friends were so critical of the government as to approach treason against their own Constitution.[11]

Yet among his friends Story was a delightful conversationalist. Lord Morpeth also said of him that he was one of the most generous and single-hearted men—an impression perhaps enhanced by the fact that Story was an enthusiastic admirer of England and especially of its lawyers. He added, "I must admit one thing, when he was in the room few others could get in a word; but it was impossible to resent this, for he talked evidently not to bear down others, but because he could not help it."[12] Timothy Walker, a former law student and at the time of Story's death editor of the *Western Law Journal*, said of him:

> If ever the term *fascinating*, would be appropriate for a man, it might be applied to him. His conversational powers were unrivalled, and made him emphatically the centre of any circle in which he moved. He could be grave without tediousness, gay without frivolity, and witty without satire. His vivacity was inexhaustible. To see him when not at

---

[10] Joseph Story to John McLean, Aug. 16, 1844, McLean Papers.

[11] Quoted in Arthur M. Schlesinger, Jr., *The Age of Jackson*, 323, n. 4.

[12] From Lord Morpeth's *Travels in America* (1851), quoted in *Am. Legal Hist.*, 2:82, 1958.

work, one might suppose he never did work, so completely did he abandon himself to the spirit of the hour.[13]

As a man who turned out work in such great volume it is only natural that he was jealous of his time and careful with whom he spent it. A stimulating younger man whom he enjoyed and under whose editorship he wrote articles on legal topics for the *Encyclopedia Americana* was a German immigrant, Francis Lieber. "I can scarcely tell you," Story wrote to Lieber, "how much I wish that you lived at Cambridge. I should not even then (so constant are my occupations) see you often; but then I could catch a lazy hour and sit down and talk straight forward with you, on all you thought and wished. I want a mind that can stir my own."[14] It seems clear that he got much of this kind of stirring from his associations at Harvard. Like most of his neighbors, he was persuaded of the superiority of his region over any other part of the country, at least for living the intellectual life. "Boston," he wrote to Lieber, " is the proper place for a literary man."[15] He was a firm Unitarian.

All in all, ornament to the Supreme Court though he might be and was, it can be seen that Story would not merge with complete harmony into the newly evolving Taney Court.

Smith Thompson, James Monroe's only appointee to the Supreme Court, had no such distinguished career as that of Story. From 1802 until 1819 he was a member of the Supreme Court of New York, holding the chief justiceship from 1814 when James Kent left it to become chancellor. To accept the appointment to the United States Supreme Court in 1823, he resigned as Secretary of the Navy. He wrote no legal commentaries or other legal works outside his official opinions. He never became well known outside the state of New York, and the immediate circle of the Supreme Court itself and of the circuit which he served. He found it hard to surrender his interest in politics and even harder to give up his position on the Court. In 1828 he was responsible for an entry in the diary of Martin Van Buren with respect to the governorship of New York in which Van Buren said, "I was elected by a plurality of more than 30,000 over my quondam friend Smith Thompson, who was run for the office without resigning his seat on the Supreme Court."[16]

---

[13] [Timothy Walker], "Death of Judge Story," *West. L.J.*, 3:45, 1845.

[14] Joseph Story to Francis Lieber, Aug. 16, 1834, Lieber Papers.

[15] Joseph Story to Francis Lieber, July 28, 1834, Lieber Papers.

[16] "The Autobiography of Martin Van Buren," J. C. Fitzpatrick, ed., *Annual Report of the American Historical Association for the Year 1918*, 2:220, 1820.

III: *Personnel of the Taney Court*

As might be expected of a man with a restless and unsatisfied political ambition, Thompson did not surrender completely to the captivating personality of John Marshall. He indicated a states' rights leaning by differing from Marshall in *Ogden v. Saunders*,[17] *Brown v. Maryland*,[18] and *Craig v. Missouri*.[19] In these cases he took the position that a state might enact bankruptcy laws relieving from the obligations of future contracts, that it could tax imports upon arrival within its borders, and might issue small-denomination loan notes which circulated as money. And yet, joined by Justice Story, he also dissented in *Cherokee Nation v. Georgia*,[20] making a broader claim for the exercise of federal judicial power than the Chief Justice was willing to make.

As a political enemy of Van Buren, Andrew Jackson's first Secretary of State, it was but natural that Thompson should be suspicious of the Jackson Administration. In 1831 he confided his uneasiness to John Quincy Adams, expressing alarm for the fate of the judiciary and for the Bank of the United States, thinking with Adams that "the leading System of the present Administration is to resolve the Government of the Union into the national imbecility of the old Confederation."[21]

In the Taney Court as in the Court of John Marshall, Thompson was to tread an uneven path. There was something symbolic in the fact that when in 1837 Taney first joined his brethren as Chief Justice, Thompson, at age sixty-nine, appeared in Washington with a new wife, and found rooms for himself and his wife in a different roominghouse from that occupied by the other members of the Court, who had left their wives at home. Thereby he promoted fragmentation in the pattern of Supreme Court living in Washington, setting, along with Justice McLean, an example gradually to be followed by other members of the Court. He continued to live apart, though at times he had to make his Washington trips alone, becoming before his death in 1843 at nearly seventy-six years of age the father of three children in his new family.

Thompson was an active Presbyterian. It is said that he was small in stature and reserved in manner and speech, but kind and affable on close acquaintance.[22] Unlike Story's, Thompson's Circuit Court opinions were in general not published, although the varied legal business of the Second Circuit was highly important. His death was deplored by New York Whigs who feared his replacement at the hands of President John Tyler, since Tyler, they felt, had betrayed the party which had put him in office.[23]

---

[17] 12 Wheat. 213 (1827).
[18] 12 Wheat. 419 (1827).
[19] 4 Pet. 410 (1830).
[20] 5 Pet. 1 (1831).
[21] *Memoirs of John Quincy Adams*,
Charles F. Adams, ed., VIII, 304.
[22] Robert E. Cushman, "Smith Thompson," *D.A.B.*, 18:471–72, 1936.
[23] See Daniel Lord to J. J. Crittenden, Dec. 16, 1843, Crittenden Papers.

John McLean, who became a member of the Court in 1829, was the first of the Jackson appointees. He served until his death in 1860, only four years before the end of the Taney period. For all the length of his judicial service, however, he is known less for the quality and volume of his work on the Bench than for the fact that he was one of the most politically minded of all the Justices. Under the Adams Administration he had held the office of Postmaster General, thereby controlling a great deal of patronage, both in employment and in contracts for carrying mail. Concerned with the welfare of his department and perhaps with his own political future, he gave Adams no support in the election of 1828, after which the Jacksonians attempted to build him into the new Administration. According to his story as told in later years when he was courting a Presidential nomination from the Whigs, he told Jackson that he had done nothing to advance his interests but had given attention only to his official duties. Jackson approved McLean's past course but clearly expected that as a member of the Cabinet he would cooperate in the placement of loyal supporters. According to McLean, "[I]t was found before his administration commenced, that I could not take one step with them. The bench was offered to me and I accepted it. I censured the course of the administration, and was denounced from time to time by the Globe." He asserted that he had never knowingly or intentionally influenced any individual to vote for Jackson, and that he had never voted a Jackson ticket.[24]

McLean's Supreme Court appointment involved service also on the Seventh Circuit, which at that time consisted of Ohio, Kentucky, and Tennessee. Then and thereafter always an aspirant for the Presidency, he flirted variously with the Jackson supporters, Anti-Masons, Whigs, Free Soilers, Know-Nothings, and Republicans. His private correspondence contains a wealth of material on American political history, disclosing the maneuvering of groups for party dominance. McLean was an abolitionist, an opponent of the annexation of Texas and of the Mexican War, a temperance man, and an active Methodist. These interests reveal themselves both in his political activities and in his judicial performance.

Like Thompson and unlike Story, McLean had had judicial experience before his Supreme Court appointment. In 1816, when he was thirty-one, the Ohio legislature had elected him a member of the state supreme court, where like Justices of the Supreme Court of the United States he had to ride circuit. He served until 1822. There he disclosed a

---

[24] John McLean to John Teesdale, July 19, 1846; see also letters of Mar. 27, Sept. 26, and Dec. 17, 1846, McLean Papers (O.H.S.). See also Francis P. Weisenburger, *The Life of John McLean*, 66–67. The *Globe* here referred to was the Jackson party newspaper in Washington.

tendency toward long opinions, toward indulging in *obiter dicta*, and toward moralizing. Quoting from one of McLean's speeches from the bench, his biographer remarks, "On such occasions the Justice's role was approximating that of the Methodist lay preacher!"[25]

At the time of McLean's appointment to the Supreme Court, Justice Story, knowing the political background of the move, wrote that "it is a good and satisfactory appointment, but was, in fact, produced by other causes than his fitness, or our advantage."[26] A year later, having observed McLean on the Bench, Daniel Webster expressed the fear that he had "his head turned too much by politics."[27] But more and more during Story's lifetime, McLean moved in the direction of the Whig-Bank of the United States group to which Story and Webster belonged. His son Nathaniel studied law at Harvard, and thereby strengthened the bond between the two Justices. From 1837 onward Story found himself in more comfortable association with McLean than with any others of his brethren. It was primarily to McLean that he wrote lamenting the passing of the old order and the inferiority of the members of the new Court. Indeed, McLean as a Justice seems to have moved as far from the camp of Jackson, who had appointed him, as did Story from that of James Madison.

For all his preoccupation with politics, McLean carried a heavy load of professional work. The Seventh Circuit, which in 1837 was shifted to include Ohio, Indiana, Illinois, and Michigan, was in 1857 the most populous of all the circuits, with more than four million people.[28] For 1856 more cases were added to the docket and more were disposed of in McLean's circuit than in the five so-called Southern circuits put together, the Fourth, Fifth, Sixth, Eighth, and Ninth.[29] McLean gave much attention to the writing of Circuit Court opinions, in contrast particularly with those of his brethren whose Circuit opinions were usually not reported and were oftentimes never written out at all. He stood virtually alone among the Justices in that he compiled reports of his own opinions, of which six volumes were published.[30] Many of the cases dealt with strictly local matters, but others dealt with critical issues of federalism, the scope of the commerce power, and slavery. In the Supreme Court likewise he wrote a goodly share of the opinions dealing with the major issues of the times.

---

[25] Weisenburger, *The Life of John McLean*, 30.

[26] *Life and Letters of Joseph Story*, I, 564.

[27] Daniel Webster to Jeremiah Mason, Feb. 27, 1830, *Writings and Speeches of Daniel Webster*, XVII, 489.

[28] *Cong. Globe*, 34th Cong., 3rd Sess., 300 (1857).

[29] See chart, *Cong. Globe*, 36th Cong., 1st Sess., 367 (1860).

[30] Weisenburger, *The Life of John McLean*, 183. Justice Curtis also reported his own opinions for the brief period of his service on circuit.

There is no doubt that at Marshall's death McLean would have liked to succeed to the Chief Justiceship. He was of a stature such that the appointment would not have been inappropriate, though as viewed through hindsight it would not have been distinguished. By this time, however, he had drifted too far away from Jackson to hope for such recognition. Indeed, at a time when Taney's appointment was generally expected but before it had been officially made, McLean, ignoring the constitutional question as to the scope of the appointing power of the President, wished that a law might be passed automatically elevating the senior Associate Justice whenever a vacancy occurred in the higher position.[31] Such elevation at this time, of course, would have given the Chief Justiceship to Story.

McLean was at once formally hospitable and friendly, and withdrawn from the rank and file of the people. On the Supreme Court he chose intimacy of association with Justice Story as against general closeness to all the members of the Court. As early as 1834 he set a precedent for Thompson in bringing his wife to Washington for the term of the Court, a step he was to take with another wife in later years as the members of the Court grew further and further apart. He entertained powerful and influential people extensively, both in Washington and on the circuit. Yet his political instincts were probably less well developed than they needed to be for success in politics. At Cincinnati in the middle 1850s he entertained distinguished counsel for both sides of the important McCormick patent case but failed to include in his invitation a relatively unknown member of the group, Abraham Lincoln.[32] Salmon P. Chase, likewise of Ohio, who had much in common though no close friendship with McLean, expressed to his wife the wish that McLean "had a little warmer manners." An able lawyer had been received so coldly as to create the impression that he had incurred McLean's displeasure. Said Chase, "I told him I was sure the Judge had no such feeling as he supposed; for his manner even to those whom he loved best was not much warmer, than towards him. It is a thousand pities that a man of such real benevolence of heart as the Judge possesses, should not allow more of it to flow out into his manners."[33]

McLean was large and somewhat statuesque in appearance, with a visage and brow not unlike that of George Washington, whom he somewhat resembled also in his manner of aloofness. Like Webster, to whom he also had some facial resemblance, he had perennial financial difficulties, not so much from rich living as from the display of a

---

[31] Ibid., 158.
[32] Albert J. Beveridge, Abraham Lincoln, 1809–1858, I, 580.

[33] Salmon P. Chase to Mrs. Chase, July 24, 1847, Chase Papers.

48

generous hand to relatives and friends in financial need.[34] There seems to have been about him a suggestion of greatness never quite attained.[35] With the more sensitive aspects of his personality normally concealed behind a massive front, he sometimes revealed his inner feeling and convictions inadvertently in his judicial opinions, as when he said for the Supreme Court in 1839, "To break down or impair the great principles which protect the sanctities of husband and wife, would be to destroy the best solace of human existence."[36]

The appointment of Henry Baldwin of Pittsburgh in January, 1830, marked Jackson's second addition to the Supreme Court. A native of New Haven and a graduate of Yale College from which he received an LL.D. degree in 1830, Baldwin studied law in the office of Alexander J. Dallas in Philadelphia.[37] He began his practice in the courts of the cities and counties of western Pennsylvania, engaged in various speculative businesses, and participated in politics. He gave vigorous support to Jackson in 1828. He and his friends were disappointed that the position of Secretary of the Treasury went not to Baldwin but to Calhoun's friend, Samuel D. Ingham of the same state, but they regarded the Supreme Court appointment as a victory over Calhoun, or at any rate over Duff Green, editor of the *United States Telegraph*, which became the Calhoun paper in Washington, and who had denounced Baldwin in his columns.[38] Apart from the matter of personal conflicts, the issues involved included attitudes toward the protective tariff, which Calhoun was fighting and on which the Jackson Administration had not taken a clear position. Baldwin's leanings were at least more protective than were those of the Calhoun group. Although the nomination was confirmed by a vote of forty to two, it was said that "many of the Jacksonians are very sore about Baldwin's appointment."[39] Daniel Webster, on the other hand, was pleased. He wrote, "This is another escape. We had given up all hope of anything but Chief Justice Gibson's[40] nomination. Mr. Baldwin is supposed to be, substantially, a *sound* man, and he is undoubtedly a man of some talents."[41]

---

[34] Weisenburger, *The Life of John McLean*, 225–26.

[35] *Ibid.*, 226–27.

[36] Stein v. Bowman, 13 Pet. 209, 223 (1839).

[37] Daniel Agnew, "Address to the Allegheny County Bar Association, December 1, 1888," *Pennsylvania Magazine of History and Biography*, 13:23, 1888.

[38] See "S. H. Jenks to Francis Baylies, Jan. 7, 1830," *Massachusetts Historical Society Proceedings*, 46: 337, 1913.

[39] "John Bailey to John Brazer Davis, Jan. 7, 1830," *Massachusetts Historical Society Proceedings*, 49: 218, 1916.

[40] John B. Gibson of the Pennsylvania Supreme Court.

[41] Daniel Webster to Jeremiah Mason, Jan. 6, 1830, *Writings and Speeches of Daniel Webster*, XVII, 192, 1903.

Justice Baldwin was not to be classified either with Marshall and Story or with people of Jacksonian sentiments who were in time to dominate the Court. He regarded Justice Story as too much imbued with civil law prejudices and was particularly opposed to the infusion of equity into American law and the curtailment of resort to juries.[42] He must have horrified Justice Story with his charge to a jury that "you have the power to decide on the law as well as the facts of this case, and are not bound to find according to our opinion of the law,"[43] even with the added statement that if the court disagreed with the jury as to the law when voting to convict, it might order a new trial.

At the 1831 term of the Supreme Court Justice Baldwin seems to have taken offense at the majority and at the Reporter for the handling of the *Cherokee Nation* case, in which the Supreme Court had been asked by the Cherokees to curb the interference of Georgia with their rights on the Indian reservation. In that case Chief Justice Marshall, speaking for a majority of the Court, held that the Cherokees had no right to sue in the Supreme Court in the exercise of its original jurisdiction and that therefore no relief could be granted. He did, however, express sympathy with the predicament of the Indians and indicate disapproval of the alleged invasion of their rights, an invasion which had the support of the Jackson Administration, by adding, "If it be true that wrongs have been inflicted, and that still greater are to be apprehended, this is not the tribunal which can redress the past or prevent the future."[44] Justice Baldwin wrote a concurring opinion avoiding all expression of sympathy for the Indians and any suggestion that their rights were being violated. But Richard Peters, Reporter of the Court, gave further offense to the Jacksonians and evidently also to Baldwin by publishing the case in a separate pamphlet, along with, in his own words, "Mr. Wirt's great argument in behalf of the Cherokees, which had been taken down by stenographers employed for the purpose." This action convinced the Jacksonians that the Court and the Reporter were engaging in political pamphleteering in opposition to the Administration.[45]

At the end of the term Justice Baldwin evidently left in deep disgust at the performance of his brethren and notified the President of his intention to resign after completion of his work on circuit.[46] By October, however, he seems to have changed his mind. Marshall, visiting his physician in Philadelphia, saw Baldwin there and remarked to Story, "He seems to have resumed the dispositions which impressed

---

[42] "The Late Mr. Justice Baldwin," *Pa. L.J.*, 6:8–9, 1846.

[43] United States v. Wilson, 28 Fed. Cas. 699, 712 (No. 16730) (C.C.E.D. Pa. 1830).

[44] Cherokee Nation v. Georgia, 5 Pet. 1, 20 (1831).

[45] "The Autobiography of Martin Van Buren," *Annual Report of the American Historical Association for the Year 1918*, 2:291–92 (1820).

[46] *Ibid.*, 578.

50

us both so favorably at the first term. This is as it should be. He spoke of you in terms not indicating unfriendliness."[47] In November he wrote, "Our brother Baldwin has called on me frequently. He is in good health and spirits, and I, always sanguine, hope that the next term will exhibit dispositions more resembling those displayed in the first than the last."[48]

If human relations on the Court got better, matters got worse for Baldwin in a personal way. Harassed by debts he was unable to pay, his conduct gave rise to reports in 1832 and 1833 that he was insane.[49] He was absent from the term of the Supreme Court beginning in January, 1833. In April he wrote to a business friend, "As my situation makes all my little money concerns dependent on the receipt of my salary as it becomes due a delay of even a few days is a matter of no small inconvenience to me."[50]

Financial difficulties continued throughout the remainder of his life. Delivery to the press in 1836 of a volume of reports for the Third Circuit, consisting of Pennsylvania and New Jersey, was probably calculated in part to relieve that distress. That volume, however, covering only the years 1828 to 1833, and listed as Volume 1, was never followed by another. In 1837, in part to set forth his own constitutional doctrines but evidently also to raise money, he published a small book entitled *A General View of the Origin and Nature of the Constitution and Government of the United States, Deduced from the Political History of the Colonies and States, from 1774 until 1788, and the Decisions of the Supreme Court of the United States, together with Opinions in the Cases Decided at January Term, 1837, Arising on the Restraints on the Powers of the States*. It was a novel experiment for a member of the Supreme Court to write a book expounding upon his views in cases decided by the Court and to market it for profit. It seems improbable that the venture paid well. With the aid of Richard Peters, the Reporter, he allocated one hundred copies to be sold at auction to help with the cost of publication. These copies sold at only about seventy cents each, thereby compelling reduction in the price of the remaining copies.[51]

More serious than this disappointment was the fact that Justice Baldwin had to raise money on his personal library, said to have been a very fine collection. His friends, unwilling to see him lose it through

[47] "John Marshall to Joseph Story, Oct. 12, 1831," *Massachusetts Historical Society Proceedings*, 2nd series, 347, 1901.

[48] "John Marshall to Joseph Story, Nov. 10, 1831," *Massachusetts Historical Society Proceedings*, 2nd series, 348.

[49] Daniel Webster to Joseph Story, Dec. 27, 1832, *Massachusetts Historical Society Proceedings*, 2nd series, 354, n. 1, and *Richmond Enquirer*, Jan. 5, 1833.

[50] Henry Baldwin to Richard Smith, April 5, 1833, Conarroe Collection (H.S.P.).

[51] Henry Baldwin to John Cadwalader, Dec. 19, 1838, Cadwalader Papers.

irrevocable sale, raised money on it and took charge of it but held the books in such a way that Baldwin could have continuing use of it. Matters grew worse, however, rather than better. His son, an attorney, also got into financial trouble, and brought his family home for support. By June, 1842, Justice Baldwin had decided to clear the record by selling the books outright. He made arrangements for sales, including allotments to the Library of Congress as books were selected by Chief Justice Taney, who annually made recommendations of purchases of law books.[52] Baldwin wrote:

> The Ch. Justice has agreed to purchase for the library of Congress such as are not there, & duplicates for the conference room to the amount of the unappropriated balance now on hand, say 900. He has made a selection of what would be wanted at all events, & will make out a list of others when he has time to examine the catalogue of those on hand.[53]

Justice Baldwin was of sturdy build and some five feet ten inches tall, with a dark complexion and a round, agreeable face. Like Chief Justice Taney, he was addicted to smoking black Spanish cigars. Debarred from smoking while on the bench, he was apt to grow restless, inattentive, and petulant.[54] When sitting as a circuit judge he sometimes had coffee and cakes brought to him on the bench. Since he often carried candy in his pockets, which he freely gave to children,[55] it is to be suspected that even in his position on the Supreme Court candy sometimes assuaged his hunger for forbidden cigars. He died of paralysis on April 21, 1844, at the age of sixty-four. His friends raised money to pay his funeral expenses.

---

[52] Daniel Agnew, "Address to the Allegheny County Bar Association," *Pennsylvania Magazine of History and Biography*, 13:25, 1888.

[53] Henry Baldwin to John Cadwalader, June 18, 1842, Cadwalader Papers.

Baldwin's financial difficulties may have promoted the somewhat frenetic character of some of his judicial opinions. To mention of this subject Chief Justice Taney replied, "I am not surprised at the temper of Judge Baldwin's opinions, and it is difficult to say what is best to be done. In his unhappy state of mind I am most unwilling to do any thing that would give him pain. But the evil will grow as the infirmity grows upon him and the reports of the Court will every year become more and more mortifying to those who wish to maintain the decorum of judicial proceedings. It will I fear be necessary before long to take some step to guard the tribunal from misconstruction." R B. Taney to Richard Peters, June 3, 1840, Peters Correspondence, II, Cadwalader Papers. The records do not show whether any attempt at restraint was actually made.

[54] David Paul Brown, *The Forum: or Forty Years Full Practice at the Philadelphia Bar*, II, 80–81.

[55] Agnew, "Address to the Allegheny County Bar Association," *Pennsylvania Magazine of History and Biography*, 13:27–28, 1888.

III: *Personnel of the Taney Court*

When Roger B. Taney first met with his brethren in January, 1837, the most recently appointed of his senior associates was James M. Wayne of Georgia, who had taken his seat two years earlier as the successor to Justice William Johnson. Born in Savannah, Georgia, in 1790, Wayne graduated from the College of New Jersey at Princeton in 1808, and began the study of law in Savannah under John Y. Noel, but upon the death of his father he was sent in 1809 to New Haven for study under Judge Charles Chauncy. He returned to Savannah early in 1811 to begin his practice, which was interrupted by the War of 1812, in which he served as an officer. Thereafter he served as a member of the state legislature and as mayor of Savannah, moving steadily upward in political influence and in mastery of his profession. His judicial experience began in 1819 when the legislature elected him judge of the Court of Common Pleas for the City of Savannah, and in 1822 he was transferred to the Superior Court for the Eastern District, where he served until his election to Congress in 1829.[56]

Wayne's experience in politics probably had much more to do with his Supreme Court appointment than did his previous judicial experience. Georgia was, of course, the neighbor state of South Carolina, where John C. Calhoun had been planting the seeds of nullification as a means of warring against the protective tariff. Georgia also had its nullificationists, but Wayne belonged to the group who had followed William H. Crawford, Calhoun's Georgia rival, and who, for all their preoccupation with states' rights were nevertheless Unionist in sentiment. In Congress from 1829 until his appointment to the Supreme Court in 1835, Wayne favored tariff reduction but he was also emphatically against nullification. In May, 1830, writing to Justice McLean, he found the political atmosphere better than when McLean had been in Washington, saying that even the Vice President, Calhoun, talked but cautiously of nullification and those who were with him now advocated it with so many modifications that it had lost most of its meaning.[57] When Calhoun resigned as Vice President and went back into the Senate to push the nullification issue, Jackson countered with the so-called Force Bill, along with a compromise modification of the tariff. Wayne voted for both measures.

In 1832 Wayne showed himself in harmony with the sentiments of Jackson with respect to getting Indian tribes out of the way of the exercise of white jurisdiction. When in *Worcester v. Georgia*[58] the Supreme Court held unconstitutional a Georgia law restricting the

---

[56] For the fullest account of Wayne's life see Alexander A. Lawrence, *James Moore Wayne, Southern Unionist*.

[57] James M. Wayne to John Mc-Lean, May 29, 1830, McLean Papers.
[58] 6 Pet. 515 (1832).

53

authority exercised by the Indians, much to the resentment of the President, Wayne, in Washington, consulted with Taney, who was then Attorney General. Wayne wrote to Georgia's Governor Wilson Lumpkin of his very satisfactory conversation with Taney, saying that Taney thought Georgia's proceedings entirely constitutional and was prepared to defend them if the Court called on the President to enforce its order. Wayne already knew the President's position but he had sought assurance that Jackson and his legal adviser were thinking in harmony.[59]

Finally, and perhaps most important from a political point of view, Wayne supported Jackson and Taney throughout the struggle with the Bank of the United States. In 1833 and 1834 there was no more precise test of loyalty to the Jackson Administration.

It is said that when Justice William Johnson died, in August, 1834, Whig leaders feared that Jackson might nominate Taney, who had been rejected a few weeks earlier for Secretary of the Treasury, even though the judicial circuit involved was the Sixth (South Carolina and Georgia), far away from Taney's home in Baltimore.[60] However that may be— and we know that more in mind for Taney was his home circuit, the Fourth, then held by Justice Duvall—Jackson waited until the following January, a few days before the Duvall resignation, to fill the Johnson vacancy. Since Johnson came from South Carolina, that state, largely dominated by John C. Calhoun, hoped for a local nomination. It had Whig candidates, who might have had trouble gaining the support of Calhoun and hence getting confirmation, in view of the practice of "Senatorial courtesy," and it had Democrats of the Calhoun stamp who were infected with the virus of nullification. When Jackson chose Wayne, a Unionist from Georgia, the Whigs sensed that from their point of view the nomination might have been much worse, and they refrained from opposing it. Webster, it is true, said privately that he would not regard it as a first-rate appointment, adding, "He is gentlemanly and amiable in private life, and respectable in general character; fitter I should think, for Speaker of the House of Representatives than for a Judge of the Supreme Court."[61] Receiving the sanction of the Senate, Wayne immediately left the hall of the House of Representatives on the main floor of the south end of the Capitol for the Supreme Court room on the basement floor of the north end.

Wayne's period of service on the Court spanned the entire Taney period, running to the time of his death in 1867. He remained a Unionist throughout his life, and during the Civil War abandoned his

---

[59] Lawrence, *James Moore Wayne*, 61–62.

[60] Charles Warren, *The Supreme Court in United States History*, II, 794.

[61] Daniel Webster to Warren Dutton, Dec. 18, 1834, Webster Papers (Dartmouth).

home in Savannah for residence in Washington. He defended the legal rights of slaveowners but was at no time a rabid proslavery man. In such matters as the scope of the commerce power of Congress he took the position that it was exclusive as against the states, yet he found in the police powers of the states sufficient authority for coping with local race problems. He was apparently highly influential in the councils of the Court, finding there outlet for most of his political energies, instead of engaging in maneuvering for the Presidency, as did his colleague McLean. Wayne was essentially politically minded, however, and McLean was sometimes irritated at his "caucusing" for management of procedures and making decisions within the Court.[62] He was handsome, courtly, and convivial. When eventually the Justices began as a matter of course to bring their wives to Washington, the Waynes took a prominent part in the social life of the capital. They had many friends and associations in the North as well as in the South. Their son, Henry Constantine Wayne, spent two years at Harvard and then went to West Point. He served in the armed forces of the United States, and later, like many other Southerners trained at West Point, served in the forces of the Confederacy.

Justice Wayne wrote no legal commentaries or other books or articles. He did not compile his Circuit Court opinions, and they are in general not available. His official public record is almost exclusively in the United States Reports. His personal papers seem not to have been preserved. Personal letters are scattered in collections throughout the country, but they are in general unrevealing as to his views on judicial institutions and the development of American law, and for illegibility they are exceeded only by those of Reverdy Johnson of Baltimore.

Philip P. Barbour of Virginia, who was nominated and confirmed along with Taney, was born May 25, 1783. Little is known of his formal education or of his preliminary training in the law. It is said that he went to Kentucky to begin practice while still in his teens, returned to spend a year at the College of William and Mary, and settled down in Orange County to a life of agriculture, politics, and law.[63] Senator Thomas Hart Benton wrote of him:

> Judge Barbour was a Virginia country gentleman, after the most perfect model of that most respectable class—living on his ample estate, baronially, with his family, his slaves, his flocks and herds—all well

---

[62] John McLean to Joseph Story, Jan. 26 and Mar. 14, 1843, Story Papers.

[63] The account written by Dumas Malone, "Philip H. Barbour," *Dic-tionary of American Biography*, I, 595–96, is more than usually full for treatment in that source, and is one of the few good summary accounts.

cared for by himself, and happy in his care. A farmer by position, a lawyer by profession, a politician of course—dividing his time between his estate, his library, his professional, and his public duties—scrupulously attentive to his duties in all: and strict in that school of politics of which Mr. Jefferson, Mr. Madison, John Taylor of Caroline, Mr. Monroe, Mr. Macon, and others, were the great exemplars.[64]

Linn Banks, a Congressman from Virginia, said of him at the time of his death in 1841, "He was a kind, tender, and affectionate husband, father, and friend, and a humane master."[65]

After a term in the Virginia House of Delegates, Barbour served in Congress from 1814 to 1825. He was Speaker from 1821 to 1823, losing the office thereafter to Henry Clay. In 1825 he was appointed to the General Court of Virginia, but returned to Congress in 1827. He was a member of the Virginia constitutional convention of 1829–1830, and was elected president after James Monroe proved unable to serve. In 1830 he was appointed United States District Judge for the Eastern District of Virginia, where in the United States Circuit Court he sat with Chief Justice Marshall.

In political theory, Barbour stood at the opposite poles from the nationalism of Marshall. He was opposed to internal improvements financed by the federal government. As early as 1827 he disclosed hostility to the Bank of the United States by proposing that the government dispose of its stock in the Bank.[66] His desire to restrict the jurisdiction of the Supreme Court, as indicated in his argument in *Cohens v. Virginia*,[67] represented a deep personal conviction and not merely a position taken for the purpose of winning a case. In 1829 he supported a bill to require the concurrence of five out of seven Supreme Court judges for the decision of constitutional questions, saying that such a measure was necessary to allay popular discontent with the Court.[68] Sensing the popularity of Barbour and of his views, John Quincy Adams dreaded the death of Chief Justice Marshall: "The terror is, that if he should now be withdrawn some shallow-pated wild-cat like Philip P. Barbour, fit for nothing but to tear the Union to rags and tatters, would be appointed in his place."[69]

A critic more analytical and less denunciatory than Adams noted

---

[64] Thomas H. Benton, *Thirty Years' View*, II, 203.

[65] *Cong. Globe*, 26th Cong. 2nd Sess. 209 (1841).

[66] Edward Everett to Nicholas Biddle, Dec. 13, 1827, Reginald C. McGrane, ed., *The Correspondence of Nicholas Biddle Dealing with National Affairs, 1807–1844*, 44.

[67] 6 Wheat. 264 (1821).

[68] Warren, *The Supreme Court in United States History*, I, 717.

[69] *Memoirs of John Quincy Adams*, VIII, 315–16.

that logical acuteness was the distinguishing characteristic of Barbour's mind:

> No man could reason from premises to conclusions with more unerring certainty, or was less liable to be diverted from his path by the chicanery of an adversary. The view which he took of a subject was never very broad, but it was always strong, and he maintained it with an ability corresponding with its natural strength. He was a most formidable adversary in argument. . . . If there was any fault to be found with the material of his public speeches, it may be said to have consisted in an inveterate habit of refining. The peculiar structure of his mind, and the skill which long habit had imparted, in handling the weapon of logic, no doubt led him into this error. From indulging in it too freely, he sometimes took what the law-books call "a distinction without a difference," and wandered through all the mazes of metaphysics, lost himself and his hearers, in a cloud of abstractions.[70]

But if in formal address Barbour pushed logical distinctions to the point of wearisome sterility, he was attractive and skillful in human relations. Even after his appointment as United States District Judge, his political friends were unwilling to permit him to retreat into judicial obscurity. In May, 1832, the Virginia delegation to the Democratic convention in Baltimore, headed by Peter V. Daniel and William H. Roane, cast its twenty-three votes for Barbour for Vice President.[71] On the Supreme Court he exercised his capacity for good human relations and came to be well liked by all members, even including those who disagreed with his states' rights views. When he died of a heart attack on February 25, 1841, at the age of fifty-eight, Justice Story wrote of him:

> He was a man of great integrity, of a very solid and acute understanding, of considerable legal attainments, (in which he was daily improving,) and altogether a very consciencious, upright, and laborious Judge, whom we all respected for his talents and virtues, and his high sense of duty.[72]

If he had lived to a more advanced age he would have exerted considerable influence on the work of the Court, helping to bend it in the direction of a states' rights emphasis, but doing so judiciously. As it

---

[70] Hugh R. Pleasants, "Sketches of the Virginia Convention of 1829–30," *Southern Literary Messenger*, 17:298–99, 1851.

[71] Joseph Hobson Harrison, Jr., "Martin Van Buren and His Southern Supporters," *Journal of Southern History*, 22:455, 1956.

[72] Story, *Life and Letters of Joseph Story*, II, 349–50.

happened, the story of the restrictive influence of Virginia sentiment must be followed out in terms of his more extreme successor, Peter V. Daniel.

The sketches presented above include the six colleagues with whom Chief Justice Taney met at his first term of the Supreme Court in January, 1837. It was obvious that the demands of Western states for judicial service comparable to that given to the older states would soon have to be met, as the admission of Arkansas in 1836 and of Michigan in 1837 brought to a total of eight the states not given such service. It will be recalled that in 1835 the Senate had passed a bill merging the Third and Fourth Judicial Circuits and transferring one judgeship to the West and creating another, to bring the total number of Justices to eight. The House of Representatives, however, after debating the bill, had failed to act on it. Then, in 1836, the Senate had passed a similar bill except that the circuits merged were the Fourth and Fifth, but again the House of Representatives failed to act. In the meantime, confirmation of the appointments of Taney of Maryland and Barbour of Virginia had rendered the Senate bill anomalous if the circuits were to be served, as hitherto, by Justices residing within their respective borders.

Finally, at the next session of Congress, beginning in December, 1836, Senator Felix Grundy of Tennessee introduced another bill providing for two additional circuits in the West without the merging of any circuits and therefore bringing the total number to nine. The bill passed the Senate on February 15 and the House of Representatives on March 3, 1837. The debates on the subject and the votes in the two houses were left unpublished. It seems clear, however, that such controversy as the bill aroused had to do not with the increase in the number of circuits and Justices to the unprecedented number of nine but with the drawing of the lines among the Western circuits. The states hitherto excluded from circuits were Alabama, Mississippi, Louisiana, Arkansas, Missouri, Illinois, Indiana, and Michigan. These states would seem to divide into two circuits, one in the North and the other in the South. But with the passing years regional divisions were becoming more and more sensitive matters, and Southern statesmen were, of course, not averse to collecting both Supreme Court judgeships. Furthermore, there was a more localized regional interest in the matter. The state of Tennessee now had as President of the United States, Andrew Jackson; as Speaker of the House of Representatives, James K. Polk; and as chairman of the Judiciary Committee of the Senate, Felix Grundy. Tennessee was quite willing to provide a Justice but was embarrassed by the fact that it was now included with Ohio and Kentucky in the Seventh Circuit, which was the province of Justice McLean. As early as 1826 a plan had been worked out to include Ohio in a new Eighth Circuit consisting of Ohio, Indiana, and Illinois, with the expectation, indeed, that McLean would be appointed by President Adams to head the new circuit. But Martin Van Buren, then chairman of the House Judiciary Committee, saw injury to his own political interests in the proposed move, and brought about changes in the 1826 bill which resulted in its defeat.[73] Now, in 1837, Van Buren's friends in Tennessee found themselves embarrassed by his earlier maneuver.

Prominent in the councils of the Jackson group in Tennessee was John Catron of Nashville, who until recently had been chief justice of the state Supreme Court. Because of the part here played by Catron, and because, more important, his career on the Supreme Court of the United States was to overlap virtually the entire Taney period, his biography has special significance for the story of the Court. It is thought that he was born about 1781 in Pennsylvania into a family of German-Swiss extraction named Kettenring. In translation into English the name was modified to Kettering and to various other forms, and during the days of his youth the future judge and other members of the family adopted the spelling of Catron. In any event, John Catron spent his boyhood on a farm in Virginia and then moved westward into Kentucky and then into Tennessee where, largely self-trained, he began the practice of law, having been admitted to the bar shortly after a campaign under General Andrew Jackson. Rough, strong, and vigorous, Catron took care of himself well on the Tennessee frontier. In part, he said in his own account of his life, as a result of his army popularity, the legislature named him attorney for the government in his part of the state. With the aid of hard work, a judge with a penchant for convictions, and "an arrogance that would have done credit to Castlereagh," he developed into a successful prosecutor.[74]

In 1818 Catron moved to Nashville where he was the unwitting beneficiary of the panic of 1819, which filled the courts with thousands of causes, and where ambition and industry made him a most successful lawyer. As was so often the case in frontier states, the land laws of Tennessee were in a state of confusion. Grants had been made without adequate records in earlier years when land had little value. As it increased in value, the grants became worth fighting for. Catron made himself an expert in the law and the facts of overlapping and imper-

---

[73] Curtis Nettels, "The Mississippi Valley and the Federal Judiciary, 1807–1837," *Mississippi Valley Historical Review*, 12:202–222, 1925.

[74] For Catron's own account of his life see "Biographical Letter from Judge Catron," *U.S. Monthly L. Mag.*, 5:145, 1852. The quotation is on p. 148. For other accounts see Josephus C. Guild, *Old Times in Tennessee*, 459–61, and William Chandler, *The Centenary of Associate Justice John Catron of the United States Supreme Court.*

fectly recorded grants and, often more important, possession acquired by virtue of occupancy and not traceable to any grant at all. He became a master in the field of the action of ejectment. At a time when, it is said, title to virtually half the state depended on judicial interpretation, a vacancy occurred on the highest court of the state, the personnel of which were chosen by the legislature. Knowing Catron's commitment to confirmation of titles to land long held by the same parties whatever the defects of records of origins of grants, the legislature put him on the court, where he served from 1824 until 1835, in the position of chief justice for the last six of those years.

In the early 1820s Catron and the rising young Tennessee politician James K. Polk married young women from the locally prominent Childress family. The two women were not sisters but they were lifelong friends, socially minded and with an instinct for politics. Eventually they became two of the shrewdest observers in Washington. In earlier years each advanced the cause of her husband and aided in keeping the two men together.[75] Both Catron and Polk made early commitments to the cause of Andrew Jackson. As supporters of Jackson they supported also Martin Van Buren, who became one of the leading lieutenants in the Jackson Administration and eventually Jackson's choice for his successor.

From the beginning of the Jackson Administration it was apparent that the recharter of the Bank of the United States might become one of the critical issues. Never one to shy away from political issues because of the judicial position he held, Catron in 1829 published in a Nashville paper a series of letters in which he denounced the Nashville branch of the Bank of the United States for its inflationary loans, for usurious interest collections, and for draining away from the state large sums of money. He noted the issue of the recharter of the Bank, and the fact that it permeated Tennessee politics in that those who were elected to the state legislature would select the United States Senators from Tennessee, who, in turn, would participate in the decision on the recharter.[76]

If on the bank issue Catron was attempting to lead as much as to follow Jackson, he tried very hard to be a loyal follower on the issue of nullification. On December 10, 1832, Jackson delivered his ringing proclamation in reply to the Nullification Ordinance of South Carolina.[77] Great excitement raged in the border states, including Tennessee. Governor William Carroll, loyal to Jackson, asked Catron to draw up resolutions for a meeting to be called in support of the proclamation.

[75] See Charles G. Sellers, *James K. Polk, Jacksonian, 1795–1843*, 94.
[76] St. George L. Sioussat, "Some Phases of Tennessee Politics in the Jackson Period," *American Historical Review*, 14:51, 64–65, 1908.
[77] J. D. Richardson, *A Compilation of the Messages and Papers of the Presidents*, II, 640.

After the meeting Catron wrote to Jackson of the adoption of the resolutions "without a dissenting voice." They denied the right of nullification and of secession, approved the doctrines maintained by the President's proclamation, and, for some reason not apparent, used the occasion to defend the right of the Supreme Court to pass on the constitutionality of Acts of Congress.

Catron thought these principles would not be seriously questioned in Tennessee but promised in any event to do what he could to sustain them. He thought that if real trouble developed, however, it should be met with overwhelming military force:

> I take it for granted the main object of the proclamation was to inspire moral courage—to fix determination, preparatory to action in the field. I state these views not to obtrude opinions, but because I am shaping my conduct to them; and because, a man situated as I am, is intimately acquainted over the State, especially with the lawyers, and his opinions have from this situation, something of weight, on subjects involving the powers of government.[78]

Such a position, no doubt taken in good faith even though Catron showed anxiety that he should not be "mistaken as to the view of the Executive," could be expected further to entrench Catron in Jackson's estimation as a sound statesman. So also could Catron's opinion in *State v. Foreman*,[79] which was decided at the July term of the Tennessee court in 1835, at around the time of Chief Justice Marshall's death. It had to do with the power of Tennessee to punish an Indian for murder committed on an Indian reservation within the state, and Catron's opinion was admittedly written with the strategy of getting the Supreme Court, on writ of error, to modify the position taken in *Worcester v. Georgia*, which had so upset Jackson. Catron sent a copy of his opinion to Van Buren, asking him to read it and "see if any Jeffersonian doctrine be violated—and say to me as a lawyer, whether my view of the Constitution meets yours."[80] Although a writ of error was issued under the hand of Justice Catron[81] and a citation served on the governor of Tennessee, and although the documents were sent to the Supreme Court, the case was never argued there—rumor has it that the prisoner escaped in the meantime—but if anything was needed to establish Catron's political orthodoxy with the Administration, this end was achieved.

At this time President Jackson, although enjoying his fullest

---

[78] John Catron to Andrew Jackson, Jan. 2, 1833, Jackson Papers.
[79] 16 Tenn. (8 Yerger) 256 (1835).
[80] John Catron to Martin Van Buren, Dec. 12, 1835, Van Buren Papers.
[81] It was marked as received Jan. 1, 1836. Clerk's Files.

popularity throughout the country, was losing his grip on politics in his home state of Tennessee. His methods were assailed as high-handed, his choice of officeholders made enemies among state leaders, and many of the latter opposed his plan to turn over the Presidency to Martin Van Buren of New York. It was believed that if Tennessee could provide one President, it could also provide another, and a group of powerful and dissident leaders began to back a local candidate, Hugh Lawson White.[82] This struggle reached even into the state constitutional convention of 1834. The new constitution reconstructed the state judiciary. In 1835, when the state supreme court was reconstituted, Catron, who with Polk and Grundy had stood by Jackson and Van Buren, found himself unemployed. He returned to private practice but gave much of his time to the Van Buren campaign for the Presidency, writing editorials and engaging in the general management of the *Nashville Union*, the paper of the Jackson forces, whose alcohol-imbibing editor, Samuel H. Laughlin, kept the local Jacksonians in despair.[83] Van Buren won the election even though he did not carry Tennessee. Catron had suffered in behalf of the victors, and Jackson and Van Buren were not men to permit their friends to go unrewarded, or at any rate to incur punishment from their enemies.

In November, 1836, after the election, Catron wrote to Polk, Speaker of the House of Representatives, not merely about the problem of operating the *Nashville Union* but also about the arrangement of federal judicial circuits. Catron hoped that either Polk or Grundy would consult with Justice McLean about the feasibility of rearranging the Seventh Circuit to permit Tennessee to be grouped with one of the new circuits. He thought McLean would prefer Indiana to Tennessee as one of the member states. Any of the states bordering on the Ohio, Catron suggested, would be more accessible by water travel than would Tennessee to a Justice traveling from Ohio.[84]

The Tennessee Jacksonians worked carefully with Catron's strategy and interests in mind. Finally, on the last day of the session on March 3, 1837, apparently toward the end of the day, the bill received from the Senate was passed by the House of Representatives and sent to the President for signature. The measure recast the Seventh Circuit so that it included not Ohio, Kentucky, and Tennessee, but Ohio, Indiana, Illinois, and Michigan. In the new Eighth Circuit were placed Kentucky, Tennessee, and Missouri. Finally, in the new Ninth Circuit were Alabama, Mississippi, Louisiana, and Arkansas.[85] The President signed

---

[82] See Powell Moore, *The Revolt Against Jackson in Tennessee, 1835–1836*, 335.

[83] See for example John Catron to James K. Polk, Sept. 6, 1836, Polk Papers.

[84] John Catron to James K. Polk, Nov. 24, 1836, Polk Papers.

[85] 5 Stat. 176.

the bill and at the very end of the day, or beyond it, submitted for the Eighth Circuit the name of John Catron of Tennessee and for the Ninth Circuit William Smith of Alabama.[86]

In the meantime Catron had gone to Washington for his first appearance as counsel before the Supreme Court, and had been admitted by Chief Justice Taney on January 19, 1837, the date on which the argument in the famous *Charles River Bridge Case* was begun. During the term he argued two cases. One was an ejectment case from Tennessee,[87] which he won, and the other was an admiralty case from New Orleans, which he lost.[88] There is an apocryphal story that Catron was a modest man satisfied with his lot who was hurried by his aggressive wife to Washington, where alone she braved Old Hickory in his home to ask for the Supreme Court position for her husband, whereupon the President declared that "By the Eternal" he would make the appointment.[89] Such a proceeding does not seem out of character with what is known of Mrs. Catron, but it hardly comports with her husband's temperament. He was ambitious and aggressive and by no means inclined to hold himself back. In the disparaging words of Justice McLean, he was "full of himself."[90] He did not require a wife's intercession.

So late was the hour of submission of the two nominations that action on them had to be postponed. The Senate reached them only on March 8, at the session called to act on executive nominations to be submitted by the new President, Martin Van Buren. Van Buren could, of course, have recalled the nominations and submitted others, but it seems clear that with respect to them he and Jackson were in full accord. The Catron nomination was confirmed by a vote of twenty-eight to fifteen and that of Smith by a vote of twenty-eight to eighteen. "And what judges they will make!" expostulated Henry Clay.[91]

It was said of Catron that he was a well-proportioned man of swarthy complexion, with black eyes and features indicative of intelligence, industry, and purpose, one who might be expected "to paddle his own canoe and ask no favors."[92] A St. Louis lawyer who saw a great deal of Catron on circuit issued to a wealthy but not too level-headed widow a warning against taking advice from the judge, saying that he was a "monstrous old humbug" and a "time serving old sensualist."[93]

---

[86] For the statement that the nominations were actually submitted after midnight on this last day of the session, see *Delaware State Journal* (Wilmington), Mar. 14, 1837.

[87] Poole v. Fleeger, 13 Pet. 185 (1837).

[88] Steamboat *Orleans* v. Phoebus, 11 Pet. 175 (1837).

[89] Rufus Rockwell Wilson, *Washington: The Capital City*, I, 314–15.

[90] John McLean to Joseph Story, Sept. 12, 1837, Story Papers.

[91] Henry Clay to Francis S. Brooks, Mar. 7, 1837, Clay Papers.

[92] Guild, *Old Times in Tennessee*, 459.

[93] Thomas T. Gantt to Mrs. Lisinka Brown, June 29, 1855, Brown-Ewell Papers.

There was no extensive newspaper comment at the time of the appointment. One article stated, "He is a well-informed, industrious man, and a tolerably good lawyer, but not exactly the person to be put on the bench of the Supreme Court. He is, however, a favorite of the Hero—that is enough!"[94] The *Nashville Union*, which Catron had helped to edit during the Van Buren campaign, gloated over the political victory and said that Jackson had paid a compliment to Tennessee which would prove highly satisfactory to the people.[95]

During his term of service from 1837 to 1865, Catron engaged in no extra-judicial legal writing. His Circuit Court opinions were for the most part not published. On the Supreme Court a large portion of the opinions assigned to him dealt with the diverse body of land laws on which he was an expert. In the midst of his first term he wrote to Jackson, now in retirement at the Hermitage, that the Court presented few of the difficulties he had apprehended. The legal questions here, as elsewhere, depended more on common sense than on any deep legal knowledge. He had had difficulty only with legal problems arising under the peculiar system of law of Louisiana, and there his brethren were equally without knowledge. Division on the Supreme Court, he remarked, was just as natural as in the Senate, and almost as common. He thought it most strange that the West had not sooner realized the need for representation on the Court—"and we must have more judges. Of this anon."[96] Chief Justice Taney wrote to Jackson concerning Catron, "The more I have seen of him the more I have been impressed with the strength of his judgment, legal knowledge, and high integrity of character. He is a most valuable acquisition to the Bench of the Supreme Court, and will I am confident continue to rise in public estimation as he becomes more generally known in those states in which he was a stranger at the time of his appointment."[97]

Catron never became so interested in law as to lose interest in contemporary politics. He continued political correspondence with Jackson until the latter's death in 1845. He was a close adviser of James K. Polk both before and during his Presidency, and was similarly close to President James Buchanan. He was a go-between with respect to members of Congress and the Supreme Court where legislation affecting the judiciary was involved, and on circuit he was a kind of news carrier about happenings in Washington. He was the complete opposite of a cloistered oracle of the law.

---

[94] *New York Commercial Advertiser*, Mar. 9, 1837.
[95] *Nashville Union*, Mar. 21, 1837.

[96] John Catron to Andrew Jackson, Feb. 5, 1838, Jackson Papers.
[97] Roger B. Taney to Andrew Jackson, Sept. 12, 1838, Jackson Papers.

In the debates on the rearrangement of the judicial circuits, legislators sometimes mentioned the need for specialized knowledge on the Supreme Court and in what became the Ninth Circuit with respect to the code law of Louisiana, which was so alien to common law judges as to be puzzling or incomprehensible. In making the appointment for the Ninth Circuit, however, Jackson paid no attention to this need. William Smith of Alabama, whom Jackson appointed along with Catron, had lived briefly in Louisiana but not long enough to equip himself with knowledge of Louisiana law—in the doubtful event that he was at all interested in the subject. He had been a lifelong friend and probably in his boyhood a schoolmate of Andrew Jackson, in his political life in South Carolina he had been a Unionist opponent of John C. Calhoun and his doctrine of nullification, and in Congress and local politics he had been one of Jackson's ardent supporters. His judicial experience had been limited to a brief period on a local state court during his early years in South Carolina. It is said that near the beginning of his Administration in 1829 Jackson offered Smith a position on the Supreme Court, but the offer was declined.[98] In 1837, at the suggestion of Van Buren,[99] who was also politically indebted to Smith, Jackson nominated him, apparently without notice to the nominee.

Before the nomination was confirmed the three members of the House of Representatives from Louisiana and one from Mississippi—which was likewise in the Ninth Circuit—sent to the Senate a protest against Smith's appointment, saying that because of his advanced age (he was then about seventy-five) and the length of time he had been withdrawn from judicial and legal pursuits, he was "disqualified from their performance."[100] The Senate nevertheless confirmed the nomination, but Smith declined the appointment, saying that when he had left the courts for the Senate he had done so with a full determination never to return.[101] Later Smith wrote a public letter saying there had been considerable inquiry why he would decline "a very dignified office, of light labors, and a permanent salary of $5,000 a year." He had done so not because he doubted his legal learning or because he was indifferent to the honor. It was because he wished to be free to continue his support and defense of Andrew Jackson, who as to his public record and

---

[98] J. G. de R. Hamilton, "William Smith," *Dictionary of American Biography*, XVII, 359–60. See also John Belton O'Neall, "William Smith," *Biographical Sketches of the Bench and Bar of South Carolina*, 106–20.

[99] "The Autobiography of Martin Van Buren," *Annual Report of the American Historical Association, 1918*, 2:199, 1920.

[100] R. Garland, *et al.*, to the Senate of the United States, Mar. 6, 1837, *Records of the U.S. Senate*.

[101] William Smith to John Forsyth, Apr. 5, 1837, Department of State Appointment Files.

even his moral rectitude was still under attack in spite of the fact that his Administration had now come to an end.[102]

One of the reasons for haste in nominating new Justices as soon as the requisite statute was enacted was the need to secure confirmation before adjournment of the Senate to enable the new Justices immediately to begin their work on circuit. Justice Catron did go at once to work on his circuit, but Smith's rejection of the appointment threatened to leave the Ninth Circuit unattended. On the day the statute was enacted a letter was sent to President Jackson by four members of the House of Representatives—two from Alabama and two from states outside the circuit—recommending John McKinley of Alabama, saying that his qualifications for the office were not surpassed by any individual in the circuit.[103] McKinley, like Smith, had been a loyal supporter of Jackson and Van Buren. He had been born in Virginia in 1780, moved to Kentucky where he read law and was admitted to the bar, practicing at Frankfort and Louisville, and then about 1818 moved to Huntsville, Alabama, and later to Florence in the same state. He entered politics, and amid a series of victories and defeats served in the state legislature and in the United States Senate and House of Representatives. At the time when the Supreme Court position was created, the Alabama legislature had elected him to the ensuing term of the United States Senate.

President Van Buren found no preferable candidate, and on April 22, 1837, gave McKinley a recess appointment.[104] The panic of 1837 having compelled Van Buren to call Congress into special session, he presented McKinley's name to the Senate on September 18 and after Senate confirmation a permanent commission was issued on September 25. In terms of mileage, including distance from Washington, McKinley had by far the largest circuit, a burden of which he perennially complained.[105] Even after he secured some reduction of his travels he was frequently absent from sessions of the Supreme Court because of what

---

[102] *Niles' Weekly Register*, 52:184, 1937.

[103] J. L. Martin, *et al.*, to Andrew Jackson, Mar. 3, 1837, Department of State Appointment Files.

[104] Down to this time this would seem to be the fourth appointment initially made to the Court while the Senate was in recess, the predecessors being Thomas Johnson, named on Aug. 5, 1791, the second John Rutledge, on July 1, 1795, and the third Henry B. Livingston, on Nov. 10, 1806. See list of nominations, in Warren, *The Supreme Court in United States History*, II, 757–58. Records thus far available do not clearly show whether Justice McKinley began his circuit work on the basis of his recess appointment or waited until after his name had been submitted to the Senate on Sept. 18, 1837, with confirmation on Sept. 25, 1837.

[105] See S. Rep. No. 50, 25th Cong., 3rd Sess. 38–39 (1838); McKinley (signature page missing) to Martin Van Buren, Nov. 6, 1839, Van Buren Papers; and S. Doc. No. 99, 27th Cong., 2nd Sess. (1842).

he regarded as his obligation to work at his Circuit Court docket. At least nominally to promote convenience of travel he moved from his Alabama home to Louisville, on the Ohio, outside his circuit, where he found time to act as a member of the firm of Clark, Churchill and Company, manufacturers of hemp bagging and rope.

Throughout his career as a member of the Court McKinley was hampered by poor health and serious illnesses, including in 1842 a paralytic attack.[106] His Circuit Court opinions were not published, and few if any of them were regarded as of such general interest as to justify printing, even in newspapers. During his fifteen years of membership he wrote for the Court only eighteen opinions, with the addition of only two concurring and two dissenting opinions; it is said that "not one of the decisions, including the dissenting opinions . . . involved a major constitutional question."[107] He made no significant contribution to legal thinking in any form. When he died in 1852 he had not made any notable imprint on the work of his profession. He was probably the least outstanding of the members of the Taney Court.

The Justices of the early Taney period included also Peter V. Daniel of Virginia, whom Martin Van Buren, at the very end of his Administration, appointed to replace the recently deceased Justice Barbour. Daniel was born in Virginia in 1784, had studied at but not graduated from Princeton, had read law with Edmund Randolph, famed as a member of the Constitutional Convention and as the first Attorney General of the United States, and had married Randolph's daughter. He moved into Virginia politics almost as soon as he was admitted to the bar, in 1808, served in the House of Delegates, and then, from 1812 until 1835, was a member of the Privy Council. He was an ardent Jackson man, writing toward the end of 1836 of "the honest and venerable old patriot Andrew Jackson, whom I cannot permit to go to the far West, without the tribute of my unfeigned respect."[108] He was an unrelenting enemy of the Bank of the United States, and an even more ardent believer in states' rights than Justice Barbour, while suspicious of Calhoun and his nullification strategy.

In 1833, when Taney was made Secretary of the Treasury to serve as Jackson's principal lieutenant in the struggle with the Bank, Daniel had been offered the vacated post of Attorney General. He declined the office, later giving as his explanation, noted above, the belief that it was the most burdensome position in the government and

---

[106] Joseph Story to Richard Peters, Nov. 27, 1842, Peters Correspondence, II.

[107] Herbert U. Feibelman, "John McKinley of Alabama," *Ala. Lawyer*, 22:424, 1961.

[108] P. V. Daniel to William Brent, Nov. 13, 1836, Cabell Papers.

not adequately compensated.[109] Thereafter in the vicissitudes of Virginia politics Daniel fell upon hard times. When Barbour resigned as United States District Judge for the Eastern District of the state, his friends urged Daniel for the vacancy, elaborately recounting his loyalty and his services to Jackson.[110] The position was offered and Daniel accepted with a vast sense of relief and with denunciation of his political enemies, doubting that there were enough honest men in Richmond to save the city from the fate of Sodom and Gomorrah.[111]

Long a voluminous correspondent with Van Buren on political matters, Daniel as a judge continued to give advice to Van Buren as President and to denounce his enemies. When Justice Barbour died, on February 25, 1841, Van Buren was near the end of his single term in the Presidency and was about to be succeeded by a Whig, William Henry Harrison. Recalling the experience of 1835 when the nomination of Taney as an Associate Justice had been defeated by resort to partial enactment of legislation to change the judicial circuits, the Whigs in the Senate now set out to block in similar fashion any appointment that Van Buren might make. Aware of the clamor of Justice McKinley about the outrageous dimensions of his circuit, the Senate passed a bill to merge the existing Fifth Circuit with adjacent circuits and permit the giving of relief in the Southwest and provision of an expert on the civil law as applied in Louisiana. Van Buren nevertheless nominated Daniel for the vacancy. Democrats forced consideration of the nomination in the face of protests of the Whigs, led by Henry Clay. When confirmation seemed inevitable Clay, with a "Good night, gentlemen," walked out of the Senate chamber followed by other Whigs, in the hope of preventing a quorum. The Whigs did not return but the sergeant-at-arms was able to round up enough Democrates to constitute a quorum and the nomination was confirmed.[112]

The Democrats, of course, gloated over their victory in filling the position with one of their own instead of leaving it to a Whig. A few days after the end of his term, Van Buren wrote to Jackson, "I had an opportunity to put a man on the Bench of the Supreme Court at the moment of leaving the government who will I am sure stick to the true principles of the Constitution, and being a Democrat *ab ovo* is not in so much danger of a falling off in the true spirit. The Federalists have

---

109 P. V. Daniel to John Y. Mason, July 19, 1845, Polk Papers.

110 See especially C. L. Morgan to Andrew Jackson, Mar. 22, 1836, Department of State Appointment Files.

111 P. V. Daniel to William Brent, July 13, 1836, Cabell Papers.

112 For an account of the proceedings and summary of the discussion see the *Washington Globe*, Mar. 5 and 10, 1841. See also *Baltimore Clipper*, Mar. 5, 1841; *Boston Daily Atlas*, Mar. 6, 1841; *Massachusetts Spy* (Worcester), Mar. 10, 1841; *Portland Eastern Argus* (tri-weekly), Mar. 19, 1841; *Baltimore Republican*, Mar. 8, 1841.

raved about the selection of our old friend Daniel of Virginia, but that did not distress me so much as some supposed it would do."[113]

The Whigs, however, got their revenge by a strategy which belongs primarily to an account of the judicial circuits rather than to this account of Supreme Court personnel. In brief, Congress merged the Fifth Circuit, then consisting of Virginia and North Carolina, with the circuits to the north and south, and constituted a new Fifth Circuit of Alabama and Louisiana. The Ninth Circuit was then to consist of Mississippi and Arkansas. The Supreme Court was directed to allocate Justices to the reconstituted circuits.[114] The Court allocated McKinley to the Fifth and Daniel to the Ninth. So it was that, maintaining his home at Richmond, he was compelled each year to travel hundreds of miles, at first primarily by stagecoach and steamboat, to reach the circuit on which he was designated to serve. In 1843 he wrote to Van Buren from Jackson, Mississippi, "I am here two thousand miles from home (calculating by the travelling route,) on the pilgrimage by an exposure to which, it was the calculation of federalist malignity that I would be driven from the Bench. Justice to my friends, and a determination to defeat the machinations of mine and of their enemies, have decided me to undergo the experiment, and I have done so at no small hazard, through yellow fever at Vicksburg and congestive and autumnal fevers in this place and vicinity. The enormity of the useage I have experienced is almost without an example, and I trust to the overruling protection of a good providence to disappoint its purposes, and to the justice and independence of my friends, and the friends of honor, magnanimity and common fairness to give me redress."[115]

In spite of his continued complaints of mistreatment, Daniel received no redress save as improvement in travel facilities made the trip easier. He continued to serve the newly-constituted Ninth Circuit until his death in 1860.[116]

On the Supreme Court Justice Daniel found it difficult to merge his judgments easily with those of his diverse colleagues. He took extreme positions on behalf of the rights of the states in cases involving the scope of the federal commerce power, the federal admiralty power, and the powers that were or could be given to corporations. In a word he much liked to use, he was "constrained" to dissent in large numbers of cases in these and related areas involving the rights of the states and particularly of the South. His correspondence showed him approaching

---

[113] Martin Van Buren to Andrew Jackson, Mar. 12, 1841, Van Buren Papers.

[114] 5 Stat. 507.

[115] P. V. Daniel to Martin Van Buren, Nov. 3, 1843, Van Buren Papers.

[116] For a further account of his experiences see Lawrence Burnette, Jr., "Peter V. Daniel: Agrarian Justice," *Virginia Magazine of History and Biography*, 62:289, 1954.

hysteria with the rising pitch of strife between the North and the South. He was deeply and bitterly intolerant on sectional and racial issues. From his portrait and from descriptions it appears that he was tall and spare, with high cheekbones, prominent nose, and full lips, and with a dark complexion.[117] He was a man of deep emotions, his eyes carrying a gleam of dry humor easily converted into sparkling or burning indignation or brooding fanaticism. He was not untypical of an extreme element in the South in his time. A great-nephew, with whom he had affectionate relations, stressed the logical character of his intellect but found that on the matter of race relations his mind was closed: "When in his house in Washington I ventured to say something favourable to the antislavery sentiment he closed the subject by saying, 'I fear those people are very wicked.' "[118]

---

[117] *Ibid.*, 295. A full biography is John P. Frank, *Justice Daniel Dissenting.*

[118] Moncure Daniel Conway, *Autobiography*, I, 223.

CHAPTER IV

The First Term and the Bridge Case

T HE SENATE'S DELAY IN acting on the Taney nomination for the Chief Justiceship, on the ground that action should be postponed until a bill reorganizing the circuits had been passed, meant that the Supreme Court had to operate without a Chief Justice during the January term of 1836. The central chair sat vacant through the term, a reminder of the nation's loss. "We could not behold his seat vacant from the beginning to the end of the term," said a brooding reporter, "without the recurrence of sober and solemn feeling."[1] As senior Associate Justice, Story presided from his position at the right of the empty chair, it was said with great ability and urbanity. A Boston reporter expressed regional and Whig sentiments by deploring the partisanship which stood "in the way of his permanently holding a station for which he is by his talents, learning and public standing, so preeminently qualified."[2] The term came to an end before the Taney nomination was confirmed.

Story himself enjoyed the experience of presiding and of being addressed by counsel. The following December, however, he wrote in a somber mood of his prospective trip to Washington for the new term of the Court, where a new order would be represented:

> I go to Washington on the 2d of January, to perform my annual routine of judicial duty. I feel little encouragement in the view of it. Public affairs seem to me in a sad way. Our Republic presents few of the features which a warm imagination in a glowing heart would de-picture. I hope it may last. But I confess my hopes are subdued, my confidence shaken, and my zeal chilled. It seems to me that the spirit

---

[1] *Washington National Intelligencer*, Mar. 1, 1836.

[2] *Boston Daily Advertiser*, Jan. 18, 1836.

of party (which is always the spirit of selfishness) is become irresistible. It is establishing a system of despotism of opinion fatal to all true ambition, and a corrupt influence and eagerness for office destructive of all liberty. I hope that I may be deceived; and I shall rejoice if I am.[3]

For Democrats, on the other hand, the meeting of the Court on January 2, 1837, marked a grand occasion. A majority of the seven members were now Jacksonians, and the Chief Justice was Jackson's principal lieutenant in defeating the Bank of the United States, a man twice rejected by a hostile Senate and now victorious as the head of one of the three coordinate branches of the government. In honor of the occasion the courtroom had been newly carpeted and much of the furniture changed, including the chairs and desks of the Justices. Noting that a reputation for presiding on circuit greatly to the satisfaction of the bar had preceded the new Chief Justice to Washington, a reporter spoke of his appearance of youth—the sprightliness and elasticity of his step and the clear black color of his hair. Story sat on his right and Thompson on his left, with the other Justices arranged according to seniority, save that Justice Wayne, who should have occupied the seat at the extreme right, was absent. There, too, were the officers of the Court, including the Reporter, Richard Peters, a man known for his racy wit and his ability to set tables in a roar, "he who could create a soul under the ribs of death,"[4] now quiet in the impressive atmosphere of the courtroom. On this first day of the term, as was the custom, the Court met but for a moment and then adjourned to pay a courtesy call on the President of the United States. The records do not tell of the pleasure either of the President or of the Chief Justice, but the inference can easily be drawn.

The docket of the Court had somewhat fewer than sixty cases.[5] They included three major constitutional controversies, involving the scope of the protection given by the Contract Clause, the effect of the Commerce Clause in restricting the power of states with respect to

---

[3] Joseph Story to Francis Lieber, Dec. 28, 1836, Lieber Papers.

Some two weeks earlier Story had written to George Ticknor, "I go to Washington on the 2d of January, to meet a new Chief Justice (Taney)— Quantum mutatus ab illo &c." Joseph Story to George Ticknor, Dec. 16, 1836, Story Papers (University of Texas). The Latin quotation, from Virgil, *Aeneid*, II, 274, was not entirely apposite. Whereas in that ac-

count Hector, horribly changed, had returned in a dream, "how altered from the man we knew," Justice Story did not expect again to meet John Marshall in any form whatsoever, but only to see in the Chief Justiceship to which Marshall had given form and dignity and power an entirely different man, Roger B. Taney.

[4] *Boston Atlas*, quoted in *Boston Statesman*, Jan. 28, 1837.

[5] *Niles' Weekly Register*, 51:320.

immigration, and the question whether the notes of state banks fell within the category of forbidden bills of credit. Land title issues were well represented, with ejectment cases based on two interstate compacts, one involving land titles in the Louisana Purchase based on Spanish grants, and a claim of title based on adverse possession. One case involved the question of the scope of the admiralty jurisdiction of the federal courts, another the power of Congress either under admiralty or the Commerce Clause to punish theft on shore of goods salvaged from a ship in distress, and another a question of marine insurance involving negligence at sea. Significant as to a future source of highly controversial litigation, one case involved interpretation of a statute prohibiting the importation of slaves.

The more important of the constitutional cases had been on the docket for some time, continued from year to year because absences of some of the Justices and differences among those present made it impossible to muster majorities of the full Court in behalf of any position. It had been the hope that the work of the Taney Court could begin immediately with argument of the famous *Charles River Bridge Case*, which had been argued in 1831 but continued year after year, along with other cases, until now when a full Court was expected to be present. For a few days the litigants and the Court suffered delay in that Justice Wayne failed to arrive from his home in Georgia, leaving to speculation the reason for his nonarrival. Especially irked by Wayne's absence was Simon Greenleaf, professor of law at Harvard, who was in Washington waiting to argue the case, and who was eager to get back to his classroom and to the more congenial atmosphere of Cambridge. He finally discovered that Wayne, although now transferred from the House of Representatives to the Supreme Court, had not yet divorced himself from politics but had remained late in Georgia, along with one of the state's Senators, to give aid at a special election for replacement of a member of the House.[6]

Until Wayne's arrival on January 19, some ten days late, the Court did little more than adjourn from day to day, disposing incidentally of a number of cases submitted on written argument. In one of these, a land case disposed of on January 16, it is significant of the attitude of the new Chief Justice with respect to solidarity of voting on the Court that instead of voting with the majority even though unable to control it, and writing the opinion of the Court, he joined in a dissenting opinion written by Justice McLean, with Justice Barbour speaking for the majority.[7]

---

[6] Charles Warren, *History of the Harvard Law School*, I, 532–33.

[7] Marlatt v. Silk, 11 Pet. 1 (1837).

Finally, on January 18, the Court began to hear arguments in cases not involving constitutional questions, in spite of the absence of Justice Wayne. On that day it proceeded with the argument and decision of one case. The question involved was whether Acts of Congress for suppression of the slave trade had been violated by transportation back to the United States of a slave woman whose New Orleans mistress had taken her on a trip to Paris. In a unanimous opinion by the Chief Justice, the Court held that no such violation had taken place.[8] On the following day, June 19, Justice Wayne was at last present, and the Court was able to proceed with the *Charles River Bridge Case*.

The *Bridge Case*, important to the Boston area where litigation had started nine years earlier, had in the intervening years developed importance for people all over the United States who were concerned with problems of transportation—and, next to those involving stability in titles to land, transportation problems were perhaps the most critical of all those the American people had to face. Sailing vessels, steamboats, turnpikes, canals, railroads, all these were subjects of constant preoccupation. A year and a half before the Taney Court heard argument in the case, the first railroad train had come puffing into the heart of Washington, immediately below the Capitol at Pennsylvania Avenue and Second Street, thereby rendering largely obsolete the once profitable stagecoach lines between Washington and Baltimore. Sponsors of the Baltimore and Ohio Railroad and the Chesapeake and Ohio Canal continued for years in competition for the privilege of opening up transportation to what was then the distant West. All over the country, turnpikes, many of the profitable toll roads, were yielding part of their traffic to the smoother travel of canals, and, even as construction of canals continued, railroads also were being built, at first often to link canals across high and rough terrain and then to compete with them on the basis of greater speed and carrying capacity and less vulnerability to freezing winters. Perennial was the search for greater speed, convenience, dependability, and economy. The old must not be permitted to stand in the way of the new.

Yet society recognized also a competing value. Progress depended on investments, and investments could be attracted only if property rights were made secure. Original construction of means of transportation always involved risks that the means would not stand up, that the anticipated traffic would not develop, or that competition would capture the hoped-for profits. States had to give guarantees in corporation charters, and had to establish and maintain the confidence in fulfillment

---

[8] United States v. The Ship *Garonne*, 11 Pet. 73 (1837).

of their obligations. The sanctity of contract must be observed, because both the interests of business and the provisions of the Constitution required it. The competing values of stability and change, of maintenance of property rights and keeping the way clear for new developments, were involved in the case of the Charles River Bridge, and the decision in the case was sure to have a tremendous impact on the economic life of the country as a whole and not merely in the Boston area.

The roots of the *Bridge Case* go back to within twenty years of the landing on Plymouth Rock, when in 1640 the colonial legislature provided a means of income for Harvard College by authorizing it to operate a ferry between Boston and Charlestown. As shown on a simplified map of the locale which was utilized by the Supreme Judicial Court of Massachusetts,[9] the site of Boston was virtually a peninsula jutting into the waters of Boston Bay and the mouth of the Charles River. Charlestown was on another peninsula jutting southward in the direction of Boston. The two towns grew in size and communication between them became increasingly important. By 1785 engineering experience in Massachusetts had developed to such a stage that, although risks were involved, it seemed a good economic venture to build a bridge at the location of the ferry. In that year the legislature authorized construction of the Charles River Bridge, giving the company the right to collect tolls for forty years, and during that time to pay Harvard College two hundred pounds annually in lieu of ferry tolls, whereafter the bridge was to become the property of the state. The bridge proved a success, leading to proposals for construction of other bridges at other points in the watery terrain. In 1792 the legislature chartered another company to build a bridge westward from Boston to Cambridge, with a much longer span. Although the ends of the two bridges inland from Boston were to be far apart, it was clear that the West Boston Bridge would collect some traffic that would otherwise pay toll to cross to Boston via the bridge from Charlestown. The proprietors of the first bridge therefore protested at the construction of the second. The legislature, without admitting a legal obligation to do so, compensated the proprietors of the Charles River Bridge by extending for thirty additional years the period over which tolls might be collected. Still other bridges were constructed in the area—with no additional concessions to the first adventurers.

The population of the area continued to increase, and with it the traffic into and out of Boston. In spite of such competition as other bridges provided, the increase in traffic greatly increased the value of

---

[9] Charles River Bridge v. Warren Bridge, 23 Mass. (6 Pick.) 376, 388 (1828).

the Charles River Bridge stock. Shares having a par value of $333.33 sold in 1805 at $1,650 and in 1814 at $2,080. Whereas the original capitalization had been $50,000, the company in 1823 claimed a value of $280,000.[10] Although the increase in value of the bridge property may not have been greater than the appreciation of the value of other property privately held in the area, customers came to regard the company as an objectionable monopoly extorting tolls which it had no right to collect. The company refused to make concessions either in the way of improved services or reduced tolls.

Repeated attempts were made to persuade the legislature to authorize construction of an immediately competing bridge between Boston and Charlestown. Finally, in a Democratic versus Whig struggle in Massachusetts, in a movement in which the masses fought to protect their interests against the holders of investment property, the battle was won. In 1828 the legislature chartered a company to build the Warren Bridge, which was to be only sixteen rods from the old bridge on the Charlestown side and fifty rods on the Boston side. The Warren Bridge was to be surrendered to the state as soon as tolls had paid for its construction, with, in any event, a maximum period for collection of tolls. Thereafter its use was to be free to the public. It was obvious that a new bridge would compete heavily for tolls with one that was both old and unpopular, and that when the new one became a free bridge it would get all the traffic, rendering the stock of the old bridge valueless.

The Charles River Bridge brought suit in the Supreme Judicial Court of Massachusetts to enjoin construction of the competing bridge, employing as counsel Daniel Webster and Lemuel Shaw, who a few years later was to become the distinguished chief justice of that tribunal. The attempt failed,[11] and the case was taken to the Supreme Court of the United States on writ of error. It was argued at the 1831 term before six Justices, Justice Duvall being absent because of the illness of his wife.[12] The Court was sharply divided. The case went over to the ensuing term, when Justice Johnson was absent because of illness.[13] Evidently Chief Justice Marshall and Justices Story and Thompson were in favor of reversing the decree of the Massachusetts court and holding that the act chartering the Warren Bridge violated the obligation of contract in the charter of the Charles River Bridge. Justice McLean was said to be doubtful as to jurisdiction. Justice Story wrote out his

---

10 See Warren, *History of the Harvard Law School*, I, 510–13.

11 Charles River Bridge v. Warren Bridge, 23 Mass. (6 Pick.) 376 (1828), 24 Mass. (7 Pick.) 344 (1829).

12 Joseph Story to J. H. Ashmun, Mar. 10, 1831, *Life and Letters of Joseph Story*, William W. Story, ed., II, 51.

13 *Ibid.*, 91.

opinion, in the hope of persuading his doubting brethren.[14] However, he was unable to win a majority of the entire Court to his position, and the case went over for eventual reargument before the Taney Court.

During the intervening years, 1831 to 1837, Webster watched anxiously over the interests of his client, the Charles River Bridge Corporation, seeking both to bring about a reargument of the case before the full membership of the Supreme Court and at the same time to secure remedial action from the Massachusetts legislature. With reargument in mind he reported in early January, 1833, to his colleague Warren Dutton on the personnel of the Court: "You may probably have heard of the breaking out of Judge Baldwin's insanity." Justice Johnson's health was thought to be mending. Justice Duvall was hearty but it was difficult for him to *hear* cases. The Chief Justice was in good health.[15] Later in the month he was still hopeful of the reargument of the case at that term. "Bring all the evidence you can," he wrote to Dutton, "to show the State, as a State, is *now enjoying the revenue of Warren Bridge*. If we can make this point to appear, I have great hopes of Ch. Jus. opinion for us, it will make so plain a case." He thought the real argument would then have to be made to Justice Duvall, "who is generally sound, on such subjects."[16]

Continued absences from the Bench having prevented the reargu-

---

[14] For summary see Charles Warren, *The Supreme Court in United States History*, I, 773, n. 2. Story first mentioned his opinion to Jeremiah Mason in a letter of Nov. 19, 1831, saying that when it was finished he would like to have Mason read it: "It is so important a constitutional question, that I am anxious that some other mind should see, what the writer rarely can in his zeal, whether there is any weak point which can be fortified or ought to be abandoned." *Memoir and Correspondence of Jeremiah Mason*, 335. Mason expressed his willingness to comment on the opinion and his relief at improvement in the health of Chief Justice Marshall and indicated his fears of the Jackson Administration by saying, "I trust and hope in divine mercy that his life and strength may be continued till the danger to the judiciary from the present dynasty shall have passed away." Jeremiah Mason to Joseph Story, Nov. 24, 1831, *ibid.*, 336. In sending his opinion for inspection Justice Story commented, "I have

written my opinion in the hope of meeting the doubts of some of the brethren, which are various and apply to different aspects of the case. To accomplish my object, I felt compelled to deal with each argument separately, and answer it in every form, since the objections of one mind were different from those of another. One of the most formidable objections is the rule that royal grants, etc., are to be strictly construed. Another is against implications in legislative grants; another is against monopolies. Another is that franchises of this sort are bounded by local limits; another that the construction contended for will bar all public improvements. I have been compelled, therefore, to re-state the arguments in different connections. I have done so hoping to gain allies." Joseph Story to Jeremiah Mason, Dec. 23, 1831, *ibid.*, 336–37.

[15] Daniel Webster to Warren Dutton, Jan. 4, 1833, Webster Papers (Dartmouth).

[16] Daniel Webster to Warren Dutton, Jan. 29, 1833, *ibid.*

ment at the 1833 and 1834 terms, Webster discussed in December, 1834, the prospect of argument in 1835, when he was anticipating the replacement of the late Justice Johnson by James M. Wayne. He assumed that it was hopeless to look for legislative intervention at home to compromise and settle the dispute. "This would be the thing most to be desired, if it could be."[17] With the prospect of Wayne's confirmation, he assumed that the argument would take place, saying, "I have heard nothing respecting Judge Duval[l], since I wrote you, but have no doubt he will be here."[18] Indeed, Webster tentatively arranged with Chief Justice Marshall that the argument should take place around the first of February.[19] Then, to Webster's dismay, occurred the Duvall resignation and the Taney nomination, on which the Senate, under Webster's leadership, delayed action until another term of the Court had expired.

In the face of these delays, Webster became more and more concerned about protecting the rights of his client through legislative compromise. He thought the bridge proprietors ought to appoint a committee to talk with the governor.[20] True, he was concerned about the possibility of irresponsible action by the legislature: "I fear that Charlestown Bridge is a dead corpse." What he hoped for was that petitions would be gotten up in all the towns having privately operated toll bridges whereby the bridges would be taken over by the state with appropriate compensation to the owners—"all my hopes of doing any good for the Proprietors of the Ch. R. B. rested on the chance of bringing them in, with others in some such general arrangement."[21]

After the Taney nomination had been defeated, only to be followed by the death of the Chief Justice, and then by the nomination of Taney for the leading position and Barbour for the Associate Justiceship, Webster again urged compromise, saying that these two nominees were undoubtedly to be the judges, "and you may therefore judge of the value of our chance for justice, in such a question."[22] It was in this context that Webster agreed with Justice Story that the Supreme Court and everything else was "gone."[23] The income from the Charles River

---

[17] Daniel Webster to Warren Dutton, Dec. 18, 1834, *ibid.*

[18] Daniel Webster to Warren Dutton, Jan. 7, 1835, *ibid.*

[19] Daniel Webster to Warren Dutton, Jan. 13, 1835, *ibid.*

[20] Daniel Webster to Warren Dutton, Jan. 26, 1835, *ibid.*

[21] Daniel Webster to Warren Dutton, Feb. 5, 7, 1835, *ibid.*

[22] Daniel Webster to Warren Dutton, Dec. 24, 1835, *ibid.*

[23] Daniel Webster to Caroline Webster, Jan. 10, 1836, Webster Papers (N.H.H.S.). To Edward Everett, Webster complained that the Whig Party was dismembered and the Senate revolutionized, and added, "The Court will be radically changed. There seems therefore nothing in which to place reliance, in any branch of the Government." Daniel Webster to Edward Everett, Jan. 27, 1836, Everett Papers (M.H.S.).

IV: *The First Term and the* Bridge Case

Bridge was indeed gone. The competing Warren Bridge had yielded enough in tolls to pay for itself, and the state then threw it open as a free bridge. The Charles River Bridge, drawing no customers at toll rates, was closed to traffic.

After the first and before the second argument of the *Charles River Bridge Case* before the Supreme Court a question of the exclusiveness of the right of a transportation company having a monopoly grant arose in another geographical area. The Camden and Amboy Railroad and the Delaware and Raritan Canal companies had persuaded the New Jersey legislature of 1832 to incorporate in charter provisions an agreement that without the consent of these companies no other company should for a stated time be authorized to build a competitive line between Philadelphia and New York. A number of eminent lawyers of the day were asked to give professional opinions as to the binding character of the monopoly provision. One of them was Roger B. Taney, at that time Attorney General of the United States. Since he was now Chief Justice, his opinion was of preeminent importance. It was later said of Taney's opinion that it "made much sensation from its imputed denial of what, without reflection, are apt to be thought not only vested but sacred rights."[24]

In his Camden and Amboy opinion Taney called it "too well settled to be disputed" that a charter of a private transportation company was a contract which could not be altered by subsequent legislation. It was clear, however, that the legislature could not bind the state beyond the scope of its own authority. In this instance the legislature sought to restrict the power of succeeding legislatures to authorize public improvements. He could find in the New Jersey constitution no authorization of such exercise of restrictive power. He thought it had no foundation in reason or public convenience and that it was inconsistent with the principles upon which all our political institutions were founded. The monopoly provision was therefore not binding. He admitted that "principles of moral justice" might require that the company be indemnified for its loss of expectations based on an authorized legislative act, but found the question of indemnity a matter for the legislature.[25]

Other professional opinions were sought, perhaps in part for the purpose of opposing the position taken by Taney. One was written by Horace Binney, a distinguished Philadelphia lawyer, and Charles

---

[24] "Speech of Charles J. Ingersoll in the Convention of Pennsylvania, on Legislative and Judicial Control over Charters of Incorporation," *Democratic Review*, 5:99, 109, 1839.

[25] "The Opinion of Mr. Taney, Attorney General of the United States, On the Validity of the Law of New Jersey, under which the Camden and Amboy Rail Road, and the Delaware and Raritan Companies Claim a Monopoly. Sept. 5, 1833," *Niles' Weekly Register*, 15:151–52, 1833.

Chauncey of New Haven. These men found that the New Jersey legislature had the power not only to charter corporations but also to determine the conditions under which they would exercise their functions, including the degree of freedom they should have over a limited time in operating with respect to competition from other corporations similarly chartered.[26] Ex-Chancellor James Kent of New York, a friend of Justice Story, Webster, and other Whigs, and having a similar attitude toward the sanctity of rights of contract, read Taney's opinion but waived discussion of Taney's point, holding, with the concurrence of Webster, that the legislative provision should be strictly construed, "as one that may be exceedingly inconvenient to the public welfare."[27] These several opinions were much discussed[28] and were available to counsel and the Court at the time of the second argument of the *Bridge Case.*

The case was argued by four Massachusetts lawyers, all of them men of great ability. With Webster, who had been in the case from the beginning in 1828 for the Charles River Bridge, was Warren Dutton. For the Warren Bridge were Simon Greenleaf and John Davis. Greenleaf was Justice Story's principal colleague in teaching law at Harvard. Although he participated regularly in the argument of cases along with his teaching, in this case he found it expedient to get the consent of his employers since defense of the interests of the Warren Bridge ran counter to the interest of the college with respect to the annual payment hitherto received from the Charles River Bridge.[29] John Davis, a conservative Whig, had been governor of Massachusetts and would later be governor again. Whether in anticipation of his appearance in this case or for some other reason, he had deserted his party leadership in the Senate ten months earlier to vote for the confirmation of Taney as Chief Justice, at a time when confirmation seemed inevitable in any event.

The Court was still in the era of long arguments, particularly in highly important cases. The debate which began on Thursday, January 19, was concluded the following Thursday. Dutton opened for the Charles River Bridge and concluded on Saturday. Greenleaf spoke two hours on Saturday and three on Monday. Davis spoke during the remainder of Monday and for three hours on Tuesday. Webster spoke through the remainder of Tuesday and on Wednesday and concluded

---

[26] *Opinion of Messrs. Binney & Chauncey, On the Subject of the Acts of the Legislature of the State of New-Jersey, relative to the Delaware and Raritan Canal, and Camden and Amboy Rail Road Companies.* (Pamphlet) Oct. 24, 1833.

[27] James Bradley Thayer, *Cases on Constitutional Law,* II, 1641.

[28] See C. C. Cambreling to Gideon Welles, Apr. 15, 1835, Welles Papers.

[29] Warren, *History of the Harvard Law School,* I, 528.

on Thursday. The courtroom was thronged with spectators, especially on the day when Webster was expected to speak. It was said that at an early hour all seats were taken within and without the bar except those to be occupied by counsel. A reporter spoke of "ladies, whose beauty and splendid attire and waving plumes gave the Court-room an animated and brilliant appearance such as it seldom wears."[30] After conclusion of the argument Justice Story wrote to his son, "We have been for a week engaged in hearing the Charles River Bridge cause. It was a glorious argument on all sides, strong, and powerful and *apt*. Mr. Greenleaf spoke with great ability and honored Dane College. Mr. Webster pronounced one of his greatest speeches. Mr. Dutton was full of learning and acute remarks, and so was Gov. Davis. 'Greek met Greek.' "[31] To Charles Sumner, who was teaching Greenleaf's classes at Harvard—at the Dane Law School there—Story wrote more at length, again praising each of the counsel while noting that "Webster's closing reply was in his best manner, with a little too much of fierté here and there." He took pride in the fact that "On the whole, it was a glorious exhibition for old Massachusetts; four of her leading men brought out in the same cause, and none of them inferior to those who are accustomed to lead here."[32]

Throughout the several arguments the central constitutional question was for the most part kept clear: Did the legislative act chartering the Warren Bridge impair the contract in the charter of the Charles River Bridge? But since each speaker had unlimited time, the discussion ranged into innumerable related questions of law and of legal and social theory. It was a legal debate reflective of disciplined reasoning but at the same time it shaded into the social and economic issues that divided the Democratic and the Whig parties. Warren Dutton, for the Charles River Bridge, contended that the charter to build that bridge and collect tolls for its use carried by necessary implication a grant of exclusiveness as to traffic between Boston and Charlestown, and that chartering the Warren Bridge, which now carried all the traffic and eliminated all tolls, impaired the first contract and violated the Constitution. The act, he contended, took the property of the plaintiffs and gave it to the public. It was an act of confiscation. "It violates all those distinctions of right and wrong, of justice and injustice, which lie at the foundation of all law, and of all government; and if men were to deal with each other as this act deals with the plaintiffs, the very framework of our civil polity would be broken down; all confidence would be

---

[30] Warren, *The Supreme Court in United States History*, II, 22.

[31] Joseph Story to W. W. Story, Jan. 28, 1837, Story Papers (M.H.S.).

[32] Joseph Story to Charles Sumner, Jan. 25, 1837, *Life and Letters of Joseph Story*, II, 266.

destroyed, and all sense of security for the rights of persons and property would be lost."[33]

Dutton asserted that in Massachusetts alone the title to more than ten million dollars in property would be determined by the principles to be established in this case. He was opposed to leaving rights of property dependent on popular prejudice and the equity and justice of the legislature. Experience had taught him not to trust legislative bodies as the guardians of private rights. Here he made his appeal directly to the Supreme Court:

> I look to the law; to the administration of the law, and, above all, to the supremacy of the law, as it resides in this court, for the protection of the rights of persons and property, against all encroachments by the inadvertent legislation of the States. So long as this court shall continue to exercise this most salutary and highest of all its functions, the whole legislation of the country will be kept within its constitutional sphere of action. The result will be general confidence, and general security.[34]

Greenleaf, for the Warren Bridge, of course contended that there was no violation of contract. The act chartering the Charles River Bridge must be read in the light of the state's power of eminent domain, which could not be contracted away. The rights of the company were entitled to protection, but not in equity or in the Supreme Court of the United States. If compensation was due, it should be recovered at law and in the courts of the state:

> If Massachusetts has taken the property of the plaintiffs for public use, her honor is solemnly pledged in her constitution to make adequate compensation. If their rights have been sacrificed for higher public good, the laws of nations equally bind her to restitution. From these obligations she could not seek to escape, without forfeiting her *caste*, in this great family of nations. Her conduct in this matter has been uniformly dignified and just. The plaintiffs have never yet met her, except in the attitude of stern and uncompromising defiance. She will listen with great respect, to the opinion and advice of this honorable court; and if her sovereign rights were to be submitted to arbitration, there is doubtless no tribunal to whose hands she would more readily confide them.[35]

---

[33] Charles River Bridge v. Warren Bridge, 11 Pet. 420, 453–54 (1837).

[34] *Ibid.*, 461.

[35] *Ibid.*, 473. Greenleaf's peroration showed anxiety lest European as well as American creditors get from this controversy the impression that states would fulfill their obligations only if subject to judicial coercion.

In addition to the summary in 11 Peters, information about Greenleaf's argument can be derived from his notes on file at Harvard University.

IV: *The First Term and the* Bridge Case

From the Reporter's summaries it appears that it was John Davis who went most deeply into the law of ferries to determine the heritage of the Charles River Bridge from the original Harvard College ferry and also to determine the principles to be applied in the interpretation of public utility charters. Using materials which were later to be restated in the opinion of the Court, he showed that "in England, contracts of this character are rigidly construed in favor of the public, and against corporators."[36] He thought it irrelevant that some of the present stockholders were said to be great sufferers in that they had bought shares at the high figure of two thousand dollars each. By its Act of 1792, when it had chartered the West Boston Bridge, the state had in effect given notice that it did not regard the charter of the Charles River Bridge as giving an exclusive right.[37] The plaintiffs sought to have traffic from Charlestown driven by a circuitous route across their own bridge and to pay tribute perpetually, "not to indemnify for the enterprise, but to add to the mass of wealth already accumulated. If the State is tied down to this burden, be it so; but let us see decisive proof of it. Let it not be by presumptions or implications."[38]

While agreeing with Dutton that the legislature ought not to violate principles of natural justice by taking property without compensation, Davis denied that the Constitution gave the Supreme Court the right to inquire whether the legislature and the state courts had disregarded principles of natural justice. But he also denied that there had been such violation. "The supposed violation of natural justice does not consist in interfering with the provisions of the act, but in refusing to recognize claims not enumerated in it—rights unauthorized by it—privileges not intended to be granted. We cannot find in the act certain provisions of which they claim the benefit. Is it a violation of natural justice to refuse them the right to add what they please to the act?"[39]

There is no record of Daniel Webster's feelings as he stood at the lectern before the Chief Justice whom he had denounced as a pliant instrument of Andrew Jackson and from whom he had drawn the countercharge that he was a pliant instrument of the Bank of the United States, the Chief Justice whom he had helped defeat as a nominee for an Associate Justiceship and opposed to the bitter end for his present position. Perhaps neither man was happy over the situation. Greenleaf wrote to Charles Sumner that Webster was observed to be very uneasy and moody during the whole defense.[40] It has been inferred that he

---

[36] *Ibid.*, 487.
[37] *Ibid.*, 495.
[38] *Ibid.*, 499.
[39] *Ibid.*, 503. Evidently a misprint, the last word of this quotation is printed as "fact."
[40] Warren, *History of the Harvard Law School*, I, 534.

expected to lose his case.[41] When he left Washington, after the case was decided, he disappointed the Reporter by failing to leave with him a statement of his argument in the case or even his notes from which a statement might have been developed.[42] In any event, listeners were impressed by his Courtroom performance. A reporter stated, for example, that "Painting could not have conveyed a better idea of the places to the mind of the spectator than his picturesque description did to the auditors."[43]

Webster himself was the subject of many verbal portraits. Three years before the argument of the Charles River Bridge Case a dilettante Philadelphia lawyer with a literary flair described him as follows:

He is a great man. With an intellect at once clear & logical stored with knowledge & alert and practical from the experience of a life of active exertion, he possesses at the same time a certain loftiness of character, which commands respect. In his oratory there is nothing dazzling or brilliant, but its character is elevated, severe, sober, and argumentative. His is the eloquence of reason. But however profound, well arranged and convincing his arguments may be, in his speeches there is much more than mere reasoning. A certain nobility of thought & feeling, an elevated patriotism, the anger, the enthusiasm, the scorn of a great mind, are perpetually flashing forth when the occasion calls for them, and over all is shed the glowing radiance of a rich imagination, elevating and warming, and adding the charm of metaphor and poetical illustration to his style. His delivery is very dignified and imposing and his appearance is very expressive of his character, and just what one would expect. He is of the middle height, rather stout, with small limbs & delicate extremities. His carriage & air are calm and severe & his manner graceful & gentlemanly. Such a face & head I never saw—a jutting, broad & lofty forehead, black & beetling brows, immense, blazing dark eyes, deep sunk, a large mouth, the smile of which at times is bland and pleasing enough, but when curled in scorn or anger, and assisted by the glaring orbs above, gives to its possessor the expression of an enraged demon, conscious of his power—these, together with a dark sallow complexion and black hair, complete an

[41] Warren, *The Supreme Court in United States History*, II, 23.

[42] 11 Pet. 514, n. 1. Webster's argument as printed in *Writings and Speeches of Daniel Webster*, J. W. McIntyre, ed., XV, 322, is but a reprint of the statement developed by the Reporter, Richard Peters, from his own notes, and first printed in 11 Pet. 514. For evidence of Peters' attempt to get from Webster a draft or notes of his argument see copy,

Richard Peters to Daniel Webster, Apr. 13, 1837, Peters Correspondence, II, Cadwalader Papers. Webster's earlier argument in the Supreme Judicial Court of Massachusetts, Charles River Bridge v. Warren Bridge, 24 Mass. (7 Pick.) 344, 427 (1829), is reprinted in *Writings and Speeches of Daniel Webster*, XV, 347.

[43] Warren, *The Supreme Court in United States History*, II, 22.

appearance the most striking that I ever saw. His voice is in accordance with the rest, deep toned & powerful but not harsh. His dress is that of a gentleman, always clean, a little careless, and composed of dark rich colors. He occupies the most eminent and influential position in the country, because he is the leader of a great state, & perhaps of more than one, & has the reputation of possessing the most powerful intellect & being the most eloquent & efficient orator in Congress. Many however doubt the soundness and purity of his political and personal integrity, and he is so reckless of money, that notwithstanding the immense emoluments of his profession, he is said to be involved in debt.[44]

An anonymous Southern writer said of him in the year of the *Bridge* decision that as a product of the cold North he shared the coldness of his native region. He never thundered with the wild vehemence of Clay or burned with the continuous warmth of Preston or Calhoun. He lacked the passion and enthusiasm necessary to the most overpowering oratory. Yet his manner suited the subject matter which he chose to discuss, and his auditors received the firm conviction of his greatness.[45]

The Reporter's notes show that in his argument in the *Bridge Case*, Webster, like the other three counsel, sought to cover the entire controversy, and in addition to counter the arguments of his opponents. He had told Greenleaf and Davis that he would tear their arguments to pieces and abuse Greenleaf.[46] As reported, Webster accused Greenleaf of saying that the legislature could completely take away the grant without making compensation.[47] This was a misstatement of Greenleaf's position, which was that compensation could be had from the state, if necessary through action at law in the state courts. Webster reminded the Court of Justice Story's question to Greenleaf:

Suppose a railroad corporation receive a charter at the hands of the State of Massachusetts, in which an express provision was inserted that no other road should be granted during the duration of the charter, within ten miles of the proposed road. The road is built and opened. Did he hold that, notwithstanding the covenant, a subsequent Legislature had the power to grant another road, within five rods of the first, without any compensation other than the faith thus given by their charter of the State of Massachusetts?[48]

Greenleaf's reply that he did so hold had struck Webster, as it must have struck the Court, as a most startling doctrine. At this point in his

---

[44] "The Diaries of Sidney George Fisher," entry of Aug. 6, 1834, *Pennsylvania Magazine of History and Biography*, 76:184–85, 1952.
[45] "Daniel Webster," *Southern Literary Messenger*, 3:759–60, 1837.
[46] Warren, *History of the Harvard Law School*, I, 532.
[47] 11 Pet. 518.
[48] *Ibid.*, 533.

record the Reporter bracketed in Greenleaf's explanation that in such a case the faith of the state was pledged to indemnify the parties for all injuries done to private rights, and that the Court would not presume that the faith of the state would be broken.[49]

Webster also challenged Davis' position that since the plaintiffs had received very large profits they had received reasonable compensation. "Nothing," he proclaimed, "is reasonable but the fulfillment of the contract. It is not reasonable that one party should judge for themselves, as to compensation, and depart from the terms of the contract, which is definite and plain in its meaning."[50] The grant was impaired, the Contract Clause of the Constitution was violated, and the Supreme Court was asked to give relief in terms of its precedents of the past thirty years in protecting individual property against legislative assumption.[51]

On January 31, five days after conclusion of the argument, Webster included in each of two private letters statements that nothing had been heard from the Court respecting the *Bridge Case*.[52] On February 3, however, he wrote to Jeremiah Mason a resentful letter stating that the case would be decided that day, and that it would be decided wrong. He explained the positions of the several judges, and the fact that he was incorrect only about the date of the announcement of the decision indicates that he had firsthand information from a member of the Court. The three old judges, he stated, Story, Thompson, and McLean, would be for reversing the judgment of the state court, and the four new ones, Taney, Baldwin, Wayne, and Barbour, would be for affirming the judgment. He remarked that McLean, not doubting the merits, had doubts about the jurisdiction, "which doubts, I believe, nobody else entertains."[53]

The Court was revolutionized, Webster continued. Politics had at last gotten possession of the Bench and it was vain to deny or attempt to disguise it. "Taney is smooth and plausible, but cunning and jesuitical, and as thorough going a party judge as ever got onto a bench of justice. He is a man who wears his robes for the purpose of protecting his friends and punishing his enemies." He regarded Baldwin as "naturally a confused strong-headed creature, very opinionated and intriguing."

---

[49] *Ibid.*, 534.

[50] *Ibid.*, 531.

[51] *Ibid.*, 536–37.

[52] *Writings and Speeches of Daniel Webster*, XVIII, 25, 26.

[53] Daniel Webster to Jeremiah Mason, Feb. 3, 1837, from a copy as sent by William D. Mitchell to Chief Justice Harlan F. Stone, filed with Harlan F. Stone to William D. Mitchell, Jan. 9, 1945, Mitchell Papers. Concerning the Webster letter, Chief Justice Stone remarked, "After all, times do not seem to have changed so much, but at least, so far as I am aware, our opinions are not public property before their delivery as the opinions of the Court seem to have been in Webster's day."

He saw Baldwin as now paying court to the new Chief Justice. Wayne was a good follower for strong men like Marshall and Story, but presumably thought he must not differ from his friends. Barbour was honest and conscientious but had an absolute devotion to states' rights. Thompson was honest but with some original bias against the powers of the federal judiciary, and was getting to be an old man. McLean, though wholly fair, was not more than half right on constitutional questions. He was a judge by compulsion, preferring "a high popular office." In this situation, Webster continued, Justice Story—presumably Webster's source of information about the Court's position on the *Bridge Case*—had decided to leave the Bench rather than remain and be voted down on all great questions. He hoped to get the presidency of an insurance company in Boston, which might pay him twenty-five hundred or three thousand dollars, and live on this salary together with his income from his professorship.[54]

Although official announcement of the decision was postponed, Story wrote to Greenleaf on February 11 to tell him that he had triumphed. He again explained the positions of the several judges and added that the Chief Justice would write the opinion of the Court.[55] Story also wrote to Mrs. Story that Greenleaf had gained his cause, and he, Story, was sorry for it: "A case of grosser injustice, or more oppressive legislation, never existed. I feel humiliated, as I think every one here is, by the Act which has now been confirmed."[56]

As counsel had taken all the time needed for presentation of the case, so the Justices took time for reading long opinions in Court. On the first day, Chief Justice Taney read the opinion of the Court and Justice McLean his concurring opinion, holding that the Supreme Court should take no action because of want of jurisdiction[57] but explaining at length his agreement with the plaintiffs on the merits. Justice Story began reading his dissenting opinion but suspended at four o'clock to resume the next day, occupying altogether upwards of three hours.[58] He proclaimed that, after hearing the new arguments and having the benefit of researches in the years intervening since the case was first presented, he adhered to his original opinion with his most firm and unhesitating conviction.

The opinion of the Court, the first important opinion to be de-

---

[54] *Ibid.*

[55] Joseph Story to Simon Greenleaf, Feb. 11, 1837, *Life and Letters of Joseph Story*, II, 267–68.

[56] Joseph Story to Mrs. Story, Feb. 14, 1837, *ibid.*, 268.

[57] Justice McLean's finding of want of jurisdiction was based on his conclusion that an action of the state which unsettled vested rights but did not operate "on the contract" was not encompassed by the Contract Clause of the Constitution, with the result that there was no federal question for review.

[58] *Boston Daily Advertiser*, Feb. 21, 1837.

livered by the new Chief Justice, was written with the limpid clarity, the "apostolic simplicity," of Taney's earlier arguments at the bar. It was simple, direct, unemotional, and seemingly almost in the form of understatement. With the materials reworked to fit his own style and personality, the content of the opinion seems to have been drawn largely from the argument of John Davis. Taney noted the Court's duty both to guard as far as possible the rights of property and to abstain from encroachment on the rights reserved to the states. He cited precedent for the position that the Constitution did not protect all vested rights against state interference, but only those covered by some constitutional provision—as claimed in this instance, the provision of the Contract Clause. The charter of the Charles River Bridge did not specifically grant exemption from competition by other bridges. The question, therefore, was whether the Court should by implication read into the charter the exemption which it did not specifically contain.

Here Taney parted company with Story, who delved deep into the common law of England to show that in terms of principles once firmly established it had been true of public grants as well as private grants that the rule was to construe them most strongly against the grantor—which in this instance would mean against the state of Massachusetts. Scoffing at the current tendency to rely on modern interpretations, Story proclaimed:

> I stand upon the old law; upon law established more than three centuries ago, in cases contested with as much ability and learning as any in the annals of our jurisprudence, in resisting any such encroachments upon the rights and liberties of the citizens, secured by public grants. I will not consent to share their title deeds by any speculative niceties or novelties.[59]

The Chief Justice, on the other hand, relied heavily on a recently decided English case in the Court of King's Bench where a canal company claimed by implication rights which had not been expressly granted. The court found the fully established rule to be that any ambiguity in the terms of the contract must operate against the "adventurers" and in favor of the public.[60] "It would present a singular spectacle if, while the courts of England are restraining, within the strictest limits, the spirit of monopoly, and exclusive privileges in nature of monopolies, and confining corporations to the privileges plainly given to them in their charter; the courts of this country should be found enlarging these privileges by implication; and construing a statute more unfavorably to

---

[59] 11 Pet. 598.
[60] Proprietors of the Stourbridge Canal v. Wheely, 2 Barn. & Adol. 792 (1831).

88

the public, and to the rights of the community, than would be done in a like case in an English court of justice."[61]

Yet not even Chief Justice Taney, cautious as he was in such matters, could avoid counsel's example of going beyond precedents into theory of government in the process of searching for the rule to govern the interpretation of public grants. His statement is particularly important in light of the fact that, by contrast with other periods, Supreme Court pronouncements of the Taney period were largely barren of philosophical discussion—even the highly pragmatic type of philosophical discussion here represented.. The object and end of all government, Taney contended, was to promote the happiness and prosperity of the community. Therefore it could never be assumed that the government intended to diminish its power of accomplishing that end. Our rapidly growing country was in constant need of new channels of communication, commerce, and trade. The whole community had an interest in preserving undiminished the power to authorize such new channels, and a state ought never to be presumed to have surrendered such power. The continued existence of a government would be of little value if by implications and presumptions it was disarmed of the powers necessary to achieve the ends of its creation. As for the obligation to protect property rights, "While the rights of private property are sacredly guarded, we must not forget that the people also have rights, and that the happiness and well being of every citizen depends on their faithful preservation."[62]

In the light of these assumptions he thought it would indeed be a strong exertion of judicial power to raise, by a sort of judicial coercion, an implied contract from an instrument in which the legislature had taken pains to avoid language giving the exclusive rights here claimed. The Court could not take away from the states by legal intendments and mere technical reasoning "any portion of that power over their own internal police and improvement, which is so necessary to their well being and prosperity."[63]

At this point the Chief Justice moved into the realm of practical considerations. The principle here involved would apply to the vast number of charters given during the past forty years to turnpike companies and which had been in some degree supplanted by charters to canals and railroads:

> Let it once be understood that such charters carry with them these implied contracts, and give this unknown and undefined property in a

---

[61] 11 Pet. 545–46. Taney further cited a number of Supreme Court decisions to show that the rule of construction now prevailing in England prevailed in the United States as well.
[62] *Ibid.*, 548.
[63] *Ibid.*, 552.

line of traveling, and you will soon find the old turnpike corporations awakening from their sleep, and calling upon this court to put down the improvements which have taken their place. The millions of property which have been invested in railroads and canals, upon lines of travel which have been before occupied by turnpike corporations, will be put in jeopardy. We shall be thrown back to the improvements of the last century, and obliged to stand still until the claims of the old turnpike corporations shall be satisfied, and they shall consent to permit these States to avail themselves of the lights of modern science, and to partake of the benefit of those improvements which are now adding to the wealth and prosperity, and the convenience and comfort, of every other part of the civilized world.[64]

The Court would not assume responsibility for such a debacle. It adhered to its doctrine that public grants must be construed narrowly. It could not come to the aid of the Charles River Bridge.

With the announcement of the decision in the *Bridge Case*, some Democratic spokesmen leaped to the conclusion that the millennium had arrived. The editor of the *Boston Advocate* joyously proclaimed that the victory was due to the democratic principles of the Administration and to democratic judges on the Supreme Bench. "Taney, Baldwin, Barbour, Wayne, are democrats, appointed by a democratic President, and to them we owe the triumph of this great principle." Had the majority of the Court been composed of Whig judges, had vacancies been filled by guardians of vested rights such as Clay and Webster, the Warren Bridge would never have been free. Judge Story had "read a book, occupying over three hours in its delivery, in which he undertook to show that the bigoted blockheads who lived in the time of the old year books and my Lord Coke, were incomparably wiser than the present race, and that we had no business to do anything which they had not sanctioned! The opinion was full of learning and exclusive argument, wrought up with great power and ingenuity, but better suited to the dark days of Dudley and Empson than to this age and this country. There was not one liberal principle in it."[65]

Simon Greenleaf, returning to Cambridge where his associations were basically conservative and admiring of Justice Story, found it

---

[64] *Ibid.*, 552–53. Justice McLean similarly noted that "The spirit of internal improvements pervades the entire country" (*ibid.*, 583), and talked of the immense amount of business with which the Supreme Court would be overwhelmed if the taking of private property as here illustrated were held to impair the obligation of contracts. His strategy was to write a defense of the rights of the plaintiffs and then hold that the Supreme Court had no jurisdiction to give relief.

[65] The Editor of the *Boston Advocate*, Feb. 14, 1837, reprinted in the *Worcester Republican*, Feb. 22, 1837.

expedient to defend his work as counsel by an anonymously published article showing that his argument had been grounded in law and not in democratic propaganda and that he had not attacked vested rights but merely sought their protection in the state rather than in the Supreme Court.[66] During the argument he had written to Charles Sumner that he and Davis had avoided everything "peoplish" in their remarks and confined themselves closely to legal views.[67] Even so, he found his argument misrepresented, "as though it was agrarian in its character, and tended to the destruction of vested rights, and justified the taking of private property for public use *without* compensation." To vindicate himself with his pupils and others he placed on file at Harvard a scrapbook containing his papers and notes in the case.[68]

Webster, in defeat, assured Justice Story that his opinion left the opposition not a foot nor even an inch to stand on. The intelligent part of the profession would be with him. The decision of the Court had completely overturned one great provision of the Constitution.[69] Eight years later, when general acceptance of the decision was apparent, Webster could still say that when over the lapse of years he read the opinion of the Court he saw all the difference between "A manly and just maintenance of the right, and an ingenious, elaborate, and sometimes shamefaced apology for what is wrong."[70] Despairing of winning, or at any rate holding, a place of influence at the bar of the Supreme Court, or even in the Senate in light of his series of defeats during the Jackson Administration, Webster talked much of resigning from the Senate and devoting his life to private affairs, but undoubtedly with an eye also to the possibility of winning the Presidency which he regarded as currently the real locus of effective power.[71] A group of New York Whigs presided over by Chancellor Kent invited him to a public dinner to be given in his honor on his way home, resolving:

> That in the judgment of this meeting there is none among the living or the dead who has given to the country more just or able expositions of the Constitution of the United States; nor who has enforced, with more lucid and impassioned eloquence, the necessity and importance of the preservation of the Union, or exhibited more zeal or ability in defending the Constitution from the foes without the government, and foes within it, than Daniel Webster.[72]

---

[66] The Correspondent of the *Boston Atlas*, Feb. 1837, reprinted in the *Worcester Republican*, Feb. 22, 1837.

[67] Warren, *History of the Harvard Law School*, I, 532.

[68] Simon Greenleaf's longhand statement in front of his scrapbook on the *Bridge Case* as filed at Harvard University.

[69] *Life and Letters of Joseph Story*, II, 269.

[70] Warren, *History of the Harvard Law School*, I, 540.

[71] *Writings and Speeches of Daniel Webster*, II, 189.

[72] *Ibid.*, 190.

Webster gave up his alleged intention to resign from the Senate but stopped in New York where he was royally entertained and where he delivered an address suggesting a campaign for the Presidency.[73] William Kent, son of the ex-chancellor, had high praise for the speech of two and a half hours but noted that Webster showed the marks of his age and high living. He had become fat, and the exciting and luscious life he lived in Washington was beginning to tell on his frame.[74] Chancellor Kent, who dined with Webster and Justice Thompson and "his new and very young and flauntingly gay wife" (as a Justice who had concurred in Story's dissent in the Bridge Case Thompson was in good standing with the Whigs), reported that Webster had made a prodigious sensation in the city.[75] His Presidential ambitions, however, were not to be fulfilled, nor was the Supreme Court to be restored to a tribunal reflective of the sentiments of Chief Justice Marshall.

Chancellor Kent wrote to Justice Story that he had read the opinion of the Chief Justice in the *Bridge Case* and dropped it in disgust. By contrast he referred to Story's "masterly and exhausting argument."[76] Later he reread the opinion of the Court "with increased disgust." To his mind it abandoned the great principle of constitutional morality and went far to destroy the security and value of legislative franchises. It injured the moral sense of the community and destroyed the sanctity of contracts. "I abhor the doctrine that the legislature is not bound by everything that is necessarily implied in a contract, in order to give it effect and value, and by nothing that is not expressed *in haec verba*, that one rule of interpretation is to be applied to their engagements, and another rule to the contracts of individuals."[77]

In spite of the fact that the Justices worked together harmoniously, that the new Chief Justice conducted himself with great urbanity and that Justice Barbour proved to be a very conscientious and painstaking judge,[78] Justice Story was in despair about the Court and his despair was driven deeper by Chancellor Kent's criticism of the *Bridge* decision. He had sent Kent the opinions without comment and waited for his

---

[73] *Ibid.*, 193.

[74] William Kent to Moss Kent, Mar. 19, 1837, Kent Papers.

[75] James Kent to Joseph Story, Mar. 20, 1837, Kent Papers.

[76] Warren, *History of the Harvard Law School*, I, 539.

[77] James Kent to Joseph Story, June 23, 1837, *Life and Letters of Joseph Story*, II, 270. In a portion of this letter withheld from publication by Justice Story's son, Chancellor Kent said, "I have just now finished a studied perusal of the 11th volume of Peters Reports and I cannot avoid venting my grief and mortification *in confidence* to you. It appears to me that the Court has fallen from its high station and commanding dignity, and has lost its energy, and spirit, and independence, and accuracy, and surrendered up to the temper of the day, the true principles of the Constitution." James Kent to Joseph Story, June 23, 1837, Story Papers (M.H.S.).

[78] Joseph Story to Charles Sumner, Jan. 25, 1837, *Life and Letters of Joseph Story*, II, 266.

independent reaction. That reaction confirmed his own judgment. He had refrained from resigning only on persuasion from his friends. "I am sick at heart," he wrote sadly, "and now go to the discharge of my judicial duties in the Supreme Court with a firm belief that the future cannot be as the past."[79] While he remained on the Court he would on important occasions come out with his own opinions but oftentimes he would remain silent from a desire not to be contentious and to refrain from weakening the influence of the Court. One of the preeminent qualifications of a great judge, Story continued, was that he should have a supreme reverence for the law and the firmness to maintain its principles against the temper of the times and the fluctuations of party spirit. It would be the shipwreck of all great principles when Mr. Jefferson's momentous dogma should be realized: that the judges should represent and be made to feel the force of public and popular opinion.[80]

To Harriet Martineau, author of a work then currently published entitled *Society in America*,[81] Story reported the addition of the two new Justices to the Supreme Court: "Mr. Taney is the Chief Justice. I am the last of the old race of Judges. I stand their solitary representative, with a pained heart, and a subdued confidence. Do you remember the story of the last diner of a club, who dined once a year? I am in the predicament of the last survivor."[82]

In Boston the opinions in the *Bridge Case* were published for the use of the legislature, from which the Charles River Bridge now sought compensation for its losses. Justice Story wrote to Justice McLean, who had been for the Charles River Bridge in all save jurisdiction, that "Your opinion I have heard spoken of by gentlemen of the profession, in very high terms, and I think it has added strength to your judicial reputation."[83] Justice Story added that the opinion of the Chief Justice had not been deemed satisfactory and that a great majority of the ablest lawyers were against the decision of the Court.[84]

---

[79] Joseph Story to James Kent, June 26, 1837, in Charles Fairman, "The Retirement of Federal Judges," *Harv. L. Rev.*, 51:397, 413, 1938.

[80] *Ibid.*, 413–14.

[81] Harriet Martineau, *Society in America* (1837).

[82] Joseph Story to Harriet Martineau, Apr. 7, 1837, *Life and Letters of Joseph Story*, II, 277.

[83] Joseph Story to John McLean, May 10, 1837, *ibid.*, 272.

[84] *Ibid.*, 272. Charles Sumner, Greenleaf's replacement at Harvard during the argument of the case, had originally been won over to Green-leaf's side. When he first read the opinion of the Court he was impressed by the clearness and distinctness with which the Chief Justice had expressed himself and by the strategy which enabled him to avoid many considerations which counsel had introduced. But upon turning to Story's opinion he admitted realization of how much had been lacking in Taney's opinion. He concluded, in a figure attributed to Lord Mansfield, that rereading Taney's opinion after reading Story's was "taking hog-wash after champagne." "Charles Sumner to Joseph Story, Mar. 25, 1837,"

At the 1837 term of the Supreme Court the *Bridge* decision was accompanied by decisions on constitutional questions in *New York v. Miln*,[85] *Briscoe v. Bank of the Commonwealth of Kentucky*,[86] and other cases of importance. None of the decisions did anything to relieve Whig depression. Democrats, on the other hand, overestimating the extent of the change in the pattern of constitutional law, were exuberant. The *Democratic Review* for January, 1838, carried an important article on the Court by an able anonymous writer with a pronounced Democratic bias. The author professed in times past to have seen the federal judiciary "grasping at jurisdiction with a covetous eagerness, and a wide stretch of embrace, which could never be satisfied within any limits short of universal dominion."[87] Emphasizing the present trend toward Americanism and toward democracy, he noted that Taney was the only Chief Justice who had not been in foreign service,[88] and that he was "the first Chief Justice of these United States, who ever so far departed from precedent, (most portentously, we submit,) as *to give judgment in trowsers!*"[89] He approved of this spirit of sansculotteism.

The writer paid Justice Story the compliment of saying that no man had contributed more to the literature of the law or left his impress more distinctly on the work of the Court, or done more distinctive work on circuit. "His works have wrought the miracle of converting English and European contempt, into admiration of American law-learning. The practice of courts, admiralty, revenue, prize and common law, equity, the lesser law of nations, as well as international law, constitutional law, in short, almost all the departments of jurisprudence have been cultivated by Judge Story with most praiseworthy labor and flattering success."[90] Nevertheless he disapproved of the trend toward judicial aggrandizement, for which he regarded Story as in part responsible, saying that no such formidable power was known to any other representative government as the judicial veto, a power to dismiss laws as the President might dismiss officers, without question.[91] But better days were now predicted.

This moderate article with a Democratic bias was perhaps more offensive to Whig sympathizers than more extreme emotional outpourings, of which there were many. The editor of the passionately Whig *New York Review* implored Justice Story to write a reply article for his publication, laying down the "true" principles and signalizing the "bad" and defending the Court where unjustly attacked: "Let us make

Proceedings of Massachusetts Historical Society, 2nd series, 15:210–11, 1902.

[85] 11 Pet. 102.
[86] 11 Pet. 257.
[87] "The Supreme Court of the United States: Its Judges and Jurisdiction," *Democratic Review*, 1:142, 146, 1838.
[88] *Ibid.*, 150.
[89] *Ibid.*, 152.
[90] *Ibid.*, 156.
[91] *Ibid.*, 166.

a lofty stand for the right, the noble, the true, against the miserable loco-focoism that rides rampant and roaring over the most sacred institutions and only defences of American freedom."[92] Story's name could be kept secret, and the editor could get Chancellor Kent to insert appropriate passages about Justice Story himself.

Justice Story declined to write the article, but expressed the wish that Chancellor Kent prepare it. The vitriolic and authoritarian ex-chancellor agreed to do so.[93] He set the tone of his anonymous article by characterizing the Supreme Court as the balance-wheel of the machinery of the Constitution and then saying that "until recently" it had contributed more than any other institution to inspire universal confidence in the stability of the Constitution and in the wisdom and integrity of the national administration of justice.[94] He summarized with high praise the contributions of the Marshall Court and then entered upon a review of the eleventh volume of Peters' *Reports* and of Justice Baldwin's *A General View of the Origin and Nature of the Constitution*. These works, he said, contained the decisions of the Supreme Court under a new dynasty; "and in reading those decisions, we perceive at once an altered tone and a narrower spirit, not only in Chief Justice Taney, but even in some of the old associates of Chief Justice Marshall, when they handle constitutional questions. The change is so great and so ominous, that a gathering gloom is cast over the future. We seem to have sunk suddenly below the horizon, to have lost the light of the sun, and to hold on our way *per incertam lunam, sub luce maligna*."[95]

At this point Chancellor Kent proceeded to pick to pieces the opinion of the Court in the *Bridge Case*, saying in lament, "What a deep injury has this decision inflicted on the Constitution, jurisprudence, and character of the United States! we are fast sinking even below the standard of Pagan antiquity."[96] He had high praise for most of Justice McLean's opinion but deplored its "astonishingly lame and impotent conclusion."[97] He concluded, "The Judges of the Supreme Court have no business to be looking with timidity and awe upon the State sovereignties, as if they were the safer and the purer sovereigns, and as if the powers arrested from them were taken from their proper place, and committed to some forbidding and dangerous sovereignty."[98]

---

[92] C. S. Henry to Joseph Story, undated (postmarked Jan. 23) 1838, Story Papers.

[93] C. S. Henry to Joseph Story, Feb. 23, 1838, Story Papers.

[94] [James Kent], "Supreme Court of the United States," *N.Y. L. Rev.*, 2: 372, 1838.

[95] *Ibid.*, 385.

[96] *Ibid.*, 390.

[97] *Ibid.*

[98] *Ibid.*, 404. For another critical but less personal and vituperative article see "Constitutional Law," *North American Review*, 46:126, 1838, said to have been written by Charles S. Davies, a member of the Portland bar and a friend of Justice Story. On the point of authorship see Fairman, "The Retirement of Federal

The *Democratic Review* answered the Kent article, but largely without resort to comparable vituperation. In extenuation it remarked that at the time the article was written the whole country was in the grip of the panic of 1837 and that even the most distinguished persons did not always escape the influences of such excitement. Of Chief Justice Taney and his opinion in the *Bridge Case,* the writer noted with deep perception:

> It is a most able document, bearing on its face those features for which all the intellectual productions of that distinguished statesman and jurist are remarkable. He clears the very intricate subject before the Court of all irrelevant matter, with the unerring instinct of genius; and as he pursues his unbroken chain of clear, logical reasoning, spreads light all around, leaving no cloud to confound or mislead those who may come after him. Indeed the present Chief Justice escapes from irrelevant matter with as much ease as Judge Marshall or the most distinguished of the English Judges. Like them he seizes the true question in the case, and never loses sight of it for a single instant. He strips off, gently but firmly, all the disguises with which forensic eloquence often veil the truth, and without fear or hesitation follows wherever she may lead.[99]

Chancellor Kent had made the mistake of asking for the pressure of public opinion upon the Court, a kind of pressure which, on its face at least, Justice Story had deplored. True, Kent was asking for pressure from people whose thinking was like his own, and which, with respect to modification of judicial trends, would inspire the Court "with a larger infusion of the spirit of moderation and forbearance." The *Democratic Review* quite naturally replied, "Yes, enlightened public opinion has already acted, and is now acting; and that man must be blind indeed to the signs of the times, who does not see that the Court has been fully sustained in those very respects about which so much complaint has been made in a certain quarter."[100]

To return briefly to the story of the Charles River Bridge itself, the competition of free traffic on the Warren Bridge meant that the collection of tolls was at an end. Rather than permit free use of the structure, the proprietors raised the draw and left it unused. When they lost their case in the Supreme Court they petitioned the legislature for compensation. The heat of partisan feeling long prevented a settlement. Finally, in 1841, the legislature appropriated $25,000 in return for

---

Judges," *Harv. L. Rev.*, 51:397, 411, n. 40, 1938.
[99] "The Supreme Court of the United States," *Democratic Review,* 7:497, 503–04, 1840.
[100] *Ibid.*, 314.

which the title of the Charles River Bridge was transferred to the state. Being in need of more highway space, the state now operated both bridges, and being in need of revenue, it converted both bridges into toll bridges. Private company tolls with high rewards for investments were abolished but government tolls took their place. Whether Massachusetts observed the good faith for which Simon Greenleaf demanded that it be trusted can be debated. Eventually Harvard College was reimbursed to the extent of $3,333.30, an amount much less than the originally anticipated payments from the Charles River Bridge.[101]

The rule announced by the Supreme Court that public grants were to be construed narrowly, so violently denounced by the critics of the Court, remained in good standing throughout the Taney period and thereafter. Speaking for the Court in 1862, Justice Clifford noted that "Judge Story dissented from the views of the majority of the judges, but the opinion of the court has since that time been constantly followed. Later decisions of this court regard the rule as settled, that public grants are to be construed strictly, and that nothing passes by implication."[102] If perchance announcement of the rule worked hardships as to grants previously made, it induced future applicants for corporate privileges to specify more clearly the scope of the privileges sought. It protected the public against inadvertent loss of property and against privileges not clearly intended to be given. For all the distress of the critics of the decision, it would seem ultimately to have been salutary.[103]

The work of the 1837 term thus marked the beginning of a new order. The transition was not a sharp one, and those who saw it as

---

[101] This statement is summarized from Warren, *History of the Harvard Law School*, I, 541–43.

[102] Rice v. Minnesota & Southwestern R.R., 1 Black 358, 380 (1862). The intervening cases on this point are cited on this page.

[103] It is to be noted that although the judicial holding was that the contract rights conveyed by charter were to be construed narrowly, it did not provide for their abolition. By legislative acts never brought before the Supreme Court such rights were often drastically impaired in ways which the Court presumably would not have justified. Of interest is the following observation of performance by the Georgia legislature:

It is a perfect mob talking spitting smoking &c &c, and what is still worse I can see but little difference between *our* people and *yours.* I was much amused yesterday at the manner of treating 'vested rights.' In 1836 the Legislature passed an act incorporating a Life & Trust company at Columbus. It was got on another bill and hurried through with some very objectionable provisions. It is not contended that they have violated their charter but a bill has been introduced to repeal it without giving the parties an opportunity to be heard and passed the House yesterday almost unanimously. There seems to be but one subject in which they all agree and that is the omnipotence of the Legislature.

Erastus Smith to Gideon Welles, Dec. 15, 1839, Welles Papers.

such were mistaken. In spite of the radical doctrines sponsored by some Jacksonians of the time, the Court was careful to adhere to traditional patterns. In the *Bridge Case*, for example, there was no challenge to the status of the charter of a private corporation as a contract. The holding of the Marshall Court in the *Dartmouth College Case* stood firm. The same was true of the other highly controversial cases of this term. The change was limited, sometimes almost infinitesimal, and yet it was there. There was a greater tendency to look to items of local welfare and to emphasize the rights of the states, a greater concern with living democracy in a rapidly changing society. The tendency was to manifest itself further in succeeding terms in other kinds of cases. There was a modification of precedent also in the fact that Taney made no attempt as Chief Justice to take upon himself the task of speaking for the Court in most of the cases decided, as Chief Justice Marshall had done. While he spoke for the Court in the *Bridge Case*, he left to other Justices spokesmanship in the other cases which brought notoriety. He did the same with respect to cases of lesser importance. It became clear, therefore, that the new Chief Justice intended to be democratic with respect to the inner workings of the Court. The Taney Court was to be genuinely a Court first of seven and then of nine members, and not a reflection of the ideas and the personality of the Chief Justice.

CHAPTER V

The Realm of Finance

IN A PUBLIC LETTER TO John Quincy Adams on November 11, 1836, Nicholas Biddle, able, shrewd, and powerful president of the Bank of the United States, wrote:

> The country five years ago, was in possession of the most beautiful machinery of currency and exchanges the world ever saw. It consisted of a number of state banks protected, and, at the same time, restrained by the Bank of the United States.[1]

Quite understandable was Biddle's nostalgia for an order that was gone. Understandable also were the ominous aspects of his statement which left the enemies of his Bank determined that the abandoned order should never be restored. For twenty years the Bank of the United States, in conjunction with banks chartered by the several states, had performed the desirable functions of a central banking system in that, directly or indirectly, it had determined the size of the stream of credit and the issue of bank note currency in terms of the needs of the United States as viewed from its own headquarters.[2] Undoubtedly it had performed

---

[1] *Niles' Weekly Register*, 51:245, 1836.

[2] For accounts of the operations of the Bank of the United States as interpreted by authors sensitive to the needs of the country for centralized control of currency and credit, see for example R. C. H. Catterall, *The Second Bank of the United States*; Fritz Redlich, *The Molding of American Banking* (1947); and Bray Hammond, *Banks and Politics in America from the Revolution to the Civil War.*

For the author's account of the bank war as Taney was involved in it, more elaborate than it is here possible to insert, see his *Roger B. Taney.* For Taney's own account as left in a rough longhand draft started in 1849, see Carl Brent Swisher, ed., Roger B. Taney's "Bank War Manuscript," *Maryland Historical Magazine*, 53, 103–30, 215–37, 1958, cited herein as Bank War Manuscript. For significant correspondence on the part of the Bank see *The Correspondence of*

great services for the country. In some instances it had even well served state banks themselves by demanding specie payments for their notes when such banks had overextended their credit. It had exercised from afar a stabilizing judgment over local interests which lacked the perspective of long-range observation.

Yet the situation involved danger, in that the state banks could exercise no reciprocal checks on the Bank of the United States if it abused its power. Neither could adequate restraint be exercised by the federal government, which, although it had chartered the Bank and owned a fifth of the stock and chose a fifth of the directors, had little to do directly with its management. In the five-year period referred to by Biddle the bank war had been fought over the recharter of the Bank. The war had been started by the Bank and won by its enemies in the Jackson Administration. All the Jackson appointees to the Supreme Court had been in some degree engaged in the Administration struggle with the Bank, and their thinking about the management of banking and currency and credit had presumably been in some degree influenced by that experience. Of the several new Justices the most deeply involved had been the Chief Justice himself, in his capacities as Jackson's Attorney General and Secretary of the Treasury.

Taney's deep involvement had begun with an official opinion of June 27, 1832, in which as Attorney General he advised Jackson to veto a bill about to be passed by Congress under Whig leadership to insure at once renewal of the Bank charter which was to expire four years later. The opinion showed Taney already committed to a narrower conception of the scope of congressional power than that which characterized the Marshall Court. He did not challenge the power of Congress to establish a national bank—here accepting the decision in *McCulloch v. Maryland*.[3] He did question whether the Court in that decision had gone beyond this general holding to approve or even to consider the constitutional questions transcending the mere matter of establishment. The Court, he contended, had not decided whether Congress could constitutionally give to the Bank exclusive banking rights, or rights for a specified period, or a particular capitalization, or whether the Bank could establish branches at its discretion. Charter provisions on these and other points were constitutional, Taney contended, only if they were "necessary and proper," a determination which a court was not in a position to make. The executive, on the other hand, in the exercise of the legislative function of approving or disapproving bills passed by Congress, ought to look to these important constitutional questions. In discussing these questions for Jackson, Taney argued that

Nicholas Biddle Dealing with National Affairs, 1807–1844, Reginald C. Mc-Grane, ed.

[3] 4 Wheat. 316 (1819).

a national bank could be constitutionally maintained only if its functions were drastically reduced below those of the present Bank and those provided for in the current bill for renewal of the charter.

In the same opinion Taney made another highly controversial point about the nature of a banking corporation and the consequent scope of the constitutional protection of its charter. While admitting that Congress had the power to create a corporation to exercise fiscal functions if doing so was found to be "necessary and proper," he refused to look upon such a corporation as a purely private organization with charter rights not subject to impairment. Instead he saw it as a public body with rights and powers subject to increase or decrease as the public interest might require. He contended that inclusion in the charter of guarantees against such adjustments in the public interest violated the Constitution and justified veto of the bill.[4] In making his point he laid the groundwork for a similar argument against the immutability of bank charters which was to be used in future years in controversies over state banks.

Congress passed the bill, and Jackson called on Taney to aid in drafting a veto message.[5] This he did, along with Amos Kendall and Levi Woodbury, then Secretary of the Treasury, who in 1845 was to be appointed to the Supreme Court to succeed Justice Story. The veto message, as submitted July 10, 1832, had much of the content of the Taney opinion, the forthrightness and vigor of Jackson, and a popular literary flair attributable to Kendall. It was a politically challenging document which threw the odds to Jackson in the upcoming presidential campaign.

Yet at one point, on a constitutional issue, the ghost-writers made a mistake in strategy of which the Whigs took full advantage. On the subject of the obligation of the President to follow constitutional interpretations by the Supreme Court the message said in part:

> If the opinion of the Supreme Court covered the whole ground of this act, it ought not to control the coordinate authorities of this Government. The Congress, the Executive, and the Court must each for itself be guided by its own opinion of the Constitution. Each public officer who takes an oath to support the Constitution swears that he will support it as he understands it, and not as it is understood by others.[6]

---

[4] Opinion of Roger B. Taney Regarding the Recharter of the Bank of the U.S., June 27, 1832, Jackson Papers.

[5] For the drafting of the message see Bank War Manuscript 226–27.

[6] J. D. Richardson, *A Compilation of the Messages and Papers of the Presidents*, II, 582.

The quotation clearly had its origin in Taney's position that although the President must enforce statutes as he found them, he must use his independent judgment on constitutionality when participating in the enactment or reenactment of statutes. But the passage in the message seemed to imply that in the enforcement of statutes as well as in their enactment the President had a right to ignore judicial interpretations of the Constitution, and Daniel Webster took full advantage of the seeming invitation to Presidential lawlessness, doing so in part through a Senate speech circulated throughout the country at the expense of the Bank.[7] Henry Clay and other Whigs joined him in denouncing the veto and the insidious constitutional doctrines they found in the message.

For decades thereafter this issue came up for renewed argument. In 1860, in connection with the preparation of his memoirs, Martin Van Buren wrote to the then aged Chief Justice for an explanation of the controversy. In a preliminary reply, which he asked Van Buren to destroy along with other confidential items because "a multitude of such evil spirits will be sure to gather about your grave and mine," the Chief Justice complained of the deliberate garbling and misrepresentation of the message, and insisted that the President was talking only about his right of independent judgment on constitutional questions when exercising his legislative function. He had claimed no right to refuse enforcement to statutes which he himself thought unconstitutional. Nevertheless, Taney admitted, "The proposition is perhaps too loosely stated in the message, and the error overlooked. You know the same thing happened in the protest[8] and from the same hand and the same cause."[9]

Perhaps for authorized use in the memoirs, Taney later wrote Van Buren a formal letter defending the message and making no admission of faulty phrasing. He there asserted that Jackson had never expressed a doubt concerning his obligation to carry into execution any Act of Congress regularly passed, whatever his own opinion on the constitu-

---

[7] *Writings and Speeches of Daniel Webster*, J. W. McIntyre, ed., VI, 165.

[8] This reference is to a "Protest" filed by Jackson with the Senate on Apr. 15, 1834, in response to a Senate resolution condemning the President for removal of government deposits from the Bank of the United States. Here again, in asserting the powers of the President, Jackson seems to have overstated his case, with the result that a supplement had to be sent disavowing any implication that Congress could not legislate on the custody and disposition of public funds. For the

Protest and the supplemental statement see Richardson, *Messages and Papers of the Presidents*, III, 69.

[9] R. B. Taney to Martin Van Buren, May 8, 1860, Van Buren Papers. Since Amos Kendall participated in the drafting of both the veto message and the protest, it is presumed that he was the man blamed by Taney for bad phrasing. For Jackson's invitation to Kendall to participate in drafting the protest see *Correspondence of Andrew Jackson*, John Spencer Bassett, ed., V, 257–58.

tional question. Indeed, at the time of the veto message he was executing all provisions of the existing charter of the Bank and he continued to do so until the act expired.[10]

Other events of the bank war remained acutely clear in the recollection of the Chief Justice. In his account of the struggle, begun in 1849 at the middle of his judicial career and near the end of the lifetime of Webster who in the meantime had argued many cases before the Taney Court, he recalled the tone and temper of the speech made by Webster in his dual capacity as United States Senator and counsel for the Bank. He referred to the princely income that Webster was receiving from the Bank, whether or not he was paid for this particular speech, and contended that the speech was prepared deliberately to deceive the uninformed. Having written the comment, Taney then struck it out, as if finding it indiscreet for a Chief Justice writing about a leading statesman of the day who might again appear before him in Court.[11]

The veto message helped to sustain the veto and to reelect Jackson to the Presidency. Thereafter the administration set a watch to prevent further abuse of power on the part of the Bank. Part of that power derived from the fact that government deposits with it served as a basis for credit and profitable business. Jackson had as one of his goals the liquidation of the entire national debt. Nicholas Biddle, as president of the Bank, could think of much more satisfying ways of using government revenues than redemption of outstanding government bonds. For a time he was able to persuade the Treasury Department to delay its call of certain issues. Then, without the knowledge of the department, the Bank arranged to prevent redemption in part by persuading Baring Brothers, the great English banking house, to hold up United States bonds held abroad instead of permitting them to be sent back to the Treasury. Since interest on the bonds was not paid by the government after they were called, the Bank itself agreed to pay the interest as a

---

[10] R. B. Taney to Martin Van Buren, June 30, 1860, Van Buren Papers. Although Van Buren preserved in his files both the formal and informal letters from Taney, he did not make direct use of them in his history but relied instead on contemporary Congressional materials. The reason may conceivably have been Taney's own unpopularity during the Civil War period resulting from his attitude toward slavery and secession. See Martin Van Buren, *Inquiry into the Origin and Course of Political Parties in the United States*, 325–31.

[11] Bank War Manuscript, 230–31. Additional evidence of belief in the widespread corruption of members of Congress attempted by the Bank is to be found in the following excerpt from a Jefferson Davis letter to William Allen: "I had but cannot now find a speech of yours showing that the U.S. Bank loaned at a time which indicated the purpose, more money to members of Congress than the amount of their pay. Can you send me a copy of that speech?" Jefferson Davis to William Allen, Mar. 25, 1844, Allen Papers.

condition of having them held back. The agent of the Bank, further-more, allegedly in excess of instructions, also arranged for the Barings to buy outright for the Bank some of the called bonds, and hold the certificates as security. In the language of the leading historian of the Bank, "The affair made a great noise, and kept the bank's advocates busy explaining for many months."[12]

This maneuvering on the part of the Bank so enraged the Jack-sonians that some of them seriously considered seeking from the United States Circuit Court in Philadelphia, the home city of the Bank, an order to forfeit the charter. A realist in the area of judicial strategy, Taney advised against such a step. He opposed it primarily on the ground that the action would have to be brought before Justice Henry Baldwin, an advocate of the recharter of the Bank. He feared that Baldwin might give way to his deep feelings on the subject, and in his charge to the jury might reply to the veto message and deliver a lecture to the Presi-dent on the subject.[13] Whatever the reasons, the Administration abandoned thought of forfeiture of the Bank's charter during the re-maining years of its life and set out to curb its powers by gradually depriving it of the use of government deposits.

From September, 1833, to May, 1834, Taney as Secretary of the Treasury faced onslaught from the Bank-Whig forces in Congress and in the business community. He nevertheless withheld government in-come from the Bank and placed it with selected state banks, while reducing government funds in the hands of the national bank by paying government expenses therefrom. The Bank and its friends continued to seek its recharter, but to no avail. While, particularly where some of his friends were involved, Taney had occasion for disillusion with state banks as well,[14] and moved in the direction of a hard money position, nothing in the experience modified his judgment of what Jackson called the "Monster," the Bank of the United States.

Among the local banks that failed to live up to the high standards

---

[12] Catterall, *The Second Bank of the United States*, 272. For a more elaborate discussion see adjacent pages in the same work and also Bank War Manuscript, 232–37.

[13] Bank War Manuscript, 234–35.

[14] For Taney's full account of the story of Taney's difficulties with his Baltimore friend, Thomas Ellicott, see Stuart Bruchey, ed., "Roger Brooke Taney's Account of His Relations with Thomas Ellicott in the Bank War," *Maryland Historical Magazine*, 53: 58–74, 131–52, 1958. Disillusionment

with state banks in other areas than Maryland developed as some of the more powerful of those banks en-gaged in political activities on a large scale. A Connecticut politician was led to ask, "Has it come to this that we have put down the U.S. Bank for interfering with our elections and ap-pointments; and are to have the little fingers of our State deposit banks, stronger than the loins of the U.S. Bank?" William H. Ellis to Gideon Welles, Dec. 31, 1835, Welles Papers.

which Taney sought to preserve were a number in the District of Columbia, which of course had their charters not from any state but from Congress. Three of them had suspended specie payments at a critical time in 1834, thereby adding greatly to the difficulties of the Treasury Department in operating its new program. Existing charters expired in 1836. In that year Congress passed a bill of eight lines extending the charters of seven district banks for two years.[15] Although Taney was by this time Chief Justice, Jackson referred the bill to him for comment. Taney advised against a veto, since, as he stated, Jackson had made a practice of vetoing bills only when he deemed them unconstitutional, but he took the occasion to denounce the banks which had suspended specie payment. To him the fact that they had to suspend was evidence that they had been mismanaged. If they had been mismanaged, they had not served the public, the reason for their existence had been nullified, and the charters ought not to be renewed.

At this point came Taney's significant statement of legal theory. Every charter, he contended, was a grant of a peculiar privilege and gave to the recipients rights and privileges not possessed by other members of the community. It would be against the spirit of our free institutions to grant such special privileges merely for the advancement of private interests. No charter should be granted on that ground: "The consideration upon which alone, such peculiar privileges can be granted is the expectation and prospect of promoting thereby some public interest, and it follows from these principles that in every case where it is proposed to grant or renew a charter the interests or wishes of the individuals who desire to be incorporated, ought not to influence the decision of the Government. The only inquiry which the constituted authorities can properly make on such an application, is whether the charter applied for, is likely to produce any real benefit to the community, and whether that benefit is sufficient to justify the grant."[16] The opinion indicated the attitude likely to be taken by the new Chief Justice not only toward banking corporations but toward other private corporations as well—as in the instance of the *Charles River Bridge Case*, already discussed.

From the time of the first meeting of the Taney Court in 1837, decisions with respect to money and banking intertwined chronologically with extra-judicial pronouncements on the subject. Awaiting action by a full Court was *Briscoe v. Bank of the Commonwealth of Kentucky*, which had been continued from the 1834 term. The case had been argued before five of the seven Justices, who apparently

---

[15] For the bill as enacted see 5 Stat. 69.

[16] From a draft in Taney's longhand, June 20, 1836, Jackson Papers.

divided three to two in holding that the notes issued by the Kentucky bank were bills of credit which states were forbidden to issue. At that time the Court entered the notation:

> As it is the practice of this court not to decide questions involving constitutional points arising under the 25th section of the act of 1789 unless with a concurrence of four Judges, and as that concurrence cannot be obtained in the present case—it is therefore ordered by the court that this cause be and the same is hereby continued to the next term of this court to be reargued before a full court.[17]

The same situation prevailed at two ensuing terms, and the reargument did not take place until 1837.

The *Briscoe* case was argued before the Taney Court from January 28 to February 1, 1837, and decided ten days later. Neither in the case nor in the counsel does there seem to have been the widespread public interest that was shown in the *Bridge Case*, even though Senator Henry Clay, who had opposed the confirmation of the new Chief Justice, appeared for the bank. If this opposition might seem to endanger his case, it was counterbalanced by the fact that another opponent, Senator Samuel L. Southard, appeared for Briscoe. Also of counsel were Joseph M. White for Briscoe and Benjamin Hardin for the bank. The bank was the victor, and Justice McLean, who wrote the opinion for the Court, seems to have made extensive use of Clay's argument.

Clay was a keen debater, of whom it was said that "on sudden occasions he utters bursts of declamatory eloquence which are very effective. He is a tall, thin man, with twinkling small grey eyes, a florid complexion, scanty sandy hair, and a wide mouth. The expression of his face is lively, intelligent and pleasing. His manner and appearance give one the impression that he is playing a part, and canvassing for popularity."[18] He was distrusted by conventional Southern politicians who regarded him as something of a parvenu,[19] and no doubt by Easterners and Northerners as well, but he nevertheless maintained himself as the leading Whig in the country over a considerable period.

The *Briscoe* case closely resembled the case of *Craig v. Missouri*,[20] decided in 1830. The *Craig* case had to do with the refusal of debtors to repay to the state sums borrowed from the state in the form of loan

---

[17] Briscoe v. Bank of Commonwealth of Kentucky, 8 Pet. 118, 122 (1834).

[18] "The Diaries of Sydney George Fisher," *Pennsylvania Magazine of History and Biography*, 76:183, 1952.

[19] See "Representative Men, Andrew Jackson and Henry Clay," *Southern Literary Messenger*, 19:585, 1853.

[20] 4 Pet. 410.

certificates issued by it, on the ground that the certificates were bills of credit which the state was forbidden to issue. The Supreme Court, with Justices Johnson, Thompson, and McLean dissenting, held that the certificates were indeed bills of credit and that the state was not entitled to recover. One of the justifications of Justice Thompson's dissent was the argument that the principle of the decision would extend also to the prohibition of the notes of state banks. The *Briscoe* case involved an attempt to avoid repayment of a debt which a debtor had incurred in borrowing state bank notes issued by the Bank of the Commonwealth of Kentucky. The bank was owned by the state and the state chose its officers. The bank was intimately related to the governmental machinery of the state but its official acts were in its own name and not in that of the state. Counsel for Briscoe and others contended that the bank notes were in essence like those of Missouri, which had been condemned as bills of credit, and that these notes too must be so classified. The Kentucky Court of Appeals denied the identity of the two cases, saying "They are distinguishable in at least one important and essential particular,"[21] but refrained from stating what that particular was.

As Whigs opposed to local inflationary measures, Hardin and Clay, for the bank, had to disavow the measure on policy grounds even as they denied that the notes were bills of credit. The state had resorted to this and other "quack medicines" because after the War of 1812 the people had incurred financial distress by excessive purchases of imported goods. The remedy had not worked, and for a time the notes of the bank had greatly depreciated, although later they had returned to par. Clay noted, furthermore, that some of the people now seeking to escape payment on the ground of the unconstitutionality of the note issues had been among the most enthusiastic advocates of establishment of the bank. He doubted that the cause of good morals would be served by giving them relief from the obligations that had been incurred. But in any event, were the notes bills of credit? He contended that they were not, since they had been issued in the name of the bank and not the state, and were not backed by the credit of the state.[22]

Apart from the *Craig* case, which had been decided by a closely divided Court, there was little guidance as to the meaning of the term "bills of credit." Except for the difficulty of distinguishing the *Craig* case, the *Briscoe* case could easily have gone either way as far as the search for verbal meaning was concerned. But even Whigs were fully aware that the country needed the currency provided by state bank

---

[21] Briscoe v. Bank of the Commonwealth, 30 Ky. (7 Marshall) 349 (1832).

[22] Briscoe v. Bank of the Commonwealth of Kentucky, 11 Pet. 257, 280 (1837).

notes, and needed it all the more now that the Bank of the United States had been reduced to the level of, or transformed into, a mere state bank in Pennsylvania. Since in 1830 Justice McLean, riding a Western circuit, had dissented from the holding that Missouri loan certificates were to be classified as the forbidden bills of credit, it was only natural that now, in a case from his circuit which then included Kentucky, he should deny that notes were bills of credit when issued by a bank and not by a state, even when the state owned the bank. He wrote the opinion of the Supreme Court in which it was stated:

> To constitute a bill of credit within the Constitution, it must be issued by a State, on the faith of the State, and be designed to circulate as money. It must be a paper which circulates on the credit of the State, and is so received and used in the ordinary business of life.[23]

The Kentucky bank notes were not to be so described, and were therefore not bills of credit.

In lone protest, Justice Story wrote a ringing dissent. He denied that to outlaw as bills of credit the notes of the Kentucky bank would classify as forbidden bills of credit the notes of all state banks. It was notes issued by states, and not by banks chartered by states, that were proscribed. In this case the state and the bank were the same. Resort to the bank was a mere subterfuge to get around the Constitution. The framers of the Constitution had been concerned not with eliminating note issues by private banks but with preventing their issue by states, after a pattern which had "constituted the darkest pages in American annals."[24]

Even more than in the *Bridge Case*, Justice Story here revealed his despair over the passing of the old order. At the first argument in the case the majority had deemed the act establishing the bank unconstitutional and void; that majority had included Chief Justice Marshall, "a name never to be pronounced without reverence."[25] He quoted from Marshall in the *Craig* case—"a voice now speaking from the dead."[26] At the close of his long and closely reasoned opinion he explained that he had written it because he was of the opinion that upon constitutional questions "the public have a right to know the opinion of every judge who dissents from the opinion of the court, and the reasons of his dissent"—a position very different from that of the Marshall Court in its early years. He then continued with respect to Marshall:

> I have another and strong motive—my profound reverence and affection for the dead. Mr. Chief Justice Marshall is not here to speak for

---

[23] *Ibid.*, 318.   [24] *Ibid.*, 348.   [25] *Ibid.*, 328.   [26] *Ibid.*, 332.

himself, and knowing full well the grounds of his opinion, in which I concurred, that this act is unconstitutional, I have felt an earnest desire to vindicate his memory from the imputation of rashness, or want of deep reflection. Had he been living, he would have spoken in the joint names of both of us.[27]

This was the prime example but not the last one wherein apostles of the old order attempted to cast the vote of a deceased Chief Justice in the decision of a case.

In any event, whoever was right as to the proper interpretation of the constitutional phrase, the Supreme Court restated again and again its position that state bank notes were not bills of credit, referring not merely to notes of private banks chartered by states but also to those of banks which were little more than arms of the states themselves.[28] The question eventually lost much of its public importance when, as a result of the financial pressures of the Civil War, the federal government chartered national banks throughout the country with the power to issue notes to circulate as money, and taxed out of existence similar notes issued by state banks.[29]

The fact that Chief Justice Taney wrote no opinion in the *Briscoe* case is not to be taken as implying that he had lost interest in financial matters after becoming a judge. Indeed, insofar as time permitted he had continued to give advice to the President while performing his judicial duties. The previous summer he had written a proposed veto message for the bill passed by Congress to deposit with the several states the surplus revenue in the federal treasury. The bill had been passed with mixed motives, some of them probably casting aspersions on Taney's system of using selected state banks as federal depositories. Beyond that, it was clear that the so-called deposit with the states was likely to turn into an outright gift, and a precedent would be established for the raising of unneeded revenue by the federal government for

---

[27] *Ibid.*, 350. Chancellor Kent concurred fully in Story's mournful sentiments. "It absolutely overwhelms me in despair, and I have no hopes left especially when I consider that we have two new Judges [Catron and McKinley]—very feeble lights added to your bench. I think that decision is monstrous. . . . I am astonished that Judge Thompson should have deserted you, but he had married a wife [a subject much gossiped about because of the advanced age of the Justice and the youth and vivacity of his new wife] and could not come to the rescue of the Supreme Court. . . . I respect it no longer." James Kent to Joseph Story, June 23, 1837, Story Papers (M.H.S.).

[28] See Woodruff v. Trapnall, 10 How. 190 (1851); Darrington v. Bank of Alabama, 13 How. 12 (1851); and Curran v. Arkansas, 15 How. 304 (1853). The credit pledged for the redemption of the notes, it is true, was the credit allocated by the state to the bank, and not the state's credit as a whole.

[29] See Veazie Bank v. Fenno, 8 Wall. 533 (1869).

support and then for coercion of the states. Presumably Taney saw also the possibility that the proposed deposit with the states would lead to increased expenditures and speed the inflationary trends that were now in evidence and that had already led the government to curb the speculative purchase of public lands by requiring payments exclusively in gold and silver.[30]

Jackson reluctantly signed the deposit bill in spite of Taney's advice but Taney nevertheless remained in good standing as a Presidential counsellor. In October, 1836, Jackson wrote to Taney to ask for help on a farewell address he planned to give, somewhat after the fashion of Washington. Among other things he wanted to stress the dangerous power of the Bank of the United States and the dangers of speculation and corruption emanating from a paper money system.[31] Taney promised to think the matter over while holding Circuit Court in Dover and then give his impressions—which he did. He noted the financial disturbances resulting from expanded note issues of the Bank of the United States shortly before its federal charter expired, with corresponding expansion by state banks. He noted the inflationary effects of the distribution of the federal surplus to the states. He thought the West had been saved from bankruptcy and ruin by the Treasury order requiring payment for public lands in specie. But he thought that the fundamental trouble lay with the paper money system. The currency would always be subject to ruinous fluctuations as long as it consisted of paper, and the only cure was to return to the constitutional currency of gold and silver. He had hoped that the state governments would institute their own currency reforms but he now feared that they would be too much influenced by speculators and that it would be necessary for Congress to act to prevent the issue of small notes, wherein much abuse was involved. He expressed the opinion that "The currency will not be entirely stable until no note under twenty dollars can be issued and for my own part I should prefer to go gradually to fifty."[32] In the light of this attitude the decision of the Supreme Court in the *Briscoe* case must have seemed at best a choice between evils, and it is to be wondered whether the Chief Justice may have considered joining Justice Story in dissent.

Jackson's farewell address of March 4, 1837, was duly given to the public,[33] the portion of it dealing with finance bearing the stamp of Taney's hand. This was his last task performed for Jackson as

---

[30] For the veto message proposed by Taney see *Correspondence of Andrew Jackson*, V, 404. For Taney's informal explanation of his position see R. B. Taney to Andrew Jackson, June 27, 1836, *ibid.*, 409.

[31] Andrew Jackson to R. B. Taney, Oct. 13, 1836, *ibid.*, 409.

[32] R. B. Taney to Andrew Jackson, Oct. 27, 1836, *ibid.*, 432.

[33] Richardson, *Messages and Papers of the Presidents*, III, 292.

President but he continued to correspond with him about public affairs. Financial news quickly became grim. On his way home to Tennessee, Jackson wrote to President Van Buren that a gigantic banking speculation in Mississippi had exploded, that as a repercussion many strong banking houses in New Orleans had collapsed, and that general bankruptcy among speculators was to be expected.[34] On his arrival at home Jackson sent a warning that the deposit banks of the West and South were in trouble, and that the Secretary of the Treasury, Levi Woodbury, should look to the safety of the public funds. In New York, Chancellor Kent wrote of the fall of great banking houses,[35] and William Kent wrote of the rage for speculation that had become universal and of the universal impression that widespread insolvencies were due in American cities.[36] Banks suspended specie payments individually here and there and then en masse all over the country. During the month of May even the deposit banks suspended, and since the governing Act of Congress forbade government deposits in banks that did not pay specie, Van Buren was compelled to call a special session of Congress to meet the following September. The country as a whole and the government were gripped in a major disaster.

On July 3, 1837, Chief Justice Taney wrote to Jackson his impressions of the causes of the panic and his proposals for remedy. To him the central weakness was reliance on a paper currency. Beyond that, the deposit law had been at fault. It had required deposit banks to pay interest to the government under certain circumstances, with the result that they had to use the money for expansion of credit in order to do sound business. His plan had been to keep the number of deposit banks small—not more than twenty while he was Secretary of the Treasury—and to have the funds held available for government use at all times. The number being small, selection was a distinction worth attainment. But now there were some ninety such banks, with the result that little distinction attached.[37]

Van Buren wrote Taney a confidential letter asking advice. Taney's reply of July 20[38] was important not because some of his advice was ultimately taken but because most of it was not, with the result that he shifted more and more to the sidelines with respect to government finance. At the plea of hard-pressed merchants, the Administration had delayed collection on bonds for import duties. Taney advised Van

[34] Andrew Jackson to Martin Van Buren, Mar. 22, 1837, *Correspondence of Andrew Jackson*, V, 465. See also *ibid.*, 473.

[35] James Kent to Moss Kent, Mar. 20, 1837, Kent Papers.

[36] William Kent to Moss Kent, Mar. 19, 1837, Kent Papers.

[37] R. B. Taney to Andrew Jackson, July 3, 1837, *Correspondence of Andrew Jackson*, V, 491.

[38] R. B. Taney to Martin Van Buren, July 20, 1837, Van Buren Papers.

Buren to make the merchants pay up, as a means of coercing banks into resuming specie payments. Congress, however, authorized further postponement.[39] In view of the prevailing financial distress, Taney advised against suspension of the fourth payment of the deposit Congress had directed to be made to the states. Congress authorized postponement.[40] Taney advised that restoration of specie currency be kept always to the fore and that the government refrain from issuing treasury notes to circulate as money during the crisis. Congress authorized such an issue.[41]

Perhaps the most important query had to do with the possibility of abandoning the use of state banks as government depositories, not in favor of a new national bank but in favor of what was commonly called a sub-treasury system, whereby the government through its own officers stored public funds in the treasury proper and at mints and various collection points throughout the country. Taney opposed the idea. It would increase public patronage and invite public corruption. The public would have more faith in corporations whose books and accounts were subject to inspection than in individuals in the government—as witness the preference of bank notes over the notes of individuals. He opposed giving ammunition to political enemies by having funds kept by persons dependent on the executive when any other safe depository could be found. His own plan was analogous to the plan he had initially followed when the deposits were removed from the Bank of the United States. He would select a few banks and have them serve as custodians of funds in a literal sense. They would give security for the faithful keeping and disbursement of money. They would not lend the money or make it the basis for extension of credit, but would merely keep it safe. Congress debated this problem for nearly two years before setting up a sub-treasury system,[42] which after another year, in the Whig Administration of John Tyler, it repealed,[43] in the midst of a fruitless struggle to restore the Bank of the United States.[44]

Justice Barbour, another Southerner fearful of the growing power of the federal government, also urged resort to special deposits in state banks rather than the building up of a bureaucracy of irresponsible individuals that would be involved in maintaining a sub-treasury system. He assured Van Buren, however, that the matter was one of legitimate

---

[39] 5 Stat. 205.
[40] 5 Stat. 201.
[41] 5 Stat. 201, 228.
[42] 5 Stat. 385.
[43] 5 Stat. 439.
[44] Taney said at the close of his letter to Van Buren (July 20, 1837, Van Buren Papers), "You say that my answer to your letter shall be as

private as I desire. You know the delicacy of my position and I submit it to your discretion and friendship and am quite sure that it will not be made known to any one who is not worthy of confidence. . . . Your letter with the one inclosed has been burnt. I keep no copy of this."

difference of opinion and that such differences would not produce estrangement among his friends.[45] He returned to the subject later by reference to "the apprehension which I feel, founded upon experience of human infirmity, of the danger . . . arising from the possession by single individuals, of large sums of public money."[46] With him as with other leading Jacksonians, however, the great fear was of the establishment of a new national bank.[47] When in 1841 President John Tyler, a Virginian who had deserted Jackson and joined the Whigs, vetoed a bill to establish a national bank, Barbour felt that Tyler's jealousy of Clay, the leading Senate sponsor of the bank, had "surely wrought a great escape of the nation."[48]

With respect to the business of the Supreme Court generally, Justice Catron may have exaggerated when he wrote to Jackson that division was just as natural and almost as common as in the Senate,[49] but the generalization was correct as far as attitudes toward the handling of public finances were concerned. Catron himself maintained his enmity toward the Bank of the United States and his suspicion of all banks, but he recognized the frailties of men and the conditioning of habit, and he was willing to make concessions. Indeed, he believed that concessions were necessary if Democrats were to remain the country's leaders. He disagreed with Taney and Barbour about placing federal money in selected state banks: that money must be kept scrupulously in the hands of the government. Writing to his close friend, James K. Polk, Speaker of the House of Representatives, he proclaimed, "I care not what private Banks you put it into, it will convert the keepers into Federalists in principle and practice in a few years."[50] The treasury was the arm of power. It must not be placed in private hands to raise up a rival power to the popular will.

But viewing the situation politically, Catron was convinced that there must be a paper currency. Habits of resort to paper currency and to credit had become deeply engrained in the cities and towns and even in the planting states. Such a system might be a mark of corruption but the Democratic Party (he still called it the Republican Party) would have to adjust to it or fall in fruitless though patriotic resistance. Therefore there should be treasury notes to circulate as money, bearing the name of the United States, the name which had given potency to Biddle's bank and promoted its circulation. With an adequate

---

[45] P. P. Barbour to Martin Van Buren, Dec. 15, 1837, Van Buren Papers.

[46] P. P. Barbour to Martin Van Buren, Jan. 6, 1837, *ibid.*

[47] See P. P. Barbour to Martin Van Buren, Dec. 4, 1840, *ibid.*

[48] P. P. Barbour to Martin Van Buren, Dec. 16, 1841, *ibid.*

[49] John Catron to Andrew Jackson, Feb. 5, 1838, Jackson Papers.

[50] John Catron to James K. Polk, Sept. 2, 1837, Polk Papers.

issue of treasury notes, Biddle would be forgotten in three years—
especially as his bank, operating now as a state institution even though
still using "United States" in its name, was likely to fail. The important
consideration was that the note issue should be sufficient to meet the
needs of the nation.[51] Catron's advice, though undoubtedly well received
by Polk, lost its identity in the political cauldron. Eventually when Polk
became President he would lead in the reestablishment of the sub-
treasury system which the Whigs had eliminated in 1841.

The Democratic Justices blamed the panic of 1837 on the Bank
of the United States and on speculation and the overexpansion of
credit generally. For Justice Story, on the other hand, as for most
Whigs, the blame belonged obviously on the Jackson Administration
for its removal of the deposits, the annihilation of the Bank of the
United States, and the treasury circular which had required payment
in specie for public lands. The effects, he wrote to Justice McLean, in
whom he had a sympathetic listener, had swept the country with the
violence and desolating impact of a hurricane. Would the people awaken
to their rights and duties? He feared not. They had become stupefied
and were led on to ruin by the art of demagoguery and the corrupted
influences of party.[52] Also to McLean he wrote, "My own belief is that
a national bank is indispensable for the *true and permanent* interests of

---

[51] John Catron to James K. Polk,
Sept. 10, 1837, *ibid.* It is impossible
to tell what influence Justice Catron
may have had at an earlier stage of
the controversy in connection with a
statute enacted under the sponsorship
of his fellow Tennesseean, Senator
Felix Grundy, to prevent the issuing
of bank notes by corporations chartered by the United States whose
charters had expired. 5 Stat. 297.
Grundy and other Democrats were
enraged at the Bank of the United
States, now chartered by the state of
Pennsylvania instead of by the United
States, which with much of the prestige derived from its earlier status
continued to issue and reissue notes.
They were further enraged by Biddle's proposal that banks should refuse to resume specie payments until
the enemy, the Democratic Administration, should be gotten out of office.
See the report made by Grundy for
the Senate Judiciary Committee on
the bill, Senate Report No. 179, 25th
Cong., 2nd Sess. (1838). See also his
speech before the Senate, *Cong. Globe*,

25th Cong., 2nd Sess., App. 299
(1838). For the bill in its various
forms see S. 211, 25th Cong., 2nd
Sess. (1838), Senate Papers. Said
United States Senator John M. Niles,
"We have past [*sic*] today Mr.
Grundy's bill for sending Nick Biddle to the penitentiary for putting
into circulation a spurious illegal
currency. Nothing has troubled Clay
and the Whigs so much; they dared
not even debate it or attempt to
defend Biddle." John M. Niles to
Gideon Welles, Apr. 20, 1838, Welles
Papers. The bill was written in general language but was clearly intended to apply to the president and
directors of the Bank of the United
States, and Senator Grundy so stated
on the floor of the Senate. The bill
was passed in the face of some doubt
whether a federal statute could reach
the president and directors of what
was now technically a new legal
entity, and not the institution created
by Congress.
[52] Joseph Story to John McLean,
May 10, 1837, McLean Papers.

the Union; and I care not where it shall be located."[53] He supposed the day of a return to a national bank to be far distant. Meanwhile he had more confidence in a few banks with large capital, for protection against the federal government, than in the present system of small banks.

If others regarded Nicholas Biddle as a complete scoundrel, Story felt quite otherwise. Through an agent in Boston, Biddle continued to help Story with the process of collecting his salary. In reply to words of praise for him, Story wrote to Biddle, "If I shall have attained a little of your approbation by my labour as a public magistrate, I shall have great consolation in the thought; for I know nothing, beyond the consciousness of the discharge of duty, which ought to gratify one more, than to have a place in the respect of the wise, the good, and the honored of our own times."[54]

The financial crisis brought its first important Supreme Court litigation in *Bank of Augusta v. Earle*,[55] decided in 1839, which dealt with the right of corporations to do business in bills of exchange in states other than those in which they were incorporated. Bills of exchange were highly important media of commercial exchange between regions which had no common currency and where the shipment of gold and silver was at least inconvenient. Since the United States had no common currency except gold and silver, with specie for the most part not available at all when banks suspended specie payments as they did during the panic of 1837, bills of exchange were essential to the continuation of trade. The bills, representing the value of goods shipped, were discounted by banking houses, which, collecting on the bills, made their profits in terms of the percentage of the discounts.

In his argument in the *Briscoe* case in 1837, Henry Clay stressed the economic importance of bills of exchange in voicing his concern lest the line of argument pursued by Briscoe lead to their classification as bills of credit, and hence forbidden by the Constitution. "The day will be disastrous to the country," Clay maintained, "when this court shall throw itself on the ocean of uncertainty, and adopt an interpretation of the prohibition of the Constitution which will apply to a constructive bill of credit. The large and prosperous commercial operations of our country are carried on by bills of exchange, notes, and bank notes, redeemable in specie, and on which suits may be brought, should they not be paid according to their tenor."[56] Clay won his case, and bills of exchange were not endangered.

---

[53] Joseph Story to John McLean, May 25, 1837, McLean Papers.
[54] Joseph Story to Nicholas Biddle, Mar. 22, 1838, Etting Collection.

[55] 13 Pet. 519.
[56] Briscoe v. Bank of the Commonwealth of Kentucky, 11 Pet. 257, 285 (1837).

Approval of use of bills of exchange as instruments of credit was, however, by no means unanimous. In September, 1837, in his message to the special session of Congress called because of the panic and the closing of the banks of the country, President Van Buren noted that bills of exchange fell into two classes. One class consisted of bills drawn for the purpose of transferring actual capital from one part of the country to another, or to anticipate the proceeds of property transmitted. Such bills were highly useful. The other class, however, consisted of bills not representing actual transfers but drawn to create fictitious capital, thereby creating undesirable inflation. Such bills had in recent years resulted in usurious profits without facilitating trade and with dangerous effects on the circulatory medium.[57] Both classes of bills, however, produced profits for the bankers who dealt in them, with resulting rivalries among bankers and among the parts of the country where they operated.

The legal controversy here under discussion arose in Mobile, Alabama, where banks from a number of other states, along with Alabama banks, kept representatives with funds for discounting bills of exchange, based particularly on the cotton delivered there for shipment to distant points. The constitution of Alabama restricted the activity of banking in the state to a state bank and such branches as the legislature might establish. Each of the seven banks so established was authorized to deal in bills of exchange. By statute the state guaranteed payment of the bills in which it dealt, and it required that all profits from the business be paid into the state treasury.[58] So it was that out-of-state banks, which through their agents in Alabama dealt in bills of exchange there, were engaged in competition in a profitable business which Alabama legislators apparently thought they had exclusively reserved to the state itself. This competition was a sore point as it involved in part rivalry between the North and the South, and it was a particularly sore point in a time of financial crisis. It was in the midst of this crisis that debtors defaulted on debts owed to banking corporations of Louisiana, Georgia, and Pennsylvania—the last being the Bank of the United States, or United States Bank, as reincorporated under the laws of Pennsylvania. The corporations brought suit in the United States Circuit Court in Mobile. In April, 1838, Justice McKinley held the corporations not entitled to recover, on the ground that they had no legal right to do business in bills of exchange in Alabama.

A few days later, from his home in Ohio, Justice McLean reported the holding to Justice Story. It struck him as a singular decision and

---

[57] Richardson, *Messages and Papers of the Presidents*, III, 329.
[58] See the dissenting opinion of Justice McKinley, Bank of Augusta v. Earle, 13 Pet. 519, 601–04 (1839).

he presumed it to be without any authority, for he doubted that the question had ever been raised before. In a time of commercial distress, he feared the decision not likely to increase the confidence of the commercial community in at least one of the members of the Supreme Court. Judge McKinley, once a violent Federalist, had changed to a states' rights politician, and, as was common in such changes, had now adopted extreme doctrines. As for himself, Justice McLean had little pleasure in association with the Court as now constituted, except for his relationship with Justice Story. "But we must trudge on in the journey of life," he wrote piously, "and take things as they come and never despond."[59]

The McKinley holding produced great excitement among commercial people all over the country. Justice Story wrote to Charles Sumner that it had "frightened half the lawyers and all of the corporations of the country out of their proprieties."[60] He wrote to Justice McLean that the decision had struck him with very great surprise. If well founded, it would ruinously affect the interests of all local state corporations throughout the Union. Many if not most state banks and manufacturing corporations carried on extensive operations involving contracts in other states. If McKinley was correct, what was to become of all these mighty interests? As for himself, he had never doubted that the Bank of England might sue and contract in any state, and that our own corporations might do the same. As for associations on the Court, except for his close relationship with McLean, he, too, took little pleasure in them.[61]

The immediately injured corporations took quick action to get their cases before the Supreme Court. In the meantime, one of them employed James Kent to write an opinion on the constitutional question for publication in an early issue of *The Law Reporter*, which was to become one of the prominent law reviews of the time. Not surprisingly, the opinion maintained that a corporation of one state might do in another state the business which corporations of that state might do: "This is a species of international law throughout the commercial world."[62] The contention that the activities of a corporation were limited to the jurisdiction in which it was created was "a new and refined distinction, without any support in English law, or in the sense and practice of commercial nations."[63] In closing, the doughty ex-chancellor, who had recently published anonymously a harsh review of the work

---

[59] John McLean to Joseph Story, May 5, 1838, Story Papers.

[60] Charles Warren, *The Supreme Court in United States History*, II, 50. For a summary of newspaper comment see the same source.

[61] Joseph Story to John McLean, May 25, 1838, McLean Papers.

[62] James Kent, "The Law of Corporations," *Law Rep.*, 1:57, 58, 1838.

[63] *Ibid.*, 60.

of the first term of the Taney Court,[64] proclaimed the duty of the judiciary in this case. All persons, natural and corporate, stood on an equal footing with respect to the right to do legitimate business. The most valuable principle of our law was the liberty of all persons to engage in legitimate business anywhere in the land. "The courts of justice are the appropriate guardians of this inestimable right, and it is their duty to give it a liberal and firm support."[65]

So eager were the corporations involved to have a Supreme Court determination of the issues and, if possible, a reversal of Justice Mc-Kinley's position, and so cooperative was the Supreme Court in the matter, that when, delayed by illness, Justice McKinley returned to Washington late in January, 1839, the cases were already being argued there. The *Washington Globe*, the Administration newspaper, treating the cases as purely political, noted that at McKinley's decision, "so strikingly just and proper," the bank press had opened its batteries of abuse, not only against the judgment but also the character and purity of the judge who gave it. Wall Street, conspicuous in these calumnies, had stimulated a great corporation to procure and publish the opinion of "an old Federal lawyer of New York," condemning McKinley's opinion in order to influence the Supreme Court. It was perhaps as well, said the *Globe*, that McKinley had not arrived when the argument was begun, for had he been present he would have heard David B. Ogden, a prominent New York lawyer, spend his breath for two hours denouncing the "monstrous" doctrine announced by McKinley and portraying the ruinous consequences thereof. But fortunately McKinley had taken his seat just in time to hear from C. J. Ingersoll, prominent Democratic lawyer from Pennsylvania, a complete vindication of his position, "and a conclusive argument against the right of these money-mongering monsters to stray from their spheres, and invade the quiet regions of distant States, there to ravage, monopolize, and destroy." What a blessing it would be, proclaimed the *Globe*, if the judiciary should interpose to enforce the law against the wrongdoers, whose rapacity had so deeply encroached on the best interests and institutions of the country.[66]

In David B. Ogden, John Sergeant, and Daniel Webster, the latter two being regularly retained counsel of the Bank of the United States, the bank interests brought to their defense three of the most able lawyers in the country in the fields of constitutional and commercial law. All of them were, of course, Whig leaders as well. Apart from Ingersoll, who had developed an extensive practice as well as a reputa-

---

[64] [James Kent]," Supreme Court of the United States," *N.Y. L. Rev.*, 2: 372, 1838.

[65] *Law Rep.*, 1:62. For an answer to Chancellor Kent, anonymous save as signed "J.R., Pennsylvania, September, 1838," see "The Law of Corporations," *Law Rep.*, 1:185, 1838.

[66] *Washington Globe*, Feb. 1, 1839.

tion for being a fighting Democratic politician, opposing lawyers were less well known and perhaps less able. The only other to deliver an oral argument, indeed, was William J. Vande Gruff of Alabama.[67] One Crawford merely submitted a written argument.

The central legal questions in the cases, variously presented by the several counsel, in terms of their respective strategies, were:

> 1. Could a private corporation, formed under the laws of one of the states, make enforceable contracts within the borders of another state?
> 2. If under any circumstances a corporation could make such a contract in another state, could another state exclude an out-of-state corporation from doing business within its borders?
> 3. If a state could exclude out-of-state corporations from such business, had Alabama excluded them from doing business in bills of exchange through its constitutional and statutory provisions which reserved banking business in the state to a state bank and its branches?

Counsel on both sides naturally sought to make the most of the propaganda possibilities of the current financial crisis. In defense of Alabama against invasion by banking corporations of other states, Ingersoll used language resembling that recently employed by Chief Justice Taney in his advice to Jackson about the recharter of the banks of the District of Columbia. Corporations, Ingersoll contended, were created only to serve the public good. Their powers were limited to that end. The public good in each state—and with it the possible scope of corporate powers—was to be determined by the legislature of that state. The judiciary had no power to extend the field of corporate operations beyond the scope of the legislative judgment.

Ogden, on the other hand, looking to the good of the business community at large, contended that "If the decision of the Circuit Court shall be sustained by this court, a deeper wound will be inflicted on the commercial business of the United States than it has ever sustained."[68] Webster could see no limit to the calamitous consequences of a decision affirming the judgment of the Circuit Court. That judgment was "new and unheard of in our system, and calculated to break up the harmony which has so long prevailed among the States and people of this Union."[69]

However, Webster concluded in a ringing peroration before an

---

[67] In a longhand statement of the case prepared by Webster, preserved in his papers and published anonymously in the *Washington National Intelligencer*, Feb. 9, 1839, he said of Vande Gruff that he "stands high among his professional brethren in Alabama." Webster Papers, No. 839158 (Dartmouth).

[68] Bank of Augusta v. Earle, 13 Pet. 519, 523 (1839).

[69] *Ibid.*, 567.

enthralled audience, it was not for counsel on either side to say that they spoke for the country. Only the Court could do that. "It is for you, Mr. Chief Justice and judges, on this, as on other occasions of high importance, to speak and to decide for the country. The guardianship of her commercial interests; the preservation of the harmonious intercourse of all her citizens; the fulfilling, in this respect, of the great object of the Constitution, are in your hands; and I am not to doubt that the trust will be so performed as to sustain at once high national objects and the character of this tribunal."[70]

With Chief Justice Taney writing the opinion of the Court, the Supreme Court reversed the judgment of the Circuit Court. Taking an intermediate position, the Chief Justice denied that the Privileges and Immunities Clause of Article IV of the Constitution gave out-of-state corporations the right to do business as they saw fit in spite of the laws of the state of operation. But he held that, as in international relations foreign corporations were by the rule of comity assumed to have the right through their agents to make contracts in other countries unless specifically forbidden, so the same right must be assumed to exist in interstate relations. Since Alabama laws had not specifically prohibited dealing in bills of exchange by out-of-state corporations, the right would be presumed to exist.

Justice McKinley, who seldom wrote opinions of any kind, here wrote an earnest dissent, contending that Alabama had indeed closed the door to financial operations by out-of-state corporations, and that, in any event, no rule of comity prevailed among the states that could make the laws of one state effective in another. Justice Baldwin, on the other hand, in an opinion not delivered to the Reporter,[71] went so far as to contend that the right in question was protected by the Privileges and Immunities Clause and could not be denied by Alabama even by specific enactment.[72]

In commercial circles the decision brought a vast sense of relief. Justice Story wrote to the Chief Justice that his opinion had given very general satisfaction to the public, and added, "I hope you will allow me to say that I think it does great honor to yourself as well as to the Court."[73] A prominent Whig newspaper in New York said, "The opinion read by Chief Justice Taney is as far from Loco Foco doctrines as Alexander Hamilton could have desired."[74] Democratic and anti-Bank newspapers, on the other hand, denounced the Court for delivering

---

[70] *Ibid.*, 567.

[71] *Ibid.*, 597.

[72] *New York Courier and Enquirer*, Mar. 12, 1839.

[73] Joseph Story to R. B. Taney, Apr. 19, 1839, Samuel Tyler, *Memoir of Roger Brooke Taney*, 288.

[74] *New York Courier and Enquirer*, Mar. 12, 1839.

a blow to the rights of the states, in language similar to that long used against the conservative Marshall Court.[75] A Pennsylvania paper prepared to battle for the inalienable rights of the people, and announced its intention to strike first at the life judiciary of the United States, the "judicial noblemen of America."[76] The *Washington Globe*, however, it was said in reply, had been repelled in its attempt to dictate to the Court, and Ingersoll's tissue of sophistries had been scattered to the wind.[77]

As far as the specific decision was concerned, both sides read too much into it. It gave protection to the bank property immediately involved, but, in light of what the Court said about the power of the state to exclude "foreign" corporations if it saw fit to do so, Alabama proceeded at once to enact the exclusionary measure.[78] If the measure had bad effects on the welfare of the state or nation, it would be very hard to particularize them in the generally depressed condition of the economic life of the country. On the other hand, other states in general did not enact such measures, and banking corporations continued to do business across state lines. An important fact was that, in the opinion of the Court, the states were not limited to permitting foreign corporations to do as they pleased or to excluding them altogether. They could admit on condition, and by means of prescribing conditions exercise local control over, corporations otherwise restrained only in the states of incorporation. It has been said that "the terse and quotable style of the opinion, its philosophical flavor, and its clear-cut reasoning combined to give even the dicta of the Chief Justice an authority which was to stand unquestioned for half a century."[79]

The bill-of-exchange cases from Alabama, involving highly important public issues, were handled with high statesmanship by the Supreme Court and without reflection of the sentiments of the Justices with respect to the Bank of the United States. Indeed, in writing the opinion of the Court, Chief Justice Taney dealt with the three cases as one and presented the facts in terms of the Georgia bank engaged in the litigation, the Bank of Augusta, and left the Bank of the United States as such largely out of the picture. In another case involving the latter bank, however, and less deeply involving the public interest, the Chief Justice and some of his brethren were less successful in excluding from consideration the stormy controversy with the Bank.

---

[75] For summaries see Warren, *The Supreme Court in United States History*, II, 57–62.

[76] *Harrisburg Pennsylvania Reporter*, Mar. 22, 1839.

[77] *New York Commercial Adver-* *tiser*, quoted in *Salem Essex Register*, Mar. 14, 1839.

[78] See G. C. Henderson, *The Position of Foreign Corporations in American Constitutional Law*, 47–48.

[79] *Ibid.*, 42.

This other case likewise had to do with a bill of exchange, one used as a means of collecting money which by treaty the government of France had agreed to pay to the United States in settlement of damages done to American shipping during the Napoleonic Wars. In 1833, on advice from Nicholas Biddle as to the best way to get the payment of more than nine hundred thousand dollars transferred to the United States, Louis McLane, then Secretary of the Treasury, sold to the Bank of the United States a bill of exchange for the amount involved. France unfortunately refused to pay—a refusal which brought relations between the two countries to the breaking point. Money which on the books of the Bank of the United States had been transferred to the government, but which as a deposit was still available to the Bank in connection with its banking operations, had to be transferred from the name of the government back to that of the Bank. One item in the bad relations between the Administration and the Bank of the United States at this time was the demand that the government pay to the Bank not merely the costs of this unfortunate transaction but also a 15 percent penalty on the amount of the bill. The claim was made on the basis of law in force in the District of Columbia, which in this instance was in the form of a Maryland statute of 1785 which remained in force when part of the District was carved out of Maryland territory.

McLane referred the matter to Taney, who was then Attorney General. On May 24, 1833, Taney replied that in his opinion the item had "no foundation in law or in equity, and ought not to be paid by the government."[80] He would state his reasons on another occasion. The controversy stalled for a time, and during this period McLane was replaced as Secretary of the Treasury by William J. Duane, who proved more friendly toward the Bank than toward the Administration. On inquiry from Biddle, Duane reported that on the basis of the records turned over to him the government would pay the expenses of the Bank in handling the abortive bill of exchange but would not pay the 15 percent penalty, and sent along a copy of Taney's letter. Biddle pressed Duane for a statement of Taney's reasons, and Duane wrote to Taney. Taney replied that whereas the executive branch of the government was entitled to his legal advice, the Bank was not, and that he would write out his opinion in his own good time.[81] Duane faithfully sent Biddle copies of all the correspondence, and the matter was suspended for a time while Jackson tried to persuade Duane to remove the government deposits from the Bank of the United States. Upon

---

[80] Bank of the United States v. United States, 2 How. 711, 716 (1844).

[81] R. B. Taney to William J. Duane, Aug. 17, 1833, printed in part in *ibid.*, 746–47.

Duane's refusal, Jackson removed him from office and appointed Taney in his place.[82]

Finally, on July 8, 1834, Biddle notified Levi Woodbury, who in the meantime had succeeded Taney as Secretary of the Treasury, that the Bank had decided to collect not only the expenses but the penalty by withholding the amount involved from a payment to be made to the United States as a dividend on that portion of the stock in the Bank owned by the government. This he thought the proper mode of getting the question decided by the courts. He sent an accompanying letter saying that the settlement of this particular bill was not to be taken as waiving the claim of the Bank for full compensation and indemnity for the violation of the charter of the Bank by removal of the government deposits.[83] Woodbury expostulated, contending that the proper way of raising the issue was not to levy on the property of the United States but rather to make application to Congress for indemnity,[84] but to no effect.

The wrangling continued. Woodbury pressed Benjamin F. Butler, Taney's successor as Attorney General, for a copy of the opinion supposed to have been filed by Taney. Butler could find no such opinion—which Taney, presumably, had never written out at all. Butler wrote to Taney, now (in late 1834) in private practice, asking for a copy of his opinion or for a statement of his grounds. Taney replied with a statement of the law and facts, contending that the Maryland statute providing for a 15 percent penalty on protested bills of exchange did not apply when the assessment was made against the government and that the Bank's claim had no support either in technical law or upon any principle of moral justice.[85] The matter was reported to Congress again and again, without solution.[86] Finally, early in 1838, the United States Attorney for the Eastern District of Pennsylvania was directed to bring suit against the Bank, now an institution chartered by the state of Pennsylvania.[87]

The litigation, slow in starting, dragged along in the courts for many years. Nicholas Biddle retired in 1839 as president of the Pennsylvania-chartered Bank of the United States. Thereafter rumors began to stir about prior mismanagement of the Bank, facts began to substantiate the rumors, and in 1841 the Bank permanently closed its

---

[82] For a fuller statement of facts see Carl B. Swisher, *Roger B. Taney* 220–23.

[83] "Two letters, Nicholas Biddle to Levi Woodbury, July 8, 1834," *Niles' Weekly Register*, 17:60, 1834.

[84] Levi Woodbury to Nicholas Biddle, July 14, 1834, *ibid.*, 60–61. See

Biddle's reply of Nov. 28, 1834, *ibid.*, 241.

[85] R. B. Taney to B. F. Butler, Nov. 25, 1834, *ibid.*, 307–08.

[86] See for example *Niles' National Register*, 52:27–29, 1837.

[87] *Niles' National Register*, 53:388, 1838.

doors. At approximately the time of Biddle's death, early in 1844, the Supreme Court decided a single aspect of a case involving the penalty on the French-protested bill. Speaking through Justice McLean, the Court held that under the Maryland statute of 1785 the federal government should be held liable to the assessment of penalties on protested bills.[88] The decision looked like victory for the now defunct enemy of the Jackson Administration. Although the case was to go back to the Circuit Court for further action, Justice McLean, with only Justice Catron dissenting and Justice Wayne disavowing the reasoning employed, wrote the opinion of the Court in such a way as to appear to settle the entire controversy.

In view of his previous connection with the case it would have been expected that Chief Justice Taney would take no part in the decision. At the time of the decision, indeed, he had to be absent because of illness, but he retained a strong interest in the matter. Attorney General John Nelson, who argued the case for the United States and lost to formidable opponents in John Cadwalader and John Sergeant, wrote to the Chief Justice about the decision. Taney immediately wrote to Benjamin C. Howard, recently installed as Reporter of the Court. Because he had given an opinion in the case when Attorney General, he wrote, he had not expected in any event to sit in the case in the Supreme Court. But, he continued, "I have always intended if the decision was in favor of the Bank to publish my opinion in the appendix to the volume. I do not mean the opinion already published, which was very brief, and prepared in some haste, but one in which the facts will be more fully stated, and the reasoning on authorities more fully set forth."[89] He therefore asked Howard to let him see the opinions written in the case, not, he said, that he might examine and answer the reasoning of the Court, but to enable him to determine whether the case dealt with the whole controversy or merely with the Maryland statute. Leaving Howard no discretion in the matter, he stated, "If the judgment of the Supreme Court settles the whole controversy, I shall immediately prepare my opinion, and must ask you to insert it in the appendix in your second volume. If nothing is decided but the construction of the act of assembly, then I should not for the present publish my opinion."[90]

After seeing the McLean opinion Taney wrote again to Howard saying that in the light of that opinion and the manner of the statement of the case in the record he had decided to publish his own opinion. It was unavoidably long, for he desired to leave no room for misrepresenta-

---

[88] Bank of the United States v. United States, 2 How. 711 (1844).

[89] R. B. Taney to B. C. Howard, Mar. 18, 1844, Howard Papers.
[90] Ibid.

tion of facts.[91] He presented an opinion which took up twenty-four pages in the volume. At the end of the case the Reporter inserted a note that because the Chief Justice did not sit in the case his opinion was placed in an appendix, but he so arranged the volume that the Bank case was the last one presented, and the appendix followed immediately with continuous paging so that readers of the opinion of the Court and of the Catron dissent were likely to see the Taney opinion as well.

Justice McLean wrote to Justice Story, evidently in outraged protest at the printing of the Taney opinion in the reports. Story replied in like vein, saying that the publication struck him as "indelicate, improper, and in a judicial view wanting in self respect as well as in respect for his brother Judges."[92] He could not conceive how Taney could have taken such a step so much at variance from his own general notions on such subjects and his criticism of Judge Baldwin's conduct in preparing dissenting opinions when the Court was on vacation. The action had greatly lessened his confidence in Taney and he thought Howard's conduct in printing the opinion inexcusable: "He has just as much right to publish regular criticisms upon all our judgments from any private person; and for one, I shall feel even more absolved from the slightest effort to aid him in his Reports."[93]

With Justice Story the conduct of the Chief Justice continued to rankle. In a long letter to Chancellor Kent discussing the 1844 term of the Court he declared that he was for the case "*totis viribus*," and he saw no reason now to doubt its correctness. "Why Chief Justice Taney, who did not sit in the cause and *never heard the arguments*, should, after the session was over, have written out an opinion assailing ours, I profess myself unable to account for."[94]

There is no way of measuring the effect of publication of the Taney opinion on the ultimate outcome of the case. The case went back to the Circuit Court for further proceedings, and there, in the light of the Supreme Court decision, the Bank was the victor. By writ of error the case was again brought back to the Supreme Court for further action in 1847, after a number of personnel changes had taken

---

[91] R. B. Taney to B. C. Howard, Apr. 20, 1844, Howard Papers. See also Taney's letter of Apr. 25, 1844, in the same collection. A letter from Taney, addressed evidently to the printers of the reports, dated June 26, 1844, and dealing with the correction of proof on the opinion, is filed at the Cornell University Library.

[92] Joseph Story to John McLean, Aug. 16, 1844, McLean Papers.

[93] *Ibid.*

[94] Joseph Story to James Kent, Aug. 31, 1844, Story Papers (MHS). The portion of the letter quoted is deleted from the letter as published, *Life and Letters of Joseph Story*, William W. Story, ed., II, 469–70.

place. There the Court, this time speaking through Justice Catron, cut the ground from under the Bank's case by holding that the Maryland statute did not embrace a bill of exchange drawn on a foreign government. Justice McLean, of course, dissented, lamenting that "the changes on the bench show the uncertainty of human hopes."[95] Justice Wayne dissented without opinion. Justice Woodbury, the former Secretary of the Treasury who for years had played a part in the controversy, refrained from sitting because he had given an official opinion on the matter in his earlier capacity. Chief Justice Taney, unrepentant about having published an opinion in the case when previously before the Court, filed the following memorandum:

> The Chief Justice withdrew from the bench in the argument of this case, having given an official opinion, when he was Attorney-General of the United States, against the claim made by the bank, and concurring altogether with the above opinion given by the court.[96]

The death of President Harrison, who presumably would have followed Whig leadership in Congress in the matter of chartering a new national bank, the defection of President Tyler, who was more Democrat than Whig, and the election of James K. Polk to the Presidency brought an end to immediate prospects of return to use of a central banking institution. The prolonged bank war had left a settled imprint on the thinking and emotionalized the attitudes of the country but the subject moved into the background. For Chief Justice Taney it was never far beneath the surface. Almost from the time of his rejection as Secretary of the Treasury, he mentioned in letters to Jackson and others his plan to write a history of the bank war, and from time to time referred to writing in progress. The principal works left by him are the account of his difficulties with Thomas Ellicott and the Union Bank of Maryland and his Bank War Manuscript. The latter document ends before the beginning of his service as Secretary of the Treasury, and both are rough and unpolished. He was given much more to adversary proceedings than to the writing of history as such, and he undoubtedly found the task difficult. Apart from this limitation on his ability as a historian, he had full-time responsibility as Chief Justice, and his health, perennially poor, left him little energy for creative work outside the demands of his office. His settled feelings about the bank war seem to have remained very much as stated to Judge Ellis Lewis of Pennsylvania in 1845, in commenting on a eulogy which Lewis had delivered after the death of Jackson. Taney wrote in part:

---

[95] United States v. Bank of the United States, 5 How. 382, 401 (1847).

[96] *Ibid.*, 400–01.

V: *The Realm of Finance*

Perhaps no topic was more difficult to manage upon such an occasion than that of the Bank, as you were addressing an assembly composed of men of all parties, many of whom were yet sore from the recollection of that violent and protracted conflict—and some of them perhaps the more sensitive from secret misgivings, arising from subsequent events, that Genl. Jackson might have been right & they in the wrong. This difficult point is I think very happily touched upon & disposed of. Yet I am persuaded that the time cannot be distant, when the honest & patriotic men of all parties, will with one accord, do justice to the men concerned in that measure; and will admit that the overthrow of *The Monster* was the greatest of all the great public services of Genl. Jackson; and that nothing but the removal of the deposites could have secured the victor. So I thought when I first advised that measure, and also when I afterwards carried it into execution—and subsequent events have confirmed that opinion. For it is now evident from the immense power displayed by the Bank in that conflict that it would have been too powerful for the government under almost any other chief; and if the deposites had not been removed & the decisive conflict thereby brought on during the administration of Genl. Jackson, the Bank would have been rechartered in spite of his successor—or rather no one could have been elected to succeed him who was not devoted to the Bank—and that corporation would at this day have been virtually governing the country;—corrupting its councils—& directing the operations of the government as might best suit the cupidity or ambition of those at the head of the corporation.[97]

Taney's statements of convictions about the dangers of monopoly power in the Bank of the United States have the power even a century after their delivery to stir the wrath of advocates of centralized banking. Yet they belong to the antimonopoly tradition of the American people. Their weakness lies in their negativism. The Jacksonians never looked much beyond the defeat of the "Monster" and close reliance on specie currency. Taney and some others, it is true, seem to have believed for a time in reliance on carefully selected state banks, but their experiences with those banks were dissillusioning. They never thought out a creative substitute. They were agrarians and capitalists on a small scale, but with respect to currency and credit they held back when it came to planning a system for the giant capitalism that was to come. The cautiousness of the Jacksonians generally became the cautiousness of the Supreme Court as Jacksonians came to provide most of its members. The distrust of monopoly power played into the thinking of the Court as it dealt further with the position of corporations and as the question of the allocation of power became regional under the dark shadow of Civil War.

---

[97] R. B. Taney to Ellis Lewis, Oct. 25, 1845, Lewis Papers.

CHAPTER·VI

Hard Times
and Contract Obligations

T HE PANIC OF 1837 and continuing economic turbulence intensified anew the problems of indebtedness which had caused stress and strain and much litigation some two decades earlier. Enforcement of state bankruptcy legislation and issues involving imprisonment for debt again came to the fore. Advocacy of a federal bankruptcy law which had failed earlier now succeeded, but with repeal following soon afterward. State legislatures enacted stay laws to prevent wholesale foreclosure of mortgages. A number of states formally repudiated or scaled down or simply refrained from paying debts incurred during more prosperous years.

The several types of interference with fulfillment of contract obligations brought indignant disapproval from creditors and from those who recognized the necessity of maintaining American borrowing power in foreign countries. In one way or another many of the issues reached the courts, including the Supreme Court. That Court, it is true, did not during this period pass on the constitutionality of state repudiation, but the subject provided background against which cases in other fields were decided. The federal bankruptcy statute furnished a great deal of work for federal district judges and for Supreme Court Justices on circuit, even for some years after the act had been repealed. The Supreme Court interpreted the measure in important decisions but its constitutionality was discussed only in lower-court cases. The legitimacy of state bankruptcy or insolvency laws, much discussed in the Marshall period, continued to be important, particularly as the cases involved the power of a state to relieve debtors from the obligation of contracts between citizens of different states. In a number of cases the Supreme Court found state stay laws unconstitutional. It did so belatedly, however, with the result that the statutes had some effect in curbing the process of economic contraction. Interwoven also was the confusion in the field of banking.

During the period of economic expansion in the 1830s, debts so heavy as to lead to talk of repudiation after the panic had been incurred by Pennsylvania, Maryland, Mississippi, Michigan, Louisiana, Indiana, and Illinois.[1] Considerably more than half the money borrowed had been expended on internal improvements such as canals, railroads, and turnpikes. In the South the funds were often invested in banking institutions which in turn extended credit for public developments.[2] The clamor over repudiation was heard most loudly in connection with the financial activities of Mississippi. Difficulties arose in part from the issuing of some millions of dollars in bonds to establish a bank, not strictly according to state law but with immediate popular approval. Under depression conditions it proved impossible to market the bonds at their face value, as the law required. They were finally sold to Nicholas Biddle, president of the United States Bank of Pennsylvania, for less than what should have been their value at the time of the sale, and partly on credit rather than exclusively for cash. Biddle marketed the bonds in Europe, his bank collapsed, and heavy losses had to be taken either by the European purchasers or by Mississippi.[3]

The threat of direct flouting of European investors by outright repudiation brought consternation to all who were interested in the maintenance of American credit. When Whigs tried to make a party issue of the matter, farsighted Democrats refused to wear the repudiation label. Said the *Democratic Review*:

> The Mississippi bonds must be paid. To the last dollar, the last cent, the last mill, every pledge of the public faith, whether by the whole of our glorious Union, or by any one of its constituent parts, must be honorably redeemed—be the consequences, be the cost what they may. Be justice done though the firmament fall.[4]

Among the Whigs also demanding payment of all legitimate debts was Benjamin R. Curtis, a friend and former student of Justice Story and later to be a member of the Supreme Court, who in an illuminating article in the *North American Review* for January, 1843, threw the whole subject into perspective. Curtis traced the development of finan-

---

[1] George T. Curtis, *A Memoir of Benjamin Robbins Curtis*, II, 99.
[2] "State Debts," *North American Review*, 51:316, 319, 1840.

[3] "State Credit," *U.S. Magazine and Democratic Review*, 10:3, 1842.
[4] *Ibid.*, 3. See also "The State Debts," *U.S. Magazine and Democratic Review*, 14:3, 1844.

cial crises in the several states and the hard times that characterized the entire country. He spoke of "farmers, owning large and well stocked farms, who could hardly get money enough to pay postage on a letter. They had scarcely any currency, and most of what they had was bad. In the commercial States, matters were little better."[5] But whatever the excuse, he contended that disgrace had fallen on the United States in the eyes of the civilized world, and that repudiation, which was another name for confiscation, must be abandoned as an instrument of state policy. The conduct of a few states had destroyed the credit of other states as well, and had made impossible the flotation of a loan authorized by Congress in 1842.[6]

In an argument which Justice Story praised in terms of "its sound constitutional views,"[7] Curtis discussed the impact of the Eleventh Amendment on the suability of states. He contended that the Amendment did not prevent foreign states from bringing suits against the debtor states in the Supreme Court,[8] "a tribunal which is our own ark of safety, and to which offended Europe may come confidently, and obtain such justice as war and reprisals never gave, and never can give."[9]

Although some of the states eventually paid their debts, in part or in full, it proved impossible to coerce, frighten, or shame others to do the same. After a century some of the debts, including those of Mississippi, were still unpaid.[10] While the Supreme Court decided in 1904 that one state might sue another and thereby determine the obligation to pay bonds, when the debt was backed by mortgaged property,[11] a state could bring such a suit only by becoming the bona fide owner of the bonds. It could not assume the role of litigant merely for the benefit of citizen owners.[12] It was not until 1934 that the Supreme Court considered the power of a foreign state to sue one of the United States in the Supreme Court. When it did so it held, contrary to the position of Curtis and presumably of Justice Story, that foreign states, in this instance the Principality of Monaco, could not sue one of the states, in this instance Mississippi, to recover on bonds issued a century

---

[5] Benjamin R. Curtis, "Debts of the States," *North American Review*, 58: 109, 121, 1844. The article was reprinted, in *Life and Writings of Benjamin R. Curtis*, Benjamin R. Curtis, ed., II, 93.

[6] Curtis, "Debts of the States," *North American Review*, 58:150, 1844.

[7] Curtis, *A Memoir of Benjamin Robbins Curtis*, I, 102.

[8] Quoting from the opinion of Chief Justice Jay in Chisholm v. Georgia, 2 Dall. 419, 476 (U.S. 1793), he

made the mistake of referring to it as the opinion of Chief Justice Marshall. Curtis, "Debts of the States," *North American Review*, 58:154, 1844.

[9] Curtis, "Debts of the States," *North American Review*, 58:155–56 1844.

[10] For figures on debts repudiated or scaled down see W. Brooke Graves, *American State Government*, 596.

[11] South Dakota v. North Carolina, 192 U.S. 286 (1904).

[12] New Hampshire v. Louisiana, 108 U.S. 76 (1883).

earlier. Said Chief Justice Hughes for the Court, "As to suits brought by a foreign State, we think that the States of the Union retain the same immunity that they enjoy with respect to suits by individuals whether citizens of the United States or citizens or subjects of a foreign State."[13] Although some of the impoverished states urged the federal government to assume their debts,[14] as it had done shortly after the adoption of the Constitution, no such action was taken. With respect to the defaulting states the holders of the bonds proved to be the losers.

While people with broad vision and widespread interests were concerned about the debts owed by the states, the mass of the people were more concerned about the debts owed by individuals and private corporations. In reminiscences of his law practice Joseph G. Baldwin recorded that in the county of Sumpter, Alabama, where there were some twenty-four hundred suable men, the number of common law suits brought in a single year ran to four or five thousand, while the federal courts in the state were equally well patronized. "It was a merry time for us craftsmen; and we brightened up mightily, and shook our quills joyously, like goslings in the midst of a shower."[15] In 1839 Justice McKinley wrote to President Van Buren of distressing and frightening experiences in holding Circuit Court in Mississippi. At each of the two terms there were some twenty-seven hundred cases for trial. "To do any thing like justice to the parties, in the short time allowed for holding the court, we were compelled to hurry over the docket as rapidly as possible, and to refuse to hear argument upon plain and well settled questions. This gave great offence to the host of debtors who thronged the court and who had employed counsel, not to maintain a meritorious defence to the suits against them; but to prevent, by all the means in their power, the rendition of judgments against them."[16]

Matters got so bad that one of the judges was subjected to gross personal indignity. Apparently without result, Justice McKinley proposed the transfer of the court from Jackson to Natchez, "where there is an old and respectable population, comparatively free from debt; and where impartial juries might be obtained."[17] In varying degrees the

---

[13] Monaco v. Mississippi, 292 U.S. 313 (1934).

[14] It was said that the suggestion of federal assumption of state debts came first from a former governor of the Bank of England and was taken up by Barings and other foreign creditors but that in general it was ridiculed by moneyed men in the United States. James Lee to Martin Van Buren, Nov. 6, 1839, Van Buren Papers.

[15] Joseph G. Baldwin, *The Flush Times of Alabama and Mississippi*, 240.

[16] John McKinley to Martin Van Buren, Nov. 6, 1839, Van Buren Papers.

[17] *Ibid.* Because of the impoverished condition of people throughout the state and the public attitude toward contract obligations, debts were hard to collect even after judgments had been won in a federal court. In 1839 one such judgment was won in the

panic conditions extended throughout the United States. The continuing crisis brought revival of the proposals of the 1820s, sponsored by Justice Story among others, for enactment of a federal bankruptcy law.[18] Although the states could enforce their own bankruptcy or insolvency laws with respect to debts incurred after the measures were enacted, such measures varied greatly from state to state, and the statute of one state, under the decision of the Supreme Court in *Ogden v. Saunders*,[19] could not give relief as against creditors in other States. Some states had abolished imprisonment for debt while others had not. So it was that a man who was free of debt under the laws of the state of his residence might find himself in prison if he traveled in other states where he had incurred obligations. With the continuing crisis, petitions for enactment of a federal uniform bankruptcy law poured in upon Congress and were referred to the respective judiciary committees. They came from both state legislatures and volunteer groups. Some were written in longhand and couched in personally persuasive terms. Others were printed in formal language. Among the more revealing was a memorial from citizens of Galena, Illinois, which stressed the conflict among state laws and the need for uniformity throughout an increasingly commercial community, and closed with the plea:

> A bankrupt law, that shall set the honest debtor free, on the surrender of all his property, and restore him to the full exercise of his industry, and faculties, would operate at once, upon a very large, active, and intelligent body of men, now paralyzed, and disheartened; and thus set in motion hearts, and arms, capable of doing much for themselves, and much for the general good.[20]

---

southern circuit by Joseph Holt, then a young attorney on his way to a prominent career. Holt sensed that collection would be a problem, particularly in view of the desire of debtors to pay debts in depreciated money. He therefore warned the marshal that only real money would be acceptable. The marshal nevertheless accepted from the debtor depreciated bank notes at their face value, and Holt and his partner took the case back to court. The case went to the Supreme Court on a certificate of division of opinion between Justice McKinley and the district judge. That Court, speaking unanimously through Justice Daniel, held that the marshal had no right to accept depreciated paper in satisfaction of a money judgment. Griffin v. Thompson, 2 How. 244 (1844). Here, however, it was the watchfulness of the attorney and the promptness of his action that saved his right to payment in sound money. In another case from the same circuit, in which the creditor seemed to have acquiesced initially in the acceptance of depreciated bank notes, and delayed action to protect his rights, the Supreme Court held that the marshal had fulfilled his duty. Buckhannan v. Tinnin, 2 How. 258 (1844).

[18] The best treatment of the subject is Charles Warren, *Bankruptcy in United States History*, of which Part II deals with the crisis of the 1840s and the federal statute of 1841.

[19] 12 Wheat. 213 (1827).

[20] "Memorial of Sundry Citizens of Galena (Illinois) for the enactment of a general Bankrupt Law," Mar. 13, 1840, Senate Papers, 26th Cong., 1st Sess.

VI: *Hard Times and Contract Obligations*

There was dispute in Congress and throughout the country over whether the proposed measure should aim primarily at the protection of creditors through involuntary bankruptcy or should also include voluntary provisions for those debtors who saw fit to make use of them. There was also dispute as to whether it should include corporations, and particularly banks which refused or were unable to redeem their notes in specie but nevertheless continued to do business. Among people hostile to banks and believing them to be responsible for the depressed state of business it was even suggested that there should be a federal bankruptcy act exclusively for the purpose of liquidating banks that failed to redeem their notes.[21]

Early in 1840, at the first session of the Twenty-sixth Congress, the Whig-dominated Senate went seriously to work to enact a federal bankruptcy statute, with Daniel Webster as one of the prime movers. According to Millard Fillmore the bill as introduced was the joint product of Webster and Justice Story,[22] and was based on the insolvency law of Massachusetts of 1838.[23] In the course of debate it underwent many modifications. Webster, who had taken a stand against inclusion of corporations,[24] was pressed sufficiently hard on the subject to seek Justice Story's opinion. The latter saw no absolutely insuperable objections to including corporations but did see practical difficulties. If banks were included, should other corporations be included too? To what extent and in what fashion should the administration of the statute reach stockholders? He was concerned about the fact that inclusion of corporations would shake confidence in corporation stock and depreciate it excessively. He admitted doubts whether a statute applying to individuals and not to corporations would meet the constitutional requirement of uniformity, but he turned immediately to the fact that no bankruptcy law in England or other country that he knew of had reached corporations, and he thought this a strong practical objection. He added a statement of doubt on the score of states' rights that had a discordant sound in terms of his known philosophy:

> Is it quite certain, that State Rights, as to the creation and dissolution of corporations, are not thus virtually infringed? I confess, that I feel no small doubt, whether Congress can regulate State Corporations by any other laws than State laws. A State Corporation is entitled to just such rights and powers, as the charter gives it, and I do not well see where Congress can get the power to alter or control them, or to suspend or extinguish them.[25]

---

[21] See James Lee to Martin Van Buren, Nov. 6, 1839, Van Buren Papers.

[22] *Cong. Globe*, 26th Cong., 2nd Sess., App. 480 (1841).

[23] Warren, *Bankruptcy in United States History*, 70.

[24] *Ibid.*, 68.

[25] *Life and Letters of Joseph Story*, William W. Story, ed., II, 332.

The bill that passed the Senate provided for both voluntary and involuntary bankruptcy but made no provision for corporations. The House did not act. During the Presidential campaign of 1840 bankruptcy legislation was made a party issue, and the Democrats, who retained control of the House during the lame-duck period, stood in the way of the measure at the session which began in December, 1840. Justice Story complained about the situation, saying that the great controversial measures—a national bank, a bankruptcy law, and the imposition of luxury taxes to meet revenue deficits—were like collegiate themes and dissertations: to be discussed but not acted on. They gave rise to long speeches, but there the matter ended.[26]

On March 4, 1841, the Whig President William Henry Harrison took the oath of office and immediately called a special session of Congress to assemble May 31, 1841. He died on April 4, and when Congress assembled, the Presidential office was occupied by John Tyler, an apostate Democrat whom the Whigs had made Vice President to assure victory for their ticket. Tyler, no particular advocate of a bankruptcy statute, made no mention of it in his message to Congress, but did forward to Congress a memorial in behalf of such a measure signed by nearly three thousand citizens of New York. In doing so he remarked that a bankruptcy law, carefully guarded against fraudulent practices and applicable to all classes in society, would afford extensive relief. Congress would decide whether to consider enactment at the special session.[27] Although Daniel Webster had now left the Senate to head the Department of State, Whig Senators quickly brought about passage of the bill that had been approved by the Senate at the preceding session. The bill was tabled in the House of Representatives, but was revived by a political deal with friends of a bill to charter a national bank and a bill to distribute to the states the income from the sale of public lands. The House then passed the bankruptcy bill, with an amendment postponing its operation until February 1, 1842—to give the ensuing Congress time to repeal it. The Senate accepted the amendment and the bill was signed August 19, 1841.[28]

During the preceding session of Congress Justice Story had urged Webster not to accept a time limitation on the statute of less than five years. Otherwise the act would expire before its just effects were seen, as had been the situation with the Bankruptcy Act of 1800.[29] The Act of 1841 was passed without a terminal date but the strategy of its

---

[26] Joseph Story to Francis Lieber, Feb. 15, 1841, Lieber Papers.

[27] Richardson, *Messages and Papers of the Presidents*, IV, 54–55.

[28] For accounts of the political deal see Thomas H. Benton, *Thirty Years'*

View, 229–34, and Warren, *Bankruptcy in United States History*, 72–79. For the statute see 5 Stat. 440.

[29] Story, *Life and Letters of Joseph Story*, II, 332.

enactment forecast that a movement for its repeal would be under way even before it went into effect, the people who changed their votes to secure votes for other measures not feeling bound beyond the stage of original enactment. Since the act remained in effect until its repeal on March 3, 1843, with continuation thereafter of judicial proceedings already instituted, its administration for that brief period becomes part of the history of the federal judiciary as a whole and to a limited degree of the Supreme Court.

The statute placed the great burden of responsibility for administration in the hands of the United States District Courts, which selected the assignees in bankruptcy and prescribed rules and regulations and forms of proceedings. Involuntary bankrupts were entitled to jury trial in the matter of their bankrupt status. In the light of the fact that some states had only one District Court, and that in any event some debtors might live a long way from the situs of the court, the act provided that:

> [I]f such person shall reside at a great distance from the place of holding such court, the said judge, in his discretion, may direct such trial by jury to be had in the county of such person's residence, in such manner, and under such directions, as the said court may prescribe and give.[30]

Bankrupts failing to get a discharge might also demand a jury trial, or might appeal to the United States Circuit Court. Circuit Courts were to have concurrent jurisdiction in various matters, and district judges might adjourn questions thereto—with the result that Supreme Court Justices on circuit became directly involved as well as incidentally engaged as advisers to district judges and carriers of information about modes of proceedings in other circuits and other districts. In view of the fact that thousands of persons throughout the United States were seeking relief, the burden of administering the act promised to be enormous. In the debate on the bill Senator James Buchanan had contended that it could never be carried into effect without increasing the judicial force at least tenfold.[31] *The Law Reporter*, published in Boston, predicted repeal because of the inordinate volume and complexity of the litigation to be thrust on the District Courts.[32]

The district judges did indeed find themselves faced with a confusing set of problems. Judge Nathaniel Pope, of the United States District Court in Illinois, for example, filed a series of questions with Justice McLean. Was it necessary that in bankruptcy cases the court sit only at the state capital or could it move about for the convenience of the parties? He would willingly do the latter, and he had seen a newspaper

---

[30] 5 Stat. 442.
[31] *Cong. Globe*, 27th Cong., 1st

Sess., App. 206 (1841).
[32] *Law Rep.*, 4:406, 1842.

statement that the district judge in Connecticut planned to do so, but no member of the Illinois bar advised that he could do so. Before what tribunal was trial to be had in cases where jury trials at a distance were permitted? The statute did not say. Did the statute confer full chancery jurisdiction? If the Supreme Court did not adopt bankruptcy rules for the sake of uniformity (which the statute did not authorize it to do), could Justice McLean get for Judge Pope a copy of the rules adopted in New York by Justice Thompson and Judge Betts?[33]

Judge H. H. Leavitt, United States district judge for Ohio, also filed with Justice McLean a long list of questions. He had thus far appointed a separate assignee for each separate bankrupt, as he believed the statute required, but in view of the large number of cases to come he wondered if an assignee could be appointed for each county in the state, a course pursued in New York and probably in other states. If this device were used, it might be necessary in some counties to appoint two assignees. If that were done, would they act jointly or severally? At that time, on March 9, 1842, more than a month after the act went into effect, only 160 cases had been filed in his court but they were coming fast. He expected to hold one term for bankruptcy cases in April and another in the summer. As was to be characteristic of later inquiries with respect to expansion of admiralty jurisdiction,[34] and related expansion of the federal judicial system and increase in salaries, he closed with a note of inquiry about "the *Court & Salary* Bill."[35]

In one way or another, whether by borrowing from one another or by local invention, the several district judges worked out rules of administration and got under way with the new task. On February 10, 1842, Justice Story remarked with a sense of relief that the statute had a breathing spell left to it, though he could not tell how long it would be suffered to live. If Congress would leave the courts to carry it into effect, he believed that it would become a most useful and salutary law. He at least would do all he could to give it a fair operation and a cheap one.[36] On April 29 he wrote to John M. Berrien of Georgia, who had defended the statute in the Senate, that the Bankruptcy Act worked well and that no immediate changes were needed.[37]

In the New England circuit full advantage was taken of the expertness of Justice Story in the law of bankruptcy by resorting to the concurrent jurisdiction of the Circuit Court. In *Ex parte Foster*,[38] sitting with Judge Peleg Sprague, Justice Story answered one of the questions put to

---

[33] Nathaniel Pope to John McLean, Feb. 13, 1842, McLean Papers.

[34] See for example H. H. Leavitt to John McLean, Jan. 29, 1845, *ibid.*

[35] H. H. Leavitt to John McLean, Mar. 9, 1842, *ibid.*

[36] *Life and Letters of Joseph Story*, II, 416.

[37] Joseph Story to John M. Berrien, Apr. 29, 1842, *ibid.*, 404–05.

[38] 9 Fed. Cas. 508 (No. 4960) (C.C.D. Mass. 1842).

Justice McLean by holding that the District Courts of the United States possessed the full jurisdiction of courts of equity in cases under the statute. He gave offense to extreme defenders of states' rights by denying to creditors the right of attachment under state laws of the property of petitioners in bankruptcy under the federal statute. In the United States James Buchanan cited the case in criticism of the Whigs who, he contended, had "made, and attempted to make, longer strides toward consolidation, within the brief space of one short year, than we have ever witnessed before, since the commencement of the present century." Only the vetoes of the President had saved the country from a national bank. A measure to distribute to the states the proceeds of the sale of public land was "a law converting these States into mere stipendiaries on the General Government, and sinking them to the level of corporations, dependent upon Congress for their daily bread." Furthermore:

> Since the present Administration came into power, we have also enacted a bankrupt law—and such a law!—which places the relation of debtor and creditor, throughout the several States, under the jurisdiction of the Federal courts, and deprives these States of the power to regulate this important domestic subject according to their own laws. I have recently seen a decision of Judge Story, in a newspaper, by which the attachment laws of Massachusetts are declared to be prostrated under our bankrupt system.[39]

Some of the language employed by Justice Story in the *Foster* case displeased other judges who looked more fully than he to the states as the source and guardian of rights of property. On October 31, 1842, Justice Baldwin, in the United States Circuit Court in the Eastern District of Pennsylvania, rejected Justice Story's invocation of Supreme Court support of the doctrine that "a judgment is no lien till an execution is issued and a levy made,"[40] and proceeded to show that the Supreme Court had taken no such position. Complaint continued, however, that the Bankruptcy Act invaded the rights of the states,[41] and the states' rights issue played an immediate part in the accumulation of unpopularity which brought about the repeal of the statute.

There were other grounds of unpopularity. One already mentioned was the great distances which parties and witnesses had to travel to reach the District Courts, the courts apparently finding that they must operate from their prescribed locations rather than from multiple points of convenience throughout the several states, as had been suggested. Many creditors resented interference with their rights under state laws

---

[39] *Cong. Globe*, 27th Cong. 2nd Sess., App. 385 (1842).
[40] Dudley's Case, 7 Fed. Cas. 1150,

1153 (No. 4114) (C.C.E.D. Pa. 1842).
[41] Warren, *Bankruptcy in United States History*, 66, 82.

to exact the maximum of payment from debtors. Some of them wanted to participate in the selection of assignees and in the decision whether bankrupts should be discharged. One such memorial concluded with the warning:

> The Bankrupt Law forms an alarming era in our commercial history. The dread of the evils which it will produce, has already depreciated the stocks of our most solvent institutions; and it depends on your honorable body whether it shall be remembered as a blessing, or a curse.[42]

Opposition to a voluntary bankruptcy act was proclaimed on the ground that bankruptcy applied only to merchants and traders and only in involuntary situations, and that a voluntary act pertained to insolvency and not to bankruptcy, and was not authorized by the Constitution.[43] Justice Story, on the other hand, in his *Commentaries* as published in 1833, had treated the terms bankruptcy and insolvency as virtually interchangeable,[44] and the advocates of a broad general measure continued to treat them as such. Running through the criticisms of the statute was the implication that people ought to pay their debts and that government had no right and no power to relieve them of that obligation. The defense of the statute, on the other hand, carried humanitarian implications but assumed further that the good order of the country required clearing the morass of economic confusion in a fair and uniform manner so that prosperity could be restored.

On December 13, 1842, the Senate called on the Secretary of State, Daniel Webster, to secure from the judicial officers of the United States information about the administration of the statute and to get from the judges opinions as to changes that might be desirable. Highly diverse replies were received from the six Justices of the Supreme Court, listed according to the chronology of the replies: Daniel, Story, Taney, McLean, Thompson, and Baldwin. All were revealing, either for what they said or for what they did not say.

Justice Daniel replied in the vein of Southern agrarians, who were in general opposed to federal bankruptcy legislation. He thought the

---

[42] The Memorial of the Subscribers, Manufacturers, Merchants, Mechanics, and others, of the City of New York, Dec. 20, 1841, Senate Papers, 26th Cong., 2nd Sess.

[43] Among contemporary discussions see "The Late Bankrupt Law of the United States," *Pa. L.J.*, 3:1, 1844, and Henry Raymond, "The Late Bankrupt Law," *Pa. L.J.*, 3:489, 1844. See also the opinion of Judge Richard M.

Young in Wattles v. Lalor, Circuit Court of Illinois, October term, 1843 in *West L.J.*, 3:315, 1846. As discussed below see also *In re* Klein, 14 Fed. Cas. 719 (No. 7866) (D.C.D.Mo. 1842) and *In re* Klein, 14 Fed. Cas. 716 (No. 7865) (C.C.D. Mo. 1843).

[44] Joseph Story. *Commentaries on the Constitution of the United States*, III, 4–15.

benefits of individual relief under the law had been "greatly over-weighed by the decay, I might, perhaps, be warranted in saying by the destruction, of confidence, and of wholesome credit, the consequent withdrawal of pecuniary facilities, and the torpor of useful energy and enterprise." He saw the remedy not in modification of the law but in unconditional repeal.[45] Justice Story, by contrast, replied in a judicious vein that in his circuit the system had worked well and had benefited the public, as a cheap and expeditious means of achieving the ends desired. It was true that returns to creditors had been small, but this was due to the fact that whole classes were insolvent and in ruin. He forebore to suggest improvements, saying that it had worked remarkably well in the twenty-six states with diverse "jurisprudence" and that "if it is now to perish, it is not worth the labor to attempt any amendment or improvement."[46]

Chief Justice Taney submitted an extremely cautious reply, sug-gesting that if the statute were to remain in force it would be well to clarify some of the difficulties of construction. But, he added, "I observe that a proposition to repeal the law is now under discussion in Congress. And while that question remains undecided, it is, I presume, not desired that I should trouble the Senate with matters which are alto-gether unimportant if the law is to be repealed."[47] Justice McLean was similarly cautious. As with Chief Justice Taney, only a few cases had reached him in the Circuit Court. He thought the provision most objected to was that for voluntary bankruptcy. If the statute were limited to traders and if banks were included, the measure would be more accept-able than it now was, and its beneficial influence would be felt more by creditors than by debtors. The reply had all the indefiniteness that was to be expected on a controversial subject from a perennial aspirant for the Presidency. Justice Thompson said that the act was certainly very artificially drawn and in many parts difficult of interpretation, no doubt as a result of the many amendments adopted to express the preferences of different legislators. He thought that judicial interpretations had been generally in a common pattern and that new amendments might give rise to new questions of interpretation.[48]

Justice Baldwin, finally, presented a thoughtful and in part a critical analysis, preserving a kind of aloofness in spite of the financial distress to which he had himself been subject. He thought that in general the effects had been beneficial.[49] Now that the emergency had passed, he was inclined to believe that the relief should be withdrawn. While benefits had been derived in the past, people should not be led

---

[45] Senate Doc. No. 19, 27th Cong., 3rd Sess. 17 (1842).
[46] *Ibid.*, 28.

[47] *Ibid.*, 51–52.
[48] *Ibid.*, 69–70.
[49] *Ibid.*, 70.

to expect similar benefits in the future—a point on which he differed from those who thought it bad policy to interfere with past contracts but legitimate to establish a policy as to future contracts. In any event, a number of modifications were needed, some of which he proposed. But as to detailed changes, he thought:

> [T]he better mode of suggesting them would be, in my opinion, a conference between the members of the judiciary committee and the judges at the ensuing term. This mode would lead to more uniformity of decision than by acting on the suggestion of the judges separately.[50]

No replies came from Justices Wayne, Catron, and McKinley. All three represented Southern or Southwestern circuits where the sentiments of constituents may well have been much like those of Justice Daniel. It may be that the Justices themselves were in favor of the statute and that they avoided political controversy by not replying.

We know something of Justice Catron's position from another source. In Missouri Judge Robert W. Wells, a jurist of considerable capacity, wrote at the September, 1842, term of the United States District Court an opinion in the case of Edward Klein holding the federal Bankruptcy Act unconstitutional as it applied to contracts made before the act was passed. He maintained that the Bankruptcy Clause of the Constitution, like other clauses, must be read in the light of the meaning the term had had in English law at the time the Constitution was adopted. In that view, the power given to Congress was the power to establish "a system for the benefit of creditors, to enable them to collect their just debts, and to prevent the frauds of debtors who might remove their property and themselves into different states."[51] Judge Wells contended that the Act of 1841 was solely for the benefit of debtors and to enable them to avoid their debts, and was therefore in opposition to the whole intent, spirit, and object of a bankruptcy law. It was therefore unconstitutional.

---

[50] *Ibid.*, 71–72. A number of United States District Judges also expressed opinions. United States Attorneys and court clerks gave some information about numbers of cases and method of handling. The same document contained copies of the rules adopted in two districts, Connecticut (p. 32) and Kentucky (p. 83). For the Pennsylvania rules see "Practice in Bankruptcy," *Pa. L.J.*, 1:8, 1842. For general treatises see George A. Bicknell, Jr., *A Commentary on the Bankrupt Law of 1841, Showing Its Operation and Effect*, and Samuel Owen, *A Treatise on the Law and Practice of Bankruptcy, with Reference to the General Bankrupt Act*. For a later report on the quantity of business under the statute see *House Doc.* 223, 29th Cong., 1st Sess.

[51] *In re* Klein, 14 Fed. Cas. 719, 721 (No. 7866) (D.C.D. Mo. 1842). The date of this decision in *Federal Cases* is given as 1843. However, in a copy submitted to Daniel Webster along with his letter of Jan. 5, 1843, Judge Wells states that the case was decided at the September term, 1842.

An appeal was taken to the United States Circuit Court, where Justice Catron sat alone. He reversed the order of the District Court, admitting that under the English interpretation bankruptcy did not include voluntary action of debtors to secure their own release but contending that such action was included in the practice of American states before adoption of the Constitution and that the Bankruptcy Clause should be read in the light of American practice. He thought a prime merit of the federal statute was the reservation of this uniform authority to the federal government and the prevention of diverse and conflicting regulations by the states.[52] Neither of these Western judges saw fit to quote Justice Story's *Commentaries* on the subject.

Justices Wayne and McKinley published no opinions revealing their attitudes toward the Bankruptcy Act. Indeed, although the position of Justice Story was, of course, well known, the Supreme Court as a whole never expressed an opinion on the constitutionality of the act, and the Circuit Court opinion of Justice Catron in the *Klein* case, discussed above, seems to have provided the only official treatment of constitutionality by any of the Justices. Because Justice Catron had sat alone in decision of the case, it was not possible to get the question before the Supreme Court on certification of division of opinion between him and Judge Wells, and the statute did not allow an appeal from the Circuit Court to the Supreme Court. Members of the St. Louis bar were interested in having a Supreme Court decision on the constitutional question and asked Justice Catron to try to bring about such a decision in another case. In the light of that request, in a case arising in the district of Kentucky, which was also in Justice Catron's circuit, certain points were adjourned from the District Court to the Circuit. Judge Thomas B. Monroe and Justice Catron sat together in the Circuit Court, and they certified to the Supreme Court certain questions on which they were divided. Unfortunately for the ends in view, the Supreme Court, in *Nelson v. Carland*,[53] held that in cases adjourned into a Circuit Court under the Bankruptcy Act the district judge could not sit as a member of that court, with the result that points could not be certified to the Supreme Court. Nor would an appeal or writ of error lie from the decision of the Circuit Court.

Only Justice Catron dissented. After returning to St. Louis for the ensuing term of the circuit there, he worked out strategy to minimize the loss and get at least his own opinion on the constitutional question before the country by sending a copy of his opinion in the *Klein* case to William Thomas Carroll, the Clerk of the Supreme Court, and asking

---

[52] *In re* Klein, 14 Fed. Cas. 716 (No. 7865) (C.C.D. Mo. 1843 [?]). See the opinion also as a note appended to

Nelson v. Carland, 1 How. 265, 277 (1843).
[53] *Ibid.*

that it be published in connection with his dissenting opinion in the *Nelson* case:

> I enclose you a copy of my opinion on the constitutionality of the Bankrupt law; which I desire shall in some way appear in your reports, in the appendix; or as a note at the end of my dissenting opinion in the Bankrupt Case brought up frankly for the purpose of this question, here. Place it anywhere your judgment may suggest—or leave it out, if you deem it in any way improper.[54]

Carroll referred the matter to the Reporter, Benjamin C. Howard,[55] and on not hearing from Howard questioned facetiously whether "you mean to pass me the responsibility of omitting Judge Catron's *Errata* in your present volume with which I apprehend he would be very much disappointed." The *Klein* opinion was published as a supplement to Catron's Supreme Court opinion in the *Nelson* case.

Comparable to the difficulty in getting the question of the constitutionality of the Bankruptcy Act before the Supreme Court was the difficulty of getting decisions on questions of interpretation. Chief Justice Joel Parker, of the Superior Court of Judicature of New Hampshire, deplored the fact that the act provided no common tribunal for its interpretation but gave final jurisdiction to between thirty and forty District and territorial courts, unless the district judge saw fit to adjourn questions into the Circuit Court, in which case final interpretation was left to nine Circuit Courts. Except by the bankrupt on a question of discharge, no provision was made for appeals, and none for writs of error. Since the district judge did not sit in cases involving questions adjourned, cases could not be brought before the Supreme Court by certificate of division.[56] Where interpretation of the statute involved questions as to the scope of state powers, there was apt to be jealousy on the part of the highest courts of the states at limitation of their powers by federal district or circuit judges without the opportunity for verification in the Supreme Court. This seems to have been particularly true in the New England states and, oddly enough in view of his prestige throughout the region, in important cases where Justice Story spoke for the United States Circuit Court.

One set of delicate questions involving issues of states' rights arose out of two sections of the federal statute. Those sections sought to prevent discriminating distributions of property among creditors before the Bankruptcy Act was invoked. However, it exempted the "lawful rights

---

[54] J. Catron to B. C. Howard, Apr. 30, 1843, Howard Papers.
[55] William Thomas Carroll to B. C.

Howard, May 11, 1843, Howard Papers.
[56] Kittredge v. Warren, 14 N.H. 509, 511 (1844).

of married women, or minors, or any liens, mortgages, or other securities on property, real or personal, which may be valid by the laws of the States respectively, and which are not inconsistent with the provisions of the second and fifth sections of this act."[57] Particularly important was the question whether attachments on mesne process, a device "peculiar in some measure to New England,"[58] fell within the area of "liens, mortgages, or other securities on property," which were protected against the operations of the Bankruptcy Act. In *Ex parte Foster*, decided in 1842 and briefly discussed above, Justice Story, to the horror of James Buchanan, held that an attachment sued out under state law before bankruptcy proceedings were instituted was not a lien and was not protected under the second section of the act. He took the same position in later cases.

In 1844, however, amid rumblings of discontent on the part of groups of adversely affected parties and of states' rights defenders, the highest court in New Hampshire, in *Kittredge v. Warren,* challenged the position taken by Justice Story, asserting that the attachment was protected and that discharge under the Bankruptcy Act could not be pleaded in bar to action on the attachment. Later in the same year Justice Story, in another Circuit Court case, *In re Bellows*, rejected the interpretation given by Chief Justice Parker and said of his own opinion in the *Foster* case that "the more I reflect upon the doctrines stated therein, the more I am satisfied, that they conform to the true intent and objects of the bankrupt law of 1841; and I adhere to them with undoubting confidence."[59] He adhered to his earlier position "toto animo," and would therefore "act upon my own judgment, until the supreme court of the United States has instructed me otherwise."[60]

Chief Justice Parker refused to yield, restating his own carefully worked out conclusions and arguing from many cases decided in New England state courts and some federal courts that his own reading of the law with respect to attachments was correct.[61] In the meantime the governor of New Hampshire entered the fray by reporting the controversy to the legislature, which responded by a set of defiant resolutions. It resolved that the Supreme Court of the United States was the only constitutional tribunal that could revise and correct the adjudications of state courts; that the Superior Court of Judicature of New Hampshire had ample power to enforce its judgments and to protect its officers in the execution of its process; and that the legislature heartily appreciated and approved the firm and decided stand taken by the state judges

---

[57] 5 Stat. 442.
[58] Kittredge v. Warren, 14 N.H. 509, 518 (1844).
[59] *In re* Bellows, 3 Fed. Cas. 138,

140 (No. 1278) (C.C.D. N.H. 1844).
[60] *Ibid.*, 143.
[61] Kittredge v. Emerson, 15 N.H. 227 (1844).

in opposition to the unwarrantable and dangerous assumptions of the Circuit Courts, and that "they ought and will be sustained in that stand, if need be, by the united voice and power of the government and people of the state."[62]

When in the summer of 1844 Justice Story announced that in applying the bankruptcy law he would act upon his own judgment until the Supreme Court of the United States instructed him otherwise, he knew that the Supreme Court had carried over from the preceding term a case involving the power of the Court to give instructions in bankruptcy cases and he probably knew what the position of the Court would be. The case came not from New England but from New Orleans and involved bankruptcy litigation that persisted in that area over a number of years. This case, *Ex parte The City Bank of New Orleans*,[63] sometimes cited as *Ex parte Christy*, arose on a motion on behalf of the City Bank of New Orleans for a prohibition directed to the United States District Court in Louisiana to curb the court's exercise of allegedly unlawful jurisdiction.[64] The bank had challenged the jurisdiction of that court to determine the validity of a mortgage held by the bank under state law, contending that such power was reserved to the state tribunals. The question was adjourned to the United States Circuit Court, where Justice McKinley held that the federal court had jurisdiction.

Since the Bankruptcy Act gave no right of appeal to the Supreme Court, the bank tried to infer from the Judiciary Act of 1789 a power to issue writs of prohibition parallel to that given in admiralty and maritime jurisdiction. In 1845 the Supreme Court decided unanimously that it was not authorized to issue the writ and that it had no revising power over the District Court sitting in bankruptcy. Justice Story wrote the opinion on this point of full agreement, and went beyond it, with Justices Catron and Daniel dissenting, to hold that the District Court was within its power in taking jurisdiction to determine the validity of mortgages under state laws. Without of course mentioning Chief Justice Parker of New Hampshire, he here continued his rivalry with that jurist by asserting on the authority of the Supreme Court the broad scope of the power of federal courts in bankruptcy cases.[65]

---

[62] "Bankruptcy," *Law Rep.*, 7:494, 1845.

[63] 3 How. 292 (1845).

[64] For discussion see Charles G. Haines and Foster H. Sherwood, *The Role of the Supreme Court in American Government and Politics, 1835–1864*, 203–04.

[65] In rejecting this portion of the opinion of the Court Justice Catron noted that in similar cases he and the district judges in his circuit had recognized the validity of sales brought about under the jurisdiction of state courts, and he inserted as a part of his Supreme Court opinion a Circuit Court opinion of Justice Baldwin, recently deceased, taking the same position. Since the Supreme Court disclaimed jurisdiction he thought its opinion mere dictum, and opposed publishing such dictum: "In this

Although in a later decision at the same term the Supreme Court through Chief Justice Taney made clear that it had not decided whether or not state courts were deprived of all jurisdiction over the property of bankrupts,[66] Chief Justice Parker, a few months later in *Peck v. Jenness*,[67] returned to the attack on Justice Story. Contending that Story's opinion in the *New Orleans* case was a misinterpretation of the act and inconsistent within itself, he continued to assert the authority of state courts with respect to the mortgaged property of bankrupts and insisted that attachments had the status of liens under state and federal law. The case was appealed to the Supreme Court. Meanwhile, in 1845, Justice Story died, and before the case was decided in 1849 various other changes in Supreme Court personnel had taken place. In a unanimous opinion delivered by Justice Grier the Court accepted Chief Justice Parker's position with respect to the continuing authority of state courts—where they took jurisdiction prior to that exercised by the federal courts—and the classification of attachments on mesne process as liens.[68] Justice Story had gone down to posthumous defeat.

True, as demonstrated by another unanimous decision a year earlier,[69] the federal courts were in no sense crippled in the exercise of their own jurisdiction. But that case, likewise involving the City Bank of New Orleans, has today more value for its human interest than for its defense of a statute then already five years repealed. It brought out distinguished counsel in the persons of Reverdy Johnson of Maryland, Henry Clay of Kentucky, and John Sergeant of Pennsylvania. Clay, then seventy-one years of age, was the lion of the group. It seemed as if the population of Washington went en masse to the Courtroom to hear him.[70] A reporter wrote that every inch of space was occupied, even to the lobbies leading to the Senate. Another noted that visitors got

---

course I cannot concur; perhaps it is the result of timidity growing out of long established judicial habits in courts of error elsewhere, never to hazard an opinion where no case was before the court, and when that opinion might be justly arraigned as extrajudicial, and a mere dictum by courts and lawyers; be partly disregarded while I was living, and almost certainly be denounced as undue assumption when I was no more. A measure of disregard awarded with an unsparing hand, here and elsewhere, to the dicta of State judges under similar circumstances: and it is due to the occasion and to myself to say, that I have no doubt the dicta of this court will only be treated with

becoming respect before the court itself, so long as some of the judges who concurred in them are present on the bench; and afterwards be openly rejected as no authority—as they are not." 3 How. 322 (1845).

[66] Nugent v. Boyd, 3 How. 426 (1845).

[67] 16 N.H. 516 (1845).

[68] Peck v. Jenness, 7 How. 612 (1849).

[69] Houston v. City Bank of New Orleans, 6 How. 486 (1848). See comment on case, *West. L.J.*, 4:432, 1847.

[70] For a summary of accounts see Warren, *The Supreme Court in United States History*, II, 168–69.

within the bar and crowded the judges in their seats, remarking that "liberty of the press" was never carried to a more dangerous extent. Clay, he said, had always been a great favorite with the ladies. The gallantry of his bearing, the dignity of his gestures, the warmth of his manners, his sonorous voice, and "the many graces with which he is ideally associated in the general imagination make him the proper favorite of the more discriminating portion of creation."[71] While the case had no deep interest for the audience it was of personal interest to Clay in that it dealt with power under the bankruptcy law which he had helped to enact. It was said of the beginning of his performance:

> His exordium as he rose to address the Court, has been represented as not less touching than beautiful. Mr. Clay's recollections and sentiments were always in harmony, and no man could better grace facts with touches of feeling. As this might be the last time he would ever appear in that place, what more natural than that he should make some allusion to the first? He did so with great pertinency and effect, and as he was a model of suavity and politeness, it was equally natural that he should pay a compliment to the Court, which, indeed, in its moral influence, was not likely to injure his client; though, far be it from us to suggest that the Court could be unduly influenced. Not a face was on that bench which was to be seen in that place when Mr. Clay first had the honor of appearing as counsel there; that was a monition of the changing scenes of life.
>
> But the Court had maintained its character and dignity. That was a compliment. After a few such like historical allusions, and touches of sentiment, done in Mr. Clay's peculiar style of pertinency, grace, and dignity, to the edification of the Court, as well as to the delight of his audience, he proceeded to open his case. His argument on this occasion was allowed to be as vigorous and as effective as any he ever made.[72]

Said a newspaper reporter, it mattered not to the audience how dry and intrinsically uninteresting the subject. "It was Mr. Clay they wished to hear, and not of Bankrupt Law or any other law. They hung upon his words, as if each was an inspiration."[73]

Clay wrote to his wife that his friends were highly gratified with his argument and that he was well satisfied. Overrun with visitors at the United States Hotel, and entertained by celebrities including President Polk, he retired to the home of a friend to await the decision of the Court. He won his case, in what proved, indeed, to be his last major appearance before the Supreme Court.

---

[71] *New York Tribune*, Feb. 15, 1848.
[72] *Works of Henry Clay*, III, 79.

[73] *New York Tribune*, Feb. 15, 1848.

VI: *Hard Times and Contract Obligations*

Since the Bankruptcy Act of 1841 was in effect only about a year, and since during a part of that year it was clear that repeal was in the offing, it might be assumed that the measure was of little importance to the country despite all the litigation to which it gave rise. Yet at a time of crisis, or of confusion resulting from economic crisis, the act did permit a vast body of debtors and creditors to begin working out resolution under the jurisdiction of federal courts.[74] If the absence of unifying supervision by the Supreme Court meant that administration would vary greatly from district to district, or at any rate from circuit to circuit, there was nevertheless a measure of uniformity, and proceedings in the federal courts were effective throughout the United States, by contrast with proceedings under state insolvency laws which could not adequately reach beyond the borders of the administering state. The value of the program may have been tacitly recognized even by many of those who successfully worked for the repeal of the statute.

Objections to the statute, it will be recalled, were numerous and interrelated.[75] The Committee on the Judiciary in the Senate, which sought to protect the ill-fated statute, offered a defense which is significant for the continuation of the story of hard times and the obligation of contracts. It contended that repeal of the statute would injuriously affect our credit abroad, since in the absence of an escape through bankruptcy the people would turn to repudiation in some form: "In some of the States repudiation has found advocates. Some have passed, and, if this law be repealed, more of them will pass what are denominated 'stay laws'—laws impeding the operations of the creditor in the collection of his debts; and the failure of individuals, under the pressure of necessity, or from whatever other cause, in the fulfilment of their pecuniary obligations, is more universal than at any former period of our history. . . . Why give this finishing blow to American credit abroad?"[76]

During the period of economic crisis relief through "stay laws" was attempted in many of the states, including Alabama, Ohio, Illinois, Indiana, Michigan, Minnesota, Mississippi, Pennsylvania, Virginia, and Wisconsin.[77] Stay laws sought to protect debtors by postponing execution on contracts, and were usually linked with valuation provisions whereby the sale of property for the payment of debts was forbidden

---

[74] For reports on the quantity of business done in the several districts see H.R. Exec. Doc. No. 223, 29th Cong., 1st Sess. (1846), and H.R. Exec. Doc. No. 99, 29th Cong., 2nd Sess. (1847).

[75] For partial discussion see S. Rep. No. 121, 27th Cong., 3rd Sess (1843).

[76] *Ibid.*, 23.

[77] For discussion see Warren, *Bankruptcy in United States History,* 87–90, and John B. McMaster, *History of the People of the United States During Lincoln's Administration,* VII, 45–46.

unless a specified fraction of the appraised value of the property was offered. The case of *Bronson v. Kinzie*,[78] decided by the Supreme Court at about the time of the repeal of the federal bankruptcy statute, involved a stay law enacted by the Illinois legislature in 1841. The statute gave a one-year period for redemption of property sold to pay debts, and provided that the property should not be sold at all unless two-thirds of the appraised value was offered. In a case involving foreclosure on a mortgage executed before the statute was passed, Justice McLean and United States District Judge Nathaniel Pope, in the United States Circuit Court for Illinois, disagreed over whether the restrictive provisions of the statute should be adopted as the rule of that court. They certified the question to the Supreme Court.

For Bronson, the creditor, the case was submitted on written argument by Isaac N. Arnold, a young Chicago attorney who was on his way to achievement of considerable prominence both at law and in politics. Although he seems to have adhered primarily to technical issues involving impairment of the obligation of contracts, Arnold in his concluding paragraph stressed the issues of public policy:

> It it not intended here to discuss the general policy of these laws, but all who have observed their operation will admit, that . . . they ultimately injure the class they are designed to relieve, and prolong and increase the distress of the whole community—that frauds abound— credit is necessarily greatly impaired, the debtor made dishonest, and the creditor extortionate.[79]

Unfortunately the case for the debtor—the defense of the constitutionality of stay laws—was not presented, either orally or on written brief. The Supreme Court heard therefore no such arguments as were to be presented long afterward during the New Deal period for the need of flexibility in constitutional interpretation to meet the stresses of economic emergencies. Since neither what we call "Brandeis briefs" nor judicial opinions in the vein of such briefs were of the order of the day, it is not surprising that in writing the opinion of the Court Chief Justice Taney dealt only with strictly legal considerations. He held the statute unconstitutional as an impairment of the obligation of contracts. "Whatever belongs merely to the remedy," he explained, "may be altered according to the will of the State, provided the alteration does not impair the obligation of the contract. But if that effect is produced, it is immaterial whether it is done by acting on the remedy or directly on the contract itself. In either case it is prohibited by the Constitution."[80]

---

[78] 1 How. 311 (1843).
[79] Quoted in a brief notice of the argument, *Law Rep.*, 6:46, 1843.
[80] 1 How. 316.

The opinion was strictly legalistic in its phraseology. It made no excursions into the history of the economic crisis and no reference to the need of impoverished people for flexibility in the enforcement of law in a time of collapsing property values. Obviously the several Justices, traveling through the country on circuit and talking with lawyers and judges wherever they went, were fully aware of the predicament in which the people found themselves. Yet they did not find it expedient to write economic considerations into constitutional law save as it could be done in strictly conventional legal terms.

Even Justice McLean, in whose circuit the case arose, and who was the only dissenter on the Court, restricted his opinion to such technical matters as the distinction between the substantive obligation of contracts and the remedy provided by law, a distinction hitherto made clear, he asserted, by Chief Justice Marshall in *Sturges v. Crownin-shield.*[81] He gave his vote, but not his powers of exposition, to the cause of harried debtors.

Justice Story, absent from the Court throughout the term because of illness, was depressed at the repeal of the federal Bankruptcy Act, which had provided an orderly means for dealing with economic distress, and by the threat of direct or indirect repudiation of debts through action of the state governments. He wrote to Chief Justice Taney that he had read his opinion in the Illinois case and entirely concurred in it. He was disturbed at the report that Justice McLean had dissented. "There are times," he remarked, "in which the Court is called upon to support every sound constitutional doctrine in support of the rights of property and of creditors."[82] Somewhat later he wrote to Justice McLean, "I have read the opinion published in the newspapers in the Illinois case, and I am entirely satisfied with the opinion of the Court." He added somberly, "I look on the future prospects of my country with utter despondency."[83]

When Justice McLean returned to his circuit he was reported as saying that where mortgages were involved he would hold stay laws unconstitutional, even though he doubted the correctness of the Supreme Court decision, but as intimating that he would not extend the logic of the decision to suits on common debt where no mortgages were involved.[84] But in 1844 the Supreme Court held unconstitutional the Illinois stay law as presented in such a case.[85] Justice Baldwin wrote the opinion of the Court. Justice McLean remained silent—whether under the persuasion of Justice Story or from a change in conviction we

---

[81] 4 Wheat. 122, 200 (1819).
[82] Samuel Tyler, *Memoir of Roger Brooke Taney*, 289.
[83] Joseph Story to John McLean, Apr. 14, 1843, McLean Papers.

[84] *Niles' National Register*, 64:245, 1843.
[85] McCracken v. Hayward, 2 How. 608 (1844).

do not know. Here, oddly enough, Justice Catron, whom the Reporter had listed as present at the decision of the Bronson case, now announced, "I have formed no opinion whether the statute of Illinois is constitutional or otherwise."[86] Yet a year later he wrote the opinion of a unanimous Court in a decision which he rested in part on the Bronson case.[87]

From debtor groups and their spokesmen the Supreme Court decisions, of course, brought sharp criticism. The Democratic Review said of stay laws, appraisal laws, and bank suspension laws:

> All are the incoherent stammerings of a principle as yet but imperfectly developed. But when a truth has even thus far wreaked itself upon expression, there is no power on earth . . . to resist its supremacy. It will agitate, it will struggle, it will writhe, but it will have utterance. It may succumb for a season, but it will not be cheated of a single fraction or tithing of the empire over the heart and mind of man. We look for the time, and that soon, when the political parties shall divide upon the expediency, if not the constitutionality of protecting contracts by law, and when the present offices of the judiciary shall in this particular be very seriously restricted.[88]

A joint resolution—which failed of enactment—was introduced in the United States Senate proposing a constitutional amendment to prohibit the Supreme Court from declaring void any state or federal act on the ground of violation of the Constitution or of a constitution of a state.[89] The widely read Western Law Journal, published in Cincinnati, carried articles voicing the criticisms in Justice McLean's dissent in the Bronson case and called attention of the legal profession to "a departure so wide from all the rules of construction known to the law."[90]

There is evidence that creditors feared not merely the postponement of collections on debts as provided for by stay laws but widespread repudiation of debts, public and private, at the hands of the states. Illinois papers discussing the Bronson case mentioned particularly the talk of repudiating state canal bonds.[91] The important question was whether state courts would follow the lead of the Supreme Court in protecting property rights—for the lower federal courts had general

---

[86] Ibid., 617–18.

[87] Gantly's Lessee v. Ewing, 3 How. 707 (1845).

[88] "Prospects of the Legal Profession in America," United States Magazine and Democratic Review, 18:27–28, 1846.

[89] Warren, The Supreme Court in United States History, II, 105.

[90] S.J., "The Obligation of a Contract—What Is It?," West. L.J., 4:254, 260, 1847, continued West L.J., 5:173, 1848. See also A.W., "Legislative and Judicial Power," West. L.J., 4:337, 1847.

[91] Springfield (Ill.) Sangamo Journal, Mar. 16, 1843.

jurisdiction at this time only in cases involving diversity of citizenship. The mass of cases arose in the state courts, and none of this immediate kind were appealed from the highest state courts to the Supreme Court. When the *Bronson* case was decided, a Baltimore newspaper correspondent wrote:

> The course of legislation upon which some of the States appear too willing to embark, of casting every impediment in the way of the collection of debts, is thus early and happily arrested; and the reasoning of the Chief Justice, by whom the opinion was delivered, is so lucid, and addresses itself so commandingly to the judgment, that I have no doubt it will receive the sanction of every intelligent mind in the country.[92]

A threat of rejection of Supreme Court leadership came in 1844 when the eminent chief justice of Pennsylvania's highest court, John Bannister Gibson, distinguished the *Bronson* case and upheld a temporary stay law of that state, saying:

> To hold that a State Legislature is incompetent to relieve the public from the pressure of sudden distress by arresting a general sacrifice of property, by the machinery of the law, would invalidate many statutes whose constitutionality has hitherto been unsuspected.[93]

Although various other state judges refused to follow the leadership of the Supreme Court, still others fell into line,[94] including, indeed, Judge Ellis Lewis of Pennsylvania,[95] then a circuit judge, who was to become chief justice of the state. Eventually the crisis passed, and although repercussions included an affirming Supreme Court decision on the eve of the Civil War,[96] the issue for a time pretty much lost its importance.

Chief Justice Taney's interpretation of the Contract Clause of the Constitution remained in good standing for nearly a century. Then, during the New Deal period when judges as well as legislators were compelled by another crisis to look anew at the pattern of our institutions, the Supreme Court, dividing five to four, distinguished the *Bronson*

---

[92] *Baltimore American*, Feb. 25, 1843.

[93] Chadwick v. Moore, 8 Watts & Serg. 49, 52 (Pa. 1844).

[94] For reference to cases of both kinds see Warren, *Bankruptcy in United States History*, 88–89.

[95] See "Political Portraits with Pen and Pencil: Ellis Lewis," *United States Magazine and Democratic Review*, 20:355, 1847. For the operation of stay laws in Pennsylvania see Louis Hartz, *Economic Policy and Democratic Thought, 1776–1860*, 231–33.

[96] Howard v. Bugbee, 24 How. 461 (1861).

decision to uphold a Minnesota stay law which was temporary in character and gave somewhat more protection to the rights of creditors than did the stay laws of the earlier period. Here, in *Home Building and Loan Association v. Blaisdell*,[97] Chief Justice Hughes, for the Court, resorted to the doctrine of emergency to justify the exercise of power that could not be exercised in normal times, while Justice Sutherland, for the dissenters, deplored the abandonment of sound constitutional principles and reminded the Court that the emergency following the panic of 1837 had been "quite as serious as that which the country has faced during the past three years."[98]

As the repeal of the federal Bankruptcy Act closed one door to better things for harassed debtors, finding stay laws to be unconstitutional closed another. True, in finding the Illinois statue unconstitutional Chief Justice Taney did say that various kinds of property could be exempted from execution on judgments, and a number of states took broad advantage of the opportunity to create such exemptions.[99] But the major remaining resort for debtors was to the varying insolvency laws of the several states.[100] Here the federal courts became involved primarily as the insolvency laws had repercussions beyond the borders of the states which enacted them. It had been held in 1819 that the obligation of contracts was impaired when state laws were employed to discharge debts incurred before the laws were enacted,[101] and that such laws were likewise unconstitutional even if their enactment antedated the contracts from which they gave relief.[102] In *Ogden v. Saunders*,[103] however, decided in 1827, the Supreme Court had left the situation badly confused. With the seven Justices dividing four to three, the Court had there held that within its own territorial jurisdiction a state could relieve debtors of the burden of debts incurred after the relief laws were passed. But by another division of four to three the Court also held in that case that a discharge of a debtor under a state insolvency law would not be valid as against a creditor resident in another state who had never voluntarily subjected himself to the laws of the state seeking to give the relief.[104] So it was that while within its borders a state might give relief with respect to the obligation of contracts made after enact-

---

97 290 U.S. 398 (1934).

98 *Ibid.*, 466.

99 Warren, *Bankruptcy in United States History*, 88.

100 For examples of the problems involved in application of insolvency laws see "The Insolvent Law of Massachusetts," *Law Rep.*, 10:385, 1848.

101 Sturges v. Crowninshield, 4 Wheat. 122 (1819).

102 McMillan v. McNeill, 4 Wheat. 209 (1819).

103 12 Wheat. 213 (1827).

104 See affirmation of this decision, Boyle v. Zacharie, 6 Pet. 348 (1832).

ment of the relieving statute, and every other state was required by the Constitution to give full faith and credit to its acts, the Court by a re-aligned majority limited possible relief to the boundaries of territorial jurisdiction. Thus long before the due process standard was made applicable to the states by the Fourteenth Amendment, the Court contrived on general principles drawn from private international law to place limits on the territorial jurisdiction of the courts of a state.

With the continued expansion of business between citizens of different states, debtors found it increasingly irksome that state relief was limited to contracts of a state's own citizens. Yet judges maintained the restriction in spite of criticism of the decision. In 1842 Justice Story in Circuit Court said of the insolvency law of Massachusetts that "the settled position of the supreme court of the United States is, that no state insolvent laws can discharge the obligations of any contract made in the state, except such contracts as are made between citizens of that state."[105]

On his circuit, in Maryland, Chief Justice Taney reluctantly took the same position because in an inferior tribunal he felt himself bound to follow the decisions of the Supreme Court. The case was *Cook v. Moffat*,[106] where in 1847 the Supreme Court affirmed the judgment of the Circuit Court. Here Justice Grier spoke for the Supreme Court, holding that a discharge under the Maryland insolvency law did not affect a contract by a Maryland citizen made with a citizen in New York and to be performed in New York. He emphasized in this case not merely the diverse citizenship but also the situs of the contract. So controversial was the subject, however, that four Justices, from as many approaches, wrote concurring opinions. Chief Justice Taney admitted that bankruptcy laws could have no force beyond the limits of the enacting states except as other states by comity gave them recognition, but he thought it should be the states and not the federal courts which determined the measure of that comity. The question, however, had given rise to so much controversy since the year 1819 that he saw no value in further argument. Justices McLean, Daniel, and Woodbury also accepted the decision of the Court but found it necessary to indicate diverse shadings of opinion.

This decision likewise brought criticism from democratic elements. Daniel Raymond, a briefless lawyer in Baltimore and a writer on constitutional law and political economy, denounced the Court's mechanical resort to *stare decisis* through the series of cases and, tracing the decisions and the multiple opinions, concluded that "Such discordant

---

[105] Springer v. Foster, 22 Fed. Cas. 1008 (No. 13266) (C.C.D. Mass. 1842).

[106] 5 How. 295 (1847).

decisions, and such discrepancy of opinion, among the members of the Supreme Court, never can settle a question of constitutional law."[107]

In spite of the criticism and in spite of the difference in patterns of judicial reasoning, the Supreme Court held to its central position. During the Civil War period it asserted that position again, basing its unanimous decision on geographical grounds and the diverse citizenship of the parties without reference to the situs of the contract. Said Justice Clifford for the Court:

> Insolvent laws of one State cannot discharge the contracts of citizens of other States, because they have no extraterritorial operation, and consequently the tribunal sitting under them, unless in cases where a citizen of such other State voluntarily becomes a party to the proceeding, has no jurisdiction in the case.[108]

In short, throughout each of these series of cases, the Supreme Court held staunchly for the protection of rights of property and the maintenance of principles giving that protection. True, some of the Justices gave full support and others cautious support to federal bankruptcy legislation protecting distressed debtors. With different theoretical approaches, apparently all of them recognized the right of states to give insolvency protection prospectively to debtors in contract relations with citizens of the same state.[109] Yet it is clear that, in spite of differences in individual positions, the Court provided the outstanding bulwark in the country against the breakdown of contract relations in times of great economic crisis and furnished legal and moral leadership for other courts, both state and federal, and for the federal and state governments as a whole and for the people at large. For the most part that leadership was written into the law of the land and was generally accepted. Broader amelioration of the conditions of debtors in crisis periods was postponed until later periods in American history when our institutions were more firmly established and when flexibility could be provided without such serious threat to the legal and economic order.

---

[107] "Constitutional Law," *United States Magazine and Democratic Review*, 23:444, 1848. The article was here published without the author's name. With his name and with some modifications it was republished, *West. L.J.*, 6:112, 1848.

[108] Baldwin v. Hale, 1 Wall. 223, 234 (1864).

[109] Though see Justice McLean's opinion that a state insolvency law relieving debtors from the payment of debts was unconstitutional even as to contracts made after the laws were passed. Concurring opinion, Cook v. Moffat, 5 How. 295, 311 (1847). Justice Story was no longer living. It is to be noted that the McLean position was approximately that of Chief Justice Marshall twenty years earlier in *Ogden v. Saunders*, in which Justice Story concurred.

CHAPTER VII

The Scope of Executive Power

T HE ACTIVITIES OF every strong leader in the Presidency—Jefferson, Jackson, Lincoln, the Roosevelts—and every national crisis, whether of internal conflict, depression, or war, raise anew the question of the proper relations among the three branches of the federal government and, particularly, of the scope of executive power. Theories of the scope of that power differ widely. At one extreme is the position that the President is elected primarily to enforce such acts as Congress sees fit to enact and, beyond that, to serve merely as a kind of passive figurehead. At the other extreme is the argument that the President is the one and only directly chosen spokesman of the American people, members of Congress being representatives only of particular regions, and that it is his right and duty not merely to command the executive branch but to infuse leadership throughout the government and among the people. Always there has been conflict, latent or open, between the President and Congress over control of the personnel and activities of the several agencies of the executive branch of the government. The Constitution provides that "The executive power shall be vested in a President of the United States of America," makes the President Commander-in-Chief of the Army and Navy, gives him a broad appointing power, and directs that "he shall take care that the laws be faithfully executed." But the Constitution also gives broad powers to the legislative branch. Congress, which by statute creates and defines the powers and duties of the executive departments and most of the other important agencies—the Senate, especially, which advises and consents to appointments—tends to regard departmental personnel and performance as very much its concern. During the time span of the Taney Court there were two widely separated periods of controversy in this field. The first was that of the Jackson Presidency and the Van Buren succession, and the second—to be discussed further along—was that of President Lincoln's strong leadership during the Civil War.

From the beginning of his first Administration President Jackson stirred up storms of controversy by his claims to executive authority and immunity from interference by the other two branches of the government. Although it was not until near the close of his second Administration that an aspect of the controversy became a matter for the courts, the background and the animus lay in his behavior and his claims throughout his eight years in office. It began with his wholesale removal of government employees and their replacement with his loyal followers, that is, his wholehearted resort to the spoils system. Involved were his forthright veto of public improvements at federal expense, his handling of South Carolina's threat of nullification of revenue laws, his veto of the bill to recharter the Bank of the United States, the strategy by which he secured removal of government deposits from the Bank, and his attack on inflationary speculation by requiring specie for the purchase of public lands.

It was the removal of William J. Duane as Secretary of the Treasury in September, 1833, and his replacement by the alleged "pliant instrument," Roger B. Taney, that most enraged the Whig leadership in Congress. Duane was a recess appointee, and the Senate had not had an opportunity to pass on his nomination at the time of his removal. Nevertheless his removal under the circumstances was treated as an outrage. It was not contended that Jackson had no power to remove Duane, but rather that Jackson had no right to use the removal power for the illegitimate purpose of coercing the Secretary of the Treasury in the performance of a duty which Congress had laid directly upon the Secretary, and not upon the President. The statute of 1816 chartering the Bank of the United States had provided that government deposits should be made in the Bank and its branches "unless the Secretary of the Treasury shall at any time otherwise order and direct," in which case the Secretary was to report his reasons to Congress.[1] Jackson had for a time tried to persuade Duane to make the removal. At first he promised to do so or to resign, but later decided to force Jackson's hand. In August, 1833, Jackson wrote wrathfully to Van Buren, "Should Mr. Duane refuse to yield to the wishes of the Executive, and retire, I pledge myself that no one superintends that Department hereafter but one whose opinions I *know* correspond with my own. I will give the agency to Mr. Taney who is right, and with me *in all points*."[2] When

---

[1] 3 Stat. 274.
[2] Andrew Jackson to Martin Van Buren, Aug. 16, 1833, *Correspondence of Andrew Jackson*, John S. Bassett, ed., V, 159.

Duane refused to act, Jackson peremptorily dismissed him and appointed Taney in his place.[3]

For the session of Congress which met in December, 1834, the Whig-Bank faction came storming back into Washington determined to have revenge on Jackson and his new Secretary of the Treasury. The Jackson forces, too, had their power, however, and by the end of the following March the opposition had achieved little that was tangible except the adoption by the Senate on March 28 of a resolution of censure against Jackson. The President called in Amos Kendall to aid in drafting his famous Protest, saying that "Mr. Taney is worn out almost" and the new Attorney General, Benjamin F. Butler, was working on the legal aspects of the Protest.[4]

The Protest condemned the Senate's denunciation of the President as an attempt at impeachment by unconstitutional means. It stressed the heavy responsibilities of the President and stated that in addition to being subject to impeachment he was "also liable to the private action of any party who may have been injured by his illegal mandates or instructions in the same manner and to the same extent as the humblest functionary."[5] In addition to the various forms of legal liability, furthermore, the President was said to be accountable at the bar of public opinion for every act of his Administration.

The executive power, the Protest noted, was vested in the President. The power of appointment, with designated exceptions, was also in him. Neither the power of nominating nor of appointing was vested in the Senate. The Senate had merely a negative power over Presidential selections. Being vested with the whole executive power, it was necessary that the President have also the power to employ agents of his own choice for whose acts he would be willing to take responsibility. The President was responsible for the faithful execution of the laws by his Secretary of the Treasury as well as by others and must therefore be able to protect himself by exercise of the removal power. Jackson had done that to Duane: "His place I supplied by one whose opinions were well known to me, and whose frank expression of them in another situation and generous sacrifices of interest and feeling when unexpectedly called to the station he now occupies ought forever to have shielded his motives from suspicion and his character from reproach."[6]

Henry Clay, in the meantime, had brought Whig sentiment to a focus by introducing in the Senate a resolution declaring that the Constitution did not vest in the President the power to remove officers whose

---

[3] See Jackson's letters to Duane and Taney, Sept. 23, 1833, *ibid.*, 206.
[4] Andrew Jackson to Amos Kendall, Apr., 1834, *ibid.*, 258.

[5] J. D. Richardson, *A Compilation of the Messages and Papers of the Presidents*, V, 71.
[6] *Ibid.*, 85.

positions had been established by law, and that Congress was authorized by the Constitution to prescribe tenure, terms, and conditions.[7]
Daniel Webster, fighting Jackson and Taney all along the line, was slow
in backing Clay on this point. Indeed, he said on one occasion, "Although
I disapprove of the removal [of Duane] altogether, yet the power of
removal does exist in the President, according to the established construction of the Constitution."[8] Later, however, he came to the support
of a bill limiting Presidential removals to the extent of requiring explanations to the Senate, thus abandoning his earlier position and the
precedent of the argument of James Madison, on which many relied.[9]

The pro-Jackson and anti-Bank forces in Congress were strong
enough to prevent enactment of any restrictions on the President's removal power, and the controversy over the scope of that power with
respect to executive officers was to continue into another era.[10] Neither
was Congress able to restore the government deposits to the Bank of
the United States nor to renew its charter. Indeed, the effectiveness of
either house of Congress was limited largely to the Senate's resolution
of censure of the President—which his friends at a later session had
expunged from the Journal—and to the rejection of the nominations of
sundry Presidential appointees, including prominently the nominations
of Taney for Secretary of the Treasury and then for the position of
Associate Justice. But the sense of legislative frustration remained,
lasting, indeed, until long after the end of the Jackson Administrations.
All this was an important part of the background of the controversy over
the obligation of Amos Kendall, as Postmaster General, to pay money
to certain contract carriers which he was convinced they had not earned.

The Kendall story begins with the efficient management of the
Post Office Department by John McLean before his appointment to
the Supreme Court, the decline of the department under Jackson's first
replacement of McLean, William T. Barry, and the attempt at restoration and rebuilding by his second replacement, Amos Kendall.[11] Because of the large number of postal employees and the amount of money
involved in contracts for carrying mail, the department was always
deeply involved in politics. Barry, an easy-going Kentucky gentleman,
was no match for the maneuverers in his department and among the
contractors. The rapid growth of the country and expansion of postal

---

[7] Senate Doc. No. 155, 23rd Cong.,
1st Sess.

[8] *Writings and Speeches of Daniel
Webster*, J. W. McIntyre, ed., VII,
105.

[9] "Appointing and Removal Power,"
ibid., 179–99.

[10] See Myers v. United States, 272
U.S. 52 (1926).

[11] For a summary of the story see
Leonard D. White, *The Jacksonians*,
251–83. For Amos Kendall's account
see *Autobiography of Amos Kendall*,
William Stickney, ed., 333–66.

services kept the work of the department in process of constant change, with opportunity for increasingly remunerative contracts. In this situation a group of established contractors were able to fight off competition and persuade Barry, or his subordinates, to expand by enormous sums the amounts to be paid to them, in loosely drawn contracts that were hard to interpret. Congress made extensive investigations and there is reason to believe that legislators of both political parties were deeply involved in the mismanagement.

The scandals grew so great that in 1835 Jackson was compelled to remove Barry from his headship of the department—via appointment to a foreign post. To succeed him Jackson selected Amos Kendall, a leading crusader for Jackson and against the Bank of the United States. The appointment was made in recess, and after months of delay was confirmed at the same time as that of Taney for the Supreme Court. In his letter of gratitude to Jackson for his office the new Chief Justice noted, in language partly repetitious of things said many times, that "it is also not a little pleasant to find that Mr. Kendall with whom I have passed through so many trying scenes and who shared with me so largely the vindictive persecutions of the panic war, was in the same session of the Senate in which I was confirmed and in the same hour, placed firmly in the high station to which you have called him, and which he is so entirely worthy to fill, and that he is no longer in the power of those who have sought and still desire to make him one of the victims of their vengeance."[12]

Against corrupt employees and corrupting contractors Kendall turned all the zeal he had used against the Bank of the United States. He eliminated gross overexpenditures and tried to terminate close contacts between contractors and department employees, and especially the provision of personal gratuities and services, which often included stagecoach transportation free of charge. He did much to restore financial order but found major difficulties with a debt alleged to be owed by his Department to the firm of Stockton and Stokes, one of the major contract carriers and coach operators between Washington, Baltimore, and Philadelphia, and between Washington and Wheeling.[13] Kendall could find no legitimate basis for the claim, and his strict honesty was

---

[12] R. B. Taney to Andrew Jackson, *Correspondence of Andrew Jackson*, V, 390.

[13] One aspect of the dispute with this firm turned on the interpretation of a very loosely drafted contract. On Jan. 17, 1835, two days after he had been nominated for the position of Associate Justice, Taney filed as counsel for Stockton and Stokes an opinion that the contract should be so interpreted as to yield the sum claimed by the firm. The opinion is eminently circumspect and does not go into related issues. The longhand opinion is filed in the manuscript division of the New York Public Library.

outraged when through an intermediary his wife was promised a carriage and a pair of horses if the claim was allowed.[14]

The facts and the equities in the case seem to be matters of utter confusion.[15] When Kendall failed to act, Stockton and Stokes appealed to Congress for the settlement of their claim. Instead of directing or refusing to direct payment of the amount claimed, Congress passed an act "for the relief of" the parties involved by which it directed the Solicitor of the Treasury to determine what "may seem right according to the principles of equity,"[16] and directed the Postmaster General to credit them with that amount. According to Kendall, the Solicitor of the Treasury, Virgil Maxcy, a friend of the claimants, without consulting with informed persons in the Post Office Department, allowed the amount claimed plus about forty thousand dollars in claims the department had never heard of. Under protest Kendall credited the amount of the original claim but refused to authorize the additional amount.[17]

Stockton and Stokes then asked President Jackson to direct payment of the remainder of the award. Jackson replied that in light of the dispute between the two officers as to the meaning of the Act of Congress, it would be well to ask Congress to interpret its own act. Taking Jackson's advice, the contractors appealed to Congress. There the House of Representatives took no action. The Senate, where according to Kendall his recommendation was not sought and where his uninvited report was buried, passed a resolution to the effect that Maxcy's recommendation should be carried out. When Kendall still failed to act on the amount left unpaid, the claimants sought in the United States Circuit Court of the District of Columbia a writ of mandamus commanding Kendall to act.

By its strategy thus far the executive branch of the government had done little to strengthen its position. First, an inefficient and inept Postmaster General had put a major department in a highly embarrassed position. Then his successor had so conducted himself in a difficult situation that Congress had taken from him a right of decision in the case at hand, and had commanded him to accept the decision of a subordinate in an adjacent department. Then the President had washed his hands of the matter by proposing that Congress interpret its own statute. And finally, a federal court was being asked to issue a writ of mandamus to an executive department head. By this time Kendall and other de-

---

[14] Kendall, *Autobiography*, 351.
[15] As evidence of the confusion see the opinion of Attorney General Benjamin F. Butler to Kendall, Oct. 10, 1835, 3 Op. Att'y Gen. 1 (1837).
[16] 6 Stat. 665.
[17] Kendall, *Autobiography*, 352.

partment heads were concerned about the loss of power and prestige that might be involved in their subjection to court orders. In response to a rule to show cause why the writ should not issue, Kendall wrote a polite letter to Chief Justice William Cranch explaining that he wished to get the opinion of the Attorney General in the matter, since he doubted the power of any court, and particularly of a court in the District of Columbia established for local purposes, to inquire into the conduct of the President or the heads of executive departments.[18] Kendall then filed an opinion by Attorney General Butler to the effect that under the Judiciary Act of 1789 a United States Circuit Court had no power to issue the writ. Thereafter he filed a long document in support of his position and a further opinion of the Attorney General.

The court was not convinced, and the case went to argument. Stockton and Stokes employed as counsel Richard S. Coxe of the District of Columbia and Reverdy Johnson of Baltimore, two of the ablest courtroom lawyers in the country. Kendall was represented by Francis Scott Key, United States Attorney for the District of Columbia and, it will be remembered, the brother-in-law of Chief Justice Taney. Using an opinion format in some respects closely resembling that of Chief Justice Marshall in the mandamus case of *Marbury v. Madison*, Chief Judge Cranch wrote the opinion of the Circuit Court holding that the court had the power to issue the writ and that it ought to do so. The case went to the Supreme Court on writ of error.

Kendall, a journalistic controversialist, infused into this postal controversy something of the excitement and emotionalism characteristic of the bank war. While the case was proceeding in the Circuit Court and thereafter, he and Virgil Maxcy, the Solicitor of the Treasury, published in newspapers documents and letters calculated to establish their respective positions. Kendall, of course, had access to the *Globe*, which he had helped to edit, and Maxcy used the Whig *National Intelligencer*. Tension continued into the argument of the case in the Supreme Court at the 1838 term. There the same counsel appeared, Key sharing the podium with Attorney General Butler. Key contended that the judiciary had here assumed a power hitherto unknown to it, a power which annihilated one of the great departments of the government and to an undefined extent transferred power to another. The court had assumed to set executive authority under the restraints of the law, thereby assuming supremacy for itself.[19]

---

[18] This letter and many of the other documents are printed in the report of the Circuit Court decision, United States *ex rel.* Stokes v. Kendall, 26 Fed. Cas. 702 (No. 15517) (C.C.D.C. 1837). Duplicate materials and some others are to be found in *Niles' National Register*, 52:229–34, 247–48, 260, 274–88, 305, 318–20, 344–51, 385, 1837.

[19] Kendall v. United States, 12 Pet. 524, 535 (1838).

Of the opposing counsel, Coxe poured out his vituperative eloquence on Kendall, stigmatizing him as a relentless persecutor of his opponents and even imputing to him in some fashion the death of one of the contractors, which had occurred during the litigation. He accused Kendall of a desire to break down the judiciary, to destroy constitutional safeguards, and to subject the legislative will to the control of the executive.[20] He declared that "this functionary has arrayed himself in an attitude of hostility against all the authorities of the government with which he has been in contact," and intimated surprise that the United States Attorney and the Attorney General had come to his defense.[21]

Attorney General Butler condemned this resort to personal attack, this pouring out of accusatory matter, in the hallowed chamber of the Supreme Court: "This hall had been regarded as holy ground; and the consoling reflection had been cherished that within these walls one spot had been preserved where questions of constitutional law could be discussed with calmness of mind and liberality of temper; where the acts of a public servant might be subjected to free and rigorous scrutiny, without any unnecessary assault upon his character; where, though his conduct were proved to be erroneous, purity of motives might be conceded till the contrary appeared; where it was usually deemed repugnant to good taste to offer as argument the outpourings of excited feeling, or the creation of an inflamed imagination, and where vehement invective and passionate appeals, even though facts existed which in some other forum might justify their use, were regarded as sounds unmeet for the judicial ear."[22]

Butler renounced the extreme positions attributed to him by opposing counsel. Had the act required of the Postmaster General been merely a ministerial act, as the Circuit Court had found it to be, he admitted that a mandamus would be a proper instrument to enforce obedience. He even went so far as to say that as to purely ministerial acts the power would extend to the President as well as to the heads of departments.[23] But in nonministerial matters the President was responsible for the acts of his inferiors. If he took part in an illegal action of a subordinate affecting a private individual he was himself subject to a civil suit, along with the inferior officer. He admitted that the President could not forbid execution of an Act of Congress and that the judiciary had the power to execute its judgments.

Butler's position, in short, was that the act required of Kendall was not merely ministerial, but that it required the exercise of judgment and discretion, and that, although the Circuit Court might be given

---

20 *Ibid.*, 564, 586.
21 *Ibid.*, 565.
22 *Ibid.*, 586.

23 *Ibid.*, 595. Compare the later decision in Mississippi v. Johnson, 4 Wall. 475 (1867).

the power to issue the writ of mandamus in cases involving ministerial acts, such power had not in fact been given.

Kendall went down to resounding defeat at the hands of the Supreme Court. Indeed, the Justices were unanimous in finding that the act required of Kendall was merely ministerial and could be coerced by mandamus. Justice Thompson, speaking for six members, held that the Circuit Court had the requisite power, with the result that its judgment was affirmed. As to the powers conferred by the Constitution, the President was "beyond the reach of any other department, except in the mode prescribed by the Constitution through the impeaching power."[24] But not every officer of the executive branch was under the exclusive direction of the President. Duties could be laid on executive officers for which the President was not responsible, and this was particularly true of duties merely ministerial in character.[25]

The opinion of the Court was coolly objective and free from the emotionalism of the arguments and the preceding public discussion. But the ensuing newspaper discussion lost none of its color. The *National Intelligencer* took pride in the "spirit of independence and of resistance to the insidious encroachments of despotism." It boasted that the opinion would "stand as a beacon to mark to demagogues in office, for all future time, the point at which their presumption and tyrannous despotism will be rebuked and effectively stayed."[26] A Democratic paper, on the other hand, asserted without detailed explanation that Chief Justice Taney and Judges Barbour and Catron did not agree with their associates and averred, "The intelligent and unprejudiced portion of the people—at least a majority of them—are of the opinion that the Supreme Court has no right to assume authority over the executive, and hence, that the ground taken by the Postmaster General was perfectly correct."[27]

Richard Peters, the Reporter of the Supreme Court, wrote to Chief Justice Taney about the misrepresentation or misunderstanding in the press of the positions of the several judges, saying that he had declined to answer the comments in any way. The Chief Justice replied that this was wise. The daily press, from the nature of things, could not be "the field of fame" for judges. When he had seen his Circuit Court opinions misstated, he had refrained from giving to the press the opinion

---

[24] 12 Pet. 610.

[25] The *National Intelligencer* many years later, in its issue of Oct. 14, 1854, carried a statement that Justice Thompson's opinion as read in Court had attributed to counsel for Kendall the argument that the Postmaster General was exclusively responsible to the President in the performance

of his duties. Butler protested that such was not his position, whereupon the statement was modified. Charles Warren, *The Supreme Court in United States History*, II, 46–47.

[26] *Washington National Intelligencer*, Mar. 13, 1838.

[27] *Boston Statesman*, Mar. 24, 1838.

really delivered because he did not think it proper for a member of the Supreme Court to use the newspapers to discuss legal questions.[28]

Newspaper publication did have one effect, however, on Taney's action in the Kendall case. Although according to the papers he had announced in Court the dissent of himself and Justices Barbour and Catron on the point of the jurisdiction of the Circuit Court, he had thereafter agreed to join in the opinion to be written by Justice Barbour. But, he said, "the publications afterwards led me to change that intention and to determine to write out my opinion."[29] He opened his opinion with the explanation for writing it that "As this case has attracted some share of the public attention, and a diversity of opinion exists on the bench, it is proper that I should state the grounds upon which I dissent from the judgment of the court."[30] He made it very clear that there was no difference of opinion about the constitutional powers of the executive and the judiciary in the case, or about the duty of the Postmaster General to make the payment to the contractors, or the ministerial character of the act. The difference was only as to the power given by statute to the Circuit Court. Perhaps for the same reasons as those of the Chief Justice, Justice Catron also wrote out his opinion, submitting it belatedly so that it had to be published in the appendix to a later volume of Supreme Court reports.[31]

Although the case was now decided, and the payment in controversy was made, neither party was ready to stop fighting. Kendall's next move is revealed in the annual message of President Martin Van Buren of December 3, 1838, which Kendall presumably aided in writing insofar as it dealt with the Post Office Department. Van Buren called attention to the seriousness of the decision and of the issues that had been debated. He urged Congress to consider withdrawing from the Circuit Court of the District of Columbia the power to issue the writ of mandamus to executive officers, a power admittedly not belonging to other federal courts throughout the country.[32] Friends of the Administration succeeded in getting a bill to that effect through the Senate[33] but it did not pass the House.

Stockton and Stokes made their next move by bringing suit against

---

[28] R. B. Taney to Richard Peters, Mar. 27, 1838, Samuel Tyler, *Memoir of Roger Brooke Taney*, 307.

[29] *Ibid.*, 307–08. The published letter refers to "Judge Baldwin's dissenting opinion," but the name is obviously a misprint for that of Barbour. For Taney's request for the printed record and other documents for use

in writing his opinion see Roger B. Taney to W. T. Carroll, Mar. 20, 1838, Clerk's Files.

[30] 12 Pet. 626.

[31] 13 Pet. 607.

[32] Richardson, *Messages and Papers of the Presidents*, III, 503–05.

[33] *Cong. Globe*, 25th Cong., 3rd Sess., 208 (1839).

Kendall in the Circuit Court of the District of Columbia for damages for his long delay in paying the money owed them by the government. While the suit was pending, Kendall resigned as Postmaster General to manage Van Buren's campaign for reelection to the Presidency. The campaign further stirred partisan antagonisms whereafter, according to Kendall, the case was tried before a jury of eleven Whigs and one Democrat,[34] and the jury awarded eleven thousand dollars in damages.[35] Said a Washington correspondent, "I believe this is the most remarkable case that has ever occurred of the prosecution of an executive officer, in his private capacity, for an official act."[36] The jury had proceeded on an instruction that Kendall was personally liable if as a public officer he had not acted in good faith or had performed with malice. Kendall's counsel persuaded the court to set aside the verdict as contrary to the evidence, and a new trial was ordered. At the succeeding trial the court held that a show of malice was not necessary, and Kendall lost again.[37]

Kendall was given twelve months in which to pay the damages awarded or go into bankruptcy. During that time he was confined to the boundaries of the county, and at the end of the period he must go to jail if he had not paid. Most of his property was in Western lands which could not be sold immediately without great loss, and in any event he had other obligations which he regarded as much more binding than the claim of Stockton and Stokes. "It rends my heart with sorrow," wrote Andrew Jackson when he heard of Kendall's condition:

This precedent must lead to make the President and all the heads of Departments, subject to be harassed by suits, by every villain who wishes to put his hands into the public crib, and is prevented by them; and we see them all with their hands folded, without an effort to relieve you, or to have this dangerous innovation set aside by the Supreme Court, and with lukewarmness and stoic philosophy see you immured in a prison for preserving the funds of the Government from the rapacious grasp of Stockton and Stokes for improvements stipulated, contrary to my express order, and, as the testimony produced before me shew, had never been performed. I still hope that the Supreme Court will set aside the Judgment and release you. Can I be of service to you in this business?[38]

Kendall replied that he was determined to go to jail rather than see his real creditors cheated by payment of this unjust judgment. From

---

[34] Kendall, *Autobiography*, 355.
[35] Stokes v. Kendall, 23 Fed. Cas. 140 (No. 13479) (C.C.D.C. 1840).
[36] *Charleston Courier*, Jan. 18, 1841.

[37] Kendall, *Autobiography*, 355.
[38] Andrew Jackson to Amos Kendall, Sept. 29, 1842, *Correspondence of Andrew Jackson*, VI, 170.

this resort he could be saved only by a decision of the Supreme Court or by a change in the law by which imprisonment for debt was authorized. Knowing the crowded condition of the Supreme Court docket, he asked Jackson to let the judges know of the importance of a decision at the coming term. He asked Jackson to take the matter up with Justice Catron and suggest to him the expediency of presenting the matter to the other judges, and also of seeing members of Congress about the law.[39] Jackson promised to attend to the matter promptly, saying that "if this precedent be not reversed, then any and all the heads of Departments may be sued and mulked in damages for preserving the public interest, and preventing frauds upon the Treasury."[40]

Jackson did talk to Justice Catron who, with Mrs. Catron, spent a day with him at the Hermitage. Catron assured Jackson that every principle of justice required that the Kendall case be heard at the next term of the Supreme Court, and that he would attend to it. The judge had been of the mistaken impression that the law requiring imprisonment for debt in the District of Columbia had already been repealed.[41] Jackson wrote also to Cave Johnson, a Tennesseean in Congress, and got assurance that something would be done about the legislation.[42] It was Johnson rather than Catron who proved immediately helpful, unless, as may well have been the case, Catron also lobbied for the proposed legislation. On March 3, 1843, the President signed a bill prohibiting imprisonment for debt in the District of Columbia for any person who had an appeal pending with respect to a judgment against him.[43] It was not until nearly two years later that the Supreme Court decided the case as brought up by writ of error.

Kendall was at last the victor. With only Justice McLean dissenting, the Supreme Court, speaking through Chief Justice Taney, reversed the judgment of the Circuit Court. Looking apparently to the long period of delay prior to the enactment of the statute requiring Kendall to accept the findings of the Solicitor of the Treasury, the Chief Justice found that Kendall was engaged in official acts which were not ministerial in character, and that he was not liable to an action for an error in judgment. As for the writ of mandamus, the opposing party had chosen it as his remedy, and he had to be satisfied with it. He could not reap its benefits and then resort to a judgment for damages.[44] Ken-

---

[39] Amos Kendall to Andrew Jackson, Oct. 7, 1842, Jackson Papers.

[40] Andrew Jackson to Amos Kendall, Oct. 26, 1842, Jackson Papers. (Printed letter.)

[41] Andrew Jackson to Amos Kendall, Nov. 3, 1842, Jackson Papers.

(Printed letter.)

[42] Andrew Jackson to Amos Kendall, Dec. 20, 1842, *Correspondence of Andrew Jackson*, VI, 180.

[43] 5 Stat. 629.

[44] Kendall v. Stokes, 3 How. 87 (1845).

dall then petitioned Congress for payment of his counsel fees and other costs, and the petition was granted.[45]

The claim of Stockton and Stokes on money alleged to be due from the United States was only one of many claims filed and held up for one reason or another by executive officers doubting their legitimacy. When the first Kendall decision by the Supreme Court, in 1838, disclosed a weapon in the form of a mandamus from the Circuit Court of the District of Columbia, it is not surprising that other claimants reached for the same weapon. One of the first was Susan Decatur, widow of Commodore Stephen Decatur, of American naval fame, who had died in 1834. In 1837, in response to a sentiment that the government should aid widows and orphans of men who had died in their country's service, the Senate had passed and sent to the House of Representatives an act to provide them with half-pay. While the bill was pending in the House and before its passage was assured, Mrs. Decatur's friends in the House had secured passage of a resolution granting a pension specifically to her for a period of five years, to assure her of support pending enactment of a general bill. Toward the end of the session her friends in the Senate brought about the passage there of the resolution granting the special pension, fearing that the general bill would not pass the House. In the rush of business it happened that both measures were enacted.[46]

It would appear that Mrs. Decatur was greedy. She petitioned for grants under both measures, seeking in effect, for a five-year period, the amount of her husband's full pay. On the advice of Attorney General Butler, Secretary of the Navy Mahlon Dickerson told her she could file a claim under either measure but not under both. She filed under the general act, without surrendering her alleged right under the special act. When she had received the pension with arrears under the general act, she applied to Dickerson's successor, James K. Paulding, for compensation under the special act. Paulding refused to reopen the case, whereupon she sought from the Circuit Court of the District of Columbia a mandamus to direct Paulding to pay the claim.

To the discomfort of the Secretary of the Navy he had to put in an appearance before Chief Judge Cranch and two associate judges to demonstrate that he had denied no right enforceable by writ of mandamus. The court refused to issue the writ, whereupon Mrs. Decatur took

[45] Kendall, *Autobiography*, 357–58.
[46] For this explanation see "Portraits with Pen and Pencil: Henry D.

Gilpin," *United States Magazine and Democratic Review*, 8:512, 518–19, 1840.

the case to the Supreme Court on writ of error, employing as one of her counsel Richard S. Coxe, who had helped win the first Kendall case.

With multiple opinions but with Chief Justice Taney writing the opinion of the majority, the Supreme Court too decided against Mrs. Decatur. Taney held that the decision which had to be made by the Secretary of the Navy was not merely ministerial, as had been the duty of Postmaster General Kendall in entering a credit as specifically directed by Congress, but that it required the exercise of official judgment. Recognizing the danger to executive independence and integrity, he declared, "The interference of the courts with the performance of the ordinary duties of the executive departments of the government, would be productive of nothing but mischief; and we are quite satisfied that such a power was never intended to be given to them."[47]

As was often true in these years, the decision had strong political overtones. The Taney position—or the position of the majority of the Court—gave a measure of comfort to the Democratic Administration which sought protection against interference with the exercise of official discretion. Justices McLean and Story, on the other hand, the two members currently in sympathy with the Whigs, agreed with the Court on the merits of Mrs. Decatur's claim but denied that the law gave the Secretary any discretion in the matter.[48] Justice Catron, on the other hand, stated the Democratic position, or at any rate the position of the Administration. In a concurring opinion that sounded like a speech in Congress he began by saying, "Between the Circuit Court of this district and the executive administration of the United States there is an open contest for power."[49] Although in this case the court had not issued its writ, it had assumed jurisdiction and compelled the Secretary of the Navy to file a long answer and to defend the United States in a tedious lawsuit. The evil lay not in the monetary cost to the government but in the assertion of the power of the court to sit in judgment on the Secretary's decision. The court had laid claim to an instrument for controlling expenditures from the treasury. This power, he contended, belonged only to the executive branch, with no right of judicial interference.

The Supreme Court adhered to its position in the Kendall case that the Circuit Court of the District of Columbia could issue the writ of mandamus to executive officers to compel performance of strictly ministerial duties, but it interpreted those duties narrowly, so that no

---

[47] Decatur v. Paulding, 14 Pet. 497, 516 (1840).

[48] Ibid., 517. Justice Baldwin filed late, for publication in the appendix to 14 Peters, a concurring opinion dealing with vast abstractions and close to incomprehensible. Ibid., 599.

[49] Ibid., 518.

great degree of judicial power could be exercised.[50] A great mass of claims against the United States were submitted to Congress, where investigations were made and appropriations authorized for those Congress saw fit to pay. The machinery was cumbersome, however, and the results often inequitable. Finally, in 1855, Congress established a Court of Claims to hear and determine claims against the United States and make recommendations to Congress.[51] At the initial stage the so-called court was nothing more than an advisory agency for Congress. In 1863, in light of the mass of claims business growing out of the Civil War, Congress went a long way toward making the court a genuine judicial tribunal, but because of inclusion of a provision that money judgments were subject to revision by the Secretary of the Treasury, the Supreme Court held that it could exercise no appellate jurisdiction over the Court of Claims.[52] To do so would in effect be an exercise of original judicial jurisdiction. Finally, in 1866, Congress gave the court sufficient independence to make it a court in fact as well as in name.[53] Resort to this institution relieved Congress of an enormous burden and also relieved the executive branch of interference in money matters by a nonspecialized court in the District of Columbia.

One of the mandamus cases coming up from the Circuit Court of the District of Columbia raised again the question of the removal power of the President, this time in connection with the removal of a territorial judge. Territorial judges were ordinarily appointed for terms of four years. The question of their status was much discussed, but it was generally assumed that they were not among those judges whose right to office during good behavior was guaranteed by the Third Article of the Constitution. On March 19, 1849, near the beginning of his term, President Zachary Taylor, with the advice and consent of the Senate, commissioned Aaron Goodrich to be chief justice of the Supreme Court of the territory of Minnesota, for a four-year term.

Goodrich proved unsatisfactory as a judge. His removal was sought on grounds of incapacity, unfitness, and want of moral character. Millard Fillmore, who at Taylor's death succeeded to the Presidency, asked his Attorney General, John J. Crittenden, for an official opinion whether he could remove Goodrich from office prior to the expiration of his four-year term. Crittenden answered that the President did have the power. He quoted from an opinion by Chief Justice Marshall that terri-

---

[50] See for example Brashear v. Mason, 6 How. 92 (1848), Wilkes v. Dinsman, 7 How. 89, 129 (1849), United States *ex rel.* Goodrich v. Guthrie, 17 How. 284 (1855), United States *ex rel.* Tucker v. Seaman, 17 How. 225 (1855).

[51] 10 Stat. 612.

[52] Gordon v. United States, 2 Wall. 561 (1865).

[53] See Williams v. United States, 289 U.S. 553 (1933).

torial courts were not constitutional courts set up under Article III, with its guarantee of tenure, but rather the power of their establishment stemmed from the power to govern territories.[54] The statutory provision for a term of four years did not mean that judges might serve out that term however they might misbehave. A statutory guarantee of a four-year term would have been in violation of a constitutional power of removal. The statute meant no more than that the appointees would be out of office at the end of that term unless reappointed. The President therefore had the power to remove the chief justice of the territory of Minnesota.[55] In short, the Whig Attorney General advised the Whig President with all the confident belief in broad executive power that had characterized the Democrats and at times so offended the Whigs.

Fillmore waited until October 22, 1851, and then had Crittenden as acting Secretary of State notify Goodrich of his removal and his replacement by another man. Goodrich challenged the President's power of removal, and at the end of what would have been his four-year term of office demanded payment of his salary for the completion of the period. When payment was refused he sought from the Circuit Court of the District of Columbia a rule directing James Guthrie, the Secretary of the Treasury, to show cause why a writ of mandamus should not issue directing payment. The court, with the experience of Supreme Court restriction of its power in case after case, refused to grant the rule, and the case was taken to the Supreme Court on writ of error.

When the case came to argument in the Supreme Court in January, 1855, a Democratic Administration was again in power and a Democratic Attorney General, Caleb Cushing, had succeeded Crittenden to present the case for the government. He presented the same strong argument in support of Presidential power, and contended that the duty involved was political and not ministerial, and that therefore the writ of mandamus was not an appropriate remedy. A majority of the Court, speaking through Justice Daniel, decided the case exclusively on the latter point,[56] and avoided discussion of the President's removal power. Justices Curtis, Campbell, and Grier insisted on a notation that they were expressing no opinion on the other question.

But Justice McLean dissented and again opened for discussion the question of the scope of the President's removal power. He challenged, apparently even as to the executive branch of the government, the assumption that the power to remove was a necessary incident to the power to appoint, and he condemned the exercise of the removal power

---

[54] American Insurance Co. v. 356 Bales of Cotton, 1 Pet. 511, 546 (1828).

[55] Executive Authority to Remove the Chief Justice of Minnesota, 5 Op. Att'y Gen. 288 (1851).

[56] United States *ex rel.* Goodrich v. Guthrie, 17 How. 284 (1855).

particularly where judicial officers were concerned. He thought that territorial judges, like judges with life tenure, should be subject to removal within their terms only by impeachment. As for the argument that the power to remove officers was based on the President's mandate to see that the laws were faithfully executed, it was his view "that the power to see that the laws are faithfully executed, applies chiefly to the giving effect to the decisions of the courts when resisted by physical force."[57]

The question of the tenure of territorial judges went unsettled, however, for another third of a century. Then, in 1891, the Supreme Court decided a case brought up from the Court of Claims with respect to a district judge in the territory of Alaska. The Court held, by a vote of six to three, that the President had the power under the Constitution and statutes to suspend the judge, that he was not entitled to receive his salary while suspended, and that the suspension became permanent on confirmation of his successor.[58]

Whereas ardent Jacksonians of the Kendall stamp were inclined to assume virtual autonomy of the executive branch from legislative and judicial interference, and had to be brought back into line by contact with harsh realities, there were others who had to be reminded of the extent to which high executives had authority over their subordinates. This seems to have been particularly true in the War and Navy Departments, where the public expected the exercise of centralized power and subordinates occasionally sought to take responsibility upon themselves. In 1840, for example, the United States brought suit against William A. Eliason, an Army officer, to recover funds allegedly illegally spent on certain fortifications. The law was sufficiently unclear that Eliason, or his administratrix, won the case in the Circuit Court of the District of Columbia[59] but lost it in the Supreme Court. The facts are not now important but statements of Justice Daniel for a unanimous Court reflect the concern of the Court about the maintenance of military authority. The power of the executive to establish rules and regulations for the government of the Army was undoubted, he explained. Furthermore such regulations could not be questioned or disobeyed by subordinates because they might be thought unwise or mistaken. Such discretion on their part would bring complete disorganization of both the Army and the Navy.[60]

---

[57] *Ibid.*, 310.
[58] McAllister v. United States, 141 U.S. 174 (1891). Compare Humphrey's Executor v. United States, 295 U.S. 602 (1935) (removal of Federal Trade Commissioner held invalid).
[59] United States v. Eliason, 25 Fed. Cas. 997 (No. 15040) (C.C.D.C. 1841).
[60] United States v. Eliason, 16 Pet. 291, 302 (1842).

Discipline was enforced again, and the Circuit Court of the District of Columbia once more reversed, in an action brought by a marine against an officer who had imposed physical punishment on him for disobedience. A unanimous Supreme Court held that it was within the discretion of the commanding officer of a ship to flog a marine to secure prompt obedience to orders,[61] and the Court failed to find the evidence that the marine was no longer obligated to serve which had apparently impressed the Circuit Court. It was clear that the Supreme Court would avoid if possible placing any barriers in the way of efficient administration of the armed forces.

Yet it was also made clear, in an important case arising out of the Mexican War, that the military would not be permitted to ride roughshod over private rights, and particularly rights of property, and that immunity for obviously unlawful acts could not be found in the fact that the acts were performed in obedience to commands of superior officers. The victim in this case, who claimed damages of one hundred thousand dollars for loss of a trading wagon train consisting of horses, mules, wagons, and goods, was Manuel X. Harmony, who was on a trading expedition from Missouri to Mexico. Harmony left Missouri in 1846 shortly after the declaration of war against Mexico but before he had heard of it. He had to hold back until American armed forces moved ahead of him, and was thereafter apparently encouraged to trade with Mexicans in conquered territory as a means of restoring good relations. On the way from El Paso to Chihuahua, Lieutenant Colonel David D. Mitchell, acting under orders from Colonel A. W. Doniphan, compelled the wagon train to move with him as a part of his advancing force and kept control of it until the property was used up, destroyed, or hopelessly scattered.

The assumption of the military seems to have been that Harmony would petition Congress for compensation for the property lost. Instead, he brought suit against Mitchell personally, in the United States Circuit Court for the Southern District of New York, before Justice Samuel Nelson, who in 1845 had succeeded Justice Thompson. Justice Nelson's instructions to the jury set forth a clear case in behalf of Harmony, and damages of over ninety thousand dollars were awarded.[62]

With dissent only from Justice Daniel, the Supreme Court affirmed the judgment. Chief Justice Taney, for the Court, rejected Mitchell's contentions that seizure was justified because Harmony was trading with the enemy and because the wagon train was in danger of falling into the hands of the enemy. The law, said the Chief Justice, did not give

---

[61] Wilkes v. Dinsman, 7 How. 89 (1849).

[62] Harmony v. Mitchell, 11 Fed. Cas. 559 (No. 6082) (C.C.S.D. N.Y. 1850).

the commanding officer a discretionary power over private property. The order given was an order to perform an illegal act. As for Mitchell's claim to immunity on the ground that he was merely obeying the order of his superior officers, "it can never be maintained that a military officer can justify himself for doing an unlawful act, by producing the order of his superior. The order may palliate, but it cannot justify."[63] Seizure would have been justified only in the face of immediate and impending danger or urgent necessity not admitting of delay. The case was to have importance in the years ahead in defining the rightful scope of military power.

These, in summary, are the central threads of the story of judicial thought about the scope of federal executive power from the Jackson period until close to the era of the Civil War.[64] Following the Jackson Administration and its immediate aftermath, this period was one of not more than modest claims for power by any of the Presidents. Incumbents of that office were usually compromise candidates chosen with an eye to placating the South, with its growing sensitivity to possible federal restriction on its "peculiar institution." The subject of the scope of executive power is related, however, to that embraced in the doctrine of "political questions," to be discussed hereafter.

---

[63] Mitchell v. Harmony, 13 How. 115, 137 (1852).

[64] For discussion of the President's pardoning power in terms of his power to grant conditional pardons, see *Ex parte* Wells, 18 How. 307 (1856).

CHAPTER VIII

The Impact of Foreign Affairs

B ECAUSE OF THE EXTENT to which the conduct of foreign affairs is the responsibility of the political branches of the federal government, involvement of the judiciary is limited and sporadic. Yet at various times during the Taney period the Supreme Court, or the Justices on circuit or at chambers, did play an important role. This role involved the development of constitutional doctrines with respect to limitations on the powers of the states, the respective jurisdictions of the state and federal governments, the status of slavery, and other important topics.

It is to be remembered that during the 1830s and for some time thereafter the United States had uneasy relations with neighbors both to the north and to the south of its borders. One of the most controversial questions, indeed, was just where our present borders lay and where our future borders ought to be. The boundary line between the United States and Canada was imperfectly defined from the Atlantic Ocean to the Rocky Mountains. West of the Rockies the two countries held jointly the vast Oregon Territory, stretching from Mexican-owned California on the south to Russian-owned Alaska on the North. Southward, United States settlers in Texas fought for and achieved independence for an area with an undetermined border on the Mexican side, and sought annexation to the United States, precipitating problems of relations with Mexico. Whereas aggressive Americans demanded scrupulous respect for borders on the part of neighbors living on the other side, adventurers among them believed that it was the manifest destiny of the United States to rule the western hemisphere, and particularly that we had an obligation to free our neighbors from the domination of European rulers.

Because in the international relations field the first important Supreme Court decision of the Taney period had to do with extradition, the story may well begin with that subject. American experience with extradition had thus far been confused and unsatisfactory. The people had no desire to see their country a dumping ground or a place of refuge for criminals, but they did not want mere allegations of crime to provide a means of capturing political refugees who had fled here. Our most extensive international relations likely to involve extradition procedures were with Great Britain. The Jay Treaty of 1794 provided for reciprocal extradition for certain crimes. Unfortunately, at the turn of the century use of the device became embroiled in Federalist-Republican politics and remained malodorous, so that for many years after the War of 1812 we had no extradition agreement with Great Britain. At the request of President John Adams, a United States district judge ordered delivery to British officials of a man whom they claimed as Thomas Nash and who, in a mutiny at sea, had committed murder. The prisoner maintained that he was not a British subject, that he was on the British ship as a result of British impressment, and that his participation in the mutiny was as an American seeking escape from unlawful control. He claimed not to be Nash at all, but to be Jonathan Robbins, a native of Connecticut. Whatever the truth of the matter, the case made good anti-Federalist and anti-British propaganda, and the Jeffersonians made the most of it.[1] Many years were to pass before the furor died down.

It was independent Americanism to protect alleged Americans against British captors and to protect also political refugees who were claimed on the basis of alleged crime, but the long absence of any extradition agreement with Great Britain meant that, other than by resort to mere expulsion beyond borders, we had no discretion in dealing with the refugees who were claimed. In 1825, for example, Charles P. Van Ness, the governor of Vermont, sent to Henry Clay, Secretary of State, correspondence with the Governor of Canada, who asked the return of two soldiers who were accused of robbery. Clay expressed his regret that the stipulation providing for the reciprocal return of fugitives from justice was no longer in force.

It would appear, however, that not all the governors of the northern tier of states were as meticulous about the exercise of constitutional powers as was Governor Van Ness, and that, without consulting Washington, they surrendered fugitives to Canada and successfully claimed American fugitives who had fled there.[2] This relationship of comity be-

---

[1] See United States v. Robins, 27 Fed. Cas. 825 (No. 16175) (D.C.D.S.C. 1799) and materials appended to the report of the case. See also Albert J. Beveridge, *The Life of John Marshall*, 458–75. For the history of that early period an important aspect of the story is the defense of the Administration by John Marshall, both in Congress and in the press.

[2] See for example the message of Governor William H. Seward to the New York legislature as published Sept. 10, 1842, in *Niles' National Register*, 63:28, 1842.

tween Canadian governors and governors of states of the American Union was disturbed by the controversy that gave rise to the Supreme Court decision in *Holmes v. Jennison*.[3] The Canadian Governor sent to Governor Silas H. Jennison of Vermont a request for the extradition of George Holmes, later shown to be native of New Hampshire resident in Canada, who had been indicted for murder. Holmes, arrested after fleeing to Vermont, sought release by means of a writ of habeas corpus, employing as his counsel Van Ness, the meticulous Vermont governor of earlier years who had discovered by correspondence with Secretary of State Henry Clay that there was no law of extradition between the United States and Canada. The Vermont Supreme Court decided, without written opinion, that Holmes was lawfully held, whereupon the case was taken to the Supreme Court of the United States on writ of error.

Because Justice McKinley was absent through the entire 1840 term, the case was presented to a Court of only eight Justices. No counsel appearing for Governor Jennison, it was argued only by Van Ness. The Justices being divided on a number of questions, Justice Catron had Van Ness write out his argument to permit careful study.[4] At the end of the term the Justices were still divided, four to four, on the disposition of the case. Chief Justice Taney wrote an opinion for one group of four—himself, Story, McLean, and Wayne. Each of the other Justices wrote his own opinion.

Chief Justice Taney answered in the affirmative the difficult question whether the Supreme Court had jurisdiction in a habeas corpus case thus brought up from a highest state court. He then reasoned that since power in the field of foreign affairs had been allocated exclusively to the federal government, and since states had been forbidden to enter into any agreement with a foreign power, the governor of a state could not agree with the head of a foreign state to surrender fugitives. For a judge bearing the label of the Democratic Party and of the South, the opinion was regarded as highly nationalistic. Senator James Buchanan lamented that some portions of the opinion of the Chief Justice, for whom he had always entertained the highest respect, were "latitudinous and centralizing beyond anything I ever read, in any other judicial opinion."[5] Justice Story, on the other hand, thought Taney's opinion a masterly performance and predicted that it would elevate his judicial reputation. He was surprised that it had not been unanimously adopted.[6]

The four disagreeing Justices either denied jurisdiction or were of the opinion that states might extradite fugitives in the absence of federal

---

[3] 14 Pet. 540 (1840).
[4] *Ibid.*, 597.
[5] *Works of James Buchanan*, John Bassett Moore, ed., V, 238.

[6] Story letter to Richard Peters, written some time in May, 1840, Samuel Tyler, *Memoir of Roger Brooke Taney*, 290.

law on the subject, or took both positions. Justice Barbour, a states' rights theorist, contended that the exercise of state power to extradite conflicted with no federal power so long as Congress failed to confer that power on the executive. It was not the mere presence of a dormant power in the federal government, but rather the exercise of that power, which was incompatible with the exercise of the same power by a state. Justice Catron came to the conclusion that, in light of the division on the Court, it was better for the country that the question should remain open.

Oddly enough, it was Justice Baldwin, often highly nationalistic in his approach, who waxed most indignant at the argument that the existence of a dormant federal power in this area automatically debarred the states from acting, seeming to assume that denial of the power to extradite was the equivalent of denial of the power to expel undesirables.[7] As later cases were to show, however, the power of states to get rid of undesirables had to be distinguished not only from the power of the federal government over extradition but also from its power over interstate and foreign commerce and its power with respect to the return of fugitive slaves.[8]

Before dealing with the indirect involvement of American judges with filibustering along the Canadian border and with the insurrection in Canada in 1837-1838, it is well to follow the story of extradition into the ensuing decades. The Webster-Ashburton Treaty of 1842 settled long-disputed questions about the border between the United States and Canada and provided also for extradition for certain specified crimes. The treaty provided that requests for extradition should be made by ministers or other authorities of the respective governments, and that the judges and other magistrates should have power to authorize commitment for deportation on presentation of proper evidence.[9] In the following year a convention providing for extradition was entered into with France, but with no mention of the officers to serve as committing magistrates.[10]

Of the two international agreements, that with France first gave rise to litigation. In 1846 the French minister to the United States called upon the executive branch of the federal government for the extradition of Nicholas Lucien Metzger, who was wanted for forgery. Presumably by James Buchanan, who was then Secretary of State, the minister was told that it would be necessary first to seek commitment by a member

---

[7] 14 Pet. 618.

[8] The *Holmes* case went back to the Supreme Court of Vermont which, after reading the opinions of the several justices, decided that the governor of Vermont had no power

to deliver Holmes to the Canadian authorities and therefore ordered his release. *Ex parte* Holmes, 12 Vt. 631 (1840).

[9] 8 Stat. 576.

[10] 8 Stat. 580.

of the judiciary. A French consular representative in New York applied for a commitment order from a Judge Drinker in a local court which was part of the state judicial system. Concerned that all should go well with the first case under the convention, and fearing that the warrant would not be issued, Buchanan called on Benjamin F. Butler, former Attorney General but now holding the lesser office of United States Attorney for the Southern District of New York, to give such help as he could with the case.[11] The warrant was issued but Metzger sought relief from Judge Worth Edmonds, in a local circuit court in New York, on the ground that the convention with France made no provision for the participation of the judiciary in the extradition proceeding. The French minister reported the matter to Buchanan, who replied that he could not interfere in a case pending before a judicial tribunal except to ask the United States Attorney to appear in behalf of the United States to uphold a proper interpretation of the convention. Should the decision be against extradition, he wrote to Butler, the minister desired that the case be brought before the Supreme Court.[12] Butler was instructed to take part in the proceeding before Judge Edmonds, and, if Edmonds should decide that the local court had not had jurisdiction to issue the warrant, to seek a warrant from Judge Samuel R. Betts, in the United States District Court for the Southern District of New York.[13]

Butler, however, was in no position to take leadership in the matter, and when Judge Edmonds held that a state court had no jurisdiction in the case the French authorities asked the President, James K. Polk, to direct the United States Marshal in New York to apprehend Metzger and then to determine whether a commitment could be authorized. This, wrote Buchanan for Polk, would be a judicial, not an executive, duty. But the President saw no difficulty in the matter, since the French authorities could apply to one of the federal judges in New York— Judge Betts or Justice Samuel Nelson, who by this time had replaced Justice Thompson on the Supreme Court.[14]

Metzger was taken into custody again and brought before Judge Betts, where his counsel contended that the court had no jurisdiction since the convention with France made no mention of judicial participation in the extradition process. If this contention were admitted, there would be no means of extraditing the alleged criminal since the President had decided that he could not take action without judicial participation. Judge Betts, however, found precedent for holding that treaties

[11] James Buchanan to Benjamin F. Butler, Oct. 15, 1846, *Works of James Buchanan*, VII, 106.

[12] James Buchanan to Benjamin F. Butler, Oct. 15, 1846, *ibid.*, 106–07.

[13] James Buchanan to Benjamin F. Butler, Nov. 13, 1846, *ibid.*, 115.

[14] James Buchanan to Benjamin F. Butler, Nov. 25, 1846, *ibid.*, 124–25.

as the supreme law of the land were enforceable without the aid of supporting statutes and that in the enforcement of the law the judiciary was properly involved.[15] Metzger then applied to the Supreme Court for a writ of habeas corpus, ably represented by Richard S. Coxe and Walter Jones, with Attorney General Nathan Clifford, a future member of the Court, representing the government. Speaking through Justice McLean, the Supreme Court decided that it had no power to issue the writ to review a decision of a judge given at his chambers.[16]

It now looked as if the extradition proceeding was nearing its end. The French minister sent to Buchanan an authenticated copy of the Betts opinion,[17] whereupon Buchanan sent to the United States Marshal at New York a warrant for the surrender of Metzger to the French authorities.[18] But Metzger now turned back to Judge Edmonds in the New York Circuit Court, seeking release from illegal detention. With a lack of decisiveness that was to characterize him as President on the eve of the Civil War, Buchanan generalized broadly about the government's predicament but was unable to devise a course of action. He wrote to Butler:

> If, after all the judicial proceedings required by our treaties of extradition have been perfected, and the President has thereupon issued his warrant, any Judge, upon a Habeas Corpus, can review the evidence presented to and taken before the committing Judge, with a view to the reversal of his judgment, and thus arrest the execution of the President's mandate, then we ought to make no more Treaties of this character, and relieve ourselves from the obligations of those which already exist as speedily as possible. In that event, we have pledged the national faith to the performance of obligations which it is in the power of any Judge who may feel the disposition to defeat, and the accused will always have it in his power to select that Judge who will the best answer his purpose.[19]

The case remained in the state circuit court from March until October, when Judge Edmonds ordered Metzger released on the ground that his commitment had been illegal.[20] Federal authorities had done nothing to prepare for this eventuality, and Metzger escaped from their hands. Buchanan, deeply discomfited, complained that the French vice

---

[15] *In re* Metzger, 17 Fed. Cas. 232 (No. 9511) (D.C.S.D. N.Y. 1847).
[16] *In re* Metzger, 5 How. 176 (1847).
[17] James Buchanan to Alphonse Pageot, Feb. 26, 1847, *Works of James Buchanan*, VII, 229–30.
[18] James Buchanan to Eli Moore, Feb. 26, 1847, *ibid.*, 230.
[19] James Buchanan to Benjamin F. Butler, Mar. 23, 1837, *ibid.*, 246.
[20] For comment see "Extradition—Case of Metzger, Under the Treaty with France," *West. L.J.*, 5:141–42, 1847.

consul had not been ready immediately to apply to the United States Circuit Court for Metzger's rearrest at the time of his release.[21] He complained about the slowness of the vice consul in New York when action could have been had by the two federal judges then sitting in the United States Circuit Court. He deplored the fact that at the very beginning the French authorities had applied to a state judge rather than to a federal judge, thereby bringing Judge Edmonds into the picture. He could see nothing else to do than to appeal the Edmonds decision to the Supreme Court of New York—a futile step since Metzger was now among the missing.[22]

One of the results of the confusion and frustration in the Metzger case was to bring about enactment of a statute enabling federal and state judges, and commissioners authorized by the federal courts, to act as committing magistrates for extradition purposes.[23] With that enactment, Congress believed that it had solved the vexing procedural problems. But litigants continued to search for loopholes. In June, 1852, Joseph Bridgham, a United States Commissioner in New York, issued a warrant as the first step in proceedings to extradite to Great Britain Thomas Kaine, who was accused of attempt to commit murder in Ireland. Among the Irish population in New York and among other groups as well large numbers of persons opposed surrendering any fugitive to Great Britain, whatever the alleged offense. Counsel with the good Irish names of Brady, Busteed, and Emmet sued out a writ of habeas corpus before Judge Betts, alleging that the executive must institute extradition proceedings before the courts could act. Judge Betts rejected the argument. He dealt only with procedural questions and not at all with the merits of the case, mindful of the popular uproar which made it inexpedient to bring the prisoner into court lest he be released by the mob.[24] The proceedings were reported to the Department of State and a warrant was issued directing that Kaine be delivered to the British consul.

But Kaine's counsel did not give up. They petitioned again for a writ of habeas corpus, this time presenting their petition to Justice Nelson at chambers at his office in Cooperstown, New York, the place of his residence, but addressing it to the several Justices of the Supreme Court. Seeing the case as important far beyond any interest he had in Kaine, Justice Nelson adjourned the case into the Supreme Court for

---

[21] James Buchanan to Benjamin F. Butler, Oct. 29, 1847, *Works of James Buchanan*, VII, 447.

[22] James Buchanan to Alphonse

Pageot, Nov. 3, 1847, *ibid.*, 448–51; Nov. 10, 1847, *ibid.*, 453–54.

[23] 9 Stat. 302.

[24] *In re* Kaine, 14 Fed. Cas. 84, 86 (No. 7598) (C.C.S.D. N.Y. 1852).

hearing at the ensuing term,[25] and at the same time the record from the Circuit Court was brought up by certiorari.

In spite of the crowded docket the case was speedily heard, but the eight Justices—Justice McKinley having recently died—afforded no relief to Kaine.[26] Justice Catron spoke for himself and Justices McLean, Wayne, and Grier, of the majority, and Justice Curtis, also of the majority, spoke for himself. Justice Nelson wrote a dissenting opinion in which he was joined by Chief Justice Taney and Justice Daniel. He argued that a committing magistrate could not act in extradition proceedings until authorization was received from the President, that the commissioner in this case had not been authorized to act in such cases, and that the commissioner had no proper evidence.

The questions seem important only in terms of the particular statute involved and the particular situation. Yet behind the technicalities lay important issues of public policy. Justice Catron rejected the contention that the judiciary should act in extradition cases only pursuant to direction of the President, stressing the Jonathan Robbins case as an example of the evil growing out of such direction. He remarked "The people of this country could hardly be brought to allow an interference of the President with the Judges in any degree."[27] He stressed the need for effective machinery of extradition and deplored obstructions allowed to prevail in this case, as in the instance of the mob that made it inexpedient to bring the prisoner into court in New York.

Justice Nelson, on the other hand, was concerned about the weight of influence to be brought on the judiciary, and particularly on lower officers acting as committing magistrates, by representatives of foreign powers. Because of the need to get quickly to a magistrate in order to prevent a refugee from losing himself in the wilds of our country, Congress had authorized state judges, variously chosen, to serve as committing magistrates, and also United States Commissioners, who were officers of the courts with strictly limited functions. Justice Nelson thought it bad public policy to put these various magistrates in a position to act or to refuse to act in the face of demands of foreign representatives. He thought that demands should be made first upon the executive who, if he thought extradition in order, could so indicate as a preliminary to a judicial determination of the strictly legal questions.

Although he spoke only for a minority of three, Justice Nelson's position was important, both for Kaine and for the development of extradition procedures. The case as he had adjourned it into the Supreme Court from his chambers at Cooperstown was returned to him in his

---

[25] *In re* Kaine, 14 Fed. Cas. 82 (No. 7597a) (C.C.S.D. N.Y. 1852).

[26] *In re* Kaine, 14 How. 103 (1853).
[27] *Ibid.*, 111.

capacity as a circuit judge. There he adhered to his position taken as a Supreme Court Justice, and ordered Kaine's release. It was important, he stated, that extradition be limited strictly to conventional crimes. Extradition should not apply at all to political offenses, even when incidentally linked to acts of crime. The line was often hard to draw:

> The surrender, in such cases, involves a political question, which must be decided by the political, and not by the judicial, powers of the government. It is a general principle, as it respects political questions concerning foreign governments, that the judiciary follows the determination of the political power which has charge of its foreign relations, and is, therefore, presumed to best understand what is fit and proper for the interest and honor of the country.[28]

At a result of the Nelson position, the federal government modified its extradition procedure to the extent that a foreign country might, if it saw fit to do so, seek from the President a mandate with respect to a fugitive in a criminal case as a means of bringing the question of extradition before a magistrate. The foreign country might go directly to a magistrate without approaching the President, but in doing so it ran the risk of having the magistrate take the Nelson position and refuse to authorize extradition. This change in procedure, Attorney General Caleb Cushing instructed the Secretary of State, did not give the President power to control a magistrate in determining whether the fugitive was to be extradited. It merely incorporated a preliminary step to meet the views of a minority of the Supreme Court.[29]

This summary indicates the difficulties with which judicial enforcement of extradition treaties got under way in the United States. There were difficulties, or at any rate there was concern, in other countries as well. Lord Ashburton, who with Daniel Webster had worked out the treaty with Great Britain in 1842, reported concern in his country among antislavery people lest extradition for robbery be used as a means for recovering fugitive slaves.[30] But just as Americans found ways of protecting political refugees, so the passengers on the underground railroad to Canada managed to make good their escape in spite of the existence of the treaty provisions.

---

[28] *Ex parte* Kaine, 14 Fed. Cas. 78 (No. 7597) (C.C.S.D. N.Y. 1853).

[29] International Extradition, 6 Op. Att'y Gen. 91 (1853).

[30] Lord Ashburton to Daniel Webster, Apr. 28, 1843, *Writings and Speeches of Daniel Webster*, J. W. McIntyre, ed., 191. For Justice Story's part in the drafting of this treaty see his reply of Apr. 19, 1842, to Webster's request of Apr. 9, 1842, *Writings and Speeches of Daniel Webster*, XVI, 367–69.

VIII: *The Impact of Foreign Affairs*

At this point the story may well return to the involvement of American citizens along the Canadian border in the Canadian rebellion of 1837–1838.[31] During the panic of 1837 and the resulting unemployment and general uneasiness, the political turmoil in Canada was for the people of northern United States the great adventure, an adventure enhanced by resort to a secret order, Hunters' Lodges, to shelter and give importance to those aiding the rebellion. In a charge to a grand jury in the United States Circuit Court for Ohio in 1838, Justice McLean told of the existence of these associations all along our northern border. He noted that, in violation of the Neutrality Act of 1818,[32] they were collecting men and materials of war, that military officers were appointed and, in anticipation of military success, civil officers as well. He called it "notorious that organized bodies of men, though, perhaps, not bearing arms, were marched through the northern part of this and other states, on our northern boundary, with the known intention of invading Canada, who were permitted to pass without molestation. And, it is believed that, in some instances, they were encouraged in their enterprise by contributions of money, provisions, and other necessaries."[33]

Justice McLean warned against violations of law which might dry up the country's prosperity and drench it in blood, and asked for effective law enforcement. On this occasion, as on others, with something of the manner of a lay preacher, he warned that the great principles of our republican institutions could not be propagated by the sword. This could be done only by moral force, not physical: "If we desire the political regeneration of oppressed nations, we must show them the simplicity, the grandeur, and the freedom of our government. We must recommend it to the intelligence and virtue of other nations, by its elevated and enlightened action, its purity, its justice, and the protection it affords to all its citizens, and the liberty they enjoy."[34]

Most of the American offenders were never called to account, but the firebrand leader of the rebellion, William Lloyd Mackenzie, who raised men and materials in New York for combat on Canadian soil, was brought to trial before Justice Thompson in the United States Circuit Court for the Northern District of New York, sitting at Rochester. Mackenzie, a spellbinding orator, addressed to the jury a ringing exposition of the oppression to be eradicated in Canada and sought to show that the cause he had sponsored was the cause of liberty everywhere

---

[31] The rebellion is dealt with in many histories. See for example Orrin Edward Tiffany, "The Relation of the United States to the Canadian Rebellion of 1837–1838," *Publications of the Buffalo Historical Society*, 8: 1, 1905.

[32] 3 Stat. 447.

[33] Charge to Grand Jury—Neutrality Laws, 30 Fed. Cas. 1018 (No. 18265) (C.C.D.Oh. 1838).

[34] *Ibid.*, 1020.

and had always been the goal of American foreign policy. In charging the jury, Justice Thompson admitted the probability that the oppression detailed actually existed, and that the acts of Mackenzie had been the acts of a patriot. As a personal opinion he might express sympathy for the defendant. But the disturbances in Canada had been of the nature of a family quarrel with which the American people had no right to interfere. The question was not one of sympathy but of law.[35]

It was said that the jury was deeply stirred by Mackenzie's appeal, but they nevertheless found him guilty. He was given a light sentence of eighteen months in jail, and was released at the end of a year.[36]

Out of one aspect of the Mackenzie venture grew the McLeod case, which for a time threatened to start a war between the United States and Great Britain and which further illustrated the difficulties caused by American federalism in the conduct of foreign affairs. A group of Mackenzie's followers in New York in December, 1837, used the steamboat *Caroline* to carry men and war materials to Navy Island, a Canadian possession in the Niagara River. In reprisal a Canadian military officer sent a band of men to capture or destroy the *Caroline*. They took the boat, killed one man in doing so, set the boat afire and let it float down the river until it sank. This reprisal stirred angry excitement throughout northern United States, but the Department of State was able to get from Great Britain neither explanation nor apology. Nearly three years later Alexander McLeod, a Canadian, was arrested in Lewiston, New York, as one of the raiding expedition, and charged with murder and arson. McLeod appealed to Canadian authorities, who alerted the proper authorities of Great Britain.[37]

---

[35] "Mackenzie's Trial, Judge Thompson's Charge," *Niles' National Register*, 56:299–300, 1839.

[36] William Kilbourn, *The Firebrand; William Lyon Mackenzie and the Rebellion in Upper Canada*, 232. In 1840 a man known as "Bill Johnson of the Thousand Isles" was convicted in the United States District Court for the Northern District of New York, presided over by Judge Alfred Conkling, for violation of the neutrality laws in setting on foot a military expedition against Upper Canada. He was sentenced to one year in the county jail and a fine of five dollars. *Niles' National Register*, 57:384, 1840.

[37] For an excellent account of the *McLeod* case see Alastair Watt, "The Case of Alexander McLeod," *Canadian Historical Review*, 12:145, 1931.

To protect the interests of the United States at the trial as originally scheduled in the New York court, President Harrison sent his Attorney General, John J. Crittenden. Crittenden stated that Governor William H. Seward "knew that the chief object of my agency in attending the trial was to see that the case was properly placed on the record in the event of a conviction, so as to enable the Supreme Court to exercise its revisory jurisdiction, if it had any. Though I do not know that the governor made any objection to the Federal government taking any part in the prosecution against McLeod, and perhaps mentioned it as an objection to the appointment of Mr. [Joshua A.] Spencer as District Attorney of the United States that he had him em-

The British now avowed the destruction of the *Caroline* as an act of their government and demanded the release of McLeod as not personally responsible according to the usages of international law. Authorities in Washington replied that they could take no direct action since McLeod was in the hands of state and not federal authorities. For a time it was hoped that William H. Seward, governer of New York, might be persuaded to get the charges dropped, but Seward, though a Whig and desirous of cooperating with the Harrison-Tyler Administration, was unwilling to incur local unpopularity. In consultation with Secretary of State Daniel Webster, McLeod's counsel sought a writ of habeas corpus in the Supreme Court of New York, on the ground that under international law as applied in the United States, McLeod, even if guilty of the act in question, was not personally responsible for what was in effect an act of the Canadian government. Indeed, the United States Attorney for the Northern District of New York appeared as one of McLeod's counsel. He did so in his private capacity, but his appearance nevertheless added to the growing impression that the federal Administration and the Whig Party were aligning themselves with Great Britain and against the state of New York.

In explaining to the British minister why the federal government could not act directly in the matter, Webster told him of the habeas corpus case, and assured him that "a tribunal, so eminently distinguished for ability and learning as the Supreme Court of the State of New York, may be safely relied upon, for the just and impartial administration of the law, in this, as well as in other cases."[38] But the case turned into a political as well as a legal battle. The attorney general of New York, Willis Hall, joined the county district attorney in fighting against McLeod's release. He denied that the court could look beyond the indictment and the plea, and he denied that by the public assumption of responsibility for individual acts a foreign country could impede the judicial processes of a state of the American Union. A murder had been committed on American soil and the prisoner indicted therefor. The lives of American citizens must be protected:

In my early days in reading the records of Roman greatness, it was not her palaces, nor her temples, nor the extent of her dominions, nor the power of her armies, that thrilled me, but it was the magic power of the exclamation, even amongst the remote and barbarous nations, "I am a Roman citizen!" And in modern times, the exclamation, "I am an Englishman," has become almost an equal passport and

---

ployed as counsel for McLeod." *The Life of John J. Crittenden*, Mrs. Chapman Coleman, ed., I, 151.

[38] Daniel Webster to Henry S. Fox,

Apr. 24, 1841, William R. Manning, *Diplomatic Correspondence of the United States, Canadian Relations, 1784–1860*, III, 140.

protection throughout the world. When will the time arrive when the exclamation, "I am an American citizen!" shall claim an equal respect? Never until we learn with equal scrupulousness to protect the lives, liberties and property of the humblest citizen of our Republic. Never while we disarrange the decent folds of the drapery of our judiciary with undignified haste to obey the irregular and illegal demands of a foreign nation.[39]

While McLeod's counsel emphasized the fact that the way to give meaning to American citizenship was to leave the federal government unembarrassed in the exercise of its constitutional powers, the dominant sentiment of local New Yorkers had its way. The Supreme Court of three justices, including as chief justice Samuel Nelson, who four years later would become a member of the Supreme Court of the United States, declined to direct McLeod's release, in a long, diffuse, and confusing opinion by Justice Esek Cowen.

While the decision pleased the so-called patriotic societies along the Canadian border, it brought consternation to national leaders concerned with preserving the peace. Webster wrote to Justice Story that Cowen's opinion was "hollow, false, and almost dishonest from beginning to end." It ought to be answered, even though the case would now have to go to trial:

> *Nobody but yourself can do this.* You must, therefore, laying aside all other things, give a day or two to the subject. This is indispensable. Send me the matter which you put together, and I will see it come forth in some semi-official manner; and I pray you let me have it within ten days. I will see that the speeches made on the subject in the Senate and House of Representatives (such as be good for any thing) be sent you tomorrow.[40]

There seems to be no record of a review of the case by Justice Story[41] but a careful and condemning analysis was written by Judge David B. Talmadge, of the Superior Court of the City of New York, published in pamphlet form, and circulated far and wide. Together with favorable comments the review was published in the current volume of New York Reports, with a reply article in a subsequent volume.[42]

---

[39] People v. McLeod, 25 Wend. (N.Y.) 483, 542 (1841).

[40] Daniel Webster to Joseph Story, July 16, 1841 (misdated 1842), *Writings and Speeches of Daniel Webster*, XVI, 379.

[41] Justice Story was reported by Charles Sumner as saying that the British were clearly within their rights in destroying the *Caroline*. Edward L. Pierce, *Memoir and Letters of Charles Sumner*, II, 177.

[42] Review of the Opinion of Judge Cowen, 26 Wend. (N.Y.) 663 (1841). For anonymous editorial publication in the *Washington National Intelli-*

In the meantime McLeod's counsel got a change of venue to a county where public excitement was less than in the county of the indictment, and he was brought to trial. Between the time of the arrest and the trial, community gossip had it that McLeod had publicly boasted of his participation in the attack on the *Caroline* and that the state had witnesses who would identify him as seen at the place of the crime. He made no such admission to his counsel, however, and at the time of his letter to Justice Story, quoted above, Webster believed that he would be acquitted. At the trial he had witnesses who provided him with an alibi, and the witnesses who were to place him at the scene of the crime failed to appear. McLeod was acquitted, to the discomfiture of enemies who long suspected that the Administration had managed to get the key witnesses out of the picture. Intervention of this kind, however, was never proved.[43]

With the release of McLeod after a verdict of not guilty, the strain in relations between the United States and Great Britain relaxed, but border tensions generally still remained, and a new crisis of the same kind might come at any time. In his annual message of December 7, 1841, President Tyler asked Congress to provide for removal to the federal courts of cases involving international relations after the fashion of the McLeod case.[44] In the following March he reported the arrest of another participant in the *Caroline* affray and again urged Congress to act.[45]

States' rights sentiments ran too deep to permit the removal of cases from state courts to federal courts for trial because of some alleged right under international law or because of a claim to be acting under the orders of a foreign power. The change needed was not to permit the federal courts to conduct trials, but merely to determine whether, because of international law involvement, the person could be tried at all in an American court. While it was true that McLeod had been found not guilty in the state court, Great Britain had claimed that he was not subject to punishment in the United States even if he had performed the acts in question, because the responsibility was not his own but that

---

gencer of Feb. 11, 1842, Webster wrote in praise of the Talmadge analysis, seeking, for some reason of strategy, to conceal the legal qualifications of the writer by saying, "Of course we are not competent to look at this production with professional eyes." Webster's longhand document, Webster Papers (Dartmouth), No. 842161. See also "The Supreme Court of New York and Mr. Webster, on the McLeod Question," *United States Magazine and Democratic Review,* 10: 487, 1842, reprinted, 3 Hill (N.Y.) 635 (1842).

[43] See Watt, "The Case of Alexander McLeod," *Canadian Historical Review,* 12:158 1931.

[44] Richardson, *Messages and Papers of the Presidents,* IV, 75.

[45] *Ibid.,* 103.

of the government for which he acted. The President and the Secretary of State were probably justified in sensing the imminence of war if McLeod were found guilty and put to death. It was to prevent such an eventuality that a new procedure was needed.

So it was that the Judiciary Committee of the Senate reported out a bill not to transfer to federal courts the trial of such cases but, on petition, to grant writs of habeas corpus to determine whether prisoners should be tried at all or should be released to their own countries. If they were to be tried, they would be returned to the state courts from which they came, though with a right of appeal from the District Court judge to whom they had applied, or from an individual Supreme Court Justice, to the Supreme Court itself before being sent back for trial. It was ironic that the man who reported the bill from the committee of which he was chairman was John M. Berrien of Georgia, a state which in many cases had scornfully resisted federal judicial encroachments on what it regarded as its rightful jurisdiction.

Berrien explained the bill,[46] and it was passed as a Whig measure pretty much by a party vote.[47] Democrats, though realizing their impotence, poured out their wrath at this further encroachment of federal power on the province of the states and at Whig knuckling under to Great Britain. James Buchanan made dire predictions of justice delayed or prevented by this device which would enable defendants to appeal to federal courts hundreds of miles distant and in infrequent session, in effect linking his argument with one of those used against bankruptcy legislation enforced through widely scattered federal courts. It was not that he wanted more federal courts. Centralization was already going too fast and too far. This bill was an insult to state sovereignty.[48]

Most new measures raised with Southerners the possibility of danger to the South's "peculiar institution." Senator Arthur P. Bagby of Alabama saw the possibility that foreigners seeking to stir up rebellion among slaves might escape state jurisdiction on the ground that, like McLeod, they were acting on orders from a foreign power. He thought the spirit of fanaticism abroad in the land might lead to this very thing. And if the state refused to surrender jurisdiction, as it probably would, how would obedience to the writ of habeas corpus be enforced.[49]

John C. Calhoun thought there was no urgent necessity for the bill. He believed the state tribunals ought to be trusted. The outcome of the McLeod trial illustrated their trustworthiness. Foreign powers had no right to make a change in the character of our institutions. The

---

[46] *Cong. Globe,* 27th Cong., 2nd Sess. 443–44 (1842).
[47] For the bill as passed see 5 Stat. 539.

[48] *Cong. Globe,* 27th Cong., 2nd Sess., App. 386 (1842).
[49] *Ibid.,* 555–56.

bill would endanger rather than promote the peace and safety of the country.[50]

As is often true of dire predictions, none of them came true. The new statute provided an important safeguard without proving a threat to our federal system or to the institution of slavery.

A year and a half after the destruction by Canadians of the steamboat *Caroline* the capture of the schooner *Amistad* by its slave passengers occurred, with an additional mass of legal disputes involving American foreign relations. In June, 1839, the *Amistad* had set out from Havana for another Cuban port, carrying cargo and more than fifty Negroes, most of whom had been captured in Africa by Spaniards in violation of treaties outlawing the slave trade. The claimant, however, had with him a document from the Governor-General of Cuba listing them as his slaves. In a successful rebellion the Negroes killed the captain and compelled the alleged owner, José Ruiz, and another Spaniard, Pedro Montez, to sail the ship for them, with directions to proceed to Africa.

For a month the Spaniards managed to outwit their captors, and the *Amistad* was taken into custody off the coast of Long Island, where some of the Negroes had gone ashore to get supplies, by Lieutenant Gedney, of the United States brig *Washington*. In the United States District Court for Connecticut claims for salvage were filed by Gedney and by certain residents of Long Island, with an eye to the value of the ship and its cargo and the alleged slaves, all of whom had been brought back on board the *Amistad*. Ruiz and Montez filed claims to all the property, including the slaves. The Spanish minister in Washington called on the Secretary of State to restore all the property to the rightful Spanish owners, and in pursuance of this request the United States Attorney for Connecticut also filed a claim in the District Court. Beyond this series of overlapping claims was the question whether the federal court had jurisdiction to try the Negroes for mutiny and the murder of the captain. Martin Van Buren, then President, tried so to conduct his Administration that the slavery question would not come to the fore, but his Secretary of State, John Forsyth of Georgia, responded to Southern sentiment that property in slaves must be protected, that Negro rebellions against white control must be suppressed, and that Negroes who won out in contests with white people must not be permitted to infiltrate the

---

[50] *Ibid.*, 557. See also the speeches of Robert J. Walker of Mississippi, *ibid.*, 611–19; Perry Smith of Connecticut, *ibid.*, 645–47; and Charles J. Ingersoll of Pennsylvania, *ibid.*, 953–57. For the contrasting and approving opinion of Chancellor Kent see James Kent to Daniel Webster, Dec. 21, 1842, *Private Correspondence of Daniel Webster*, Fletcher Webster, ed., II, 160–61.

population of the country. The several claims and the several questions of law were entangled in proceedings of the District Court and of the Circuit Court, with the further question of the jurisdiction of this District Court, turning on whether the *Amistad* had been seized in the waters of Connecticut or of New York.

United States Judge Andrew P. Judson went aboard the *Amistad* to conduct a court of inquiry with respect to the jurisdiction of his court to deal with the mutiny. He directed that most of the male Negroes be held in jail at Hartford to be brought before the Circuit Court for trial for the crime of murder committed within the admiralty and maritime jurisdiction of the United States, and that one man and four girls be held as witnesses.[51] In the several cases which arose, no lower-court decision was officially reported, with the result that the happenings are not clear. A committee of abolitionists was formed to protect the Negroes, who were the subject of much curiosity. Theodore Sedgwick, Jr., and Roger S. Baldwin of Connecticut sought the release of the Negro girls on habeas corpus, presenting the petition to Justice Thompson in the Circuit Court. Thompson dismissed the petition pending determination of the judicial district in which the capture had taken place, or of whether it took place within any judicial district. He gave only an oral opinion. His personal feelings were as abhorrent to slavery as those of any man present, but his feelings were irrelevant: "If a seizure is made within the limits of a state the jurisdiction of the district court is local. If it is made on the high seas, *any* district court may take cognizance of the matter."[52]

Here Justice Thompson noted an intermediate proceeding of which we have no other record. Under the directions of the court the grand jury had disposed of the charge of murder on the ground that there was no criminal offense cognizable in the courts of the United States. If a murder had been committed on a foreign vessel with a foreign crew and foreign papers, the offense was not against the laws of the United States but against the laws of the country to which the vessel belonged. True, our federal courts had jurisdiction of offenses against the law of nations, but the murder of the captain of the *Amistad* was not such an offense.[53] The cases pending, therefore, were based on the conflicting claims to property and not on alleged crime.

The Spanish minister in Washington continued to press for the surrender of the *Amistad* with its cargo and the alleged slaves. Felix Grundy of Tennessee, who was now Attorney General of the United States, gave Secretary of State Forsyth an official opinion that the

---

[51] H.R. Doc. No. 185, 26th Cong., 1st Sess., 52–54 (1840).

[52] "Decision of Judge Thompson," *Niles' National Register*, 57:75, 1839.
[53] *Ibid.*

request should be granted in light of a treaty with Spain providing for restoration of ships that might have been seized by pirates or robbers.[54] It would have been an extreme action for the Administration to take the personnel away from the courts, but the opinion may well have prevailed in Administration circles that the courts would decide in harmony with Administration sentiment. Because the *Amistad* was in bad condition the Spanish minister asked the President to provide a ship for delivery of the slaves. The President directed that the schooner *Grampus* be made available for that purpose by naval officers.[55] The United States Attorney for Connecticut, who in a letter that was expurgated when a copy was called for by the House of Representatives had said, "I should regret extremely that the rascally blacks should fall into the hands of the abolitionists, with whom Hartford is filled,"[56] asked whether he should enforce the President's order whatever the court decision might be.[57] Forsyth replied that if Holabird lost the case he should take an immediate appeal, whereas if he won it he should send off the Negroes immediately and not wait to see whether their counsel would appeal.[58]

But the Administration was disappointed, both by the United States District Court for Connecticut, which was found to have jurisdiction, and by the Circuit Court, to which the United States Attorney appealed. Salvage on the *Amistad* and cargo was awarded to certain claimants and not to others, and it was directed that all the Negroes, except one who was admittedly a slave, should be turned over to the President, not for delivery to the claimants but for return to Africa, pursuant to a statute of 1819 providing for the removal of Negroes illegally brought into the United States.[59]

In the meantime, in the House of Representatives, John Quincy Adams had brought about a call for and the publication of the official correspondence dealing with the *Amistad* captives. He and other abolitionists made the most of Van Buren's—or Forsyth's—conniving with the Spanish minister to ship the Negroes out of the country and back into slavery. He was able to get original copies as well, or at any rate to see them, and to demonstrate that some of the embarrassing passages in the correspondence had been dressed up for publication. The rights of Negroes being a major preoccupation with him, he agreed to join their counsel before the Supreme Court even though long years had passed since he had last appeared before that tribunal and he realized

---

[54] 3 Ops. Att'y Gen. 484 (1839).

[55] See Van Buren's order dated Jan. 7, 1840, H.R. Doc. No. 185, 26th Cong., 1st Sess., 69 (1840).

[56] *Memoirs of John Quincy Adams*, Charles F. Adams, ed., X, 398.

[57] W. S. Holabird to John Forsyth, Jan. 11, 1840, H.R. Doc. No. 185, 26th Cong., 1st Sess., 56 (1840).

[58] John Forsyth to W. S. Holabird, Jan. 12, 1840, *ibid.*, 56.

[59] 3 Stat. 532.

that he was better at dynamic invective in the House of Representatives than at cool argument before the Court. He was not half prepared, wrote the seventy-four-year-old ex-President a few days before the beginning of the argument. He went to the Court with a heavy heart, full of un-digested thought, sure of the justice of his cause but despairing of his ability to sustain it.[60]

As Roger S. Baldwin pointed out at the beginning of his argument on behalf of "the humble Africans," the record showed that these simple people had two powerful governments arrayed against them—the United States and Spain. Adams tried to remedy the balance by utilizing the support of Great Britain on the other side, not in Court but for pub-licity purposes. Great Britain had gradually abandoned slavery for eco-nomic penetration, which was regarded as at once more humane and more profitable, and had become the world's leading opponent of the institution to which the American South clung so stubbornly. Henry S. Fox, British minister in Washington, was instructed to interpose his good offices in behalf of the *Amistad* Negroes and also to intervene with Spain.[61] Fox consulted Adams, saying that he had recently heard with great surprise that the decision of the Supreme Court would be to "deliver up these unfortunate men."[62] He promised to prepare a letter and to show it to Adams before it was sent. The two men had a conver-sation of an hour and a half on the *Amistad* case.[63]

Fox wrote to Forsyth that he knew that the Negroes had been imported into Cuba from Africa in a Portuguese ship and sold in Havana and put aboard the *Amistad* to be carried to another port of Cuba, in violation of Spanish law made in pursuance of a treaty of 1817. The United States and Great Britain, by the Treaty of Ghent, had agreed to do their best to suppress the slave trade. His government therefore hoped that the President would take measures to secure the liberty of the captives. In reply, Forsyth called attention to the fact that the President had neither the power nor the disposition to control the courts in the matter. But he indicated the same belief that Fox seems to have held, namely, that the Supreme Court would decide against the Negroes, and that they would be delivered to Spain and taken back to Cuba, where the British government could negotiate with Spain about the observance of treaty stipulations.[64]

The argument in the *Amistad* case was spread over eight days in the latter part of February and early March, 1841, being interrupted

---

[60] *Memoirs of John Quincy Adams,* X, 399.

[61] See W. Fox Strangways to Wil-liam P. Patton, Dec. 23, 1839, *Niles' National Register,* 58:140, 1840.

[62] *Memoirs of John Quincy Adams,* X, 400.

[63] *Ibid.,* 401.

[64] The correspondence between Fox and Forsyth is summarized in John B. McMaster, *History of the People of the United States,* XI, 609.

by the death of Justice Barbour. Attorney General Henry D. Gilpin presented the case for the United States, contending that since the papers of the *Amistad* were in good order the United States was obligated to surrender the schooner and her cargo, human and otherwise, without inquiring into background facts concerning the legal status of the Negroes. Roger S. Baldwin, who had been with the case from the beginning, contended that the Court must look at the entire record, which showed that the Negroes were rightfully free men in whose enslavement the United States should not participate, and that they ought to be set free.

Adams wrote in his memoirs that "in commenting upon the insurrection of the blacks, Mr. Baldwin firmly maintained their right of self-emancipation, but spoke in cautious terms, to avoid exciting Southern passions and prejudices, which it is our policy as much as possible to assuage and pacify."[65] But if Adams himself was on this exceptional occasion in any sense "pacific" toward Southern feelings, there was nothing pacific at all in his denunciation of the Administration for its strategy of cooperation with Spain in keeping the Negroes in slavery. Justice Story called his argument extraordinary, "extraordinary, I say, for its power, for its bitter sarcasm, and its dealing with topics far beyond the record and points of discussion."[66]

Adams recorded in his memoirs that he spoke four and a half hours on February 24 and four hours on March 1, stopping even then before he had used much of his accumulated material. On the first day he was still troubled with the sense of agitation which the case had aroused in him for weeks, and he felt that he did not do his best in the well-filled courtroom. He had concentrated on one fundamental principle, the ministration of justice. "I then assigned my reason for inviting *justice* specially, aware that this was *always* the duty of the Court, but because an immense array of power—the Executive Administration, instigated by the Minister of a foreign nation—has been brought to bear, in this case, on the side of *injustice*. . . . I did not, I could not, answer public expectation; but I have not yet utterly failed. God speed me to the end!"[67]

Because of the absence of Justice McKinley and the death of Justice Barbour in the midst of the argument, the case was presented to a Court of only seven Justices. The Court, speaking through Justice Story, pleased Adams and disappointed the Administration by deciding that the fact of the illegal enslavement of the Negroes, admitted even by the United States Attorney, had to be recognized, that they were right-

---

[65] *Memoirs of John Quincy Adams,* X, 430.
[66] William W. Story, ed., *Life and*

Letters of Joseph Story, II, 348.
[67] *Memoirs of John Quincy Adams,* X, 431.

fully free men, that they were not pirates or robbers in spite of their mode of asserting their freedom, and that nothing in the treaty with Spain called for their restoration to the Spanish claimants.[68] The Negroes were ordered to be set free and not delivered to the President for deportation to Africa, as the decree of the lower court had provided.[69] Only Justice Baldwin dissented, without written opinion.

Abolitionists were delighted with the decision. The New York committee of the Anti-Slavery Society requested that public thanks be given in all the churches of the land.[70] Justice Story, of course, had not turned his opinion into an antislavery tract or into an assault on the Administration, in spite of the fact that his sentiments were Whig and abolitionist. Speaking for a Court which included Democrats and slaveholders, he had to limit the opinion to the matter actually decided. Richard Peters, in preparing to report the arguments in the case, apparently sought to limit them somewhat to the area of points discussed in the opinion of the Court. It would appear that he asked Adams to delete from his presentation his rough treatment of the Administration, which the Court did not discuss. Adams replied that if Peters left out his flagellation of the Secretary of State and of the man from Kinderhook (Van Buren), then he might put in what he pleased. The important comment on Van Buren's performance was that the Negroes were now free.[71] The result was that Adams submitted to Peters no document at all. In his explanation Peters noted sardonically, "As many of the points presented by Mr. Adams, in the discussion of the cause, were not considered by the court essential to its decision, and were not taken notice of in the opinion of the court, delivered by Mr. Justice Story, the necessary omission of the argument is submitted to with less regret."[72] Instead of shortening his argument for publication by Peters, Adams lengthened it to include materials not presented to the Supreme Court and published it as a pamphlet of 135 pages,[73] in which form it

---

[68] United States v. The . . . Amistad, 15 Pet. 518 (1841).

[69] The Negroes, or such of them as had survived imprisonment, were eventually transported back to their homeland under the kindly supervision of missionaries. See Niles' National Register, 61:224, 1841.

[70] Salem Register, Mar. 29, 1841.

[71] J. Q. Adams to Richard Peters, May 19, 1841, Peters Papers.

[72] 15 Pet. 566.

[73] "Argument of John Quincy Adams, Before the Supreme Court of the United States, in the Case of the United States, Appellants, vs. Cinque, and Others, Africans, Cap-

tured in the Schooner Amistad. By Lieut. Gedney, Delivered on the 24th of February and 1st of March, 1841. With A Review of the Case of the Antelope." Reported in the 10th, 11th and 12th Volumes of Wheaton's Reports (1841).

The materials Adams had had to omit from his oral argument had primarily to do with the Antelope case as a precedent. Francis Scott Key, who had been the losing counsel in that case, predicted that Adams would lose the Amistad case on the basis of it, probably thereby leading to much research in that area. See Memoirs of John Quincy Adams, X,

was circulated as an item in the abolitionist propaganda of the times. In the meantime he wrote to the New York committee which had financed the defense of the Negroes a letter listing questions of human liberty that had been involved in the decisions of the lower courts but not dealt with by the Supreme Court, with the implication that these questions ought to have been answered.[74]

The *Amistad* story has an odd sequel in the continued refusal of the executive branch of the government to accept the Supreme Court's interpretation of the treaty with Spain. In spite of the decision the Spanish government demanded reparations and repeated the demand year after year. In February, 1843, President Tyler recommended that some kind of payment be made, evidently in reimbursement of salvage.[75] Tyler seems not to have strongly pressed the matter but pressure came in earnest in the Polk Administration with James Buchanan as Secretary of State. In 1846 Buchanan recommended to Charles J. Ingersoll, chairman of the House Committee on Foreign Affairs, the payment of the claim, evidently including compensation to Spain for the liberated Negroes. He expressed to the committee the firm belief that the claim deserved prompt attention and serious consideration,[76] and sent a copy of his letter to the Spanish legation.[77] In doing so he in effect notified the Spanish government that the executive branch of our government repudiated the decision of the Supreme Court.

At the 1846–1847 session of Congress the Senate included in a general appropriation bill an appropriation of $50,000 to pay the Spanish claims. In an attempt to get the approval of the House of Representatives, Buchanan wrote to the chairman of the Committee on Ways and Means, "I have given the question a thorough and deliberate consideration, and cannot avoid the conclusion that the claim is well founded, under . . . our Treaty with Spain of the 20th October, 1795."[78] This letter also he sent to the Spanish legation, giving assurance that it had the cordial support of the President.[79]

396–97. Key, then a colonizationist and United States Attorney for the District of Columbia, thought that in any event it would not do to send the Negroes back to Cuba. It would be better to make up a purse to finance their return to Africa.

It is worth noting that the milder and shorter argument made by Roger S. Baldwin was also published in pamphlet form, with a similarly long title, for use in the antislavery campaign.

[74] John Quincy Adams to Simeon S. Jocelyn *et al.*, Mar. 17, 1841, *Niles' National Register*, 60:116, 1841.

[75] Richardson, *Messages and Papers of the Presidents*, IV, 232.

[76] James Buchanan to Charles J. Ingersoll, Mar. 19, 1846, *Works of James Buchanan*, VI, 426.

[77] James Buchanan to Don A. Calderon de la Barca, Apr. 17, 1846, *ibid.*, 453.

[78] James Buchanan to James J. McKay, Mar. 2, 1847, *ibid.*, 232.

[79] James Buchanan to Don A. Calderon de la Barca, Mar. 19, 1847, *ibid.*, 242.

The measure stirred the wrath of the aged Adams. As a member of the House described the scene:

> My venerable and ever-lamented friend, John Quincy Adams, was then just lingering upon the confines of life; he was pale and trembling under the weight of nearly fourscore years; his voice was so weak that he was able to make himself heard at the distance of only a few yards; he had ceased to mingle in the debates of this Hall; he had, however, been familiar with all the details of this pretended claim, and when he saw his country about to be disgraced by contributing the public funds to the payment of these Spanish slave dealers, for the failure of their anticipated speculations in human flesh, his spirit was stirred within him, and he once more, and for the last time, rose in defense of his country's honor, in defense of humanity. Members from the distant parts of the Hall left their seats and gathered around him, in order to catch the last words of the venerable statesman. The reporters, unable to hear him, rushed into the seats of members, and crowded near, to give to the country as much as possible of the last speech of the greatest man then living. He spoke briefly, but continued his remarks until his physical system appeared to sink under the effort.[80]

At least in part because of the Adams opposition, the measure completely failed. Buchanan continued to press for the appropriation, and Polk officially supported it,[81] but without avail.

The matter seems to have slipped into the background during the Administrations of Presidents Tyler and Polk, but President Pierce again supported the Spanish claim, contending that "good faith requires its adjustment."[82] He, too, failed to get the desired appropriation. When Buchanan himself became President, in his first three annual messages he reiterated the duty and the desirability of paying the claims, saying that it was important in connection with the settlement of other disputed claims between the two countries.[83] In his last annual message, in 1860 after the election of Abraham Lincoln and when the Civil War was in sight, Buchanan in effect admitted defeat. The *Amistad* claim had been referred along with other claims to a joint commission, the commission had rejected it, and even the Spanish government had ceased to insist on its validity.[84] So ended at last the futile attempts of the executive branch to flout a treaty interpretation given by the Supreme Court.

---

[80] From the speech of J. R. Giddings of Ohio, *Cong. Globe,* 33rd Cong., 1st Sess., App. 53 (1853). For what was gathered of the Adams speech see *Cong. Globe,* 29th Cong, 2nd Sess., App. 437 (1847).

[81] Richardson, *Messages and Papers of the Presidents,* IV, 551.
[82] *Ibid.,* V, 209.
[83] *Ibid.,* 446, 511, 561.
[84] *Ibid.,* 641.

In the experience with another ship, the *Creole*, the United States found itself further embroiled with Great Britain. In October, 1841, the *Creole* set out from Hampton Roads, Virginia, carrying a cargo of tobacco, a few passengers, and 138 slaves. The destination was New Orleans, where presumably the slaves were to be marketed as one of Virginia's profitable products. Whether or not the slaves had heard of the *Amistad*, they conducted themselves after the fashion of that other human cargo. A group of some nineteen of them, led by one with the imposing name of Madison Washington, mutinied and killed one of the slaveowners and wounded the captain and the first mate and forced the second mate to take the brig to Nassau, in the island of New Providence, one of the British-owned Bahamas. There the mass of the slaves were told that they were free and the owners were not permitted to resume control of them.[85] In an atmosphere deeply hostile to slavery it would appear that the American consul, unable to get the slaves sent to the United States, sought to have the mutineers tried in a local British court as pirates. The attempt failed, leading the Chief Justice of the Bahama Islands to express doctrines and sentiments which, according to Daniel Webster, Secretary of State in the Tyler Administration, went so far as to be "absolutely ferocious."[86]

The *Creole* incident stirred immense excitement in the United States. Slavery spokesmen were ready to go to the verge of war about it, while abolitionists hailed the event as a victory for freedom. A resolution, as summarized in the *Congressional Globe*, declared that the slaves had "acted in accordance with the decision of the Supreme Court in the case of the *Amistad*, and proved themselves worthy of their freedom," and it trusted that their example would be followed by others.[87] The resolution, of course, ignored the important difference that while the Negroes aboard the *Amistad* had been kidnapped without any semblance of law, those aboard the *Creole* had been legally slaves in Virginia and were on a ship flying the American flag. To deal with this point an Ohio abolitionist in the House of Representatives, Joshua R. Giddings, offered a resolution to the effect that slavery, being an abridgment of the natural rights of man, had the support only of municipal law; that the laws of Virginia by which the Negroes on the *Creole* had been enslaved had no operation on an American ship; that their resumption of their natural rights violated no law of the United States and called for no penalty; and that attempts on the part of the

---

[85] For a good running account of the experience see the Protest signed by Zephaniah C. Gifford, *et al.*, Dec. 7, 1841, *Niles' National Register*, 61: 323–26, 1842.
[86] Daniel Webster to Edward Everett, May 16, 1842, *Writings and Speeches of Daniel Webster*, XVI, 374.
[87] *Cong. Globe*, 27th Cong., 2nd Sess. 116 (1842).

United States to maintain commerce in slaves or to reenslave those set free were subversive of the rights and injurious to the feelings and interests of the free states, and unauthorized by the Constitution.[88] The proposed resolutions stirred such hostility that Giddings was persuaded to withdraw them, and then he was censured by the House. He resigned, returned to Ohio, and was reelected to Congress.[89]

Webster tried unsuccessfully to have the mutineers sent back to the United States for trial, urged on by President Tyler, who as a Virginian and a slaveowner was much excited by the incident.[90] Webster wrote to Justice Story that he had not seen fit to "demand" the return of the mutineers because he did not wish by making such a demand to weaken a claim for compensation for the rest of the slaves. He asked Justice Story whether the law of nations did not make a difference between the case of ordinary fugitives from justice and that of persons committing offenses on the high seas, and what he remembered of cases of the returning for trial of fugitives of the latter kind.[91]

Justice Story replied that he knew of no distinction between the two kinds of cases except as to piracy. Apart from piracy, offenses committed on the high seas were cognizable in the courts of the countries to which the ships belonged, and not elsewhere. But when a ship was taken over by pirates it lost its national character, and piratical acts were punishable in the courts of any country. He thought such offenders had sometimes been sent back for trial in the country to which the ship had originally belonged, but such action had been understood to be a matter of comity and discretion and not of national duty.

Here he plumbed to the weakness of Webster's case for the return of the Negroes who had been aboard the *Creole*. It involved their dual status as persons and as property, with differing rules of law in different parts of the world:

> The real question, however, in the Creole Case is not a question as to the delivering up of fugitives from Justice, as of property, and property coming by the vis major and involuntarily into a foreign port. Suppose the case had been one of shipwreck, and the Cargo had been ordinary goods, no one could well doubt that in the present state of civilization every nation would feel itself bound by the general doctrines of comity and humanity and justice to protect and restore such property, and to give right of reclaiming it from wrong doers. The question then is reduced to this, whether there is a sound distinction between that case,

---

[88] *Ibid.*, 342.

[89] McMaster, *History of the People of the United States*, VII, 55.

[90] See Wilbur Devereux Jones, "The Influence of Slavery on the Webster-Ashburton Negotiations," *Journal of Southern History*, 22:48, 1956.

[91] Daniel Webster to Joseph Story, Mar. 17, 1842, *Writings and Speeches of Daniel Webster*, XVI, 364.

and the case of Slaves, who are property and held as property by their owners, in America, and are by the vis major, or by shipwreck found in a foreign port. It is certainly true, that no nation held itself bound to recognize the State or the rights of slavery, which are recognized and allowed by any other Country. And if slaves come *voluntarily* into a Country with the consent of their masters, they are deemed free. The only point left of my argument seems to be whether the like privilege applies, where they are in such a Country by the vis major, or by shipwreck. I have always inclined to think that this must be deemed matter of comity, which a nation was at liberty to concede or refuse, and not a right of another nation to claim or enforce, as strictly arising under the Law of nations.[92]

In short, he thought the United States had no basis for a claim on the fugitives in the absence of commitments made by treaty between the two countries—and here there were none. For illumination of the subject he referred Webster to the *Amistad* case and to the recently decided case of *Prigg v. Pennsylvania.*[93]

Great Britain was obdurate in the matter. The slaves were not recovered and the mutineers went unpunished. Because mutiny had been excepted from the risks covered, the owners were not even able to collect insurance on their slave property.[94]

Sporadically but often dangerously throughout the Taney period, or at any rate down to the Civil War, bands of Americans continued to engage in predatory expeditions touching outlying territory of other nations. Operations along the Canadian border have already been mentioned. To the south of us, and long before the Taney period, adventurous and predatory Americans engaged in expeditions to free Mexico from Spanish dominion.[95] In the middle 1830s, people from the United States were pouring into Texas, then a Mexican possession, settling that rich farm country, and preparing to declare independence from Mexico with the hope of admission as a state of the Union. John Catron of Tennessee, then in the interim between his state and federal judicial positions, was most actively concerned with the fight for Texan independence. He wrote to President Jackson about the excitement in

---

[92] Joseph Story to Daniel Webster, Mar. 26, 1842, *ibid.*, 365.

[93] 16 Pet. 539 (1842).

[94] For the case and for an extensive account of the Creole incident see McCargo v. The New Orleans Insurance Co., 10 Rob. (La.) 202 (1845).

[95] For evidence in the Taney period of the activities of the largely illfated Baltimore Mexican Company of 1816, for the destruction of which Mexico by a treaty of 1839 was persuaded to pay, and for disputes among claimants, see Gill v. Oliver's Executors, 11 How. 529 (1850); Williams v. Oliver, 12 How. 111 (1851); and Deacon v. Oliver, 14 How. 610 (1852). Extensive records of the disputes are filed at the Maryland Historical Society.

his part of the country over Mexican outrages committed in the war with Texas, and warned that for a member of Congress failure to support the independence of Texas would bring political ruin. He hoped for immediate recognition before Mexico called Great Britain to her aid and involved us with that country.[96] He wrote in similar fashion to Daniel Webster, then in the Senate.[97]

The question of the annexation of Texas to the United States deeply involved slavery issues, although not all Southern statesmen advocated it or thought that slavery would be aided by it. In 1844 Justice Daniel, returning from traveling his circuit "from the immediate confines of Texas itself," indicated that annexation was not generally desired and that its advocacy was limited largely to the Tyler-Calhoun faction of the Democratic Party. He had seen many persons who were strenuously opposed to the acquisition of Texas, "regarding it as a measure which must injuriously affect the price of lands and the progress of improvement in the Southern Country."[98] Justice Catron, however, remained an enthusiast, and advised President Polk on this matter as on many others. He was not disturbed at the thought of a war with Mexico except that we might get in too deep, with vaunted effort to acquire territory all the way to California, and thereby court trouble with Great Britain, when we were having enough trouble already over Texas and Oregon.[99] Justice McLean, on the other hand, with an eye to the slavery issue, was an ardent opponent of the annexation of Texas and the waging of the Mexican War.[100]

After the Mexican War, with the acquisition of territory all the way to the Pacific and northward to Oregon, restless groups looked for new realms to conquer in the achievement of the "manifest destiny" of the American people, offering an outlet for bands of men recently trained for battle who had not had their fill of adventure. Next in sequence, therefore, came a series of filibustering expeditions southward, to Cuba and to Nicaragua. The more important were the three Lopez expeditions to Cuba, from 1848 to 1851, which drew adventurous and predatory men from all over the United States but principally from the South.[101] Federal judges all the way from New York to New Orleans were compelled to deliver to grand juries charges condemning acts of war on the

---

[96] John Catron to Andrew Jackson, June 8, 1836, *Correspondence of Andrew Jackson*, John S. Bassett, ed., V, 401.

[97] George T. Curtis, *Life of Daniel Webster*, I, 523.

[98] Peter V. Daniel to Martin Van Buren, June 11, 1844, Van Buren Papers.

[99] John Catron to James K. Polk, Aug. 16, 1845, Polk Papers.

[100] Francis P. Weisenburger, *The Life of John McLean*, 108.

[101] See Robert Granville Caldwell, *The Lopez Expeditions to Cuba, 1848–1851*.

territory of our neighbors and the violation of our neutrality statute.[102] So strong were the sympathies of juries with the offenders that prosecutions both in New York and in New Orleans, from which the expeditions set out, failed to bring convictions.[103] Justice McLean, on his circuit in Ohio, poured out denunciation of the violators of law, but without appreciable effect on public opinion.[104]

Although Justice Catron had expressed no disapproval of the private efforts of Americans in Texas to take that country from Mexico and had advocated annexation after Texas was recognized, he assailed the Cuban expeditions in the Circuit Court in Nashville. He noted that "recent acts and demonstrations, too prominently notorious to have escaped general attention, have been committed in this city, and which acts were professedly done in violation of the treaties and laws of the United States. Our streets have been paraded by military music, accompanied with banners, for the purpose of exciting the vicious, the idle, the young, and the thoughtless to enlist as soldiers for the purpose of invading the island of Cuba, and aiding there a portion of its population to overthrow the present government."[105] He directed the grand jury to indict, on evidence known to any member and especially on evidence submitted by the United States Attorney. Here again, however, there is no evidence that any substantial change was made in public sentiment. The sense of manifest destiny still prevailed.

The Supreme Court as a body dealt with the subject by indirection. The government finding it impossible to get convictions of Americans for violation of our neutrality statute, no relevant cases came up on appeal. But a case did come up involving a contract made many years earlier with respect to land in Texas, after Texas had declared its independence but before its independence had been recognized by the United States. It seems clear that the Supreme Court, speaking through Chief Justice Taney, used the case of *Kennett v. Chambers*[106] not merely to determine the controversy at hand but also to let filibustering Americans know where they stood with respect to the law. In the midst of the Texas rebellion, General T. Jefferson Chambers, of the Texas army, had

---

[102] For a charge delivered by United States District Judge Samuel R. Betts, in New York City, see "Cuban Expedition," *West. L.J.*, 7:510, 1850.

[103] See "The Late Cuba State Trials," *United States Magazine and Democratic Review*, 30:307, 1852. For an article in defense of attempts to "liberate" Cuba see "The Neutrality Law: What Does It Mean, What Prohibit and What Permit?," *ibid.*, 497.

[104] Charge to Grand Jury—Neutrality Laws, 30 Fed. Cas. 1021 (No. 18267) (C.C.D. Oh. 1851). See also the charge of Justice Curtis in Boston, 30 Fed. Cas. 1024 (No. 18269) (C.C.D. Mass. 1851).

[105] "The Cuban Expedition," *West. L.J.*, 9:39, 1852. For further instructions to the grand jury by Justice Catron see "Duty of Grand Jurors," *Law. Rep.*, 14:523, 1852.

[106] 14 How. 38 (1852).

gone to Cincinnati to raise troops and buy supplies for military purposes. The bait for enlistment and for the provision of funds was the prospective value of Texas land after independence and perhaps after annexation to the United States. General Chambers received from a group of Cincinnati men $125,500, pledging for the money a tract of land which he held in his own name.

Independence was won and annexation achieved, and the anticipated increase in property values came about. Instead of completing the transfer of the land described in the agreement, General Chambers held on to it, contending that the contract was invalid because it was made in violation of our treaty with Mexico and the Neutrality Act of 1818. The United States District Court in Texas upheld his contention, and an appeal from the decree was taken to the Supreme Court.

The Supreme Court affirmed the decree, on the same grounds, and held the contract illegal and void. Chief Justice Taney took occasion to say not only that the parties had entered into an unlawful contract on which they were not entitled to recover but that in lending the money they had been liable to criminal prosecution for violating the neutrality laws of the United States. The statement stood as a warning to men who in the 1850s were putting up money for the invasion of Cuba in the hope of future gains.

In demonstrating the illegality of the contract to help get supplies for the Texas rebellion against Mexico, with which country we had a treaty of peace, Chief Justice Taney took occasion indirectly to answer a current argument about the responsibility of individuals as distinguished from the federal government in the field of foreign affairs. It was contended that the federal government had no power to govern the acts of individuals as it had attempted to do by neutrality legislation.[107] Chief Justice Taney made it clear that in the Constitution the people had placed the conduct of foreign affairs in the government and that its decisions were binding on every citizen of the Union:

> He is bound to be at war with the nation against which the war-making power has declared war, and equally bound to commit no act of hostility against a nation with which the government is in amity and friendship. This principle is universally acknowledged by the law of nations. It lies at the foundation of all government, as there could be no social order or peaceful relations between the citizens of different countries without it. It is, however, more emphatically true in relation to citizens of the United States. For as the sovereignty resides in the people, every citizen is a portion of it, and is himself personally bound

---

[107] See for example Speech of John A. Quitman, of Mississippi, on the Subject of the Neutrality Laws: Delivered in Committee of the Whole House on the State of the Union, Apr. 29, 1856.

by the laws which the representatives of the sovereignty may pass, or the treaties into which they may enter, within the scope of their delegated authority. And when that authority has plighted its faith to another nation that there shall be peace and friendship between the citizens of the two countries, every citizen of the United States is equally and personally pledged. The compact is made by the department of the government upon which he himself has agreed to confer the power. It is his own personal compact as a portion of the sovereignty in whose behalf it is made.[108]

With all the forthrightness and clarity that language could provide, the opinion demonstrated the illegality of any participation in private wars against the territory of friendly countries. The effect may have been somewhat limited by the fact that Justices Daniel and Grier dissented, but they did so without writing opinions. The mode of reporting the decision suggests that Justice Catron was in a situation of peculiar difficulty. As indicated by his charge to a grand jury, quoted above, he was much concerned about the stirring up of Americans to participate in forays against Cuba. Yet he had enthusiastically approved our mode of acquisition of Texas. In a strictly legal sense this case dealt with Texas and not at all with Cuba. His feelings might therefore be expected to be divided. He was prevented by illness from participating in the decision. Instead of mentioning his absence at the end of the opinion of the Court the Reporter stated at the very beginning, immediately following the headnotes, that Justice Catron had been absent and had taken no part[109]—as if this were the key item in the case.

This case, *Kennett v. Chambers*, marked the peak Supreme Court pronouncement on American foreign relations for the Taney period prior to the Civil War. The decision was not, of course, a corrective of all misbehavior with respect to the rights of other nations, and Justices on circuit continued to have difficulties. This was particularly true of Justice John A. Campbell, who in 1853 replaced Justice McKinley. In spite of the fact that as a Southerner he understood the complex motivations of the filibustering groups, he took a firm stand against the outbursts of illegal behavior, following in his instructions to grand juries the recent Supreme Court decision.[110] In the light of the difficulty of stopping filibustering expeditions by getting convictions in court, he haled some of the distinguished leaders before him, including Governor John A. Quitman of Mississippi, and required them to give bond for good behavior.[111]

At Mobile, in Alabama, his own state, Justice Campbell faced the

---

[108] 14 How. 50.
[109] *Ibid.*, 39.

[110] Henry G. Connor, *John Archibald Campbell*, 90–92.
[111] *Ibid.*, 94–100.

same kind of problem in connection with the plans of William Walker, the "grey-eyed man of destiny," to "colonize" Nicaragua with Southerners and thereby add to the slave area of the United States.[112] The story shades into the story of the mobilization of the South for separation from the Union. The judiciary did what it could to preserve the rule of law in the conduct of the foreign affairs of the United States, but what it could do was limited by the division of popular sentiment over the proper boundaries of the country, a division which turned to a considerable degree on the pervasive issues of slavery.

---

[112] *Ibid.*, 100–02.

CHAPTER IX

Politics and Personnel

AT THIS POINT an interlude in the account of legal proceedings is called for, to sketch more coherently the political background of the business of the Court and to present its personnel during the middle of the Taney period.

It was inevitable that the several courts throughout the country, particularly state and local courts but also to some extent the federal courts, should feel the impact of Jacksonian democracy. This broad social movement enhanced the influence of the masses of the people over their government, or at any rate of the leaders who made their appeal to widespread democratic support. It carried the influence of local political sentiments deeper and deeper into American political institutions. Jacksonian Democrats scorned the aristocratic sentiment that undistinguished people should leave matters of high policy to their betters. They demanded that legislators and administrators, and even judges, be subject to popular control. To achieve these ends they broadened the electoral base by eliminating most of the remaining property qualifications for voting and by increasing the percentage of offices which were filled by election rather than appointment. They acted on the assumption that within a considerable range one man was as good as another and that the public was better served, by and large, if offices were passed around at relatively frequent intervals rather than held for long periods by a favored few. This they deemed especially true because of the tendency of prolonged officeholding to become linked with powerful economic interests, at the expense, they were convinced, of the masses of the people.

Although the selection and tenure of judges varied greatly from state to state and from level to level, the tendency during the early years was to appoint the judges of the highest courts for long terms or for life during good behavior. The democratic impetus brought curtailment of terms in many states, particularly in new states being admitted to the Union, and a shift from appointment to election, with widespread popular discussion of the need for responsiveness of the courts to the popular will on the one hand and for independence and responsibility only to the law on the other. One of the most extensive debates of this kind occurred in the Pennsylvania constitutional convention of 1837–1838, with a resulting change from life appointment of state supreme court judges to appointments for fifteen years. Democratic ferment continued in that state, with the result that in 1850 popular election was substituted for appointment. By its constitution of 1846 New York turned to popular election. The trend remained dominant, although Massachusetts provided an exception in refusing to make the change to election of judges which was proposed by its constitutional convention of 1853.

It is ironic that changes in mode of selection and tenure which were calculated to make courts more responsive to the popular will seemed to reduce the stature of judges in the eyes of the people, and that this occurred even when selection and tenure were not changed. In the new states judicial salaries were established at low levels and in the older states they were kept low or were even reduced. The Massachusetts legislature in 1842 deeply slashed the salaries of all the state judges.[1] The act was challenged as unconstitutional as well as bad public policy, and it was said that Chief Justice Lemuel Shaw, of the Supreme Judicial Court, refused to receive any salary whatever from the state treasury until the earlier salary level for his court was restored,[2] as it was the following year. The restoration, made by a legislature with a majority of Whigs, was opposed by all the Democrats and even by some of the Whigs.[3] An attempt to restore the salaries of the judges of the court of common pleas was defeated.[4] A retrenchment statute of 1844 enacted by the Ohio legislature reduced the salary of supreme court judges by a third, with only partial restoration made soon afterward.[5] That judicial salaries were in general not so munificent as to require reduction in the public interest is indicated by the fact that in 1846 the level of the salaries of the chief justices of the highest state courts ranged from $650 in Rhode Island to $3,667 in Pennsylvania, with the exception that in Louisiana the chief justice received the much higher figure of

---

[1] See "The Attack on the Judiciary of Massachusetts," *Law Rep.*, 6:241, 1843.

[2] "The Power of the Legislature to Create and Abolish Courts of Justice," *Law Rep.*, 21:65, 72, 1859.

[3] "Legislation in Massachusetts,"

Law Rep., 6:553, 1844.

[4] *Ibid.* See also "The Resignation of the Judges," *Law Rep.*, 7:113, 1844.

[5] See extracts from a speech made by Thomas J. Gallagher in the Ohio House of Representatives, "Judicial Salaries," *West. L.J.*, 3:265, 1846.

$6,000 while the associate justices received $5,500.[6] Indeed, the level of judicial salaries, as of public salaries generally, seems to have been partly determined by the fact that there was intense competition for offices whatever the salaries, and it was assumed to be unnecessary to pay high salaries if officers could be secured with low ones.

Legislative debates and other public discussion, of course, presented also the allegedly antidemocratic argument, which was that the judiciary had to be independent and secure if it was to serve the public as the public ought to be served. Much more was expected of the courts than that they give expression to the will of the legislatures. Legislatures touched the body of the law only at its fringes. The courts were there to give effect to the maxims of the common law which in large part had been incorporated by state constitutions and to hold legislative performance within constitutional bounds. This they could not be expected to do if their positions or their salaries were in jeopardy, and the men whom the community needed as judges could not be expected to seek or accept judicial office under such circumstances.[7] In arguing a case before the Supreme Court, Henry Clay expressed his personal position and the conservative position generally by saying, "I hope never to live in a State where judges are elected, and where the period for which they hold their offices is limited, so that elections are constantly recurring."[8]

Democrats, on the other hand, contended that independence of the judiciary was a kind of misnomer in the United States. In England it had meant independence of the king, not of the people. Such independence had met a great need, although it was not to be forgotten that judicial power had itself often become a source of tyranny. "Power," expounded the *Democratic Review*, "long and arbitrarily exercised, without check or restraint, has too often transformed her judges into tyrants, and instead of being protectors, they have become the scourges of the human race."[9] Noting that we had borrowed what was termed the independence of the judiciary from England, the author asked whether we, under very different circumstances, had need of the same institution: "If it be important in England that the judiciary should be

---

[6] "Judicial Salaries," *West. L.J.*, 3: 180–82, 1846.

[7] See for example "The Independence of the Judiciary," *North American Review*, 57:400, 1843. See also "An Elective Judiciary," *Am. L. Rev.*, 8:1, 1873; and "The Elective Principle as Applied to the Judiciary," *West. L.J.*, 5:127, 1847; and "The Independence of the Judiciary," *Democratic Review*, 23:37, 1848.

[8] Groves v. Slaughter, 15 Pet. 449, 486 (1841). In 1850, two years before Clay's death, his state of Kentucky adopted a new constitution which provided for the election of the court of appeals for terms of eight years.

[9] "Elective Judiciary," *Democratic Review*, 22:199, 200, 1848.

appointed for life, in order to render them independent of the crown, does it follow, therefore, that our judiciary should be appointed for life, when we have neither king nor aristocracy to dread?"[10]

Although the federal Constitution, less easily amended than many state constitutions, provided life tenure for federal judges and prohibited reduction of the salaries of those who had been appointed, the attitudes of Jacksonian democracy made themselves felt with respect to the federal courts as well. This was particularly true with regard to the federal District Courts. The salaries of the district judges were notoriously uneven, ranging in 1844 from $1,000 in Ohio, Indiana, and Illinois to $3,500 for the southern district of New York.[11] Variation in salary levels was presumed necessary because of the difference in work loads, amount of expenses, and inconvenience of travel. But the situation was always unstable. New states were being admitted from time to time, new districts were being set up either in new states or by the division of older districts, and the amount of business in particular districts was on the increase. Although given salaries, or the salaries of given individuals, once established could not be diminished, they could be raised, and there was often good reason for increasing them in the light of changed circumstances. But salary levels were issues of politics as well as of merit, and representatives in Congress were under pressure to protect federal judges in their own states against alleged discrimination when the salaries of judges in other states went up or when raises were proposed. In the repeated debates over salary levels and over the division of districts to create new judicial positions the issue of the democratic versus the aristocratic theory of judicial performance came to the fore.

Such a debate took place in the United States Senate in 1844 in connection with a bill to increase the salary of the federal district judge in Tennessee from $1,500 to $2,000. Senator Spencer Jarnigan of

---

[10] *Ibid.*, 201. See also "Election of Judges," *Am. L.J.*, 8:481, 1849; "The New Constitution of Kentucky," *West. L.J.*, 7:321, 1850; "Judges—Interesting Statistics," *West. L.J.*, 7:402, 1850; "Pennsylvania Judiciary," *Am. L.J.*, 10:333, 1851; "Report of the Judicial Department," *West. L.J.*, 8:282, 1851; "The Election of Judges," *West. L.J.*, 8:423, 1851; "Some of the Provisions of the Original and Recent Constitutions of the Several States Relating to the Judiciary," *Law Rep.*, 14:649, 1852; "The Power of the Legislature to Create and Abolish Courts of Justice," *Law Rep.*, 21:65, 1858; "An Elective Judiciary," *Law Rep.*, 23:385, 1860.

[11] *Cong. Globe*, 28th Cong., 1st Sess. 468 (1844). For salary figures see H.R. Rep. No. 113, 29th Cong., 1st Sess. 1–2 (1846). Senator John M. Berrien of Georgia noted that "Since the foundation of the Government there had been no such thing as a classification of salaries. Congress had always legislated in individual cases, as was proposed by this bill—taking into consideration the change of the circumstances by the advancement of the country since the judges were appointed, the increase of duties, and the increase of the expenses for the necessaries to support life." *Ibid.*, 455.

Tennessee, a Whig and the sponsor of the bill, explained that the amount of labor required of the judge had doubled since his appointment and that the proposed increase would not give more than a fair compensation. Senator Benjamin Tappan of Ohio, where the salaries of state judges had recently been reduced, a Democrat and an advocate of the democratization of the courts, opposed the increase, observing that the federal district judge in Ohio received only $1,000. He noted the tendency of federal judges in recent years to find additional places to hold court within their districts and then apply to Congress for increased salaries. When the judges accepted federal office they were obligated to give full service and were not entitled to additional compensation with increase in the amount of their work: "If the judge was satisfied that he did not receive sufficient pay for his services, he could resign, and there would be no difficulty in filling his place at the same salary."[12]

Ephraim H. Foster, the other Senator from Tennessee and likewise a Whig, replied cogently that if the judge resigned it would indeed be possible to find a successor, with an actual reduction in the salary offered to $1,000 or even to $500. "The question involved was not whether they could, for a certain sum, get a *man*, but whether for such a sum they could get a *judge*. He had had experience enough to know that the lowest priced labor was not always the cheapest."[13] The bill for an increase failed to pass, however, and the salary was left at its existing figure.

Any argument for an increase in the salaries of district judges on the basis of expansion of duties would have been equally valid for the Supreme Court. Yet the figures of $5,000 for the Chief Justice and $4,500 for the Associate Justices remained unchanged from 1819 until 1855, presumably in part because of Democratic opposition to the development of a judicial aristocracy. Abortive efforts were made to eliminate life tenure and to reduce salaries. The *Pennsylvania Reporter*, for example, a newspaper organ of Democrats who had won a victory over the life judiciary in Pennsylvania, promised a battle for the inalienable rights of the people and proclaimed, "The first blow that we strike is against the life judiciary of the United States—the judicial noblemen of America." People selected to enforce and interpret the laws should be "of the people and not above them." Having in mind the recent decision of the Supreme Court in *Bank of Augusta v. Earle*,[14] applying the rule of comity to hold that banking corporations of one state could enter into contracts in other states, the editor denounced the Court for such extensions of power:

---

[12] *Ibid.*, 453.
[13] *Ibid.*, 453. For continuation of

the debate see *ibid.*, 453–54, 468.
[14] 13 Pet. 519 (1839).

The danger in America proceeds from incorporated credit, and paper mints. All lawyers who regard wealth as the great god of their idolatry, are the friends and advocates of these scrip aristocracies. They are fed and nurtured by them. Out of these lawyers, judges are made, or if by chance one is appointed who has not been a pet of these great establishments, as soon as he mounts the bench he is hired into the fold— *by his associates*—by the bought heads of the bar, and by the honied accents of those who control by paper the destinies of the speculators of this western world. Friends thus made, are friends for life—in a judiciary life—and are even friends beyond the grave, for their decisions live after them.[15]

The article was picked up and answered by the pro-Whig and pro-Bank *National Intelligencer* in Washington, which found the attack on the judiciary too serious to be treated with the ridicule and contempt befitting the distempered ravings of Tammany Hall. The article was a declaration of war against the Constitution. Defending the supremacy of the judiciary, the *National Intelligencer* argued that if the representative principle was the foundation of the government, the judiciary was the keystone, the imparing of which would bring down the whole edifice in a mass of crumbling ruins:

> In one word, the *only* security which we have for the sufficiency of the restraints, as well as for the rights recognized by the Constitution, whether as regards States or individuals, is the very feature of the Judiciary against which "the first blow" of successful Locofocoism is to be aimed. Without that guard over all, the reservations to the States and to the People, contained in the Constitution, would be of no more worth than the strip of parchment on which they are engrossed, and our Government would become one vast illimitable and unfathomable Despotism.[16]

The attack on the life-term provision for the federal judiciary was pointed up by a joint resolution introduced in the Senate by Benjamin Tappan of Ohio, proposing an amendment to the Constitution which would reduce the terms of all federal judges to seven years, or to good behavior within that period.[17] Judges sitting at the time of the adoption of the constitutional amendment and who had served for twenty years were to leave the bench at the end of one year. Those who had served for ten years were to leave at the expiration of three years. Senator Tappan's defense of his proposal was not recorded. It was said of Senator Truman Smith of Connecticut, a Whig but evidently an apostate

---

[15] (Harrisburg) *Pennsylvania Reporter*, Mar. 22, 1839.
[16] *Washington Daily National Intelligencer*, Apr. 18, 1839.
[17] S. J. Res. 1, 27th Cong., 3rd Sess. (1842).

in this matter, that he "followed in a speech of much research . . . showing that the independence of the judges in Great Britain was proper against the sovereign power; but only proper here against the executive and legislative power, returning to the people at stated times their legitimate control."[18] The measure failed of adoption in the Senate by a vote of eleven to twenty-four. It was brought up in the ensuing Congress[19] but failed again.

Although no large-scale attempt was made to reduce the salaries of members of the Supreme Court, as distinguished from preventing increases, there was at least a token attempt to that end. William H. Haywood, a Democratic Senator from North Carolina, introduced a bill for the reduction of each of the salaries by one thousand dollars annually.[20] Actually a constitutional amendment would have been necessary to reach the salaries of Justices already sitting. The bill was referred to the Judiciary Committee and no further action was taken on it.

In various ways, and particularly in the filling of vacancies, partisan and factional politics penetrated into the Supreme Court during the Administrations of Presidents Tyler and Polk. With the installation of William Henry Harrison as President and John Tyler as Vice President on March 4, 1841, the Whigs looked forward to a new order in which the titular head of government would be guided by the established leaders of the party—Webster, Clay, and others—and the country would return to prosperity with a new national bank, a program of internal improvements, and other items on the Whig agenda. Their hopes were dashed when Harrison died a month after taking office and the Presidency passed to Tyler of Virginia, a states' rights Whig who had been nominated only to insure more votes for the ticket and whose sympathy with the Whig Party consisted largely in disaffection from Andrew Jackson and his followers. So great was the gap between Tyler and the Whig leadership in general that most of Harrison's Cabinet resigned. Daniel Webster, it is true, remained for a considerable time to perform important duties as Secretary of State.

In helping to reconstitute the President's Cabinet Webster asked Justice McLean if he would accept the position of Secretary of War, assuring him that the Senate would confirm the nomination. As he saw it, McLean was needed both on the Court and in the Cabinet. "You cannot be in both places; but if you are tired out by long journeys, and sick of bills, and answers, and demurrers, no one will be happier than

---

[18] *Cong. Globe*, 27th Cong., 3rd Sess. 162 (1843).

[19] *Cong. Globe*, 28th Cong., 1st Sess. 307 (1844).
[20] *Ibid.*, 431.

myself to meet you in the circle of heads of departments."[21] McLean decided against leaving his secure position on the Supreme Court for the precarious life in the Cabinet of a President who had already been disavowed by his party. Furthermore, McLean as a nationalist and an advocate of a national bank, and as a man opposed to the expansion of slavery interests, was likely to find himself at odds with Tyler. It would be better to remain where he was.

As President Tyler became more and more estranged from the Whigs, he became increasingly friendly with the Democrats, including many who had been ardent Jacksonians. Justice Daniel, a fellow Virginian and directly familiar with partisan and personal strife in his state, was willing to accept such benefits as could be derived from Tyler's jealousy of Henry Clay, as in the President's veto of a bill to charter a national bank, but he remained uneasy about policies based on jealousy rather than principle: "Men with honest and patriotic feelings can accomplish little good without system or cardinal principles; what then can be expected from those who are vacillating or designing when associated with the craft, duplicity, and heterodoxy of such men as Daniel Webster and others of the same school?"[22] Chief Justice Taney, however, was less suspicious, or at any rate he became so before the end of the Tyler Administration. On the occasion of a party given by the Tylers the Chief Justice wrote to Mrs. Taney, "You know the President and I are good friends, and he and Mrs. President received me with great kindness."[23]

Whig leaders, at first hopeful of being able to place members of their own party on the Supreme Court, began to express hopes that no vacancies would occur until Tyler's successor was in office. When in the latter part of 1843 Justice Thompson fell ill, Daniel Lord wrote, "If we could keep him alive for a couple of winters, even if unable to sign his name, we would hold fasts and prayers for it. The change we fear, at his death now, is fearful to us in every prospect. We are sure of one thing, however, that the judge is as resolute in holding on to life as we can be earnest in wishing him to be."[24] Justice Story, who shared the concern of other Whigs, wrote to his son early in 1844 about Chief Justice Taney that "His constitution is exceedingly feeble and broken; but I trust and hope that he will be spared until times assume a better

---

[21] Daniel Webster to John McLean, Sept. 11, 1841, McLean Papers.

[22] P. V. Daniel to Martin Van Buren, Dec. 16, 1841, Van Buren Papers.

[23] Samuel Tyler, *Memoir of Roger Brooke Taney*, 472. For Tyler's words of praise for Chief Justice Taney expressed some years later see Lyon G. Tyler, *Letters and Times of the Tylers*, I, 497–98, note.

[24] Daniel Lord, Jr., to John J. Crittenden, Dec. 16, 1843, Crittenden Papers.

aspect."[25] He continued with a discussion of the bright prospects for the election of Henry Clay to the Presidency.

Chief Justice Taney survived this and many other crises in health, but Justice Thompson did not. Thompson died December 19, 1843, leaving a Supreme Court vacancy for the Second Circuit, which consisted of New York, Connecticut, and Vermont. Then Justice Baldwin died, on April 21, 1844, leaving a vacancy for the Third Circuit, consisting of Pennsylvania and New Jersey. So it was that President Tyler had two Supreme Court positions to fill. In considering men for each of the positions, Tyler seems to have been torn between the desire to aid himself politically and the desire to appoint distinguished lawyers or judges with a record of sound experience. One of his first steps with respect to the position on the Second Circuit seems to have been to investigate the possibility of appointing Martin Van Buren of New York, who was still regarded as the leader of the Democratic Party in spite of his defeat for reelection in 1840 and in spite of serious party factionalism in his own state. If Van Buren could be elevated to the Supreme Court at this time it would remove a rival to Tyler's nomination by the Democratic Party for the ensuing term. According to Senator Silas Wright, a leading New York Democrat, Tyler unofficially sent to him an intermediary, a General Mason from Michigan, to ask about the advisability of nominating Van Buren. Wright's reply was, "Tell Mr. Tyler for me that if he desires to give to this whole country a broader, deeper, heartier laugh than it ever had and at his own expense, he can effect it by making that nomination."[26]

Sensing that his strategy would not work, Tyler abandoned it and instead sent to the Senate the name of John C. Spencer, likewise of New York. Spencer was an able lawyer with scholarly leanings, having edited an edition of Tocqueville's *Democracy in America*. As a Whig, Tyler had appointed him Secretary of War. His acceptance of office under Tyler and his conduct therein had offended Whig leaders, and he drifted with Tyler in the direction of the Democratic Party. In 1843 Tyler shifted him from the position of Secretary of War to that of Secretary of the Treasury. Tyler naturally wished to reward Spencer for his loyalty, but he threatened to become an embarrassment, in that while Tyler was eager to bring about the annexation of Texas, Spencer was opposed.[27] Public attitudes toward Spencer seem to have been further complicated in that in December, 1842, while he was Secretary of War,

---

[25] Joseph Story to W. W. Story, Jan. 30, 1844, Story Papers (M.H.S.).
[26] Silas Wright to Martin Van Buren, Jan. 2, 1844, Van Buren Papers.

[27] See Spencer's letter of Sept. 12, 1847 to the editor of the *Washington National Intelligencer, Niles' National Register*, 73:69, 1847.

his son, a midshipman in the Navy, had been put to death aboard the brig *Somers* for the crime of mutiny. The execution brought attempts at court action against the commanding officer, Captain Alexander S. Mackenzie, with much division in public sentiment over the merits of the case.[28]

Spencer's disloyalty to the Whigs was the principal object of discussion. Solomon Van Rensselaer, a Whig politician in New York, called him "the most finished scoundrel I know."[29] Henry Clay, who had left the Senate to campaign for the presidency, said, "If Spencer be confirmed, he will have run a short career of more profligate conduct and good luck than any man I recollect."[30] Francis Granger, another Whig politician in New York, said that "the removel of faithful Whigs often appointing, yea, re-instating the most violent *locos* and his general course of action at Washington have developed a character that should not be approved, by an appointment to one of the most dignified positions in the world."[31] Willie P. Mangum, Whig Senator from North Carolina and president of the Senate, said of another man that "J. C. Spencer always excepted, I regard him as the meanest of the mean."[32] Charles F. Mayer, a Whig lawyer in Baltimore, was more cautious. He thought the public might say that Spencer's sin was no more flagrant than that of Chief Justice Taney, and that his rejection might reflect upon the Whigs, who had the power in the situation. It might show the Whigs to be more concerned with political matters than with fitness for a judicial position. He added, "It may be a fair inquiry whether a judicial station would not be a proper disposition of Mr. Spencer even if he be politically restless, and might not be the appropriate sedative of the temperament, he may be supposed to have."[33]

Mangum admitted that Spencer was a man of eminent intellectual ability, "inferior to no man in New York," and that he had "the talent and cunning of the Devil himself." But he was relieved at the rejection of his nomination,[34] which was accomplished by a vote of twenty-one

---

[28] See United States v. Mackenzie, 26 Fed. Cas. 1118 (No. 15690) (D.C. S.D. N.Y. 1843); United States v. Mackenzie, 30 Fed. Cas. 1160 (No. 18313) (C.C. S.D. N.Y. 1843); *Niles' National Register*, 64:83–87, 107–11, 1843; William M. Meigs, *The Life of Charles Jared Ingersoll*, 260, note. Justice Story was quoted to the effect that the execution was clearly legal. See Edward L. Pierce, *Memoir and Letters of Charles Sumner*, II, 255.

[29] Solomon Van Rensselaer to J. J. Crittenden, Jan. 20. 1844, Crittenden Papers.

[30] Henry Clay to J. J. Crittenden, Jan. 24, 1844, Crittenden Papers.

[31] Francis Granger to J. J. Crittenden, Feb. 3, 1844, Crittenden Papers.

[32] Willie P. Mangum to Paul C. Cameron, Feb. 10, 1844, *The Papers of Willie Person Mangum*, Henry Thomas Shanks, ed., IV, 41.

[33] Charles F. Mayer to J. McPherson Berrien, Jan. 12, 1844, *ibid.*, 11–12.

[34] Willie P. Mangum to Paul C. Cameron, Feb. 10, 1844, *The Papers of Willie Person Mangum*, Henry Thomas Shanks, ed., IV, 41.

to twenty-six.[35] Gloating over Spencer's defeat, Thurlow Weed proposed publication in the *National Intelligencer* and throughout New York of a letter of the Whig members of the New York legislature offering congratulations to the Whigs in the Senate on their action. Spencer had boasted that the Senators from New York had been for him; Weed wanted it known that "The Whig members of the legislature and the Whig press throughout the state, are with the Senate and against Mr. Spencer."[36]

There was something highly erratic about President Tyler's attempts to fill the Supreme Court vacancy on the Second Circuit. Van Buren was the leading man in the Democratic Party. Spencer had in effect followed Tyler out of the Whig Party. Both resided in the judicial circuit to be served. But after the rejection of Spencer's nomination, if in general we may believe an account written long afterward which contains at least one serious and obvious error, Tyler offered the position first to John Sergeant and then to Horace Binney, both of them dyed-in-the-wool Whigs and political enemies of Tyler, and both of them residents of Philadelphia, in the Third Circuit. The story was told long afterward in a memoir of Tyler written by his friend Henry A. Wise and published in 1872 under the title *Seven Decades of Union*.

The occasion of the offers to Sergeant and Binney was that of the argument before the Supreme Court of the famous *Girard Will Case*.[37] Stephen Girard had left to the city of Philadelphia a large sum of money to found a school for "poor white male orphans." Girard prescribed in detail the kind of school he wanted maintained, and expressed the desire that "by every proper means a pure attachment to our republican institutions, and to the sacred rights of conscience, as guaranteed by our happy constitutions, shall be formed and fostered in the minds of the scholars."[38] But while he also desired that the school should instill the

---

[35] *Niles' National Register*, 65:388, 1844. As indicative of the political considerations involved in dealing with Tyler's appointments, John J. Crittenden had written as follows on Jan. 28, 1844, to Governor R. P. Letcher of Kentucky: "Tyler, there is no doubt, is now chiefly hostile to the Van Burenites, and may probably give the Whigs a preference over them during the balance of his administration, but there is no anticipating his vascillations or where he will settle down. *We* will certainly do nothing to repel his preference; *we* will even do what we can to cherish him in any return-

ing sense of kindness to the Whigs; but we intend also to hold on our course firmly and act our part in such a manner as to be satisfied with ourselves in any event that may happen. I think [James M.] Porter will be rejected as Secretary of War, and Spencer, as Judge of the Supreme Court. *The Life of John J. Crittenden*, Mrs. Chapman Coleman, ed., I,. 216.

[36] Thurlow Weed to Willie P. Mangum, Feb. 15, 1844, *Papers of Willie P. Mangum*, IV, 48.

[37] Vidal v. Philadelphia, 2 How. 127 (1844).

[38] *Ibid.*, 132.

purest principles of morality, he introduced the extraordinary requirement "that no ecclesiastic, missionary, or minister of any sect whatsoever, shall ever hold or exercise any station or duty whatever in the
said college; nor shall any such person ever be admitted for any purpose,
or as a visitor, within the premises appropriated to the purposes of the
said college."[39] He made this restriction, he said, not to cast reflection
upon any sect or person, but because he wanted the children protected
against the excitement of clashing doctrines and sectarian controversies.

This making of a huge and highly publicized charitable bequest
in the nature of a public affront to organized religion was taken by the
warring sects as a red flag waved at all of them. Such sects, of course,
had no economic interest to make them parties to a suit to challenge
the validity of the will, but the interest was provided by relatives of
Girard who hoped to break the will and get the money for themselves.
The case was decided against them in the United States Circuit Court
in Philadelphia, and was appealed to the Supreme Court. There Daniel
Webster and Walter Jones represented Girard's relatives and Sergeant
and Binney represented the executors under the will. The case, involving
deep investigation into the law of charitable trusts in England and the
United States, and treated with an overlay of religious sentiment, was
argued for ten days. According to newspaper and other reports as compiled by Charles Warren,[40] people came to the courtroom in droves
to enjoy the forensic display, and hundreds had to be turned away. It
was said that more than two hundred women were present, crowding
in even behind the judges. Among the spectators, "with a cluster of
handsome girls," were the two sons of President Tyler.

Webster and Jones attempted to show the illegality of the trust,
and Webster, perhaps sensing the weakness of his case on technically
legal grounds, emphasized the necessarily Christian ingredients of charitable trusts. Here the sick were denied the comforts of their religion
and children were to be reared in the pattern of the infidel. While tears
poured from the eyes of sentimental observers, hardened reporters
smirked about "the Gospel according to Webster." The sharp-tongued
John Quincy Adams went into the courtroom "to see what had become
of Stephen Girard's will, and the scramble of lawyers and collaterals
for fragments of his colossal and misshapen endowment of an infidel
charity-school for orphan boys." He had heard reports that if Webster
won he was to have "fifty thousand dollars for his share of the plunder."[41]

As for the other side, Justice Story wrote to his wife that Binney
had made "a most masterly argument." From his later opinion for a

[39] Ibid., 133.
[40] Charles Warren, The Supreme
Court in United States History, II,
124–33.
[41] Memoirs of John Quincy Adams,
Charles F. Adams, ed., XI, 510.

unanimous Court finding the will valid we know that he found Binney and Sergeant's position the more persuasive. Binney and Sergeant insisted that exclusion was necessary because of the difficulty of keeping ministers from being controversialists and teaching the doctrines of their divisive sects. "I was not a little amused," Story wrote, "with the manner in which, on each side, the language of the Scriptures, and the doctrines of Christianity, were brought in to point the argument; and to hear the Court engaged in hearing homilies of faith, and expositions of Christianity, with almost the formality of lectures from the pulpit."[42] In the opinion of the Court he found that the exclusion of ecclesiastics was not tantamount to an attack on the Christian religion and that the will was not thereby invalidated.[43]

Since the case caused great excitement in Washington, particularly the argument of Webster, who had recently resigned as Secretary of State and was thought now to be making a bid for the Whig nomination for the Presidency, it is plausible that at this time Tyler conceived the idea of appointing one of the opposing lawyers to the Supreme Court, Whig and political enemy though he might be, and from another circuit than that of the vacancy. So it was that Tyler sent Henry A. Wise to Sergeant's hotel to ask him to accept the position. Sergeant declined, confidentially giving the reason that being past sixty years of age he ought not to accept, and that he regarded Binney, more robust than himself, as the more acceptable candidate. The position was then offered to Binney, who declined in the same fashion and proposed the appointment of Sergeant, neither of the two ever being informed that the other had been approached.[44]

---

[42] *The Life and Letters of Joseph Story*, 468.

[43] For involvement of the Supreme Court and certain District Courts and certain judges individually in the controversy over the division of property between the northern and southern branches of the Methodist Church, which had divided on slavery issues, see Smith v. Swormstedt, 16 How. 288 (1854), Smith v. Swormstedt, 22 Fed. Cas. 663 (No. 13112) (C.C.D. Ohio 1852). For the part in the controversy played by Justice McLean, see Francis P. Weisenburger, *The Life of John McLean*, 175–80. See also John N. Norwood, *The Schism in the Methodist Church, 1844; a Study of Slavery and Ecclesiastical Politics*. Although the Supreme Court decision turned on interpretation of the plan of separation and distribution of

church property, and on the power of a governing organization to make the arrangement, counsel before the Court discussed at length the agitation of the slavery question in the church which had led to the separation. As to this material the Reporter noted, "The argument upon this branch of the subject is omitted." 16 How. 298.

[44] Henry A. Wise, *Seven Decades of the Union*, 219. The element of doubt about the story of the attempted appointment of one or the other of these two men lies in the fact that Wise wrote about it in connection with the filling of Justice Baldwin's place, whereas at the time specified Justice Baldwin was still living. On the other hand, if the offers were made in connection with the vacancy created by the death of Justice Baldwin the following April, they could

Whatever the truth of this story, President Tyler turned back to New York in his search for a replacement for Justice Thompson. On the basis of many recommendations he sent to the Senate the name of Reuben H. Walworth, chancellor of that state. Thurlow Weed of New York wrote to John J. Crittenden, a Whig member of the Senate from Kentucky, that Walworth had been recommended because of a desire to get rid of a "querulous, disagreeable, unpopular chancellor." If the nomination were confirmed, New York would get a Loco Foco chancellor, while if it were left unacted upon, the nation would get from another source a better judge and New York a better chancellor as soon as Walworth reached the retirement age.[45]

While the Walworth nomination was pending, Justice Baldwin died, leaving the Third Circuit vacant. "He had generous impulses," wrote Justice Story of the man with whom he and most of his brethren had had difficulties over the years, "but his mind was unhappily organized for the exercise of the social virtues, in a continued intercourse; and he had other faults, but these should be forgotten in the reflection that he has gone to his final account. We shall miss him on the bench." Story thought that either Binney or Sergeant should be appointed to the vacancy. He wanted to see the Bench elevated from its present depressed state.[46] "How nobly it might be filled!" he wrote to Chancellor Kent. "But we are doomed to disappointment." As for the vacancy on the Second Circuit, he wished he might have either William Kent, Chancellor Kent's son, or Daniel Lord, as his new colleague. He had thought them the only candidates whom as to age, character, and professional qualifications a President ought to select for office. "But what can we hope from such a head of an administration as we now have but a total disregard of all elevated principles and objects. I dare not trust my pen to speak of him as I think. Do you know (for so I was informed at Washington) that Tyler said he would never appoint a Judge 'of the school of Kent'?"[47]

President Tyler first offered the position on the Third Circuit to James Buchanan, then a prominent Democratic Senator from Pennsylvania. Justice McLean said of Buchanan that he was an able man and

---

have had no direct connection with the argument of the *Girard Will Case*, as Wise contended. See Charles C. Binney, *The Life of Horace Binney*, 229–32, for further expression of doubt as to the authenticity of the story. Charles Warren, however, finds that the account "seems in the main to be accurate." Warren, *The Supreme Court in United States History*, II, 113.

[45] Thurlow Weed to J. J. Crittenden, Mar. 17, 1844, Crittenden Papers.

[46] Joseph Story to Richard Peters, May 15, 1844, Peters Correspondence, II, Cadwalader Papers.

[47] "Joseph Story to James Kent, Apr. 25, 1844," *Proceedings of Massachusetts Historical Society* (2d), 14: 424, 1901.

would make an able judge: "Take him from politics, and his ambition and pride are sufficient guaranties that his course will be elevated and just."[48] Buchanan declined, for reasons not disclosed.[49] Tyler then sent to the Senate the name of Edward King, a Democrat who was judge of the Court of Common Pleas in Philadelphia.[50] This nomination Justice Story regarded as one of an extraordinary series of exhibitions on the part of President Tyler. He knew nothing of Judge King except his name: "But I do know Binney, Sergeant, J. R. Ingersoll, Chauncey, and many others, the lights and ornaments of the law."[51] With support lacking both from Whig Senators and from Democrats who wished to see the office filled by their nominee, Polk, the nomination waited in vain for confirmation.[52]

Toward the end of the session, noting that the Senate had laid on the table the nomination of Walworth for the position on the Second Circuit, Tyler withdrew it and submitted again the name of John C. Spencer (who meanwhile had resigned as Secretary of the Treasury), saying, "The circumstances under which the Senate heretofore declined to advise and consent to the nomination of John C. Spencer have so far changed as to justify me in my again submitting his name to their consideration."[53] It was reported that action on the nomination on the last day of the session required unanimous consent and that unanimity could not be achieved. Tyler therefore withdrew Spencer's name and reinstated that of Walworth.[54]

When Congress reassembled in December, 1844, the Presidential race had been run between Henry Clay and James K. Polk, and Clay had gone down to defeat. The lame-duck President who was more Democrat than Whig but who had been rejected by both parties, and the lame-duck Senate, now with a Whig majority but about to be replaced by a Democratic one, still had rights and duties with respect to the Supreme Court vacancies. The political picture had greatly changed

---

[48] John McLean to Richard Peters, Dec. 8, 1844, Peters Correspondence, II, Cadwalader Papers.

[49] Warren, *The Supreme Court in United States History*, II, 116.

[50] See Richard Rush to William Allen, June 4, 1844, and Henry Horn to William Allen, Nov. 29, 1844, Allen Papers.

[51] Joseph Story to Richard Peters, July 6, 1844, Peters Correspondence, II, Cadwalader Papers.

[52] After the Polk election Justice Story wrote to Richard Peters, "You speak of the nomination of Judge King. I have little doubt that there are many movements from *certain* quarters against him. The friends of Mr. Polk are desirous to give him the appointment, and I have very little doubt, that the gentlemen, whom you name, are active in that direction. Mr. Buchanan, from all I can hear, now desires the appointment, and will eagerly embrace it." Joseph Story to Richard Peters, Dec. 25, 1844, *ibid.*

[53] J. D. Richardson, *A Compilation of the Messages and Papers of the Presidents*, IV, 328.

[54] *Washington National Intelligencer*, June 18, 1844.

but there had been no restoration of good will. Politicians in both parties reassessed the situation in the light of future prospects. For a time President Tyler continued to support King and Walworth for the two positions.[55] With respect to King, Richard Peters, a Whig from Philadelphia and until recently Reporter of the Supreme Court, wrote to Justice McLean of his hope that the nomination would be confirmed. Had Clay been elected to the Presidency he would have felt differently about it, but if King were rejected the next nominee would be John M. Read, "as suited for a Judge as I am for an admiral."[56]

The Senate refused to act on King's nomination, and in February, 1845, Tyler withdrew his name and presented that of Read, a Democrat and a friend of Buchanan who had formerly been a United States Attorney for the Eastern District of Pennsylvania. On this nomination, too, the Senate failed to act, and the vacancy was left to be filled by Tyler's successor.

With respect to the vacancy on the Second Circuit, President Tyler was at last more fortunate. He withdrew the name of Chancellor Walworth and presented that of Samuel Nelson, chief justice of the Supreme Court of New York. Nelson, born in 1792, was a Democrat of Scotch-Irish heritage. Planning initially to go into the ministry, he was graduated from Middlebury College, supported, it is said, by funds raised by his father through the sale of a Negro girl.[57] His interests shifted from the ministry to law. He studied in the office of Savage and Woods in Salem, moved to Madison County with Judge Woods, was admitted to the bar in 1817, and began his independent practice in Cortlandt, New York. He entered politics, served as a postmaster for three years, and in 1823 was appointed judge of the Sixth Circuit in New York. He held that position until 1831 when he was appointed an associate justice of the Supreme Court of New York. He was promoted to the chief justiceship in 1837.

Judge Nelson was brought to widespread public attention early in

---

[55] On Jan. 24, 1845, Senator John M. Niles reported that "The two nominations for the Supreme Court have been reported to the Senate with the recommendation that they lie on the table *for the present.* I think we can lay them on the table, or not take them up until the fourth of March if we desire it, and probably shall." John M. Niles to Gideon Welles, Jan. 24, 1845, Welles Papers.

[56] Warren, *The Supreme Court in*

United States History, II, 118. Justice McLean replied to Peters that he should have no fears about the appointment of Read. The Whigs and many Democrats would go against him. John McLean to Richard Peters, Dec. 8, 1844, Peters Correspondence, II, Cadwalader Papers.

[57] John Bigelow, Diary, May 10, 1851, manuscript, p. 222, New York Public Library.

1845 when a Democratic group in the legislature tried but failed to bring about his election to the United States Senate. President Tyler submitted Nelson's name to the Senate early in February, 1845, and the nomination was confirmed after a lapse of only ten days. The new Justice took the oath of office before Judge Samuel R. Betts in the United States District Court in New York City, and hurried to Washington to take his seat on the Supreme Court just as the term was ending, and presumably to attend the inauguration of the incoming President.[58] Then he returned to his circuit to catch up on work accumulated since the death of Justice Thompson two years earlier.

In the courts of New York and as a Supreme Court Justice, Nelson was generally known as a stable, sound, and unspectacular judge. The *American Law Journal* said of him, "His learning, his high judicial integrity, and the masculine energy of his mind, will be held in perpetual remembrance."[59] He was not a man of deeply philosophical bent or soaring imagination. His meticulous opinions as chief justice in New York tell little of what might be expected of him as a federal judge. An unwillingness to stretch the law to make it conform to local moral sentiments is suggested by his opinion for the court in a two-to-one division holding not indictable the leasing of property for use as a house of prostitution.[60] Yet he showed a capacity for indignation in a divorce case involving a man's abuse and neglect of his wife.[61] Sensitivity to issues of public policy was shown by his dissenting opinion in a case in which the majority of the court held that a New York statute violated due process and a just compensation clause in providing for the laying out of private roads without the consent of the landowner. Said Judge Nelson, "Works of this nature are indispensable to the prosperity of the country."[62] In the Supreme Court and on circuit he was preoccupied with matters of international relations, extradition, prize law, admiralty, and many common law questions, but he never became a leading spokesman in the field of constitutional law.

The campaign of 1844 brought sorrow and distress to the Whigs and joy to the Democrats, who in James K. Polk succeeded in electing a bona fide member of their own party. In the midst of a rough-and-tumble campaign involving issues of corruption and of the rights of foreigners and Catholics, Justice Story wrote to Justice McLean of his despair of republican government: "My heart sickens at the proflig-

---

[58] *Washington National Intelligencer.* Feb. 18, Mar. 4, 1845.
[59] *Am. L.J.*, 8:335, 1849.
[60] Brockway v. The People, 2 Hill (N.Y.) 558 (1842).

[61] Burr v. Burr, 7 Hill (N.Y.) 207 (1843).
[62] Taylor v. Porter, 4 Hill (N.Y.) 140, 149 (1843).

acy of public men, the low state of public morals, and the utter indifference of the people to all elevated virtue and even self respect. . . . Is not the theory of our government a whole failure?"[63] He was bitterly disappointed at the failure to elect Clay, for he had hoped to give Clay the opportunity to appoint his successor. Now he would have to decide whether to resign during Polk's Administration or wait for the more distant future. He now expected to do the former.[64]

Justice Story wrote in similar fashion to Clay himself, who forwarded the letter to John J. Crittenden with the remark that he was not surprised at Story's disgust with his service on the bench of the Supreme Court: "Among the causes of regret, on account of our recent defeat, scarcely any is greater than that which arises out of the consequences that the Whigs cannot fill the two vacancies in the Supreme Court."[65]

Chief Justice Taney, on the other hand, was elated, and sent warm congratulations to Polk. He had never before seen a combination of such dangerous influences as those united in support of Clay. Polk's triumph had given him increased confidence in the intelligence, firmness, and virtue of the American people and in the stability of our institutions.[66] The Chief Justice wrote to Jackson that the spirit of 1828 and 1832 had been abroad in the election: "You will imagine what pleasure I shall feel in administering the oath of office to the 'Young Hickory' as he has been called. It will remind me of the proud day when in your presence, and that of thousands of friends I administered it to Mr. Van Buren."[67]

On New Year's Day, 1845, Taney joined the throng at the President's mansion who went to give the season's greetings to the Tylers and to one another. He went back to his room and wrote to ex-President Jackson about his pleasure in visiting where he used to see Jackson and where soon again he would see one of his most firm and faithful friends: "You know that since I have been on the Bench I have abstained from taking part in political movements; but the sincere regard I entertain for Mr. Polk and the trying times through which he and I passed together, made it more difficult for me to remain quiet when he and Mr. Clay were the opposing candidates. And now that Mr. Polk has been so triumphantly elected, I feel the more anxious for the suc-

---

[63] Joseph Story to John McLean, Aug. 16, 1844, McLean Papers.

[64] Joseph Story to Ezekiel Bacon, Apr. 12, 1845, *Life and Letters of Joseph Story*, II, 527.

[65] Henry Clay to John J. Crittenden, Jan. 7, 1845, *Life of John J. Critten-*den, Mrs. Chapman Coleman, ed., I, 225.

[66] Roger B. Taney to James K. Polk, Nov. 20, 1844, Polk Papers.

[67] Roger B. Taney to Andrew Jackson, Nov. 20, 1844, Jackson Papers.

cess of his administration, because I see the difficulties which will beset him the moment he enters upon the duties of the high office to which he has been chosen."[68]

Taney and other members of the Supreme Court advised Polk on appointments and other matters, the Chief Justice going so far as to seek the appointment of his son-in-law, J. Mason Campbell, as United States Attorney for Maryland. He made the uncomfortable discovery that judges, largely divorced from politics, had little influence in the distribution of the spoils of office.[69] The member of the Court who definitely had not withdrawn from politics and who was most in contact with Polk was Justice Catron. Polk and Catron had seen a great deal of each other since the 1820s when they had married members of the prominent Childress family and when Polk was a member of the Tennessee legislature and Catron a member of the state supreme court. When in the 1830s part of the Jackson following in Tennessee deserted him and supported a local candidate for the Presidency in place of Van Buren, who was Jackson's candidate, Catron and Polk remained stalwart Jackson men. By 1836 Polk was Speaker of the House of Representatives, and Catron, having lost out on the state supreme court by virtue of the political enemies he had made, was helping edit a Jackson paper in Nashville and probably waiting for a federal Supreme Court appointment when additional circuits were created in the West. The two men engaged in voluminous correspondence about political matters, and the correspondence continued after Catron became a member of the Court. Both were opposed to a monopoly national bank and to a high protective tariff, and both favored the annexation of Texas, a step which Tyler was unable to bring about.

In the summer of 1844 the Polks were to stay with the Catrons at their home in Nashville and receive political friends there. Catron promised to engineer private interviews as well as the meeting of groups: "I'll make it work like the old clock, and with less noise." As for embarrassment because of his judicial position, "Don't believe that I have any squeamishness on the Judgeship score." One of his brethren, he explained, with obvious reference to Justice McLean, "is openly seeking the Presidency—and founds himself on this ground as a Judge,

---

[68] Roger B. Taney to Andrew Jackson, Jan. 1, 1845, *Correspondence of Andrew Jackson*, John S. Bassett, ed., VI, 354. Taney saw one of Polk's most immediate responsibilities as that of getting rid of John C. Calhoun, who was Secretary of State in Tyler's Cabinet and who, it was feared, would want to continue in office: "You always said that with all his talents, he had no judgment, and I am every day more and more convinced of the correctness of your opinion."

[69] See Carl B. Swisher, *Roger B. Taney*, 438–40.

and is praised for his patriotism." Other judges played a prominent part in politics. Thus entertaining friends for Polk would not be taken amiss.[70]

Catron continued in close communication with Polk through the election and made arrangements for his living quarters in Washington on arrival. Through the Polk Administration Catron kept in close touch with the President when in Washington and corresponded with him when on circuit, keeping him posted on political developments. He attended parties and receptions, occasionally went to church with him, and he and Mrs. Catron visited at the President's mansion with complete informality. Mrs. Catron and Mrs. Polk, as two beautiful and accomplished women unburdened with children, married to important men, and themselves skilled in the art of politics, were the talk of the social set in Washington. For all their friendship they may have been in some degree social rivals. On his arrival in Washington, Vice President George M. Dallas of Philadelphia wrote to his wife that Mrs. Polk made a most favorable impression when she received company, although her dress was too showy for his taste—"silk, with broad stripes of brown figured with white." He added that "She certainly eclipsed Mrs. Catron very far."[71] On a later occasion he wrote, "The lovely Mrs. Judge Catron is here; and at the drawing room on Tuesday last, had very much the aspect of a vinegar cruet."[72] But if perchance there was a bit of feminine rivalry, the families remained good friends. Within a few days of the close of his Administration Polk wrote in his diary, "After night Judge and Mrs. Catron called. A heavy storm came on. My coachman was absent, and it being Sunday night no hack or carriage could be procured, and Mrs. Catron remained with us all night. Judge Catron returned to his lodgings."[73]

After Polk's election, Richard Peters wrote to Justice McLean of his growing apprehension about the Supreme Court: "May heaven in its tenderest mercy preserve the life of our good Chief Justice. Catron will succeed him, if he should, while Polk is President, be called to a better world."[74] Chief Justice Taney did not make way for Catron as his successor, but at the beginning of the Polk Administration the position on the Third Circuit remained to be filled, and the First Circuit also was to become vacant, giving Polk two appointments to the Supreme Court. Polk had almost as much trouble filling the Third Circuit vacancy

---

[70] John Catron to James K. Polk, July 23, 1844, Polk Papers.

[71] George M. Dallas to Mrs. Dallas, Feb. 16, 1845, "The Library: The Mystery of the Dallas Papers," *Pennsylvania Magazine of History and Biography*, 73:349–61, 1949.

[72] *Ibid.*, Dec. 10, 1848, 483.

[73] *The Diary of James K. Polk*, Milo M. Quaife, ed., I, 351–52. (1910).

[74] Richard Peters to John McLean, Dec. 6, 1844, Warren, *The Supreme Court in United States History*, II, 117.

as did Tyler, though he moved with great leisure in the matter instead of with the precipitateness of his predecessor. For many weeks he took no steps at all, giving his attention to political appointments, to the tariff question, the question of the annexation of Texas and other problems, while records were built up for candidates for the judicial position. The competition for the position and the variety of considerations advanced make the story one of exceptional interest in the history of the Court.

Upon the President were urged the qualifications of candidates from both eastern and western Pennsylvania, and also from New Jersey, which, it was emphasized, had had no Supreme Court representation since the death of Justice William Paterson some forty years earlier. New Jersey sponsors stressed the fact that whereas Pennsylvanians were dividing their advocacy among many people, New Jersey was advancing only one, Peter D. Vroom of Trenton, who had been governor and chancellor and a member of Congress from that state. Vroom's claims were urged with particular vigor by Senator Garrett D. Wall, his father-in-law.[75] The matter was in no sense a family affair, however, support being given by the Democratic State Committee for New Jersey,[76] by the members of the Supreme Court of New Jersey,[77] and by many others. The judges emphasized the fitness of the candidate for the position, while the politicians emphasized the rights of the state to a share in political appointments. Yet Vroom also had his critics in New Jersey. Polk was told that he lacked political courage, and that while Vroom was the first choice of the people of the state, their second choice would be John M. Read of Philadelphia,[78] whom President Tyler had nominated without avail.

Read had support from Philadelphia and he had backing from James Buchanan, Polk's Secretary of State, who was well entrenched in Pennsylvania politics. Wilson McCandless of Pittsburgh, however, whom many years later President Buchanan was to appoint to a district judgeship, reminded Polk that politically Read had no influence in or out of Philadelphia, "and I have yet to learn of any extraordinary services rendered by him in 1840 or '44."[79] McCandless was himself a supporter of Robert C. Grier, then a local judge in the Pittsburgh area.

In the meantime, on September 29, 1845, Buchanan went to Polk with an involved story of a false rumor that he himself was seeking the Supreme Court appointment. He had long preferred such a position

---

[75] See Garrett D. Wall to James K. Polk, Aug. 17, 1845, Dec. 2, 1845, June 29, 1846, Appointment Papers, State Department Files.

[76] J. C. Volts, *et al.* to James K. Polk, Mar. 8, 1845, *ibid.*

[77] See Joseph C. Hornblower, *et al.*, Nov. 15, 1844, O. S. Halsted *et al.*, Jan. 24, 1846, *ibid.*

[78] John R. Thomson to James J. Polk, Nov. 25, 1845, *ibid.*

[79] Wilson McCandless to James K. Polk, Dec. 10, 1845, *ibid.*

to any other in the government, but it had not been offered in such circumstances that he could accept. He feared, however, that he would not be able to control the Pennsylvania delegation in Congress and insure support of Polk's tariff program. His position in the Cabinet might therefore be an embarrassment to the President, and a Supreme Court appointment might provide relief from that embarrassment. Polk, telling the story in his diary, noted, "It was manifest from the whole tenour of the conversation that Mr. Buchanan was very desirous to go on the Bench, though he expressed entire satisfaction with the President and with the course of his administration."[80] On November 19, Buchanan told Polk he had decided not to ask for the Supreme Court appointment, though he still preferred such a position to any other in the government and would rather be Chief Justice than President.[81] It seems obvious that though he was looking toward the Presidency at that time, he was also conscious of the possibility that the Chief Justice, always in poor health, might vacate the highest judicial office.

On December 23, without consulting Buchanan, Polk sent to the Senate the name of George W. Woodward of Wilkes Barre, Pennsylvania. He did so on the advice of Vice President Dallas, who was himself from Philadelphia, and of David Wilmot and other Pennsylvania Representatives in Congress. He wrote in his diary that he had great confidence that Woodward was "a sound, original, and consistent democrat, of the strict construction school, that he was a man of fine talents and well qualified."[82] He had not felt that he could yield to Buchanan's plea and appoint Read, who had been a Federalist and whose constitutional doctrines he distrusted: "I have never known an instance of a Federalist who had after arriving at the age of 30 professed to change his opinions, who was to be relied on in his constitutional opinions. All of them who have been appointed to the Supreme Court Bench, after having secured a place for life became very soon broadly Federal and latitudinarian in all their decisions involving questions of Constitutional power."[83]

Buchanan heard the news and went to the President's mansion seeming to be "in a pet," and then left before the President could see him. Polk sensed the reason and noted that he could not appoint Read, and that Woodward was appointed for the reasons given and "because the friends of other candidates had gotten into an excited state between each other. Mr. Woodward did not apply for the office, but was warmly recommended by Mr. Dallas and the other Gentlemen I have named above."[84] When Buchanan did see Polk he complained that the nom-

---

[80] *Diary of James K. Polk*, I, 47.
[81] *Ibid.*, 97–98.
[82] *Ibid.*, 138.
[83] *Ibid.*, 136.
[84] *Ibid.*, 139.

ination had been made without informing him. Polk replied that he was responsible for his own appointments, that Buchanan could have had the position had he wanted it, that he knew of Buchanan's desire for the appointment of Read, and that he was determined to do otherwise. He therefore thought Buchanan had nothing to complain about.[85]

But it was one thing to nominate and another to get confirmation. Woodward was politically vulnerable, on grounds of which Polk had been informed before the nomination was made. He had started on a promising career as a country lawyer and as a Democrat. But in the Pennsylvania constitutional convention of 1837–1838 he had antagonized the immigrant population of Pennsylvania by proposing broad disfranchisement of foreigners, and giving impetus to the American or "Know-Nothing" Party movement which had defeated loyal Democrats in ensuing elections. He had been appointed to a minor judicial position by Governor Porter, "that corrupt bad man." One of the leading judges in the state told Polk's informer that "it would shock the bar, the bench and the public, to learn that a judge of an inferior court in the woods without any evidence of great legal condition, had been translated to the Supreme Court of the United States."[86]

Polk, indeed, had had a forerunner of trouble over Woodward at the beginning of his Administration. Buchanan's resignation to become Secretary of State had left a vacancy in Pennsylvania's representation in the Senate. The Democrats held control of the Pennsylvania legislature by a narrow margin. Woodward was the nominee of the party. But Simon Cameron, who was long to be a powerful, turbulent, and untrustworthy figure in Pennsylvania politics, bolted the party and with the aid of Whig votes brought about his own election to the Senate. According to the perhaps superficial interpretation of James G. Blaine, "The President endeavored to heal Judge Woodward's wounds by placing him on the bench of the Supreme Court as the successor of the eminent Henry Baldwin."[87]

But Woodward's troubles were not to be blamed solely upon Cameron. Judge James Campbell of the court of common pleas in Philadelphia, who as a Catholic was sensitive to antiforeign attitudes, wrote to Polk that Woodward's course in the Pennsylvania constitutional convention would never be forgotten. Many influential Democrats believed that if Woodward had been elected to the Senate the state would have been lost to the party at the next election. As for nominating Woodward to the Supreme Court, "It would place the whole body of

---

[85] *Ibid.*, 143–46.
[86] Benjamin H. Brewster to James K. Polk, Dec. 15, 1845, Appointment Papers, State Department Files.
[87] James G. Blaine, *Twenty Years of Congress*, I, 196.

naturalized citizens, Germans and Irish, in a most hostile array against the Administration. I need not say to you how strong the feeling is at this time against all holding native doctrines."[88]

Being vulnerable on political grounds and having an enemy in Senator Cameron, Woodward was in a dangerous position. Polk was evidently surprised, however, when, on January 22, 1846, six Democrats, including Cameron, joined the Whigs to reject the nomination. Since some of the six were close to Buchanan, Polk suspected him of interference, and was sure that at the very least Buchanan had determined the course of events by not actively using his influence in support of the nomination.[89] The nature of relations between Buchanan and Woodward is not clear. Woodward was quoted as having made comments about Buchanan's going on the Bench which were unpleasant enough that Woodward denounced them as a "malicious fabrication." He had expressed the belief to Buchanan that the position was there for him to take himself or to dispose of as he saw fit. He thought that Pennsylvania would be sorry to lose Buchanan from the Cabinet, and recommended for the Supreme Court position Judge Joel Jones of the District Court of Philadelphia.[90] If in fact Buchanan was responsible for the defeat of the nomination it may have been because of suspected enmity on the part of Woodward, or a desire to keep the position available for himself, or to have the disposition of it in his own hands.

In any event, after Woodward's rejection, Buchanan inquired through an intermediary whether the position was still available to him. Polk replied that he desired that Buchanan continue with his duties as Secretary of State and that he could give no intimation as to whom he might appoint to the Supreme Court.[91] Buchanan was kept confused by the silence of the President and by the conflicting counsels of his friends, some of whom urged him to go on the Court where he could be a leader and others of whom implied that it would be near treason to the people who had put him in office if he left the domain of politics.[92]

Evidently not worrying at all about the vacancy on the Supreme Court or the accumulation of Circuit Court business in the Third Circuit, Polk kept quiet on the subject from January, 1846, until June. Then he called in Buchanan to talk about the vacancy on the United States District Court at Philadelphia occasioned by the death of Judge

---

[88] James Campbell to James K. Polk, Dec. 15, 1845, Appointment Papers, State Department Files.

[89] Diary of James K. Polk, I, 186–90, 194–97.

[90] George W. Woodward to James Buchanan, Oct. 30, 1845, Buchanan Papers.

[91] Diary of James K. Polk, I, 196. For related items see pp. 197, 200–03, 210–12, 216–18, 234–36.

[92] Such letters are scattered through the Buchanan papers for the period.

Archibald Randall. Buchanan, having learned the lesson of proper subordination, professed to have no candidate. Polk then announced his intention of nominating John K. Kane. Buchanan said Kane would make a respectable judge and he would not object, although Kane would not be his choice. The subject led to that of the Supreme Court vacancy, and Polk said he would appoint Buchanan after the Oregon question had been settled, if Buchanan so desired. The promise restored good relations between the two men.[93] Buchanan left to think the matter over.

From the way in which the subject was bandied back and forth it is hard to tell whether Polk wanted Buchanan to take the Court position or whether he wanted him to reject it and continue to exercise his very considerable political power in behalf of the Administration. When Buchanan indicated his willingness to accept if appointed immediately, Polk found him indispensable in the Cabinet for a longer period.[94] When eventually, on August 1, 1846, Buchanan announced that after all he preferred to remain in the Cabinet, Polk replied that in that event he would submit to the Senate the name of Robert C. Grier—which he may have been intending to do for quite some time.

Robert C. Grier was born in Cumberland County, Pennsylvania, on March 5, 1794, the son of a Presbyterian minister. He received a fine classical education from his father and from Dickinson College, where he graduated in 1812. He taught at Dickinson and then at Northumberland Academy, studied law in his spare time, and was admitted to the bar in 1817. In 1833, he was appointed president judge of the District Court of Allegheny County, in the vicinity of Pittsburgh. He was active in politics prior to his judicial appointment, apparently at first with Federalist leanings but then drifting toward the Democrats. In this respect, as President Polk admitted, he was subject to the same criticism as John M. Read, though to a lesser degree.[95]

Grier was an active participant in the work of the Presbyterian Church, but he was something of a rough character nevertheless. It was said of him:

> He was a man of quick perceptions, decided convictions, and positive opinions, and like all men of that cast, inclined to be arbitrary and dictatorial. In the trial of a cause, when he believed injustice was attempted, he was most emphatic in his charge, not unfrequently arguing the cause to the jury as an advocate. His contempt for hypocrisy and cant, his love of the right and hatred of the wrong, with his

---

[93] *Diary of James K. Polk*, I, 463–65.

[94] See *ibid.*, II, 1–2, 4–6.
[95] *Ibid.*, I, 138.

stern, decided character, made him sometimes appear on the District bench despotic. But he was seldom wrong in his convictions or opinions.[96]

Elsewhere he was described:

Judge Grier is a man of large proportions; upwards of six feet high; apparently of great muscular power, and iron constitution, and somewhat corpulent; of sanguine temperament; ruddy complexion, and a most agreeable and good-natured face. Notwithstanding an occasional roughness of manner, and harshness of voice, no one can fail to perceive that this is the result of the situations into which, in early life, he was thrown, rather than of any want of gentleness and kindness of nature. If he happens to give the slightest offence, he atones for it so soon, and so willingly, that he secures a friend, where some men would make an enemy.[97]

At least as early as the beginning of the Polk Administration, and perhaps even earlier for a period of which records are not available, judges and practitioners at the bar in and around Pittsburgh collaborated in urging the appointment of Judge Grier to the Supreme Court. Prominent among them was Judge Benjamin Patton, of the Court of Common Pleas of Pittsburgh, who knew Grier intimately and had also known Polk since the early 1830s when he had spent some time in Nashville. Patton had worked with Grier in support of Andrew Jackson for the Presidency, and he knew of Grier's indirect aid to the party after he had gone on the Bench. Another leader was Charles Shaler, who for a time had been a colleague of Grier's on the bench. It was said that Shaler went to Washington to urge Grier's appointment, that while there he was himself offered the position, but that he rejected it out of loyalty to Grier.[98] Another was Wilson McCandless, as mentioned above. Patton said of McCandless, "He has the most extensive practice at this Bar. He exerted a more potent influence—rendered more effective services—spent more time, and more money in the late political contest than any man of our party in this state."[99]

Apart from factors of legal ability and industry, integrity and service to the Democratic Party, Grier's friends stressed two important points. One was that the candidate should know the peculiar and diffi-

---

[96] J. F. W. White, "The Judiciary of Allegheny County," *Pennsylvania Magazine of History and Biography*, 7:143, 175, 1883.

[97] David Paul Brown, *The Forum: or Forty Years' Full Practice at the Philadelphia Bar*, II, 99–100.

[98] J. F. W. White, "The Judiciary of Allegheny County, *Pennsylvania Magazine of History and Biography*, 7:164, 1883.

[99] Benjamin Patton to James K. Polk, Mar. 21, 1845, Appointment Files, State Department Papers.

cult law of Pennsylvania, and particularly the law of real estate, and the other was that he must be "right" on issues of slavery, or of abolitionism. The first was used as an argument in part for the selection of a man from Pennsylvania rather than from New Jersey, but it seemed nevertheless to have the ring of validity. The appointment of a candidate from New Jersey would be an outrage, wrote Luther Kidder of Wilkes Barre to Judge Patton. He had already joined the group backing Judge Joel Jones of Philadelphia, but he felt that in any event, "The great questions connected with our land titles demand a Pennsylvania lawyer in place of Judge Baldwin."[100] But the point made variously by a number of people was stated most fully by A. V. Parsons in a letter to Patton:

> Most of the cases in the western district are ejectments, and I understand from the gentlemen of the bar in this city, that very many of the cases now in the Circuit Court of the United States here, are those testing the validity of land titles which are situated in those counties where there are valuable coal lands. You know that the land law in this state is peculiar to Pennsylvania, and no one until he has spent years in this state and become familiar with our land titles is in any respect qualified to try an ejectment. In fact there are but few lawyers at the present day residing among us, who are profound in that branch of the law. I knew Judge Grier well when at the bar; have tried many causes with him, and I think there are but few men his superior in that, or any other branch of the law in the Commonwealth; and but few who would so well fill the office now vacant as that Gentleman.
>
> There is another reason why I hope the President will not fill the vacancy by the appointment of a gentleman out of the state and it is this, we have had no court of chancery in this state; and none possessed of chancery powers till within a few years past, hence a system of law and equity has become blended together, and is peculiar to Pennsylvania and none but a Pennsylvania lawyer can *well* administer the same.[101]

On the subject of abolition, Patton assured Polk that Judge Grier was "a warm if not violent opponent." He told of an instance in which an abolitionist elder in the Presbyterian Church of which Grier was also an elder sent to the pulpit an announcement of an abolitionist meeting to be read to the congregation. After the service and before the people had left, Grier arose and demanded to know who had sent the notice. The pulpit, he proclaimed, was not to be made a town crier's office for such purposes—purposes which were unconstitutional and seditious and were to be repudiated by all good Christians and loyal

---

[100] Luther Kidder to Benjamin Patton, Feb. 5, 1845, *ibid.*

[101] A. V. Parsons to Benjamin Patton, Apr. 11, 1845, *ibid.*

231

citizens.[102] An unsigned confidential letter written from the executive chamber at Harrisburg, presumably by Governor Francis R. Shunk, assured Polk that "The rights guaranteed by the Constitution to the states—the republican doctrine of state rights—opposition to a national bank—all the cardinal principles of the democratic party, and I may add hostility to the mad spirit of abolitionism, will in him, you may rest assured, find a sincere, and steadfast advocate."[103]

Sentiments in the adjoining slave state of Maryland are well disclosed in the following letter, written by a member of the House of Representatives from that state and signed also by three others:

> I am urged by several letters from my constituents to call your attention to the importance, especially to citizens of Maryland, of filling the vacancy on the bench of the Supreme Court, occasioned by the death of Judge Baldwin, with a gentleman who acknowledges the constitutional guarantees of the right of the master to his slave and will enforce it irrespective of the clogs from time to time attempted to be thrown around it by state legislation.
>
> . . . The modes of escape of this species of property from Maryland into Pennsylvania have been so multiplied by abolition societies organized along the line and by facilities afforded by railroad and canal communications, as to render it quite important to the owners of slaves in Maryland to look to the means of enforcing compensation against those who decoy, rescue, or secrete them, as the adoption of rigorous measures to prevent their escape.
>
> And I am happy to add that while making inquiries in regard to the opinions of Judge Grier upon this subject, I received the most undoubted assurance of his eminent talents and extensive acquirements, and believe that his appointment will be gratifying to Maryland and valuable to the Union.[104]

The position had now been vacant for more than two years. Judge Grier's nomination was sent to the Senate August 3, 1846. It apparently pleased almost everyone, or at any rate the fact was obvious that the position must be filled without further delay. The nomination was confirmed on the following day. Grier served until 1870 when, because of obvious evidence of senility, a committee of colleagues had to persuade him to resign.[105] Through most of his career, however, he served with industry and vigor, both in Washington and on circuit, taking time off each year for his favorite sport of trout fishing. As for his outlook as

---

[102] Benjamin Patton to James K. Polk, Mar. 30, 1845, Polk Papers.

[103] [Francis R. Shunk?] to James K. Polk, Nov. 28, 1845, Appointment Papers, State Department Files.

[104] Albert Constable to James K. Polk, Dec. 10, 1845, *ibid*.

[105] See Charles Evans Hughes, *The Supreme Court of the United States*, 75–76.

a judge, his friends had appraised him well, particularly with respect to abolitionism, as later chapters will show. At once generous of heart and rough and outspoken in manner, he probably found himself closer to Justice Catron, whom in these respects he resembled, than to any other of his colleagues. "Judge Catron has for twenty years been my intimate friend," he wrote at the death of the latter in 1865. "There was no man on our bench for whom I had so much personal atttachment."[106]

In the meantime a vacancy had occurred on the First Circuit and had been quickly filled. That vacancy had been expected for some time, but as a result of the resignation rather than the death of Justice Story. Ever since the death of his beloved Chief Justice Marshall, Story had lamented the passing of the old order and had expressed the desire or the intention of leaving the Bench at some undesignated date. When in the election of 1844 Polk defeated Clay, he realized that his resignation would have to be postponed another four years if a Whig President was to fill his place. Such a period seemed intolerable. He spoke of the fact that he was the last of the old Court and that the doctrines of that Court were no longer in the ascendancy. He had to choose between continuous dissent and yielding in the face of his own convictions. Neither alternative seemed tolerable.[107]

Although apparently no date of resignation was announced, political rumors credited the probability that he would take such a step, and advocacy of candidates began. In the summer of 1845, he fell ill with an intestinal ailment that had plagued him for some time.[108] For a while he was reported to be recovering. "Why, why, why does he resign," protested Benjamin Douglas Silliman of New York. "He cannot so long as life lasts have an adequate excuse."[109] But the Justice took a turn for the worse, and on September 10, 1845, he died.[110]

The death of the distinguished jurist brought widespread public mourning and expression of admiration and deference second only to that which had followed the death of Chief Justice Marshall. "What a

---

[106] R. C. Grier to Samuel Treat, June 27, 1865, Treat Papers.

[107] Joseph Story to Ezekiel Bacon, *Life and Letters of Joseph Story*, II, 527–28.

[108] "Death of Mr. Justice Story," *Law Rep.*, 8:241, 245, 1845.

[109] "Benjamin Douglas Silliman to Charles Sumner, Sept. 8, 1845," *Proceedings of Massachusetts Historical Society*, 50:288, 1917.

[110] There are grounds for speculation as to whether the cause of his death was cancer. Timothy Walker, his friend and former student and editor of the *Western Law Journal*, said in an obituary notice that the cause was "stoppage of the intestines, or intestinal strangulation, the same disease which caused the death of Hugh S. Legaré, Attorney General of the United States, at Boston, in 1843." "Death of Judge Story," *West L.J.*, 3: 44, 1845.

loss the Court has sustained in the death of Judge Story," wrote Chief Justice Taney to Richard Peters. "It is irreparable, utterly irreparable in this generation, for there is nobody equal to him. You who have seen me sitting there for so many years between Story and Thompson will readily understand how deeply I feel the loss of the survivor of them, especially so soon after the death of the other.[111] "I cannot realize the distressing fact," wrote Justice McLean. "I loved Story, as a very dear brother, and no one could know him as I knew him, and not love him. . . . But now I go to Washington without hope and full of melancholy. There is indeed but little in this world that is worth living for."[112] "I mingle my grief with yours," wrote Henry Clay, lamenting that "a great light of law and learning was extinguished by his death."[113]

Yet on the part of the Polk Administration there was no time for lamentation, and indeed no inclination to lament. The old order had passed. With the Presidency in the hands of a Jacksonian Democrat from Tennessee, it was not to be expected that the vacancy would be filled by another conservative Whig from the Boston aristocracy, and it does not appear that this group even seriously tried to bring about such a replacement. The letters sent to Polk were largely from Democrats, and they concentrated on Levi Woodbury of New Hampshire, Ether Shepley of the Supreme Court of Maine, and Governor Marcus Morton of Massachusetts. Bron Bradbury of Eastport, Maine, wrote that the appointment of Woodbury would "be a source of high gratification to all of those who desire to see sound principles of constitutional law established by the highest judicial tribunal of the United States. They will feel that his name affords a sure guaranty that no doctrines of *expediency* or *latitudinarian construction* would be brought to aid, by judicial decisions, in the subversion of the true principles of the Constitution—those principles upon which depend, as they believe, the perpetuity of the Union and the future strength and glory of the Republic."[114]

Woodbury was said to be a better politician than Governor Morton and a more faithful partisan than Judge Shepley. Samuel Cushman of Portsmouth, New Hampshire, made against Judge Shepley what was to him the horrible accusation that in the election of 1844 he did

---

[111] R. B. Taney to Richard Peters, Nov. 14, 1845, Peters Correspondence, II, Cadwalader Papers. Quotation printed in Tyler, *Memoir of Roger Brooke Taney*, 290–91. For official tributes at the time of death, including one eloquently phrased by Daniel Webster, see *Life and Letters of Joseph Story*, II, 613–47.

[112] John McLean to Richard Peters, Sept. 17, 1845, Peters Correspondence, II, Cadwalader Papers.

[113] Henry Clay to Richard Peters, Sept. 20, 1845, *ibid.*

[114] Bron Bradbury to James K. Polk, May 22, 1845, Appointment Papers, State Department Files.

not even cast his vote! "If so, his political character *cannot receive my approbation*."[115]

Woodbury was, of course, well known at Democratic headquarters. Born at Francestown, New Hampshire, on December 22, 1789, educated at Dartmouth College, trained in law in the office of Judge Jeremiah Smith, he had led a life of service in the state and federal governments. He had served in the highest offices in each of the three branches of the government of his state. He had served the United States government as Senator, Secretary of the Navy, and Secretary of the Treasury. In the last position he had replaced Roger B. Taney in 1834 and fought courageously and quietly against the pressures of the national banking interests. He remained in that position until the expiration of the Van Buren Administration, when he was elected to the Senate. As a Senator he was suspected by Van Buren's friends of developing aspirations for the Presidency, but he did not come to the fore as a rival in the 1844 election, and hence remained acceptable to Polk, whom he knew well, as a candidate for the Supreme Court.

In his diary for September 20, 1845, Polk noted:

> The Cabinet met today, it being the regular day of meeting, all the members present. Nothing of importance occurred. The President announced his intention to appoint the Hon. Levi Woodbury to be Judge of the Supreme Court of the U. States in place of Judge Story, deceased. All members of the Cabinet approved the appointment.[116]

The appointment was made when the Senate was in recess. It was submitted to the Senate December 23, 1845, and confirmed January 3, 1846.

Woodbury's term of service on the Supreme Court was brief, terminated by his death in 1851. Either because of his political activities or those of his friends, his transition from politics to the judiciary seems to have been incomplete. He was continually suspected of being a Presidential candidate, a Northern man with pronounced Southern leanings, or at least, leanings toward slavery.[117] He was an advocate of the annexation of Texas.[118] When his party failed to nominate him in 1848, William H. Seward wrote to Salmon P. Chase to say, "I am quite sure that Judge Woodbury has lost the last nomination that was open

---

[115] Samuel Cushman to James K. Polk, Sept. 13, 1845, *ibid.* See also Levi Morrill to James K. Polk, Sept. 15, 1845, *ibid.*

[116] *Diary of James K. Polk*, I, 37.

[117] See for example Joseph G. Rayback, "The Presidential Ambitions of John C. Calhoun, 1844–1848," *Jour-* *nal of Social History*, 14:331, 355, n. 85, 1948; Joseph G. Rayback, ed., "Martin Van Buren's Desire for Revenge in the Campaign of 1848," *Mississippi Valley Historical Review*, 40:707, 714, 1954.

[118] *New York Tribune*, Jan. 29, 1848.

to a Judge of the Supreme Court who regarded Emancipation as Fanaticism."[119]

By his colleagues on the Supreme Court, Woodbury and to some extent his family were regarded as highly reticent and enigmatic persons. On one occasion Justice Catron, an inveterate political gossip, made to James Buchanan the frustrated comment, "My Brother Woodbury has never in word or motion shown any symptoms as to what side he is on, in the present aggitation [sic] going forward, and is the most valuable example of prudence, in the Court, or in all society I think. Nor do his women leak anything."[120] Chief Justice Taney wrote of Woodbury:

He had been much engaged in public life and was familiar with all the proceedings of the general government. But he was a singularly wary and cautious man; unwilling to commit himself upon any opinion upon which he was not obliged immediately to act and never further than that action required. And if he expressed an opinion upon a measure he most commonly added to it so many qualifications and limitations and doubts, that he sometimes appeared to take it back again. He was a man of a strong and astute mind: of great industry, which carefully gathered together all the information that could be obtained upon any subject before him; even to the smallest matters of detail. He had I presume his own opinions and views well defined in his own mind— bu did not deem it prudent to disclose them too distinctly even to his friends and associates.[121]

Woodbury was described as nearly six feet tall, solidly built, with a manner of keen alertness. He was strict in self-discipline, imbibing only cold water and working with great speed and earnestness.[122] "While anything remained to be done," wrote a commentator at the time of his death, "his motto was 'Onward, onward, work, work, work.' "[123] Even his recreation was work in another form, consisting mostly of "collecting statistical and archaeological information, forming cabinets of specimens in botany, conchology, mineralogy, and other branches of natural science, studying questions connected with engineering, naval

[119] William H. Seward to S. P. Chase, June 12, 1848, Chase Papers (L.C.).

[120] John Catron to James Buchanan, undated (penciled date "1849?"), Buchanan Papers.

[121] Bank War Manuscript, 126–27. Although Chief Justice Taney wrote this appraisal of his colleague in connection with his discussion of the Bank War, he did so in 1849 or later, when Woodbury was a member of the Supreme Court and when his possible candidacy for the Presidency had recently been to the fore. It is therefore probable that the judgment expressed was derived in part from contemporary events as well as from those of the Jackson period.

[122] New York Tribune, Feb. 4, 1850.

[123] "Mr. Justice Woodbury," Law Rep., 14:349, 358, 1852.

ROGER B. TANEY, ESQ.
As a member of the Maryland Bar
(Reproduced by permission of Villanova University)

Members of the Court

ROGER B. TANEY
Chief Justice 1836–1864

JOSEPH STORY
Associate Justice 1811–1845
(*Library of Congress*)

SMITH THOMPSON
Associate Justice 1823–1843
(Library of Congress)

JOHN McLEAN
Associate Justice 1829–1861
(*Library of Congress*)

HENRY BALDWIN
Associate Justice 1830–1844
(Library of Congress)

JAMES M. WAYNE
Associate Justice 1835–1867
(Library of Congress)

Philip P. Barbour
Associate Justice 1836–1841
(*Library of Congress*)

architecture, and the application of science to the useful arts generally," with occasional fishing and some work at experimental farming.[124]

In his professional work, "His style of writing was turgid and obscure, doing little justice to his acknowledged clearness of intellect."[125] His judicial opinions were often enormously long. For all the brevity of his service, they dealt with such important topics as the scope of the commerce power, admiralty, slavery, prohibition, and "political questions."

From the appointment of Justice Grier in August, 1846, until the death of Justice Woodbury in September, 1851, the Supreme Court had full membership. All members were Democrats except Justice McLean who, although appointed by President Jackson, was now known generally as a Whig but one who seemed willing to accept a Presidential nomination on any ticket on which he might have a chance to be elected. Meanwhile the election of 1848 had brought to the Presidency a Whig, Zachary Taylor. This time the party did not make the mistake of 1840 in choosing a dissident Democrat as Vice President, but gave that office to Millard Fillmore, a Whig from New York, who was to become President in 1850 on the death of Taylor.

At Justice Woodbury's death, Fillmore wrote to Daniel Webster, his Secretary of State, seeking advice about refurbishing the Whig position on the Court to the extent of this vacancy. He explained, "I am therefore desirous of obtaining as long a lease, and as much moral and judicial power as possible, from this appointment. I would therefore like to combine a vigorous constitution with high moral and intellectual qualifications, a good judicial mind, and such age as gives a prospect of long service."[126] Several distinguished names had occurred to him but he inquired particularly about Benjamin R. Curtis of Boston.

On the day Fillmore's letter was written, Webster, in Boston, wrote to him recommending Curtis, saying that support for him was almost universal there. "Mr. B. R. Curtis is of a very suitable age, forty-one; he has good health, excellent habits, sufficient industry and love of labor, and, I need hardly add, is in point of legal attainment and general character in every way fit for the place."[127] Since Rufus Choate, an older man, was more extensively known and had led quite a distinguished life it would be necessary to confer with him, but it was not to be supposed that Choate would accept the place. Because of the

[124] *Ibid.*, 360.
[125] "Death of Judge Woodbury," *West L.J.*, 9:43, 44, 1851.
[126] Millard Fillmore to Daniel Webster, Sept. 10, 1851, *Memoir of Benjamin Robbins Curtis*, George T. Curtis, ed., I, 155.
[127] Daniel Webster to Millard Fillmore, Sept. 10, 1851, *ibid.*, 154–55.

pressures likely to develop, Webster thought it best to dispose of the matter as quickly as possible. He expected claims to be advanced in behalf of Judge Peleg Sprague of the United States District Court for Massachusetts, who was now on his way home from Europe. Judge John Pitman of the United States District Court for Rhode Island was a learned lawyer, an able judge, and an excellent man. If an appointment were to be made by promotion from the federal bench it would be very difficult to overlook him, since he had been on the bench much longer than Judge Sprague and working at a much smaller salary. But Webster thought it much better to appoint Curtis.

As in 1845, with Polk in the Presidency, it would have been unrealistic to expect the appointment of a conservative Whig from Boston, so in 1851, with Fillmore as President, it would have been unrealistic to expect the appointment of a Democrat of the stamp of the deceased Justice Woodbury. When Rufus Choate, colorful Whig leader of the Boston bar, had been consulted and had indicated the belief that he was not temperamentally fitted for the Supreme Court position and did not desire it,[128] Fillmore speedily issued Curtis a recess appointment, eighteen days after Woodbury's death, renewing the nomination when the Senate assembled in December. Confirmation was secured without difficulty.

Benjamin R. Curtis was born at Watertown, Massachusetts, in 1809, the son of a ship captain. The Curtis family was one of the oldest in the state, dating back to 1632. Many members of the family had been professional people, with college education. Curtis graduated from Harvard College in 1829, with the financial aid of his wealthy and distinguished uncle, George Ticknor. Brilliant in mind, poised and reserved and with a fine capacity for lucid reasoning, Curtis was attracted to the legal profession. He began the study of law under Justice Story, the Dane Professor at Harvard, and became one of his outstanding students even though he left for private practice before completing his course of training. He began practice in Northfield in 1831, and in 1834 became a partner of Charles P. Curtis of Boston, a distant relative and the father of the woman who was to become his second wife.

At the bar Curtis relied not at all on the flamboyant oratory of the day, but rather on precision and clarity of thought and expression. He enjoyed the competitive life of his profession and the financial rewards flowing from it, and he gave to it virtually all his time and energy save that spent with his family. In 1837, he wrote to his uncle:

---

[128] Among the several sources see Warren, *The Supreme Court in United States History*, II, 227, Richard H. Leach, "Benjamin Robbins Curtis: Judicial Misfit," *New England Quarterly*, 25:507, 513, 1952.

I would most gladly shake off the cares and thoughts of business often, if it were in my power, and find relaxation in literature; but I cannot. In the first place, I am of an earnest temperament, and can do nothing well without a strong devotion of my mind to it. In the next place, I have no dislike to the practice or study of the law, nay, I believe I may say without affectation that I have a strong love for its rough chances; and last, but most important, I am in the very midst of the tide, where its current is strongest and most rapid, and nothing would be easier than to be thrown out into comparatively still water, but in this eager community of the bar I am sure I should never get back again. It has been truly said, that a lawyer can no more regulate the amount of business he will do, than an engineer can blow a barrel of gun powder half-way down; so I think of those who are dependent on me, and, blessing my stars for my good fortune, rejoice in the clients who make me work so hard, but withal pay me so well.[129]

Curtis was a firm defender of contract rights and of property rights generally, as illustrated by his article on the obligation of the states to pay their debts in the face of popular pressure for repudiation. His defense of property rights included property in slaves. As early as 1835 he saw the preservation of the Union as dependent on checking the abolitionists and convincing the South that the great body of Northern people were unsympathetic to the abolitionists.[130] In 1836 he defended before the Supreme Court of Massachusetts the right of a slaveholder to hold a slave while visiting in a free state and to take the slave home against his will—a subject of much controversy between the slave and free states. The court, speaking through Chief Justice Shaw, held that the slaveholder had no such right.[131] Curtis joined with Webster in supporting the Compromise of 1850, which included a greatly strengthened Fugitive Slave Act.

Curtis thus stood aligned with the more conservative interests of his community. He differed with most members of the Supreme Court in that he did not move easily in the activities of political life. He had served in the Massachusetts legislature on two occasions, but he had accepted membership only in order to advocate reforms in the practice of the law of the state.[132] Perhaps it was this very lack of mellow partisanship that led a contemporary writer to characterize his mind as "eminently of a judicial cast," and to "regard it as a most fortunate circumstance, that he has consented to devote the rest of his days to dispensing justice on the highest tribunal in the world."[133]

---

[129] *Memoir of Benjamin Robbins Curtis*, I, 78.
[130] *Ibid.*, 72.
[131] Commonwealth v. Aves, 35 Mass. (18 Pick.) 193 (1836).
[132] "The Appointment of Mr. Curtis," *Law Rep.*, 14:332, 1851.
[133] *Ibid.*

To the great disappointment of the people who had taken delight in his appointment, Justice Curtis did not "devote the rest of his days" to his work on the Supreme Court. Although he had the long life that was hoped for him—he died in 1874—he left the Supreme Court in 1857, after the debacle and intra-Court wrangle over the Dred Scott case. But even before that event, his discontent was apparent to close friends. Although he was a craftsman of great skill and immensely useful to the Court both in the conference room and as the author of opinions, he was more advocate than judge. He had no such dedication to even-handed justice as was needed to make him endure the reduction in income and the consequent hardship for himself and his family. He was committed to an aristocracy of wealth as well as of the mind, and at that time there was nothing aristocratic about the salaries and the burdens of work expected of members of the Supreme Court.[134] The Dred Scott case, therefore, may have provided more the occasion than the cause of his return to private practice.

Although in 1851 President Fillmore had no difficulty in getting Senate confirmation for a distinguished Whig appointment to the Supreme Court, the political situation became distinctly unfavorable to the Whigs by the time of the death of Justice McKinley in 1852. Here again, of course, the President was desirous of adding to Whig membership. The Fifth Circuit, vacated by Justice McKinley, consisted at that time of Alabama and Louisiana, with judicial duties to be performed primarily at Mobile and New Orleans. Because he had business interests at Louisville, Kentucky, and because its location on the Ohio made it a convenient travel point between Washington and his circuit, Justice McKinley had taken up residence there. In recognition of this fact, Congress in 1849 gave him a limited amount of judicial responsibility there by authorizing the judge of the Fifth Circuit to hold Circuit Court in Kentucky in the absence of the judge of the Eighth Circuit, to which Kentucky officially belonged.[135] Alabama and Louisiana, therefore, and to a limited extent Kentucky, had some claim on the vacated position.

New Orleans, a thriving commercial city, had a goodly assortment of able lawyers of whom many were Whigs. On August 16, 1852, some two weeks before the current session of Congress was to come to an end, President Fillmore nominated Edward A. Bradford of New Orleans, "a scholarly New Englander, with a splendid mind."[136] The Democratic majority in the Senate, looking forward to the election of Franklin

---

134 For discussion see Richard H. Leach, "Benjamin Robbins Curtis: Judicial Misfit," *New England Quarterly*, 25:507, 1952.

135 9 Stat. 403.
136 Pierce Butler, "Judah Philip Benjamin," in *Great American Lawyers*, VI, 257, 275.

Pierce to the Presidency and hoping for a Democratic appointment, failed to act on the nomination. The President had been urged to nominate Humphrey Marshall, a prominent Kentucky Whig in the Senate, but because Kentucky was technically out of the circuit served by the Justice to be appointed, Fillmore appointed him minister to China instead.

From the adjournment of Congress at the end of August until early in 1853, many names were discussed for the Supreme Court position, including prominent persons not residing in the circuit of the vacancy. One of the most outstanding was Thomas Ruffin, chief justice of the Supreme Court of North Carolina, who as a state judge ranked in public estimation with Lemuel Shaw of Massachusetts and John B. Gibson of Pennsylvania. Judge Ruffin had announced his resignation from the North Carolina court at the age of sixty-five, but his friends discovered that he would welcome the more distinguished position on the Supreme Court of the United States. His background was that of a Jeffersonian Republican but he was much more judge than partisan and, given the Democratic complexion of the Senate, his friends hoped to bring about his appointment. Memorials were drafted with the signatures of prominent lawyers and judges of the state for submission to the President. A friend wrote to Ruffin to say, "I expect to see you on your way to Mississippi soon, to teach the natives to pay their debts— to New Orleans to punish Filibustering—and anywhere out there, to prove we have a national Government."[137]

But things went badly for Ruffin's cause, for the reasons that he lived outside the circuit of the vacancy and was not a Whig, and also that the Senator from North Carolina who was to submit the memorials and press for his nomination, George E. Badger, was a Whig and himself became a candidate for the position. The memorials were never submitted to the President, and Badger himself was nominated.[138] Badger was at once attacked from other parts of the South because he resided outside the circuit, because he supported the Wilmot Proviso, which had been denounced throughout the South, and, perhaps more covertly, because he was a Whig and not a Democrat. He had great prestige as a lawyer and as a Senator, but this prestige was not sufficient to win the necessary votes. The Senate in effect rejected the nomination by postponement of action.[139] Returning to the Fifth Circuit in search of a candidate, Fillmore nominated William C. Micou of New

---

[137] Frederick Nash to Thomas Ruffin, Dec. 27, 1852, *The Papers of Thomas Ruffin*, J. G. De Roulhac Hamilton, ed., II, 370–71.

[138] For a summary of events see

Thomas Ruffin to Joseph B. G. Roulhac, Feb. 7, 1853, *ibid.*, 386–88.

[139] Warren, *The Supreme Court in United States History*, II, 242–45.

Orleans, but the Senate failed to act on the nomination, and the vacancy was left to be filled by Fillmore's successor, Franklin Pierce.

President Pierce sought advice from members of the Supreme Court itself, and received it in the form of letters taken to him by Justices Catron and Curtis, a Democrat and a Whig.[140] Their candidate was John A. Campbell of Alabama, who had recently appeared before them in one of their recurrent bouts with the celebrated Gaines case.[141] Campbell, of Scotch-Irish descent, was born in Georgia in 1811, was graduated from Franklin College, studied law in the office of his uncle, John W. Campbell, and was admitted to the bar at the age of eighteen. Soon afterward he moved to Alabama, practicing law first in Montgomery and then in Mobile.

In Alabama Campbell had a distinguished career both in law and in politics. In the state legislature in 1836 he came into contact with McKinley, whom he would suceed on the Supreme Court, and apparently aided in electing McKinley to the United States Senate. At that time he had little respect for McKinley, saying that he was "an unspeakably weak man,"[142] and "He is a feeble man—not much superior to a Methodist preacher."[143] He made shrewd comments on the course of political events but remarked that he did not wish to continue in public life—" *The law* furnishes that kind of employment most congenial to my disposition." Yet from time to time he was drawn into political activity of one kind or another, especially with respect to the issues of slavery and relationships between the North and the South. He seems to have been close to John C. Calhoun, who had been a friend of his father, even though not always in agreement with him as to extremity of position. He distrusted the judgment of James Buchanan as Polk's Secretary of State and joined with Calhoun in denouncing the declaration of war against Mexico. He was opposed to the Wilmot Proviso to exclude slavery from the territories to be acquired from Mexico, but, realizing the impracticality of maintaining slavery in some of the acquired areas, his inclination would have been to refuse any annexation beyond the boundaries of Texas. In November, 1847, he wrote to Calhoun:

> I regard the subject of the acquisition of New Territory mainly as it may affect the *balance* of power in the federal government. What will be the effect of any large acquisition? Will it be to preserve the balance of power as it now exists? The territory is wholly unfit for a negro

---

[140] 20 Wall. ix (1873) (Memorial address of Campbell on Curtis).

[141] Gaines v. Relf, 12 How. 472 (1852). The protracted litigation is discussed in Chapter XXX, "Property in Land."

[142] J. A. Campbell to Henry Goldthwaite, Nov. 20, 1836, Groner Papers.

[143] J. A. Campbell to Henry Goldthwaite, Nov. 22, 1836, Groner Papers.

population. The republic of Mexico contains a smaller number of blacks than any of the old colonies of Spain and tho' this is not conclusive yet it is a persuasive argument that negro labor was not found to be profitable.[144]

The growing storm over slavery in the territories and the strengthening of the Fugitive Slave Law deepened the sectional rift. At a convention of representatives of the southern states held in Nashville in June, 1850, Campbell as a delegate from Alabama drafted the resolutions which condemned the Wilmot Proviso and demanded the protection of Southern rights—without, however, pressing the threat of secession.[145] It was therefore clear that Campbell as a Supreme Court Justice would be safely in the Southern and proslavery camp, for all that he had differences with some of the leaders in the Democratic Party.

Even as President Fillmore, toward the end of his term, was trying to fill the Supreme Court vacancy with a man of his own choosing, it was reported that all the Southern states except Louisiana and Texas —the former with a spate of candidates of its own—had recommended Campbell to President-elect Franklin Pierce for the position.[146] Pierce submitted the nomination on March 21, 1853, and the Senate quickly confirmed it. The *New York Times* explained that there had been much difficulty about this important appointment, "a life estate in $4500 a year." Fillmore, a lame-duck Whig President, had not been permitted to fill it. Pierce had considered former United States Senator Solomon W. Downs of New Orleans, who, however, had lacked professional eminence by comparison with Campbell.[147]

---

[144] John A. Campbell to John C. Calhoun, Nov. 20, 1847, "Correspondence of John C. Calhoun," J. Franklin Jameson, ed., *Annual Report of the American Historical Association for the Year 1899*, 2:1139, 1140, 1900. A month later Campbell wrote to Calhoun about the strategy of getting rid of Buchanan as a Presidential candidate and preventing the building up of Justice Woodbury. He said of the latter that he "has reached quite as high a place as Nature ever intended he should fill." He thought the best strategy for the South was to support General Taylor, on the theory that Taylor would not be a man of either political party. He repeated his argument that the Southern people should not insist on the acquisition of territory. *Ibid.*, 1155. A few months later Campbell expressed to Calhoun the belief that, as to the territory

that was acquired, Congress could determine what was to be held as property—a position which he renounced in his opinion in the Dred Scott case. He again spoke of "Mr. Polk's war" as likely to produce disastrous consequences for the South and noted his opposition to the lust for territory which Polk had encouraged. J. A. Campbell to John C. Calhoun, Mar. 1, 1848, "Correspondence Addressed to John C. Calhoun, 1837–1848," Chauncey S. Boucher and John P. Brooks, eds., *Annual Report of the American Historical Association for the Year 1929*, 431, 1930.

[145] See Farrar Newberry, "The Nashville Convention and Southern Sentiment of 1850," *South Atlantic Quarterly*, 11:259, 266–67, 1912.

[146] *New York Times*, Jan. 1, 1853.

[147] *New York Times*, Mar. 23, Apr. 4, 1853.

Campbell possessed vast professional learning. As a man of cultivation he ranked with Justice Story.[148] Outside the legal profession it was said that "he is as well read in Theology as any one whose business it is to produce divinity every week." He was a man of the finest personal character, amiable, gentle, strictly temperate and inflexibly just. "Anomalous as it seems in gentlemen of the Green Bag, he is delicate almost to tremulousness, and with tremendous intellectual power, as shy as a young lady."[149]

Although on the Supreme Court Justice Campbell stood as a defender of the rights of the states and of proslavery interests, he was no such agrarian extremist as Justice Daniel. On circuit he did all that a judge could do in a hostile atmosphere to bring about punishment of violators of our neutrality laws in relations with Nicaragua and Cuba. He left the Supreme Court in 1861 only after failure of efforts to bring about a compromise that might save the Union. During the Civil War he served as Assistant Secretary of War for the Confederate government, in a position of little influence. After the war he was imprisoned for a time as one of the war leaders, later returning to the practice of law to appear from time to time before the Supreme Court as one of the most distinguished of its practitioners. He lived until 1889, twenty-eight years after his resignation from the Court.

The filling of still another pre-Civil War vacancy requires mention here. On September 1, 1857, after an irritating exchange of letters with Chief Justice Taney over access to opinions in the Dred Scott case, which had been decided the preceding March, Justice Curtis submitted his resignation as a member of the Court, leaving the First Circuit vacant. President James Buchanan could be expected to fill the vacancy with a loyal Democrat, or at any rate with a man sympathetic to the slaveholding interests of the South. Howell Cobb of Georgia, Buchanan's Secretary of the Treasury, reported twelve days after the resignation that the President was inclined toward Isaac Toucey of Connecticut, his Secretary of the Navy. The name of Rufus Choate had come up again, but Cobb voiced doubt as to "his soundness on the constitutional questions of so much interest and importance at this time." He could find no evidence of such soundness in Choate's recent speeches. He was sure that the President would "appoint no man who is not known to be perfectly sound on those questions."[150]

---

[148] For further comments see Warren, *The Supreme Court in United States History*, II, 245–47.

[149] *New York Times*, Apr. 4, 1853.

[150] Howell Cobb to Alexander H. Stephens, Sept. 12, 1857, "The Correspondence of Robert Toombs, Alexander H. Stephens, and Howell Cobb," Ulrich B. Phillips, ed., *Annual Report of the American Historical Association for the Year 1911*, 2:422, 1913.

IX: *Politics and Personnel*

Friends strongly recommended John J. Gilchrist, former chief justice of New Hampshire and now chief justice of the United States Court of Claims,[151] and Buchanan for a time considered going all the way to the South and appointing a man from Alabama, William L. Yancey. But he finally fixed on Nathan Clifford of Maine.[152] Clifford was born in New Hampshire in 1803. He was admitted to the bar in 1827 after studying law in the office of Josiah Quincy, and thereafter moved to western Maine to begin practice. In 1830 he began a political career as a Democrat in the Maine legislature. He was at one time state attorney general, and he served two terms in the House of Representatives.[153] In 1846 President Polk made him Attorney General of the United States.

Provincial in his training and interests until this time, it was in Polk's Cabinet that Clifford began to develop as a national statesman. At first he was intimidated at the thought of representing the government before the Supreme Court. One December Sunday in 1846, on returning from church, Polk was astonished to find Clifford awaiting him with a letter of resignation. Polk gave his assurance of confidence and warned that resignation at this time would be taken as evidence of unfitness, whereupon Clifford was persuaded to remain in office. Polk wrote in his diary:

> I think Mr. Clifford an honest man and a sincere friend. He feels in his new position somewhat timid, fears that he will not be able to sustain the reputation of his predecessors, and had therefore brought himself to the conclusion that he had better resign. He finally concluded not to tender his resignation, and retired apparently well satisfied at the interview I held with him.[154]

Presumably his self-confidence was restored when at the ensuing term of the Supreme Court he argued and won a long contested case against the now defunct Bank of the United States.[155]

A modest man who stirred no sense of rivalry in either Polk or Buchanan, Clifford got along well with the two of them. At the close

---

[151] Judge Gilchrist wrote to Pierce that Toucey was being recommended because of a desire to get him out of the Navy Department. Apart from Toucey he thought the competition was between himself and Nathan Clifford. He thought Clifford not his superior. He explained that "I should prefer a seat on the Bench of the Supreme Court to my present position because I do not think it so anscious [*sic*] a place, the salary is better, and the thing is more fixed and permanent." J. J. Gilchrist to Franklin Pierce, Sept. 16, 1857, Pierce Papers.

[152] Warren, *The Supreme Court in United States History*, II, 322.

[153] For an account of his early career see Philip G. Clifford, *Nathan Clifford, Democrat*.

[154] *Diary of James K. Polk*, II, 275.

[155] United States v. Bank of the United States, 5 How. 382 (1848).

of the war with Mexico, along with A. H. Sevier of the Senate Committee on Foreign Relations, he was sent to Mexico to resolve difficulties resulting from Senate modifications of the treaty drafted with that country. According to Vice President George M. Dallas, the two inexperienced diplomats got themselves into difficulties by signing a certification that the Senate changes in the treaty left the treaty with its original meaning. It would have been well, wrote Dallas in his diary, to have argued this point orally, but the two "were verdant and silly enough to put into the shape of a formal document what, in effect, was a repudiation or retraction of the amendments of the Senate.[156] However, the matter was worked out and Clifford remained as minister to Mexico until the end of the Polk Administration.

Returning to Maine, Clifford practiced law in Portland for eight years. In the light of his friendship with Buchanan, his party affiliation, his residence in the First Circuit, and the southern sympathies he was known to hold, it is not surprising that he was nominated for the Supreme Court vacancy. Neither is it surprising that abolitionist critics of the Administration poured out their wrath at the nomination.[157] The New York Tribune attacked Clifford's qualifications by contrasting them with those of Caleb Cushing. Clifford, it said, was "just about equal to the trial of a case of assumpsit upon a promissory note in the court of a Justice of the Peace. Whatever else may be said of Gen. Cushing, he certainly does know a little law."[158] A Boston paper, on the other hand, came to Clifford's defense by saying:

He happily combines the qualities of a lawyer, trained to aid in the administration of justice between individuals, and those of a statesman accustomed to move in that higher domain of jurisprudence, where more especially are considered and determined the rights of nations and governments. For the proper and acceptable discharge of the function of Judge of the Supreme Court of the United States, there is required a kind of qualification different from that demanded in the Court of one of the States. The training to which we refer can be had only in the executive department of the Government.[159]

---

[156] "The Library: The Mystery of the Dallas Papers," Pennsylvania Magazine of History and Biography, 73:475, 507, 1949.

[157] For summary see Warren, The Supreme Court in United States History, II, 322–24.

[158] New York Tribune, Dec. 23, 1857.

[159] Boston Post, quoted in Pitts. L. J., 5:271, 1857. One of Clifford's political friends wrote to him that the carping of Greeley and others of that "ilk" was itself evidence that a good selection had been made, adding that "there is nothing which these fellows more dread than a Judiciary who will fearlessly and impartially expound the meaning of the Constitution. Their chief reliance is, and has ever been, in confering upon that Instrument the Protean Elasticity which characterizes their own Political Creed." Samuel A. Burns to Nathan Clifford, Jan. 12, 1858, Clifford Papers.

IX: *Politics and Personnel*

The nomination, submitted December 9, 1857, was confirmed by a narrow margin on January 21, 1858, and Justice Clifford took the seat he was to occupy until his death in 1881. Stocky and phlegmatic, and meticulous and thorough in his work, he never stood out as a leader on the Court. He wrote no majority opinions on important constitutional questions. His specialties were commercial and maritime law, the law of Mexican land grants, and procedure and practice. He remained a firm Democrat on a Court which before his death became largely Republican.

This account of appointments and activities of members of the federal judiciary illustrates the depth of continuous political involvements. It was taken as a matter of course that political ideas and interests would influence the scope of judicial activity, the rewards received therefor, and the trends of judicial decisions. While the country was committed to maintenance of a federal system and a tripartite division of powers, it was nevertheless subject to a pronounced drift in the direction of practical democracy, minimizing the power to be left in the hands of an aristocratic judiciary. This drift represented the convictions of the Democratic Party, which except for brief periods was in power from the Jackson period until the Civil War. But if the Democratic Party used its political power to determine judicial appointments and influence the course of judicial operations, the Whig Party did likewise to the extent of its opportunities, justifying its attitude as protecting the conception of the judiciary entrenched by the Marshall Court. Apart from partisan considerations, nominees were selected in terms of their supposed attitudes on critical problems, such as the protection of property in general, the protection of slavery, and the allocation of power within the federal system. This is not to imply that Americans of the Taney period were without reverence for the body of the law or for the mystique of it. During this period, as Roscoe Pound said of the latter part of the nineteenth century, we were in some respects "a lawridden people."[160] The permeating character of the law was to be taken for granted, but the similarly permeating factor of politics was also to have its appropriate degree of attention. Because politicians were apt to be more at home with politics in its infinite variety than with the law, or, at least, could more easily communicate about it in public performances, politics at times seemed to conceal the law within its shadow.

---

[160] Roscoe Pound, "Organization of Courts," *Journal of American Judica-* *ture Society*, 11:69, 1927.

CHAPTER X

The Judges and the Circuits

THROUGHOUT THE TANEY PERIOD the members of the Supreme Court, like those of earlier periods, spent more than half their working time holding Circuit Court in their respective circuits and traveling from place to place for the purpose. At the beginning of the Taney period there were seven circuits, with one Justice assigned to each. The work of the Circuit Courts was coordinated with that of the District Courts. Each state constituted at least one district, to which a district judge was appointed, and as of 1836 each of two states, Pennsylvania and New York, had two districts; other states would be divided with the increase of population and federal judicial business. In addition to holding the District Courts, district judges in areas within the seven circuits sat with Supreme Court Justices to hold the Circuit Courts. When a Supreme Court Justice was unable to attend at a term of the Circuit Court, the district judge might hold it sitting alone. In states not yet incorporated within any of the circuits, district judges were required to perform circuit duties as well as district duties. In 1852 a popular journal described the interrelations between the two sets of courts and the two classes of judges:

> [I]n each one of the districts into which the United States are divided, there is a District Judge, who presides singly in the District Court, and who is also associated with one of the Supreme Court Judges in holding within his district the term of the Circuit Court, which is a court of higher grade than the District Court. It often happens that the Circuit Judge is unable to hold the required terms, in which case the District Judge holds the Circuit term by himself, precisely as he holds his District term. The two are distinct courts, with different calendars, jury panels, &c, though it very commonly happens that the same District Judge presides singly in both, and often within five minutes is sitting, now in the one capacity and now in the other, ad-

248

journing the District and opening the Circuit Court, or *vice versa*, according to convenience.[1]

Although the Constitution contained no requirement of geographical representation on the part of members of the Supreme Court, it was tentatively assumed that each new appointment should be made from within the circuit where there was a vacancy. Proposals to depart from this practice always brought loud protests from politicians in the vacant circuit. As already discussed in connection with the appointments of Chief Justice Taney and Justices Catron and McKinley, the addition of new states to the Union created pressing problems in the readjustment of circuits to include new areas, and the politics of appointments was closely linked with the politics of the arrangement of circuits.

When in 1836 Chief Justice Taney became a member of the Court the arrangement of circuits and the allocation of justices were as follows:

First: Maine, New Hampshire, Massachusetts, Rhode Island	Story
Second: Vermont, Connecticut, New York	Thompson
Third: Pennsylvania, New Jersey	Baldwin
Fourth: Maryland, Delaware	Taney
Fifth: Virginia, North Carolina	Barbour
Sixth: South Carolina, Georgia	Wayne
Seventh: Ohio, Kentucky, Tennessee	McLean

The statute of 1837 which increased to nine the number of circuits and Justices and rearranged the Seventh Circuit left the last three circuits as follows:

Seventh: Ohio, Indiana, Illinois, Michigan	McLean
Eighth: Kentucky, Tennessee, Missouri	Catron
Ninth: Alabama, Mississippi, Louisiana, Arkansas	McKinley

In the 1830s, as during the first decade in the history of the Court, Justices complained about the wear and tear of travel and the burden of work to be done on circuit. The loudest complaints at this time came from the two new Justices, Catron and McKinley, who had the greatest distances to cover and the most backward conditions of travel to endure. It was probably at McKinley's request that on February 13, 1838, Senator Clement C. Clay of Alabama made a motion "That the Committee on the Judiciary be instructed to inquire into the expediency of making allowances for mileage to the judges of the circuit courts of the United States in such manner as to equalize their compensation."[2] Since

---

[1] "The Late Cuba State Trials," *Democratic Review*, 30:307 n., 1852.

[2] *S. Jour.*, 25th Cong., 2nd Sess. 226.

members of Congress received travel allowances it must have seemed reasonable to the judges that they, too, should be reimbursed for the expenses of travel extending in some instances to thousands of miles. The Senate committee, finding that it needed more information as a basis for action, dropped the compensation proposal for the time being[3] and secured adoption of a resolution asking the Secretary of State to ascertain and report the state of the dockets of the Circuit Courts and the mileage required of the Justices in their travels.[4] Some time later Justice McLean reported to Justice Story, on circuit, that "Our mileage bill made no progress in the Senate. The committee to whom the subject was referred asked leave to be discharged from a further consideration of it. The truth is that our two South Western brothers have no great weight with their political friends."[5]

Although the report assembled for the Senate by Secretary of State John Forsyth brought no important immediate changes it did provide for posterity illuminating data on the Circuit Courts and the duties required of the traveling Justices. The mileage summary was as follows:[6]

Taney	458	miles
Baldwin	2,000	
Wayne	2,370	
Barbour	1,498	
Story	1,896	
Thompson	2,590	
McLean	2,500	
Catron	3,464	
McKinley	10,000	

The individual reports showed varying degrees of meticulousness on the part of the reporting justices. Chief Justice Taney, accounting for round trips to New Castle and to Dover, Delaware, got mileage figures from the post office. He gave the shortest routes possible for public transportation but volunteered the information that he had once traveled by a longer route. Justice Story gave mileage figures as he supposed them to be, and suggested that any error could be corrected by reference to figures in the Post Office Department at Washington. Justice McKinley arrived at his enormous total of ten thousand through only the roughest sort of estimate.

The Justices traveled by stage coach or steamboat, depending on the region and the time of year, and took advantage of railroad transportation as it developed. Journeys were often hazardous. When in

---

[3] Ibid., 299.
[4] Ibid., 288.
[5] John McLean to Joseph Story,

May 5, 1838, Story Papers.
[6] S. Rep. No. 50, 25th Cong., 3rd Sess. 32 (1839).

X: *The Judges and the Circuits*

March of 1836 Justice Story returned to Cambridge after the end of the term of the Supreme Court, Daniel Webster learned from his son that the judge had "met with various disasters, upsets and breakdowns, &c.; but came at last in safely."[7] Webster explained that his own difficulty in getting home by water was caused not by ice off the New England coast but in more southern waters. "No boat runs yet from Baltimore—both the Chesapeake Bay and the Delaware river are covered with thick-ribbed ice."[8] In his report on circuit travel Justice McLean included a notation that "on no inconsiderable part of my route through Indiana in May last, the road was so deep as to be almost impassable to a carriage of any description. The mails and passengers had to be conveyed in common wagons."[9] Justice Wayne explained that except for his trips to Washington he had had to travel "altogether by land, and without the facilities of steamboats or railroads." He based his total computation "upon that of the General Post Office, and upon the present stage, steamboat, and railroad route from Savannah to Washington, which is the shortest."[10] Justice McKinley could offer only a loose estimate of mileage for two annual visits to each of his courts:

> The shortest practicable route by which the travelling can be performed, according to the best information I can obtain, is about six thousand five hundred miles. But upon some of the roads there are no public conveyances, and the time allowed for holding the courts would render it impossible to perform the travelling by any private mode. I have never yet been at Little Rock, the place of holding the court in Arkansas; but, from the best information I can obtain, it could not be conveniently approached in the spring of the year, except by water, and by that route the distance would be greatly increased. If the courts of this circuit were properly arranged, the travelling would be diminished considerably. . . .[11]

Although not itself giving totals by circuits, the Senate document carried figures to show that in addition to having by far the greatest mileage to travel, the Justice assigned to the Ninth Circuit had nearly two-thirds of the cases at that time pending in all the Circuit Courts of the country. Much of the accumulation was the product of the panic of 1837 and of the inability of the district judges to handle the circuit business that had been allotted to them before the Ninth Circuit was created, but explanations did not solve the problem of the work load any more than that of mileage and travel.

---

[7] Fletcher Webster to Daniel Webster, Mar. 10, 1836, Webster Papers (N.H.H.S.).

[8] Daniel Webster to Fletcher Webster, Mar. 14, 1836, *ibid.*

[9] S. Rep. No. 50, 25th Cong., 3rd Sess. 35 (1839).

[10] *Ibid.*, 35.

[11] *Ibid.*, 39.

But fault as well as misfortune appears to have been involved in the accumulation of business. In June, 1838, Henry Johnson of Louisiana complained in the House of Representatives about the operation of the federal judicial system in his state over a period of years. In the summer of 1837 the incumbent district judge had died and had been replaced by the appointment of Philip K. Lawrence. Desiring to have a personal friend as clerk of the District Court, Judge Lawrence had appointed John Winthrop and sent a letter of dismissal to the incumbent clerk, Duncan U. Hennen. When in May, 1838, Justice McKinley came to New Orleans to hold Circuit Court sitting with Judge Lawrence, Hennen challenged the power of the judge to remove him, and the question was argued by counsel. Judge Lawrence held to his position while Justice McKinley took the opposite position, with the result that no business could be done by the Circuit and District courts until after the question had been decided by the Supreme Court of the United States. Thus, said Congressman Johnson, "the mass of business in both courts is to be postponed, and the interests of the people sacrificed, because the district judge wishes to remove a clerk who is eminently qualified for the situation, and against whom he has no cause of complaint, with the view of bestowing the office on an intimate friend."[12] Johnson believed that the district judge ought to be impeached and dismissed from office.

To clear the impasse as quickly as possible an attempt was made to get from Chief Justice Taney at the vestigial August term of the Supreme Court a writ of mandamus to protect Hennen's position as clerk. Taney decided that he had no power at this term to issue the writ,[13] whereupon the case was ordered presented to the full Court at the January term in 1839. There, perhaps in part because of the general importance of the question of the control of judges over the appointment and removal of court officers, the case was argued by four of the leading lawyers of the country: Richard S. Coxe, Samuel L. Southard, Henry D. Gilpin, and Walter Jones. In an opinion by Justice Thompson the Supreme Court decided unanimously, presumably with at least the reluctant concurrence of Justice McKinley, that the district judge had the power to remove the clerk of the District Court, an officer whose status had not been changed by the Act of 1837 creating the Ninth Circuit except for the fact that he now had duties in the Circuit Court as well as in the District Court.[14]

---

12 *Niles' National Register*, 54:251, 1838.

13 *Ex parte* Hennen, 13 Pet. 225 (1839).

14 *Ex parte* Hennen, 13 Pet. 230 (1839). The minutes of the Court indicate that argument of the case was postponed until McKinley's arrival, which, as often happened, was late. He was present on the three days of argument and on the day of the decision. No dissent was recorded.

X: *The Judges and the Circuits*

Congress, evidently irritated with Justice McKinley's inability to get his work done, was struggling with the problem of what to do about it. A bill was brought up to eliminate northern Alabama, the place of his residence, from the Ninth Circuit, returning its circuit business to the District Court which had formerly been responsible for it. Before the bill was passed Senator Ambrose H. Sevier of Arkansas expressed the resentment of his state by offering an amendment providing that if the judge should neglect or fail to hold court in the places designated he should except in case of illness be held guilty of a high misdemeanor.[15] The bill was passed without the amendment.[16]

Justice McKinley found the relief given insufficient. He talked with President Van Buren, and thought the President agreed to deal with the matter in a message to Congress. When Van Buren failed to do so, McKinley, from his new home in Louisville, Kentucky, sent the President a letter of complaint, calling attention to the revelations of the Senate report. He thought it obvious that a judge could not attend to all the business of the Ninth Circuit even by giving it his full time. And how, he asked, could full performance be expected of him when New Orleans and Mobile, where two of the most important courts were held, were subject to yellow fever from late autumn until winter almost every year? Furthermore, "by the peculiar mode of proceeding under the laws of Louisiana it takes double the time to try a cause that it would to try one, of like character, by the rules of the common law."[17]

Justice McKinley was also having trouble in Mississippi. At each of the last two terms the court had had upwards of twenty-seven hundred causes. The court had been compelled to hurry over the docket and refuse to hear argument on plain and well-settled questions, to the great resentment of throngs of debtors who were involved, and who were determined to prevent the execution of judgments against them. "These circumstances finally led to a gross personal indignity being offered to one of the members of the court." McKinley thought the court was being held in the wrong city—in Jackson, where there were many debtors and desperate men who would not permit justice to be done. He favored moving it to Natchez, where there was a more stable population and less indebtedness.[18]

Complaints from Justice McKinley and perhaps from other Justices who thought themselves overworked, and from constituencies which thought themselves inadequately served, kept alive in the Supreme Court and in Congress the subject of the rearrangement of circuit

---

[15] *New York Commercial Advertiser*, Mar. 23, 1838.
[16] 5 Stat. 210.
[17] John McKinley to Martin Van

Buren, Nov. 9, 1839 (signature page missing), Van Buren Papers.
[18] *Ibid.*

253

boundaries. Early in 1840 both houses reported bills to remove Mississippi from the Ninth Circuit to the Eighth. To compensate Justice Catron for the extra work in Mississippi, Missouri was to be transferred to the Seventh Circuit, and in turn Michigan was to be transferred from the Seventh to the Third. When the Supreme Court adjourned for the 1840 term most of the Justices evidently expected this arrangement to be adopted. But some weeks later Chief Justice Taney discovered that the Senate bill had been changed to make drastic modifications in most of the circuits and to add vastly to the duties of his own, and that work loads had been lightened for Justices Baldwin and Catron of the Third and Eighth Circuits, who had remained in Washington pending the revision of the bill. He assumed that they had therefore been responsible. He wrote in protest to his friends in Congress, and informed Justice McLean and perhaps others of the absent Justices. According to the proposed arrangement all of New Jersey and eastern Pennsylvania would be added to the Fourth Circuit, then consisting of Maryland and Delaware. The Chief Justice told McLean that "Under this arrangement our Brother of Pennsylvania will have but little to do, while my duties are more than doubled. . . . No man can perform the duties of the circuit intended to be assigned to me, in the manner in which they ought to be performed."[19]

The proposed changes aroused so much protest that the matter went over to the ensuing session of Congress, when, on February 25, 1841, occurred the death of Justice Barbour, to whom was assigned the Fifth Circuit, including Virginia and North Carolina. This event seemed to clear the way for the merging of eastern circuits and the creation of a new circuit in the West. Whatever grief he may have felt about the death of his colleague, Justice Catron on the day of Barbour's death rushed into consultation with the Chief Justice and Justice Wayne and then wrote to Garrett D. Wall, chairman of the Senate Judiciary Committee, to propose circuit changes:

> The death of our lamented, and excellent friend, Judge Barbour, will supersede the necessity of leaving the seaboard circuits as they now are. By adding Virginia to Maryland and Delaware, (the Chief Justice's circuit,) and North Carolina to South Carolina and Georgia, (Judge Wayne's,) the valley of the Mississippi, will command, the vacant situation to fill a new circuit: Say Mobile, and New Orleans. This will make a fair division of labour, and *render it possible*, to have the southern and western business done. . . .
>
> The most delicate, and difficult matter that has occurred since I have been on the Bench, has been, the attempt, on part of the Court,

---

[19] Roger B. Taney to John McLean, May 5, 1840, McLean Papers.

to arrange the circuits; and as the occasion now presented, removes all difficulty so far as the Court is concerned, it is ardently hoped Congress will embrace it.[20]

On February 27 Senator Wall brought up the bill and Senator Clement C. Clay of Alabama offered an amendment conforming to an agreement among the Justices. Senator William H. Roane of Virginia made a stirring protest against taking a Justiceship away from Virginia and separating that state from North Carolina, with which she had traditionally been linked. He warned against shifting circuits to the West where the deranged state of the currency and the rage for speculation had clogged dockets. The time might well come when the dimensions of admiralty and maritime business might call for restoration of the old arrangement of circuits along the east coast.[21] Senator Thomas Hart Benton of Missouri opposed the amendment because he thought the number of Justices and circuits ought to be increased, and not merely shifted westward.[22] But Senator James Buchanan of Pennsylvania thought that even nine was too large a number if it could be avoided, and believed this the ideal time for a readjustment—when there was a vacancy on one of the Eastern circuits. With a grass-roots knowledge of the politics involved, he confidently predicted that as to men appointed to the Court from an Eastern circuit none would ever be shifted from East to West by Congress against his will.[23]

The bill passed the Senate by a substantial majority,[24] but the House of Representatives failed to act. Rather than leave the appointment to his Whig successor, President Van Buren filled the vacancy on the unmodified Fifth Circuit by the appointment of Peter V. Daniel of Virginia, and in a stormy session the lame-duck Senate confirmed the nomination.

When another year had passed without Congressional action to modify the circuits, Justice McKinley resorted to the unusual expedient of preparing a petition to the two houses of Congress setting forth and explaining his grievances and asking for relief. Senator William R. King of Alabama presented the petition, told of the complaints against McKinley because of his failure to perform all his prescribed duties, and asked that the petition be printed and sent to lawyers and judges to

---

[20] John Catron to Garrett D. Wall, Feb. 25, 1841, Dreer Collection. A postscript added the following day carried a message that the Chief Justice was unwilling to take the court for the western part of Virginia. Catron's solution was that "Judge McKinley *must* take it, or do anything else to obtain relief—so that

this trifle should not for a moment stand in the way of an arrangement, to last with slight alterations for forty years; as it must."

[21] *Cong. Globe*, 26th Cong., 2nd Sess. 213 (1841).

[22] *Ibid.*, 214.

[23] *Ibid.*, 215.

[24] *Ibid.*, 216.

enable them to know the cause of delays in the business of the courts.[25] The petition was therefore published as a Senate document. In the petition McKinley explained, in terms of the earlier Senate report, that nearly two-thirds of the pending cases were in the Ninth Circuit, that about one-third of the total necessary travel by the Justices was required there, and that the inequality extended also to expenses. He questioned the fairness of this arrangement.

> Is it proper that a judge should have no time allowed him for attending to his private concerns? no time for relaxation? no time for reading and study? Is it just to suitors in the ninth circuit to deprive them of the services of the judge, by requiring more of him than he can possibly perform? Is it just to the judge to require as much service of him as of four or five others of the judges? Your petitioner believes that all the other judges are convinced that it is impossible for him to perform the duties required of him; but they have not the power to relieve him, nor can they agree upon a plan for doing it.
> He believes, however, that they are all of the opinion that the judges of the Supreme Court ought not to be required to hold more than one term of the circuit courts a year in each district, as is now the case in some of the circuits; and that they ought to be allowed to interchange circuits, or any one or more of the courts thereof, whenever convenience or necessity requires it.[26]

Once again Congress took up the problem. On July 23, 1842, the Senate completed discussion of a bill eliminating the existing Fifth Circuit by attaching Virginia to the Fourth Circuit and North Carolina to the Sixth, and erecting a new Fifth Circuit of Alabama and Louisiana and leaving in the Ninth only Mississippi and Arkansas. As James Buchanan had predicted, Congress avoided the unpopular task of exiling an eastern judge westward—or southward. But it did seek to attain the same ends and avoid responsibility on its own part by leaving circuit allotments to the Supreme Court, in a situation such that Justice Daniel would obviously have to move. The bill left to the Supreme Court itself the difficult question of deciding the placement of Justices Daniel and McKinley as between the two Southern or Southwestern circuits.[27]

In the House of Representatives John W. Jones of Virginia made a final stand in behalf of Virginia's claim to the Fifth Circuit and tried to prevent the exile of his friend Justice Daniel to the Gulf Coast. He

---

[25] *Cong. Globe*, 27th Cong., 2nd Sess. 213 (1842).

[26] Petition of John McKinley, Praying an alteration in the Judicial circuits of the United States, S. Doc. No. 99, 27th Cong., 2nd Sess. 3 (1842).

[27] *Cong. Globe*, 27th Cong., 2nd Sess. 781 (1842).

proposed an arrangement which would have made changes in eight of the nine circuits but left the Fifth as it was but for the addition of South Carolina. Assuming that Justice Daniel would be assigned to the new Fifth Circuit, he protested the transfer "at the sacrifice of all the social ties which bind him, and which have been going on through life—and a transfer from a climate which they knew to be salubrious, to the pestilential atmosphere of New Orleans and Mobile; presenting the alternative of great risk or resignation, which he hoped was not the object of any gentleman. He could not believe that such motives influenced any gentleman of that body; he would not suppose it, because it would be to suppose that gentlemen were aiming a deadly blow at the independence of the judiciary itself."[28]

For the Whigs, Daniel D. Barnard of New York offered the reminder that the change in circuits met the needs of the judiciary and that protest would not have come but for the involvement of the interest of a particular judge. The judges themselves were to decide which of their number would occupy the two southern circuits. The bill was passed by a vote of 115 to 68.[29]

Although Congress avoided responsibility by directing the Supreme Court to allocate the Fifth and Ninth Circuits among the Justices, attempts were made to influence the Court from behind the scenes. Justice McLean reported that at the time the allocation was to be made Chief Justice Taney received letters from all the members of the Senate Judiciary Committee saying that in passing the law it was expected that Justice Daniel would take the Fifth Circuit, consisting of Alabama and Louisiana. McLean, anticipating political maneuvers on the Court in which he was likely to be in the minority, and "suspecting that this allotment would be made by caucus, in which Judge Daniel would have his choice," asked Senator Robert J. Walker of Mississippi if Daniel would be acceptable in the Ninth Circuit, and was told that he would be acceptable and that his allocation there was expected. The competition for Justice Daniel's services may or may not have been the result of Justice McKinley's reputation for getting into trouble and for not getting his work done. In any event, Justice McLean wrote to Justice Story that "by five votes Daniel was allocated to the ninth circuit, Baldwin and myself voting against it."[30]

Justice Catron had his own unique explanation of the allocation. He had been told by William Thomas Carroll, Clerk of the Supreme Court, that Robert J. Walker preferred McKinley for the Ninth Circuit.

---

[28] *Ibid.*, 877.
[29] *Ibid.*, 878. For the text of the statute see 5 Stat. 507.

[30] John McLean to Joseph Story, Jan. 25, 1843, Story Papers.

He wrote to Walker that Senator Sevier of Arkansas had had the opposite preference. In any event, he preferred to make the allocation in such a way as eventually to throw a new Supreme Court appointment to the western area. With Catron's abbreviations written out into words, his letter read in part as follows:

> Should a vacancy occur the appointment will come from your circuit—and we need it on our principles very much.
>
> The Chief Justice is exceedingly frail—indeed he will hardly outlast the next three years, I think clearly not. If he dies, then Judge Daniel will of course be retained in the Virginia circuit.
>
> Then again; Daniel is a feebler man than McKinley, and not likely to last as long. Then we get another Western judge.[31]

The prime defect of Justice Catron's strategy was that the three men died in exactly the reverse order of that which he predicted.

Justice Daniel, the chief sufferer from the rearrangement of circuits, regarded the whole arrangement as an attack on the part of his enemies. On his first trip south he wrote from Jackson, Mississippi, to Martin Van Buren, who had appointed him, saying:

> I am here two thousand miles from home (calculating by the travelling route,) on the pilgrimage by an exposure to which, it was the calculation of federal malignity that I would be driven from the Bench. Justice to my friends, and a determination to defeat the machinations of mine and their enemies, have decided me to undergo the experiment, and I have done so at no small hazard, through yellow fever at Vicksburg and congestive and autumnal fevers in this place and vicinity. The enormity of the usage I have experienced is almost without example, and I trust to the overruling protection of a good providence to disappoint its purposes, and to the justice and independence of my friends, and the friends of honor, magnanimity and common fairness to give me redress.[32]

Redress never came. Since Justice Daniel was ardently pro-Southern, the only other circuits on which he would have been comfortable were the Fourth, held by Chief Justice Taney, and the Sixth, held by Justice Wayne, and both those Justices lived well beyond the time of his death in 1860. He seems never to have stopped complaining about his hard lot. He found life in Arkansas particularly uncomfortable. He told of a hotel consisting of a beached and converted steamboat where he was housed in a room six feet by four and tormented by Buffalo gnats, and

---

[31] "John Catron to Robert J. Walker, Jan. 26, 1843," *Legal Historian*, 1:51, 1958.

[32] Peter V. Daniel to Martin Van Buren, Nov. 9, 1843, Van Buren Papers.

where, even for all the discomfort, Yankees flocked in almost as numerous as the insects and flourished and fattened among them.[33]

Like other Justices traveling westward, until the completion of the Baltimore and Ohio Railroad to the Ohio River at Wheeling in 1853, Justice Daniel was accustomed to taking a stagecoach over the Cumberland Road to the Ohio and then proceeding by steamboat down the river to his destination. Completion of the railroad promised greater speed and greater comfort. His first trip was a disillusioning experience. He set out with the handicap of a swollen ankle where a dog had bitten him, so that wearing a boot was exceedingly painful. The company had promised completion of the trip in nineteen hours, but it required two nights and a day, with frequent stops along the way but none for food or refreshment, restaurant facilities along the line not yet having been established. His discomfort threatened to continue even on the boat trip down the Ohio. He was at first offered only a portion of a stateroom in an undesirable area near the boilers. But fortunately the boat was owned in Wheeling, and the captain, recognizing his name, came to Daniel's aid and provided a commodious stateroom all to himself in the "Lady's Cabin." This special kindness was the result of his dissenting opinion in the first of the *Wheeling Bridge* cases, where he had protested that Pennsylvania could not in the Supreme Court attack the validity of the construction of a bridge which would make Wheeling rather than Pittsburgh a main port for traffic between the Ohio and the East.[34] The boat served an excellent table, "except that they do not supply you with wines of any kind, as they do on the best New Orleans boats." This boat belonging to the Baltimore and Ohio Railroad Company, "and not to the Cincinnati or Pittsburg *boors*," the managers had "some notions of decent living."[35]

For all of Justice Catron's prediction that the 1842 readjustment in circuit boundaries would "last with slight alterations for forty years,"[36] suggestions of further changes were made as new states were added to

---

[33] Peter V. Daniel to Elizabeth Daniel, Apr. 17, 1851, "Justice Daniel in Arkansas," William D. Hoyt, ed., *Arkansas Historical Quarterly*, 1:160–61, 1942.

[34] See Pennsylvania v. Wheeling and Belmont Bridge Co., 9 How. 647, 659 (1851), 13 How. 518, 593 (1852). The litigation is discussed in Chapter XVII, "The Developing Pattern of the Commerce Power."

[35] For the letter in full see "Travel to Cincinnati in 1853," William D. Hoyt, Jr., ed., *Ohio Archaeological and Historical Quarterly*, 51:62, 63–64, 1942. For all his complaints,

Justice Daniel was impressed with the stupendous achievement in the construction of the Baltimore and Ohio Railroad. He spoke of the many bridges and tunnels, was thrilled at traveling across a viaduct at giddy heights, and speculated on the possibility of cars being precipitated hundreds of feet downward into the abyss. Building and maintenance of the road, he thought, required great strength and vigilance, and great courage was required of those who traveled over it. *Ibid.*, 64.

[36] John Catron to Garrett D. Wall, Feb. 25, 1841, Dreer Collection.

the Union. Texas and Florida were admitted in 1845, Iowa was to follow in 1846, and other new states soon afterward. Early in 1846 Gideon I. Pollard, from President Polk's home town of Columbia in Tennessee, wrote to Polk about a bill to create a new circuit. He thought that existing circuits might be moved eastward and westward to create a new one of Alabama and Mississippi, and that he, as a "floating resident" of Mississippi by virtue of planting interests there, might be appointed to the new circuit.[37] But now, as in earlier years, conflicting interests stood in the way of easy adjustments of circuits to incorporate new states. And now, as earlier, the problem was partly solved in temporary fashion by establishing District Courts and giving Circuit Court jurisdiction to the district judges. The solution was only partial because although there were many highly competent district judges their level was by no means that of Justices of the Supreme Court; and while a Circuit Court consisting of a Supreme Court Justice and a district judge could send cases on to the Supreme Court by way of certificate of division of opinion, a district judge sitting alone as a circuit judge could not give litigants the benefit of that procedure for securing review in Washington. Although there was much discussion of abandonment of circuit riding for Supreme Court Justices and their replacement on circuit by judges appointed specifically as circuit judges, this device was resorted to only on the West Coast,[38] where special needs were created by the necessity of settling California land claims amounting to many millions of dollars and involving immense litigation. Major reorganization of old circuits and creation of a tenth Supreme Court Justiceship for the circuit on the West Coast did not come until the period of the Civil War.

During the early years under the Constitution, when the federal system was but vaguely understood by many of the people and when the contents of federal statutes were not widely known, the Supreme Court Justices on circuit served as educators by expounding the law, especially in their charges to grand juries. The charges were often received with real gratitude, and requests to publish them in local newspapers or journals were granted save when the Justices lacked time to write them out or avoided publication because they wished to use with apparent freshness the same charge at the different places of holding court. Yet charges delivered by Justices with Federalist sympathies were often thought to have a political slant, and the use of this judicial prerogative may well have been suspect in Democratic circles.

In any event, when in April, 1836, Chief Justice Taney addressed

---

[37] Gideon I. Pollard to James K. Polk, Jan. 22, 1846, Polk Papers.

[38] 10 Stat. 631.

in Baltimore his first grand jury, his charge was largely in the nature of an explanation of the fact that in the future he would ignore the custom of delivering such a charge:

> It has been usual for this court, at the opening of the term, to deliver a charge to the grand jury; and you will probably expect one from me, in conformity with this practice. As I doubt much the necessity of continuing the custom, and may not hereafter adhere to it, my address to you will be a brief one, and its chief object to explain why I am disposed to depart from the former practice.[39]

He admitted that there might have been a time when precise and detailed instructions were required for the purposes of justice, but with the present state of public enlightenment he thought it no longer necessary. It was not essential that the court survey the broad field of criminal jurisprudence when it was known that the action of the grand jury would be limited to a very small portion of it. He closed his charge with a general request for diligence in inquiry in consideration of the rights of the accused.

If the Taney address to the grand jury brought warm approval from Democrats, as it may well have done, it aroused scorn in Charles Sumner, close friend and former law school student of Justice Story, who liked to provide admonitions for the people on such occasions. Sumner called it a "jacobin speech." He thought it the speech of a demagogue to proclaim that the people were now so well informed as not to need the instruction of charges.[40]

Although Chief Justice Taney's first grand jury charge did not mark the end of all such charges, and it cannot be said definitely that no more were delivered even by him, they came to attract less attention and to be published only when they dealt with subjects of peculiar importance such as enforcement of neutrality laws or fugitive slave laws. Thus in 1838, as discussed elsewhere, Justice McLean, who was given to the kind of sermonizing resorted to in earlier years, urged vigilant enforcement of neutrality laws against participants in filibustering expeditions in Canada: "I invoke in behalf of the tribunals of justice, the moral power of society. I ask it to aid them in suppressing a combination of deluded or abandoned citizens, which imminently threatens the peace and prosperity of the country."[41] Other charges continued to be delivered on this subject both before and after the Civil War.

---

[39] Charge to Grand Jury, 30 Fed. Cas. 998 (No. 18257) (C.C.D. Md. 1836).

[40] Charles Sumner to Richard Peters, Nov. 23, 1836, in Vol. II of the bound volumes of the Correspondence of Richard Peters, deposited in the Cadwalader Papers.

[41] Charge to Grand Jury—Neutrality Laws, 30 Fed. Cas. 1018–19 (No. 18265) (C.C.D. Ohio 1839).

In northern states charges in considerable numbers were delivered after enactment of the Fugitive Slave Law of 1850. In Georgia Justice Wayne delivered a memorable charge with respect to the outlawing of the slave trade.[42] With the coming of the Civil War, many charges were delivered on the law of treason. But in general the educative and evangelistic functions of the Supreme Court Justices gradually declined with the passing years.

As for the judicial opinions delivered on circuit by Supreme Court Justices, some were published and others were not. Justice McLean, during his long period of service, edited and published his own opinions. Justice Curtis did the same for his shorter period. Justice Baldwin published one volume covering only the early years of his service. Justice Story delivered his circuit opinions to a series of reporters for publication, his last reporter being his son and biographer. Justice Woodbury used his son as one of the reporters of his massive opinions. After Chief Justice Taney's death, his son-in-law published a volume of selected circuit opinions. Some but by no means all of Justice Grier's opinions were published.

Other Justices published few or none of their Circuit Court opinions. There were probably several reasons. The task of preparing written opinions for the scrutiny of the bench and bar added to the already heavy burden of the circuit work. There were times when it was more comfortable to avoid publication of opinions on critical issues—which in part may explain Justice Swayne's failure to continue the practice maintained by his predecessor, Justice McLean. In some instances refraining from writing opinions may have been a convenient means of avoiding display of sheer lack of ability—with Justice McKinley as an example. Justice Catron, whose pre-Civil War circuit opinions were almost never offered for publication, provided still another reason for abstinence. He thought it undesirable that a Supreme Court Justice commit himself to writing on circuit in a matter which might be passed upon by the Supreme Court. It was said of him:

> He was opposed to the publication of circuit opinions, because he thought the Justices of the Supreme Court should meet, *in banc*, with minds perfectly open to conviction. He was apprehensive that the natural desire to vindicate one's published views on circuit, or in the more imposing shape of text-books, would induce pride of opinion or of consistency to sway the final judgment. In only one instance, so far as known, did he wish a circuit opinion of his, or of his colleagues, published. That was on a department of law comparatively but little

---

[42] Charge to Grand Jury, 30 Fed. | Cas. 1026 (No. 18269a) (C.C.D. Ga. 1859).

known in the West at that time. But even then he insisted upon his colleague's writing and delivering the opinion; simply adding that he concurred in the result.[43]

With the coming of the Civil War, it is true, his convictions on behalf of the Union were so dynamic that he found it necessary not only to announce the law but also to explain its "wisdom, justice and beneficence."

Apart from the publication of opinions and charges to grand juries, the federal courts attracted widespread public attention. In these times of restricted entertainment and diversion it was a great occasion in many areas when the Supreme Court Justice and the district judge came to town to hold federal court.[44] Important cases brought the public crowding into courtrooms as they did into the Supreme Court room in Washington. The meeting of federal courts, like meetings of state courts and of state legislatures, brought spectators from far and wide and precipitated social gatherings. The visiting judges were entertained by distinguished members of the bar and by other social leaders in the community. The judges carried political and social news from Washington and from other parts of their circuits.

In the nature of their social life the Justices varied greatly. Justice Story, for all his faithfulness to judicial duties and his extensive private writing, took ample time for enjoyment of friendly companionship. It was said that "while he was in the room few others could get in a word," but his was a rich flow of conversation sought rather than resented by his companions.[45] Justice McLean entertained extensively and made wide contacts on circuit with an eye to the realization of his political ambitions, but by some was thought too rigid and austere for good companionship. Because of physical frailty, Chief Justice Taney had to keep himself largely withdrawn from social life, recuperating in his home or at his boarding house while on circuit. The exceptional period seems to have been at the beginning of his travels to Richmond, in 1843. On his first trip there he wrote to Mrs. Taney that on the morrow he was to dine with Justice Daniel—who lived in Richmond—and meet friends there, but that he expected to do no more dining out and would

---

[43] "The Late Mr. Justice Catron," *Legal Intelligencer*, 23:132, 1866.

[44] When in November, 1838, United States District Judge John Pitman wrote to Justice Story that a new courtroom was to be dedicated at the ensuing term of the court to be held in Providence he predicted that the room would "probably be thronged by the citizens and not a *few ladies* under the expectation that something

Dedicatory may be said by you in your charge or in some other way." He hoped that Mrs. Story could accompany her husband. John Pitman to Joseph Story, Nov. 13, 1838, Story Papers (M.H.S.).

[45] A quotation from Lord Morpeth, *Travels in America*, "The Letters of Joseph Story," Howell J. Heaney, ed., *Am. J. Legal Hist.*, 2:68, 82, 1958.

willingly forego this experience, pleasant as the company was sure to be.[46] A week later he wrote, "I am working hard and dining out every day with most pleasant and hospitable people, who with one accord seem disposed to make my term as agreeable as I could desire."[47]

In later years Chief Justice Taney found it necessary to protect his health by holding himself pretty much in isolation when on circuit. In 1848 he wrote from Richmond that he had been unfit to pay visits and had been nowhere except to Judge Daniel's and Judge Hallyburton's. He found the travel wearing and his experience in court had been strenuous:

> I was very near making myself sick on Thursday by sitting in court from ten o'clock in the morning until five in the evening without leaving my chair. It could not however be avoided, for I was trying a man upon a charge of having been engaged in the slave trade, and as the punishment would have been death if he had been found guilty, I could not permit the jury to separate until the case was decided. I therefore remained in session until the case was finished, rather than confine the jury until the next day. But I was very much fatigued. I feared that night I had made myself sick. . . . The fellow was acquitted—but I am satisfied he was guilty and deserved to be punished. Still however I was not sorry that the jury acquitted him, for it would have been no pleasant duty to pass sentence of death upon him.[48]

---

[46] R. B. Taney to Mrs. Taney, May 2, 1843, Howard Papers.

[47] R. B. Taney to Mrs. Taney, May 10, 1843, *ibid.* The following item of local color with respect to one of Taney's trips to Richmond was attributed to the editor of the *Barre Gazette* and reprinted June 14, 1845, in *Niles' National Register*, 68:229:
The U.S. circuit court is now in session here, held by Chief Justice Taney. I was present at the opening of the court on Monday and observed an aged negro dressed in a long black coat, small clothes and stockings, knee buckles and other characteristics of fashion "sixty years old." As the chief justice entered the door, the old fellow rose and was greeted by the head of the judiciary with as much civility as if he had been the "chief executive magistrate." The chief justice and the district judge shook him cordially by the hand and made inquiries for his health. On inquiry I found he was the slave and favorite body servant of the late Chief Justice Marshall, whose memory the faithful negro cherishes in most affectionate remembrance. He is but a nominal slave, now, preferring like many others here, not to be free. He dresses in precisely the style of his former distinguished owner, and insists on being at the door of the court house, as in days of yore, to tender his services to the esteemed successor of his old master. He takes the hat of the chief justice, fills his glass of water, and does several other offices as proudly as if he were the titled chamberlain of a king, and is treated with as much consideration by the very urbane and popular jurist as his old master could have been.

[48] R. B. Taney to Mrs. Anne Taney, May 7, 1848, B. C. Howard Papers.

X: *The Judges and the Circuits*

At New Castle, Delaware, the Chief Justice complained of his living quarters somewhat as Justice Daniel lamented his quarters in Napoleon, Arkansas, in a six-by-four room in a converted steamboat. Of his room Taney complained that "in size, and furniture and cleanliness, it is very little better than a well kept pigpen." For his parlor at night he had the room in which the court and members of the bar had their meals during the day. These included Wilmington lawyers and Judge Willard Hall, who went home at the end of each day. But for the use at night of this dining room, "I hardly know how I could write you a letter, for I have no table in my room—nor is it big enough to hold one without taking out the bed."[49]

Justice Catron, who as a member of the bar had been accustomed to camping out when traveling circuit with hard-drinking, hard-fighting, gun-toting fellows, was probably not distressed by uncomfortable living quarters when he began his tours as a circuit justice. But he was disturbed by the combination of envy and lack of respect with which he was received in Kentucky. Gossip had it there that he and James K. Polk, whose wives were Childresses, had married heiresses, and that they were now independently wealthy, and that "things in Tennessee are ruled with a golden rod." It had also been reported, presumably through Senator John J. Crittenden, a Kentucky Whig ("Poor man! He has forgotten Blackstone, and is getting too old to declaim"),[50] that Catron was wanting in legal skill. This criticism from a bar like that of Kentucky filled Catron with derision: "Where the most important causes are heard and decided without reference to a single book, and any knowledge where the law is to be found. The best lawyers here we have never heard of; these are sore at the repute [of] their brethren, whose fame is based on stump oratory, and they are content with any judge who is capable and does his duty: nor do the Seniors presume to complain, for whether the judge is right or wrong they have no knowledge."[51]

Worse than that, as Justice McKinley got into a controversy with Judge Lawrence in New Orleans over the appointment of the court clerk, so Justice Catron was disrespectfully treated by Judge Thomas B. Monroe in Frankfort. Justice McLean, in whose circuit Kentucky had formerly been included, had called Monroe the most impractical man he had ever seen. Catron wrote to McLean that he had had more

---

[49] R. B. Taney to Mrs. Anne Taney, May 25, 1848, *ibid.*

[50] Apart from the personal and political animus here disclosed there is nothing to show why Catron spoke thus disparagingly of Crittenden, who in 1837 was only fifty years of age,

with a quarter of a century of his distinguished career at the bar, in Congress, and as Attorney General still ahead of him.

[51] John Catron to James K. Polk, May 8, 1837, Polk Papers.

annoyance with Monroe in three weeks than he had experienced in twelve years on the Tennessee bench:

> I feel very sure that but one course is left me, either tamely to follow, and permit the man to preside in the court, and decide every cause in his own way, or to act independently of him, with little or no consultation. How did you get along? and especially on the Bench. There he submits to no judgment I give, though we agree in the consulting room, and he informs me he has at all times delivered his opinion *first* on all occasions, and which I have no means of preventing without a direct and open rupture, so far as I can now see. What is your practice with the District judges? I imagined it to be as I had seen the practice in Tennessee, for the presiding judge to consult the other judge on the Bench in all cases, and then deliver the conclusion, but here I consult, and Judge Monroe instantly delivers the judgment of the Court—giving all directions to the clerk, counsel, &c. The Bar and the officers of the Court—especially the latter, are so annoyed that I will be compelled at the next term to take a stand for the helm—for two thirds of the time is talked and trifled away, and angry contentions grow up, that it is a duty to prevent, and I should be very much obliged for your advice, which shall be entirely confidential, and which you alone can give.[52]

McLean's reply to Catron's plea is not known. Presumably the Supreme Court Justice and the District judge worked out a means of accommodation, for there is no clear record of continuing strife. The relationship marked the diversity likely to characterize judicial associations on circuit. Judge Monroe was operating in his home area and was well known there as a Kentucky lawyer and politician who had been elevated to judicial office by President Jackson in 1834. Justice Catron had been elevated by the same President to an even higher office, but he was from Tennessee, a community far more distant than it seems today. Catron was an inveterate politician, rough and vigorous and outgiving in association. Monroe had scholarly inclinations and much less of a feel for practical politics. He liked working with young men, and, along with his judicial work, spent part of several years teaching law in his home, at the University of Louisiana, at the Transylvania Law School, and at Western Military Institute. He received honorary degrees from Centre College in Kentucky and from Harvard University. Both men had proslavery sentiments. But while Catron tried to keep his state in the Union at the time of secession, Monroe was an ardent secessionist. When threatened with military arrest he sent President Lincoln a letter saying, "I have determined to emigrate and hereby resign the

---

[52] John Catron to John McLean, May 19, 1837, McLean Papers.

office I have held of judge of the United States in and for the District of Kentucky."[53] He set out for Nashville, where before a Confederate judge he made a declaration as of an alien announcing his intention to become a citizen of the Confederate States.[54] Catron in turn followed Union forces back to Nashville and resumed there the functions of the federal judiciary.

Circuit Court problems were also illustrated by Catron's report on his first visit to St. Louis to hold court there. The district judge for Missouri was Robert W. Wells, an able lawyer with whom Catron apparently got on well in spite of major differences on some legal questions, as in the field of bankruptcy. But having made the trip, by steamboat down the Ohio and then up the Mississippi to St. Louis, Catron found that the marshal of the court had not yet received his commission and so was not able to act. Furthermore, the necessary court records had not yet been transferred to St. Louis from Jefferson City, the capital of the state. For this term, therefore, the court did not sit at all. Catron limited his activities to sizing up the lawyers, the people, and the political situation. He found that the lawyers were usually poor and dependent on the merchants for support. They were generally critical of their United States Senator, Thomas Hart Benton, an ardent Jacksonian, and of the "rabble" running the government whom they stigmatized as "Jackson Boys." Although he was told that the lawyers were well informed, Catron had little opportunity to ascertain this fact.[55] In later years he found St. Louis the center of important legal business with able lawyers in charge. Yet personnel problems continued to keep operations uncertain. In 1844, for example, it was reported that the United States District Court for the adjustment of land titles in St. Louis was obliged to adjourn for want of a marshal, and that for the same reason the ensuing term of the United States Circuit Court would be canceled.[56]

As between the two sets of lower federal courts, it seems in general to have been the Circuit Courts rather than the District Courts which experienced delays because of congestion of business, or at any rate in the cooperation between Supreme Court and District Court justices it was the District Court judges who came to the aid of the members of the Supreme Court on circuit. But even here there were exceptions. In 1843, presumably with the approval of Justice Catron, Congress came to the rescue of District Judge Morgan W. Brown in

---

[53] Thomas B. Monroe to Abraham Lincoln, Sept. 28, 1861, Attorney General Papers.
[54] Impeachment of West H. Humphreys, H.R. Rep. No. 44, 37th Cong.,

2nd Sess. 9 (1862).
[55] John Catron to James K. Polk, Apr. 16, 1837, Polk Papers.
[56] *Niles' National Register*, 67:65, 1844.

Tennessee, by providing that in his absence in the District Court the circuit judge might exercise District Court jurisdiction.[57] When in 1853 the district judgeship in Tennessee fell vacant, Catron called the attention of President Franklin Pierce to his District Court power and urged delay in filling the vacancy until the selection of a new district judge could be fully considered. He was, he wrote, "in the constant habit of doing the duties of a District Judge in addition to those of a Circuit Judge."[58] Pierce, however, refused to delay the appointment, selecting West H. Humphreys, a lawyer of presumed competence but one who soon became a fire-eating secessionist.[59]

Personal relations among judges inevitably varied from circuit to circuit and from district to district. In general those relations appeared good, and conflicts which went beyond legitimate differences on matters of law were infrequent. District judges tended in various ways to be dependent on their colleagues from the Supreme Court. The latter had the greater prestige, they were usually although by no means always more capable, in appealed cases they had the final say in the Supreme Court, and they had political associations in Washington which were apt to be important to the district judges. The district judges, with salaries varying from district to district, always wanted more money. If the Supreme Court Justices on their circuits were of the "right" political persuasion they might exercise political influence in behalf of increases, and in any event they could collect important political information. They could play a part in the perennial discussion as to whether the growth in business in particular districts justified dividing the districts and creating new judgeships.

A good example of a highly dependent relationship was that of District Judge Hugh H. Leavitt of Ohio to Justice McLean. Leavitt served the district for Ohio from 1834 until 1855 when the state was divided into two districts, and served the southern district thereafter until 1871. His sense of professional subordination to Justice McLean is indicated by a letter written in December, 1844, when he had to hold Circuit Court alone because the beginning of the Supreme Court term had been moved backward to the first of December, thereby overlapping the term of the Circuit Court. At the end of the month he wrote to Justice McLean:

> I am now near the close of the term. I have felt not a little embarrassment, in my new position, as the sole judge of the Circuit Court. I have been so long in the habit of looking to, and relying upon, your

---

[57] 5 Stat. 610.
[58] John Catron to Franklin Pierce, Mar. 10, 1853, Attorney General Papers.

[59] Impeachment of West H. Humphreys, H.R. Rep. No. 44, 37th Cong., 2nd Sess. 9 (1862).

greatly superior learning and judgment, that I scarcely knew how to encounter the responsibility thrown upon me. I have however gone on comfortably; and, have endeavored at least, to do the best I could. How far I may have given satisfaction, I have not the means of knowing. There have been a good many trials; though the more important cases of ejectment, and in chancery, have been continued.[60]

On at least two scores Judge Leavitt desired the help of Justice McLean. First, he hoped to have his salary raised above the inadequate annual figure of one thousand dollars—in the face of the tendency to restrict government salaries wherever possible rather than to raise them. In the second place, he hoped for the division of Ohio into two districts, for which a bill was drafted by William Miner, clerk of the court, and shown to Justice McLean before being submitted for introduction in Congress. It was this same clerk who, with McLean's and Leavitt's approval, was pushing the fight for the extension of the admiralty jurisdiction of the federal courts to the lakes and rivers of the United States, believing that the increase in the work of the District Court would promote division of the district and add to the fees of court officers.[61] It was hoped that Justice McLean could advance these measures through his contacts in Washington, in return for which Leavitt kept McLean posted on political happenings in Ohio.

As far as the salary increase was concerned, Leavitt faced the opposition of members of the Ohio delegation in Congress,[62] including Senator Benjamin Tappan, sponsor of a bill to reduce the terms of federal judges to seven years—which in view of Tappan's hostility to Leavitt would presumably have eliminated Leavitt altogether from the federal judiciary. So although he desired division of the judicial district, Leavitt wrote to McLean of his fears that it might be done in such a way as to eliminate his position altogether:

Indeed, I have heard from a source entitling it to credence, that it is in contemplation by some of the fierce radicals as a part of the plan, to cut off my judicial legs. This, I understand, they propose to accomplish by a repeal of the law creating the District of Ohio—which they suppose will repeal my commission—and then to provide for the division of the state into two Districts, conferring on the President the power to appoint a Judge, Attorney and Marshal for each. This though a bold project, and savouring of the extremest radicalism, involving as I think, a virtual infraction of the Constitution, may be attempted. There are some rabid politicians in this state, as you are well apprized, who will stop at nothing, to accomplish their purposes.

---

60 H. H. Leavitt to John McLean, Dec. 10, 1844, McLean Papers.
61 H. H. Leavitt to John McLean,

Dec. 19, 1844, *ibid.*
62 See H. H. Leavitt to John McLean, Jan. 10, 1840, *ibid.*

And, I thought I could take the liberty of requesting you to keep an eye to the movements at Washington, in relation to this matter, with a view to counteract the machinations of those who may lend themselves to the accomplishment of the proposed plan, should it be attempted.[63]

The plan to divide Ohio into two federal judicial districts contemplated the holding of courts at Cleveland and Cincinnati, rather than at Columbus, as hitherto, and therefore incurred opposition from lawyers and businessmen in Columbus. To protect its interests that city sent to Washington Noah H. Swayne—who in 1862 would be appointed to the Supreme Court by President Lincoln to replace Justice McLean. Judge Leavitt wrote to Justice McLean:

I am sure, there is no man in the state, whose interests I should be more disposed to regard, or who, I should more reluctantly disoblige, than Col. Swayne. But, in the first place, I can not believe, that his *individual* interests are greatly concerned, in the matter. I have very little doubt, that he would have quite as good a practice in the federal courts, if located at Cincinnati, as he has, under the existing arrangement. And, as it relates to the interests of the owners and keepers of hotels in Columbus, that may be supposed to be, to some extent, affected by this measure, I do not know that Col. S____ need feel any apprehensive degree of anxiety.[64]

Although no return correspondence is available to show clearly the part played by Justice McLean with respect to the districts and the jurisdiction of federal courts in Ohio, it seems clear that he served faithfully as an ambassador in the matter. The admiralty jurisdiction was expanded, by enactment and by interpretation, and in 1855 the state was divided into two districts as had long been sought,[65] Judge Leavitt being allocated to the southern circuit. Increasingly in that state and throughout the Seventh Circuit, the district judges performed circuit duties both with Justice McLean and independently when he was unable to appear. On the part of none of them was there such an assertion of independence and prerogative as that made by Judge Monroe of Kentucky with respect to control of the Circuit Court in the presence of Justice Catron.

Judicial relationships varied similarly on other circuits. Toward Justice Story the district judges of the First Circuit showed affection and great respect. The mutuality of such feeling is demonstrated by mis-

---

[63] H. H. Leavitt to John McLean, Dec. 19, 1844; see also H. H. Leavitt to John McLean, Dec. 30, 1844, and William Miner to John McLean, Dec.

31, 1844, *ibid.*
[64] H. H. Leavitt to John McLean, Feb. 6, 1845, *ibid.*
[65] 10 Stat. 604.

cellaneous correrespondence and such other items as Justice Story's dedication of his *Commentaries on the Law of Agency* to Judge John Davis, long the United States district judge for Massachusetts. We have the story of a hot professional dispute between Justice Story and Chief Justice Parker of New Hampshire over the application of the federal Bankruptcy Act, but no such dispute between him and district judges seems to have been recorded. On the other hand, on the Second Circuit, Justice Nelson so enraged Judge Alfred Conkling by some of his admiralty decisions that Conkling, after leaving the bench, scathingly denounced Nelson in a revision of his admiralty treatise. There may be some truth to the generalization that the ablest and the most influential Justices were treated with respect by their subordinates whereas other Justices were not, but the generalization should not be overemphasized.

The subject matter of Circuit Court work varied considerably from circuit to circuit and from region to region. Unsettled land titles on the frontier called for specialization in this subject and, as has been noted, Justice Catron's principal claim to distinction derived from such specialized knowledge. Justice Grier's appointment to the Third Circuit was justified in part because of his knowledge of the peculiar land laws of Pennsylvania and because he had the approved sentiments toward the responsibility of the courts for the return of fugitive slaves. The appointments of other Justices seem to have been scrutinized in the light of their attitudes on the latter subject, with Circuit Court work as well as work of the Supreme Court in mind.

In 1859 a significant if possibly biased article in the *New York Tribune* discussed the circuits in terms of the kind and extent of the work to be done. It noted that the result of the addition of the Eighth and Ninth Circuits in 1837 was to give predominance to slavery interests, in spite of the fact that the population and legal business of the North exceeded that of the South, with the disparity steadily increasing. The North had four circuits and the South had five. The writer noted that the business of the Circuit Courts was chiefly of two kinds. They were suits on patents for inventions, and civil cases arising out of maritime business and the revenue laws. Nearly all the patents were issued in the North, and most of the litigation occurred there. As for shipping, during the preceding year the four Northern circuits had produced more than four million tons whereas the five Southern had produced less than nine hundred thousand tons.[66] The article ignored the unusually large amount of debtor litigation that occurred in the Ninth Circuit in the South as originally established, especially in the years immediately following the panic of 1837, and it ignored the greater distances that had

---

[66] *New York Tribune*, Mar. 26, 1859.

to be traveled in the Southern circuits and the greater difficulties of travel. Nevertheless its judgment may in the main have been justified. The situation is confused by the fact that both the quantity and character of the work of the Circuit Courts varied with time and circumstances—with periods of hard times or of prosperity and expanding business, with developments taking place in business and in transportation, and with the periodic involvement of the nation in war.

There were still other areas of difference. At least throughout Justice McKinley's term, from 1837 to 1852, the interrelation of common law and civil law procedures in Louisiana created difficulties.[67] Practices varied from state to state even where rootage was completely in the common law, as in the extent to which judges attempted to guide the verdicts of juries. An illustration was provided by the decision of the Supreme Court in *Mitchell v. Harmony* where, speaking through Chief Justice Taney, the Court upheld vigorous guidance by Justice Nelson on circuit in interpreting facts to the jury as well as the law. Said the Chief Justice:

> The practice in this respect differs in different states. In some of them the court neither sums up the evidence in a charge to the jury, nor expresses an opinion upon a question of fact. Its charge is strictly confined to questions of law, leaving the evidence to be discussed by counsel, and the facts to be decided by the jury without commentary or opinion by the court.
>
> But in most of the states the practice is otherwise; and they have adopted the usages of the English courts of justice, where the judge always sums up the evidence and points out the conclusions, which in his opinion ought to be drawn from it; submitting them, however, to the consideration and judgment of the jury.
>
> It is not necessary to inquire which of these modes of proceeding most conduces to the purposes of justice. It is sufficient to say that either of them may be adopted under the laws of Congress. And as it is desirable that the practice in the courts of the United States should conform, as nearly as practicable, to that of the state in which they are sitting, that mode of proceeding is perhaps to be preferred, which from long-established usage and practice, has become the law of the courts of the state.[68]

Justice Daniel, however, with long quotations from Blackstone and Coke, contended in dissent that the charge should be limited to statement of points of law and to the competency or relevancy of testimony.

But in this matter succeeding Justices even from the same state

---

[67] See John McKinley to Martin Van Buren, Nov. 9, 1839, Van Buren Papers.

[68] Mitchell v. Harmony, 13 How. 115, 130–31 (1852).

tended to differ. Justice Baldwin of Pennsylvania had told a jury that they had the power to decide on the law as well as the facts and were not obligated to accept the judge's opinion as to the law.[69] By contrast, Justice Grier, who succeeded Baldwin, was apt to be "most emphatic in his charge, not unfrequently arguing the cause to the jury as an advocate."[70]

As is discussed elsewhere, the Justices on circuit differed on many other subjects, such as the scope of the federal bankruptcy power and admiralty jurisdiction. Yet in the main, for all the regional and personal diversity, their functions were pretty much the same. As courts of original jurisdiction, the Circuit Courts applied federal law in cases involving the criminal law of the United States and in other areas where such jurisdiction was given in connection with particular statutes, as in the act for chartering the Second Bank of the United States.[71] Part of the jurisdiction of the Circuit Courts was original and a limited amount of it was appellate from the United States District Courts. In cases resting on diversity of citizenship, the Circuit Courts applied state law, save that what was regarded as a general federal common law was developed and applied by these courts where there was no applicable local statute and where the controversy involved general problems of commercial law. If the circuit work of the Justices often appeared to be more that of local courts than of courts of the nation as a whole, the Justices nevertheless gave shape to the developing body of federal law, and in doing so gained the knowledge of local law and local conditions necessary to appropriate action as members of the Supreme Court.

A further fact is important. The amount of work which came to the Circuit Courts, or at least that part of it which involved diversity of citizenship, tended to vary in terms of the despatch with which it was done and the confidence which the bar and the people had in the respective courts. For a time, for example, as a result of the excellent work of Justice Baldwin, the Circuit Court in Pennsylvania had high prestige and tended to draw the kind of cases appropriate to it. From this work Justice Baldwin himself published one volume of reports, and he arranged with John William Wallace, many years later the Reporter of the Supreme Court, for the publication of another. But during his later years Justice Baldwin was absent from court a great deal because of illness, and the illness or his critical financial situation led him to take up residence in one of the remote counties of the state. After his death the position was vacant for more than two years before it was

---

[69] United States v. Wilson, 28 Fed. Cas. 699, 712 (No. 16730) (C.C.E.D. Pa. 1830).

[70] J. F. W. White, "The Judiciary of Allegheny County," *Pennsylvania*

Magazine of History and Biography, 7:143, 175, 1883.

[71] See for example Osborn v. Bank of the United States, 9 Wheat 738 (1824).

filled, in 1846, by the appointment of Justice Grier. In the eastern part of Pennsylvania, furthermore, continuity was interrupted by personnel changes in 1842 and again in 1846. A law journal in 1850 reported:

> [W]hen the present Judges took their places on the bench, the business of the Court had so largely departed from it, so much of what remained was fallen into decay, and indeed, the Court itself had become so unfamiliar to the bar, that notwithstanding the well known character of the new Judges, and their readiness to attend to the business of the Circuit, it was impossible for some time, to bring anything to a condition in which it could be either heard or disposed of. A jurisdiction entirely new would have had less to contend with in this respect, than one thus fallen into desuetude. It is only now, indeed, that the confidence which the new Court so justly inspired, begins to shew itself in the increase of its business and the revival of its ancient importance.[72]

Yet for all the temporary effect of this hiatus, the problem worked itself out within a few years after the appointment of Justice Grier, as did most circuit problems deriving from personnel changes or the peculiar characteristics of particular Justices. For all the diversity, there was a steady drift in the direction of uniformity.

The Justices resided primarily within the circuits to which they were assigned rather than in Washington, gave much of their time to their circuit work, and in some instances perhaps felt a closer allegiance to individual circuits than to the Supreme Court itself, for which they assembled in Washington for only a few months each year. Certain it is that their circuit work gave them an earthy knowledge of local law and local conditions, even as their work on the Supreme Court played its part in efforts to complete the forging of a nation. If the interplay of the two kinds of responsibility was to prove inadequate to the achievement of the final goal of unity without trial by battle, the fault may have lain not so much in the judicial system or in the personnel as in the impossible dimensions of the task to be performed.

---

[72] From a review of the first volume of Wallace's reports for the third circuit, *Am. L.J.*, 9:431–32, 1850.

CHAPTER XI

The Expanding Work Load

ALTHOUGH FROM THE TIME OF the establishment of the federal judicial system members of the Supreme Court complained about the burden of circuit riding, nearly half a century passed before the work of the Court itself came to be regarded as unduly heavy. As of the middle 1820s the Court met each year on the first Monday in February and sat until the middle of March or perhaps until the end of the third week, after which the seven Justices dispersed to their respective circuits. Congress in 1826 provided that from 1827 onward the term should begin the first Monday in January rather than the first Monday in February,[1] presumably because of the more than one hundred cases left on the docket annually, but the matter seems not to have been regarded as of stirring importance in comparison with the more intricate problem of rearranging the circuits. In any event, the lengthening of the term reduced substantially the number of cases left in arrears.

When Chief Justice Taney first presided over the Court, at the January term of 1837, the docket seemed of manageable proportions. It was said that every case on the docket was called,[2] and only twenty-nine were left unargued. The Court found it possible that year to adjourn as early as March 16, leaving Taney ample time for additional work on President Jackson's farewell address. But during the years immediately following, the Court found itself under increasing pressure. In 1838 Justice Story complained about the effect of the increased size of the Court on its deliberations:

---

[1] 4 Stat. 160.

[2] Joseph R. Ingersoll, *Cong. Globe*, 30th Cong., 1st Sess. 398 (1848); for the status of the docket from 1823 to 1846 see *ibid.*, App. 351. For figures through 1848 see *U.S. Monthly Law Mag.*, 1:84, 1850.

You may ask how the Judges got along together? We made very slow progress, and did less in the same time than I ever knew. The addition to our numbers has most sensibly affected our facility as well as rapidity of doing business. "Many men of many minds" require a great deal of discussion to compel them to come to definite results; and we found ourselves often involved in long and very tedious debates. I verily believe, if there were twelve Judges, we should do no business at all, or at least very little.[3]

Through most of the Taney period members of the Court and their friends in Congress worked at the task of relieving the Court of the pressure of an ever expanding load of work. A minor but specific attempt at relief came in 1839 when Congress repealed the Act of 1802 requiring that the Justice allocated to the Fourth Circuit should attend Court in Washington on the first Monday in August to make orders with respect to the business of the Court.[4] Although for many years Justice Duvall had not seen fit to be present, but had left it to the Clerk of the Court to announce continuance of cases, Chief Justice Taney appeared regularly at the time designated. In 1838 the attention of Congress was called to this term when the clerk of the District Court in Louisiana contested his removal by Judge Lawrence in the face of opposition from Justice McKinley. Chief Justice Taney announced that he had no power to deal with such a matter at the August term,[5] while the full Court in 1839 decided that the district judge under existing statutes had full power of removal.[6] Congress at this time abolished the August term and, incidentally, provided that the Circuit Courts should have the power of appointment of their own clerks and that in the event of a disagreement between the judges the appointment should be made by the presiding judge[7]—the Supreme Court Justice on circuit. But the abolition of the August term did no more than save a day of time for one member of the Court.

As elderly men, the members of the Court were harassed by illness, and absences from the Bench were frequent. Throughout his judicial career Justice McKinley, reputedly always in poor health, attended Court only sporadically, in Washington as well as on circuit. If his nonattendance was relatively unimportant as far as his intellectual contribution is concerned, his absence sometimes meant that cases on which his brethren were evenly divided had to be reargued, at great expense in terms of the time of the Court. Because of illness Justice

---

[3] Joseph Story to Charles Sumner, Mar. 15, 1838, *Life and Letters of Joseph Story*, William W. Story, ed., II, 296.

[4] 2 Stat. 156; 5 Stat. 322.

[5] *Ex parte* Hennen, 13 Pet. 225 (1839).

[6] *Ex parte* Hennen, 13 Pet. 230 (1839).

[7] 5 Stat. 322.

Story was absent during the entire term of 1843. Chief Justice Taney, who had always had serious health problems, found that they increased with the passing years. In 1841 he wrote to Andrew Jackson, "I have become so liable to sudden and severe attacks upon my lungs, that I can hardly expect again to have health enough to justify me in venturing upon the journey to visit you, which I have so long hoped to make."[8]

In 1843, the term of Justice Story's absence, Chief Justice Taney wrote to express his regret, noting that the daily discussions of the Court involved questions of great interest and that large amounts of property were at stake:

> And I felt your absence the more sensibly because Brother Thompson was obliged to leave early in the Term. And I have been so accustomed to have you on the one side and him on the other, that with the sincerest respect for my other Brethren, I must acknowledge that it was sometimes uncomfortable to feel that you were both absent. After Judge Thompson left us there were only six attending, and it several times happened that we were reduced to a mere Court, from the indisposition of some one or other of the Judges. We however worked on to the usual time of adjourning. Yet I am sorry to tell you that at the close of the session we found that we had not been able to dispose of the cases which stood for argument at the last Term—some fifteen or twenty I believe not having been reached in the call of the docket—and two which were argued, and took up two weeks in argument, being ordered to be reargued at the next Term, on account of differences of opinion among the attending Judges, and in the hope of a full Bench at the next term.[9]

As indicated by Chief Justice Taney's letter, the 1843 term was critical in the matter of falling behind in numbers of cases and important issues left undecided. The 1844 term saw a further regression. Justice Story was back in action but soon after the beginning of the term Chief Justice Taney fell ill and was absent the remainder of the term. Justice Story, who presided in the absence of the Chief Justice, wrote to his son that Taney's constitution was exceedingly feeble and broken. He reported that the work of the Court was going on slowly and tediously, with long arguments and long speeches, "which of course must combine much reflection and still more irrelevant matter."[10]

Justice Catron, listening to long arguments in the *Girard Will Case*,[11] was much less tolerant than Justice Story. To relieve his feel-

---

[8] R. B. Taney to Andrew Jackson, Apr. 24, 1841, *Correspondence of Andrew Jackson*, John S. Bassett, ed., VI, 106.

[9] R. B. Taney to Joseph Story, Mar. 18, 1843, Story Papers (M.H.S.).

[10] Joseph Story to W. W. Story, Jan. 30, 1844, Story Papers (M.H.S.).

[11] Vidal v. Philadelphia, 2 How. 127 (1844).

ings he wrote to James Buchanan of Pennsylvania about the consumption of time by his Philadelphia friends. He yearned to see as Chief Justice such a bully as old Kenyon[12] was, or old Spencer,[13] tossing out with a pitchfork two-thirds of a speech. Spencer had reduced the New York bar to speeches of not more than an hour. If John Sergeant of Pennsylvania were told that fifteen of his twenty heads were too familiar for discussion, and Walter Jones of Virginia were told the same, all such refuse would become unfashionable in a month. But in the Supreme Court not the slightest control was exercised or even claimed. The Chief Justice should suggest the needed curtailments to counsel and then consult with the Court. In most instances his brethren would assent. A single term would set the fashion of brevity. Catron had discussed the subject with the Chief Justice and his brethren to the point of boredom but without result. He suggested that if the Court were required each term to end its docket rather than merely to serve some two months of time, the Chief Justice would be quickly pressed into action.[14]

In asking the Chief Justice to take responsibility for suppression of irrelevant oratory, Catron was asking him for an authoritarian type of performance that was out of character with Taney's gentle and courteous if sometimes highly persistent personality. In asking the Court as a whole to take such action he was asking the tribunal to run counter to the tradition of oratory that still characterized public functions in American government. The maximum that was to be had at this time was a polite appeal to the bar on February 1, 1844, spoken through Justice Story in the absence of the convalescent Chief Justice. He called attention to the congested state of the docket "arising from the great increase of the business of the country, and the magnitude and importance of the interests involved in it." The Court could do but little to dispose of the mass of causes without the cooperation of the bar. He noted that litigants seeking speedy settlements could bring cases before the Court on printed arguments which the Court could examine when not listening to oral presentations. Moreover, while admitting that some cases required lengthy arguments, he urged condensation wherever possible and stressed the need that "where there were two counsel, one of whom was immediately to follow the other in argument, much time would be saved in cases embracing different points, if the counsel were to divide those points and each should argue, when practicable, the points not occupied by the other."[15]

---

[12] Lloyd Kenyon, first Lord Kenyon (1732–1802), master of the rolls.

[13] Judge Ambrose Spencer (1765–1848), of the New York Supreme Court.

[14] John Catron to James Buchanan, Jan. 28, 1844, Buchanan Papers.

[15] "Supreme Court of the United States," *Law Rep.*, 6:523, 524, 1844.

This plea for condensation of arguments had insufficient effect, and Chief Justice Taney could not be persuaded to curb unnecessary oratory. Finally, to take effect at the December term, 1849, the Court adopted over the protest of Justices Wayne and Woodbury its Rule No. 53 whereby it was ordered that no counsel be permitted to speak in the argument of any case for more than two hours without the special permission of the Court given in advance. It was required also that counsel submit in advance a printed abstract with points to be made and books and cases to be cited, and reference in argument to other books or cases was forbidden.[16]

In the meantime, in 1844, as a result of the frustrations of the Supreme Court that year in coping with the docket, the Court and Congress worked out an arrangement for giving more time to the Court in Washington. The beginning of the annual term was again shifted back, from the first Monday in January to the first Monday in December, and each Justice was freed from the obligation to attend more than one term of the Circuit Court in any district during any year, the term attended to be that of his own selection.[17] To this limited extent, therefore, the problem of the Supreme Court was solved at the expense of work on circuit. Since circuit work was likewise expanding in quantity, the change meant that more of it had to be done by district judges.

But mere addition of a month to the term of the Supreme Court, a month in which occurred the Christmas holidays, did little to help the Court with its basic problem. The Court continued to fall behind with its work. By January of 1846 Senator Henry Johnson of Louisiana was seeking elimination of circuit duties or the establishment of a new circuit consisting of Louisiana and the new state of Texas.[18] According to Justice Catron, by early 1846 most members of the Court had reached the conclusion that since with the carrying of circuit duties not more than a third of the work of the Supreme Court could be done, the Court must ask that all circuit work be allocated to the district judges and the membership of the Supreme Court thereafter reduced to seven as deaths occurred. Appeals to the Supreme Court were to lie in all cases of judgments and decrees involving more than five hundred dollars.

To protest against this plan and provide a counterproposal, Justice Catron wrote a long letter to Milton Brown, a Tennessee member of the Judiciary Committee of the House of Representatives. If the plan were

---

[16] 7 How. v (1849).
[17] 5 Stat. 676. As if to placate Justices or other persons disapproving of the arrangement, it was provided, however, that any Justice might at his discretion attend other terms when in his opinion the public interest required it.
[18] *Cong. Globe*, 29th Cong., 1st Sess. 182, 261–62 (1846); Senate Doc. No. 91, 29th Cong., 1st Sess. (1846).

adopted, he argued, within five years all the Justices would reside in or near Washington, they would eventually come to be selected from the great departments of the government, and they would be destitute of knowledge of the terrain, the habits, the practice, and the local statutes of the states: "All the common sense of the Court would be lost, to a great extent. No legal knowledge I care not how high it is can supply the humble information that country life teaches, and on which most decisions affecting property (to say no more) must depend in some degree."[19] The district judges not usually being first-class in the legal profession, and the dollar value at which appeals could be taken being fixed so low, the Supreme Court would be flooded with appeals in unimportant cases and would lose all dignity and force.

Justice Catron's counterproposal was that, with the current Circuit Court work transferred to the District Courts, the district judges in each circuit should meet annually at central points, with the Supreme Court Justice of the circuit presiding, to serve as an intermediate court of appeals, each such court to sit until its docket was cleared. Writs of error and appeal were to lie to the Supreme Court only in cases involving constitutional questions or property to the amount of from two to five thousand dollars. By this arrangement he thought that only great causes would come to the Supreme Court, and only after they had been sifted by local lawyers familiar with the local law and the facts. The great mass of legal business would stop with what Catron preferred to call conference courts. Under this arrangement the Supreme Court "will be one of dignity and force; the Bar will be brought together and be improved by ambition, exertions and high preparations—the Judges[20] will also learn much and become different men in mind; have higher aspirations, and will exert themselves to produce superior opinions. These should be required in every case, they would be reported of course; men would be anxious to do so as the Court would be of a high grade and its judgments authoritative."[21]

It would appear that Justice Catron won at least some of his brethren over to his position. The records of the Court preserve a draft of a bill, in his longhand, marked as sent to the Judiciary Committee on February 18, 1846, which embodies his proposals with the notation that the intermediate courts were to be renamed courts of appeals at the request of Justice Nelson, and that the amount of three thousand dollars be fixed as the point permitting writs of error and appeals to the

---

[19] John Catron to Milton Brown, Feb. 12, 1846, draft, Clerk's Files.
[20] It would appear from the context that Justice Catron is referring to the district judges rather than primarily to members of the Supreme Court.
[21] Ibid.

Supreme Court at the request of Justice Woodbury.[22] The effort bogged down, however, amid problems growing out of the war with Mexico, sectional rivalry, and other issues. It is recorded that on August 4, 1846, Edwin H. Ewing of Tennessee introduced in the House of Representatives a bill "to alter and amend the judicial system of the United States," which was referred to the Judiciary Committee,[23] but no action was taken on the bill. Justice Catron's proposal was left merely to provide grist for further discussion in later years.

An entanglement of docket problems with problems of the jurisdiction of the federal courts led Chief Justice Taney in 1846 to a discussion of the former in an opinion of the Supreme Court. In 1844 John A. Barry, a British subject resident in Nova Scotia, sought from the Supreme Court a writ of habeas corpus to gain custody of his daughter, who like her mother was American born, and who was with her grandmother in New York, the parents having been separated since 1838 and the courts of New York having refused to surrender the child to the father. The unanimous Supreme Court, speaking through Justice Story, found that it had no jurisdiction, and left Barry to seek redress "in such other tribunal of the United States as may be entitled to grant it."[24] Barry then sought the writ in the United States Circuit Court in New York. The writ was denied and the case taken back to the Supreme Court by writ of error. Barry returned to the United States to represent himself before the Supreme Court at the term beginning in December, 1844, but the case was not reached on the docket. He returned the following year, but fell ill in New York, and did not reach the Supreme Court until the day after the case had been called and sent back to the foot of the docket. In February, 1846, Barry filed with the Court a petition explaining his predicament and asking to be heard at that term. In response to this petition Chief Justice Taney filed for the Supreme Court a unanimous opinion regretting that the case must go over but saying that more was involved than a mere departure from established rules:

> In four or five weeks, at farthest, the court will be compelled to close its session, in order to enable its members to perform their duties at the circuits; and several important cases, some of which cannot be continued without producing much public inconvenience in three or more of the States, have already been specially assigned for argument, and the order in which they are to be taken up announced from the bench;

---

[22] First draft of the Judiciary bill of 1846—sections altered, others left in. Submitted draft sent to Judiciary Committee Feb. 18, 1846, Clerk's Files.

[23] H.R. 530. H.R. Jour., 29th Cong., 1st Sess. 1216 (1846).

[24] *Ex parte* Barry, 2 How. 65, 66 (1844).

and in obedience to this notice counsel have been for some time past, and still are, attending to argue them; it is very doubtful whether enough remains of the term to enable the court to dispose of these cases, and it is probable that one or more of them may of necessity be continued.[25]

In these circumstances the Court felt unable to make a place for the insertion of Barry's case. The case went over to the ensuing term, when the Court decided that under existing statutes it could review the judgments of a Circuit Court only when the matter in dispute had a known value, and when the amount involved exceeded two thousand dollars. In this case no specified value was in dispute, and the writ of error had to be dismissed for want of jurisdiction.[26]

The middle to late 1840s was the period of extensive turnover on the Court, with delays in filling vacancies attributable variously to Presidents Tyler and Polk and to the Senate. It was the period of multiple arguments involving the scope of the commerce power in the *License Cases* and the *Passenger Cases*, and the cases growing out of the Dorr Rebellion, and others that were highly important. Congestion on the docket was therefore an increasingly serious matter. On February 29, 1848, Joseph R. Ingersoll of Pennsylvania told the House of Representatives that as of January 7 there had been 198 cases on the docket. The Court was at the moment hearing No. 39, and it would adjourn the following week. He offered a bill to provide a temporary remedy—that for two years the Justices be freed from all circuit responsibilities so that the accumulation of cases could be cleared.[27]

The proposal aroused discussion of all the usual points. A two-year exemption would be extended into permanent exemption. The Justices would lose contact with the people and the Court would lose prestige. Leaving the circuit work to district judges would multiply appeals to the Supreme Court and defeat the purpose of the act. Along with debate on these matters ran criticism of a life judiciary and threats of change to

---

[25] Barry v. Mercein, 4 How. 574 (1846).

[26] Barry v. Mercein, 5 How. 103 (1847). As illustrated by letters of John Sergeant to John Cadwalader in connection with argument of a case in which they were appearing for the Bank of the United States, the Court was apt to be ruthless in dropping to the foot of the docket cases which counsel were not prepared to argue when called. Even so, the tardiness of counsel tended to create confusion and the Court was compelled to do a considerable amount of skipping about over the docket to get at cases which counsel were ready to present. John Sergeant to John Cadwalader, Dec. 12, 17, 18, 19, 1846, Cadwalader Papers.

[27] *Cong. Globe*, 30th Cong., 1st Sess. 398 (1848). For elaboration of the speech see *ibid.*, App. 351–55.

the elective process. James B. Bowlin of Missouri, in Justice Catron's circuit, immediately offered a proposal similar to Catron's for a system of intermediate appellate courts.[28] The Bowlin substitute was rejected and the Ingersoll bill, modified to give only one year of exemption from circuit work, passed the House by a vote of eighty-nine to sixty.[29]

For some reason the Senate was less sympathetic than the House. Senator Benton of Missouri thought the question was whether the Supreme Court should forever be cut loose from the states, a question already frequently decided by both houses of Congress. The issue was brought up again, not directly and openly but "by a sapping and mining process." Grant one year of exemption from travel and two more years would be sought, and the exemption would become permanent. "From that moment the states would degenerate into mere provinces. The central power would be always here, the judges would always reside here in view of the Capitol."[30] William Allen, an extremist Democrat from Ohio who favored the election of Supreme Court Justices for a specified term, likewise predicted that an exemption from travel of one year would mean permanent exemption, and that if for twenty-five years the Court remained exclusively in Washington it would become the prevailing power of the government.[31]

Although in the Senate the Court had its mild defenders,[32] the selective reporters of Senatorial debates picked up no such encomiums on its performance as were delivered during a later period. Even Senator George E. Badger of North Carolina, later an advocate of increased salaries for the Justices and other relief measures, remarked at this time—in 1848, prior to announcement of the rule limiting arguments of counsel—that instead of deciding 40 cases during a term the Court might decide 140, if it met "with the resolute purpose of confining the argument of counsel to the questions on record, and refusing to listen to any discussion of any points which the court considered to be clear and settled."[33] This criticism, indeed, may well have played a part in

---

[28] For the full statement of Bowlin's position see *ibid.*, App. 350–51.

[29] *Ibid.*, 433.

[30] *Ibid.*, 581.

[31] *Ibid.*, 594.

[32] One of the principal defenders was Senator John J. Crittenden of Kentucky, who noted that although the bill was labeled as "for the relief of" the Supreme Court it merely prescribed for the Court a year of work in Washington, where its tasks, or the tasks of the individual Justices, were presumably no less arduous than those performed on circuit. He noted

also that in extending the term of the Court for the year in question the bill merely did something which the Court could do for itself, since the length of each term was now limited only by the discretion of the Court. *Cong. Globe*, 30th Cong., 1st Sess. 595–97 (1848). It was true, however, that the beginnings of the terms of the several circuits were set by statute, and in order to be present on circuit the Justices had to adjourn the Supreme Court.

[33] *Cong. Globe*, 30th Cong., 1st Sess. 594 (1848).

persuading the Court to institute the limiting rule which went into effect in 1849.

In any event, by a vote of twenty-three to seventeen[34] the Senate rejected the bill to relieve the Justices of circuit work for a year. Furthermore, it refused to adopt the milder measure proposed by Senator Badger that the term of the Court beginning in December, 1849, should be extended until the first Monday in the following July to permit the Court to make at least limited inroads on the work load, with permission to adjourn for the month of April if the public interest or the Court's own convenience required it.[35]

Yet from the Badger proposal, which may itself, like other such proposals, have been inspired by the Court, a means was developed of getting at least some of the extra work done. According to the minutes of the Court, instead of adjourning during the first or second week in March, 1850, the Court continued in session until March 29—giving the Reporter, Benjamin C. Howard, his first opportunity to publish two volumes of reports within the same term of the Court. In 1851 the Court adjourned on March 11, but in 1852 it remained in action until May 27, apparently without the benefit of any Act of Congress. In 1854 it held an adjourned term from April 3 to May 26, following an adjournment from March 1. It held similar adjourned terms in 1858 and 1859, with a merely prolonged term in 1860.

Since there was no statutory limit on the length of the term or prescribing the date of adjournment, the Court was not violating any statute by sitting longer than had been its custom. However, the duties on circuit remained also to be performed, and like the duties of the Supreme Court they were expanding year by year. When there were vacancies in the district judgeships, or when judges were temporarily incapacitated, the circuit as well as the district work had to go undone. While refusing to sanction further absence of Supreme Court Justices from the circuits, Congress gave indirect sanction for what the Court decided to do by authorizing the Justices to shift district judges about within their respective circuits in order to see that work accumulating because of vacancies or illness would eventually be done. In the event of a vacancy in the circuit judgeship itself—the equivalent of a vacancy on the Supreme Court—the Chief Justice was to make any necessary reallocation of district judges.[36] Piecemeal attempts were thus made to deal with the problem of the judicial work load, even as Congress picked up from time to time and then dropped various proposals for dealing with the problem more fundamentally.

---

[34] *Washington National Intelligencer*, Apr. 19, 1848.

[35] *Cong. Globe*, 30th Cong., 1st Sess. 656 (1848).

[36] 9 Stat. 442.

While congestion of the Supreme Court docket was thought to encourage some litigants to appeal cases merely for delay,[37] it may have encouraged others to present cases on written argument alone. Justice Catron, however, thought it dangerous to decide important questions, and particularly constitutional questions, without the benefit of oral argument. With the warm approval of Justice Wayne, he refused to participate in the decision of an admiralty case involving constitutional questions merely on the basis of written argument,[38] although Chief Justice Taney later convinced Justice Wayne that it had been the custom of the Court to decide constitutional as well as other questions on this basis.[39] The majority of the Court was apparently in no mood to require additional oral arguments when time to hear arguments was already at a premium.

In general the Court was watchful of attempts to crowd onto its docket cases coming from the lower federal courts with legal issues not properly sifted there. In 1848, for example, it dismissed a case where it appeared that under the cover of certifying a division of opinion between two Circuit Court judges the entire case, and not merely certified legal questions, had been sent up for decision by the Supreme Court.[40] Yet with somewhat different procedure involved the Court seemed sometimes to forget the element of consistency. In 1850 it decided a case appealed from Chief Justice Taney's circuit in Maryland where the reporter stated that "a decree pro forma was entered," and where Justice Catron stated that the case had not been heard in the Circuit Court.[41]

---

[37] See statement of Samuel F. Vinton of Ohio in the House of Representatives as paraphrased by the clerk: "He had a cause on the docket himself, which had been there for three years without being reached; and this fact, he was of the opinion, was an inducement with some parties to carry up their cases, as thereby they availed themselves of the delay which an appeal produced. To appeal to the Supreme Court of the United States was in many cases an absolute denial of justice, and something should be done to remedy the existing evil." *Ibid.*, 433.

[38] Cutler v. Rae, 7 How. 729 (1849).

[39] Cutler v. Rae, 8 How. 615, 617 (1850). Among the cases decided with written arguments alone on one or both sides were Bronson v. Kinzie, 1 How. 311 (1843) and Nathan v. Louisiana, 8 How. 73 (1850).

[40] Nesmith v. Shelton, 6 How. 41 (1848).

[41] As summarized by the Reporter: Mr. Justice Catron stated from the bench, that he objected to a decree being made by this court on the bill, because the cause came here by a transfer from the Circuit Court, never having been heard there. It was only prepared for hearing, and is now presented and heard as an original cause in this court. We have appellate and not original jurisdiction in such cases, both by the Constitution and by the Judiciary Act of 1789. Before an appeal can be prosecuted, something must be adjudged to appeal from. And in the second place, if it be once established that causes can be sent here by mere transfer, nothing having been decided below, we must be overwhelmed by such causes, there being now thirty courts and more that may send them up. This is one evil

Justice Nelson, speaking for an otherwise unanimous Supreme Court, dealt with the constitutional question by the simple expedient of ignoring it.

Although after the submission in 1846 of Justice Catron's bill for reorganizing the federal judiciary a number of years passed before Congress got down to the discussion of specific reorganizing measures, continued complaints about delays in Supreme Court litigation and proposals for reform kept the subject in ferment. One such proposal came to the Senate in 1849. It was drafted by John Henderson, a former Senator from Mississippi, who thereafter practiced in New Orleans, which was included in Justice McKinley's circuit, by whom, indeed, it may well have been inspired. Henderson noted the congestion of the Supreme Court docket, the effect upon the Circuit Courts of the statute of 1844 which took Supreme Court Justices away from the Circuit Courts for one of the two terms each year, the admission of four new states—Texas, Florida, Iowa, and Wisconsin—and the prospective admission of others, and the need for circuit service in the new states and for more adequate service in the old ones. He therefore proposed a rearrangement of the circuits to include the new states, elimination of circuit riding for Supreme Court Justices, the appointment of judges for the Circuit Courts as such, and the retention of important original jurisdiction by the Circuit Courts. The unique feature was the division of the nine circuit judges into three groups, each of which was to sit for a specified time each year as a court of errors and appeals, thereby relieving the Supreme Court of much of its appellate work involving property valued at less than thirty thousand dollars.[42]

intended to be avoided by the framers of the Constitution, when the Supreme Court was excluded from the exercise of original jurisdiction in cases like the present.

Tayloe v. Merchants' Fire Insurance Co., 9 How. 390, 406 (1850).

The facts about the case are not entirely clear. Chief Justice Taney wrote about it to the Reporter:

I mentioned to you the other day that I wished the report of the case of Tayloe vs. The Merchants' Fire Insurance Co. to show that the decree in the circuit court was pro forma. The mode you then suggested seemed to me at the time free from objection. But it occurred to me afterwards that it would be better to state the record precisely as it is. You will find that the record states that the decree was pro forma and made at the request of counsel. But in whatever form it appears in the record please state it in the same words in your report, and say nothing as to what was orally said by me in court. It has you know been agreed among the judges that nothing should be inserted in the reports, but what was reduced to writing and read in court when the judgment was pronounced, and I prefer adhering literally to the rule even in this small matter.

R. B. Taney to B. C. Howard, May 31, 1850, Howard Papers.

[42] Memorial of John Henderson, Submitting a Plan for the Reorganiza-

XI: *The Expanding Work Load*

Since the debate of 1848 on the proposal to suspend temporarily the circuit-riding requirement, with its alleged implications for permanent suspension, nothing had happened to convince legislators of the desirability of such action except the continued accumulation of cases on the Supreme Court docket. Congress was preoccupied with the slavery problem and other regional questions, which were to find a measure of temporary solution in the Compromise of 1850, and was in no mood for judicious consideration of the problems of the courts. The Supreme Court, less closely identified with slavery interests than it was later to seem, was in some degree suspect in the South as in the North. Indeed, Senator William R. King of Alabama gave notice in January, 1850, that he would ask leave to introduce a bill to repeal the twenty-fifth section of the Judiciary Act of 1789,[43] the section conferring appellate jurisdiction on that tribunal.

The Congressional mood with respect to the Court was perhaps best revealed by the consideration of a joint resolution which evidently came from some member or members of the Supreme Court calling for the appointment of what came to be called an "investigating clerk." The resolution had been handed to and was introduced in the Senate by Arthur P. Butler of South Carolina. It called for the appointment by the Court of a clerk whose duty it would be to "do such copying of opinions and other matters, and to make such researches, as the Chief Justice or either of his associates may require in the progress of the business of the said court."[44] Senator Butler asked immediate enactment, "because there are now before the Supreme Court cases in litigation involving an amount equal to at least four millions of dollars, which cases depend mainly upon proofs contained in papers in the Spanish language, correspondence, and otherwise; and it is impossible for the Court to act upon those cases satisfactorily without the aid of an officer such as is here proposed. The number of judgments that are to be pronounced cannot be written out by the judges without such aid and assistance."[45]

The Senate gave but cursory attention to the joint resolution and passed it by unanimous consent.[46] The House of Representatives, on the other hand, gave it more extended treatment. In presenting the resolution Thomas H. Bayly of Virginia explained that in writing their opinions the Justices frequently interlined them very much, so that they had to be copied. Some of them wrote bad hands. It would be impossible for them to do their own copying, and bad economy were it possible. There was need for a clerk who was himself a lawyer and who would under-

---

tion of the Judicial System of the United States, S. Misc. Doc. No. 4, 31st Cong., 1st Sess. (1850).

[43] *Cong. Globe*, 31st Cong., 1st Sess. 197 (1850).

[44] *Ibid.*, 334.

[45] *Ibid.*

[46] *Ibid.*, 344.

stand technical legal terms and abbreviations. Furthermore, it was contemplated that the clerk would make investigations into legal matters as requested by the Justices, "which would save much more drudgery of labor on their part, and enable them to dispatch their business more expeditiously."[47] Bayly admitted that he had no great respect for the opinions of a majority of the Court, though he did for the opinions of some. He thought the Court would not ask for the appointment unless it were needed.

David K. Carter of Ohio brought the House to roars of laughter when he ridiculed the proposal to hire a clerk to do for the Court thinking it was not able to do for itself, to furnish the Justices with "auxiliary brains." The way to correct the evil was not to provide what was in effect a supplemental judge, but to amend the Constitution to cut off the judges when old age, debility, or bad habits disabled them for investigating for themselves. But Chauncey F. Cleveland of Connecticut deplored the ridicule, and reminded the House that more clerical help was deserved, now that the Court had limited long-winded debate on the part of counsel and was covering more cases. In the end, with little serious consideration of the measure, the House passed it by a vote of ninety to seventy-three.[48]

But on the following day the House did give serious if not very imaginative consideration to this first effort to give the Supreme Court a bit of professional research assistance. Lucius B. Peck of Vermont moved reconsideration of the vote, on the basis of the overnight discovery that although a majority of the Justices favored the plan, a minority opposed it. If the judges were not agreed on so novel a measure he thought the House ought not to support it. Other legislators followed suit, prominent among them being William Strong of Pennsylvania, who in 1870 was to be appointed to the Court which he now viewed most critically. He was utterly unable to perceive any necessity for the appointment of an investigating clerk for the Court. The nine judges decided only from forty to sixty cases a year, which meant only five or six cases for each judge. The highest court in Pennsylvania decided more than five hundred cases a year without resort to such aid. Indeed, he had had some experience with courts of error, and knew of none that had the kind of assistant here discussed. He had still another objection:

> It is, that the proposed additional clerk would inevitably give character to the opinions emanating from the Court. Judges are but men. With an officer under their control, whose duty it would be to investigate the questions referred to him, it is too much to hope that they would not roll off upon him the labor from which all naturally

---

[47] *Ibid.*, 351.   [48] *Ibid.*, 351, 352.

shrink. His researches would give tone to the opinions, and doubtless, in many cases control the judgments of the Court. His peculiar opinions would tinge all the opinions of the Court. His mind, his hand would be visible in them all. I am unwilling for one to transfer the important duties of the court to a clerk, and I trust, therefore, that the vote by which the resolution was passed will be reconsidered.[49]

Andrew Ewing of Tennessee contended that it was the duty of Congress to give the Justices the aid they needed and scoffed at the idea that the clerk would infuse his own views and opinions into the decisions of the Court. If that could happen with respect to any judge, it was time for that judge to leave the bench. The tide of sentiment, however, had gone in the opposite direction; the vote was reconsidered, and the bill was laid on the table.[50] The Court was thereby saved from the threat of subversion by an investigating clerk.

Amid the weighty controversies which were leading to the "irrepressible conflict" the basic problems of the federal judiciary could receive little attention. One more attempt, however, was made to secure broad reorganization before the outbreak of war. In his first annual message to Congress, in December, 1853, President Pierce called attention to the fact that five new states and parts of older states were now denied the full benefits of the judicial system, and invited a request for a reorganization proposal.[51] Congress requested the proposal, and it was put forward in the form of a message to the President by Attorney General Caleb Cushing, who submitted an analysis of the problems of the judicial system and of the several proposals for reform that were being considered.[52] He made one of his own, which is important primarily because of its close resemblance to the act passed in 1869,[53] when the war was over and adequate attention could be given to the subject. He proposed to relieve the district judges of their circuit duties, to appoint Circuit judges for nine reorganized circuits (California later to be included in a Tenth Circuit), with Circuit Courts to be held by Supreme Court and circuit judges or either of them. Supreme Court Justices, in other words, were to continue to ride circuit to the extent possible, but in their absence circuit work would be done by judges appointed at a higher level than that of district judges.

Cushing's plan was revised in the Senate Judiciary Committee, which reported a bill to relieve Supreme Court Justices of circuit duties, to appoint independent circuit judges, and to have Circuit Courts held

---

[49] *Ibid.*, 356.
[50] *Ibid.*, 357.
[51] J. D. Richardson, *A Compilation of the Messages and Papers of the* *Presidents*, V, 218.
[52] Courts of the United States, 6 Op. Att'y Gen. 271 (1854).
[53] 16 Stat. 44.

by circuit and district judges.[54] Yet along with the committee bill came the proposal of a complete substitute by Stephen A. Douglas of Illinois. The Douglas amendment resembled the Catron proposal of 1846 in leaving to the district judges the original jurisdiction hitherto vested in the Circuit Courts and setting up in each circuit a court of appeals consisting of the Supreme Court Justice assigned thereto and the district judges.[55] Again the difference was primarily between those willing to free Supreme Court Justices from circuit duties and those opposed. The committee thought such exemption necessary to get the Supreme Court work done. Douglas, with many adherents, voiced the old refrain:

> I think it is good for the country, and for the good of that court, that its judges should be required to go into the country, hold courts in different localities, and mingle with the local judges and with the bar. I think that, if the judges of that court be released from all duties outside the city of Washington, and stay here the whole year round, they will become, as a Senator remarked to me a moment ago, mere paper judges. I think they will lose the weight of authority in the country which they ought to have, just in proportion as they lose their knowledge of the local legislation, and of the practice and proceedings of the courts below.[56]

The bill and the proposed amendments were discussed on a much higher level than had been the minor proposal to give the Supreme Court an investigating clerk. In some instances, in connection with this bill and a contemporary bill to raise the salaries of the Justices, the Court received high praise.[57] Yet the insistence on ensuring that the Justices would have to travel out of Washington and scatter among the circuits implied not merely a desire to educate them but a fear of their concentrated power. William H. Seward of New York, who voted against the salary increase, expressed the belief that of all the departments of the government the judiciary was the only one that approached the absolute in form.[58] Yet some Senators frankly recognized the fact that, desirable as it might be to have the Justices do circuit work, they could not do all the work of the Supreme Court and of the circuits too. Said Senator Andrew P. Butler of South Carolina:

> Why is not the fact before us that they cannot do it, and do not do it? Judge Daniel is required to hold circuit courts in Arkansas. When

---

[54] *Cong Globe*, 33rd Cong., 2nd Sess. 191–92 (1855).
[55] *Ibid.*, 193–94.
[56] *Ibid.*, 194.

[57] See the speeches of George E. Badger, *ibid.*, 41; Salmon P. Chase, *ibid.*, 217; and Lewis Cass, *ibid.*, 298.
[58] *Ibid.*, 299.

was he in Arkansas or Mississippi? He cannot be there and here at the same time. The same remark may apply to any judge who may be required to go to Texas. . . . They cannot do it; and yet gentlemen talk about requiring these judges to go on circuit.[59]

Among the Senators who sought to relieve the Justices of their circuit duties was Salmon P. Chase of Ohio, who in 1864 was to be appointed Chief Justice to succeed Taney. With this relief he proposed an additional arrangement whereby no vacancies on the Court should be filled until the membership was reduced to six[60]—a device which was to be used during his Chief Justiceship to prevent the filling of vacancies by President Andrew Johnson.

The Douglas amendment to the committee bill was rejected after long debate,[61] and action on the bill itself was in effect put off indefinitely by a vote to postpone until the following December.[62] Congress at the same session did raise salaries from the 1819 level by the amount of fifteen hundred dollars for each Justice, so that the Chief Justice would receive sixty-five hundred dollars and the Associate Justices six thousand. Even on this measure, however, the vote of the Senate was thirty to fifteen, the minority including such dignitaries as Stephen A. Douglas, William P. Fessenden, Hannibal Hamlin, William H. Seward, and Charles Sumner.[63]

Although the organization of the judiciary remained fundamentally the same, Congress during 1855 enacted one measure with a portent for the future. Unwilling to increase the membership of the Supreme Court to ten, and made vividly aware of the need for Circuit Court services in California where the discovery of gold and other wealth had given rise to a mass of litigation, Congress created for California the office of a circuit judge who was not a member of the Supreme Court.[64] Although in 1863 a tenth position on the Supreme Court was created, with an assignment to the Pacific circuit,[65] the eight years of experience with an independent circuit judge pointed the way of the future.

The Court itself continued to struggle with its docket without legislative relief. In March, 1859, it was announced that the Court had adjourned after having cleared less than half the calendar.[66] In November of 1859 it was announced that the docket of the Court was crowded, the government alone having ninety cases.[67] As the ensuing term progressed,

---

[59] *Ibid.*, 213.
[60] *Ibid.*, 216–17.
[61] *Ibid.*, 300.
[62] *Ibid.*, 308.
[63] *Ibid.*, 742.
[64] 10 Stat. 631.

[65] 12 Stat. 794.
[66] *New York Tribune*, Mar. 12, 1859.
[67] *New York Tribune*, Nov. 16, 1859.

it was made known that the Court would prolong its term into the spring to cope with its work load,[68] obviously at the expense of time to be spent on circuits;[69] the same reports carried references to illness among the Justices with consequent delays in achievement. The coming of the war, to be discussed hereafter, converted judicial problems into crises.

---

[68] *New York Tribune*, Feb. 14, 17, 27, Mar. 3, 5, 12, 20, 1860.

[69] Individual Justices sometimes absented themselves from the Supreme Court during its regular term because of the importance of cases to be tried on circuit. Shortly after his appointment to the Court, Justice Clifford wrote to Chief Justice Taney for advice in such a situation. Taney replied in part:

In relation to the subject you mention, there is no settled practice of the court and the Judge has exercised his own discretion upon the matter. In cases where important questions of law arise in a Capital case, he has remained to try it. Judge Grier some years ago was absent the first week or two from the Supreme Court, having remained in the circuit court to try some persons who were charged with treason, for combining to prevent by force the execution of the fugitive slave law. And Judge Wayne has now gone south to try the parties who were engaged in the slavers lately sent into Charleston by Capt. Moffit. He will not be in Washington before the middle of December, perhaps not so soon.

Some years ago two men were indicted for piracy and murder in the Virginia district. But the cases did not involve any new or important question of law, and I went to the Supreme Court, and left them to be tried by the District Judge sitting in the circuit court.

These are all the cases that I can now recall to mind, and I mention them particularly to show you the principles upon which the Judges have acted in exercising their discretion. It may perhaps properly be influenced in some degree by the wishes and opinions of the Bar, and of the community among whom the trial is to be had.

I should greatly regret your absence from the Supreme Court, especially for so long a period as you speak of. It is usual where there is likely to be a difference of opinion upon an important constitutional question, to postpone it, until we have a full court. But very interesting questions are continually recurring upon which we shall desire your aid and assistance. . . .

R. B. Taney to Nathan Clifford, Nov. 13 (?), 1858, Clifford Papers.

CHAPTER XII

The Clerk and the Reporter

T HE PRINCIPAL AIDES OF the Supreme Court were the Clerk and the Reporter. The position of the Clerk was designated by the Court through its first formal rule, adopted in February, 1790, which named the first Clerk and provided that he should keep his office at the seat of the government, and forbade him to practice law before the Court while in office.[1] This rule continued to provide the pattern of the office throughout the Taney Period, during which it was occupied until the 1860s by William Thomas Carroll, of the distinguished Carroll family of Maryland. The office of the Reporter had a less tangible beginning at about the same time, when Alexander J. Dallas of Pennsylvania, without initial connection with the Supreme Court and before there were any Supreme Court decisions to report, compiled a volume of decisions of various Pennsylvania courts which became the precursor of the early volumes of Supreme Court reports compiled by him. Until after the close of the Taney period the Reporter's connection with the Court was less than that of the Clerk. Unlike the Clerk, he was not required to keep an office at the capital, doing much of the work of compiling opinions at his home, wherever he might reside. He was not forbidden to practice before the Court, but rather used his position to advertise his availability for the handling of cases for litigants residing far from the capital.[2]

The Supreme Court was also served by the Marshal of the district in which the Court was located. After Washington became the capital site, the Marshal of the District of Columbia served as Marshal of the Court during the few weeks of each annual term, and occupants of the

---

[1] Rules and Orders, 1 How. xxiii (1843).

[2] A Card, to His Professional Brethren and the Public Generally, 1 How. v (1843).

293

office changed with political party shifts in the office of President. In spite of early informality of the procedure of the Court there was in 1853 a crier, mentioned in unsigned minutes of the Court by an anonymous wag as "oppressed by a relapse into sobriety, a state inconsistent with his wont."[3] Justice Catron remarked in 1843 that the Clerk had "three or four deputies, constantly employed at salaries to support families."[4] When in 1855 Congress directed the Marshal to pay three dollars a day to messengers of the Court, Chief Justice Taney by direction of the Court told the Marshal that the Court had no such officers as messengers. The Court thought the word *messenger* should be construed *officer* and that the resolution was intended to embrace officers hitherto allowed two dollars per diem. The man who had moved the resolution assured the Court that such had been the intention. There were still other employees whom the Chief Justice referred to as "servants about the Court." These the Court thought should receive an additional fifty cents a day in view of increased living costs and increased allowances generally made to public employees.[5] Of these miscellaneous employees and their salaries no systematic records seem to have been kept.

With respect to the compensation of the Clerk, the ruling statute was an Act of 1799, passed when the capital was still in Philadelphia. It provided:

> That the compensation to the clerk of the supreme court of the United States, shall be as follows, to wit: for his attendance in court, ten dollars per day, and for his other services, double the fees of the clerk of the supreme court of the state in which the supreme court of the United States shall be holden.[6]

The records do not show whether compensation in Washington was measured by that of the clerk of the highest court in Maryland, from which the occupied portion of the District of Columbia had been carved, or by some other standard. Congress showed from time to time what the Court regarded as unwelcome inquisitiveness about costs and expenditures in the office of the Clerk. In 1843, for example, Justice Catron wrote to H. L. Turney, a Representative from Tennessee, asking the source of information of any person contending that the matter required Congressional attention: "The office has been a good deal

---

[3] Longhand notes among the papers of the clerk, Jan. 26, 1853, Clerk's Files.

[4] John Catron to H. L. Turney, Feb. 16, 1843, *ibid.*

[5] Copy, R. B. Taney to J. D. Hoover, Mar. 10, 1855, McLean Papers.

[6] 1 Stat. 624, 625.

examined by me, and I think it is as well kept, almost, as it is possible: and you need not be informed, that I am particular in such official duties."[7] Answering complaints that Supreme Court fees were higher than those of state courts, he contended that they had to be higher because the cases were at once fewer in number and required a great deal more work.

In public thinking the question of fees in the Supreme Court was confused with that of fees in the lower federal courts. As to the latter there was much debate over whether they should be uniform throughout the United States or should conform to figures in the state courts. In 1842 Congress had authorized the Supreme Court to prescribe regulations for the purpose of reducing costs in the District and Circuit courts.[8] According to Justice Catron the law gave the Supreme Court the power "to regulate all the fees of every court officer in the Union." The task was a heavy one and he did not want interference. He ended his letter to Congressman Turney with the demand, "Let us alone."[9]

The Supreme Court never did get around to establishing on its own a uniform system of fees and costs, but presumably it had a great deal to do with the content of the so-called Fee Bill enacted by Congress in 1853.[10] That measure dealt only with the lower federal courts and not with the Supreme Court. There being at this time no Department of Justice, administration of matters with respect to the federal judiciary lay with the Department of the Interior. In his annual report to President James Buchanan, made in December, 1857, the Secretary of the Interior complained:

> The clerk of the Supreme Court cannot, by the received construction of the law, be required to make a return of the fees and emoluments of his office, nor is his compensation limited; yet the policy and spirit of the law includes this officer, as well as the clerks of the circuit and district courts. If the existing law be wise and ought to be maintained, then no valid reason exists why this officer should be made an exception.[11]

To prevent a repetition of this criticism the following year, Justice John A. Campbell wrote to Attorney General Jeremiah S. Black saying that he thought the subject ought not to be discussed. "The Chief Justice is sensitive," he explained, "and I think myself the Court ought not to be overhauled in Executive reports. I will bring the subject to the Chief

---

[7] John Catron to H. L. Turney, Feb. 16, 1843, Clerk's Files.
[8] 5 Stat. 516, 518.
[9] John Catron to H. L. Turney,

Feb. 16, 1843, Clerk's Files.
[10] 10 Stat. 161.
[11] Senate Ex. Doc. No. 11, 35th Cong., 1st Sess. 73 (1857).

Justice's notice and to that of the Judges on my return and it will be easy to rectify whatever is wrong about the matter."[12]

The subject of the Clerk's fees and of his compensation remained largely outside the control of Congress until the enactment of a regulatory measure in 1883.[13] Until that time, according to Chief Justice Waite, "the clerk collected the fees of his office, paid the expenses, and kept what remained as his own compensation. He was not accountable to the government or to anyone else for the income."[14] There are no records adequate to show how lucrative the office of Clerk may have been.

If indeed the office of Clerk was lucrative, it also had its hard work and its irritations. Since he was the one responsible employee of the Court who was always available, the Clerk was called upon to handle all sorts of problems. They dealt with the courtroom, the library, the subordinate employees, the collection of the salaries of the Justices, and the location of satisfactory rooms for the Justices when they came to Washington—the last always a difficult task and one calling for much diplomacy, and especially difficult in the period of congestion and high prices during the Civil War. The duties of the Clerk and the Reporter overlapped and intertwined, creating still other problems of diplomacy. Yet the task had its rewards, particularly for members of old families who relished associations with such dignitaries as members of the Supreme Court and Congress and leading members of the bar. The office would seem to have been conducive to good health. William Thomas Carroll served from 1827 until his death in 1863, when he was replaced until 1880 by Daniel W. Middleton, who as early as 1843 had been with him as his assistant.

While the Clerk of the Supreme Court was a kind of business manager and errand boy for the Justices and for practitioners before the Court, the Reporter was responsible only for the task of getting the decisions of the Court published in a form acceptable to the Court and to the bar, for sale at a reasonable price. There was widespread disagreement, however, as to the subject matter to be included in the reports. The question was much discussed in law journals and other learned journals which made it their practice to review volumes of judicial reports as they appeared. Reviewers varied all the way from those who wanted to save money for lawyers by limiting publication to selected opinions, to those who advocated publication of all opinions together with arguments of counsel and other relevant documents. Most critics advocated a compromise arrangement whereby arguments

---

[12] J. A. Campbell to J. S. Black, Nov. 14, 1858, Black Papers.
[13] 22 Stat. 631.

[14] Bean v. Patterson, 110 U.S. 401, 402 (1884).

of counsel were summarized and opinions were explained in analytical headnotes rather than in what were sometimes merely summaries drafted by Reporters, but they differed as to when proper standards had been observed.[15]

Although there seems to have been a lack of clear and discriminating thinking on the subject, theoretical differences went deep. There were differences of opinion whether Court decisions as rationalized in official opinions themselves constituted the law, or whether the decisions were merely evidence of law preexisting as a body of abiding principles, evidence which had its parallels in other sources than the opinions of the Court[16] and which might be in conflict with those opinions. If the opinions themselves constituted the law, then there was little need for publishing more. On the other hand, if the opinions were merely evidence of independently existing law, then the arguments of distinguished counsel might be worth more to the bar than the opinion of a mediocre judge, even if for the moment the judge happened to be speaking for

---

[15] Reviews of state court reports during the Taney period are themselves worthy of independent study. Apart from those which are merely perfunctory the following are the sources of some noteworthy reviews:
Alabama: *Am. Jurist*, 25:252, 1841
Connecticut: *Am. L. J.*, 8:272, 1848
Georgia: *U.S. Monthly L. Mag.*, 3:272, 1851
Indiana: *West. L. J.*, 1:476 (1844); *U.S. Monthly L. Mag.*, 3:115, (113) 1851
Illinois: *Am. L. Reg.* (N.S.), 1:701, 1862
Iowa: *Am. L. Reg.* (N.S.), 1:191 1862; *ibid.*, 639, 1864
Maine: *Am. Jurist*, 25:249, 1841; *U.S. Monthly L. Mag.*, 3:113, 1851
Massachusetts: *Am. Jurist*, 17:471, 1837; *ibid.*, 20:224, 1838; *Am. L. Reg.* (N.S.), 2:191, 1863; *ibid.*, 3:382, 1864
Michigan: *Am. L. Reg.*, 7:383, 1859
New Jersey: *Am. L. Reg.*, 8:62, 1859
New York: *Am. L. J.*, 8:273, 1848
North Carolina: *U.S. Monthly L. Mag.*, 3:117, 1851
Ohio: *Livingston's Monthly L. Mag.*, 2:744, 1854
Pennsylvania: *Am. Jurist*, 18:521, 1838; *Pa. L. J.*, 1:22, 1842; *ibid.*, 2:69, 1843; *ibid.*, 2:129, 1843;

ibid., 6:398, 1847; *ibid.*, 6:540, 1847; *Am. L. Reg.*, 7:639, 1859; *Am. L. Rag.*, 9:317, 1861; *ibid.*, 9:572, 1861; *Am. L. Reg.* (N.S.), 1:447, 1862; *Pittsburgh Legal J.*, 6:478, 1859; *ibid.*, 11:178, 1863
Rhode Island: *Am. L. Reg.*, 8:64, 1859
South Carolina: *Am. Jurist*, 22:488, 1840
Tennessee: *Am. Jurist*, 25:243, 1841; *U.S. Monthly Mag.*, 3:117, 1851
Virginia: *Southern Literary Messenger*, 14:255, 1848
First U.S. Circuit: *West. L. J.*, 5: 140, 1847
Third U.S. Circuit: *Pennsylvania Magazine of History and Biography*, 8:xiii, 1884; *Am. L. J.*, 9:431, 1850
Second U.S. Circuit: *Am. L. Reg.*, 1:60, 1852
Seventh U.S. Circuit: *West. L. J.*, 9:191, 1852
[16] See for example Julius Goebel, Jr., "The Common Law and the Constitution," in W. Melville Jones, ed., *Chief Justice John Marshall, A Reappraisal*, 101–23; Frederick G. Kempin, Jr., "Precedent and Stare Decisis: The Critical Years, 1800 to 1850," *Am. J. Legal Hist.*, 3:28–54, 1959.

the majority of the Court. Indeed, the analyses or summaries of the Reporter might be of greater worth and reliability than the opinions—and it might be the duty of the Reporter to prune and correct the opinions before their publication. Although there is little evidence that the judges faced these questions squarely, they were implicit in much that was said and done.

Richard Peters of Philadelphia, who became Reporter of the Court in 1828, ran into difficulties because of these differing conceptions of what the reports should contain and on other grounds as well. In a period when the Jacksonians were in power in Washington he permitted himself to be juggled into a position of defending Whig interests or strategy,[17] he had to fight competitors for the privilege of publishing the opinions of the Court, he got into disputes with the Clerk over the handling of the opinions, and he found himself at odds with individual Justices over the handling of their opinions.

Reservations about Peters and his office were indicated in 1830 when Congress refused to make the customary triennial renewal of the statute providing the Reporter with an annual salary of one thousand dollars and prescribing the conditions of publication of the reports.[18] Thereafter until 1842 Congress merely made annual appropriations for the necessary expenses, making no advance commitment to the Reporter. One of the factors making for friction was probably jealousy on the part of the Clerk over the matter of handling the opinions and the desire of competitors to share in the profits of publishing the opinions. In 1834 the Clerk had explained his inability to provide a copy of an opinion by saying, "The opinions of the Court are neither recorded nor filed in this office, but when pronounced they have been always delivered to the Reporter and taken by him to Philadelphia and treated as his

---

[17] One of Peters' offenses against the Jacksonians was his advertising of Chief Justice Marshall's rebuke to Administration Indian policy by publishing in pamphlet form the opinion of the Court in Cherokee Nation v. Georgia, 5 Pet. 1 (1831), in such a way as to highlight William Wirt's argument on behalf of the Indians. For criticism see "The Autobiography of Martin Van Buren," John C. Fitzpatrick, ed., *Annual Report of the American Historical Association, 1818*, 2:292, 1920. Whether because of the criticism aroused or for some other reason, Peters found it expedient to omit the Wirt argument from the official edition of the reports. Further-

more, at a time when the Jacksonians were engaged in a war to the death against the Bank of the United States, Peters was aligned with its friends. When the Taney nomination for the Chief Justiceship was pending in the Senate, Peters wrote to Nicholas Biddle, "I congratulate you on the character of the Bank. All your friends have seen with the highest satisfaction the just sense of your services declared and testified by the Stockholders." Richard Peters to Nicholas Biddle, Mar. 1, 1836, Jurists, Etting Collection.

[18] See 3 Stat. 376, 606, 768, 4 Stat. 205.

property."[19] The letter made no mention of an order of the Court adopted some six weeks earlier, on March 14, 1834, providing that upon publication of each volume of the reports the original opinions should be filed in the office of the Clerk for preservation.[20]

This requirement of eventual filing of the opinions of the Court with the Clerk failed to satisfy those who hoped to get immediate access to the opinions in order to publish them. On a number of occasions bills were introduced in Congress to require initial filing with the Clerk for recording before their delivery to the Reporter.[21] Congress failed to pass the bill, perhaps forestalled by the action of the Court in issuing a new rule, later listed as Rule No. 42,[22] requiring that opinions be first delivered to the Clerk for recording and then sent to the Reporter. Peters refrained from printing the new rule in the current volume of his reports and protested against it to Justice Story, who for a time after the death of Chief Justice Marshall served as the administrative spokesman of the Court, [23] but the Court declined to modify the rule.[24]

Although the controversy intensified the strife between the Clerk and the Reporter there is no evidence that Peters was greatly damaged by such independent publication of opinions as took place as a result of their availability in the Clerk's office. More disturbing as a threat to Peters' position was a resolution of Joseph R. Ingersoll adopted by the House of Representatives to inquire whether the decisions of the Court were being reported "with accuracy and fidelity."[25] The resolution evidently led Peters to seek assurance from such of the Justices as he could trust in this matter. Important was a reply from Justice Story, who thought the duty of the Reporter required him to exercise a sound discretion. The Reporter was to abridge arguments, state facts, and give the opinions of the Court "substantially" as they were delivered. When the Court itself provided a statement of the facts, it was better that the Reporter merely insert this statement than that he duplicate it or replace it with one of his own. As for the correction of verbal and grammatical

---

[19] Copy, William Thomas Carroll to C. Allen, Apr. 26, 1834, Clerk's Files.

[20] 8 Pet. vii (1834), published as Rule 41, 1 How. xxxv (1843).

[21] For the maneuvering of Duff Green, editor of the *United States Telegraph*, in this matter, and his desire to have Richard S. Coxe edit the opinions to be published by him in advance of publication by Peters, see the letters by Peters and others for 1835 in Correspondence of Richard Peters, 1835–1847, II, a bound volume of Peters letters deposited in the Cadwalader Collection, Historical Society of Pennsylvania.

[22] 1 How. xxxv (1843).

[23] Richard Peters to Joseph Story, Jan. 23 (or 24), 1836, Peters Correspondence, II. See also Richard Peters to Joseph R. Ingersoll, Jan. 25, 1836, *ibid.*

[24] Joseph Story to Richard Peters, Jan. 26, 1836, *ibid.*

[25] *Cong. Globe*, 24th Cong., 1st Sess. 321 (1836).

errors in the opinions, which would occasionally occur even with the most accurate writers, he thought the correction of such blemishes did the judges a favor. He had always been grateful for it.[26]

Justice Thompson indicated full satisfaction with Peters' work, in spite of criticism by Benjamin Hardin of Kentucky on the floor of the House of Representatives.[27] But when after congratulating Chief Justice Taney on his appointment Peters sought from him also a letter of assurance,[28] Taney responded warmly to the congratulation but replied that a member of the Court could not with propriety interfere in a Congressional investigation whether the Court had continued in office one who had shown himself to be a negligent, incompetent, and unfaithful officer and whether, therefore, Congress should continue his salary.[29]

Chief Justice Taney and Peters came to deal with each other on a plane of mutual respect and seemingly even of affection, but Taney refused to become involved in the running controversy between the Reporter and the Clerk over early access to the opinions, accuracy in copying, and other matters, or to become an intermediary between Peters and members of the Court who were critical of Peters' reporting.[30] Justice Story remained one of Peters' principal sponsors, wrote to him freely about his difficulties with the Clerk and with Justice Baldwin, who created hardships for Peters by the lateness of his opinions and annnoyed Justice Story by criticism of his *Commentaries*,[31] and he gave Peters advice with respect to the organization of a comprehensive digest of American law.[32] In a Boston newspaper publication of opinions in the *Charles River Bridge Case* thought to have been provided by Carroll, Justice Story found an abundance of errors. He expressed to Justice McLean the hope that Carroll would in the future be indulgent with the errors in Peters' reports, "for if these opinions had been printed from his copy verbatim, it would have exhibited the Court in a very sad

---

[26] Joseph Story to Richard Peters, May 7, 1836, *Life and Letters of Joseph Story*, William W. Story, ed., II, 231–32. A similar attitude on the part of Justice McLean is indicated by the following: "I had not time to revise the opinion, after it was written, and I wish you to correct any errors of language which in haste, have been overlooked by me." John McLean to Richard Peters, Mar. 16, 1840, Peters Correspondence, II.

[27] Smith Thompson to Richard Peters, May 2, 1836, Peters Corre-spondence, II.

[28] Richard Peters to R. B. Taney, Apr. 19, 1836, *ibid.*

[29] R. B. Taney to Richard Peters, April 26, 1836, *ibid.*

[30] See R. B. Taney to Richard Peters, Mar. 20, 27, 1838, Dec. 27, 1838, May 8, June 3, 1840, Mar. 22, 1841, *ibid.*

[31] See Joseph Story to Richard Peters, May 12, June 14, 21, 1837, June 17, 1838, *ibid.*

[32] See for example Joseph Story to Richard Peters, Apr. 13, 1839, *ibid.*

way."[33] But in a letter to Chief Justice Taney, Carroll hotly denied that he had been responsible for sending out botched copies of the opinions: "Being pretty tenacious of my character for accuracy in such matters allow me to ask at your hands the favor to make the above fact known to the Judges of the Court."[34]

Whether this example of inaccuracy stemmed from the Clerk or the Reporter or from some other source, rumors were in circulation that a change in the Reporter's office was in prospect. Justice Barbour seems to have given this information to Francis Scott Key, Chief Justice Taney's brother-in-law, and promised to bear in mind for the position J. Mason Campbell, Taney's son-in-law: "I can perceive no injury, which can result to the public from the fact that the reporter stood in that relation to one of the members of the Court."[35] Key sent Barbour's letter to Campbell and promised to write to Justices Catron and McKinley. He had discussed the matter with Benjamin C. Howard, of the prominent Maryland family of that name, who had promised to speak to Justice Wayne.[36] Howard at this time may or may not have been an aspirant to the position, which he was later to occupy.

There is no evidence that the Chief Justice took part in the maneuvering of his relatives. He worked diplomatically with both Peters and Carroll, and, in spite of periodic irritations, Peters continued to serve until 1843. Many of his difficulties arose from the emotional imbalance of Justice Baldwin, who in 1837 published some of his opinions as a booklet of his own in the hope of adding to his income,[37] and thereafter wrote independent opinions which he submitted too late for inclusion in the volumes in which they belonged or failed to submit them at all.[38] When Justice Catron received a copy of Peters' twelfth volume, for the 1838 term, he wrote to Peters deploring omission of his dissenting opinion in *Kendall v. United States*,[39] on which, he said, he had bestowed much care.[40] Peters published the opinion in the appendix to the ensuing volume with an explanatory note that it had not been received from the Clerk with the opinions for the 1838 term and had been received directly from Justice Catron on March 6, 1839.[41] Whether

---

[33] Joseph Story to John McLean, May 10, 1837, McLean Papers.

[34] Unsigned copy, William Thomas Carroll to R. B. Taney (undated), Clerk's Files.

[35] P. P. Barbour to F. S. Key, Aug. 28, 1837, Etting Collection.

[36] F. S. Key to J. Mason Campbell, Sept. 5, 1837, *ibid.*

[37] Henry Baldwin, *A General View of the Origin and Nature of the Constitution and Government of the United States.*

[38] See Bank of Augusta v. Earle, 13 Pet. 519, 597 (1839); Holmes v. Jennison, 14 Pet. 540, 599 (1840); Decatur v. Paulding, 14 Pet. 497, 599 (1840).

[39] 12 Pet. 524 (1838).

[40] J. Catron to Richard Peters, July 20, 1838, Peters Correspondence, II.

[41] 13 Pet. 607.

this delay was the fault of the Reporter or the Clerk or the Justice himself, Catron came to be one of Peters' major critics on the Court.

Peters may have gotten into further trouble in the crossfire among the Justices about concurring and dissenting opinions. The rule of the Court as announced in 1835 required the filing with the Clerk of opinions of the Court but made no mention of other opinions. As explained by Chief Justice Taney in 1841, "A fashion has lately grown up, to examine after Term, opinions delivered in court, and to write answers to them to be published in the reports." He did not like the practice. He would not complain of it insofar as it involved opinions of the Court written by him; but as to his separate opinions, that was another matter. He did not wish to write answers to the opinions of his brethren or even to see them until they were published, but neither did he intend to give them his separate opinions. In an important case he therefore proposed to deliver his separate opinion to Peters only when it was needed for immediate publication, in order to prevent its advance circulation among the Justices for the writing of answers. He did not wish to bring Peters into collision with any member of the Bench through a refusal to communicate his separate opinion, and indeed he admitted that once the opinion was put on record any other Justice was entitled to a copy.[42] The situation was difficult in that even though the Chief Justice was responsible for withholding his opinion until the time when it had to be submitted for immediate publication, Peters was likely to draw the blame of Justices desiring an advance look at the opinion.

With the appointment in 1841 of Justice Daniel, always a carping critic, Peters' troubles were further increased. In his first volume to include Daniel's opinions he offended the Justice by making the rather common mistake of adding an "s" to his name and recording it as Daniels, and making on his own part or through his printer still other mistakes. The Justice disapproved.[43] The accumulation of disfavor was ominous.

An excuse for making a change in the Reporter's office began to appear in 1842 when Congress set out to regularize appropriations in a number of fields by providing for preliminary authorizations of expenditures before the actual appropriations were made. One of the items in a bill dealing with a great mass of diverse appropriations made provision for the appointment and payment of the Reporter of the Supreme Court.[44] The bill provided for a salary of $1,250 as against

---

[42] R. B. Taney to Richard Peters, Mar. 22, 1841, Peters Correspondence, II. The Taney opinion under discussion was that in Groves v. Slaughter, 15 Pet. 449, 508 (1841).

[43] P. V. Daniel to Richard Peters, Oct. 10, 1842, Peters Correspondence, II.

[44] An act legalizing and making appropriations for such necessary objects as have usually been included in the general appropriation bills without

the earlier figure of $1,000, required presentation of 150 copies of the reports to the government, and publication within four months after adjournment of the Court.[45]

While this omnibus bill was pending, Senator John M. Berrien introduced an independent measure concerning the office of the Reporter. Justice Catron read an announcement of this bill in the *Washington Globe* and saw in the situation the means of getting a new Reporter. He dashed off a letter to his friend Senator James Buchanan of Pennsylvania, asking him to have the bill amended to require Court action on an appointment soon after the beginning of the next term, with provision for reconsideration every four years, or more often if the Court saw fit. He pointed out there had been no change in occupancy of the office since his own appointment to the Court, and expostulated about the "errors, blunders, and great defects" in Peters' sixteenth volume. Implying, probably erroneously, that Justice Story was one of Peters' critics, he wrote:

> My Brother Story [is] very tremblingly alive to the great fears that we would not appear well in *England*. He lectures on it. I have read none but my own opinion in the 16 P.—only two days here—and God help *me* in England, or the Cherokee courts, if I am to be judged by Mr. Peters' prints of my opinions. Some wag said of Sheridan he was a great author that could not spell. I hope that John Bull will be equally indulgent to my brother Story: For my poor self, I have written so little that any one will have occasion to read, that I have less fear, at home, or abroad—and in sober truth it is no small comfort.[46]

Perhaps with a thought to getting support from the Chief Justice, he remarked that if it could do no better the Court could make "Frank" Key the Reporter.

Catron's letter came too late, and in any event this was no time for Democratic leadership in political matters. The bill was passed without his proposed changes, and it added to the prevailing confusion by putting the salary at thirteen hundred dollars, requiring publication within six months "after the said decisions shall be made," and limiting to five dollars the market price to the public.[47] Clearly the Congressional mind needed ordering as well as the mind of the Court.

When the Supreme Court assembled January 8, 1843, for a new term, only five members were present, and action on such an important

---

authority of law, and to fix and provide for certain incidental expenses of the Departments and offices of the Government, and for other purposes. 5 Stat. 523.

[45] 5 Stat. 524.
[46] John Catron to James Buchanan, Aug. 4, 1842, Buchanan Papers.
[47] 5 Stat. 545.

matter as selection of a Reporter was not to be immediately undertaken. Two of the Justices arrived later, but Justices Story and McKinley were prevented by illness from attending at that term.[48] On January 11 occurred the death of Mrs. Taney's brother, Francis Scott Key, and the Chief Justice, ill with a cold, was compelled to return to Baltimore for a few days pending recovery.[49] Richard Peters came to Washington as usual, assuming continuation of his status as Reporter, and did such work as was to be done at the beginning of the term. On the evening of January 25 four members of the Court, constituting a majority of the seven present, insisted on dealing at once with the appointment of a Reporter. The four, Wayne, Baldwin, Catron, and Daniel, voted for Benjamin C. Howard of Maryland, a former member of Congress who had been a friend of Justice Wayne's since their college years at Princeton. Chief Justice Taney and Justices Thompson and McLean urged Peters' retention throughout the current term, after which he might be encouraged to resign, but his critics insisted on his immediate replacement. Justice McLean, who refused to vote on the selection when he saw that the result had been arranged in advance, blamed the precipitate action on Justice Wayne, perhaps not realizing the extent of Justice Catron's maneuvering in the matter. In complaining of the action to Justice Story he remarked that he knew nothing of Howard's qualifications, but "He will certainly make a capital Reporter if he caucuses as well as our brother Wayne, with whom he was educated."[50]

Justices Story and McLean, vigorous defenders of Peters, had hoped for his replacement by Charles Sumner when eventually a change had to be made, and young Sumner, for a time the reporter of Justice Story's Circuit Court opinions, was eager to have the post but rebellious at the thought of having to lobby for it.[51] Justice Story was deeply wounded at what he regarded as the discourtesy of his colleagues in acting on the matter without consulting him and removing Peters without notice. It was uncalled for, he insisted, both by the language and the object of the Act of Congress. "For myself I can only say that I know of no reason for Mr. P.'s removal and I think it a most ill ad-

---

[48] "We are likely to have a crippled Court this Term. I have told you McKinley is unable to attend, and today we have a letter informing us that Judge Story is sick again, and we fear he will not be strong enough to be present during the Term." R. B. Taney to Mrs. Taney, Jan. 11, 1843, Howard Papers.

[49] John McLean to Joseph Story, Jan. 11, 1843, Story Papers.

[50] John McLean to Joseph Story, Jan. 25, 1843, Story Papers. McLean later wrote of the work of the term that "We have had more caucusing than usual; Mr. Wayne always being the chief Manager. I am ashamed to say this much, even to you, to whom I can speak respecting the Court." John McLean to Joseph Story, Mar. 14, 1843, ibid.

[51] See Charles Sumner to John McLean, Feb. 2, 1843, McLean Papers.

vised and rash step, which will bring the Court into odium—as having been governed by peculiar motives."[52] Although this subject was not mentioned, some report of Justice Story's sense of disillusionment with the conduct of his brethren may have occasioned the warm and kind letter which the Chief Justice wrote to Story at the end of the term telling him how much he had been missed in the disposition of important cases.[53]

Peters, angered and hurt at his summary removal, determined to continue reporting the decisions of the Supreme Court in competition with Howard, evidently assuming that he could sell enough copies to make it a profitable venture without salary or patronage from the government. For the 1843 term of the Court, therefore, he published a little-known seventeenth volume of his series. In the preface he revealed bitterness at his mistreatment and boasted that if two Justices had not been absent because of illness he would not have been removed. In the same volume he published correspondence with the foreman of the establishment which did his publishing about a list in Howard's first volume of what were for the most part certainly minor errors in Catron's opinions in five volumes of the Peters reports.[54] The manuscripts of Justice Catron's opinions, he wrote, were "often obscure, and sometimes illegible," and a great deal of skill had been required to read them.

---

[52] Joseph Story to John McLean, Feb. 9, 1845, *ibid*. Story had first expressed his sympathy to Peters through a letter from Charles Sumner, who deplored the fact that the demon of party had entered the sacred precincts where Marshall had once presided with such serenity and justice. Charles Sumner to Richard Peters, Peters Correspondence, II. Story later wrote to Peters directly expressing his grief at the unceremonious manner in which the dismissal had taken place: "Let it be your consolation that you had the warmest attachment of the old Court of Ch. Justice Marshall and his Brethren." Joseph Story to Richard Peters, Feb. 7, 1843, *ibid*. Justice McKinley, confined to his home at Louisville by a paralytic stroke (Joseph Story to Richard Peters, Nov. 27, 1842, *ibid*.), wrote to Peters expressing his surprise at the action of the Court, which he likened to the Court allocating to him a circuit other than that in which he had his home and property. He had never heard the slightest complaint about

Peters from any member of the Court. John McKinley to Richard Peters, June 6, 1843, *ibid*.

[53] R. B. Taney to Joseph Story, Mar. 18, 1843, Story Papers.

[54] 1 How. xv–xix (1843). The Peters Correspondence includes an inconclusive interchange about the matter of errors in the Catron opinions. Catron refused to disclose the record of the proceedings at which Peters had been removed, saying that it was a judicial act and covered by the rule of secrecy which applied to the decision of cases. J. Catron to Richard Peters, June 27, 1843, Peters Correspondence, II. For the *Philadelphia North American* Peters wrote anonymously and in the third person a defense of himself and an account of his removal casting aspersions on his enemies on the Court, carrying the date of Feb. 3, 1842, an obvious misstatement of the year, which should have been 1843. For the longhand copy see Peters Correspondence, II. Evidence of publication has not been found.

Furthermore, "To correct some of the pages as required by the learned judge would be offensive to the rules of grammar," and to follow his specific directions "would be to exhibit irregularities and inconsistencies without number." Howard's publication of the "errata" seemed to him an unprovoked and undeserved injury.[55]

Continued publication of reports without official sponsorship proved not to be feasible, and the seventeenth volume was the last in Peters' series. He was subject to criticism on other grounds, even though these were seldom clearly set forth. Part of the difficulty lay in his conception of the Reporter's responsibility. He stated his conception in the preface to his seventeenth volume:

> In the preparation of this volume for the press, much labour has been given to exhibit the facts and circumstances of each case in the syllabus, and thus to enable the profession to use and apply the principles of law decided in each cause, without a more particular examination of the whole of the report. This has been done in conformity with the plan pursued by the Reporter in the sixteen volumes of reports which have preceded this volume.[56]

But there were lawyers and judges who regarded the opinions of the Court as themselves the law, or at very least better evidence of the law than any summary the Reporter could provide, and who were therefore disgruntled at the space and time-consuming summaries with which Peters introduced each case. These critics hoped for something better with the selection of a new Reporter.

Benjamin Chew Howard was a man with fine family connections, in a region where family was extremely important. His father was John Eager Howard of Baltimore, of Revolutionary War fame, and his mother a member of the Chew family of Philadelphia. His wife, Jane Gilmor, came from a prominent mercantile family of Baltimore. Through

---

[55] Richard Peters to Thomas McKellar, Aug. 8, 1843, Correspondence, 17 Pet. v (1843).

[56] 17 Pet. iv (1843). Although Peters' seventeenth volume was the last to be published in this series, he continued with other projects, receiving advice from Justice Story. One was the compilation in five volumes of the laws of the United States, which stand at the beginning of the official series of the *United States Statutes at Large*. For this project he needed support from Congress. In his efforts to get that support he believed, and persuaded Justice Story to believe, that Carroll, the Clerk of the Supreme Court, was acting as his opponent. Said Justice Story, "I should be surprised at the gross and improper interference of Mr. Carroll with your projected edition of the laws of the U. States, if I could be surprised at any thing from him. And I need not say how utterly without apology or excuse such conduct is. I have not the slightest doubt that the main object is to *defeat you*." Joseph Story to Richard Peters, Apr. 4, 1844, Peters Correspondence, II.

the Keys he was indirectly related to the family of Chief Justice Taney. He graduated from Princeton, studied law in the office of a Baltimore firm, held high military rank in action in the War of 1812, served the governments of both Baltimore and Maryland, served four terms in Congress as a Democrat, and was one of the peace emissaries of the federal government to settle a territorial dispute between Ohio and Michigan. A letter to his wife in March, 1835, when he was on that mission, carries a reminder of his continued association with James M. Wayne, who had recently become a member of the Supreme Court. The Wayne family had evidently visited in his home during his absence. "I suppose," he wrote, "the Waynes have gone and left you to your desolations."[57]

Howard stood well with Democratic leaders, and it was said that he was freely mentioned as a successor to Justice Barbour[58] on the death of the latter in 1841—for the position to which Peter V. Daniel was appointed. Yet for all his connections of family and friends, he seems not to have been able to do well in a professional or business way. Neither high offices nor big retainers came his way. With expert economy and in a beautiful and precise longhand his wife, in forwarding to him a letter of congratulation on his appointment as Reporter, gave her own congratulations and also a warning. She felt "so deeply to my very heart's core the misery and degradation of being in debt." Men did not feel these things as women did, she believed, for they were not so deeply sensitive. She had been brought up to feel it a disgrace to owe a debt that could not be paid, and she had been made to feel that disgrace. She pitied Mr. Peters, for she knew how "the iron enters the soul," but his misfortune had not been her husband's fault, and she knew that her husband was equal to his newly appointed task.[59]

On the night of the Supreme Court's action, Justice Wayne wrote to Howard that the Court had selected him as Reporter in a way altogether pleasing to his feelings, and that the Chief Justice would send him a notice of appointment.[60] Howard received warm congratulations from Gouverneur Kemble, a prominent and convivial New York industrialist with whom he had served in the House of Representatives, on the ground that the position would add not only to his resources but also to his reputation. He had little respect, said Kemble, for the fleeting

---

[57] Benjamin C. Howard to Mrs. Howard, Mar. 29, 1835; William D. Hoyt, Jr., "Benjamin C. Howard and the 'Toledo War': Some Letters of a Federal Commissioner," *Ohio State Archaeological and Historical Quarterly*, 60:297, 300, 1951.

[58] Jonathan Elliot to B. C. Howard,

Feb. 26, 1841, Howard Papers.

[59] Mrs. Howard to B. C. Howard, on margin of a letter, Gouverneur Kemble to B. C. Howard, Feb. 1, 1843, Howard Papers.

[60] James M. Wayne to B. C. Howard, Jan. 25, 1843, Howard Papers.

character of a politician. Even those who shone brightest in the House of Representatives and the Senate could effect little toward permanent fame. But he thought the position of Reporter very different, and he explained why:

> There is probably no position under our government, not even except-ing the presidency or Chief Justiceship, where a man can so engraft his name upon the laws and constitutions of our country, as the one that you have accepted; and when we consider that the Supreme Court by its decisions, are at this time establishing a code of common and constitutional law which is hereafter to govern this great continent, with its countless millions of inhabitants, and that what you now write will one day become legal authority from Hudson's Bay to Mexico, and must extend itself with the march of Anglo-Saxon blood even be-yond it, I consider that a more glorious ambition was never opened to the mind of man.[61]

Howard, perhaps with a sense of his own limitations, had professed doubt as to whether he ought to accept the position, but Kemble assured him that he had nothing to fear if a "trifler like Peters" could maintain himself as Reporter. It would give him a little trouble in the beginning to develop a concise and plain literary style in the analysis of arguments, but he had it in him, and circumstances would bring it out.

With Justice Wayne as a guest in his home and presumably giving advice,[62] and with specific requests from Justice Catron for the inclusion of subject matter, Howard compiled his first volume of reports. Justice Catron insisted on inclusion of the list of errors as they had appeared in Peters' reports, and apparently required Howard and Carroll to compile the list for him.[63] In order to secure public attention for one of his bankruptcy opinions in the Circuit Court, Catron also persuaded Howard to publish the opinion as an appendage to a Supreme Court decision.[64] To fill out the volume for a term at which little business had been done, Howard published also the rules and orders of the Court issued down to that time, and also the rules of practice for the Circuit Courts as courts of equity which had been worked out by the Supreme Court, and a list of all previously published decisions of the Court. Beyond that he resorted to what seemed an amazing example of bad taste by adver-tising his availability for the argument of cases that might be brought from a distance when it proved inconvenient for counsel to follow them.

---

[61] Gouverneur Kemble to B. C. Howard, Feb. 1, 1843, Howard Papers.

[62] B. C. Howard to William Thomas Carroll, Apr. 3, 1843, Clerk's Files.

[63] See B. C. Howard to William Thomas Carroll, Mar. 29, Apr. 3, May 18, 1843, *ibid.*

[64] Nelson v. Carland, 1 How. 265, 277 (1843).

XII: *The Clerk and the Reporter*

Justice Catron, back in his home town of Nashville and as usual keeping his ear to the ground for public sentiment, wrote to Howard that his first volume was looked for with a good deal of interest west of the mountains. Lawyers were worn out with grumbling about Peters' volumes: "Any report from Mr. Peters will not sell." He had made some inquiry and was of the opinion that double the number of volumes could be sold in the West if the price were reduced to three dollars.[65]

Reviewers of Howard's volumes were at first inclined to be cautious. As for the first volume, the *American Law Magazine* was scornful of the "unfortunate and absurd epistle of Mr. Justice Catron correcting errors of the press," and the advertisement of professional services. In the second volume it saw signs of improvement from the reports of earlier years, though lamenting Howard's lack of facility for condensing the arguments of counsel. It found his statements of cases generally succinct and clear, approving the brevity of syllabi, and dissenting from the position put forth by Peters that the syllabus ought to be an abridged report of the case. The Peters practice was out of harmony with almost any other reports, English or American.[66]

Readers found themselves disappointed in their hopes that Howard would improve in skill with additional experience. By 1846 *The Law Reporter* was complaining that his fourth volume, which ran to about 750 pages, might have been reduced to 550 "by making the statements of the cases and the reports of the arguments as condensed as is done by the most approved reporters."[67] Yet if Howard on the whole tended to publish too much, he was at times guilty of ruthless curtailment. In 1849, for example, in a suit between two states, he explained the brevity of reporting, saying, "he is admonished, by the size which this volume has already attained, that he must reduce the cases which are yet to be reported to as small a compass as possible."[68] In a case decided in 1854, where the decision of the Court was controversial enough to bring dissents from three Justices, he altogether omitted arguments of counsel, with the explanation that:

> The arguments of counsel upon both sides were in such an unbroken train of reasoning, that the reporter cannot compress them into a mere report; and as together, they made upwards of sixty pages in print, he cannot publish them entire. The reader who desires to examine into the case thoroughly, can consult the opinion of the Supreme Court of Arkansas, delivered in November, 1851. In that opinion the court maintains its doctrines with great earnestness.[69]

---

[65] John Catron to B. C. Howard, June 7, 1843, Howard Papers.
[66] *Am. L. Mag.*, 4:226, 1844.
[67] *Law Rep.*, 9:229, 1846.

[68] Missouri v. Iowa, 7 How. 660, 663 (1849).
[69] Curran v. Arkansas, 15 How. 304, 305 (1854).

The honeymoon period between Howard and some of the Democratic Justices gradually came to an end. Opinions were handed to the Clerk for recording and sent to the Reporter for publication, often in the varied longhands of the several Justices with consequent difficulties of accurate reading. The Reporter linked the opinions with his syllabi and digests of arguments and other documents included and sent them to the printer, after which they were to be returned to the Clerk for filing. The Justices sometimes wished to make changes in their opinions at various stages after delivery, thereby complicating the procedure. There is reason to wonder whether all the opinions were actually recorded by the Clerk before they were sent to the Reporter, and it is clear that the Reporter was extremely slow in returning the original opinions to the Clerk, if indeed some of them were ever returned at all. In 1850, for example, Carroll formally notified Howard that none of the original opinions for the December terms of 1845 through 1848 had been filed in his office, and unless they were supplied he would have to lay the matter before the Court.[70]

A letter from Justice Nelson at the close of his first term on the Court illustrated the problem of literary accuracy, at a time when the Reporter was changing publishers for the reports. He gave Howard instructions for the handling of materials in reporting certain cases in which he had written opinions, adding:

> And I would ask you, generally, to examine the opinions with care and make clear any obliteration or obscurity in the hand writing. The opinions were written under such a pressure for time, and no opportunity to review them with deliberation myself. I must rely on you.
>
> I am the more anxious about this, as the manuscripts are going into the hands of persons unacquainted with the character of our hand writing, and as you do not read the proof sheets, they will be exposed to blunders. Indeed unless the press in Boston has an Examiner of the proofs who is a good lawyer, familiar with legal language, he will be very apt to blunder. The old printer, I suppose, was familiar with the hand writing of the judges.[71]

With the kind of procedure here implied it is not surprising that mistakes were made which could not be corrected until volumes had been reprinted. In 1850, for example, Chief Justice Taney wrote to Howard in exasperation after learning from Justice Nelson that in a newly published volume the printer had crisscrossed headnotes in two

---

[70] Copy, William Thomas Carroll to B. C. Howard, Jan. 24, 1850, Clerk's Files.

[71] Samuel Nelson to B. C. Howard, Mar. 4(?), 1846, Howard Papers.

cases, one of them highly important, with one opinion written by Justice Nelson and the other by Justice Catron. Taney protested, "How the publisher could have fallen into the mistakes he has committed, and mixed up these headnotes in such singular fashion is to me incomprehensible."[72] A law review comment was that "the Reporter has either neglected his duties or employed some incompetent to discharge them."[73] Although the increase in the work of the Court done at adjourned terms in order to keep up with the docket added to Howard's compensation with the addition of new volumes of cases,[74] it also added to the pressure and to the likelihood of error.

At about this time it appears that printer's proofs of the opinions began to be sent to the Justices who wrote them. In 1851, for example, Chief Justice Taney wrote courteously to Howard to say:

> I am sorry that my carelessness in revising the printed opinion in Bennett–vs–Butterworth has given you so much trouble—& presume it was revised by me, although at this time I have no recollection of it.— The error in the printed copy consists in inserting the word *established* in place of the word *abolished*.[75]

He thought that if Mr. Carroll would look at the manuscript again he would find the word as it should be though so badly written as to be mistaken.

Although the Justices did not get from Congress the authorization sought in 1850 for employment of an "investigating clerk," one of whose duties would be to copy opinions, it seems that thereafter Justices were allowed to use clerks working in Carroll's office for that purpose, at least as far as opinions of the Court were concerned.[76]

Dissenting opinions, however, seem sometimes to have been handled separately[77] and with greater proneness to error. Justice Daniel expostulated to Carroll that he could see no reason why dissenting opinions could not be published with the same care and accuracy as opinions of the Court. His last four opinions had abounded with blunders and absurdities. He was determined thereafter to withhold his opinions from publication unless he himself could correct the proof.[78] But he

---

[72] R. B. Taney to B. C. Howard, June 10, 1850, *ibid*.

[73] *Am. L. J.*, 10:47, 1850. The cases were Menard's Heirs v. Massey, 8 How. 293 (1850), and Bissell v. Penrose, 8 How. 317 (1850).

[74] See for example 9 Stat. 532 and 9 Stat. 608.

[75] R. B. Taney to B. C. Howard, Sept. 24, 1851, Howard Papers.

[76] Justice Catron so wrote to Carroll, saying that the copying was to be done at the expense of the fund to defray the expenses of the Court. John Catron to William Thomas Carroll, Jan. 23, 1851, Clerk's Files.

[77] "Judge Wayne delivered to me the package of Dissenting opinions. . . ." B. C. Howard to William Thomas Carroll, May 20, 1851, *ibid*.

[78] P. V. Daniel to William Thomas Carroll, Mar. 17, 1853, *ibid*.

evidently failed in his determination, for in 1854 a serious error appeared in a printed volume. Justice Daniel had written one of his frequent dissents at permitting corporations to sue and be sued in federal courts on the basis of diversity of citizenship, admitting the futility of minority protest but saying melodramatically that "the effort can never be foreborne to raise that humble voice in accents of alarm at whatever is believed to threaten even the sacred bark in which the safety both of the States and of the United States is freighted."[79] Instead of getting credit in the published volume for his flow of eloquence, he found that it had been tacked on as a concluding part of another dissenting opinion by Justice Catron, who wrote in a very different style. Daniel wrote to Howard indignantly about the "ridiculous and mortifying attitude" in which the error had placed both Catron and himself, and said that since he had no other means of preventing such mistakes he was considering refusal to publish at all the dissenting opinions which he might read in Court.[80]

Howard apologized profusely for the error, indicating that in assembling the several opinions he must have failed to notice that Justice Daniel had not placed his name at the top of his longhand opinion and had himself failed to supply that item, with the result that the printer had proceeded from the Catron opinion to that of Daniel without a break in the page. With this explanation he proceeded to suggest a way in which the Justice could aid in preventing future errors:

> Permit me, my dear Sir, to mention that several of the Judges frequently direct their dissenting opinions to be copied under the supervision of the Clerk (which is paid for under order of the Court as a part of the Court expenses) and then review them before they are filed; and to suggest that if you could find it convenient to adopt the same course, thus co-operating as suggested in your note, I can but indulge the belief that with increased diligence on my part, you would have less reason hereafter to regret the errors of the press.[81]

Howard's gentle suggestion that Justice Daniel might himself share the responsibility for the error in handling the opinion proved a mistake in diplomacy. The irascible judge replied that it was the business of the Reporter and the Clerk to know the judges to whom the several opinions were to be ascribed. As for having his opinions copied at the expense of the Court, even if it were convenient he knew of no authority under which it could be sanctioned, and in any event mistakes

---

[79] Northern Indiana R.R. v. Michigan Central R.R., 15 How. 233, 251 (1854).

[80] P. V. Daniel to B. C. Howard, Jan. 22, 1855, Howard Papers.

[81] Copy, B. C. Howard to P. V. Daniel, Jan. 23, 1855, *ibid.*

from printing were scarcely less frequent than from difficult manuscript. He ended his outburst by saying, "Until further reflection, I shall direct my mere dissent to be recorded"[82]—that is, he would withhold the opinions themselves from publication. In some way, however, Justice Daniel was persuaded to continue to submit his dissenting opinions for inclusion in the reports,[83] without which his contribution to the grist of published materials, particularly in his later years, would have been small indeed.

The files do not show Justice Catron's reactions to the merging of one of his dissenting opinions with that of Justice Daniel, but the absence of his earlier friendly feeling for Howard was disclosed a year later when after consultation with Chief Taney he peremptorily refused to make corrections in an opinion he had written for the Court, corrections evidently suggested by Howard, adding, "nor shall my name be involved in instructions that leave you nothing to report."[84]

In his exuberance at getting Richard Peters removed as Reporter of the Supreme Court, Justice Catron seems to have inspired from Tennessee and Kentucky petitions to Congress for the republication of the earlier reports and to have given advice about the handling of Congressional strategy.[85] The project fell through, however, and the field was open when Justice Benjamin R. Curtis decided in the early 1850s, shortly after his appointment to the Supreme Court, that he would reprint all previously decided cases, without arguments of counsel and other documentary material and with only the most concise headnotes, to sell in competition with the more bulky reports then in circulation. Justice McLean, after ten years still smarting at the way in which his colleagues had replaced Peters with Howard, was enthusiastic about Curtis' plan. He hoped that Curtis would not merely republish back reports but would provide a continuing series:

I have never heard a member of the profession speak well of Howard's reports. They are made up of matter uninteresting to any one, with the view, it would seem, of increasing the size and number of volumes.

---

[82] P. V. Daniel to B. C. Howard, Jan. 24, 1855, *ibid.*

[83] See for example his dissenting opinion in Fontain v. Ravenel, 17 How. 369, 396 (1855), the request for which had sparked the angry controversy—see P. V. Daniel to B. C. Howard, Jan. 22, 1855, Howard Papers. See also at the same term Williams v. Gibbs, 17 How. 239, 271 (1855).

[84] John Catron to B. C. Howard, Apr. 4, 1856, Howard Papers. The case was Nutt v. Minor, 18 How. 287 (1856). In the interchange between the reporter and the judge it is hard to tell which came off best, since in reporting the case Howard limited to a few lines his inserted material.

[85] See John Catron to William Thomas Carroll, Mar. 20, 1844, Clerk's Files.

Your edition, I have no doubt, will supersede all others, in a short time; and such a result will be creditable to the Court, and highly beneficial to the bar.[86]

For advertising purposes all members of the Court signed in advance of publication a letter expressing approval of the plan. After publication of the first three volumes Chief Justice Taney and Justices McLean, Catron, Grier, and Daniel wrote letters of praise, likewise to promote the reception of the work. Chief Justice Taney called it one of the most useful publications that had issued from the American press. Justice McLean said, "The correction of the errors of the press in the present editions and the reference to subsequent cases where the decisions have been doubted, modified, overruled, or affirmed, as proposed in this edition, will give it increased value." Justice Catron noted, "He has disencumbered the reports of cases of useless matter, reducing them to form and size convenient to the student and comfortable to the lawyer and the judge; and then the price is reasonable." Justice Grier praised the work because it eliminated "the diffuse syllabuses, the superflous statements, and other mass of useless matter in which many of the cases (as now reported) are enveloped and concealed." Justice Daniel made the same point in other language. Along with this high praise from the Court went the notice that whereas in the old Reporter series fifty-eight volumes were priced at $222, Curtis' twenty-two volumes, covering the same body of opinions, sold for $66.[87]

From reviewers the Curtis volumes received praise similar to that which came from the other members of the Court, with, however, some reservations based on his exclusions. The Law Reporter stressed the fact that a case consisted of much more than the opinion of the Court—history, pleadings, and arguments of counsel. Especially important were the arguments of counsel on the losing side. The art of a Reporter was in knowing what to take and what to reject: "Brevity, the soul of wit, is sometimes the parent of obscurity."[88] It was feared that Justice Curtis had gone too far.

Although the Curtis volumes were well received, the Justice, about to leave the Supreme Court for private practice, did not continue the series. The spotlight therefore continued to be on Howard's reports until 1861 when he resigned because of involvement in Maryland politics. In 1856 The Law Reporter considered Howard's eighteenth volume an improvement on its predecessors in that the compiler had refrained from including with the more important opinions "a confused mass of

---

[86] John McLean to B. R. Curtis, Jan. 1, 1853, Curtis Papers. See B. R. Curtis, A Memoir of Benjamin Robbins Curtis, I, 188–91.

[87] These materials were published in the Washington National Intelligencer, Feb. 1, 1856.

[88] Law Rep., 9:113, 1856.

documents, of but little service to the reader, and occupying a great deal of valuable room."[89] But the *American Law Register* found the nineteenth volume a hopeless mess, with inaccurate headnotes, inept statements of facts, poor digests of arguments, and much extraneous material. It characterized Howard as a gentleman of the old school with deserving social and political connections, who ought to be taken care of because "they infuse a tone of placid respectability into the Government, which is necessary to temper the rude progress of Democracy," but it thought that if Howard were to be so employed some really competent lawyer ought also to be employed to do the necessary work.[90]

In his condensed reports Justice Curtis tended to be uniformly cryptic, sometimes to the extent of giving but little clue as to the content of a decision. In the *Charles River Bridge Case*, for example, with its manifold implications, he merely said, "The rules of construction of public grants of franchises, explained and applied."[91] In the *Passenger Cases*, with all the diversity of opinions and no opinion of the Court as such, he was pardoned for having little to say, "because we fancy it would puzzle a Philadelphia lawyer to make anything more out of them."[92] There even Howard was constrained to brevity, merely saying that New York and Massachusetts taxes on alien passengers arriving in those states were found unconstitutional, and adding:

> Inasmuch as there was no opinion of the court, as a court, the reporter refers the reader to the opinions of the judges for an explanation of the statutes and the points in which they conflicted with the Constitution and laws of the United States.[93]

Perhaps it was this lack of clarity that led the Senate, on the motion of Daniel Webster,[94] to order the diverse opinions published for the Senate's own use.[95] Perhaps Howard's agreement in sentiment with his fellow Marylander, Chief Justice Taney, who dissented in those cases, made it more difficult to state the position of the majority and expedient to omit such a statement.

However that may be, the situation was different in important cases which Chief Justice Taney was interested in having properly introduced. In the famous Dred Scott case,[96] where there was not a

---

[89] *Law Rep.*, 9:473, 1856.

[90] *Am. L. Reg.*, 5:755–59, 1857.

[91] For comment see *Law Rep.*, 9: 114, 1856.

[92] *Ibid.*

[93] Passenger Cases, 7 How. 283 (1849).

[94] *Cong. Globe*, 30th Cong., 2nd Sess. 550 (1849).

[95] Senate Misc. Doc. No. 60, 30th Cong., 2nd Sess.

[96] Dred Scott v. Sandford, 19 How. 393 (1857).

unanimous majority as to all that was said but where Chief Justice Taney was determined to have his own intricate opinion stand as the opinion of the Court, he took over for Howard the task of writing the elaborate headnote that was published.[97] Further concerned about having the several opinions in that case published only as they would stand in the context of the whole case and with introduction by his headnote, and perhaps wishing also to protect Howard's prospect of sales of the pamphlet of the opinions and the volume containing them, he even went so far as to deny access to the opinions to Justice Curtis, who as a result of his opinion and the reaction of the public had lost with the majority of the Court the high standing he had had when he first published his own series of reports. In the matter of the *Booth Cases*[98] the Chief Justice, whether or not he himself wrote the headnote, thought there would be a public demand for copies of his discussion of the nature of federalism and of the constitutionality of the Fugitive Slave Act, and urged upon Howard the desirability of publishing the unanimous opinion in a separate pamphlet as well as in the official volume of reports, and relaxed his rule preserving the privacy of Court records to the extent of giving the Attorney General access to the manuscript opinion.[99]

On September 13, 1861, Howard sent Chief Justice Taney his resignation as Reporter of the Supreme Court, saying he had accepted the nomination of the Friends of Peace—an anti-Administration and antiwar group—for the governorship of Maryland.[100] The Chief Justice withheld his answer a few days and then replied that he would have answered sooner but for the report that Howard had been imprisoned by the military, in which event a reply would not reach him. He could not accept the resignation, since the appointment was by the Court and not by the Chief Justice. Howard was therefore still Reporter until the Court accepted his resignation.[101]

Howard lost the election and Chief Justice Taney tried without avail to persuade the Court to keep him as Reporter, but got no support from any other member of the Court. He therefore announced the resignation,[102] writing to Howard, "I need not tell you how much I am disappointed and mortified at the result of this matter."[103]

---

[97] Taney's longhand draft is preserved in the Howard Papers.

[98] Ableman v. Booth, 21 How. 506 (1859).

[99] See Alfons J. Beitzinger, "Chief Justice Taney and the Publication of Court Opinions," *Cath. U. L. Rev.*, 7:32, 1958.

[100] B. C. Howard to R. B. Taney, Sept. 13, 1861, Bayard Papers.

[101] R. B. Taney to B. C. Howard, Sept. 17, 1861, *ibid*. Howard's brother Charles had been so imprisoned. See B. C. Howard to William D. McKim, Nov. 16, 1861, *ibid*.

[102] *Baltimore Sun*, Dec. 6, 1861; *Washington National Intelligencer*, Dec. 5, 1861.

[103] R. B. Taney to B. C. Howard, Dec. 5, 1861, Bayard Papers.

XII: *The Clerk and the Reporter*

The Supreme Court lost little time in selecting a new Reporter. On December 16, 1861, a journal known as the *Maryland News Sheet* announced that "Hon. Jeremiah S. Black, formerly Attorney General and last Secretary of State under the Buchanan Administration was yesterday elected by the Judges Reporter of the United States Supreme Court, in the place of Benjamin C. Howard, who resigned on account of his secessionist proclivities."[104] As chief justice of the highest court in Pennsylvania Black had shown himself a jurist of high stature. He added to his reputation in the office of Attorney General. At the end of the Buchanan Administration he had been nominated for a position on the Supreme Court, but had failed of confirmation because many friends of the Administration were already withdrawing from the Senate in preparation for secession. He was left without a means of immediate support, and was glad for a time to have the office of Reporter while he reestablished himself at the bar.

Although Black did not resort to Howard's stratagem of advertising his availability to argue cases, he soon found himself swamped with private business. Much of it involved California land claims, running to many millions of dollars in value. Black had become thoroughly familiar with the legal questions as Attorney General and was fortunate enough to have on the West Coast a son-in-law with whom he collaborated in handling the business. In one of these cases he received a fee of $180,000,[105] and others that he handled provided a flow of high income throughout the remainder of his life.

With such opportunities for independent achievement it is not surprising that he resigned as Reporter of the Supreme Court after publishing only two volumes of reports. He was far superior to either Peters or Howard, and was at least the equal of any of his predecessors. A friendly reviewer said of his first volume:

> The statement of facts, which in cases in this Court must be condensed from documents of more than usual complexity and extent, is, in general, clear, succinct, and intelligible to a noticeable degree. Nothing is inserted which is not necessary to a correct understanding of the decision; and, on the other hand, nothing important to that end is omitted. The arguments of counsel are well reported. The points and authorities are brought out with perfect distinctness, and at the same

---

[104] On the same day Justice Grier wrote to Judge Cadwalader, "We elected Judge Black unanimously, on Saturday, as reporter. There were about twenty candidates. We were overwhelmed with letters of recommendation, and personal importunity. We determined to elect no one unless personally known to the court. I have no doubt B. will make a good reporter, and if there are any profits, [he] will need them as much as any one." R. C. Grier to John Cadwalader, Dec. 16, 1861, Cadwalader Papers.

[105] William N. Brigance, *Jeremiah Sullivan Black*, 143.

317

time, diminished to the proper focus, with due literary skill. There is often, indeed, a freshness and epigrammatical turn in the language used, which shows that the Reporter has not contented himself with a mere reduction by scale, so to speak.[106]

For all this praise, however, a correspondent sent him a list of "several errors in the citation of cases, caused most probably by the carelessness of the proofreaders."[107] It is quite possible, therefore, that had he remained Reporter for a number of years he would have encountered at least some of the criticism faced by Peters and Howard.

During the December, 1863, term of the Court, Black let it be known that he must give up his work as Reporter in order to devote all his time to his private practice. In discussing the qualifications of candidates for the office, Chief Justice Taney wrote in a letter to Justice Clifford a shrewd comment on the subject:

> I have some misgivings as to gentlemen who have mixed much in politics or been members of Congress. When they come to Washington they meet old political associates, and generally find the excitement of political life pleasant and the duty of a Reporter mere labor, and would rather be in one of the lobbies, instead of plodding at the Reporter's desk.[108]

The majority of the Court selected a man who was not Taney's choice but who met the standards of his letter. On March 21, 1864, they accepted Black's resignation and appointed John William Wallace of Pennsylvania. He was the Reporter of the Circuit Court for the Third Circuit and an author and librarian.

Wallace, whose story belongs essentially to the post-Taney period, began his work under the handicap of having to report a considerable mass of decisions handed down before his appointment and therefore not under his observation at the time of their announcement. Congress extended from six months to one year the time in which he must deliver his first volume,[109] but he nevertheless delivered it within the shorter period. He demonstrated on the first page of a garrulous and flowery

---

[106] Henry Wharton, reviewing 1 Black, *Am. L. Reg.*, 1:702, 1862. Justice Nelson wrote to Black that the volume was all he could wish: "The headnotes which are, perhaps, the best test of the soundness of a law report, appear to me not only clear but accurate, showing that the case has been studied and comprehended— the *head* used instead of the *shears*.

There is also a condensation and neatness in the statement of the case deserving all praise." Samuel Nelson to J. S. Black, Sept. 25, 1862, Black Papers.

[107] C. J. Hoadly to J. S. Black, Dec. 20, 1862, Black Papers.

[108] R. B. Taney to Nathan Clifford, Feb. 11, 1864, Clifford Papers.

[109] 13 Stat. 405.

preface his normal proneness to error by misstating by one year the date of his appointment.[110] With Wallace as Reporter until 1875, and Daniel W. Middleton as Clerk until 1880, the office administration of the Court moved into a new regime, though one not essentially different from its predecessor. Errors continued to be made, and critics continued to differ as to the precisely correct techniques for reporting the decisions of the Court.

---

[110] Preface, 1 Wall. vii (1864). By implication, though not specifically, Wallace on p. ix treats Wheaton as the recipient of the letter of Justice Story discussing the duties of the Reporter. See *Life and Letters of Joseph Story*, II, 231.

CHAPTER XIII

Federal Courts and the Common Law

U NDER THE EDITORSHIP OF his young friend Dr. Francis Lieber, recently arrived from Germany, Justice Story in the early 1830s wrote anonymously a series of articles on legal topics for the *Encyclopaedia Americana*.[1] In one of them he described the hierarchy of federal courts and explained as to the Supreme Court that the general mass of its business consisted of "private controversies respecting property, or personal rights and contracts." But although such private controversies constituted the mass of Supreme Court business, he noted that questions of national and public law were also finally discussed and settled there, and asserted that the most important function of the Court was "the decision of the great constitutional questions, which, from time to time, arise in the different parts of the Union."[2]

Justice Story retained his conviction as to the importance and interest of public law cases in contrast to ordinary cases of private rights. Concerning the work of the 1838 term of the Court, for example, which had a large proportion of private law cases, he wrote to Charles Sumner, "There were few causes of general interest argued, and still fewer which gave rise to very comprehensive researches into nice or recondite law."[3] Only a boundary dispute between Rhode Island and Massachusetts[4] and a case involving a writ of mandamus to compel the

---

[1] For an account of the authorship of the articles see John C. Hogan, "Joseph Story's Anonymous Law Articles," *Mich. L. Rev.*, 52:869, 1954. Mr. Hogan has edited the republication of various of the Story articles in scattered law reviews. A full judicial biography is Gerald T. Dunne, *Justice Joseph Story and the*

Rise of the Supreme Court.

[2] *Encyclopaedia Americana*, III, 596 (new ed., 1835).

[3] Joseph Story to Charles Sumner, Mar. 15, 1838, *Life and Letters of Joseph Story*, William W. Story, ed., II, 295.

[4] Rhode Island v. Massachusetts, 12 Pet. 657 (1838).

Postmaster General to obey an Act of Congress[5] had really captured his attention. Justice Catron, who through his private practice and as a member of the Tennessee Supreme Court was well grounded in common law rules, remarked about the same term, his first on the Court, that the strictly judicial work was not more difficult than that of the Tennessee court, and that the legal questions, here as elsewhere, depended "more on common sense than any deep legal knowledge."[6] His principal difficulty seems to have been with the public law questions in the mandamus case, in which he submitted his dissenting opinion more than a year late.[7]

But even if it sometimes produced tedium, or in any event, seemed easy work, the preoccupation of the Supreme Court with private litigation during much of its time had important implications. In private law was to be found the source of most of the principles and rules of practice to be applied in the public law field. Anchorage in private law subject matter tended to curb the drift into current politics which preoccupation with public law issues tended to invite. Beyond that, private law issues at times proved important enough to rival those of public law in their significance for the public welfare. It was in the private law field, furthermore, that the Supreme Court Justices were expected to render to the country much of their Circuit Court service, by taking over from the state courts the handling of cases between citizens of different states.

While it may have seemed possible that the Supreme Court Justices, with their high prestige and their travels through the states on circuit duties, would achieve leadership over the state courts in the application of common law and equity in cases of diversity of citizenship, such leadership never became pronounced. During the Taney period the commentaries, the cases reprinted, digested, or commented on in the law journals of the time, were predominantly cases in the highest courts of the states. Supreme Court and Circuit Court opinions were not entirely absent but they never stood out to mark the achievement of leadership.

The explanation of this failure in leadership was doubtless complex. The states and the state courts were jealous of their prerogatives and fearful of the "alien" encroachments of the federal government. Each slow step in the evolution of the common law tended to have its explanation in the community in which it was taken, and state judges were assumed to have a familiarity with local needs and customs not to be gained by federal justices moving rapidly through their circuits.

---

[5] Kendall v. United States, 12 Pet. 524 (1838).
[6] John Catron to Andrew Jackson, Feb. 5, 1838, Jackson Papers.
[7] Kendall v. United States, 13 Pet. 607 (1839).

Another explanation lay in the congestion of federal court dockets and the tendency of harried federal judges to give most of their attention to jurisdiction that was peculiarly theirs rather than to that shared with the states and allowed to federal courts only in cases involving diversity of citizenship. This predicament was highlighted in 1851 in an address given before the Law Academy in Philadelphia by John William Wallace, then reporter for the Third Federal Circuit. Wallace contended:

> [W]hile the same jurisdiction over commercial cases exists [in the federal courts], constitutionally, as of old, practically it is not at all so exercised. The decisions of the Supreme Court of the United States instead of being referred to for the commercial law of the country, are hardly known to the profession, now, except as settling patent, admiralty, or revenue cases, as reviewing the opinions of State tribunals on constitutional questions, and as containing the great practical exposition of the powers of the State and National Governments. All questions of commercial law go, therefore, to the State Courts.[8]

That all questions of commercial law went to the state courts was of course an overstatement. Within limits the federal courts made a fight for jurisdiction which, if it may be said to have been given up at all, was not abandoned until after the first third of the twentieth century. It was made partly in the field of commercial law but it extended into other areas as well. The story had its background, indeed, in the Marshall period when the Court had considered whether the federal courts had common law jurisdiction in criminal matters. At a time when Chief Justice Marshall was still fighting hard to maintain in the Supreme Court unanimity both of decision and opinion, he achieved it at the expense of permitting Justice William Johnson to say for the Court that such common law jurisdiction did not exist.[9] Of the several members of the Court, at least Justice Story, who was usually expansionist with respect to the jurisdiction of federal courts, was reluctant to consider the question as settled.[10] Unable to carry the Supreme Court with him, he turned to Congress for the expansion of jurisdiction over crimes. He drafted a bill of more than seventy sections, based on a careful revision of the criminal code of England, which passed twice in the Senate but failed in the House of Representatives. Finally, in 1825, a limited version of it was enacted.[11]

---

[8] John William Wallace, *The Want of Uniformity in the Commercial Law Between the Different States of Our Union,* 27.

[9] United States v. Hudson and Goodwin, 7 Cranch 32 (1812).

[10] United States v. Coolidge, 1 Wheat. 415, 416 (1816).

[11] 4 Stat. 115. For Justice Story's account of the bill see Joseph Story to John M. Berrien, Feb. 8, 1842, *Life and Letters of Joseph Story,* II, 402.

XIII: *Federal Courts and the Common Law*

Story continued to work for the expansion of the criminal jurisdiction of the federal courts. In 1842, at the time of the important decision in *Swift v. Tyson* in the field of commercial law,[12] and shortly before he was to draft a bill for the extension of admiralty jurisdiction to inland waters, he submitted to Congress a section of a bill to extend the criminal jurisdiction of the federal courts to offenses committed on the high seas and elsewhere within the admiralty jurisdiction of the United States.[13] He was much disappointed when Congress dropped the section from a much broader measure dealing with the federal courts.[14]

In other areas Justice Story was more successful in maintaining and expanding the jurisdiction of the federal courts, or in shaping the law that they must apply. The thirty-fourth section of the Judiciary Act of 1789 provided with reference to cases coming into the federal courts by diversity of citizenship that "in trials at common law" the rules of decision, with certain exceptions, should be "the laws of the several states."[15] Unfortunately the statute did not define the scope of the "laws of the several states" which the federal courts were required to follow. Years later Charles Warren discovered and published draft material showing that at one stage in the formulation of the Judiciary Act it was proposed that in diversity cases the federal courts must follow not only state statutes but also the state "unwritten or common law." Draftsmen dropped the references to statutes and to unwritten or common law and used merely "laws of the several states," without indicating whether they had meant to narrow the requirement or merely to compress the language.[16] Warren saw the strategy as merely one of compression of language without limitation of scope; it would result in the federal courts being required in diversity cases to follow not merely state statutes but the "unwritten or common law" as well.

Having apparently no access to the documentary history of the statute, Justice Story reached the opposite conclusion from that later reached by Warren. The underlying assumptions of his thinking are to be found in Circuit Court decisions with respect to the sources of the law of equity to be applied by federal courts, as distinguished from the common law. When a federal court exercised equity jurisdiction, based on diversity of citizenship of the parties and not because of responsibility for enforcement of a federal statute, he contended that the federal court had no obligation to look for guidance to equity law as developed

---

[12] 16 Pet. 1 (1842).

[13] *Life and Letters of Joseph Story*, II, 403–04. For discussion see Chapter XVIII, "Admiralty and Maritime Jurisdiction."

[14] *Ibid.*, 405–06. For the measure enacted see 5 Stat. 516.

[15] 1 Stat. 73, 92.

[16] Charles Warren, "New Light on the History of the Federal Judiciary Act of 1789," *Harv. L. Rev.*, 37:49, 86, 1923.

323

in the courts of any state or states. Although he would not have used the language, it is evident that for him equity was something that Justice Holmes later insisted the common law was not, namely, a kind of "brooding omnipresence in the sky."[17] Equity, for him, was an all-pervasive body of principles of justice, to be discovered by reference to the opinions of distinguished chancery judges in England without necessary reference to the fumbling attempts of American state judges to expound the meaning of those principles.

So it was that in 1836, in an equity case in a United States Circuit Court in Maine, Justice Story could slough off an objection that his interpretation of equity differed from that of the courts of Maine. He remarked that "the equity jurisdiction of this court is wholly independent of the local laws of any state; and is the same in its nature and extent, as the equity jurisdiction of England, from which ours is derived, and is governed by the same principles."[18] A year later he remarked with respect to views expressed in the highest court of Massachusetts that "these views, not being founded upon local law, but upon general principles of interpretation applicable to courts of equity, are not, and cannot from their nature be, conclusive upon this court, in a suit in equity addressed to its general jurisdiction."[19]

The position of Justice Story on circuit became the position of the Supreme Court. One of many instances was a case arising in Louisiana where state practice, based on the civil law, ignored the distinction between law and equity. The title to land of great value depended on whether the United States courts for Louisiana, in determining the validity of titles, would observe state practice or would adhere to the distinction between law and equity, and in determining the content of equity would hark back to English principles. For the Supreme Court Chief Justice Taney declared that in the courts of the United States "the distinction between courts of law and of equity is preserved in Louisiana as well as in the other States."[20] Senator Solomon W. Downs of Louisiana immediately introduced a bill to require local federal courts to conform to the practice of the state.[21] The proposal was challenged, however, by Senator Samuel S. Phelps of Vermont, who preferred that practice should be uniform throughout the system of federal courts in all the states rather than in harmony with the separate state patterns:

---

[17] Southern Pacific Co. v. Jensen, 244 U.S. 205, 222 (1917).

[18] Gordon v. Hobart, 10 Fed. Cas. 795, 797 (No. 5609) (C.C.D. Me. 1836).

[19] Flagg v. Mann, 9 Fed. Cas. 202, 223 (No. 4847) (C.C.D. Mass., 1837).

[20] United States v. King, 7 How. 833, 844 (1849).

[21] An act to amend "An act to regulate the mode of practice in the courts of the United States for the District of Louisiana," approved May 26, 1824. See *Cong. Globe*, 30th Cong., 2nd Sess. 626 (1849). See S. 421, 30th Cong., 2nd Sess.

XIII: *Federal Courts and the Common Law*

"I think it all-important that citizens of the United States, resorting to the jurisdiction of the United States, should find one and the same remedy, and one and the same course of proceedings in every court."[22] The bill had been brought up as one not likely to cause much debate. Upon show of a great deal of opposition it was laid on the table.[23] Soon afterward, in another case from Louisiana, Chief Justice Taney for the Supreme Court drove home the point by saying that when an injunction was applied for in the federal Circuit Court in Louisiana the court would grant it or not, according to the principles of equity, and not according to the laws and practice of the state, in which there was no court of chancery.[24]

Thereafter, in 1852, speaking through Justice Curtis, the Supreme Court stated the principle more broadly. In a case from Georgia where equity was in fact recognized and where the state supreme court professed to apply the same equitable principles, stemming from the High Court of Chancery in England, as were applied in the federal courts, Justice Curtis announced that the Supreme Court did not feel obligated to follow the interpretation of equity principles given by the Supreme Court of Georgia.[25]

Thus the "brooding omnipresence" of equity, severed from any necessary connection with state court decisions, was now firmly established. True, the state courts were no more obligated to follow federal doctrines of equity than were the federal courts to follow the state courts, but within the range of such cases as came to the federal courts by virtue of diversity of citizenship the federal courts were free to go their own way. The power of Congress to legislate on the subject had been exercised simply to authorize the Supreme Court to promulgate rules of equity practice.[26]

In seeking to narrow the range of state authority to which the federal courts were required to defer by the thirty-fourth section of the Judiciary Act of 1789, Justice Story went beyond equity to exclude also what he called general law or general jurisprudence, treating the act as if it applied only to state statutes and perchance to state court decisions on matters strictly local in character. In 1836, in a Circuit

---

[22] *Cong. Globe*, 30th Cong., 2nd Sess. 626 (1849).

[23] See the statement of Senator Charles G. Atherton, *ibid.*, 626.

[24] Bein v. Heath, 12 How. 168, 179 (1852).

[25] Neves v. Scott, 13 How. 268 (1852). For discussion of the principle here involved by the author of the opinion see Benjamin R. Curtis,

Jurisdiction, Practice, and Peculiar Jurisprudence of the Courts of the United States, 240–43.

[26] See 5 Stat. 516, 518. See also: Rules of Practice for the Courts of Equity of the United States, Promulgated by the Courts of the United States, January Term, 1842, 1 How. xxxix–lxxx (1843).

Court case in Massachusetts, he voiced the *obiter dictum* that "questions of commercial law are generally considered, as not justly included in that branch of local law, which the courts of the United States are bound to administer, as the state courts hold it to be."[27] In 1838, in summing up a case for a jury in the United States Circuit Court for Maine, he took what seemed an even longer step in arrogating discretion to the federal courts. Although the soundness of land titles seemed a matter peculiarly dependent on the application of state law, he nevertheless chose to interpret the language of a deed as if it were not a matter of "purely local law," but subject to interpretation according to the rank and ability of the judicial interpreter.[28]

Story's next step was to persuade the Supreme Court itself that in diversity of citizenship cases not merely equity but the great body of "general law," as distinguished from state statutes and laws having strictly local application, was to be found directly by federal judges without obligation to accept state court interpretations as rules of decision. In thus seeking to expand the jurisdiction of federal courts, Justice Story manifested neither a hunger for power nor any high degree of intellectual subtlety. It is to be remembered that he supported fully the broad interpretation of federal constitutional powers of Chief Justice Marshall and that he had reorganized the Marshall materials into a work of commentaries on the Constitution. With the transition to the Taney Court he believed that the old constitutional doctrines were fast fading away, and feared that within his day the Supreme Court would not again assert itself to the extent of declaring unconstitutional any law either of a state or of Congress.[29] He felt an obligation to do what he could to preserve the old order and to maintain the power of the Court.

Furthermore, in writing huge volumes of commentaries not merely on the Constitution but also on bailments, conflict of laws, equity jurisprudence and pleading, agency, partnership, bills of exchange, and promissory notes, Story assumed a position of authority with respect to vast fields of law, including areas in which state court interpretations were scattered in all directions, leaving the law as a whole in confusion. He was concerned with maintaining the federal judicial system as the guide and harmonizer to minimize the growing confusion. Long afterward John Chipman Gray, Austinian and ardent positivist, and unsympathetic with Story's natural law tendencies, offered a biting psychological explanation. He saw Story as "a man of great learning," and "of reputation for learning greater even than the learning itself." He

---

[27] Donnell v. Columbian Ins. Co., 7 Fed. Cas. 889, 893 (No. 3987) (C.C.D. Mass. 1836).

[28] Thomas v. Hatch, 23 Fed. Cas. 946, 949 (No. 13899) (C.C.D. Me. 1838).

[29] *Life and Letters of Joseph Story,* II, 272.

noted the fact that Story was writing his work on bills of exchange, with necessary concern about the confusion among the states—which "would lead him to dogmatize on the subject." He pointed to Story's success in extending admiralty jurisdiction, with the implication that the success had expanded his appetite for more. He asserted that Story "was fond of glittering generalities; and he was possessed by a restless vanity."[30]

Much of Story's thinking was consistent with theories of an over-shadowing body of natural law to which judicial decisions and even statutes must conform. Yet the reader will search in vain for more than incidental treatment of such a subject. Story was a recorder and a purveyor of the law, and not an expounder of systematic and abstract theory. While he could engage in "very comprehensive researches into nice or recondite law,"[31] and present the results in voluminous opinions, volume did not imply intellectual luminosity. He was pedestrian, and thorough, and determined. But the point should not be made too pointedly. As Justice Holmes said of Marshall as well as of Story, it was "the mark of the time, a god-fearing, simple time that knew nothing of your stinking twisters but had plain views of life. . . . They were an innocent lot and didn't need caviare for luncheon."[32] Justice Story was much concerned with correct discovery of "the law," and with applying that law through the federal courts in such a way as to maintain a strong federal union.

Justice Story's opportunity to marshal the entire Supreme Court for the position that a federal court need not conform its decisions to those of the states in matters of "general commercial law" came with *Swift v. Tyson.*[33] The case came up from the United States Circuit Court for the Southern District of New York, on a certificate of division of opinion between Justice Thompson and Judge Samuel R. Betts. It involved the rights on a bill of exchange, with important ramifications into American history well beyond the range of the technical legal question in dispute.

During the 1830s timbered and undeveloped land still constituted one of the most important areas of profitable speculation. It was an area also of much fraudulent enterprise. In 1836 George W. Tyson of New York bought a tract of allegedly valuable land in Maine from two men, Nathaniel Norton and Jarius S. Keith, for something over eighteen hundred dollars. Tyson paid for the land by a bill of exchange, drawn to the order of Norton and due six months after date. Before the bill be-

---

[30] John C. Gray, *The Nature and Sources of the Law,* 253.

[31] Joseph Story to Charles Sumner, Mar. 15, 1838, *Life and Letters of Joseph Story,* II, 295.

[32] *Holmes-Laski Letters,* Mark De Wolfe Howe, ed., II, 1015.

[33] 16 Pet. 1 (1842).

came due, Norton endorsed it to John Swift, apparently a resident of Maine.

Tyson proved to have been gullible, and Norton and Keith treacherous. After committing himself to payment by way of the bill of exchange, Tyson discovered that the two men had no land to sell. Had Norton held the bill of exchange for the six months' period and then attempted to collect from Tyson, he would have been unable to do so because of want of consideration, in that he and Keith were never able to deliver title to the land. But Swift claimed that the situation was now different, since he had acquired the bill in payment of a debt which Norton had owed to him, and he had received it without notice of the initial fraud.

In the foreground in the *Swift* case was the importance of bills of exchange as a medium of intrastate, interstate, and foreign commerce, a matter that had recently been given careful attention by the Supreme Court in *Bank of Augusta v. Earle*.[34] In his *Commentaries on the Law of Bills of Exchange*, in preparation at the time of the decision in the *Swift* case, Justice Story found it to be the custom of the commercial world to hold bills of exchange "as in some sort sacred instruments" in favor of bona fide holders for a valuable consideration without notice.[35] Whatever might have been the business relations of the original parties, when the bill passed by lawful means into the hands of a third person, in this case Swift, it transferred rights without reference back to the original transaction. By shutting out defenses arising out of the earlier transaction, "the instrument has, for many practical purposes, become equivalent to, and a representative of, money; and it circulates through the commercial world, as an evidence of valuable property, of which any person, lawfully in possession, may avail himself, to make purchases, to pay debts, and to pledge, as a security or indemnity for advances."[36]

Justice Story was interested in protecting the commercial community in this use of bills of exchange, and so, apparently, were the other Justices and most of the courts of the states as well. The general rule as to the exemption of purchasers for value of bills of exchange from defects that might have destroyed the value of the bill as between the original parties was recognized in New York, where the bill here involved was accepted; but according to some New York decisions, the rule applied only when the bill was transferred "in the usual course of business or trade." There was a question whether a transfer made to pay a preexistent debt, such as that between Norton and Swift (which

---

[34] 13 Pet. 519 (1819). For discussion see Chapter V, "The Realm of Finance."

[35] Joseph Story, *Commentaries on the Law of Bills of Exchange*, 17.

[36] *Ibid.*

in theory at least might have involved collusion between these two parties to defraud Tyson), was a transfer made in the usual course of business or trade. When Swift sued Tyson in the Circuit Court in New York, Tyson argued that under New York law the bill was infected with the fraud of the original transaction. He contended further that under the thirty-fourth section of the Judiciary Act of 1789 the federal court in New York was obligated to follow the law of New York—the decisions of the New York courts—in deciding the case. The judges certified to the Supreme Court the question whether Tyson could assert the defenses which would have been available had the suit been one between the original parties.

The case was first submitted to the Supreme Court at the January term, 1840, with Daniel Webster arguing the case for Swift and either Amasa Dana or Alexander H. Dana of New York[37] submitting a written argument for Tyson. The Supreme Court in 1840, in the absence of Justice McKinley, consisted of only eight members, and in the *Swift* case the eight proved to be equally divided "as to the manner of stating the question."[38]

The case was not presented again until 1842, by which time Webster was Secretary of State. He turned the case over to William P. Fessenden of Maine, a brash young lawyer and a member of Congress who at that time was one of his aides and admirers and to whom he had been godfather. Fessenden and Dana presented the case on written briefs, without oral argument. Fessenden, whether using Webster's argument or his own, called on the Supreme Court to preserve its own consistent interpretation of commercial law and not to follow the differing courts of the several states "with vacillating inconsistency." How, he asked, could the Court in so doing preserve its control over the reason and affections of the people? "In what light will the judicial character of the United States appear abroad, under such circumstances?"[39] Perhaps Fessenden knew, as Justice Catron recorded, that Justice Story was "tremblingly alive" to the impression which the Court made in England, and that he lectured his brethren on the importance of the subject.[40]

Fessenden pointed out that "By all without the United States, this court is looked to as the judiciary of the whole nation known as the United States, whose commerce and transactions are as widely diffused as is the use of bills of exchange."[41] He asked the Court to adopt a

---

[37] 16 Pet. 1, 9.
[38] John Catron to James Buchanan, Aug. 4, 1842, Buchanan Papers.
[39] *Ibid.*, 9.

[40] Catron to Buchanan, *supra* note 38.
[41] 16 Pet. 8.

reasonable interpretation of the Judiciary Act to the effect that it was required to follow only the legislative enactments of the states. Dana, on the other hand, emphasized the fact that, for all the influence of the common law on the American constitutional system, there was no common law to be enforced by the courts except the common law of the several states, and that in deciding common law cases with parties who were citizens of different states the federal courts could rely only on the law of the relevant states for rules of decision.

Whether the federal judges in New York had better stated the certified question, or whether some members of the Court were influenced by the written arguments, or whether Justice Story had done persuasive work between the presentations of the case in 1840 and 1842, his position was now unanimously victorious. In writing the opinion of the Court he asserted that the "laws of the several states" which federal courts were required to follow could not include state court decisions, since decisions did not constitute laws. "They are, at most, only evidence of what the laws are, and are not of themselves laws."[42] The Court had "uniformly" supposed that the laws to be followed were state enactments and their interpretations and rights and titles to things having a permanent locality. "It never has been supposed by us, that the section did apply, or was designed to apply, to questions of a more general nature . . . as, for example, to the construction of ordinary contracts or other written instruments, and especially to questions of general commercial law."[43]

By its decision in the *Swift* case the Supreme Court committed itself to the position that the common law was, again in Justice Holmes' phrase, a "brooding omnipresence in the sky," that it was something more than "the articulate voice of some sovereign or quasi sovereign that can be identified,"[44] that it was a body of independent law to be discovered by the trained reasoning capacities of federal judges. The decision left the country with two unanswered questions: How far would the federal judiciary carry the assertion of its independence of the state courts in applying the common law in the several states? And would the state courts, immediately or eventually, accept the leadership of the federal courts and so bring about the development of a harmonious body of common law in the several states instead of riding off in all directions as the state courts were now tending to do?

That the Court was not likely to be chary in the exercise of its newly asserted independence was further indicated at the same term, and indeed in part in the same case. In writing the opinion in the *Swift* case Justice Story went beyond the facts of the case to say that

---

[42] *Ibid.*, 18.
[43] *Ibid.*, 18–19.

[44] Southern Pacific Co. v. Jensen, 244 U.S. 205, 222 (1917).

bills taken by way of security for an antecedent debt, no less than those taken in payment, were free of prior defenses. In a concurring opinion Justice Catron objected to this. The state courts, some of which had already taken different positions from that here asserted unnecessarily by the Supreme Court, could not be expected to yield to "a mere expression of opinion of this court." It would have been better, Catron argued, to wait until a case involving a further extension of doctrine came before the Court, when a decision either way would settle it.[45] But Justice Story was not one to delay or show diffidence in such matters.

At the same term of the Court Justice Story extended to the interpretation of insurance policies the practice of determining questions without reference to state court decisions. The case came up on writ of error from the United States Circuit Court for Rhode Island. John Whipple, a distinguished Rhode Island lawyer, argued the case for a property owner, who had suffered fire damage, against an insurance company. The company was represented by similarly distinguished counsel in Richard W. Greene of Rhode Island and John Sergeant of Pennsylvania. Whipple sought to persuade in terms of relevant state court decisions,[46] and Green and Sergeant challenged those decisions, supporting the position the Court was now taking as to the irrelevance of state court decisions in a vast but undefined field. Justice Story refrained from discussing the state decisions, again finding that the case depended on "general commercial law," involving construction of a contract of insurance, which was "by no means local in its character, or regulated by any local policy or customs." While the decisions of state tribunals were entitled to great respect, they could not conclude the judgment of the Supreme Court.[47]

The Court continued to expand the area of its independent operation. In 1845, in the absence of Justice Story, Justice McLean took the lead in refusing to follow the highest court of Mississippi with respect to the construction of a will. The decision was too much for Justice McKinley, who ordinarily had little to say in the pages of the *United States Reports*. With the concurrence of Chief Justice Taney he disagreed both with the reasoning of the Court and with its assertion of independence. He thought the decision likely to bring a struggle for power between federal and state courts. To avert that contest he thought the federal courts ought to follow state decisions establishing rules concerning title to real estate.[48] This dissent, however, marked no crusade

---

[45] 16 Pet. 23.

[46] Whipple's brief was preserved with the record but not that of opposing counsel.

[47] Carpenter v. Providence Wash-ington Ins. Co., 16 Pet. 495, 511 (1842).

[48] Lane v. Vick, 3 How. 464, 482 (1845).

on the part of either Justice McKinley of Chief Justice Taney for abandonment of the doctrine of the *Swift* case. Indeed, in a case decided on circuit, the Chief Justice later specifically stated his commitment to the doctrine.[49]

So the development proceeds from case to case.[50] It is hard to tell how confident were the expectations of the Supreme Court that state courts would choose to conform their own common law decisions to those of the Supreme Court, and thus produce uniformity of decision by contrast with the growing diversity. A year after the decision in the *Swift* case Chancellor Reuben H. Walworth of New York let it be known that for all his respect for Justice Story as an expert in commercial law he felt no obligation to modify the law of his state to conform to the Supreme Court interpretation.[51] Similar expressions of respect were made by other courts, which, if they followed the Supreme Court, did so out of the persuasiveness of Justice Story's reasoning rather than from a sense of obligation to yield to superior authority. John William Wallace, in the 1851 address mentioned above, found a dearth of state citation of Supreme Court decisions and noted the predicament:

> The Supreme Court of the United States has declared that on commercial questions it will not follow the State Courts; and the State Courts in turn declare that on such questions, they will not follow the decisions of the Supreme Court of the United States; and both have a constitutional right to say so; for both are courts of final and co-ordinate jurisdiction. With such causes of discord, it is remarkable that so great uniformity exists. The evil, however, is increasing and must continue to increase.[52]

Wallace saw a possible solution through giving a writ of error to the Supreme Court in all commercial cases, but he admitted that this could not be done without a constitutional amendment,[53] and he must have known how impossible it would be to secure the necessary amendment in this period of sectional rivalries and assertion of the doctrine of states' rights.

---

49 Meade v. Beale, 16 Fed. Cas. 1283, 1291 (No. 9371) (C.C.D. Md. 1850).

50 For the sequence and for discussion of many of the cases see Robert H. Jackson, "The Rise and Fall of Swift v. Tyson," *A.B.A.J.*, 24:609, 1938.

51 Stalker v. McDonald, 6 Hill (N.Y.) 93 (1843).

52 Wallace, *The Want of Uniformity in the Commercial Law*, 27.

53 *Ibid.*, 29. Wallace suggested also that under the Commerce Clause a code of commercial law might be framed which would be uniform throughout the United States, after the fashion of the famous Hanseatic code. He admitted, however, that such codification would be difficult or impossible. *Ibid.*, 30.

XIII: *Federal Courts and the Common Law*

The story of the further development of the doctrine of *Swift v. Tyson* belongs in large part to other periods of the history of the Supreme Court, down to and after the time when, in 1938, in *Erie Railroad v. Tompkins*,[54] the *Swift* case was overruled. Within the Taney period, however, certain other developments of at least temporary significance took place in logical extension of the doctrine of the *Swift* case; they further illustrated the indefiniteness of judicial thought about the nature of law and the nature of interrelations between state and federal judiciaries. The Supreme Court began to challenge not merely state court interpretations of the common law but also state statutes violating principles or practices in which the Court believed—as if in anticipation of the weapon of due process which the Fourteenth Amendment was later to put into judicial hands. Justice Daniel, for example, for all his jealous concern about the rights of the states, spoke for a unanimous Court in refusing to apply a Mississippi statute limiting a right of recovery on a bill of exchange. "A requisition like this," he explained, "would be a violation of the general commercial law, which a state would have no power to impose, and which the courts of the United States would be bound to disregard."[55]

Even in the matter of statutes concerning title to land, a majority of the Supreme Court in 1850 went so far as to refuse to follow what had been Chancellor Kent's interpretation of private statutes enacted by the New York legislature specifically with respect to the disposition of a particular estate, for the care and education of infant heirs. To Justice Wayne, as spokesman for the majority, the steps taken were not to be justified, and he refused to admit that the requirement to follow the decisions of the highest courts of the states with respect to state statutes "comprehends private statutes or statutes giving special jurisdiction to a State court for the alienation of private estates."[56]

Justice Nelson, who had been for many years chief justice in New York, challenged the Supreme Court decision and reminded the Court of its obligation to follow the laws of the states in matters of titles to real property. The federal courts, he said for himself and Chief Justice Taney and Justice Catron, were "obliged to adopt the local law, not only because the titles are founded upon it, but because these courts have no system of jurisprudence of their own to be administered, except where the title is affected by the Constitution of the United States, or by acts of Congress."[57] The sentiments expressed by Justice Nelson were also those of the courts of New York. They refused to give way to the

---

[54] 304 U.S. 64.
[55] Watson v. Tarpley, 18 How. 517, 521 (1856).

[56] Williamson v. Berry, 8 How. 495, 543 (1850).
[57] *Ibid.*, 558.

Supreme Court. Eventually, a decade after its first decision, the Supreme Court itself gave way and, speaking unanimously through Justice Campbell, agreed to accept the interpretation by the New York courts of New York's own statutes.[58]

In one instance the Supreme Court refused to accept as the law of a state the interpretation given by the state's own courts to its constitution. A provision of the Mississippi constitution was interpreted by the Supreme Court in *Groves v. Slaughter* in 1841, at a time when there was no existing interpretation of that provision by the highest state court. The Supreme Court there held that a constitutional provision forbidding the importation of slaves from other states into Mississippi would be effective only after adoption of an implementing statute.[59] But thereafter in a number of cases the highest court in Mississippi held that the state constitution debarred importation of its own force. When a later case involving the same question arose in the United States Circuit Court in Mississippi, that court followed the state court interpretation, and the case went to the Supreme Court on writ of error.

Justice Daniel, from whose circuit the case came to the Supreme Court, was the only dissenter when the Supreme Court, in *Rowan v. Runnels*, decided to follow its own earlier decision rather than those of the Mississippi courts. Speaking through Chief Justice Taney, the Court refused to void contracts for the purchase of slaves made in good faith on the basis of its earlier decision. Although he admitted that as to future contracts the decisions of the state courts must govern, the Chief Justice asserted that the Supreme Court could not be required, "by any comity or respect for the State courts," to surrender its judgment as to matters previously decided.[60] It seems not to have occurred to him that in the interpretation of state constitutions and statutes the Supreme Court was a tribunal inferior to the courts of the states, and that it was controlled not by "comity or respect for the State courts" but by an Act of Congress, the thirty-fourth section of the Judiciary Act of 1789. Here again, the prevailing feeling seems to have been that law derived from an abiding principle which preserved the rights of property and promoted trade. Not even the sanctity of state sovereignty was to stand in the way of the Court when the protection of commercial continuities was involved. Again there can be sensed the presence of due process restrictions not yet officially adopted, or not yet articulated.

The subject of the nature and source of the law to be applied by the federal courts in cases involving diversity of citizenship merges

---

[58] Suydam v. Williamson, 24 How. 427 (1861).
[59] Groves v. Slaughter, 15 Pet. 449 (1841).
[60] Rowan v. Runnels, 5 How. 134 (1847).

with other topics discussed elsewhere, including that of the position of business corporations in American law which needs in part to be stated here. It is to be remembered that during the 1840s and 1850s the people alternated between approval of aid to private corporations, particularly banking and railroad corporations, and hostility to corporations which failed to do all that was expected of them or proved to be the enemies rather than the friends of the investing public. These alternating attitudes of the people found expression in state statutes and, to a lesser extent, in court decisions. In an 1854 decision in which there was no single opinion for the Court, Chief Justice Taney announced for himself and Justice Grier the position that if a contract when made was valid under the laws of a state, its validity and obligation could not be impaired by either a subsequent legislative act of the state "or decision of its courts, altering the construction of the law."[61] This position, that a state court decision and not merely an act of a legislature, might violate the constitutional provision that no state should "pass any law" impairing the obligation of a contract, stood in the record for adoption by the majority of the Court when a case arose calling for its use. Court decisions, which in Story's opinion in the *Swift* case had been labeled as not law but merely the evidence of law, were now categorized as law when they violated prohibitions levied directly not against the courts but against the legislature.

The Taney position was to be adopted by the Court ten years later, in 1864, in *Gelpke v. Dubuque*, an important municipal bond case which came up from Iowa. The people of Iowa, like the people of other states, had become enthusiastic about railroad building, and allowed themselves to indulge in overly sanguine financing to promote construction. Although the Iowa constitution limited to one hundred thousand dollars the amount of debt to be incurred by the state and forbade the state to own stock in private corporations, the legislature authorized municipal governments to issue bearer bonds to aid railroad construction, not only within the limits of the municipalities but throughout the state. This device of permitting subdivisions of the state to do what the state government itself could not do was aimed at circumventing the constitutional limitation.

The money was oftentimes wastefully spent, the prosperity expected from railroad operations failed to arrive, and taxpayers within the municipalities found themselves taxed to pay off the bonds, which were now circulating far and wide after having been used to buy railroad stocks. Taxpayers challenged the proceedings on the ground that the bond issues had violated the prohibitions in the state constitution. Early state court decisions upheld the measures taken, but eventually public

---

[61] Ohio Life Ins. & Trust Co., 16 How. 416, 432 (1854).

sentiment forced a change in judicial attitudes, and the Iowa Supreme Court held that the state authorization was unconstitutional.[62]

Soon afterward a suit to recover interest on bonds was brought against the city of Dubuque in a federal court in Iowa. The court, in its attempt to follow Iowa interpretations of the Iowa constitution, had to decide whether to follow the several earlier decisions or the final one which was the reverse of these. It elected to accept the latest decision and held that the holder of interest coupons on bonds issued by the city of Dubuque could not collect. The case went to the Supreme Court on writ of error.

The case had far-reaching implications for the American economy, involving financial strategy in many other states as well as Iowa. Counsel for the creditors proclaimed, "It concerns the honor, not of Iowa only, but of all the States; the value of millions of securities issued by nearly every State of the Union, and by cities and counties and boroughs in them all. Yet more: we shall ask this court to treat as contradicting precedents made by the Supreme Court of Iowa itself, and so subversive of regard for authority,—as erroneous, therefore, in the law, and of no obligation,—the latest decision of a State of this Union . . . and any decisions which, to the disregard of earlier and settled precedents, follow it."[63]

Counsel claimed, in short, that the obligation to pay debts went beyond the law of any particular state and had a kind of universal existence, which was to be demonstrated by examination not only of Iowa decisions but also those of other states. With the convenient vagueness that in courts of law tends to accompany arguments having a natural law tinge, counsel apparently regarded the obligation to pay interest and redeem bonds as supported by a kind of "general law" as discussed

---

[62] Former Justice Benjamin R. Curtis later discussed the situation as follows:

The bonds were issued and sold in the market, were taken in good faith by those who had occasion to invest capital, or who were induced by other reasons to take the bonds, and the question arose whether that was a constitutional act, authorizing those municipal bodies to issue these bonds. It was held by the Supreme Court of the State that it was a constitutional act. Thereupon the sale of the bonds proceeded, and, under the authority of this decision, confiding in its soundness, very large amounts of these bonds were issued. They finally became very burdensome to the people of Iowa and those communities that had issued them, and there was a great change in the popular sentiment of the State; and in consequence of that, their judges being elective, new judges were elected, and a different decision made,—that the legislature of the State had no constitutional power to authorize the cities and towns and counties to issue those bonds.

Benjamin R. Curtis, *Jurisdiction, Practice, and Peculiar Jurisprudence of the Courts of the United States*, 237.

[63] Gelpcke v. Dubuque, 1 Wall. 175, 179 (1864).

in the *Swift* case, a body of general law now so well established that decisions of the Iowa courts could not change it. As for the interpretation of the Iowa constitution, "Whether, in view of the Constitution of Iowa, it was or was not rightly settled in the first instance, is a matter not at all important to inquire into. It was settled by a tribunal which had power to settle it; and on the faith of judicial decisions the bonds were sold."[64]

Counsel for the city too ranged far and wide in the search for arguments, noting as to the earlier state court decisions that "In many of the decisions, the courts seem to have been imbued with the frenzy of the day, and to have lost sight of the well-defined distinction between the powers and liabilities of municipal and private corporations."[65] Counsel added that Iowa decisions in favor of the bonds were never quite unanimous, "and have never given satisfaction to either profession or courts."[66] In any event the matter was now at last unanimously decided in Iowa, and the federal courts should follow that decision.

A year before the *Dubuque* case was decided by the Supreme Court and while the litigation was pending, Justice Swayne, who in 1862 had replaced Justice McLean on the Supreme Court, decided a case from another state court in another field of law by saying that under the thirty-fourth section of the Judiciary Act of 1789 the Supreme Court gave the laws of the states the same construction and effect as were given by local tribunals. That construction, said Justice Swayne, was regarded as a part of the statute and as binding upon the federal courts. He added: "If the highest judicial tribunal of a State adopt new views as to the proper construction of such a statute, and reverse its former decisions, this court will follow the latest settled adjudications."[67]

In including this reference to the latest "settled adjudications," Justice Swayne forged for himself and a majority of his brethren an instrument for rejecting the single most recent Iowa decision, even though unanimously reached, and going back to the series of earlier decisions. Yet having created the weapon, he seemed to avoid direct reliance on it, saying it was not necessary to decide whether the *Dubuque* case came within that category. He declared that the Supreme Court could not be expected to "follow every such oscillation, from whatever cause arising, that may possibly occur," and then proceeded to approve the earlier decisions as "sustained by reason and authority," and in harmony with the adjudications of sixteen states of the Union. He rested the case on the position taken by Chief Justice Taney and Justice Grier in the Ohio case mentioned above, to the effect that when contracts

---

[64] *Ibid.*, 187.
[65] *Ibid.*, 197.
[66] *Ibid.*, 198.

[67] Leffingwell v. Warren, 2 Black 599, 603 (1862).

were made on the basis of trust in past judicial decisions those contracts could not be impaired by any subsequent construction of the law.[68]

The opinion of the Court, based on a confusion of concepts of natural law and common law and the obligation of contracts, closed with the emotional outburst, "We shall never immolate truth, justice, and the law, because a state tribunal has erected the altar and decreed the sacrifice."[69]

Justice Samuel F. Miller, a new member of the Supreme Court, and himself from Iowa, castigated the decision of the majority and the use of "language as unsuited to the dispassionate dignity of this court, as it is disrespectful to another court of at least concurrent jurisdiction over the matter in question."[70] He predicted that the action of the Supreme Court of the United States would not win over the Iowa Supreme Court to its position but would lead the latter court to adhere to its position with all the more tenacity—a prediction which proved to be correct.[71]

By the end of the Taney period, therefore, the Supreme Court had not managed to resolve the confusion deriving from a notion of the "brooding omnipresence" of the common law, with natural law overtones, and with restraining effects on the interpretations to be given to state statutes and even to state constitutions. Parallel confusion in the body of thought about the attempts at codification of state law also had at least peripheral significance for the work of the Court during this period.

---

[68] 1 Wall. 175, 206 (1864).

[69] *Ibid.*, 206–07.

[70] *Ibid.*, 209.

[71] For discussion of the case as seen in terms of Justice Miller and in terms of future developments in other cases see Charles Fairman, *Mr. Justice Miller and the Supreme Court,* 207–36. A full account is given in Charles Fairman, *Reconstruction and Reunion, 1864–88: Part One, Holmes Devise History of the Supreme Court,* VI, chs. 17, 18.

CHAPTER XIV

Fringes of the Codification Movement

T HE STRUGGLE TO BRING ABOUT the codification of the common law
began before the Taney period and continued beyond it. Although the movement as a whole is not a part of the history of the
Supreme Court, in a number of ways the Court was peripherally involved.

Charles Warren attributed to five intermingling factors the desire to
replace the common law with codes drafted to meet American needs.
Briefly stated they were: continuing hostility to the common law because
of its English origin; jealousy of lawyers who entrenched themselves in
positions of power by means of the abstruseness of the common law; the
growing number of law reports; the success in Europe of the Napoleonic
Code; and the influence of Jeremy Bentham.[1] The factors were not
completely consistent one with another, as, for example, hostility to all
things English, and acceptance of the influence of the English Jeremy
Bentham. It is also to be noted that Justice Story, one of the American
leaders in the movement for a limited degree of codification, was anything but hostile to English institutions and was not at all an admirer
of the supposed radicalism of Bentham.

Nevertheless, hostility to things English probably remained an appreciable factor down into the Taney period, accentuated now and then
by strife over filibustering on the Canadian border, the slave trade, and
the Oregon question. A scholarly mixture of anti-English feeling and
criticism of the content of the common law is apparent in a Maryland
reformer, Daniel Raymond, who wrote in 1846:

> The foundations of the common law of England were laid in the
> twilight of modern literature and science, when scholastic philosophy

---

[1] Charles Warren, *A History of the American Bar*, 508.

and school divinity pervaded and perverted the intellect of Europe. Hence the common law, as we should expect, is full of metaphysical abstractions, scholastic subtilties, arbitrary distinctions, and intangible or incorporeal rights to things, separate from the things themselves.[2]

With the development of the Democratic Party under the leadership of Andrew Jackson, and the Whig Party in opposition, the Democrats proved to be the more radical advocates of reform and the more severe critics of both the common law and Great Britain, the Whig Party moving into the position of defense. This fact may help to explain what seems to have been a growing coolness on the part of Justice Story toward the codification movement which had greatly interested him in earlier years.

The jealousy of laymen toward the big-name and the more pontifical of the lawyers, those who collected the largest fees and exerted the greatest influence, also expanded with the influence of Jacksonian democracy. The character of the bar itself was changing. The old-fashioned lawyer had won respect even from his critics. He was remembered for "the powdered hair, the small-clothes, the silver knee-buckles, the silk stockings, the gold-headed cane, the solemn countenance. . . . Moderation and gravity were the two words most strongly written on the faces of the venerable men who walked quietly into court in the morning, spoke, when they had anything to say, earnestly and to the point, and then walked home as serene as when they came." These dignitaries had now given way to bustling and restless men, a new race characterized by feverishness and strain.[3]

---

[2] Daniel Raymond, "Law Reform in Regard to Real Estate," *West. L.J.*, 3:385, 1846. Another writer said of the common law that "It is an artificial, complex, technical system, inherited from our forefathers, and now grown so obsolete, and so burdensome, as no longer to command the respect or answer the wants of society. Its principal characteristics are a great many forms of an antique phraseology, according to which every controversy in the ordinary courts must be carried on; forms, the reasons of which perished long ago, and which are now become inadequate, uncouth, and distasteful. By reason of the prevalence of these forms in the ordinary courts, another system of courts has grown up, called courts of equity, practising upon another plan, professing to supply the deficiencies of the former, and yet become themselves so artificial, and withal so dilatory, that their delays and expense have passed into a proverb." *Democratic Review*, 14:345, 349, 1844.

See also the following: "The blind devotion of the English for every thing they peculiarly possess, has descended upon the children of the colonists in the matter of the Common Law—a system of jurisprudence in many respects unfitted to our peculiar institutions." *Democratic Review*, 18:19, 1846. See Perry Miller, "The Common Law and Codification in Jacksonian America," *Proceedings of the American Philosophical Society*, 103:463, 1959. See also Perry Miller, *The Life of the Mind in America*, Book II, Ch. VII.

[3] "The Study and Practice of Law," *Democratic Review*, 14:345, 1844.

XIV: *Fringes of the Codification Movement*

Democratic spokesmen welcomed the passing of the old order and boasted that the practice of law had degenerated from a liberal art to a trade, that artists had become artisans and scholars had become clerks. This they claimed was the natural result of the growth of individualism. "Thereby we know that we no longer enjoy our liberties at the discretion of others. No haughty proconsul, the proxy of a despot, armed with double licensiousness or unrestrained authority and unbridled appetites, can now impoverish our provincial cities, riot upon our substance, and violate our most sacred sentiments and rights. . . . His professional talents can never distinguish or dignify the position of the lawyer, in a society where the people are denied no important rights."[4]

It was said that the age was gone when the chief end of a system of jurisprudence was the establishment of an abstruse science and the creation of a special order of men to administer it. The prime end of law was now seen as the meting out of speedy justice, in disregard of the technicalities and crotchets of a scholastic age. Forms must yield to substance. Outmoded precedents must be abandoned. It was necessary to eliminate the defects in the machinery of justice which had created the widespread impression that "the law, and especially the practice of the law, is a system of chicanery, or, at the best, of quackery, and that every lawyer is by profession either a knave or a charlatan, or a compound of both."[5] While these sentiments were by no means universal, they played their part in developing sentiment for the codification and simplification of law so that it might be understood by laymen as well as by specially trained and specially favored members of the bar.

The influence of the Napoleonic Code and its interpreters found expression in citations of French authorities in American courts[6] and in the influence of the codes drafted by Edward Livingston for the state of Louisiana, which circulated throughout the United States even though they were not officially adopted.[7] By 1840 it was said that the work, completed in 1825, had proved a treasury of provisions from which many systems and codes had derived important improvements: "The criminal laws of New York, Massachusetts, Georgia, and Illinois, which have been revised since the publication of the Louisiana project, are indebted to the labors of Mr. Livingston for very many useful and humane suggestions, which they have adopted to a greater or less

---

[4] "Prospects of the Legal Profession in America," *Democratic Review*, 18: 26, 28, 1846.

[5] "The American Bar," *Democratic Review*, 28:195, 197, 1851.

[6] See Roscoe Pound, "The Place of Judge Story in the Making of Ameri-

can Law," *Am. L. Rev.*, 48:676, 686–89, 1914.

[7] See Charles H. Hunt, *Life of Edward Livingston*, 255–81; William B. Hatcher, *Edward Livingston*, 245–88.

extent."[8] The French contribution was, of course, diluted with American materials, with some of the heritage of the common law, and with suggestions from Jeremy Bentham and others whom Livingston consulted; nevertheless much of the European continental influence remained.

Although Jeremy Bentham died at the age of eighty-four, some four years before Roger B. Taney became a member of the Supreme Court, some of his books continued to appear thereafter under the editorship of the Frenchman Stephen Dumont, and his works and ideas continued to be discussed in law journals and other publications of the period. To many Americans, indeed, he may have been more "alive" during the two or three decades after his death than he had been earlier. As an Englishman, Bentham was a scathing critic of the law of his native land. He scorned the eclectic system or lack of system of Sir William Blackstone, who through his *Commentaries on the Laws of England* had provided a kind of bible on the common law—at least in terms of the thinking of American lawyers.[9] Although Bentham evolved a kind of natural law theory of his own without use of the label, he was sharply critical of natural law theory as Blackstone expounded it to give sanctity to the body of English law. He was at opposite poles from the German historical jurist Frederick von Savigny, who saw law as evolving out of the dynamics of society and as something to be changed by legislation only at society's peril. Bentham was quite ready to wipe the slate clean and write complete codes of new law based on the concept of the greatest good of the greatest number. Indeed, he confidently offered to perform that function for rulers as greatly different as the Czar of Russia, the American President, and the governors of a number of the states of the American Union.[10]

Bentham had, at first, all the ineffectiveness of a crusader who overstates his position and oversimplifies his subject matter, but his almost monomaniacal zeal for reform of the law worked its way into the thinking of people less drastic in their desires and plans for change in a period when change had to come both in his own country and abroad. His ideas on penology, on the law of real property, and on other sub-

---

[8] Luther S. Cushing, "Livingston's Penal Codes," *Am. Jurist*, 22:395, 398, 1840. See also "Edward Livingston and His Code," *Democratic Review*, 9:3, 1841. See also review of Livingston's penal code in *North American Review*, 43:295, 1836.

[9] For background on Bentham, apart from his own voluminous works and other sources, see Sir William Holdsworth, "Bentham's Place in English Legal History," *Cal. L. Rev.*, 28:568, 1940; C. W. Everett, "Bentham in the United States of America," in George W. Keeton and George Schwartzenberger, *Jeremy Bentham and the Law*; Charles E. Stevenson, "Influence of Bentham and Humphreys on the New York Property Legislation of 1828," *Am. J. Legal Hist.*, 1:155, 1957.

[10] See William Plumer, Jr., to Joseph Story, Sept. 28, 1841, and Jeremy Bentham to William Plumer, Nov. 14, 1819, *Am. Jurist*, 27:62, 1842.

jects began to infiltrate the law of various American states. Discussing this contribution in 1838 an American commentator said there was no question that Bentham was "the most profound and original of law reformers."[11] While rejecting Bentham's utilitarian theory, Luther S. Cushing of Massachusetts, who worked closely with Justice Story in an appraisal of the common law of that state, agreed.[12] "There may be more dazzling, but there are no more honorable or useful spheres of exertion than in the department of LAW REFORM," said the *Democratic Review* in a laudatory account of Bentham's *Theory of Legislation*.[13] As late as 1862 an American law journal, in discussing Bentham's contribution to the law of evidence, said of him that he was certainly a very remarkable man, and "there was so much common sense in his conclusions upon legal reform, that in spite of very strong prejudices they have been gradually making their way both in England and the United States, and in England faster than the United States."[14]

The third of the five reasons which Charles Warren offered in explanation of the codification movement was that the mass of reports flowing from the courts of the several states was soon likely to become unmanageable. Justice Story had discussed this problem as early as 1821 in an address before the Suffolk bar. He then thought the only remedy was a gradual digest, under legislative authority, of the growing body of settled law, to reduce the text to exact principles and avoid the necessity of appealing to volumes containing jarring and discordant opinions. The way might thereby be paved to a general code for the guidance of the lawyer, the statesman, and the private citizen.[15] Story paid deference to the code in force in Louisiana which, he said, gave complete relief without trammelling itself with prescribed forms, which often perplexed and sometimes defeated the ends of justice.[16] Some years later he referred approvingly to the infusion of large extracts from the civil, the French, and other foreign law and again noted the merits of codification in Louisiana.[17] He did not, however, follow other admirers of codes and friends of codification in the United States to the extent of proposing

---

[11] Arthur James Johns, "On the Legal Arguments Urged in England for a Continuation of the Separation of the Law and Equity Jurisdictions," *Am. Jurist*, 20:111, 115, 1838.

[12] Luther S. Cushing, "The Greatest-Happiness Principle," *Am. Jurist*, 20: 332, 1839.

[13] *Democratic Review*, 8:251, 271, 1840. For comment on the popularity of Bentham's views with Jackson Democrats see Arthur M. Schlesinger, Jr., *The Age of Jackson*, 330–31.

[14] G. S., "Competency of Witnesses," *Am. L. Reg.* (N.S.), 1:257, 1862.

[15] For discussion herein of the reporting of cases in state and federal courts see Chapter XII, "The Clerk and the Reporter."

[16] Joseph Story, "Progress of Jurisprudence," in *Miscellaneous Writings*, 198, 237.

[17] *Ibid.*, 217.

drastic simplification of practice and pleading. Here he condemned American practitioners as far behind the English bar in knowledge and performance. The forms of pleading, he contended, were not mere trivial forms. Study of them, more than any other employment, "leads the student to that close and systematic logic, by which success in the profession is almost always secured."[18] For him, "special pleading contains the quintessence of the law, and no man ever mastered it, who was not by that very means made a profound lawyer."[19]

It seems probable that with the coming of Jacksonian democracy and the identification of legal reform with the democratic movement Justice Story became increasingly cautious in his attitude. Nevertheless, when he wrote an article on the subject for the 1835 edition of Francis Lieber's *Encyclopaedia Americana*, he continued to advocate codification in areas where the common law principles were largely settled but where uniformity of statement was needed to make the law clear without extended research in large numbers of volumes. He noted that every state in the Union had resorted to legislation to codify varying classes of its laws. The criminal code had almost everywhere received legislative attention. Virginia had taken important steps. New York had recently gone much farther, making alterations in the common law as well as statute law. As for the areas of law ready for legislative statement, "Our

---

[18] "Digests of the Common Law," *ibid.*, 404–07. Justice Story's occasional preferences for Roman law principles over those of the common law are illustrated by a Circuit Court decision in 1837 in which he discussed the problem of allocating indefinite payments to various debts owed to the same creditor: "There is no doubt that the doctrine of the common law, as to the appropriation of indefinite payments, has generally been borrowed from the Roman law; and it is deeply to be regretted that there has been any departure in any of the authorities from its true results. The Roman law is equally simple, convenient, and reasonable upon this subject; and, for most cases, will furnish an easy and satisfactory solution." Gass v. Stinson, 10 Fed. Cas. 72, 77 (No. 5262) (C.C.D. Mass. 1837).

About this case, Chief Justice John Bannister Gibson of Pennsylvania remarked, "For everything that comes from Mr. Justice Story, I feel a def-erential respect; and had not the weight of his name been thrown into the scale, I should not have felt called on to vindicate the rule of the common law. But in saying that as regards the application of payments, the Roman law is more rational and consonant to the presumed intention of the parties, than the common law; that it is equally simple and convenient; and that it is, or ought to be, the law of the subject in this country; it seems to me, his partiality for his favorite code has carried him too far. In the American courts, the question is not an open one; and it would require some intolerable mischief—certainly more than an equality in point of simplicity, convenience and reasonableness—to justify us in overturning the decisions of more than two centuries." Logan v. Mason, 6 W. & S. (Pa.) 9, 11 (1843).

[19] Story, "Progress in Jurisprudence," in *Miscellaneous Writings*, 198, 232.

commercial law is generally in this state. The law of bills of exchange and promissory notes, of insurance, of shipping and navigation, of partnership, of agency and factorage, of sales, of bailments, and many kindred titles, admits of codification to a very high degree of certainty."[20]

The discussions of legal reform continued in terms ranging all the way from proposals to recast the entire body of law, perhaps according to some formula such as Bentham's "greatest good of the greatest number," to others which provided merely for a restatement, in whole or in great or small part, of the law as it was deemed to stand at the time of the restatement. The more conservative members of the bar wanted no legislative changes in the structure of the common law, and those who were merely less conservative wanted such redrafting of the principles of case law as would improve the efficiency of legal administration in areas of special difficulty. As indicated above by Justice Story, piecemeal changes had long been in the making in a number of states, unaccompanied by the radicalism of Bentham or the zeal for reforming not merely legal administration but society itself which was feared in some of the Jacksonians.[21] The time was to come when participation in the reform movement could be explained either in terms of a desire to further reform or to keep control of developments to insure that reform did not go too far.

Justice Story's motives may have been mixed when in 1836 he was made chairman of a committee appointed by Governor Edward Everett of Massachusetts to report on the practicability of codifying the common law of Massachusetts or any part of it. The report, obviously written by Justice Story himself, elaborated on his position taken in the *Encyclopaedia Americana*. It favored codification of law with respect to the civil rights of persons in their interrelations, titles to real and personal property, contracts, crime, and evidence. The report made clear that the proposed code was to be "deemed an affirmance of what the common law now is, and not containing provisions in derogation of that law, and therefore subject to a strict construction."[22] It renounced the idea of a detailed code of the entire body of the common law, and left undiscussed the need for reform in practice and pleading.[23]

Indicating his measured attitude at that time toward codification, Justice Story on December 26, 1836, wrote:

---

[20] *Ibid.*, 233.

[21] "Law, Legislation, Codes," in *Encyclopaedia Americana*, VII, 576, 591 (1835).

[22] For an example of more radical attacks on judge-made law as seen by a friend of labor, see Robert Rantoul, Jr., *Memoirs, Writings and Speeches* (1854), as quoted in *Readings in Legal History*, Mark DeWolfe Howe, ed., 472–78.

[23] Story, "Codification of the Common Law," in *Miscellaneous Writings*, 698, 716.

We shall report favorably to the codification of some branches of the commercial law. But the report will be very qualified and limited in its objects. We have not yet become votaries to the notions of Jeremy Bentham. But the present state of popular opinion here makes it necessary to do something on the subject.[24]

He wrote to Francis Lieber that the report was subdued and qualified because they wanted to win public favor for it.[25] His young protégé, Charles Sumner, then editing the *American Jurist*, wrote to Story's Heidelberg correspondent, Professor Karl Joseph Anton Mittermaier, in the hope of getting an article on codification for his journal. Sumner emphasized the fact that in the United States codification was mere revision and reduction of the text of the law; he thought the error of Jeremy Bentham and John Locke was "in supposing that they, in their closets, could frame *de novo* a code for a people."[26]

It is not clear whether Story's committee refrained from mentioning the reform of procedural law because of division among the members or because mention was deemed inexpedient in terms of getting legislative acceptance of the report. However that may have been, Luther S. Cushing, a member of the committee, immediately wrote for the *American Jurist* an article criticizing both the historic forms of action which complicated practice at common law and the administration of remedial justice through the different channels of law and equity.[27] Justice Story, whether from the point of view of political strategy or from differing convictions about the merging of law and equity, questioned whether Cushing's paper would not "press against any scheme of codification."[28]

---

[24] Charles Warren, *History of the Harvard Law School*, 504.

[25] Joseph Story to Francis Lieber, Jan. 14, 1837, Lieber Papers.

[26] Charles Sumner to K. A. J. Mittermaier, Mar. 27, 1837, *Memoir and Letters of Charles Sumner*, Edward L. Pierce, ed., I, 189.

[27] Luther S. Cushing, "Reform in Remedial Law," *Am. Jurist*, 17:253, July, 1837. The *North American Review*, in general no radical journal, said in reviewing a reprint of Cushing's article that "Mr. Cushing recommends nothing less than the amalgation of the two systems of law and equity, and the construction or revival from the two of a sort of *tertium quid*, in the language of the chemists, which shall have the great advantage of unity and consistency. . . . Now it

can hardly be questioned that our system would be preferable to what it is now, if it were divested of its present Janus-face, and made to assume but one countenance." *North American Review*, 46:545, 1838.

[28] Joseph Story to Charles Sumner, Jan. 25, 1837, *Life and Letters of Joseph Story*, William W. Story, ed., II, 267. Justice Story's continuing sensitiveness on the subject of procedural reform is indicated by a letter to a friend in England saying, "I have been examining, with a good deal of attention, the working of your new rules of Pleading, which have demolished the general issue. At present, I am not entirely satisfied that in the full extent the change has been so beneficial as was anticipated. I perceive the Reports are beginning to be

XIV: *Fringes of the Codification Movement*

It proved possible to get from the Massachusetts legislature an authorization to proceed only with the law of crimes. On the ground of professional engagements Justice Story declined to serve as chairman of the board of commissioners.[29] In 1839 the commission submitted a sample of codified law in the form of materials on the law with respect to murder.[30] The legislature failed to take action and the commission suspended its efforts. The movement for reform of substantive law in Massachusetts gradually lost much of its force.[31] It has been suggested that one of the reasons was the demonstration by the highest court of the state, led by Chief Justice Lemuel Shaw, that the common law could advance with the times and meet the needs of the current era without drastic changes or codification, as in the notable decision in *Commonwealth v. Hunt*,[32] in which organized labor was given a measure of protection against the law of conspiracy.[33]

In any event, Justice Story, in the later years of his life, had lost most of his own zeal for reform in the law. The scene of codification activity shifts elsewhere before Benjamin R. Curtis, one of Justice Story's ultimate successors on the Supreme Court from the First Circuit, took the leadership in the cause of procedural reform in Massachusetts.

Thereafter for a time the principal area of codification activity was the state of New York, where the major leadership was provided by David Dudley Field. At that time Field had no connection with the Supreme Court of the United States. His connection remained limited, but extended to practice before the Court and, after 1863, to having a brother on the Court, Stephen J. Field, who became a member, in part with his aid. This brother brought about the adoption of the Field codes in California and facilitated the spread of their use to other new states as well. Field had the use of materials produced by Bentham, Livingston, and Story. He differed from Bentham in that he had a practical knowledge of the practice of law, and was concerned centrally with improvement of legal administration and not with the reform of society as a whole. He differed from Justice Story in that, although not interested in codifying law down to the last detail, he did propose to operate

---

crowded, not to say overloaded with special pleadings, which present a great variety of intricate questions of no great general importance." Joseph Story to James John Wilkinson, Nov. 3, 1837, *ibid.*, 292. For discussion of the 1836 remedial statute in Massachusetts see Warren, *A History of the American Bar*, 534.

[29] Joseph Story to Edward Everett, Mar. 28, 1837, *ibid.*, 251.

[30] "Preliminary Report of the Criminal Law Commissioners of Massachusetts," *Am. Jurist*, 21:286, 1839.

[31] See Warren, *A History of the American Bar*, 531.

[32] 45 Mass. (4 Met.) 111 (1842).

[33] For discussion see Leonard W. Levy, *The Law of the Commonwealth and Chief Justice Shaw*, 196–206.

over the whole field of the law, both substantive and remedial. Following after these earlier reformers, furthermore, Field had the benefit of continuing and active discussion and experimentation with legal reform in England.[34]

In New York itself reform activities had been taking place. In 1829 an extensive codification primarily of statutes had been done, not for the purpose of making drastic changes but, where statutes covering common law subject matter were concerned, for the purpose of authoritatively declaring the common law.[35] Even the limited reform undertaken stirred opposition, particularly as changes were made in the law of real property.[36] But Field planned to go far beyond anything that had already been done to reform the basic structure of both substantive and procedural law.[37] Operating as a powerful politician as well as a lawyer, he

---

[34] The following excerpt is from a newspaper article written by Theodore Sedgwick to stir interest in codification in the forthcoming constitutional convention in New York:

It is a mortifying, though not a very surprising fact, that there is far more earnest and systematic discussion of the subject of Legal Reform in England, than in this country. We have abundant denunciation of the legal profession —abundant, hap-hazard legislation, aimed in general at "fees and costs," but as for any careful consideration of the causes which lead to good or evil in the system, we have it not. The reverse of this, in England, is very strikingly the case. Various causes conduce to this result: the very magnitude of the abuses has there turned the minds of all men to the subject. Law Reform has, for ten or fifteen years, incessantly occupied the labors of Parliament. While here, one class of our people is too constantly occupied in the pursuit of wealth, and another too agreeably immersed in the political game, to permit them any leisure for a subject so trifling as the administration of justice.

Theodore Sedgwick, "Law Reform," *West. L.J.*, 3:145, 1846.

[35] See E. P. S., "Judiciary System of New York," *Am. Jurist*, 26:38, 1841; J. Louis Telkampf, "On Codi-

fication or the Systematizing of the Law," *Am. Jurist*, 26:113, 143, 1841.

[36] "The true lesson to be learnt from this example is, to avoid all fundamental changes, and especially such as affect rules of property and such as leave the system incongruous and impracticable." S.F.D., "Codification and Reform of the Law," *Am. Jurist*, 21:352, 372, 1839; "We regard most of the reforms, by the revisers of the New York statutes, as fundamental, and many of them as subversive of the law of real property." S.F.D., "Codification and Reform of the Law," *Am. Jurist*, 22:282, 1840; "The Rules of property under the system of the common law were founded upon principles of mathematical truth, and a departure from those rules necessarily implied a subversion of true principles." "The Law of Real Property as Affected by the Revised Statutes of the State of New York," *Am. L. Mag.*, 4:310, 1845.

[37] For source materials dealing with Field's codification program see "Law Reform—State and International," in *Speeches, Arguments, and Miscellaneous Papers of David Dudley Field*, A. P. Sprague, ed., I, 219–583. For discussion of Field and his work in distant perspective see *David Dudley Field, Centenary Essays*, Alison Reppy, ed. For a somewhat personalized account, see Henry M. Field, *The Life of David Dudley Field*, 68–96.

worked on his project from 1847 to 1865. As Livingston had discovered, however, it was one thing to draft codes and another to secure their adoption. After adopting in 1848 the Code of Civil Procedure, New York lost much of its interest, with the result that others of his codes became law in newer states to the westward while being rejected at home. Even in other states, the most immediate and extensive use was made of the Code of Civil Procedure, which abolished common law forms and merged common law and equity in greatly simplified procedure, in general the procedure of equity. One commentator said of the code that it was a "bold work" which bore marks of "a wise and skilful, although daring hand," one which perhaps manifested "too much of that impatience of legal forms which is natural to some minds."[38] Another noted, "The science of special pleading, and the learning therein which the most eminent professors have acquired by long years of laborious study, are swept away as 'needless distinctions, scholastic subtleties and dead forms which have disfigured and encumbered our jurisprudence.' "[39]

Justice Story was now no longer living, and no other member of the Supreme Court seems to have been taking an active interest in the codification movement. In Missouri, however, United States District Judge Robert W. Wells, a jurist of considerable competence, was waging the fight for his state. He published in 1847 a pamphlet on the pleadings and practice of the courts of Missouri in which he portrayed the confusion and delay resulting from resort to complicated and obsolete procedures and from the division of the remedial field between law and equity.[40] As a result he was asked to draft for the legislature a bill providing for the needed reforms. Using the materials of the New York commissioners, English statutes, and the statutes of Missouri and other states, he drafted a measure which, like the New York code, abolished special pleading and merged the procedures of law and equity.[41] The measure, which went into effect July 4, 1849, was hailed as "another Declaration of Independence, as to the forms, and technicalities, and quibbles, which too often defeat justice."[42] Judge Wells was quoted as saying:

---

[38] "The New York Code of Procedure," *Law Rep.*, 11:97, 112, 1848.
[39] "The New York Code of Procedure," *Am. L.J.*, 8:188–89, 1848. See John Worth Edmonds, "An Address on the Constitution and Code of Procedure (1848)," as reviewed and excerpted, in *Law Rep.*, 11:232–35, 1848. For a number of years articles on the subject continued to appear in the relatively small number of law journals then being published, with some discussion in other journals as well.
[40] For discussion of the pamphlet see "Law Reform," *Democratic Review*, 21:477, 1847.
[41] See "Law Reform in Missouri," *West. L.J.*, 6:445, 1849.
[42] Timothy Walker, "Law Reform in Missouri," *West. L.J.*, 6:431, 1849.

I shall always deeply regret, that, instead of spending my time in the study of law, as a most extensive, enlightened, and liberal science, and in the acquisition of general literature, and arts and sciences, I was compelled to spend one half of the best seventeen years of my life in the study of special pleading, and the distinctions and niceties with which it is connected. I desire most earnestly to see the profession relieved from that, which, in my own case, I deem a misfortune.[43]

Massachusetts in 1850 returned to the task of legal reform, when a commission headed by Benjamin R. Curtis was directed to investigate the need for procedural reforms. The commission paid deference to the art of special pleading, but deemed it outmoded for state practice either in its original form or as recently modified, and proposed further modifications. The future Supreme Court Justice then accepted election to the lower house of the legislature primarily to see enactment of the proposed measure to completion. The changes were substantial but were less drastic than those adopted in New York, Missouri, and other states.[44] Changes such as the merging of common law and equitable remedies were not even contemplated.

In the constitutional convention held in Maryland in 1852 the abolition of special pleading was opposed. Chief Justice Taney's friend, and later his biographer, Samuel Tyler, won adoption of a compromise proposal merely to simplify common law pleading instead of abolishing it. Thereafter he was selected as one of three commissioners to report a proposal for the simplified procedure. He sent a copy of the report to the Chief Justice, but found him unwilling to make the detailed study necessary for more than a general comment. Taney warned that the task of reforming the system of pleading, which was interwoven with the common law itself, was one of extreme difficulty and delicacy. He was by no means satisfied with experiments made in other states or in England. He observed that there were as many or more cases upon pleading now than before the changes were made. He admitted that some procedural reforms ought to have been made long ago, reforms which the courts themselves were empowered to make but which they had obstinately refused to undertake. He thought legislative action would be necessary, but warned that the legislation should be drafted to preserve the full

---

[43] Quoted from Judge R. T. Wells, "Law of the State of Missouri, Regulating Practice in the Courts of Justice (1849)," in "Law Reform in Missouri," *West. L.J.*, 6:445, 453, 1849.

[44] See "Report of the Commissioners Appointed to Revise and Reform the Proceedings in the Courts of Justice in this Commonwealth," in *A Memoir of Benjamin Robbins Curtis*, Benjamin R. Curtis, ed., II, 149. See also "Reform in Pleading—Massachusetts," *Law Rep.*, 13:601, 1851.

vigor of the principles of the common law and trial by jury, without which no free government could long exist.[45]

The leading American historian of common law pleading wrote near the end of the century:

> The change from common law pleading to code pleading . . . came, when it did come, as suddenly as a barbarian invasion; and for many years it was hotly resisted as something barbarous by a host of able practitioners. Conservative lawyers have scarcely yet ceased to ascribe the change to a "love of innovation," to "barbaric empiricism," to the "suggestions of sciolists, who invent new codes and systems of pleading to order."[46]

Because, at first, state codification and simplification of procedure had little effect on the operations of the federal courts, Supreme Court attitudes are to be discovered from a relatively small number of cases. The effects were small because the Acts of Congress governing procedure in the federal courts tended to prescribe for the federal courts in a state the rules of practice of the courts of that state, not as currently in force but as of some prescribed date, such as the date of admission to the Union. Federal practice therefore remained fixed, while that of a state might be changed by succeeding acts of legislation or of the state courts. The Act of Congress in 1842 which authorized the Supreme Court to promulgate rules in equity gave the same power with respect to practice at common law, but the Court, presumably preferring to follow the unchanged rules of the several states, took no action.

In most states the slowly developing differences between changeable state practice and fixed federal practice worked little harm until the drastic changes which came with the new codes, departing widely from the common law and often merging the procedures of law and equity. In some states the result was to split the bar. The larger number of practitioners became familiar primarily with the code practice of individual states, while a smaller group specialized in practice in the federal courts according to the old forms. The difficulties of following

---

[45] Roger B. Taney to Samuel Tyler, June 12, 1854, Samuel Tyler, *Memoir of Roger Brooke Taney*, 322–24. See Samuel Tyler, *A Treatise on the Maryland Simplified Preliminary Procedure and Pleading in the Courts of Law* (1857). Tyler also prepared for the Maryland legislature a report on a simplified equity practice. See

Samuel Tyler to J. S. Black, Oct. 24, 1857, Black Papers.

[46] Charles M. Hepburn, *The Historical Development of Code Pleading in America and England*, 18. For the sequence of the adoption of codes see *ibid.*, Chapter 4. See also Robert W. Millar, *Civil Procedure of the Trial Court in Historical Perspective*, 54–55.

cases and areas of litigation in the several tribunals became so great that in 1872 Congress passed what has come to be called the Conformity Act,[47] which required for the most part conformity of practice in the federal courts with that of the states in which the courts were held. The federal courts thereby became subject to the procedural provisions of the state codes.[48]

During the Taney period, however, the Supreme Court had to deal with the products of state codifiers only in cases coming from states which, like Texas, had never at any time adopted common law practice, or from states where the federal judges had been persuaded to follow simplified procedures in spite of the provisions of federal law. Texas came into the Union with a heritage of Spanish law. Although the leaders of the government, themselves largely of American heritage, adopted the common law as the basis for rules of decision, they adopted the Spanish system of pleading and abandoned the distinction between law and equity. This step has been tentatively explained in terms of the frontier impatience with the forms and technicalities of law.[49] The first United States district judge in Texas was John C. Watrous, who was born in Connecticut and practiced law in Tennessee and Alabama before going to Texas in 1842. He became Attorney General of the Republic of Texas, and was presumably committed to the Texas position with respect to legal procedure. When in 1846 he became a federal district judge, with circuit judge powers as well, he adopted the Texas forms of practice in his court.

The Supreme Court did not direct Judge Watrous to abandon Texas innovations for common law principles of practice and pleading, but in a number of decisions it disclosed its revulsion at such innovations. The case of *Toby v. Randon*[50] involved a suit to recover money due for the purchase of slaves, the debtor asserting in part that the debt was not collectible because the importation of slaves into Texas had been illegal at the time the purchase took place. If Texas procedure was supposed to expedite litigation, the handling of this case disclosed inexpertness on the part of counsel or the court, or both: more than two years was required for a series of petitions, answers, and demurrers. The case was eventually decided for the defendant, who took it to the Supreme Court on writ of error.

---

[47] 17 Stat. 196, 197.
[48] See Millar, *Civil Procedure of the Trial Court in Historical Perspective*, 58–59. See also Nudd v. Burrows, 91 U.S. 426, 441 (1875); Lamaster v. Keeler, 123 U.S. 376, 388 (1887); Chicago & N.W. Ry. v. Kendall, 167 Fed. 62 (1909).

[49] Samuel H. Lowrie, *Culture Conflict in Texas, 1821–1835*, 179. For more extended discussion see Joseph W. McKnight, "The Spanish Legacy to Texas Law," *Am. J. Legal Hist.*, 3:222, 1959.
[50] 23 Fed. Cas. 1349 (No. 14072) (D.C.D. Tex. 1849).

XIV: *Fringes of the Codification Movement*

The important factor here with respect to *Randon v. Toby* is not the reversal of the decision of the District Court but rather Justice Grier's unanimous opinion excoriating the District Court for its choice of procedure. Had the case been conducted according to the principles and practice of the common law, he began, it would have been a simple matter to prepare it for trial on the merits:

> But, unfortunately, the District Court has adopted the system of pleading and code of practice of the State courts; and the record before us exhibits a most astonishing congeries of petitions and answers, amendments, demurrers, and exceptions—a wrangle in writing extending over more than twenty pages, and continued nearly two years—in which the true merits of the case are overwhelmed and concealed under a mass of worthless pleadings and exceptions, presenting some fifty points, the most of which are wholly irrelevant, and serve only to perplex the court, and impede the due administration of justice.[51]

In reversing a Watrous decision in *Bennett v. Butterworth*, decided at the same term, a case also involving a debt connected with the purchase of slaves, Chief Justice Taney for the Court denounced the attempt, as far as appeals to the Supreme Court were concerned, to bring about in one suit the blending of legal and equitable claims. The distinction between law and equity, he pointed out, was established in the Constitution. Legal claims might be pursued at law, and according to the forms of practice in the state court. But equitable claims must be presented according to the equity rules prescribed for the courts of the United States. The two roads could not be traveled at the same time.[52]

In 1857, dissenting in an admiralty case, Justice Campbell reaffirmed his faith in the traditional accoutrements of the common law by offering a quotation from James Kent, a judge and commentator not then much quoted by Democrats and Southerners. "General rules will sometimes appear harsh and rigorous," said Kent, then chief justice of the supreme court of New York, "but I entertain a decided opinion that the established principles of pleading, which compose what is called the science, are rational, concise, luminous, and admirably adapted to the investigation of truth, and ought, consequently, to be very cautiously touched by the hand of innovation."[53]

A year later Justice Grier returned to the attack against distortion of sound procedure, speaking for a unanimous Court in *McFaul v.*

---

[51] Randon v. Toby, 11 How. 493, 517 (1851).
[52] Bennett v. Butterworth, 11 How. 669, 674–75 (1851).
[53] Malcolm v. Bayard, 1 Johns. (N.Y.) 453, 471 (1806). For Justice Campbell's use of part of the quotation see Dupont v. Vance, 19 How. 162, 175 (1857).

Ramsey. This case came up from the United States District Court in Iowa, where the court had adopted the state's simplified procedure with the merging of law and equity. Iowa, like Texas, was at that time not included within any circuit, with the result that the district judge seems to have been in position to select the remedial procedures to be followed. From the point of view of history the importance of the case lies not in the settlement of a controversy over the sale of some eight hundred hogs but in Justice Grier's lecture to the bar and to the lower federal courts about the preparation of records in cases to be taken to the Supreme Court. The parties had been permitted to frame their pleadings, he said, not according to the simple and established forms of action in courts of common law, but according to the system of pleadings and practice adopted by the state, which had abolished technical forms of action and set its own standards. He proceeded to extol the common law as providing the proper method for the achievement of justice. It committed questions of law to courts which were supposed to be learned therein, and questions of fact to the jury. It provided pleadings for the identification of the points at issue. At one time the system of pleading had been brought into disrepute by the overelaboration of subtle distinctions and the introduction of cumbrous forms, fictions, and contrivances, but all this had been changed in more modern times. The system had been trimmed of its excrescences, and pleadings had been simplified:

> This system, matured by the wisdom of ages, founded upon principles of truth and sound reason, has been ruthlessly abolished in many of our States, who have rashly substituted in its place the suggestions of sciolists, who invent new codes and systems of pleading to order. But this attempt to abolish all species, and establish a single genus, is found to be beyond the power of legislative omnipotence. They cannot compel the human mind not to distinguish between things that differ. The distinction between the different forms of actions for different wrongs, requiring different remedies, lies in the nature of things; it is absolutely inseparable from the correct administration of justice in common law courts.[54]

The result of these experiments had been to destroy the certainty and simplicity of all pleadings, and to introduce on the record an endless wrangle which perplexed the court and delayed and impeded the administration of justice.

He had made these introductory remarks, said Justice Grier, in order that the bar and the lower federal courts might make their records conform to these views.[55] It may well be that his strictures on code plead-

---

[54] McFaul v. Ramsey, 20 How. 523, 525 (1858).   [55] *Ibid.,* 526.

ing had some effect in keeping the federal courts and bar in line. Yet two years later, in a case arising in Judge Thomas H. Duval's court in the western district of Texas, he declared that this added "another to the examples of the utter perplexity and confusion of mind introduced into the administration of justice, by practice under such codes."[56] The District Court had permitted counsel to turn the case into a written wrangle, "instead of requiring them to plead as lawyers, in a court of common law."[57] He returned to the subject two years later, again as in the earlier cases speaking for a unanimous Supreme Court. Here he remarked, "It is no wrong or hardship to suitors who come to the courts for a remedy, to be required to do it in the mode established by the law. State Legislatures may substitute, by codes, the whims of sciolists and inventors for the experience and wisdom of ages; but the success of these experiments is not such as to allure the court to follow their example."[58]

If it was not apparent to Justice Grier, however, it must have been manifest to others, and it is evident from the point of view of history, that the Supreme Court was fighting a losing battle to preserve the rituals of the common law in the trial of cases in federal courts. It was becoming increasingly difficult in the growing number of code states for lawyers to practice in both state and federal courts—and few able and ambitious lawyers cared to be segregated according to the courts in which cases arose. New district judges were coming to be appointed in code states from among lawyers who knew code practice much better than they knew practice according to the antiquated procedures of the common law. If code practice initially caused confusion even in the courts of the enacting states, as it gradually matured it achieved greater efficiency. The 1860s saw appointment to the Supreme Court itself of men from code states. These included Noah H. Swayne, from Ohio, Samuel F. Miller, from Iowa, and Stephen J. Field, from California. Justice Field, it will be recalled, had adapted his brother's codes of civil and criminal procedure to the needs of California and had brought about their adoption.[59] With complete freedom from personal modesty he said as chief justice of the Supreme Court of California in 1860, "It is not within the wit of man to devise more simple rules of pleading than those prescribed by the Practice Act of this State, and there is no excuse for any departure from them."[60] Such emphatic acceptance of codified procedure would at least break the solidity of ranks on the Supreme

---

[56] Green v. Custard, 23 How. 476, 486 (1860).

[57] *Ibid.*, 525–26.

[58] Farni v. Tesson, 1 Black 309, 315 (1862).

[59] Stephen J. Field, *Personal Reminiscences of Early Days in California*, 65.

[60] Coryell v. Cain, 16 Cal. 567, 571 (1860).

Court and make tolerable or even desirable the Conformity Act of 1872 requiring federal courts to conform practice and pleadings in the common law area to the patterns currently prescribed in the states for their own courts.

In the area of substantive as distinguished from remedial law, legislation and codification proceeded more slowly, with most of the successful activity taking place near the end of or after the Taney period. The Benthamite zeal for complete rewriting of the whole body of law gradually dissipated. Experiments began to show that the ideal of rewriting all law so fully and clearly as to make "every man his own lawyer" was hopeless. Justice Story, while advocating codification in certain areas, helped to make it less essential by making available his huge commentaries in many fields. Other authors poured out commentaries and textbooks and compiled digests in increasing numbers. Nevertheless many of the states found it necessary to compile and simplify their statutes and to cover in codes and statutes increasing areas hitherto left to the common law. Because their statutes and codes themselves gave rise to litigation, the simplification that reformers had sought did not materialize, but the reform measures nevertheless helped with the task of keeping up with the growing body of legal materials.

Because it was in general admitted that with respect to the written law of each state the federal courts must follow the interpretations given by the state courts, the codification of substantive law brought no such disputes as those which arose over pleading and practice. Although in implementing its devotion to the common law the Supreme Court was fighting a losing battle, it may have served the country well in holding on to the best of the old until the new achieved discipline and refinement.

CHAPTER XV

The Control of Commerce

J USTICE STORY, it will be recalled, had said during the early 1830s that while the great mass of Supreme Court business consisted of private controversies respecting property, or personal rights, or contracts, the most important function of the Court was the decision of great constitutional questions.[1] Some of the most important of these constitutional issues during the Taney period involved interpretation of the Commerce Clause, giving Congress the power to regulate commerce with foreign nations and among the several states.[2] The cases coming to the Court did not ordinarily involve challenges to the exercise of Congressional power to regulate commerce, but rather to the exercise of state powers in the commerce field which were alleged to encroach on federal regulatory statutes or on dormant federal commerce power. The scope of the power of Congress was a subject of hot debate, it is true, but it took place largely in the political branches of the government. Congress and the President were concerned with the scope of the power of the federal government to make so-called internal improvements, which were talked of primarily in terms of the power to tax and spend for the public welfare rather than the commerce power, but which facilitated interstate commerce. They were concerned about the clearing of rivers and harbors, an enterprise often necessary for the development of the commerce of the country, which on a vast scale was operated by water. But because Congress was hesitant to use its commerce power or because the Presi-

---

[1] "Courts of the U. States," *Encyclopaedia Americana*, III, 594, 596 (1835).

[2] Among the discussions of commerce cases of the Taney period see Felix Frankfurter, *The Commerce Clause under Marshall, Taney, and Waite*, and F. D. G. Ribble, *State and National Power over Commerce*. As is true in other fields, the relevant chapters in Charles Warren, *The Supreme Court in United States History*, are illuminating.

dent vetoed its more extreme measures, the courts were not much called upon to exercise a restraining influence.

With respect to federal regulation of foreign commerce, indeed, even the more extreme defenders of states' rights on the Supreme Court seem to have had no fears of the excessive exercise of the power of Congress. In 1850, for example, the Court was asked to hold that Congress had no power to prevent importation of counterfeit coin and its circulation in the states—in light of the fact that the Court had already held that a state might punish cheating by means of counterfeit coin.[3] But Justice Daniel, anything but a nationalist, rejected the argument for a unanimous Court. Since the passage of the Embargo and Nonintercourse acts, he wrote, and the repeated judicial sanctions of those statutes, it could scarcely be open to doubt that every subject falling within the legitimate sphere of commercial regulation might be partially or wholly excluded when the interests or the safety of the nation required it:

> Such exclusion cannot be limited to particular classes or descriptions of commercial subjects; it may embrace manufactures, bullion, coin, or any other thing. The power once conceded, it may operate on any and every subject of commerce to which the legislative discretion may apply it.[4]

The commerce power was therefore permitted to anticipate or to render unnecessary, or even to duplicate, the exercise of state power with respect to fraudulent transactions.[5]

The area of internal commerce, or of state legislation with respect

---

[3] Fox v. Ohio, 5 How. 410 (1847).
[4] United States v. Marigold, 9 How. 560, 567 (1850).
[5] The issue of prohibition by two governments of the same act had been dealt with in the earlier case. There Justice Daniel had said for the Court, "It is almost certain, that, in the benignant spirit in which the institutions both of the State and federal systems are administered, an offender who should have suffered the penalties denounced by the one would not be subject a second time to punishment by the other for acts essentially the same, unless, indeed, this might occur in instances of peculiar enormity, or where the public safety demanded extraordinary rigor. But were a contrary course of policy and action either probable or usual, this would by no means justify the

conclusion, that offenses falling within the competency of different authorities to restrain or punish them would not properly be subjected to the consequences which those authorities might ordain and affix to their perpetration." Fox v. Ohio, 5 How. 410, 435 (1847). Justice McLean dissented on this point, contending that a state could not punish under its own laws an act identical with one which the federal government had also outlawed. He concluded by saying, "I stand alone in this view, but I have the satisfaction to know, that the lamented Justice Story, when this case was discussed by the judges the last term he attended the Supreme Court, and, if I mistake not, one of the last cases which was discussed by him in consultation, coincided with the views here presented." Ibid., 440.

to internal problems, provided a much more fertile field for judicial controversy. Some of these problems involved the influx of European immigrants. Although Americans took pride in their country as a haven for the oppressed and the adventuresome, the growing stream of immigrants brought local hazards and discomforts. Immigrants were often carriers of diseases, some of them contagious and not subject to any known means of control. Furthermore, impoverished immigrants were often unable either to find local employment or to finance their transportation into the interior. They became burdens on the seaport communities and possible sources of crime. They also became competitors of local workers for employment. The border states having seaports began to demand the submission of information about immigrants landed on their shores, the exclusion of undesirable immigrants, and that the stream of immigration as a whole should in some way pay the costs of pauperism deriving from it. The exercise of police powers therefore began to encroach on the area of foreign commerce.

With expanded consumption of alcoholic beverages some states began to restrict manufacture and sale, by direct prohibition, local option, or restrictive licensing systems. Although enforcement in many communities was difficult enough in strictly local operations, state laws applied not merely to liquor locally produced but also to that imported by distributors in interstate and foreign commerce. Here again, the powers of police became enmeshed with that commerce which Congress had power to regulate.

In various ways the states also exercised power with respect to navigation. Congress willingly left to the states the regulation of their own harbors even though interstate and foreign commerce were involved. At times the states authorized construction of dams which impeded the navigability of streams. They authorized the construction of bridges over navigable streams, thereby often obstructing navigation at their foundations or by their superstructures, and bringing about conflict between rival means of transportation over water and over land.

Always in the background of judicial reasoning with respect to these controversies were the issues of slavery. Did the transportation of slaves across state lines constitute interstate commerce? Could Congress regulate it as such? Could the states regulate such interstate commerce in the absence of federal regulation? In any event, could the states exercise their police powers with respect to transportation of slaves across state lines? Whether or not the carrying of slaves or of other persons across state lines constituted interstate commerce, could the states in the exercise either of a concurrent power over such commerce or of their police powers exclude free Negroes from slave states to prevent the stirring up of trouble among slaves? Could the states constitutionally require—as some of them did—that Negroes brought into the harbors

359

of slave states as seamen be imprisoned for the period of the stay of the ships in port, and that unless the shipmasters paid for the costs of imprisonment the Negroes be sold to pay these costs?

In point of time, cases alternated among the several fields, and decisions served reciprocally as authorities. So it is that the story of the Supreme Court and the control of commerce must place emphasis on chronology as well as upon the fields of the several cases.

The first of the important commerce cases of the Taney period, *New York v. Miln*,[6] was argued January 27–28, 1837,[7] during the first term of the Taney Court. Like *Charles River Bridge v. Warren Bridge* and *Briscoe v. Bank of the Commonwealth of Kentucky*, this case was first argued before the Marshall Court in 1834. Because of the absence of two of the Justices and division among the others, so that the majority did not constitute a majority of the entire Court, the case was continued.[8] It was continued again in 1835.[9] Between that term and the ensuing term occurred the death of Chief Justice Marshall. The vacancy and that caused by the resignation of Justice Gabriel Duvall remained unfilled until after the 1836 term, with the result that the case remained to be heard by the Taney Court.

The *Miln* case had to do with a New York statute of 1824 entitled "An act concerning passengers in vessels arriving in the port of New York." Strictly speaking, the case involved only the first section of the statute, which required the masters of vessels to make detailed reports on passengers brought into the port of New York from foreign countries or from other states. The case was argued primarily in the light of this section, but, as often happens, those whose argument would thereby be aided sought to show the broader purpose of the statute by recourse to other provisions. The master of the vessel was required to give bond for each foreigner brought in, and to remove at his own expense any foreigner whom the mayor designated as liable to become chargeable to the city.

The case came up on a certificate of division from the United States Circuit Court in New York, where, from the nature of his opinion in 1837, it would appear that Justice Thompson had found the first section of the statute constitutional. The city of New York was represented before the Supreme Court by David B. Ogden, who with Daniel Webster and William Wirt in *Gibbons v. Ogden* had successfully challenged the constitutionality of the New York steamboat monopoly

---

[6] 11 Pet. 102.
[7] See Charles Warren, *The Supreme Court in United States History*, 25–26.

[8] See Chapter IV, "The First Term and the Bridge Case," and Chapter V, "The Realm of Finance."
[9] 9 Pet. 85.

statute, and by a man who in the record stands only as Mr. Blount. Facing a Court on which only Justice Story sat as a representative of the old order, Blount stressed the local need for regulation of migration in the light of the annual influx of 65,500 persons into the port of New York alone. While admitting that Congress had supreme power in the regulation of commerce, he contended that the power was concurrent with the states, and that the states might regulate in the absence of federal control. He contended further that the New York statute was "not a commercial regulation in the sense contemplated in the Constitution, but a police regulation,"[10] which the state was not forbidden to enact.

Ogden noted of George Miln, the opposing party, that he was an alien, and remarked in lofty fashion that "although a stranger among us, he has undertaken to teach us constitutional law."[11] Apparently highly nationalistic in his thinking and probably more at home with his nationalist argument in *Gibbons v. Ogden* than with his defense of the current New York statute, he observed, as summarized by the Reporter, that:

> he did not belong to that school of politicians or lawyers who are in favor of giving the Constitution of the United States a construction restricted to its words. All his reflections and all his habits of thinking had induced him to give a more liberal interpretation and application to that instrument. Give to it all its fair, proper, and essential powers. . . . On this occasion it is not, therefore, proposed to advocate a restricted, limited, and narrow construction of the Constitution. But while this is properly and necessarily to be avoided, it is not to be stretched beyond its proper limits, or, like everything else, it will break and be destroyed.[12]

In a broad gesture he referred to "Mr. Chief Justice Marshall, to whose every word upon constitutional questions great attention is most justly due, and from whose expositions of the Constitution everyone who reads will derive instruction."[13] Yet he contended that the states had the power to regulate commerce in the absence of federal regulation, and that the decisions cited to the contrary, *Gibbons v. Ogden* and *Brown v. Maryland*, struck down state statutes only where there were competing federal regulations. He, too, contended that the New York statute was a police regulation which the state had the power to enact.

Appearing for Miln and arguing against the constitutionality of the New York statute were Walter Jones, a prominent Virginia lawyer now residing in Washington, and Joseph M. White of Florida, who chose to look at the statute as a whole rather than at a single provision, and to

---

[10] 11 Pet. 110.   [11] *Ibid.*, 121.   [12] *Ibid.*, 122–23.   [13] *Ibid.*, 127.

see it as a regulation of commerce rather than a police measure. Said Jones, "The law of New York is a prohibition of emigration, and if carried into full effect will entirely prevent the entrance of all persons from abroad into the city of New York, the great throat of emigration."[14] He contended that in the light of *Gibbons v. Ogden* the statute was necessarily invalid.

The Supreme Court lacked the guidance of a clear precedent for the decision. Chief Justice Marshall may have been persuaded by Daniel Webster's argument in *Gibbons v. Ogden* that the power of Congress over interstate and foreign commerce was "exclusive, from the nature of the power,"[15] and that the "doctrine of a general concurrent power in the states is insidious and dangerous."[16] However, Marshall had said in the opinion of the Court:

> In discussing the question, whether this power is still in the states, in the case under consideration, we may dismiss from it the inquiry, whether it is surrendered by the mere grant to Congress, or is retained until Congress shall exercise the power. We may dismiss that inquiry, because it has been exercised, and the regulations which Congress deemed it proper to make, are now in full operation. The sole question is, can a state regulate commerce with foreign nations and among the states, while Congress is regulating it?[17]

However Chief Justice Marshall and his fellows may have felt about the exclusiveness of Congressional power, all remained at that time officially silent except Justice Johnson, who asserted that "the power to regulate foreign commerce is necessarily exclusive,"[18] and that "the language which grants the power as to one description of commerce, grants it as to all."[19]

In *Brown v. Maryland*, where a state statute was found unconstitutional as an invasion of the power of Congress to regulate foreign commerce, there was also federal law with which the state measure came in conflict, so that no precedent for *New York v. Miln* was provided. Furthermore, in a later case, *Willson v. Black Bird Creek Marsh Co.*, Chief Justice Marshall, choosing to ignore a federal coasting license like that which had been stressed in the *Gibbons* case, had spoken for a unanimous Court in saying that if there had been an Act of Congress regulating commerce on navigable creeks along the Atlantic coast, a Delaware statute authorizing erection of a dam on such a creek would have been unconstitutional, but the Court did not think that the act "to

---

[14] *Ibid.*, 120.
[15] 9 Wheat. 16.
[16] *Ibid.*, 17.

[17] *Ibid.*, 200.
[18] *Ibid.*, 228.
[19] *Ibid.*, 229.

place a dam across the creek, can, under all the circumstances of the case, be considered as repugnant to the power to regulate commerce in its dormant state, or as being in conflict with any law passed on the subject."[20]

So it was that the Taney Court lacked a definitely controlling precedent. It knew that Chief Justice Marshall, at the time of the first argument of the *Miln* case, had thought the New York statute unconstitutional, but of the Justices of that period now sitting only Justice Story was committed to that position. Justice Thompson, the only other appointee of the pre-Jackson period on the Court, had in the Circuit Court apparently aligned himself with the other side. It could hardly be expected that Taney and Barbour, two ardent Jacksonians committed to the defense of states' rights, would follow Story's leadership.

Actually the Court, consisting in 1837 of seven members, finally divided six to one in finding the New York statute constitutional. The critical question proved not to be centered on the decision but on the way it would be rationalized. The brief term of the Court brought decisions in three important cases, along with others of less importance and difficulty. Chief Justice Taney himself wrote the opinion of the Court in the *Charles River Bridge Case* and assigned to Justice McLean the *Bank of Kentucky* case. The account of what happened in the *Miln* case must be taken in part from Justice Wayne's opinion delivered twelve years later in the *Passenger Cases*.[21] According to Wayne, the opinion of the Court in the *Miln* case was originally assigned to Justice Thompson. The written opinion, however, aroused some protest from other Justices because, in addition to calling the statute a police measure which was justified as such, he went on to make comments on the scope of the police power with which not all the Justices agreed. Justice Thompson declined to make proposed changes in the opinion, whereupon it was agreed that he should read it merely as his own, and Justice Barbour was asked to write the opinion of the Court.

Justice Barbour framed an opinion in which he said that the New York statute was "a regulation not of commerce but of police."[22] This was the point on which the majority Justices were agreed, and it seemed to free the Court, at least semantically, from taking a position with respect to the exclusiveness of the power of Congress under the Commerce Clause. In justifying his position, however, Justice Barbour differentiated between the carrying of goods, which was commerce, and the carrying of persons, which, he said, was not commerce: "the goods are the subject of commerce, the persons are not." Of persons he said again, "They are not the subject of commerce; and not being imported goods,

---

[20] 2 Pet. 252.   [21] 7 How. 429–36.   [22] 11 Pet. 132–33.

cannot fall within a train of reasoning founded upon the construction of a power given to Congress to regulate commerce, and the prohibition to the States from imposing a duty on imported goods."[23]

Justice Wayne stated that Justice Barbour read his opinion to the Court at the conference held the night before the last day of the term, apparently implying that under the pressure of completing the work of the term the opinion did not receive the full and discriminating attention it might otherwise have received. It was read in Court the next morning. Justice Baldwin, who was not present at the morning session, looked the opinion over, saw the statement that persons were not subjects of commerce, and went in search of Justice Barbour to ask that the statement be eliminated from the official opinion. By this time, however, Barbour had hurried away to the steamer that was waiting to take him down the Potomac to his Virginia home, and could not be reached. The Court was now adjourned, and the opinions, including that in the *Miln* case, were turned over to the Reporter for publication. Justice Baldwin relieved his own sense of responsibility by publication of a long document setting forth his "General View of the Origin and Nature of the Constitution and Government of the United States," in which he discussed four of the cases decided at the 1837 term, including the *Miln* case, and his document has in the Lawyers Edition been incorporated as an appendix to the eleventh volume of Peters' reports. There he made the point with respect not to persons as persons but paupers as paupers, that they were not "articles of merchandise or traffic, imports, or exports,"[24] and that Congress could not compel a state to receive them. He did not attempt to refute the Barbour statement, but merely to draw the line where he thought it ought to be. Two other Justices, Wayne and McLean, who wrote nothing to explain their positions, thereafter in case after case heard counsel quote as the opinion of the Court the statement that persons were not subjects of commerce, much to their discomfort as nationalists.[25]

Justice Story dissented alone. While admitting that the Court could look only to the question certified, which had to do with the first section of the statute requiring reports from masters of ships, he discussed the statute as a whole to demonstrate the intention to regulate interstate and foreign commerce. Relying heavily on *Gibbons v. Ogden* and *Brown v.*

---

[23] 11 Pet. 136–37.

[24] 9 Law. Ed., 11 Pet., App. 185.

[25] Chief Justice Taney noted some disagreement with Justice Wayne's recollection. See 7 How. 487–90. The one factor in the *Miln* opinions to cast some doubt on the strict accuracy of the Wayne account is the fact that Justice Thompson's concurring opinion, said to have been written first as the opinion of the Court, is written in part in the first person, as presumably it would not have been had it been intended in that form to speak for the Court as an institution. Of course it may have been recast by Thompson.

Maryland, he implied, without clearly saying, that in those cases the Court had held that the power of Congress was exclusive even in the absence of federal regulation. He used such phrases as "If the power to regulate commerce be exclusive in Congress . . . ,"[26] and "The power given to Congress to regulate commerce with foreign nations and among the States has been deemed exclusive. . . ."[27] He then concluded by saying:

> In this opinion I have the consolation to know that I had the entire concurrence, upon the same grounds, of that great constitutional jurist, the late Mr. Chief Justice Marshall. Having heard the former arguments, his deliberate opinion was that the act of New York was unconstitutional, and that the present case fell directly within the principles established in the case of *Gibbons* v. *Ogden* (9 Wheat. R.,1) and *Brown* v. *The State of Maryland* (12 Wheat. R.,419).[28]

Issues of commerce and of slavery were locked in a titanic struggle in *Groves* v. *Slaughter,* which was decided four years after the decision in the *Miln* case. As was the custom in some slave states, Robert Slaughter in 1836 entered the state of Mississippi with a group of slaves, and marketed them there. As was also customary, he accepted in partial payment notes amounting in this case to seven thousand dollars. The notes fell due but remained unpaid, and the spread of the panic of 1837 and hard times in Mississippi made it ever more difficult to collect debts. When in 1838 and 1839 suits were brought in the United States Circuit Court in Louisiana to collect on the notes, the district judge, sitting as a circuit judge and evidently in the absence of Justice McKinley in whose circuit the controversy arose, held that Slaughter was entitled to recover the amount of the contract.

The situation was complicated, however, by the fact that the new Mississippi constitution of 1832 provided that after May 1, 1833, the introduction of slaves into the state as merchandise or for sale should be prohibited. No implementing statute was enacted by the legislature until 1837, after the sale here involved took place, but the makers of the notes contended that the constitutional provision, without the aid of a statute, made the sale invalid and the notes uncollectible. Slaughter in turn contended that state action to prevent the bringing of slaves from another state was an unconstitutional encroachment on the commerce power of Congress.

The case had importance far beyond the immediate controversy, for during the middle 1830s large numbers of slaves had been brought into Mississippi and sold on credit. According to Henry Clay as counsel for Slaughter, the slave population of Mississippi had risen from about

---

[26] 11 Pet. 157. [27] *Ibid.,* 158. [28] *Ibid.,* 161.

65,000 in 1830 to about 195,000 in 1840. Indirectly involved, said Clay, was more than three million dollars, due by citizens of Mississippi to citizens of Virginia, Maryland, Kentucky, and other slave states. The reasons for the constitutional restriction, and for the supporting statute eventually enacted in 1837, were evidently mixed. The state was concerned about the outward flow of funds, the importation of slaves depressed the market value of those already held in the state, and the operations of slave traders brought to Mississippi slaves who had been "sold South" because they were troublemakers or in other respects undesirable. In any event, men who had bought slaves stood to gain by a judicial holding that their debts did not have to be paid.

In the Supreme Court the amount of money indirectly involved and the interesting constitutional issues brought to the case some of the ablest lawyers in the country. For the makers of the notes appeared Henry D. Gilpin, Attorney General of the United States, and Robert J. Walker of Mississippi, who was on his way to a distinguished career in national politics. Walker delivered an argument that ran to eighty-eight pages of fine print. The Reporter, Richard Peters, finding it too long to include in the text of his fifteenth volume and too valuable to compress, printed it in full in the appendix. Walker received high praise from Justice Baldwin, an old friend whom he warmly complimented in the course of his argument,[29] and from Justice Story.[30]

For Slaughter, the vendor, appeared Walter Jones, who had argued in the *Miln* case, and Daniel Webster and Henry Clay, whom he characterized as "The Ajax and the Achilles of the bar."[31] At the time of Webster's argument the New York observer Philip Hone wrote that the Supreme Court presented a sublime and beautiful spectacle: "The solemn temple of justice was filled with an admiring auditory consisting of a large proportion of well-dressed ladies who occupied the seats within the bar." Hone thought that Webster was "not remarkably correct in his costume, nor graceful in his action, but commanding by the force of his giant intellect and irresistible control over the minds of all who heard him, and enchaining all their faculties to one point of observation and attention."[32] Of Clay's argument a newspaper reporter noted, "Mr. Clay spoke for more than three hours in one of the most forcible legal arguments that I ever heard. . . . Before he had done he established the position

---

[29] See 15 Pet., App. lxxviii.
[30] See Robert J. Walker, *United States Magazine and Democratic Review*, 16:162–63, 1845. See also Joseph Story to R. J. Walker, July 3, 1841, manuscript letter, New York

Historical Society, thanking Walker for copies of his argument.
[31] 15 Pet. 477. For a description of Jones see John E. Semmes, *John H. B. Latrobe and His Times*, 369–70.
[32] *The Diary of Philip Hone, 1828–1851*, Allan Nevins, ed., II, 523.

fully, to my satisfaction, and I am inclined to believe also, to that of most of his auditors, whatever effect it might have had upon the Court."[33]

Because of the illness of Justice Catron and the death of Justice Barbour between the dates of the argument and the decision of the case, only seven Justices participated in the decision. With Justices Story and McKinley dissenting, Justice Thompson for the majority held that the provision in the Mississippi constitution of 1832 did not become effective until a supporting statute was enacted, with the result that the contracts in question were not invalidated by it.[34] Justice Story explained his own position in a letter to Robert J. Walker:

> I was not present at the delivery of the opinion of the Court in your Mississippi Case. My ordinary habit is when I do not agree in the opinion of the Court to content myself with a silent dissent. Indeed, I very rarely express any dissenting opinion, except where it involves Constitutional principles. Mr. Justice McKinley has, however, truly expressed my opinion, and as far as my present recollection goes, I believe that we entirely agreed in our views of the questions argued. I deemed (1) That the constitution of Mississippi contained in itself a positive, present, operative prohibition of slaves and without any legislative act to aid it. (2) That such a prohibition was not in violation of the Constitution of the United States, (especially as interpreted in the late decisions of the Supreme Court,) upon the ground that the power to regulate commerce was exclusive, and admitting it to be exclusive. (3) That the notes given upon the sales in violation of the constitution of Mississippi were utterly void. Whether these views were expressed by Mr. Justice McKinley, I do not know. At all events, as he openly expressed his dissent in Court, and affirmed also that I concurred in the same dissent, I now wish that Mr. Peters would insert in the volume of Reports as follows: "Mr. Justice Story also dissented."

---

[33] *The Massachusetts Spy*, Feb. 24, 1841.

[34] 15 Pet. 449 (1841). The Supreme Court was able to determine independently this point with respect to the Mississippi constitution because there was at that time no settled determination of the question by the Mississippi courts. When in Rowan v. Runnels, 7 How. 134 (1847), the Supreme Court decided another case involving the same issue, but after the Mississippi courts, differing from the Supreme Court, had held that the constitutional provision was self-enforcing, the Supreme Court, speaking through Chief Justice Taney and with only Justice Daniel dissenting, refused to change its position. Undoubtedly, said the Chief Justice, the Supreme Court would always feel itself bound to respect the decisions of the state courts, and would regard them as conclusive in the construction of their own constitutions and laws. "But we ought not to give them a retroactive effect, and allow them to render invalid contracts entered into with citizens of others States, which in the judgment of this court were lawfully made." *Ibid.*, 139. See Chapter XIII, "The Federal Courts and the Common Law."

If you will do me the favour to write to Mr. Peters on the subject I shall be much obliged to you, as that will supersede the necessity of my writing to him.[35]

Justice Thompson stated that in view of the way in which the case was decided it was "unnecessary to inquire whether this article in the constitution of Mississippi is repugnant to the Constitution of the United States,"[36] and that, indeed, such inquiry was not properly in the case. But the Justices had listened for hours to arguments that the commerce power was exclusive in Congress, that it was concurrent with the states, that persons were not subjects of commerce, that commerce included the carrying of passengers, that Congress had no power over slavery, and that the police power of the states did or did not extend to prohibition of interstate slave trade. The pressure for self-expression on these topics was too much for Justice McLean, who stated:

> [A]lthough the question I am to consider is not necessary to a decision of the case, yet it is so intimately connected with it, and has been so elaborately argued, that under existing circumstances I deem it fit and proper to express my opinion upon it.[37]

John Quincy Adams, who at this term of the Supreme Court had argued the famous slavery case of the *Schooner Amistad*, and who was closely following the decisions of the Court, made the following diary entry about the decision in *Groves v. Slaughter*:

> The Chief Justice read an opinion upon the Mississippi slavery case, whereupon Judge McLean took from his pocket and read a counter-opinion, unexpectedly to the other Judges, to which Judges Thompson, Baldwin, and McKinley severally replied, each differing from all the others.[38]

It seems probable that Adams wrote his entry some time after the event and that he mistakenly crossed the names of Thompson and Taney. This seems especially true since the opinion of the Court to which Thompson's name remains attached includes the statement that the commerce inquiry is not properly in the case. It is possible, however, that here, as in the *Miln* case, a shift took place in the authorship of the opinion of the Court. As the opinions stand in the permanent record, Taney wrote a concurring opinion in which he discussed the scope of

---

[35] Joseph Story to R. J. Walker, May 22, 1841, manuscript letter, New York Historical Society.
[36] 15 Pet. 503.

[37] 15 Pet. 504.
[38] *Memoirs of John Quincy Adams*, Charles F. Adams, ed., X, 442.

state power over slavery, even though he specifically declined to discuss the exclusiveness or concurrence of the federal commerce power.

At any rate, into an atmosphere heated by the slavery controversy Justice McLean injected excitement by tacitly rejecting the holding that persons were not subjects of commerce and saying that as to navigation, "it is immaterial whether the cargo of the vessel consists of passengers or articles of commerce."[39] Yet he also held that as states could outlaw slavery altogether, so also they could limit it by prohibiting the introduction of slaves by citizens of other states as merchandise:

> The power over slavery belongs to the States respectively. It is local in its character, and in its effects; and the transfer or sale of slaves cannot be separated from this power. . . . Each State has a right to protect itself against the avarice and intrusion of the slave dealer; to guard its citizens against the inconveniences and dangers of a slave population.[40]

Chief Justice Taney said he had not intended to express an opinion as to the power of Congress to regulate traffic in slaves between the states, "But as my brother McLean has stated his opinion upon it, I am not willing, by remaining silent, to leave any doubt as to mine."[41] Although his sentiments as to slavery were far from those of McLean, he, too, held that the states had exclusive power over the bringing of slaves within their borders, and that state action could not be controlled by Congress, by virtue either of the commerce power or any other power. But he declined to express an opinion as to the exclusiveness of the commerce power, suggesting most inaccurately that no situation was likely to arise involving state regulations of commerce that might be regulated by Congress.[42]

Justice Baldwin likewise lamented the discussion by other Justices of questions not necessary to be decided: "But since a different course has been taken by the judges who have preceded me, I am not willing to remain silent, lest it may be inferred that my opinion coincides with that of the judges who have now expressed theirs."[43] He held that the power of Congress to regulate interstate commerce was exclusive of any interference by the states, and cited *Gibbons v. Ogden* and *Brown v. Maryland.* Yet he emphasized the importance of drawing a line between regulations of commerce and exercise of the police powers of the states, and held that the introduction of slaves was under the exclusive jurisdiction of the states. He saw slaves not only as persons but as property, and believed that in so doing he stood alone among the members of the

---

[39] 15 Pet. 506.
[40] *Ibid.*, 508.
[41] *Ibid.*, 508.

[42] *Ibid.*, 509–10.
[43] *Ibid.*, 510.

Court;[44] and he regarded them as subjects of commerce, but he saw the question of the fact and degree of slavery in a state as to be determined by the state.

Sandwiched between the opinions of Chief Justice Taney and Justice Baldwin is an odd statement that four Justices, Story, Thompson, Wayne, and McKinley, concurred with the majority of the Court in the opinion that the Commerce Clause did not interfere with the provision in the Mississippi constitution. Justice Story elaborated his position in the letter to Robert J. Walker quoted above. Into it can be read a suggestion that he got wry pleasure from the fact that the limited interpretation of the Commerce Clause in the *Miln* case opened the door for state restriction of interstate commerce in slaves. Justice Thompson had said at the end of the opinion of the Court that the inquiry as to the commerce power was not properly in the case. The record does not show why Justices Wayne and McKinley, feeling deeply on the subject as they apparently did, limited themselves to concurrence in this brief statement.

Although technically speaking *Groves v. Slaughter* merely determined the fact that during the period from 1833 to 1837 the state of Mississippi had not prohibited the introduction of slaves for sale as merchandise, the several opinions demonstrated to the country the diversity of attitudes and the depth of feelings of the Justices toward Commerce Clause issues. The sequence of commerce cases now shifted to a vastly different area, that of local control over the sale and consumption of alcoholic beverages.

During the early years of American history the consumption of such beverages was respectable, accepted, and practiced freely even among the clergy. It was discovered, however, that making liquor accessible to Indians was at once demoralizing and dangerous.[45] Also for the protection of the white population against slaves, the "black codes" in the slave states severely restricted the sale of liquor to black people.[46] Gradually a body of sentiment developed in favor of restricting or prohibiting the sale of intoxicating beverages even to white persons.[47]

The temperance movement became important to the Supreme Court when it gave rise to questions involving the commerce power. The first case to reach that Court had to do with the so-called Twenty-eight Gallon Law of Massachusetts. The statute forbade the retail sale of liquor in amounts of less than twenty-eight gallons, unless the retailer had received a license for which he must pay the nominal fee of one

---

[44] *Ibid.*, 512–13.
[45] See John Koren, *Economic Aspects of the Liquor Problem*, 26.
[46] *Ibid.*, 59.
[47] For broad discussion of the sub-

ject see John A. Krout, *The Origins of Prohibition.* For discussion specifically of prohibition in Pennsylvania see Louis Hartz, *Economic Policy and Democratic Thought*, 204 *ff.*

dollar.[48] With respect to both the state and the federal Constitution, the distinguished chief justice of the Supreme Judicial Court of Massachusetts upheld the measure as an exercise of the police power, doing so in the same year as the police power decision of the Supreme Court of the United States in the *Miln* case, and relying on Chief Justice Marshall's opinions in *Gibbons v. Ogden* and *Brown v. Maryland*. The power to regulate the sale of liquor, said Chief Justice Shaw, had been exercised in Massachusetts and other states since before the Constitution of the United States was adopted. "It is not to be presumed, that the constitution was intended to inhibit or restrain the exercise of so useful a power, unless it shall so appear by plain words, or necessary implication."[49] He saw the measure as falling within "that large class of powers necessary to the regulation of police, morals, health, internal commerce, and general prosperity of the community, which are fully subject to State regulation."[50] It has been said, "While deeply conceived standards cannot be extracted from Shaw's opinion, its suggestion of an empirical test enriched constitutional theory in a day of absolutist formulas."[51]

The Massachusetts decision upholding the state regulation encroached upon powerful social and economic interests, and it was not to be accepted as long as there was a possibility of reversal in Washington. *Thurlow v. Massachusetts*[52] was one of an important group known as the *License Cases*. Here counsel for the state in defense of the statute faced an imposing array of talent consisting of Webster, Rufus Choate, and Benjamin Hallet, the first two of whom filed a composite brief. The *Thurlow* case was argued from January 29 to January 31. Counsel for the state defended that statute as a legitimate police measure, while Webster and his colleagues attacked it as an unconstitutional encroachment on the power of Congress to regulate interstate commerce. Furthermore, said a reporter:

> Mr. Webster took occasion to make some allusion to the laws of the States affecting the rights and privileges of persons, and expressed the hope that the Court would give its view of the question. Mr. Webster desired an opinion no doubt upon such laws as those of South Carolina affecting the privileges of persons of another State visiting that State. He spoke of the excitement which prevailed upon important subjects in the country, and thought it time—high time—that the Court should give an opinion upon questions of so much interest.[53]

---

[48] For discussion of Massachusetts litigation concerning the statute see Leonard W. Levy, *The Law of the Commonwealth and Chief Justice Shaw*, 232 *ff.*, 259 *ff.*

[49] Commonwealth v. Kimball, 41 Mass. (24 Pick.) 359, 361 (1837).

[50] *Ibid.*, 363.

[51] Levy, *The Law of the Commonwealth and Chief Justice Shaw*, 236.

[52] License Cases—Thurlow v. Massachusetts, 5 How. 504 (1847).

[53] *Charleston Courier*, Feb. 5, 1845.

At the time of this argument, Justices Thompson and Baldwin had died, and because of the inability of President John Tyler and the Senate to agree upon new appointments, their places had not been filled. The argument was heard, therefore, by only seven Justices. No agreement could be reached, and on February 14 the Court ordered the case to be continued and reargued at the next term.[54] Before the beginning of the next term Justice Story had died, leaving the Court still further depleted. The case was not reargued until January, 1847, and even then the Court lacked one of its members by virtue of the absence of Justice McKinley, who, under pressure from Circuit Court litigants, had notified Chief Justice Taney that he was going to New Orleans for circuit work instead of coming to Washington.[55] Three new members were present, however, in the persons of Justices Nelson, Woodbury, and Grier, each of whom had his own notions about the relation of the commerce power of Congress to the police power of the states. In the meantime, other cases involving the same statute and the same constitutional questions had been piling up in the Massachusetts courts, and cases were arising in other states involving similar measures. At the time of the reargument of the Massachusetts case the Court ordered *Fletcher v. Rhode Island* and *Peirce v. New Hampshire* to be argued along with it. Each of these was presented independently by its own counsel. In the *Rhode Island* case Samuel Ames and John Whipple appeared against Richard W. Greene—all distinguished men of the law— and in the *New Hampshire* case John P. Hale opposed Edmund Burke. Of the original counsel in the Massachusetts case only Webster reappeared, in opposition to John Davis, who brought prestige to the position of the state.

The Massachusetts and Rhode Island cases were much alike in that, as stated by Chief Justice Taney, "the question is how far a State may regulate or prohibit the sale of ardent spirits, the importation of which from foreign countries has been authorized by Congress."[56] The sales involved in these two cases were made retail, not in the original packages but in "broken" packages. The New Hampshire case was somewhat like the other two but differed in that it involved the sale of a barrel of liquor exactly as it was brought in from another state, that is, in the "original" package. Here the distinctions of the original package doctrine as announced in *Brown v. Maryland* came into play and provided the basis for further diversity in argument.

The Massachusetts case, the record of which had been filed in the Supreme Court as early as 1843, was finally decided March 6, 1847,

---

[54] See Warren, *The Supreme Court in United States History*, II, 153.
[55] R. B. Taney to Mrs. Anne Taney,

Dec. 6, 1847, Howard Papers.
[56] License Cases, 5 How. 504, 574 (1847).

along with the cases from the other two states. The eight Justices all agreed to uphold each of the three statutes involved but were unable to agree on a line of reasoning. Six of them wrote opinions. Justice McLean wrote separate opinions for each of the three cases. Justice Catron wrote opinions in two cases and brought the third case within the province of one of them. Justice Nelson concurred in the Taney and Catron opinions. Only Justice Wayne remained completely silent, as he had in *Groves v. Slaughter*. It was clear that if there had been a carry-over from the Marshall period of the tradition of seeking unanimity among the Justices and speaking through one voice, that ideal had now, by 1847, been largely abandoned with respect to critical constitutional issues.

The commentator on the opinions of the six Justices can no more bring them into harmony than could the Justices themselves. Some of the positions, nevertheless, are worth stating to illuminate the developing theory of the commerce power. Chief Justice Taney was able to dispose of the Massachusetts and Rhode Island cases in terms of the original package doctrine in *Brown v. Maryland*. While he had argued that case on the Maryland side and had lost it by virtue of the holding that the state could not collect a license tax on the sale of imported goods until after the original sale had taken place or until after the original package had been broken, further and more mature reflection had convinced him that the rule laid down by the Supreme Court was a safe and just one.[57] He was now willing to accept that line of demarcation. Since the Massachusetts and Rhode Island statutes applied in these cases only to liquor in "broken" packages, they did not constitute regulations of interstate or foreign commerce.

But in the New Hampshire case the situation was different. Here the liquor, shipped from one state to another and sold in the original package, was not protected by the doctrine. Here, if he was to uphold the statute, the Chief Justice had the option of relying on the police powers of the state as exercised to curb drunkenness, or taking the position that the states had concurrent power to regulate interstate commerce—a question which in *Groves v. Slaughter* he had thought unlikely to arise. He chose the latter alternative. He stated:

> The controlling and supreme power over commerce with foreign nations and among the several States is undoubtedly conferred upon Congress. Yet in my judgment, the State may nevertheless, for the safety or convenience of trade, or for the protection of the health of its citizens, make regulations of commerce for its own ports and harbors, and for its own territory; and such regulations are valid unless they come in conflict with a law of Congress.[58]

---

[57] *Ibid.*, 575.   [58] *Ibid.*, 579.

The Chief Justice was not persuaded of the validity of the police power argument. It seemed to him that if a state, with a view to its police or health, might make valid regulations of the subject matter of commerce which yet fell within the controlling power of the general government, the state was regulating commerce as commerce, and the power derived nothing of substance by being labeled police power: "Upon this question the object and motive of the State are of no importance, and cannot influence the decision. It is a question of power."[59]

Justice McLean had more respect than Chief Justice Taney for the category of police power. Again differing from the Chief Justice, he believed that the commerce power was exclusive in Congress. He looked to the motive of the legislature, which in this instance was inspired by a "great moral reform, which enlisted the judgments and excited the sympathies of the public."[60] Although the police power and the federal commerce power could come into direct conflict, as in the instance of excluding merchandise likely to carry communicable disease, each power had its own legitimate source, and the source of the state police power was to be found in the public need and not in a concurrent power to regulate commerce as such. He admitted that under *Brown v. Maryland* a state could not forbid an importer to sell in the original package. But in the cases from two states the controversies were over the sale of broken packages, to which the power of Congress did not extend, while in the other case only interstate, not foreign, commerce was involved, and here he denied that states were forbidden to require licenses. True, in *Brown v. Maryland* Chief Justice Marshall had said, "It may be proper to add, that we suppose the principles laid down in this case, to apply equally to importations from a sister state."[61] Justice McLean disapproved of this dictum, remarking, "It must have been made with less consideration than the other points ruled in that important case."[62] Yet for him the act of licensing, engaged in with police motives, did not imply regulation of commerce as such and therefore did not mark an unconstitutional encroachment on the commerce power, which as a power was exclusive in Congress.

The opinions of the other Justices in the *License Cases* further illuminate the controversy, but in their diversity they also confuse. Justice Daniel, preoccupied as usual with states' rights, rejected the original package doctrine which Chief Justice Taney had now come to accept, remarking that with some commodities shipped there was no such thing as the breaking of original packages:

---

[59] *Ibid.*, 583.
[60] *Ibid.*, 588–89.

[61] 12 Wheat. at 449 (1827).
[62] 5 How. 594 (1847).

With respect to the phrase above mentioned, it may be retorted, that a person may import a steam engine, a piano, a telescope, or a horse, and many other subjects, which could not be broken up in order to be mingled with the general mass of property.[63]

Justice Grier thought the question of the exclusiveness of the commerce power did not have to be decided. Justice Catron thought that in light of the disagreement over the interpretation of the decisions in *Gibbons v. Ogden* and *Brown v. Maryland* the question of exclusiveness should be treated as an open one, and he felt free to take a position on the question similar to that of the Chief Justice. Justice Woodbury, who at the time of this decision was working out a long opinion on the Commerce Clause in a Circuit Court case,[64] marked the course of the future by suggesting that exclusiveness or nonexclusiveness of the power of Congress might depend on whether the interstate or foreign commerce was essentially national in character[65] or was essentially local, permitting diversity of regulation; but he thought that in the *License Cases* the states were exercising their police powers and were not regulating commerce at all. No other Justice concurred in his opinion.

The riot of diversity in judicial opinions in the *License Cases* seems not to have been related to individual sentiments about drinking. Taney correspondence during the Civil War period indicates that the Chief Justice had a liking for good wine only second to his attachment to long black cigars. Justice McLean believed in temperance rather than in prohibition, and thought that forbearance was to be engendered more by religion than by law.[66] Justice Wayne, who remained silent but apparently joined in the decision of the Court, was a temperance advocate.[67] While all the Justices were believers in public order, and no doubt opposed selling liquor to slaves, it is hard to conceive of any of them as prohibitionists. Indeed, while the temperance battle continued to rage in many of the states (until the Civil War temporarily shifted reformist attention away from the subject), and while some judges vigorously supported the movement, there were opposing reactions of the nature of that of Judge Samuel E. Perkins of the Indiana Supreme Court. Citing "the inspired psalmist" to the effect that man was made to laugh as well as to weep, he contended that stimulating beverages had been created by the Almighty to promote hilarity and enjoyment. Prohibition was based on the misuse of a sound legal maxim:

---

[63] *Ibid.*, 612–13.

[64] See United States v. New Bedford Bridge, 27 Fed. Cas. 91 (No. 15867) (C.C.D. Mass. 1847).

[65] 5 How. 625 (1847).

[66] Francis P. Weisenburger, *The Life of John McLean*, 224–25.

[67] Alexander A. Lawrence, *James Moore Wayne, Southern Unionist*, 95.

It is based on the principle that a man shall not use at all for enjoyment what his neighbor may abuse, a doctrine that would, if enforced by law in general practice, annihilate society, make eunuchs of all men, or drive them into the cells of monks, and bring the human race to an end, or continue it under the direction of licensed county agents.[68]

By contrast Orville H. Browning of Illinois, who during the Lincoln Administration was to aspire ardently to a position on the Supreme Court, wrote in 1855:

How is the land filled with misery, and wretchedness and crime by the monstrous vice of drunkenness—and yet there are those among us who think no laws should be passed to dry up the fountains of the evil.[69]

It was said that after the decision of the Supreme Court in the *License Cases* there was increased excitement on the subject, particularly in Massachusetts where the power to license was often used as a power to withhold a license and therefore to convert temperance legislation into prohibition.[70] Experience varied from state to state. In Ohio, between 1854 and the outbreak of war, the temperance movement "grew progressively weaker as the moralists abandoned it to join the anti-slavery agitation. The movement languished during the war, but following the internecine struggle it was revived and Presbyterians once again took up the temperance standard."[71]

It was obvious that in the *License Cases* the Supreme Court Justices were thinking on a level very different from that of the desirability or the undesirability of liquor licenses. Given a substantial public sentiment with respect to laws to enforce temperance, it would have been hard to strike down the statutes without imperiling state power in adjacent regulatory fields. Referring to the argument of Daniel Webster, the *New York Tribune* noted:

Overwhelming as is the power of the leading counsel on the beaten side, it was morally impossible that he should prevail in this case without subverting the powers of the State to regulate the sale of poisons, of gunpowder, and all dangerous substances whatever. Regarding the decision as inevitable from the outset, we have regretted the delay in pronouncing it only as giving a sort of countenance to a

---

[68] Herman v. The State, 8 Ind. 545, 563 (1856).

[69] *Diary of Orville H. Browning,* I, 169–70.

[70] License Laws, *West. L.J.,* 4:525 (1847).

[71] Donald G. Gorrell, "Presbyterians in the Ohio Temperance Movement of the 1850's," *Ohio State Archeological and Historical Quarterly,* 60:296, 1951.

state of anarchy and pernicious license, which could not fail to prove injurious to public morals and that salutary reverence for law which should be cherished in every community.[72]

For people who were interested in getting from the Supreme Court not merely a determination of the constitutionality of licensing laws but a determination of the exclusiveness or nonexclusiveness of the commerce power and the relation of that power to the police powers of the states, the tandem array of individual opinions in the *License Cases* must have been frustrating and exasperating, even though the decision itself was unanimous. The questions, of course, were enormously complex and shot through with implications both clear and unclear. If perchance it would have been better to leave the issues to be worked out in some other forum rather than have the Supreme Court speak with virtually every member set in some way against each and all of the others, it is nevertheless hard to say what that forum should have been. The problems were too intricate for people merely of general competence and for the literary reviews and similar periodicals which provided much of the grist of public discussion. Presidents and members of Congress were too much involved with the actual phenomena of commerce and slavery and with the conflicts among groups and interests to deal adequately with matters of constitutional doctrine. The law reviews of the period published cases en masse, but provided only a limited amount of such learned discussion as they were to be carrying a century later. However great the yearnings for judicial synthesis after the fashion of that provided for the Marshall Court, it may be that publicly displayed judicial ferment had to precede the arrival of such synthesis. At any rate, the condition was one of ferment par excellence. Had Thomas Jefferson been living at this time, with his love for seriatim opinions and maximum individual expression, he ought to have been very happy over the performance of the Supreme Court. It remained to be seen whether manifold diversity would mark the pattern of future Court performance or whether a return to agreement on principle and institutional expression was in the offing.

---

[72] *New York Tribune*, Mar. 13, 1847.

CHAPTER XVI

The Continuing Struggle over Commerce

FROM THE *License Cases*, decided in 1847, the commerce story shifts back to the transportation of persons and involves the *Passenger Cases*, which were pending along with the *License Cases* but, because here the Justices were divided over the decision as well as the reasoning behind it, were not decided until 1849. Although in the *Passenger Cases* as in *New York v. Miln* the immediate issue was that of state regulations at major ports of entry and involved white people coming from abroad, the growing tensions with respect to slavery kept internal issues to the fore during the five years in which the cases were before the Supreme Court. The landing of immigrants on American shores created problems primarily for the ports to which they came, but the interstate movement of Negroes, whether free or slave, raised problems for the entire Union.

For more than three decades, Negro seamen acts of North Carolina, South Carolina, Georgia, Florida, Alabama, and Mississippi disturbed diplomatic relations with Great Britain and stirred abolitionists in the North. Every uprising or threat of uprising of slaves reminded slaveowners that the presence among them of free Negroes fostered yearnings and could provide leadership for slave revolts. Presence of free Negroes may also have troubled owners who sought to keep alive in their own minds the belief that Negroes were beings of an inferior order fit only to be held as property, but the fear of rebellion may alone have been sufficient to motivate their efforts to exclude free Negroes. In 1834 Chief Justice Catron of the Tennessee Supreme Court, later to be a Justice of the Supreme Court of the United States, noted the belief that all slaveholding states and some free states as well had adopted a policy of excluding free Negroes. He was opposed to a policy of manumission in Tennessee that was dependent on the expulsion of the freed persons into adjacent states that were unwilling to receive them:

> Would it not be treating the non-slaveholding states unjustly to force our freed negroes upon them without their consent? and would it not be treating the slaveholding states cruelly? We are ejecting this description of population, fearing it will excite rebellion among the slaves; or that the slaves will be rendered immoral to a degree of depravity inconsistent with the safety and interests of the white population. These are fearful evils. But are they not more threatening to Virginia (just recovering from the fright of a negro rebellion), to the Carolinas, to Georgia, Alabama, Mississippi, and Louisiana than to us? . . . How can we then, as honest men, thrust our freed negroes on our neighbors of the South?[1]

The Negro seamen acts restricted the activities of colored seamen while in port, usually required imprisonment during that period, and as in the instance of the South Carolina statute for a period, required that such imprisoned sailors be sold into slavery to pay the costs of their detention unless the costs were paid by the masters of their ships. The measures were drastic and their enforcement brought innumerable British protests to Washington and local negotiations between consuls and state officials.[2]

The South Carolina statute was challenged before Justice William Johnson in the United States Circuit Court in South Carolina as early as 1823.[3] At this time, a year prior to the decision in *Gibbons v. Ogden*, Justice Johnson expressed the opinion that, "the right of the general government to regulate commerce with the sister states and foreign nations is a paramount and exclusive right,"[4] but he was unable to find anything that his court could do about it. In 1824, shortly after the decision in *Gibbons v. Ogden*, Attorney General William Wirt gave the Secretary of State an official opinion that the South Carolina statute was unconstitutional, saying that "the power of regulating commerce with foreign nations and among the States is given to Congress; and this power is, from its nature, exclusive."[5] In 1831, however, the year of the Nat Turner slave rebellion in Virginia, President Jackson asked another

---

[1] Fisher's Negroes v. Dabbs, 14 Tenn. (6 Yerger) 119, 129 (1834).

[2] For a detailed account of diplomatic experience with such measures see Philip M. Hamer, "Great Britain, the United States, and the Negro Seamen Acts, 1822–1860," *Journal of Southern History*, 1:3–28, 138–68, 1935.

[3] For discussion of the handling of the case see Donald G. Morgan, *Justice William Johnson, The First Dissenter*, 192–202.

[4] Elkison v. Deliesseline, 8 Fed. Cas. 493, 495 (No. 4366) (C.C.D.S.C. 1823).

[5] 1 Op. Att'y Gen. 659 (1824).

Attorney General, John M. Berrien of Georgia, for an opinion on the same statute. Berrien, deeply committed to the institutions of his state, disagreed with Wirt. He took the position that the power to regulate their own internal police was reserved to the states and that Congress might not encroach upon that power; he found the statute a legitimate exercise of the police power.[6]

The issue continued to make trouble in diplomatic relations. Later in the same year Berrien was replaced as Attorney General by Roger B. Taney. The Secretary of State called on Taney for an opinion on the same measure. Taney postponed his reply, and in the meantime gave an opinion on a statute of a free state setting free any slave brought into the state. He found that the Pennsylvania statute violated no treaty with Great Britain, which was again the protesting country. He added, significantly, that "It is, perhaps, unnecessary now to inquire whether the United States could, by treaty, control the several States in the exercise of this power. I think they could not."[7]

When on May 28, 1832, Taney responded to prodding from the Secretary of State by giving his opinion on the South Carolina measure, he wrote a voluminous document discussing the degraded status of the Negro, the reserved powers of the states, the nature of judicial power, the scope of the treaty power, and other topics, with, however, little specific discussion of the commerce power.[8] Concerning the colored population, he said:

> Every slaveholding state it is believed has prohibited their migration and settlement within their limits, and in the absence of evidence of their freedom presumes them to be slaves and subjects them to imprisonment without any offence being charged against them, and has forbidden all persons of that colour from keeping or carrying arms. Did the slaveholding states mean to surrender the right to enact such laws? It is impossible to imagine that they could have so intended, and the uniform course of their legislation since the adoption of the Federal Constitution shows that they did not so understand that instrument. The slave holding states could not have surrendered this power, without bringing upon themselves inevitably the evils of insurrection and rebellion among their slaves, and the non-slave holding states could have no inducement to desire its surrender.[9]

Since the states had not surrendered this power to the federal government, neither the treaty power nor any other power could frustrate its exercise by the states.

---

[6] 2 Op. Att'y Gen. 427 (1831).
[7] 2 Op. Att'y Gen. 476 (1831).
[8] For the location of this unpublished opinion and extensive quotation therefrom see Carl B. Swisher, *Roger B. Taney*, 151–58.
[9] Manuscript opinion, May 28, 1832, Attorney General Papers.

Taney admitted, however, that there were conflicting opinions on the subject. He was aware that the Supreme Court had maintained doctrines on it to which he could not yield his assent, and he was aware that his opinion might not be sanctioned by the Court: "Indeed, judging by the past I think it highly probable that the Court will declare the law of South Carolina null and void if contrary to the stipulations in the treaty whenever the subject comes before it. And believing that such is likely to be the case it is my duty to apprise you of it. It is unnecessary now to say what in that event ought to be done."[10]

Unable to secure a remedy through the federal government, British representatives turned to negotiations with the offending states to protect their mariner citizens. By 1843 a committee of the House of Representatives found that the application of the offending laws had been largely suspended as to foreign vessels. They were enforced, however, with respect to colored persons on vessels from the Northern states. The House Committee on Commerce considered a protest from more than 150 citizens of Boston and joined in condemning the state laws as violations of the privileges and immunities of citizens and as encroachments on the commerce power of Congress. "This power is, from its very nature, a paramount and exclusive power, and has always been so considered and so construed."[11] A minority report, however, made effective use of the comments about the police power expressed in *Gibbons v. Ogden, Brown v. Maryland,* and *New York v. Miln,* and defended the rights of the states to enact police measures for their internal defense.

In 1844 the United States District Court in Massachusetts struck a propaganda blow at the seamen's acts, though an ineffective one. Under a Louisiana statute a colored seaman aboard the *Cynosure* was imprisoned during his stay in New Orleans and the master of the vessel was compelled to pay the costs of his detention. The mariner claimed damages from the master of the vessel for taking him into the port, and the master, in his turn, sought to deduct from the mariner's wages the costs of detention. Judge Peleg Sprague held that "A state cannot thus interfere with the navigation of the United States, nor dictate to the owners of an American vessel the composition of her crew."[12] Though Southern statesmen were in no mood to listen to federal judges in Northern states, no vital Southern interest was involved in the case and no appeal was taken.

The Massachusetts legislature tried another expedient. It directed the governor to employ counsel to test the constitutionality of the seamen

---

[10] *Ibid.*
[11] Free Colored Seamen—Majority and Minority Reports, H.R. Rep. No.

80, 27th Cong., 3rd Sess. 2 (1843).
[12] *The Cynosure,* 6 Fed. Cas. 1102, 1103 (No. 3529) (D.C.D. Mass. (1844).

laws, presumably in the area of actual conflict. The governor could find no reputable Southern lawyer to handle the litigation. He therefore sent the venerable Samuel Hoar from Boston to undertake such a case in Charleston. On Hoar's arrival at Charleston the legislature passed a resolution demanding his expulsion. Before orderly expulsion could be attempted a mob assembled to drive him out of the city and he was compelled to board a ship and return northward.[13] Henry Hubbard was sent from Massachusetts to New Orleans in 1845 to attempt to bring a suit to test the Louisiana statute. He, too, was compelled to make a hasty departure amid a roar of hostile excitement. The two unsuccessful missions added to the sectional strain and stiffened the South's determination to enforce against Northern ships its discriminatory legislation.[14]

The excitement and anger aroused by controversies over the seamen's acts merged with similar emotions over other slavery cases yet to be discussed, over the annexation of Texas, the Mexican War, tariff disputes, and trade rivalries between the North and the South. In the midst of the sectional turmoil, in 1843 and 1844, the two *Passenger Cases, Norris v. City of Boston* and *Smith v. Turner*, the latter from New York, were docketed in the Supreme Court. Inevitably they absorbed within themselves much of the tension of the slavery issue. Yet they had other important elements, and these, too, are essential to their comprehension. They included the problems of white immigration that were involved in *New York v. Miln*, in exaggerated proportions. The port of New York, which in 1837 had received a stream of more than sixty-five thousand immigrants, now received some two hundred thousand per year.[15] Other Eastern port cities saw similar increases. In large numbers the new Americans seeking a land of opportunity moved immediately westward toward the frontier to occupy new land and settle new cities.

It seems evident that the port cities were not averse to taking their toll from the moving stream during their brief period of opportunity. But it was also true, now as earlier, that in considerable numbers the immigrants settled in the Eastern cities themselves, where with their own customs and their own drives and interests, and sometimes through their religious affiliations, they stirred hostility on the part of the established population, giving rise in politics to the "native American" or "Know-Nothing" movement. Furthermore, again now as earlier, many hopeful immigrants landed on American shores without adequate resources to

---

[13] George F. Hoar, *Autobiography of Seventy Years*, I, 24–27.

[14] Hamer, "Great Britain, the United States, and the Negro Seamen Acts, 1822–1860," *Journal of Southern History*, 1:23, 1935. See *Niles' National Register*, 65:217, 1843; *Niles'*

National Register, 67:315–17, 394–99, 1845; *Niles' National Register*, 68:55, 1845.

[15] Statement of David B. Ogden, Passenger Cases—Norris v. City of Boston, 7 How. 283, 314 (1849).

take them westward or the skills and knowledge of American ways of life necessary to earning a livelihood at the points of arrival. Some of them became charges on the communities, which had to choose between caring for them or letting them die or find subsistence through crime. In addition there was always the problem of illness, including contagious diseases such as yellow fever and cholera, which took lives by the hundreds and thousands, and which were still largely medical mysteries. There was still no adequate regulation of immigration by the federal government. The Eastern states therefore felt that they had the duty and the right to do what they could to alleviate the evils, and to collect the necessary costs from the incoming population. Such was the purpose of the statutes involved in the two cases.

The New York statute, focusing on the establishment of a marine hospital, provided for the collection of "hospital moneys" by authorizing the health commissioner to collect from the masters of vessels from foreign ports one dollar and fifty cents for each cabin passenger, and one dollar for each steerage passenger, and from the master of each coasting vessel twenty-five cents for each passenger. The Massachusetts statute, an act "relating to alien passengers," required inspection of incoming ships to prevent the landing of any person found to be a "lunatic, idiot, maimed, aged, or infirm person," unless a bond was given to insure that the person did not become a public charge. Passengers were not to be landed until two dollars should be collected from each of them, "to be appropriated as the city or town may direct for the support of foreign paupers."

The two states, of course, attempted to justify their statutes as police measures rather than basically as regulations of commerce. In the Boston case Chief Justice Shaw noted the necessary interaction of state and federal powers. The states had the power to make health laws. He suggested that if state laws were found to be oppressive, the proper mode of relief would be for Congress to supplant them rather than for the courts to strike them down as violations of a dormant federal power.[16] He cited *New York v. Miln* in support of the statute now being tested, and proved that the statute was not a regulation of imports by citing Justice Barbour's statement that persons were not the subject of commerce.

The *Passenger Cases*, like the *License Cases* with which they partly overlapped, were before the Supreme Court during the period in the 1840s when vacancies and absences of members were numerous and prolonged. Originally argued separately, the two cases gave rise to a total

---

[16] Norris v. City of Boston, 45 Mass. (4 Met.) 282 (1842). For discussion of the Shaw opinion see Leonard W. Levy, *The Law of the Commonwealth and Chief Justice Shaw*, 237–40.

of six arguments, each case being presented three times. The New York case was first argued in December, 1845, and the Boston case in February, 1847. Both were reargued in December, 1847, after the *License Cases* had been decided, and again in December, 1848. The decisions were announced February 7, 1849. During the course of the several arguments eight men appeared as counsel. Outstanding among them were Daniel Webster, who appeared in the two cases and followed them from beginning to end, David B. Ogden, Rufus Choate, John Davis, and John Van Buren, the son of the former President. In presenting the arguments of counsel Benjamin C. Howard, Reporter of the Supreme Court, explained that it would be impossible to present them all, since if this were done these cases alone would require a volume. He therefore resorted to the doubtful expedient of presenting only such sketches of arguments as had been furnished to him by the counsel themselves, and mentioning only the names of the others. This meant that for Webster and Choate, who may well have shared the prevailing conservative opinion of Howard as a Reporter, nothing was presented except a brief statement of three points with citations of cases, whereas arguments of other counsel were presented at great length. Because of the changes in personnel from case to case, Howard admitted that "some of these counsel never heard the arguments to which, from this collocation they might be supposed to reply, arising from the different terms at which the arguments were made."[17]

Webster considered the constitutional issue in the *Passenger Cases* the most important he had argued since the *Steamboat* case, *Gibbons v. Ogden*, in 1824. He thought it likely to be his last[18]—and indeed it did prove to be his last great constitutional case. It was said that at the argument in December, 1847, he wore the clothing in which he dressed on great occasions and which he was remembered as having worn in 1830 when he delivered his famous "reply to Hayne": "He wore a blue coat, a buff vest with brass buttons. This was the old Fox colors in England over fifty years since. The followers of Charles James Fox wore them, to distinguish themselves from the Pittites."[19] He seems to have needed the support of striking garb, for with respect to these cases his mood was depressed. It was strange to him that the legislature of Massachusetts could have passed such a law, he wrote to his son in connection with the argument of the Massachusetts case in February, 1847. In the days of Marshall and Story it could not have stood one moment. Yet the present judges were, he feared, "quite too much inclined to find

---

[17] 7 How. 288 (1849).
[18] Daniel Webster to R. M. Blatchford, Feb. 3, 1849, *Writings and* *Speeches of Daniel Webster*, J. W. McIntyre, ed., XVIII, 294.
[19] *New York Tribune*, Dec. 27, 1847.

apologies for irregular and dangerous acts of State Legislation." There was just about an even chance, but he believed the act would be pronounced unconstitutional.[20] In connection with the argument of the New York case in December, he wrote, "In the cases, I have no doubt, whatever, that the law is with us; but where the Court will be, I know not."[21] He wrote grimly of an argument in December, 1848, when the temperature in the courtroom rose to ninety degrees, after which the doors and windows were thrown open, giving him a cold and leaving him with a stiff back: "I argued my cause well enough, and if I were not always unlucky, now a days, in such cases, I should think I saw a glimmering of success."[22] Concerning the Massachusetts statute Webster argued that it regulated commerce, which Congress had the exclusive power to regulate, that it was a prohibited impost or duty on imports, and that it was repugnant to the actual regulations and the manifested will of Congress.[23]

From some argument in behalf of New York Webster picked up and replied to the thesis that from this source came rich financial resources for the federal treasury and great contributions generally to the Union. All this he admitted. Yet much of the wealth of New York, he contended, derived from the fact that she was so placed as to be a distributing agent for the government and for the producers and consumers of the country. Without the rest of the country, New York "would be as nothing, *a caput mortuum*, and nothing more."[24] New York was the beneficiary of commerce, which Congress had exclusive power to control, and that commerce included the carrying of passengers, in spite of arguments to the contrary. As for the slavery issue which was in the minds of many, he called slavery a peculiar institution which the Constitution recognized and declared that he had no wish to disturb it.[25] Knowing the sensitivity of Southerners on the subject, he clearly sought to underplay the issue as much as possible.

David B. Ogden, arguing alongside Webster for broad interpretation of the federal commerce power as he had done long ago in *Gibbons v. Ogden*, was apparently much more comfortable with this type of

---

[20] Daniel Webster to Fletcher Webster, Feb. 7, 1847, *Writings and Speeches of Daniel Webster*, XVI, 470.
[21] Daniel Webster to Fletcher Webster, Dec. 7, 1847, *ibid.*, 488. In a letter in which the bracketed date as published seems to be incorrect, since it treats as undecided the *License Cases*, which had been decided before the date given, Webster said that nobody could tell what would be done with the license laws, so great was the difference of opinion on the Bench.

It was his prediction that the license laws would be sustained and that the passenger law of Massachusetts would not be sustained. *Ibid.*, 490.
[22] Daniel Webster to Fletcher Webster, Dec. 26, 1848, *ibid.*, 509.
[23] 7 How. 281–88.
[24] Report published in the *Baltimore American*, reprinted in the *National Intelligencer*, and later reprinted in *Writings and Speeches of Daniel Webster*, XV, 403.
[25] *Ibid.*, 404.

argument than he had been in defending state power in *New York v. Miln*. His argument was recorded at length, in sharp contrast with that of Webster. In a preliminary statement he offered to the Court a thinly veiled warning against permitting law to drift with the times, and particularly against surrender to the sentiments of localism that were widely held by Jacksonian Democrats, who included among their leaders Martin Van Buren and Van Buren's son, here appearing as counsel for New York. In public law as in private law, he contended, judges were bound by the law and were not permitted to change it. Constitutional rights should not depend on "the whims and caprice of the judges who may happen to be on the bench of this court."[26] Ogden saw danger to the Union in the fact that of the new constitutions of the original states, and those of the new states, only one required legislative, executive, and judicial officers to take an oath to support the Constitution of the United States. He noted the warning of James Madison that there was less danger of encroachment by the general government on the states than of encroachment of the latter on the former, and that of the two processes state encroachment was the more dangerous.[27]

Counsel arguing for the constitutionality of the two state statutes made the familiar police power argument, which embraced the power to exclude undesirable persons, such as paupers and the insane, and to admit immigrants under conditions such that the port cities were protected against dangers to health and welfare. They cited *New York v. Miln* to the effect that persons were not subjects of commerce, and contended that if the statutes were deemed to regulate commerce, the power was concurrent in the states. Among the arguments cutting down to the sore issue of slavery was that of John Davis, who asked pointedly:

> If we cannot meet and control by suitable regulations the introduction of such persons, on what principle can the laws expelling or forbidding the introduction of free negroes be sustained? Such laws exist, and I apprehend it will be found difficult to sustain them on the ground of color alone.[28]

It was the Democratic and antislavery John Van Buren who attracted the sharper criticisms from people holding nationalist sentiments. The *New York Tribune*, which praised Webster's dress and appearance, deplored "the appearance of his young opponent, who, both yesterday and today, presented himself in undress frock coat,"[29] and added that if the Justices took the trouble to put on gowns, those who appeared before them should exhibit a corresponding care in dress. It was Van Buren who

---

[26] 7 How. 292.
[27] *Ibid.*, 295.
[28] *Ibid.*, 333.

[29] *New York Tribune*, Dec. 27, 1847. See also *ibid.*, Dec. 24, 1847.

irked Webster by reference to the vast contributions made by New York to the resources of the Union, with little counterclaim on either its justice or its bounty; indeed, she had suffered at the hands of that government. Her insolvent laws had been prostrated by the judgment in *Sturges v. Crowninshield*. The commerce power, here urged as a curb on her activities, had not been used to dig her canals or produce her other internal improvements. She had proceeded on her own. Yet that power was now being used to make her the victim of judicial condemnation. She hoped the power would not be used to prostrate her institutions of public health.

Here Van Buren proclaimed that New York "saw with unaffected concern the prodigious strides made by this power to regulate commerce towards engrossing and consolidating the power of the Union. This may well be regarded as the mastodon of construction, starting from this bench, and in its giant strides trampling upon the rights of the States and their sovereignty. Fortunately it is only known to the present day by its colossal bones, scattered through the reports of the early opinions of the members of this court."[30] *New York v. Miln* and the *License Cases* had put an end to judicial encroachment. He warned of the jealousy felt toward the Court, with the life tenure of its Justices which removed it from the direct effect of public opinion. He thought it desirable that the Justices should secure the affections of the people and he regarded the recent decisions as evidence that "popular and liberal impulses" had reached the Bench.[31] Webster, superbly skilled as a platform strategist, praised Van Buren for the skill and legal knowledge displayed in his argument, then turned to Van Buren's compliment to the Court for yielding to "the popular impulses of the day." This, he said sternly, was a compliment which he would not address to this Court or to any court for which he entertained feelings of respect. Thus, said the correspondent of the *New York Tribune*, "he set John Van Buren up and then knocked him down."[32]

Although privately Webster deplored the fact that the Court at that time lacked "a strong and leading mind,"[33] he chose publicly to speak of the sanctity of its decisions.[34] In May, 1847, he made a trip through the South and in Savannah was introduced at a public reception by Justice Wayne, who lauded his contribution to American constitutional development. Webster depreciated his own influence, praised the tradition of the Court, and voiced the hope "that its future may resemble its past, and that the same learning and dignity—the same

---

[30] 7 How. 378–79.
[31] *Ibid.*, 379.
[32] *New York Tribune*, Dec. 27, 1847.
[33] Daniel Webster to Franklin Haven, Dec. 28, 1847, *Writings and Speeches of Daniel Webster*, XVI, 489.
[34] *Ibid.*, XV, 403.

integrity and firmness which have characterized its decisions in times past may also distinguish them in times to come."[35]

The final arguments of the two *Passenger Cases* were the only ones made before a full Court. Before decision was announced, on February 7, 1849, it was widely known that the decision would be made by a closely divided Court and that the presence of Justice McKinley had been necessary to the arrival at a decision.[36] Voting five to four, the Justices found the two state statutes unconstitutional. Apart from the introductory material inserted by the Reporter, the Justices occupied 180 pages of Howard's reports. Eight Justices wrote opinions in one or both of the cases. Although some of them concurred in the opinions of brethren, they did not in general regard opinions other than their own as saying all that should be said. The one exception was Justice Nelson, who concurred fully in the dissenting opinion of Chief Justice Taney and had nothing to add to it. The majority consisted of Justices McLean, Wayne, Catron, McKinley, and Grier; the minority of Chief Justice Taney and Justices Daniel, Nelson, and Woodbury. As was characteristic of him during his brief stay of less than six years on the Court, the longest opinion, fifty-four pages, was written by Justice Woodbury in dissent.

The opinions, whether majority or minority, were so diverse that attempts to summarize could only confuse. Beyond stating that the statutes in question were found to be unconstitutional, the bewildered Reporter of the Court could only say, "Inasmuch as there was no opinion of the court, as a court, the reporter refers the reader to the opinions of the judges for an explanation of the statutes and the points in which they conflicted with the Constitution and laws of the United States."[37] Within his own opinion Justice Wayne summarized the points on which he deemed the majority to be in agreement, but although there is some evidence of modification of opinions after the initial reading, no other Justice announced concurrence in the Wayne summary. It does seem safe to say that the majority here abandoned the position taken in *New York v. Miln* that persons were not subjects of commerce—and it was here that Justice Wayne, with some protest from Chief Justice Taney, exposed the circumstances under which the *Miln* case had been decided, as discussed above in connection with *Groves v. Slaughter*.

As for the exclusiveness of the commerce power of Congress, Justice McLean reaffirmed his belief that the power was exclusive in Congress as settled by *Gibbons v. Ogden* and *Brown v. Maryland*,[38] although he admitted that as to *Willson v. Black Bird Creek Marsh Co.*,

---

[35] *Savannah Republican*, May 29, 1847.
[36] See the dispatch of Jan. 22,

1849, to a New York newspaper, *Law Rep.*, 11:478, 1849.
[37] 7 How. 283.
[38] 7 How. 400.

"the language of the eminent Chief Justice who wrote the opinion is less guarded than his opinions generally were on constitutional questions."[39] Justice Wayne asserted his own belief that the power was exclusive, but agreed with Justice Catron that the state statutes conflicted with Acts of Congress regulating commerce and with treaties with Great Britain, so that the question of exclusiveness was not pertinent. Justice Grier seemed to take the same position. Justice McKinley appeared to agree at once with McLean, who found that the commerce power was exclusive, and with Catron, who withheld judgment.[40] He then proceeded to argue that the state laws fell afoul of federal laws classified under those regulating "migration and importation," a point that had not been argued before the Court. Chief Justice Taney, although dissenting as to the cases at hand which involved only the tax measured by foreigners brought in, made the point, noted with pleasure by Webster,[41] that a tax collected on passengers brought from other parts of the United States would have been unconstitutional. The Constitution, he said, was intended to secure the freest intercourse between citizens of the United States. In sentences in which he continued thereafter to take pride,[42] he said:

> For all the great purposes for which the federal governmnt was formed, we are one people, with one common country. We are all citizens of the United States; and, as members of the same community, must have the right to pass and repass through every part of it without interruption, as freely as in our own States.[43]

Since the majority found the state measures unconstitutional, any defense of the police powers of the states in these cases might be expected to occur in the dissenting opinions. Chief Justice Taney, however, as illustrated by his opinion in the *License Cases*, had no particular liking for that term, and thought it merely synonymous with the sovereign powers of the states. In the *Passenger Cases* he upheld the attempts of states to deal with the needs of paupers and prevent the spread of infectious diseases by means of the taxes and other provisions of the statutes, but he did little for the development of doctrine. Justice Daniel placed his emphasis on the narrowness of federal power over commerce and warned, "Once let the barriers of the Constitution be removed, and

---

[39] *Ibid.*, 397.
[40] *Ibid.*, 452.
[41] Daniel Webster to J. Prescott Hall, Feb. 10, 1849, *Writings and Speeches of Daniel Webster*, XVI, 512.
[42] In a matter of choice of phrases from opinions for some purpose he wrote to his son-in-law of this statement that "Perhaps I like it rather better than the other, because this opinion is supposed to be the best I have delivered from the Bench." R. B. Taney to J. Mason Campbell, Feb. 22, 1850, Campbell Papers.
[43] 7 How. 492.

the march of abuse will be onward and without bounds."[44] Justice Woodbury used police power terminology only briefly, saying that a police measure in common parlance often related to something connected with the public morals, but that in law the word was much broader, and included "all legislation for the internal policy of a State."[45] So it was that the phrase, so important for the future development of constitutional law, was little affected by the dissenting opinions in the *Passenger Cases*. Furthermore, as far as coping with disease and pauperism as the products of immigration was concerned, the subject was eventually to be recognized as a responsibility of the federal government rather than of the states.

The more significant discussion of the police power, indeed, came from Justice Wayne in his majority opinion, as it related to the critical issue of slavery. Wayne admitted that police powers and sovereign powers were the same. He contended that the states had retained all the police powers necessary for their internal government.[46] The states had a right to turn away paupers, vagabonds, and fugitives from justice, and, he contended, "the States where slaves are have a constitutional right to exclude all such as are, from a common ancestry and country, of the same class of men."[47] As if speaking to persons deeply anxious about the implications of the decision for the slave states, Justice Wayne declared that Congress had no power to treat as subjects of legitimate commerce paupers, vagabonds, suspected persons, fugitives from justice —and, he seemed to imply also, free Negroes seeking to enter slave states:

> That is a very narrow view of the Constitution which supposes that any political sovereign right given by it can be exercised, or was meant to be used by the United States in such a way as to dissolve, or even disquiet, the fundamental organization of either of the States.[48]

He promised that should the matter of introducing free Negroes into the Southern states ever become a subject of judicial inquiry a guard against it would be found in the Constitution. It would not be necessary for the states to resort to extreme measures: "They may rely upon the Constitution, and the correct interpretation of it, without seeking to be relieved from any of their obligations under it, or having recourse to the *jus necessitatis* for self-preservation."[49]

The Wayne opinion stood as a notice to the South that Southerners did not have to choose between admitting free Negroes and seceding

---

[44] See Swisher, *Roger B. Taney,* 400–02.
[45] 7 How. 518.
[46] *Ibid.,* 523.

[47] *Ibid.,* 424.
[48] *Ibid.,* 426.
[49] *Ibid.,* 428–29.

from the Union or otherwise violating the Constitution. Yet the voice was the voice of only one member of the Court. In large part the other Justices avoided the question.[50] But Justice Woodbury warned that it was not possible to put aliens in one category and slaves, free blacks, convicts, and paupers into another. For him, nationalism as to commerce, and states' rights as to Negroes, were incompatible.

Justice Wayne's ability to separate the concept of slaves as slaves, and indeed of Negroes as Negroes, from the concept of commerce as Congress had the power to regulate it, explained in part how it was that as a Southerner he could accept what seemed a Federalist-Whig position on the exclusiveness of the power of Congress. A reason why he found such a position patriotic and desirable in terms of Southern welfare may be found in his introduction of Daniel Webster at the public reception in Savannah. Referring to Webster's argument in *Gibbons v. Ogden*, he said:

> The Court felt the application and force of your reasoning, and it made a decision, releasing every creek and river, lake, bay and harbour, in our country, from the interferences of monopolies, which had already provoked unfriendly legislation between some of the States, and which would have been as little favorable to the interests of Fulton as they were unworthy of his genius.[51]

His position, therefore, seems to have been an antimonopoly position, one opposed to state action which contributed to the building up of aggregations of irresponsible power. It was not clear that he, any more than Chief Justice Marshall or Justice Story, sought positive federal intervention in the internal affairs of the states. Indeed, if he favored extensive federal regulation even of immigration, and federal efforts to curb the consequent evils of pauperism, crime, and disease, that fact has not been disclosed in the limited records of his career. But he, together with his fellow Southerner Justice McKinley, may have been moved by the growing power of business corporations spawned by the states of the North and inadequately controlled by the states of their origin, corporations which bled the South in commercial interchange and, rightly or wrongly, got a share of the blame for the fact that prosperity in the South was outstripped by that of the North.

When constitutional questions were so complicated that eight of the nine Justices found it necessary to write independent opinions, it is not surprising that the people at large showed similar diversity both as to the constitutional issues and as to the performance of the Court.

---

[50] *Ibid.*, 429.   [51] *Savannah Republican*, May 29, 1847.

Commentators deplored the lack of unity on the Court, the diversity of opinions, and the closeness of the five-to-four decision, which stood as a mark of the instability of constitutional law in critical areas.[52] The Senate, in the midst of acrimonious debates over slavery issues, ordered printings of large numbers of copies of the thick pamphlet of opinions for distribution to constituents. It was true, said Senator Daniel Webster, that the opinions would be printed in the annual volume of Supreme Court reports. But the reports reached but a small part of the legal profession and scarcely any part of the people at large. These opinions dealt with a subject of vast importance. They were valuable and interesting to everyone who wished to possess knowledge on questions of constitutional law.[53]

Senator William H. Seward of New York used the occasion to expound upon the problems of New York City with its inadequately supervised stream of immigration, including the frauds practiced on immigrants themselves. The state had adopted a system of regulation for their protection and the Supreme Court decision had subverted that system, leaving the immigrants in a state of hopeless destitution. He wished to make the opinions immediately available to enable the New York legislature to discover how they might constitutionally remedy the evils.[54] Senator George E. Badger of North Carolina, who would later receive an unconfirmed nomination to the Supreme Court, thought the opinions should be circulated because the decision would necessitate action by Congress, and "it was important that the community should be aware of what was the precise position of the constitutional law which the majority of the Supreme Court had assumed."[55]

Senator John M. Berrien of Georgia, President Andrew Jackson's first Attorney General, perceived in the comments of Seward the suggestion that the opinions were to be printed to enable the New York legislature to find means of circumventing the decision. He thought New York could get its own copies without the intervention of the United States Senate. As for general circulation of the opinions, "the object was, as he took it, to take an appeal from the decision of the Supreme Court of the United States to the people of the United States."[56] Senator Badger replied soothingly that he had no intention of advocating such an appeal, and he did not see how it could be taken.[57]

---

[52] For discussion see Charles Warren, *The Supreme Court in United States History*, II, 178–82.

[53] *Cong. Globe*, 30th Cong., 2nd Sess., App. 353 (1849).

[54] *Ibid.* For Webster's irritation at attempts of the New York and Massachusetts legislatures to "get around the decision of the Supreme Court," see *Letters of Daniel Webster*, C. H. Van Tyne, ed., 392.

[55] *Cong. Globe*, 30th Cong., 2nd Sess., App. 353 (1849).

[56] *Ibid.*, 354.

[57] *Ibid.*

In view of the diversity and volume of the opinions in the *Passenger Cases* it is not surprising that members of Congress, newspapermen and the public at large were confused about the implications of the decision. Had the country, and Congress in particular, not been in such turmoil over slavery issues—the "package deal" known as the Compromise of 1850 was now only a year ahead—it is possible that Senator Badger's prediction of comprehensive federal legislation respecting immigration would have come true. As it was, the growing Southern fear of strength in the federal government in view of the possibility that that government might soon fall under the domination of the North curbed the development of statesmanlike thinking on the subject. It was not to be dealt with in comprehensive fashion until the slavery controversy was out of the way.

In spite of Justice Wayne's assurance that the police powers of the states for dealing with both slave and free Negro problems were fully protected, many Southerners read the opinions—or at any rate read about the decision—in the light of their fears rather than in terms of that assurance. The correspondent of the *Charleston Mercury* wrote from Washington that "your inspection laws are virtually annulled."[58] Later the same paper remarked dismally:

> The intellectual as well as judicial weight of the Court was clearly against the decision, but numbers prevailed. If we correctly understand the points decided, they sweep away our inspection laws, enacted to prevent the abduction of our slaves in northern vessels. They sweep away also, all our laws made to prevent free colored persons—"citizens of Massachusetts," or whatever abolition region—from entering our ports and cities. Thus it seems as if the Union is to be so administered as to strip the South of all power of self-protection, and to make submission to its rule equivalent to ruin and degradation.[59]

The comment was picked up by the Washington press,[60] and probably by newspapers elsewhere, as evidence of the far-reaching effect of the decision on the "peculiar institution" of the South.

In general the policy of South Carolina, and doubtless also of other Southern states, seems to have been to prevent wherever possible tests in the Supreme Court of the United States of their various statutes discriminating against Negroes.[61] While the states had no direct control over the federal courts where diversity of citizenship was involved, local

---

[58] *Charleston Mercury*, Feb. 12, 1849.
[59] *Charleston Mercury*, Feb. 14, 1849.
[60] *Washington Daily National In-*

telligencer, Feb. 28, 1849.
[61] See the speech of Thomas J. Turner of Illinois in the House of Representatives, *Cong. Globe*, 30th Cong., 2nd Sess. 222 (1849).

lawyers were unwilling to incur the unpopularity of handling such cases, and in the notorious instance of Samuel Hoar in 1844, the state resorted to legislative expulsion and mob violence to prevent such litigation. For some reason, however, according to an account from the *Charleston Courier* of April 22, 1853, reprinted by *The Law Reporter*,[62] published in Boston, it proved possible to institute a test case before the United States Circuit Court in Charleston. The suit, an action for damages, was brought against Jeremiah D. Yates, sheriff of Charleston, by Reuben Roberts, a free Negro from Nassau, who had been imprisoned during the stay of a British ship in the Charleston port. It may well have been the diplomacy of the British consul in Charleston that led to the filing of the suit and agreement on the facts, which were presented without argument and not controverted even though there was a distinguished array of counsel on both sides. Justice Wayne not being present at the trial, the proceedings took place before District Judge Robert Budd Gilchrist, sitting alone. Judge Gilchrist charged the jury that the position of the case required him only to give his opinion without argument or statement of reasons. He considered the statutes involved to be valid and constitutional.[63] The case was scheduled to go to the Supreme Court on a bill of exceptions to the judge's charge. Somewhat later, however, it was reported that, probably acting on instructions from his government, British Consul Mathews had withdrawn the appeal and the suit was dropped. The validity of the statutes seemed as far from determination as ever.[64]

There for the most part the matter stood until the Civil War wiped out the issue. Incidental light was thrown on the question in 1855 through a decision by District Judge Peleg Sprague, the eminent blind jurist in the federal court in Massachusetts. The master of a ship had signed on free colored seamen in Halifax, Nova Scotia, at twenty-four dollars a month, to make a trip to Europe and back to a "port of discharge" in the United States. The ship returned to New Orleans, where local law required that free Negroes be kept on board or, if they came on land, that they be imprisoned. The master used their predicament as a means to compel the Negroes to agree to work then and on the continuing voyage for only fifteen dollars a month. On arrival in Boston they brought suit for compensation at the original figure. Judge Sprague held that a port in which the seamen could land only to be imprisoned could not be treated as a port of discharge for colored seamen and that they were entitled to compensation at the original figure.[65]

---

[62] *Law Rep.*, 16:49, 1853.

[63] Roberts v. Yates, 20 Fed. Cas. 937, 938 (No. 11919) (C.C.D. S.C. 1853).

[64] *Law Rep.*, 16:178, 1853.

[65] Stratton v. Babbage, 23 Fed. Cas. 255 (No. 13527) (D.C.D. Mass. 1855).

XVI: *The Continuing Struggle over Commerce*

In the meantime questions as to the nature and scope of the commerce power continued to grow in importance and to demand clearer definition than the Supreme Court had thus far provided. They continued to involve slavery, but they became increasingly important apart from that overshadowing issue.

CHAPTER XVII

The Developing Pattern
of the Commerce Power

T HE CONCEPT OF COMMERCE goes to the roots of social behavior and permeates basic patterns of human relations. If in the commerce cases of the Taney period the South's "peculiar institution" was always in the offing, it is also true that other issues were present, and that they would have been there in some form even in the complete absence of slavery issues. Immigration, for example, raised problems of its own, quite apart from the fact that lawmaking for transportation or exclusion of white alien passengers had implications for the transportation or exclusion of free Negroes and slaves. Restrictions on the transportation and sale of alcoholic beverages likewise had their own implications. Although commercial rivalries between New York and New Orleans involved competition between Northern and Southern interests, and therefore between slave and free areas, the two regions would in any event have been commercial competitors. Slavery issues were not usually important in rivalries between New Orleans and Charleston, or Philadelphia and New York, or New York and Boston, yet such rivalries did exist, and they gave rise to conflict in the constitutional field.

Speaking more broadly, in the conflict of political theory between nationalism and localism slavery was only one of the critical factors. In general, the defenders of slavery came to be the defenders of states' rights, while the free states were the advocates of a more concentrated nationalism, but there were nevertheless large and important exceptions, with the Southern states at times leaning toward concentration of power and the North and West proclaiming the rights of the states. For many individuals and groups the issues of nationalism versus localism gradually cut themselves loose from the particular conflicts of interest that gave rise to them, and came to appear as matters of principle in and of themselves, often having more relation to political party affiliations than

396

to the interests involved in their origin. Both the interests and the theories had their impact on the interpretation of the Commerce Clause.

Throughout its history the country, with its vast tracts of rich and undeveloped territory, had been obsessed with plans for improving transportation by what were called internal improvements. These included the dredging and clearing of harbors for ships, the removal of obstructions in the form of shoals and snags in major navigable rivers, and the building of turnpikes and canals, and then of railroads. Because of inadequacy in the body of corporation law and the lack of experience in using private corporations for large ventures, the states initially played an extensive part in financing internal improvements. Beginning with the Administration of Thomas Jefferson the federal government took an extensive part even with respect to internal improvements on land, particularly in connection with the building and repair of the Cumberland Road (also known as the National Road), which across Maryland, Pennsylvania, Virginia, and Ohio marked the line of the "U.S. 40" of the present day. Other major projects were under consideration when President Monroe called a halt through a veto message which maintained that only after an authorizing constitutional amendment could the federal government build and operate a highway system across the several states.[1] Public sentiment was too much divided to support the suggested constitutional amendment.

The Monroe veto was not, of course, the equivalent of a Supreme Court decision, and Congress continued to make sporadic efforts to advance public improvements. When in 1830 Congress passed and sent to President Jackson the Maysville Road Bill authorizing a subscription to the stock of a turnpike company in Kentucky, Jackson vetoed the bill on the ground that it was purely local in character. Technically speaking, the project was indeed local, but the road met at the Ohio River the terminal point of a road running up through Ohio as far as Zanesville, and the two roads taken together had long been thought of as a single highway known as Zane's Trace. The local designation, however, permitted Jackson to differentiate between local projects such as this and national projects or projects of general interest, which might possibly be subject to federal jurisdiction. Even as to such national projects, however, Jackson voiced a warning. He pointed to the Cumberland Road, for which appropriations were sought year after year, and sometimes granted and sometimes not. Such fluctuations he thought fatal to any scheme of national improvement.[2]

---

[1] J. D. Richardson, *A Compilation of the Messages and Papers of the*

Presidents, II, 142.
[2] *Ibid.,* 483, 492.

Differences over the power of the federal government to make public improvements tended to become differences between political parties. Henry Clay, who had been one of the major sponsors of the Cumberland Road, became a leader of the newly formed Whig Party. The party of Andrew Jackson became the Democratic Party after Jackson ceased to lead it, and Martin Van Buren and other Democratic Presidents adhered to the restrictive position. Clay was popular along the road which he helped to build, while Van Buren, traveling the road, had the axle of his carriage sawed partway through so that it broke where the mud was deepest.[3]

As is true of many constitutional issues, that of public improvements underwent much discussion in other quarters before it reached the Supreme Court, and only piecemeal did it ever reach that tribunal at all. The Justices were, of course, highly conscious of it. Since all of them had to travel hundreds, and some of them thousands, of miles each year, they were well informed on matters of transportation, whether on water or on land, and some of them regularly used the Cumberland Road to reach their Western circuits. One of Chief Justice Taney's early important cases on circuit had to do with injuries to passengers due to negligence of the driver of a major stagecoach line running from Baltimore to Wheeling. The passengers on a coach along the line in western Maryland on a cold December day in 1836 included Francis W. Saltonstall and his wife. The driver, exposed to the weather outside the coach, had been drinking to keep himself warm, so that at the point of a change of horses he was seen to be drunk. He proceeded nevertheless and continued to drink as he drove. The coach ran off the road. Saltonstall leaped from his seat, evidently in an attempt to get control of the horses. Mrs. Saltonstall also leaped out, and just as she did so the coach overturned and fell on her, injuring her badly.

The suit brought by the Saltonstalls against the owners of the coach line, Stockton and Stokes, was brought in the United States Circuit Court in Baltimore not by virtue of any Act of Congress but on the basis of diversity of citizenship. The case had more than a personal and temporary interest because of questions to become vitally important in future years in the development of the law of public carriers, including the question of the responsibility of the carrier for injuries resulting from the negligence of his employee, and the legal effect of a contributing act of the injured passenger, in this instance Mrs. Saltonstall's leaping from the coach. In giving his instructions to the jury Chief Justice Taney ruled, with respect to the driver, that "the law requires of him a high degree of caution and prudence, and the least negligence on his part, which pro-

---

[3] A. P. Hulbert, *The Cumberland Road*, 183.

duces bodily injury to the passenger, will render the carrier liable."[4] As for Mrs. Saltonstall's contribution to her own injury by leaping from the coach, Chief Justice Taney noted that the agent of the carrier was responsible if he put her in the dilemma of being injured in the coach or outside of it.

The Saltonstalls were awarded damages. The proprietors of the stage line, aware of the implications of the decision, took the case to the Supreme Court on writ of error, where it was submitted on printed and written arguments. The Supreme Court unanimously affirmed the Circuit Court decision, in an opinion by Justice Barbour.[5] The case was to be widely cited in future years.

The federal government constructed the Cumberland Road in the several states only after the legislatures had given their consent. The commerce power was only one of the asserted sources of power, the postal power being one of the others prominently listed. Constitutional doubts coupled with the reluctance of people to pay taxes made it hard to secure federal appropriations to keep the road in repair. Congress eventually turned the road over to the states, who were to keep it in condition with the aid of tolls for its use, with the reservation that tolls should not be collected from wagons or carriages laden with the property of the United States. While the other states exempted from tolls the coaches which carried United States mail, Pennsylvania collected such a tax from the line of Stockton and Stokes, which was involved in the case discussed above. The line challenged the assessment as a levy on the property of the United States. The majority of the Supreme Court, speaking through Chief Justice Taney, held that "the United States have unquestionably a property in the mails,"[6] and that tolls could not be collected on the transportation. On this point disagreement came from Justice McLean, himself a former Postmaster General, who knew not merely the problems but the personnel involved, and who denied that the mails were federal property within the meaning of the statute.

Both Chief Justice Taney and Justice McLean were careful to explain that the constitutionality of the construction of the Cumberland Road was not involved in the case. Justice Daniel, however, ardent in his defense of the rights of the states, insisted on discussing the subject. He declared that "neither Congress nor the federal government in the exercise of all or any of its attributes possesses the power to construct roads, nor any other description of what have been called internal im-

---

[4] Saltonstall v. Stockton, 21 Fed. Cas. 275, 277 (No. 12271) (C.C.D. Md. 1838).

[5] Stokes v. Saltonstall, 13 Pet. 181 (1839).

[6] Seawright v. Survivors of Stockton, 3 How. 151, 169 (1854).

provements, within the limits of the States."[7] The scope of power could not be changed merely with the consent of the states: "Neither the federal government separately, nor conjointly with the State of Pennsylvania, could have power to repeal the Constitution."[8]

It seems probable that other members of the Court felt as did Justice Daniel about federal construction of public improvements but, amid heated public discussion of the subject, deemed it inexpedient to say so in a case where such a statement was not necessary to the decision. A year later President Polk curbed federal expenditures for the improvement of rivers and harbors by vetoing on constitutional grounds a huge appropriation for that purpose.[9] Justice Daniel immediately wrote him an enthusiastic letter of approval, citing his own opinion in the *Cumberland Road* case. He said in part:

> I have considered this bill a source of more serious alarm, than was the probability of war with Britain or Mexico; and its passage and sanction as constituting a greater calamity than would be actual war with either of those powers; for without principles and public integrity what are we and what security have we for our liberty and the permanence of our institutions? With virtue and political integrity we can overcome any external evils. The growing lack of principle and conduct in many of our public men, and their seeming inability to resist the temptation of dipping into the treasury on every occasion, and their facility in putting by all constitutional restraint under such temptation, have for some time been viewed with deep alarm and mortification. In proportion to the intensity of these feelings is the gratification felt at finding in the Executive a sternness of principle which meets and rebukes the growing and dangerous delinquency just mentioned.[10]

Although Justice Daniel's personal position had long since been taken and publicly stated, it was not until 1853 that he was able to have it embodied in a unanimous opinion of the Supreme Court. A statute of the state of Maine had granted exclusive navigation rights on the Penobscot River, which was exclusively within the state, to a single corporation. The Court held that the statute did not invade the commerce power of Congress. The correct rule of interpretation, said Justice Daniel, "excludes from the regulation of commerce between the States and the Indian tribes the control over turnpikes, canals, or railroads, or the clearing and deepening of watercourses exclusively within the States, or the management of the transportation upon and by means of such im-

---

[7] *Ibid.*, 180.
[8] *Ibid.*, 181. See also Neil, Moore & Co. v. Ohio, 3 How. 720 (1845), and Justice Daniel's dissent therein. See also Achison v. Huddleson, 12 How. 293 (1851).
[9] Richardson, *Messages and Papers of the Presidents*, IV, 460.
[10] P. V. Daniel to James K. Polk, Aug. 5, 1846, Polk Papers.

provements."[11] Within this sphere of operations it now appeared that the Supreme Court had surrendered to the most restricted interpretation of the Commerce Clause.

Yet there were conflicting tides of sentiment throughout the country and even within the region of the South with respect to the commerce power, so that each case needed to be read in the light of its peculiar facts and not merely in terms of the generalizations of its spokesman. The Erie Canal had linked the Great Lakes with the Hudson River and so with the Atlantic Ocean, turning eastward traffic that would otherwise have gone down the Mississippi. The Cumberland Road established a link at Wheeling, as later also did the Baltimore and Ohio Railroad. Other railroad connections were to be established at Pittsburgh. In the face of this threat to the Mississippi trade the Southern spokesman, John C. Calhoun, turned nationalist to the extent of seeking federal development of the Mississippi transportation area. Of the Memphis commercial convention held the preceding winter, De Bow's *Commercial Review*, published in New Orleans, said in September, 1846:

> We shall never forget the deep burst of approbation and applause which rung through the hall when he made from his seat the remarkable and unexpected declaration that the Mississippi and its great tributaries were to be regarded as an "inland sea," and as much entitled to the protection and care of the federal government as the Atlantic coasts. The effect was electrical.[12]

The February, 1847, issue of the same journal proclaimed:

> A contest has been going on between the North and South, not limited to slavery, or no slavery—to abolition or no abolition, nor to the politics of either whigs or democrats, as such, but a contest tendered by our Northern brethren, whether the growing commerce of the great West, shall be thrown upon New Orleans, or given to the Atlantic cities—which shall receive, store, sell and ship the immense products, of that great country, lying between the Appalachian and Rocky mountains? Shall Boston, New York, Philadelphia and Baltimore do it, or shall our own New Orleans?[13]

The author spoke hungrily of sufficient federal appropriations to open every river and tributary of the Mississippi, by the removal of snags,

---

[11] Veazie v. Moor, 14 How. 568, 574 (1853).
[12] *De Bow's Commercial Review*, 2:83, 1846.

[13] "Contests for the Trade of the Mississippi Valley," *De Bow's Commercial Review*, 3:75, 98, 1846.

shoals, and bars, so as to afford at New Orleans an outlet for the vast productions of the West.

In 1847 a convention was held in Chicago to discuss river and harbor improvements, bringing together, it was said, from five thousand to eight thousand persons, some from long distances. Issues of constitutional doctrine and conflicts of commercial interest became so entangled that little could be said about the convention beyond the fact that each individual and group sought to phrase doctrine so as to make it serve its own interest.[14] In 1851 a Democratic journal published in New York praised the Democratic members of Congress who at the last session "so fearlessly resisted at all hazards a scheme of internal improvements, which would ultimately abstract hundreds of millions from the treasury, and consolidate the federal government as the moneyed head of the nation."[15] If the Supreme Court had been inclined to look to the general public for guidance, there was little guidance to be found.

In the limited areas in which Congress did act on commerce it provided the courts with opportunities for shaping the course of constitutional interpretation. An example was provided by the act to punish crimes against the United States,[16] which in one of its sections dealt with thefts from vessels which were in distress or which had been wrecked, lost, or stranded. A case decided by the Supreme Court in 1838 had to do with the theft of property from a wrecked ship, the property having been taken ashore and left above the high-water mark. Justice Story, speaking for a unanimous Court, admitted that, according to established interpretation, admiralty jurisdiction did not extend above the ebb and flow of the tide, but held that jurisdiction could be based on the Commerce Clause. The commerce power of Congress did not stop at the mere boundary line of a state, but extended to such acts done on land as interfered with, obstructed, or prevented the due exercise of the commerce power.[17]

In 1838 Congress attempted to curb a holocaust of steamboat disasters on the navigable waters of the United States by requiring new enrollment and new licenses of all steamboats, providing for safety inspection, and prescribing rules of operation.[18] Competition among owners and carelessness of operation had resulted in the bursting of boilers, fires, collisions, and other disasters. United States district judges were required to appoint inspectors of boats and equipment and periodic inspection

---

[14] See H. G., "River and Harbor Improvements," *De Bow's Commercial Review*, 4:291, 1847, and "Chicago Convention," *Democratic Review*, 21: 89, 1847.

[15] "The Thirty-First Congress," *Democratic Review*, 28:289, 1851.
[16] 4 Stat. 115.
[17] United States v. Coombs, 12 Pet. 72 (1838).
[18] 5 Stat. 304.

was required. Owners and masters were required to employ competent engineers and to see that certain routines were observed, such as the opening of safety valves whenever vessels stopped for any purpose whatever.

Judicial attitudes were illustrated by a grand jury charge of United States District Judge Theodore H. McCaleb of Louisiana. He deplored the "frightful loss of life and property annually sustained by our community" and urged vigorous enforcement. He said of the twelfth section of the act:

> It was designed to punish the captains, engineers and pilots of steamboats for their negligence or inattention.
>
> There is too much reason to believe that there has hitherto been a shameful remissness on the part of both owners and captains generally, in the performance of this duty; and those who from parsimonious motives have failed in their duty to the public, should be promptly made to feel the consequences of their criminal cupidity and their indifference to the rights of others. The only manner pointed out by the law by which owners can be made to suffer is by civil action for damages, as set forth in the last section of the act.[19]

The statute gave rise to important decisions by the Supreme Court, usually with entanglements over the subject of the scope of admiralty jurisdiction.[20] The Court did not question the statute where interstate or foreign commerce was concerned, but federal judges grew hesitant when the statute was applied to ferries, which were regarded as essentially local even though operated on interstate navigable streams. When an attempt was made to penalize the operation of a ferry across the Missouri River without a federal license, United States District Judge Robert W. Wells held that the statute did not apply. He admitted that the ferry might be covered by the comprehensive language of the statute but held that Congress had no jurisdiction over commerce which was completely internal and confined to one state.[21] Justice Catron affirmed the decision in the United States Circuit Court, remarking that three Supreme Court judges had handed down similar decisions on their circuits.[22] Judge Wells took the same position with respect to a ferry across the Mississippi River. He admitted that Congress might regulate interstate transit by ferries but seemed to believe that in order to do so it would be necessary to separate interstate from intrastate commerce:

---

[19] Charge to Grand Jury, 30 Fed. Cas. 990, 991 (No. 18253) (D.C.E.D. La. 1846).

[20] See for example Waring v. Clarke, 5 How. 441 (1847).

[21] United States v. *The James Mor-* rison, 26 Fed. Cas. 579 (No. 15465) (D.C.D. Mo. 1846).

[22] United States v. *The William Pope*, 28 Fed. Cas. 629 (No. 16703) (D.C.D. Mo. 1852).

Congress have not yet undertaken to separate the purely internal trade and intercourse of the people of a state on its roads, from the commerce among the several states. They have not yet undertaken to regulate, either on the roads or over the ferries, the passage of every market man with his chickens and pigs; or a man going to mill or to church, although passing from one state into another state.[23]

Here the matter stood until in later years Congress saw fit to extend its control by additional statutes.

On the subject of the exclusiveness or nonexclusiveness of the power of Congress within admitted areas of interstate and foreign commerce the Supreme Court, in a series of cases which culminated in the *Passenger Cases* of 1849, already discussed, had divided in bewildering fashion. In the case of *Cooley v. Board of Wardens of the Port of Philadelphia*[24] in 1852, the Court had to return to the subject. The Board of Wardens provided pilots for incoming and outgoing vessels at the port of Philadelphia, including extensive interstate and foreign shipping. A Pennsylvania statute of 1803 required that masters of vessels refusing to employ pilots in the port must nevertheless pay half the regular pilotage fee, the money to be allocated "for the relief of distressed and decayed pilots, their widows and children."

The levy bore at least a distant resemblance to the taxes collected by Massachusetts and New York to take care of impoverished immigrants, which by a vote of five to four had been held unconstitutional in the *Passenger Cases*. The levy was attached, however, to the operation of ships in the harbor, and was not directly connected with either passengers or commodities shipped. The situation also differed in that whereas in the *Passenger Cases* no Congressional support for the state enactments could be found, counsel for the Philadelphia pilots could point to an Act of Congress in 1789 providing:

That all pilots in the bays, inlets, rivers, harbors and ports of the United States, shall continue to be regulated in conformity with the existing laws of the States respectively wherein such pilots may be, or with such laws as the States may respectively hereafter enact for the purpose, until further provision shall be made by Congress.[25]

Of this statute Chief Justice Taney had said in the *License Cases* that Congress undoubtedly had the power to adopt existing state laws as its own, but it could not give the status of federal law to whatever measures the states might enact at some future time. If the Constitution deprived the states of power to regulate interstate and foreign commerce,

---

[23] *Ibid.*, 630.   [24] 12 How. 299.   [25] 1 Stat. 54.

Congress could not change the Constitution by conferring that power.[26] Unless in the *Cooley* case the Supreme Court were to reject this position and hold that Congress might delegate its own commerce power to the states, it could hardly uphold the Pennsylvania statute on the basis of the Act of Congress which had preceded it. Unless there were occasions on which the states of their own force might regulate interstate and foreign commerce, the Pennsylvania statute must be unconstitutional.

Shortly before the decision in the *Cooley* case Justice Woodbury, a Democrat and in general inclined toward a states' rights position, had been replaced by Justice Benjamin R. Curtis, a Whig with nationalist leanings. Although on the subject of the commerce power Justice Curtis' position resembled that of Justice Woodbury as expressed in the *License Cases*,[27] he did bring to the subject the freshness of a new personality— he was not among those who had endlessly belabored the subject in earlier cases. Eight Justices were present, Justice McKinley being absent because of the illness that was soon to terminate in death. Four of the eight, including three who had hitherto insisted on expressing their individual opinions in commerce cases, and Justice Nelson who had not, joined in an opinion of the Court by Justice Curtis, leaving Justices McLean and Wayne to dissent at the nationalist extreme, and at the other pole, Justice Daniel to write a concurring opinion expressing states' rights sentiments. Shortly before the case was decided Justice Curtis wrote to George Ticknor that his opinion would excite surprise, "because it is adverse to the exclusive authority of Congress, and not in accordance with the opinions of McLean and Wayne, who are the most high-toned Federalists on the bench. But it rests on grounds perfectly satisfactory to myself, and it has received the assent of five judges out of eight, although for twenty years no majority has even rested their decision on either view of this question, nor was it ever directly decided before."[28]

The gist of Curtis' solution of the conundrum of the exclusiveness or nonexclusiveness of the commerce power of Congress was to restate the question. He divided interstate and foreign commerce into two categories to which separate rules applied. He explained one of these categories by saying that "Whatever subjects of this power are in their nature national, or admit of only one uniform system, or plan of regulation, may justly be said to be of such a nature as to require exclusive legislation by Congress."[29] The second category was that of aspects of interstate and foreign commerce which were essentially local, as in the

---

[26] License Cases, 5 How. 504, 580 (1849).
[27] *Ibid.*, 627–30.

[28] *A Memoir of Benjamin Robbins Curtis*, George T. Curtis, ed., 168.
[29] Cooley v. Board of Wardens, 12 How. 299, 319 (1852).

instance of pilots in the harbors where different conditions required or at least permitted different regulations. Here, the Court held, the mere existence of the grant of power to Congress did not prevent the states from regulating. Although in this field there was federal legislation, the import of the legislation was to leave the subject to the states. The Pennsylvania statute was therefore constitutional.

Justice Catron, watchdog in Washington for James Buchanan as he had been for James K. Polk, wrote to Buchanan about the decision. He told of the holding rather than of the finer shadings of the opinion, and noted that Justice Grier, like Buchanan a Pennsylvanian, had concurred in upholding the Pennsylvania measure even though he had hitherto leaned toward the position that Congress had the sole power to regulate the commerce involved. Catron continued:

> Curtis is a first rate lawyer—exceedingly fair-minded—and writes smoother than any man on the Bench. Of the truth of the doctrine held, I have not doubted for 25 years. I expressed my opinion in 5 Howd. 600 & 601, in the License Cases. Will you do me the favour to read my views as there stated. the Ch. Justice & I concurred on that occasion—& have stood by each other since. McLean & Wayne hold that Congress has the sole power, & that *all* the pilot laws are void. Dnl. of course holds that Congress has no power on the subject, & all regulations made by Congress are void. But the question is now settled.[30]

It seems probable that Justice Catron—and with him also Chief Justice Taney—was elated at the victory implied in the holding that at times the states might regulate interstate and foreign commerce, and that he gave little thought to the distinction between national and local commerce. Here as in many other cases the concurring Justices may have paid little attention or given little weight to the incidental remarks of the Justice writing the opinion of the Court. Outstanding, rather, was the defeat of McLean and Wayne, the "most high-toned Federalists on the bench."

Commentators differ concerning the value of the distinction between that commerce subject to the jurisdiction of Congress which is national and that which is local. Certain it is that the opinion provides little guidance for distinguishing between the two beyond classifying pilotage as local. It left unanswered the question whether the Court would find to be local any interstate or foreign commerce other than that which Congress had designated as such, and whether Congressional designation was sufficient to classify a particular segment of commerce as local—as,

---

[30] J. Catron to James Buchanan, Mar. 3, 1852, Buchanan Papers.

for example, when Congress differentiated among states in terms of their outlawing the manufacture and sale of alcoholic beverages[31] or the competitive sale of prison-made goods.[32] If it was in a sense an eloquent statement of indefiniteness, with the statement the indefiniteness came to seem in some way manageable, by contrast with the confusion of multiple opinions as in the *License Cases* and the *Passenger Cases*. The opinion promised to give a more pragmatic, less conceptual and categorical direction to the Court's thinking concerning state regulation of commerce.

Yet between the word and the act there may be a gulf. State courts not sympathetic to particular constitutional holdings of the Supreme Court were often slow to fall into line or flatly refused to do so. With respect to the doctrine of the *Cooley* case, even a member of the Supreme Court itself, Justice McLean, on circuit later in the same year ignored the doctrine, saying, "That the exclusive power to regulate commerce among the states, is vested in congress, in my judgment, is not now a debatable question."[33]

There were litigation-breeding conflicts between the interests of navigation and of highway traffic that required the bridging of navigable streams, and there were the special interests of railroads as lines were constructed throughout the country. The early conflicts arose mostly along the eastern seaboard, where geological depression of the land brought tidewater far up the beds of rivers and made them navigable farther or for larger ships than they otherwise would have been. The geological factor meant that coastwise land traffic had to proceed far inland or required numerous and long bridges over the rivers or the inland arms of the ocean. In Massachusetts alone, Justice Woodbury said in an outstanding federal case in 1847 challenging obstruction of navigation by a bridge, fourteen or fifteen acts of incorporation had been passed since that for the Charles River Bridge in 1785.[34] Other states with similar enactments included Maine, New Hampshire, Connecticut, New York, Pennsylvania, and Delaware; and Congress had taken the same step by authorizing the bridging of the Potomac in the District of Columbia.[35]

---

[31] See Clark Distilling Co. v. Western Maryland Ry., 242 U.S. 311 (1917).

[32] See Whitfield v. Ohio, 297 U.S. 431 (1936).

[33] Rogers v. Cincinnati, 20 Fed. Cas. 1111 (No. 12008) (C.C.D. Ohio 1852). See also his later concurring opinion on the Supreme Court: "Every voyage of a vessel between two States is subject to the admiralty jurisdiction, and not to any State regulation. A denial of this doctrine is a subversion of the commercial power of Congress, and throws us upon the Confederation." Jackson v. Steamboat *Magnolia*, 20 How. 296, 304 (1858).

[34] United States v. New Bedford Bridge, 27 Fed. Cas. 91, 94 (No. 15867) (C.C.D. Conn. 1847).

[35] *Ibid.*, 127.

407

The New Bedford Bridge, built across the Acushnet River, obstructed navigation between the Atlantic Ocean and the ports of New Bedford and Fairhaven. Robert Rantoul, a crusading Democrat and free trade advocate appointed United States Attorney for Massachusetts by President Polk, secured an indictment against the proprietors of the bridge for obstructing navigation in alleged violation of maritime law.[36] His associate in the case was Charles L. Woodbury, the son of the Justice. Opposing counsel were Benjamin R. Curtis, who in 1851 would replace Justice Woodbury on the Supreme Court, Rufus Choate, and J. H. W. Page.

In a widely ranging opinion now covering some thirty-six fine-printed pages of *Federal Cases*, Justice Woodbury held that the grant of admiralty jurisdiction in the Constitution carried with it no body of criminal law for enforcement in the admiralty courts, and that obstructive bridging of navigable streams could be punished in such courts only if Congress, in the exercise of the federal commerce power, enacted criminal legislation. Rantoul therefore failed in his attempt to use a federal court to clear the navigation channel by elimination of the obstructing bridge. He did not take the case to the Supreme Court.

Even though it was only a Circuit Court decision the New Bedford decision attracted attention in the West,[37] where bridges across freshwater navigable streams created similar problems. Important among them was the bridge across the Ohio River at Wheeling, in what was then a part of Virginia but is now West Virginia. The bridge connected the Virginia part of the Cumberland Road with its counterpart in Ohio. The road was completed to Wheeling as early as 1818, but thereafter until the completion of the bridge in 1849 the crossing had been by ferry. Crossings had often been delayed by ice and floods, and efforts were made for many years to secure from Congress appropriations for the construction of a bridge. The efforts were defeated by sectional rivalries. Whereas Virginia and Ohio were eager to have the bridge erected, Pennsylvania was opposed to it because of the rivalry between Wheeling and Pittsburgh and the rivalry also between Philadelphia and cities to the south over the control of Western trade. The Cumberland Road had done much to bring Wheeling to prominence. The plan to make it the western terminal of the Baltimore and Ohio Railroad promised greater things. Pittsburgh was naturally unwilling to see river traffic from the Mississippi Valley, and specifically from the Ohio River, turned eastward at Wheeling and toward Baltimore, rather than going on to

---

[36] See "Political Portraits with Pen and Pencil: Robert Rantoul, Jr. of Massachusetts," *Democratic Review*, 27:348, 1850.

[37] *West. L.J.*, 5:93–94, 1847.

Pittsburgh, which hoped to be connected by railroad with Harrisburg and Philadelphia. The bridge, it was feared, in addition to standing as the means and the symbol of east-west traffic to the south of Pittsburgh, would be an actual obstruction. To get more steam power for the movement of larger and larger boats, builders were erecting higher and higher smokestacks. It was feared that the bridge, however high over the river it might be constructed, would interfere with the passage of the larger boats.[38]

In March, 1847, sensing the fact that the opposition of Pennsylvania coupled with lethargy in Congress would prevent a federal grant within the reasonable future, the Virginia legislature authorized the previously chartered Wheeling and Belmont Bridge Company to construct a wire suspension bridge and to collect tolls from traffic thereon. It provided further that the bridge must not obstruct navigation "in the usual manner" and that if it did so it might be abated as a common nuisance.

In September, 1847, contracts were let for construction of a bridge ninety-three and one-half feet above the low-water mark of the river. While construction proceeded, work also went forward on the Baltimore and Ohio Railroad, which was to terminate at that point and draw eastern traffic from down the Ohio River and by means of the bridge from the interior of the state of Ohio. At the same time Pennsylvania was extending its own system of internal improvements, including both canals and railroads, to take advantage of the trade potential of east-west traffic.

Western Pennsylvania, and Pittsburgh in particular, looked askance at the construction of the Wheeling Bridge, but not until the summer of 1849 was an attempt made to block the project. At that time Edwin M. Stanton of Pennsylvania, who was to play a prominent part in this series of cases before the Supreme Court and also in other cases, both as private counsel and as Attorney General of the United States, made the first move, acting for the attorney general of Pennsylvania. Stanton appeared before Justice Grier in the room of the United States Circuit Court at Philadelphia, to address him not as a circuit justice but as a Justice of the Supreme Court at chambers. Stanton asked for an injunction against completion of the construction of the

---

[38] This account is summarized from James Morton Callahan, "The Pittsburgh-Wheeling Rivalry for Commercial Headship on the Ohio," *Ohio Archaeological and Historical Quarterly*, 57:40, 1913. The situation was complicated by the fact that for crossing the Ohio River from Wheeling to Bridgeport, Ohio, two bridges were necessary. The river divided at that point, flowing around Zane's Island. In 1836 a wooden bridge was constructed from Zane's Island to the Ohio shore. The wire suspension bridge, which gave rise to so much controversy, was to extend across the wider or main channel of the Ohio from Wheeling to Zane's Island.

bridge on the ground that it would obstruct river traffic between Wheeling and the headwaters of the Ohio, some fifty miles of which ran through the state of Pennsylvania itself. Notice of the bill was served on the bridge company.[39]

Stanton filed an amendment to the bill in equity to show that curtailment of Ohio River traffic above Wheeling would detrimentally affect canals and railroads constructed at the expense of the state in anticipation of connection with that traffic. The company, complaining that Pennsylvania had postponed action until the expenditure on the bridge was nearly completed, of course denied that the bridge would constitute any appreciable interference with navigation, and contended that Pennsylvania had "no corporate capacity to become a party to a suit in the Supreme Court, to protect or vindicate the rights of her citizens."[40] Perhaps referring to the main tributaries of the Ohio River in Pennsylvania, it noted that Pennsylvania had itself set an example by bridging the same stream at a height no greater than that of the Wheeling Bridge.

After hearing arguments in the case Justice Grier noted that the question of Pennsylvania's right to prosecute the case was new, that the Supreme Court—for which he at chambers was asked to act—would not have original jurisdiction unless Pennsylvania was entitled to prosecute the action, that the injury threatened was not imminent or certain, and that in any event there was an adequate remedy at law. Instead of deciding the case he therefore ordered the essential documents to be filed in the Supreme Court.[41]

In the Supreme Court supplemental documents were filed, among them the charge that in November a steamboat traveling from Pittsburgh to Cincinnati had to stop at the bridge to cut seven and a half feet from its chimneys in order to pass. Another boat, traveling from Cincinnati to Pittsburgh, had to stop at Wheeling, "a port of entry of Virginia," and there discharge passengers and cargo.[42] The Virginia legislature, sensing the danger of legal action against the bridge as a nuisance, modified the 1847 statute to render the nuisance provision inapplicable to the bridge as it now stood. So it was that the states of Virginia and Pennsylvania ranged themselves in combat in judicial and legislative halls.

It is said that the leading members even of the Pennsylvania bar thought that Pennsylvania could show no such legal interest in the obstruction created by the Wheeling Bridge as would enable it to bring

---

[39] Pennsylvania v. Wheeling and Belmont Bridge Co., 9 How. 647 (1851).

[40] *Ibid.*, 652.
[41] *Ibid.*, 654.
[42] *Ibid.*, 655.

the suit, and that Virginia lawyers treated the suit with derision.[43] The case was presented, however, by Stanton and by Robert J. Walker, a prominent Mississippi lawyer formerly from Pennsylvania, and by Pennsylvania's attorney general, C. Darrah. Opposed were Alexander H. H. Stewart and Reverdy Johnson of Maryland, who had a lucrative private practice along with serving as Attorney General of the United States. Pennsylvania won at that time at least an implied victory on the question of jurisdiction in that, without discussing the jurisdictional question, the Supreme Court ordered that the cause be referred to former Chancellor R. H. Walworth of New York, to take testimony as to the obstruction of navigation and the means of eliminating it. To this reference only Justice Daniel dissented. He did so on the ground that Pennsylvania had no such interest as to entitle it to sue, and that in any event the question of nuisance was one to be settled by a court of law and not of equity.[44]

The order of the Court was issued in May, 1850. The report was filed a year later and the case was argued in December, 1851, at the same term at which the *Cooley* case was argued and decided. Making effective use of Walworth's report of more than seven hundred pages demonstrating that while the bridge did not obstruct navigation by sailing vessels, it did obstruct steam navigation, Stanton quoted from the *Passenger Cases* to show the McLean and Wayne position that the power of Congress to regulate interstate and foreign commerce was exclusive, the Grier and Catron position that the inaction of Congress implied a determination that commerce should be free from regulation, and the Taney and Daniel admission that the control of commerce extended to the control of the ships used in navigation. Defendants' counsel continued to challenge the right of Pennsylvania to bring the suit, the original jurisdiction of the Court, and the contentions that since the bridge interfered with the passage of some boats without modification of chimneys, while permitting the great body of traffic to pass, it could be called an obstruction to commerce and abated as a nuisance. Bias in the Walworth report was suggested by the fact that the engineer selected to make measurements was a brother-in-law of one of the counsel for complainant.[45]

On December 27, 1851, Justice Curtis, in his first term as a member of the Supreme Court, wrote to his uncle, George Ticknor, that although he had been obliged to dissent in one case, the *Wheeling*

---

[43] George C. Gorham, *Life and Public Services of Edwin M. Stanton,* I, 40.

[44] Pennsylvania v. Wheeling and

Belmont Bridge Co., 9 How. 647 (1851).

[45] Pennsylvania v. Wheeling and Belmont Bridge Co., 13 How. 518, 556 (1852).

Bridge case was the first in which the Court was likely to be sharply divided.[46] On January 24, 1852, Justice Catron wrote a gossipy letter to James Buchanan, saying that at this term things had gone along so smoothly that only once had his "delectable temper" been disturbed. That was by "your damd Wheeling Bridge Case." Catron disclosed the fact that a majority of the Court considered the bridge an obstruction of commerce and would give the company the option of removing it or raising it high enough that it would no longer be an obstruction. The undecided question among the majority had been as to the distance above the low-water mark to which the bridge should be raised. Catron wrote jokingly:

> I had to pull the Bridge down, but flatly refused to raise over 20 feet higher—& in effect bringing Steam Boat Chimneys to 80 feet above the water: & as I held a strong position among half formed, & divided opinions, *forced* the majority to my 110 feet level. The Bridge is now ninety feet above low water. This is secret gossip for the nonce, as no opinion is yet delivered in Court. McLean writes the opin. & a scattering thing he'll make of it. Grier fought with the stubbornness of a Bull for 30 feet rise, & 120 above low water, but was forced into my terms. The Chief & Dnl went against jurisdiction, & think, the old Dominion & the Keystone, shd. be left to fight it out—& so the Ch. & Barbour thought, & said in the Book, when Rhode Island & Massatts. were at law about their State boundary. Towit:—That the question then and now, was political, & not of judicial cognizance. As the States are not allowed to treat or fight, & have a right of outlet on the great rivers by law-pact—making the right a perfect one—it is hard to see what they can do, if they cannot sue for the right of using a comn highway, plainly made common, by compact among all the States. To the (US) judicial power there is no exception; it extends to *all controversies*, between States; & a State, & citizens of another State. But enough of husky law.[47]

Although, in Catron's language, the decision of the Court was still in the category of "secret gossip," the gossip spread. On January 28, 1852, the *New York Tribune* reported that the Supreme Court had decided the case against the bridge company. The Court would order that the bridge be removed as a nuisance or elevated so as to permit boats to pass. Judge McLean would deliver the opinion of the Court.[48]

Justice McLean officially announced the decision February 6,

---

46 *A Memoir of Benjamin Robbins Curtis*, I, 165.
47 J. Catron to James Buchanan, Jan. 24, 1852, Buchanan Papers.
48 *New York Tribune*, Jan. 28,

1852. The *New York Journal of Commerce* had also reported the decision well in advance of the date of its official announcement. See quotation in *Baltimore American*, Feb. 9, 1852.

1852, with Chief Justice Taney and Justice Daniel dissenting. If Justice Catron continued to regard the McLean opinion as "a scattering thing" he nevertheless refrained from presenting a concurring opinion. It is possible, indeed, that here as in other instances he used private correspondence to relieve the pressure of personal sentiments that might otherwise have found expression in concurring opinions.

The Court found that Pennsylvania was not a party to the suit by virtue of its sovereignty, as it would be in a question of disputed state boundaries, and that it was not suing to protect the rights of its citizens —as would seem to have been the implication when the case was first presented to Justice Grier. Rather, it was appearing because of injury to its own interests in that the obstruction at Wheeling would curtail the use of canals and railroads in which the state had invested many millions of dollars. Justice McLean admitted that an indictment at common law could not be sustained in the federal courts in the absence of a federal statute, but held that resort to equity might nevertheless be had. On the basis of the Walworth report the Court found that the bridge obstructed navigation and gave the company the option of raising it or removing it.

Chief Justice Taney's dissenting opinion had a sharp clarity not possessed by the opinion of the Court. He could find no law, either common or statute, state or federal, under which the bridge could be dealt with as a nuisance. The bridge had the sanction of the Virginia legislature. Congress might have legislated on the matter of the height of bridges over this navigable stream, but it had not done so. Undoubtedly the Supreme Court had original jurisdiction when a state was a party, but it could not exercise that jurisdiction without a law to govern the proceeding. As for such interference with navigation as was provided by the bridge, he thought the subject was governed by *Willson v. Black Bird Creek Marsh Co.,* where the Supreme Court, speaking through Chief Justice Marshall, had refused to strike down a Delaware statute providing for a dam across a navigable stream. Even apart from any past decision, he did not see how the mere grant of the commerce power to Congress could give the judicial branch power to define unlawful obstructions. He could not see how, in any event, a court of equity could order demolition of a structure that had cost more than two hundred thousand dollars to save a state from speculative and questionable and inconsiderable loss, in connection with a stream of river commerce that was still growing in spite of the alleged obstruction, particularly in light of the fact that the structure served the public by greatly facilitating the commerce of which it was an instrument.

Justice Daniel dissented with even greater vigor. He spoke disparagingly of the Walworth report, regarding part of it as irrelevant and part of it as contrary to the testimony on which it was supposed to be based. Pennsylvania had no property in this structure, which was exclusively within the state of Virginia, and no sufficient interest in the matter to make it a party to a suit. Unlike the Chief Justice, he denied that the commerce power was sufficient to enable Congress to determine the flow of commerce by water or by land instruments as determined by the people of the states in which the commerce took place.

Apart from the strictly legal points, the McLean and Daniel opinions threw light on conflicting attitudes toward different forms of transportation, which had some relation to the interests of the regions from which the Justices came. Justice McLean had lived most of his life in Ohio where the eastern and southern borders were marked by a giant navigable stream from which the state derived much of its prosperity. Interior rivers had performed much the same function, and he had seen the state crossed by a network of canals to facilitate interior transportation. Only gradually were the railroads breaking into the picture at the middle of the century, and McLean continued to envisage water as providing the major amount of transportation. He noted:

> We have an extent of river coast, counting both shores, exceeding twenty-five thousand miles, through countries the most fertile on the globe. This is a greater distance than the combined railways of the world. That our railroads, as avenues of commerce, may develop our resources in a greater degree than is now anticipated, must be the desire of everyone. But the great thoroughfares, provided by a beneficient Providence, should neither be neglected nor abandoned. They will still remain the great arteries of commerce.[49]

Justice Daniel, although as a Virginian fully aware of the importance of water transportation, also knew of the need of Virginia for connections with her own western regions and with Western states, connections across mountains which water could not easily provide. Beyond that, as a highly sensitive Virginian he felt the tensions of the competitive interstate struggle with Pennsylvania, even though it was McLean rather than Grier who spoke for the Court. So it was that Daniel, in the language of a critic, "intoxicated with the recent effects of the development of railroads,"[50] rushed to their defense. For all the improvement in navigation by steam and sails, he contended, it was railroads that were connecting the remote sections of the country, even in areas where water transportation was feasible. They had the superiority of greater speed and safety and freedom from dependence on wind or depth of

---

[49] 13 How. 576.
[50] Callahan, "The Pittsburgh-Wheeling Rivalry for Commercial Headship on the Ohio," *Ohio Archaeological and Historical Quarterly*, 57:47, 1913.

water, and lines could be constructed longitudinally or latitudinally at will, without reference to the meandering of vessel-carrying streams. This progress must not be arrested by a fiat of the Court, with retreat into a system of narrow local monopoly.[51]

When in February, 1852, the opinions of the Justices were read, Reverdy Johnson asked for another engineering inquiry to discover whether there was some alternative to removing or elevating the Wheeling Bridge. At the end of the term the Supreme Court, after studying the resulting report, somewhat modified its decree but left the company faced with the task of making greater changes or removing the bridge at the end of a year.

The varied interests defending the bridge now shifted the battle to Congress. With unsuccessful opposition from Pennsylvania and from certain other interests Congress was persuaded to attach to a post office appropriation bill provisions by which the bridge was declared to be a lawful structure in its existing position and elevation and was declared to be a post road for the passage of mails.[52] The bill was passed in the face of the Pennsylvania protest against this move to "reverse, or render inoperative, the solemn adjudications of the Supreme Court."[53] Sentiment against the Supreme Court decision and in favor of the protecting statute was strong, and Pennsylvania seemed inclined to give up attempts to enforce the decree. In December, 1853, a motion previously filed for enforcement of the decree was dismissed when counsel for Pennsylvania failed to appear.[54] It seemed that the controversy was now at an end.

The conflict took on renewed life, however, when nature intervened. In May, 1854, a windstorm hurled the bridge into the river, to the great glee of Pittsburgh interests, some of which taunted Wheeling by having steamboats lower their chimneys in mockery at the point where the bridge had been, with the consequent threat of mob violence in return. The company quickly cleared away the wreckage and began rebuilding. Pennsylvania, claiming that the decree of the Supreme Court was still effective in spite of the statute, got from Justice Grier at chambers an injunction against the reconstruction. The Wheeling press denounced the action of "the Pittsburgh judge of the Supreme Court," the bridge company asked Congress to investigate bribery charges, and

---

[51] 13 How. 603–04.
[52] 10 Stat. 112. For discussion see Callahan, "The Pittsburgh-Wheeling Rivalry for Commercial Headship on the Ohio," *Ohio Archaeological and Historical Quarterly*, 57:48, 1913.
[53] *Cong. Globe*, 32nd Cong., 1st

Sess., App. 967 (1852). For contemporary discussion of the legal issues see "The Wheeling Bridge Case," *West. L.J.*, 9:529–30, 1852.
[54] See comments, *Washington Daily National Intelligencer*, Dec. 17, 1853.

the engineer on whom the injunction was served ignored it and in mid-summer had the bridge back in place.[55] In December, 1854, Stanton and Reverdy Johnson were back before the Supreme Court in renewed conflict.[56]

The case was not decided—or the decision was not officially announced—until April 21, 1856, but more than two months earlier the *New York Tribune*, which seems to have had a trustworthy pipeline to the Supreme Court, told what the decision would be. By a considerable majority the Court would hold that the protecting statute was constitutional, and in effect this holding would reverse the former decision. This was the first instance in the history of the government, said the *Tribune*, when Congress had interposed to arrest a decree of the Supreme Court. The precedent might lead to future embarrassment and to further conflict between the judicial and legislative branches of the government, "for if the law settled by the highest judicial tribunal be not the accepted law of the land, and is liable to review by demagogues in Congress, of their own motive or by the inspiration of worse ones out of doors, the Court of last resort becomes but a mockery."[57]

The *Tribune* was well served by its new source—from the nature of the comment apparently one of the dissenting Justices. The Court upheld the power of Congress to give legal status to the bridge which the Court itself had classified as a nuisance. Declining to say whether the statute could be justified under the postal power, on which Congress had placed emphasis, the Court upheld it as an exercise of the commerce power. Said Justice Nelson for the Court and with only three Justices dissenting:

> The regulation of commerce includes intercourse and navigation, and, of course, the power to determine what shall or shall not be deemed in judgment of law an obstruction of navigation; and that power, as we have seen, has been exercised consistent with the continuance of the bridge.[58]

The Court admitted that a judgment for damages in an action at law would have been beyond the reach of Congress, and adhered to its position that the bridge company must pay the cost of past litigation; but it noted that the decree directing abatement of the obstruction was executory, a continuing decree, and held that by regulating commerce Con-

---

[55] See Callahan, "The Pittsburgh-Wheeling Rivalry for Commercial Headship on the Ohio," *Ohio Archaeological and Historical Quarterly*, 57: 52–53, 1913.
[56] See *New York Times*, Dec. 14, 15, 1854.
[57] *New York Daily Tribune*, Feb. 19, 1856.
[58] Pennsylvania v. Wheeling and Belmont Bridge Co., 18 How. 421, 431 (1856).

gress could here make lawful what was not lawful before the act was passed.

The decision on this central point was unacceptable to Justices McLean, Wayne, and Grier. For the first two, who in the *Cooley* case had continued to insist that the commerce power of Congress was exclusive, dissent seemed, on its face, somewhat puzzling. Yet the issues were complex and matters of personal and judicial pride were involved. Justice McLean, who had written the opinion of the Court in the basic case, wrote a long dissenting opinion in which neither of his colleagues expressed full concurrence. He restated evidence to show that the bridge had been found to obstruct navigation and was therefore a nuisance. He contended that nuisance was a matter of fact, and that fact could not be changed by an act of Congress. Continuing to regard commerce as virtually synonomous with navigation and exclusive of land transportation, he seemed to treat the power of Congress as limited to prevention of obstructions.[59] If Congress could build a bridge over a navigable stream it could construct a railroad or a turnpike as it saw fit. The settled opinion was now against the existence of this power. He admitted that the states had the power to bridge navigable streams but contended that the power must always be exercised so as to avoid material obstruction to navigation.

Justice Wayne, concurring with "many of the views" expressed by Justice McLean, promised later to give his opinion fully on the action of the Court and of Congress in the case—a promise that was never fulfilled. He knew of no power in Congress to interfere with the judgment of the Court, whether in terms of the commerce or the postal power. His brief statement indicated obvious discomfort. His biographer remarks that this was "one of those rare occasions when Wayne failed to correlate constitutional power with the necessities of a fast growing nation."[60] Justice Grier concurred with Justice McLean that Congress could not annul or vacate any decree of the Court. He found the assumption of the power without precedent, and as a precedent for the future, dangerous.

Other issues in the case than that of the commerce power caused difficulty and divisions along different lines, and may have been responsible for the delay in handing down the decision. Although the arguments of counsel were but sketchily reported, it was apparently hotly contended on one hand that Justice Grier had usurped power in June, 1854, in issuing an injunction against rebuilding the bridge, and on the

---

[59] "It may, under this power, declare that no bridge shall be built which shall be an obstruction to the use of a navigable water. And this, it would seem, is as far as the com-mercial power by Congress can be exercised." *Ibid.,* 442.

[60] Alexander A. Lawrence, *James Moore Wayne, Southern Unionist,* 101.

other hand that attachments should issue against those who disobeyed the injunction. The majority opinion said nothing about the power of a single judge to issue an injunction in the name of the Court, but merely ordered the injunction dissolved in the light of the statute legalizing the bridge. Justice Grier concurred "with the majority of this court, that in cases where this court has original jurisdiction, an interlocutory or preliminary injunction may be awarded in vacation, by any judge of the court."[61] Quite naturally he disagreed with the majority in "declining to punish a wanton contempt of the process of the court."[62] On this point he had the concurrence of Justices Wayne, Nelson, and Curtis.

It was Justice Daniel who provided the stormy part of the two-and-a-half-hour session[63] required for delivery of the opinions. He agreed, of course, with the majority that the motion for the attachment should be denied and the injunction dissolved, but he also took occasion to denounce Justice Grier's participation in the case from the very beginning. He could not comprehend by what warrant a circuit judge could issue at chambers an interlocutory order relative to rights of person and property beyond the bounds of his jurisdiction and transfer the controversy to the Supreme Court. Still more irregular was the issuing of an injunction at chambers to control persons and property beyond his legitimate power, and out of harmony with a decree already issued by the Supreme Court:

> According to my interpretation of the Constitution of the United States, the Supreme Court is a distinct, aggregate, collective body—one which can act collectively, and in term or in united session only. It cannot delegate its functions, nor can it impose its duties upon any number of the body less than a quorum, constituted of a majority of its members; much less can a single judge be clothed with its joint powers, to be wielded by him at any time or in any place, or to any extent to which his individual discretion may point.[64]

The case came once more before the Court when the bridge company, having its legality now established, sought to escape the costs of litigation which had been assessed against it. The Court denied the motion for review, saying, "There must be an end of litigation."[65]

For all the time and effort that went into the argument and decision of the several cases involving the Wheeling Bridge, the cases settled very little beyond the fact that this bridge, specifically protected by

---

[61] 18 How. 449.
[62] *Ibid.*
[63] For reference to the length of time required see "Decision in the Wheeling Bridge Case," *Pittsburgh*

L.J., 4:428, 1856.
[64] 18 How. 452.
[65] Pennsylvania v. Wheeling and Belmont Bridge Co., 18 How. 460, 463 (1856).

a federal statute, was to remain in use where it was built. Although the cases were cited as precedents in various other cases involving other bridges across other streams, the facts always differed enough to leave issues in doubt. With the expansion of highways and railroads all over the country more and more bridges were built across navigable streams. Although their construction as drawbridges became virtually the rule rather than the exception, drawbridges caused delays and therefore impeded navigation. Merchant ships, jealous of expanding railroads, fought bridge construction wherever possible. As the Wheeling Bridge involved rivalry between Wheeling and Pittsburgh and between Philadelphia and Baltimore and other cities to the south, so other bridges involved other regional conflicts. Supreme Court Justices on circuit, and district judges sitting either in District or Circuit courts, found themselves involved in case after case of this kind.

In 1855, for example, while final action with respect to the Wheeling Bridge still remained to be taken, Justice McLean had to decide a Circuit Court case with respect to a railroad bridge crossing the Mississippi at Rock Island, almost due west of Chicago. The bridge, if constructed at that point, would promote east-west trade, in competition with trade up and down the Mississippi—thereby involving North-South rivalries. On the basis of legal entanglements arising from the earlier status of Rock Island as a federal military post, the Attorney General of the United States brought suit to enjoin construction of the bridge across the island pursuant to a charter granted by Illinois. Justice McLean found no violation of any federal right, and beyond that he discussed the commerce issue involved. While reasserting his old position that "Congress has the exclusive power, under the constitution, to regulate commerce between two or more states,"[66] he held that the state-authorized bridge, with draws on both sides of the island, did not sufficiently endanger or restrain interstate commerce to call for judicial interference. If the hidden parties to the suit were Southern interests rather than the United States, they suffered defeat.

The controversy was renewed in 1856 when the steamboat *Effie Afton* collided with one of the bridge piers, overturned stoves and caught fire, and was destroyed along with the draw of the bridge. The boat owners brought suit for damages, the bill of complaint averring that the bridge was a permanent obstruction to navigation. The suit was brought in the Circuit Court before Justice McLean, with Abraham Lincoln as one of the distinguished counsel defending the bridge company.[67] The trial, held in September, 1857, demonstrated the intensity

---

[66] United States v. Railroad Bridge Co., 27 Fed. Cas. 686, 688 (No. 16114) (C.C.N.D. Ill. 1855).

[67] For a summary account see Albert J. Beveridge, *Abraham Lincoln, 1809–1858*, 598–605.

of rivalry between regions and between kinds of traffic. The burning of the bridge, said Lincoln, had caused shouting and ringing of bells among steamboat men, a jubilee greater than the excitement that followed an election.[68] He did not ask for the obstruction of the river but contended that traffic must be permitted to move east and west as well as north and south. Justice McLean's long charge to the jury made clear that the decision of the jury should depend in large part on facts concerning currents and eddies in the vicinity of the piers.[69] The jurors divided irreconcilably, however, and their dismissal marked another victory for Chicago and the railroad interests.[70]

In the United States Circuit Court in Pennsylvania and in New Jersey Justice Grier had to decide cases involving the bridging of navigable streams carrying interstate and foreign commerce but without the regional implications of those in the West. He issued an injunction against the construction of a bridge about a mile above the mouth of the Schuylkill River and below the port of Philadelphia, even though the bridge was to be equipped with a draw for the passage of river traffic. He held that "In every investigation of this kind the question is relative, not absolute. Whether a certain erection be a nuisance must depend upon the peculiar circumstances of each case,—when the trade of the channel is of great amount and importance and that across it trifling, the same rule cannot apply, as to a case where the conditions are contrary."[71]

By this decision Justice Grier protected the river commerce of Philadelphia much as in the *Wheeling Bridge* case the Supreme Court had protected the river commerce of Pittsburgh until Congress intervened. Yet when the scene of litigation shifted to New Jersey, Justice Grier's action well illustrated his point that decisions in this field must turn on the peculiar circumstances of each case. The New Jersey cases involved the construction of certain bridges in the vicinity of Newark. Here Justice Grier looked to the peculiar merits of railroad transportation. As against an earlier time,

Newark has become a great city. Locomotives moving at a velocity of forty miles an hour, which were then considered but the dream of the projectors, are now established facts. Curves have given way to straight lines, and the notion that railroad cars darting through the

---

[68] *Ibid.*, 603.

[69] See *Chicago Daily Democratic Press*, Sept. 25, 1857.

[70] It is said, however, that in 1859 the bridge was declared an obstruction to navigation, to be rebuilt after the Civil War in such a way as to reduce the obstruction. Louis C. Hunter,

Steamboats on the Western Rivers, 594. See also Ernest Howard Ruffner, *Practice of Improvement of the Non-Tidal Rivers of the United States*, 15, 46.

[71] Devoe v. Penrose Ferry Co., 7 Fed. Cas. 566, 568 (No. 3845) (C.C.E.D. Pa. 1854).

more frequented streets of a city are neither a convenience nor a benefit, has become obsolete. The conflicting interests which inexperience and ignorance had originally produced, need no longer be propitiated for the sake of peace.[72]

Here he thought the question of the public interest was best determined by the people of New Jersey, and the people had spoken through their legislature. As for the commerce question, he thought the case governed by *Willson v. Black Bird Creek Marsh Co.* The New Jersey cases marked a drift even from Justice Grier's own earlier interpretation of the *Wheeling Bridge* case, narrowing the scope of federal equity powers to curb obstructions to navigation by bridges when constructed by state authority. The facts and the legal issues were highly complex, and powerful economic interests were involved. The cases were appealed to the Supreme Court. A long array of counsel protected the interests of the railroads, including William H. Seward and Joseph P. Bradley, whom President Grant would appoint to the Supreme Court. In the Supreme Court the litigants had trouble getting the cases heard because of the periodic absences of Justices and a series of vacancies. Early in January, 1860, it was announced that the cases had been postponed until February because of the illnesses of Judges Taney and Daniel.[73] In February they were again postponed. They were finally called up for argument in December, 1860, in spite of the fact that the intervening death of Justice Daniel had left a vacancy, the *New York Tribune* noting that they had "enlisted some of the ablest talent in the country."[74] The arguments took place over five days—and the Supreme Court proved to be evenly divided! The Court adjourned for the term without announcing a decision. Justice McLean died in April, 1861, and Justice Campbell resigned. The Court was apparently still evenly divided. Finally, on January 27, 1862, it affirmed the decision of the Circuit Court by virtue of its equal decision.[75]

Justice Nelson had a similar case on circuit, involving the construction of a bridge across the Hudson River at Albany. In 1857 he issued a preliminary injunction.[76] When in 1859 argument was heard on making the decree permanent, the long array of counsel included Reverdy Johnson for the bridge company and William H. Seward for the steamboat interests. The arguments were heard by Justice Nelson and United States District Judge Nathan Kelsey Hall. Justice Nelson

---

[72] Milnor v. New Jersey Railroad, 17 Fed. Cas. 412, 423 (No. 9620) (C.C.D. N.J. 1857).

[73] *New York Tribune*, Jan. 2, 1860.

[74] *New York Tribune*, Dec. 8, 1860.

[75] Milnor v. New Jersey Railroad, 16 L. Ed. 799 (1862). (Not reported in Howard's *Reports.*)

[76] Silliman v. Hudson River Bridge Co., 22 Fed. Cas. 116 (No. 12851) (C.C.N.D. N.Y. 1857).

favored the decree and Judge Hall opposed, and the case went to the Supreme Court on certificate of division of opinion.[77] The case was argued in the Supreme Court at the same time as the New Jersey case and was decided at the same time, again by an equally divided Court.[78] Ironically, it was argued again in January, 1865, after there had been substantial changes in Court personnel, and was again decided by an equally divided Court.[79]

The equal division of the Court in the later bridge cases suggests the broad scope of unsettlement in interpretation of the Commerce Clause at the end of the Taney period. It can be said in summary that at the beginning of the period the Court was concerned both with the specific and often highly charged facts of commercial conflicts and with matters of constitutional theory such as the exclusiveness and the non-exclusiveness of Congressional power and the relation of the commerce power of Congress to the police powers of the states. The constitutional issues were stated again and again in highly diverse situations, with vast differences of opinion concerning them. In the *Cooley* case in 1852 a majority of the Court seemed to agree on a matter of principle—that some interstate and foreign commerce was essentially local in character and could be regulated locally in the absence of regulation by Congress, whereas some commerce was national in character and required a national rule if it was to be regulated at all, and therefore could never be regulated by the states. Only six Justices, however, seemed to concur in this statement, and it has appeared that several of them made no very deep commitment to it.

The doctrine of the *Cooley* case may have been the beginning of wisdom, but it required still more appreciation of questions of degree, questions of the extent of local need measured against the effects of local laws on interstate commerce. The cases themselves, as well as the history of the country, reflect a recession in the comparative importance of river and canal transportation with the expansion of long lines and networks of railroads. Constitutional law had to be stated in the light of the evolving pattern of economic life. The Court was striving to deal with this evolution in a sensible way, without having itself evolved constitutional principles sufficiently sensitive for the task.

---

[77] Silliman v. Hudson River Bridge Co., 22 Fed. Cas. 120 (No. 12852) (C.C.N.D. N.Y. 1859).

[78] Silliman v. Hudson River Bridge Co., 1 Black 582 (1862).

[79] Coleman v. Hudson River Bridge Co., 2 Wall. 403 (U.S. 1865).

CHAPTER XVIII

Admiralty and Maritime Jurisdiction

W HILE IT IS TRUE that during the Taney period Congress exercised but little of its constitutional power to regulate commerce among the several states, the federal judiciary was extensively involved in commercial controversies through exercise of its admiralty and maritime jurisdiction. In a provision in Article III which was quite independent of the Commerce Clause in Article I, the Constitution provided that the judicial power of the United States should extend "to all cases of admiralty and maritime jurisdiction." Although this area of jurisdiction tended to merge with that originating in the Commerce Clause, and the two areas tended at times to be confused with each other, admiralty and maritime jurisdiction had its own independent source and its own independent history, the history including a prolonged struggle for power and prestige between the common law and admiralty courts of England. Pursuant to the Admiralty Clause, the Judiciary Act of 1789 gave to the United States District Courts exclusive original cognizance of all civil causes of admiralty and maritime jurisdiction,[1] with appellate jurisdiction in the Circuit Courts where the amount involved was more than three hundred dollars,[2] and further appellate jurisdiction in the Supreme Court where the amount involved was more than two thousand dollars.[3]

Although the statute reserved to litigants the right to a common law remedy where the common law was competent to give it,[4] and thereby left to state courts a measure of jurisdiction affecting water transportation, admiralty jurisdiction as such was taken away from state courts and given to the federal courts. In this area, therefore, the national government was in effect empowered to bring about through its courts the uniform development of a body of admiralty law. Yet here,

---

[1] 1 Stat. 77.　　[2] 1 Stat. 83.　　[3] 1 Stat. 84.　　[4] 1 Stat. 77.

as in other areas, defenders of the rights of the states deplored the curtailment of state power and criticized Acts of Congress and judicial interpretations which implemented and threatened to expand the federal prerogative.

During the Taney period the controversies in admiralty which reached the Supreme Court involved not only the substantive law but also the territorial extent of admiralty jurisdiction—whether it was limited to areas within the ebb and flow of the tide, as held in English and early American cases; and, beyond that, whether even on tidewater admiralty jurisdiction was debarred from arms of the sea extending inland and must there give way to state laws and to the jurisdiction of the state courts. During this period the admiralty decisions of the Supreme Court and of the lower federal courts were often inconsistent one with another and with earlier decisions during the Marshall period. In a comprehensive survey of admiralty cases published in 1871, Richard Henry Dana, Jr., remarked:

> After seventy years of baffling winds and cross currents in the region of admiralty jurisdiction, the Supreme Court of the United States has sailed out into deep water. Before this was accomplished, principles were affirmed, disaffirmed, and re-affirmed, many decisions overruled, a good deal of reasoning corrected, and numerous dicta retracted.[5]

Involved particularly in the controversies were five of the Justices: Story, Taney, Daniel, Campbell, and Nelson. Story adhered to a long-held position that admiralty jurisdiction stopped with the ebb and flow of the tide, but he drafted, seemingly on the basis of the Commerce Clause, a statute to give jurisdiction over inland commerce largely according to the forms of admiralty. Taney spoke for the Court in shifting the constitutional base of Story's statute, overruled decisions on which Story had relied, and extended admiralty jurisdiction to navigable lakes and rivers. Daniel fought relentlessly against every move that might be interpreted as an extension of admiralty jurisdiction at the expense of the powers of the states. Campbell also defended the rights of the states and, with his impressive legal scholarship, attacked positions taken as a result of Story's leadership. Nelson accepted the extension of admiralty jurisdiction to freshwater areas, but at first succeeded and then failed in preventing its exercise where the commerce took place only within one state. He eventually failed, in other words, in his effort to establish the boundary of admiralty jurisdiction at the line which marked the

---

[5] [Richard Henry Dana, Jr.], "History of Admiralty Jurisdiction in the Supreme Court of the United States," *Am. L. Rev.*, 5:581, 1871.

periphery of the federal commerce power. These positions suggest the nature of the issues to be canvassed.[6]

It was said of Justice Story that "if a bucket of water were brought into his court with a corn cob floating in it, he would at once extend the admiralty jurisdiction of the United States over it."[7] If the comment was apt, it is nevertheless true that for many years he played a leading part in preventing the extension of admiralty jurisdiction to freshwater lakes and rivers. In 1825, in *The Thomas Jefferson*,[8] he had spoken for a unanimous Supreme Court in holding that admiralty jurisdiction did not support a suit for recovery of wages earned on a voyage on the Missouri River. Admiralty, he held, could exercise jurisdiction in suits for seamen's wages only when the services were performed "upon the sea, or upon waters within the ebb and flow of the tide."[9] It thus appeared that the thousands of miles of river and lake traffic moving on the internal waters of the United States would have to find protection not in admiralty law as applied exclusively by federal courts but in meager federal legislation based on the Commerce Clause and in the common law and statutes of the several states.

Significantly, however, Justice Story did include in the opinion a comment which may have derived from the thinking of the Supreme Court a year earlier when it decided the famous commerce case of *Gibbons v. Ogden*.[10] He remarked:

> Whether, under the power to regulate commerce between the states, Congress may not extend the remedy, by the summary process of admiralty, to the case of voyages on the western waters, it is unnecessary for us to consider. If the public inconvenience, from the want of a process of an analogous nature, shall be extensively felt, the attention of the legislature will doubtless be drawn to the subject.[11]

This suggestion of a remedy via the Commerce Clause but with process like unto that of admiralty was to lie fallow for some twenty years, before Story himself turned to the drafting of a bill for Congressional action.

---

[6] For summary of many of the events herein discussed see, in addition to the Dana article cited above, "From Judicial Grant to Legislative Power: The Admiralty Clause in the Nineteenth Century," *Harv. L. Rev.*, 67: 1214–37, 1954, and materials therein cited. See also George C. Sprague, "The Extension of Admiralty Jurisdiction and the Growth of the Sub- stantive Maritime Law in the United States Since 1835," *Law: A Century of Progress*, 3:294–341, 1937.

[7] "Extension of Federal Jurisdiction Over State Canals," *Am. L. Rev.*, 37:911–16, 1903.

[8] 10 Wheat. 428.

[9] *Ibid.*, 429.

[10] 9 Wheat. 1.

[11] 10 Wheat. 430.

When in 1837 Chief Justice Taney first presided over the Supreme Court, the precedent in the case of *The Thomas Jefferson* was still in good standing. It had been discussed in a case decided in 1833, but had not been effectively challenged. At this earlier date the Court had upheld the exercise of admiralty jurisdiction at New Orleans, but it had done so only upon a finding that the waters of the Mississippi were appreciably affected by the tide.[12] At the 1837 term Justice Story, in a case, *Steamboat Orleans v. Phoebus*,[13] in which the substantive issues are not here important, restated for a unanimous Court the jurisdictional point made in *The Thomas Jefferson*. Apart from this restatement the case is noteworthy in the history of the Court only on two grounds. One was the roster of counsel. Present on one side was John Catron, a husky and energetic lawyer from Nashville, who was here making his first appearance (or one of his first two appearances at about the same time) before the Court of which within a few weeks he was to become a member. One of the two victorious opposing counsel was John J. Crittenden of Kentucky, already distinguished in Congress and at the bar and yet to win greater distinction, whom Catron a few weeks later was to accuse of having forgotten his Blackstone and being too old to declaim. The other opposing counsel was Samuel F. Vinton of Ohio, who in Congress later became a leading advocate of extending admiralty jurisdiction to freshwater lakes and rivers.[14]

Since the doctrine of *The Thomas Jefferson* as to the outer limits of admiralty jurisdiction was to be abandoned after much controversy even though unanimously reasserted in the *Phoebus* case in 1837, the other important aspect of the case was the discussion by Crittenden and Vinton of the public policy issues involved in the delimitation of admiralty jurisdiction. They stressed the disadvantages of the exercise of admiralty jurisdiction with respect to a vessel having New Orleans as the southern terminal point of its voyages, but traveling northward over diverse river waters unaffected by the tide for as much as two thousand miles. If admiralty reached any part of such a voyage, they contended, it reached to all of it. The effect would be to exclude common law jurisdiction with respect to such navigation, and with respect to contracts connected with navigation, only the courts of the Union could be called upon for relief. Yet because federal courts were spaced far apart and some of them were located at great distances from the navigable fresh waters on which disputes arose, the settlement of controversies through admiralty courts would be far more difficult than in the state courts.

---

[12] Peyroux v. Howard, 7 Pet. 324 (1833).
[13] 11 Pet. 175 (1837).

[14] See Daniel Webster to S. F. Vinton, Feb. 19, 1844, House of Representatives Papers.

Moreover, it was argued, there was less need for admiralty in the interior, since there, in contrast with vessels on the seas, the vessels and the owners could always be found. Although suits *in rem*, that is, suits brought against vessels themselves as distinguished from those brought against the owners *in personam*, were not part of the procedures of the common law, counsel assumed that such procedures could be provided for by state statutes and could be carried out in state courts. In some states, counsel noted, liens similar to those of admiralty had already been given by statute, and this procedure could be resorted to universally.[15] As they saw it, practically everything that could be done in the admiralty courts of the federal government with respect to maritime transactions could be done by the courts of the states with respect to transactions on interior waters.

At all events, the expansion of interior and exterior navigation in the years following the depression of 1837 forced the rethinking of many matters. Business in the federal admiralty courts and in the state courts rapidly increased and revealed conflict and disorder. To eliminate unnecessary diversity in the handling of admiralty cases in the federal courts, Congress in 1842 asked the Supreme Court to adopt a series of uniform rules of procedure.[16] The rules adopted in 1845, included in the third volume of Howard's reports, were said to have been the work largely of Justice Story,[17] in whose circuit the largest body of admiralty cases arose. Through use of the rules and the basic body of admiralty principles a much higher degree of order was achieved in the federal courts than in state courts applying diverse state laws. As a result, busi-

---

[15] Uncertainty prevailed both as to the scope of admiralty jurisdiction and as to the substance of maritime law. With respect to proceedings in rem on waters over which admiralty courts may exercise jurisdiction, state statutes may give to state courts jurisdiction to enforce liens against vessels for nonmaritime torts, as in the instance of a collision between a vessel and a supporting pier of a bridge. Such jurisdiction cannot be given, on the other hand, in connection with controversies which are genuinely maritime. Martin v. West, 222 U.S. 1911. The latter limitation is relevant, however, only where admiralty jurisdiction may be found to exist. Crittenden and Vinton were concerned with commerce on waters where, as of 1837, according to the 1825 decision in the *Thomas Jefferson*, admiralty jurisdiction could not be exercised. Since there was no jurisdiction in admiralty, admiralty placed no limitations on the state legislatures in respect of in rem procedures in state courts. While it had been held that admiralty jurisdiction might be exercised concerning maritime controversies on the tidewater Mississippi at New Orleans, the Court found that the controversies involved in the *Phoebus* case had to do with a vessel operating primarily on fresh water, so that it was not engaged in maritime trade or navigation.

[16] 17 Stat. 516, 518.

[17] See Judge H. H. Leavitt in Ward v. *The Ogdensburgh*, 29 Fed. Cas. 199, 206 (No. 17158) (D.C.D. Ohio 1853).

nessmen making use of Western lakes and rivers felt aggrieved at their disadvantage by contrast with those engaged in interstate commerce on the Atlantic Ocean who had the right of resort to admiralty. Shipowners against whom claims were asserted often lived in distant states and were hard to hale into court. Since a navigable stream might run through and between many states, the rightful state jurisdiction was often difficult to determine. Furthermore, if perchance shipowners at times welcomed obscurity as to jurisdiction to escape enforcement of contracts against them, in cases of collision on navigable waters the litigants on at least one side of each controversy wished to know definitely of a place of redress. In addition, whatever their capacity to do so, many of the states had failed to supplement the common law by authorizing proceedings *in rem* against vessels themselves.

Although interest in the subject was developing on the Western rivers and on the Great Lakes at the same time, it was pressure from the lake area that brought Congressional action. A typical petition to Congress read as follows:

> Your petitioners, residents of the City of Chicago, and of the State of Illinois bordering on Lake Michigan would respectfully represent, that much inconvenience has been experienced by those engaged in the commerce, shipping and navigation of the Northern Chain of Lakes, in consequence of the want of any general laws and provisions of Congress regulating the same and such matters therewith connected which ordinarily come with maritime jurisdiction. Your petitioners would represent that the navigation of the Lakes, the nature of the perils and the length of the voyages thereon, the character of the shipping and the contracts growing out of such navigation, are similar, in most respects, to those of the high seas, and especially, to those of the coasting trade, now under the regulations and subject to the maritime law of the United States.
>
> Your petitioners would therefore pray that the commerce, shipping and navigation of the Northern Chain of Lakes, from Lake Ontario to Lake Michigan inclusive, and the matters therewith connected may be embraced under the general provisions of the United States on such subjects, so far as the same are applicable, or under suitable maritime provisions and that they may be placed under and regulated by the maritime law of the United States.[18]

A petition submitted from Detroit, said to be signed by "the principal vessel men, vessel masters, forwarders, merchants, landholders & lawyers of Detroit, as well as by the United States Dist. Attorney, Mar-

---

[18] Petition dated Dec. 8, 1843, House of Representatives Papers. An identical petition was presented by citizens of St. Joseph, Michigan.

shall, Collector & Grand Jury in their official capacity,"[19] was even more explicit as to the need. It spoke of the inconvenience to commerce and navigation on the Great Lakes "from the want of a certain and defined legal jurisdiction over civil controversies, offenses and crimes." It stated:

> The line through the middle of the lakes separates the territories and dominions of the United States from those of Great Britain; and this increases the embarrassments and difficulties with regard to jurisdiction and the operation of law upon these inland seas.[20]

Citizens of Buffalo, New York, calling attention to their residence on the American border of Lake Erie, and no doubt concerned with expansion of the traffic which the Erie Canal had made possible, filed a similar petition.[21]

At this stage the sequence of events becomes unclear. In April 1844 Timothy Walker of Cincinnati published in his *Western Law Journal* a statement that Justice McKinley, on his way down the Ohio to perform his circuit duties, had reported the drafting of a bill to extend admiralty jurisdiction. As Walker printed the statement it was that "Mr. Justice Story, at the request of one of the judiciary committees of Congress, has prepared a bill for extending admiralty jurisdiction over all the lakes and rivers of the U. States."[22] Walker hoped that the bill would pass and that the same learned judge would prepare another bill, based on the commerce power, which would render uniform throughout the country the law of commerce as well as of navigation.[23] Justice Daniel, who clearly would not have approved of any act to extend admiralty jurisdiction, said thirteen years after the act was passed that Justice Story "has the reputation of being the author of the Act."[24] At the same time Justice Campbell, who had not been a member of the Court when the bill was drafted, stated that the act was passed "upon an application of a portion of this Court,"[25] and spoke indignantly of "this interference by the Legislative Department of the Government, elicited, too, by the Judiciary Department."[26]

---

[19] John Chester to Augustus S. Porter, Jan. 20, 1844, Senate Papers.

[20] Filed with the Chester letter, *ibid.*

[21] Referred to Committee Mar. 5, 1844, House of Representatives Papers.

[22] "Admiralty Jurisdiction Over Our Lakes and Rivers," *West. L.J.*, 1:336, 1844.

[23] Walker later reported that Story's bill had been submitted to and had received the sanction of all the members of the Supreme Court who were in Washington at the time of the drafting. Timothy Walker, "The Project of Extending Admiralty Jurisdiction Over the Lakes and Rivers," *West. L.J.*, 2:563, 1845.

[24] Jackson v. Steamboat *Magnolia*, 20 How. 296, 342 (1858).

[25] *Ibid.*, 315.

[26] *Ibid.*, 316.

We know that on May 24, 1844, Stephen A. Douglas, a new member of the House of Representatives from Illinois who was interested in building up the commerce of his state, reported a bill from the House Committee on the Judiciary. The bill, H.R. 380, was entitled "An Act extending the jurisdiction of the District Courts to certain cases upon the Lakes and navigable waters leading into or connecting the same."[27] The bill was read twice and referred to the Committee of the Whole House, but no further action was taken. At the following session, Henry Johnson of Louisiana introduced in the Senate S. 36, which was evidently identical with H.R. 380. The Senate Committee on the Judiciary reported the bill after making some minor changes to restrict the scope more definitely to the lakes and the connecting waters, and the bill was passed almost or entirely without debate, while the country was concerned with such major issues as the annexation of Texas and relations with Mexico. S. 36 passed the House also, and was signed by President Tyler on February 26, just before the end of his term. It was passed with the title, "An Act extending the jurisdiction of the district courts to certain cases, upon the lakes and navigable waters connecting the same."[28]

In drafting the bill, Justice Story failed to indicate whether it was to mark an exercise of the commerce power or whether it was based on the Admiralty Clause. It provided that in matters of tort and contract the remedies, forms of process, and modes of proceeding should be *the same as* those that were or might be used in cases of admiralty and maritime jurisdiction. It provided that the maritime law of the United States should constitute the rule of decision. But it nowhere stated that the Admiralty Clause was the source of power. Furthermore, the extended jurisdiction was limited to vessels of twenty tons or more licensed in the coasting trade and engaged in commerce and navigation "between ports and places in different States and Territories upon the lakes and navigable waters connecting said lakes." The restriction to interstate commerce seemed to imply a basis in the commerce power, but did not so assert. Again, while the statute provided that the maritime law of the United States should constitute the rule of decision, it also provided for saving "to the parties the right of trial by jury of all facts put in issue in such suits." Jury trial had its rootage not in admiralty but in the common law. Its absence from admiralty, indeed, was one of the prime bases for protest against the expansion of admiralty jurisdiction. It might therefore be suggested either that the inclusion of the provision for jury trial marked an attempt to make admiralty

---

[27] H. R. See *Journal of the House of Representatives*, 28th Cong., 1st Sess. 966, and the text of the bill, House of Representatives Papers.
[28] 5 Stat. 726.

jurisdiction less unpalatable to its critics or that it was evidence of action on the basis of the Commerce Clause where its use would be appropriate.

There may be a clue to Justice Story's thinking in a letter written by Daniel Webster, evidently in reply to an inquiry about the jury trial provision from Samuel Finley Vinton, a Representative from Ohio:

> I suppose the provision for trial by Jury may save this Bill from Constitutional objection. Our existing laws, are, in one respect quite questionable; that is, in subjecting to trial, without Jury, goods seized on any waters navigable from the sea for vessels of 10 tons &c. There is no pretense to say that admiralty jurisdiction extends so far. In England seizures for violation of the revenue laws are always tried by Jury. But our laws have been [with]out it from the beginning.[29]

Webster seems to have believed at this time that admiralty jurisdiction extended only to the sea, and not also inland on "waters navigable from the sea." In any event, it seems reasonable that for him as the advocate in *Gibbons v. Ogden* of sweeping power under the Commerce Clause, the latter clause would seem a most appropriate source of power for the regulation here provided for. On matters of this kind he and Chief Justice Marshall and Justice Story had been wont to think alike. It therefore seems probable that Justice Story as a draftsman had his own eye on the Commerce Clause, as suggested in his opinion in *The Thomas Jefferson*, while so phrasing the statute that persons opposed to expansion of the commerce power and not averse to the inland extension of admiralty could regard the Admiralty Clause as the source of power. There is unfortunately no record of the discussion among the Justices of the Court when Story submitted his draft for their consideration. When the act was passed Justice Story was about half a year from the time of his death. Formal judicial sanction would have to be worked out without his aid and counsel.

Some Westerners with interest in river transportation as well as transportation on the Great Lakes were under the impression that Justice Story's bill extended jurisdiction both to the rivers and to the lakes. There was interest in the matter quite apart from the interests of shippers. The extension of admiralty jurisdiction would mean more business for the United States District Courts, and perhaps smaller districts and higher salaries. William Miner, clerk of the United States District Court in Columbus, Ohio, wrote to Justice McLean saying that

---

[29] Daniel Webster to Samuel Finley Vinton, Feb. 19, 1844, House of Representatives Papers.

"if the Admiralty Bill passed I supposed the State would be districted as a matter of course."[30] United States District Judge H. H. Leavitt, who had all of Ohio as his district, was also interested in the extension of admiralty jurisdiction and in the division of his state into two districts, with himself as the judge of the southern district. He, too, had been of the impression that the Story bill would extend jurisdiction to navigable rivers as well as to lakes, with the consequent addition of a great deal of business from the Ohio River, which lined both the eastern and southern border of his state. When he saw the new statute he wrote to Justice McLean about it, expressing the belief that it extended only to lakes and seeking verification: "If I am wrong in this view of the law, will you have the goodness to set me right? Having been at Washington, when the act was under discussion, you are no doubt apprized of the intention of Congress in its passage."[31]

The people who wanted the extension of admiralty jurisdiction over river traffic did not give up easily. From 1846 through 1850, members of Congress from various Western states introduced memorials, resolutions, and bills asking the extension of admiralty jurisdiction to all navigable waters of the United States. William Miner called Justice McLean's attention to a bill introduced by Senator Charles S. Morehead of Kentucky. He thought Morehead might consult the Justice about it. "I hope the Supreme Court will before they adjourn establish for the Bill. It would be a great saving and prevent great abuse and give uniformity in the Taxation of costs, save the accounting officers much trouble."[32] Still interested in the division of Ohio into two judicial districts, Miner wrote about it to Salmon P. Chase, then United States Senator from Ohio. He asked about the prospect of extension of admiralty jurisdiction, and added:

> I understood from Judge McLean that there was doubt among the Justices of the Supreme Court as to the power of Congress to extend the Jurisdiction, that the Bill giving the Jurisdiction on the Lakes was drawn up by Judge Story and submitted to his associates and that they approved of it, and that the Bill as originally proposed gave the Jurisdiction over the Rivers but was amended in the House by adding between the words Lakes and Rivers *"connecting the same."*[33]

If Justice Story did include a provision for river jurisdiction in his original draft, the change was made before the formal introduction of the bill by Stephen A. Douglas, but such an earlier change may well

---

[30] William Miner to John McLean, Jan. 29, 1845, McLean Papers.
[31] H. H. Leavitt to John McLean, Mar. 19, 1845, McLean Papers.

[32] William Miner to John McLean, Dec. 25, 1847, McLean Papers.
[33] William Miner to Salmon P. Chase, June 2, 1850, Chase Papers.

have been made. In any event, Justice McLean was much interested in the extension of jurisdiction. He, too, wrote to Chase about the matter, saying:

> I am told that the Committee of the Senate have reported that it would be unconstitutional. The courts have thought otherwise as to the law which has been extended over the Lakes and the rivers falling into them. We wanted nothing more than the extension of the same law. I suppose there can be no doubt of the constitutionality of this law. A jury is given which obviates all possible objection to the law.[34]

Nevertheless the bills for the extension of admiralty jurisdiction to freshwater rivers failed to make any headway in Congress. In addition to concern about constitutional questions, Southern members were by this time suspicious of any steps that might add to the power of the federal government. Significantly, it was A. P. Butler of South Carolina who in February, 1850, submitted the Senate Judiciary Committee report against enactment of the proposed measure, doing so not only on grounds of constitutionality but of expediency as well.[35]

It now seemed clear that advocates of the extension of admiralty jurisdiction to the rivers of the country could expect no help from Congress. Their remaining resort was to the courts.

Since a decision was not reached by the Court on the Act of 1845 until 1852, it is well to drop back to analyze the developing American attitude toward admiralty jurisdiction and to trace certain cases in terms of which the courts shaped their thinking. The vitality of thinking was suggested in 1838 by George T. Curtis in the preface to a digest of American admiralty cases, where he remarked:

> That the Admiralty Jurisdiction will not only become more and more important, in this country, upon the whole extent of the Atlantic coast, but that it will ultimately be extended over the inland waters of the West, is perhaps more than a mere speculation.[36]

Curtis steered away from the constitutional question, but neither judges nor commentators were long able to avoid it. Straws in the wind were indicated by the same author in 1841 when he noted the recent enactment in England of a statute enlarging admiralty jurisdiction in that

---

[34] John McLean to Salmon P. Chase, July 18, 1850, Chase Papers.

[35] Senate Report No. 48, 31st Cong., 1st Sess. See also House Report No. 72, 31st Cong., 1st Sess.

[36] George Ticknor Curtis, *A Digest of Cases Adjudicated in the Courts of Admiralty and in the High Court of Admiralty in England*, viii.

country to an extent that would have been horrifying to Lord Coke,[37] who in English legal history was the prime defender of the common law against the encroachments of admiralty:

> If we compare this outline of jurisdiction with that held and practised in this country, we shall find no material difference; and it affords no small compliment, in effect, to the learning of our judges, who have affirmed that the admiralty jurisdiction formerly held in England, and rightfully belonging to us, covered the ground which parliament have now impliedly affirmed it had all along covered, but for the encroachments of the courts of law.[38]

In Cincinnati Timothy Walker, editor of the *Western Law Journal*, urged that the internal commerce and navigation of the country were of at least equal importance with the external, and were equally entitled to the benefits of admiralty jurisdiction. The principles of admiralty law, he urged, had a universality which belonged to no other branch of the law. They embodied the wisdom of all ages and nations in the field of their operation. This embodiment was in sharp contrast with the diversity of state laws and of the decisions of state courts—and it was to be noted that on a voyage from Pittsburgh to New Orleans a steamboat passed through eleven distinct jurisdictions, administering perhaps as many distinct systems of law. He noted, "The remedies provided by the admiralty are more simple, less technical, more equitable, and more efficient, than those of the common law."[39]

Yet there were also objections, as Walker noted, including the expansion of the power of the federal judiciary, to which some people were opposed, and resort to a system of practice with which common law lawyers were not generally familiar. The widely popular *Democratic Review*, much more critical of the federal courts than was the *Western Law Journal*, stressed also the escape from the requirement of jury trial by resort to admiralty. It believed that the admiralty courts had from the beginning usurped the decision of questions which were not for them to decide, and that the usurpation had now become the settled law of the courts.[40]

This criticism by the *Democratic Review* reflected the body of attitudes of those who distrusted strength and vigor either in govern-

---

[37] See 3 and 4 Victoria, Aug. 7, 1840, Chap. 63.

[38] George Ticknor Curtis, "Enlargement of the Admiralty Jurisdiction in England," *Am. Jurist*, 24:405, 407, 1841.

[39] Timothy Walker, "The Project of Extending Admiralty Jurisdiction over the Lakes and Rivers of the United States," *West. L.J.*, 2:563, 566, 1845.

[40] "Judicial Encroachment," *Democratic Review*, 26:243, 245, 1850.

ment or in business corporations, believing in a minimum of government and in a maximum of popular participation and intervention in such government as was authorized. Furthermore, some state judiciaries distrusted admiralty jurisdiction because of the fear that it would enhance the power of the federal courts at their expense.[41] Many lawyers, judges, and commentators, however, welcomed the expansion of admiralty by judicial interpretation and by statute. A perhaps extreme example was the ecstatic approval of the *Monthly Law Reporter* in 1849 in reviewing a volume of reports of cases decided in the United States District Court for Maine, which, as might be expected, included many admiralty opinions:

> We are peculiarly gratified with the learned exposition of admiralty principles and practice contained in this volume and its predecessor, as since the passage of the act of congress of February 26, 1845, extending the jurisdiction of the district courts of the United States to cases upon the lakes and the navigable waters connecting the same, and the rapidly increasing commerce which has sprung up on our distant Pacific coast, this important branch of the law will be felt in its liberal and beneficent operations wherever the tide ebbs and flows on our almost unlimited sea-coast, or wherever upon our inland seas the white sails of our vessels or the smoke of our steamers, show that traffic and commerce administer to the convenience and necessities of civilized life. Let the foundations of this branch of our jurisprudence now be laid broad and deep, for they are to last as long as winds blow and waters flow.[42]

The increase in the number and complexity of admiralty cases meant that federal district judges had to expand their knowledge of the field. Indeed, enactment of the Act of 1845 meant that federal judges in the districts bordering on the Great Lakes had suddenly to familiarize themselves with a jurisdiction hitherto completely unfamiliar to them. There were works such as George T. Curtis' digest of cases and there were a few commentaries based largely on admiralty practice in England, but it was said that the only work commonly on the shelves of the legal profession in the United States was Dunlap's *Admiralty Practice*, a book already out of print.[43] The United States District Judge for the Northern District of New York, Alfred Conkling, therefore met a very real need when in 1848 he brought out the first edition of his *The*

---

[41] For indirect evidence on this point see the several opinions in People v. William Tyler, 7 Mich. 160 (1859), and William Tyler v. People, 8 Mich. 319 (1860).

[42] *Law Rep.*, 2:610, 1850.

[43] *Am. L.J.*, 8:276–77, 1848. Judge Conkling's work was followed by Henry Flanders, *A Treatise on Maritime Law*, and by Theophilus Parsons, *A Treatise on Maritime Law*.

Jurisdiction, Law and Practice of the Courts of the United States in Admiralty and Maritime Causes, Including Those of Quasi Admiralty Jurisdiction Arising Under the Act of February 26, 1845. The work came into widespread use, and was revised in 1857 to take into account later decisions, some of which require attention here.

In the continuing battle over the scope of admiralty jurisdiction litigants on one side were little concerned about what the scope of admiralty jurisdiction had been in England and argued that in terms of American needs the jurisdiction should be extended to all navigable waters whether or not connected with the sea. Opposing litigants contended that under the Constitution the jurisdiction was limited to what it had been in England at the time of the adoption of the Constitution and the Judiciary Act of 1789, and that such limitation excluded it not only from fresh waters but also from tidewater rivers over which jurisdiction might be exercised by the governments of the states to which the adjacent lands belonged, and even from deep-sea harbors and other projections of the sea which were to some extent land-locked. In any event, these litigants contended, admiralty jurisdiction could be exercised on land-hemmed tidewaters only by proceedings *in rem* and not *in personam*, in the light of the provisions of the statute which reserved to litigants the right to a common law remedy where the common law was competent to give it. In other words, even if injured parties could sue vessels in admiralty courts they would have to go to the courts of the states in order to sue the owners.

These jurisdictional questions were raised and heatedly argued during the early 1840s in two admiralty cases which arose in the widely separated judicial districts of eastern Louisiana and Rhode Island and which reached the Supreme Court for argument in 1847. The Louisiana case, *Waring v. Clarke*,[44] originated in a collision on the Mississippi River above New Orleans between the steamboats *De Soto* and *Luda* by which the *Luda* was sunk. In material facts the story differed little from those of many other collisions on American rivers. On the night of November 1, 1843, some ninety-five miles above New Orleans, and some two hundred miles above the mouth of the river, the *Luda* pushed her way northward against the current on a regular commercial trip to Bayou Sarah, traveling, as the law required, as close to the east bank as safety permitted. Steaming southward with the current on a similar trip between Bayou Sarah and New Orleans, and allegedly without warning lights or a proper lookout, came the *De Soto*. When the pilots sensed the imminence of a collision the *De Soto* turned in the

---

[44] 5 How. 441 (1847).

wrong direction, the boats collided, and the *Luda* went to the bottom, with two men lost. The master of the *Luda*, Thomas Clarke, brought suit in admiralty against the owners of the *De Soto*, Nathaniel S. Waring and Peter Dalman.

The suit was brought in the United States District Court in New Orleans, before Judge Theodore H. McCaleb, one of the more distinguished jurists of the South and a legal educator as well as a judge, with admiralty as one of his specialties. As a thriving port for both inland and oceangoing trade, New Orleans was deeply concerned about the applicability of the uniform principles of admiralty in river trade. The collision took place prior to the expansion of admiralty jurisdiction by the Act of 1845, which in any event applied only to the lakes and their connecting rivers. Admiralty jurisdiction in this case, therefore, would have to depend on a determination that the river at the point of collision was affected by the tide. It would depend also on whether, even on tidewater, admiralty jurisdiction could be exercised, as variously phrased, *infra corpus comitatus*—"within the body of a county"—or *infra fauces terrae*—that is, on water jutting inland where state jurisdiction was exercised on adjacent territory.

Judge McCaleb took note of Justice Story's opinion in *The Thomas Jefferson* that admiralty jurisdiction could not be exercised beyond the tidewater area, but he accepted evidence that the tide affected the level of the stream at the point of the collision, and held that the court had jurisdiction in admiralty.[45] The decision was affirmed soon afterward by the United States Circuit Court.[46]

It was while this case was on its way through the federal courts in Louisiana that Justice Story was consulting with members of Congress and at least some of his brethren about the language of a bill to expand admiralty jurisdiction. The subject undoubtedly remained prominent in the minds of the Justices while the measure was in process of enactment in 1845, and thereafter until 1847 when the case of *Waring v. Clarke* was argued and decided—the delay being attributable to the deaths of three members of the Court, Baldwin, Thompson, and Story, and the delays involved in their replacement by Grier, Nelson, and Woodbury.

In the Supreme Court the case was argued for the owners of the *De Soto* by Reverdy Johnson, whom Chief Justice Taney is said to have called the greatest lawyer in Maryland "and probably in the United

---

[45] For Judge McCaleb's opinion on the subject of jurisdiction see "Jurisdiction of the Courts of Admiralty in Cases of Collision on Tide-Waters within the Body of a Country: The Case of the *Luda* and *De Sota*, on the Mississippi," *De Bow's Commercial Review*, 2:179–92, 1846.

[46] See Waring v. Clarke, 5 How. 441, 451 (1847).

States."[47] John J. Crittenden of Kentucky presented the case for the owners of the *Luda*. Justice Wayne, who wrote the opinion of the Court and to whom the Reporter left the statement of Johnson's argument, noted that Johnson had presented two grounds for denial of admiralty jurisdiction. First he had contended that admiralty jurisdiction was limited to the dimensions of that jurisdiction in England at the time of the Revolutionary War or of the adoption of the Constitution, which did not reach to collisions on tidewater rivers. Secondly, he had contended that the statutory reservation of a common law remedy debarred the exercise of admiralty jurisdiction. The Supreme Court rejected both contentions, through an opinion which indicated that the Court as well as counsel had dug deep into the history of admiralty and its conflict of jurisdiction with the common law. The Court concluded that "the grant of admiralty power to the courts of the United States was not intended to be limited or to be interpreted by what were cases of admiralty jurisdiction in England when the Constitution was adopted."[48] It denied that reservation of concurrent jurisdiction at common law where the common law provided a remedy was the equivalent of a denial of admiralty jurisdiction at the point of overlapping.[49] The Court held, in short, that admiralty jurisdiction could be exercised on inland tidewater without reference to its limitations in English law—a position which, incidentally, Justice Wayne had already taken three years earlier with respect to the Savannah River in a Circuit Court opinion.[50]

The vote of the Justices stood five to three, Justice McKinley being absent and Justice Catron writing a cautious concurring opinion in which he indicated sympathy with portions of the dissenting opinion written by Justice Woodbury, a strict constructionist who in succeeding Story brought none of that distinguished jurist's love of admiralty. For Woodbury, "the law as it existed in England at the time of the Revolution, as to admiralty jurisdiction over torts, is the only certain and safe guide."[51] He was distressed at the thought of taking from the states and giving to federal courts of admiralty jurisdiction in "personal quarrels between seamen in the coasting trade and our vast shore fisheries, and timber men on rafts, and gundalo men, and men in flat boats, workmen in the seacoast marshes, and half the injuries to their property," which took place "where the tide ebbs and flows in our rivers, creeks and ports, though not on the high seas."[52] In addition, there was

---

[47] Notes of Washington Perine, 1936, filed with a series of Reverdy Johnson letters, Perine Papers.

[48] 5 How. 459.

[49] *Ibid.*, 460-61.

[50] Bulloch v. *The Lamar*, 4 Fed. Cas. 654 (No. 2129) (C.C.D. Ga. 1844).

[51] 5 How. 476-77.

[52] *Ibid.*, 490.

the matter of jury trial, involving "principles dear to freemen of the Saxon race—preferring the trial by jury, and the common law, to a single judge in admiralty, and the civil law."[53]

In this case Justice Daniel, who later was to criticize bitterly the extension of admiralty jurisdiction, merely concurred in the Woodbury dissent. Justice Grier also concurred in it and, further, announced his belief that the weight of evidence was against the existence of a tide at the place of collision, though he refrained from commenting sarcastically about "an occult tide," as he was to do in another case.[54]

Parallel with the case from Louisiana and raising some of the same questions of admiralty jurisdiction was the *Lexington* case from Rhode Island, *New Jersey Steam Navigation Co. v. Merchant's Bank of Boston*. The *Lexington* case grew out of the burning of the passenger and freight-laden steamboat of that name, with great loss of life and property. The disaster took place when the *Lexington*, operating as a common carrier between New York and Stonington, Connecticut, caught fire from bales of cotton which had been stacked too close to a hot chimney, negligence which was compounded by defective arrangements for dealing with fire. The event provided tragic drama which carried through the years to a Supreme Court decision in 1848, when Justice Woodbury said of it:

> Beside the great amount of property on board on this occasion, they had in charge from one to two hundred passengers, including helpless children and females, confiding for safety entirely to their care and fidelity. All of these, except two or three, were launched into eternity, during that frightful night, by deaths the most painful and heart-rending.[55]

The case arose in the form of a suit on a contract for the delivery of several thousand dollars in gold and silver lost in the disaster. Since the *Lexington*, like the *Luda*, had been completely destroyed, it was not possible to recover the value of the gold and silver by a suit *in rem*, against the ship itself. The suit, bristling with difficult questions of contract and tort liability, had to be brought against the owning company, with further argument of the question whether the suit could be brought in admiralty because of the reservation of a common law remedy. The

---

[53] *Ibid.*, 490.
[54] Jackson v. Steamboat *Magnolia*, 20 How. 296, 302 (1858).
[55] New Jersey Steam Navigation Company v. Merchant's Bank, 6 How. 344, 427 (1848). For Justice Story's personal account of the accident see *Life and Letters of Joseph Story*, William W. Story, ed., II, 322.

suit was instituted in the United States District Court in Rhode Island. In October, 1842, Judge John Pitman, with the consent of the parties, rendered a pro forma decree dismissing the libel, and an appeal was taken to the United States Circuit Court, where the trial would be before Judge Pitman and Justice Story. On November 15, 1843, the Circuit Court awarded something over twenty-two thousand dollars and costs, after which an appeal was taken to the Supreme Court. There this case, like that resulting from the sinking of the *Luda*, was delayed because of congestion of the docket and changes in personnel. Its first argument took place at the term beginning in January, 1847, and it was returned to the calendar and reargued the following December. For the owners of the *Lexington* the case was argued by Samuel Ames and John Whipple of Rhode Island, and for the bank by Richard W. Greene of Rhode Island and Daniel Webster.

Here again, in addition to other jurisdictional and substantive questions, counsel debated the question whether admiralty jurisdiction could be exercised even on seawater when the area was hemmed in by land,[56] although the Long Island Sound marked no such extension inland as did the tidewater portion of the Mississippi River. By the time of the second argument of the *Lexington* case the decision in *Waring v. Clarke* was on the record, and the argument against jurisdiction seemed unlikely to prevail.

Whether the change resulted from a change in conviction on the legal point or from strategy likely to help with his case, it is noteworthy that Webster here saw possibilities in the inland extension of admiralty jurisdiction which he had not seen at the time of the drafting of the Act of 1845. Then he had seemed to find a basis for jurisdiction only in the Commerce Clause.[57] Now, early in 1848, he referred to the statute as based on a finding that admiralty jurisdiction was indispensable on the interior lakes and rivers. He added, almost derisively if correctly quoted:

> The only objection to this necessary law seems to be, that Congress, in passing it, was shivering and trembling under the apprehension of what might be the ultimate consequence of the decision of this court in the case of *The Thomas Jefferson*. It pitched the power upon a wrong location.
>
> Its proper home was in the admiralty and maritime grant, as in all reason, and in the common sense of a mankind out of England, admiralty and maritime jurisdiction ought to extend, and does extend, to all navigable waters, fresh or salt.[58]

---

[56] 6 How. 356.
[57] See Daniel Webster to Samuel

Finley Vinton, Feb. 19, 1844, House of Representatives Papers.
[58] 6 How. 378.

Webster had somewhat deplored the necessity of arguing the case a second time, thinking that nothing good would come of it. He remarked that he would be required to listen to other counsel and take notes for at least five days. Although his colleague Greene saw the *Lexington* case helped by the decision in *Waring v. Clarke*, Webster was doubtful. In any event, "I look for much division and diversity. The Court wants a strong and leading mind."[59]

When the reargument, lasting some eight days, was completed, however, he was glad that it had taken place. He now thought that a greater or less majority of the Court would decide:

1. That it *is* a case of Admiralty jurisdiction.
2. That the owners of the Boat are common carriers, and so answerable, at all events, for the loss, without going into any proof of actual negligence.
3. That the Bank has a right to call on the owners of the Boat, directly; and cannot be turned over to Harnden, by virtue of the notice.[60]

The prediction proved to be right, with the result that Webster won his case. He was right also in predicting diversity among the Justices. Justice Nelson wrote an opinion concurred in by Chief Justice Taney and Justices McLean and Wayne. Justice Catron wrote a cautious concurring opinion, as he had done in *Waring v. Clarke*. Justice Woodbury wrote a long opinion in which he concurred as far as the award to the bank was concerned, but he did so not in terms of the contract of shipment, which was made on land and in his estimation could not therefore be enforced in admiralty, but on the ground that the bank was entitled to damages in tort for the negligence of those in charge of the *Lexington*. Justice Daniel dissented in a long opinion denying that admiralty could exercise jurisdiction. According to the minutes of the Supreme Court, Justice Grier joined in the Daniel dissent. The manuscript opinion book of the Court shows no record of such concurrence, however, nor does the published report. It would seem, therefore, that he escaped without official expression of opinion.[61] Justice McKinley was absent for the entire term, and did not participate.

[59] Daniel Webster to Franklin Haven, Dec. 28, 1847, *Writings and Speeches of Daniel Webster*, J. W. McIntyre, ed., XVI, 489.

[60] Daniel Webster to Franklin Haven, Jan. 8, 1848, *ibid.*, 489. See also Charles Warren, *The Supreme Court in United States History*, II, 160–61.

[61] Twelve years later, however, Justice Grier wrote an opinion of the Court in which he implied agreement with the basic point involved in the *Lexington* case. Noting that the case had been twice argued at very great length, he added that "The whole subject was most thoroughly investigated, both by counsel and the Court. Everything connected with the history of courts of admiralty, from the reign of Richard II to the present day— everything which the industry, learn-

For all the division among the Justices, one effect of the decision was to determine that admiralty jurisdiction extended not merely to torts which took place on water and to contracts made on water but also to contracts made on land when the purpose was essentially maritime. The decision was important also in determining that common carriers were responsible for damages resulting from negligence in spite of general disclaimers to the contrary.

The *Lexington* decision had repercussions in a variety of directions. It extended the liability of American owners beyond that of English owners as determined by the laws of their own country and put American shipping at a competitive disadvantage. In 1851, largely through the efforts of eastern seaboard men in Congress,[62] an act was passed limiting liability roughly to that of English ships, with a qualification, insisted on by Westerners, that the act should not apply "to any vessel of any description whatsoever, used in rivers or inland navigation."[63] The definition of "inland navigation" was to provide still further difficulties for the Supreme Court.[64]

In the meantime, in 1847, litigation got under way through which the interpretation of the Act of 1845 would be worked out and its constitutionality determined. The litigation resulted from a collision on Lake Ontario between a schooner, the *Cuba*, which was loaded with wheat and traveling between Sandusky, Ohio, and Oswego, New York, and a steam-driven propeller, the *Genesee Chief*. The *Chief* ran afoul of the *Cuba* and sank her, with resulting loss of both ship and cargo. The owners of the *Cuba* brought suit in admiralty under the Act of 1845. The cause was tried in April, 1848, in the United States District Court for the Northern District of New York, before Judge Alfred Conkling—in the year in which Conkling completed the first edition of his work on admiralty jurisdiction. Neither party called for a jury trial, which the statute made optional. Delivering an opinion which, if written out at all, has apparently been nowhere published, Judge Conkling issued a decree in favor of the owners of the *Cuba*. In July, 1849, Justice Nelson affirmed the decision in the United States Circuit Court. The way was now paved for a decision by the Supreme Court.

---

ing, and research of most able counsel could discover, was brought to our notice. We then decided that charter-parties and contracts of affreightment are 'maritime contracts' within the true meaning and construction of the Constitution and act of Congress and cognizable in courts of admiralty by process either *in rem*

or *in personam*." Morewood v. Enequist, 23 How. 491, 493 (1860).

[62] See *Cong. Globe*, 31st Cong., 2nd Sess. 713 *ff*.

[63] 9 Stat. 635, 636. For discussion of the statute see "The Limitation of the Liability of Ship-Owners by Statute," *Am. L. Rev.*, 1:597, 1867.

[64] See Moore v. American Transportation Co., 24 How. 1 (1861).

XVIII: *Admiralty and Maritime Jurisdiction*

According to his statement in the 1857 edition of his treatise on admiralty jurisdiction, Judge Conkling had applied the Act of 1845 in this case as an exercise of power based not on the Admiralty Clause but on the Commerce Clause of the Constitution, finding the Admiralty Clause excluded because of the position taken by the Supreme Court in *The Thomas Jefferson*. Conkling found support for his position in Webster's statement in the argument of the *Lexington* case, that Congress in seeming to base the statute on the Admiralty Clause had "pitched the power upon a wrong location"—that is, that it should have been based on the commerce power.[65] Justice Nelson had presumably heard that argument in the Supreme Court before affirming the Conkling decision in the Circuit Court.

We know that Justice McLean was deeply interested in the extension of admiralty jurisdiction not merely to the lakes but also to the great Western rivers, and that in Washington, with its crosscurrents of political gossip, the several Justices must have been aware of the Congressional discussion of the subject. Linkage of the Supreme Court with the Act of 1845 must have been kept in the minds of the judges by such items as the memorial, introduced in the Senate in 1850 by Senator Thomas Corwin, asking for an expansion of the act. The memorial, pretty much in the language of an article published in the *Western Law Journal* in 1845,[66] told of Justice Story's preparation of the bill and about its receiving "the approbation of all the Judges of the Supreme Court then in Washington." It set forth the subject of admiralty jurisdiction in terms of Story's *Commentaries on the Constitution*,[67] and his opinion in *The Thomas Jefferson*. Praising the principles of admiralty for their universality, their certainty, and their stability, it argued that since both the Supreme Court and Congress had found that they had admiralty jurisdiction on the lakes, "they must have it also with respect to the rivers, since the objection that there is no ebb and flow of the tide, is the same to both."[68] When amid the political turmoil of 1850 the Senate Committee on the Judiciary put aside memorials concerning river jurisdiction by saying that "aside from all constitutional objections which may exist against legislation upon the subject embraced in said memorials, the committee are of the opinion that legislation is inexpedient thereon,"[69] the advocates of extended

---

[65] See Alfred Conkling, *The Admiralty Jurisdiction, Law and Practice of the Courts of the United States*, I, 11–13. See also Judge Conkling's opinion in Merrit v. Sackett, 17 Fed. Cas. 140 (No. 9484) (D.C.N.D. N.Y. 1849).

[66] Timothy Walker, "The Project of Extending Admiralty Jurisdiction over the Lakes and Rivers of the United States," *West. L.J.*, 2:563, 1845.

[67] See Joseph Story, *Commentaries on the Constitution of the United States*, III, 525–36.

[68] The memorial, submitted Jan. 3, 1850, is in the Senate Papers.

[69] Senate Report No. 48, 31st Cong., 1st Sess.

jurisdiction, and probably some of the Justices themselves, were driven to wonder what could be done judicially without the intervention of Congress.

When at the December term, 1851, the Supreme Court heard arguments in *Propeller Genesee Chief v. Fitzhugh*,[70] Abraham P. Grant of New York, counsel for Fitzhugh, one of the owners of the sunken *Cuba*, argued that the Act of 1845 was constitutional; but unfortunately, the Reporter, who was often accused of dumping masses of irrelevant material into his volumes, here recorded only the citation of a few cases. He made no mention of the argument of William H. Seward for the *Genesee Chief*, but he summarized the points made by Seward's colleague, Selah Mathews, who contended that since the collision did not occur on tidewater there was no basis for admiralty jurisdiction, that the Act of Congress was one merely for extension of judicial jurisdiction and not for the regulation of commerce, and that Congress could not so legislate under the guise of a commerce regulation. Here he employed the "parade of horrors" argument likely to impress the devotees of states' rights:

> If this law can be sustained, it is not perceived why Congress may not extend the jurisdiction of the federal courts to every case of contract or tort, growing out of the extensive trade and commerce, now carried on, by land and water, among the States of the Union; and thus draw within the cognizance of these courts one half of the litigation of the country.[71]

Chief Justice Taney took responsibility for guiding the Court through the confusion of argument. No friend of any expansion of the commerce power of Congress that would take power away from the states, he nevertheless knew the merits of admiralty jurisdiction on the Chesapeake Bay and other inlets along the Atlantic Coast, and he was able to sense the need for the exercise of such jurisdiction on the vast expanses of navigable fresh water in the North and West. He disavowed a Commerce Clause basis for the Act of 1845, though its operation was limited to commerce involving more than one state, and asserted that an act defining the jurisdiction of the federal courts could not be based on that clause. If Congress on the basis of the Commerce Clause could extend proceedings in admiralty to transportation on water, the clause, which applied also to land transportation, might be used to extend admiralty proceedings to land cases as well—a type of extension he deemed unthinkable.

---

[70] 12 How. 443.   [71] *Ibid.*, 448.

444

The Chief Justice found the statute constitutional, however, on the basis of the Admiralty Clause. It was true, he admitted, that in England navigable waters had been virtually only those in which the tide ebbed and flowed, with the result that admiralty jurisdiction had been limited to tidewater areas. In the United States the identification of the boundaries of admiralty jurisdiction with the boundaries of tidewater had continued to be assumed, until the development of freshwater commerce had demonstrated the incongruity of this limitation. The limiting decision in the Supreme Court, that of *The Thomas Jefferson*, had been handed down in 1825, "when the commerce on the rivers of the west and on the lakes was in its infancy, and of little importance, and but little regarded compared with that of the present day."[72] He concluded that "as we are convinced that the former decision was founded in error, and that the error, if not corrected, must produce serious public as well as private inconvenience and loss, it becomes our duty not to perpetuate it."[73]

Taney noted that by providing the option of jury trial the Act of 1845 avoided the principal objection to admiralty jurisdiction, that the expansion of the content of maritime law had its parallel in contemporary expansion in England, and that a concurrent remedy at common law was available where the common law was competent to provide it.

When *The Genesee Chief* was decided, in March, 1852, Story's successor, Woodbury, who was hostile to the expansion of admiralty jurisdiction, had died and had been replaced by Benjamin R. Curtis, who had no such hostility. Chief Justice Taney was able to carry with him all his brethren except Justice Daniel, who, as in the *Lexington* case, strongly opposed any extension of admiralty jurisdiction. Daniel, relying for support on the opinions of judges of whose positions he seldom spoke with approval, remarked:

My opinions may be deemed contracted and antiquated, unsuited to the day in which we live, but they are founded upon deliberate conviction as to the nature and objects of limited government, and by myself at least cannot be disregarded; and I have at least the consolation—no small one it must be admitted—of the support of Marshall, Kent, and Story in any error I may have committed.[74]

Since in the *Genesee Chief* case the collision involved had taken place on one of the Great Lakes, Chief Justice Taney formally limited his discussion to the area of the lakes and their connecting waters as covered by the Act of 1845. The overruling of *The Thomas Jefferson*

---

[72] *Ibid.*, 456.   [73] *Ibid.*, 459.   [74] *Ibid.*, 465.

as to the restriction of admiralty jurisdiction to tidewater eliminated any constitutional question about extension of admiralty jurisdiction to navigable freshwater rivers, but such jurisdiction in the United States District Courts could extend only if given by Congress. The Act of 1845 applied only to lakes and their connecting waters. Could such jurisdiction be exercised on a freshwater river without further action by a Congress which had hitherto refused to act? Or, since *The Thomas Jefferson* had now been overruled, could it be said that admiralty jurisdiction was conferred on the federal courts by the Judiciary Act of 1789, and that the Act of 1845 was now superfluous? The latter act had been passed to extend jurisdiction. If the provision for extension was superfluous, what was the status of its restrictive provisions, such as those giving the option of jury trial and limiting jurisdiction on the lakes to interstate commerce? If those limitations were now effective as to the lakes, and if admiralty jurisdiction now extended to rivers by virtue of the Act of 1789, did the restrictions, which applied in terms only to lakes and connecting waters, now apply to commerce on the rivers?

Obviously the situation was still confused. *The Genesee Chief* clarified only one point, albeit a central one, in the confusion. At the same time the Court decided *Fretz v. Bull*, which involved a collision between a steamboat and a raft on the Mississippi far enough upriver so that not even what Justice Grier called "an occult tide" could be detected. There Justice Wayne, speaking for the Court, with only Justice Daniel dissenting, said the *Genesee Chief* case had decided that admiralty jurisdiction "was not limited by tide water, but was extended to the lakes and navigable rivers of the United States."[75] The exercise of admiralty jurisdiction in this case, where interstate commerce was involved, was upheld. The other questions remained unanswered. In any event, commerce in vast amounts was involved, and a great expansion of the business of the federal courts was assured. Justice Catron wrote to James Buchanan, "In their practical consequences these decisions have more in them than any fifty others ever made by the Supreme Court."[76] A law journal noted:

This will bring within the range of the Admiralty, the Mississippi to the Falls of St. Anthony, and Pittsburgh, the Susquehanna, and in fact every stream of any importance in the United States. As questions of

---

[75] Fretz v. Bull, 12 How. 466, 468 (1852).

[76] John Catron to James Buchanan, Mar. 3, 1852, Buchanan Papers. The Court decided at the same time the important commerce case, Cooley v. Board of Wardens, 12 How. 299, and one of the colorful Gaines Cases, Gaines v. Relf, 12 How. 472. Both are discussed in the Catron letter here cited.

collision and on the law of carriers are daily arising, especially on our Western waters, our readers will see the very important character of this decision.[77]

The extension of admiralty jurisdiction probably was responsible for the expected division of Ohio into two judicial districts,[78] and a like division in Illinois.[79] It may also have brought about increases in judicial salaries, which took place piecemeal in different districts. As measured by tons of shipping, it is true, the preponderance of admiralty business continued to be in the New England—New York area. With the allocation of Supreme Court circuits in terms of slavery and non-slavery areas in mind, the *New York Daily Tribune* noted in 1859 that in the four circuits of the free states shipping in the previous year had measured over four million tons, whereas in the five circuits of the slave states it had measured less than nine hundred thousand tons.[80] Yet admiralty business added substantially to the work of the federal courts in most sections of the country.

Much admiralty litigation had to do not primarily with the jurisdictional questions with which we are here primarily concerned but with the substance of the law. The newspapers of the time indicate its importance even for general readers through its involvement of the activities of commercial communities. Announcing Justice Curtis' opinion for the Supreme Court in an important case in 1856 involving the responsibility of masters of vessels for repairs and supplies, the *Tribune* stated that "Judge Taney occupied an hour in the delivery of his views, regarding the subject as highly important, and containing points for the first time brought before that tribunal."[81] Such cases abound in the records of the District and Circuit Courts, and no small number of them reached the Supreme Court.

Jurisdictional questions continued to preoccupy the courts and to cause disagreements among state and federal judges. An unusual example was a decision of Justice Nelson in the United States Circuit Court in New York half a year after the decision in the *Genesee Chief* case. Justice Nelson reversed a decree handed down by Judge Alfred Conkling[82] in a matter of a maritime lien created by state law.[83] Unlike

---

[77] *Am. L. Reg.*, 1:58, 1852.

[78] 10 Stat. 604.

[79] 10 Stat. 606. For discussion see the remarks of Senator John B. Weller, *Cong. Globe*, 33rd Cong., 2nd Sess. 667 (1855).

[80] *New York Daily Tribune*, Mar. 26, 1859.

[81] *Ibid.*, Dec. 30, 1856. The case was Thomas v. Osborn, 19 How. 22 (1856).

[82] *The Globe*, 10 Fed. Cas. 480 (No. 5484) (D.C.N.D. N.Y. 1850).

[83] 10 Fed. Cas. 477 (No. 5483) (C.C.N.D. N.Y. 1852).

most judges in lower courts who must submit silently to being overruled by higher tribunals, Conkling resigned from his court to serve for a brief period as President Fillmore's minister to Mexico, and then turned to revision of his widely used work on admiralty. Scathingly and in a highly personal vein he denounced Justice Nelson's performance, saying that apart from two or three sentences the reader would find Nelson's opinion to consist "of matters as inapplicable to the question before the court as the law of copyright, and in the excepted sentences, he will find only bold assumptions in conflict with 'the first principles of natural justice,' and contradicted by the highest judicial authorities."[84] Declaring that Nelson violated judicial duty and decorum by ignoring the published reasons for the contrary opinion, he turned to generalized denunciation:

> No judge has a right thus to trifle with his high functions. They furnish scope for the highest intellectual endowments and the profoundest legal learning. However great may be the abilities of a judge, he is bound to devote them conscientiously and strenuously to the public service; and especially is this duty incumbent on a judge of humble capacity. *He* is bound to strive as far as in him lies, to supply this deficiency, by extra-ordinary exertions. But unfortunately judges of this character are precisely those who are apt to be blinded by conceit and self-complacency, and thus to be rendered incapable of apprehending the responsibilities of their office. I believe this to be the only highly civilized country in the world where such men are elevated to the highest judicial stations. They require to be watched; and he, who, regardless of their displeasure, proclaims their delinquencies, and arouses them to the better performance of their duty, entitles himself to be regarded as a public benefactor.[85]

Although Judge Conkling's work on admiralty was widely respected and widely used, there is no evidence that he was regarded as a public benefactor for his denunciation of a member of the Supreme Court. Since the amount involved in the suit was less than two thousand dollars, no appeal to the Supreme Court was possible. An eminently reputable law journal thought that Conkling was probably right on the question in admiralty but deplored his use of harsh language in criticism, noting that "it does not comport with the dignity of the parties or of the subject to retort by a reflection upon the general qualities and fitness for office of a mistaken superior."[86]

---

[84] Conkling, *The Admiralty Jurisdiction, Law and Practice of the Courts of the United States*, I, 102.
[85] *Ibid.*, 102–03. For other attacks by Judge Conkling on Justice Nelson see *ibid.*, 417–26, and *ibid.*, II, 593–610.
[86] *Law Rep.*, 20:356–57, 1857.

Justice Daniel, even when he had to stand alone, continued to insist on limiting admiralty jurisdiction to tidewater, and to that tidewater which was outward to the sea and was not within the body of any county. He dissented when all the other Justices found admiralty jurisdiction in tort growing out of a boiler explosion on the tidewater portion of a voyage between Sacramento and San Francisco. He thought it absurd that admiralty jurisdiction could extend wherever the ebb and flow of the tide was found, using as an illustration the creek called the Tiber which at that time backed up from the Potomac at high tide to stream across Pennsylvania Avenue not far from the Capitol.[87]

Justice Daniel had company in dissent, however, when the Court, in *Jackson v. Steamboat Magnolia*,[88] went further and upheld the exercise of admiralty jurisdiction in a case of collision on the Alabama River, above the ebb and flow of the tide. To Justice Grier, who wrote the opinion of the Court, the controlling jurisdictional consideration seemed to be that the Alabama was "a public navigable water on which commerce is carried on between different states or nations."[89] The question of the exercise of admiralty jurisdiction within the body of a county, he held, had been adjudicated ten years earlier in *Waring v. Clarke*. The Court had not since been called on by the bar to review that decision, nor had it heard of "any complaints by the people of wrongs suffered on account of its supposed infringement of the right of trial by jury."[90] The use of the ebb and flow of the tide as a measure of admiralty jurisdiction had been dealt with in *The Genesee Chief*.

The Court had here to deal with the question whether the Act of 1845, in extending admiralty jurisdiction to the lakes, with the restrictions that the commerce involved should be interstate and that jury trial should be available, had the effect of extending the restrictions to river commerce as well. Justice Grier noted that by the Judiciary Act of 1789 admiralty jurisdiction had been conferred on the federal courts on ocean waters and on waters "navigable from the sea," but had not then been conferred as to lake traffic, so that the Act of 1845 was needed for the lake areas. But the statute did not, he held, serve as a limitation on the admiralty jurisdiction on rivers which were "navigable from the sea." Jurisdiction over the great navigable rivers of the West was not "claimed under the Act of 1845, or by virtue of anything therein contained."[91]

Justice McLean, friend of the extension of admiralty jurisdiction on the Western rivers, wrote a concurring opinion to reinforce the opinion of the Court, saying, "If this jurisdiction has been found salutary

---

[87] Steamboat *New World* v. King, 16 How. 469, 479 (1854).
[88] 20 How. 296 (1858).

[89] *Ibid.*, 299.
[90] *Ibid.*, 299.
[91] *Ibid.*, 300.

in that part of our country which is most commercial, it cannot be injurious or dangerous in those parts which are less commercial."[92] Justice Daniel, however, again indignantly insisted on the narrowest possible range for admiralty jurisdiction, quoting another judge as to "the silent and stealing progress of the admiralty in acquiring jurisdiction to which it has no pretensions."[93] He criticized the Court as well for intervention in the legislative process in advocating enactment of the Act of 1845.[94]

Justice Daniel had the support, furthermore, of Justice Campbell, who next to Justice Story was probably the outstanding scholar on the Court during the Taney period. With evidence of learning that matched that of Story, Campbell delved deep into the history of the development of admiralty jurisdiction, perhaps motivated by fealty to his own state of Alabama, which was involved in the case. Of Story's opinion in *De Lovio v. Boit*,[95] which was much relied on by those who favored expansion of admiralty jurisdiction in the United States, Campbell wrote accusingly that it was "celebrated for its research, and remarkable, in my opinion, for its boldness in asserting novel conclusions, and the facility with which authentic historical evidence that contradicted them is disposed of."[96] Finally, as to the case at hand, Justice Campbell said:

> I consider that the present case carries the jurisdiction to an incalculable extent beyond any other, and all others, that have been pronounced, and that it must create a revolution in the admiralty administration of the courts of the United States; that the change will produce heart burning and discontent, and involve collisions with state legislatures and state jurisdictions. And, finally, it is a violation of the rights reserved in the Constitution of the United States to the states and to the people.[97]

How it was that Justices Daniel and Campbell carried with them Justice Catron, who in the light of his comments on the *Genesee Chief* case and its companion case might have been expected to vote with the majority, the record does not show. It seems apparent, however, that the growing sectional strife over states' rights was forcing upon the Supreme Court extreme care in the development of legal doctrines affecting those rights. In *Taylor v. Carryl*,[98] decided at the same term

---

92 *Ibid.*, 305.
93 *Ibid.*, 307.
94 *Ibid.*, 315–16.
95 7 Fed. Cas. 418 (No. 3776) (C.C.D. Mass. 1815).
96 20 How. 336. For discussion of Justice Campbell as a legal theorist

see John R. Schmidhauser, "Jeremy Bentham, the Contract Clause and Justice John Archibald Campbell," *Vand. L. Rev.*, 11:301, 1958.
97 20 How. 342–43.
98 20 How. 583.

of the Court, involving claims against a vessel based on conflicting state and federal jurisdiction, Justice Campbell carried with him a bare majority of the Court in favor of the claimants under state jurisdiction. It was left to Chief Justice Taney to say in dissent, and in defense of admiralty jurisdiction:

> The Constitution of the United States is as much a part of the law of Pennsylvania as its own Constitution, and the laws passed by the General Government pursuant to the Constitution are as obligatory upon the courts of the states as upon those of the United States; and they are equally bound to uphold the acts and process of the courts of the United States, when acting within the scope of its legitimate authority.[99]

Taney deplored treatment of the controversy as a conflict between two sovereignties, as Campbell treated it and as innumerable controversies in the late 1850s were coming to be viewed. To him it was merely a question of the relative powers of a court of admiralty and a court of common law.[100]

State courts as well as federal judges criticized the expansion of federal control. Criticisms were directed particularly at proslavery holdings, and in some instances, as in the *Booth Cases* in Wisconsin, state courts asserted their authority to curb that of the federal courts. Some of the judges of the Supreme Court of Michigan were particularly critical of the extension of federal admiralty jurisdiction over the adjacent lakes, for all the earlier efforts of Michigan citizens to bring about enactment of the Act of 1845. In 1858 a dissenting judge, Randolph Manning, denounced the assertion of federal power over the lake property of the state. If such control were valid, then about one-quarter of the state was withdrawn from state jurisdiction and made subject to the uncontrolled legislation of Congress.[101]

---

[99] *Ibid.*, 605.

[100] *Ibid.*, 601. In a letter to Justice Clifford, Chief Justice Taney predicted that the majority Justices would find more trouble with the opinion of the Court than they anticipated, as a result of the confusion of common law and admiralty, as illustrated by an inquiry about the position of the Supreme Court which he had had from the federal district judge in Virginia in a case involving seamen's wages. Said Taney, "We shall have much difficulty in going back from the admiralty jurisdiction where state laws give the lien. Look at the 12th rule passed by this court in express terms to regulate the proceedings in the admiralty courts. It authorizes the court in express terms to proceed *in rem* where the state law gives the lien, and the District courts have all acted under this rule. Yet the rule is clearly wrong, but I do not see how a District court can disregard it, until it is repealed (as it must be) by the Supreme Court." R. B. Taney to Nathan Clifford, June 18, 1858, Clifford Papers.

[101] American Transportation Co. v. Moore, 5 Mich. 368, 404 (1858).

The same year saw the origin of another controversy which brought from Michigan judges sharp criticism of the exercise of federal power with respect to navigable waters. William Tyler of Detroit, a United States Deputy Marshal, was sent by the United States District Court for Michigan to serve a writ of attachment and take possession of the brig *Concord*, which flew the American flag and engaged in lake and river commerce. Tyler apprehended the brig on the St. Clair River, which links Lake Huron with Lake St. Clair, and ultimately with Lake Erie. The river constitutes part of the boundary between the United States and Canada, the line running with the middle of the stream. There is in the record an unverified suggestion that Henry Jones, the master of the brig, took the vessel to the Canadian side of the stream in the hope of avoiding legal service of the writ. However that may be, Tyler attempted to serve the writ, and Jones attempted to fight him off. Thereupon Tyler, in the language of a subsequent federal indictment, "not having the fear of God before his eyes, but being moved and seduced by the instigation of the devil," shot Jones and inflicted a mortal wound. Jones died after being landed at Port Huron in Michigan.

Tyler was indicted by a federal grand jury and brought to trial for manslaughter at a special term of the United States Circuit Court, pursuant to the Crimes Act of 1857. The act, which provided for punishment of nonmalicious killing on waters within the admiralty jurisdiction of the United States and out of the jurisdiction of any state, had been drafted by Justice Benjamin R. Curtis of the Supreme Court of the United States, after a case tried before him in the United States Circuit Court of his district had revealed an undesirable limitation in existing statutes.[102] Although the statute provided for punishment of imprisonment up to three years and fine up to one thousand dollars, Tyler received from the federal judge a surprisingly light sentence of one month in the Wayne County jail and a fine of one dollar.

But it also appears that, prior to the federal indictment and trial, Tyler had been indicted in the Circuit Court for the county of St. Clair, on the basis of the common law doctrine that a crime resulting in death was punishable at the place where the death took place. If Tyler was not to be punished twice for the same act of killing—and it seems not to have been thought that the same act could constitute separate offenses against two sovereigns—then the federal conviction, if legally brought about, would stand as a bar to trial in the county court. Indeed, it is possible that the purpose of the federal prosecution of the federal deputy was to prevent trial in the county court where a harsher

---

[102] 11 Stat. 250. See People v. Tyler, 7 Mich. 160, 181, 216 (1859). See also United States v. Armstrong, 24 Fed. Cas. 864 (No. 14467) (C.C.D. Mass. 1855).

penalty might be applied. The key question, therefore, was whether the United States had the power to try Tyler for an act done aboard an American ship while in Canadian waters not navigable from the sea. Tyler was brought to trial in the county court, and the question was taken to the Michigan Supreme Court on demurrer.

The four Michigan justices, each speaking separately, held that the federal statute—and federal admiralty jurisdiction—did not extend to navigable waters on an inland river in a foreign country, and that the county was therefore not estopped from bringing Tyler to trial. They referred to the relevant decisions of the Supreme Court as if that tribunal was at most no higher than a coordinate body with their own court. Chief Justice George Martin rejected Chief Justice Taney's opinion in the *Genesee Chief* case and contended that if the federal courts had admiralty jurisdiction on the lakes and rivers at all they had it only by virtue of the commerce power.[103] Justice James V. Campbell said of Taney's opinion that it was "not only unsupported by any satisfactory proof, but is in direct opposition to the most overwhelming evidence, historical and judicial, both in this country and in England."[104] Justice Manning pronounced the Act of 1845 unconstitutional and void.[105]

Tyler was therefore brought to trial in the county court, convicted of murder in the second degree, and sentenced to six years of imprisonment. The case went back to the Michigan Supreme Court. That court again held that the United States Circuit Court had had no jurisdiction to try Tyler and that the circuit court of the county did have jurisdiction, with the result that the judgment of the local court was affirmed.[106]

In the face of state criticism of the expansion of federal power via admiralty jurisdiction the Supreme Court drew a wavering line. For a number of years it drifted in the direction of limiting admiralty jurisdiction not only on lakes, as covered by the Act of 1845, but also on rivers, to such commerce as was interstate. The leading advocate of this position was Justice Nelson, who had suggested it in the *Lexington* case.[107] In the *Magnolia* case Justice McLean disclosed similar leanings, saying, "The admiralty and maritime jurisdiction is essentially a commercial power, and it is necessarily limited to the exercise of that power by Congress."[108] In 1859, with three Justices silently dissenting, Justice Nelson held for the Court that under the Act of 1845 admiralty jurisdiction did not extend to the carriage of goods on Lake Michigan

---

[103] 7 Mich. 164.
[104] *Ibid.*, 241.
[105] *Ibid.*, 250.
[106] Tyler v. The People, 8 Mich. 320 (1860).

[107] New Jersey Steam Navigation Co. v. Merchants' Bank, 6 How. 344, 392 (1848).
[108] Jackson v. Steamboat *Magnolia*, 20 How. 296, 304 (1858).

between two points in Wisconsin, even though the vessel used was at that time on its way to Chicago.[109] At the same term it held through the same Justice and with only one Justice dissenting that admiralty did not extend to enforcement of a state lien in California to recover for coal used for navigation exclusively in California.[110] In 1860 Justice McLean, speaking for the Court, said of admiralty that "This law is commercial in its character, and applies to all navigable waters, except to a commerce exclusively within a state."[111] In 1861 Justice Nelson said for the Court, of the Act of March 3, 1851, that it "can apply to vessels only which are engaged in foreign commerce, and commerce between the states."[112]

By 1862, however, the Civil War was under way, Southern statesmen had lost their influence on national policy, new judges with nationalist sentiments were being appointed to the federal courts, and court-created restrictions on admiralty jurisdiction were being ignored.[113] The Supreme Court, too, losing membership by death and about to be reconstituted through new appointments, began to give way. Unanimously it upheld exercise of admiralty jurisdiction in a collision case on the Hudson River in spite of the fact that only intrastate commerce was involved.[114] Although the question was as to jurisdiction in tort, and not in contract, where the restriction of jurisdiction had been most severe, the decision marked a new trend that was to extend to contracts as well. It was but a matter of time—four years after the close of the war—until the restrictive trend was entirely repudiated.[115] The restriction in the Act of 1845 limiting admiralty jurisdiction to interstate commerce was assumed to be valid for approximately the same period, and then was likewise repudiated. For the Court Justice Nelson said

---

[109] Allen v. Newberry, 21 How. 244 (1859).

[110] Maguire v. Card, 21 How. 248 (1859).

[111] Nelson v. Leland, 22 How. 48, 56 (1860).

[112] Moore v. American Transportation Co., 24 How. 1, 39 (1861).

[113] For summary see "From Judicial Grant to Legislative Power," *Harv. L. Rev.*, 67:1214, 1228–30, 1954.

[114] Commercial Transportation Co. v. Fitzhugh, 1 Black 574 (1862).

[115] See *The Belfast* v. Boon, 7 Wall. 624, 641–42 (1869). For explanation of the Supreme Court's modification of its controversial Admiralty Rule XII to terminate enforcement in admiralty of state liens and leave their enforcement to state courts see Chief Justice Taney's opinion for the Court in Meyer v. Tupper, 1 Black 522 (1862). Of that decision the *New York Times* for May 15, 1862, said in part, "We congratulate the Bar on the determination of this vexed question. And if they find any difficulty in harmonizing the views of this decision with those of the past few years, it can hardly be as great as the difficulty of harmonizing those decisions with others of yet earlier date." For discussion of the historical roots of the problem, and particularly of another of Justice Story's controversial decisions in admiralty, *The General Smith*, 4 Wheat. 438 (1819), see Fitz-Henry Smith, Jr., "The Confusion in the Law Relating to Materialmen's Liens on Vessels," *Harv. L. Rev.*, 21:332, 1908.

from the time of the *Genesee Chief* decision admiralty jurisdiction might be thought of as stemming from the Judiciary Act of 1789 rather than from the Act of 1845.[116] The latter statute was to be regarded as obsolete except for the optional clause with respect to jury trial.[117]

And so throughout the Taney period decisions of the Court with respect to admiralty jurisdiction followed a meandering course. Still to be determined were a variety of questions, such as the legal definition of navigability, the continuing interrelation of admiralty and the commerce power, and the use of the Admiralty Clause of the Constitution as the basis of legislative as well as judicial power. The difficulties of interpretation and the pattern of inconsistencies were due to a number of factors: the uncertainties of fact and interpretation in the European history of admiralty, the contemporary expansion of admiralty jurisdiction in England, the problem of determining the spirit as well as the letter of the law in reasoning from English precedents to very different American experience, the pressures coming from Western interests for the extension of the uniform jurisdiction of admiralty to subject matter hitherto dealt with diversely in different state jurisdictions, aspirations toward a more tightly knit nationalism on the one hand and on the other hand fear of national encroachments on states' rights through the admiralty jurisdiction.

Various members of the Supreme Court played their part in shaping the meandering course. Justice Story, the original great educator in the field of admiralty in the United States, at once aided in expanding the content of maritime law and in limiting jurisdiction to tidewater. He attempted to circumvent his limitation by way of the Commerce Clause, but his former colleagues and successors on the Court rejected his original limitation along with his designated route around it. Chief Justice Taney, for all his defense of states' rights in other areas, played in one critical case a leading part in establishing admiralty jurisdiction on lakes and rivers and opposed generally the restriction of admiralty jurisdiction at the hands of his colleagues. Justice Nelson chose a middle course, for a time successfully identifying the outer limits of admiralty jurisdiction with those of the commerce power in the field of interstate and foreign relations. Justice Daniel's hostility to admiralty was so extreme as to render him of little direct influence with respect to it, though his opinions may have played a part in shaping restrictive opinion generally. Justice Campbell brought impressive legal scholarship to attempts to restrict admiralty jurisdiction, even though he made but

---

[116] *The Eagle* v. Frazer, 8 Wall. 15 (1869).
[117] For discussion of resort to that clause see *Harv. L. Rev.*, 67:1229–30, 1954.

limited headway in undermining the scholarly reputation of Justice Story in that field.

Apart from the influence of personalities and of the factors suggested above there were, of course, still broader considerations. The development of admiralty must be seen in the light of the growth of the United States as a major commercial and industrial power. Expanded jurisdiction in admiralty during the Taney period made sense in the light of beliefs about our national destiny, as did the expansion of the commerce power in later decades.

CHAPTER XIX

The Rights of Corporations

A<small>N IMPORTANT TASK</small> of the Supreme Court, related to that of interpreting the Commerce and Admiralty clauses and clauses having to do with money, banking, and credit, was the delineation of the constitutional position of private corporations. Corporations were spawned in great numbers by state legislatures, at first by means of special acts and special provisions for each corporation chartered, and then by general laws, which varied considerably from state to state. Corporations were chartered to provide transportation on natural waterways and for the construction and operation of canals, turnpikes, and railroads; they were chartered for manufacturing and for the mining and shipment of coal; and they made up most of the banking and insurance institutions of the country.

Although the corporation device had been known for centuries, during this period of rapid expansion of enterprise governments had to experiment extensively and sometimes painfully with the development of an adequate body of controlling legislation and relevant principles of the common law. It was necessary to protect corporations in the performance of their functions and to protect stockholders, customers, and employees against the misuse of the aggregate of corporate power. Since most corporations were formed under state laws and performed functions usually regarded as subject to local control, the responsibility for the development and application of law was in large part that of the states. State action varied all the way from the making of grants and stock subscriptions to drastic encroachments on charter provisions.[1] On

---

[1] For works illuminating the experience of various states in chartering and controlling corporations see the following: Joseph G. Blandi, *The Maryland Corporation*; John W. Cad- man, Jr., *The Corporation in New Jersey, Business and Politics, 1791–1875*; Edwin M. Dodd, *American Business Corporations until 1860, with Special Reference to Massachusetts*;

the whole, state experience in this field throughout the Taney period was pretty chaotic, with implications to be discovered only by highly detailed studies.

Yet the federal government was also involved, because of the Commerce Clause, the Contract Clause, and other parts of the Constitution, and because of the jurisdiction of the federal courts deriving from diversity of citizenship. On various grounds corporations became involved in litigation in federal courts. That involvement entailed definition of the status of private corporations within the constitutional system, a definition rendered difficult by the fact that the Constitution nowhere made mention of such a device.

Since corporations were created by the states they might have been classified as in effect public bodies, arms of the states themselves. But in terms of nineteenth-century constitutional thought, the power of any arm of a state, such as a city or town or county, could at any time be reabsorbed by the state itself. The charter of a public corporation did not constitute a contract which the states by the Contract Clause were forbidden to impair.[2] The *Dartmouth College Case* assured to private corporations this important protection. On the other hand, as public corporations these bodies would presumably have been entitled to have their grants construed broadly, a privilege which Daniel Webster and others sought for them in the *Charles River Bridge Case* but which the Supreme Court denied to them.[3]

As for the analogy with persons, Chief Justice Marshall gave recognition to that legal status in the *Dartmouth College Case*, saying that "A corporation is an artificial being, invisible, intangible, and existing only in contemplation of law."[4] But although status as persons gave to corporations certain protections, such as those of the Fifth Amendment, it did not give the right to sue in federal courts by virtue of diversity of citizenship. That right was granted not to mere persons but to citizens. Could a corporation be a citizen within the meaning of the Jurisdictional Clause? The difficulty here lay in the tendency to identify citizenship with voting privileges, which presumably no one wished to grant to or even to claim for corporations and, more important, if a corporation was a citizen for the purpose of suing or being sued in a federal court it could with equal logic be held to be a citizen within the provision of

---

George Heberton Evans, *Business Incorporations in the United States, 1800–1943*; Oscar Handlin and Mary Flug Handlin, *Commonwealth, A Study of the Role of Government in the American Economy: Massachusetts, 1774–1861*; Louis Hartz, *Economic Policy and Democratic Thought: Pennsylvania, 1776–1860*;

James Neal Primm, *Economic Policy in the Development of a Western State—Missouri, 1820–1860*.

[2] See the implications of this position in Dartmouth College v. Woodward, 4 Wheat. 518 (1819).

[3] Charles River Bridge v. Warren Bridge, 11 Pet. 420 (1837).

[4] 4 Wheat. 518, 636 (1819).

XIX: *The Rights of Corporations*

Article IV, Section 2 of the Constitution—"The citizens of each state shall be entitled to all privileges and immunities of citizens in the several states." This provision was a troublemaker in another field in that it provided basis for the claim of the right of free Negroes to move from state to state and be treated as equals with white citizens, a right which Southern states were determined not to grant. Those states hostile to the influence of Northern capital exercised through corporations were likewise opposed to a definition of citizenship which would permit corporations to range at will through states other than those by which they were incorporated.

The first Supreme Court pronouncement on the subject had come in 1809 in *Bank of the United States v. Deveaux*, in which Chief Justice Marshall said flatly for the Court, "That invisible, intangible, and artificial being, that mere legal entity, a corporation aggregate, is certainly not a citizen; and, consequently, cannot sue or be sued in the courts of the United States, unless the rights of the members, in this respect, can be exercised in their corporate name."[5] Nevertheless, by looking at what he called "the rights of the members," he concluded that a corporation whose "members" were citizens of another state might bring suit in a federal court against a citizen of a state on the basis of diversity of citizenship. Chancellor Kent explained the case in his *Commentaries* by saying, "The court can look beyond the corporate name and notice the character of the members, who are not considered, to every intent, as placed out of view, and merged in the corporation."[6] The vagueness of the author's language indicates the difficulty which the Court had faced in giving limited jurisdiction over corporations without going so far as to incur serious opposition.[7]

The decision was handed down during the period of Jeffersonian democracy, which was hostile to the federal courts and to large-scale business enterprise. To assert federal jurisdiction at all was to take a considerable step. To limit jurisdiction to cases in which all the "members" of a corporation could be reached in one state was consistent with the slightly earlier decision in *Strawbridge v. Curtiss*,[8] where the Court had held that under the Judiciary Act of 1789 suits involving multiple parties could be brought in a federal court only when each of the plaintiffs was a citizen of a state other than that of each of the defendants. The result was to deny jurisdiction in suits of group against group of persons who might for the most part reside in different states but

---

[5] Bank of the United States v. Deveaux, 5 Cranch 61, 86 (1809).
[6] James Kent, *Commentaries on American Law*, I, 348.
[7] For reassertion of the position by Justice Story on circuit in 1839 and for the relevant intervening cases see Bank of Cumberland v. Willis, 2 Fed. Cas. 648 (No. 885) (C.C.D. Me. 1839).
[8] 3 Cranch 267 (1806).

where one of the joint plaintiffs might be a citizen of the same state as one of the joint defendants. Since in the corporation case the Court looked to the "members" as the basis for jurisdiction, it was naturally assumed that jurisdiction would not exist if one of the "members" proved to be a citizen of the same state as the opposing party.

As indicated hereafter, Chief Justice Marshall and other members of his Court came to deplore the limitations which they had set up to jurisdiction in cases involving corporations. In 1839 Congress modified the Judiciary Act to remove the limiting effect of the *Strawbridge* case by authorizing jurisdiction in cases involving multiple parties as if some adversaries in the groups involved were citizens of different states, even though some might be citizens of the same states. Judgments and decrees were to be valid as to the citizens of different states but were not to reach the persons who were citizens of the same states.[9] Although the statute did not specifically say so, some people believed that a citizen of one state might now sue a corporation of another state, even though one or more "members" of that corporation might reside in the state of the plaintiff. The argument was first presented to the Taney Court in *Commercial and Railroad Bank of Vicksburg v. Slocumb*, decided in 1840.[10]

The Bank of Vicksburg was incorporated in Mississippi and had its principal place of business there, but it happened to have two stockholders in Louisiana as well. When in the United States Circuit Court in Mississippi other Louisiana citizens won a judgment against the bank, the bank took the case to the Supreme Court, contending that jurisdiction was lacking since the plaintiffs had a common citizenship with two of the stockholders. The original plaintiffs, now defendants in error, argued that the Act of 1839 made it possible for the Circuit Court to take jurisdiction in spite of the limited amount of common citizenship. Although, as noted below in discussion of the *Letson* case, the Supreme Court acted most reluctantly, it decided unanimously that the existence of the limited common citizenship, or the absence of complete diversity of citizenship, meant that the Circuit Court had no jurisdiction in the case. The statute of 1839, said Justice Barbour for the Court, did not extend to this case of a corporate defendant. The position taken was incidentally reaffirmed in another case decided at the same term, Justice Baldwin remarking in a unanimous opinion that the line of decisions had "settled this point definitively."[11]

---

[9] 5 Stat. 319.

[10] 14 Pet. 60 (1840).

[11] Irvine v. Lowry, 14 Pet. 293, 299 (1840). For discussion of the cases both before and after this date see Gerard C. Henderson, *The Position of Foreign Corporations in American Constitutional Law*, 50–76.

JOHN CATRON
Associate Justice 1837–1865
(Library of Congress)

Etched by Albert Rosenthal Phila. 1890

JOHN McKINLEY
Associate Justice 1837–1852
(Library of Congress)

PETER V. DANIEL
Associate Justice 1841–1860
(Library of Congress)

SAMUEL NELSON
Associate Justice 1845–1872
(*Library of Congress*)

LEVI WOODBURY
Associate Justice 1845–1861
(Library of Congress)

ROBERT C. GRIER
Associate Justice 1846–1870
(*Library of Congress*)

BENJAMIN R. CURTIS
Associate Justice 1851–1857
(Library of Congress)

JOHN A. CAMPBELL
Associate Justice 1853–1861
(Library of Congress)

XIX: *The Rights of Corporations*

Yet there was growing discontent with respect to the limitation of the jurisdiction of the federal courts in corporation cases. Corporations were growing larger as well as more numerous and stock was more and more widely held, with the result that there was frequent overlapping citizenship between stockholders and opposing parties, with consequent curtailment of federal jurisdiction. The panic of 1837 and the economic turmoil of the ensuing years increased the volume of litigation. Although Congress refused to include corporations among the beneficiaries of the short-lived bankruptcy statute, those interests which felt that more adequate justice could be attained in the federal than in the state courts were anxious to see federal jurisdiction expanded. Within a four-year period from the date of the *Bank of Vicksburg* decision, the Supreme Court unanimously, or with seeming unanimity, reversed its position.

The reversal was brought about in connection with a suit brought by Thomas W. Letson, a citizen of New York, against the Louisville, Cincinnati, and Charleston Railroad Company, a South Carolina corporation, in the United States Circuit Court for South Carolina, before Justice Wayne and District Judge Robert B. Gilchrist. The company was one of the many ventures of its kind which were started with high hopes of wealth and achievement and ended in frustration and disappointment. Organized under the presidency of the ardent Southerner and advocate of states' rights Robert Y. Hayne, it had been intended to link Charleston with Louisville and Cincinnati and promote a stream of commerce between the South and the West in competition with Northern trade. "The South and the West," Hayne proclaimed in a toast in Knoxville in 1836. "We have published the banns—if any one know aught why these two should not be joined together, let him speak now, or forever hold his peace."[12]

Unexpectedly and tragically for Hayne, the voice of the gyrating business cycle spoke the unwelcome words. The panic of 1837 and the business turbulence which followed, and the death of Hayne himself, brought collapse of the major part of the venture. Letson's suit against the company, where he won damages of some eighteen thousand dollars, was merely one of the innumerable steps toward final settlement.

Had all the stockholders of the company been citizens of South Carolina there would have been no doubt that Letson, as a citizen of New York, could sue the company in a federal court in South Carolina. But the situation was confused in that two of the stockholders were citizens of North Carolina; and one of the stockholders was the Bank of

---

[12] Ulrich B. Phillips, *A History of* | *Transportation in the Eastern Cotton Belt to 1860*, 184.

Charleston, two of whose own stockholders were citizens of Letson's state of New York; and, to make matters even more complicated, stock in the railroad corporation was held by the state of South Carolina itself, which by the Eleventh Amendment was protected against suits brought directly against it by citizens of other states. Clearly the time had come when the citizenship or the personality of the corporation needed to be defined more precisely for purposes of determining the jurisdiction of the federal courts.

The court records in the *Letson* case are exasperatingly sparse. In writing the opinion of the Court Justice Wayne referred to "the really distinguished ability of the arguments of the counsel"[13] in the case. Since the docket of the Supreme Court shows the cases as having been presented only on written arguments, it is hard to tell whether Justice Wayne's reference is merely to the written arguments or also to the oral arguments in the court below. With respect to the filing of reply briefs, the docket entries seem to be deficient. The Reporter, however, Justice Wayne's friend Benjamin C. Howard, noted that on account of the great importance of the case "the reporter has thought it proper to insert these arguments in extenso,"[14] and he did so accordingly.

Deciding the jurisdictional question without a written opinion, the Circuit Court found the necessary diversity of citizenship, whereupon the case was taken to the Supreme Court exclusively on that question. In presenting the case for the appellant railroad, Alexander Mazyck of Charleston, evidently an able lawyer though now one largely unknown to history, had the solid support of a long line of Supreme Court decisions. The attack on that line of decisions was made in a brief by the firm of Petigru and Lesesne of Charleston. James L. Petigru was a distinguished Whig and an opponent of the political leadership of Hayne and Calhoun. An additional brief was filed by Hugh S. Legaré, another distinguished Whig from South Carolina who at this time was in Washington as Attorney General of the United States. Justice Story regarded him as a profound legal scholar, and his loss—his death occurred in Boston in 1843 between the time of the submission and the decision of the *Letson* case—as irreparable.[15]

Petigru and Lesesne attacked the position long held by the Supreme Court that jurisdiction of the federal courts in corporation cases depended on what Chief Justice Marshall had called the "members" of the corporation, which had been held to mean the stockholders. They contended that at most the only persons whose citizenship was relevant were the corporate officers, who acted for the corporation, and

---

[13] Louisville, Cincinnati and Charleston R.R. v. Letson, 497, 555 (1844).

[14] *Ibid.*, 498.
[15] *Life and Letters of Joseph Story*, William W. Story, ed., II, 452–58.

against whom in any case it would be necessary to proceed. The stockholders who were not officers could not be proceeded against in any suit against the corporation as such and could not sue in its name; therefore their citizenship was irrelevant to the jurisdictional question. A corporation was "but a state in miniature,"[16] and in a corporation as in a state the real authors of official acts were the heads of administration.

Attorney General Legaré began his argument by stating a general consideration that was likely to weigh heavily with the Supreme Court. It was that if a citizen of New York could not thus be protected in his dealing with a corporation whose place of business and whose officers were located in South Carolina, "everybody will admit that there is somewhere a great chasm in our laws, and a serious grievance in our practice."[17] He stressed the fact that ours was a country where "the spirit of association goes hand in hand with that of commerce; and all great enterprises, without exception, throughout the whole extent of this vast confederacy, are carried on by incorporated companies, local in nothing but their name and origin."[18] He contended that a corporation was a personification of certain legal rights, and that "the whole is essentially and unchangeably different from all the parts, which are as completely merged and lost in it as the ingredients are in a chemical compound."[19] It was essential, he contended, that this distinction between the corporation and its constituent members should always be kept in view. He deplored as "a deviation from clear principles" the line of decisions in which the courts had determined jurisdiction by looking to the citizenship of corporate members.[20] Yet, perhaps wary lest he uproot all justification of federal jurisdiction in this type of case by excluding the factor of the citizenship of stockholders, he stated that he did not "desire any judicial innovation on a rule so well established,"[21] and tried to show that with a correct interpretation of the 1839 statute the Court could take jurisdiction in this case.

The case was submitted to the Supreme Court in February, 1843, at a time when Justices Story, Thompson, and McKinley were absent. At the end of the term it was continued under advisement. At the 1844 term a vacancy resulted from the death of Justice Thompson, Chief Justice Taney was absent most of the term because of illness, and Justice McKinley's attendance was never more than sporadic. The entry in the Supreme Court docket dates the judgment of the Court as March 7, 1844, but the minutes show no action on that date, carrying the entry as of March 15, 1844. As of that date only Justices Story, McLean, Baldwin, Wayne, and Catron were present. Since there was no record of

---

[16] 2 How. 510.
[17] *Ibid.*, 515.
[18] *Ibid.*

[19] *Ibid.*, 520.
[20] *Ibid.*, 523.
[21] *Ibid.*

dissent, it is important to note the presence of Justice Catron and the absence of Justice Daniel, both of whom later found much to criticize in the opinion of the Court.

In the opinion of the Court Justice Wayne stated that the early cases had never been satisfactory to the bar or even to the Court and that they had been followed most reluctantly and with dissatisfaction: "By no one was the correctness of them more questioned than by the late Chief Justice who gave them. It is within the knowledge of several of us, that he repeatedly expressed regret that those decisions had been made, adding, whenever the subject was mentioned, that if the point of jurisdiction was an original one, the conclusion would be different."[22] The recent decision in the *Bank of Vicksburg* case, in 1840, had been most reluctantly given, "upon mere authority." The Act of 1839 had been passed to rid the courts of the *Strawbridge* case, and it would be possible to decide the *Letson* case on that basis, but the Court preferred to rest it on a broader ground.

That broader ground Justice Wayne stated as follows: "It is, that a corporation created by and doing business in a particular State, is to be deemed to all intents and purposes as a person, although an artificial person, an inhabitant of the same State, for the purposes of its incorporation, capable of being treated as a citizen of that State, as much as a natural person."[23] It is to be noted that he found the basis of corporate citizenship in the place of incorporation and the place of doing business, and not, as Petigru had urged, in the citizenship of the officers of the corporation. The Court, said Justice Wayne, could not reconcile the corporate qualities of residence, habitation, and individuality with a requirement that jurisdiction was to be had only if all the corporators were citizens of the state in which the suit was brought: "When the corporation exercises its powers in the State which chartered it, that is its residence, and such an averment is sufficient to give the circuit courts jurisdiction."[24]

Five years before the decision in the *Letson* case, in *Bank of Augusta v. Earle*,[25] the Supreme Court had rejected Daniel Webster's argument that a corporation of a state was in a broad sense a citizen of a state and, under the Privileges and Immunities Clause, was entitled in other states to the privileges accorded to citizens there. In that case Chief Justice Taney held that a corporation of one state might have in another state only such privileges of doing business as the latter state might see fit to give to it. But with the statement in the *Letson* case that a corporation was capable of being treated as a citizen of the state of its incorporation "as much as a natural person,"

---

[22] *Ibid.*, 555.　　[23] *Ibid.*, 558.　　[24] *Ibid.*, 559.　　[25] 13 Pet. 519 (1839).

464

and with the assumption of jurisdiction in federal courts thereafter as a matter of course in diversity of citizenship cases involving corporations, pressure began to be exerted once more to give to corporations the rights of citizens in other states as well as in their own. In the argument of a case before the New Jersey Supreme Court, counsel cited opinions of Webster and other authorities to the effect that a state could not levy on a foreign corporation taxes which it did not levy on its own corporations.[26] The court rejected the argument but its presentation was evidence of a movement which the courts would have to take seriously.[27]

Presumably it was the growing power of corporations and the increase in their pretensions which led Justice Daniel in 1853 to challenge the decision in the *Letson* case, in which for some reason he had not taken the trouble to dissent even though it had been before the Court for a full year. Contending that within the meaning of the Constitution only a natural person could be a citizen, he extended his criticism back even to *Bank of the United States v. Deveaux*, where the Court had limited jurisdiction to cases in which, according to the averments, all "members" of the corporation were citizens of a state other than the state of the opposing party. He contended that if a corporation could be treated as a citizen for any purpose it might be so treated for all purposes, including the right to aspire to the Presidency.[28]

The case, involving a suit by citizens of Pennsylvania against a canal company in Delaware, brought no substantive disagreement among the Justices but difference only on the jurisdictional question. Justice Daniel having brought up that subject, Justice Catron also decided to take a position on it, even though the majority wholly ignored the question. It appears that he had understood the *Letson* case not as Justice Wayne had written the opinion but as Petigru had argued it, namely, as holding that a corporation could sue and be sued in a federal court when its officers were citizens of a state other than that of the opposing party. Justice Catron thus stood with Justice Daniel in desiring to prevent expansion of the rights of corporations by classifying them

---

[26] Tatem v. Wright, 23 N.J.L. 429, 435–36 (1852).

[27] See also Commonwealth v. Milton, 51 Ky. (12 B. Mon.) 212, 227 (1851), where the Kentucky Court of Appeals said of the *Letson* case that "There are, it is true, some expressions in the opinion which indicate that corporations may be regarded as citizens to all intents and purposes. But in saying this, the Court went far beyond the question before them, and to which it must be assumed, their attention was particularly directed. They make no reference to the clause of the Constitution now under consideration. There is no reason to suppose that they deliberated upon it, or looked to the effect of its application to corporations regarded as citizens. They certainly did not undertake to construe this clause."

[28] Rundle v. Delaware & Raritan Canal Co., 14 How. 80, 101 (1853).

as citizens, but wished equally to preserve the right of suit in federal courts. He thought the preservation of federal jurisdiction essential to the protection of the rights of litigants who must contend with corporations.[29]

At the following term Justice Catron restated his interpretation of the *Letson* decision and contended that jurisdiction could not be based on the assumption that a corporation was a citizen of the state in which it was incorporated. There must be an averment of the citizenship of the president and directors.[30] Justice Daniel reiterated his position that jurisdiction could not be derived either from the citizenship of persons or from an alleged citizenship of the corporation itself.[31] In this case was heard a new voice, that of Justice Campbell of Alabama, who noted that the case had been decided without recourse on the part of the majority to averments as to the citizenship of the parties. He warned that from this decision no inference was to be drawn as to his position in the matter.[32] It was evident that the majority of the Court would have to reassert and perhaps to reformulate its position with respect to jurisdiction in corporation cases.

The restatement was made in a case involving the Baltimore and Ohio Railroad Company, a case which in other respects than that of jurisdiction illustrates the problems created by the growing power of corporations. The case was a suit by Alexander J. Marshall of Virginia against the Baltimore and Ohio, for fifty thousand dollars for lobbying in the legislature to grant the railroad a right of way through western Virginia. There were in Virginia competing railroad and canal interests that were opposed to the extension of the line of the Maryland corporation, and Marylanders had not learned how to make themselves effective in the legislature at Richmond. The president of the railroad during the late 1840s was Louis McLane, who as Secretary of the Treasury and then as Secretary of State had been a rival of Attorney General Roger B. Taney for leadership in the Jackson Cabinet.

Marshall visited McLane to discuss a project for lobbying legislation through the legislature for a huge contingent fee, and then wrote out his plan in a letter of amazing frankness. The legislation had thus far been defeated by logrolling, which, he explained, had been developed into a system in the Virginia legislature. Members openly avowed and acted on it, and never concealed their bargains except where dis-

---

29 *Ibid.*, 95. For Justice Daniel's brief reaffirmation of his own position at the same term see Philadelphia & Reading R.R. v. Derby, 14 How. 468, 488 (1853).

30 Northern Indiana R.R. v. Michigan Central R.R., 15 How. 233, 249 (1854).
31 *Ibid.*, 251.
32 *Ibid.*, 251–52.

closure would jeopardize success. The secret of the success of opposition to the right of way lay in propinquity: the opposition was on the ground and in position to make itself effective, whereas the corporation was not. Marshall proposed to remedy this defect by employing a group of well-known and well-liked people to associate in friendly fashion with Virginia legislators and talk favorably about the project without disclosure of their purpose. He noted that the mass of the legislators were "a thoughtless, careless, light-hearted body of men, who come there for the 'per diem,' and to spend the 'per diem.' For a brief space they feel the importance and responsibility of their position. They soon, however, engage in idle pleasures, and on all questions disconnected with their immediate constituents, they become as wax, to be molded by the most pressing influences."[33]

The company agreed to Marshall's proposal, and concurred later in certain modifications of the proposed right of way. Within four months after the Marshall letter was written the measure was enacted. The company then seems to have tried to settle Marshall's bill for a mere six hundred dollars. He brought suit in the United States Circuit Court in Baltimore for the full fifty thousand, which was to be paid in bonds of the company at par value. In the trial of the case before Chief Justice Taney he gave instructions which in terms of the facts would render the contract void as contrary to public policy, and the jury returned a verdict for the company.[34] Marshall took the case to the Supreme Court on writ of error.

Revealing a sense of nausea at the whole performance, the Supreme Court affirmed the judgment. All persons had a right to advocate legislation, said Justice Grier for the majority, but persons who appeared for that purpose must do so honestly and in their true characters: "Any attempts to deceive persons intrusted with the high functions of legislation, by secret combinations, or to create or bring into operation undue influences of any kind, have all the injurious effects of a direct fraud on the public."[35] Bribes in the shape of high contingent compensation, he reasoned, must necessarily lead to the use of improper means to secure the desired ends. "The use of such means and such agents will have the effect to subject the state governments to the combined capital of wealthy corporations, and produce universal corruption, commencing with the representative and ending with the elector. Speculators in legislation, public and private, a compact corps of venal solicitors, vending their secret influences, will infest the capital of the Union and

---

[33] Marshall v. Baltimore & Ohio R.R., 16 How. 314, 317 (1854).
[34] Marshall v. Baltimore & Ohio R.R., 16 Fed. Cas. 828 (No. 9124) (C.C.D. Md. 1852).
[35] 16 How. 335.

of every State, till corruption shall become the normal condition of the body politic, and it will be said of us as of Rome—'omne Romae venale.' "[36]

Justice Grier felt it necessary to reassert, as against three dissenters, the right of the federal courts to take jurisdiction in suits between citizens of one state and corporations of another. He noted that the published report of the *Letson* case, "whatever the fact may have been," disclosed no dissent in that case from the opinion of the Court. It had now for ten years been regarded as settling the question, and the practice and forms of pleading in the federal courts had been conformed to it. Cases involving large amounts had been decided on the basis of it. For this reason alone, even if the Court were not now inclined to approve the *Letson* decision, the rule should not be abandoned.

But in reaffirming the jurisdiction of the federal courts, Justice Grier resorted to a very different line of argument from that taken by Justice Wayne in the *Letson* case. He admitted that a corporation itself could not be a citizen, and he reasserted the position of *Bank of Augusta v. Earle* that a corporation could have no existence outside the bounds of the sovereignty that had created it—thereby countering the argument that a corporation might be a citizen of other states with all the privileges and immunities of such citizens. He rested jurisdiction once more upon the citizenship of the persons acting through or for the corporation, not saying specifically whether he relied on the citizenship of the directors or on that of all the stockholders, but seeming to rely on the former. Taking this position, he introduced an enormously important fiction:

> The persons who act under these faculties, and use this corporate name, may be justly presumed to be resident in the state which is the necessary habitat of the corporation, and where alone they can be made subject to suit; and should be estopped in equity from averring a different domicil as against those who are compelled to seek them there, and can find them there and nowhere else.[37]

This fiction was necessary, he said, because otherwise a corporation could deprive its adversaries in other states from access to federal courts by the device of electing a director from the state in question. The necessary averment for jurisdiction was that the corporation was formed under the laws of a given state. He deplored the interpretation of the Jurisdictional Clause of the Constitution with the narrowness of a penal statute. The right of choosing an impartial tribunal was a privilege

---

36 *Ibid.*   37 *Ibid.*, 328.

of great importance, both for persons contending with powerful corporations and for corporations in places where local prejudices or jealousy might affect them.

The *Marshall* decision brought another long dissenting opinion in Justice Daniel's colorful language. He welcomed Justice Grier's concession that a corporation was not itself a citizen but he made no concessions of his own. The case of *Bank of the United States v. Deveaux* had been "ignis fatuus No. 1." The *Letson* case had been "ignis fatuus No. 2." The *Marshall* decision was "indeed the chef d'oeuvre among the experiments to command the action of the spirit in defiance of the body of the Constitution."[38]

In language hardly more temperate Justice Campbell also dissented, with the concurrence of Justice Catron. Corporations had not been in the minds of the framers when they delegated jurisdiction in controversies between citizens of different states. He deplored the attempts to extend the rights of corporations beyond the borders of their own states and he was opposed to enlarging the connections between corporations and the federal courts. Reflecting the dislike of many Southerners for business corporations, he observed scathingly:

> Their revenues and establishments mock at the frugal and stinted conditions of state administration; their pretentions and demands are sovereign, admitting impatiently, interference by state legislative authority. And from the present case we learn that disdainful of "the careless arbiters" of state interests, they are ready "to hover about them" in "efficient and vigilant activity," to make them a prey; and, to accomplish this, to employ corrupt and polluting appliances.[39]

For all its vigor, the opposition of the dissenters proved ineffective. The lower federal courts, with the approval of the Supreme Court, continued to take jurisdiction of corporation cases based on diversity of citizenship. Justice Curtis wrote the next opinion of the Supreme Court in such a case, stating that an averment that a corporation was a citizen of a state made no sense but that the defect was remedied by an allegation that a corporation was created under the laws of a state and had its principal place of business there.[40] Although by a kind of verbal

---

[38] *Ibid.*, 344. The opinion continued, "It is compelled, from the negation of that instrument, by some necromantic influence, potent as that by which, as we read, the resisting Pythia was constrained to yield her vaticinations of an occult futurity. For in this case is manifested the most entire disregard of any and every quali-fication, political, civil or local." *Ibid.*, 344–45.

[39] *Ibid.*, 353.

[40] Lafayette Insurance Co. v. French, 18 How. 404 (1856). See also Chief Justice Taney in Covington Drawbridge Co. v. Shepherd, 20 How. 227 (1858); and Justice Catron in Covington Drawbridge Co. v. Shepherd, 21 How. 112 (1858).

shorthand there was a tendency to talk about the citizenship of a corporation, Chief Justice Taney explained in 1862 that when a corporation sued in a federal court the suit was in contemplation of law "the suit of the individual persons who compose it."[41] He refrained from saying whether "persons" included all stockholders or merely the president and directors. During the Taney period the Court drew the line only at attempts of corporations having charters from two or more states to claim a kind of universal right to sue in a federal court, even when the opposing party was a citizen of one of the states by which a charter was conferred. In such a situation, said Chief Justice Taney, the corporation could not bring suit in the federal Circuit Court in either of the states of its incorporation.

By the end of the Taney period the right of corporations to sue in federal courts by virtue of diversity of citizenship, and the right of persons to sue them there, were well established. For the most part during this period corporations seem to have tried as hard to escape that jurisdiction as to have it confirmed. It was in later decades that "forum shopping" came to be associated with corporations and federal courts came to be looked upon as their special refuge. As for other rights of citizenship than those of suing in federal courts, the efforts of Daniel Webster and others to secure them to corporations were permanent failures.

In many other contexts the Court played a part in defining the rights of corporations. It had to act in light of the fact that, glamorous as were the prospects of achievements and profits through use of the corporation device, a justifiable attitude of popular suspicion was often reflected in legislation. It was widely felt that large holdings of land must not be permitted to fall into corporate hands, and many states legislated to that end, often limiting even their own corporations to the ownership of only such tracts as were essential to the enterprise for which they were chartered.[42] The Court noted on one occasion that in Pennsylvania, although both domestic and foreign corporations might acquire land, land held without a license from the state was subject to forfeiture.[43]

Although the *Charles River Bridge* decision had asserted the principle that the charters of private corporations were to be construed strictly in the determination of the rights conferred, the application of the principle remained to be worked out in many highly controversial

---

[41] Ohio & Mississippi R.R. v. Wheeler, 1 Black 286, 297 (1862).

[42] Cadman, *The Corporation in* *New Jersey, Business and Politics, 1791–1875*, 232–33.

[43] Runyan v. Lessee of Coster, 14 Pet. 122 (1840).

cases. It remained to be determined, for example, whether a state could take by eminent domain a franchise which it had given to build and operate a toll bridge. In 1848 Daniel Webster and Jacob Collamer of Vermont represented before the Supreme Court the West River Bridge Company, from which a bridge at Brattleboro had been taken, opposing Samuel S. Phelps of that state. Webster and Collamer contended that the act impaired the obligation of the contract. The power of eminent domain, they asserted, only recently recognized and "naturalized" in this country, was unknown to the Constitution, and to the constitutions of the states. It had been adopted by writers "on other and arbitrary governments," and was based on the premise that all sovereign powers were vested in some department of state authority—an assumption that was far from true. The only security lay in the Supreme Court of the United States to keep the newly asserted power within safe and well-defined limits and protect private citizens from unlimited despotisms. Otherwise the state legislatures and their agents would become the sole judges of what might be taken and for what purpose, and "the most levelling ultraisms of Antirentism or Agrarianism or Abolitionism may be successfully advanced."[44]

Webster lost his case. With only Justice Wayne dissenting, the Court held that the property represented by the charter was subject to the power of eminent domain, a power not surrendered to the United States by the states, and that the taking by this process did not violate the obligation of contracts. This defense of states' rights gave Justice Daniel one of his relatively infrequent opportunities to speak for the Court. The decision established the principle that, for all the sanctity of the contracts in corporation charters, the property rights conferred could be recaptured by the states through the eminent domain process just as other property could be so taken.

Situations sometimes changed so that corporations found it expedient to claim rights which had not been specified in their charters. An example was the charging of tolls on passengers carried back and forth on the Chesapeake and Delaware Canal on a route between Baltimore and Philadelphia. At the turn of the century both cities had been rivals for the trade of the interior of the country, and Pennsylvania had wanted construction of an inland water link with the Chesapeake Bay in order to trade with that region, which was then pretty much monopolized by Baltimore. Construction was authorized only after agreements for other developments to aid Baltimore, such as improvement of the Susquehanna for inland trade. Cargo in the form of goods was almost exclusively in mind, and it was only after the development of steam navigation and the considerable increase in population that

---

[44] West River Bridge v. Dix, 6 How. 507, 520–21 (1848).

the company tried to read into its charter the power to charge passenger tolls.

The company attempted to collect passenger tolls, the collection was challenged, and the constitutional question was certified to the Supreme Court from the United States Circuit Court in Delaware, where Chief Justice Taney was one of the two federal judges. The Supreme Court in a Taney opinion refused to read into the charter a power not there given. It was the province of the Court to expound the law as it stood, said the Chief Justice, and not to determine whether larger powers would have been given if the legislature had anticipated subsequent events.[45] The privilege of constructing the canal had been given without any compensation except that of public use of the canal. The states and the United States had contributed to the expenses. The Court was called upon to "decide whether the States who chartered this company have authorized it to exact any amount of toll it may think proper from its own citizens, as well as others, for the privilege of passing over it; or may, if such be its interest or policy, refuse altogether the permission to pass."[46] He could find no such authorization.

Many of the controversies over the scope of charter grants had to do with banking corporations. If it was hard to control corporations chartered to deal with relatively tangible materials such as transportation facilities, it was even harder to control those whose milieu consisted of the intangibles of banking. The public and the legislatures granted banking privileges in the hope of providing much needed currency and credit and promoting local prosperity. They clamored for restrictions and revenge when privileges were abused or when depressions came instead of prosperity. After the panic of 1837 debtors in Mississippi had the frustrating experience of seeing state banks refuse to receive their own depreciated notes in payment of debts due them.[47] In 1840 the legislature, responding to public resentment, tried to eliminate this subterfuge by denying to banks the right given by their charters to transfer bills and notes.

The highest court in Mississippi upheld the 1840 measure, and certain banks took cases to the Supreme Court on writ of error. In

---

[45] Perrine v. Chesapeake & Delaware Canal Co., 9 How. 172, 189 (1850).

[46] *Ibid.*, 192. Justice McLean, for himself and Justices Nelson and Woodbury, agreed that the canal company had no existing power to charge tolls on passengers, as distinguished from cargo and empty boats, but contended that the company was under no obligation to permit the passage of a line of passenger boats, charging for them as empties. Evidently the assumption was that the legislature could be persuaded to authorize the charging of passenger tolls.

[47] For discussion see Charles Warren, *The Supreme Court in United States History*, II, 161–63.

Planters' Bank v. Sharp[48] Justice Woodbury for the Court found that the assignment or selling of notes was granted by the bank charter and was essential to conducting the business of banking, and that the restricting statute impaired the obligation of contract. It was left to Justice Daniel in typical dissent to defend the rights of the states and to criticize a combination, "the effects and manifest purposes of which were to deny to the holders of the notes of these banking corporations the power of making payment to them in their own currency, and to enable the latter to seize or to appropriate to themselves or their favorites the substance of those very note holders to whom such right of payment was denied. A proceeding thus subversive of justice has not heretofore been sanctioned by this court."[49]

The Court also curbed the state of Arkansas in dealing with a bank chartered and owned by the state. A provision of the chartering statute provided that the notes of the bank should be received in payment of debts to the state. After the funds of the bank had been depleted by withdrawal or dissipation, the legislature repealed the provision requiring the state to accept its notes. For a majority of five members of the Court, Justice McLean held that the provision had constituted a contract, between the state and the holders of the paper of the bank, and that the contract could not be impaired.[50] By a series of statutes the state also took over the property of the bank instead of leaving it for payment of its debts. The Court held that such withdrawals likewise impaired the obligation of contracts with creditors.[51] These restrictions on the state of Arkansas, it is true, were not of a piece with those protecting the contract rights of corporations as such, but were rather defenses of the public and of customers and creditors of the bank chartered and owned by the state. As such they had characteristics different from most of those here under discussion.

Some of the most important cases involving the rights of corporations came from Ohio. For many years the state was embroiled in difficulties with its railroad, canal, and banking corporations. Its legislature was no more immune to unprincipled lobbying than that of Virginia—as in the instance of the Baltimore and Ohio right of way—or any other state. Until adoption of the constitution of 1851, most corporation

---

[48] 6 How. 344 (1848).

[49] *Ibid.*, 341. Chief Justice Taney and Justice McLean also dissented. Among the imposing array of counsel it is an odd fact that Daniel Webster appeared in opposition to the banking interests and the claims based on bank charters, and again found himself on the losing side.

[50] Woodruff v. Trapnall, 10 How. 190 (1851). The dissenters were Justices Catron, Daniel, Nelson, and Grier, with the last writing the dissenting opinion.

[51] Curran v. Arkansas, 15 How. 304 (1854). Justice Curtis wrote the opinion of the Court. Justices Catron, Daniel, and Nelson dissented.

charters were drawn by the interested parties and accepted by special acts of the legislature under circumstances which usually prevented careful consideration. In the language of Chief Justice Taney in connection with one of the Ohio cases:

> [I]t is a matter of public history, which this court cannot refuse to notice, that almost every bill for the incorporation of banking companies, insurance and trust companies, railroad companies, or other corporations, is drawn originally by the parties who are personally interested in obtaining the charter; and that they are often passed by the Legislature in the last days of its session, when, from the nature of our political institutions, the business is unavoidably transacted in a hurried manner, and it is impossible that every member can deliberately examine every provision in every bill upon which he is called on to act.[52]

Sentiment in the state was particularly divided over banking corporations. In general the Whigs were the friends of corporate enterprise and the Democrats the critics, but there were sharp divisions even among the Democrats.[53] It so happened that during the aftermath of the panic of 1837 and during the early 1840s many bank charters expired. Democrats were opposed to the extensive granting of charters and to the issuing of bank notes of low denominations, but in 1845, when the Whigs were temporarily in power in the legislature, they passed a general banking act under which banks throughout the state might be formed as branches of the State Bank of Ohio. One of the important provisions of the act required the bank to pay to the state 6 percent of its profits, "in lieu of all taxes to which such company, or the stockholders thereof, on account of stock owned therein, would otherwise be subject." When the Democrats came back into power to find the state harried in its search for needed revenues, they looked jealously on wealthy institutions which paid taxes only on their profits while individuals were paying on the value of their property whether they earned profits or not.

The constitutional convention which sat in 1850 and 1851 adopted a provision directing the legislature to provide for the taxation of all bank property, "without deduction," so that all property employed in banking should always bear a burden of taxation equal to that

---

[52] Ohio Life Ins. & Trust Co. v. Debolt, 16 How. 416, 435 (1854).

[53] Among the sources see C. C. Huntington, "History of Banking and Currency in Ohio Before the Civil War," *Ohio Archaeological and Historical Quarterly*, 23:235, 1915; Ernest L. Bogart, "Financial History of Ohio," *University of Illinois Studies in the Social Sciences*, 1: 1912; Edgar A. Holt, "Party Politics in Ohio, 1840–1850," *Ohio Archaeological and Historical Quarterly*, 37:439, 1928; Eugene H. Roseboom, *The Civil War Era, 1850–1873*; Francis P. Weisenburger, *The Passing of the Frontier, 1825–1850*.

imposed on the property of individuals.[54] In its enthusiasm for making the banks pay their equal burden of taxation, the legislature, before the new constitution was voted on, enacted "An act to tax banks and bank and other stocks, the same as other property is now taxable by the laws of this State."

The Ohio Life Insurance and Trust Company, one of the banks chartered under the Act of 1845, challenged the validity of the measure as a violation of the obligation of contract in the Act of 1845. The Ohio Supreme Court, reorganized under the new constitution, held that the earlier tax provision had not constituted a contract binding on subsequent legislatures, and that the enacting legislature had had no constitutional power thus to bind future legislatures.[55] This and other decisions involving the same question were taken to the Supreme Court.

It was important for Ohio to discover whether in this instance one legislature had granted a tax exemption which could not be repealed by another, and it was even more important for the country as a whole to discover whether in general one legislature could tie the hands of another with respect to taxation. The questions were argued in the Supreme Court on April 19–21, 1854, by Henry Stanbery, later to be Attorney General of the United States, and one Vinton for the Piqua Branch of the State Bank of Ohio, and by Rufus P. Spalding and George E. Pugh for Jacob Knoop, county treasurer. On the broad question of constitutional power, counsel dug deep into constitutional theory. On the question of the broad or narrow interpretation of the provision in the Act of 1845 which was claimed to give exemption from additional taxation, they relied respectively on the majority and minority opinions in the *Charles River Bridge Case*.[56]

With three Justices dissenting and Chief Justice Taney writing a brief and restrictive concurring opinion, the Court, on May 24, 1854, held the 1851 tax measure unconstitutional. Justice McLean, speaking for the majority, held that the Act of 1845 gave a contract right to exemption from taxation other than the 6 percent on profits. He rejected the argument that the power to tax was like the power of eminent

---

[54] Ohio constitution of 1851, Art. XII, Sec. 3.

[55] Debolt v. Ohio Life Ins. & Trust Co., 1 Ohio St. (1853).

[56] They relied also on the majority and minority opinions in Richmond, Fredericksburg & Potomac R.R. v. Louisa R.R., 13 How. 71 (1852). That case involved the question of impairment of the obligation of contract in the chartering of a railroad which in some measure competed with an earlier line which had been guaranteed freedom of competition as to passenger traffic. The question was difficult enough to bring about a four to three decision, in which the majority gave a restrictive interpretation to the grant. Justice Grier wrote the opinion of the Court and Justice Curtis spoke for the minority, which included also Justices McLean and Wayne.

domain in that it could not be contracted away by the state. Under eminent domain property might be taken, but it had to be paid for. Taxes collected contrary to contract yielded no such compensation.

In writing the opinion, Justice McLean expressed the dislike of general theory which characterized the Taney Court, but which it usually demonstrated only by example and not by critical statement:

> In the discussion of the principles of this case, we have not felt ourselves at liberty to indulge in general remarks on the theory of our government. This is a subject which belongs to a convention for the formation of a constitution; and in a limited view, to the law-making power. Theories depend so much on the qualities of the human mind, and these are so diversified by habit as to constitute an unsafe rule for judicial action. Our prosperity, individually and nationally, depends upon a close adherence to the settled rules of law, and especially to the great fundamental law of the Union.[57]

Justice Catron began his dissenting opinion by saying, "This is a contest between the State of Ohio and a portion of her banking institutions,"[58] then noted that the interests of some fifty banks were at stake, and said that their taxable property amounted to about eighteen million dollars. In the contest his sympathies were clearly with the state. He argued that the provision in the Act of 1845 did not constitute a contract, and that the power to tax, like the power of eminent domain, could not be contracted away. Justice Campbell too argued that the 1845 provision did not constitute a contract, advocating narrow interpretation partly on the ground that "The nature of legislative authority is inconsistent with an inflexible stationary system of administration."[59] Justice Daniel took an even more extreme position. Although the case had come up from a state court, he contended that a corporation was not a kind of entity of which the Court could take judicial notice, and that "one of the parties to this controversy being a corporation created by a State, this court can take no cognizance, by the constitution, of the acts, or rights, or pretensions of that corporation."[60] This was perhaps the most extreme position taken by any member of the Court in behalf of restriction of the rights claimed by corporations.

Ohio banks chartered by special act before 1845 were also taxed by the Act of 1851, and they, too, claimed violation of their rights under earlier statutes. The Supreme Court agreed with the Ohio courts that these banks were protected by no contract, but the six majority

---

[57] Piqua Branch of the State Bank of Ohio, 16 How. 369, 392 (1854).
[58] *Ibid.*, 393.

[59] *Ibid.*, 407.
[60] *Ibid.*, 405.

Justices divided so many ways that there was no opinion of the Court. Chief Justice Taney, writing more at length than he had done in the preceding case, discussed for himself and Justice Grier some of the issues of policy involved, particularly with respect to the scope of the freedom of the state to legislate. On the one hand, he agreed that there were "fixed and immutable principles of justice, sound policy and public duty" which no state could disregard without serious injury to the community or its citizens, and he admitted that states sometimes acted incautiously in the making of contracts. But on the other hand, he insisted that whether such contracts should be made was a matter exclusively for state decision. Over the making of such contracts the Supreme Court had no control. Even in the matter of making ruinous contracts the states were limited only by the provisions of the Constitution: "The principle that they are the best judges of what is for their own interest, is the foundation of our political institutions."[61] In the instance of these older banks, however, he could not find that any contract had been made.

The three dissenters in the preceding case naturally made up part of the majority in this one. Justice Catron referred ominously to "the unparalleled increase of corporations throughout the Union within the last few years; the ease with which charters, containing exclusive privileges and exemptions are obtained; the vast amount of property, power, and exclusive benefits, that are vested in and held by these numerous bodies of associated wealth."[62] Justice Daniel condemned the "suicidal doctrine" that one legislature had power to bind another by acts "however mischievous or destructive," and again asserted that a corporation could not be a proper party in a case before the Supreme Court.

In view of the amount of capital involved and also in view of the statement of constitutional principle, it was the first of these two cases that was most important, both in Ohio and in the country at large.[63] Banking interests were pleased but Democratic spokesmen were critical. The *Cincinnati Daily Enquirer* observed that this was not the first decision in which the doctrine of states' rights had met with little favor before the Court: "It has always leaned strongly to the Federal idea of a *strong* National Government, and has been very conservative in maintaining and carrying out the old English common law principle of the sacredness of corporations and their immunity from legislation."[64] The decision, said the *Enquirer*, was a great outrage against states'

---

[61] Ohio Life Ins. Co. v. Debolt, 16 How. 416, 429 (1854).
[62] *Ibid.*, 442–43.
[63] For discussion of the public reception of the Piqua Bank decision

see Warren, *The Supreme Court in United States History*, II, 249–53.
[64] *Cincinnati Daily Enquirer*, May 26, 1854.

rights. Its effect would be to release the wealthy chartered banks from their share of the burdens of government and to impose that share on the people.[65]

The Ohio Supreme Court seems to have been equally indignant at what it regarded as federal invasion of state prerogatives. For more than two years it refused to enter the mandate of the Supreme Court of the United States in the *Piqua Bank* case. Then, after the question had been argued before it, by Henry Stanbery, who initially argued the case for the bank, and by the current attorney general of Ohio, a majority of the state court decided to acquiesce. It did so over the objection of the chief justice, Thomas W. Bartley, who contended that the acts of 1845 and 1851 were merely state revenue laws, "in no way whatever affecting the operation of the federal government and wholly unconnected with the affairs of the United States."[66] Chief Justice Bartley pro-

---

[65] *Ibid.*, June 2, 1854.

In attempts by way of a new constitution and new statutes to solve tax problems, the people of Ohio added to their difficulties. The constitution provided that bank property should be taxed "without deduction." The Ohio Supreme Court found a tax on all banks to be constitutional. The legislature passed an act with respect to taxation on individuals and some corporations other than the banks in question and permitting the deduction of debts. The Ohio Supreme Court then held that the phrase "without deduction" which applied specifically to banks was to be applied by interpretation also to individuals. Exchange Bank of Columbus v. Hines, 3 Ohio St. 1 (1853). Then, with the holding of the Supreme Court of the United States that the major group of banks in Ohio could be taxed only to the extent of 6 percent on their profits, the people, who had been accustomed to deduction of debts from the tax base, found themselves in a worse position than ever in comparison with the banks. Said the *Enquirer*, "The shrewd and able attorneys for the Banks, in order to release the latter from the rates of taxation to which they were subject, saw no better way of doing it, than to place the people who had no chartered privileges, and who therefore ought not to be subject to high

taxation, upon the same platform with them. They argued in favor of so doing before the Court, and a majority of that body made its decision in accordance with their wishes, to the surprise of almost everybody in the State." *Cincinnati Daily Enquirer*, Apr. 28, 1854.

After the decision of the Supreme Court of the United States in the *Piqua Bank* case the same paper said, "The banks, therefore, have slipped off the constitutional platform of taxation, having managed, however, previously, by the cunning of their lawyers in influencing the Ohio Supreme Court, to get the people elevated to the same high standard, although it was not intended so to be by the framers of that instrument, and it is manifestly against both its letter and spirit. For the people there is no relief except through a change in the organic law of the State. Although, in the opinion of our highest judicial tribunal, the Constitution prescribes uniformity of taxation, the *banks only*, and *not the people* get rid of their burdens by this decision. This fact will render our present tax system more odious and iniquitous than before, and will greatly increase its unpopularity with the people." *Ibid.*, May 26, 1854.

[66] Piqua Branch of the State Bank of Ohio v. Knoup, 6 Ohio St. 342, 345 (1856).

ceeded to argue the negative side of the question, long since affirmatively settled by the Supreme Court, whether the appellate jurisdiction of the Supreme Court extended to the review and reversal of judgments of a state court. His, indeed, was a states' rights position argued with all the fervor of the Southern defenders of that position.[67]

In the meantime, in 1853, probably knowing that their cause would receive more sympathy in the federal courts than in the courts of Ohio, the banks organized under the Act of 1845 sought to get as much as possible of their litigation transferred to those courts. A county treasurer, George C. Dodge, entered certain Cleveland banks and took from them the money claimed for the taxes in controversy. The banks knew that recovery through the state courts was not to be expected. They therefore assigned to John C. Deshler of New York their claim to the seized money, whereupon Deshler sought recovery on a writ of replevin in the United States Circuit Court for Ohio, claiming diversity of citizenship. In spite of a provision in the Judiciary Act of 1789 which arguably prevented resort to such strategy,[68] the Circuit Court took jurisdiction, and the question was taken to the Supreme Court on writ of error.

With four Justices dissenting, the Supreme Court upheld the exercise of jurisdiction. The strategy of the banks was highlighted by the dissenting opinion of Justice Catron, who spoke resentfully of "a very disreputable proceeding" and "the grossness of this transaction," and insisted that "the Constitution did not contemplate this mode of acquiring jurisdiction to the courts of the Union."[69]

But for the banks it was naturally not enough to be able to sue to recover taxes after transfer of claims thereto to some person outside the state. They wanted to prevent the initial collection. John M. Woolsey of Connecticut became the owner of thirty shares of stock in a Cleveland bank. Woolsey sought in the United States Circuit Court for Ohio an injunction against the same county treasurer and against the

---

[67] Chief Justice Bartley also took the negative on another long-settled constitutional question by saying in another case, "I must be permitted to say, with all due deference, that I consider this doctrine, that the charter of a corporation is a contract, grossly preposterous, and most unjust and oppressive in its tendency." Citizens' Bank of Steubensville v. Wright, 6 Ohio St. 318, 341 (1856).

[68] "Nor shall any district or circuit court have cognizance of any suit to recover the contents of any promissory note or chose in action in favour of an assignee, unless a suit might have been prosecuted in such court to recover the said contents if no assignment had been made, except in the case of foreign bills of exchange." 1 Stat. 73, 79.

[69] Deshler v. Dodge, 16 How. 622, 634, 635 (1854).

officers of the bank to prevent the exaction and the payment of the taxes claimed. Justice McLean as circuit judge issued the injunction, denouncing the county officer's annual entry into the bank to seize funds to collect an illegal tax. "What a spectacle!" he wrote indignantly. "What a spectacle to a law-abiding people! Is there no preventive remedy? What stronger ground than this can be imagined for an injunction?"[70]

Once again the Supreme Court heard about the problems of bank taxation in Ohio, the bank being represented in this as in other cases by Henry Stanbery and also by a well-known Whig lawyer, Samuel F. Vinton, with Rufus P. Spalding representing the tax collector. With Justices Campbell, Catron, and Daniel dissenting, the Court, speaking through Justice Wayne, affirmed the decision of the Circuit Court. That the case was improperly brought in the Circuit Court as a "contrivance" to give that court jurisdiction, said Justice Wayne, was something to be proved in proper form in the case and not merely asserted in the argument. On the record it was a bona fide suit between citizens of different states. The purpose of the jurisdiction of the federal courts in suits between citizens of different states was to make the people think and feel, though residing in different states of the Union, that their relations to each other were protected by the strictest justice, administered in courts independent of all local control or connection with the subject matter of the controversy between the parties to the suit.[71]

As for the validity of the tax involved, the question was identical with that in the *Piqua Bank* case save that there the measure had been enacted under the old constitution of Ohio and this measure had been enacted under the new. "A change of constitution," said Justice Wayne, "cannot release a state from contracts made under a constitution which permits them to be made." The constitution permitted the making of the contract. Under neither constitution could the contract be impaired: "The moral obligations never die. If broken by states and nations, though the terms of reproach are not the same with which we are accustomed to designate the faithlessness of individuals, the violation of justice is not the less."[72]

The opinion of Justice Campbell, who spoke for the three dissenters, revealed him as the ablest of the Court's defenders of states' rights, at a time when the Dred Scott case was already under consideration and when civil war was only five years away. This, he said, was a suit not merely against the county treasurer but also against directors of

---

[70] Woolsey v. Dodge, 30 Fed. Cas. 606, 607 (No. 18032) (C.C.D. Ohio 1854).

[71] Dodge v. Woolsey, 18 How. 331, 354 (1856).
[72] *Ibid.*, 360.

the corporation, and hence a suit against the corporation itself. He now contended, as Justice Daniel had done in many cases, that a corporation could not be a citizen in the sense in which the term was used in the Constitution, and that therefore it could not be sued in a federal court. The Court having nevertheless taken jurisdiction, he contended that the case was not one where a court of chancery could provide a remedy—it was one not of redress of grievances but of supplying prudence and discretion requisite to successful corporate management.

On the merits of the case, he contended that the state had the right to make and interpret its constitution without supervision by the federal judiciary, and that alleged conflicts between constitutions and statutes or contracts included therein were matters for state solution. As for the claim for the Supreme Court as the final arbiter of these questions, he said, "I can imagine no pretension more likely to be fatal to the constitution of the court itself. If this court is to have an office so transcendent as to decide finally the powers of the people over persons and things within the state, a much closer connection and a much more direct responsibility of its members to the people is a necessary condition for the safety of the popular rights."[73] The people of Ohio had never deposited with the Court the authority to overrule their own judgment upon the extent of their powers over institutions created by their government. The fundamental principle of American constitutions was that to the states belonged all questions of municipal government and that the states were the judges of the exercise of their own powers.[74]

As for corporations, Justice Campbell argued, their "extraordinary pretensions" were well known far back in history, including those of ecclesiastical corporations acknowledging supremacy to the Pope, with their claims to inviolable rights of property. He believed that the principle of corporate policy, the dictate of corporate ambition, which had dominated in Europe and led to strife and devastating wars, was the same as that now being ratified by the Court. These creatures of the state were elevated above the legislatures which had created them. This interposition of the Court between the corporations and the people of Ohio would "establish on the soil of every State a caste made up of combinations of men for the most part under the most favorable conditions in society, who will habitually look beyond the institutions and the authorities of the State to the central government for the strength and support necessary to maintain them in the enjoyment of their special privileges and exemptions. The consequence will be a new element of alienation and discord between the different classes of society, and the

---

[73] *Ibid.*, 373.   [74] *Ibid.*, 374.

introduction of a fresh cause of disturbance in our distracted political and social system. In the end, the doctrine of this decision may lead to a violent overturn of the whole system of corporate combinations."[75]

There is no doubt that jealousy of the growing power of corporations and their arrogance in exercising that power did, in the language of Justice Campbell, provide an additional element of alienation and discord in an already disturbed and distracted political system. But the outbreak of violence, already in the offing, was not more than indirectly aimed at the overthrow of corporate power. The Supreme Court, while adhering to its position of guardianship of the rights given by charters, did something, as cases arose, to curb the illegitimate exercise of corporate power. Justice Campbell spoke for a unanimous Court in upholding the right of a stockholder to sue in a federal Circuit Court to restrain a corporation from performing acts not authorized by the charter. "A corporation," he said, "quite as much as an individual, is held to a careful adherence to truth in their dealings with mankind, and cannot, by their representations or silence, involve others in onerous engagements, and then defeat the calculations and claims their own conduct had superinduced."[76] The Court restated the same position in 1863,[77] some two years after Justice Campbell had left it to give aid to the Confederacy. Furthermore, the Court restated from time to time the position of the *Charles River Bridge Case* that rights given by charter were to be construed narrowly.[78]

The Taney period came to a close, however, without illumination by the Court of one problem of corporate responsibility which was to become important in the following decades. It dealt only sporadically with the tort liability of corporations for damage to property and injuries to persons, whether passengers, employees, or persons who happened to be in the vicinity of operations. In *Stokes v. Saltonstall*,[79] decided in 1839, it decided one of its first cases defining the duties of passenger carriers. It held that a carrier was obligated to use all possible foresight for the protection of passengers, and that in an action against a carrier the occurrence of an injury-producing accident was prima facie evidence of negligence on the part of the carrier. It held elsewhere that a railroad company was responsible for injuries to a passenger resulting from the gross negligence of an employee, even though the passenger

---

[75] *Ibid.*, 373.
[76] Zabriskie v. Cleveland, Columbus and Cincinnati R.R., 23 How. 381, 400–01 (1860). Also see Justice Campbell in Bacon v. Robertson, 18 How. 480 (1856).
[77] Moran v. Board of Commissioners of Miami County, 2 Black, 722 (1863).
[78] See for example Minturn v. La Rue, 23 How. 435 (1860); Rice v. Minnesota & Northwestern R.R., 1 Black 358 (1862).
[79] 13 Pet. 181 (1839).

had not paid his way but was a guest of the president of the company.[80] It held a corporation responsible for libelous publication of materials collected in a report of directors with respect to the conduct of its officers.[81] But in general the development of the law in this area, as far as the Supreme Court was concerned, was to come in a later period.

---

[80] Philadelphia & Reading R.R. v. Derby, 14 How. 468 (1853).

[81] Philadelphia, Wilmington & Baltimore R.R. v. Quigley, 21 How. 202 (1859).

CHAPTER XX

Patent Rights and Free Enterprise

DURING THE TANEY PERIOD the country bristled with excitement over the changing face of the country: the acquisition and settlement of new territory and the admission of new states, as well as discoveries and inventions which made possible new ways of life. New mechanisms and devices gave rise to new forms of industry, transportation, and communication, demonstrating the superior merits, so it was felt, of American democracy. Although public sentiment and legal theory recognized the peculiar virtues of free and competitive enterprise and assumed even in pre-Darwinian days that worth was measured by ability to survive in the competitive struggle, it was also recognized that progress might be promoted by rewards of temporary monopolies to inventors and discoverers. From this recognition came the statutory protection of patent rights and the litigation that they engendered.

The Constitution, following English practice dating from the Statute of Monopolies of 1624, had sought to "promote the progress of science and useful arts" by authorizing Congress to "secure for limited times to authors and inventors the exclusive right to their respective writings and discoveries." Congress promptly enacted such a measure in 1790 and replaced it with another in 1793. The latter remained in force for more than forty years, and was undergoing critical survey preparatory to its own replacement at the time of the appointment of Chief Justice Taney in 1836. The report of a special committee of the Senate, dated April 28, 1836, gave the setting of the patent problem and presented the replacement statute of 1836, which with amendments was to constitute the legislation on the subject until after the Civil War. The committee approved of the patent grant as the best mode of encouraging and rewarding inventors: "It is not at this day to be

484

doubted that the evil of the temporary monopoly is greatly overbalanced by the good that the community ultimately derives from its toleration."[1]

In the interpretation of patent rights, said the committee, American judges had followed the decisions of English courts, though with a more liberal application of equitable principles for the protection of patentees, "in a just endeavor to sustain patents for meritorious inventions, instead of seeking to find, in the technicalities of law, a pretext for setting them aside."[2] At the same time, in the granting of patents American policy had been so liberal that the country was flooded with patents which were worthless and void, either because they infringed on other patents or because lacking novelty or invention they covered unpatentable items. The Secretary of State, under whose jurisdiction the subject fell until creation of the Department of the Interior, had no authority or facilities for investigation of patentability. As a ministerial duty he issued the patents applied for when applications were made in the prescribed form and the requisite fees were paid. Indeed, the lack of control was so complete that people were said to have copied models in the patent office and secured their own patents on them, with the result that speculation in patent rights became a business involving hundreds of thousands of dollars and producing, for the time, an enormous amount of litigation. The courts, indeed, rather than the Department of State, became the primary agencies for determining patentability and the validity of patents issued. The committee recommended expansion of the facilities of the Patent Office in the State Department to determine novelty before a patent was granted, with power to reject applications where novelty could not be shown to exist. "The present law waits till infringements and frauds are consummated —nay, it even aids them; and then it offers an inadequate remedy for the injury, by giving an action for damages. It ought, rather, by refusing to grant interfering patents, to render prosecutions unnecessary. Instead of sanctioning the wrong by granting the privilege to commit it, it should arrest injury and injustice at the threshold, and put an end to litigation before it begins."[3]

By the Act of 1836[4] and by subsequent amending statutes,[5] Congress attempted to eliminate the evils discussed by the Senate committee and to transfer as much as possible of the decision-making process from the courts back to the Patent Office. The attempt was only partly successful. Personnel in the Patent Office were no doubt able to

---

[1] S. Rep. No. 338, 24th Cong., 1st Sess. 1 (1836).
[2] *Ibid.*, 2.
[3] *Ibid.*, 6.

[4] 5 Stat. 117.
[5] See especially 5 Stat. 191, 353, 543 (1837, 1839, 1842).

eliminate obvious frauds but there was a limit to which they could simplify a complex problem. The question of novelty in a new device for which a patent was sought and of infringement on an existing patent involved highly intricate considerations. Like other political agencies, the Patent Office was subject to political pressures from those seeking its aid. It was often easier to issue a patent of doubtful validity and permit its validity to be determined by the courts than to deny an application. Conversely, on rare occasions interests holding a patent already granted might be so influential as to make expedient the denial of a competing patent in an adjacent field, leaving to judicial or quasi-judicial determination the question of the appropriateness of the denial. And so the federal courts continued to find themselves deeply involved in the technicalities of patent litigation, with many of the cases decided finally in the Supreme Court.

Before the close of the Marshall period the Court had made clear the fact that the exclusive right which Congress was authorized to "secure" to authors and inventors was a right derived from the Constitution itself and implemented by statute, and not one deriving from the common law, settling the question in the famous suit between Henry Wheaton and Richard Peters over the copywriting of the reports of the Supreme Court itself.[6] Chief Justice Taney, it is true, speaking for the Supreme Court in 1851, imported common law and natural law overtones by saying that "the discovery of a new and useful improvement is vested by law with an inchoate right to its exclusive use, which he may perfect and make absolute by proceeding in the manner which the law requires."[7] Justice Daniel in dissent characterized as "mischievous and alarming an attempt to introduce a quasi and indefinite, indefinable, and invisible estate, independently of the Constitution and acts of Congress, and unknown to the rules and principles of the common law."[8] Six years later Chief Justice Taney, again speaking for the Court, eliminated the unwelcome overtones by saying that the right which a patentee had in his invention and his right to exclusive use derived altogether from statutory provisions.[9]

The judicial task, therefore, became that of applying the provisions of the statute, which in turn derived its force from the relevant provision of the Constitution. As a matter of principle the question of the validity of a patent was a question of law. Yet since, almost by definition, a discovery or an invented device must border on the fron-

---

[6] Wheaton v. Peters, 8 Wheat. 591 (1834).
[7] Gayler v. Wilder, 10 How. 477, 493 (1851).

[8] Ibid., 504. For discussion see E. Burke Inlow, The Patent Grant, 78–81.
[9] Brown v. Duchesne, 19 How. 183, 195 (1857).

tiers of the unknown, the question of patentability, or the question of infringement of a valid patent, often seemed more a matter of the discovery and arrangement of facts than of inquiry into the law. Judges had to acquire or pretend to knowledge in scientific fields far from the areas of their professional competence. Though with important exceptions, the counsel who argued patent cases before them tended to be specialized lawyers with an unusual knowledge not merely of patent law but also of the interrelations of law with the gadgetry of current invention, and to be as much interested in applied science as in law. They were accustomed to dramatizing their cases, not through the oratory of the period but through the fascination of patent models set up and operated in the courtroom.

A notable exemplar, in the Supreme Court, was George Harding of Philadelphia, who during the Taney period became one of the leading patent lawyers in the country. One case he argued,[10] from February 11 to February 18, 1864, had to do with alleged infringement on a patent for the manufacture of hats, and millions of dollars were said to depend on it.[11] A reporter, closely following the progress of the case, wrote, "In the hat body machine case today in the Supreme Court, Harding, of Philadelphia, closed his argument. He illustrated it impressively by making hats from fur cut from skins right in Court, in the short space of two minutes. Six Negroes drove the different machines, while the nine gowned judges leaned over their benches among the most interested of the spectators."[12] The reporter later wrote that the opinion in the case, by Justice Grier, was "considered the most important opinion on patent law ever decided in the Court."[13] With the operation of the machinery in mind, Justice Grier dealt with one of the most important distinctions to be made in patent cases, that between invented machinery on the one hand and a scientific principle on the other. The former could be monopolized by patent, the latter could not: "A machine is not a principle or an idea. The use of ill defined abstract phraseology is the frequent source of error. It requires no great ingenuity to mystify a subject by the use of abstract terms of indefinite or equivocal meaning. Because the law requires a patentee to explain the mode of operation of his peculiar machine, which distinguished it from others, it does not authorize a patent for a 'mode of operation as exhibited in a machine.' "[14]

The subject matter of patent litigation ranged all the way from items never very important and long since forgotten to inventions which transformed the whole economy. The litigation struggles over the more

---

[10] Burr v. Duryee, 1 Wall. 531 (1864).
[11] *New York Times*, Feb. 15, 1864.
[12] *New York Times*, Feb. 18, 1864.
[13] *New York Times*, Mar. 29, 1864.
[14] 1 Wall. 570.

important inventions may be illustrated by two of the most outstanding, the Morse telegraph and the McCormick reaper.

In 1844, as a government-financed experiment, the first telegraph line was constructed between Washington and Baltimore, with the transmission not only of the famous initial message, "What hath God wrought?" but also reports of the activities of national political party conventions. The construction made use of a patent issued in 1840 to Samuel F. B. Morse, a portrait painter with a bent for natural science. The telegraph marked a long step beyond earlier forms of telecommunication such as semaphores and sound drums, and even cannons set at spaced intervals and fired to indicate the consummation of some anticipated event. Knowledge of electricity had been accumulating for many decades, and the development of the telegraph had been in prospect for some time. Yet its commercial success was by no means a foregone conclusion. Although the government-financed line was subject to private use free of charge, little use was initially made of it, and the government declined to spend more money on its development, or for the purchase of the patent.

Morse therefore turned to private interests for the exploitation of his invention. For business and legal advice he relied on Amos Kendall, Postmaster General under Presidents Jackson and Van Buren, who had from his former government office extensive knowledge of lines of communication throughout the country. For the raising of funds and the construction of telegraph lines, regional rights to use the Morse invention were given to Francis O. J. Smith of Maine, who as a member of Congress had become much interested in the telegraph, and to other persons as well. An extensive construction contract was entered into with Henry O'Reilly, an enthusiastic and adventuresome if somewhat unpractical New York Irishman with a newspaper background, who in the midst of a great deal of litigation over contract and patent rights confused the records by reversing the vowels in his name, changing O'Reilly to O'Rielly. The partners and contractors fell out among themselves and also got involved in litigation over the use of competing patents in the telegraph field.

The story as it involves scientific developments is too long and complex even for summarization here, and the summary of the legal episode itself must be brief.[15] Yet the latter involved immense time

---

[15] The best-developed account of the invention and exploitation of the telegraph is Robert Luther Thompson, *Wiring a Continent: The History of the Telegraph Industry in the United States, 1832–1866.* Apart from original sources as cited herein, other important sources are Edward Lind Morse, ed., *Samuel F. B. Morse: His Letters and Journals,* and Samuel I. Prime, *Life of Samuel F. B. Morse.*

and effort on the part of federal judges. Before a major case was decided by the Supreme Court in 1854, United States Circuit Court litigation had involved Justices Catron, Grier, McKinley, Nelson, and Woodbury. Involved also were District Judges Kane, Leavitt, and Monroe. Future members of the Supreme Court employed as counsel were Salmon P. Chase and Benjamin R. Curtis.

The litigation began in January, 1847, in the United States Circuit Court in Philadelphia, before Judge John K. Kane. Here, in the name of Morse and others, although apparently under the instigation not of Morse and Kendall so much as of the predatory F. O. J. Smith and his brother-in-law, Eliphalet Case, an application was made for a special injunction to void O'Reilly's construction contract in a region which the Smith interests wanted to control. But Judge Kane held that the Morse interests could not bring the suit because they had previously transferred their rights to Case, and that, furthermore, the contract could not in any event be thus voided by injunction.[16]

The decision in Philadelphia was regarded as an important propaganda victory for the O'Reilly interests, which by the opposition of Smith and others had been driven to strike out for themselves and which, using other patents than those given to Morse, were planning and building lines in competition with those using Morse equipment. While it is not to be presumed that potential financiers knew much about technical legal issues, they were highly sensitive to adverse court decisions and injunctions that might cut off all prospects of profits.

One of the patents to which O'Reilly turned was that of Royal E. House, which covered a mechanism much more complicated than that covered by the Morse patent and used letters instead of the dots and dashes of the Morse code. Making use for themselves of available propaganda, the Smith-Kendall interests published statements that use of the House invention would infringe the Morse patent. House, protesting that the statement was false and injurious to him, challenged them to bring suit against him to test the accuracy of their assertion.[17] O'Reilly at the same time printed for distribution circulars denouncing attempts at monopoly on the part of the people using the Morse patents and asserting that they had not dared to prosecute in the United States courts for violation of patent rights.

In the struggle with O'Reilly the Morse interests were in position to bring litigation in the region and in the court of their own choosing. O'Reilly was pressing them most severely through his construction of a line intended to run from Louisville to Nashville and thence to New

---

[16] Morse v. O'Reilly, 17 Fed. Cas. 867 (No. 9858) (C.C.E.D. Pa. 1847).

[17] Draft, Royal E. House to F. O. J. Smith and Amos Kendall, Sept. 28, 1847, O'Reilly Papers.

Orleans, on which equipment was being used that was allegedly invented by still other people, Edmund F. Barnes and Samuel K. Zook. Morse sought an injunction from the United States Circuit Court in Kentucky, which was in the Eighth Circuit, presided over by Justice Catron. However, in August, 1848, to permit District Judge Thomas B. Monroe to teach law during the winter at the University of Louisiana, Congress changed the terms of the United States courts in Kentucky in such a way that it was impossible for Justice Catron to be present at the time when the patent case would come up.[18] As a result Morse's motion for an injunction was brought before Judge Monroe at chambers.

The case was presented over a total of fifteen days. Seven were taken for the reading of pleadings and other relevant documents and eight for the delivery of arguments. Three counsel appeared on each side, and it may or may not be relevant that one of the counsel for Morse was Benjamin Monroe, the brother of the judge. Morse himself was present, as was Kendall. Counsel fought their battles in court in the daytime and met with one another and with clients in one large group for fun and delightful conversation in the evening.[19]

Morse attempted to show infringement of his patent, as originally issued in 1840 and as reissued in 1846 and 1848. O'Reilly not only denied infringement but went to great lengths to show that Morse had not been the inventor of the telegraph at all but had merely used the accumulated discoveries and inventions of others, so that his patent was invalid. At the close of the argument O'Reilly wrote, "The Judge is no doubt a well-meaning man; but it remains to be seen how far he has made up his mind under the benevolent efforts of Kendall and other benevolent friends to enlighten his understanding."[20]

O'Reilly had good grounds for concern. Judge Monroe handed down a decision sustaining the validity of the Morse patents and holding that they were infringed by the inventions of Barnes and Zook. His brother published the opinion in a sixty-five page pamphlet entitled *The Great Telegraph Case*, which he marketed at three dollars a copy.[21] O'Reilly, already in a financial crisis such that he had put his business into the hands of three competent financiers, found himself now in the midst of disaster. It proved impossible to get funds for an enterprise that was tied up in litigation. Since the mere transmission of electric current over wires was not itself subject to patent, but only the transmitting and receiving instruments, O'Reilly tried to circumvent the injunction by changing instruments so as to use sound. His agent was cited for con-

---

18 9 Stat. 282.

19 Prime, *Life of Samuel F. B. Morse*, 561–62.

20 Henry O'Rielly to James S. Wallace, Sept, 6, 1848, O'Reilly Papers.

21 A copy is in the O'Reilly Papers. For a brief digest see Morse v. O'Reilly, 17 Fed. Cas. 871 (No. 9859) (C.C.D. Ky. 1848).

tempt for violation of the injunction. The line was then extended across the Ohio River to Indiana and the instruments moved there in order to operate across but not within Kentucky. The court ordered the marshal to seize enough of the line to prevent further operation in Kentucky. O'Reilly was thereby compelled to suspend operations.[22]

Such was the breadth of Judge Monroe's injunction, as enforced by him, that it clearly applied to House's writing telegraph as well as to other devices. The remaining hope of O'Reilly in terms of new instruments lay in a different invention by Alexander Bain. Henry Pirtle, one of O'Reilly's counsel and a professor of law at the University of Louisville, saw Judge Monroe about the matter as the latter was on his way to his own professorship at the University of Louisiana. Judge Monroe replied that he did not have the materials on Bain's patent, and that the only thing to be done at that time was to apply to Justice Catron for leave to use Bain's invention on the line through Kentucky.[23] Such a move was discussed from time to time but no action seems to have been taken.[24] Meanwhile, without going into the federal court in Tennessee for action there, the Morse interests decided to present to Justice Catron in Washington their argument for an injunction against O'Reilly in Tennessee. Kendall sent word that Morse should be there and have all his patent papers with him.[25] Judge Catron, who had agreed to hear the case at chambers on a Saturday, seems to have given at least three days to it. Prominently discussed was a technical question whether, under the statute, an injunction could be granted without a bill having been actually filed.[26] On some ground the judge decided against taking action.

Defeated by the drastic enforcement of the Monroe injunction, O'Reilly presented a memorial to Congress demanding impeachment of the judge and, in letters to members of Congress, he criticized the judge and Congress itself for activities bearing directly or indirectly on the patent struggle. He urged upon a New York Congressman an investigation which would either clear Judge Monroe of charges or bring about his removal for cupidity, fanaticism, or malfeasance. For evidence, he urged, Congress should look beyond the report of the case, which was prepared by the counsel of O'Reilly's adversaries and also the brother of the judge. O'Reilly demanded that legislators look into the handling of

---

[22] For a summary of these events see Thompson, *Wiring a Continent*, 154–55.

[23] Copy, Henry Pirtle to Henry O'Reilly, Nov. 29, 1848, O'Reilly Papers. See also E. F. Barnes to Henry O'Reilly, Nov., 1848, O'Reilly Papers.

[24] See Henry Pirtle to C. B. Moss, Dec. 20, 1848; Henry Pirtle to R. H. Gillet, Dec. 22, 1848, O'Reilly Papers.

[25] George Wood to S. F. B. Morse, Dec. 16, 1848, Morse Papers.

[26] R. H. Gillet to Messrs. Gholson and Miner, Jan. 29, 1849, O'Reilly Papers.

certain bills affecting patents at the last session, and particularly an iniquitous measure "for revolutionizing the Federal Courts in Kentucky, by altering the time of holding those courts so as to prevent the *Circuit* Judge from being present to overrule the 'injunctions' and 'contempts' of the District Judge."[27]

Senator Joseph R. Underwood of Kentucky presented the O'Reilly memorial to Congress but insisted that wrong motives had been ascribed to the measure changing the time for holding the federal courts in Kentucky. In presenting that bill, "I had no other object in view than to accommodate the judge of the district court who had received an appointment to preside over a law school in Louisiana. Thinking that the change would accommodate him, and that it would not compromise the public service, I cordially supported the bill."[28] Morse, Kendall, and others published a pamphlet criticizing in turn the O'Reilly attack on Judge Monroe and further setting forth their own position, so that the attack on the judge was made to redound to their own benefit.

During the latter part of 1848 some efforts were made to bring the litigation to an end. Kendall proposed that the issues be referred to arbitration by three members of the Supreme Court. O'Reilly's counsel in Washington, R. H. Gillet, pointed out that for all the effort to get acceptance of an arbitration decision by all the parties with interest in telegraphic communication, there would be still other parties who might come into the picture with new controversies. His counterproposal was that a case should be built up for the United States Circuit Court in Maryland involving as many of the patent issues as could be brought to a head, tried there before Chief Justice Taney, and then appealed to the Supreme Court by the losing party.[29]

But things were happening too rapidly to permit the orderly planning of litigation. Alexander Bain secured from the patent office in December, 1848, a patent for a telegraphic device but he was denied a patent on a further improvement on the ground that the improvement infringed one of Morse's patents. As permitted by statute,[30] Bain appealed the denial to the chief justice of the United States District Court for the District of Columbia, then Judge William Cranch. Bain was represented by R. H. Gillet, counsel for O'Reilly, in opposition to Amos Kendall. O'Reilly's strategy was to establish the validity of the Bain inventions and use them on the line from Louisville to New Orleans,

---

[27] Draft, Henry O'Rielly to Washington Hunt, Jan. 20, 1848, O'Reilly Papers. Other items of correspondence in the O'Reilly Papers deal with the same subject.

[28] *Cong. Globe*, 30th Cong., 2nd Sess. 253 (1849).

[29] Draft, R. H. Gillet to Amos Kendall, Dec. 29, 1848; draft, Henry O'Rielly to James K. Moorhead, Dec. 30, 1848, O'Reilly Papers.

[30] 5 Stat. 354.

where on the Kentucky part of the line he had been stopped by Judge Monroe's injunction from using other devices. An overtone of the controversy was the belief on the part of the O'Reilly interests that the Patent Office was biased in favor of Morse, particularly in that an examiner in the office was Leonard D. Gale, a former colleague and partner of Morse. One of the men called to testify by Gillet was Joseph Henry, secretary and head of the Smithsonian Institution,[31] with whom in earlier years Morse had had friendly relations but who more recently had been piqued by Morse's neglect.

Judge Cranch reversed the decision of the Commissioner of Patents and ordered the patent issued to Bain, saying as to one of the points stressed by Kendall, "If this were a doubtful question I should think it my duty to render the same judgment, so as to give Mr. Bain the same right to have the validity of his patent tested by the ordinary tribunals of the country which Mr. Morse would enjoy as to his patent, and finally, to obtain the judgment of the supreme court of the United States upon it."[32]

O'Reilly's counsel in full array, and now including Salmon P. Chase of Ohio, went back before Judge Monroe for a determination that the injunction previously issued did not cover the use of the Bain patent which Judge Cranch had authorized. Judge Monroe so held, but reserved a number of other questions for determination at a later date,[33] when presumably he would hold Circuit Court along with a member of the Supreme Court. That Justice, it appeared, would be McKinley, and not Catron, whom the O'Reilly interests seemed to want. Congress left the terms of the federal courts in Kentucky scheduled for the convenience of Judge Monroe in his teaching of law in Louisiana, but provided that Justice McKinley, the presiding officer of the Fifth Circuit, who, however, lived in Louisville, in the Eighth Circuit, might hold Circuit Court in Kentucky in the absence of the judge of that circuit.[34] Gillet feared that the arrangement was "some trick," and he hoped that effort would be made to have Justice Catron present when the case came up for final hearing in the fall of 1849.[35]

From this time onward court proceedings in the United States Circuit Court in Kentucky, although important in the history of the case, are but skimpily recorded. It would appear that Justice McKinley was asked to enjoin O'Reilly operations in Tennessee as well as Kentucky. Salmon P. Chase contended that McKinley had no right to offici-

---

[31] Henry O'Rielly to Joseph Henry, Feb. 7, 1849, O'Reilly Papers.
[32] Bain v. Morse, 2 Fed. Cas. 394, 407 (No. 754) (C.C. D.C. 1849).
[33] *Louisville Courier*, June 16, 1849, as reprinted in an O'Reilly circular, Chase Papers, item no. 3467.
[34] 9 Stat. 403.
[35] R. H. Gillet to Henry O'Rielly, March 30, 1849, O'Reilly Papers.

493

ate in Tennessee, which was in Justice Catron's circuit and not linked with Kentucky in the permission recently given by Congress.[36] However, Kendall reported to Morse that Justice McKinley, being in feeble health, had adjourned the Tennessee case northward to Kentucky where he lived.[37] There he issued a temporary injunction protecting the Morse claims on lines through the state of Tennessee. Morse and Kendall were delighted, Morse wrote, that "Judges Monroe and McKinley are the judges before whom the main case will be tried in the fall and both of them have already decided on merits; that is, have had the whole case before them, as much so as it could be on the final hearing and they are strong on the subject and in my favor. Judge Monroe more so than ever."[38]

In October, 1849, the case in Kentucky came up for final hearing, before Judge Monroe, Justice McKinley apparently not being present. Chase outlined the O'Reilly case in advance as asserting the invalidity of Morse's patent, the noninfringement of Morse's patent by O'Reilly's "Columbian Telegraph," and the practicability of working O'Reilly's line with Bain's instruments without interference with any right or claim on the part of Morse.[39] In September Chase and others went to a summer place near Boston to get from Joseph Henry a deposition which would show the extent of the work done by others toward the invention of the telegraph and help to demonstrate that Morse was not the true inventor.[40] The deposition revealed more of the personal activities of Henry than of the history of the telegraph generally, but along with other depositions proved to be of use to the O'Reilly interests.[41] Nevertheless, by the time Kendall and his fellow counsel had finished presenting their case it was clear that as far as the Circuit Court was concerned the O'Reilly interests were destined to lose. Chase informed Kendall that the O'Reilly counsel did not intend to argue the case unless O'Reilly directed them to do so, or unless the judge requested it, thinking that they would suffer less loss of prestige in losing the case without argument than with it.[42] The Morse interests won their case as expected, though with qualifications that from their point of view left something to be desired. To the extent that they had not won, they expected the

---

[36] S. P. Chase to Henry O'Rielly, July 3, 1849, O'Reilly Papers.

[37] Amos Kendall to S. F. B. Morse, June 22, 1849, Morse Papers.

[38] See "The Telegraph Case," *West. L.J.*, 7:148, 1849. See Amos Kendall to S. F. B. Morse, July 14, 1849, Morse Papers. S. F. B. Morse to Sidney E. Morse, July 10, 1849, Morse Papers.

[39] S. P. Chase to Henry O'Rielly, June 20, 1849, O'Reilly Papers.

[40] Charles T. Smith to Henry O'Rielly, Sept. 2, 1849, O'Reilly Papers. Statement of S. P. Chase, *Annual Report of the Board of Regents of the Smithsonian Institution . . . for the Year 1857*, 90 (1858).

[41] Reproduced in *ibid.*, 107–17.

[42] Amos Kendall to S. F. B. Morse, Oct. 22, 1849, Morse Papers.

Supreme Court to support them. In practical effect the O'Reilly enterprises in the West were already stopped by the litigation.[43] As far as the McKinley injunction against operations in Tennessee was concerned, Justice Catron was said to have characterized the proceedings as irregular and the result therefore as a nullity,[44] but it nevertheless had its effect in persuading capitalists not to invest in O'Reilly's projects.

The case from Kentucky did not appear on the docket of the Supreme Court until early in the December term of 1850 and was not argued until two years later. In the meantime other telegraph patent cases were decided in federal Circuit Courts in other parts of the country, in areas where the Morse patent rights had devolved upon F. O. J. Smith of Maine, mentioned above as one of the early promoters. Shrewdly distrustful of Smith in all business and legal relations, Kendall advised Morse that they should keep aloof from the Smith suits, while making available all possible information, and take one of their own suits to the Supreme Court.[45] This policy of aloofness was observed.

One of the Smith cases, involving not a matter of infringement but of the contract of 1845 between Morse and O'Reilly, was brought before Justice Nelson in the United States Circuit Court in northern New York. The court refused to enjoin O'Reilly's operations.[46] Smith brought an infringement suit against O'Reilly interests in Ohio before Justice McLean and Judge Leavitt. The case was approaching decision when the parties and the two judges decided to certify certain key questions to the Supreme Court as a means of getting the major issues settled there. In the meantime, however, Justice McLean, who for some time had evidently felt free to discuss the issues informally with counsel,[47] decided immediately to publish an opinion in the case. In doing so he pointed up two weaknesses of the Morse claim: The Morse patent purported to run for fourteen years from the date of issue in 1840, whereas under the statute it could run only from the date of an earlier patent given to Morse in 1838 in France, and it was void if it specified a longer term; and, comparably important, although under the statute it was possible to patent a discovery or an invention, the patent could not run beyond the scope of invention so far as to give monopoly rights to a principle in nature, but only to a device for utilizing a principle.[48] The latter point in particular was to make trouble for Morse at a later date. There seems to have been no published discussion

---

[43] Amos Kendall to S. F. B. Morse, Nov. 12, 1849, Morse Papers.

[44] See Henry O'Rielly to S. P. Chase, Dec. 9, 1849, Chase Papers.

[45] Amos Kendall to S. F. B. Morse, Apr. 6, 1850, Morse Papers.

[46] Smith v. Selden, 22 Fed. Cas. 652 (No. 13104) (C.C.N.D. N.Y. 1849).

[47] See Amos Kendall to S. F. B. Morse, Jan. 3, 1850, Morse Papers.

[48] Smith v. Ely, 22 Fed. Cas. 533 (No. 13043) (C.C.D. Ohio 1849).

of Justice McLean's eagerness to get into print an opinion in a case not yet decided.

More serious was Justice Woodbury's decision in the United States District Court for Massachusetts refusing Smith's application for an injunction against use of the House telegraph instrument, the so-called printing telegraph. Like Justice McLean, Justice Woodbury held that a principle, as distinguished from an invention, was not patentable. He interpreted narrowly the patent grant to Morse and held that it was not infringed by use of the House device. Much of the information used by Morse had antedated his invention: "He came into the world too late for truly claiming much as new. A large galaxy of discoverers on this subject had preceded him."[49] George Wood, who was prominent in the Morse organization, sputtered about the "corrupt judge" and said of the opinion, "It is a most miserable parade of apparent learning and confusion of facts."[50] Kendall saw it as the product of "the Judge's *compromising mind*."[51]

In the United States Circuit Court in Philadelphia still another hard-fought battle took place before Justice Grier and Judge Kane. Assignees of Morse rights challenged here the use of the Bain patent, or modifications of it. Each side was represented by four counsel. Seeking protection of Morse interests were Amos Kendall, George Gifford of New York, St. George T. Campbell of Pennsylvania, and George Harding of Pennsylvania, all experts in patent law. For the opposition were William M. Meredith, R. H. Gillet, William Schley, and Peter McCall. The writing of the opinion was allocated to Judge Kane, with Justice Grier concurring.[52] The court carefully appraised and upheld the several Morse patents. It disposed of the McLean challenge to the Morse patent of 1840 on the ground of proper dating from the earlier French patent by showing that the statutory provision did not apply since Morse had applied for an American patent before his French patent was issued. The victorious counsel were authorized to draft a decree for the protection of the Morse interests.[53]

In the meantime the case appealed from the United States Circuit Court in Kentucky awaited its turn on the docket of the Supreme Court. In April, 1852, George Wood wrote to Morse at his home in

---

[49] Smith v. Downing, 22 Fed. Cas. 511, 513 (No. 13036) (C.C.D. Mass. 1850). See also Smith v. Clark, 22 Fed. Cas. 487 (No. 13027) (C.C.D. Mass. 1850).

[50] George Wood to S. F. B. Morse, Dec. 26, 1850, Morse Papers.

[51] Amos Kendall to S. F. B. Morse, Dec. 2, 1850, Morse Papers.

[52] See Prime, *Life of Samuel F. B. Morse*, 578–80.

[53] French v. Rogers, 9 Fed. Cas. 790 (No. 5103) (C.C.E.D. Pa. 1851). For a briefer report of the case see Morse & Bain Tel. Case, 17 Fed. Cas. 873 (No. 9861) (C.C.E.D. Pa. 1851).

Poughkeepsie, saying that the argument was imminent and that Morse should come to Washington. He thought the auspices were favorable. Gillet, like Goliath, defied the armies of Israel, but though no stone could penetrate his skin, it was not his brains but those of the supreme judges that were to be reached. All these were capable of seeing black from white and truth from fraud. Since Justice Woodbury, who had died recently, had "gone to be judged for his judgments and actions," he thought the decision would be unanimous.[54] Kendall reported to Morse a "most singular incident" in the office of the Clerk of the Supreme Court. An unexplained fire had occurred there during the night, burning papers dealing with the Morse patent case but burning nothing else.[55] He was concerned about the original of a sketchbook prepared by Morse. George Wood followed with another letter urging Morse to be present at the argument, saying that George Harding, the brilliant young patent lawyer from Philadelphia, thought it most important. He explained, "Why I don't precisely see; except that Judges are men, and are influenced no little by your presence. . . . This point is the pivot of all your life's affairs, and you must be here."[56] But soon afterward Wood wrote again that Gillet had "shown the white feather" and had had the argument postponed until the following term. He thought the unwillingness of the O'Reilly interests to meet their opponents ought to give new prestige to stock in the Morse telegraph.[57]

During the intervening summer of 1852 a great many mergers took place between Morse and O'Reilly lines,[58] perhaps indirectly indicating a Morse victory even without a Supreme Court decision. By the fall of 1852 there was talk of further postponement of the case before the Supreme Court. Some interests remained undetermined, however, and Morse urged that the case be pressed, rather than postponed to permit the less adequately prepared Smith case from Ohio, in which Justice McLean had written an opinion without a decision, to determine crucial patent issues.[59]

It was finally decided to proceed with the case. Argument was begun on December 24, 1852, with the allotment of six hours to each side,[60] later further extended. Seven Justices were present. Justice Curtis, who had recently replaced Justice Woodbury, did not sit since he had been counsel in the Morse patent case before Justice Woodbury

---

[54] George Wood to S. F. B. Morse, Apr. 20, 1852, Morse Papers.

[55] Amos Kendall to S. F. B. Morse, Apr. 21, 1852, Morse Papers.

[56] George Wood to S. F. B. Morse, Apr. 20, 1852, Morse Papers.

[57] George Wood to S. F. B. Morse, Apr. 27, 1852, Morse Papers.

[58] *New York Herald*, June 23, 1852. From a clipping in the O'Reilly Papers, Box 17, Vol. 55.

[59] S. F. B. Morse to Amos Kendall, Dec. 7, 1852, Morse Papers.

[60] S. F. B. Morse to Mrs. Morse, Dec. 25, 1852. See also *The New York Times*, Dec. 28, 1852.

in Massachusetts. Justice McKinley had recently died and his position had not yet been filled. Gillet and Chase appeared in O'Reilly's name, and Campbell, Harding, and Gifford represented Morse, with Kendall apparently operating as the master of strategy. It was said that Harding "gave a highly interesting explanation of the scientific principles of the Morse machine, putting three instruments in operation in the court-room."[61]

Although Morse and newspaper reporters had been confident that a decision in *O'Reilly v. Morse* would be reached in two or three weeks, the weeks passed without any report of action. At the end of January, 1853, Morse was told that Justice Wayne had requested and secured an interview with Kendall and made an appointment to visit a Morse telegraph office to see the operation of the instruments. Kendall got the impression that the Court had decided on all except what was much discussed as Morse's "eighth claim," in which Morse, in connection with the reissue of his patent in 1848, had said that he did not propose to limit his patent claim to specific machinery or parts of machinery, but:

> the essence of my invention being the use of the motive power of the electric or galvanic current, which I call electro-magnetism, however developed, for marking or printing intelligible characters, signs or letters, at any distances, being a new application of that power of which I claim to be the first inventor or discoverer.[62]

O'Reilly's counsel had attempted to show that by this claim Morse had gone beyond invention to assert possession of a principle, which was not subject to patent, and that this excessive claim, which had not subsequently been disavowed, had invalidated the whole patent. Kendall sensed that this question was involved in the Court's delay in arriving at a decision.[63] He reported to Morse that Justice Wayne was entirely with them but that other Justices had doubts on the "eighth claim" because of the deposition of Joseph Henry, which had seemed to narrow the range of discovery or invention left to Morse at the time when he began to experiment in the field.[64] The Justices were so confused or so much at odds about the matter that, to the disappointment of the Morse group, the decision was postponed until the ensuing term, though with assurance from Justice Wayne that they had little to worry about.[65]

---

[61] *The New York Times*, Dec. 28, 1852.

[62] O'Reilly v. Morse, 15 How. 62, 112 (1854).

[63] George Wood to S. F. B. Morse, Jan. 31, 1853, Morse Papers.

[64] Amos Kendall to S. F. B. Morse, Feb. 1, 1853, Morse Papers.

[65] George Wood to S. F. B. Morse, Feb. 4, 1853; Amos Kendall to S. F. B. Morse, Feb. 5, 1853, Morse Papers.

XX: *Patent Rights and Free Enterprise*

At this time occurred an interesting flurry in the competition between counsel for the two sides. Of the several counsel it would appear that only Gillet had given to the Court a printed summary of the points presented in his argument. After the argument Chase, his colleague, sensed that the Court was undecided on important points and perhaps confused by the history of intricate scientific developments, which had their background in a number of countries of Europe as well as the United States. Chase therefore printed and delivered to the Court a pamphlet of forty-five pages as a summary of his oral argument, attempting to show that Morse's patents were void for want of invention and that, in any event, they were not infringed by the instruments used by O'Reilly. Chase closed with a flourishing gesture to the Court:

> Supplying by your learning the omissions of counsel, and by your disciplined judgments, the defects of their arguments, unmoved from established principles of law by the novelty and wonderful characteristics of the subtle element, the applications of which are the subject of controversy, and only stimulated to more diligence in investigation and carefulness in conclusion by the difficulty of some of the questions involved, you will, I am sure, endeavor to do impartial justice between these parties, by so administering the law as to protect at once the rights of individuals and of the public. In behalf of my clients I ask no more.[66]

The Chase argument was sent to the Court without notice to opposing counsel. Disturbed at this tactic, Kendall conferred with co-counsel about the publication of their own arguments for the use of the Court. He wrote to Morse that the counsel would probably provide him with outlines which he would fill out: "I think we can manage Chase."[67] Kendall thought it better to give the substance of the arguments rather than pretend to give them just as delivered. This would give them more latitude: "As Chase's speech is printed for the public we can print for the public also and annex in our appendix such additional material as we may think useful. Campbell proposes that we

---

[66] *The Electric Telegraph, Summary of the Argument of S. P. Chase Before the Supreme Court of the United States, . . . O'Reilly v. Morse,* 45. This document was not filed with the Record of the case in the Supreme Court. A copy was preserved in the Morse Papers, annotated in Morse's hand. On p. 33 Morse noted as "folly" a point taken from the Woodbury opinion in the United States Circuit Court in Massachusetts, and on p. 43 he asserted that a point attributed to Joseph Henry was not true and was not made by Henry. Another copy of the Chase argument is on file in the library of the Johns Hopkins University.

[67] Amos Kendall to S. F. B. Morse, Feb. 5, 1853, Morse Papers.

each prepare what we please and then meet together and consolidate."[68]

Kendall had trouble getting for publication a written argument from Gifford, who as a condition demanded that he be paid five hundred dollars of his contingent fee. Kendall refused, but he eventually got from Gifford, or prepared in Gifford's name, a document running to ninety-four pages, more than twice the length of the Chase pamphlet. Kendall told Morse, "My argument is in the hands of Judge Wayne who promised me his remarks upon it. He previously told me, he had made up his mind in our favor."[69]

The Gifford argument denied that Morse had attempted to patent a mere principle in nature but had rather patented a newly discovered use of the principle. He thanked the Court for extending the time of argument and stressed the need for still more time: "We are not unmindful of the other important duties of this Court, nor of how great is the value of its time to the country; but we cannot avoid remembering also, how small is the value of a few days of the time of this or any other court, compared with the vast amount of time which Morse's Telegraph is daily saving to the country and to the world."[70] Gifford closed his book with another reference to the lack of adequate time and with a gesture to the Court similar to that of Chase. Being compelled to stop:

> I therefore submit the cause, with the hopes, labors, and merits of this benefactor, Professor Morse, to the custody of the learned members of this distinguished tribunal, not doubting but that his merits will be appreciated, his rights be protected, and justice be done.[71]

Further informal argument or demonstration of the case seems to have continued throughout the year. Justice and Mrs. Wayne visited at the Morse home in Poughkeepsie. Harding deplored the fact that he had not had advance knowledge of the visit. Had he known, he would have had a working model at Morse's home. He felt pride in his model, "regarding it as the prettiest child of my brain." He hoped that an early opportunity would be afforded to exhibit it to Justice Wayne, for

---

[68] Amos Kendall to S. F. B. Morse, Feb. 7, 1853, Morse Papers.

[69] Amos Kendall to S. F. B. Morse, Apr. 4, 1853, Morse Papers. Since Kendall was not officially of counsel in this case it is not clear to what document this reference is made.

[70] *Argument of George Gifford, Esq., of New York, . . . O'Reilly v. Morse*, 3. The only copy of this

pamphlet thus far located is in the New York Public Library. It was evidently given by Henry O'Reilly, to whom it was inscribed.

[71] *Ibid.*, 94. Although the correspondence indicates that Campbell too was preparing a written argument, no copy attributed to him or to Harding has been located.

from the interest he had shown during the argument of the case he was sure that the Justice would appreciate it. However, "I am also anxious that he should not see it until it is in all respects a worthy representation of the great invention which it is intended to illustrate."[72]

Returning to Washington in December, Justice Wayne took up quarters in a house on Pennsylvania Avenue with Chief Justice Taney and Justice Grier, and set out to keep Morse posted on developments in the Court, telling him when the first consultation on the case would take place. He wanted to see Morse as soon as he should arrive in Washington.[73] The task of decision proved difficult. At a party in Washington on January 10, Kendall met Gifford and Justice McLean. Gifford told Kendall, from the Justice, that there would be a decision in a few days, with an opinion by Chief Justice Taney. He was of the impression that no decision would be given with respect to Morse's "eighth claim," it not being necessary to the case.[74]

The decision was announced on January 30, 1854, thirteen months after completion of the formal argument. The Court decided unanimously that Morse had been entitled to his patents as the first inventor of the telegraph, but by a vote of four to three rejected his "eighth claim." Chief Justice Taney wrote the opinion of the Court. Taking indirectly into account the contentious rivalry between Morse and Joseph Henry—who in a sense was an employee of the Chief Justice in that the latter was *ex officio* the chancellor of the Smithsonian Institution of which Henry was the effective head—Taney wrote of Henry that "it is due to him to say that no one has contributed more to enlarge the knowledge of electromagnetism, and to lay the foundations of the great invention of which we are speaking, than the professor himself."[75] Even so, and in spite of the work of Henry and that of physicists in many parts of Europe, the Court reached the conclusion that Morse had been the first to develop an operating electric telegraph, so that he was entitled to his patent. For all the clarity of Taney's presentation, it can be said of his treatment of the historical and scientific facts not so much that he determined the truth in an area of hot dispute as that he affixed to the facts the interpretation on which legal rights were to depend, whether or not it was correct. From this time onward there would be no point in further raising questions of priorities of past discoveries or inventions in this field, whatever opinions might be held about them.

Chief Justice Taney also spoke for the full Court in holding that

---

[72] George Harding to S. F. B. Morse, Sept. 28, 1853, Morse Papers.
[73] James M. Wayne to S. F. B. Morse, Dec. 12, 1853, Morse Papers.

[74] Amos Kendall to S. F. B. Morse, Jan. 11, 1854, Morse Papers.
[75] O'Reilly v. Morse, 15 How. 62, 107 (1854).

the telegraphic instruments used by the O'Reilly interests sufficiently resembled the instruments covered by Morse's patents as to infringe those patents, so that Morse was entitled to the injunction which he sought. The differences between the four majority Justices and the minority of three lay in reaction to Morse's "eighth claim." The majority saw the claim as extending beyond any invented instrument to a principle of nature apart from any invention. "In fine," said Taney, "he claims an exclusive right to use a manner and process which he has not described and indeed had not invented, and therefore could not describe when he obtained his patent. The Court is of opinion that the claim is too broad, and not warranted by law."[76]

For the three minority Justices, Justice Grier contended that Morse's "eighth claim," read in the light of his first claim, was not as broad as the majority found it. Furthermore, he contended that in promoting "the progress of science and useful arts," in the constitutional phrase, and in rewarding "any person who has discovered or invented any new and useful art," in the language of the statute of 1836, it was possible to award a patent for the fullness of Morse's "eighth claim."

Although the decision gave Morse his injunction against O'Reilly, he lost in certain important respects. The majority of the Court held that since the one claim was invalid, the costs of the litigation would have to be borne by both parties and not assessed exclusively against O'Reilly. Furthermore, in order to protect his patent, Morse would within a reasonable time have to disclaim the invalid "eighth claim." Finally, since Morse's rights to telegraphic communication were thus limited, he might continually have to resort to litigation against other inventors in the telegraphic field to prevent infringement on his patent, with no advance assurance that some new device would not be found sufficiently different from his own to receive judicial support as an independent invention.

To put the matter differently, the decision may be regarded as a compromise in three directions. It read to Morse's benefit a body of confused scientific history so unclear that it might have been interpreted in any of a variety of ways. The decision thereby demonstrated the willingness of the Court to protect major patent claims, yielding great profits to inventors, and to settle the confusion of claims for the sake of the country as well as of the inventors themselves. But the rejection of Morse's "eighth claim" demonstrated that the Supreme Court would insist on actual invention or discovery, and would not sanction a monopoly of something that might be deemed merely a first claim upon a principle of nature itself, as distinguished from the development of an instrumentality for its use. The third direction of the com-

---

[76] *Ibid.*, 113.

promise was indicated by the gesture in behalf of Joseph Henry. Originally a friend of Morse and a professor at Princeton, Henry had left Princeton to head the newly established Smithsonian Institution in Washington. His preoccupation was with scientific experiment in general rather than with reaping the benefit of particular inventions, and he was committed, in the face of opposition in the government, to developing the Smithsonian as a scientific institution of high rank. In this aim he had the support of Chief Justice Taney as chancellor of the institution. His prospect of success depended in part on the maintenance and development of prestige. Morse and his friends, more concerned with practical achievement than with pure science or with scientific reputation, pretty much ignored Henry in their accounts of developments in telegraphic communications. On both personal and professional grounds, Henry was irked at this neglect. He did not voluntarily involve himself in the controversy, but when Salmon P. Chase, interested in showing that Morse was not the inventor of the telegraph, insisted on a deposition from Henry, his deposition emphasized his own researches and experiments and tended to narrow the range of Morse's contribution, much to the disgruntlement of the Morse people.[77] The praise given to Henry in the opinion of the Court tended to enhance his professional reputation and that of the Smithsonian Institution, and to protect the institution against shortsighted people who wanted immediately to use its funds for the aid of American farmers.

The text of the decision was slow in reaching the interested parties.[78] Nine days after the case was decided, Kendall reported to Morse, "It seems the Judges are in the habit of revising their Opinions after they are delivered, and then the Clerk gives out no copies until all that may have been ordered are ready. We are yet without any copy of the late Opinions in your case."[79] In eleven more days Morse was in Washington, had read the opinion of the Court and of the minority, and had discussed the case with Justice Wayne. He thought the minor-

---

[77] For discussion see Morse, *Samuel F. B. Morse: His Letters and Journals*, 260–66; Thomas Coulson, *Joseph Henry, His Life and Work*, 208–34; for early relevant documents see Alfred Vail, *Description of the American Electro Magnetic Telegraph Now in Operation Between the Cities of Washington and Baltimore*; *Annual Report of the Board of Regents of the Smithsonian Institution*, H.R. Misc. Doc. No. 135, 35th Cong., 1st Sess. (1858).

[78] As noted above, only seven Jus-

tices sat in the case. Justice Wayne intimated that if Justice Curtis had sat he would have supported Morse's "eighth claim," and he thought it possible that Justice Campbell, who had joined the Court since argument of the case, might also have done so. At any rate, the point remained an item of uncertainty. Amos Kendall to S. F. B. Morse, Jan. 31, 1854, Morse Papers.

[79] Amos Kendall to S. F. B. Morse, Feb. 8, 1854, Morse Papers.

ity opinion "a masterly, unanswerable argument, and to this judgment both the Supreme Court and the public at large will eventually come, or I am greatly mistaken."[80] He wrote later that he hoped eventually to derive some benefit from the decision but that "the reckless and desperate character" of his opponents might defeat him. Such was the reward he had purchased for himself by his invention.[81] Actually the days of his prosperity were only beginning, and from this time onward both he and Kendall seem to have done well for themselves. The case long since brought up on certificate from Justice McLean's circuit in Ohio, and still on the Supreme Court docket, was now remanded to the Circuit Court without argument,[82] and nothing more was heard of it. The consolidation of competing telegraph lines and operations worked out to the benefit of Morse interests and they were now in a position to exploit the economic benefits of the invention.

A remaining item in the O'Reilly-Morse saga in the Supreme Court is worthy of mention. Benjamin C. Howard, the Court Reporter, for whom intricate cases often caused trouble, faced in this major patent case a task of reporting that was completely beyond him. He began his statement by saying, "It is difficult to make a fair report of this case without writing a book. The arguments of counsel would fill a volume by themselves."[83] Fortunately he had access to the complex history of the case as drawn up by Judge Monroe—or by Monroe's brother as reporter in the court below. With Judge Monroe's permission he published as a preface to the Supreme Court opinion a long extract from the Monroe opinion, explaining that although Monroe's narrative was occasionally interspersed with the opinions which led to the decree, "yet the history is given with great precision and clearness."[84] Among arguments of counsel, Gillet's presentation was fortunately arranged according to numerical points which Howard could follow. With little more than the combination of Monroe and Gillet materials he was content. Such expositions as those of Chase and Gifford seem to have received no attention at all.

As the telegraph revolutionized communication and, indirectly, the business life of the country, so the reaper, invented by Cyrus McCormick, revolutionized farm life where wheat and other grains were major products. It took a long time to harvest an acre of wheat by hand sickle or by the swinging of a cradle. The need for better equipment led

[80] S. F. B. Morse to Mrs. Morse, Feb. 19, 1854, Morse Papers.

[81] S. F. B. Morse to Mrs. Morse, Mar. 4, 1854, Morse Papers.

[82] Smith v. Ely, 15 How. 137 (1854). For praise of the telegraph as

a new necessity see "The Telegraph," De Bow's Review, 16:251–62, 1854.

[83] O'Reilly v. Morse, 15 How. 62, 63 (1854).

[84] Ibid., 63.

to experimentation by many individuals and to conflicting claims as to invention. The first patent for a reaper drawn by the power of horses was issued in 1834 to Cyrus McCormick of Virginia.[85] According to evidence presented twenty years later before Justice Nelson in the United States Circuit Court for the Northern District of New York, the machine first invented was not successful, and few were manufactured. It was said that only seven were sold down to 1842. Indeed, for many years McCormick permitted the period of his patent rights to slip by without exploitation, giving his attention to other things. Then he turned back to the reaper. Some twenty-nine machines were sold for the harvest of 1843, on McCormick's warrant of successful operation. Some fifty were sold for the harvest of 1844, and between one hundred and two hundred for 1845.[86] By this time the patent was within three years of its expiration. In 1845 McCormick secured a patent for an improvement on his 1834 machine, but it was not until 1847 that, with another patent, providing satisfactorily for the seat of the raker, he began to make extensive sales and his machinery came greatly into demand. Now within one year of the expiration of his basic patent, he sought renewal of it for the statutory period of seven years, confident that the renewal would be granted.

But by this time other inventors were operating in the field, and manufacturers had learned from McCormick's experience that the sale of reapers could be a profitable business. Farmers, interested in buying reapers at the lowest possible price and not all interested in paying tribute to McCormick, were opposed to the curtailment of competition by the renewal of the patent. Battles over the subject were fought in the Patent Office and in Congress. The expiration of McCormick's basic patent in 1848 permitted other manufacturers to enter the field, with improvements of their own, raising questions as to whether their improvements infringed McCormick's improvement patents of 1845 and 1847. McCormick warned manufacturers not to produce and farmers not to buy, under penalty of the law; his competitors hooted at his threats and promised to give users of their reapers full protection.

Early litigation developed with the firm of Seymour and Morgan of Brockport, New York, which from 1845 to 1849 manufactured reapers under a license from McCormick. Seeking for itself the benefit of

---

[85] For background discussion of the McCormick reaper story, including the story of the litigation, see especially William T. Hutchinson, *Cyrus Hall McCormick, Seed-Time, 1809–1856.* See also Herbert N. Casson, *Cyrus Hall McCormick, His Life and Work,* and Cyrus McCormick, *The Century* *of the Reaper.* Many of the facts presented hereafter, however, are taken directly from opinions in the several cases.

[86] McCormick v. Seymour, 15 Fed. Cas. 1329 (No. 8727) (C.C.N.D. N.Y. 1854).

McCormick's 1834 patent, the firm was said to have opposed the renewal of that patent. After 1849, making some changes which they claimed to be important and sufficiently different from McCormick's improving patents to avoid infringement, it began to produce and sell reapers resembling McCormick's without paying the license fee. In the United States Circuit Court for the Northern District of New York, McCormick asked Justice Nelson for an injunction against further manufacture. Justice Nelson refused to grant the petition but ordered a full accounting of all machines made and sold. McCormick then sued for damages, and, pending trial, an injunction against further manufacture was granted. The firm made further changes, changed the name of their reaper, and continued production.[87]

McCormick appeared in court with four counsels, Samuel Stevens, Charles M. Keller, Edwin W. Stoughton, and Samuel Blatchford, the last the reporter for the Second Circuit and a future member of the Supreme Court. Seymour had Ransom H. Gillet and Henry Selden, both of whom were involved to some extent in the telegraph patent litigation. Pursuant to Justice Nelson's charge, and after a second trial, the jury found a verdict for McCormick for more than seventeen thousand dollars.[88] On writ of error the case was then taken to the Supreme Court, which in a unanimous opinion by Justice Grier found that the damages assessed were excessive and sent the case back for a new trial.[89]

The litigation had to do with McCormick's patent of 1847 dealing with the raker's seat on his reaper. Before the Supreme Court had decided the case, McCormick had secured a reissue of that patent in a modified form. When he went back to the Circuit Court for the redetermination of damages, he learned that the process of having the patent reissued had terminated his right to any damages incurred before the date of the reissue. Determined to find some way to make his opponents pay for their invasion of his right and, if possible, to stop their doing so in the future, he now based his claim to damages on his 1845 patent, which had to do not with the raker's seat but with mechanisms called dividers and reel-bearers. Once more in charging the jury Justice Nelson had to discuss problems of novelty of invention in terms of highly intricate mechanisms which had to be examined through models and drawings. Once more the jury found infringement of McCormick's patent. This time damages of $7,750 were assessed, together with the costs of the litigation.[90]

---

[87] Hutchinson, *Cyrus Hall McCormick*, 423–25.

[88] McCormick v. Seymour, 15 Fed. Cas. 1322 (No. 8726) (C.C.N.D. N.Y. 1851).

[89] Seymour v. McCormick, 16 How. 480 (1854).

[90] McCormick v. Seymour, 15 Fed. Cas. 1329 (No. 8727) (C.C.N.D. N.Y. 1854).

Again Seymour took the case to the Supreme Court, where he was represented by Henry R. Selden, Peter H. Watson, Edwin M. Stanton, and George Harding. McCormick was represented by Edward N. Dickerson, who had made his start in things scientific with Joseph Henry at Princeton, and Reverdy Johnson. McCormick won his case, save for the fact that the Court, speaking through Justice Nelson with Justice Grier dissenting, decided that costs could not be assessed against Seymour.[91] After these years of litigation Seymour and Morgan were eventually driven from the reaper market in the United States.[92]

It had become increasingly apparent that the best place for use of the reaper was on the broad prairies of the West. McCormick was manufacturing in Chicago, where he now lived and made shrewd investments in real estate. But other adventurers also saw the rich prospects. One John H. Manny of Illinois made numerous changes from the McCormick reaper and began production. McCormick bought and analyzed a Manny machine, and brought suit for infringement. Justice McLean, in the United States Circuit Court, required Manny to post bond to secure accurate accounting of sales and satisfy any judgment the court might hand down. Both sides made lavish preparations for the contest.[93]

McCormick was represented by Reverdy Johnson and Edward N. Dickerson. Manny's leading counsel were Edwin M. Stanton and George Harding. The selection of Harding was deemed important not only because he had demonstrated his ability as a patent lawyer in Morse telegraph cases but also because the case was to be tried before Justice McLean, who was his father-in-law.[94] In addition they associated with them Peter H. Watson of Washington, who was said to have an amazing amount of influence with the Patent Office. The manipulation engaged in included location of an old model of a McCormick machine and the patenting of one of the devices used, to show that McCormick's patented machine, presented at a later date, had not been a new invention.[95] In this and other respects the handling of the case was a game of wits which had little to do with traditional practice of law.

Although, like Watson, his name was not used in the reporting of the case, another of Manny's counsel was Abraham Lincoln of Illinois. The story of Lincoln's employment as passed down by Harding was told by Albert J. Beveridge in his biography of Lincoln. It had

---

[91] Seymour v. McCormick, 19 How. 96 (1857). The assessment of costs was dropped, as in *O'Reilly v. Morse*, because the patent in question included a claim which could not be supported.

[92] Hutchinson, *Cyrus Hall McCormick*, 429–30.
[93] *Ibid.*, 434–42.
[94] *Ibid.*, 435.
[95] *Ibid.*, 436–37.

originally been supposed that the case would be tried before United States District Judge Thomas Drummond in Chicago. It was thought advisable to add to Manny's counsel a local lawyer who knew the judge and had his confidence. Harding sent Watson to Springfield to look at Lincoln. Watson was not impressed by the lank Midwesterner, and, while paying Lincoln a retainer, advised Harding to employ Stanton and keep Lincoln in the background, especially since it had been decided not to hold the trial in Chicago but to move it to Cincinnati, where Judge Drummond would go but where he would sit with the more impressive Justice McLean of Ohio.

At Cincinnati Stanton and Harding ignored their unknown Illinois colleague. At the opening of court Reverdy Johnson, calling attention to the fact that Manny was represented by three counsel, proposed to equalize the situation by an agreement that Dickerson would speak twice. Harding and Stanton, to prevent Dickerson from speaking both before and after Harding, put Lincoln in position where he had to withdraw. He did withdraw but remained for the argument of the case. He sent to Harding through Watson his manuscript in the case but Harding did not even look at it. When during the period Justice McLean entertained at his home counsel from both sides, Lincoln was not invited.

Yet, as if completely without envy or hurt feelings, Lincoln sat through the argument, sized up a man who was to be a member of his Cabinet in a little more than half a decade, and learned a great deal about the practice of law. He was reported as saying to Ralph Emerson, one of Manny's partners, that he was going home to study law. When Emerson remarked that that was what he had been doing he replied that he had not studied it as these college-bred men had. These men had reached Ohio and would soon be in Illinois, and he would be ready for them.[96]

McCormick lost his case. Justice McLean wrote that the case had been "argued on both sides with surpassing ability and clearness of demonstration. The art involved in the inquiry was traced in a lucid manner, and shown by models and drawings, from its origin to its present state of perfection."[97] There had been no time after the argument for consultation with Judge Drummond, but the latter had transmitted his views on the points in question and there was no difference between them. At this point Justice McLean launched into a technical discussion

[96] For the account see Albert J. Beveridge, *Abraham Lincoln*, I, 575–82. See also Emerson Hinchliff, "Lincoln and the 'Reaper Case,'"

Illinois State Historical Society, *Journal*, 33:361–65, 1940.
[97] McCormick v. Manny, 15 Fed. Cas. 1314, 1316 (No. 8724) (C.C.N.D. Ill. 1856).

of the McCormick patents and competing patents. He found McCormick's patents valid but held that Manny's devices were sufficiently different not to infringe. The decision was written in such a way as to sound like a compromise, or the result of arbitration between parties with legitimate but opposing interests:

> Having arrived at the result, that there is no infringement of the plaintiff's patent by the defendant, as charged in the bill, it is announced with greater satisfaction, as it in no respect impairs the right of the plaintiff. He is left in full possession of his invention, which has so justly secured to him, at home and in foreign countries, a renown honorable to him and to his country—a renown which can never fade from the memory, so long as the harvest home shall be gathered.[98]

Once again McCormick went back to the Supreme Court. That Court, speaking through Justice Grier and with only Justice Daniel dissenting, affirmed the decision of the court below, finding that Manny had patented an improvement and that the McCormick patent had not been infringed.[99] The decision demonstrated that McCormick would have to produce his reapers in competition with other producers and not with the benefit of a monopoly. Indeed, McCormick, seeking to improve his reapers as manufacture continued, found himself on the defensive in the courts when he was sued by Obed Hussey in the United States Circuit Court in Chicago for a patent infringement, before Justice McLean and Judge Drummond. Here his earlier enemies at law, Peter H. Watson and George Harding, turned up against him again.[100] Hussey won his case, an injunction was issued against McCormick's further use of the improvements involved, and substantial damages were assessed against him.[101] Nevertheless he continued to prosper, though his prosperity arose from shrewd land speculation as well as from his production of reapers. The courts for him had been a battleground in the competitive struggle, but only one of a number of battle-

---

[98] *Ibid.*, 1321.

[99] McCormick v. Talcott, 20 How. 402 (1858). In this case McCormick was represented by Johnson and Dickerson. An ironic item is the fact that McCormick had been dissatisfied with Dickerson and had thought instead to employ Benjamin R. Curtis, who had recently resigned from the Supreme Court. Johnson, who probably knew a great deal about inner Court sentiment, advised against making a change, saying that because of the friction over the Dred Scott decision it would be unwise to employ Curtis to appear before his recent associates. Hutchinson, *Cyrus Hall McCormick*, 447.

[100] Hussey v. McCormick, 12 Fed. Cas. 1063 (No. 6948) (C.C.N.D. Ill. 1859).

[101] Hutchinson, *Cyrus Hall McCormick*, 450–51. See also Hussey v. Whitely, 12 Fed. Cas. 1067 (No. 6950) (C.C.S.D. Ohio 1860).

grounds. Although it is said that he took personal charge of counsel in the management of his cases, he was much more successful in business than in litigation. As far as the courts were concerned, the litigation with respect to reaper patents, like that with respect to telegraph patents, reflected more in the way of expedient compromises than of development of legal principles. The "rightness" of decisions seems to have been less important than the fact that decisions eventually terminated litigation and eliminated it as an obstruction to manufacture.

In the cases dealing with vast numbers of inventions or alleged inventions there was often the question how far the development of new knowledge must proceed before it could be classified as invention or discovery and therefore subject to patent, and at the other end the scope of the protection which patents gave against the exploitation of alleged additional novelty by others. It cannot be said that the mass of decisions of the Taney period greatly clarified these questions other than as experience with the cases familiarized the judges with constantly recurring problems in ever differing settings.

One interesting question, it is true, a question of timing and novelty, did get threshed through with some resulting illumination. The leading case had to do with a safe, made by Daniel Fitzgerald in such a way as to be fire-proofed by the use of plaster of Paris. The vulnerability of Fitzgerald's patent lay in the fact that, a few years before it was issued, one James Conner had constructed and used in his own office a similar safe. Conner had not sought to patent his safe, or to manufacture safes for others, and as far as the records were concerned his own safe had eventually disappeared. The validity of Fitzgerald's patent was challenged on the ground that he had produced nothing new. In the United States Circuit Court in New York Justice Nelson charged a jury that if Conner had not made his discovery public but merely used it for himself and if it had finally been forgotten or abandoned, it was no obstacle to the validity of Fitzgerald's patent.

The Supreme Court, speaking through Chief Justice Taney and with Justices McLean, Daniel, and Grier dissenting, took the same position. It was in this situation as with the lost arts, said the Chief Justice:

It is well known that centuries ago discoveries were made in certain arts the fruits of which have come down to us, but the means by which the work was accomplished are at this day unknown. The knowledge has been lost for ages. Yet it would hardly be doubted, if anyone now discovered an art thus lost, and it was a useful improvement, that, upon a fair construction of the act of Congress, he would be entitled to a patent. Yet he would not literally be the first original inventor. But he would be the first to confer on the public the benefit of the invention. He would discover what is unknown, and communicate knowledge which the public had not the means of obtaining without his invention.[102]

The principle, urged on the Court by Daniel Webster as counsel,[103] was by this case well established in American patent law.[104]

Although this position seems to have been first taken by Justice Nelson on circuit, its eloquent statement for the Supreme Court was the work of Chief Justice Taney, as was the position taken in *O'Reilly v. Morse* that a principle in nature, as distinguished from an invention utilizing a principle, was not subject to patent—a position which remained entrenched in patent law. This is not to imply, however, that in any considerable degree any member of the Court became its authority on patent law. Justice Nelson heard many patent cases in Circuit Court, but this was because many inventions were made within the boundaries of the Second Circuit. The same was true of Justice Grier in the Third Circuit. Justice Story was highly articulate on patent matters, and produced many quotable statements,[105] but it cannot be said that his contribution during the Taney period was substantial. For his brief period on the Court Justice Woodbury found himself embroiled in patent cases but he established no leadership. Justice Curtis was of counsel in patent cases both before and after his term on the Court and as a judge had some cases in this field, but his term was too short for the establishment of leadership. Justice McLean wrestled with patent cases ably but seemingly also with an eye to public sentiment where such popular inventions as that of the reaper were concerned. If leadership were said to exist at all it might have to be located in the Chief Justice, but for the most part the Court seemed too concerned with working its way out of the intricacies of individual and highly complex cases to involve itself centrally with the body of patent law.

---

[102] Gayler v. Wilder, 10 How. 477, 497 (1851).

[103] *Ibid.*, 491–92.

[104] For discussion by Justice Grier on circuit see Rich v. Lippincott, 20 Fed. Cas. 672, 675 (No. 11758) (C.C.W.D. Pa. 1853). For reiteration by the Supreme Court see Seymour v. Osborne, 11 Wall. 516 (1871).

[105] See Frank D. Prager, "The Changing Views of Justice Story on the Construction of Patents," *Am. J. Legal Hist.*, 4:1, 1960.

CHAPTER XXI

Political Questions and Judicial Power

ALTHOUGH DEMOCRATS of the Jackson period complained that the federal judiciary exercised too much power and ought to be more directly subject to popular control, the Marshall Court had set some limits to the power of the judiciary where the prerogatives of the other two branches of the government were concerned. Key decisions opened the way for the Taney Court to disclaim responsibility for matters said to belong within the purview of the executive or of Congress rather than of the courts. For the Marshall Court this was particularly true where Indian affairs and foreign affairs were concerned, with implications respecting powers to be exercised by the states.

Certain Indian cases had been perhaps the more highly charged with emotion. It will be recalled that in *Cherokee Nation v. Georgia*, decided in 1831, the Indians had sought from the Supreme Court protection against inroads by the state of Georgia upon rights secured by treaties with the United States, in a situation where the sympathies of the Jackson Administration were with the state rather than with the Indians. The Supreme Court denied the injunction sought, on the ground that the Cherokee Nation, not being a "foreign state" within the meaning of the Constitution, could not bring an original suit in the Supreme Court. But in writing the opinion of the Court, Chief Justice Marshall, while making sympathetic comments about the plight of the Indians that angered Georgians and Jacksonians, made a further significant comment about jurisdiction:

The bill requires us to control the Legislature of Georgia, and to restrain the exertion of its physical force. The propriety of such an interposition by the court may be well questioned. It savors too much of the exercise of political power to be within the proper province of the judicial department.[1]

The comment had pleasing implications for those persons, judges or otherwise, who were eager to narrow the scope of judicial power.

With respect to treaties with foreign states, Chief Justice Marshall had already somewhat circumscribed the powers of the judiciary. In *Foster and Elam v. Neilson,* dealing with the boundaries of the Louisiana Purchase as determined by treaty, Marshall stressed the fact that a Congressional determination of the boundary was not to be denied by the courts: "A question like this respecting the boundaries of nations, is, as has been truly said, more a political than a legal question; and in its discussion, the courts of every country must respect the pronounced will of the Legislature."[2] Although in the United States a treaty was not merely an agreement between foreign powers but was also the supreme law of the land, a contract stipulation in a treaty addressed itself "to the political, not the judicial department; and the Legislature must execute the contract before it can become a rule for the court."[3]

Although in this case there was nowhere a definitive discussion of political questions,[4] the Taney Court used the concept again and again in discussing the limits of judicial power. During his second term on the Court Chief Justice Taney applied the principle of the *Foster and Elam* case, quoting at length from the Marshall opinion.[5] Yet the extension of the concept to other areas immediately involved controversy. Taney himself would have extended it to a denial of jurisdiction in suits between states to determine disputed boundary lines. The question came up in the celebrated case of *Rhode Island v. Massachusetts* over border territory which had been in dispute since early colonial days. Here James T. Austin, Democratic attorney general of Massachusetts, contended:

This court has no jurisdiction, because of the nature of the suit. It is in its character political; in the highest degree political; brought by a sovereign, in that avowed character, for the restitution of sovereignty.[6]

His point was that a suit for the restitution of sovereignty was not a case in law or equity—which a suit must be if it was to be brought in a federal court.

---

[1] Cherokee Nation v. Georgia, 5 Pet. 1, 20 (1831).
[2] Foster & Elam v. Neilson, 2 Pet. 253, 309 (1829).
[3] *Ibid.,* 314.
[4] See Charles Gordon Post, Jr., *The Supreme Court and Political Questions.*
[5] Garcia v. Lee, 12 Pet. 511 (1838).
[6] Rhode Island v. Massachusetts, 12 Pet. 657, 685 (1838).

This case, involving a conflict between two states, indeed abounded with difficulties. Justice Barbour identified one of them when he asked Benjamin Hazard, counsel for Rhode Island, if he could point to any process by which the Court could enforce a decree in such a case,[7] a question which almost always makes trouble in suits against states. Hazard could go little beyond his contention that a decree in this case was fundamentally like decrees in other cases, and expressed the belief that when the boundary line was settled by decree, "the rights of jurisdiction and sovereignty will necessarily follow."[8]

Although this decision did nothing more than determine the fact that the Court could take jurisdiction, it did determine that fact, Justice Baldwin as the Court's spokesman rejecting the contention that the case should be dismissed because the question was political. The determination, he said, depended on a fact and on the law of equity. He saw the controversy as one of ordinary judicial nature, as frequently occurred in suits between individuals. "This controversy, then, cannot be a political one, unless it becomes so by the effect of the settlement of the boundary; by a decree on the fact, or the agreement; or because the contest is between States as to political rights and power, unconnected with the original, or compact boundary."[9] He was convinced that the framers of the Constitution had intended to give the Supreme Court jurisdiction in suits of this kind.

The case brought a dissenting opinion from Chief Justice Taney, which stood alone but nevertheless highlighted the continuing importance of the doctrine of political questions. He did not question the power of the Court to decide boundary disputes when property rights were the subject in controversy, but he denied jurisdiction to determine sovereignty, as in the present case. He contended that "the powers given to the courts of the United States are judicial powers; and extend to those subjects only which are judicial in their character; and not to those which are political."[10] Quoting from Chief Justice Marshall's opinion in *Cherokee Nation v. Georgia*, he argued that the questions involved here did not belong to the judicial department.[11]

After the Supreme Court found that it had jurisdiction in the suit brought by Rhode Island against Massachusetts, the case moved through a series of interlocutory proceedings to final determination, when the Court decided that Rhode Island's bill should be dismissed. Chief Justice Taney took part in those interlocutory proceedings but, adhering to his conviction that the Court had no jurisdiction, he absented himself from the elaborate arguments on the merits. When the Court

---

[7] *Ibid.*, 694.
[8] *Ibid.*, 706.
[9] *Ibid.*, 736.

[10] *Ibid.*, 752.
[11] *Ibid.*, 753–54.

dismissed the bill on the merits, he merely reasserted his position that the Court had had no jurisdiction and avoided expression of opinion on the merits.[12] By the time of this decision, in 1846, another case, involving the Dorr Rebellion in Rhode Island, was on its way to consideration by the Supreme Court, yielding a much more elaborate development of the doctrine of political questions and of constitutional limitations on the power of the federal judiciary.

As an important event in American history, though without particular emphasis on its important judicial aspects including that of political questions, the story of the Dorr Rebellion has been told many times.[13] Apart from its judicial aspects it can be repeated here only in brief summary. Rhode Island, unlike other original states of the Union, had not adopted a constitution at the time of the separation from Great Britain, but treated as its constitution the charter granted by Charles II in 1663. Amendment of this charter-constitution was badly needed for expansion of the base of suffrage, which was by act of the legislature limited to freeholders, and for a more equitable basis of legislative representation among cities and towns and other parts of the state. Entrenched interests were strong enough repeatedly to defeat plans for adoption of a new constitution in orderly fashion, or more simply for modification of the suffrage provision.

At sessions of the legislature held in January and June, 1841, concerted efforts were made to bring about suffrage reform. When the efforts failed a loosely organized reform association, under the leadership of Thomas W. Dorr, extra-constitutionally called a convention which met October 6, 1841, to draft a new constitution to include the desired changes. The resulting constitution was approved at a referendum held in late December, the voters apparently including many persons who were disfranchised under the charter. On April 18, 1842, a slate of officers was selected under the new constitution, with Dorr as governor. In the meantime the charter government continued in opera-

---

12 Rhode Island v. Massachusetts, 4 How. 591, 639–40 (1846). For detailed discussion of this and other suits between states during the Taney period see Charles Grove Haines and Foster H. Sherwood, *The Role of the Supreme Court in American Government and Politics, 1835–1864*, 245–86. About the interlocutory proceedings in the case it is of interest to note that Daniel Webster, as counsel for Massachusetts, was extremely unhappy. He was "ashamed of the Court," he wrote to John Davis. The last two

questions had been decided *flagrantly* wrong. Yet there was nothing to do but conform to the orders of the Court in the filing of a required answer, even though it would entail a great deal of work. Daniel Webster to John Davis, Aug. 16, 1841, *Writings and Speeches of Daniel Webster*, XVI, 341.

13 The most elaborate account is Arthur May Mowry, *The Dorr War, or the Constitutional Struggle in Rhode Island*.

tion and in possession of state offices and other facilities, and under it a Whig legislature and a Whig governor, Samuel Ward King, were chosen. The charter legislature provided severe penalties for voting in any election held by the Dorr government and for serving as an officer of that government.

The strife in Rhode Island received nationwide attention and Dorr was apparently led to believe that he would receive extensive volunteer support if he had to resort to violence to establish his government in power.[14] On May 17, 1842, Dorr and his party made an abortive attempt to seize the arsenal in Providence. His group was poorly organized and their equipment ineffective, with the result that it had to disband without actual violence and Dorr fled from the state. Rumors that Dorr was about to invade the state with outside forces led the legislature on June 24 to adopt a resolution declaring martial law, which Governor King issued as an executive proclamation. The governor also asked President Tyler for military aid, under the fourth section of the Fourth Article of the Constitution, which provided for protection of the state against insurrection or domestic violence. Tyler replied that he could take no action in the absence of actual insurrection, but made it clear that if that event occurred he would do so, but without involving the federal government in political issues which were to be settled by the people of Rhode Island themselves. In short, the federal government would not permit the violent overthrow of a state government, whatever the need for internal reform, even though assertion of its power must await an actual display of force.

Presumably the position taken by the President played a part in bringing about the collapse of the Dorr movement. The charter government, however, bombarded by nationwide criticism, called a constitutional convention and adopted a new constitution making some but not all of the desired reforms. There remained the punishment of Dorr and others who had participated in the collapsed government. The entire movement took place in a setting of partisan politics. Although Dorr was initially supported by both Democrats and Whigs, Democrats outside the state in general came to Dorr's defense whereas Whigs supported "law and order" in the form of the charter government. Indeed, a great deal of the historical material connected with the rebellion was compiled as a result of a memorial from Rhode Island Democratic legislators asking the federal House of Representatives to inquire into the suppression of the Dorr movement through "the interference and

---

[14] Arthur May Mowry, "Tammany Hall and the Dorr Rebellion," *American Historical Review*, 3:292, 1898.

assistance of the President of the United States."[15] On the other hand, the Rhode Island legislature as a whole, called into special session for the purpose, adopted a protest against Congressional inquiry into the affairs of the state.[16]

The Dorr case became an item of controversy in the Presidential election of 1844. Henry Clay told an audience at Raleigh, North Carolina, that Whigs everywhere disapproved of the Dorr movement and that all the sympathy and encouragement had come from Democrats. He noted the possible results in the South if Dorrism should become popular:

> Any unprincipled adventurer would have nothing to do but to collect around him a mosaic majority, black and white, aliens and citizens, young and old, male and female, overturn existing governments, and set up new ones at his pleasure or caprice! What earthly security for life, liberty, or property would remain, if a proceeding so fraught with confusion, disorder, and insubordination were tolerated and sanctioned?[17]

During the period of the campaign Dorr was convicted of treason against the state of Rhode Island and sentenced to life imprisonment at hard labor. Andrew Jackson, although no lover of disorder, was persuaded to say for his party that as he understood it Dorr had committed no offense except that of endeavoring to supersede the royal charter by a constitution emanating from the people, and that even if he had erred in his means it was difficult to conceive how such severe punishment could be justified.[18]

Indignation meetings at Dorr's imprisonment were held in various parts of the country. The National Reform Association of New York sent Francis C. Treadwell of Maine, a counsellor at law, to Rhode Island to start proceedings for Dorr's liberation.[19] Certificates entitled "Dorr Liberation Stock" were issued, certifying over Treadwell's signature that the person named had contributed ten cents to the Dorr Liberation Fund.[20] Treadwell found that the Rhode Island Supreme Court had refused to suspend sentence pending an attempt to get the case before the Supreme Court of the United States by writ of error, and prison authorities denied him access to Dorr to get his signature

---

[15] Rhode Island—Interference of the Executive in the Affairs of, H.R. Rep. No. 546, 28th Cong., 1st Sess. 1 (1844).

[16] *Niles' National Register*, 66:86–87, 1844.

[17] *Ibid.*, 297.

[18] *Niles' National Register*, 67:23, 1844.

[19] *Niles' National Register*, 66:390, 1844.

[20] See reproduction, Mowry, *The Dorr War*, 258.

to a petition for the writ. Treadwell then petitioned the Supreme Court for a writ of habeas corpus, contending that the writ was necessary to protect Dorr's constitutional right to have his defense examined by the Supreme Court. He contended that Dorr was being unconstitutionally punished for treason since treason could be committed only against the United States and not a state; that Dorr had acted lawfully as governor under the rightful constitution of Rhode Island; and that if Dorr had actually levied war it had been against the United States and not against the state, and therefore could not be inquired into by any state court.[21]

On December 27, 1844, the Supreme Court denied the writ of habeas corpus, speaking unanimously through Justice McLean. No federal court or federal judge, it said, could issue a writ of habeas corpus to bring up a prisoner who was in custody under a sentence of execution of a state court for any other purpose than to be used as a witness. As for the requested writ of error, said the Court, it was clear that since counsel did not act under the authority of Dorr but at the request of his friends the prayer could not be granted.[22]

Although the Supreme Court decision was flatly negative as to both writs, the publicity of the case may have brought some benefit for Dorr. On January 4, 1845, a petition for a writ of error was filed— indicating that in some fashion Dorr's signature had been secured— and the writ was allowed by Justice Story three days later, effective as of the December term of 1845. The judges of the Rhode Island Supreme Court seem to have been slow in sending the record in the case—it did not arrive until January 23, 1846. In the meantime, on June 27, 1845, Dorr was released pursuant to an act of amnesty passed by the Rhode Island legislature. The case remained on the docket of the Supreme Court until December 5, 1849, when it was dismissed without ever having come to argument.

Meanwhile the issues of the Dorr Rebellion were moving toward the Supreme Court from another direction. With more optimism than the situation seems to have justified, certain of Dorr's friends and followers, seeing that they had no chance of victory in the state courts, initiated suits against state government officers in the United States Circuit Court. One of the litigants was Martin Luther, who had served as a moderator for the Dorr government at a meeting in the town of Warren in violation of an act of the legislature of the charter government. Claiming residence in Fall River, Massachusetts, evidently to give the necessary diversity of citizenship, Luther brought an action of

---

[21] *Niles' National Register*, 67:242, 1844.

[22] *Ex parte* Dorr, 3 How. 103 (1844).

trespass against Luther M. Borden and others who, in the execution of commands under martial law, had invaded his home in Warren, Rhode Island, and searched it without a warrant, failing to capture him only because he had taken warning and absented himself. The other action was brought by Luther's mother, Rachel Luther, who was at home at the time of the search and was the victim of allegedly high-handed procedures.

The Circuit Court consisted of Justice Story and District Judge John Pitman. Both these judges, conservative in their leanings, had expressed themselves as in opposition to the Dorr Rebellion before the litigation began. In January of 1842 Judge Pitman published a pamphlet addressed to the Rhode Island legislature in which he warned that an attempt by a single political party to force a change in the law with respect to suffrage might be followed by another making inroads on property rights.[23] He sent a copy of the pamphlet to Justice Story, who, reading it in bed during a severe illness, expressed his warm approval. If ever there was a case requiring a judge to write and speak openly and publicly, said Justice Story, this was it. He trusted that the state might be saved from having all its best institutions shaken, if not destroyed, by the Free Suffrage Party. "What is a Republican government worth if an unauthorized body may thus make, promulgate, and compel obedience to a Constitution at its own mere will and pleasure?"[24]

In a letter to Daniel Webster, then Secretary of State, Justice Story on April 26, 1842, displayed a similar bias in behalf of the charter government. He was fearful that the free suffrage constitution would be forced upon the people by intimidation and military force, in which event the charter government would fight back. There could be no doubt, he asserted, that the proceedings of the free suffrage convention and the constitution made by it were without law and against law. He urged upon Webster the need for additional protective measures on the part of the federal government, in the form of placement of federal troops and a proclamation of warning by the President.[25]

[23] Mahlon H. Hellerich, "The Luther Cases in the Lower Courts," *Rhode Island Historical Review*, 2:33, 43–44, 1952.

[24] Joseph Story to John Pitman, Feb. 10, 1842, *Life and Letters of Joseph Story*, W. W. Story, ed., II, 416.

[25] Joseph Story to Daniel Webster, Apr. 26, 1842, Webster Papers, N.H.H.S. Webster sought to allay the strife by resort to diplomacy as well as threat of use of force. He wrote to John Whipple, an influential Rhode Island lawyer, that since the United States pledged support to the existing constitution and since the rebels were not in power, it was time for conciliation, and urged that there be no more arrests. (Daniel Webster to John Whipple, May 9, 1842, *Ibid.*) Webster was told, however, that this was a political movement, and that no compromise was possible: "I am not willing that Dorr, Pearce and Anthony should make capital for Mr. Van

When on June 15, 1842, at the height of the excitement, Justice Story delivered a charge to a Rhode Island grand jury, he discussed the issues of treason involved in the rebellion. While admitting that treason against the United States and against the state might be closely intertwined, he distinguished between the two, making it clear that treason might be "aimed altogether against the sovereignty of a particular state,"[26] thereby aiding the state courts by making it clear that they too had a function to perform where treason was involved. At a time when the sending of federal troops to suppress an insurrection was still a possibility, he warned that armed resistance to those troops would constitute a levying of war against the United States, and implied that such action would constitute treason. Such were the convictions of the judges before whom Luther and his mother brought actions of trespass against officers of the charter government for their execution of martial law.

Luther's case was initiated at the November term of 1842 and continued to the term of a year later. His counsel contended that the people had a right to change their government, that they had done so by the Dorr constitution, that the Dorr government was the legitimate government of Rhode Island at the time of the alleged trespass, and that Borden had had no right of entry into Luther's home. Borden in turn contended that the charter government was at that time the legitimate government and that he had acted pursuant to constitutional authorization. Presumably under the guidance of the judges, the jury found a verdict for Borden, and, as had been intended, arrangements were made to take the case to the Supreme Court on writ of error.

The convictions of Justice Story had remained as stated in 1842. In his grand jury charge of November, 1843, he gave high praise to the old charter of Rhode Island even though it had now been superseded by a new constitution, and warned against resort to untested theories of government: "The most beautiful theories of government have been found to fade away at a single touch of practice, at a single test of experience."[27] At the argument of the Rachel Luther case Justice Story fought plaintiff's counsel as a partisan.[28] When Benjamin Hallett contended that although martial law existed in the cities of conflict, it did not extend to Warren where such conflict did not exist, Justice

---

Buren out of our domestic disturbances. . . . They have roused the passions of the people to that degree that we are almost daily threatened with the torch and with the sword." W. Channing Gibbs to Daniel Webster, May 12, 1842, *Ibid.*

[26] Charge to Grand Jury—Treason,

30 Fed. Cas. 1046, 1047 (No. 18275) (C.C.D. R.I. 1842).

[27] Extract from Judge Story's Charge to the Grand Jury in Providence, Delivered in November, 1843, 1 West. L.J. 201, 202 (1844).

[28] See Hellerich, "The Luther Cases in the Lower Courts," *Rhode Island Historical Review*, 2:43, 1952.

Story replied that "as martial law was declared by the State, it extended all over the State."[29]

Hallett denied that the legislature had the power to proclaim martial law, contending that the power was a military power not subject to legislative authorization, and that in any event it could exist only where troops were in the field. He found himself stopped again:

> Judge Story said, that, as far as the questions of law were concerned, he was ready to decide them now, as he should be at the end of the trial. In the first place, he had no sort of doubt of the power of the legislature of Rhode Island to declare martial law. It was a legislative power, and was one of the acts of their sovereign authority. . . . The legislature of Rhode Island was the sole judge of the necessity of the case within their territory; and, having the power to provide for the occasion, they exerted it, and the declaration of martial law was a proper legislative act.[30]

As for the finding of the President of the United States that the situation did not require federal intervention, the President was the proper judge within his sphere, "but he is no judge of the necessity of such action on the part of the State." Rhode Island was a sovereign state and must have the right to maintain her own sovereignty. Summarizing his points, Justice Story added that "These views he had formed upon mature deliberation, and he could not change them until they were reversed by the Supreme Court. He apprehended that he should be very slow in being taught there, that a State could not maintain its own sovereignty and the supremacy of its laws by all necessary means, or that a State must follow its army, and declare martial law only on its route."[31]

As if he felt that his case was being very well handled by the judge, it was said of counsel for the defendant that "Mr. Whipple dwelt shortly on the testimony adduced, and closed after a very brief address."[32] In his charge to the jury Justice Story repeated the points he had already made and proceeded to argue the case for Borden as if he himself were of counsel.[33] But for all the help given from the bench the jury divided in Mrs. Luther's case, endangering the plan to take it to the Supreme Court along with the case of her son. The judges then tried to send it along by the strategy of certifying a series of twenty-nine points on which they were alleged to be divided.

---

[29] Rhode Island Memorial, H.R. Rep. No. 581, 28th Cong., 1st Sess. 158 (1844). This report had been reprinted from the *Providence Journal*. *Ibid.*, 43.

[30] *Ibid.*, 159.
[31] *Ibid.*, 160.
[32] *Ibid.*, 163.
[33] *Ibid.*, 163–67.

Although the record in Martin Luther's case was received and filed in the Supreme Court, the case, for one reason or another, was continued from term to term for nearly four years before it was argued, and it was nearly five years before it was decided. In the meantime the government of Rhode Island under the constitution of 1843 was well entrenched as the legitimate successor to the charter government. In addition to a fine of five hundred dollars, Martin Luther served a jail sentence of six months for his aid to the Dorr government.[34] A number of changes took place on the Supreme Court, including the death of Justice Story and his replacement by Justice Woodbury. In short, by the time the Supreme Court argument began, on January 21, 1848, the Dorr Rebellion looked somewhat like ancient history. The specific issues concerning the government of Rhode Island had shaded into theoretical questions about the rights of the people to change their governments at will and political issues by means of which Democratic and Whig parties sought election to office.

Even after the passage of so much time, the case was argued before only six judges, Justices Catron, McKinley, and Daniel being absent because of illness. Although during this period the Court was behind with its work and wrestling with the problem of clearing the docket and keeping up with the stream of new cases, it permitted the argument to proceed for a total of six days.[35]

The leading argument for Dorr was made by Benjamin F. Hallett, who in addition to being a lawyer was a newspaper editor and a crusader for the rights of people as against oppressive governments. Benjamin C. Howard said of his argument that "the Reporter is much at a loss how to give even a skeleton of the argument, which lasted for three days, and extended over a great variety of matter."[36] Hallett's strategy was to establish the right of the people of Rhode Island, in the face of the power of the minority who were in control of the charter government, to adopt their own constitution and establish their own government. According to Howard's summary he proceeded to an analysis of fundamentals, examining definitions of the state and of the people, finding the ultimate power of sovereignty in the people and justifying the right of the people to establish their own government. He contended that the Dorr constitution, and not the royal charter which had never been adopted by the people, had been in 1842 the legitimate instrument of government in Rhode Island. He noted that in Dorr's trial for treason in the Rhode Island court there had been no determina-

---

[34] H.R. Rep. No. 546, 28th Cong., 1st Sess. 322–24 (1844).

[35] The argument was begun on Jan. 21, 1848, and continued on Jan. 24–28.

[36] Luther v. Borden, 7 How. 1, 21 (1849).

tion of which was the valid constitution of the state. "It was made a political question, and not a judicial construction, as far as it entered the case."[37]

A few weeks later, when discussing in the Senate the possibility of limiting the arguments of counsel to enable the Court to keep up with its work load, Reverdy Johnson remarked:

> I heard pamphlet after pamphlet, fourth of July speech after fourth of July speech, written and delivered years ago, read before that tribunal, to prove that a free people have the right to establish that form of government they deem best. Sir, I imagine that if the Chief Justice, speaking for himself and his associates, had said that no such authority should be cited, the press of the country would have run mad, particularly if the result had been, as in all probability it will be, that on the unanimous judgment of that tribunal, the Dorr revolution was nothing but naked and inexcusable rebellion.[38]

Hallett was aided only by Nathan Clifford, then Attorney General and later to be a member of the Supreme Court. According to Howard, who had no record of Clifford's argument, he dealt almost exclusively with the point that a state had no right to declare martial law.[39] The *New York Tribune*, considering that Clifford had missed the important issues, said that "Mr. Attorney General Clifford, in the Supreme Court, undertook to defend Dorrism. If he was no more successful in making the Court understand it than he seemed to comprehend it himself, the defense must have recoiled upon the author."[40]

John Whipple, who like Hallett had argued the case in the Circuit Court, left the discussion of broad principles primarily to his new associate, Daniel Webster. He denied the legitimacy of the Dorr constitution as adopted, or at any rate voted on, without the authorization of law, and insisted that constitutional reform must start with the legislature. He praised the royal charter as a wise instrument of government and commented on the voting irregularities for the adoption of the Dorr constitution. He insisted that the right to vote, where it existed, was a political and not a natural right, and that "political rights are matters of practical utility."[41] Even the Dorr constitution had excluded men under the age of twenty-one and people of residence of not more than one year. If the state could thus limit the right, it could confine the right of voting to freeholders, as well as adults or residents for a year.[42]

---

[37] *Ibid.*, 26.
[38] *Cong. Globe*, 30th Cong., 1st Sess. 587 (1848).
[39] 7 How. 34.
[40] *New York Tribune*, Jan. 31, 1848.
[41] 7 How. 28.
[42] *Ibid.*, 29.

Webster made the case the occasion of a tremendous effort. In a voluminous argument shaped to the use of techniques of oratory he fully admitted that the people were the source of all political power, but he denied that any assemblage of people, even one claiming to represent a majority of the people, could interject itself in place of the existing government of the state. The American people in all the states had committed themselves to acting through their existing governments, and particularly through their legislatures, when making constitutional changes. The people limited the power of their governments but they also set limits on themselves, limits which were exceeded by the procedures of the Dorr Rebellion.

In any event, said Webster, the facts involved in determining which of two legislatures was the rightful legislative body were not facts which the Supreme Court could inquire into or which the court below could try. The purpose of allegation of the facts was "the establishment of a new sovereignty; and that is a question to be settled elsewhere and otherwise. From the very nature of the case, it is not a question to be decided by judicial inquiry."[43] Insofar as it was capable of being determined by the government of the United States it had already been determined by the President in execution of an Act of Congress to fulfill the obligation to guarantee each state a republican form of government and protect it against domestic violence. Furthermore, "according to our system, it devolves upon the executive to determine, in the first instance, what are and what are not governments."[44] This was true of the governments of states as well as of foreign countries.

The *New York Tribune* reported that "In the Supreme Court of the United States Daniel Webster used up the last remnant of Dorrism. The court room was crowded with ladies and distinguished gentlemen, to listen to the great effort."[45] The *Washington National Intelligencer* reported that the argument established "by a train of reasoning as incontestable as it is profound, the lawless and untenable nature of the Dorr Government and proceedings, and, by consequence, the constitutional right and authority of the charter government."[46] After completion of his argument Webster himself wrote to his son that "I believe we have pretty effectively suppressed the Rhode Island insurrection."[47]

The six Justices who heard the arguments in *Luther v. Borden* failed to reach a decision, or at any rate to agree upon an opinion of

---

[43] "The Rhode Island Government," *Writings and Speeches of Daniel Webster*, XXI, 217, 238.

[44] *Ibid.*, 237.

[45] *New York Tribune*, Jan. 29, 1848.

[46] *Washington National Intelligencer*, Feb. 3, 1848.

[47] Daniel Webster to Fletcher Webster, Jan. 29, 1848, *Writings and Speeches of Daniel Webster*, XVIII, 267.

the Court, at the term at which the case was argued, with the result that the case was continued under advisement until the ensuing term. It is hard to tell whether the delay resulted from difficulties with the case, or from the burden of work, or from a desire to keep the decision from playing a part in the Presidential election of 1848, in which Zachary Taylor, of the Whig Party, contended with Lewis Cass, of the Democrats. The decision was announced on January 3, 1849, with Chief Justice Taney writing the opinion of the Court and speaking for five of the six Justices, Justice Woodbury dissenting on a single point.

As indicated by the Chief Justice, the weight of time—more than six and a half years had passed since the Dorr Rebellion—stood as a barrier to judicial examination at this time of the legal status of the rival governments. The charter government had continued as the operating government of Rhode Island until replaced by government under a new constitution which had stemmed from the operations of the charter government. For the Supreme Court to reach back to 1842 and hold that the real government of the state had been the abortive government headed by Dorr would create vast confusion in the laws and finances of the state and in the pattern of rights related to governmental operations. When the decision of the Court might lead to such results, it became the duty of the Court to examine carefully its own powers before undertaking to exercise jurisdiction.

The Court found that it had no such jurisdiction, making extensive use of the line of argument pursued by Webster. The courts of Rhode Island had already held that within the state the determination of the legitimacy of a government was to be made by the political power and not by the judiciary—a position which Chief Justice Taney thought obvious since the authority of the judiciary itself depended upon the question to be determined. In interpreting the constitution and laws of a state the federal courts, according to a well-settled rule, followed the decisions of the state courts. Furthermore, the question of fact as to the adoption of the Dorr constitution by an alleged majority of the people was one into which the judiciary could not possibly go. It was a question of fact which could be determined by no proper judicial proceeding.

Moreover, said Taney, the fourth section of the Fourth Article of the federal Constitution, which provided for federal interference in the concerns of the state to preserve a republican form of government and to repel invasion and suppress domestic violence, had "treated the subject as political in its nature, and placed the power in the hands of that department."[48] Here he followed the Webster argument in expounding on the responsibilities of Congress and the President and the ina-

---

[48] 7 How. 42.

bility of the judiciary to interfere. If the judicial power did extend to such interference, then "the guarantee contained in the Constitution of the United States is a guarantee of anarchy, and not of order."[49]

Assuming the legitimacy of the charter government as determined by the political branches of the governments of Rhode Island and the United States, the Court held that, even though the President had not found the kind of crisis that justified federal military intervention, Rhode Island had acted within its own powers in exercising its own military authority, including its action in breaking and entering Luther's house.

On the latter point Justice Woodbury wrote a seemingly interminable opinion. (The *New York Tribune* noted that "Mr. Woodbury's report this morning was long beyond the patience of most listeners, and nearly two hours were occupied in the delivery."[50]) Ignoring the decision by which the Supreme Court of Rhode Island had in the Dorr trial upheld the exercise of military power, and the obligation of the Supreme Court to follow the state court in matters of state law, he insisted that according to general principles and in terms of the charter constitution of Rhode Island, the exercise of military power in this case was unconstitutional. With the exception of Justice McLean, all the members of the Supreme Court at this time were Democrats, but Justice Woodbury was the only active Democratic aspirant for the Presidency. It is impossible to tell to what extent his opinion was the product of the political sentiments of his party, which in general had been favorable to the cause of Dorr and his followers.

But Justice Woodbury stated specifically that the difference between him and his brethren extended only to the points in issue concerning martial law. He accepted the holding of the Court that the question of the legitimacy of a state government was a political question and not one to be answered by the judiciary. Already committed to the principle that the judiciary must not express itself on political questions,[51] he exercised self-denial here, noting, however, that before coming to the Bench he had frequently and publicly avowed his opinion as to the legitimacy of the charter government.

With its decision in *Luther v. Borden*[52] the Supreme Court firmly

---

[49] *Ibid.*, 43.

[50] *New York Tribune*, Jan. 5, 1849.

[51] See Jones v. Van Zandt, 5 How. 215, 231 (1847).

[52] The case of *Rachel Luther v. Borden*, which was a parallel case to that of Martin Luther and was brought up on what was clearly a fictitious certification of differences between Justice Story and Judge Pitman, received short shrift in the Supreme Court. Chief Justice Taney noted that the division was "merely formal" and that the whole case had been transferred to the Supreme Court by the certification of a multitude of points. The Court had repeatedly decided that such a mode of proceeding was not warranted and the case

entrenched the principle that certain kinds of questions deeply involving the activities of the political branches of government were to be treated as political and not to be inquired into by the judiciary. Such questions were referred to from time to time during the remainder of the Taney period.[53] The concept achieved its prime importance, however, in the period after the close of the Civil War, when resort to it enabled the Supreme Court to avoid disastrous conflict with Congress and the executive over the constitutionality of reconstruction legislation. Its development marked one of the important contributions of the Taney Court.

---

was sent back to the Circuit Court, the Chief Justice remarking that the material points had nevertheless been decided in the case involving Martin Luther. (7 How. 47.)

[53] See for example Doe v. Braden, 6 How. 635 (1854). See also Chief Justice Taney dissenting in Pennsylvania v. Wheeling Bridge Co., 13 How. 518, 587, 592 (1854). For development of the doctrine of political questions down to 1962 see Baker v. Carr, 369 U.S. 186 (1962).

CHAPTER XXII

Sectionalism and Slavery

I SSUES OF SLAVERY and of the status and rights of free Negroes in the United States dogged the judiciary from the beginning to the end of the Taney period, bursting finally into the flames of civil war. With respect to these issues, as with respect to those involved in the development of commerce, the maintenance of sound currency, the giving of relief in bankruptcy, and the handling of international crises, the judiciary operated only at the periphery, even though its peripheral action in a case involving the claim to freedom on the part of a Negro named Dred Scott was to precipitate violence affecting the entire nation. For the study of judicial performance in this area it is necessary at once to have in mind, and yet to subordinate in discussion, the highly emotionalized moral issues which cut deeper than the body of prevailing law and which in turn provided the basis on which new law was eventually to be evolved. It is necessary to face the fact of the man-made degradation enforced on an entire race, including those members who were nominally free, and to comprehend the self-deception which convinced most white men of their own inherent superiority and enabled large numbers of them to live relatively at peace with themselves even as they served as the instruments of or gave sanction to oppression of blacks. It is necessary to know how Negroes were treated—a spectrum ranging from the kindness that might be shown to untutored members of reputable white families (which occasionally, though unadmittedly, they actually were) to individual gross brutality and the calculated working to death of masses of slaves on large plantations in the process of getting maximum returns from slave property. It is necessary to remember that although some slaves might and did become nominally free, they had little prospect of rising to higher economic and cultural levels. While they ran the same grim risks as lower-class white men that they might collapse in the economic struggle for survival, they could not share the same dream of rising to the top, of seeing a son, for example, become President of the United States or hold other office of honor or profit.

All these things most people of both races (but never all) took for granted. There were always "agitators" who broke through the lethargy encompassing a life of slavery to remind Negroes of the wrongs they had to endure, and who reminded otherwise comfortable white people of the injustice stemming from their way of life. The agitation threatened the nice balances of the law.

At the beginning of the Taney period an uneasy peace had been preserved for more than a third of a century between the North and the South by reliance on the Fugitive Slave Clause of the Fourth Article of the Constitution and the Fugitive Slave Act of 1793 based on it. Always with exceptions here and there, slavery became more anathema in the North, where it was unprofitable, and more highly approved in the South, where an evolving economic system was based upon it. Sectional antagonism flared in the 1830s. The Nat Turner rebellion of slaves in Virginia in 1831 convinced slaveowners of the validity of their hitherto latent fears of such uprisings and led to drastic restrictive measures. These included prohibitions against education of slaves that might render them more accessible to abolitionist propaganda from the North and prepare them to develop aspirations for freedom. During the same year William Lloyd Garrison of Massachusetts established his crusading and vitriolic abolitionist magazine, *The Liberator*, and aided in founding the New England Anti-Slavery Society. He traced the roots of the hated institution to the fabric of the Constitution itself, and persuaded the Massachusetts Anti-Slavery Society to adopt what became a notorious declaration to the effect that the compact between the North and the South was "a covenant with death and an agreement with hell," and that it "should be immediately annulled."[1]

The abolitionist movement split into two factions the previously consolidated, more generally supported colonization movement. While the colonizationists had included abolitionists, they had included also men at the opposite extreme who desired the colonization of free Negroes in Liberia or some other far-off place to prevent their living reminder to slaves that they too might be free and to prevent their participation in possible slave rebellions or escapes. But the leaders among the abolitionists were not satisfied with mere deportation of free Negroes. They demanded freedom for slaves as well, and seem in some instances to have urged free Negroes to stand their ground and not be intimidated into emigrating.

---

[1] Archibald H. Grimke, *William Lloyd Garrison*, 310–11.

Members of the Supreme Court, making annual tours through their circuits and returning to Washington when Congress was in session, were naturally conversant with the race problem, and some of them were directly engaged in efforts at solution. Justice Bushrod Washington, for example, had been first president of the American Colonization Society at its organization in 1817. In 1833 Chief Justice Marshall was president of the Virginia component of the society. In 1835, in a letter to such an organization in Philadelphia, he praised its activities and indirectly contrasted them favorably with those of abolitionists. The object of the society, he wrote, ought to be "dear to every American bosom, and particularly so to our fellow citizens of the south." He expressed the hope that the efforts of the society would "go far in counteracting the malignant effects of the insane fanaticism of all those who defeat all practical good, by the pursuit of an unattainable object."[2]

Justice Story, in his *Commentaries on the Constitution*, published in 1833, noted that the fugitive slave provision of the Constitution was "introduced into the constitution solely for the benefit of the slave-holding states,"[3] and emphasized the concession which it represented on the part of the Eastern and Middle states. He remarked further that "This forms no just subject of complaint; but it should for ever repress the delusive and mischievous notion, that the South has not at all times had its full share of the benefits of the Union."[4] On the other hand, like Webster, Story was much concerned about the preservation of the Union, he feared the disunionist tendencies of the abolitionists, and he was concerned about the fact that their extremism played into the hands of the Democratic Party and injured the Whigs. In 1842, along with deploring specifically the tactics of abolitionists, he expressed concern about "the inroads of a low and mischievous Democracy," and added that "For my own part I think, that we have fully tried the Experiment of a Representative Republic; and that it is a failure on our part. The vital principles of the Constitution are uprooted and disregarded in the blind fury of a party spirit."[5]

His concern continued to deepen, and in 1843 he delivered a lecture to his law school class on the subject of the abolitionist threat of disunion, which was described by one of his students, Rutherford B. Hayes, as "the most eloquent lecture I ever heard." He reminded his class of the existence of the fugitive slave provision of the Constitution, and warned that if one part of the country might disregard one part of the Constitution, other sections might disregard other provisions and the

2 *Niles' Weekly Register*, 48:162, 1835.
3 Joseph Story, *Commentaries on the Constitution*, III, 676.

4 *Ibid.*, 677.
5 Joseph Story to Richard Peters, Nov. 27, 1842, Peters Correspondence, II, Cadwalader Papers.

Union would become a mere rope of sand, or be severed into four, six, or eight little confederacies, or fall under the control of a despot. The Constitution had been the product of compromise and the spirit of concession and forbearance, and it would come to an end when that spirit died in the hearts of the people.[6] Shortly before the Presidential election of 1844 he wrote that the abolitionists as usual were against the Whigs, simply to defeat Clay, even though in doing so they would aid Polk's election. "But that is nothing to them," he added bitterly. "They are for dissolving the Union."[7]

But while Justice Story would grant to the South the full benefit of the Fugitive Slave Clause, he refused to grant other benefits not clearly given. On some points his position was obscure. Although he must have been aware of the controversy over whether free Negroes benefited from the constitutional guarantee that "citizens of each state shall be entitled to all privileges and immunities of citizens in the several states," he mentioned the subject only by indirection. The purpose of the clause, he explained, was to confer on citizens of each state "a general citizenship; and to communicate all the privileges and immunities, which the citizens of the same state would be entitled to under the like circumstances."[8] When in 1833 Chief Justice David Daggett of Massachusetts instructed a jury that Negroes could not be citizens within the meaning of the federal Constitution,[9] Justice Story is said privately to have "treated the decision as utterly untenable, and, indeed, worthy of little more than ridicule."[10] This comment, communicated privately to a member of Congress, was apparently not published until long after the slavery controversy had been settled by civil war and constitutional amendment.

In the meantime, as previously remarked in connection with the regulation of commerce, Roger B. Taney as Attorney General had officially expounded on the inherently degraded status of the Negro and his incapacity for citizenship and on the power of the states to control the interstate movements of free Negroes, to prevent their carrying arms, and otherwise to limit their freedom. John Catron, as chief justice of the Supreme Court of Tennessee, had warned against the indiscriminate manumission of slaves because of the miserable status of free Negroes and the danger involved in their association with slaves. "Degraded by their color and condition of life, the free negroes are a

---

[6] *Diary and Letters of Rutherford Birchard Hayes*, Charles Richard Williams, ed., I, 131.
[7] Joseph Story to Richard Peters, Sept. 1, 1844, Peters Correspondence, II, Cadwalader Papers.
[8] Story, *Commentaries*, III, 675.

[9] Crandall v. Connecticut, 10 Conn. 339, 344 (1834).
[10] Charles Sumner to Robert C. Winthrop, Feb. 3, 1843, *Memoir and Letters of Charles Sumner*, Edward L. Pierce, ed., II, 257.

very dangerous and most objectionable population where slaves are numerous; therefore no slave can be safely freed but with the assent of the government where the manumission takes place."[11]

Justice Wayne, although much more of a nationalist than Catron, was apparently committed to the preservation of the institutions of his state, among which slavery was included. Justice Barbour operated a large Virginia plantation with slaves, and his successor, Justice Daniel, apparently had an even deeper emotional commitment to slavery as an institution. Justice McKinley was no rebel against Southern institutions. Justice Baldwin seems to have had no special commitment beyond the normal commitment of a judge to law enforcement, but at his death he gave place to Justice Grier, one of whose prime qualifications was his zeal for protection of property in slaves, where he stood companionably with Justice Woodbury as the successor to Justice Story. Justice Thompson seems to have had no special commitment on the subject, but he gave way to Justice Nelson, a warm defender of the rights of slaveholders. Even the friendliness of Justice McLean to the rights of the Negro was limited by his oath of office as a judge, which was to enforce the law as it stood, including the provisions of the Constitution and of federal statutes which protected the institution of slavery.

To summarize and to state the matter somewhat differently, no member of the Supreme Court during the early part of the Taney period was so friendly to the Negro as to assume that there was a "higher law than the Constitution" to protect the rights of Negroes, and that his duty lay to that higher law. All of the Justices admitted as a matter of course the obligation to enforce fugitive slave legislation. Such differences among them as there were probably lay in differing conceptions of the status of Negroes as persons and as citizens, with implications as to the protection to which free Negroes were entitled in law enforcement, and possibly other differences as to the merits of slavery as an institution, which could reveal themselves in borderline decisions in various branches of the law.

While by the middle 1830s abolitionists were attacking slavery wherever it might be found in the United States, the most vulnerable point of attack was slavery and the slave trade in the District of Columbia. The District was the location of the government for the entire nation. Opponents of slavery contended that this disgraceful institution should not be permitted to exist there, under virtual sponsorship by the federal government. The South, on the other hand, contended that slavery was justified by the inherent inferiority of the Negro and by the Constitution, and pointed out that the District of Columbia itself was

---

[11] Fisher's Negroes v. Dabbs, 14 Tenn. (6 Yerger) 118, 126 (1834).

532

carved from two slave states, Maryland and Virginia, and continued to be governed in part by the bodies of law which had existed in those states at the time when the District was created. At the time when Roger B. Taney was anxiously awaiting action by the Senate on his nomination as Chief Justice, Martin Van Buren, the Jackson-chosen Democratic candidate for the Presidency, was writing a long letter to a group of North Carolina Democrats to explain his position on the issues of slavery in the District. He refrained from offending the opponents of slavery to the extent of saying that Congress could not interfere with slavery in the District, but he did contend that its abolition there would "violate that spirit of compromise of interests which lies at the basis of the social compact."[12]

During the first term of the Taney Court in its basement chamber in the Capitol in Washington, the calm debates in the courtroom stood out in sharp contrast to the angry debates over slavery in the Senate chamber just overhead and in the chamber of the House of Representatives on the south side of the building. Into both chambers were pouring petitions from Northern constituencies for abolition of slavery in the District, a movement which marked but the beginning of the war on slavery in general.[13] In the Senate John C. Calhoun and other Southerners were opposing even the reception of these petitions and denouncing the disturbance of social order and the invasion of rights of property which they represented. Men had no right, said Calhoun, to petition to deprive others of what belonged to them. Slaves were as much property as stocks, houses, or lands.[14] The House of Representatives gagged the petitioning process, but abolitionist leader John Quincy Adams raised even more of a furor over the rejection of the petitions than would have taken place had they been received and buried in committee. A resolution to censure him for insisting on being heard merely gave him the opportunity to speak in behalf of freedom of speech and particularly of the right of petition which, he proclaimed, derived not merely from the Constitution but from God himself.[15] By means of the newspapers and the *Congressional Globe* the debate echoed angrily throughout the country and carried forebodings of increasing strife.

---

[12] Martin Van Buren to Junius Amis *et al.*, Mar. 6, 1836, *Niles' National Register*, 50:126–28, 1836.

[13] *Cong. Globe*, 24th Cong., 2nd Sess. 265 (1837). In the language of Waddy Thompson of South Carolina, "They regard abolition in the District as a first but decisive step to abolition in the States. So do I. So does the whole slaveholding country." For broad discussion of the subject see Russel B. Nye, *Fettered Freedom: Civil Liberties and the Slavery Controversy, 1830–1860*.

[14] *Cong. Globe*, 24th Cong., 2nd Sess. 122 (1837).

[15] *Ibid.*, 261–62.

Although the differences between the North and the South over slavery had given rise to a constitutional provision for its protection and to an early statute for enforcement of the return of fugitive slaves, the settlement resembled as much an agreement between sovereigns as it resembled establishment of a body of law for enforcement in the courts. While some of the slaves who escaped into free states were captured and returned to their owners by means of legal process, it was not until after the close of the Marshall period that important litigation on the subject reached the Supreme Court.

For the Taney Court, however, it was a portent of the future that on its docket at its first term was a case involving slavery issues, even though giving rise to less stirring emotions than the controversy raging in Congress over proposals to abolish slavery in the District of Columbia. The constitutional prohibition against interference with the slave trade—the importation of slaves from abroad—had come to an end in 1808, and Congress had exercised its power to prohibit the trade. An Act of 1818 forbade bringing into the United States "in any manner whatsoever" any colored person to be held or sold as a slave and provided for the confiscation of any vessel by means of which the statute might be violated.[16]

On casual reading it would seem that the statute was intended only to prevent bringing blacks into the United States for their initial introduction into slavery and not to prevent owners who had gone abroad with their slaves from bringing them back again. Nevertheless, in New Orleans, in the heart of slave country, a district attorney libeled two vessels on the ground that they had violated the statute in bringing back to the United States female domestics who had visited France with their owners. The United States District Court for Louisiana dismissed both the libels and the United States prosecuted appeals to the Supreme Court. Attorney General Benjamin F. Butler contended that the statute should be applied in terms of its language whatever might have been the intention of Congress, and that as properly interpreted it had been violated by the vessels bringing the slaves back to New Orleans. Walter Jones, on the other hand, contended that the interpretation was incorrect, and that in any event it would be "a direct interference with the rights of those owners, and is against the Constitution of the United States."[17]

The Supreme Court apparently had no difficulty in arriving at a decision. For a unanimous Court, Chief Justice Taney held that the statute must be interpreted in the light of its object of putting an end to the slave trade, and that it did not apply to bringing back to the United States slaves owned by residents here. He made another point

---

[16] 3 Stat. 450.   [17] United States v. *The Garonne*, 11 Pet. 73, 76 (1837).

534

which is important in the light of later cases. It had apparently been contended also that the slaves had become free by virtue of their temporary residence in France, and that their transportation back to the United States violated the statute in that it reintroduced them into a state of slavery. The Chief Justice held that whatever had been the status of the Negroes while in France in terms of French law, the slaves had continued to be inhabitants of Louisiana in terms of the laws of that state, and the statute did not prevent their being returned to the United States as slaves.

In the two succeeding terms of the Supreme Court no slavery cases were decided and the 1840 term saw only one such decision. This case had to do with what was clearly the slave trade, or was intended to be such. It involved a criminal action against one Isaac Morris for participation in the slave trade. Morris commanded a vessel fully equipped for the trade which set out from Havana but was captured before slaves were taken aboard. He contended that there had as yet been no violation of the statute, whatever the evidence of intention. The judges of the United States Circuit Court for the Southern District of New York certified questions to the Supreme Court to determine this point. Speaking unanimously through Chief Justice Taney, the Court held that Morris had violated the statute even though the purpose of the voyage had not been fulfilled.[18]

It was in the following year, 1841, that the Court found itself in the thick of the slavery discussion, from which it did not actually escape until the close of the Civil War period, even though there were intervening years in which no such cases were actually decided. The 1841 cases, two in number, have been discussed in connection with other legal categories. *Groves v. Slaughter*[19] revealed the entanglement of slavery issues with questions as to the scope and exclusiveness of the federal power over interstate commerce, with multiple divisions among the Justices in the matter. The *Amistad* case,[20] deeply involving problems in American foreign relations, had to do with the status of recently captured Negroes who had seized command of the ship transporting them into slavery and sailed it into an American port hoping to attain their freedom there, with consequent important litigation. From this time onward the eyes of the people were on the Supreme Court as well as on Congress when issues of slavery were discussed.

The year 1842 brought the decision of one of the critical cases of the period, that of *Prigg v. Pennsylvania*, which dealt with the scope

---

[18] United States v. Morris, 14 Pet. 464 (1840).
[19] 15 Pet. 449 (1841).

[20] United States v. *The Amistad*, 15 Pet. 518 (1841).

of federal and state responsibilities in connection with the capture and return of fugitive slaves. The background of the case is important. With the growth of abolitionist sentiment in the North and the organization of abolitionists for aid to fugitives, the northward escape of slaves became more and more frequent. Of the many who fled to Pennsylvania, some traveled onward to permanent refuge in Canada, while others chose to make their homes in the Keystone State and take their chances on recapture. Owners or their agents often pursued fugitives into the state, but found detection and recovery difficult because of the sympathies of abolitionists and the aid given by them. The situation was complicated by the fact that in some instances slaveholder agents were suspected of coming to Pennsylvania not to recapture fugitives but to capture free Negroes, claim them as fugitives, and transport them southward into slavery at handsome profits to the captors.

The Fugitive Slave Act of 1793 provided that in order to recover possession of a fugitive slave the owner or his agent should "take him or her before any judge of the circuit or district courts of the United States, residing or being within the state, or before any magistrate of a county, city or town corporate, wherein such seizure or arrest shall be made, and upon proof to the satisfaction of such judge or magistrate, either by oral testimony or affidavit taken before and certified by a magistrate of any such state or territory," the official in question should issue a certificate authorizing removal.[21] Since there were only two United States District judges in all Pennsylvania and since the Supreme Court Justice riding circuit was there only part of the time, it was often inconvenient or impossible to take an alleged slave before a federal judge to get the desired certificate. Furthermore, in the light of extensive public hostility to the recovery of fugitive slaves and the possible kidnapping of free Negroes, local magistrates were often slow to act or refused altogether to give aid.

Pennsylvania sentiment with respect to slavery was by no means wholly abolitionist. Rather it was very mixed, with considerable numbers of the propertied people sympathetic to the rights of slaveowners. In 1826 the legislature enacted a statute which was calculated at once to aid slaveowners in recovering their property and to protect free Negroes against kidnapping. It required owners or their agents to present full credentials for themselves and clear evidence of ownership. In connection with any claim to ownership of a slave it required a local judge or other magistrate to issue a warrant to apprehend the fugitive, but the certificate authorizing removal must come from a judge and not from an alderman or justice of the peace. In short, it provided full opportunity for the detention of alleged fugitives, but postponed

---

[21] 1 Stat. 302.

removal until more careful determination of the claim had been made. It forbade local magistrates to act pursuant to the federal statute as well as the state statute.

The *Prigg* case arose in connection with a claim to a slave, Margaret Morgan, who in 1832 fled from the home of her owner, Margaret Ashmore, in northern Maryland, to a point a few miles northward in southern Pennsylvania. The record does not show why the escaped slave remained unmolested for five years, or why at the end of that period four Marylanders went to Pennsylvania to recover the slave and her children, one of whom had been born in the latter state. However, they did go, and they got from a justice of the peace a warrant directing a county constable to take the woman into custody.

Pursuant to the restriction in the Pennsylvania statute, however, the justice of the peace refused to issue the certificate of removal. Apparently having some difficulty in finding a judge from whom the certificate might be secured, the captors took the Negroes to the county seat of Harford County, Maryland, some seven or eight miles away, where after some three days of investigation the county court certified as to their status as slaves.[22]

Nevertheless the removal of the Negroes from Pennsylvania had been in violation of the Pennsylvania statute, the captors were indicted in a Pennsylvania court, and the governor of Pennsylvania demanded of the governor of Maryland that they be surrendered for trial. The situation was complicated, it being noted that

> the very law of Pennsylvania, the operation of which is now complained of, was passed by the legislature of that state in compliance with the request of the state of Maryland, who deputised very talented members of her own legislature to go to Harrisburg, and urge that their laws should be so altered as to prevent a mere justice of the peace from having the power to decide, as to the property of *our* citizens in slaves that are fugitives in that state.[23]

In other words, the captors, men of prestige in Maryland, had now fallen afoul of the statute enacted at the request of a deputation from the Maryland legislature.

Thomas W. Veazey, governor of Maryland at the time when the kidnapping took place, was reluctant either to grant or to refuse the demand of Joseph Ritner, then governor of Pennsylvania, that the captors be surrendered for trial. He sent Thomas Culbreth, secretary of the Maryland Council, to Harrisburg to negotiate, hoping to get the prose-

---

[22] "Delicate and Interesting Case," *Niles' National Register*, 56:298, 1838.
[23] *Ibid.*

cution dropped. Ritner's secretary contended that if Culbreth was right in believing that the captors had acted without criminal intent they should submit to trial and count on a verdict of not guilty. Neither Culbreth nor William P. Maulsby, a member of the Maryland legislature and counsel for the captors who accompanied Culbreth to Harrisburg, was able to get any concession from the Pennsylvania governor.[24] Governor Veazey finally directed that the surrender be made, although the leader of the group, Nathan S. Bemis, had been willing to return the Negroes to the place from which they were taken if doing so would ward off the prosecution.

At this point the confusing story becomes even more confused. The Maryland legislature, at its December session in 1837, enacted a resolution directing the appointment of a commission "to repair to Harrisburg, Pennsylvania, and endeavor to procure the dismissal of the prosecutions pending against Nathan S. Bemis, Jacob Forward, Edward Prigg, and Stephen Lewis, Citizens of Maryland," the four captors who were under indictment, and "to make such arrangements as may be necessary to refer the questions involved to the Supreme Court of the United States without compromitting the liberty of the accused, and obtain such modification of the Laws of Pennsylvania as will preserve the rights of slave holders and cherish good will between the two states."[25] On appointment approved by the state senate, Governor Veazey sent Jonathan Meredith of Baltimore to Harrisburg, but Meredith found it necessary to postpone action until the ensuing session of the Pennsylvania legislature because of the political turmoil in the state.

Finally, by an act of May 22, 1839, the Pennsylvania legislature arranged for a trial at which by a special verdict Edward Prigg, one of the captors, would be found guilty and the case, challenging the constitutionality of the 1826 statute, would be handled in such a way that it could be taken to the Supreme Court.

The *Prigg* case was argued in the Supreme Court on February 8, 9, and 10, 1842, and decided March 1, 1842, each side being represented by two counsel: Prigg by Jonathan Meredith and John Nelson of Maryland, and Pennsylvania by its attorney general, Ovid F. Johnson, and by a deputy attorney general, Thomas C. Hambly, who had been involved in the case from the beginning. The arguments of counsel, like the correspondence of executive and legislative officers about

---

[24] See Thomas Culbreth to Thomas W. Veazey, June 28, 1837, *Maryland Executive Proceedings, 1834–1839.*

[25] Message of Governor Thomas W. Veazey to the Maryland legislature, Jan. 2, 1839, at page 19 of the document as it appears in longhand near the middle of the otherwise unpaged *Executive Proceedings, 1834–1839.*

the case, gave indications of the tensions produced by it. Meredith characterized the case as "one of vital interest to the peace and perpetuity of the Union itself," and referred to "that exasperation of public sentiment which unhappily prevailed upon a subject that seemed every day to assume a more malignant and threatening aspect."[26] Hambly asserted that no constitutional question decided by the Court involved greater results for the good or ill of the nation than that now before it:

> An all absorbing subject is incidentally involved in it—a subject which is even now heaving the political tides of the country, which has caused enthusiasm to throw her lighted torch into the temples of religion, and the halls of science and learning, whilst the forum of justice, and the village bar-room have equally resounded with the discussion. Its influences have been calculated by political economists; its consequences and determinations by political prophets; until all, from the statesmen in the hall of legislation to the farmer at his fireside, are found arrayed on one side or the other of this, great question, so that, whilst it has become "sore as a gangrene" in one region, it is the football of the enthusiast in another.[27]

It is ironic that counsel representative really as much of Maryland and other Southern interests as of Prigg contended that the power here involved, the power to provide for the return of fugitive slaves, was exclusive in the federal government, while counsel for Pennsylvania and Northern interests sought to preserve the power of the states. It is ironic that Jonathan Meredith, for Prigg and the sponsors of slavery, articulated for the Supreme Court and for Justice Story as its spokesman the doctrine that would justify the Northern states in refusing to aid in the return of fugitive slaves, and that his argument dovetailed with Hambly's contention that the federal Fugitive Slave Act was unconstitutional to the extent that it sought to impose judicial duties on state magistrates.

Meredith was concerned about the fact that if the states were to exercise any jurisdiction over fugitive slaves they might, as in this instance, seek to punish as kidnapping any recapture that did not conform to their own laws, and might thereby greatly interfere with the recapture of lawful property. Hambly was concerned about the fact that, in the absence of protection by the states, free Negroes might be seized by people who were no more than alleged agents of lawful owners and converted into slaves. He noted that in the absence of state protection and pursuant to the constitutional provision, claimed Negroes were to be surrendered to claimants on the claim being made

---

[26] Prigg v. Pennsylvania, 16 Pet. 539, 559 (1842).   [27] *Ibid.*, 572.

known, and that "under this clause a power is contained, in virtue of which, anyone may step into a crowd and seize and carry off an alleged slave, 'just as he would a stray horse,' or any other article of personal property."[28]

Perhaps because Nelson's argument in behalf of Prigg was not submitted to the Reporter, we have no direct statement of the Prigg position here taken with respect to the limitations on the rights of Negroes under the Constitution, even when they were not slaves. From Hambly's reply, however, we know that they contended, as Taney had when Attorney General, that "slaves are not parties under the Constitution," and that they were not included among "we, the people."[29] Hambly made no claim as to the rights of slaves but he did emphasize the rights of free Negroes. He contended that free men could not be subjected to "unreasonable seizure" or "deprived of liberty without due process of law."[30] He proposed a hypothetical case where on the streets of Philadelphia a man was seized simultaneously by citizens of Virginia and South Carolina, each claiming him as their slave. According to the position of Prigg's counsel, the state could do nothing to protect him even if he had satisfactory evidence that he was legally free:

> What is to be done? Allow these parties to wrangle it out in the streets, to settle the question with dirk and bowie knife, to execute the judgment of Solomon? No, the answer will be; hand them over to the District Court, and there let them settle the right to property? Yes, but there you meet an unexpected difficulty. The District Court can try the right of property as between the claimants, but not the right of liberty as between them and the arrested free man; therefore it follows that because the party out of possession of the alleged slave cannot prove his right to take him, the party in possession restrains him, and carries a free man into slavery. Possession of a slave, in the absence of proof, is sufficient evidence of title.[31]

In denying to the arrested party the right to demonstrate his freedom, Hambly contended, the constitutional right of the privileges and immunities of citizens of the several states was also being denied him. He was subject to arrest and detention in jail, and to sale for jail fees even though he had been free. If his rights were left to be determined by the state into which he was taken he was denied the constitutional right of trial in the state in which the offense was committed, and if tried in the state of his captors he would have the body of public opinion against him. "Better a thousand slaves escape," reasoned Hambly, "than that one free man should be thus carried into remediless slavery!"[32]

---

[28] *Ibid.*, 573.   [29] *Ibid.*, 576.   [30] *Ibid.*, 577.   [31] *Ibid.*, 578.   [32] *Ibid.*

The argument in the *Prigg* case presented to the Supreme Court for the first time the issues involved in the fugitive slave controversy. The Court was fully aware of their inflammable character. Justice Story, according to the account written by his son, would have been glad to avoid participation in the decision, hostile as he was to the institution of slavery, and would have been particularly glad to avoid the position of spokesman of the Court, but was "urged to this position by the strenuous request of his brother Judges."[33] He did write the opinion of the Court, and, given his predilections in the matter, it is not surprising that the opinion contained arguments objectionable to slaveholders generally and to some members of the Court.

For all the growth of abolitionist sentiment in the North and particularly in New England, the opinion offered no challenge to the legality of slavery or to the right of owners to recapture fugitive slaves. As Justice Story stated in a letter to a friend about another slave case, "You know full well that I have ever been opposed to slavery. But I take my standard of duty *as a Judge* from the Constitution."[34] He demonstrated the constitutionality of the federal Fugitive Slave Law, found the Pennsylvania statute of 1826 to be in conflict therewith, and so reversed the judgment of the lower court and relieved Prigg from his predicament. But in arriving at this decision he went far beyond the points here stated. He held that the jurisdiction of the federal government over the return of fugitive slaves was complete, and that the states were estopped from giving aid as well as from interfering with the process. They were entirely without responsibility in the matter, and they could not assume responsibility. Here he was following the argument of Jonathan Meredith that under the cover of giving aid the states might enact diverse and hampering regulations and so in effect interfere with, and thereby frustrate, the constitutional purpose. He agreed also with Hambly, at least by implication, that the federal government could not make use of state magistrates in the performance of its exclusive function. The task was that of the federal government alone.

Chief Justice Taney and Justices Thompson and Daniel, and apparently also Justice Baldwin, denied that the existence of federal jurisdiction prevented the states from aiding in the return of fugitive slaves, and Taney and Daniel, both Southerners, were particularly vigorous on this point. The Chief Justice spoke highly of the practice of Maryland of apprehending fugitives on the way northward and holding them until claimed by their owners. If the officers of the state could not act in this fashion, he contended, "the territory of the State must

---

[33] *Life and Letters of Joseph Story*, W. W. Story, ed., II, 391.

[34] Joseph Story to Ezekiel Bacon, Nov. 19, 1842, *ibid.*, 431.

soon become an open pathway for the fugitives escaping from other States."[35] He seemed to feel that the state had not only a moral but also a constitutional obligation to refrain from becoming such a pathway.

It is an interesting fact that in spite of all that was said in argument about the kidnapping of free Negroes in the Northern states, nothing was said in the several opinions about the fact that border states might become pathways not for escaping slaves but for kidnappers and their captives. For some of the Justices, Taney and Daniel particularly, the conception of Negroes as essentially degraded people with lesser rights than those of white men may have kept the subject out of focus. Justice Story may have seen his opinion as rendering the maximum of possible service by invalidating state laws calculated to aid in the recapture of fugitives and withdrawing state services in connection with enforcement of the federal statute, thereby greatly crippling federal enforcement. He made another point, indeed, which he may have regarded as even more important in resistance to the entrenchment of slavery. As part of the device of showing that the protection of slavery was based exclusively on provisions in the Constitution, he asserted that it was protected only by municipal law and not by international law:

> By the general law of nations, no nation is bound to recognize the state of slavery, as to foreign slaves found within its territorial dominions, when it is in opposition to its own policy and institutions, in favor of the subjects of other nations where slavery is recognized. If it does it, it is as a matter of comity, and not as a matter of international right. The state of slavery is deemed to be a mere municipal regulation, founded upon and limited to the range of the territorial laws.[36]

Soon after the decision was handed down Justice Story told Charles Sumner of this point in the opinion of the Court, stressing the holding that by the law of nations we could not require the surrender of fugitives, thus, said Sumner, "throwing the weight of our highest tribunal upon that of the English House of Lords."[37] In later years Sumner deplored Story's connection with the *Prigg* case but spoke of the judge's belief that his opinion was "a triumph for Freedom." Sumner wrote to Salmon P. Chase, ardent defender of Negro rights, that "He was happy in obtaining from the Supreme Court a recognition of the locality of slavery, as the creature of municipal law. I think that his mind was so much occupied with this idea, that he did not reflect upon

---

[35] 16 Pet. 632.
[36] *Ibid.*, 611.

[37] Pierce, *Memoir and Letters of Charles Sumner*, II, 203.

the tyrannical power which he placed in the hands of a slave hunter."[38] To still other people in the Boston area Justice Story referred to his opinion as "a triumph of freedom,"[39] thereby protecting his reputation with his antislavery friends and adding to dislike or suspicion of the decision on the part of slavery sympathizers.

Without seeing the text, the *Baltimore Sun* reported that the decision was "all that Maryland can desire, and will be particularly agreeable to the slaveholders of the South."[40] The *National Intelligencer* commented fretfully on the anomalies of legislation, that the law as laid down by the highest judicial tribunal was a sealed book to the people upon whom it operated.[41] A Newark paper deplored the unavailability of the opinion and suggested that the Reporter, "as a mere matter of pecuniary speculation," should publish it as a pamphlet. The case was particularly important in the North because it would seem to nullify the laws of New York and other states which allowed the removal of alleged slaves only after jury trial to determine that they were really slaves[42]—a determination often hard to get from liberal-minded juries. "If we do not misapprehend the decision," said the *Massachusetts Spy*, "even the taking of a claimed fugitive before a justice and identifying him to the satisfaction of that functionary, is unnecessary and idle. The slaveholder may take his slave wherever he may find it, without application or appeal; and the citizen of the free State may, or must not aid him in so doing, but cannot question his assertion of property. At any rate, all free State legislation designed to prevent abuses of the slaveholder's constitutional right of reclamation, are hereby declared null and void, and the trial by jury law of this State, as well as that of Pennsylvania, is henceforth a dead letter."[43]

Although it was stated by the *North American Review* that there was "hardly a whisper against the fidelity and even-handed justice"[44] with which the Supreme Court acted in the *Prigg* case, there was loud protest from the abolitionist press and from abolitionist leaders through-

---

[38] Charles Sumner to S. P. Chase, Mar. 12, 1847, Chase Papers.

[39] See *Life and Letters of Joseph Story*, II, 392–93. Justice McLean seems to have feared that in terms of the opinion of the Court owners might seize and remove fugitive slaves in other states even without conformity with the Act of Congress. As if recognizing the unfeasibility of relying exclusively on federal machinery he took the position that in the matter of recapturing fugitive slaves Congress might impose duties on state officers as provided in the Act of 1793, and that lawful removal could be made only by use of the prescribed machinery.

[40] *Baltimore Sun*, Mar. 3, 1842.

[41] *Washington National Intelligencer*, Mar. 3, 1842, as quoted, *Charleston Courier*, Mar. 8, 1842.

[42] *Newark Daily Advertiser*, Mar. 5, 1842.

[43] *Massachusetts Spy*, Mar. 9, 1842.

[44] "The Independence of the Judiciary," *North American Review*, 57: 400, 419, 1843.

out the country. *The Philanthropist* of Cincinnati, to note a single example, found the decision "revolting," and proclaimed that it made a wreck of state sovereignty and did more to centralize power than all the acts of the government since its establishment.[45] So unconcerned were the abolitionists about adherence to the Constitution where it was out of harmony with their specialized commitments that Justice Story delivered to his law class the eloquent appeal, already noted, for full commitment to the Constitution. That instrument, he maintained, was the product of the spirit of concession and forbearance, and it would end when that spirit died in the hearts of the people. If one section disregarded one provision of the Constitution and other sections ignored others, the Union would disintegrate or become the instrument of a despot. He condemned "those mad men who even now are ready to stand up in public assemblies and in the name of conscience, liberty, or the rights of man, to boast that they are willing and ready to bid farewell to that Constitution under which we have lived and prospered for more than half a century."[46]

Some Northern journals, however, saw less intemperateness of work and conduct on the part of the North than of the South. The *Portsmouth Journal* remarked that if the decision had borne down as hard on the South as it did on the North, the nation would have heard at once the threat of nullification, secession, and disunion. But the North was more temperate, for there was a peaceful remedy, that of amendment to the Constitution.[47]

Richard Peters, in his last year as Reporter of the Supreme Court —and his action here may have had something to do with the fact that it was his last year—took the advice to make capital out of the decision by publishing it as a pamphlet. He brought out an impressive document of 141 pages with the voluminous title:

> Report of the Case of Edward Prigg against the Commonwealth of Pennsylvania. Argued and Adjudged in the Supreme Court of the United States, at the January Term, 1842. In which it was decided, that all the Laws of the several States relative to Fugitive Slaves are Unconstitutional and Void; and that Congress have the exclusive Power of Legislation on the Subject of Fugitive Slaves escaping into other States. By Richard Peters, Reporter of the Decisions of the Supreme Court of the United States.[48]

---

[45] *Cincinnati Philanthropist*, Mar. 30, 1842.

[46] From the notes of Rutherford B. Hayes on a lecture by Justice Story, delivered Dec. 21, 1843. (*Diary and Letters of Rutherford Birchard Hayes,* I, 131.)

[47] *Portsmouth Journal*, quoted, *The Liberator*, Mar. 18, 1842.

[48] For announcement of the publication see *North American Review*, 55:270, 1842.

Both Northern and Southern interests attempted to use the decision to their advantage or to find ways of avoiding its implications. Governor William H. Seward of New York, for example, contended in a message to the legislature that the authority of the decision could not be extended to cases with materially different facts, and that the privilege of habeas corpus and the right of trial by jury remained unimpaired.[49] At the same time many of the Northern states withdrew their facilities from aid to slaveholders seeking to recapture fugitives, and the controversy added to the growing pattern of lawlessness whereby hostile groups interfered with the recapture of fugitive slaves and aided in their escape.

On the other hand, the Southern states continued to aid in the recapture and return of fugitive slaves in spite of the holding of the Court that they had no power to do so. Such action continued on the part of friendly officials even in the Northern states. Judge Ellis Lewis of Pennsylvania, for example, first a state district judge and later chief justice of the Pennsylvania Supreme Court, continued enforcing that part of the Act of 1826 which aided in the return of fugitive slaves.[50] Long afterward, on the eve of the Civil War, Judge Lewis wrote to Chief Justice Taney in criticism of the opinion of the Court in the *Prigg* case, saying, "It was this unfortunate opinion which induced the northern states to repeal their state legislation in favor of surrendering fugitives from labor, and to enact laws prohibiting the use of their jails, and the action of State officers, in aid of such surrender."[51] He added that in his *Criminal Law of the United States*, in his judicial opinions, and in actions everywhere, he had always repudiated that por-

---

[49] *Niles' National Register*, 63:28, 1842.

[50] "Political Portraits with Pen and Pencil: Ellis Lewis," *Democratic Review*, 20:355, 361, 1847.

In an article published in the *American Law Journal* for April, 1850, which seems to have been written by Judge Lewis, it is said that "The *authority* of the decision has been confined, as it should be, *to the question upon the record*—to wit— whether a State could constitutionally pass a law to convert the act of recaption of *property* by the owner or his agent, into the crime of kidnaping." Reprinted, "Fugitive Slaves," *Democratic Review*, 27:57, 1850. But Pennsylvania seems to have taken the instrument of enforcement from the judge's hands by repealing the Act of 1826. Judge Lewis referred to Chief Justice Taney's "clear and unanswerable argument," and added, "His great ability as a jurist, and his tried integrity as a man, give to his opinion a weight with the American people which is enjoyed by no man now living." *Ibid.*, 60. He thought it not surprising, however, that in the light of the decision of the Court the Northern states should have repealed their enforcement laws. For the original article see "The Slavery Question," *Am. L.J.*, 9:433, 1850.

[51] Ellis Lewis to Roger B. Taney, Dec. 8, 1860, Lewis Papers. For a similar statement see Ellis Lewis to James Buchanan, Feb, 15, 1861, Buchanan Papers.

tion of Justice Story's opinion as unsound and not properly presented in the case. Chief Justice Taney replied:

> I have always thought that the decision in the case of Prigg vs. the Commonwealth of Pennsylvania [was] an unfortunate one and not sufficiently considered by the Court. And I am persuaded that some of the Judges who formed the majority did not view the case in the same light, with Judge Story, nor intend to accomplish such an object. It certainly gave an impulse to the abolition feeling in the non-slave-holding states and perhaps laid the foundation for all the mischief which has since followed. The decision I still think, was an erroneous one, and contrary to the plain words of the Constitution.[52]

Albert J. Beveridge has said of the *Prigg* case that historically it was one of the most important decided by the Supreme Court.[53] Certain it is that the case became immediately a part of the developing struggle between the North and the South. It played a prominent part in federal and state judicial decisions, in federal and state legislative debates, and in the outpourings of newspapers, law journals, and public journals generally. Because while upholding the power of the federal government to provide for the return of fugitive slaves, it nullified the obligation and seemed to nullify the power of the states to aid in the process, it at once gave incentive to abolitionist activities and led the South to demand enactment of a Fugitive Slave Act which could be effectively administered without the aid of the states. Thereby it added to the furor of sectional conflict and the hysteria of competing parties. Heavy irony seemed relatively moderate, as in a petition presented by John Quincy Adams, alleged to be from a group of citizens of Gettysburg, Pennsylvania, characterizing slavery as a "continual and eternal blessing to the Union," and asking that "immediate measures may be taken and legislation matured for the annexation of the Continent of Africa, including the Barbary States and the Country of the Hottentots and all of the interior and the Coasts; this immense Territory to be appropriated to the purpose of breeding and raising negro slaves for the Southern States and Texas, when annexed, so as to supply the South in accordance with the above construction of the Constitution with the numerous blessings and the perpetuity of the Institution of Slavery."[54]

The reactions of the *Prigg* case tied in with controversies over

---

[52] R. B. Taney to Ellis Lewis, Dec. 24, 1860, Lewis Papers.
[53] Albert J. Beveridge, *Abraham Lincoln, 1809–1858*, II, 68.
[54] Petition of George E. Buehler *et al.*, Feb. 18, 1845, Referred to the Committee on the Judiciary of the House of Representatives, House of Representatives Papers.

the internal and external slave trade, the recapture of fugitive slaves, the maintenance of slavery and slave trade in the District of Columbia, the acquisition of new territory in which slavery might be expected to flourish, the allocation of powers between the states and the federal government, the position of free Negroes within American society, and the right of discussion of public issues, however disturbing to the public peace and to national stability such discussion might prove to be. It is difficult indeed to appraise the case apart from its involvement with these other factors. Given the clarity of the fugitive slave provisions of the Constitution, the knowledge of the conditions of their adoption, and the commitment to lawfulness on the part of the members of the Supreme Court as of most other courts, it is hard to conceive that the Court might have decided that Congress could not provide for the return of fugitive slaves or that the states might enact legislation interfering with the recapture of known fugitives. On the other hand, it would have been possible for the Court merely to strike down the Pennsylvania statute of 1826 as interfering with the recapture of fugitives, without generalizing about the constitutionality of state statutes and state officials and state proceedings which gave aid to the process. If it was well that the sectional issues should be brought to a head, that controversy be stirred to a point of precipitating a climax even in the form of civil war in order to achieve the moral end of freedom, then the expanded scope of the opinion of the Court may well have served a desirable purpose. If, on the other hand, it was the function of the Court to limit itself to the points necessary to be decided and to avoid as much as possible repercussions in the body politic, then the breadth of the opinion was to be regretted. In deciding the case broadly the Court did no more than the Marshall Court had done on many occasions toward the building of an important body of constitutional law. At the same time, what the Taney Court did here, through the spokesmanship of Justice Story, was highly similar to the strategy of the same Court fifteen years later in the *Dred Scott* decision, which more immediately precipitated the Civil War. On that occasion the Court defended the claims of slavery, in contrast with the limitations on the rights of slavery interests in the *Prigg* case.

From the time of the *Prigg* decision in 1842, fugitive slaves moved in increasing numbers into the Northern States, to find harbor there or to continue onward into Canada. With the aid of organized enemies of slavery, many fugitives escaped permanently without detection. Others were caught and taken back into slavery, oftentimes in spite of local and violent opposition, and with the benefit of violence some were set free again to make permanent their escape. Many cases involving the return of fugitives or the punishment of free men for aiding in their escape arose in the third and seventh judicial circuits, which stretched from the coast of New Jersey across Pennsylvania, Ohio, Indiana, and Illinois, to the banks of the Mississippi.

One case, which arose in the United States Circuit Court in Cincinnati and eventually reached the Supreme Court, illustrates the complicated pattern of experience. In April, 1842, nine Negroes owned by Wharton Jones, who lived in Kentucky a few miles south of Cincinnati, escaped into Ohio and began their trek northward. On a road leading out of Cincinnati they were picked up by John Van Zandt, a farmer who was driving a covered wagon home on the road to Lebanon. Van Zandt rode inside the wagon with eight of the Negroes and permitted the ninth to drive the wagon.

While the northern tier of border states had many abolitionists they had also along their southern borders many friends of slavery, some of whom had come in from the slave states or had friends and relatives there. Beyond that, since there were stipulated rewards for the recovery of fugitive slaves, there were always men eager to collect these rewards. On this occasion two men, named Hefferman and Hargrave, recognized Van Zandt's wagon in spite of the fact that he himself was concealed, rode after it, and in spite of the driver's attempt to outrun them pursuant to Van Zandt's instructions, seized all the Negroes except one, who escaped, and took them to Covington, Kentucky, where they were placed in jail pending identification and restoration to their owner.

From the owner Hargrave and Hefferman collected a reward of four hundred fifty dollars. In Warren County, Ohio, they were indicted for kidnapping, but they kept out of the way of trial. Others who aided them and who were brought to trial were acquitted.[55] Van Zandt, in turn, was subjected to a series of actions in the United States Circuit Court for having harbored and concealed escaping slaves despite notice of their status, in violation of the federal Fugitive Slave Law.

Both Justice McLean and District Judge H. H. Leavitt were present for the term of court held in Cincinnati in July, 1843, the former, of course, presiding. "I have been attending the Circuit Court of the United States today," wrote James Wickes Taylor, a youthful observer. "Judge McLean presides with dignity and is a man of imposing presence. Leavitt is associated with him, although by no means a man of such mark."[56] It was said that several of the court's cases had grown out of the common practice of helping slaves escape from their

[55] J. W. Schuckers, *The Life and Public Services of Salmon Portland Chase*, 54.

[56] James Wickes Taylor, *A Choice*

Nook of Memory: The Diary of a Cincinnati Law Clerk, 1842–1844, James Taylor Dunn, ed., 29.

Kentucky masters. Escape was usually successful and the Van Zandt case was one of the exceptions. The city and the courtroom were crowded, as was usually true at the meeting of the Circuit Court.

The three counsel on each side included former United States Senator Thomas Morris for Jones and Salmon P. Chase, inveterate enemy of slavery, for Van Zandt. In the trial, which lasted more than a week, witnesses were permitted to break the tedium of technical arguments with provocation of outbursts of humor. One witness at the capture of the Negroes had told Van Zandt that "it didn't look well, for a man that belonged to the meeting, to be running horses on Sunday. He was always lecturing me for my bad deeds, and I thought I'd lecture him." Chase tried to find out what the witness's bad deeds were but the witness assured the court that that subject would take at least a week. Justice McLean therefore cut the narrative short. Another witness told the court, "I am afraid I cannot make myself heered by your Honor. Since I've been here, I've caught this *Cincinnati distemper*, and I am very hoarse."[57]

The important questions in the case had to do with what constituted harboring and concealment of fugitive slaves and due notice of their status within the meaning of the Fugitive Slave Act, but the trial was a jury trial, and counsel were not content to limit themselves to technical questions and relieving outbursts of humor. They ranged further into discussion of the law of nature and of the rights of Negroes as the rights of man, implying on one side that in spite of constitutions and statutes the Negroes were entitled to their freedom and Van Zandt was within his rights in aiding them to escape. In charging the jury—in such a way as to show that Van Zandt's conduct came within the prohibitions of the federal statute, with a resulting verdict for Jones —Justice McLean warned against reliance on such vague concepts as laws of nature or of conscience. Under great excitement conscience might mislead, and it always did mislead when it urged violation of the law. "Paul acted in all good conscience, when he consented to the death of the first martyr; and, also, when he bore letters to Damascus, authorizing him to bring bound to Jerusalem all who called upon the name of Jesus."[58] The Constitution and the Act of Congress "form the only guides in the administration of justice in this case."[59]

Chase at once moved for a new trial and for an arrest of judgment. On the ground that the award of twelve hundred dollars might be excessive in the light of the counts referred to by the jury, Justice

---

[57] *Ibid.*, 30.
[58] Jones v. Vanzandt, 13 Fed. Cas. 1040, 1045 (No. 7501) (C.C.D. Oh. 1843). (The "Vanzandt" name is so spelled in the Circuit Court reports, but elsewhere it is Van Zandt.)
[59] *Ibid.*, 1046.

McLean allowed the new trial, with costs to be paid by Van Zandt.[60] The succeeding steps in the proceedings are obscure. It would seem that, quite possibly because of the costs involved, Van Zandt did not take advantage of the right to a new trial, and that he died before proceedings came to an end, leaving to his administrator the settlement of the financial obligation.

Nevertheless, although no new trial was held, the judges in the Circuit Court seem to have been persuaded that it would be well to have the questions involving interpretation of the federal Fugitive Slave Act passed upon by the Supreme Court. They therefore converted the points made in behalf of a new trial and arrest of judgment into questions to be certified to the Supreme Court on pretense that there was difference of opinion between the two of them. The division was merely pro forma, there being no real difference between the justices, but the Supreme Court recognized the legitimacy of the device, saying through Justice Woodbury that it was used "in conformity to what is understood to have been the usage in the circuits," whereby the judges "accommodated the parties by letting a division *pro forma* be entered on all the points presented."[61]

The case was to be presented to the Supreme Court by United States Senator James T. Morehead of Kentucky for Jones, and by Chase and William H. Seward for Van Zandt, the latter two donating their services, as seems to have been their custom in slavery cases, with some of the expenses paid by interested members of the public. The period was the middle 1840s, when the Supreme Court docket was running behind because of the increased load and the absence of some of the Justices, and when Chase and Seward were extremely busy with other duties. The *Van Zandt* case therefore seemed to slip into the background with both the Court and counsel for the defendant.[62] Chase and Seward were apparently much more concerned with general advancement of the cause of freedom than with the few hundred dollars that were at stake in their case. They thought that their cause was improving with the passage of time. Seward agreed with Chase that it was desirable to postpone the Supreme Court argument as long as possible: "Every year enables us to assume higher ground and ripens the sentiments of moral justice and the opinions of national policy to be invoked."[63]

When either for this reason or because of their involvement in other litigation Chase and Seward sought further postponement of

---

[60] Jones v. Vanzandt, 13 Fed. Cas. 1047 (No. 7502) (C.C.D. Oh. 1843).
[61] Jones v. Van Zandt, 5 How. 215, 224 (1847).

[62] See Seward to Chase, Jan. 10, 1846, Chase Papers.
[63] Seward to Chase, Dec. 26, 1846, Chase Papers.

the argument, Justices McLean and Nelson told Seward there could be no continuance and that the choice was between a default and submission on a printed argument.[64] Seward later wrote to Chase that "The Court manifestly does not desire an *oral argument*, of this great case," but "by directing a submission by printed arguments they give us an opportunity to argue the constitutional question."[65]

Chase devoted more than half his written argument of 108 pages to the pleadings and to the interpretation of the Fugitive Slave Act of 1793. He challenged the position that driving slaves across the countryside in a wagon, with one of them as the driver, constituted harboring and concealment. He denied that mere admission on the part of the Negroes themselves that they were slaves constituted "notice" under the statute, stressing the point already much discussed by abolitionists that in Ohio the testimony of a Negro could not be received in court against a white man.[66]

Chase then turned from technical legal argument to a presentation that was clearly in part propaganda for the abolitionist cause. He contended that the Ordinance of 1787 with respect to the Northwest Territory remained in force with the adoption of the Constitution and that it invalidated the federal Fugitive Slave Act. He contended further that the Constitution conferred on Congress no power to legislate on the subject, and that in any event the act was unconstitutional since it authorized unreasonable search and seizure and seizure without due process of law. He made broad appeal to the Declaration of Independence and to the Bill of Rights, and, in terms of natural law principles, asserted:

No Legislature is omnipotent. No Legislature can make right wrong; or wrong right. No Legislature can make light, darkness; or darkness, light. No Legislature can make men, things; or things, men. Nor is any Legislature at liberty to disregard the fundamental principles of rectitude and justice. Whether restrained or not by constitutional provisions, there are acts beyond any legitimate or binding legislative authority.[67]

Seward was especially pleased that Chase had fully discussed the pleadings in the case, saying as to his own constitutional argument

---

[64] Seward to Chase, Jan. 15, 1847, Chase Papers.

[65] Seward to Chase, Feb. 2, 1847, Chase Papers.

[66] See Daniel Raymond, "Remarks on the Case of Jones v. Van Zandt," *West. L.J.*, 2:245, 248, 1845.

[67] S. P. Chase, *Reclamation of Fugitives from Service. An Argument*

for the Defendant, Submitted to the Supreme Court of the United States, at the December Term, 1846, in the case of Wharton Jones vs. John Vanzandt, 93. The available copy of Chase's written argument was found at the library of the Johns Hopkins University.

that "I was looking continually over the Court to the People, in preparing my argument, and endeavoring chiefly to prevent them from saying they could not endure the technicalities of the case."[68] It was said of Seward's argument that he "made a bold exposition of what northern radicals desired to see accepted as constitutional law."[69]

The briefs by Chase and Seward were widely circulated among antislavery people, both at home and abroad.[70] Chase expressed gratitude for the reception of his argument. Of that reception he wrote, "I hail it as an auspicious augury of approaching deliverance from the despotism of the slave power and of pro-slavery construction."[71]

But if antislavery counsel managed to achieve wide circulation of their written arguments for propaganda purposes, Benjamin C. Howard refused to cooperate with them by giving their productions extended notice in the *United States Reports*. This Reporter, who often incurred widespread criticism for dumping into the reports materials of all kinds to expand the size of his volumes, here reversed his usual custom. He wrote that it was impossible to insert the arguments because of their length, saying that that of Chase ran to upwards of one hundred pages and that of Seward to forty pages.[72]

Furthermore, the Supreme Court seems to have minimized the propaganda effect of its own decision by speaking through only one member, Justice Woodbury, and by answering the certified questions in such a way as firmly to uphold the position taken by Justice McLean in the court below. It held that Van Zandt's transportation of the slaves constituted harboring and concealment within the meaning of the statute, and that Van Zandt's knowledge that the Negroes were slaves constituted or fulfilled the requirement of the "notice" prescribed by the statute. There being no dissenting or concurring opinions, Justice Woodbury was not driven to detailed discussion of the arguments presented by Van Zandt's counsel. He briefly reaffirmed the constitutionality of the federal statute and held that the Northwest Ordinance constituted no impediment.

In closing, Justice Woodbury did take brief notice of the argument that the Constitution and the statute should give way to the principle of the inexpediency and invalidity of all laws recognizing slavery

---

[68] Seward to Chase, Feb. 18, 1847, Chase Papers.

[69] Frederic Bancroft, *The Life of William H. Seward*, I, 181. Much of Seward's argument was reprinted in the *New York Tribune* of Mar. 10, 1847.

[70] See Seward to Chase, Dec. 7, 1848, Chase Papers.

[71] Chase to John P. Hale, May 12, 1847, Robert B. Warden, *An Account of the Private Life and Public Services of Salmon Portland Chase*, 312.

[72] Jones v. Van Zandt, 5 How. 215, 223 (1847).

or any right of property in man. This, he said, was a political question, settled by each state for itself. The federal power over the subject was the product of one of the "sacred compromises" of the Constitution which the Court was bound to enforce. "Their path is a straight and narrow one," he wrote piously, "to go where that Constitution and the laws lead, and not to break both, by traveling without or beyond them."

While the case was pending in the Supreme Court, Justice McLean wrote to Francis Lieber criticizing the development of extreme positions both in the North and in the South. "We should never forget the principle on which the Constitution was adopted," he wrote. "We must stand by that sacred instrument and maintain it in all its parts."[73] Shortly after the case was decided and apparently before the opinion was published he wrote anonymously and in the third person a letter to one Matthews of the *Herald*, presumably of Cincinnati, protesting criticism of the decision and the accusation that with respect to the Supreme Court and slavery issues it was possible to apply the Scotch maxim, "Show us the subject of controversy and we will show you the decision."[74] He showed that the decisions of the Court had not always been against the alleged slaves,[75] as was contended, and restated his position in the *Van Zandt* case. He used the revered name of Justice Story and to a lesser extent the names of Justices Thompson and Baldwin to refute any possibility of corruption in the *Prigg* case, and, still writing in the third person, he explained and defended his own different position in that case.

Neither the opinion of the Court nor defenses such as those of McLean carried weight with abolitionists generally or with Chase, the current "attorney general for runaway Negroes," as he was denominated in Kentucky,[76] and the future Chief Justice. It was strange, he wrote, that the proslavery construction of the Constitution, so utterly indefensible by history or by reason, should be so tamely acquiesced in by the courts. He agreed that, at the bar and elsewhere, men should be "bold, indignant, and emphatic" in denunciation of this construction.[77] Four years after the decision in the *Van Zandt* case, in sending out a copy of his written argument, he remarked that the case was worthy of exami-

---

[73] John McLean to Francis Lieber, Nov. 9, 1846, Lieber Papers.

[74] A longhand draft is in the McLean Papers, beginning on folio 3097a. An abbreviated quotation is printed in Charles Warren, *The Supreme Court in U.S. History*, II, 157–58.

[75] Citing Fenwick v. Chapman, 9 Pet. 461 (1835), Wallingford v. Allen, 10 Pet. 583 (1836), and Rhodes v. Ball, 2 How. 397 (1844).

[76] Schuckers, *The Life and Public Services of Chase*, 52.

[77] Chase to John P. Hale, May 12, 1847, Warden, *An Account of . . . Chase*, 312.

nation "as illustrative of the facility with which the federal judges reach conclusions adverse to freedom over obstacles apparently insurmountable." He thought it a remarkable sign of the times that "the late latitudinarian construction of Story and such as he, should now be resorted to by democrats to justify usurpation of power by Congress."[78]

The Supreme Court decisions in *Prigg v. Pennsylvania* and *Jones v. Van Zandt* firmly asserted the right of slaveowners to recover fugitive slaves from other states and the power of Congress to legislate on the subject, although the *Prigg* case demonstrated the inadequacy of the existing federal statute in the light of the inability of the states to give aid. The basic position of the two cases remained undisturbed in spite of the attacks of abolitionists. But there were related questions to provide additional litigation, particularly with respect to slaves who were not fugitives but who were taken by owners or agents into free states. The Fugitive Slave Clause of the Constitution had reference to a "person held to service or labour in one state, escaping into another." It said nothing about slaves who had not escaped but who had been taken into states where slavery was prohibited.

It was apparent that if slaveowners were able to take slaves into free states and keep them there in permanent enslavement the prohibitions against slavery would be largely nullified. So it was that, in the South as well as in the North, it was generally recognized that such a change in permanent residence conferred freedom. Much of the litigation took place over the status of Negroes taken into free states for temporary periods, often as body servants, or merely passing through a free state between two points at each of which slavery was lawful.

As to temporary residents, Chief Justice Lemuel Shaw of the Supreme Judicial Court of Massachusetts set the pattern for the Northern states in 1836 by his opinion in *Commonwealth v. Aves*.[79] The case marked the efforts of Massachusetts abolitionists to win freedom for a black girl who had been brought into the state on a visit by the wife of her Louisiana owner. The case was argued at length before the highest court in the state. Ellis Gray Loring of the Massachusetts Anti-Slavery Society presented the case for the girl's freedom, along with Rufus Choate and Samuel E. Sewall. The leading counsel for defense of the rights of the owner was Benjamin R. Curtis, then twenty-seven years of

---

[78] Typewritten copy, Chase to ———, Jan. 5, 1851, Chase Papers. (On folio 5876a). For reference to a jury charge by Justice Grier resulting in conviction of a Pennsylvanian, a Dr. Mitchell, merely for giving employment to a fugitive slave, see *Niles' National Register*, 73:221, 1847.

[79] 35 Mass. (18 Pick.) 193. For discussion of this and related cases see Leonard W. Levy, *The Law of the Commonwealth and Chief Justice Shaw*, 62–71.

age, who by his argument won admiration from his profession[80]—and, no doubt inadvertently, the approval of people who would ultimately consider his appointment to the Supreme Court.

For a unanimous court Chief Justice Shaw rejected Curtis' contention that according to the rule of comity among nations the right of private property in a slave should be recognized in Massachusetts as to slaves brought by visitors from slave states. Slavery was contrary to natural right and to numerous provisions of the state constitution and laws. For its force and effect where it was lawful it depended on local laws. Slaves brought into Massachusetts, as distinct from fugitives, became free on arrival there.

Although the decision carried the prestige of one of the most distinguished courts in the country it was nevertheless a state decision and therefore not necessarily to be followed in other states. Some of the free states seem not to have been averse to permitting slaves to be transported across their territory or even to make temporary sojourns without change of status. These differences did not extensively concern the federal courts save as they became involved in cases implicating allegedly fugitive slaves. One such case was tried before Justice McLean in 1845 in the United States Circuit Court for Indiana. The suit was brought by one Vaughan, a citizen of Missouri, against Owen Williams of Indiana. Vaughan had bought a number of slaves in Missouri, but they escaped into Indiana. Williams had been a leader of a large group of men who aided the slaves in escaping from Vaughan. Vaughan brought suit for damages under the Fugitive Slave Act of 1793.

Under ordinary circumstances Vaughan would have been able to collect damages on the finding of a jury that the defendant had indeed aided slaves to escape. The complicating factor in this case lay in the background of the alleged slaves. In the middle 1830s they had been owned by one Tipton in Kentucky. Tipton moved to Illinois and took his slaves with him. Evidently there was resentment among the people of Illinois at the holding of slaves there and discussion of their right to their freedom. There is implication that because of this public attitude and his desire not to lose the value of his property, Tipton left his home in the dark of night and took his slaves to Missouri where he sold them, thereafter himself returning to his residence in Illinois. The Negroes escaped into Indiana, where their new owner recaptured them and where Williams aided in their reescape.

---

[80] Justice Story wrote to Loring that "I have rarely seen so thorough and exact arguments as those made by Mr. B. R. Curtis and yourself." *Life and Letters of Joseph Story*, II, 235.

For Curtis' argument in full see "The Case of the Slave Med," *Memoir of Benjamin Robbins Curtis*, II, 69–92.

In the light of these facts, Justice McLean charged the jury that these Negroes, held in Illinois for six months by an owner who had transferred his residence there, were entitled to their freedom. Since they had not been slaves at the time when Williams had helped them escape, Williams was not subject to the penalty.[81]

In the case of *Vaughan v. Williams* the question was raised whether the title to the slaves might not be good in light of the contention that in going to Missouri with Tipton they had voluntarily returned to slavery. Justice McLean said the question was not relevant because there was no evidence that they had gone voluntarily. The implications of temporary residence of a slave in free territory followed by voluntary return to the state of enslavement were to be raised again, in the courts of Kentucky and then in the Supreme Court in the case of *Strader v. Graham*. Here again the Negroes in question had been slaves in Kentucky and lived in free territory to the north, but the parallel was not complete. In this instance a Dr. Christopher Graham of Harrodsburg, Kentucky, owned three Negro men who were musicians and whom he wished to have further trained by the experience of playing to audiences throughout the country. To one Williams, a free man of color, Graham gave a letter by which he was permitted to take the three into other states for musical performances. Williams spent time with the three in Ohio and Indiana, after which they were returned to Kentucky, where presumably they continued to serve their master in the same capacity.

Having lived in free territory and been treated essentially as free men, the Negroes were discontented with their lot as slaves in Kentucky, and, of their own volition or under persuasion of others, they escaped across the river into Ohio and were lost to their owner. Under Kentucky law an owner was entitled to damages for the loss of slaves transported out of the state without authorization. Dr. Graham therefore filed a bill in chancery in a Louisville court against the steamboat *Pike*, on which the men had escaped, making the Ohio owners and the captain parties to the suit. The case in due time reached the Kentucky Court of Appeals. That court admitted, in terms of its own decisions,[82] that a slave taken by its owner into Indiana, a part of the Northwest Territory which by the Ordinance of 1787 was to be free territory, and kept as a permanent resident there, became a free person. But in this case, where the slaves were taken into Ohio and Indiana for only a temporary purpose, the court held that they had not become free, with the result

---

[81] Vaughan v. Williams, 28 Fed. Cas. 1115 (No. 16903) (C.C.D. Ind. 1845).

[82] Rankin v. Lydia, 9 Ky. (2 A.K. Marshall) 467 (1820).

NATHAN CLIFFORD
Associate Justice 1858–1881
(Library of Congress)

NOAH H. SWAYNE
Associate Justice 1862–1881
(Library of Congress)

SAMUEL F. MILLER
Associate Justice 1862–1890
(Library of Congress)

DAVID DAVIS
Associate Justice 1862–1877
(Library of Congress)

STEPHEN J. FIELD
Associate Justice 1863–1897
(*Library of Congress*)

Officers of the Court

RICHARD PETERS,
Reporter 1828–1843
Portrait by Rembrandt Peale
(Library of Congress)

BENJAMIN C. HOWARD,
Reporter 1843–1861
Watercolor by T. W. Wood
(Courtesy of Mr. John Eager Howard
of Baltimore, through the
Maryland Historical Society)

JOHN WILLIAM WALLACE,
Reporter 1864–1875
(Library of Congress)

WILLIAM T. CARROLL,
Clerk 1827–1863
(Library of Congress)

DANIEL MIDDLETON,
Clerk 1863–1880
Portrait by Thomas Hicks
(Supreme Court of the United States)

Attorneys General

FELIX GRUNDY,
Attorney General 1838–1839
(Library of Congress)

HENRY D. GILPIN,
Attorney General 1840–1841
(Library of Congress)

JOHN J. CRITTENDEN,
Attorney General 1841, 1850–1853
(Library of Congress)

ISAAC TOUCEY,
Attorney General 1848–1849
(Library of Congress)

REVERDY JOHNSON,
Attorney General 1849–1850
(Library of Congress)

CALEB CUSHING,
Attorney General 1853–1857
(Library of Congress)

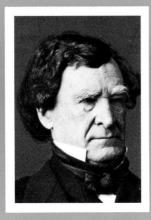

JEREMIAH S. BLACK,
Attorney General 1857–1860
Reporter 1861–1864
(Library of Congress)

EDWIN M. STANTON,
Attorney General 1860–1861
(Library of Congress)

EDWARD BATES,
Attorney General 1861–1864
(Library of Congress)

Celebrated Litigants and Eminent Counsel

SAMUEL F. B. MORSE
(Library of Congress)

CYRUS H. McCORMICK
(Library of Congress)

DRED SCOTT, about 1858
*(Reproduced by permission of the
Missouri Historical Society)*

MYRA CLARK GAINES
(Library of Congress)

that their owner was entitled to damages from those who had aided their escape.[83]

This case, decided by the Kentucky court in 1844, was like other cases of the period in that it was a long time in reaching the Supreme Court, or at any rate a long time elapsed before a decision was handed down from that Court. It was there decided at the December term, 1850, after the years of public and Congressional debate over the territorial and slavery items that went into the Compromise of 1850. Included in that debate was the question of the power of Congress to exclude slavery from the territories, a subject at least indirectly involved in the case in the question of the effect of the Ordinance of 1787. That ordinance had dealt with a series of topics ranging from a guarantee of freedom of worship to freedom of navigation on the Mississippi, and included a prohibition of slavery throughout the Northwest Territory. It declared itself to be a compact between the original states and the people and the states created in the territory and to be forever unalterable unless changed by common consent. Although it appeared that compact status and legislative status were intermingled, the fact that among other things the Ordinance was legislation carried the suggestion that its subject matter was appropriate for legislation by Congress under the Constitution.

The Supreme Court's decision was centrally important for its holding that while they were in Kentucky the status of the Negroes in question was determined by the laws of Kentucky and not by those of Ohio, where for a time the Negroes had been employed, or by the laws of the United States. Hence they were slaves, and the people who had aided in their escape might be penalized as provided by Kentucky statutes. In so deciding, indeed, the Court provided a pattern which for the good of the country it might have been well to follow seven years later in the Dred Scott case.

But apart from the decision as here stated, Chief Justice Taney also said for the Court that the Ordinance of 1787 could not confer jurisdiction on the Supreme Court, that it was superseded by the adoption of the Constitution which placed all states on a plane of equality, and that so much of the Ordinance as was now operative was so because of reenactment by Congress or by the constitutions and laws of the states. From the text of his discussion it is impossible to tell what limitations on legislative power Taney intended to imply, or what his purpose was in thus obliterating the Ordinance. It is significant, however, that Justice McLean, the one member of the Court who was drifting toward an abolitionist position, was skeptical of the Chief Justice's language. He admitted that the slavery provision of the Ordinance

---

[83] Graham v. Strader & Gorman, 14 Ky. (5 B. Monroe) 173 (1844).

was adopted into the constitution of Ohio and that the Ohio constitution had received the sanction of Congress, so that the original parties to the compact might be said to have substituted the constitutional provision for that of the Ordinance, but he would not say more: "Anything that is said in the opinion of the court, in relation to the ordinance beyond this, is not in the case, and is, consequently, extra-judicial."[84]

A battle was shaping up for the courts which was already being waged in the political branches of the government and which was to divide the country more and more and lead eventually to civil war.

---

[84] Strader v. Graham, 10 How. 82, 97 (1851). Justice Catron, who presumably had no reservations about what was said concerning the Ordinance and slavery, did voice a reservation that the Ordinance ought to be considered as still in effect with respect to the free navigation of the Mississippi.

CHAPTER XXIII

Soil for Slavery

A LTHOUGH SUPREME COURT JUSTICES watched from the sidelines, they were vitally interested observers of the process of American territorial expansion during the 1840s. On their circuits they became somewhat involved in coping with filibustering expeditions for the seizure of new territory during that and the ensuing decade.[1] They became deeply involved in the slavery controversy as it intertwined with territorial questions, bringing together the fugitive slave controversy with that of the exclusion of slavery from the territories. In June, 1836, less than a year before his appointment to the Supreme Court, John Catron wrote to President Jackson from Nashville in great perturbation over the cruelty practiced by Mexicans in the war with Texas in which Texas was fighting for its independence. He told of excitement throughout the Southwest and the desire of men under thirty-five, "and all the women," to have Santa Anna shot and the Texas Eagle planted over the Mexican capitol. He urged that the United States immediately recognize Texas and bring an end to the war before England used it as an excuse for intervening and governing Mexico as she did India.[2] To Daniel Webster, in the Senate, Catron wrote in a similar vein, saying that the "object of this scrawl is to give the state of temperament in the West—uncontrollable as the Mississippi."[3]

Webster, however, was conscious of difficulties of an entirely different kind. The active forces in the Texas rebellion had come origi-

---

[1] See for example Charge to Grand Jury—Neutrality Laws, 30 Fed. Cas. 1018 (No. 18265) (C.C.D. Ohio 1838), and other similar charges reprinted in the same section of *Federal Cases*.

[2] John Catron to Andrew Jackson, June 8, 1836, *Correspondence of Andrew Jackson*, John S. Bassett, ed., V, 401–02.

[3] John Catron to Daniel Webster, June 12, 1836, George T. Curtis, *Life of Daniel Webster*, I, 524.

nally from the United States, and they desired not merely independence from Mexico but annexation to the United States. Webster feared that the addition of so much new territory on the southern borders would drastically affect the center of gravity of the Union and might result in its breaking apart.[4] People throughout the country saw the implications for slavery in the annexation of Texas, and the petitions pouring into Congress on the latter subject were mixed with petitions on behalf of the rights of Negroes. Justice Story, so much a nationalist in many respects, provided abolitionists and other Northerners with a constitutional argument against the admission of Texas, contending that the Constitution did not provide for the admission of a foreign state into the Union. We could no more admit Texas to the Union than we could admit Great Britain. Furthermore, on grounds of expediency and propriety, he could not contemplate the admission of Texas without feeling that it was full of dangers of all sorts—moral, political, and sectional.[5] The constitutional argument was picked up by the memorialists to Congress.[6]

The debate over Texas continued until its admission to the Union in December, 1845, by the device of a joint resolution of Congress after it had proved impossible to secure the necessary two-thirds majority of the Senate for admission by treaty. Among the odd items was the opposition of Justice Daniel, during the Tyler Administration in 1844, because he deemed the movement for annexation a part of a surge for power by John C. Calhoun, Tyler's Secretary of State. In touring his circuit, which bordered upon Texas, he had come to believe that the excitement in behalf of annexation had been worked up by a few interested managers of the Tyler and Calhoun factions, and that the matter was not an important political issue with the people generally.[7]

Yet Justice Daniel, as always, was supersensitive on regional issues as well as local politics, and was writing soon afterward a tirade of denunciation of Northern assumptions of superiority over Southern slaveholders:

> Can anything be more galling to the spirit of honorable men than to be told that it is enough to justify the condemnation of any measure, that its effect may be the promotion of their peculiar interests and

[4] *Ibid.*, 523.

[5] Joseph Story to Joseph Tuckerman, July 25, 1837, Fulmer Mood and Granville Hicks, "Letters to Dr. Channing on Slavery and the Annexation of Texas, 1837," *New England Quarterly*, 5:593–94, 1932.

[6] Resolutions of the Legislature of Rhode Island, S. Doc. No. 80, 25th Cong., 2nd Sess. 1 (1838). Resolutions of the Legislature of Massachusetts, S. Doc. No. 432, 25th Cong., 2nd Sess. 1 (1838).

[7] See P. V. Daniel to Martin Van Buren, June 11, 1844, Van Buren Papers.

welfare: that it may prove advantageous to the holders of slave property? Are we to be placed under permanent and unrelenting ban of the Federal Government? To be held as less than the *equals* of our miscalled *fellow citizens*? To be regarded as the plague-spot upon our nation, and then required by our oppressors and revilers to shout for our *blessed Union*? A blessed Union indeed it would be upon such terms. No—No—The most temperate amongst us, would not hesitate to decide, if things have come or are to come to this complexion, to go with our imputed blemishes, our crimes and defilements, apart to ourselves; and leave these exclusively beautiful and moral and clean and immaculate, to their own purity.[8]

Although both political parties were somewhat divided on the Texas issue, Henry Clay, as Whig Presidential candidate in 1844, took a stand against annexation,[9] while Polk was for it. Andrew Jackson predicted that Clay, then in the Senate, would avoid the question as a campaign issue by abandoning his opposition to annexation, but Justice Catron shrewdly observed that Clay was exceedingly proud of his opinions and that he and his friends were too fully committed to recant. They would therefore reject the treaty.[10] The treaty was rejected, with Clay's help. Catron later remarked that as a result of this action Clay could have been beaten only by Polk.[11] Webster, seeing the inevitability of annexation with Polk's election, remarked gloomily on the depths of disgrace into which the country was sinking when national peace and perhaps the peace of the world was disturbed "by its greediness for more slave Territory, and for the greater increase of Slavery!"[12]

In August, 1845, Justice Catron wrote to Polk from Nashville about the rumor that war with Mexico was imminent. His only fear was that the United States would not stop short of doing too much and thereby excite European jealousy. He was especially disturbed by newspaper boasting about adding to United States territory California and Mexico this side of the Cordilleras. He considered such boasting to be folly at this time when the country had the Texas and Oregon questions on its hands and when Whig papers were reiterating charges about the grasping ambition of the Democratic Party. As for the disputed Texas boundary with Mexico, he preferred that little be said about it until the state was in the Union. Catron recommended study of British strategy in India. The English, he said, never talked of what they intended to do.

---

[8] P. V. Daniel to Martin Van Buren, Oct. 17, 1844, Van Buren Papers.

[9] See his letter of opposition, *Niles' National Register*, 66:152–53, 1844.

[10] John Catron to J. K. Polk, June 8, 1844, Polk Papers.

[11] John Catron to J. K. Polk, Nov. 23, 1844, Polk Papers.

[12] Daniel Webster to R. C. Winthrop, Dec. 13, 1844, Winthrop Papers.

They acted first, and with ample force, and negotiated afterward. "I shall set you down (one and all) as bunglers, if you fail to follow the English example."[13]

When Texas was admitted to the Union in December, 1845, its border with Mexico was still in dispute, as had been expected. When Mexican troops entered the disputed area and blood was shed, the United States treated the invasion as an act of war and in May, 1846, the conflict was on, though ends and aims and motives were fantastically blurred. Before it was over, various Americans advocated steps all the way from the mere fixing of the Texas-Mexican boundary to the absorption of all of Mexico. In August, 1846, Polk asked Congress for an appropriation to carry on the war, and to the resulting bill in the House of Representatives David Wilmot sought to attach the famous Wilmot Proviso, which provided for exclusion of slavery from any territory acquired from Mexico. The amendment, adopted by the House but not acted on by the Senate, further heated the flames of the slavery controversy. Further attempts were made to win its adoption at the ensuing session, with still further sectional strife even though the amendment failed. Positions ranged from that of the Wilmot Proviso, through the provision of the Missouri Compromise that slavery should not be permitted north of thirty-six degrees and thirty minutes, to the position now being taken by Calhoun and other extreme Southerners that Congress had no power to enact any such measure as the Missouri Compromise or the Wilmot Proviso for the exclusion of slavery from any United States territory. Furious debates continued until the war ended in 1848 with the acquisition of New Mexico and California on the basis of a cash settlement and through the working out of the Compromise of 1850.

Justice Daniel, for all his dislike of Calhoun, agreed with him that Congress had no power to exclude slavery from the territories. "I have ever regarded what has been called the Missouri Compromise," he wrote to Van Buren, "as utterly without warrant from the Constitution." The people might observe such a compromise as long as they pleased, but there was no constitutional basis for its requirement. The power of Congress to govern territories was the power to govern for general and national purposes only. Every state and its citizens had an equal right in whatsoever belonged to the United States. He repeated his attack on the insolence of the North in assuming its superiority and projecting a degrading inferiority onto the South: "Here is at once the extinction of all fraternity, of all sympathy, of all *endurance* even: the

---

[13] John Catron to J. K. Polk, Aug. 16, 1845, Polk Papers.

creation of animosity fierce, implacable, undying. It is the immitigable outrage, which I venture to say, there is no true Southron from school-boy to octogenarian, who is not prepared for any extremety in order to repel it."[14]

Justice Catron at this time felt very differently about the matter, and as far as the President was concerned his advice was much more important. Of him and Mrs. Catron, indeed, F. P. Blair remarked that they were "the right and left hands of Old Buck and Polk."[15] Catron had read approvingly in the *National Intelligencer,* he wrote to Polk, a speech delivered in the House of Representatives by Julius Rockwell of Massachusetts in which Rockwell argued that Congress had the power to govern territories and to exclude slavery therefrom. In that speech[16] Rockwell had been concerned primarily with the need for a territorial government for Oregon. Proslavery leaders recognized the fact that slavery was not likely to prosper in the Oregon climate, but since they were increasingly taking the position that Congress had no power to prevent slaveowners from taking their property into any territory of the United States, many of them were opposing formal exclusion in the provision for territorial government. Rockwell admitted that free Negroes occupied a degraded position in the United States, and indeed in demonstration of that fact he quoted at length from Catron's opinion on the subject written when he was chief justice of the Supreme Court of Tennessee.[17] But the free Negroes were here, he contended, not because Negroes had sought to come here but because the people of their race had been brought here as slaves. He was opposed to spreading the evil to Oregon or to any other newly organized

---

[14] P. V. Daniel to Martin Van Buren, Nov. 1, 1847, Van Buren Papers.

In the correspondence in question Justice Daniel was apparently attempting to get his old friend Van Buren committed to his own position of hostility to the Wilmot Proviso. He did not succeed. If he understood Van Buren's position, he wrote, he contemplated it with deepest sorrow and alarm. "I shall have been constrained to perceive on the part of those, on whom of all the public men in the nation I reposed the greatest trust, what my deliberate convictions compel me to view as the overthrow of the great national compact; as the extreme of injury and oppression; oppression in its most galling form,

because it declares to me that I am not regarded as an equal; the sharer of a common birth right—that the compatriots of Washington, Jefferson, Madison, Monroe, of Henry, of Mason, of the Randolphs, the Lees, of Giles, of Brent, and of many other worthies, are a disfranchised or degraded caste. Oppression which all that is holy in duty and obligation binds the patriot to repel at any and every cost." P. V. Daniel to Martin Van Buren, Nov. 19, 1847, Van Buren Papers.

[15] F. P. Blair to Martin Van Buren, Nov. 16, 1848, Van Buren Papers.

[16] *Cong. Globe,* 30th Cong., 1st Sess., 790–94 (1848).

[17] Fisher's Negroes v. Dabbs, 14 Tenn. (6 Yerger) 119 (1834).

territory. Since the question of admission or exclusion was one of justice and expediency, and not of constitutionality, he would always vote for exclusion.

Catron fully agreed with Rockwell that slavery should be excluded from Oregon, saying that were he in Congress he would not hesitate a moment to vote for such exclusion. He differed only as to Southern territory, where he thought the true line of division between slave and free territory should be an extension westward of the Missouri Compromise line. He thought this the best compromise in view of sentiment in both the North and the South, and also in view of the division within the Republican (Democratic) Party.[18] Fortunately for Catron's reputation for consistency this correspondence was not published, and was not available to embarrass him when he wrote his opinion in the Dred Scott case saying that the Missouri Compromise "violates the most leading feature of the Constitution—a feature on which the Union depends, and which secures to the respective States and their citizens an entire equality of rights, privileges and immunities."[19]

If Justice Daniel took an extreme position and Justice Catron a moderate one with respect to expansion of slave territory at the time of the Mexican War, that of Justice McLean was highly critical. McLean expressed to Francis Lieber the opinion that the war was unjust on our part and unprovoked by Mexico. Having already enough space for two hundred million people, we did not need more. He believed that further expansion might lead to an overthrow of the government, and he was concerned about the extreme positions on slavery being taken in the North and in the South. He would regret to see the Presidential election turn on this subject. A fanatic on either side would ruin us.[20] Early in 1848 he wrote for publication a letter saying that the war had been unnecessarily and unconstitutionally commenced by marching our army into disputed territory in possession of Mexico, and urging that Congress put an end to the war. Congress should agree upon the terms for a treaty and call upon the executive to negotiate and to suspend hostilities while doing so. If the President refused, Congress should cut off military appropriations.[21]

In the Senate the McLean letter brought a tirade of criticism from Henry S. Foote of Mississippi, who denounced both the "unpatriotic views" announced and the attempt of a judge to dictate to Congress. He deplored the fact that the high tribunal where Marshall once presided with majestic dignity had been discredited "by a Presidency-seeking

---

[18] John Catron to J. K. Polk, July 12, 1848, Polk Papers. See also Catron to Polk, July 24, 1848, Polk Papers.
[19] Dred Scott v. Sandford, 19 How. 393, 529 (1857).

[20] John McLean to Francis Lieber, Nov. 9, 1846, Lieber Papers.
[21] John McLean to ———, Jan. 7, 1848, *Niles' National Register*, 73: 354, 1848.

official."[22] In spite of the criticism stirred by his proposal, McLean, with the 1848 election in mind, refused to stay out of the political picture. After the annexation of the new territory he wrote that in harmony with the principles of the Constitution and according to sound procedure the people might prevent the extension of slavery to the free territory annexed. They could do it by the simple expedient of refraining from giving slavery in the territory a legal sanction: "Without the sanction of law, slavery can no more exist in a territory than a man can breathe without air. Slaves are not property where they are not made so by the municipal law. The legislature of a territory can *exercise no power which is not conferred on it by act of Congress.*"[23]

While current members of the Supreme Court were working out their positions on the sectional crisis so also was John A. Campbell, who was to become a member in 1853. In November, 1847, from his law office in Mobile, Alabama, he wrote to Calhoun that he viewed the acquisition of new territory mainly as it affected the balance of power in the federal government. He thought the territory to be acquired not particularly good for slave occupancy, and in any event the larger portion to be acquired would fall to the nonslaveholding states. If the Missouri Compromise line were extended, the North would be the principal beneficiary. But even apart from the slavery issue, he was opposed to the acquisition of new territory. Mexico had been the victim of an unprovoked war on our part and there was no just ground for the dismemberment of her territories. Furthermore, he feared that the expansion of territory would be too much for the government of the United States. He was concerned about the wild and turbulent conduct of the Western members and their greediness with respect to federal appropriations. He would not increase the number of states until the new ones already in the Union became more civilized.[24]

Writing again to Calhoun in March, 1848, after further correspondence and after reading debates in Congress, Campbell, like

---

[22] *Cong. Globe,* 30th Cong., 1st Sess. 597 (1848).

Senator Reverdy Johnson, a Whig residing in a proslavery environment, likewise regretted McLean's intervention in affairs and thought that McLean himself, in cooler judgment, would come to regret an appeal that cast a shade on the purity of the bench. He added, "In my opinion, Mr. President, a judge should be separated not only while he is upon the bench, but forever, from all the agitating topics of the day. Once a judge, he should be ever a judge. The ermine should never be polluted, nor suspected of pollution; it should be the very type of Justice herself—pure, spotless, faultless." *Cong Globe,* 30th Cong., 1st Sess., 587 (1848).

[23] "Territorial Government," *Democratic Review,* 23:189, 191–92, 1848.

[24] J. A. Campbell to John C. Calhoun, Nov. 20, 1847, Calhoun Correspondence, *Annual Report of the American Historical Association for the Year 1899,* 2:1139–45, 1900.

Catron, took a position which he was to reject as a member of the Supreme Court in the Dred Scott case. He here asserted that Congress, having the power to organize the people of a territory into a body politic, could as an incident to that power "decide what shall be held and enjoyed as property in that territory, and that persons should not be held as property." In the absence of Congressional changes in local law in the territories, they were governed by the same laws applicable therein prior to the cession, and in the absence of such earlier laws providing for slavery, the institution could not exist unless and until positively provided for by Congress, for, he agreed, it was a purely municipal institution.[25]

In writing this letter, Campbell deemed the best mode of protection of the South to be that of preventing the acquisition of territory from Mexico, and his strategy was to persuade Calhoun and others to oppose acquisition because the new territory would not become slave territory. He was deeply concerned about the future and predicted gloomily that "we at the South will come out of these conflicts with the loss of everything—I fear honor—as well as influence, stability, strength."[26] When the territory had been acquired in spite of his opposition he shifted his ground and argued that slavery could not be excluded from it. He took this position in the convention of representatives of the Southern states which met in Nashville in June, 1850. Here he presented resolutions contending that the territories of the United States belonged to the people of the several states and that the people of any of the states might migrate there with their property. By contrast with his previous assertion that the law prevailing in the territories when acquired from Mexico dictated that the territories would be free unless Congress legislated positively to authorize slavery, he now contended that the acquisition was made in the light of the existence of slavery in the United States, with the result that slavery could not be excluded. He declared the assault upon the rights of the slaveholding states and territories to be blows aimed at the Constitution itself. Nevertheless, if a majority refused to recognize the full constitutional right here asserted, he proposed to compromise on the Missouri Compromise line of division, "as we did on a former occasion upon considerations of what is due to the stability of our institutions."[27]

---

[25] J. A. Campbell to John C. Calhoun, Mar. 1, 1848, "Correspondence Addressed to John C. Calhoun, 1837–1849," Chauncey S. Boucher and Robert P. Brooks, eds., *Annual Report of the American Historical Association for the Year 1929*, 431–34, 1930.

[26] *Ibid.*, 434.

[27] For Campbell's resolutions as reprinted from the *Republican Banner* and *Nashville Whig*, June 6, 1850, see George W. Duncan, John Archibald Campbell, *Transactions of the Alabama Historical Society 1904*, 5: 107, 122–25, 1906. For a discussion of the Southern convention at Nashville see St. George L. Sioussat,

XXIII: *Soil for Slavery*

In the Congressional debates on territorial and slavery issues which took place between 1847 and 1850 the Supreme Court came into the discussion again and again. In some instances the work of the Court was lauded and its ability to settle disputes was praised, as in the *Prigg* case and *Groves v. Slaughter*. In the House of Representatives Thomas H. Bayly of Virginia urged that an arrangement be made to get from the Supreme Court a decision on the right of slaveowners to take their slaves into United States territories, and derided the Whigs for their unwillingness to put their faith in the result. "It is a new position with the Whig party," he asserted, "that the Supreme Court is an unfit tribunal to decide such a question as this."[28] Now that a vast area to the west of Texas had been taken away from Mexico, though with compensation, of course, the question of the western boundary of Texas remained important. That western border touched upon or reached into territory called New Mexico, which included the present state of that name, Colorado, Nevada and Utah, most of Arizona and part of Wyoming. Any part of that territory that could be treated as part of Texas would be governed by the law of Texas, which gave protection to slavery. Proslavery people sought inclusion of as much territory as possible within the Texas domain, in spite of the fact that most of it had hitherto been considered as separate from Texas.

To settle the controversy Samuel F. Vinton of Ohio proposed in the House of Representatives that the matter be determined through a suit in the Supreme Court. The abolitionist opposition to this strategy was voiced by Horace Greeley of New York, the editor of the *New York Tribune*, who happened at this time to be serving his brief term as a member of the House.[29] Knowing that the question of liberty or slavery was involved, he said, and that a decision of the Court favorable to Texas would carry slavery over a territory larger than the whole of New England, he was unwilling to commit the question to such a tribunal, composed as it was of a majority of slaveholders.[30] The method proposed, he insisted, failed to take into account the desires of the people of New Mexico. If those people were permitted to pass on the question he would be willing to abide by their decision. "But to authorize five slaveholders (forming a majority of our Supreme Court) to decide this momentous question on grounds and under rules which silence entirely the voice of the people of New Mexico, is what I can never agree to."[31]

"Tennessee, The Compromise of 1850, and the Nashville Convention," *Mississippi Valley Historical Review*, 2:313–47, 1915.

[28] *Cong. Globe*, 30th Cong., 1st Sess., 1085 (1848).

[29] *Cong. Globe*, 30th Cong., 2nd Sess., 610 (1849).

[30] *Ibid.*

[31] *Cong. Globe*, 30th Cong., 2nd Sess., 249 (1849).

Congressional debate and public debate generally continued with ever mounting tension through 1848, 1849, and the summer of 1850. Until that time, only the provision in 1848 for the government of the territory of Oregon, with the restrictions of the Ordinance of 1787,[32] disposed of a then critical issue. The abolitionist demand grew in power and shrillness, as did Southern anger and hysteria. Moderate positions became harder and harder to hold, and unpopular with increasing numbers of people. Nevertheless the bonds of the Union were still strong, and under the leadership of Henry Clay a group of moderate leaders began the formulation of what came to be called the Compromise of 1850.[33] Among the more important provisions were those granting the request of California for admission as a free state; establishment of territorial governments for New Mexico and Utah, including all the newly acquired territory west of Texas except California, without the much-sought restriction of the Wilmot Proviso; termination of the slave trade in the District of Columbia (of the use of the District as a marketplace for slaves to be disposed of in the slave states) without interference with slavery as such in the District unless Maryland and the people of the District gave their permission; and finally, the enactment of a more effective fugitive slave law.

In his famous "Seventh of March" speech Daniel Webster defended the compromise despite its provision for a new fugitive slave act, so much hated by the growing number of abolitionists of New England. His was a speech not for slavery but in behalf of the Union, to whose building he had given much of his life. He spoke, he said, "not as a Massachusetts man, nor as a northern man, but as an American, and as a member of the Senate of the United States."[34] He had been opposed to the annexation of Texas, which had nevertheless been brought about, with the result that we had another slave state. We now had the territory of New Mexico. He saw no point in insisting on a Wilmot Proviso with respect to it, for the reason that its physical geography took care of the matter. It could not in reason be thought of as slave territory. As for the return of fugitive slaves, he had always thought of the constitutional provision as binding upon the state legislatures. The Supreme Court decision to the contrary (in the *Prigg* case) "may not have been a fortunate decision."[35] In any event, Congress

---

[32] 9 Stat. 323, 329.

[33] The subject is fully discussed in most general histories of the period. For special articles see for example Robert R. Russel, "What Was the Compromise of 1850?" *Journal of Southern History,* 22:292–309, 1956; F. H. Hodder, "The Authorship of the Compromise of 1850," *Mississippi*

Valley Historical Review, 22:525–36, 1936; Holman Hamilton, "Democratic Leadership and the Compromise of 1850," *Mississippi Valley Historical Review,* 41:403–18, 1954.

[34] *Cong. Globe,* 31st Cong., 1st Sess., 269 (1850).

[35] *Ibid.,* 274.

was obligated to make the constitutional mandate effective. Again and again he came back to the necessity for preserving the Union: "Never did there devolve, on any generation of men, higher trusts than now devolve upon us for the preservation of this Constitution, and the harmony and peace of all who are destined to live under it."[36]

While the strength of the leadership of Clay and other sober-minded men brought about the adoption of the several provisions of the compromise as independent measures, Webster lost caste with the growing body of abolitionists in New England and in other parts of the country, and came to be regarded by them virtually as a traitor to his country. It was the voice of a younger man, William H. Seward of New York, that sounded the wave of the future. Denouncing concessions to slavery, Seward asserted that although we had acquired the public domain we held it in trust rather than by arbitrary power. The Constitution regulated our stewardship, devoting the domain to union, to justice, to defense, to welfare, and to liberty. And here, perhaps inadvertently, he articulated an idealistic battle cry for those who would make no compromise with evil even in the name of the Constitution, proclaiming that "there is a higher law than the Constitution, which regulates our authority over the domain, and devotes it to the same noble purposes."[37]

Although Seward proposed to restrict slavery by interpretation of the Constitution rather than by violation of it, his appeal to a higher law gave a slogan to those who were far more concerned with ends than with constitutionality, and further antagonized Southerners by the implication that they were guilty of violation of the law of nature.[38] As the flames fanned hotter it became increasingly doubtful whether this new Clay compromise would bring about the long era of regional peace it was proposed to ensure.

Alongside Seward stood his colleague at what might be called the abolitionist bar, Salmon P. Chase, recently elected to the Senate from Ohio, who delivered a speech entitled "Union and Freedom, without Compromise."[39] Important among his remarks, particularly in view of the fact that fourteen years later he was to occupy the office of Chief Justice, was his discussion of sectionalism on the Supreme Court. Discussing the occupants of high federal offices in terms of region, he

---

[36] *Ibid.*, 276.

[37] *Ibid.*, 265.

[38] See the attack on "his Holiness of the Senate" in "The Doctrine of the 'Higher Law,' Mr. Seward's Speech," *Southern Literary Messenger*, 17:130–42, 1851. See also reference to "The 'Higher Law' which a political demagogue had declared superior to our Constitution," in "The Higher Law," *Democratic Review*, 27:508–19, 1850. See also appropriate references in "Vermont 'Democratic' State Convention, Speech of Mr. Van Buren," *Democratic Review*, 29:72–77, 1851.

[39] *Cong. Globe*, 31st Cong., 1st Sess., 468–80 (1850).

pointed out that "Thirteen of the Judges of the Supreme Court have been taken from the slave states; from the free states, twelve. No northern man has filled the office of Chief Justice during this century; and, notwithstanding the population of the free States is more than double the free population of the slave states, the latter have always been represented by a majority of the Judges upon the Supreme Bench."[40]

The imbalance of history, he noted, continued to the present day —the slave States had now, as ever, a majority of the Justices of the Supreme Court. While he cordially agreed as to the probity, learning, and ability of the present judges, he insisted that, "eminent and upright as they are, they are not more than other men exempt from the bias of education, sympathy, and interest." He thought it only natural that Southern statesmen should desire that judges should have interests like those which they would desire to maintain, and he presented a population chart of the several circuits to show that the Southerners had been eminently successful in realizing their aspirations.[41]

While Chase, a prospective Chief Justice, was fighting compromise of the cause of freedom, Benjamin R. Curtis of Massachusetts, soon to be an Associate Justice, was aligning himself with Webster in behalf of law and order and the defense of the Union. When on April 29, 1850, following the month of the delivery of his "Seventh of March" speech, Webster returned to Boston, Curtis was selected to give the welcoming address. Taking into account the bitter attacks being made on Webster by the abolitionists of his own state, Curtis hailed Webster as the expounder and defender of the Constitution and assured him that confidence, slowly given, was "not to be uprooted by any gusts of passion or prejudice, nor blasted by the breath of suspicion."[42] About the time of the adoption of the new Fugitive Slave Law, in September, 1850, Curtis in a private letter deplored the fact that many people did

---

[40] *Ibid.*, 473.

[41] *Ibid.*, 474. In a private letter dated Dec. 21, 1850, to an undesignated recipient, Chase said of the Fugitive Slave Law that the Supreme Court would surely find it constitutional: "They were appointed to do so. The slaveholders have seen to it for years that every Judge was sound on the slavery question. But their decision won't make it constitutional. Nor is it Constitutional. An argument cannot be framed in support of its Constitutionality which would not be derided by a Common Law Jurist acquainted with our Institutions and under notice growing out of our habitudes in respect to slavery. I go for the Strict Construction Doctrine and against implied powers, not clearly essential to the execution of powers expressly granted. And I defy any man to show any power in Congress to legislate except upon the most latitudinarian principles of the Constitution." (Chase Papers.)

[42] *Memoir of Benjamin Robbins Curtis*, I, 115–16.

not seem to take into account the fact that the Constitution was a law, each of its clauses binding on every person, and that organized resistance was rebellion.[43] In November Curtis wrote for the United States Marshal in Boston an opinion upholding the Fugitive Slave Law. Webster, now Secretary of State, informed President Fillmore that the opinion was "well drawn, and argues well that which hardly seems to require argument. The opinion, however, will do good. Mr. Curtis' reputation is high, and his opinion will silence the small lawyers. It will be published in the Courier tomorrow at my request."[44]

On November 26, 1850, Curtis delivered an address at Faneuil Hall urging loyalty and obedience to the Constitution. He referred disparagingly to "good men among us, with very tender consciences but not very sound practical judgments."[45] He defended the Fugitive Slave Clause as one of the necessary compromises of the Constitution and urged the people to live up to their commitments, and to preserve the Union. As for the rights of the colored people coming into the state, he firmly believed that Massachusetts had nothing to do with them:

> It is enough for us that they have no right to be *here*. Our peace and safety they have no right to invade; whether they come as fugitives, and, being here, act as rebels against our law, or whether they come as armed invaders. Whatever natural rights they have, and I admit those natural rights to their fullest extent, *this* is not the *soil* on which to vindicate them. This is *our* soil, sacred to *our* peace, on which we intend to perform *our* promises, and work out, for the benefit of ourselves and our posterity and the world, the destiny which our Creator has assigned to *us*.[46]

In short, Curtis took the middle-of-the-road position, the law-abiding position, which placed the Union and the compact obligations of the Constitution ahead of the natural rights of an oppressed and, to him, essentially alien people. Like Webster, he had been driven to establish his position in existing constitutional law and not in theories of natural right. At this time, of course, he could not have known that within a year Justice Woodbury would have vacated the position on the First Circuit through death, and that he would be chosen for the vacancy, with as much approval from the South as any Northern appointment could be expected to bring, although confirmation was delayed by abolitionist pressure.

---

[43] *Ibid.*, 122.
[44] Daniel Webster to Millard Fillmore, Nov. 15, 1850, *Writings and Speeches of Daniel Webster*, XVI, 577.
[45] *Memoir of Benjamin Robbins Curtis*, 124.
[46] *Ibid.*, 136.

The Fugitive Slave Act of 1850 brought a broad expansion of the responsibilities of the federal judiciary. By the Act of 1793[47] the only federal officers authorized to direct removal of captured fugitives from the states to which they had fled were the federal judges. Since these included only a Supreme Court Justice during the period when he might be riding circuit within a given state, and one or at most two district judges, the task of commitment was left largely to other officers listed, namely, any magistrate of a county, city, or town where the seizure or arrest was made. Since under the Supreme Court decision in *Prigg v. Pennsylvania* these officers were eliminated, or at least the states were not required to permit such service on their part, enforcement of the statute had been greatly hampered.

To remedy this defect in administration, the 1850 statute[48] not only listed federal judges as committing magistrates but empowered United States Commissioners to perform this function and authorized Circuit Courts to appoint additional commissioners as they might be needed for this purpose. The commissioners were to be paid through an extraordinary system of fees. Issuing certificates of removal of fugitives was encouraged by the allowance of a fee of ten dollars if a certificate was issued, whereas only five dollars was allowed if the evidence was found insufficient to issue a certificate.

Efforts were made to whip United States Marshals into line by providing for a fine of one thousand dollars in each instance of refusal to execute warrants. If a captured fugitive was permitted to escape, intentionally or otherwise, the marshal or his deputy was made subject to suit by the claimant for the value of the fugitive. Furthermore, in order to insure an adequacy of arresting agents, commissioners were authorized to appoint persons to execute warrants. The fugitive, once captured, was to be taken before a judge or commissioner, who would issue a certificate authorizing removal of the fugitive to the state from which he had fled if the evidence was found to justify such action. No claim of false arrest or title to freedom on the part of the fugitive was to be taken into account. The statute provided specifically that "In no trial or hearing under this act shall the testimony of such alleged fugitive be admitted in evidence." The statute throughout, indeed, was drafted solely as an effective instrument for enforcing the claims of alleged owners. It was only natural that in making it into such an instrument and leaving the rights of blacks virtually unprotected, Congress stirred the wrath not only of all enemies of slavery but also of those who took a fatalistic attitude toward lawful slavery but were determined to protect free Negroes in the North against kidnappers from the South.

---

[47] 1 Stat. 302.   [48] 9 Stat. 462.

With enactment of the statute, members of the Supreme Court in Northern and border states became immediately involved through charges to grand juries urging enforcement and charges to trial juries in a stream of cases. Less than a month after the act was passed, Webster reported to the President that Justice Woodbury had recommended in the strongest terms the enforcement of its provisions. Webster hoped to have the charge published.[49] Fillmore replied that he had received a copy of the charge,[50] and he was considering it along with a request from Justice Grier and Judge Kane for military support in connection with enforcement of the statute in Pennsylvania.

Justice Grier continued to be at the center of conflict with respect to the return of fugitive slaves. In April, 1850, while the new federal statute was still pending, he wrote to James Buchanan of a Pennsylvania statute of 1847 which had apparently been used as an excuse for the rescue of fugitives when captured by their alleged owners or their agents. He thought the legislators had not been aware of the "evil consequences" the measure would have. He had had occasion to say judicially that when such legislation was construed to encourage and protect citizens of Pennsylvania in intervening to rescue fugitive slaves it could have no effect but to injure and mislead the people, since it would be treated as "entirely *unconstitutional, null,* and *void*" in the courts of the United States. It set an evil example for the community in that it compelled state officers to disregard the injunction of the Constitution, which was binding on all who had sworn to uphold that Constitution.[51]

It was said that the first case under the new Fugitive Slave Law arose in Justice Grier's court in Philadelphia on October 18, 1850. The alleged owner brought a fugitive before Grier to seek authorization for his removal. Counsel for the fugitive asked for postponement of the case. Justice Grier used the occasion to denounce public agitation against enforcement of the law. Although this was a summary proceeding, he said, he desired to give the prisoner an adequate opportunity for defense, and his only ground for proceeding in a summary manner would be the ill advice the colored population were now receiving. He had read of a meeting at which resolutions were adopted advising the colored race to arm themselves against law enforcement and shoot

---

[49] Daniel Webster to Millard Fillmore, Oct. 19, 1850, *Writings and Speeches of Daniel Webster*, XVI, 569.

[50] Millard Fillmore to Daniel Webster, Oct. 23, 1850, *ibid.*, 571.

[51] R. C. Grier to James Buchanan, Apr. 2, 1850, Buchanan Papers.

Justice Grier said he had taken this position in a charge to a jury with respect to a Dr. Mitchell, but had not reduced his opinion to writing. This was apparently a case involving prosecution for employment of a fugitive slave. See *Niles' National Register*, 73:221, 1847.

down officers of the law. If such advice were taken, the killing of the first officer would be a signal for extermination of the black race. White men who would give such advice were the colored people's worst enemy.

He was concerned lest adjournment of the case from day to day lead to the assemblage of thousands of black people, perhaps to resist the laws. "This would compel him to send to the Navy Yard for the whole military force, and as true as God liveth, and my soul liveth, said the Judge, I will maintain the law, though I have to order every man who puts himself in armed position to its execution to be shot down. I will execute the law as I find it, at all hazards." The detention of the prisoner was a problem, since Pennsylvania law denied the use of local prisons for the purpose. The marshal had agreed to keep the prisoner in his personal custody. Justice Grier promised that if a mob, black or white, should assemble to resist the laws it would be repelled, "even to the shedding of blood."[52]

But Justice Grier showed a determination to be fair to the prisoner as well as to protect property rights and preserve order. When he issued the warrant for the prisoner's detention he warned the claimant that papers showing ownership must be in order. At the hearing he decided the evidence of title and identity was inadmissible because of the informality of the papers and the interest of the witness. The claimant then asked for an adjournment of the hearing to enable him to get legal vouchers, but Justice Grier denied the request. The fugitive was discharged and, amid a noisy demonstration, a great crowd of friends hurried him away, so that the filing of a later claim would be without avail.[53]

It was apparently this experience which led Justice Grier and Judge Kane to ask President Fillmore for a general order authorizing the employment of troops if needed to preserve order in fugitive slave controversies. Fillmore sensed the danger of authorizing the use of troops in strife which carried the threat of civil war, but, he wrote to Webster, "Nullification can not and will not be tolerated." He had sworn to uphold the Constitution, and he knew no higher law in conflict with it. "God knows that I detest Slavery, but it is an existing evil, for which we are not responsible, and we must endure it, and give it such protection, as is guaranteed by the constitution, till we can get rid of it without destroying the last hope of free government in the world."

---

[52] Fugitive Slave Case, *West L.J.*, 8:93–94, 1850. See also R. C. Grier to William Robinson, Nov. 22, 1850,

Washington National Intelligencer, Dec. 12, 1850.
[53] *New York Tribune*, Apr. 12, 1856.

He enclosed a copy of Justice Grier's letter and asked for Webster's advice.[54]

Apparently without waiting for Webster's counsel, however, Fillmore and such of his Cabinet as were in Washington decided to give military aid wherever a federal judge should certify that it was necessary. He was making this authorization only as a last resort, Fillmore wrote to Webster, but if necessary he would not hesitate to bring the whole force of the government to sustain the law. He admitted of no right of nullification, either in the North or the South.[55]

In the meantime other cases involving slavery were coming before the United States Circuit Court for the Third Circuit. A few days after the release of the prisoner mentioned above, Justice Grier charged a jury in a case arising under the Fugitive Slave Law of 1793. He expressed the opinion that the "moral disease engendered by this moral epidemic" had infected but a small number. He denounced conventions plotting disunion for defiling the graves and maligning the memories of the patriots of the Revolution. The good citizens of Pennsylvania were opposed to slavery, he said, but they revered the Constitution and laws of their country. He praised associations which since the days of Franklin had sought to protect colored people against kidnappers, but contended that "these friends of religion and humanity have no connection with those unhappy agitators who infest other portions of the Union, and, with mad zeal, are plotting its ruin."[56]

The federal courts were continually made to feel the impact of interstate strife over slavery whether or not the strife resulted in cases brought before them. One such event, occurring in 1850, somewhat resembled that which had given rise to *Prigg v. Pennsylvania*. In 1845 a slave woman had escaped from her owner, James S. Mitchell of Cecil County, Maryland, fled to Delaware, where she was married, and moved to New Jersey where in 1849 a son was born. The mother and father were accustomed to visiting Philadelphia to sell herbs in the markets there. Mitchell got in touch with George F. Alberti, an agent for the recapture of fugitive slaves, and asked him to bring the woman back to Maryland. The woman was decoyed to Alberti's home, along with her infant son, who according to Pennsylvania law was a free person. In spite of a provision in the Pennsylvania statute of 1847 which forbade state officers to aid in the removal of slaves an officer gave a

---

[54] Millard Fillmore to Daniel Webster, Oct. 23, 1850, *Writings and Speeches of Daniel Webster*, XVI, 571–72.

[55] *Letters of Daniel Webster*, C. H. Van Tyne, ed., 439.

[56] Oliver v. Kauffman, 18 Fed. Cas. 657, 661 (No. 10497) (C.C.E.D. Pa. 1850). See also Justice Grier's charge at Pittsburg in Van Metre v. Mitchell, 28 Fed. Cas. 1036 (No. 16865) (C.C.-W.D. Pa. 1853).

certificate of removal for the woman, without mention of the child. Then secretly, and in alleged conformity with another provision of the Act of 1847 which forbade recapture of slaves in a tumultuous manner so as to disturb the peace, Alberti and J. Frisby Price took the mother and child back to her owner in Maryland.[57]

Alberti, Price, and Mitchell were indicted in a Pennsylvania court for kidnapping. Alberti and Price were tried and convicted. The governor of Pennsylvania asked the governor of Maryland to surrender Mitchell for trial, but Governor Lowe refused the requisition on the ground that Mitchell himself had not been on Pennsylvania soil, and had therefore not violated the Pennsylvania law. A constitutional convention then in session in Maryland adopted a report praising the governor for his "refusal to deliver a citizen of Maryland to an unjust and unconstitutional demand made by the Governor of Pennsylvania."[58] The convention also asked the governor to start proceedings to have the case involving the conviction of Alberti and Price brought before the Supreme Court of the United States. The resolution was vigorously supported by Benjamin C. Howard, Reporter of the Supreme Court, who was also a member of the convention. Maryland, he thought, had an obligation to try to rescue "those two poor miserable men incarcerated in a jail in Pennsylvania for committing no crime."[59] Howard admitted that there might be difficulty in getting the case before the Court since the record did not show that a constitutional point had been raised and decided, the indictment not having certified the specific nature of the crime. "But he hoped and thought the court would, in such a case as this, receive evidence beyond the record, because it would be perfectly manifest to every body, that if they chose in the free states to make their indictments general, there would be no way of getting it on the record."[60]

Whether or not Howard was in some sense speaking for some members of the Supreme Court, the case seems never to have been docketed there, but the controversy added to interstate tensions.

In September, 1851, public sentiment in Maryland and Pennsylvania was whipped to a frenzy by the murder in Pennsylvania of Edward Gorsuch of Maryland while attempting to recapture fugitive slaves in Pennsylvania pursuant to the federal statute of 1850. Having

---

[57] This part of the story is summarized in a letter of Mar. 17, 1851, written by William E. Lehman, Jr., counsel for Alberti and Price, to E. Louis Lowe, governor of Maryland. *Maryland Letter Book, 1845–1854,*

pp. 219–23.
[58] *Debates and Proceedings of the Maryland Reform Convention to Revise the State Constitution,* II, 550.
[59] *Ibid.,* 552.
[60] *Ibid.,* 552.

procured the prescribed warrants from a United States Commissioner, Gorsuch and other members of his family sought his slaves at the home of a Negro, William Parker, at Christiana, taking with them to make the arrest Deputy Marshal Henry H. Kline. Kline was evidently a man of no great capacity for leadership in a dangerous situation, it being said of him that he was "pronounced by all parties as the most consummate coward ever seen in battle."[61] It seems that Negroes in the community had advance information that slave hunters were on their way to Parker's house, and that they had gathered in large numbers both outside and in the house, equipped with firearms and other weapons. At least two white men, Castner Hanway and Elijah Lewis, put in an appearance outside the house. They showed sympathy for the Negroes but took no direct part in violent activities. Violence broke out when Gorsuch entered the house and demanded the surrender of his slaves, and he was killed and other members of his party were injured.

Marshal Kline proved helpless. The farmers of the community refused to give aid. Finally, under the leadership of another officer, a group of some one hundred railroad workmen at Parksburg, Pennsylvania, was persuaded to help round up the rioters.[62] The prisoners, a large number of Negroes and a few white men, including Hanway and Lewis, were arraigned before a county officer, Alderman J. Franklin Reigart of Lancaster County.

Excitement in Maryland over the murder of a slaveholding citizen while pursuing his lawful rights was reflected in an almost hysterical letter from Governor Lowe to President Fillmore. Proclaiming that the people were deeply and justly exasperated, he demanded "thorough and severe retribution upon the Murderous treason recently committed." He was glad to know that "those worthy and patriotic Judges Grier and Kane have expressed the opinion that the crime amounted to treason against the Federal Government, cognizable, therefore, by the Federal Courts and punishable under the Federal Laws." This gave him confidence that justice would be done, speedily and fully. But if passion and prejudice should control the verdict of Pennsylvania juries, he trembled for the Union. Maryland would not remain in the Union one day if it became assured that the federal government could not or would not protect the rights, the liberties, and the lives of her citizens.[63]

At first there was a dispute over whether the prisoners should be

---

[61] Thomas Whitson, "The Hero of the Christiana Riot," *Lancaster County Historical Society—Historical Papers and Addresses*, 1:30, 1896.

[62] Robert J. Brent to E. Louis Lowe, Sept. 25, 1851, *Maryland Governor's Letter Book, 1845–1854*, 321.

[63] E. Louis Lowe to The President of the United States (Millard Fillmore), Sept. 15, 1851, *ibid.*, 253–55.

tried for murder in a local court—there was no question that murder had been committed—or tried for the less easily defined crime of treason in a court of the United States. Because of the abolitionist sentiment in Lancaster County it was questioned apparently whether a murder conviction could be secured in a local court. The United States Attorney for the Eastern District of Pennsylvania, J. W. Ashmead, asked that the prisoners be surrendered for trial in the federal court at Philadelphia.[64] In any event, if the crime could be officially labeled as an offense against the Union rather than merely against the state and the victim, the outraged feelings of Southerners would be more fully appeased.

On September 29, 1851, clearly with the expectation that indictments for treason would be found against the prisoners, Judge Kane delivered to the grand jury a charge on the subject in the United States Court in Philadelphia. He pointed out that "levying war" as used in the Constitution applied not merely to war formally declared but also to any combination forcibly to prevent or oppose the execution or enforcement of the Constitution or a statute. In treason, he warned, there were no mere accessories—"to instigate treason, is to commit it."[65]

Amid the excitement the impression seems to have been conveyed by Maryland newspapers that the federal judges in Pennsylvania, and particularly Justice Grier, were not sufficiently precise in bringing the crime committed within the purview of treason. Some such impression seems to have been conveyed to Chief Justice Taney by his lifelong friend, William Carmichael of the eastern shore of Maryland. Taney replied that the papers had done injustice to Judge Grier. The charge had been delivered by Judge Kane, and did not go to the length imputed to him and Judge Grier. According to the interpretation of the Chief Justice:

> He charged that it was treason if there was a design, premeditated, to prevent by force the execution of this law of the United States and an overt act in pursuance of that design, as in the case of the whiskey insurrection in Pennsylvania, and he distinguishes such a case, from a sudden outbreak to resist legal process or a public officer, and also from a design to prevent the execution upon that particular individual only, without any intention of preventing altogether and by force of arms the execution of that act of Congress.[66]

---

[64] W. U. Hensel, "The Christiana Riot and the Treason Trial of 1851," *Lancaster County Historical Society—Historical Papers and Addresses*, 15: 1, 40, 44, 1911.

[65] Charge to Grand Jury—Treason, 30 Fed. Cas. 1047, 1048 (No. 18276) (C.C.E.D. Pa. 1851).

[66] R. B. Taney to William Carmichael, Oct. 17, 1851, manuscript letter in possession of Dr. R. Carmichael Tilghman, of Baltimore, Md.

Taney added that he had not looked into the many cases cited by Judge Kane, "for I think it very probable that the case may be certified to the Supreme Court, and that I may be obliged to decide upon the question, and prefer doing so without forming a decided opinion until I hear the argument."

Hanway and Lewis were duly indicted by the federal grand jury, along with two other white men and twenty-five Negroes, the total said to be "indictment of more persons for treason than were ever before or since tried for that crime in the United States."[67] The proceedings are recorded and discussed, however, primarily in the name of Hanway. Although the proceedings took place in a federal court, Maryland officials assumed that as a matter of right they should take the lead in prosecuting the case. Maryland's attorney general, Robert J. Brent, so notified John W. Ashmead, the United States Attorney in Philadelphia. Ashmead, unwilling to surrender leadership in this dramatic and important case, told Brent he might appear in the case but that its control and management would remain with the officers of the United States government and that he himself would make the closing address to the jury for the prosecution. Brent protested, "as the official representative of the State whose Citizens have been outraged and one of them murdered on Pennsylvania soil."[68]

When Ashmead failed to reply promptly Brent wrote to Governor Lowe, Lowe wrote to the President, and Ashmead consulted his superiors in Washington. Sending a copy of his letter to Governor Lowe, Daniel Webster, then Secretary of State, told Ashmead that he was to represent the government of the United States, and that he should open the case for the government, but that Maryland counsel should be invited to make the closing address to the jury.[69] Governor Lowe, pleased with the arrangement, then employed a Pennsylvanian, United States Senator James Cooper, to serve along with Brent, saying that "Many reasons of policy, as well as propriety, looking solely to the desired result of these prosecutions, induced me to pass over the distinguished claims of the Maryland Bar, and to seek the assistance of some able advocate of our common cause, from amongst the patriotic Counsellors of your State."[70]

When counsel got together in Philadelphia it was agreed that Cooper, who was at once a Pennsylvanian, a Senator of the United

---

[67] W. U. Hensel, "The Christiana Riot and the Treason Trial of 1851," *Lancaster County Historical Society—Historical Papers and Addresses*, 15: 19, 1911.

[68] Robert J. Brent to John W. Ashmead, Oct. 18, 1851, *Maryland Governor's Letter Book, 1845–1854*, 263.

[69] Daniel Webster to John W. Ashmead, Nov. 8, 1851, *ibid.*, 265.

[70] E. Louis Lowe to James Cooper, Oct. 4, 1851, *ibid.*, 259.

States, and counsel for Maryland, should occupy the leading position for the prosecution. Thereafter the relationships seem to have been fully cooperative. The prosecution was nevertheless concerned about antislavery bias on the part of jurors. Brent found evidence of such bias in the fact that the defense accepted fifty-nine of eighty-three jurors who appeared for challenge, and noted that of these the United States rejected fifty.[71] The trial proceeded with four counsel for the prosecution and five for the defense, the latter including James M. Read, whom President Tyler had vainly nominated for a position on the Supreme Court, and Thaddeus Stevens.

As amid intense excitement the trial proceeded before a jury and Justice Grier and Judge Kane, it became increasingly clear to the judges that for a conviction of treason the evidence did not sufficiently link Hanway, the leading defendant, with a preconcerted plan for illegal action and did not sufficiently show an attack on the United States, as distinguished from a private resistance to the law, to constitute levying war against the United States. But concerned as they were about the threat to the Union resulting from resistance to law enforcement, the judges were reluctant to so charge the jury and bring about an acquittal. Justice Grier did so charge the jury, and an acquittal did result, but his long opinion constituted a diatribe against violation of the Fugitive Slave Law in general and this violation in particular. It was said that "it will never be forgotten with what vigor and venom the learned and ordinarily temperate Judge Grier, in his shrill, piping voice, hurled his anathemas."[72] He denounced "the most horrible outrage upon the laws of the country,"[73] whether the legal category be riot, treason, or murder. The fault, he said, was not merely with the perpetrators of this act or with the people of this region:

It is not in this hall of independence that meetings of infuriated fanatics and unprincipled demagogues have been held to counsel a bloody resistance to the laws of the land. It is not in this city that conventions are held denouncing the constitution, the laws, and the Bible. It is not here that the pulpit has been desecrated by seditious exhortations, teaching that theft is meritorious, murder excusable, and treason a virtue. The guilt of this foul murder rests not alone on the deluded individuals who were its immediate perpetrators, but the blood taints with even a deeper die the skirts of those who promulgate doctrines subversive of all morality and all government. This mur-

[71] Robert J. Brent to E. Louis Lowe, Dec. 22, 1851, *ibid.*, 232.
[72] W. U. Hensel, "Thaddeus Stephens as a Country Lawyer," *Lancaster County Historical Society—Historical Papers and Addresses*, 10: 274.
[73] United States v. Hanway, 26 Fed. Cas. 105, 122 (No. 15299) (C.C.E.D. Pa. 1851).

derous tragedy is but the necessary development of principles and the natural fruit from seed sown by others, whom the arm of the law cannot reach.[74]

In reporting to Governor Lowe on the charge and the verdict, Senator Cooper admitted that "the evidence of a design to obstruct and *nullify* the law was not as conclusive as it ought to have been, though it was pretty clear that the design of the prisoner and his accomplices was to obstruct its execution in this particular instance." He thought that Grier's opinion was a very able one and that it would be satisfactory to the South and to the people of Pennsylvania who did not recognize the doctrine of a "higher law" than the Constitution and laws of the country: "The Judge rebukes in the most pointed manner the criminal conduct of all those who inculcate sentiments adverse to the performance of the obligations of the Constitution and the laws."[75]

Attorney General Brent, however, was outraged by the charge, and said so to Governor Lowe in a long and bitter report. He particularly resented classification of Hanway's acts as involving merely private resistance to law rather than "a general and public resistance" to a law of the United States, which could be classified as levying war and therefore treason.[76]

Brent noted that the District Attorney of Lancaster County had demanded that the defendants be tried there for murder. But although Brent admitted that a majority of the people of that county were law-abiding and loyal citizens, he said he would be much astonished to hear that justice was vindicated at last against the efforts of sympathizers and fanatics. If justice did at last triumph, then Pennsylvania would have redeemed herself, and Maryland could once more regard her as a sister state. In the meantime he advised that Maryland take no further part in prosecuting cases in the courts of that state.[77] He seems to have been right in his prediction that in this case no convictions would take place.

Illegal activity connected with slavery continued throughout Pennsylvania, and tension continued to mount. Although the 1850 statute provided machinery for the recovery of fugitive slaves without the cooperation of state officers—except that prisons were not available for temporary detention—mounting antislavery sentiment, perhaps coupled with the tendency toward lawlessness that lurks beneath the surface of any society, made it hard for federal officers to perform their lawful

---

[74] *Ibid.*, 122–23.
[75] James Cooper to E. Louis Lowe, Dec. 11, 1851, *Maryland Governor's Letter Book, 1845–1854*, 272–73.

[76] Robert J. Brent to E. Louis Lowe, Dec. 22, 1851, *ibid.*, 339.
[77] *Ibid.*, 470.

duties. Even when United States Commissioners had issued warrants for the arrest of Negroes who had undoubtedly escaped from masters in some Southern state, the fugitives did not always surrender peaceably, and the arrests were occasions of violence and public excitement. Under the Pennsylvania statute which forbade the recapture of fugitives in such a way as to cause public tumult, state officers sometimes took action against federal deputies who, in their own terms, were merely enforcing federal law.

This type of conflict between federal and state jurisdictions occurred in 1853, when, pursuant to a warrant issued by a local magistrate in Wilkes Barre, two United States Deputy Marshals were arrested for causing a riot and making an assault on an alleged fugitive slave. A writ of habeas corpus was sued out for their release before Justice Grier in the United States Circuit Court in Philadelphia. The right of intervention was based on the Act of Congress of March 2, 1833, which had been enacted to cope with South Carolina's threat of nullification of federal revenue laws. It authorized federal judges to issue writs of habeas corpus for prisoners held by state officers when they were in custody for performance of duties under federal laws.[78] Now the measure, enacted to restrain Southern misconduct, was being employed in Southern interests.

Justice Grier heard argument in the habeas corpus case in obvious resentment of what he regarded as lawlessness on the part of state officers. The facts were in dispute. The federal deputies claimed that they had used only such force as was necessary to arrest the fugitive. State officers contended, to the contrary, that the arrest was a barbarous performance carried out in a riotous manner. Justice Grier, told that the warrant for the arrest of the deputies had been sworn out by William C. Gildersleve, whom a federal marshal characterized as "an abolitionist of Wilkes Barre," expostulated, "I will not have the officers of the United States harassed at every step in the performance of their duties by every petty magistrate who chooses to harass them, or by any unprincipled interloper who chooses to make complaints against them; for I know something of the man who makes this complaint."[79]

Grier threatened that if Gildersleve failed to make out the facts set forth in the warrant of arrest he would ask the county prosecuting

---

[78] 4 Stat. 632, 634. By means of the writ of habeas corpus, a device to be much in controversy during the Civil War period, a federal judge in the type of situation here presented directed the custodian of the prisoner to bring him before the judge at a specified time. On that occasion the judge determined the legality of the detention. If the prisoner was held by a state for violation of a state law in performance of duties laid upon him by a federal statute, the federal judge might order his release in the face of the claims of the state.

[79] The Wilkesbarre Slave Case, 16 Law Rep. 468, 469 (1853).

attorney to prosecute him for perjury. He knew that the United States had a limited authority, but where it existed it was clear and undoubted and conclusive: "If any two-penny magistrate or any unprincipled interloper can come in and cause to be arrested the officers of the United States whenever they please, it is a sad state of affairs. After the man against whom the United States warrant was issued has run away, some fellow intervenes and runs to a State Judge for his interference, and has the United States officer arrested. . . . I speak of what is daily done to thwart the United States in the exercise of their lawful authority. I will see that my officers are protected."[80]

At the application for the writ one David Paul Brown appeared along with counsel for the constable of Wilkes Barre, as amicus curiae, to oppose the granting of the writ. The petition having been granted, Brown appeared to be heard on the merits. On being asked whom he represented, he replied that he appeared for the constable. The court informed him that his duty there had already been performed, and that, as already announced, he could be heard on the merits only if he represented the governor or the attorney general or the attorney general's deputy. None of those officers having countenanced the arrest of the federal deputies, the court would not permit mere volunteers to interfere for the purpose of embroiling the state against her will. Brown, it appeared, had no such authority, but rather was employed by abolitionist organizations in Philadelphia. The case was presented by the United States Attorney, without representation from the state, and Justice Grier ordered the prisoners discharged.[81]

Though perhaps to a lesser extent than Justice Grier, Justice McLean was also involved in the decision of slave cases. In the summer of 1850, while the Great Compromise was under discussion in

---

[80] *Ibid.*, 470.

[81] *Ex parte* Jenkins, 13 Fed. Cas. 445 (No. 7258) (C.C.E.D. Pa. 1853). For the fantastic continuation of this case see further proceedings under this citation with opinions by Judge Kane. See also *Am. L. Reg.*, 3:207, 208, 1854, and *Livingston's Monthly L. Mag.*, 3: 267, 1855.

Abolitionists in Pennsylvania sometimes interfered to liberate slaves on passage through the state in the custody of their masters. A notable instance was that of Passmore Williamson, an abolitionist who aided in taking slaves from John H. Wheeler, United States Minister to Nicaragua. Wheeler, a citizen of North Carolina, was on his way from Washington to his post, taking with him three slaves. He had to stop in Philadelphia to pick up family possessions. In this interval Williamson took his slaves away. For opinions by Judge Kane in habeas corpus proceedings see United States *ex rel.* Wheeler v. Williamson, 28 Fed. Cas. 682 (No. 16725) (D.C.-E.D. Pa. 1855) and (No. 16726) (D.C.E.D. Pa. 1855). See also Williamson's Case, 26 Pa. St. (2 Casey) 9 (1855) and Williamson v. Lewis, 39 Pa. St. (3 Wright) 9 (1861). See also "Contempt of Court, Habeas Corpus," *Livingston's Monthly L. Mag.*, 3:596, 1855.

Congress, he delivered to a jury in the Circuit Court in Indiana a charge in a case involving the harboring of fugitives which resulted in a substantial award of damages to the owner.[82] Salmon P. Chase wrote that although he reposed great confidence in McLean's personal integrity, he could not sanction that decision. Furthermore, McLean was now quoted as "authority for Webster's Fugitive Slave bill." He was glad that McLean was out of the Presidential election for the ensuing term. He could not have been elected, but if he could have been, "who can say that he would have stood the test better than Webster or Fillmore."[83]

In addition to being a perennial aspirant for the Presidency, and therefore concerned about public reactions to his expressions of opinion, Justice McLean, like Justice Grier, was deeply concerned about law enforcement and the preservation of order. In 1853, in the process of deciding that a Negro who had escaped from Kentucky into Ohio and had lived there a number of years as a free man should be returned to his master, he presented an elaborate discussion of the constitutional position of slavery. He had no regrets, he said, that he had been the means of inducing the Supreme Court decision in *Groves v. Slaughter*, which had limited slavery to the jurisdiction of the states sanctioning it.[84] But the constitutional commitment to return fugitive slaves was nationwide and extended to all states and all people, even though there was no power in the federal government to force any legislative action on a state.[85]

Like Justice Grier, though under less dramatic circumstances and with less dramatic action, Justice McLean had to deal with conflicts of jurisdiction between state and federal officers. In Ohio, as in Pennsylvania, a marshal, having a warrant from a United States Commissioner, took into custody an alleged slave, ran afoul of a state court which held that the Negro was unlawfully held, and found himself in jail. On habeas corpus Justice McLean ordered the marshal released.[86] When the same marshal found himself again in state jail for a similar

---

[82] Norris v. Newton, 18 Fed Cas. 322 (No. 10307) (C.C.D. Ind. 1850).
[83] S. P. Chase to E. S. Hamlin, Aug. 22, 1850, *Annual Report of the American Historical Association for the Year 1902*, 2:219, 1903. Chase wrote to Edwin M. Stanton asking him to take a case for one D. Putnam, Jr., who was being sued for concealing a slave in violation of the Act of 1793. "I want you to become familiar with the judicial slave code of the

United States, which McLean, unfortunately, I think for his fame has so largely aided in constructing." (S. P. Chase to E. M. Stanton, July 16, 1850, Chase Papers, H.S.P.)
[84] Miller v. McQuerry, 17 Fed. Cas. 335, 337 (No. 9583) (C.C.D. Ohio 1853).
[85] *Ibid.*, 338.
[86] *Ex parte* Robinson, 20 Fed. Cas. 973 (No. 11935) (C.C.S.D. Ohio 1855).

offense he was again ordered released, this time by United States District Judge Leavitt.[87]

In New York Justice Nelson dealt with the fugitive slave issue in a long and deeply analytical charge to a grand jury. He cited the constitutional provision and the supporting federal statutes and deplored the fact that some fifteen states had enacted measures interfering in some way with the constitutional requirement. It was the sober enactment of state laws, he contended, rather than occasional riotous assemblies, that had forced the Southern states to face the question whether the Union was a blessing or a curse and whether it should be dissolved. The survival of the Union would depend on public sentiment in the free states bringing about enforcement in good faith of the measure recently enacted by Congress. If anyone believed that the Union could be preserved after a material provision of the fundamental law had been broken and thrown to the wind by one section of the country, "he is laboring under a delusion which the sooner he gets rid of the better."[88]

Later, in a grand jury charge delivered in northern New York, he called ominous attention to the forcible rescue by a large crowd of a fugitive slave from federal authorities. The rescue had taken place in the midst of local police and local authorities and after ample threats and other evidence that the attempt at rescue would be made. He demanded a grave and serious inquiry, asserting that the rescue struck at the very foundation of a government of laws and substituted in its place brute force and anarchy. No government was worth preserving that did not or could not enforce obedience to its laws.[89]

A year later a hard fought case involving this rescue was before Justice Nelson and Judge Nathan K. Hall on a motion to quash the indictment because of alleged irregularities.[90] The motion was denied, but this and other attempts to stem the tide of resistance to the return of fugitive slaves proved largely futile.

As for events in the First Judicial Circuit, Justice Woodbury, as has been noted, delivered a vigorous grand jury charge in support of

---

[87] *Ex parte* Robinson, 20 Fed. Cas. 965 (No. 11934) (C.C.S.D. Ohio 1856).

[88] Charge to Grand Jury—Fugitive Slave Law, 30 Fed. Cas. 1007, 1014 (No. 18261) (C.C.S.D. N.Y. 1851). Since Justice Nelson submitted no list of the offending statutes, or even of the fifteen states said to have en-

acted them, it is impossible to determine the scope of such state offenses as seen by him.

[89] Charge to Grand Jury—Fugitive Slave Law, 30 Fed. Cas. 1013 (No. 18262) (C.C.N.D. N.Y. 1851).

[90] United States v. Reed, 27 Fed. Cas. 727 (No. 16134) (C.C.N.D. N.Y. 1852).

the new Fugitive Slave Act immediately after its enactment. The charge did not render the measure popular or even acceptable. In February, 1851, a mob took from the courtroom and aided in the escape of a Negro, Shadrach, who had been taken there for examination before a United States Commissioner. Soon afterward, in the United States District Court in Boston, Judge Peleg Sprague demanded submission to the law as a moral duty, and called attention to the penalties of the law while differentiating the action of a temporary mob from the levying of war which constituted treason.[91] Bostonians were not impressed and soon were in the thick of a complicated fight to prevent the return of Thomas Sims to his master in Georgia, with proceedings before George T. Curtis as United States Commissioner, Justice Woodbury, and the Supreme Judicial Court of Massachusetts, with Chief Justice Lemuel Shaw as its spokesman.[92] Here Curtis, Woodbury, and Shaw held the line against abolitionist attack and in behalf of law enforcement. By the device of barricading the courthouse and ringing it with chains beneath which even the judges had to stoop to gain entrance, and the use of some hundreds of armed men as an escort to a ship in the middle of the night, they were able to send Sims on his way back to slavery.

Justice Woodbury died September 4, 1851, and on September 22 President Fillmore nominated for the vacancy Benjamin R. Curtis, whose support of the Fugitive Slave Act had become well known. His was a recess appointment. Before the Senate could act upon it Judge Sprague remitted to the Circuit Court an indictment against Robert Morris, a Boston lawyer, for aiding in the escape of the Negro Shadrach mentioned above. The issue was inflammatory and might have repercussions on confirmation of the appointment. In addition to important technical questions connected with the indictment and its transfer from the District to the Circuit Court, Justice Curtis had to face the demand of counsel that the jury be permitted not only to determine the facts but also the law of the case. A Boston jury might well find that the Fugitive Slave Act was unconstitutional, as counsel asked it to do. Justice Curtis firmly asserted that "it is the duty of the court to decide every question of law which arises in a criminal trial."[93] He had considered all the authorities cited by the defendant's counsel and others as well. He was convinced that if the question of law entered

---

[91] Charge to Grand Jury—Fugitive Slave Law, 30 Fed. Cas. 1015 (No. 18263) (D.C.D. Mass. 1851).

[92] See "The Case of Thomas Sims," Law Rep., 14:1, 1851; Sims' Case, 61 Mass. (7 Cush.) 285 (1851). For sum-

mary discussion see Leonard W. Levy, The Law of the Commonwealth and Chief Justice Shaw, 93–104.

[93] United States v. Morris, 26 Fed. Cas. 1323, 1333 (No. 15815) (C.C.D. Mass. 1851).

into the issue and formed a part of it, the jury was to be told what the law was and was bound to assume that the statement of the court was correct. In this fashion he tightly closed one of the doors through which abolitionists hoped to get around the Fugitive Slave Act. While the decision may have stirred enough abolitionist hostility to postpone briefly confirmation of Curtis' appointment, at this time the support of the South and of advocates of law enforcement was more important than that of the enemies he made. In any event, the attacks on members of the Supreme Court from various directions, which made him most uncomfortable,[94] were under way at the beginning of his judicial career and continued throughout his six years of service, probably having an effect on his decision in 1857 to return to private practice.

Antislavery violence in New England grew more intense. In May, 1854, a Negro, Anthony Burns, was brought before a United States Commissioner in Boston with the demand that his removal as the property of a Virginia claimant be authorized.[95] A mob stormed the courthouse, carried away the fugitive, and killed one of the deputy marshals. In charging a federal grand jury which met soon afterwards, Justice Curtis once more earnestly demanded enforcement of the law. The crime of murder was the responsibility of the state, but the obstruction of a federal process was a matter for the federal courts. Recognizing the fact that citizens otherwise law-abiding were attempting in good conscience to nullify one particular statute, he urged the jury not to make discriminations between one law and another. To do so would destroy liberty, which depended on the fact that ours was a government of laws and not of men. One part of the country found odious the return of fugitives from labor; another the return of fugitives from justice; and another the enforcement of tariff laws. While our government stood, all its laws must be enforced or it would become the mere tool of the strongest faction of the place and the hour.[96]

Nevertheless, in spite of the earnestness of judicial leadership, there was no successful prosecution of offenders involved in the Burns case. The one case involving an instigator which was brought in the Circuit Court was dismissed because of a defective indictment.[97]

---

[94] "It cannot be doubted that the position of the judges of the Supreme Court, at this time, is in a high degree onerous; and that while it exposes them to attack, such as no honest judiciary, in any country within my knowledge, have been subject to, they have not the consideration and support to which they are entitled." B. R. Curtis to George Ticknor, Dec. 20, 1854, *Memoir of Benjamin Robbins Curtis*, I, 175.

[95] See "The Case of Anthony Burns," *Law Rep.*, 17:181, 1854.

[96] Charge to Grand Jury, 30 Fed. Cas. 983, 985 (No. 18250) (C.C.D. Mass. 1854).

[97] United States v. Stowell, 27 Fed. Cas. 1350 (No. 16409) (C.C.D. Mass. 1854).

Since the announcement of Justice Story's opinion for the Supreme Court in *Prigg v. Pennsylvania* in 1842, that decision had been under attack by slavery people and others concerned about indiscriminate law enforcement for its holding that the states could not constitutionally act on their own initiative or aid the federal government in the return of fugitive slaves. About the time of that decision Richard Eells was indicted and convicted before Judge Stephen A. Douglas in a Circuit Court in Illinois and fined four hundred dollars for violating a state statute forbidding the secreting of slaves. In 1843 the Illinois Supreme Court upheld the decision by a divided vote. Justice James Shields, who wrote the opinion of the court, thought Justice Story's reasoning as to the exclusiveness of the power of Congress "not entirely conclusive." He thought Chief Justice Taney's concurring opinion "more consonant with that nice and delicate principle, which must be applied to the adjustment of the boundaries of jurisdiction between the state and federal governments."[98]

The case was taken to the Supreme Court on writ of error, but it followed such a leisurely course that it was nine years before a decision came down. The record and a written argument for Eells were filed in September, 1845. An argument for Illinois was filed in February, 1846. Eells died and the case was continued from term to term until December, 1851, when Salmon P. Chase, now a United States Senator in Washington and always interested in slavery questions, took the case and brought about substitution of the name of the executor, Thomas Moore. The case was argued still another year later by Chase for Moore and for Illinois by another United States Senator, James Shields, who had written the opinion of the Illinois Supreme Court in 1843.

Whether because Chase relied in his oral argument on a brief previously submitted by another counsel rather than one of his own, or because of the Reporter's bias against abolitionists and the abolitionist cause, Benjamin C. Howard made no report of Chase's position beyond saying that it rested on the decision in the *Prigg* case that all state legislation upon the subject of fugitive slaves was void. He quoted at length from the argument of Shields, however, to the effect that in the exercise of its police powers a state could protect itself against undesirable immigration: "Negroes have been and continue to be regarded as constituting a vagabond population; and to prevent their influx into the State, restrictive laws have been from time to time passed."[99] Here he was able to rely on Justice Barbour's statement in *New York v. Miln* about the use of the police power to exclude paupers and vagabonds

---

[98] Eells v. Illinois, 5 Ill. (4 Scammon) 498, 511 (1843).

[99] Moore v. Illinois, 14 How. 13, 15, (1852).

and to quote Justice Story in the *Prigg* case that that decision was not intended to interfere with the police powers of the states.

On December 21, 1852, Justice Grier, speaking for all members of the Court except Justice McLean, devitalized the relevant part of the *Prigg* decision by accepting the Shields argument. The restriction on state laws in the *Prigg* decision was treated as dealing only with state laws interfering with the recovery of fugitive slaves; the part holding that the states could not even aid in the process was ignored. Judge Ellis Lewis of Pennsylvania, who disagreed with Justice Story and agreed with Chief Justice Taney's position in the *Prigg* case, wrote to the latter that "I rejoice that my views have since been confirmed by the unanimous judgment of the Court over which you preside, in the recent case of *Moore v. The People of Illinois.*"[100]

It was too late, however, for the Moore decision to have much effect. In the decade between the two decisions such states as wished to use the *Prigg* decision as an excuse for repeal of laws aiding in the return of fugitive slaves had already done so. They were not likely to reenact such measures merely because another Supreme Court decision indicated that they could constitutionally do so. In the Northern and border states, indeed, the trend, as has been seen, was mostly the other way. With public sentiment making it harder and harder to enforce the federal statute, the states were not likely to enact new measures of their own or to be vigilant in the enforcement of old ones.

From many directions events were pushing toward an ever deepening crisis. The Compromise of 1850 had been in effect less than four years when the superficial regional harmony attributable to it gave way. The Northern states were outgrowing the Southern states in population and wealth, and the South sensed the coming struggle for power in the federal government. Abolitionist sentiment, revealed in innumerable ways but illustrated by the publication and wide sale of Harriet Beecher Stowe's highly emotional *Uncle Tom's Cabin*, whipped Southern sentiment to a mounting fury. The South felt a desperate need for slave territory and for new populations sympathetic to slavery in order to hold its position of equality in the Union and protect itself from Northern domination. It was too much to expect that politicians on either side would refrain from using the tides of sentiment in political operations.

There was more territory to be opened up, some of it in the northern part of the original Louisiana Purchase. Stephen A. Douglas, the ambitious United States Senator from Illinois, proposed setting up

---

[100] Carbon copy, Ellis Lewis to R. B. Taney, Dec. 8, 1860, Lewis Papers.

territorial governments for Kansas and Nebraska in a measure that assumed the Compromise of 1850, in leaving the determination of slavery or freedom to the peoples of the New Mexico and Utah territories, had abrogated the Missouri Compromise provisions for Louisiana Purchase lands. Abolitionists challenged this assumption and denounced the move as the violation of a sacred compact. Salmon P. Chase and Charles Sumner were the initial signers of a denunciatory appeal of independent Democrats which carried such language as:

> We arraign this bill as a gross violation of a sacred pledge; as a criminal betrayal of precious rights; as part and parcel of an atrocious plot to exclude from a vast unoccupied region immigrants from the Old World, and free laborers from our own States, and convert it into a dreary region of despotism, inhabited by masters and slaves.[101]

Douglas responded in a tearing rage at the attack made upon him,[102] and the fight was on. Over and over again members of Congress threshed the question of the validity and scope of the Missouri Compromise, the effects upon it of the Compromise of 1850, the merits and indeed the fundamental democracy of what came to be called "squatter sovereignty," and other topics which had been the subject of angry debate four years earlier. While the debate consolidated Northern abolitionist sentiment for the establishment of what was to be called the Republican Party, it met defeat on the issue at hand. A single statute provided for the organization of territorial governments for Nebraska and Kansas, with the provision that upon admission as a state in the Union each should be received with or without slavery, as its constitution at the time of admission might provide.[103]

Particularly as to Kansas, enactment of the statute brought a competitive struggle between slavery and abolitionist interests to settle the new region and determine the pattern of its government. Events in "Bloody Kansas," a story well known to history, made it seem desperately important that the nationwide controversy be settled. If Congress had had the power to exclude slavery from the region in question, and if the Missouri Compromise was an irrevocable compact, as abolitionists contended, then indeed the North had a legitimate grievance. But if Congress had never had the power to exclude slavery from the territories, then the current controversy had no legitimate grounds. It appeared that many of the slavery people were willing to entrust the question to the Supreme Court, and perhaps others more concerned

---

[101] "Shall Slavery Be Permitted in Nebraska," *Cong Globe*, 33rd Cong., 1st Sess. 281 (1854).

[102] For Douglas's speech as revised by him see *ibid.* at 275–80.
[103] 10 Stat. 277, 284.

about the stability of law and of the Union. But abolitionists looked askance at that idea. According to Horace Greeley it would mean submitting the question to five slaveholders, with three of the remaining four Justices violent proslavery men: "For one, I may say, with every respect for those Judicial dignitaries, that I would rather trust a dog with my dinner."[104] And in the meantime, moving inexorably toward a Supreme Court decision, there was the case of a then unknown Negro named Dred Scott.

---

[104] *New York Tribune*, Dec. 19, 1855.

CHAPTER XXIV

The Dred Scott Case

ALTHOUGH HORACE GREELEY did not stand alone in believing that it would make more sense to trust a dog with one's dinner than to trust the Supreme Court with the settlement of slavery questions, Southerners were coming more and more to advocate reference to the Supreme Court of matters which hitherto both they and people of the North had regarded as primarily political. Congressional discussion of this subject is relevant to an appraisal of the strategy which led the Court, in the fateful *Dred Scott* case, to risk a plunge into the depths of the slavery controversy in spite of the fact that the case could have been disposed of without comment on the major controversial issues.[1]

During the debate on the Compromise of 1850 various Southerners indicated a desire to bring slavery issues before the Court. They professed willingness to abide by the Court's decisions, whatever the decisions might be. Northerners, on the other hand, resisted this strategy. Senator Roger S. Baldwin of Connecticut, for example, denied that a great political question could be turned over to the Court. The judges, he contended, should be kept free from political agitation and from suspicion of sectional bias. Congress must first declare the law, after which the Court might be asked to determine constitutional questions.[2] Henry Clay, approaching the subject from another direction in search of compromise, leaned toward the Southern position. Because of the diversity of opinion, he argued, Congress could not settle the question. "When the question comes before the Supreme Court of the United States, that tribunal will declare what the law is."[3]

---

[1] For quotation of such material more at length see Wallace Mendelson, "Dred Scott's Case—Reconsidered," *Minn. L. Rev.*, 38:16, 1953.

[2] *Cong. Globe*, 31st Cong., 1st Sess. 1147 (1850).
[3] *Ibid.*, 1155.

XXIV: *The Dred Scott Case*

Aware that Southerners were asserting the ultimate responsibility of the Supreme Court as an excuse for urging immediate enactment of legislation favorable to the South, Senator Samuel S. Phelps of Vermont countered with a proposal for immediate adoption of the Wilmot Proviso, noting that its constitutionality could thereafter be tested before the Court. He trusted that all parties would be willing to submit the constitutional question to the Court rather than begin immediately to talk of dissolution of the Union.[4] Senator David S. Yulee of Florida seemed to fall into Phelps' trap, asserting that the South was ready to submit basic questions to the Court even in advance of legislation.[5] Sensing danger to the South in this commitment, Senator Arthur P. Butler of South Carolina rejected it by saying that whereas a year earlier the position would have been tenable, it was no longer so in light of the fact that the North now had an advantage from the organization of governments in California and New Mexico; he was now unwilling to commit fourteen sovereign states—the Southern states—to the decision of the Court.[6] Senator Jefferson Davis of Mississippi demanded that slavery be permitted to pursue its natural course, taking or not taking root in new territories depending on regional adaptability to slavery, and that the South be given the benefit of a Supreme Court decision on the constitutional question.[7] On the whole it appeared that willingness or unwillingness to submit to Court decisions depended on estimates as to what the Court was likely to do and not on deference to principles of fundamental law. In light of the vigor with which the Justices supported the Fugitive Slave Act of 1850, it seems clear that the strategy of the Southern politicians was sound.

Much the same kind of discussion took place in debates prior to enactment of the Kansas-Nebraska Act of 1854 by which the Missouri Compromise was repealed. Many Congressmen from the South, like Justice Daniel, contended that the compromise had been unconstitutional in that Congress had no power to exclude slavery from the territories. Some of them cited cases in support of the contention that the Supreme Court agreed with them,[8] arguing that once a new state was admitted to the Union it had all the privileges of the original states and could not be prevented from maintaining the institution of slavery. Complaining about the invasion of states' rights, Senator Stephen A. Douglas, a leading sponsor of the Kansas-Nebraska bill, contended that

---

[4] *Cong. Globe*, 31st Cong., 1st Sess. 95.

[5] *Ibid.*, 95–96.

[6] *Ibid.*, 96.

[7] *Ibid.*, 154.

[8] See the speech of Senator R. M. T. Hunter of Virginia, *Cong. Globe*, 33rd Cong., 1st Sess. 222–24 (1854). The cases cited were Pollard v. Hagan, 3 How. 212 (1845), Permoli v. Municipality No. 1 of the City of New Orleans, 3 How. 589 (1845), and Strader v. Graham, 10 How. 82 (1851).

Missouri had been subjected to a humiliating and unconstitutional condition in that admission was denied until the state agreed not to interfere with movement into the state of free Negroes who were citizens: "Missouri came in under a humiliating condition—a condition not imposed by the Constitution of the United States, and which destroys the principle of equality which should exist, between all the States of the Union."[9] A committee headed by Douglas which reported on the bill noted approvingly that all cases involving title to slaves and questions of personal freedom were referred to adjudication by local tribunals with right of appeal to the Supreme Court.[10]

As in 1850, the Supreme Court was discussed from many angles. Senator Albert G. Brown of Mississippi emphasized the fact that he would trust the determination of the Supreme Court only if Congress left the matter to the Court and refrained from expressing an opinion of its own: "I have too often seen the Court sustaining the intentions of Congress, to risk a decision in my favor, after Congress has decided against me. The alien and sedition laws, the bank law, the tariff law, have all been decided constitutional. And why? Not, in my opinion, because they were so, but because the Supreme Court, as a coordinate Department of the Government, was disinclined to clash with the other Departments. If this question is allowed to go before the Supreme Court, free from the influence of congressional pre-judgment, I will abide the result, though it be against me."[11] Senator Butler, while maintaining that the South had lost by governmental compromises, asserted magnanimously that there were some Northern men to whom he could appeal with confidence. He would as soon trust a Northern man when he was honest as anybody else. "I say so of the Supreme Court. I would as soon trust the northern members of the Supreme bench, who are sworn to administer the law and observe the Constitution of the United States, as I would the southern judges who sit upon it."[12]

Senator Richard Brodhead of Pennsylvania noted that there were only 350,000 slaveowners in a population of over 23,000,000. He thought free people likely to penetrate territory even south of the Missouri Compromise line and prohibit slavery where it was not consistent with the character of the soil and climate. Therefore, if the Southern states were willing to repeal the Missouri Compromise, he thought that the North should be willing too. The question whether the Constitution gave protection to slave property in Nebraska was

---

[9] *Cong. Globe*, 33rd Cong., 1st Sess. 331 (1854).

[10] S. Rep. No. 15, 33rd Cong., 1st Sess. 4 (1854).

[11] *Cong. Globe*, 33rd Cong., 1st Sess. 232 (1854).

[12] *Ibid.*, 240. See also *Cong. Globe*, 33rd Cong., 3rd Sess. 217 (1855).

"left an open question for the Supreme Court of the United States to decide."[13] Senator Robert Toombs of Georgia delivered an outraged counterblast against Charles Sumner and other Northern leaders who denounced the violation of the compact in the Missouri Compromise, charging that the compromise was unconstitutional. Seeking no support from the Supreme Court, he cast aspersions on the Court, evidently as of the Marshall period, when it had talked vaguely of the doctrine of the sovereignty of the federal government: "I attach but little importance to the political views of that tribunal. It is a safe depository of personal rights; but I believe there has been no assumption of political power by this Government which it has not vindicated and found somewhere."[14]

After the Kansas-Nebraska Act was passed the Supreme Court continued much in the eye of Congress. In discussing a proposed raise in salary for the Justices, Senator George E. Badger of North Carolina praised Chief Justice Taney as a revered judge of profound judicial knowledge with singular capacity and admirable patience: "He is a noble specimen of what the judicial character should be. Every Senator knows that he has discharged all the duties of his high office with an integrity unimpeached, with unsurpassed learning, and with a decorum, a courtesy which has never, in a single instance, been swerved from its propriety. He has labored on without complaining; he has asked nothing; but there, looking only to his country and his duty, and meeting increasing demands upon his time and strength with new exertions of energy and perseverance, he continues to preside in that high court, which is the sheet anchor of our institutions, a worthy successor of that illustrious man who immediately preceded him."[15] Senator Salmon P. Chase said he concurred cheerfully and heartily in Badger's eulogy of the Chief Justice and his associates, even though, hoping to relieve the Justices from the duty of circuit riding, he advocated reduction of the Court to a membership of six rather than nine.[16]

Senator Lewis Cass of Michigan praised the Court as an impressive and almost sublime spectacle, establishing great principles essential to private and public prosperity and to the duration of the government, whose influence was felt throughout the entire Union and whose decrees were implicitly obeyed. To him it symbolized the triumph of moral as distinguished from physical force, in sharp contrast with experience on the continent of Europe.[17] Senator William H. Seward proposed to amend a bill providing for a bust of Chief Justice John Rutledge by

---

[13] *Cong. Globe*, 33rd Cong., 1st Sess. 247.
[14] *Ibid.*, 347.

[15] *Cong. Globe*, 33rd Cong., 2nd Sess. 41 (1854).
[16] *Ibid.*, 217.
[17] *Ibid.*, 298.

providing also for a bust of Chief Justice Taney, in spite of the custom of making such gestures only after the death of the person to be portrayed. He thought the honor should be awarded while the Chief Justice was still living.[18]

The debates reveal the merging of two kinds of praise for the Supreme Court. One rested upon its substitution of law and morality for physical force and the other on partial assurance of the Southerners that the Court, if given the opportunity, would protect their vital interests. In May, 1856, while the Dred Scott decision was pending before the Court, Senator Judah P. Benjamin of Louisiana called attention to the fact that in the Kansas-Nebraska Act Congress had left the question of slavery in the territories to the people of the territories, with the right of appeal to the Supreme Court on the issue on which the nation was divided.[19] He asked rhetorically, "What man, confident of his title, ever hesitated to submit it to the Supreme Court of the United States? What man, conscious of the weakness of his pretensions, did not dread to submit those pretensions to that tribunal? Let the people of the country compare the attitude of the two sections of the Confederacy on this subject, and let them draw their own inference."[20]

Resistance to the Fugitive Slave Act of 1850 provoked further cleavages. Senator Benjamin told of widespread nullification in Ohio, Vermont, Michigan, Wisconsin, and Connecticut. He analyzed particularly a nullifying statute in Michigan, requiring state officers to use all lawful means to bring about the release of any person arrested as a fugitive slave. It provided that all persons arrested and claimed as fugitive slaves should be entitled to the benefits of the writ of habeas corpus and trial by jury—in the face of the summary procedures prescribed by the federal statute. This interference with the enforcement of federal law, Benjamin contended, marked a gross violation of the rights of owners.[21]

Some of the Northern states not only obstructed in this fashion the recovery of fugitive slaves but also prosecuted in federal courts federal officers and other persons aiding in their recovery, or entertained civil suits against them. To prevent this use of state courts, slavery interests supported a bill, reported in the Senate by Isaac Toucey of Connecticut, "To protect officers, and other persons, acting under the authority of the United States." As introduced, the bill provided for transfer from state courts to local United States Circuit Courts of suits against federal officers or other persons acting under any law of the United States if the persons involved filed petitions to that

---

[18] *Cong. Globe*, 34th Cong., 1st Sess. 365 (1856).
[19] *Ibid.*, 1093.

[20] *Ibid.*, 1094.
[21] *Cong. Globe*, 33rd Cong., 2nd Sess. 219–20 (1855).

effect, after which the trials were to proceed in the federal courts. The bill had a precedent in a statute of 1815 which provided for searches and seizures in connection with trading with the enemy in the War of 1812, and authorized collectors, naval officers, and other agents of the United States to remove to federal courts suits and prosecutions brought against them for performance of their duties under the statute.[22] Congress had passed that act in recognition of the fact that in some states, with minimal commitment to the waging of the war, the state courts might lend themselves to interference with performance of the duties of federal officers. It was common knowledge that many of the most effective nullifiers of the 1815 period were residents of New England. Another precedent, significantly not much referred to by Southerners in the debates of 1855, was the so-called Force Act of 1833, passed to prevent Southern nullification of tariff legislation and providing for removal from state to federal courts of suits or prosecutions brought against federal revenue officers for acts in performance of their duties under the federal revenue statute.[23]

The proposed statute of 1855 was drafted with an eye to protecting persons aiding in enforcement of the Fugitive Slave Act of 1850, but it was phrased in general language to apply to acts "done under any law of the United States, or under color thereof."[24] The bill, giving jurisdiction to federal courts at the expense of the states, was supported by the traditional defenders of states' rights and opposed by many traditional nationalists. Its critics in the Senate attacked it both as an encroachment on states' rights generally and as a stratagem on the part of slave power to extend its influence. It marked the third of three successive surges on the part of that power, proclaimed Senator William H. Seward of New York, the predecessors being the Fugitive Slave Act of 1850 and the Kansas-Nebraska Act. It was an innovation, a thing unknown in the laws of the country. The correct mode of procedure was that now in use—proceeding in state courts with cases arising under state laws, with right of appeal to the Supreme Court. It was not necessary in the interest of justice to take jurisdiction from state courts of original jurisdiction and give it to federal courts.[25]

In defense of the bill and of the slavery cause, Senator James A. Bayard of Delaware described the turmoil in law enforcement stirred by

---

[22] 3 Stat. 198.
[23] 4 Stat. 633.
[24] S. 675, 33rd Cong., 2nd. Sess. For the text of the bill as reported to the Senate, see *Cong. Globe*, 33rd Cong., 2nd Sess. 241 (1855). For the text as amended and passed by the Senate see the corrected draft in the Senate Papers. The only victory won by the opponents of the bill was an amendment sponsored by Salmon P. Chase limiting the bill to "any civil suit," which thereby eliminated its application to criminal cases. *Ibid.*, 212.
[25] *Ibid.*, 240–43.

resistance to the recovery of fugitive slaves. A number of states had nullified a federal law which some of the ablest state courts and most of the Supreme Court judges on circuit had found constitutional. The whole purpose of the federal judiciary, he maintained, was to decide cases in which local excitements or jealousies might prejudice the rights of citizens of other states or get in the way of persons acting under the authority of the Union. This measure had the same justification as the earlier measure which had to do with enforcement of federal revenue laws. It was therefore no innovation.[26]

Charles Sumner entered the debate with one of his blistering attacks on slavery, prophesying that enforcement of the Fugitive Slave Law would in the end be defeated. He saw a vast difference between the slaveholder and a slave-hunter, and he saw the purpose of the bill before the Senate as aid in the chase of slaves. The effort would be in vain. No legislation could accomplish the purpose. "Courts, too, may come forward and lend it their sanction. All this, too, will be in vain. I respect the learning of judges; I reverence the virtue, more the learning, by which their lives are often adorned. But nor learning nor virtue, when, with mistaken force, bent to this purpose, can avail. . . . The act cannot be upheld. Anything so entirely vile, so absolutely atrocious, would drag an angel down. Sir, it must drag down every court which in an evil hour ventures to sustain it." The states, he held, were within their rights in challenging it at every point, and the Supreme Court, in the *Prigg* case, had recognized the right of a state "to withdraw its own officers from this offensive business."[27]

The bill to transfer suits against federal officers from state courts to federal courts passed the Senate by a vote of twenty-nine to nine, with Seward, Sumner, and Salmon P. Chase among those voting in the negative.[28] The vote took place near the close of the Thirty-third Congress, however, and the House of Representatives took no action on the bill. While the right of transfer of suits against federal revenue officers from state to federal courts remained on the statute books,[29] this form of protection was not extended to federal officers generally.

Congressional debates indicate that with respect to the federal judiciary, and the Supreme Court in particular, in dealing with slavery issues there were at least three groupings. At opposite extremes, represented by Charles Sumner at one end and Robert Toombs of Georgia at the other, there was profound skepticism about entrusting final decisions to courts. The skepticism extended somewhat into the middle group as well, but nevertheless belief was growing that as to disputes which in Congress were becoming more and more intense and threaten-

---

[26] *Ibid.*, 243–44.　　[27] *Ibid.*, 245.　　[28] *Ibid.*, 246.　　[29] See 36 Stat. 1094.

ing the survival of the Union there might be some point in turning to the judiciary in the hope that it could resolve a conflict which Congress was proving unable to settle. Many Southerners hoped and expected that the judiciary would decide their way and perhaps give a security which politics could not provide. Many Northerners hoped that courts could in some way find a pattern of rightness not too different from the pattern of their own beliefs. In any event, it appeared to be only a matter of time before the irritating issue of slavery in the territories would be brought before the Supreme Court. It made its appearance in the case of Dred Scott.

It does not seem probable that the Dred Scott case was deliberately initiated for the purpose of getting a Supreme Court decision on the constitutional status of slavery in the territories. It started as but one of many routine cases dealing with the alleged right to freedom on the part of a Negro and his family who had resided for a time in free territory, and evolved in seemingly accidental fashion to become one of the critical court decisions of American history and to give to the name of an illiterate Negro a notoriety and a place in history denied to innumerable statesmen, scientists, and scholars.

The story of the Dred Scott case has been told again and again in histories, biographies, monographs, and articles. Although hitherto unused items are unearthed from time to time—some of which are presented here—the story remains much as it has been told on many occasions.[30] The author of the most extended historical monograph tells us that the original name of the slave, owned by Peter Blow, a Virginian who moved to Alabama and then back to Virginia, was merely "Sam," and not "Dred Scott," with its romantic ring and faintly ominous overtones.[31] When or why his name was changed, and why by contrast with most lowly Negroes, whether slave or free, Dred Scott was so widely referred to by his full name and not merely by his Christian name, seems not to be known.

Peter Blow died in 1832, and in 1833 Dred Scott was sold to Dr. John Emerson, a surgeon in the United States Army. Keeping Dred Scott

---

[30] Among the important accounts presenting significant materials on the early history of the case are Vincent C. Hopkins, S.J., *Dred Scott's Case*; F. H. Hodder, "Some Phases of the Dred Scott Case," *Mississippi Valley Historical Review*, 16:3, 1929; *American State Trials*, John D. Lawson, ed., XIII, 233; Charles Warren, *The Supreme Court in U.S. History*, 279;

Harry V. Jaffa, *Crisis of the House Divided*. All constitutional histories of the period deal with the case, and most biographies of contemporary statesmen. With this as with most other important experiences in the life of the Chief Justice the present author has dealt in his *Roger B. Taney*.

[31] Hopkins, *Dred Scott's Case*, 2.

with him, Dr. Emerson was stationed from 1833 to 1836 at Rock Island, Illinois. In Illinois slavery had been forbidden, first by the Ordinance of 1787 and then by the state constitution. In 1836, again taking Dred Scott with him, Dr. Emerson was transferred to Fort Snelling, in the northern part of the Louisiana Purchase, where, according to the Missouri Compromise, slavery was not to be permitted to exist. At this place Dr. Emerson purchased a Negro woman, Harriet, and with his permission Dred Scott married her—or quite possibly Dr. Emerson purchased her in order that Dred Scott might marry her. The Negroes were taken back to Missouri in 1838, and one child, Eliza, was born on the trip, on the Mississippi north of the Missouri Compromise line. Another child, Lizzie, was born in Missouri.

In 1843 Dr. Emerson died, leaving the Scotts as a part of his estate. Scott tried unsuccessfully to purchase his freedom, and then, with the aid of members of the Blow family to which he had originally belonged, brought suit to win his freedom by virtue of his temporary residence in free territory. The case was tried twice, and at the second trial Dred Scott was the victor, the trial court following a long line of Missouri decisions in holding that residence in free territory at the instigation of the owner gave the right to freedom.

But Mrs. Emerson appealed to the Missouri Supreme Court, and that court, departing from the long line of earlier decisions, voted two to one to reverse the judgment, reflecting as it did so the growing tension over slavery issues. "The courts of one State," said Judge William Scott for the majority, "do not take judicial notice of the laws of other States. They, when it is necessary to be shown what they are, must be proved like other facts. So of the laws of the United States, enacted for the mere purpose of governing a territory. These laws have no force in the States of the Union, they are local, and relate to the municipal affairs of the territory. Their effect is confined within its limits, and beyond those limits they have no more effect, in any State, than the municipal laws of one State would have in another State."[32]

Every state, said the judge, had the right to determine how far in the spirit of comity it would respect the laws of other states. No state was bound to carry into effect enactments conceived in a spirit hostile to that pervading its own laws. Since the time of Missouri decisions recognizing the freedom of slaves lawfully taken into free territory, "not only individuals but States have been possessed with a dark and fell spirit in relation to slavery, whose gratification is sought in the pursuit of measures, whose inevitable consequences must be the overthrow and destruction of our government. Under such circumstances it does not behoove the State of Missouri to show the least countenance

---

[32] Scott, a Man of Color, v. Emerson, 15 Mo. 577, 583 (1852).

to any measure which might gratify this spirit."[33] Dred Scott therefore lost his claim to freedom.

A possible step would have been to take the case to the Supreme Court on writ of error. But here the case of *Strader v. Graham*[34] stood squarely in the way, the case in which the Court had held that the status of Kentucky musicians who had visited north of the Ohio and then voluntarily returned to Kentucky was determined by Kentucky law and not by the law of any free state in which they had visited. Roswell M. Field, Dred Scott's counsel, hoped, however, to get a Supreme Court determination of the questions involved by approaching the Court from another direction. Mrs. Emerson had in the meantime moved to Massachusetts and had there been married to Dr. Calvin C. Chaffee, a man with abolitionist sympathies, leaving administration of her former husband's estate in the hands of her brother, John F. A. Sanford[35] of New York.[36] So it was that Field instituted an entirely new case by filing suit in the United States Circuit Court for Missouri before Judge Robert W. Wells.

Represented by Field, Scott on November 2, 1853, brought an action of trespass against Sanford, with respect to himself, his wife, and his children. On April 7, 1854, Sanford, represented by Hugh A. Garland, took a step which was to have repercussions throughout the entire case and throughout decades of history thereafter. He filed a plea in abatement—a term to appear again and again in the opinions of the Supreme Court, to the puzzlement of laymen[37] and seemingly to the

---

[33] *Ibid.*, 586.

[34] 10 How. 82 (1851).

[35] In the name of the case and in the official records generally Sanford is incorrectly spelled "Sandford."

[36] It is often said that for the purpose of bringing a suit in the federal court in Missouri with the necessary diversity of citizenship, and to avoid embarrassing Dr. Chaffee, a fictitious sale of Dred Scott to Sanford was arranged. See for example F. H. Hodder, "Some Phases of the Dred Scott Case," *Mississippi Valley Historical Review*, 16:7, 1929. Hopkins, *Dred Scott's Case*, 23–24, 29–30, contends that there was no evidence of such a sale since Sanford was the administrator against whom in any event the suit would be brought, Mrs. Emerson being debarred by law from serving as the administratrix of her first husband's estate by virtue of the fact that she had now entered into a second marriage. Montgomery Blair

stated that Sanford had "purchased Dred Scott and his family." *Washington National Intelligencer*, Dec. 24, 1856.

[37] A plea in abatement was one of the so-called dilatory pleas which a defendant might file in answer to the plaintiff's declaration or statement of cause of action. Its challenge was to the jurisdiction of the court, rather than to the merits of the plaintiff's cause. If this and other dilatory pleas were overruled, the defendant would then, as in the Dred Scott case, be compelled to answer the plaintiff's declaration on the merits. The answer on the merits might be in the nature of a plea in bar, a so-called peremptory plea, the device used in the Dred Scott case to demonstrate that Dred Scott had no cause of action against Sanford, or that at any rate did not have this particular cause of action—that he did not on the merits have the particular right claimed. Dis-

confusion of lawyers as far as this particular plea was concerned—a plea denying that the United States Circuit Court could take jurisdiction in the case. The ground of the plea was that Dred Scott was "not a citizen of the State of Missouri, as alleged in his declaration, because he is a negro of African descent; his ancestors were of pure African blood and were brought into this country and sold as negro slaves."[38] The implication of the plea, in other words, was that no pure-blooded Negro of African descent and the descendant of slaves could be a citizen in the sense of Article III of the Constitution, which gave jurisdiction in cases involving diversity of citizenship of the parties. If accepted it would serve as another instrument for downgrading the status of free Negroes in the United States.

Field filed a demurrer to the plea in abatement, contending that the fact of Negro blood and slave and African ancestry was not sufficient to deny citizenship. Counsel argued this question before the court, and Judge Wells sustained the demurrer and rejected the ground for denial of jurisdiction. Then, it is said, pursuant to an agreement between the parties whereby a case would be shaped for appeal to the Supreme Court, Field filed for Sanford pleas in bar of the action for trespass against the Scotts. Sanford contended that he was not guilty of trespass, that Scott was a slave whom he had a right to restrain, and that the same was true of his family.[39] On an agreed statement of facts the case was brought to trial before a jury. In a statement of which no complete record is available, Judge Wells instructed the jury that it should find a verdict for Sanford, and the jury obeyed the instruction. On May 15, 1854, an appeal was taken to the Supreme Court, the date coinciding roughly with completion of the debate on the Kansas-Nebraska Act abrogating the Missouri Compromise.

The initial difficulty of getting the case presented to the Supreme Court was one of finance. The abolitionists and the friends of the Scotts in Missouri evidently felt that they had now done their part. An interesting historical item is a twelve-page pamphlet containing the Circuit Court record in the case with a preface allegedly in the language of Dred Scott and signed with his mark, pleading for help with the case in Washington. It said in part:

---

cussed hereafter will be the disagreement among members of the Supreme Court over whether, the case in the Circuit Court having proceeded beyond disposition of the plea in abatement to a decision on the merits, an appellate court could recur to and redetermine the jurisdictional ques-

tion dealt with in connection with the plea in abatement. For explanation of the pleas here involved see Benjamin J. Shipman, *Handbook of Common-Law Pleading*, 3rd ed., Henry J. Ballantine, ed., 29–31.

[38] 13 Am. St. Trials 247–48 (1921).
[39] *Ibid.*, 248.

Last fall I brought my present freedom suit in the Circuit Court of the United States at St. Louis. The judge who tried the case read from the constitution of Illinois, made in 1818, that neither slavery nor involuntary servitude should be introduced into that State; and that any violation of this provision should effect the emancipation of the person from his obligation to service. He also read from an act of Congress passed in 1820 that in all the territory north of Missouri slavery and involuntary servitude should be forever prohibited. The judge said that according to these laws While I was in Illinois and Wisconsin I was a free man—just as good as my master—and that I had as much right to make a slave of a white man as a white man to make a slave of me. I was sorry that nobody ever told me that while I was there. Yet I was glad to have the judge talk so for I thought he would set me free. But after a little while the judge said that as soon as my master got me back this side of the line of Missouri, my right to be free was gone; and that I and my wife and children became nothing but so many pieces of property. . . . So I appealed to the Supreme Court of the United States. My case will be heard at the next term, beginning in December. I am now in the hands of the sheriff of this county. I have no money to pay anybody at Washington to speak for me. My fellow-men, can any of you help me in my day of trial?[40]

More helpful if less dramatic, Field, Scott's counsel in St. Louis, wrote to Montgomery Blair, the son of the still politically influential Francis P. Blair of Silver Spring, Maryland, and a recent resident and local judge in St. Louis who had moved to Washington in 1853, asking for his help. The case, he said, involved the much vexed question whether the removal by the master of his slave to Illinois or Wisconsin worked an absolute emancipation. If Blair or any other lawyer in Washington would bring the case to a hearing the cause of humanity might be served, and in any event it was important that the question be settled.[41] For some time the Blair family had been moving toward the abolitionist camp in spite of their Southern heritage, and they were aligning themselves with the newly established Republican Party and supporting John C. Frémont for President.

Montgomery Blair consulted Gamaliel Bailey, editor of the abolitionist and Republican *National Era* in Washington, about the financial problem. He was willing to argue the case without compensation but not to pay the court costs. Bailey replied that he would be responsible for the costs and Blair proceeded with the case. (After the case had been decided, Bailey wrote to seventy-five Republican members of Congress

---

40 *Ibid.*, 244.   41 Bernard C. Steiner, *Life of Roger Brooke Taney*, 331.

asking each to contribute two dollars toward the total costs of $154.68.[42]) In the course of the litigation Blair explained his taking the case by saying that in Missouri and generally in the Southern states every lawyer felt bound to give his services in such a case, and that therefore he had not hesitated to do so:

> As I perceived that the cause involved important issues, which might possibly be engulphed in the great political controversy then just emerging in relation to the power of Congress over the territory of the United States, I felt it my duty to seek assistance, especially as when I found arrayed against me the Senator from Missouri (Mr. Geyer) and the late Attorney General, (Mr. Johnson,) among the first men of the profession of the East and the West.[43]

For the first argument of the case, however, he had had to proceed without assistance.

The case had been on the Supreme Court docket for more than a year when it was argued by Blair against Henry S. Geyer, a former Marylander and now a United States Senator from Missouri who had managed to unseat Thomas H. Benton, a good friend of the Blairs, and also against Reverdy Johnson of Maryland. In the meantime Blair had been in consultation with Roswell Field in St. Louis about the implications of the case. Field noted the importance of the refusal of Judge Wells to hold that Negro blood and a slavery heritage necessarily debarred a Negro from citizenship and from suing as a citizen in a federal court. An important further implication was that if a Negro could bring suit on an averment of citizenship a fugitive slave might be able to demand a jury trial, with the result that sympathetic juries in the North might be expected to prevent enforcement of the Fugitive Slave Law. It was therefore important to support Judge Wells' decision on the plea in abatement.[44] It was, of course, equally important to Southerners that the decision be overthrown.

But beyond the plea in abatement was the question whether residence in free territory gave rights which could be enforced in a federal court after voluntary return to the state of enslavement, and whether, beyond that, territory could be made free by an Act of Congress such as the Missouri Compromise. Judge Wells seems to have followed *Strader v. Graham*, the case of the Negro musicians from Kentucky, in holding that the Scotts were slaves in Missouri if Missouri law so provided,

---

[42] Gamaliel Bailey to Lyman Trumbull, May 12, 1857, Trumbull Papers. A notation on the letter shows that Trumbull, at least, accepted the assessment. See Horace White, *The Life of Lyman Trumbull*, 83.

[43] Montgomery Blair's "Letter to the Editor," *Washington National Intelligencer*, Dec. 24, 1856.

[44] Hopkins, *Dred Scott's Case*, 27.

even though they had been free in free territory. The hope was that since the Dred Scott case came from a United States Circuit Court, and not from a state court as in the instance of *Strader v. Graham*, the Court would go to the merits of Dred Scott's claim and not rely merely on what the Missouri court said about Missouri law.

It is hard to tell to what extent the Supreme Court was aware of the implications or potentialities of the Dred Scott case prior to its argument. Justice McLean mentioned it in a letter to John Teesdale, an Ohio editor, in November, 1855, saying that a case would be argued which involved the right of a slaveholder to bring his slave into a free state for any purpose whatsoever. He proceeded to tell Teesdale his views with respect to slavery in the territories. The Supreme Court, he said, had decided that slavery existed only by virtue of municipal law, and was local. Since the Constitution gave Congress no power to institute slavery, and since only Congress could legislate for the territories, slavery could not exist there: "Squatter sovereignty is not a part of our Government." Although the people of a territory could decide for slavery or freedom when they became a state, the free states would populate the territories five to one as against the people of the slave states, so that new states could be expected to exclude slavery.[45] The other Justices may or may not have been similarly aware of the controversy in prospect. Justice Catron, with his instinct for things political and his knowledge of events occurring in his circuit, in which Missouri was included, might be expected to have known of it, but the records supporting his knowledge remain to be discovered.

In October, 1855, Caleb Cushing, Attorney General in the Pierce Administration, rendered an official opinion anticipating a part of the Dred Scott decision. Citing earlier Supreme Court decisions he held that the Ordinance of 1787 had no continuing weight in its own right, and reasoned further that the Missouri Compromise was null and void from the date of its enactment, apart from the fact that it had been repealed by the Kansas-Nebraska Act.[46] It is to be noted that Cushing and Chief Justice Taney thought much alike in matters of race relations.

At the time of the first argument in the case, in February, 1856, Reverdy Johnson got from the Court an allocation of three hours' time for each counsel. Blair presented a brief of only eleven pages,[47] a

---

[45] John McLean to John Teesdale, Nov. 2, 1855, "Letters of John McLean to John Teesdale," *Bibliotheca Sacra*, 56:717, 737–38, 1899.

[46] 7 Op. Att'y Gen. 571, 576 (1855).

[47] A copy of this and the later briefs presented by Blair can be found in the Blair Papers in the Library of Congress. The later briefs are preserved by the Supreme Court.

document much inferior to that presented for a second argument, and not too revealing of the presentation in Court. Senator Geyer's brief for this argument is not available. Judge Wells, to whom Blair sent a copy of his brief, characterized it as incomplete and therefore unfair to himself and the Court, and proceeded to suggest improvements.[48] At this stage the newspapers, with the exception of the *New York Tribune*, gave the case little attention, preoccupied as they were with the Presidential campaign and other political issues. At completion of the argument the *Tribune* referred to it as a most important case, involving the validity of the now repealed Missouri restriction on the right of slaveholders to hold slaves in bondage after having taken them into free states and territories. It suggested that the case was not strongly put on either side, especially on the "right" side, deploring the fact that the cause of freedom was not more adequately presented.[49]

The *Tribune*, which had in William E. Harvey a confidant of Justice McLean and in James S. Pike an observant crusader against slavery, reported a stream of rumors as the Justices deliberated on the case. It predicted at first that the Court would decide merely that the present status of the Scotts was determined by the laws of Missouri, to which they had voluntarily returned,[50] but suggested thereafter that a more extended decision might be reached.[51] The Court recessed for a month and then reassembled, and for a week the *Tribune* presented almost daily reports on the discussions in conference, giving the positions of individual Justices.[52] It is apparent that the Justices were in disagreement over whether they could reexamine the holding of Judge Wells on the plea in abatement—his refusal to deny jurisdiction on the ground that no Negro could be a citizen. If the Court decided that they could redetermine this question, and if it held that no Negro could sue as a citizen, then it was hard to see how the Court could get at the merits of the case, which involved the effects on slaves of residence in free states and in territories made free by Act of Congress. The Court was not supposed to decide cases in which it found that it had no jurisdiction.

Harvey reported on April 10 that a majority now favored jurisdiction and that an additional conference would be held to determine in what mode the judges who denied jurisdiction could give opinions on the merits. This, he said, would not prove a serious dilemma for minds sufficiently ingenious to find ways for always uniting on the slavery side of every question. The majority would hold against Dred Scott:

---

[48] Hopkins, *Dred Scott's Case*, 40.
[49] *New York Tribune*, Feb. 15, 1856.
[50] *New York Tribune*, Feb. 20, 1856.

[51] *New York Tribune*, Feb. 23, 26, 29, 1856.
[52] *New York Tribune*, Apr. 9, 10, 11, 12, 1856.

But there is such a thing as a Minority left on the Bench, notwithstanding the Court has been denounced as the "Citadel of Slavery;" and unless all the impressions are erroneous, Judge McLean will fortify these positions with an opinion that cannot fail to confound those who are prepared to repudiate the judgments of Southern courts and the practice of Southern States. Judge Curtis, it is believed, will also contribute a powerful exposition of the case, and of all the incidental questions connected with it, and Judge Grier will concur with both. Of course the South will go as a body, and probably carry Judge Nelson with them.[53]

But still the decision was delayed. A month later the *Tribune*, still watching, noted that the sectional bias of Chief Justice Taney had increased with his increasing infirmities, but wondered what might happen if Taney and other members of the Court provided vacancies which would be filled by the present Administration. It said of Justice Campbell, one of the newer Justices, that though pure and unexceptionable in his private life, he was filled with all the dogmas and mad metaphysics of Calhoun, and his best conception of the Constitution was that it was the aegis of slavery. Packing the Court in this fashion to protect executive usurpation would lead to disaster.[54]

Apart from the gossip on the case leaked by Justice McLean to the *Tribune*, we have summary accounts of how it was handled in the spring of 1856 in letters written many years later by Justices Nelson[55] and Campbell.[56] Both Justices recorded the major difficulty as that of the disposition of the plea in abatement. Both Chief Justice Taney and Justice Curtis, who were at opposite poles as far as slavery in the territories was concerned, argued warmly that the Supreme Court had a right to inquire into alleged error in Judge Wells' decision on the plea in abatement. Justices Wayne and Daniel took the same position, and Justice Nelson was inclined in the same direction. Justices McLean, Catron, Grier, and Campbell, on the other hand, in Campbell's words, "were unwavering and some denounced the plea, and denounced also the authors of the plea as unscrupulous lawyers who had been astute to frame a plea to catch an opinion upon a mooted question which the facts of the case did not call for." So it was that the Justices, dividing

---

[53] *Ibid.*

[54] *New York Tribune*, May 14, 1856.

[55] Samuel Nelson to Samuel Tyler, May 13, 1871, Samuel Tyler, *Memoir of Roger Brooke Taney*, 385.

[56] John A. Campbell to Samuel Tyler, Nov. 24, 1870, *ibid.*, 382–84, and typewritten copy, John A. Campbell to George Ticknor Curtis, Oct. 30, 1879, Groner Papers. The letter was written in part to correct an alleged misstatement about the case in *Memoir of Benjamin Robbins Curtis*, I, 201–05.

one way with respect to slavery in the territories, divided in another way, or in other ways, with respect to the technicalities of judicial procedure.

When the matter was put to a vote, a bare majority decided to discuss the plea. Before any Justice was designated to write the opinion of the Court, Justice Nelson, the least assured of any of the members, asked for a reargument on the questions on which the Court was divided. There was no dissent, and the case went over to the succeeding term. The record does not show how important may have been the factor that postponement of the decision would project it beyond the forthcoming Presidential election and prevent use of it by either side in the campaign.

Postponement of the decision deprived the newly organized Republican Party of what might have been grist for campaign oratory in its first Presidential campaign. In particular, it deprived Justice McLean of the opportunity to deliver a ringing dissent, with a denunciation of the Kansas-Nebraska Act, as a means of getting the nomination. While the Court was discussing the Dred Scott case in conference McLean, working and being promoted for the nomination, was receiving and answering letters about the issues of the day. One of his letters was refurbished and published as if in reply to a request for a statement of his views from Joseph C. Hornblower, formerly chief justice of New Jersey and now the head of the New Jersey delegation to the Republican National Convention. Therein McLean explained that he could not properly say anything about the Dred Scott case, since it had been held over for reargument. He nevertheless expressed deep concern about dwindling public interest in the guarantee of liberty provided by the Ordinance of 1787, which extended even to a challenge of its constitutionality. He deplored the repeal of the Missouri Compromise and the resulting struggle over slavery in Kansas, and urged the admission of Kansas as a free state. Then, in the somber mood in which he was wont to express himself he added:

> No intelligent observer can fail to see that the tendency of our institutions is now rapidly downward, and all history and experience show that no free Government with such tendencies was ever arrested in its declining career without a revolution, either by a peaceful change of its policy and rulers or by the bloody arbitrament of the sword.[57]

---

[57] John McLean to Joseph C. Hornblower, June 6, 1856, *Washington National Intelligencer*, June 16, 1856. The letter was widely reprinted in other newspapers as well. See Francis P. Weisenburger, *The Life of John McLean*, 147–49.

McLean and his friends failed in their efforts to get the nomination for him, leaving him in even darker despair about the survival of our institutions. Of the three men nominated, he had little confidence in Frémont, the Republican, or Buchanan, the Democrat, or Fillmore, the nominee of a composite of old-line Whigs and the Southern wing of the American or "Know-Nothing" Party.[58]

From his vacation spot at Fauquier White Sulphur Springs in Virginia, Chief Justice Taney watched the campaign with similar foreboding. He read daily three newspapers, the *Baltimore Sun*, the *Baltimore Republican*, and the *Washington Star*. As a Catholic he viewed with alarm the grim prospect that the Know-Nothings might carry both Baltimore and the state of Maryland. He was more and more doubtful of Buchanan's success for the Presidency. He thought the appearance of division between the Northern and Southern Know-Nothings a mere subterfuge. The primary concern of all of them was to obtain possession of the government.

As far as the South was concerned, Taney wrote to his son-in-law, J. Mason Campbell, it mattered little whether Frémont or Fillmore was chosen. His reasons for this opinion show how far the thinking of the Chief Justice had gone by the summer of 1856 with respect to the sectional controversy. The letter has significance even though he considered his thoughts imperfectly expressed and had "half a mind to burn this letter" when it was written. His despair derived from the belief that whether the next President was Frémont or Fillmore, the Union would not be dissolved. In either event the Constitution would be trampled underfoot. The Union would be one of power (the North) and weakness (the South), like the Union of England and Ireland, or Russia and Poland.

"But how can the southern states divide, with any hope of success," he asked rhetorically, "when in almost every one of them there is a strong and powerful party, acting in concert with the Northern Know Nothings, and willing to hold power from the North, if they may be enabled thereby, to obtain the honors and offices of the general government, and domineer in their own states." He therefore concluded that "The South is doomed to sink to a state of inferiority, and the power of the North will be exercised to gratify their cupidity and their evil passions, without the slightest regard to the principles of the Constitution."

There were many bold and brave men in the South, he continued, who had no vassal feeling toward the North. They would prob-

---

[58] See *Diary of Orville Hickman Browning*, Theodore Calvin Pease, ed., I, 244–46.

ably take up arms if Frémont was elected, or if further aggressions were made under Fillmore. But how effective could they be with a powerful enemy in their midst? "I grieve over this condition of things, but it is my deliberate opinion that the South is doomed, and that nothing but a firm united action, nearly unanimous in every state can check Northern insult and Northern aggression. But it seems this cannot be."[59]

Taney's predicted oppression of the South by the next Administration was warded off by the election of James Buchanan, who had once undergone an agony of decision over whether to remain in President Polk's cabinet or accept an appointment to the Supreme Court. Immediately after the election Justice Grier, who had received the Supreme Court position which Buchanan might have had, sent his congratulations along with his recommendation for an appointment to office. Grier was pleased that their state, Pennsylvania, in supporting Buchanan had stood firmly between the Northern fanatics and Southern secessionists.[60] Buchanan's reply indicated his belief that the election constituted a mandate to save the Union by repression of the abolitionist movement: "The great object of my administration will be if possible to destroy the dangerous slavery agitation and thus to restore peace to our distracted country."[61]

The outgoing President, Franklin Pierce, read Buchanan's mandate in similar fashion. The voice of the people, he said in his message to Congress on December 2, 1856, had rebuked the attempt of a portion of the states, by sectional organization and movement, to usurp control of the government.[62] He condemned the North for a "long series of acts of indirect aggression." He denounced the Missouri Compromise, saying that it was originally acquiesced in rather than approved by the states of the Union, and that the North had virtually abrogated it by refusing to extend the line westward through the territory later acquired from Mexico. Without citing cases, though perhaps with unofficial reports of judicial attitudes in the Dred Scott case in mind, he asserted that "In a long series of decisions, on the fullest argument and after the most deliberate consideration, the Supreme Court of the United States had finally determined [the unconstitutionality of the Missouri Compromise] in every form under which the question could arise, whether as affecting public or private rights—in questions of the

---

[59] R. B. Taney to J. Mason Campbell, Oct. 2, 1856.

[60] R. C. Grier to James Buchanan, Nov. 10, 1856, Buchanan Papers.

[61] Draft, James Buchanan to R. C.

Grier, Nov. 14, 1856, Buchanan Papers.

[62] J. D. Richardson, *A Compilation of the Messages and Papers of the Presidents*, I, 399.

public domain, of religion, of navigation, and of servitude."[63] All that the repeal had done was to "relieve the statute book of an objectionable enactment, unconstitutional in effect and injurious in terms to a large portion of the States."[64]

Once the proslavery Democrats had won a victory over abolition through the election of Buchanan and the defeat of the Republican Party, it remained to be seen what the Supreme Court would do about slavery issues when it heard the reargument of the Dred Scott case. The reargument was ordered on May 12, 1856. Two days later, in deciding a case having nothing to do with slavery directly, *Pease v. Peck*,[65] the Court, speaking through Justice Grier, kept open for the Dred Scott decision the question of the obligation of the Supreme Court to follow the decision of the highest state court in matters of state law. It did so by saying that while in general the Supreme Court followed the settled pattern of a state's decisions, it was not bound to do so when that pattern was not consistent. Thereby, since Missouri had changed the pattern of its own decisions with respect to the status of Negroes who had lawfully resided in free territory, the Court freed itself from the obligation to follow its course in *Strader v. Graham*, where it had said that it must defer to the decisions of the state court.[66]

In directing reargument of the case, Chief Justice Taney framed for counsel two questions for special attention. They had to do with whether the Supreme Court could go behind the Circuit Court decision on the merits of the case to the question of the jurisdiction of the Circuit Court, and with the question whether Dred Scott was a citizen of Missouri in light of the facts appearing in the record.[67] Montgomery Blair, stirred to more intense effort by the attention the case had received from the Court and part of the press, seems to have gone off to his wife's former home and the home of his late father-in-law, Justice Levi Woodbury, for further development of his argument. He took time out to write to his father that Frémont would surely be elected President and to discuss measures to be taken thereafter. He believed:

> steps ought to be taken to facilitate the pacification of the country and put down effectually the design of the nullifiers to produce the rupture of the Union which they have threatened in that event. My own idea is that nullification is odious to the whole people of the

---

[63] *Ibid.*, 401.
[64] *Ibid.*, 403.
[65] 18 How. 595 (1856).
[66] For the statement of this matter, which went from Justice Grier to Edwin N. Dickerson and from him to George T. Curtis, see *Memoir of B. R. Curtis*, I, 210.
[67] *Ibid.*, 205.

North and South. Calhoun you know never had any party which was able to command a single state, till by the treachery of Polk and Pierce he was given the command of the Democratic organization and the controul of the general government.[68]

Later, having seen Frémont in New York, he wrote to his father that he had seen "the next President."[69] Doomed to disappointment in the election, he had to concentrate on the argument of the case, which was scheduled to begin December 15, 1856, shortly after President Pierce's diatribe against the Republicans and the Missouri Compromise.

Blair opened the case before the Supreme Court, again opposing Geyer and Reverdy Johnson. For some reason he filed two briefs, in addition to that filed at the preceding term.[70] Blair contended that the question involved in the plea in abatement, whether any Negro could sue in a federal court as a citizen, could not be reached on appeal since the Circuit Court had decided it and proceeded to the merits of the case. If the Supreme Court decided to look into the question, he provided a mass of evidence to show that Negroes had exercised rights of citizenship in many states, and that the laws of Missouri in some instances made reference to them as citizens. Going to the merits, he contended that residence in Illinois and in the area covered by the Missouri Compromise—which he argued Congress had had the power to enact—gave Dred Scott his freedom, a freedom he had a right to sue to recover when reenslaved in Missouri, and that the child born on the waters of the Upper Mississippi was free by right of birth.

Senator Geyer, for Sanford, took the opposite side on these questions. He argued that citizens were either natives or naturalized. Among the natives, citizenship was denied to the children of ambassadors, Indians, and persons of color: "True blacks are not citizens."[71] A slave, who is not a citizen, cannot become such by virtue of a deed of manumission.[72] The Illinois law did not convey freedom but merely forbade slavery in that state. As for the Missouri Compromise, the con-

---

[68] Montgomery Blair to F. P. Blair, Sept. 12, 1856, Blair-Lee Papers.

[69] Montgomery Blair to F. P. Blair, Sept. 16, 1856, Blair-Lee Papers.

[70] One of these briefs, running to eight pages, had subheadings as follows: On the Power of Congress Over the Territories; Rules and Regulations; Exercise of Power for Sixty Years; References to Acts of Congress on the Subject of Slavery in the Territories; Authorities; Cases Decided; The Question not Judicial; Equality of the States and Rights of Property. The headings of the longer brief, running to forty pages, included the following: Statement of Case; Whether Question of Jurisdiction is Waived by Answering Over; Citizenship; On the Question of Emancipation; Case of the Oldest Child; Question of Residence; *Ex parte* Grace, Commonwealth vs. Aves, Mahoney vs. Ashton; Comity; On the Power of Congress Over the Territories.

[71] Geyer's brief, 5.

[72] *Ibid.*, 5–6.

stitutional power of Congress to make rules and regulations respecting the territory or other property belonging to the United States referred only to the disposition of land, and did not authorize the establishment of territorial governments. Such power of government as Congress possessed derived from necessity, and necessity did not extend to the prohibition of slavery.[73] The *New York Tribune* said of Geyer that "his efforts did not meet the public expectation, though decorous in tone and sentiment."[74]

In reporting for the *Tribune* Reverdy Johnson's argument for Sanford, James S. Pike proclaimed emotionally that "the temper of the slaveholder within the bar and without the bar, to say nothing of the bench, is roused to crush the rebellious spirit of the North, and a decision of the Supreme Court is eagerly desired which will promote this end."[75] Pike had a measure of admiration for Johnson's strategy and a profound dislike for some of his content. He quoted Johnson as saying that "Slavery promises to exist through all time, so far as human vision can discover," and it might turn out that "the extension of Slavery on the continent is the only thing which will preserve the constitutional freedom we now enjoy." George T. Curtis, whom only three days before the beginning of the argument Blair had persuaded to aid him in the case,[76] said in later years of Johnson's argument that it was "the forcible presentation of the southern view of our Constitution, in respect to the relation to slavery to the territories and of the territories to the nation, that contributed more than anything else to bring about the decision that was made in the case."[77]

Curtis, the brother of Justice Curtis, came into the case for the final hour of the argument, saying that he did so only from an impulse of duty in the light of Blair's inability to get assistant counsel.[78] In conciliatory fashion he argued for the power of Congress to govern territories and to deal with slavery therein. The *Tribune* praised his performance, saying that "There was a force of manner and phrase in his effort which gave additional emphasis to his reasoning, together with a frank admission of views upon collateral points apparently somewhat in conflict with the great principle upon which the others

---

[73] *Ibid.*, 11–12.

[74] *New York Tribune*, Dec. 17, 1856.

[75] *New York Tribune*, Dec. 20, 1856. Because there has been some controversy as to which reporter presented particular *Tribune* dispatches, it is to be noted that this one is signed "J.S.P."

[76] See *Memoir of B. R. Curtis*, I, 240–41.

[77] From a memorial speech after Johnson's death, quoted, Bernard C. Steiner, *Life of Reverdy Johnson*, 38. Johnson's brief, if there was one, is not preserved in the Supreme Court records.

[78] Argument of George T. Curtis, Esq., in the Case of Dred Scott, Plaintiff in Error, vs. John F. A. Sanford 40 (1856).

rested, that commended it strongly in particular quarters."[79] Justice Curtis reported that his brother had conducted himself in a manner exceedingly creditable to himself and to the bar of New England, and quoted Justice Catron as saying that his was the best argument on a question of constitutional law he had heard in the Court.[80] Alexander H. Stephens, zealous Georgia patriot, sent a copy of the speech to his brother, characterizing it as "chaste, eloquent, forensic," but not convincing.[81]

For several weeks after the conclusion of the argument of the case on December 18, 1856, little was known about the Court's consideration of it. There were fragments of inquiry and of prediction. Justice Catron, after hearing Geyer argue that an army officer under orders had no legal residence at the posts to which he was sent, wrote to Jefferson Davis, Secretary of War, to ask whether the articles of war had anything to say about the carrying of servants into the Indian country north of Missouri. Davis replied that there was no special provision on the subject but that officers had been permitted to take servants there at government expense.[82]

Newspaper comment on the case as involved in national politics led Blair to publish an account of the case and of the mode of his involvement as counsel in the *Washington National Intelligencer*.[83] The *New York Herald* remarked editorially that although officially this was a case involving "the freedom of a nigger of the name of Dred Scott," the people were beginning to say that the United States Supreme Court was on trial before the people and the Constitution.[84] On January 1, 1857, Alexander H. Stephens reported that from what he heard sub rosa the decision would be according to his own opinions on every point. He had heard that the judges were writing seriatim opinions, with an elaborate one by the Chief Justice.[85] Although the case had not at this time been officially discussed, the Stephens report was to be astonishingly close to correct.

On January 3, 1857, the *Tribune* reported that there was no truth in the statement that the case had been decided and that all the

---

[79] *New York Tribune*, Dec. 19, 1856.

[80] *Memoir of B. R. Curtis*, I, 194. The several letters of Catron and Grier cited in this sequence are printed in Philip Auchampaugh and James Buchanan, "The Court and the Dred Scott Case," *Tennessee Historical Magazine*, 9:231, 234–38, 1926.

[81] Richard Malcolm Johnston and William Hand Browne, *Life of Alexander H. Stephens*, 318 (rev. ed., 1884).

[82] Hopkins, *Dred Scott's Case*, 52.

[83] *Washington National Intelligencer*, Dec. 24, 1856.

[84] *New York Herald*, Dec. 25, 1856.

[85] Johnston and Browne, *Life of Stephens*, 318.

Court but two had pronounced against the constitutionality of the Missouri Compromise. The case had not yet been even considered.[86] A few days later the *Tribune* remarked that it would be better that the decision come quickly if it was to be proslavery. Congress, the Court, and the executive would then take their place as confederates in the work of extending slavery. "When a political scheme is to be furthered by judicial action, it is a thousand times better that the action should be taken boldly, when every man, woman and child have their eyes upon the Court, than to have that body steal silently and stealthily in the same direction. Judicial tyranny is hard enough to resist under any circumstances, for it comes in the guise of impartiality and with the prestige of fairness. If the Court is to take a political bias, and give a political decision, then let us by all means have it distinctly and now. The public mind is in a condition to receive it with the contempt it merits."[87]

On January 3 a tragedy occurred in the home of Justice Daniel which further delayed official consideration of the Dred Scott case. His young wife's sleeve caught fire from a candle and she was burned to death, almost in his presence.[88] As late as February 27 Justice Curtis wrote that Justice Daniel had been prostrated by what was a sufficient cause, and the rest of the judges, in the language of Justice Story, had been kept at the oar "double tides."[89]

But governmental activities had to proceed in spite of personal tragedies. On January 27 James Buchanan came to Washington to plan for the beginning of his Administration and for the inauguration which was to take place on March 4.[90] On February 3, hoping in his inaugural address to show that the three branches of the government were solidly together in their efforts to suppress abolitionist agitation, he wrote to Justice Catron to ask whether the Dred Scott case would be decided before the inaugural date. Catron replied that it rested entirely with the Chief Justice to move in the matter, and that thus far Taney had said nothing to him about it. When the case had been before the judges in conference on two occasions a year earlier the positions of all the Justices were thereafter stated in the *New York Tribune*. Such publication was a gross breach of confidence on the part of a member of the Court, and that circumstance had "made the Chief more wary than usual." Catron thought the death of Mrs. Daniel no longer an occasion for delay, remarking that "that Judge will surely deliver his own opinion in the case, *at length*." He thought Buchanan was entitled to know when

---

[86] *New York Tribune*, Jan. 3, 1857.
[87] *New York Tribune*, Jan. 9, 1857.
[88] *New York Tribune*, Jan. 5, 13, 23, 1857; *Washington National Intelligencer*, Jan. 6, 7, 1857.

[89] *Memoir of R. B. Curtis*, I, 193–94.
[90] *New York Tribune*, Jan. 28, 1857.

the case would be decided and promised to find out and let him know.[91] A *Tribune* dispatch of February 8 from Justice McLean's friend Harvey announced that Justice Daniel was about to resume his seat and that the Court would at once proceed with consultations in the Missouri case and deliver the decision "within a few weeks."[92]

On February 10 Catron wrote to Buchanan that the Dred Scott case would be decided on the following Saturday, four days hence, but that the positions of the Justices would be highly diverse and would settle nothing.[93] From Catron's letter it is apparent that the Justices were already engaged in informal discussion of the case, whether or not it had been taken up in official conference. Catron proceeded to give Buchanan his own opinion on the power of Congress to govern territories. He thought it clear that Congress had this power, as the Court had held a few years earlier with respect to the government of California prior to the giving of statehood.[94] To hold otherwise after a practice of sixty-eight years would shock all the substantial lawyers of the country and subject the Supreme Court to ridicule. That such was the intention of the framers of the Constitution he found the same evidence as stated by George T. Curtis' speech printed in the *National Intelligencer* of January 1, 1857.

But here Catron, who had advocated extension of the Missouri Compromise westward to the Pacific for the government of territory acquired from Mexico, departed from the position of Curtis and perhaps in part from his own earlier position. He contended that the Missouri Compromise had been void, not for want of power in Congress to govern territories but because of violation of the third article of the Treaty of 1803 by which Louisiana had been acquired. He read that article as guaranteeing preservation of all rights of property in the newly acquired territory, including the right to hold slaves. Perhaps taking his cue from the abolitionists who denounced repeal of the Missouri Compromise as violation of a sacred compact, he treated the compact in the treaty as restrictive upon statutes which Congress might subsequently enact.[95]

Developments in Supreme Court conference proved somewhat more favorable to Buchanan than Catron had predicted. On February 19 he wrote to Buchanan that the case had been before the Court

---

[91] John Catron to James Buchanan, Feb. 6, 1857, Buchanan Papers.

[92] *New York Tribune*, Feb. 13, 1857.

[93] John Catron to James Buchanan, Feb. 10, 1857, Buchanan Papers.

[94] See Cross v. Harrison, 16 How. 164 (1854).

[95] The position subsequently taken by the Supreme Court is that although the provisions of treaties conveying private rights are part of the supreme law of the land, they are subject to subsequent modification or repeal by Act of Congress. See Edye v. Robertson, 112 U.S. 580 (1884).

several times since the preceding Saturday, and he outlined a statement which he thought Buchanan might safely make in his inaugural address:

> That the question involving the constitutionality of the Missouri Compromise line is presented to the appropriate tribunal to decide; to wit, To the Supreme Court of the United States. It is due to its high and independent character to suppose, that it will decide and settle a controversy which has so long and seriously agitated[96] the country, and which *must* ultimately be decided by the Supreme Court. And until the case now before it, (on two arguments) presenting the direct question, is disposed of, I would deem it improper to express any opinion on the subject.[97]

Catron then predicted that a majority of his brethren would be forced to give the desired decision by two dissentients, whom he did not then identify but who were probably known to Buchanan as McLean and Curtis. Catron urged Buchanan to drop Justice Grier a line saying how necessary it was and how good the opportunity was to settle the agitation one way or the other. He argued that Grier ought not to occupy so doubtful a ground as that whatever the status of Dred Scott while out of Missouri, his present status was determined by Missouri law, in terms of which he was not free. "He has no doubt about the question on the main contest, but has been persuaded to take the smooth handle for the sake of repose."

On Saturday, February 21, Buchanan wrote Catron another prodding note, and on Monday, February 23, Catron replied, saying that he concurred in the necessity Buchanan was under. He had been trying to get the opinion delivered before March 3, the day preceding the inauguration. Most of the Justices were ready, or nearly ready. "I want Grier *speeded*. I think whatever you wish may be accomplished."[98]

Although both Justices Catron and Grier seem to have thought of themselves as close to the President-elect, the correspondence suggests that neither knew of the other's letters to and from Buchanan and that Buchanan protected the confidence of each. On February 23 Justice Grier received and replied to a letter from Buchanan, which he showed to "our mutual friends Judge Wayne and the Chief Justice," but apparently not to Catron. In view of Justice Campbell's statement many years later that he had not the slightest information of any connection between Buchanan and the discussions of the Court or the confer-

---

[96] Catron spelled the word "aggitated."

[97] John Catron to James Buchanan, Feb. 19, 1857, Buchanan Papers.

[98] John Catron to James Buchanan, Feb. 23, 1857, Buchanan Papers.

ence,[99] we may suspect that such knowledge was limited to the four Justices mentioned above.

Grier told Buchanan that he and Wayne and Taney appreciated and concurred in his views as to the desirability of having an expression of the Court's opinion on the troublesome question of slavery in the territories, and proceeded to give him in confidence the history of the case with the probable result. When after the delay occasioned by Justice Daniel's absence the Court took up the case, the majority were of the opinion that the question of the right of a Negro to sue in a federal court did not arise on the pleadings, and that it was necessary to give an opinion on the merits. A majority decided that the merits could be dealt with without passing on the constitutionality of the Missouri Compromise—by holding that the status of Dred Scott was a matter of Missouri law in terms of which he had been found to be a slave—and Justice Nelson had been designated to write the opinion of the Court.

But then, said Justice Grier, it appeared that the two dissenting Justices intended to discuss the troublesome points. Those who held different opinions felt obligated to express their counteropinions, Justices Nelson and Grier remaining silent. A majority of the judges, including all from south of the Mason-Dixon line, agreed in the result but not in reasons. Being anxious that latitude should not appear to divide the Court, Grier, after discussion with Taney, agreed to concur with him, and Grier and Wayne would try to get Daniel, Campbell, and Catron to do the same. But Grier expected some extreme views from some of his Southern brethren. Six if not seven Justices (Nelson perhaps remaining neutral) would hold the Missouri Compromise unconstitutional. Those in communication with Buchanan would not let the others know of the cause of their anxiety to produce this effect and, "though contrary to our usual practice we have thought it due to you to state to you in candor and confidence the real state of the matter." Grier closed with a postscript saying the weak state of the Chief Justice's health would postpone the announcement of the decision until about March 6, two days after the inauguration.[100]

Although differing in some particulars, the Grier statement of events is not fundamentally inconsistent with two statements made many years later by Justice Campbell. According to Campbell, a major-

---

[99] J. A. Campbell to Samuel Tyler, Nov. 24, 1870, Tyler, *Memoir of R. B. Taney*, 384.

[100] R. C. Grier to James Buchanan, Feb. 23, 1857, Buchanan Papers. Except for the postscript the letter is reprinted, Warren, *The Supreme Court in U.S. History*, II, 295–97. This letter and Catron's letter of Feb. 19, 1857, are printed in *Works of James Buchanan*, John Bassett Moore, ed., X, 106–08.

ity of five decided that the plea in abatement was not a part of the case, having been joined by Justice Nelson since the time of the first argument, leaving Chief Justice Taney and Justices Wayne, Daniel, and Curtis in the minority on this point. On the merits Justice Nelson was designated to write the opinion of the Court to the effect that Dred Scott was not a citizen and not entitled to sue.

Justice Nelson wrote his opinion, and Justice Campbell heard him read it in his room, but it was not read at conference and not adopted as the opinion of the Court. At this point Justice Wayne made a motion that the Court refrain from limiting its decision in this fashion, but pass also upon the constitutional question with respect to slavery in the territories. According to Campbell his reasons were that the case had twice been thoroughly argued, that the public had been led to expect a decision on the question, and that the Court would be condemned as failing to do its duty if it avoided the question. Thereupon, without debate although with the disapproval of some, the scope of the decision was broadened and the Chief Justice took upon himself the writing of the opinion of the Court.[101]

While the case was before the Court, rumblings of discontent continued among abolitionists in spite of their recent defeat in the Presidential election. In the House of Representatives Benjamin Stanton, an Ohio Whig, introduced a resolution aimed at reorganization of judicial circuits so as to equalize population and business and "give to all sections of the Confederacy their equal and just representation in the Supreme Court of the United States." Stanton said that if the Supreme Court decided that Dred Scott was a slave he would not resist execution of the judgment, but he would not recognize the principle of the decision if another case arose. He presented statistics to show that by far the larger portion of the population was in the Northern circuits, and noted that five states were not in any circuit. He contended that if the Supreme Court was to aid in settling the great questions which agitated the country its organization was a matter of paramount importance. If the present sectional emphasis was maintained, the Court could not command the confidence and respect and obedience of the free states.

---

[101] Typewritten copy, John A. Campbell to George T. Curtis, Oct. 30, 1879, Groner Papers. See also the briefer statement, Nov. 24, 1870, Tyler, *Memoir of R. B. Taney*, 382–84. According to George T. Curtis, who presumably got his information from Justice Curtis, Justice Wayne told his brethren of his belief that it would be possible to quiet agitation on the constitutional questions by dealing with them in this case. He thereafter regarded it as a matter of great good fortune for his own section of the country that he had been able to bring the Court to this decision. *Memoir of B. R. Curtis*, I, 206.

Nothing could do more to weaken the Union than a decision that Congress could not legislate with respect to slavery in the territories.[102]

But the South was for the time being the victor, and the Supreme Court had many times faced threats that did not culminate in disaster. On this occasion, instead of heeding portents of disaster it listened, probably with pleased and complacent attention, to a farewell address by the retiring Attorney General, Caleb Cushing, in which he portrayed the position of the Court in the Union and lauded the sitting members. Cushing, as has been recounted, had given an official opinion to the effect that the Missouri Compromise was unconstitutional, and there is an implication that the Chief Justice discussed the matter with him before writing his Dred Scott opinion.[103] In view of this possibility and the stream of gossip about the forthcoming decision it may well be that, when on the morning of March 4, just preceding the hour for the inaugural ceremony, he addressed the Court as "the incarnate mind of the political body of the nation," he knew approximately what the fateful decision was to be. Heartily agreeing with the sentiments of the Court, he could well say:

> In the complex institutions of our country you are the pivot point upon which the rights and liberties of all, Government and people alike, turn; or rather you are the central light of constitutional wisdom around which they perpetually revolve. Long may this Court retain the confidence of our country as the great conservators, not of the private peace only, but of the sanctity and integrity of the Constitution.[104]

Soothed by oratorical flattery, on this deceptively Indian summer–like winter day, the Court adjourned to participate in the inauguration of James Buchanan as President. On the platform in front of the Capitol Chief Justice Taney found himself in the presence of President James Pierce and President-elect James Buchanan. In view of the

---

[102] Cong. Globe, 34th Cong., 3rd Sess. 300 (1857). See also Warren, The Supreme Court in U.S. History, II, 289–90.

[103] Claude M. Fuess, The Life of Caleb Cushing, II, 154. As indicative of the stream of rumor about the forthcoming decision, on March 2 John M. Read of Philadelphia wrote to Charles Sumner that "We are to hear two speeches, I learn by report in a day or two, the inaugural of our new President, and the inaugural of the Supreme Court announcing the commencement of a new administration of the Laws and a new construction of the Constitution of the United States. A majority of nine men directly interested in the question they are to decide, are to overturn the settled policy of the country and a uniform construction of nearly seventy years." John M. Read to Charles Sumner, Mar. 2, 1857, Sumner Papers.

[104] Washington National Intelligencer, Mar. 5, 1857.

audience, he spoke with Buchanan on some matter, perhaps having to do with the ceremony. The exchange was unfortunate, for out of it grew the naive story that here, on the inaugural platform, the Chief Justice whispered to Buchanan a statement as to what the Dred Scott decision was to be, enabling him to modify his prepared address to make political use of the information. The story was naive because it ignored the fact that if Taney or any of the other Justices wanted to give information to Buchanan they could do so much more effectively by letter—as we now know that Catron and Grier had done—or by some other private means than by whispered conversation in front of a vast audience.

In his inaugural address Buchanan attributed his election to the inherent love for the Constitution and the Union which still animated the hearts of the American people and noted happily that the tumult of the election period had given way to submission and calm. He thought it a "happy conception" that Congress, in the Kansas-Nebraska Act, had in the light of American democratic principles left to the people of the territories the determination of slavery issues. A difference of opinion had arisen as to the point at which the decision should be made. That he thought a matter of little importance. "Besides," he continued, inserting a paraphrase of the statement Catron had drafted for him, "it is a judicial question, which legitimately belongs to the Supreme Court of the United States, before whom it is now pending, and will, it is understood, be speedily and finally settled. To this decision, in common with all good citizens, I shall cheerfully submit. . . ."[105]

By and large the people who attend an inauguration are there to enjoy the fruits of a political victory rather than to criticize the performance of the new leader, and this was doubtless true of those who heard Buchanan's address. Yet representatives of his critics were also there. Yes, Buchanan might "cheerfully submit," scoffed the *New York Tribune*, "to whatever the five slaveholders and two or three doughfaces on the bench of the Supreme Court may be ready to utter on the subject; but not one man who really desires the triumph of Freedom over Slavery in the Territories will do so. We may be constrained to obey as law whatever that tribunal shall put forth; but, happily, this is a country in which the people make both the laws and judges, and they will try their strength on the issues here presented."[106] From this example of abolitionist preparation for the decision of the Court it

---

[105] *Messages and Papers of the Presidents*, V, 431.

[106] *New York Tribune*, Mar. 5, 1857.

should have been evident that both the Court and the new Administration were in for rough treatment when the decision was announced.

On March 5 it was reported that Chief Justice Taney had remained at home to work on his opinion in the Dred Scott case.[107] On Friday, March 6, "in a tone of voice almost inaudible," which brought derisive comment from the *Tribune*, he read his opinion in Court,[108] taking about two hours,[109] and Nelson and Catron read their concurring opinions. On the following day, Saturday, Justices McLean and Curtis read their dissenting opinions, taking some five hours.[110] It was said that Justices Campbell and Daniel had withheld their concurring opinions until after the dissenting opinions were read, "with the view of rebutting their arguments,"[111] but when McLean and Curtis had finished it was as if everybody had had enough of Dred Scott and his case, and Justices Wayne, Grier, Campbell, and Daniel submitted their opinions without reading them in Court.[112]

All of the nine Justices expressed themselves on some of the points involved, although Justice Grier's opinion was only one paragraph. The nine opinions, running to two hundred forty pages in Howard's *Reports*, defy full analysis in any treatment short of a monograph. Many of the points discussed, however, already made in connection with the arguments of counsel, can be treated in a summary of the opinion of Chief Justice Taney, called by him and by other majority Justices the opinion of the Court, with incidental mention of other opinions.

In one respect the Taney opinion was simple. It reached the conclusion that the Circuit Court should have dismissed the case for want of jurisdiction. In no other element can simplicity be found, although much of the opinion is written with the deceptive clarity characteristic of Taney's literary style. In getting at the subject of jurisdiction, Taney dealt first with the plea in abatement as presented to Judge Wells, and with the highly technical question whether, Judge Wells having rejected the plea and the case having been heard on its merits, the Supreme Court could now inquire into the validity of his decision on the plea. Supported by Justices Wayne and Daniel, who agreed with him on substantive matters, and by Justice Curtis, who did not, Taney asserted that error with respect to the plea was error on the face of the record, and could be dealt with by the Supreme Court.

---

[107] *New York Tribune*, Mar. 6, 1857.

[108] *New York Tribune*, Mar. 9, 1857.

[109] *Washington Evening Star*, Mar. 7, 1857.

[110] *New York Tribune*, Mar. 9, 1857.

[111] *New York Tribune*, Mar. 7, 1857.

[112] *New York Tribune*, Mar. 9, 1857.

XXIV: *The Dred Scott Case*

Having concluded that the Supreme Court could reexamine this original jurisdictional question, Taney could now deal with a question broader than that of the status merely of Dred Scott and his family, the question whether any Negro with slave ancestors could be a citizen of the United States within the meaning of the clause of the Constitution which gave jurisdiction to federal courts in cases involving diversity of citizenship. The question was important for those who favored, and also for those who opposed, relegating free Negroes to a position not merely of second-class citizenship but of no citizenship at all.

It is a fact well known to history that Taney held here, as he had held as Attorney General in 1832,[113] that Negroes had always been regarded in the United States as a degraded people never having had the status of citizens. At the time of the adoption of the Constitution they were considered as "a subordinate and inferior class of beings, who had been subjugated by the dominant race, and whether emancipated or not, yet remained subject to their authority, and had no rights or privileges but such as those who held the power and the government might choose to grant them."[114]

Taney admitted that for its own local purposes a state might confer such rights of citizenship as it chose. But as he saw it the concept of citizenship as employed in the federal Constitution did not change. No state could introduce any person or class of persons into the nation-wide political family. He emphasized the fact that at the time of the adoption of the Constitution Negroes had been "regarded as beings of an inferior order; and altogether unfit to associate with the white race, either in social or political relations; and so far inferior, that they had no rights which the white man was bound to respect."[115] That is, since at the time of the adoption of the Constitution the Negro "had no rights which the white man was bound to respect," he now had no *constitutional* rights which the white man was bound to respect, however much sentiments with respect to the status of Negroes might have changed in some quarters. The text of the Constitution remained unaltered and "it must be construed now as it was understood at the time of its adoption."[116] Since Dred Scott was a Negro and a Negro could not sue as a citizen in a federal court, the case in the Circuit Court should have been dismissed for want of jurisdiction.

But, said Taney, even if the plea in abatement were not before the Supreme Court, as some of its members believed, the question of jurisdiction of the Circuit Court was elsewhere presented on the face of

---

[113] For discussion and quotations illustrating Taney's position in 1832 see Carl B. Swisher, *Roger B. Taney*, 151–55.

[114] Dred Scott v. Sandford, 19 How. 393, 404–05 (1857).
[115] *Ibid.*, 407.
[116] *Ibid.*, 426.

the record, since the bill of exceptions by which the case was brought to the Supreme Court showed that Dred Scott and his family were born slaves, and that their claim to citizenship, the basis of their right to sue in a federal court, derived from temporary residence outside Missouri, which was followed by return thereto. If the Circuit Court had erred on jurisdictional grounds here as well as in connection with the plea in abatement, the Supreme Court was empowered to look into this error as well.

Taney thereby cleared the ground for determining whether Dred Scott had become free by virtue of his residence in territory covered by the Missouri Compromise. It was the judgment of the Court, he said, that the constitutional grant to Congress of power to "make all needful rules and regulations respecting the territory and other property belonging to the United States" applied only to property owned at the time when the Constitution was adopted.[117] The power to govern territory subsequently acquired was based on the power to acquire territory, which was in turn derived from other provisions of the Constitution.[118]

The Constitution did not authorize the establishment and maintenance of colonies. Territory could be acquired only for the purpose of being developed into states. The people in the territories, therefore, could not be governed merely as colonists. Territory was acquired for the benefit of all the people, and the people governed must be protected in all their constitutional rights. Here Taney brought forward one of the constitutional guarantees hitherto not much relied on by the Supreme Court, the provision of the Fifth Amendment that life, liberty, or property should not be taken without due process of law. True, the Court had discussed the clause a year earlier in a unanimous opinion by Justice Curtis in connection with a strictly procedural matter, and had said that the article was a restraint on the legislative as well as the executive and judicial powers of the government.[119] The case seems not to have been cited in the briefs of counsel in the Dred Scott case, however, nor were the relevant state cases dealing with the interpretation of due process clauses in state constitutions.[120] Chief Justice Taney's due process comment in the Dred Scott case, not developed as to its implications, marked on this point a beginning for the development of doctrine. His statement was that "an Act of Congress which

[117] *Ibid.*, 432.
[118] *Ibid.*, 442–46.
[119] Murray v. Hoboken Land & Improvement Co., 18 How. 272 (1856).
[120] See Edward S. Corwin, "The Doctrine of Due Process of Law Before the Civil War," *Harv. L. Rev.*, 24:366, 60, 1911, especially discussion of Wynehamer v. the People, 13 N.Y. 378 (1856), pp. 467–71. For briefer treatment see the same author's *The Doctrine of Judicial Review*, 144–54.

deprives a citizen of the United States of his liberty and property, merely because he came himself or brought his property into a particular Territory of the United States, and who had committed no offense against the laws, could hardly be dignified with the name of due process of law."[121]

Taney therefore reached the conclusion that the Missouri Compromise had been unconstitutional, that Dred Scott could not have become a free man by virtue of it, and therefore could not have become a citizen of a state with the right to sue in a federal court. He dealt more briefly with the effect of residence in the state of Illinois. Here he noted that in Missouri Dred Scott had been found to be a slave, and that the Supreme Court was bound to follow the settled decisions of the state courts. He found adequate record of settledness of decision to justify accepting the decision of the Missouri Supreme Court with respect to Dred Scott. So here again it was determined that Dred Scott was a slave and hence could not be a citizen, and, not being a citizen, could not sue in a federal court on the basis of diversity of citizenship.

Any decision that requires the expression of eight concurring or dissenting opinions reflects a great deal of turmoil among members of the Court. Taking the opinions in the order of their arrangement by the Reporter, it is to be noted that the two-and-a-half-page opinion by Justice Wayne is the only one that defers completely to the opinion of the Chief Justice. Wayne indicated that he had written an opinion in full but had decided not to read it or file it. He therefore limited himself to saying some things in support of the opinion of the Court.[122] He emphasized that the opinion had his "unqualified assent."[123]

Justice Nelson filed as his personal opinion the draft written earlier as the opinion of the Court. He left the plea in abatement undiscussed, and contended that the Supreme Court must follow the law of Missouri, after the pattern of *Strader v. Graham*, finding Missouri's recent decisions sufficiently settled to determine the pattern. Instead of dismissing the case for want of jurisdiction in the Circuit Court, he

---

[121] 19 How. 450.

[122] A recent commentator suggests that the lost Wayne opinion is to be found in the opinion of the Court. Making a syntactical analysis of opinions definitely written by Taney, Wayne, and Grier, he finds sufficient family resemblances with portions of this opinion of the Court to lead him to believe that Taney, feeble at the time, adopted as his own some of the writing of his colleagues. John Charles Hogan, "The Role of Chief Justice Taney in the Decision of the Dred

Scott Case," *Case & Com.*, 58:3, 1953. While it may well be that Taney borrowed some materials from his brethren, as judges often do, the parallels here with his earlier writings, and particularly with what he had had to say about Negro citizenship, together with our knowledge of his work on the opinion after it had been announced (as discussed in the following chapter), lead to doubt as to the extent of the borrowing.

[123] 19 How. 456.

favored affirming the decision of that court, with the same effect as far as Dred Scott was concerned. He left the Missouri Compromise undiscussed.

In a single paragraph Justice Grier concurred with Taney's opinion on the constitutionality of the Missouri Compromise. He seemed to disagree as to the plea in abatement, but he said it made no difference whether the judgment was affirmed or whether the case was dismissed for want of jurisdiction.

Justice Daniel wrote a completely independent opinion making the same major points as the Chief Justice. The extremity of his position is indicated by his defense of property in slaves: "the only private property which the Constitution has imposed as a direct obligation both on the States and the Federal Government to protect and enforce, is the property of the master in his slave; no other right of property is placed by the Constitution upon the same high ground, nor shielded by a similar guaranty."[124]

Justice Campbell concurred in the judgment announced by the Chief Justice, but did not say that he concurred in the opinion. In his own opinion he left the plea in abatement undiscussed in order to go directly to the matter of the effect of Dred Scott's residence in what was allegedly free territory. He showed a commitment to slavery hardly less fervent than that of Justice Daniel. He ignored the position he had taken nine years earlier in a private letter to John C. Calhoun, where he had said that "As an incident to this power [the power to govern territory] I think that Congress may decide what shall be held and enjoyed as property in that territory, and that persons should not be held as property."[125] Now he found the sentiment general if not universal that Congress had no such power.[126] He inveighed against claims for "boundless power" in Congress over the territories, and contended that the federal government must recognize as property whatever the constitutions and laws of the states determined to be property.[127]

Justice Catron flatly disagreed with the Chief Justice that the plea in abatement was before the Supreme Court, and went directly to the merits of the case. Ignoring, as mentioned above, his earlier advocacy of the extension of the Missouri Compromise line to the Pacific Coast, he found in a loosely written opinion that the Compromise was invalid as a violation of the treaty by which the territory had been acquired, and also that it violated "the most leading feature of the Constitution—a feature on which the Union depends, and which secures

[124] Ibid., 490.
[125] J. A. Campbell to John C. Calhoun, Mar. 1, 1848, "Correspondence Addressed to John C. Calhoun, 1837–1849," Annual Report of the American Historical Association for the Year 1929, 431, 1930.
[126] 19 How. 508.
[127] Ibid., 515.

to the respective states and their citizens an entire equality of rights, privileges and immunities."[128] Andrew Jackson Donelson had said of Catron that he had been for many years a wire-puller for Buchanan.[129] It is hard to explain his Dred Scott opinion on any other ground.

From this diversity of opinions among the majority of the Court we now come to the two dissenting opinions, by Justices McLean and Curtis. Despite their linkage in this case, the two men were very different. McLean's orientation all his life had been political, with the Presidency as his ultimate goal; he was accustomed to appraising political parties and political issues in the light of his personal aspirations. Curtis had little interest in party politics, and did not like the involvement of one of his colleagues in major partisan activity.[130] Although a nationalist of the Webster school, Curtis was a jurist rather than a political partisan. McLean had long had leanings toward abolitionism, and his drift toward the Republican Party, that had a check upon slavery as one of its principal tenets, took him still further in that direction. Curtis had been suspect among the abolitionists of his region, with good reason, and had been regarded by the South as one of the most trustworthy Northerners where the preservation of Southern rights was concerned. In all probability both sides missed the point that he was primarily a lawyer, concerned with things legal, and not a partisan of any interest.[131] It was perhaps inevitable that the differences between the two men should result in vast differences between their opinions.

In his thirty-six-page dissenting opinion McLean lashed out at the opinion of the Court, as a politician and a moralist no less than a judge. Unlike Curtis he denied that the plea in abatement was before the Supreme Court, and remarked that the Court's method of handling the jurisdictional question was "rather a sharp practice, and one which seldom, if ever, occurs."[132] For him the most appropriate definition of "citizen" was "a freeman." A slave who was American-born automatically became a citizen upon becoming free.[133] Whereas to members of the majority slave property was a kind of absolute, to McLean it existed only where positively authorized.[134] Whereas Taney had talked about the degraded status of the Negro race, McLean talked

---

[128] *Ibid.*, 529.
[129] William Ernest Smith, *The Francis Preston Blair Family in Politics*, I, 368.
[130] In 1856 Curtis had said that "Judge McLean hopes, I think, to be a candidate for the office [of President]. He would be a good President, but I am not willing to have a judge in that most trying position of being a candidate for this great office." Curtis, *Memoir of B. R. Curtis*, I, 180.
[131] Among the sources see Richard H. Leach, "Justice Curtis and the Dred Scott Case," *Essex Institute Historical Collections*, 94:37, 1958.
[132] 19 How. 531.
[133] *Ibid.*, 531.
[134] *Ibid.*, 535.

about "the degradation of negro slavery in our country."[135] Needless to say, McLean found the Missouri Compromise within the constitutional powers of Congress, and found that because of the unsettledness of the course of decisions in the Missouri courts the Supreme Court was not bound to follow the latest decisions of that state's court with respect to former Missouri slaves brought back there from free territory.

Justice Curtis delivered a dissenting opinion of sixty-seven pages which bore throughout the stamp of the disciplined jurist. Avoiding plays to the political galleries and jabs at his colleagues, he produced a document which as a work of legal craftsmanship was enormously persuasive, and impressive to those who refused to be persuaded. While pursuing his own line of argument, he took the position taken by Taney that the plea in abatement was before the Supreme Court. But he rejected the grounds of the plea, and adduced an enormous amount of evidence to show that at the time of the adoption of the Constitution Negroes had been regarded as citizens in a number of the states. It was this devastating display of evidence, derived largely from state court decisions and statutes, that goaded Chief Justice Taney to make the additions to the opinion of the Court which are discussed hereafter. While considering citizenship oftentimes in terms of voting, he emphasized that citizenship under the Constitution was "not dependent on the possession of any particular political or even of all civil rights."[136] As he saw it, "citizens" as referred to in the Constitution were to be identified with "free inhabitants."[137] Free colored people were citizens in some of the states, were therefore citizens of the United States, and were therefore entitled to sue and be sued in federal courts. The plea to the jurisdiction was therefore bad, and the Circuit Court had correctly overruled it.[138]

Like McLean, Curtis found that Congress, which had enacted the Ordinance of 1787 and the later supporting statute, and which had outlawed the slave trade and otherwise restricted slavery, had the power to enact the Missouri Compromise. He noted the point, often made, that "Slavery being contrary to natural right, is created only by municipal law."[139] There was no denial of due process in a prohibition against bringing slaves into a territory.[140] As for the status of a former slave brought from a free area back into a slave state, he thought the Supreme Court should follow the rules of international law and decide independently, after the fashion of its decision in *Swift v. Tyson*,[141] and not follow the erroneous decision of the Supreme Court of Mis-

---

[135] *Ibid.*, 537.
[136] *Ibid.*, 583.
[137] *Ibid.*, 584.
[138] *Ibid.*, 588.

[139] *Ibid.*, 624.
[140] *Ibid.*, 626–27.
[141] *Ibid.*, 603.

souri.[142] As for the effect of the Treaty of 1803 in protecting slavery in the Louisiana Purchase, he thought the treaty did not protect it, and argued that even if it did the Court would not invalidate a later statute because of the conflict. The matter would be not a judicial issue but a political and legislative question.[143]

Justice Benjamin Cardozo encouraged those who now read the Curtis dissenting opinion to "feel after the cooling time of the better part of a century the glow and fire of a faith that was content to bide its hour. The prophet and the martyr do not see the hooting throng.

---

[142] It will be noted that Justice McLean got rid of the precedent of *Strader v. Graham*, on which Justice Nelson fully relied and on which other majority Justices relied in part, by the expedient of largely rejecting it; and Justice Curtis got rid of it by the expedient of largely ignoring it. It is true that the *Strader* case and the Dred Scott case were by no means parallel. In the former the Supreme Court had merely held that it had no jurisdiction to review a decision in a Kentucky case wherein Strader had been sued for a penalty for aiding slaves to escape from Kentucky and wherein Strader had defended himself on the ground that the Negroes aided were no longer slaves since they had previously resided in Ohio with the consent of their master and had attained their freedom by virtue of such residence. The Supreme Court had answered the contention by holding that whatever the status of the Negroes had been while residing in Ohio, in Kentucky their status was determined by Kentucky law. The case did not involve a suit for freedom on the part of a colored person claimed as a slave. Yet the principle asserted seemed immediately relevant, unless residence in a territory governed by the United States had in a state into which a colored person might go a potency not given by residence merely in a free state, so that Dred Scott not only gained freedom from residence in free territory but retained that freedom and the right to sue as a citizen on his return to Missouri where Missouri courts held him to be a slave. Some writers have apparently so contended, as for example Harry V. Jaffa, *Crisis of the House Divided*, 443–44. But there is difficulty here, since at the time of the decision residence in a territory of the United States, as distinguished from residence in a state different from that of the opposing party, did not give the right of suing in a federal court by virtue of diversity of citizenship. *New Orleans v. Winter*, 1 Wheat. 91 (1816). In order to be able to sue in a federal court in Missouri by virtue of diversity of citizenship after his return there, Dred Scott would have had to possess in Missouri rights in addition to those he might have possessed in a territory of the United States—and in the face of Missouri law, which as currently interpreted by Missouri courts held that he was not a citizen of Missouri at all.

In short, Dred Scott's venture into a lower federal court in an attempt to get on appeal a Supreme Court decision on the merits of his claim to freedom was, strictly as a matter of law and quite apart from matters of politics, somewhat of a desperate venture taken as a last and unpromising resort. The two dissenting Justices were able to find jurisdiction only by ignoring the right of a state to determine citizenship within its borders. As of a decade later it was, of course, one of the purposes of the Fourteenth Amendment to make national citizenship dominant—which Justice Curtis came close to assuming in the Dred Scott case—and to guarantee state citizenship to all national citizens residing within a given state. The difficulty was that as of 1857 there was no Fourteenth Amendment to give national citizenship this dominance.

[143] 19 How. 629–30.

Their eyes are fixed on the eternities."[144] If this encomium was deserved it was because the opinion was written out of the warp and woof of the law itself and not because it was intended to ignite a crusade for freedom. As a performance in juristic art it resembled that of the Chief Justice himself, who, recognizing the artist in his specialized field, reacted strongly to the probing of his own vulnerability. In terms of judicial craftsmanship the performances of Taney and Curtis, among the nine highly diverse performances, were outstanding. The clash of judicial strategists had its repercussions through much of the aftermath of the decision, which is now to be traced.

---

[144] Benjamin N. Cardozo, *Law as Literature*, 36.

CHAPTER XXV

Aftermath of the Scott Case

WRITING IN 1927, in the interlude between his own two periods of service on the Supreme Court, Charles Evans Hughes referred to the Dred Scott decision as one of three notable instances in which the Court suffered severely from self-inflicted wounds.[1] The decision has gone down in history as a major disaster, degrading the Court and the Constitution and precipitating the Civil War, after which it was necessary to amend the Constitution to eliminate important legal effects of the decision and incorporate the results of the military victory.

It is clear that in writing their seven opinions in the case the majority Justices had no awareness they were doing anything of the kind. The Court was, of course, fully aware of the fact that decisions on important public issues had an impact on public affairs. To limit the generalization to the Taney Court alone, that Court, with full awareness of what it was doing, had handed down at its very first term three decisions shaping the trend of events with respect to contracts, commerce, and banking. It had taken similar steps at other terms. In the area of race relations Justice Story, speaking for the majority of the Court in the *Prigg* case, had taken the Court a long way into the realm of critical political issues by holding that the states not only need not but under the Constitution could not aid the federal government in the return of fugitive slaves. That decision won a great deal of disapproval, especially in the South, but it was regarded as an aberration from the normal course of judicial performance and not a typical abuse.

In the Dred Scott case the majority, although fully aware of the

---

[1] Charles Evans Hughes, *The Supreme Court of the United States*, 50. The other two decisions so characterized were Hepburn v. Griswald, 8 Wall. 603 (1870) and Pollock v. Farmers' Loan & Trust Co., 157 U.S. 429, 601 (1895).

631

political implications of their work, persuaded themselves that they were resting their decision on the original meaning of the Constitution, and that in doing so they were merely performing their duty. The Constitution, said Chief Justice Taney, "must be construed now as it was understood at the time of its adoption. It is not only the same in words, but the same in meaning . . . ; and as long as it continues in its present form, it speaks not only in the same words, but with the same meaning and intent with which it spoke when it came from the hands of its framers, and was voted on and adopted by the people of the United States."[2] Their decision was intended to stand as a rebuke to the abolitionists who had been attempting to distort the constitutional pattern. The majority were clearly convinced of the correctness of their position, for all its political implications. They assumed that it would be generally accepted, in spite of the opinions of two dissenting colleagues. On the political side, the Buchanan victory at the polls had seemed to support their position. They were no doubt sufficiently practical-minded, furthermore, to note that the adjournment of Congress until the following December left the Court less vulnerable to effective attack than it would have been had Congress remained in session, and that the adjournment of the Court until the same time also removed the Court somewhat from the focus of attention. Since the executive branch was more than pleased with the decision, they had nothing to worry about over an eight-month span, at the end of which they assumed the decision would be a matter of established history.

To most thoughtful persons such an estimate would have seemed reasonable, and, indeed, it was partly fulfilled. The full flood of attacks on the decision did not come immediately after its announcement. It required the reassembling of Congress, which encountered unexpectedly difficult problems connected with the admission of Kansas, and political events such as the 1858 Senatorial campaign in Illinois, to bring the case to the fore. Yet from the beginning there were grounds for anxiety. The two dissenting opinions provided not merely the abolitionist press but also thoughtful Northern people generally with devastating criticism of the use of law and history in the decision. Chief Justice Taney may well have been appalled at the presentation in the opinion of Justice Curtis of a mass of evidence that in many states at the time of the adoption of the Constitution Negroes had the status of citizens. This opinion was not only read in Court but was immediately given to a Boston newspaper for publication and extra copies were distributed widely throughout the country. Because of his desire to keep the Court out of the arena of debate, Chief Justice Taney might in any event have withheld the opinion of the Court from newspaper publication.

---

[2] Dred Scott v. Sandford, 19 How. 393, 426 (1857).

Because of the refutation of his historical argument he did withhold it for some weeks while adding to it some eighteen pages of historical documentation of his position.[3] Incidental correction of opinions after announcement in Court had been the custom, but such drastic revision was unusual.[4] It led to an interchange between the Chief Justice and Justice Curtis which has become an important segment of the history of the case.

At some early stage Curtis heard that Taney was revising the opinion of the Court. His first step was to tell William Thomas Carroll, the Clerk of the Court, by letter from Pittsfield, Massachusetts, that although he had filed his own opinion he did not desire to have it printed for any purpose until he had had an opportunity to correct it.[5] Quite possibly he expected to see the revised opinion of the Chief Justice in some newspaper and then would plan his own revision in terms of it. On April 2, not having seen it, he wrote to Carroll asking for a copy. Carroll replied that the opinion had not yet been printed, nor had the opinions of Curtis, Wayne, Nelson, and McLean. He hoped to have the opinions in about ten days. In the meantime the Chief Justice had instructed him not to furnish a copy of his opinion to anyone.[6] Taney gave this instruction at first orally, and then on April 6, as he was getting ready to leave Washington, he put it into writing over his signature and got two supporting signatures from Justices Wayne and Daniel, the only Justices still in Washington. The record does not show why these two had remained at the capital for a month instead of leaving for work on their circuits. Taney was apparently writhing under comparisons made by the abolitionist press between his opinion and that of Curtis. The *New York Tribune* had said, for example, that "If epithets and denunciation could sink a judicial body, the Supreme Court of the United States would never be heard of again," and "Chief Justice Taney's opinion was long, elaborate, and jesuitical. His arguments were based on gross historical falsehoods and bald assumptions, and went the whole length of the extreme southern doctrine."[7] "Alas! that the character of the Supreme Court of the United States, as an impartial judicial body, has gone! It has abdicated its just functions and descended into the political arena. It has sullied its ermine; it has dragged and polluted its garments in the filth of Pro-Slavery politics. . . . That Court, instead of planting itself upon the immutable principles

---

[3] *Memoir of B. R. Curtis*, I, 229. This estimate of added pages is made in notes left by Justice Curtis.

[4] For criticism of drastic changes in opinions made after reading in conference or in Court see the opinion of Justice Daniel in the Passenger Cases, 7 How. 283, 515–16 (1849).

[5] B. R. Curtis to William T. Carroll, Mar. 14, 1857, Clerk's Files.

[6] Curtis, *Memoir of B. R. Curtis*, I, 212.

[7] *New York Tribune*, Mar. 7, 1857.

of justice and righteousness, has chosen to go upon a temporary and decaying foundation. . . . And while Judge Curtis did not tell his legal Chief that he was guilty of falsehood, he did say that his statements would be received with *very great surprise*, and proceeded to demonstrate his gross historical misrepresentations."[8]

From these sample comments it is possible to understand what Taney meant when he said in his order to the Clerk that "the opinion of the court has been greatly misunderstood and grossly misrepresented in publications in the newspapers." Neither the Court nor any member of the majority, having a proper regard for their judicial positions, could become involved in attempts to correct newspaper statements. The opinion must be allowed to speak for itself and not be subjected to garbling and mutilation and false glosses. It must make its appearance only through the appropriate medium, that is, the Reporter of the Court.[9]

Curtis, unable to believe that denial of access to the opinion was intended for a member of the Court, wrote to Carroll again, but was told that the Chief Justice so intended. He then wrote to Taney. Taney, holding Circuit Court in Baltimore, waited ten days to reply, and then, on April 28, wrote a long letter enclosing a copy of the order. His letter reflected the bitterness he felt at the public reception of the decision, the political use of opinions, and the resulting distortion. He scolded Curtis for the newspaper publication of his dissenting opinion and implied that Curtis wanted a copy of the opinion of the Court only to make political use of it.[10] Clearly the Chief Justice, now eighty years of age, for two years a widower and continuously in poor health, had lost with respect to the Dred Scott decision the judicial calm for which he was publicly noted.

Curtis replied May 13 with an even longer letter justifying his conduct and his claim to a copy of the opinion of the Court, and citing the rule of the Court which required the filing of the opinion with the Clerk. He had supposed that in this country it was impossible to keep from the public what passed in an open court of justice, especially in the Supreme Court, where the interests of the nation were discussed. He had asked for the opinion because of the report that it had been revised and materially altered.[11]

On June 11 Taney replied in a letter running to five pages of fine script deploring the necessity of continuing the "unpleasant correspondence." He denied that any fact or principle of law stated in the opinion had been changed, and contended that the only changes had been in

---

[8] *New York Tribune*, Mar. 10, 1857. For elaborate quotations from newspapers and other sources see Warren, *Supreme Court in U.S. History*, 302–19 and Beveridge, *Abraham Lincoln*, II, 486–99.

[9] Curtis, *Memoir of B. R. Curtis*, I, 216.

[10] *Ibid.*, 214–15.

[11] *Ibid.*, 217–20.

the nature of support for facts and principles which he had not thought required such support until he had heard Curtis' opinion. As for withholding the opinion of the Court from the public, it was true that it had not been given to a partisan, political journal for political and partisan purposes, but it had been delivered in open court and had now been published in the manner of publication used by the Court for more than fifty years. Although on other occasions an opinion of the Court had been politically assailed, this was the first instance in which the assault had been begun by the publication of an opinion of a dissenting judge.[12]

Referring to this correspondence in conversation with his friend David M. Perine of Baltimore, Taney had predicted that Curtis would not reply to his earlier letter. Perine had thought that he would do so, in the tone of a demagogue. Taney now wrote to Perine that his prediction had been correct. Curtis had written such a letter as he predicted, "covering more than two sheets . . . very closely written upon large sized letter paper." The letter was of such a character as to call for a reply, "and it was worse than useless to reply unless I replied fully, and in doing so I found my letter necessarily ran out as long as his to me." Taney would have liked to send Perine a copy of his letter to Curtis but he had no clerk by whom a copy could be made. He predicted that Curtis would answer again. "But every attempt to justify what cannot be justified, can only plunge one in further difficulties. Yet he cannot feel comfortable in his present position."[13]

That the last comment might have been applied to the performance of the Chief Justice himself seems never to have occurred to him. His enlargement of the opinion of the Court and his later supplement to the opinion which the Court refused to permit him to file demonstrated that he too went on endlessly in futile attempt to justify a position which, in the light of the changing thinking of his times, could not be justified.

Curtis did write again but with obvious self-restraint. He said that he was not replying at length both because carrying on the discussion without bitterness would seem to be impossible and because it was not necessary. He did defend himself to the extent of saying, "I have no connection whatever with any political party, and have no political or partisan purpose in view, and no purpose whatever, save a determination to avoid misconstruction and misapprehension, from which I have suffered enough in times past."[14] Taney replied in a brief terminal note, stiff and formal in tone, in which he said that he was aware of

---

[12] *Ibid.*, 221–25.
[13] R. B. Taney to David M. Perine, Perine Papers.

[14] Curtis, *Memoir of B. R. Curtis*, I, 228.

nothing in either of his letters that was not strictly defensive in its character.[15] Curtis, finally, wrote out a set of observations for his own files in defense of his position.[16]

The fact that even in private correspondence Chief Justice Taney could be driven from his traditional professional decorum into accusations that a colleague was playing politics (a colleague who was the least political of all his fellows) and into sheer petulance was in itself indicative of something beyond the usual in the Dred Scott case and was suggestive of more trouble to come. Although until now he had got along well with his associates, Justice Curtis had found it hard to adjust his living standards from those of a prosperous lawyer to the income of an Associate Justice, even though in 1855 the salary had been increased to six thousand dollars.[17] There were financial and other difficulties in the way of moving his family to Washington for the period of the Court's term and then moving them back to Massachusetts again, especially with the problem of educating his children. Apparently he had already given some thought to returning to private practice. Now, with the development of bad relations with the Chief Justice and of doubts whether in the future he could respect the performance of the Court on constitutional questions, he gave more serious thought to resigning.[18] Indeed, his position was uncomfortable in almost every respect. People who lacked discrimination and understanding in legal matters were now classifying him with the abolitionists, or at any rate Free Soilers, for whom he had little sympathy. "I am told that he does not much relish the necessity which is making him famous," wrote Charles Francis Adams, "and that his friends groan here at the ammunition he has been obliged to furnish those rascally freesoilers. The last stroke that I heard of was that they were getting up a sum of money to print an edition of the opinion for circulation in the *Southern States*."[19]

---

[15] *Ibid.*, 228–29.

[16] *Ibid.*, 229–30.
In a letter bearing the date only of the year, 1857, but obviously written in March, 1857, George T. Curtis wrote to John J. Crittenden to ask what he and George E. Badger thought of the decision. He was pained to see reports of a squabble among the judges as to who should have the last word. He supposed Daniel and Campbell would anticipate flings from McLean and would wish to pay him back, but he was sure they could not anticipate any "bunkum" from his kinsman (that is, from Justice Curtis), though they might like to answer his law. He thought Buchanan fortunate that the case had not been decided a year earlier, for in that event nothing could have prevented Fremont's election. *The Life of John J. Crittenden*, Mrs. Chapman Coleman, ed., 137.

[17] 10 Stat. 655. The salary of the Chief Justice was increased to sixty-five hundred dollars.

[18] For materials on the resignation as assembled by his brother, George T. Curtis, see Curtis, *Memoir of B. R. Curtis*, I, 243–63.

[19] Charles Francis Adams to Charles Sumner, Apr. 7, 1857, Sumner Papers.

On July 12, shortly after the conclusion of the Taney-Curtis correspondence, Justice McLean replied to a note from Justice Curtis with a plea that the latter not resign until he had attended another term at Washington. The Court could never retrieve what it had lost. But should they abandon it? They might do the country some service by remaining at least another term.[20] Curtis replied with a statement of his reasons and McLean wrote again. He thought Congress might further increase salaries to eight or ten thousand dollars, and he thought the Justices might be relieved of circuit duties because of a desire of the Buchanan Administration to entrench their constitutional views by the creation of independent circuit judgeships. McLean doubted whether Curtis would now feel comfortable at the bar after having served on the Supreme Court. Furthermore, the country was in a great crisis. Being in a minority, he and Curtis from the Bench could at least do something by maintaining the great principles of the Constitution.[21]

Curtis submitted his resignation on September 1, 1857, explaining briefly that his private duties were inconsistent with a longer continuance in public service. Two weeks later he received from Jeremiah S. Black, Buchanan's Attorney General, a chilly letter saying that the President had received his letter and caused it to be filed in Black's office.[22] Black, a competent jurist who had been chief justice of Pennsylvania, evidently included some words of professional praise in a draft of a letter to Curtis which he submitted to Buchanan for his approval. Buchanan struck out the words of praise, saying, "I know I entertain no such opinion of him as is therein expressed, and your communication to me of what had passed between him and the Chief Justice does not serve to enhance him in my estimation."[23] And so the Dred Scott case further deepened its impact of ill will, and on the Supreme Court an able jurist withdrew to be replaced for more than two decades by a mediocre Buchanan appointment.

Most of the Justices sent letters of sincere regret at Curtis' resignation. Chief Justice Taney, however, expressed no regret. He merely remarked that his own experience had long shown him the inadequacy of the salary, and that Curtis was no doubt wise to resign while he had many years of remunerative professional labor ahead of him.[24]

An ironic sidelight appeared in correspondence between Curtis and Reverdy Johnson. Johnson, close to the Chief Justice and desirous of protecting the reputation of the Supreme Court, regretted that Curtis'

---

[20] Curtis, *Memoir of B. R. Curtis,* I, 258.
[21] *Ibid.,* 258–59.
[22] *Ibid.,* 250.

[23] James Buchanan to J. S. Black, Sept. 15, 1857, Black Papers.
[24] Curtis, *Memoir of B. R. Curtis,* I, 254.

resignation had not been postponed for another term because, coming at this time, it would be attributed to other causes than the financial explanation given. He had therefore taken steps to get an editorial published in the *Courier* and *Enquirer* in New York, giving the truth of the matter. "You know how sincerely, with yourself, I value the high character of the court, and how deeply we should feel at the loss of it, in public opinion. The sooner, therefore, that every misrepresentation is corrected, the better."[25] But Curtis noted on the back of the letter that he was replying to say that no one was authorized to deny that his regrets at leaving the Court were diminished by the state of the Court, and that he could not deny it.[26]

As the Curtis opinion was well received by antislavery people who heard it read and who received copies of it, so also was that of Justice McLean. On the Sunday following the day of its delivery, Montgomery Blair heard it read in church. He wrote to McLean that its exalted and Christian spirit made it worthy of meditation even there. He made some suggestions for incidental modification of the opinion before publication.[27] But McLean did not see the need of changes[28] and, in any event, before they could be made the opinion had been published in the *Cincinnati Gazette* and he was circulating copies far and wide throughout the country. The reply letters brought high praise. Typical was that of Orville H. Browning, who said, "I hope to live to see the opinions of the majority of the Judges spurned by the people, and by the people's representatives—by the bar, and by the bench, and yours universally acknowledged as the law of the land. Rooted, as it is, in the everlasting principles of Truth, it must ultimately command the respect, admiration, and obedience of the entire country."[29]

United States Senator Jacob Collamer of Vermont predicted that those men, both on and off the Bench, would find themselves egregiously mistaken who supposed that the extrajudicial dicta of the Supreme Court would settle the questions that divided the country. It betrayed a deep desperation in any political cause or party to enlist the judges of the Supreme Court as endorsers of political positions. The judges had been praised for their moral courage in thus hazarding their reputations. Senator Collamer thought that because of their personal immunity their performance did not take much courage, and regarded

---

[25] *Ibid.*, 261.
[26] *Ibid.*, 262.
[27] Montgomery Blair to John McLean, Mar. 8, 1857, McLean Papers.
[28] See Montgomery Blair to John McLean, Mar. 24, 1857, McLean Papers.
[29] O. H. Browning to John McLean, Mar. 23, 1857, McLean Papers.

as most serious the fact that they had done much to undermine public confidence in this great tribunal.[30]

Writing at the end of March to Montgomery Blair, Justice McLean commented that the reported modification of the opinion of the Court appeared to him to be unusual if not improper, and said that if there had been a different result in the Presidential election there would have been no such decision as that in the Dred Scott case. Commenting on Southern attitudes, he remarked, "My brethren of the South were anxious to give the decision, as it would settle the question involved, and tranquilize the public mind. I did not suppose it was possible for some of my Southern brethren to evince that entire indifference to historical facts, and the rulings of the Court, as is shown in the opinion of the Chief Justice." Illustrating in terms of a speech recently delivered in Boston by Senator Robert Toombs of Georgia, McLean said that "With very few exceptions the Southern mind appears to be incapable of treating any question which involves their interests with ordinary fairness. They supply all defects of facts by bold assertions, and by throwing a large amount of chivalry in the scale, make up the deficiencies in their logick."[31] Beliefs of this kind, held not merely by McLean but widely throughout the North, were bound to make inroads on the prestige of the Supreme Court where sectional issues were concerned.

Chief Justice Taney worked on the opinion of the Court for nearly a month before it was ready for publication. On April 3 James E. Harvey of the *New York Tribune* wrote to Justice McLean that Taney's opinion had been twice copied for revision. He added:

> That clause in Catron's, rebuking the discussion of the merits of the case, after the denial of jurisdiction, has been expurgated. But a single copy has been printed for his own use. Campbell's has been printed privately, but not for circulation. He forbade the printer from showing it to any body, but especially Grier, which was the unkindest cut of all.[32]

Harvey added that McLean's dissenting opinion was receiving high praise in the North, while the Southern papers were giving their attention to lauding the majority of the Court and largely ignoring the minority.

The continuing interest of the judges in separate publication of their individual opinions was shown at the end of May, after the official publication in Howard's volume, by a letter from Justice Catron to United States District Judge Samuel Treat of Missouri. Returning to

---

[30] J. Collamer to John McLean, Apr. 1, 1857, McLean Papers.
[31] John McLean to Montgomery Blair, Mar. 30, 1857, Blair Papers.
[32] James E. Harvey to John McLean, Apr. 3, 1857, McLean Papers.

Nashville from Frankfort where he had been holding Circuit Court, Catron found Howard's volume awaiting him, and also found that the latest issue of the *Washington Union*, the Administration newspaper, had printed, presumably from Howard, the opinion of the Chief Justice. The editor had promised to publish one more of the opinions of the majority and one of the minority opinions. Catron thought that his own opinion would hardly be allowed to appear, since he had disagreed with the Chief Justice as to whether the plea in abatement was in the case and also as to the source of the constitutional power of Congress to govern territories. Indeed, as to the plea in abatement the position of the Chief Justice was a minority position and what he said was reduced to the level of a dictum. Since his own opinion was not likely to be separately published in the *Union*, Catron asked Treat to get it published in a St. Louis paper and to correct the proof on it, having the bill made out to him if there was a charge for the publication.[33]

That Justice Daniel's opinion was privately printed before publication of the official report is indicated by a letter of March 18 to Carroll saying, "I have attempted to correct the proof of my opinion in the case of Scott vs. Sandford, but I have found the impression so very inaccurate, that I cannot correct it without comparing it with the manuscript."[34] On May 4, having lost track of events because illness had confined him to his room, Daniel reminded Carroll that Howard had promised to have a few copies of his opinion which he wished to present to friends who were not likely to see the reports of the Supreme Court. He wished also to obtain a few copies of the opinion of the Court for the same persons, "as a means of giving them *historical* rather than *professional* information." If Howard had forgotten the matter he wished to know whether the copies could be procured and at what cost.[35]

The practice of official printing of the opinions, as well as individual printing in newspapers and pamphlets, came into focus. The Reporter, who received at that time a salary of only thirteen hundred dollars a year,[36] derived most of his income from the sale of copies of the reports. A decision capturing as much public attention as that in the Dred Scott case constituted a kind of windfall for him, from the sale of the volume and, in this instance, separate publication of the deci-

---

[33] John Catron to Samuel Treat, May 31, 1857, Treat Papers. The Catron opinion was, however, published in the *Washington Union*, June 2, 1857, and, presumably at his instigation, in the *Nashville Daily Union and American*, June 11, 12, 1857.

[34] P. V. Daniel to William Thomas

Carroll, Mar. 18, 1857, Clerk's Files. In the manuscript the word "so" is erroneously written "to."

[35] P. V. Daniel to William Thomas Carroll, May 4, 1857, Clerk's Files.

[36] For the then current appropriation see 11 Stat. 218.

sion in pamphlet form. At the extra session of the Senate in March, 1857, which was held over to act on Presidential appointments, Senator Judah P. Benjamin of Louisiana offered a resolution calling for the printing of a pamphlet edition of the opinions of which twenty thousand copies would be printed for the use of the Senate, the cost to be paid out of the Senate contingent fund. When Howard protested this invasion of his source of income, the resolution was amended to allocate fifteen hundred dollars additional for the purchase of the Reporter's copyright.

In the press of business the Senate adjourned without acting on the resolution. At that time a group of Democratic Senators arranged to have the printing done anyway, and to pay the bill themselves if the Senate at the next session declined to authorize the payment.[37] Howard cooperated with the representative of the Senate printer in getting copies but he insisted that the Senate pamphlet not be published before his volume of reports or his own separate pamphlet, which was being brought out by a New York publisher. He insisted also that the Senate issue be limited to twenty thousand copies, that the copies be given only to Senators for their own distribution, and that Senators receiving copies should not give them out ahead of his own publications.[38] At the ensuing session the Senate voted to pay the bill, along with some disclaimers that such payment was intended to reflect approval of things said in the opinions. It was admitted that Howard had no copyright in the opinions, but it was deemed equitable to compensate him for the loss of sales likely to result from the competing publication.[39]

Still other competing editions went on the market. The *New York Tribune* published a pamphlet containing the full opinions of Chief Justice Taney and Justice Curtis and abstracts of the opinions of other judges, a document running to 104 pages which it sold for twenty-five cents. The pamphlet was being reprinted as late as 1860. Vice President John C. Breckenridge printed and circulated copies of the decision throughout his state of Kentucky.[40] In 1860 the Taney opinion was separately printed along with an essay by Dr. Samuel A. Cartwright upholding Taney's argument as to the inferior status of the Negro. There were undoubtedly other editions.

The Senate edition of the opinions was published with a brief historical statement and without an analysis of the points made. For

---

[37] See report of the Senate Committee on Audit and Control, *Cong. Globe*, 35th Cong. 1st Sess. 665 (1858).

[38] See in the files of the clerk of the Court memoranda of Apr. 1 and Apr. 23, 1857, of conversations between Howard and Cornelius Wendell, who was referred to as agent for the printer of the Senate.

[39] *Cong. Globe*, 35th Cong., 1st Sess. 665–67 (1858).

[40] John G. Nicolay and John Hay, *Abraham Lincoln*, II, 73–74. n 1.

the official report Chief Justice Taney, perhaps irked at newspaper statements that much of what he said was not concurred in by a majority of the Court, himself drafted a unique headnote. Running to five major divisions and thirty-one subdivisions, and covering in fine print three pages of Howard's volume, it provided a thorough outline not of the positions clearly taken by the majority but of the so-called opinion of the Court written by the Chief Justice, wherein at least as to the plea in abatement he did not have a majority with him.[41] This headnote, even though the authorship was not generally known, provided one of the points of Northern attack.

In addition to comments on the decision in newspapers all over the country and the publication of opinions in some of them, learned journals dealt with it, some of them reviewing pamphlet publications after the fashion of long book reviews. One of the ablest reviews appeared in *The Law Reporter* for June, 1857,[42] and was later reprinted as a pamphlet of sixty-two pages.[43] It was written by two bright young members of the Boston bar, Horace Gray, who in years to come would be chief justice of Massachusetts and later a member of the Supreme Court, and John Lowell, then editor of *The Law Reporter* and later to be a United States district judge and then a United States circuit judge. The authors dealt roughly with the majority of the Court and asserted that by common consent of the profession and of the public the opinion of Justice Curtis was "the strongest and clearest, as well as the most thorough and elaborate of all the opinions delivered in this case."[44] They noted the strictures on newspaper publication of opinions but said that since most judges in this Court were accustomed to file their opinions with the Clerk on delivery, after which copies were sent to the parties, and since there was no copyright, there was no reason why the opinions should not be published immediately. They criticized the holding back of opinions for alteration after their announcement, and deplored the headnote which was merely a synopsis of the opinion of the Chief Justice, contrasting it unfavorably with the headnote in the *Passenger Cases*, in which Howard had taken one sentence in which to say that certain statutes were held unconstitutional and another to say that since there was no opinion of the Court the reader must look to the several opinions for further information.[45]

---

[41] The headnote in Taney's long-hand is preserved in the Howard Papers.

[42] The Case of Dred Scott, 20 Law Rep. 61 (1857).

[43] [Horace Gray and John Lowell],

A Legal Review of the Case of Dred Scott.

[44] *Ibid.*, 57.

[45] Passenger Cases, 7 How. 283 (1849).

Chief Justice Taney was of course insistent that his opinion was the opinion of the Court, but Gray and Lowell differed with him and showed the extent of the disagreement among the majority Justices. They admitted that the opinion bore the mark of great labor but contended that "in its tone and manner of reasoning, as well as in the position which it assumes, it is unworthy of the reputation of that great magistrate, who for twenty years has maintained the position of the intellectual, as well as the nominal head of the highest tribunal of the country, and to whose grasp of mind, logical power, keen discrimination, and judicial wisdom, the people have been accustomed to look, with a confidence rarely disappointed, in cases involving great principles of the Constitution of the United States, of the law of nations, and of conflict between different systems of jurisprudence."[46] With a great deal of persuasiveness, although with what Taney would have regarded as a Northern bias, they concluded that had it maintained its consistency with sound principles the Court could not have decided that a free Negro could not be a citizen, or that Congress could not exclude slavery from the territories, or that a master might hold his slave in any free state, or that the one-time slave would necessarily become a slave again if he returned with his master.[47]

Timothy Farrar, another able Boston lawyer, wrote for the *North American Review* an analysis of twenty-three pages. He too dissected the majority opinions to show the differences among them and denounced the characterization of the Taney opinion as the opinion of the Court. He criticized those Justices who decided in connection with the plea in abatement that the Circuit Court had not had jurisdiction, and then proceeded to decide the merits of the case, including the constitutionality of the Missouri Compromise. He contended that by grasping at too much the Court had lost the whole. Yet as a political manual or textbook, "an authorized registration of the political heresies of the dominant party of the day, it will be all it was intended to be."[48]

As for the practical influence of the decision, Farrar thought both parties likely to be disappointed. Its primary impact would be on the Court itself. It would result in "the loss of confidence in the sound judicial integrity and strictly legal character" of the country's tribunals. This might well be accounted "the greatest political calamity which this country, under our forms of government, could sustain."[49]

---

[46] Gray and Lowell, *A Legal Review of the Case of Dred Scott*, 9.

[47] *Ibid.*, 57.

[48] [Timothy Farrar], "The Dred Scott Case," *North American Review*, 85:392, 414, 1847.

[49] *Ibid.*, 415. For a longer but less precise attack upon the decision see Thomas Hart Benton, *Historical and Legal Examination of . . . the Dred Scott Decision* (1857).

There were of course defenses of the decision as well as attacks, although defenses of most decisions are harder to phrase pungently and dramatically than attacks, and in this instance were made more difficult by the differences among the majority Justices themselves. One of the defenses came in the supplement to the fifth edition of *Slavery and the Remedy; or, Principles and Suggestions for a Remedial Code,* published in the summer of 1857 by Samuel Nott, a Massachusetts clergyman. Nott was an apostle of gradualness in dealing with the problems of slavery, which he regarded as an evil but one that could not be eradicated by the simple expedient of emancipation. He thought that on the whole the Supreme Court had properly understood the attitude of the American people toward slavery and that, given all the circumstances, the decision was sound and wise.

Nott sent a copy of his book to Chief Justice Taney, who from his vacation place at Fauquier White Sulphur Springs replied in grateful acknowledgment. Taney felt that on the whole, Negroes, whether slaves or free, had been kindly treated in their subordinate position to the white race, and that the relationship had been the best that was possible to the two peoples under the circumstances and had not been felt as painful degradation by the black race. Further improvement of the position of the Negro had been impeded by efforts in recent years to produce discontent in the subject race. Negroes, he said, were for the most part credulous and easily misled by stronger minds. In the face of the current agitation it would be unwise to weaken the authority of the masters. Asking that his letter not be published, Taney noted that he was not a slaveholder, that he had emancipated all his slaves more than thirty years ago except two who were too old to provide for themselves.

He thought Nott's review of the Dred Scott decision a fair one and hoped it would correct some misapprehensions which had so industriously been made, oftentimes by people who had known better. But he did not mean to publish any vindication of his opinion: "For it would not become the Supreme Court, or any member of it, to go outside of the appropriate sphere of judicial proceedings; and engage in a controversy with any one who may choose from any motive to misrepresent its opinion. The opinion must be left to speak for itself."[50]

In writing to Franklin Pierce a few days later Taney remarked that he was passing through a conflict much like that which followed the removal of the deposits. While he would have enjoyed finding that the irritating strifes of this world were over for him, the mind was less apt to feel the torpor of age when it was thus forced into action. He had

---

[50] R. B. Taney to Samuel Nott, Aug. 19, 1857, *Proceedings of the Massachusetts Historical Society, 1871–1873,* 447, 1873.

an abiding confidence that this act of his judicial life would stand the test of time and sober judgment by the country, as had his political act with respect to the Bank of the United States. He noted symptoms of discord in the Buchanan Administration, but he attributed them to the way in which offices were filled and not to policies. Because of the need for friends of the Administration to stand together, "to prevent the government from falling to pieces," he was unwilling to find fault.[51]

Justice Wayne received from his friend Benjamin Rush of Philadelphia an account of the drafting and adoption of resolutions by a Democratic state convention in Harrisburg in support of the decision. Rush, though not himself a member of the convention, had been in Harrisburg for a day, and had been asked to draft such a resolution. He had done so, in language which said:

> Resolved that the recent decision of the Supreme Court of the United States in the case of Dred Scott v. Sandford, is a model of Constitutional wisdom, of sound legal learning, and of calm unanswerable reasoning; that as such it meets the hearty acquiescence of the judgment of the Democratic citizens of Pennsylvania, and is as much commended to the whole People of the United States by the force of truth and patriotism, as it is equally binding on all by the highest sanctions of Law.

Although the primary task of this convention was the nomination of candidates for positions on the state supreme court, it deemed appropriate such a statement on a constitutional issue, and adopted the Rush resolution in a somewhat modified form.[52]

---

[51] R. B. Taney to Franklin Pierce, Aug. 29, 1857, *American Historical Review*, 10: 359, 1905.

[52] Benjamin Rush to James M. Wayne, June 10, 18, 1857, Wayne Papers.

In a letter to a political friend written three years later, Rush, calling attention to Justice Wayne's wholehearted support of the opinion of the Court in the Dred Scott case, recommended his nomination for the Presidency: "The name of Judge Wayne of Georgia, which was mentioned when you were here, has been mentioned a good deal since. *It takes.* He seems to unite in himself, it is thought, what is now most essential to the harmony and success of the Party.

A Southern man, and from the extreme South; moderate but firm in his views; for a quarter of a century an expounder of the Constitution; appointed by Jackson; prominent in early life in Congress as a Conservative Statesman; educated at the North; a man of honor and a gentleman; his name never heretofore mentioned in connection with the Chief magistracy, and the Presidency never yet given by the Democratic party to any State south of Virginia; what more, it is said, do we want, to unite the Party and ensure its triumph." (Longhand copy, Benjamin Rush to an undesignated person, June 7, 1860, enclosed with Benjamin Rush to James M. Wayne, June 9, 1860, Wayne Papers.)

Thus the Dred Scott decision worked its way not only into the publications of the day but also into political strategy. Because the decision held that Congress could not exclude slavery from the territories, it gave some plausible support to the Kansas-Nebraska Act and to the "popular sovereignty" or "squatter sovereignty" so warmly supported by Stephen A. Douglas, Senator from Illinois. In the face of the newly organized Republican Party on the one hand and ultra-slavery Democrats on the other, Douglas was on his way to the Presidency, with his reelection to the Senate in 1858 a politically essential intermediate step. In a speech delivered at Springfield, Illinois, on June 12, 1857, three months after the Dred Scott decision was announced, Douglas fully endorsed the decision.[53]

Two weeks later the Douglas position was challenged by Abraham Lincoln, Republican competitor for the Senatorial position. "Judge Douglas," said Lincoln, "does not discuss the merits of the decision; and, in that respect, I shall follow his example, believing I could no more improve on McLean and Curtis, than he could on Taney."[54] Judge Douglas denounced all who questioned the correctness of the decision or offered violent resistance to it. No resistance was offered to the decision as far as Dred Scott was concerned, said Lincoln, but it was believed to be erroneous, and its validity as a precedent was challenged. Quoting from Andrew Jackson's veto of the bank bill, perhaps without knowledge of how much the present Chief Justice had had to do with that message, Lincoln urged that "Mere precedent is a dangerous source of authority, and should not be regarded as deciding questions of constitutional power, except where the acquiescence of the people and the States can be considered as well settled."[55] He challenged the Taney position that the Declaration of Independence did not apply to the colored race, and contended that when it said that all men were created equal it meant what it said. The framers knew, he said, the proneness of prosperity to breed tyrants, and "they meant when

---

[53] Nicolay and Hay, *Abraham Lincoln*, 82–84. As Lincoln clearly pointed out, the Douglas "squatter sovereignty" argument was vulnerable as far as control of slavery by the territories was concerned, as distinguished from the states which the territories were to become, in that if Congress had no power to deal with slavery in the territories it was hard to see how territories created by Congress and deriving all their power from Congress could exercise power with respect to slavery. If, as held in the *Prigg* case, slavery was merely a municipal institution, it was hard to see how a territory could protect it. If it derived support from "natural law," it was hard to see how a territory could avoid the obligation to protect it. The Douglas argument, like most others, had its serious defects.

[54] Lincoln's speech at Springfield, June 26, 1857, *Collected Works of Abraham Lincoln*, Roy P. Basler, ed., II, 398, 400.

[55] *Ibid.*, 402.

such should re-appear in this fair land and commence their vocation they should find left for them at least one hard nut to crack."[56]

Lincoln's speech indicated the line of attack which he was to take a year later in the famous debates with Douglas, where he lost the Senatorial contest but achieved the publicity that was to secure him a Presidential nomination and election and further mark the Dred Scott decision as a political instrument. In the meantime, on March 3, 1858, in a debate in the Senate on Kansas, William H. Seward made an attack on the Supreme Court in the Dred Scott case that was to have a wide impact, using in a harsh fashion materials that Lincoln was to use with a lighter touch and greater deftness. Seward told of the adoption of the Kansas-Nebraska Act and the subsequent strife in Kansas and the refusal of President Pierce to remove "a partial and tyrannical judge." A new President was elected. This President, Buchanan, intervened more subtly in the interest of slavery in Kansas: "Before coming into office, he approached or was approached by the Supreme Court of the United States." On the docket was the Dred Scott case, wherein the Court had reached the conclusion, contrary to the Declaration of Independence and to the Constitution, that a Negro could not sue his imputed master in a federal court. The case had been argued between volunteer counsel and counsel paid by slavery interests. After a mock debate the Court had used this idle forensic discussion as an occasion for striking down the Missouri Compromise and holding that Congress could not exclude slavery from the territories: "In this ill-omened act, the Supreme Court forgot its own dignity which had always been maintained with just judicial jealousy. . . . And they and the President alike forgot that judicial usurpation is more odious and intolerable than any other among the manifold practices of tyranny."

Then, continued Seward, came the day of inauguration, a great national pageant. The President arrived and took his seat. "The Supreme Court attended him there, in robes which yet exacted public reverence. The people, unaware of the import of the whisperings carried on between the President and the Chief Justice, and imbued with veneration for both, filled the avenues and gardens far away as the eye could reach." Then came the Presidential address, in which the President referred vaguely to the forthcoming decision and pledged his submission to it. It had cost the President little to make to Kansas a promise of self-determination on the slavery issue, a cheap promise uttered only to be broken.

The pageant had ended. On the following day the judges had paid their courtesy call on the President. On the day thereafter it had

---

[56] *Ibid.*, 406.

decided the Dred Scott case, disposing of a private action for a private wrong on the ground of want of jurisdiction, and then deciding the issues as if they had had jurisdiction. A few days later the Senate's press had broadcast the opinions over the land in the name of the Senate. Simultaneously Dred Scott, who had unwittingly played the hand of dummy in this interesting political game, had been voluntarily emancipated, receiving as a reward from his master the freedom which had been denied to him as a right. The new President, "having organized this formidable judicial battery at the Capitol, was now ready to begin his active demonstrations of intervention in the Territory."[57]

Seward's attack on the Court so enraged the Chief Justice as to lead him to say privately that if Seward had been elected President, he would have refused to administer the oath of office.[58] Although some of the insinuations were either false or exaggerated, this part of the speech provided effective material for campaign purposes among people who had little knowledge of judicial processes. With that fact in mind, Reverdy Johnson attempted refutation in a letter written to be read at a public meeting held in Baltimore, denying the conspiratorial character of the decision and saying, among other things, that counsel for Sanford as well as for Dred Scott had served without compensation and in the public interest.[59] But innuendoes are hard to defeat by refutation, and it cannot be assumed that the attempt at refutation was particularly effective here.

Three months later Lincoln resorted to somewhat the same kind of conspiratorial attack, or the same kind of suggestion of conspiracy. Showing the integration of the proslavery efforts of Douglas, Pierce, Taney, and Buchanan, he hinted at preconcert among "Stephen, Franklin, Roger and James." Collaboration in strategy could not be proved, he said, but when the pieces fitted so well together, "we find it impossible not to *believe* that Stephen and Franklin and Roger and James all understood one another from the beginning, and all worked upon a common *plan* or *draft* drawn up before the first lick was struck."[60]

Lincoln made his accusation again and again, getting the point into the minds of his hearers and attempting to compel Douglas to answer it. Douglas was driven briefly to state that the charge was "in all its bearings an infamous lie," but refused to be driven into detailed discussion of a charge Lincoln admitted he could not prove,[61] knowing that an attempt at detailed refutation would even more deeply affix the charge in people's minds.

---

[57] *Cong. Globe*, 35th Cong., 1st Sess. 941 (1858).

[58] Tyler, *Memoir of Roger Brooke Taney*, 391.

[59] *Ibid.*, 385–91.

[60] Address at Springfield, June 16, 1858, Lincoln, *Collected Works*, 461, 465–66.

[61] *Ibid.*, 34–35.

XXV: *Aftermath of the Scott Case*

In speech after speech Lincoln attacked Douglas for his support of the Dred Scott decision, contending among other things that it was incompatible with the position of an advocate of popular sovereignty such as Douglas. It determined that Congress could not exclude slavery from the territories, but by implication it also determined that territorial governments, established by Congress, were similarly impotent. President Buchanan had taken that position on February 2, 1858, in recommending the admission of Kansas under the proslavery Lecompton constitution. He had said:

> It has been solemnly adjudged by the highest judicial tribunal known to our laws that slavery exists in Kansas by virtue of the Constitution of the United States. Kansas is therefore at this moment as much a slave State as Georgia or South Carolina.[62]

Douglas was therefore fighting not merely Lincoln and the Republican Party but also President Buchanan and the more ardent slavery men. While he did not directly admit that Buchanan was right in his interpretation of the Dred Scott decision, he was driven to sponsor the weak position that if slavery was to prosper it had to have positive support from government, and the people opposed to slavery could withhold that support and in effect defeat slavery.[63]

Lincoln also charged, in the light of his conspiracy theory, that the Supreme Court, in conjunction with slavery interests, having fastened slavery upon the territories, could now by another decision fasten it upon the states as well, however great their love of freedom. Experience with enforcement of the Fugitive Slave Law in some of the states demonstrated how difficult it would be to maintain slavery in the face of local public hostility, but the debates nevertheless kept the minds of the people fixed on the menace of the decision and on the alleged misuse of judicial power by the Supreme Court. Lincoln himself was like Douglas walking a political tightrope between the friends and enemies of slavery or of Negro equality in Illinois and was trying to avoid extremes of position. While predicting that a house divided against itself could not stand, and that the national house would cease to be divided, he did not advocate abolition in the South. He indicated personal opposition to conferring state citizenship upon Negroes. He asserted his opposition to the mixing of races—which, he implied, took place primarily under slavery, by means of the power which white owners had over slave women. But he did insist on equality under the Declaration of Independence and on the right of states to make Negroes citizens if they preferred to do so.

---

[62] *Messages and Papers of the Presidents,* V, 479.

[63] See *Cong. Globe,* 35th Cong., 2nd Sess. 1258-59 (1859).

Lincoln failed to oust Douglas as United States Senator, but the Lincoln-Douglas debates, with the Dred Scott decision at their core, led to his nomination and election as President in 1860, and thereby precipitated the Civil War. In that sense, at least, the Dred Scott decision played its part in what Seward called "the irrepressible conflict." It contributed also, as indicated above, by diminishing respect for the Supreme Court, which hitherto as a supposedly nonpolitical and unbiased spokesman for law and order had had a restraining influence on groups that were not already completely out of control. While the South had the Presidency, in the person of a Northerner with deep Southern sympathies, and while it had in the Supreme Court a nationally revered institution devoted to law and order with pronounced tenderness toward Southern interests and viewpoints, it had some assurance of protection in the Union. But when the Supreme Court became anathema to growing numbers of people in the North because of a proslavery decision, the South, however great its own reverence for the Court—and Southern extremists had their own doubts about it from their own point of view—could no longer count on effective judicial protection. When it lost the Presidency too, and also Congress, the ties that bound the Union together were too weak to hold.

While most of the remaining materials connected with the Dred Scott decision belong more appropriately in other contexts, certain additional items must be stated here. For example, a number of state legislatures treated the decision with heated denunciation. The New York legislature passed resolutions saying that the state would not allow slavery within her borders in any form or for any time however short and that the Supreme Court, by reason of its affiliation with an aggressive sectional party, had impaired the confidence and respect of the people of the state.[64] The Maine legislature sent to Congress resolutions denouncing the Court for its "extra-judicial" opinion. It found the opinion conclusive proof of the determination of the slaveholding states to subvert the principles upon which the Union was formed and to degrade it by the perpetuation of slavery. It demanded that the Court be reconstituted, and that further acquisition of territory be resisted until the opinion was reversed.[65] The legislature of Massachusetts sent copies of resolutions to the President, to the governors of each of the states and territories, and to each of its Senators and Representatives in Congress. It declared that no part of the Dred Scott decision was binding which was not necessary to the decision of the case. It stated that while the people recognized the rightful authority of the Court, they would

---

[64] *Harper's Monthly Magazine*, 15: 117, 1857.

[65] H.R. Misc. Doc. No. 31, 35th Cong., 1st Sess. (1858).

never consent to the impairment of their rights or invasion of their liberties "by reason of any usurpations of political power by said tribunal." It proclaimed that all citizens of Massachusetts were citizens of the United States, that nonalien Negroes residing there were citizens of the state, and that they were entitled to all the rights, privileges, and immunities of citizenship, in the federal courts and elsewhere. It declared that slavery existed nowhere except by positive law and denied that slavery in the territories was protected by the Constitution. It opposed acquisition of more territory to provide more slave representation in Congress.[66] At no previous time, indeed, had the Supreme Court received from the states such a hostile bombardment.

Chief Justice Taney watched with turbulent feelings the public treatment accorded the Dred Scott decision. He saw in the newspapers a report of a decision in the United States Circuit Court in Indiana that a Negro born in the United States of nonslave ancestry might sue as a citizen in a federal court. In September, 1858, at his home in Washington, he wrote a supplement to his Dred Scott opinion to demonstrate from English authorities the inferior position of the Negro whether or not the individual had slave ancestry. He was doing it, he said, because the case of Dred Scott was among the most important in the judicial history of the Supreme Court. If the question came before the Court again in his lifetime, his supplement would save the trouble of again investigating and annexing the proofs. To that end he prepared a document that ran to some thirty printed pages.[67] He concluded with a comment on the misrepresentations and perversions to which the opinion of the Court had been subjected, saying that he would not deal with them because refutations would merely bring other misrepresentations. He added that most of them were carefully put together in a volume published in Boston soon after the opinions were officially published[68]—thereby perhaps taking an additional jab at Justice Curtis.

It is apparent that the Chief Justice hoped to make more effective use of his supplemental opinion than merely to file it away. His chosen biographer stated that Taney hoped to have it published in Howard's reports, but that the other judges denied him the privilege.[69] Two and a half years after it was written he commented on it in a letter to his son-in-law, saying that it had been his wish to publish it while the subject was still exciting attention but that he had never seen how it could be done with judicial propriety. He would have been glad

---

[66] S. Misc. Doc. No. 231, 35th Cong., 1st Sess. (1858).

[67] Tyler, *Memoir of R. B. Taney*, 578–608.

[68] *Ibid.*, 607.

[69] Samuel Tyler to F. M. Etting, Nov. 18, 1870, Howard Papers.

to publish it in the reports, but since that could not be done his executors must in some form bring it before the public.[70] The opinion first made its appearance in the official biography.

The largely forgotten man amid all this controversy was Dred Scott himself. Eventually someone in Congress investigated the matter and found that title to the Negro was in Dr. Calvin C. Chaffee, now an abolitionist member of Congress, by virtue of the fact that he had married Mrs. Emerson, the former wife of the doctor with whom Dred Scott had taken his historic tour into free territory. Dr. Chaffee, embarrassed by the affair and perhaps surprised to hear about his property, transferred Dred Scott and his family for a nominal sum to a member of the Blow family in St. Louis, by whom they were manumitted.[71] "Being a freeman, in spite of Chief Justice Taney," said the New York Tribune sardonically, "we suppose he now has rights which white men are bound to respect."[72] He died within a year, however, and his wife soon afterward, while the storm over the litigation rolled on.

---

[70] R. B. Taney to J. Mason Campbell, Feb. 18, 1861, Howard Papers.
[71] Hopkins, Dred Scott's Case, 176.

[72] New York Tribune, May 27, 1857.

CHAPTER XXVI

The Booth Cases and Northern Nullification

Paralleling the course of the Dred Scott case through the courts, efforts increased in Northern states to hamper the capture and return of fugitive slaves. Part of the interference took place through the enactment of so-called personal liberty laws;[1] part of it through the action of state courts; and part through outright violence whereby fugitives were taken from federal authorities and aided to escape, usually northward into Canada, where they were safe. Deeply involved were the issues not only of slavery but also of the pattern of American federalism. Both sets of issues were involved in the *Booth Cases*, which arose in the abolitionist area of Wisconsin and brought from Chief Justice Taney, as spokesman for the Supreme Court, one of the outstanding statements in all American history on the relations of the federal government and the states and on the position of the Supreme Court in the American constitutional system.

In a sense this story, like that in the Dred Scott case, had its start in Missouri. On a farm just outside of St. Louis Benammi S. Garland had a slave, Joshua Glover, whom he had purchased in 1849 and who worked as his foreman. In 1852 Glover escaped and fled to Wisconsin. According to the description circulated:

---

[1] Perhaps because of lack of agreement as to what constituted personal liberty laws, there is lack of agreement as to which states had them. It is agreed that they were enacted by all the New England states and by a number of states in the Middle West. See Allan Nevins, *The Emergence of Lincoln*, II, 29; Charles Warren, *The Supreme Court in United States History*, II, 345.

Joshua was about forty-four or forty-five years of age, about five feet six or eight inches high, spare built, with rather long legs, very prominent knuckles, had large feet and hands, had a full head of wool, eyes small and inflamed, was of dissipated habits, was of rather an ashy color, had one of his shoulders stiff from dislocation, and had stooping shoulders, and a slow gait.[2]

Whatever his physical limitations, Glover maintained his freedom for some two years and was employed at a sawmill near Racine, Wisconsin. He seems to have been betrayed eventually to his owner by another Racine Negro, who visited in St. Louis. On March 10, 1854, Garland came to Glover's home with two United States Deputy Marshals and four assistants, captured Glover after a struggle in which he was seriously injured, manacled him, and drove him to a jail in Milwaukee.[3]

Immediately an excited meeting at the courthouse square in Racine passed resolutions denouncing this seizure of "one of our citizens" who was characterized as "a faithful laborer and an honest man." It demanded a fair and impartial trial by jury and promised that the people would attend for the purpose of aiding Glover to secure unconditional release. Reflecting bitterness over the recent action by the Senate with respect to the Kansas-Nebraska Bill, it further resolved:

> That inasmuch as the Senate of the United States has repealed all compromises heretofore adopted by the Congress of the United States, we, as citizens of Wisconsin, are justified in declaring *and do hereby declare the slave-catching law of 1850 disgraceful and also repealed.*[4]

While the people of Racine prepared to implement their nullifying resolution, abolitionists in Milwaukee were notified of the event. One of the leaders there was Sherman M. Booth, firebrand editor of the Milwaukee *Free Democrat*. A native of Connecticut and a graduate of Yale, he had been a lifelong abolitionist of the Garrison and Phillips type. It is said that he had the courage of his convictions but was as impolitic and unpractical as John Brown himself.[5] Booth mounted a horse and rode through Milwaukee, stopping at each street corner to

---

[2] Description in indictment of Sherman M. Booth, on p. 14 of the Supreme Court Record in United States v. Booth, 18 How. 476 (1856).

[3] Vroman Mason, "The Fugitive Slave Law in Wisconsin, With Reference to Nullification Sentiment," *Proceedings of the State Historical Society of Wisconsin . . . 1895*, 117, 122–23, 1896.

[4] *Ibid.*, 123.

[5] George W. Carter, "The Booth War in Ripon," *Proceedings of the State Historical Society of Wisconsin . . . 1902*, 161, 1903.

rise in his saddle and shout, "Freemen! To the rescue! Slave catchers are in our midst! Be at the court-house at two o'clock!"[6]

Before the meeting assembled, local authorities made their first attempt at nullification of federal action. A county court judge issued a writ of habeas corpus for the release of Glover. But the sheriff was persuaded not to serve the writ by United States District Judge Andrew G. Miller, who had authorized Glover's arrest and who was to play a prominent part in further proceedings. Miller was a native of Pennsylvania who had kept close contact with Pennsylvania politicians, including James Buchanan, since his appointment by Martin Van Buren in 1838 to be an associate justice of the Supreme Court of the territory of Wisconsin. When in 1848 Wisconsin was admitted as a state, James K. Polk appointed him a federal judge for the district. The state not being included in any federal circuit until 1862, Judge Miller was not subject to control or influence by any Supreme Court Justice on annual tour. Cases could not go up from his court on certificate of division, and appeals in criminal cases were not yet authorized. In these circumstances a federal district judge with a sense of authority and determination was a powerful figure, and Judge Miller possessed these characteristics. On the enforcement of the Fugitive Slave Law and similar measures he had convictions like those of Buchanan. In later years a Wisconsin abolitionist described him thus:

> I remember my surprise at seeing Judge Andrew Miller of the United States District Court at Milwaukee when a guest at my father's dinner table, and finding him a gracious and courtly gentleman! That a judge who had sentenced a man to jail for breaking a law of the United States that gave a runaway slave back to his master should not have horns and hoofs and breathe blue flames from his nostrils—was inexplicable to me![7]

Concerned with the growing hostile crowd assembling in Milwaukee, which was joined by a delegation from Racine, Judge Miller postponed for two days the hearing at which it was expected that he would authorize Garland to take Glover back to Missouri as his slave.

---

[6] Mason, "The Fugitive Slave Law in Wisconsin, With Reference to Nullification Sentiment," *Proceedings of the State Historical Society of Wisconsin . . . 1895*, 124, 1896. Booth contended many years later that he had not been guilty of any offense, since he had not used the word "rescue" in the sense of violation of the Fugitive Slave Law. "Communication," *Wisconsin Magazine of History*, 20:233, 1936. See also S. S. Gregory, "A Historic Judicial Controversy and Some Reflections Suggested by It," *Mich. L. Rev.*, 11:179, 183–84, 1913.

[7] Appleton Morgan, "Recollections of Early Racine," *Wisconsin Magazine of History*, 2:431, 432, 1919.

In the meantime the United States Attorney made a futile attempt to assemble military aid.[8]

On the evening of March 10 a huge crowd assembled outside the courthouse to listen to an emotional harangue by Booth in behalf of liberty and against the return of fugitive slaves. The mob, headed by John Rycraft,[9] then demanded the prisoner. When he was not surrendered they battered in the jail door and removed him, driving him down Clinton Street in the presence of a huge demonstration, Glover excitedly lifting his manacled hands and shouting "Glory! Hallelujah!" Thereafter he was put aboard a schooner clearing for Canada.[10]

In the wave of abolitionist enthusiasm, local authorities added insult to injury by arresting Garland and the federal deputies for kidnaping and assault and battery. Here Judge Miller again intervened, bringing about their release.[11]

Far and wide, in Wisconsin and elsewhere, abolitionists hailed the delivery of Glover. A month after his release an abolitionist convention in Milwaukee asserted the right of independent judgment of the states in such matters, in the language of the Kentucky and Virginia Resolutions of 1798. Here a state which only six years earlier had been a creature of the Constitution described the Constitution as a compact between the federal government and the states, a compact which each party had a right to interpret for itself. It is said that at this meeting a league was formed which was a forerunner of the Republican Party in Wisconsin.[12]

On March 15, 1854, Booth as the leader of the group and a number of other men as well were arrested on a warrant from a United States Commissioner for having aided in the escape of a fugitive slave. At the hearing Booth, as if inviting martyrdom, proclaimed that rather than see the writ of habeas corpus and the right of trial by jury stricken

---

[8] A. J. Beitzinger, "Federal Law Enforcement and the Booth Cases," *Marq. L. Rev.*, 41:7, 10–11, 1957. This article brings together a great deal of the earlier materials used in the story with materials not hitherto used.

[9] The name is spelled interchangeably in the records as "Rycraft" and "Ryecraft."

[10] Mason, "The Fugitive Slave Law in Wisconsin, With Reference to Nullification Sentiment," *Proceedings of the State Historical Society of Wisconsin . . . 1895*, 125, 1896.

[11] *Ibid.*, 125. In his opinion Judge Miller said, "I view this warrant of the mayor to have been obtained by an officious intermeddler, for the same purpose as the habeas corpus— to effect the rescue of the fugitive Glover." And again, "I cannot but consider the imprisonment of the relator, or of the marshal, (who was also prosecuted in Racine,) a greater outrage than the rescue." United States *ex rel.* Garland v. Morris, 26 Fed. Cas. 1318, 1319 (No. 15811) (D.C.D. Wis. 1854).

[12] Mason, "The Fugitive Slave Law in Wisconsin, With Reference to Nullification Sentiment," *Proceedings of the State Historical Society of Wisconsin . . . 1895*, 127–28, 1896.

down by the Fugitive Slave Law he would "prefer to see every Federal officer in Wisconsin hanged to a gallows fifty cubits higher than Haman's."[13] The court was addressed in his behalf by Byron Paine, a promising young lawyer who was also in the abolitionist camp and who had done some writing for Booth's *Free Democrat*. Booth was held for trial, with Paine as his counsel.

On May 27, 1854, the Supreme Court of the state being in vacation, Booth applied to Associate Justice Abram D. Smith for a writ of habeas corpus, asking release on the ground of the unconstitutionality of the Fugitive Slave Law which he was charged with violating. Paine devoted a day and a half to an argument against the constitutionality of the law.[14] On June 7, reading a long opinion, Justice Smith ordered Booth's release, asserting the right of the state to intervene and the unconstitutionality of the statute on the ground that it denied trial by jury to fugitive slaves and took liberty without due process of law, ignoring the various charges of Supreme Court Justices to juries and Circuit Court decisions maintaining the constitutionality of the act. He demanded that the states assert their rightful authority, that the slave states be content with the execution of the constitutional compact as originally intended, and that the federal government limit itself to the exercise of its just powers. Until these things were done, "I solemnly believe that there will be no peace for the state or the nation, but that agitation, acrimony and hostility will mark our progress, even if we escape a more dread calamity, which I will not even mention."[15]

Booth was released. Federal authorities took the case on certiorari to the full Supreme Court of three members, retaining as counsel a distinguished Wisconsin lawyer, Edward G. Ryan. The Supreme Court unanimously upheld Justice Smith's decision, and Chief Justice Edward V. Whiton and Justice Smith reaffirmed the unconstitutionality of the Fugitive Slave Law. On this point Justice Samuel Crawford dissented, thereby paving the way for his defeat at the polls when he came up for reelection in 1855.[16] The decision of the majority was hailed by abolitionists all over the country. Charles Sumner trusted that Wisconsin would not retreat from her grand position. She would help to make history.[17]

---

[13] *Ibid.*, 129.

[14] Beitzinger, "Federal Law Enforcement and the Booth Cases," *Marq. L. Rev.*, 41:12, 1957.

[15] *In re* Booth, 3 Wis. 1, 48 (1854).

[16] See John B. Sanborn, "The Supreme Court of Wisconsin in the Eighties," *Wisconsin Magazine of History*, 15:3, 5, 1931; Timothy Brown, "The Wisconsin Supreme Court," *Wisconsin Magazine of History*, 36:3, 4, 1952. For Ryan's part in the case see Alfons J. Beitzinger, *Edward G. Ryan, Lion of the Law*.

[17] Mason, "The Fugitive Slave Law in Wisconsin, With Reference to Nullification Sentiment," *Proceedings of the State Historical Society of Wisconsin . . . 1895*, 133, 1896.

This, the first decision of the Wisconsin Supreme Court in the matter, was now appealed to the Supreme Court of the United States on writ of error. Attorney General Caleb Cushing wrote to the Solicitor of the Treasury that the case would afford a convenient opportunity for obtaining the opinion of the Supreme Court on the limits of the jurisdiction of state courts to release federal prisoners on habeas corpus and on the constitutionality of fugitive slave legislation. The decision would relieve the federal courts of conflicts of jurisdiction which had arisen not only in Wisconsin but also in Ohio, Pennsylvania, and New York.[18]

In the meantime, at the term of the United States District Court in Wisconsin held in July, 1854, Judge Miller delivered to a grand jury a vigorous charge demanding indictment of the rescuers of Glover.[19] If the people, and courts and juries, did not support the marshals in law enforcement, it would be necessary to resort to outright force.[20] Presumably under pressure from the judge the grand jury indicted Booth and Rycraft, and they were arrested. Booth again sought release on habeas corpus from the Wisconsin Supreme Court. This time the application was denied, the Supreme Court holding that when a court had obtained jurisdiction of a case no other court of concurrent jurisdiction could interfere.[21] It now appeared that the defendants would have to stand trial.

When time came for the trial, Booth was seriously ill. Rycraft was therefore tried alone. Judge Miller fought hard to protect the court against the tides of public sentiment. He refused permission to a local newspaper to report the evidence in the case as given day by day, "respectfully requesting" editors to postpone such publication until the case had been determined. He cautioned the jury against "outdoor influences," explaining that this was a national court which local attitudes should not be permitted to influence. Citing jury charges and decisions of Supreme Court Justices on circuit, he upheld the constitutionality of the Fugitive Slave Law and rejected higher-law doctrines as a means of arriving at a different determination. The law was not to be disregarded because it was distasteful or unpopular. "To ask the judge to withhold the prescribed sentence, or the jury to find a verdict in disregard of the evidence, because they or the community looked upon a law with disfavor, is asking a commission of moral perjury. Such a corrupt prin-

---

[18] Constitutionality of the Law for the Extradition of Fugitives, 6 Op. Atty Gen. 713 (1854).

[19] Beitzinger, "Federal Law Enforcement and the Booth Cases," *Marq. L. Rev.*, 41:13, 1957.

[20] For the charge see *Madison Argus and Democrat*, July 6, 1854.

[21] *Ex parte* Booth, 3 Wis. 145 (1854).

ciple can not be advanced without a rebuke commensurate to its enormity."[22]

Yielding to this very strong charge, the jury found Rycraft guilty. His counsel then moved to arrest judgment, on the ground that to justify conviction it would be necessary not only to prove that Rycraft had participated in the release of the prisoner but also that Glover was a slave. Such proof had not been adduced before the court. Judge Miller deferred sentence in order to write to Justices Nelson, Grier, and Curtis about this point.[23] Apparently he got replies supporting him in the position he had taken,[24] leaving him free to administer the sentence.

In January, 1855, Booth and others of the rescuers were the subject of new bills of indictment. The Booth trial, which began January 10 and lasted for three days, was a hard-fought battle on both sides, with Paine leading for the defense and Ryan aiding the prosecution. Judge Miller, concerned about the possible breakdown of federal law enforcement, charged the jury as if he himself were one of the instruments of the prosecution.[25] Once again he warned a jury not to commit "moral perjury" by ignoring the law as interpreted by the court and adhering to its own interpretation. He made clear his own belief in Booth's guilt and virtually told the jury what the verdict should be.[26]

As if reluctantly responding to pressure from the judge, the jury found Booth guilty on two counts. Judge Miller, who himself on the eve of the trial had had to put up bail of five thousand dollars in the Milwaukee county court on the charge of false imprisonment of Booth, now, in the face of motions from Booth's counsel, proceeded to sentence Booth and to prescribe also the previously deferred sentence of Rycraft. Booth was sentenced to a month in jail and a fine of one thousand dollars plus costs, and Rycraft to ten days in jail and a fine of two hundred dollars.[27]

The conviction created great excitement throughout the state, with newspapers and resolutions of public meetings denouncing the proceedings. Resolutions adopted at Milwaukee repudiated all obligation to obey the "unlawful and unconstitutional requirements" of the Fugitive Slave Law and asked the legislature to forbid state officers to give aid in enforcement and to forbid the use of state jails and prisons in connec-

---

[22] United States v. Rycraft, 27 Fed. Cas. 918, 921 (No. 16211) (D.C.D. Wis. 1854).

[23] Beitzinger, "Federal Law Enforcement and the Booth Cases," *Marq. L. Rev.*, 41:14, 1957.

[24] "As to the correctness of the indictment I consulted Judges of the U.S. Sup. Court by letter." A. G.

Miller to J. S. Black, Nov. 25, 1857, Black Papers.

[25] See Beitzinger, "Federal Law Enforcement and the Booth Cases," *Marq. L. Rev.*, 41:15, 1957.

[26] For the charge see *Milwaukee Daily Wisconsin*, Jan. 16, 1855.

[27] Beitzinger, "Federal Law Enforcement and the Booth Cases," *Marq. L. Rev.*, 41:15, 1957.

tion with enforcement of the statute. A resolution of another town said of Judge Miller that "we regard him as a disgrace to the name of judge, a tyrant when clothed with a little brief authority, *an old Granny and a miserable Doughface.*"[28] At another place a resolution promised to see Booth and Rycraft out of their troubles, "*if we have to do it at the point of the bayonet.*"[29]

Since the federal government relied on the state for prison facilities in Wisconsin as elsewhere, Booth and Rycraft were committed to the county jail of Milwaukee County. By habeas corpus they again sought release at the hands of the state Supreme Court. That court unanimously, but with the three judges basing opinions on somewhat different grounds, found that the prisoners were unlawfully held and ordered their release.[30] Nullification by state judiciary now seemed well under way.[31] Charles Sumner sent Byron Paine his warm congratulations: "God grant that Wisconsin may not fail to protect her own rights and the rights of her citizens in the exigency now before her! To her belongs the lead which Massachusetts should have taken. Of the final result I have no doubt."[32]

Judge Miller defended the federal court decision in a statement read in his own court,[33] but in view of the pressures of local sentiment it was obvious there was nothing more he could do about it. If federal law was to be enforced, help would have to come from Washington.

The case involving Booth's original release had already gone to the United States Supreme Court but had not yet been argued. The government's strategy was now to get the second release before the high tribunal. Suspecting that the Wisconsin Supreme Court, growing more and more obstreperous, would in this case refuse to recognize the writ of error and send up the record in the case, the United States

---

[28] Mason, "The Fugitive Slave Law in Wisconsin, With Reference to Nullification Sentiment," *Proceedings of the State Historical Society of Wisconsin . . . 1895,* 135, 1896.

[29] *Ibid.,* 136.

[30] *In re* Booth and Rycraft, 3 Wis. 157 (1855).

[31] The Wisconsin courts extended their nullification of federal process to other areas than that of the recovery of fugitive slaves. In one instance Judge Miller issued a warrant for the arrest of Benjamin Bagnall, a citizen of Michigan who was under indictment in Michigan for timber thefts in that state. A county court issued a writ of habeas corpus and

ordered Bagnall's release. The United States Marshal rearrested him, whereupon he brought suit to recover the penalty which a state statute provided for rearrest of a person for the same offense after he had been discharged on habeas corpus. The Wisconsin Supreme Court held that the rearrest had been unlawful. Bagnall v. Ableman, 4 Wis. 163 (1855).

[32] Mason, "The Fugitive Slave Law in Wisconsin, With Reference to Nullification Sentiment," *Proceedings of the State Historical Society of Wisconsin . . . 1895,* 138, 1896.

[33] Beitzinger, "Federal Law Enforcement and the Booth Cases," *Marq. L. Rev.,* 41:17, 1957.

Attorney on instructions from Washington asked for and got a certified copy of the record without disclosing his purpose. True to expectations, when the Wisconsin court received the writ of error it instructed the clerk to ignore it.[34] Attorney General Caleb Cushing asked the Supreme Court to hear the case on the record previously secured from the clerk, but the Court, hoping to avoid a serious clash and trusting that the clerk might respond to a rule directing him to obey the writ of error, decided to postpone action. The Court stated, however, through Chief Justice Taney, that the refusal of the clerk could not prevent the exercise of the appellate powers of the Court.[35] The earlier appeal was likewise postponed so that the two cases could be argued together.[36]

The election of 1856 brought a change in Administration in Washington and changes in the offices of United States Attorney and United States Marshal in Wisconsin. In November, 1857, Judge Miller wrote a long letter to Attorney General Jeremiah S. Black, giving him the background of the Booth Cases. He would have ordered Booth's rearrest and imprisonment, he explained, but no jail was available. After his discharge on the order of the Wisconsin Supreme Court, no jailor or sheriff in the state would have received him. Meanwhile the Wisconsin legislature had passed personal liberty bills and bills for the relief of Booth to enable him to recover by replevin his property which had been seized in execution in favor of Garland, the owner of the escaped slave.

Judge Miller remarked that Negro politics at this time had become less exciting for want of nourishment. He thought the rearrest of Booth would be inexpedient in that it would provide material for reviving the controversy. He thought a decision of the United States Supreme Court would be of great importance in that it would show state tribunals that they should not interfere with federal prisoners. Even so, the value of the decision would be restricted in that, apparently because of the unavailability of prison facilities, no effective mandate could issue from a judgment of reversal. On the other hand, if the United States had a jail, it would not be necessary to await a Supreme Court decision in order to reimprison Booth. It had been hoped, he said, that this question of the clash of federal and state jurisdictions could be dealt with in some case other than a slave case, and Attorney General Cushing had thought such a case was on the way, he believed from Georgia.[37]

---

[34] *Ibid.*, 18.

[35] United States v. Booth, 18 How. 476 (1856).

[36] Ableman v. Booth, 18 How. 479 (1856).

[37] A. G. Miller to J. S. Black, Nov. 25, 1857, Black Papers. Judge Miller felt close enough to the Buchanan Administration to give detailed advice on the filling of numerous federal offices in Wisconsin. See his letters to Black dated Dec. 16, 1857, Feb. 5, 1858, and May 29, 1858, Black Papers.

No nonslavery case involving this question reached the Supreme Court in this period. The Court, undergoing the criticism flowing from the Dred Scott case, did not hear argument in the *Booth Cases* until January 19, 1859. At that time Attorney General Black appeared for the United States and, nominally, in the other case for Ableman, who had long since left the office of United States Marshal. Black, an orator at the bar as well as a former state judge, defended the position of the federal government on all questions and faced no opposition, since Booth and the state of Wisconsin did not deign to recognize the proceeding. Black talked of attaching the Wisconsin Supreme Court for contempt, reported the *New York Tribune*, "but said that the Government would magnanimously refrain from doing so."[38] George W. Woodward, who had been a colleague of Black's on the Pennsylvania Supreme Court, wrote to him saying that "A more atrocious case than that Wisconsin proceeding is not on record. I am glad you chastized it and very glad that it fell into your hands for chastisement. But I fancy their Honors of that old fogy Court never had their ears tickled before with such ringing periods. What did they say to it?"[39]

What the Court had to say appeared on March 7, 1859, as the unanimous opinion of the Supreme Court, written by Chief Justice Taney. The appearance of full unanimity stood in strong contrast with the Dred Scott decision. It marked a reaction to the rough experience of the Court and gave the Chief Justice the opportunity to make unhampered a supreme effort at portrayal of the position of the Supreme Court in relation to the judiciaries of the states. The *Booth* opinion marked the Chief Justice at his best, without any of the striving after extreme effect or the rewriting of American history for the making of a constitutional point which had characterized his derided treatment of Dred Scott. It was thoughtful, measured, and disciplined to the last degree.

Having set forth the interference of the Wisconsin Supreme Court with federal judicial proceedings, Taney stressed the fact that the Constitution had been adopted not merely to guard against dangers from abroad but mainly to secure union and harmony at home. To that end it had been necessary to transfer to the general government many of the rights hitherto possessed by the states, and to make that government supreme within its sphere of action, in order to prevent local interests, passions, and prejudices from becoming dominant.

To maintain that supremacy the federal government had to be clothed with judicial power equally paramount in authority with the

---

[38] *New York Tribune*, Jan. 20, 1859.

[39] George W. Woodward to J. S. Black, Feb. 18, 1859, Black Papers.

other branches of the government; "for if left to the courts of justice in the several states, conflicting decisions would unavoidably take place, and the local tribunals could hardly be expected to be always free from the local influences of which we have spoken."[40] It was essential to the very existence of the government that it should have the power of establishing independent courts of justice and a tribunal where all federal questions should be decided, whether arising in state or federal courts. The Constitution had therefore provided for such a tribunal and conferred upon it the requisite jurisdiction:

> In organizing such a tribunal, it is evident that every precaution was taken, which human wisdom could devise, to fit it for the high duty with which it was intrusted. It was not left to Congress to create it by law; for the states could hardly be expected to confide in the impartiality of a tribunal created exclusively by the general government, without any participation on their part. And as the performance of its duty would sometimes come in conflict with individual ambition or interests, and powerful political combinations, an act of Congress establishing such a tribunal might be repealed in order to establish another more subservient to the predominant political influences or · excited passions of the day. This tribunal, therefore, was erected, and the powers of which we have spoken conferred upon it, not by the Federal government, but by the people of the states, who formed and adopted that government, and conferred upon it all the powers, legislative, executive, and judicial, which it now possesses. And in order to secure its independence, and enable it faithfully and firmly to perform its duty, it engrafted it upon the Constitution itself, and declared that this court should have appellate power in all cases arising under the Constitution and laws of the United States. So long, therefore, as this Constitution shall endure, this tribunal must exist with it, deciding in the peaceful forms of judicial proceeding the angry and irritating controversies between sovereignties, which in other countries have been determined by the arbitrament of force.[41]

It was in terms of such constitutional provisions that Congress had enacted measures concerning the courts of the United States and provided modes of appeal from state courts to the Supreme Court. The prescribed writ of error had here been refused obedience by the Supreme Court of Wisconsin, which had annulled the judgment of a United States District Court and the relevant constitutional provisions as well. True, a state court had the right to inquire by habeas corpus into the lawfulness of the detention of any person held in the state, but it had no power to order release when the person was held under the authority of the United States. Such detention was subject to the control only of federal

---

[40] Ableman v. Booth, 21 How. 506, 517–18. [41] *Ibid.*, 521.

judicial tribunals. The supremacy of the general government within its sphere provided no occasion for jealousy or hurt pride on the part of the states, for the jurisdiction had been given by the Constitution, which was the voluntary act of the people of the several states.

Since in no event did a state court have the power to correct proceedings in a federal court, it was not here necessary to discuss the constitutionality of the Fugitive Slave Law. To avoid misunderstanding, however, the Court said briefly that in its judgment the act was in all its provisions fully authorized by the Constitution.

It is to be noted that whereas the first public pronouncements of the Supreme Court in the *Booth Cases* came in May, 1856, at the time of the decision to call for reargument of the Dred Scott case, the opinion discussed above was not handed down until 1859, two years after the Dred Scott decision. Throughout those two years the Court had been under bombardment for its aid to the slavery cause in the Dred Scott case. In January, 1858, a member of Congress, wearied by the discussion of that case, found it expedient to begin remarks on another subject by announcing that he had not risen to discuss the Dred Scott decision. He offered the comment of a colleague that the House might save time by setting aside one day each month for discussion of the decision, and the comment of another that the day should be called "black Friday."[42] Between the time of the argument of the *Booth Cases* on January 19, 1859, and the decision on March 7, Stephen A. Douglas was still engaged in a hot debate in the Senate over the implications of the Dred Scott case for slavery in the territories.[43] Senator John P. Hale of New Hampshire was denouncing the decision as worthy of less respect than a political platform, especially since "it was not the business of the Supreme Court to make platforms, and they went out of their way to make one." He declared that the decision would never win the assent of the country. It would "stand as one of those unfortunate decisions which courts have frequently made when they have undertaken to mold eternal principles of justice and law to suit the purposes of power."[44]

Philemon Bliss of Ohio, in whose state a clash was taking place between federal and state judiciaries comparable to that in Wisconsin, deplored in the House of Representatives the tendency to clothe the Supreme Court in robes of majesty. He poured out sarcasm on the teaching that people should "bow without question as the faithful to the decrees of the Great Lama" when "from yon mysterious vault the enrobed nine send forth their tomes, befogging by their diffuseness even

---

[42] John A. Gilmer of North Carolina, *Cong. Globe*, 35th Cong. 1st Sess. 214 (1858).

[43] See for example *Cong. Globe*, 35th Cong., 2nd Sess. 1254–60 (1859).
[44] *Ibid.*, 1265.

when announcing the plainest principles."[45] He admitted that the Constitution and laws of the United States were the supreme law, but denied that the Supreme Court had appellate jurisdiction over the state courts. State judges as well as federal judges were sworn to uphold the federal Constitution and laws, and he had no reason to believe that the state courts were behind the Supreme Court in learning, integrity, and fidelity to the admitted principles of our government. It was ironic that, just as decades earlier states'-rights Democrats had sought to terminate or limit Supreme Court jurisdiction on writ of error to state courts, so now abolitionist Republicans in Congress, more deeply devoted to abolition than to nationalism, attempted, though vainly, to withdraw that jurisdiction by repealing the twenty-fifth section of the Judiciary Act.[46]

In such an atmosphere there was reason for doubting whether the profoundly reasoned opinion of the Court in the *Booth Cases* would receive the thoughtful attention it deserved. It did receive a measure of high praise, both from Democrats and from moderate Republicans who sensed its constitutional soundness.[47] But radical Republicans and abolitionists generally viewed the opinion as one more political document improperly emanating from the judiciary. The *New York Tribune* thought it destined "to become quite as famous as the Dred Scott case, and forming a part of the same system of usurpation tending to the concentration of all power in the Federal Judiciary."[48]

Chief Justice Taney expected the opinion of the Court in the *Booth Cases* to attract a great deal of attention. To prevent its distortion in the newspapers or to assure to the Reporter his rightful income from sales, he directed the Clerk of the Court to give out no copies until it had been officially published. Attorney General Black, for whom the decision represented a victory, needed a copy of the opinion, apparently for use in connection with advice as to the handling of similar cases in lower federal courts. On April 26, some six weeks after the case was decided, he asked for a copy. Carroll being temporarily absent from the Clerk's office, subordinate employees refused to give out a copy. Black heatedly addressed to the Clerk a demand for a copy, "In the name and by the direction of the President and for the public use in a matter of great and pressing importance," and saying that "Regarding this as a public record I respectfully suggest that I have a legal right to have it for the purpose referred to."[49]

---

[45] *Cong. Globe*, 35th Cong., 2nd Sess., App. 73 (1859).

[46] *Ibid.*, 74. For discussion of attacks on the Judiciary Act see Charles Warren, *The Supreme Court in United States History*, II, 333–36.

[47] See Warren, *The Supreme Court*

in *United States History*, II, 338–43.

[48] *New York Tribune*, Apr. 1, 1859.

[49] Copy, J. S. Black to the Clerk of the Supreme Court, Apr. 26, 1859, Appellate Case File No. 3202, Clerk's Files. For discussion see Beitzinger,

D. W. Middleton, Carroll's assistant clerk, wired to Taney in Baltimore for instructions. Taney wired back tersely, "Give the opinion to the Attorney General."[50] A copy was sent to Black, who thereupon asked for copies of the mandates in the two cases and apparently also for an additional certified copy of the opinion. Carroll, disturbed by the controversy, took a train to Baltimore to discuss the matter with Taney, taking with him a copy of Black's original peremptory demand. On April 28 Taney formalized his instructions in a letter to Carroll. He assured Carroll that he and his clerks had acted properly in refusing to give out the opinion without his instructions and that they had his full support. As for Black's demand, it was probably written on some sudden impulse and on further thought Black would probably withdraw it. If not, it would be Taney's duty at the ensuing term of the Court to file a vindication of his order and to bring the matter to the attention of the Court. He asked Carroll to explain to Black that he had authorized giving him a copy of the opinion for official use only, and not for publication in advance of publication by the Reporter. He here disclosed the fact that with the same restriction he had given an advance copy of the Dred Scott opinion to Robert J. Walker, who at the time had been about to depart for Kansas as governor of the territory.[51]

Carroll thereupon delivered copies to the President and to Black, and to Black he quoted Buchanan as saying that "the Supreme Court and the Executive should stand shoulder to shoulder in such a crisis, that united they might be able to resist the fanaticism of both the North and the South and that he had determined to execute the decrees of that Court with all the force and power that the Constitution and laws placed at his disposal."[52] Black seems to have been persuaded to withdraw from Carroll's office the draft of his demand for a copy of the opinion in order to avoid further controversy with the Chief Justice, but before releasing it the Clerk made a copy for the record.

For some reason Howard seems to have been extremely slow in publishing the volume of reports containing the *Booth Cases*. On May 12, three months after the Court had handed down its final opinions for the term, Taney wrote to Carroll a letter to be shown to Howard stating that "its object is to recommend strongly to him a pamphlet edition of the Wisconsin case, published as early at least as his volume

---

"Federal Law Enforcement and the Booth Cases," *Marq. L. Rev.*, 41: 23–24, 1957. See the same author, "Chief Justice Taney and the Publication of Supreme Court Opinions," *Cath. U. of America L. Rev.*, 7:32, 1958.

[50] Telegram, R. B. Taney to D. W. Middleton, Apr. 26, 1858, Appellate Case File No. 3202, Clerk's Files.

[51] R. B. Taney to William T. Carroll, Apr. 28, 1859, *ibid.*

[52] Carroll penciled memorandum, *ibid.*

of reports, announcing it as his publication as was done in the Dred Scott Case. Thousands wish to read this decision who feel no interest in any other case in this volume, and who cannot afford or are unwilling to buy the book for the sake of this case. I think the public will expect a pamphlet edition, and Mr. Howard will lose nothing by it—most probably a gainer."[53] If the pamphlet was published he asked that a copy be sent to him at Richmond, where he was going to hold Circuit Court.

Howard's political intuition, in this instance sounder than that of the Chief Justice, told him that there would be no such demand for the opinion as to justify a pamphlet edition. He wrote, "I think the Chief Justice is mistaken with respect to the desire felt by the public to see the Wisconsin decision. Those only wish to read it who would purchase the volume to find it. Nevertheless, his language is so strong that it leaves me no alternative."[54] If such a pamphlet was published, however, it received no such widespread attention as that in the Dred Scott case.

It was not until August 4, 1859, nearly five months after the decision, that Black sent copies of the Supreme Court mandates to A. J. Upham, the new United States Attorney for Wisconsin. His letter reflected awareness of the difficulty of making the mandates effective. Upham was directed to bring the matter to the attention of the United States District Court and move for an order upon the marshal "to re-arrest Booth, and keep him safely and closely until he complies with the sentence by serving out his term of imprisonment and paying his fine." Without stating how it was to be done in a state where there was no federal prison, Black directed that the marshal be instructed to keep Booth where no effort at another rescue could be successful. He was to ignore any writ of habeas corpus issued by any state judge or state court, and defend himself against any attempt to take the prisoner out of his custody. Nevertheless the federal officers were to show no wanton disrespect to the Wisconsin authorities or do anything to furnish an excuse for opposition to the laws. Upham was further directed to lay the mandates before the Supreme Court of Wisconsin and call the attention of the justices to the action of the Supreme Court of the United States but to make no motion, merely asking that they be filed, and to say that he acted under instructions from the Attorney General.[55]

On September 3 Upham wrote that he would file the mandates

---

[53] R. B. Taney to W. T. Carroll, May 12, 1859, Files of the Clerk of the Supreme Court.
[54] Benjamin C. Howard to William

Thomas Carroll, May 13, 1859, *ibid.*
[55] J. S. Black to A. J. Upham, Aug. 4, 1859, Attorney General's Letter Book B-3, 94-96.

when the Wisconsin court met on September 20. He thought it would be well to file the mandates before Booth was again arrested.[56] On September 22, H. C. Hobart, Democratic candidate for governor of Wisconsin, wrote to Black that the mandates had been filed but urged that the arrest be postponed. He thought there was every prospect of success for the party, but feared that Booth's arrest would be seized upon by the enemies of the Administration as an effective campaign item.[57] Hobart wrote also to Secretary of the Interior Jacob Thompson, who pressed his request upon Black.[58] Black also received a visit from the United States Marshal, who notified Upham that Black would not object to a delay in making the arrest. With a note of desperation Upham wrote to Black on November 12 that he would not apply for the order of arrest until the special term of the District Court in November unless instructed otherwise, and that "I think it very desirable that the marshal should be here when the arrest is made, and for this reason as well as the fact that the State Court has not yet decided whether or not to allow the mandates to be filed."[59]

The political atmosphere in Wisconsin was such as understandably to impress federal officers seeking to enforce laws protecting rights in slavery. After announcement of the Supreme Court decision in the *Booth Cases* the state legislature adopted resolutions condemning what it called the assumption of power and authority on the part of the Supreme Court to become the final arbiter of the liberty of citizens and override and nullify the judgment of state courts. The Court was condemned as prostrating the rights and liberties of the people under the foot of an unlimited power. The resolutions were approved by the governor.[60]

In the election of a member of the state supreme court even the faithful services of Justice Abram D. Smith in the abolitionist cause proved to be not enough. On the Republican ticket he gave place to Byron Paine, the man who had defended Booth at the bar in Wisconsin. In the campaign Carl Schurz, a rising politician from the German community in Wisconsin, demanded to know whether the spirit of liberty in the Wisconsin Supreme Court was to be sacrificed: "Will you see Judge Miller's opinions and pretensions infest the highest court of this state?

---

[56] D. A. J. Upham to J. S. Black, Sept. 3, 1859, Attorney General Papers.

[57] H. C. Hobart to J. S. Black, Sept. 22, 1859, Black Papers. See Beitzinger, "Federal Law Enforcement and the Booth Cases," *Marq. L. Rev.*, 41:25, 1957.

[58] J. Thompson to J. S. Black, Oct. 3, 1859, Black Papers.

[59] D. A. J. Upham to J. S. Black, Oct. 12, 1859, Black Papers.

[60] S. S. Gregory, "A Historic Judicial Controversy and Some Reflections Suggested by It," *Mich. L. Rev.*, 11:179, 191, 1913.

Will you see the dirty fingermarks of Buchanan's administration on the Supreme Bench of Wisconsin? If not, place a man there who dares to be himself. Let the friends of liberty and self-government present an unbroken front. Their banner bears the inscription, 'State rights and Byron Paine.' "[61]

This judicial election took place early in 1859, shortly after the Supreme Court decision in the *Booth Cases*. Paine triumphed. Political sentiment remained at fever pitch throughout the summer and autumn—which may account for the leisure with which Washington and Wisconsin federal officials sought to make the decision effective. In the campaign for the governorship in the autumn attacks on Judge Miller and his "cutthroat" court continued, with the prediction that if Hobart were elected the state judiciary would be brought under Judge Miller's control and the governor would put pressure on the Wisconsin Supreme Court to file the mandates in the *Booth Cases*. Hobart was defeated, and the incumbent, Alexander Randall, who had signed the nullifying resolutions of the legislature, was reelected.[62]

Abolitionist sentiment in Wisconsin as in the rest of the country had been further inflamed by the raid on Harper's Ferry by the fanatic John Brown, and his speedy trial and execution took place to the accompaniment of outraged protest. It was in such an atmosphere that United States Attorney Upham made application to Judge Miller's court for the recommitment of Booth and for a warrant to carry the order into execution. On December 6, 1859, Judge Miller wrote to Attorney General Black that because of excitement over the Harper's Ferry affair and in the hope that the excitement might be allayed by the forthcoming message of the President, he had deferred proceedings with respect to Booth until the next term of his court, to be held the first Monday in January. Furthermore, he had thought it better to delay a few days to

---

[61] *Ibid.*, 192. Schurz later characterized the address to which this quotation was the peroration as the most enthusiastically received of all his addresses. He excluded it from his published works, however, because of the extremity of its doctrines for a man who became a prominent Republican leader. See James L. Sellers, "Republicanism and State Rights in Wisconsin," *Mississippi Valley Historical Review*, 17:213, 227, 1930; Carl Schurz, *Reminiscences of Carl Schurz*, II, 113. Charles Sumner wrote Paine from Rome in warm congratulation on his election: "God bless the people of Wisconsin who know their rights, and knowing dare maintain! God bless the cause! To the people, to the champion, and to the cause, an American citizen far away in foreign land sends the best wishes of his heart." Mason, "The Fugitive Slave Law in Wisconsin, With Reference to Nullification Sentiment," *Proceedings of the State Historical Society of Wisconsin . . . 1895*, 141, 1896.

[62] Beitzinger, "Federal Law Enforcement and the Booth Cases," *Marq. L. Rev.*, 41:25.

see whether the supreme court of the state might not in the meantime "make some order tending to show their approval of the action of the Supreme Court of the United States."[63]

On December 15, 1859, the Wisconsin Supreme Court refused to file the mandates. The mandates, merely requiring that further proceedings be in harmony with the opinion of the Supreme Court, called for no positive action by the Wisconsin tribunal, but their filing would have constituted recognition of their validity and of the validity of Booth's conviction. The chief justice favored their filing, but one justice was opposed, and Justice Paine, having been of counsel for Booth, did not sit, with the result that there was not a majority in favor of filing.[64]

The United States Attorney reported the matter to Black and predicted that on Booth's rearrest an attempt would be made to have him released once more on writ of habeas corpus by one of the judges, thereby bringing state authorities directly into collision with those of the United States. Wisconsin, he said, was in the lamentable position of having a judiciary and an executive in the hands of a party which did not appear to be governed by principles of law, or by the decisions of the higher courts, either of the United States or of other states. The marshal and his deputies would do their utmost but they might be overpowered, and besides, they had no place to keep prisoners except in the state jails, which were in charge of state sheriffs.[65]

Federal authorities in Wisconsin could derive little of the aid that Judge Miller had hoped to get from President Buchanan's annual message to Congress. The President deplored "the recent sad and bloody occurrences at Harper's Ferry," warned of the dangers of disunion, and implored mutual forbearance as "an old public functionary whose service commenced in the last generation, among the wise and conservative statesman of that day, now nearly all passed away, and whose first and dearest wish is to leave his country tranquil, prosperous, united, and powerful."[66] It appeared as if the President who had earlier been ready to bludgeon his way to victory had now been driven back to plaintive appeals in terms of his age. Yet the iron hand of his determination still showed in his reassertion that the Supreme Court had settled the question of slavery in the territories and assured the right of every citizen to take his slave property into the territories: "The supreme judicial tribunal of the country, which is a coordinate branch of the Government, has sanctioned and affirmed these principles of constitutional law, so manifestly just in themselves and so well calculated to promote peace

---

[63] A. G. Miller to J. S. Black, Dec. 6, 1859, Black Papers.

[64] Ableman v. Booth, 11 Wis. 498 (1859).

[65] D. A. J. Upham to J. S. Black, Dec. 16, 1859, Black Papers.

[66] Richardson, *A Compilation of the Messages and Papers of the Presidents*, V, 553.

and harmony among the States."[67] But neither his plaintiveness nor his dogmatism was likely to carry much influence among the abolitionists of Wisconsin.

Booth was finally arrested on March 1, 1860, nearly a year after the date of the Supreme Court decision, and imprisoned in the United States customs house in Milwaukee, under the jurisdiction of the United States Marshal. On March 6 he filed in the Wisconsin Supreme Court a petition for a writ of habeas corpus. Justice Paine declined to sit because of his earlier connection with Booth, and the remaining two justices differed in opinion, with the result that the writ was not granted.[68] Another writ of habeas corpus was issued by a state court commissioner, but the marshal refused to surrender the prisoner, and after an appearance of the United States Attorney before the commissioner the proceeding was dismissed.[69]

Booth's official jail term expired on March 21, but he was kept in custody because he refused to pay his fine. Because he had access to the press he was able to create the impression not only that he had been imprisoned for violation of an unconstitutional law but also that now he was imprisoned in violation of his sentence. Although during the preceding year Booth had lost prestige by being subject to trial for seduction of a fourteen-year-old girl, of which he was acquitted by a divided jury,[70] he was still in a position to create an impression of political martyrdom, and he made the most of it. Federal authorities in Wisconsin were thoroughly sick of Booth and wanted to get him off their hands. A group of his friends applied for a pardon, but he himself refused to apply, and Attorney General Black refused to pay attention to the matter until Booth himself applied.[71] Judge Miller had the United States Attorney publish an explanation of Booth's status to show that Booth was now in prison at his own option, to minimize the propaganda value of the subject for the coming election.[72]

On August 6 a band of men rescued Booth from his imprisonment. For a time he went about the state insulting or annoying the United States Marshal at every opportunity, but with so much popular support that little could be done. Finally, on August 8, he was recaptured and returned to the customs house at Milwaukee. After the election Booth applied to Buchanan for a pardon, only to find his desires frustrated by the exasperated Attorney General. When toward the end of Bu-

---

[67] *Ibid.*, 554.

[68] See note appended to Ableman v. Booth, 11 Wis. 498 (1859), p. 555 of the revised and annotated edition published in 1873.

[69] Jehu N. Lewis to J. S. Black, Apr. 6, 1860, Attorney General Papers.

[70] Beitzinger, "Federal Law Enforcement and the Booth Cases," *Marq. L. Rev.*, 41:22–23, 1957.

[71] *Ibid.*, 27–28.

[72] A. G. Miller to J. S. Black, July 20, 1860, Attorney General's Papers.

chanan's Administration Black was succeeded by Edwin M. Stanton, the pardon was arranged and Booth became a free man shortly before Buchanan himself went out of office.[73]

In his final annual message, on December 3, 1860, when the Union was already beginning to crumble, President Buchanan lamented that the "long-continued and intemperate interference of the Northern people with the question of slavery in the Southern States has at length produced its natural effects."[74] He deplored the factious temper of the times which had led to the impugning of the Dred Scott decision and given rise to angry political conflicts. Although the most palpable violations of constitutional duty had taken place with respect to the Fugitive Slave Law, it was to be remembered that neither Congress nor the President was responsible, and that with the exception of Wisconsin, all the courts, state or federal, which had passed upon that statute had found it constitutional. The Wisconsin decision had been reversed by the Supreme Court, and had met with such universal reprobation that there was no danger from it as a precedent. "The validity of this law has been established over and over again by the Supreme Court of the United States with perfect unanimity."[75]

Wisconsin courts found it hard to give up with respect to the constitutionality of the Fugitive Slave Law. Booth had not yet been able to recover the printing press that had been seized to satisfy the judgment against him. He brought suit in the circuit court for Milwaukee County, which held that the sale of the property in execution of the judgment of the United States District Court was not a sufficient defense to prevent recovery. The purchaser of the press appealed to the state supreme court at the June term of 1861. Justice Paine again refused to sit because of his previous involvement as counsel. Justice Orsamus Cole, who had hitherto taken the extreme abolitionist position, still expressed the belief that the Fugitive Slave Law was unconstitutional, but since that question was not before the court in this case he reluctantly gave the opinion for the majority that the sale resulting from a judgment of a federal court in a case in which the court had jurisdiction was a bar to an action to recover the property.[76] As for Booth, with Republicans in power in Washington as well as Wisconsin and with the Civil War well under way, he was soon to be lost in the companionship of friendly associations. He wrote to Secretary of the Treasury Salmon P. Chase that he was about

---

[73] Beitzinger, "Federal Law Enforcement and the Booth Cases," *Marq. L. Rev.*, 41:28–32, 1957; Carter, "The Booth War in Ripon," *Proceedings of the State Historical Society of Wisconsin . . . 1902*, 166–72, 1903.

[74] Richardson, *A Compilation of the Messages and Papers of the Presidents*, V, 626.

[75] *Ibid.*, 630.

[76] Arnold v. Booth, 14 Wis. 180 (1861).

to launch in Milwaukee a daily, triweekly and weekly newspaper and to ask for a government printing contract,[77] but not much was heard of him thereafter.

The story of the *Booth Cases* and the struggle over the return of fugitive slaves between federal and state authorities in Wisconsin is to some extent linked with a similar struggle in Ohio. Much more than Wisconsin, Ohio was divided on slavery issues. Unlike Wisconsin, it provided major highways for the underground railroad. It had citizens who were ready to betray escaped slaves to federal authorities or to owners for a price, or as a matter of principle. It had others who devoted much of their time to the cause of freedom for unfortunate blacks. Although anything but advocates of slavery, Justice McLean and the two United States district judges in Ohio enforced the Fugitive Slave Law as cases came before them, without such interference as that met by Judge Miller in Wisconsin.

But a threat of serious trouble arose in September, 1858, when a professor at Oberlin College and a number of students pursued to the adjacent village of Wellington federal authorities who had captured a fugitive slave from Kentucky. People from Oberlin and Wellington released the slave, and a number of them were arrested for violation of the Fugitive Slave Law. Two were convicted and sentenced to fines and imprisonment, to the accompaniment of excited protests from mass meetings held throughout northern Ohio.[78]

Simeon Bushnell and Charles Langston, the two prisoners, challenged their detention in a county jail, not by having friends attempt forcible rescue but by petitions for writs of habeas corpus addressed to the Ohio Supreme Court. Perhaps puzzled as to whether they should ignore the proceeding on the ground of its gross illegality or resort to full argument, the United States Attorney, G. W. Belden, and his special counsel in the case, Noah H. Swayne, who in 1861 was to become a member of the Supreme Court on an appointment from President Lincoln, compromised by filing memoranda on the principal legal points and refraining from arguing the case orally. The Ohio attorney general, C. P. Walcott, delivered an elaborate oral argument in which he challenged the constitutionality of the Fugitive Slave Law and denounced the bias of the Supreme Court, saying that it was "a sectional court, composed of sectional men, judging sectional questions upon sectional influences."[79]

---

[77] S. M. Booth to S. P. Chase, July 9, 1861, Chase Papers.

[78] Emilius O. Randall and Daniel J. Ryan, *History of Ohio*, IV, 134.

[79] *Ex parte* Bushnell, 9 Ohio St. 77, 161–62 (1859). Walcott implied that the appointment of Justice Nelson to the Supreme Court in 1845 had been confirmed, and the earlier nominations of John C. Spencer and Reuben H. Walworth rejected because of attitudes toward slavery. Chancellor Walworth

The Ohio Supreme Court consisted of five members. Two members from the northern part of the state found the Fugitive Slave Law unconstitutional. Two from the southern part found it constitutional. The Chief Justice, Joseph R. Swan, residing at Columbus,[80] at the central part of the state, joined the southerners and wrote an eloquent and highly persuasive opinion holding that state tribunals could not interfere with enforcement of a statute in the federal courts which the Supreme Court of the United States had found to be constitutional. One of the dissenting judges stormed that "The federal legislature has usurped a power not granted by the constitution, and a federal judiciary has, through the medium of reasoning lame, halting, contradictory, and of far-fetched implications, derived from unwarranted assumptions and false history, sanctioned the usurpation."[81]

By virtue of the three-to-two decision, an appeal to the Supreme Court in a case paralleling the *Booth Cases* was rendered unnecessary. Chief Justice Swan, however, paid a high price for his vote and his opinion. He was near the end of the term for which he had been elected. Although he was opposed to slavery, and had been elected by the group out of which the Republican Party in Ohio had been formed, the abolitionist leaders of the Republican Party took revenge for his action by refusing him a renomination.[82] In his opinion he had tried to protect himself and make his position clear. He remarked that the sense of justice of the people of Ohio had been shocked by unjust provisions of the fugitive slave acts. But the abuses were to be remedied by Congress. The statute had been found constitutional by "some of the soundest and wisest judges that have adorned the American bench," and the question must be regarded as settled. For himself as a member of the Ohio Supreme Court, "I disclaim the judicial discretion of disturbing the settled construction of the constitution of the United States; and I must refuse the experiment of initiating disorder and governmental collision, to establish order and even-handed justice."[83]

---

had found unconstitutional a provision in the Fugitive Slave Act of 1793 which provided for the participation of a state magistrate in the return of fugitive slaves. Jack v. Martin, 14 Wendell (N.Y.) 507, 524 (1835). Samuel Nelson, on the other hand, had found the measure constitutional. Jack v. Martin, 12 Wendell (N.Y.) 311 (1834).

[80] For the statement concerning the residence of the Ohio judges see Eugene H. Roseboom, *The Civil War Era, 1850–1873*, 346.

[81] *Ibid.*, 227.

[82] Randall and Ryan, *History of Ohio*, IV, 135–36; Warren, *The Supreme Court in United States History*, II, 344–45.

[83] 9 Ohio St. 198. While this case was pending in the Ohio Supreme Court, plans were under way for taking to that court another case from the southern district of Ohio. Attorney General Black sent to the United States Marshal firm instructions that the body of the prisoner was not to be surrendered: "The State Court have no authority to meddle with this business. If it seems probable

XXVI: *The Booth Cases and Northern Nullification*

The statement was persuasive in terms of doctrines committed to the preservation of law and order. The reception of the Ohio cases, however, as of the *Booth Cases* in Wisconsin, demonstrated that law and order was about to take second place to public policies more and more zealously sponsored by larger and larger elements of the populace. The time was growing nearer when the rule of law was to give way to the enforcement of sentiments not yet embodied in law.

---

that the jailer is disposed to produce the prisoner at Columbus you [the Marshal] must take him into your own custody, and keep him safely. In case of an attack upon you by State Officers, you must defend yourself, and maintain the rights of the United States, against all lawless aggressions. I have sent to the District Attorney a copy of the Opinion delivered by the Chief Justice and unanimously assented to by all the Judges in *Ableman vs. Booth*, at the last term of the Supreme Court of the United States." J. S. Black to Lewis N. Gifford, May 21, 1859, Attorney General's Letter Book A–3, 20. See also J. S. Black to Stanley Matthews, May 21, 1859, *ibid.*, 21, and J. S. Black to Stanley Matthews, May 23, 1859, *ibid.*, 22.

CHAPTER XXVII

Fugitives from Justice

WHILE QUESTIONS involving the restoration of fugitive slaves to their owners embroiled the federal courts in difficulties year after year throughout most of the Taney period, questions involving the return of fugitives from justice, usually though not always white men, who had escaped into other states came only occasionally into either state or federal courts. For all their importance, indeed, they were not dealt with in the Supreme Court until the decision of *Kentucky v. Dennison*, in 1861.[1] The problems were important because states were apt to become embroiled in difficulties when used as havens by criminals from other states, and because these problems were frequently entangled with the return of fugitive slaves. Yet because of the relevant provision of the Constitution and the statute based upon it, statement of the law was left primarily to the governors of the states involved. Contentious gubernatorial arguments in troublesome cases led to frequent discussion of transferring administration to the hands of federal officers or having determinations made by federal courts.

The constitutional provision was in Article IV, Section 2, next preceding the Fugitive Slave Clause. It stated that "A person charged in any State with treason, felony, or other crime, who shall flee from justice, and be found in another State, shall on demand of the executive authority of the State from which he fled, be delivered up, to be removed to the State having jurisdiction of the crime." Congress prescribed the method of enforcing the provision in the statute of 1793 which also provided for the return of fugitive slaves, thereby more closely linking the two subjects. When the executive authority of a state made a demand for the return of a fugitive from justice, he was to provide an authenticated indictment or affidavit charging the accused

---

[1] 24 How. 66 (1861).

676

with treason, felony, or other crime. Thereupon, "it shall be the duty of the executive authority of the state or territory to which such person shall have fled, to cause him or her to be arrested and secured, and notice of the arrest to be given to the executive authority making such demand, or to the agent of such authority appointed to receive the fugitive, and to cause the fugitive to be delivered to such agent when he shall appear."[2]

Controversies arose among the governors with respect to the adequacy and form of indictments and affidavits and, more important, over the nature and seriousness of the offenses which could be labeled crimes within the meaning of the constitutional and statutory text. A governor demanding the return of a fugitive would contend that the definition of an act as a crime by the laws of his own state was sufficient. A governor upon whom the demand was made was apt to look askance unless the act alleged was a crime under the laws of his own state or at any rate was regarded as criminal throughout the civilized world or treated as criminal under the common law. It was agreed that the offense must be serious rather than trivial, but there was no agreement on the line between the two. During the Taney period it was natural that the major question should be whether aiding a slave to escape from his master was a crime for which the offender should be surrendered for punishment in the state in which the offense was committed.

The principal controversy in this field raged from 1839 to 1842 between Governor William H. Seward of New York and the governors or acting governors of Virginia and Georgia, with the legislatures of these and various other states chiming in. Both Virginia and Georgia were seeking from New York the delivery of persons alleged to have aided in the escape of slaves. Seward was a highly independent governor with a proneness for literary and legal controversy. Soon after he took office he was asked by the governor of Pennsylvania to deliver a fugitive charged with fornication. The governor of New Hampshire asked for a fugitive charged with adultery.[3] Seward, unable to believe that the framers of the Constitution and of the statute had had in mind offenses of this kind, had no judicial guidance except such as could be found in a case decided in 1832 by the New York Supreme Court, of which Samuel Nelson, eventually to join the Supreme Court of the United States, was a member. Rhode Island had sought the return of a fugitive charged with fraud as an officer of a bank. In a habeas corpus case the New York court rejected the contention that the constitutional provision was intended to apply only to crimes of greater atrocity than

---

[2] 1 Stat. 302.

[3] *Works of William H. Seward,* George E. Baker, ed., II, 479 (1853).

that here alleged. That might be true in international extradition depending on the comity of nations, but the comity of nations was not here involved. In the Constitution "the word crime is synonomous with misdemeanor, . . . and includes every offense below felony punished by indictment as an offense against the public."[4]

The decision seemed to leave the governor little discretion if the requisition of the demanding state was in order, but Seward, perhaps with the prospect in mind of exercising discretion when fugitives were demanded for aiding slaves, took the position that with respect to extradition the definition of crime was not a matter merely for the demanding state, and refused to surrender persons charged with fornication and adultery.

The storm over interstate extradition of persons charged with promoting the escape of slaves began in the summer of 1839. When a schooner manned by a captain and three black seamen arrived in New York from Norfolk, a slave, a ship carpenter, who had been employed aboard at Norfolk, was found concealed amid the cargo. The slave was recaptured and returned to his master. But Virginians, concerned with making examples of any persons, particularly free Negroes, who aided in the escape of slaves, persuaded the acting governor of Virginia to demand the three seamen. The only disclosed evidence of involvement of the three in the escape was the statement of the slave that one of them had told him that he was foolish to remain in Virginia when he could get good wages in the North, and suggested that he run away.[5] The three men were arrested and held for extradition. Amid great public excitement they applied to the recorder of New York, a judicial officer, for release on habeas corpus. That officer, finding the evidence of crime insufficient, ordered their release.[6]

Virginia pressed its demand for the surrender of the three men. Seward, at his leisure, replied in a long letter of refusal. He questioned incidentally the form of the requisition and, more important, denied that the offense alleged was one covered by the constitutional provision. He contended that the provision applied "only to those acts which, if committed within the jurisdiction of the state in which the person accused is found, would be treasonable, felonious, or criminal, by the laws of that state."[7] It was true, he admitted, that each state could determine what acts should be treated as criminal within its own borders. However, "I believe the right to demand and the reciprocal

---

[4] In the Matter of Clark, 9 Wendell (N.Y.) 212, 222 (1832). For citation of this case in a fugitive slave case by Justice Nelson see Jack v.

Martin, 12 Wendell (N.Y.) 311, 323 (1834).
[5] Seward, *Works*, II, 504.
[6] *Ibid.*, 467–68.
[7] *Ibid.*, 452.

obligation to surrender fugitives from justice between sovereign and independent nations, as defined by the law of nations, include only those cases in which the acts constituting the offence charged are recognized as crimes by the universal laws of all civilized countries."[8] The offense charged was not a crime under the laws of New York or under the relevant provision of the Constitution.

The lieutenant governor of Virginia wrathfully replied that one state could not rightfully interfere with the institutions of another, asserted that the three men were accused of stealing a slave worth some six or seven hundred dollars, and remarked that "I understand *stealing* to be recognized as *crime* by all laws human and Divine." Seward countered with the assertion that "the general principle of civilized communities is in harmony with that which prevails in this state, that men are not the subjects of property, and of course that no such crime can exist in countries where that principle prevails as the felonious stealing of a human being considered as property."[9]

In both New York and Virginia the correspondence was laid before the ensuing sessions of the state legislatures. In the Virginia legislature it was said that the conduct of the governor of New York appeared to be dictated by a desire to conciliate the abolitionists. A select committee was appointed to investigate and report.[10] It was not surprising that the committee report, adopted early in 1840 by both houses of the Virginia legislature, denounced Seward's refusal to comply as "a palpable and dangerous violation of the constitution and laws of the United States," urged renewal of negotiations, asked the governor of Virginia to ask the cooperation of each of the slaveholding states in enforcing such measures of redress as Virginia might have to adopt, and asked that copies of the report be sent to the governors of the several states with the request that they be laid before the several legislatures.[11]

The committee, like the Virginia governor and, at a later date, the governor of Georgia, made full use of the decision of 1832 in which the New York Supreme Court had held that interstate extradition extended to any offense made a crime by the state in which the offense was committed. It ridiculed the suggestion that in adopting the Constitution Virginia and other Southern states had understood that the Northern states, by abolishing slavery within their limits, would "take the felony of stealing a slave out of the operation of the 2nd section of

---

[8] *Ibid.*, 452.
[9] *Ibid.*, 466.
[10] *Niles' National Register*, 57:272, 1839.

[11] The copy here analyzed is printed in *Votes and Proceedings of the Sixty-Fifth General Assembly of the State of New Jersey*, 46–65, 1841.

the 4th article of the constitution." Had they so understood it they would not have adopted the Constitution.[12] The committee contended that Seward's action violated both the letter and the spirit of the Constitution and restated the belief that he had acted either under the influence of "the fanatical feelings of northern abolitionists" or for the purpose of conciliating those enemies of domestic tranquillity.[13]

Apart from seeking support from other states, the committee discussed other courses of action. One was an appeal to the Supreme Court of the United States. This step it decided to be entirely out of the question—quite understandably in the light of Southern concern about the growth of federal power. The Supreme Court, it contended, would have no jurisdiction. This was of the nature of a political question, not of a case in law or equity over which the Court would have authority. Furthermore, the remedy would be ineffectual. The governor of New York had already disregarded a decision of the supreme court of his own state and he would probably show no greater deference toward a decision of the federal judiciary. Beyond that, the committee could not see how the judgment of the Court could be enforced, and in any event it preferred to avoid a course which would bring the authorities of the federal government and of the states into collision.[14]

The committee rejected another proposal, which had apparently been made by the state of Georgia. It was that Congress change the statute on the subject so that the demand for the return of fugitives would be made not on the governor, a political officer, but on the circuit judge of the United States in the asylum state. Such a step would abandon sound public policy and violate the Constitution by transferring to the judiciary a duty which was properly that of the executive of the state. It would add another to the list of instances, already too long, in which state and federal authorities were brought into collision. But above all, sending the subject to Congress would give to abolitionists there the long-desired opportunity "of denouncing in the national legislature an institution of such peculiar character and paramount importance, and of franking their incendiary effusions to the four quarters of the Union."[15]

Apart from an appeal to New York itself, the committee considered two other proposals. One was to provide for the inspection of all vessels trading with the North to see that no slaves were secreted, and the other was to require security for good behavior from all citizens of New York coming into Virginia. The former it thought worthy of consideration, though it would be difficult to enforce effectively. The

---

[12] *Ibid.*, 58.   [13] *Ibid.*, 58.   [14] *Ibid.*, 59–60.   [15] *Ibid.*, 61.

latter it rejected as of doubtful constitutionality and also because of hope of amicable settlement of the question.[16]

Governor Thomas W. Gilmer of Virginia transmitted the report of the committee to Seward with the request that it be laid before the New York legislature, and further challenged Seward's arguments. Seward's resort to the law of nations to determine principles applicable in international extradition would be justified only in instances where there was no treaty governing the subject. Where there was a treaty, the treaty must apply. Was the provision of the Constitution less obligatory upon New York or less beneficial to Virginia than a treaty would be? In any event, he thought it would be exceedingly difficult to determine what was the "universal law of all civilized countries" upon which Seward proposed to rely in determining the offenses for which criminals could be extradited. Had the framers of the Constitution intended to rely on any such vague concept they would have said so.[17]

At Gilmer's request, Seward referred his letter and the committee report to the New York legislature. The Senate took no action. A committee of the House of Assembly was discharged after making a report generally concurring in Seward's views but recommending against the giving of legislative advice.[18] Seward replied to Virginia with another voluminous letter restating the facts and the arguments of the controversy and again contending that the constitutional provision was intended to incorporate the principles of the law of nations.[19]

While the situation was at a stalemate a man charged with forgery in New York fled to Virginia. Using the prescribed forms, Governor Seward asked for his surrender. Governor Gilmer replied that the demand would be complied with whenever Virginia's earlier demand for the three fugitives had been met. Seward answered, this time relatively briefly, that he saw no reason for reversing his earlier decision.[20] The Virginia legislature, refusing to support their governor in this act of retaliation, adopted a resolution to the effect that the fugitive from New York ought to be surrendered, "notwithstanding the refusal of the governor of New York so to act in a similar case."[21] Governor Gilmer responded with an indignant letter about the way in which New York

---

[16] *Ibid.*, 61–62.

[17] "The Extradition of Fugitives," *Pa. L.J.*, 6:412, 423–24, 1847.

[18] Seward, *Works*, II, 469–70.

[19] See especially *ibid.*, 472. In reply to the accusation that he was disregarding a decision of the Supreme Court of New York he replied, "The question whether the alleged offence was a crime recognized by the laws

of New York, was not even raised in the case, and was not discussed by the court. In fact, the offence was one familiar to our laws, and there was therefore no occasion to examine the nature of the crime charged." *Ibid.*, 485.

[20] *Ibid.*, 492–94.

[21] *Niles' National Register*, 60:69, 1841.

had "placed herself beyond the pale of the constitution," and resigned his office because the legislature had refused to support him. The lieutenant governor thereafter surrendered the forger for delivery to New York.[22]

Virginia used the occasion of the surrender of the forger as an opportunity to reopen its demand for the surrender of the three men freed in New York.[23] Seward remained adamant, indignantly illustrating the causes for bad relations between the two states by such facts as that the governor of Virginia had offered large rewards for kidnaping the three fugitives in New York and conveying them to Virginia.[24]

In the eyes of Virginia, New York had given further offense by enacting a statute granting the right of jury trial to persons claimed as fugitive slaves. On March 13, 1841, the Virginia legislature enacted a measure entitled "An act to prevent the citizens of New York from carrying slaves out of the commonwealth of Virginia, and to prevent the escape of persons charged with any crime," suspending operation of the statute until May 1, 1842, to give New York opportunity to repeal its own offending statute and surrender the three fugitives.[25] Seward refused to be intimidated, reminding Virginia that her enactment was probably an unconstitutional regulation of interstate commerce in its requirement of state inspection of that commerce, and that in any event if Virginia could enact discriminatory legislation New York could do the same.[26]

In 1842, Seward's last year in the governorship, the New York legislature, now under Democratic control, adopted a resolution disapproving of Seward's position with respect to the surrender of fugitives from justice and asserting that the stealing of a slave within the jurisdiction and against the laws of Virginia was a "felony or other crime" within the meaning of the Constitution. Seward replied that while he welcomed advice from the legislature, the matter was one exclusively of executive responsibility. He noted retaliatory action by Virginia and South Carolina,[27] which had also enacted a measure discriminating against the commerce of New York. In view of the involvement of principles of civil liberty and of the stand already taken, he refused to attempt to conciliate Virginia by transmitting a copy of the resolution.[28]

Among the many warm supporters of Virginia in the controversy with New York was Charles J. McDonald, governor of Georgia. Mc-

---

[22] *Ibid.*, 69–70.
[23] *Ibid.*, 150–51.
[24] Seward, *Works*, II, 498.
[25] *Ibid.*, 510.
[26] *Ibid.*, 512–13.
[27] For presentation of a South Caro-lina memorial on the subject by John C. Calhoun in the United States Senate see *Niles' National Register*, 61:372, 1841.
[28] *Niles' National Register*, 62:117, 1842.

Donald voiced the position much maintained in the South that New York had no claim to a superior morality on the ground of having abolished slavery, for she had done so primarily because of the conviction that it could no longer minister to her interest. This change in the policy of New York could not affect the rights of other states or release New York from the obligation to surrender fugitives. Abandoning the traditional states' rights position of the South, as Southerners were wont to do when abandonment would aid their cause, he argued that "Congress should be required to execute this provision of the Constitution by its own officers. It should no longer rely on State functionaries, over whom it can exercise no control. If it should refuse when the subject is fairly brought to its consideration, the law of self preservation which is paramount to all constitutions will require of us a resort to any measures necessary for our safety."[29]

Governor McDonald was himself soon engaged in a comparable controversy with Governor Seward. He made a demand for the surrender of John Greenman, a seaman, who according to affidavits signed by a plantation owner, "did feloniously steal, take, and carry away, three blankets, two shawls, three frocks, one pair of ear-rings, and two finger-rings, all of the value of fifty dollars, of the goods and chattels of this deponent, contrary to the laws of this state," and, as charged in comparable language, stole a Negro woman named Kezia.[30]

With an eye to the realities of such situations, Seward sensed the fact that instead of stealing the tangible property and the slave, Greenman had no more than persuaded the slave to seek her freedom and that she had taken with her such personal belongings as she had. In terms of what could be regarded as felonious taking under the laws of New York, Seward found the affidavits defective and refused to surrender Greenman. McDonald replied that the laws involved were the laws of Georgia and not those of New York, and that he could not admit the principle that the executive of a state on whom a demand was made could "organize himself into a Court and hear accusatory and defensive testimony to ascertain whether there are circumstances manifesting a felonious intent on the one hand, and the absence of it on the other."[31] He saw the duty of the governor of New York as merely ministerial and not discretionary.

Seward replied that though he could not try the case as a court he was obligated to pass on the sufficiency of the affidavits, and reminded McDonald that although proper affidavits were acceptable under the

---

[29] Charles J. McDonald to Thomas W. Gilmer, Jan. 27, 1841, Georgia Governors Letter Book, Jan. 1, 1841–May 31, 1843, 32.

[30] Seward, *Works*, II, 519.

[31] Charles J. McDonald to William H. Seward, June 28, 1841, Georgia Governors Letter Book, Jan. 1, 1841–May 31, 1843, 136.

law, there was a wide difference between an affidavit and an indictment.[32] The dispute continued until Greenman was indicted by a county grand jury, after which McDonald made his demand on the basis of the indictment. But again Seward refused to act, contending that harboring and concealing a slave did not constitute larceny for which Greenman's surrender was sought, and that the indictment was defective in form.[33] McDonald rejected the argument and warned Seward that he was "the first to break that instrument which has heretofore been a ligament to hold together the states of the Union."[34] Seward replied by summarizing the story of this controversy and of that with Virginia, and refused to change his position.[35]

Over even a longer period successive governors of Georgia had been engaged in a similar controversy with successive governors of Maine, with similar frustrating results. In 1837 Daniel Philbrook and Edward Kelleran, master and mate of the schooner *Susan* and citizens of Maine, sailed away from a Georgia port and, according to their story, found aboard a slave, Atticus, who was owned by James and Henry Sagurs of Georgia. On the affidavit of James Sagurs, Governor William Schley demanded the surrender of the two men as fugitives from justice. Governor Robert P. Dunlap of Maine refused to direct the surrender, contending that the men were not fugitives within the meaning of the Constitution and that the papers did not properly show the commission of a felony. Correspondence followed which somewhat resembled that between Seward and the governors of Virginia and Georgia, except that Maine did not challenge the right of Georgia to determine what conduct within her borders was criminal in the sense of the Constitution.[36] This controversy led the Georgia legislature to ask Congress to transfer to United States district judges the responsibility for surrendering fugitives from justice.[37]

The Georgia legislature also enacted a measure which would have suspended all intercourse between the two states. Governor McDonald refused to sign the measure, and used his self-restraint as a ground for further discussing the question with the governor of Maine, but apparently without avail.[38]

---

[32] Seward, *Works*, II, 528.
[33] *Ibid.*, 537–40.
[34] Charles J. McDonald to William H. Seward, Nov. 22, 1841, Georgia Governors Letter Book, Jan. 1, 1841–May 31, 1843, 214. See resolutions of the Alabama legislature, Senate Report No. 127, 26th Cong., 2nd Sess. (1841).

[35] Seward, *Works*, II, 541–46.
[36] Much of the correspondence is to be found in Senate Doc. No. 273, 26th Cong., 1st Sess. (1840).
[37] *Ibid.*, 2.
[38] See Charles J. McDonald to Edward Kent, Oct. 4, 1841, Georgia Governors Letter Book, Jan. 1, 1841–May 31, 1843, 198–200.

The strictly legal merits involved in these controversies are hard to discover. It is clear that in most instances of interstate rendition involving slavery, attitudes toward that institution had a great deal to do with interpretation of the law. Chancellor Kent, although in most respects an ardent Whig and the enemy of the newly developing Democratic order in the United States, concurred with the Democratic legislature of New York that Virginia was within its rights in demanding the surrender of the three fugitives whose fate so deeply engaged the attention of Governor Seward.[39] Yet it was also true that demands were sometimes made on mere suspicion and without proper papers. In 1843, for example, Judge Nathaniel Pope, in the United States Circuit Court for Illinois, found it necessary to release on habeas corpus the Mormon evangelist, Joseph Smith, who was about to be surrendered to Missouri authorities without evidence that he had been in Missouri at the time when a crime was committed or had participated in the crime.[40] In general, when the fugitives claimed had no such unpopularity as characterized Joseph Smith, or when public or official sympathy was with them for the acts of which they were accused, the governors themselves saw to it that proper procedures were followed. When the governors failed to order release promptly or to order it at all for fugitives claiming to be improperly held, resort was occasionally had to habeas corpus petitions, as in the Smith case.

With the growing intensity of the abolitionist sentiment in the North it is not surprising that Congress enacted no legislation to facilitate recapture of fugitives from justice. The absence of federal authority in such matters was noted in 1857 by Attorney General Black in a letter to a federal officer. A man indicted for bigamy in Iowa had fled to Massachusetts. The governor of Massachusetts had at first authorized his delivery to Iowa authorities but had then revoked his warrant. The Iowa agent arrested the fugitive nevertheless, and was then indicted and convicted for an attempt to kidnap the fugitive. Attorney General Black assured the United States Marshal that "There is no law which authorizes any interference by the federal government in the affair. . . . Your obligation to see the laws faithfully executed does not compel you to rejudge the justice of the judicial tribunals, or to right all the wrongs committed by State Executives."[41]

Yet on this as on other questions related to the slavery controversy,

---

[39] "The Extradition of Fugitives," *Pa. L.J.*, 6:412, 428–29, 1847. See *Kent's Commentaries* (5th ed.), I, 37, n.

[40] *Ex parte* Smith, 22 Fed. Cas. 373 (No. 12968) (C.C.D. Ill. 1843).

[41] J. S. Black to Watson Freeman, May 25, 1851, Attorney General's Letter Book A–3, 1–2.

feelings grew more and more intense. As Seward, the spokesman of the "higher law than the Constitution," became more and more the spokesman of abolitionists, the Southern people were kept reminded of his refusal to surrender a fugitive from justice on the ground that stealing a slave was not a crime in New York.[42] William Dennison, governor of Ohio at the beginning of the Civil War, who had campaigned for office on the promise that he would permit no fugitive slave to be returned South even if he had to prevent it with bayonets,[43] at first followed Seward's pattern with respect to returning a fugitive from justice to Tennessee. Then, finding that the alleged criminal had not merely stolen a slave but jewelry as well, he reversed his position. But in a case that made history because it did reach the Supreme Court, Dennison refused to return a fugitive demanded by Governor Beriah Magoffin of Kentucky.[44]

The case of *Kentucky v. Dennison* had its origin in plans whereby a slave girl held in Louisville, Kentucky, was to be permitted to visit her mother, who lived in Wheeling, Virginia. The owner, C. W. Nichols,[45] was going there, and decided to take the girl with him. Nichols traveled to Cincinnati with the expectation of completing the journey by railroad. There the girl was seized by abolitionists who took her before a state court, where she was declared free. Nichols, in turn, found himself tied up in litigation in the Ohio courts for depriving the girl of her liberty contrary to the laws of that state.[46]

Kentucky entered the picture when Governor Magoffin demanded of Governor Dennison the surrender of Willis Lago, a "free man of color," who was alleged to have aided in the escape of the slave girl, and who had been indicted by a county grand jury for that offense "against the peace and dignity of the Commonwealth of Kentucky."[47] Governor Dennison moved slowly in the matter. The demand was dated February 10, 1860. He asked for an opinion of the attorney general of Ohio, Christopher P. Wolcott, which was dated April 14. It was not until May 31 that he sent a copy of the opinion to Governor Magoffin with a rejection of the demand. Wolcott took a position closely resembling that long since taken by Governor Seward, and evidently taken since that time by many Northern officials. He argued that the act of which Lago was accused was certainly not treason according to the laws

---

[42] See "Disfederation of the States," *Southern Literary Messenger*, 32:118, 128, 1861.

[43] Allan Nevins, *The Emergence of Lincoln*, II, 31.

[44] "Disfederation of the States," *Southern Literary Messenger*, 32:118, 128, 1861.

[45] In some parts of the record the name is spelled Nuckols.

[46] For this portion of the story see "Python," Feb. 9, 1860, *De Bow's Review*, 28:367, 370–71, 1860.

[47] Kentucky v. Dennison, 24 How. 66, 67 (1861).

of any country, and was not a felony or other crime under the laws of Ohio. He argued that the right rule for determining when a claimed fugitive should be surrendered was "that which holds the power to be limited to such acts as constitute either treason or felony by the common law, as that stood when the Constitution was adopted, or which are regarded as crimes by the usages and laws of all civilized nations."[48] Though to no effect as far as the conduct of Ohio was concerned, Governor Magoffin made a challenging reply criticizing the distortion of the Constitution by such interpretation and reminding Governor Dennison that "the Constitution was the work of slaveholders; that their wisdom, moderation, and prudence gave it to us. Non-slave-holding states were the exception, not the rule."[49]

Ohio remained adamant, and Kentucky planned another move, this time determined if possible to get a decision from the Supreme Court on the question long disputed between Northern and Southern governors. It petitioned the Supreme Court, in the exercise of its original jurisdiction, to direct Governor Dennison to show cause why a mandamus should not issue directing him to surrender Lago, the alleged fugitive from justice, to the agent of Kentucky. When the case came up for argument, on February 20, 1861, the petition was read in open court by Thomas B. Monroe, Jr.,[50] secretary of state of Kentucky, the son of the ardent Southerner of the same name who was United States District Judge for Kentucky and the son-in-law of Justice Grier.

Counsel for Kentucky,[51] in addition to presenting the substantive arguments presented again and again by Southern governors to show that the governor upon whom an extradition demand was made had no discretion in the matter, had to show that this was a proper case for the exercise of the original jurisdiction of the Supreme Court—that it was a case to which a state was a party—and that a writ of mandamus directed to a governor was the appropriate remedy.[52] They contended that by the Constitution the state of Ohio was committed to the delivery

---

48 *Ibid.*, 69.
49 Record, 11.
50 Record, 2.
51 Supreme Court records are sparse as to the participation of the several individuals. The printed brief carries the names of Cooper, Marshall, and J. W. Stevenson. The docket does not mention Cooper, but lists as counsel Crittenden, Marshall, Stevenson, and Thomas B. Monroe, Jr. The full names were presumably John J. Crittenden, Humphrey Marshall, and John W. Stevenson. The *Lawyers' Edition of the Supreme Court Reports*

gives the date of argument as Feb. 20, 1861. The docket entry shows that the argument extended at least until the following day.
52 Some of the procedural strategy is reflected in the full title to the case, which in the official reports reads *Ex Parte. In the Matter of the Commonwealth of Kentucky, one of the United States of America, by Beriah Magoffin, Governor, and the Executive Authority thereof, Petitioner, v. William Dennison, Governor and Executive Authority of the State of Ohio.*

of fugitives and that Governor Dennison was improperly assuming the discretion of a judge and refusing to perform a ministerial duty laid upon him by the Constitution and the statute. They were clearly fearful that the Supreme Court would draw upon the dictum in *Prigg v. Pennsylvania* to the effect that the obligation to return fugitive slaves was exclusively federal and would say the same thing with respect to fugitives from justice.[53] They rejected that argument and appealed to Justice McLean by special reference to his opinion in the *Prigg* case.[54] They made no reference to the opinion of Chief Justice Taney, perhaps sensing that no special effort would be required to win his concurrence in the matter.

Attorney General Wolcott, for Ohio, denied that this was a proper case for the exercise of original jurisdiction or for the issuing of mandamus. He contended that the federal statute providing for the surrender of fugitives from justice was unconstitutional, and that in any event this was not a case in which a state was a party but that if the writ were granted in this case it would be a proceeding instituted by the United States of America against the governor of Ohio. With a reference to the sectional strife which was soon to culminate in civil war, he insisted that "The power to compose this national and political strife does not reside in this tribunal; the pursuing party cannot cross its threshold; the party pursued is without the reach of its arm; the subject of the difference has been excluded from its action; and the writ which it is solicited to grant has been denied to it as a method for the exercise of its original jurisdiction."[55]

At the time when this case was argued, during the third week in February, 1861, and when it was decided, March 14, there was an element of unrealism in considering coercion of the states, or of their governors, by the hands of the federal judiciary. The states of the Deep South had already proclaimed their secession from the Union, their representatives in Congress had said their farewells, and other states and representatives were about to go. Kentucky was on the edge of indecision. Thomas B. Monroe, Jr., was soon to become a Confederate officer and to lose his life in the cause of the Confederacy, and his father resigned his federal judgeship and "emigrated" into the South. Between the dates of the argument and the decision of the case Abraham Lincoln traveled secretly through Baltimore to avoid the dangers of mob violence and was sworn in as President. The Supreme Court, discredited in the North by the Dred Scott decision, drew much of its

---

[53] For the argument see 24 How. 79–83.

[54] See *Prigg v. Pennsylvania*, 16 Pet. 539, 658 (1842).

[55] 24 How. 95.

support from men with Southern leanings. The aged Chief Justice was sympathetic toward the South. Justice Daniel had died and the ailing Justice McLean was to die soon after the date of the decision. Justice Campbell was working as a peace agent between the South and the Lincoln Administration, but his resignation was predicted and was soon to occur.

It is therefore impossible to predict the extent of the consideration given to the Kentucky-Dennison case, in which the decision was handed down on the last day of the term. We have the opinion of the Court, written by Chief Justice Taney, but no concurring or dissenting opinions. The Chief Justice held that although the respective governors were the effective agents, the suit was by one state against another, so the Supreme Court might exercise original jurisdiction. He held that the writ of mandamus, nothing more than an ordinary process of a court of justice, was in this case the appropriate means, and the only one, by which the desired object might be accomplished.

Furthermore, without mentioning the historic performance in this field of William H. Seward, who by this time was personally anathema to the Chief Justice, he took the position of the Southern governors that the crimes for which persons might be extradited extended to crimes at all levels, including mere misdemeanors, and that for the purpose of extradition the definition of crime was governed by the laws of the demanding state. The sufficiency of the indictment also was a matter exclusively for the demanding state, and not for the state in which the fugitive was found. Northern governors were put completely in the wrong for making themselves judges of the sufficiency of indictments and of the offenses which under the Constitution might be classified as crimes. From reading the opinion down to this point it would appear that the Supreme Court was about to issue a writ of mandamus directing Governor Dennison to deliver Willis Lago to an agent of Kentucky, a writ which most certainly would have been disregarded or publicly flouted by the abolitionist governor.

But Chief Justice Taney did not stop here. He turned now to the federal statute of 1793 which said as to the surrender of fugitives from justice that "it shall be the duty of the executive authority of the state." He drew a distinction here between authorization to perform a duty and the giving of a command:

> It is true that Congress may authorize a particular state officer to perform a particular duty; but if he declines to do so, it does not follow that he may be coerced, or punished for his refusal. And we are very far from supposing, that in using this word "duty," the statesmen who framed and passed the law, or the President who approved and signed it, intended to exercise a coercive power over the state

officers not warranted by the Constitution. But the general government having in that law fulfilled the duty devolved upon it, by prescribing the proof and mode of authentication upon which the state authorities were bound to deliver the fugitive, the word "duty" in the law points to the obligation on the state to carry it into execution.[56]

So it was that with respect to Northern governors Chief Justice Taney performed much as Chief Justice Marshall had performed with respect to the Jefferson Administration in *Marbury v. Madison* in 1803. He showed them to have been completely in the wrong in their insistence on the exercise of a kind of judicial power of their own with respect to the surrender of fugitives from justice, but refrained from applying to governors a coercive power which the federal government did not possess.

The strategy of Chief Justice Taney offended Northerners, just as that of Chief Justice Marshall had offended Jefferson. The *New York Evening Post*, for example, dealt with it in an editorial entitled "Judicial Twaddle," in which, reminiscent of the Marshall experience, the editor condemned Taney for saying more than that the Supreme Court did not have jurisdiction: "We fear that the Chief Justice has been spoiled by the flatteries which his southern friends heaped upon him after what is called his decision in the Dred Scott case, when he went out of his way in the same manner to make a parade of what he thought on collateral subjects."[57] The *Nashville Republican Banner* remarked that Kentucky got the decision on the merits, while the Court was not authorized to grant the required remedy. Whether or not with tongue in editorial cheek, it added the presumption that the governor of Ohio would conform his action to the decision.[58]

Whatever may be thought of the strategy of the opinion itself, the decision, divorced of its connection with the slavery issue, still stands as determining that although it is the duty of governors to surrender fugitives from justice on properly authenticated demands, they may not be coerced into doing so. In the great mass of such requests the surrenders are made as matters of routine, but in some instances, and for various reasons, the demands are rejected and there is nothing that the demanding states can do about it.

---

[56] *Ibid.*, 108.
[57] *New York Evening Post*, Mar. 16, 1861.

[58] *Nashville Republican Banner*, Mar. 21, 1861.

CHAPTER XXVIII

The Widening Breach

For all the extremist advocacy of nullification or secession and for all the heat of the controversy, the great body of the people both in North and South yielded most reluctantly to the thought of dissolution of the Union. Although warring factions each sought to determine national policies, most of them hoped to preserve the nation as a nation. Yet with growing tensions the conflict came more and more to appear "irrepressible." Evidence of the widening breach showed itself not merely in the determination of the North to prevent the return of fugitive slaves and the expansion of slave territory but also in Southern flouting of laws forbidding the slave trade, in filibustering attempts to acquire new slave territory southward, and in increased Southern restrictions on the rights of free Negroes and threats of their actual enslavement.

Even before the year 1808, prior to which the Constitution forbade outlawing the slave trade, Congress had enacted measures to take effect as soon as constitutionally possible, with others to follow in later years. The measures forbade the outfitting of ships for the slave trade and decreed the confiscation of ships illegally equipped and the fine and imprisonment of persons responsible. They declared the slave trade to be piracy punishable by death.[1] In the face of the statutes, Northern shipbuilders did a thriving business constructing and equipping ships for the nefarious business. In the hope of rewards also authorized by statute, informers often brought about prosecution of actions in federal courts in Northern districts. When the vessels outfitted were brought into actual use, the traffic was variously between Africa at one end and Brazil or

---

[1] For the statutes primarily involved in the slave trade cases of the Taney period see 3 Stat. 450, 510, 600.

Cuba or some part of the United States at the other, with the United States usually the intended final destination. Since the delivery of slaves to the United States took place in the South, such prosecutions for engaging in the slave trade as were instituted took place in federal courts in that area. Southern juries might be expected to be largely unsympathetic to the purpose of the law, and prosecuting officials and judges often shared their sentiments. A minority of such cases reached Northern or Middle Atlantic courts but even here, often for similar reasons, enforcement was far from effective.

When brought to trial, slave traders exposed limitations and loopholes in the statutes. While for the purpose of controlling the conduct of its own citizens on the high seas the United States could define the slave trade as piracy and enforce the death penalty, it could not for other nations change the rules of international law to outlaw the conduct of foreigners which their sovereigns did not forbid or did not treat as piracy. Traders therefore developed the strategy of having different persons act as captains and other officers depending on which nation challenged their activities, and perjury and other forms of deceit often made it hard to prove that given individuals had been employed on vessels with the knowledge that they were to engage in the slave trade. Defendants might claim to have been merely passengers without responsibility for the ship, or to have been deceived as to the purpose of the voyage when they accepted employment.

Similar strategy was employed with respect to the ownership of vessels. They would operate with American papers and fly the American flag when American protection was desired. But by means of papers showing transfers of ownership, in whole or in part and real or fictitious, they managed so to confuse the picture as to prevent convictions for involvement in the slave trade when brought to trial in American courts. Owners themselves sometimes escaped responsibility for the action of their vessels by letting them be taken for slave trade voyages without official authorization. Persons arrested for involvement in the trade were often released on bail at low figures and never brought to trial.

In 1848 the United States consul at Rio de Janeiro, Gorham Parks, complained to Secretary of State James Buchanan of lack of support from American courts and juries. For example, he had sent back to Philadelphia for trial in the United States Circuit Court William Brown, one of the mates of the *Fame*, a vessel caught in the slave trade. On the basis of a charge delivered by Justice Grier, the jury had rendered a verdict of not guilty. The consul got the impression that no evidence could be introduced to prove the American character of the vessel other than the original register. He correctly surmised that "there must have been some mistake in the statement as to what Judge Grier decided the law to be."[2] What Grier seems to have held was that there was sufficient evidence of foreign ownership to rebut a prima facie case of ownership by a citizen.[3]

What Justice Grier thereafter held was that although registration of the vessel might be evidence for some purposes it was not even prima facie evidence in a criminal prosecution against a third party. It was true that testimony as to American ownership was necessary to secure American registration, but the man so swearing might have sworn to an untruth, and in any event the American ownership might have come to an end between the date of registration and the date of the act of piracy. American ownership must be proved by competent evidence before a conviction depending on it could be secured.[4] The jury chafed at Justice Grier's rigid demands. In partial defiance it returned a verdict of "Not guilty under the charge of the court; but guilty in point of fact." But Justice Grier, never one to tolerate obstruction, required that the verdict be changed to "not guilty."[5] He continued in other cases to insist that prosecution penetrate confusion to determine American ownership when the verdict depended on it.

In other courts as well the government had difficulty enforcing slave trade legislation. An important series of cases grew out of the activities of the *Porpoise*, which was owned by G. Richardson of Maine and commanded by Cyrus Libby of the same state. The *Porpoise* sailed to Rio de Janeiro where it was chartered to a Brazilian, Pinto de Fonseca, Libby remaining in command. A mass of evidence indicates that the *Porpoise* was used extensively in the slave trade between the African coast and Brazil, while operating under the American flag.[6] It was betrayed to American naval personnel in the harbor of Rio de Janeiro in

---

[2] Gorham Parks to James Buchanan, Aug. 25, 1848, H.R. Exec. Doc. No. 61, 30th Cong. 2nd Sess. 29 (1848).

[3] United States v. Brown, 24 Fed. Cas. 1245 (No. 14656) (C.C.E.D. Pa. 1848).

[4] United States v. Brune, 24 Fed. Cas. 1280 (No. 14677) (C.C.E.D. Pa. 1852). In a note appended to the case John William Wallace said that the case was reported from notes given to him by others and not on the basis of personal knowledge. Confusion as to Justice Grier's position may have arisen from a statement later quoted from him by Judge Kane in which he said, "But the court think it their duty to observe, in a case of

such awful and solemn consequences to the defendant, that the jury should be cautious how they deal with mere probabilities. What hindered the government from sending to New London, and bringing here the register, and the very owners themselves, to establish this fact beyond a doubt?" Quoted in United States v. Darnaud, 25 Fed. Cas. 754, 764 (No. 14918) (C.C.E.D. Pa. 1855). While he had asked for the register, he had asked also for the owners themselves so that ownership might be authenticated.

[5] United States v. Brune, 24 Fed. Cas. 1280, 1281 (No. 14677) (C.C.E.-D. Pa. 1852).

[6] See H.R. Exec. Doc. No. 61, 30th Cong., 2nd Sess. 87–160 (1848).

January, 1845, when a note signed by three members of the crew was dropped into a boat saying that the *Porpoise* was a slaver and that two slaves then aboard were about to be disposed of.[7] Accompanied by Brazilian port authorities, Commodore Daniel Turner boarded the ship and placed there a guard of United States marines from the frigate *Raritan*. Thereafter extended negotiations took place to secure the release of the vessel with officers and crew to be sent to the United States for trial. Amid the negotiations Henry A. Wise, United States envoy, protested against Brazil's blatant neglect of duty with respect to the slave trade. "The African slave traders, Brazilian, English, American, Portuguese, are all well known, and their offences can, by the proper authority of Brazil, be easily proved; and yet many of them, wealthy and influential by their illicit gains, walk abroad in Rio Janeiro unwhipped of justice. Vessel after vessel under the United States flag sails out of the ports of Brazil, is sold on the coast of Africa, after taking out a cargo of English goods for a Brazilian charterer, and returns with a cargo of slaves to Brazil under the imperial flag."[8]

After initial refusal and protest against American invasion of Brazilian sovereignty, the *Porpoise* with its officers and crew was released to the United States, and in the May term of 1846 Captain Libby was brought to trial in the United States Circuit Court in Maine before Justice Woodbury. Counsel for Libby, one of whom was William Pitt Fessenden, cast doubts on the situation not at all apparent in the nonjudicial record. It was made to appear that the carrying trade to Africa was or could have been perfectly innocent, that the two slaves were "freed men," that the captain did not necessarily know of their presence aboard his ship when it left the African port, and that the free colored man who had testified against Libby was taking revenge because he had been punished for taking a boat ashore without permission.

Justice Woodbury reviewed plausibly for the jury the doubts which counsel advanced. In breaking up the slave trade, he expounded, the courts of the United States could go and were disposed to go as far as the laws would permit. "But they cannot go farther without exercising judicial legislation, without usurpation, and infidelity to their oaths. We are mere agents of the law, to execute, and not to enlarge or add to them."[9] Under Justice Woodbury's leadership the gallows were cheated again. Although he did not mention in his charge the ground for bias on the part of the free colored witness, his son incorporated the item in his preface to the report of the case.[10]

Under the laws there was a right of action not merely against the

---

[7] *Ibid.*, 95.
[8] *Ibid.*, 125.
[9] United States v. Libby, 26 Fed. Cas. 928, 934 (No. 15597) (C.C.D. Maine 1846).
[10] *Ibid.*, 929.

men in command of the *Porpoise* but also against the vessel itself. A libel was filed against the vessel, evidently in the United States District Court in Massachusetts. For some reason the suit remained there until December, 1848, when it was taken to the United States Circuit Court on an appeal from a decree dismissing the libel, said to have been made without a formal hearing. Having taken three years to get that far, the case took seven more years to reach a Circuit Court decision. Justice Curtis, who had replaced Justice Woodbury, disclaimed responsibility for the court, attributing the delay to the mislaying of some deposition by Robert Rantoul when he had been United States Attorney. Justice Curtis would not say whether any blame was to be attributed to any prosecuting officer. Ten years after the vessel had been seized at Rio de Janeiro, the Circuit Court decreed its forfeiture.[11] It is not apparent that the owner benefited by the delay, but delay so much extended minimized the gains often sought by informers if forfeiture was ordered.

Far to the south, excitement was stirred when, in August, 1858, the United States brig *Dolphin* captured on the northern coast of Cuba the brig *Echo*, of New Orleans, with more than three hundred slaves on board, which was sent into Charleston. A United States Commissioner ordered the commitment of the crew pending examination of the facts, and Southerners heatedly debated what should be done with the valuable black property. By people never publicly concerned about the cruelty toward and torment of Negroes captured in Africa and shipped to the western hemisphere under the most horrible conditions, it was piously argued that it would be inhumane to ship them back to be dumped somewhere along the African coast. Since they could not be liberated in South Carolina, the only thing to be done was to select "upright and high-minded masters" for them.[12]

If the Negroes were to be considered free, their shipment into a South Carolina port could be considered a violation of the South Carolina statute forbidding the bringing in of free colored persons. Under that statute they could be imprisoned during their stay in port, and if the costs were not paid the imprisoned Negroes could be sold to recover the amount of the costs. The local sheriff, advised by his solicitor that he had a right to assume jurisdiction of the Negroes, demanded that the United States Marshal surrender them to him in spite of a contrary opinion submitted by the attorney general of South Carolina, Isaac W. Hayne. The demand was refused on the ground that the Negroes were in federal custody. They were originally held at Castle Pinckney, near

---

[11] *The Porpoise*, 19 Fed. Cas. 1064 (No. 11284) (C.C.D. Mass. 1855).
[12] See the *Richmond Enquirer*,

quoted in *Annual Report of the American Anti-Slavery Society . . . for the Year Ending May 1, 1859*, 50–51.

the Charleston wharves. To prevent their seizure by state authorities they were removed to Fort Sumter, several miles down the harbor.[13] In Washington Attorney General Black concurred in the opinion of Attorney General Hayne, and instructed the United States Attorney that "If any attempt should be made, no matter on what pretense, by the State authorities, to take these negroes out of the hands in which they are now placed by the federal government, in pursuance of the laws of the United States, such attempt must be resisted by all lawful and proper means."[14] He stated that measures had been taken to remove the Negroes out of the country as soon as possible, and, indeed, such of them as survived were eventually transported to Liberia by the American Colonization Society, at the expense of the federal government.[15]

The crew of the *Echo* applied to the United States Circuit Court in South Carolina for writs of habeas corpus for release from their commitment, but Judge A. Gordon Magrath, himself no opponent of slavery, found that they were legally held.[16] The United States Attorney informed Attorney General Black that conviction would be difficult in a community where the traders had public sympathy and where a movement was under way to legalize the slave trade. Black exhorted him to diligence, saying that politics need not intervene and telling him of the appointment of Attorney General Hayne as special counsel in the case. He admitted, however, that there were difficulties in law enforcement in both the North and the South.[17]

Although detention of the crew of the *Echo* for examination had been upheld, a grand jury at Columbia refused to indict. They were indicted at Charleston at the April term of 1859. At the trial their counsel sought to persuade the jury that jurors were judges of the law as well as of the facts, and contended that the term "piracy" applied only to robbery on the high seas and, in spite of the federal statute, could not be made to extend to the slave trade. The sympathetic jury voted for acquittal.[18]

Captain Townsend, who had been in charge of the *Echo* when it was captured, was sent south to Key West for trial. The federal district judge there, presumably William Marvin, proved highly skeptical about the certified copy of the registry of the *Echo* which was to prove that

---

[13] *Ibid.*, 51–52.

[14] J. S. Black to James Conner, Sept. 9, 1858, Attorney General's Letter Book A–3, 293.

[15] See *Annual Report of the American Anti-Slavery Society . . . for the Year Ending May 1, 1859,* 52; John B. McMaster, *History of the People of the United States,* VIII, 348–50.

[16] *In re* Bates, 2 Fed. Cas. 1015 (No. 1099a) (D.C.D. S.C. 1858).

[17] J. S. Black to James Conner, Oct. 6, 1858, Attorney General's Letter Book A–3, 297–99.

[18] *Annual Report of the American Anti-Slavery Society . . . for the Year Ending May 1, 1859,* 52.

Townsend owned the vessel, and about the handwriting on the document marking the sale to him.[19] He directed the jury to bring in a verdict of not guilty. He appeared anxious, said the *New York Tribune*, to put such a construction upon the acts for the suppression of the slave trade as would effectually prevent convictions. The *Charleston Mercury* thought the verdict the result of the belief that "it would be inconsistent, cruel, and hypocritical for members of a community where Slaves are as much articles of commerce as sugar and molasses, to condemn men to death for going to a far country to bring in more of these articles of trade."[20] Captain Townsend was soon on an outward voyage in command of another slave trade vessel.[21]

In April, 1859, at the mouth of the Congo River, the British steamer *Triton* boarded and took charge of the bark *Orion*, which had an American register and was flying the American flag, suspecting that the papers were fraudulent and that the vessel was engaged in the slave trade. The *Orion* was turned over to an American war vessel, after which it was sent back to the United States for confiscation. In the face of much evidence in the form of equipment for imprisoning and feeding slaves, a new captain protested the seizure to the Secretary of State, contending that "The captain of the 'Orion' died of a broken heart, caused by threats and insults from the British officers, as will appear by the claims that will be made against the British government for our detention."[22] On looking into the matter, American officials decided not to concern themselves about the alleged invasion of American rights. Indeed, they admitted that without British intervention the *Orion* might have got away with a cargo of slaves.

In the United States Circuit Court for the Southern District of New York Judge Nathaniel Kelsey Hall, of northern New York, presumably sitting in aid of Judge Betts, found the evidence sufficient to justify a decree of condemnation.[23] Yet for some reason the *Orion* was released by the court, and in a few months it was back on the coast of Africa in pursuit of another cargo of slaves. It was again visited by a suspicious British vessel but was permitted to go its way. It loaded a cargo of some eight hundred slaves, and was then captured by the British steamer *Pluto*, doubtless, said an American naval officer, after

---

[19] Allan Nevins, *The Emergence of Lincoln*, I, 434–35.

[20] *Annual Report of the American Anti-Slavery Society . . . for the Year Ending May 1, 1860*, 27–28.

[21] *Ibid.*, 26.

[22] *American Slave Trade*, H.R. Exec. Doc. No. 7, 36th Cong., 2nd Sess. 353 (1860). See this document for extensive correspondence about the Orion and other slave trade ventures.

[23] *The Orion*, 18 Fed. Cas. 817 (No. 10575) (D.C.S.D. N.Y. 1859).

"having thrown her colors and papers overboard, as is the practice in such cases."[24] An American vessel was sent to pick up the officers and crew to bring them back to the United States[25] in another futile attempt to secure death penalties for the act of piracy.

Among the most notorious instances of illegal resort to the slave trade was the voyage of a fast yacht, the *Wanderer*, which one night in November, 1858, landed on the coast of Georgia a cargo of recently enslaved African Negroes. The *Wanderer* had been built and outfitted in New York. For a time it had been held there on suspicion as intended for the slave trade, but had been released and in brazen fashion had set out for a supply of human loot. The usual care was taken to confuse the picture of legal ownership. One of the principal owners was Charles A. L. Lamar, of a family prominent in Georgia and from a branch of which were to come two members of the Supreme Court. Charles Lamar was himself a ruthless buccaneer. Another alleged owner was the captain, William C. Corrie, a member of the New York Yacht Club, where the *Wanderer* was registered—although he lost his membership in the club because of this venture.[26]

The landing of the *Wanderer's* cargo and its dispersal in the slave states quickly became notorious throughout the country. The United States Senate asked President Buchanan for official information on the subject. The President referred the inquiry to Attorney General Black. Black replied that it was well known that a cargo of some three hundred Negroes had been landed. He stated that effective measures were being taken to execute the laws and punish the offenders, but he advised against publication of information.[27]

Determined in this instance to vindicate the government against accusations of laxness, the Buchanan Administration appointed Henry R. Jackson, a prominent Georgia lawyer, as special counsel to work with the United States Attorney, gave them virtual authority to pardon individuals to be used as witnesses in order to secure testimony needed

---

[24] *African Slave Trade*, H.R. Exec. Doc. No. 7, 36th Cong., 2nd Sess. 585–586.

[25] *Ibid.*, 586–88.

[26] For summary statements or incidental data with respect to the *Wanderer* see Frederick Bancroft, *Slave Trading in the Old South*, 359–60; W. E. B. Du Bois, *The Suppression of the African Slave Trade*, 181, 185; Nevins, *The Emergence of Lincoln*, I, 435–37; McMaster, *History of the People of the United States*, VIII, 350–51; John R. Spears,

The American Slave Trade . . . , 202–07; "A Slave Trader's Letter Book," *North American Review*, 143: 447, 1886.

[27] J. S. Black to James Buchanan, Jan. 10, 1859, Attorney General's Letter Book A–3, 341–42. A similar reply was made to a House inquiry. J. S. Black to James Buchanan, Feb. 1, and Feb. 15, 1859, *ibid.*, 353, 361. See also Importation of Africans, H.R. Exec. Doc. No. 90, 35th Cong., 2nd Sess.

for conviction,[28] and otherwise assured full support. Professing surprise at reports that local people were opposed to enforcement of the law, Black warned that unpunished violation in the South would be but an invitation to the North to continue violating the Fugitive Slave Law: "If the two sections of the Union will emulate one another in the violation of law, and the impunity they give to criminals of different classes, it will not be very long before we shall cease to have any law at all."[29]

Black told the United States Attorney that if he found any federal officers slack in their duty or too much disposed to conciliate the enemies of the law, he should report them for removal.[30] Such slackness was discovered at a key point, in the United States Marshal, Donald H. Stewart, as the slave traders were permitted to spread their cargo inland and get it into other hands. Acting Attorney General Howell Cobb, a Georgian who was then Secretary of the Navy, reported on April 2, 1859, that Stewart had been removed, but by that time much of the damage had been done.[31] Cobb told of the report that some of the imported Africans had already been taken into Alabama and asked that federal agents report information to the United States Attorney in that state. He wrote to the United States Attorney in Mobile that the executive department was determined that its full duty should be discharged in the effort to enforce the laws and that his cordial cooperation was confidently expected.[32]

Prosecuting officers were slow in getting indictments. In November, 1859, Justice Wayne gave aid to the cause in a notable charge to a grand jury. He traced the steps taken to suppress the slave trade and carefully mentioned the Southern statesmen in Congress who had supported the several statutes. He explained and defended the strategy whereby Congress, in 1820, had declared the slave trade to be piracy and subject to the extreme penalty enforced against it, plainly answering the critics not only of 1820 when the statute was enacted but also of the 1850s when advocates of resumption of the slave trade as lawful commerce were denouncing and deriding the Congressional strategy. Such criticism, he insisted, had no sound reason to sustain it. The law of nations, which applied to conduct on the seas, was in part natural and in part conventional. The consent of nations could make piracy of any offense on the high seas. The kidnapping of Africans on land could, when consummated on the high seas, become piracy.[33]

---

[28] See J. S. Black to Joseph Ganahl, Jan. 27, 1859, Attorney General's Letter Book A-3, 352.

[29] J. S. Black to Joseph Ganahl, Jan. 31, 1859, *ibid.*, 349.

[30] *Ibid.*, 350.

[31] Howell Cobb to Henry R. Jackson, Apr. 2, 1859, *ibid.*, 399.

[32] Howell Cobb to A. J. Requier, Apr. 2, 1859, *ibid.*, 398-99.

[33] Charge to Grand Jury, 30 Fed. Cas. 1026, 1031 (No. 18269a) (C.C.D. Ga. 1859).

Whatever may have been the attitude of United States District Judge John C. Nicoll, who presumably sat with Justice Wayne, the senior jurist had sufficient prestige in his native state to secure indictments. However, as proslavery men and perhaps as advocates of the legalization of the slave trade, the grand jury found bills of indictment under protest. With smugness about their own right to freedom and utter blindness to the comparable rights of colored people, they voiced their protest in a public statement:

> We feel humbled, as men, in the consciousness that we are freemen but in name, and that we are living, during the existence of such laws, under a tyranny as supreme as that of the despotic governments of the Old World. . . . Longer to yield to a sickly sentiment of pretended philanthropy and diseased mental aberration of "higher law" fanatics, the tendency of which is to debase us in the estimation of civilized nations, is weak and unwise. Regarding all such laws as tending to encourage such results, and consequently as baneful in their effects, we unhesitatingly advocate the repeal of all laws which directly or indirectly condemn this institution, and those who have inherited or maintain it; and think it the duty of the Southern people to require their legislators to unite their efforts for the accomplishment of this object.[34]

Among those indicted in Georgia was Captain Corrie. Evidently anticipating more lenient treatment in Judge Magrath's court in South Carolina than in Georgia, even though South Carolina was also in Justice Wayne's circuit, Captain Corrie went to South Carolina, where he was taken into custody. When his surrender was demanded for return for trial in the federal court in Georgia, Judge Magrath refused to surrender him. In South Carolina Justice Wayne delivered a charge to the grand jury presumably after the fashion of his charge to the Georgia grand jury, but here the jury refused to indict. Then, as if having been informed that an indictment in South Carolina would be helpful in preventing Captain Corrie's return to Georgia, the foreman of the grand jury asked that the bill against Corrie again be committed to it. Justice Wayne, in disagreement with Judge Magrath, prevented this step, but Captain Corrie continued under the jurisdiction of the court in South Carolina while at large on bail.

Subsequent South Carolina grand juries likewise refused to indict. Acting at the request of the Attorney General of the United States, the district attorney asked that a nolle prosequi be entered in South Caro-

---

[34] *Harper's Monthly Magazine*, 19: 255, 1859.

lina in order that Captain Corrie might be sent to Georgia for trial,[35] but Judge Magrath, sitting alone, refused permission. In doing so he wrote a long opinion challenging in effect Justice Wayne's interpretation of the statute providing for the punishment of the slave trade as piracy. He contended, among other things, that in order to be piracy under the statute the offense must include the enslavement of free men, and that, in view of the legality of slavery in the United States and Brazil and Cuba, the free status of the Negroes carried was not to be presumed. Their enslavement in their native land may have been in violation of other statutes of the United States carrying lesser penalties, but the statute with respect to piracy did not apply.[36] Judge Magrath's reasoning was farfetched, but it was effective for its purpose. With respect to Captain Corrie the controversy dragged on until the Civil War rendered it moot.

In the federal court in Georgia Charles A. L. Lamar was also indicted, as one of the owners of the *Wanderer*, though under a slave trade statute providing a lesser penalty. For a time he contemplated fleeing to Cuba. He was enraged when a member of Congress whose name he could not read addressed a letter to him "In Jail." He wrote to his cousin, L. Q. C. Lamar, then in Congress and later to become a member of the Supreme Court, asking him to discover the name of the writer and to issue a challenge if offense was intended: "I am *not* in jail, and the damned Government has not the power to put and keep me there. I am in my own rooms, over my office, and go home every night, and live like a fighting-cock *at the expense of the Government*; for we notified the Marshal, at the beginning, that, unless he furnished us, we would not stay with him, but dissolve all connection that exists or might exist between us. He submitted the same to the Judges, and they told him to supply us. I can *whip* the Government any time they make the issue, unless they raise a few additional regiments."[37] Lamar's case too blurred into the Civil War.

It was the strategy of the slave traders to dispose of their slave booty as quickly as possible in order to reap their profits and escape the penalties of the law. It was the belief, or at least the hope, of interested Southerners that the slave trade laws would be held inapplicable to persons who had nothing to do with the importation of slaves but who did a local merchandising business in them. In 1860 a case in-

---

[35] J. S. Black to James Conner, Mar. 17, 1860, Attorney General's Letter Book B-3, 247-48.
[36] United States v. Corrie, 25 Fed.

Cas. 658, 664-65 (No. 14869) (C.C.-D. S.C. 1860).
[37] A Slave Trader's Letter Book," *North American Review*, 143:447, 460, 1886.

volving the sale of one of the victims of the *Wanderer* by a local trader was tried in southern Alabama before United States District Judge William G. Jones. Judge Jones had only recently been appointed to the court, and at the time of his appointment had been counsel for another defendant charged with a like offense. He indicated no disposition to withdraw from the case because of a possible bias, though he did remark on the seriousness of the fact that since he was disposing of the case while sitting alone in the District Court there was no right of appeal from his decision. Following the analogy of certain commerce cases, and particularly of *Brown v. Maryland*,[38] he took the position that federal slave trade laws ceased to apply after the point of the first sale of imported Negroes, and that since the defendant had not been connected with the importation he was not subject to punishment under federal law, but only under state law.[39]

Judge Jones' decision did not settle the legal question, however, for the case of the man who had been his client remained to be tried. His own involvement being so obvious that he could not sit in the case, it was only natural that it should be tried in the United States Circuit Court before Justice Campbell, whose rank and reputation were such that he would not feel obligated to defer to the position previously taken by the district judge. Although a defender of slavery as "confined to the existing race of slaves,"[40] Justice Campbell was opposed to new enslavements. In the United States Circuit Court in New Orleans in 1858 he had delivered to a grand jury an elaborate charge explaining the history and the contents of the slave trade laws and urged their enforcement.[41] In April, 1859, he delivered a similar charge in southern Alabama.[42] There he denounced the "piratical efforts lately made to make Slaves of Africans, in despite of the treaties and laws of the United States."[43]

It was therefore not surprising that in trying a man charged with marketing an illegally imported slave Justice Campbell showed, as did Justice Wayne in his grand jury charge in Georgia in the same year, the same disposition to enforce law and order in the face of hostile public opinion as had Justices Grier and Curtis in abolitionist areas in the North. He held that Congress had full power to deal with the evils of the slave trade, whether acting upon it externally or within our borders.

---

[38] 12 Wheat. 419 (1827).

[39] United States v. Gould, 25 Fed. Cas. 1375 (No. 15239) (D.C.S.D. Ala. 1860).

[40] John A. Campbell, "Slavery in the United States," *Southern Quarterly Review*, 12:91, 98, 1847. For the credit of this anonymous article to Campbell see Henry G. Connor, *John Archibald Campbell*, 105.

[41] Connor, *John Archibald Campbell*, 103–04; *Washington National Intelligencer*, Jan. 10, 1859.

[42] *Washington National Intelligencer*, Aug. 25, 1859.

[43] *Annual Report of the American Anti-Slavery Society . . . for the Year Ending May 1, 1859*, 48 (1860).

XXVIII: *The Widening Breach*

The power did not necessarily derive from the Commerce Clause, but rather from the power to define and punish offenses against the law of nations. But even if the power was one of commerce, Congress was "clothed with powers adequate to the accomplishment of their policy. They are not dependent upon the state governments for ancillary legislation, nor can they be obstructed by their inaction or opposition."[44] In spite of his states' rights proclivities, Justice Campbell here articulated the scope of federal power after the fashion of the most ardent nationalists in any of the federal courts.

While litigation involving the officers and crew of the *Wanderer* extended over months and years, the vessel itself was condemned and sold. Lamar brazenly appeared at the sale, contended that the vessel belonged to him, and bought it for what was said to be less than a quarter of its value. He then assaulted the one man who seriously attempted to bid against him, "amid general applause."[45] Some time afterward a new captain of the vessel, nominally against orders and without proper papers and pursued by Lamar, headed out to sea on another slave-hunting voyage. When in the Canaries the captain and four aids boarded a French vessel to obtain supplies, the rest of the crew, who had no heart for operating a slaver, set sail for Boston. They carried with them, it was said, two Portuguese women whom the captain had decoyed aboard at one of the Azores with the intention of exchanging them in Africa for Negroes.[46]

In Boston the *Wanderer* was libeled for seamen's wages and proceeded against as a slaver. In the United States District Court Judge Peleg Sprague was unimpressed by Lamar's demand that the vessel be returned as one stolen from him, and by his presentation of an indictment of the captain in the federal court in Georgia for piratical seizure of the vessel. Wages were allowed and forfeiture of the *Wanderer* was decreed.[47]

Before the end of the Buchanan Administration the expansion of the unlawful slave trade became so extensive that even that slow-moving Administration had to provide additional funds and additional patrols to curb it.[48] With the beginning of the Lincoln Administration, the secession of Southern states, and the outbreak of war, the federal government concentrated in the Secretary of the Interior the administrative re-

---

[44] United States v. Haun, 26 Fed. Cas. 227, 231 (No. 15329) (C.C.S.D. Ala. 1860).

[45] *Annual Report of the American Anti-Slavery Society . . . for the Year Ending May 1, 1859*, 48 (1860).

[46] *Annual Report of the American Anti-Slavery Society . . . for the Year Ending May 1, 1860*, 25–26 (1861).

[47] *The Wanderer*, 29 Fed. Cas. 150 (No. 17139) (D.C.D. Mass. 1860).

[48] See W. E. B. Du Bois, *The Suppression of the African Slave-Trade*, 187.

sponsilibity for repressing the slave trade. Enforcement, however, continued to be a grindingly difficult task. Some of the problems were revealed in connection with the forfeiture of the *Augusta*, which in September, 1861, was decreed in the United States District Court for Southern New York,[49] with District Judge William D. Shipman of Connecticut sitting in this New York case. The owners appealed to the United States Circuit Court, and persuaded government officials to accept bond for the vessel in lieu of holding it, so that it might continue to be used. For the bond a low figure of two thousand dollars was at first proposed. The bond agreed upon was substantially higher, and after the guarantee was provided, the vessel was released, reportedly again to involve itself in the slave trade. It was reported that the attempted leniency of the government was the result of the efforts of an assistant to the United States Attorney, who consorted unduly with a representative of the owners and who employed his father-in-law as one of the appraisers. The Secretary of the Interior asked Judge Shipman to make an investigation. The judge reported that while there might have been some indiscretion there was no evidence of corruption in the matter.[50]

It continued to be difficult to secure piracy convictions for participation in the slave trade. In November, 1861, Justice Nelson, sitting with Judge Shipman in the United States Circuit Court for the Southern District of New York, charged a jury with respect to their verdict on the guilt of Minthorne Westervelt, third mate on the slave vessel *Nightingale*. Westervelt had shipped with the vessel from Liverpool. Justice Nelson closed his charge with the statement that while evidence of previous good character would not overcome proof of guilt, it was entitled to weight in the explanation of the evidence. The jury disagreed on the verdict.[51]

The first conviction for the capital offense took place in the same month in the same court before the same judges. It involved Captain Nathaniel Gordon of Portland, Maine, the son of a seafaring family, who had long been involved in the slave trade. Indeed, as early as 1851 Gordon arrived in Rio de Janeiro with a cargo of hides from California, and in the following year set out for the coast of Africa where he loaded a cargo of Negroes for sale in Brazil. The cargo was landed, the ship was burned, presumably to destroy evidence, and the officers and crew dispersed.[52]

The venture for which Gordon fell afoul of the law took place in

---

[49] United States v. *The Augusta*, 24 Fed. Cas. 892 (No. 14447) (D.C.S.D. N.Y. 1861).

[50] For the correspondence see Senate Exec. Doc. No. 40, 37th Cong., 2nd Sess. (1862).

[51] United States v. Westervelt, 28 Fed. Cas. 529 (No. 16668) (C.C.S.D. N.Y. 1861).

[52] Slave and Coolie Trade, H.R. Exec. Doc. No. 105, 34th Cong., 1st Sess. 56–57 (1856).

1860, when in an American ship he sailed from Cuba on an ostensibly legitimate voyage but, as was widely suspected, really to bring from Africa a cargo of slaves. The American Secretary of State, Lewis Cass, had been apprised by the consul general in Havana of Gordon's probable purpose and of the inability of that officer to interfere. Cass seems to have asked Attorney General Jeremiah S. Black whether an American consul in a foreign port might interfere by impounding the papers of vessels suspected as destined for the slave trade. Black replied that such power had not been given by Congress and could not be supplied by departmental regulation. In enumerating the grounds on which a consul might retain papers of a ship, this one had been omitted, "no doubt for good reasons."[53] The ship, the *Erie*, proceeded on its way.

Arriving off the coast of Africa, Gordon sailed up the Congo where he delivered a cargo of liquor. Then he took on board nearly nine hundred Negroes rounded up for the purpose, a large number of them children, whom he packed in tight quarters for shipment to Cuba. Unfortunately for him a United States warship overtook him as he was leaving the Congo, took the Negroes to Liberia, and sent Captain Gordon and the *Erie* to New York. The vessel was forfeited, bringing a handsome sum to the captors, and Gordon went on trial for piracy.[54]

This time the court thrust aside the many impediments that in earlier cases had prevented convictions. In view of his Maine heritage there was no doubt of Gordon's citizenship. Gordon had not taken the usual trouble to conceal the fact that the *Erie* was an American vessel. He had failed at a strategic moment to shift command of the vessel to another person and claim himself to be a mere passenger without responsibility for the detention of slaves. From beginning to end he had stood to the fore as the responsible person. In view of all the facts, charging the jury was an easy task and the jury had no difficulty in finding him guilty.[55]

Gordon moved for an arrest of judgment and a new trial. The two judges agreed on rejection and announced their decision through Judge Shipman sitting alone. When the verdict of guilty was announced it attracted much attention, and the courtroom was crowded on the date set for sentencing. The judge recited the facts of the case, told the prisoner that as he had shown no mercy for his victims he could expect none from the court, and sentenced him to be hanged on February 7, 1862.[56]

---

[53] African Slave Trade, H.R. Exec. Doc. No. 7, 36th Cong., 2nd Sess. 598–99 (1860).

[54] For a summary account see John R. Spears, *The American Slave-Trade*, 218–19.

[55] United States v. Gordon, 25 Fed. Cas. 1364 (No. 15231) (C.C.S.D. N.Y. 1861).

[56] Spears, *The American Slave-Trade*, 220. Spears says that the sentence was pronounced by Justice

Although the two judges were in agreement in the case, Gordon's counsel tried to persuade them to certify a difference of opinion in order to bring the case before the Supreme Court. While this device of certifying a difference that did not actually exist was sometimes utilized, the judges refused to use it here. Gordon then applied to the Supreme Court for a writ of prohibition to restrain the court and its officers from further proceedings and for a writ of certiorari directing the submission of papers, process, and proceedings. The date set for the execution was approaching. To provide time for the Supreme Court to act, he sought a respite from President Lincoln. The President asked Attorney General Edward Bates whether he could give Gordon a respite of the sentence without relieving him altogether of the death penalty. Bates assured him he could,[57] and a reprieve of two weeks was granted.

The Supreme Court heard argument in the case on February 14, 1862, and decided it three days later. For a unanimous Court, Chief Justice Taney denied the petition. The Supreme Court, he held, had no power to revise or control criminal proceedings in a Circuit Court or to express an opinion on the proceedings except where there was a certificate of division of opinion. More particularly, the Supreme Court could not go beyond the Circuit Court, from which the power to recall the decision had now passed, and interfere with the performance of a ministerial officer.[58]

The controversy was not permitted to end even with the Supreme Court decision. The President received a petition for commutation of the sentence signed by more than eleven thousand persons,[59] among them "lawyers and laymen, clergymen and citizens," the last including senators and members of the assembly from New York City. On the other hand

---

Nelson. The report of the case, however, says that it was pronounced by Judge Shipman, who brushed aside the objection that a valid sentence required the presence of the two judges.

[57] Bates wrote in part, "A reprieve does not annul the sentence, as a pardon does. It only prolongs the time, and fixes a day for execution, different from and more distant than the day fixed by the court. . . . My answer is confined to the single question of your lawful power to do the thing, which is clear and plain. I say nothing about the justice or expediance of using the power, because upon that branch of the subject, no question is propounded to me." Edward Bates to Lincoln, Feb. 4, 1862, Lincoln Papers.

According to his diary, however, Bates did give oral advice against granting a reprieve unless the President meant to give a pardon or commute the sentence, believing that such action would be made use of by Lincoln's political enemies. He was convinced that a reprieve would be taken as an implied promise of pardon or commutation even though he might asseverate to the contrary. "The Diary of Edward Bates," Howard K. Beale, ed., *Annual Report of the American Historical Association for the Year 1930*, 4:229–30, 233–34, 1933.

[58] *Ex parte* Gordon, 1 Black 140 (1862).

[59] Rhoda E. White to Lincoln, Feb. 17, 1862, Lincoln Papers.

a letter was published, allegedly signed by the United States Attorney in New York City, saying that local public opinion was earnest and almost unanimous against commutation. Gordon's counsel, Gilbert Dean, appealed to the President for a review that the Supreme Court had denied: "Where the title to property is in question the Writ of Error is a writ of right—not so here—human life is of less consequence than Bales of Cotton—or Boxes of Dry Goods."[60]

The President referred the documents to the Attorney General, who advised against intervention.[61] A last-minute appeal from the governor of New York was without avail. Gordon's rescue by a mob of Southern sympathizers was threatened, but a guard of United States marines was provided to preserve order. On the morning of his execution Gordon swallowed poison and then gloated to the guards that he had cheated them, but physicians saved him for the gallows.[62] He was the first to die pursuant to a statute which had been on the books for more than forty years.

In November, 1862, the United States Attorney in New York City, E. Delafield Smith, wrote to Montgomery Blair that three things were needed to end slave trade activities in the port of New York. The first was to stop the outfitting of ships for the trade. The second was to restrain American officers and seamen from serving on slave ships. The third was to stop the putting up of "straw bail" as a result of which vessels were released to their holders. A step had been taken toward meeting the first need when one Albert Horn had been convicted and imprisoned for fitting out a slave trade vessel.[63] The second was met by the execution of Gordon. The third would be met by the punishment of one Rudolph Blumenberg, who had been convicted and was currently in Sing Sing prison but who was seeking release. Blumenberg had a brother in Maryland who was prominent in the Union cause,[64] and whom Blair, likewise from Maryland, had evidently wanted to serve by giving aid to his brother. Smith explained to Blair the "straw bail" device in the hope of persuading him to give up his effort to get Blumenberg pardoned:

> It is remarkable that no money was ever collected upon one of these bonds, and no conviction but this was secured. Twelve such cases,

---

[60] Gilbert Dean to Lincoln, Feb. 18, 1862, Lincoln Papers.

[61] Edward Bates to Lincoln, Feb. 19, 1862, Lincoln Papers.

[62] Spears, *The American Slave-Trade*, 221–23.

[63] See United States v. Horn, 26 Fed. Cas. 373 (No. 15389) (C.C.S.D. N.Y. 1862).

[64] According to Edwin M. Stanton the loyal Union servant, Leopold Blumenberg, was charged with "cruelty in gagging men to make them confess they were deserters." Abraham Lincoln, *Collected Works*, VIII, 238.

pending on my appointment, occur to me; and in one of the vessels not yet disposed of, the lawyer recently told me that the case might as well be abandoned as the sureties were not good and never were.[65]

Smith wrote that Blumenberg's transfer to Sing Sing had operated "to give us good bondsmen, which were never offered before," and that "the pardon of Blumenberg would do more to revive the waning hopes of slave traders here than any thing of which you can conceive."

The records of the United States pardon attorney show that on October 22, 1862, the President denied a pardon, but that on July 24, 1863, the pardon was granted. By this time the war and the emancipation movement were so far advanced that the slave trade belonged largely to history, even though a few cases involving the trade were yet to come before the courts.[66]

In holding Circuit Court Justice Campbell continued through the middle and late 1850s to have trouble with the sponsors of filibustering expeditions against Cuba and other present or former Spanish possessions to the south. The expeditions were conducted with mixed motives, involving the hopes of some to acquire additional slave territory and of others, as in the instance of the perennial troublemaker, William Walker, to create a federation of independent republics with himself prominent as a leader.[67] Although personnel and funds for filibustering expeditions came from various parts of the country, New Orleans and Mobile, both in Justice Campbell's circuit, were the points of assemblage and departure.

In New Orleans in the spring of 1854 Justice Campbell, for all his Southern sympathies never an advocate of southward territorial expansion, delivered a grand jury charge denouncing the violation of neutrality laws by filibustering expeditions and reminding the people of that area that the people of the North could not be expected to support the Fugitive Slave Law while Southerners violated other laws through such expeditions. The charge, published in full in New Orleans newspapers, stirred deep resentment.[68] Receiving from the grand jury a report on preparations for further expeditions, he called in three prominent Southerners, John A. Quitman, J. S. Thrasher, and A. L. Saunders,

---

[65] E. Delafield Smith to Montgomery Blair, Nov. 17, 1862, Lincoln Papers.

[66] See United States v. Isla de Cuba, 26 Fed. Cas. 548 (No. 15447) (C.C.D. Mass. 1864); United States v. Kelly, 26 Fed. Cas. 697 (No. 15515) (D.C.D. Mass. 1863); Brig Kate v. United States, 2 Wall. 350 (1865);

Couilliard v. United States, 2 Wall. 366 (1865); Morris v. United States, 2 Wall. 375 (1865).

[67] See William O. Scroggs, *Filibusters and Financiers: The Story of William Walker and His Associates*, 228–29.

[68] Connor, *John Archibald Campbell*, 91–93.

and required them to post bond to guarantee good behavior, to the accompaniment of loud protest from them and their friends.[69] One of the investors in Quitman's Cuban project was Charles A. L. Lamar. To Thrasher, Lamar wrote that the collector of the port was a Lone Star man and could be sent away for a few days to prevent interference with the expedition. He asserted that the United States circuit judge, presumably referring to Justice Campbell, would not trouble himself or do anything more than his duty required. He himself had no fear of the consequences of violating the neutrality laws. If President Pierce and all his Cabinet were there, they could not convict him or his friends.[70]

The Cuban expedition was not carried out but in 1857, in spite of the bond required of him which was intended to guarantee his good conduct, William Walker slipped away to establish himself in Nicaragua with an armed force. The correspondence of State Department, Treasury Department, and court officials disclosed confusion and ineptitude in attempts to prevent such expeditions or to punish the persons involved when apprehended.[71] American naval forces landed in Nicaragua, seized Walker, and brought him home, but he was not punished and was soon engaged in planning another expedition. On October 30, 1858, President Buchanan issued a proclamation calling attention to rumors that another expedition against Nicaragua was being planned and enjoining all government officers to take steps to prevent it.[72] Plans were being openly made, though under the subterfuge of organizing a commercial company entitled the Mobile and Nicaragua Steamship Company.[73]

At the direction of the President, Attorney General Black called the matter to the attention of the United States Attorneys at New Orleans and Mobile,[74] and he appointed special counsel to assist them with any prosecutions that might be undertaken.[75] He appointed a special agent to give secret assistance to the United States Marshal in Mobile, directing him to aid in breaking up the expedition said to be on foot against Nicaragua. He believed this could be done only by the arrest of the leaders and their commitment to await trial.[76]

In November, 1858, Justice Campbell arranged for a special term of the Circuit Court in Mobile, nominally to catch up with the docket

---

[69] *Ibid.*, 91–102.

[70] "A Slave-Trader's Note Book," *North American Review*, 143:447, 448, 1886.

[71] See H.R. Exec. Doc. No. 24, 35th Cong., 1st Sess. (1858); Senate Exec. Doc. No. 63, 35th Cong., 1st Sess. (1858).

[72] Richardson, *A Compilation of the Messages and Papers of the Presidents*, V, 496.

[73] See Clearance of Vessels at the Port of Mobile, H.R. Exec. Doc. No. 25, 35th Cong., 2nd Sess. (1859).

[74] J. S. Black to Thomas I. Semmes and A. J. Requier, Nov. 6, 1858, Attorney General's Letter Book A–3, 309.

[75] J. S. Black to Robert H. Smith, Nov. 12, 1858, *ibid.*, 313.

[76] J. S. Black to Henry C. Wilson, Nov. 24, 1858, *ibid.*, 323–24.

but actually to deal with the projected expedition. On his arrival there he wrote to Attorney General Black, the *Mobile Register* published an article denouncing him and his purpose in holding the court, and threatening dire consequences if he charged the jury as he had done in New Orleans. He reported that the United States Attorney had been absent for three months and was timid to the point of helplessness. Yet as a contrasting circumstance, the clerk of the court had summoned both grand jurors and petit jurors. This embarrassed the judge, since the Act of Congress did not allow for a petit jury at the special term, and he could hardly find a foundation for a grand jury. Under the circumstances he at first feared to charge the grand jury, noting that "without any district attorney and with such limited powers I fear the nakedness of the court may be exposed. I shall probably dismiss the grand jury in a day or two, after charging them at large." What was most needed, he thought, was efficient police detection, possibly with the arrest of the leaders. "The courts are too clumsy for the exigencies of such a case. At all events, the preparation of the material upon which the courts have to act cannot be left to any person connected with the government that I know of here."[77]

Apparently advised by Black to offer the leaders immunity from past misconduct in return for future good behavior, Campbell replied that they were an energetic lot who felt more like hanging the officers of the United States than receiving a pardon from them. They were handicapped by the withholding of clearance from the port, and there was strife resulting from the fact that some employees had not been paid, for the reason that the dispensing of money might be used in evidence at the trial. "If I had the power to go on with the court I think they might be dispersed by it. But I fear that the disclosure of the impotence of the court may do some harm."[78]

Deciding to charge the grand jury specifically with respect to violation of the neutrality laws, Justice Campbell did so at great length. He traced the history of the legislation and set forth the responsibility of the federal government for the conduct of foreign affairs and the absence of right to interfere on the part of the states or of private individuals. He set forth the proclamation of the President in the matter. He asked the jury to go behind the ostensible purpose of the expedition to determine its actual purpose.[79]

On the following day Justice Campbell reported to Attorney General Black that he had charged the grand jury with a good deal of

---

[77] J. A. Campbell to J. S. Black, Nov. 22, 1858, Black Papers.
[78] J. A. Campbell to J. S. Black, Nov. 24, 1858, Black Papers.

[79] Charge to Grand Jury (C.C.S.D. Ala. Nov. 26, 1858), Minute Book 423, 430–31.

effect and had provided for publication in full "in the only two papers that observe common decency to the court." It was now his impression that the expedition would vanish upon the attempt of the grand jury to make the investigation, even though privately he still expressed doubt whether at a special term the court had authorization to do more than take care of unfinished business.[80] Four days later Campbell reported that the investigation was under way and that Walker and another of the leaders had been examined at great length. The "immigrants" had returned home, and the expedition for the time being was abandoned. He had decided to remain in Mobile until the grand jury made its report, saying that his presence there operated as a restraint on one class and a support to those who were disposed to do their duty.[81] In mid-December a Washington newspaper, announcing the coming of a band under the heading "The Campbells are coming," said in derision that "We trust that none of our Filibuster friends will start at this announcement. We have no allusion to his Honor the dreaded and dreadful judge of the Supreme Court of the United States. He is now safely and comfortably ensconced in the Judicial ermine, in the gloomy lower story of the Federal Capital at Washington."[82] William Walker continued his filibustering activities, but in 1860, in Honduras, he died before a firing squad.[83]

As strife over the expansion and possible legalization of the slave trade and over filibustering expeditions into Latin American territory emphasized the growing sectional differences, so also did intensified Southern opposition to the education and liberation of slaves and Southern restrictions on the rights of free Negroes. Slaveholders liked to claim as great benefits for Negroes imported into the United States their alleged education and Christianization. In 1853, for example, a local judge in Louisiana, in charging a grand jury, boasted that "The three million Africans in this country are elevated far above the naked heathen their ancestors were, when they first landed on these shores."[84] Yet in enumerating the laws to be enforced he had to include one which penalized any person "who shall teach, or permit, or cause to be taught, any Slave in this State, to read or write."[85] He mentioned this statute regretfully, he said, but attributed its necessity to unwise agitation in the free states.

In the slave states, although manumission was extensively prac-

---

[80] J. A. Campbell to J. S. Black, Nov. 27, 1858, Attorney General's Papers.

[81] J. A. Campbell to J. S. Black, Dec. 1, 1858, Black Papers.

[82] *Washington National Intelligen-* cer, Dec. 18, 1858.

[83] Scroggs, *Filibusters and Financiers*, 390–91.

[84] "Slavery in Louisiana," *Law Rep.*, 16:291, 292, 1853.

[85] *Ibid.*, 293

ticed, extreme elements and sometimes legislative majorities increasingly opposed it, not merely because some heirs were thereby deprived of rights to property but because the hope of attainment of freedom made slaves restless and reduced their value. This position was vigorously taken by Judge Joseph H. Lumpkin of the Georgia Supreme Court:

> We may not be able to prevent expatriation of the living—to restrain the master in his lifetime from removing whithersoever he pleases with his property; but when the owner has kept them as long as he can enjoy them, shall he, from an ignorance of the scriptural basis upon which the institution of slavery rests, or from a total disregard to the peace and welfare of the community which survive him, invoke the aid of the Courts of this State to carry into execution his false and fatal views of humanity?[86]

Although Judge Lumpkin admitted that his view of manumission by removal did not reflect the law of his state, a Mississippi judge quoted his dictum as a guiding principle for determining the law of Mississippi. A white man, one Edward Wells, had taken his half-colored daughter to Ohio and secured her emancipation—local emancipation being forbidden under the laws of Mississippi—and then brought her back to Mississippi and made her his heir. But the highest court in Mississippi held that manumission in Ohio could not confer in Mississippi either freedom or the right to acquire, hold, or sue for property. The court rejected the argument based on the rule of comity. It posed the possibility that Ohio, "still further afflicted with her peculiar philanthropy," should confer citizenship on the chimpanzee or the ourangoutang, "the most respectable of the monkey tribe"; would comity "require of the States not thus demented, to forget their own policy and self-respect, and lower their own citizens and institutions in the scale of being, to meet the necessities of the mongrel race thus attempted to be introduced into the family of sisters in this confederacy?"[87]

Predatory eyes were fixed on free Negroes as well. For offenses committed they were from time to time sold into slavery for temporary periods, and there is reason for believing that those sold were sometimes sent into other states for permanent enslavement. During the years just before the war proslavery zealots vigorously urged the enslavement of such free Negroes as had the temerity to remain within their respective states. In Chief Justice Taney's state of Maryland a meeting held on the Eastern Shore brought about the calling of a state convention to devise some plan for regulation of the Negro population and suggested giving free colored people a choice between leaving the

---

[86] Cleland v. Waters, 19 Ga. 35, 43–44 (1855).

[87] Mitchell v. Wells, 37 Miss. 235, 264 (1859).

state or accepting enslavement. Although in the western part of the state there was enough antislavery sentiment and sense of fairness toward free Negroes to bring about in the state convention a rejection of the Eastern Shore proposal, this extreme proslavery sentiment was widely expressed.[88]

Other states either took or seriously considered measures for forcing free Negroes into slavery. A bill introduced in the Tennessee legislature to enslave free Negroes was taken seriously enough to bring about publication of a letter of protest by Justice Catron. He denounced the proposal as unconstitutional and an outrageous attempt to perpetuate oppression and cruelty. He denounced it also on grounds of expediency, warning that the victims would preach rebellion wherever they might be driven, whether in Tennessee or on the cotton and sugar plantations of the states to the south or in abolitionist meetings in the free states. Negro women fleeing to the North would preach a crusade when begging money to relieve their children left behind in Tennessee. Returning to the merits of the bill, he challenged the claim that it was popular:

> Where is it popular? In what nook or corner of the State are the principles of humanity so deplorably deficient that a majority of the whole inhabitants would commit an outrage not committed in a Christian country of which history gives any account? . . . Numbers of the people sought to be enslaved or driven out are members of our various churches, and in full communion. That these great bodies of Christian men and women will quietly stand by and see their humble co-workers sold on the block to the negro-trader is not to be expected; nor will any set of men be supported, morally or politically, who are the authors of such a law.[89]

Fortunately the good sense of Justice Catron and other thoughtful leaders turned public sentiment against the bill. The discussion of such proposals, however, in Tennessee, Maryland, and many other states, and actual pressure in some states to compel free colored people to accept enslavement,[90] exposed the ever widening rift which culminated in the secession movement.

---

[88] *Annual Report of the American Anti-Slavery Society . . . for the Year Ending May 1, 1860*, 206–12 (1861).

[89] *Ibid.*, 215–16.

[90] For further discussion see *ibid.*, 216–21.

CHAPTER XXIX

The Court on the Eve of the War

T HE CITY OF WASHINGTON, where the Supreme Court assembled each December, despite its population of some sixty thousand people and a constant stream of transients, was still something of a rural settlement on the edge of a swampland, although its broad, unpaved streets and unutilized stretches of land pointed to the possibility of an attractive national capital. The only long stretch of pavement was Pennsylvania Avenue, whose cobblestones, under the weight of omnibuses and wagons, gave way to a pattern of deep ruts filled with mud and water and slime. This was the only street lighted at night. Parallel and cross streets were muddy or dusty thoroughfares usually resembling country lanes. Boyhood memories of a resident told of a way of life bearing no resemblance to the Washington of a century later:

> When we lived on 4th Street, opposite Judiciary Square, every evening we watched the cows passing along the street and over the common at the side of our house, to their home in Swampoodle for their milking, so that in uncovered tin pails and ladled out with a long dipper, their more or less bacteria infested milk might be peddled from door to door. Long files of solemn geese did their goosestep on their way homewards; but best of all were the pigs which also made up the procession, for we boys liked to jump astride and ride those unwilling and squealing steeds. You will see thus, that Washington was a very democratic city, where domestic animals and people lived in perfect equality, with equal and undisturbed rights.[1]

At the beginning of the war the city had only one railroad, the Baltimore and Ohio, which had served it since 1835. Its station had

---

[1] Joseph T. Kelly, "Memories of a Lifetime in Washington," *Records of* *the Columbia Historical Society*, 31: 117, 125, 1930.

been moved back from Pennsylvania Avenue at Second Street to a dingy, damp, and dark location at New Jersey Avenue and Second Street, with the passenger terminal much below the level of the street and reached by a flight of rickety stairs. The train to the South reached Virginia by creeping slowly across the "long bridge" over the Potomac, a bottleneck for traffic with serious implications for movement of troops and supplies during the war. The war necessitated a second railroad, the Pennsylvania, with a station at Sixth and B streets.[2] An obsolescent canal still ran along the mall in the general area of the present Constitution Avenue, with bridges at a number of cross streets. The canal reeked with odors from sewage, refuse, dead animals, and, it was said, occasional human derelicts who, too drunk to walk across the bridges, fell into the canal and drowned.[3]

On the landscape the President's House (increasingly called the White House though on official stationery it was designated the Executive Mansion) still stood out, and at the opposite end of Pennsylvania Avenue the nation's Capitol. Since the beginning of the Taney period the Capitol itself had been undergoing great changes. Increases in population and the admission of new states had resulted in increased membership in Congress with resultant overcrowding of legislative halls. Acoustics in the hall of the House of Representatives had always been bad, and overcrowding made matters worse. As for the Senate chamber, located just above the dark and gloomy basement home of the Supreme Court, overcrowding and poor ventilation rendered the air fetid and unhealthy for members and visitors.[4] The Library of Congress was outgrowing its Capitol quarters. Better accommodations were needed for the Supreme Court, although less seems to have been said about its needs than about those of the other agencies.

Plans for enlarging the Capitol and incidentally providing more space for the Supreme Court by turning over to it the old Senate chamber were submitted by Robert Mills, architect of the federal government from 1836 until 1852. Mills reported that members of the Court had suffered much from the inconvenience of the basement chamber and that it had proved injurious to health. Without mentioning names he stated that "The death of some of our most talented jurists has been attributed to this location of the court-room."[5] The plans for construction were developed by Thomas U. Walter, Mills' successor in office. In presenting them to the Senate from the Committee on Public

---

[2] *Ibid.*, 120–21.

[3] *Ibid.*, 119. For further details see the relevant chapters in W. B. Bryan, *A History of the National Capital*, II.

[4] *Cong. Globe*, 31st Cong., 1st Sess. 1425, 1944 (1850).

[5] *Documentary History of the Construction and Development of the United States Capitol Building and Grounds*, H.R. Rep. No. 646, 58th Cong., 2nd Sess. 433 (1904).

Buildings, Jefferson Davis explained the plans for north and south wings to house the Senate and the House of Representatives, respectively, and a western extension to take care of the Congressional library. Indicating that relocation of the Supreme Court was not yet fully worked out, he remarked that "The desired accommodations for the Supreme Court and its officers may be obtained in the basement story of the north wing."[6]

In 1850 Congress provided one hundred thousand dollars to begin construction.[7] President Millard Fillmore laid the cornerstone on July 4, 1851, and Daniel Webster, then Secretary of State, delivered an address appealing for preservation of the Union and of our free institutions.[8] The new south wing was completed to a point where it could be occupied by the House of Representatives in December, 1857, and the Senate moved into the north wing in January, 1859. To the Supreme Court was allocated the old Senate chamber with adjacent space. Senator James A. Bayard described the plan for the suite of rooms as drawn in accordance with the wishes of the Court:

> The old cloak-room of the Senate, which is nothing more than a passage way, together with the corridor and passage from the wing through the main building, are entirely devoted to the court. Crossing that, there is a small strip or a small room lying by the corridor which was formerly part of the reception room. This is to be the robing-room of the judges. Next to that comes the Vice President's room, which is to be the conference room of the court. Adjoining that is the former Secretary's office, which is to be converted into an audience room, where the judges will receive any person whom it is necessary to see during the sitting of the court. Adjoining are the offices of the clerks of the Secretary of the Senate, which are appropriated, first, to the clerk of the Supreme Court, and the other to the deputy clerk of the Supreme Court. The former Finance Committee Room is appropriated, under this amendment, to the marshal's room. The small cloak-room, on the south side of the Senate chamber, is appropriated for the reporter's office. Descending to the lower story, the present Supreme Court room is to be converted into a library with iron shelves, and the same system as the present general library of Congress, to be fitted up for the law library of Congress in the same manner. When so fitted up, it will be fire proof, and capable of containing nearly twenty-two thousand volumes. The former conference room of the Supreme Court is to be used as the judges' study in connection with the library.[9]

---

[6] *Ibid.*, 447.
[7] 9 Stat. 523, 538.
[8] "The Addition to the Capitol," in *Writings and Speeches of Daniel Webster*, J. W. McIntyre, ed., IV, 293, 301.

[9] *Documentary History of the Construction and Development of the United States Capitol Building and Grounds*, H.R. Rep. No. 646, 58th Cong., 2nd Sess. 433 (1904).

HENRY CLAY
(Library of Congress)

DANIEL WEBSTER
(Library of Congress)

MONTGOMERY BLAIR
(Library of Congress)

WILLIAM H. SEWARD
(Library of Congress)

RUFUS CHOATE
(Library of Congress)

RICHARD HENRY DANA
(Library of Congress)

CHARLES RIVER BRIDGE, 1789
(Library of Congress)

National Hotel and first telegraph office
(Watercolor by A. Meyer, 1860)

Supreme Court Chamber,
1860–1935, former Senate Chamber
(*Architect of the Capitol*)

Plan of Courtroom, 1819–1860,
shown at lower right
(*Library of Congress*)

BASEMENT STORY OF THE CAPITOL, U.S.

CHIEF JUSTICE TANEY
administering oath of office
to PRESIDENT LINCOLN, 1861
(Library of Congress)

ADJUTANT-GENERAL THOMAS
Addressing the Negroes in Louisiana
on the Duties of Freedom.
From *Harpers Weekly*.
(Library of Congress)

In the matter of the United States Appellants

vs

Singua and others severally claimants and appellees

J. Q. Adams, of Counsel for the said Africans, moves the Court for a certiorari to the Judges of the Circuit Court of the United States, for the District of Connecticut, to amend the Record of the proceedings in the said Circuit Court in this case, by sending up copies of the following papers.

1. The proceedings of the Court of Enquiry holden by the honourable judge of the District Court on board the Schooner Armistad on the 29th of August 1839. and particularly the Indictment against the said Africans for the murder of the captain and mate or cook of the said Schooner. The warrant of Seizure issued by the said District Judge on the said 29th of August 1839. directed to the Marshal of the said District, together with the monitions and other process according to Law and the return made by the said Marshal made on the 30th of August aforesaid to the said warrant of Seizure, and the return to the said monitions.

2. The two warrants of Seizure issued by the said District Judge on the 18th of September 1839. and the returns of the Marshal thereon with the process of monition and returns thereon

MOTION FOR CERTIORARI:
of John Quincy Adams, counsel
for the Africans in *U. S.* vs.
Schooner Armistad, Jan. 23, 1842.
(Library of Congress)

Senator Bayard noted that under this arrangement it would be possible to consolidate the work of the Court in the Capitol so as to dispense with a consultation room hitherto rented "up town" at the cost of two hundred dollars a month, in an area convenient to the temporary residences of the Justices. There would be some library consolidation as well, since a duplicate library of some fifteen hundred volumes was then maintained in connection with the uptown conference room.[10]

While Congress was discussing appropriations for the renovated chamber, Thomas Walter reported to William Thomas Carroll, Clerk of the Court, that he had plans drawn in lead .and was ready to talk about proceeding.[11] The initially suggested appropriation was for fifty thousand dollars, which was reduced in successive stages to twenty-five thousand dollars, much of which would go toward construction of a stairway down to the law library in the old Court chamber. The appropriation was made in June, 1860.[12]

Hearing that the renovation was now to go forward, Justice Catron wrote to Carroll that the information was "truly gratifying to me, who has been greviously [*sic*] annoyed by the dampness, darkness, and want of venliation [*sic*], of the old basement room; into which, I have always supposed, the Sup. Court was thrust in a spirit of hostility to it, by the Political Department. That the $25,000, will do all that is needful, is not expected; but I was for beginning last year, *on credit*, with the old carpet."[13]

While work proceeded on the new and greatly enlarged dome of the Capitol—it was not completed until 1863, in the midst of the war period—and on other parts of the building, the Supreme Court, at the beginning of the December term, 1860, moved into its new chamber and adjacent rooms. The chamber, like the basement chamber previously occupied, was semicircular. It was forty-five feet long and the same distance wide at the widest point. The ceiling was a low half-dome, architecturally figured, with a suspended chandelier. As in the lower chamber, the bench was arranged with judicial backs to the east wall. Ionic columns of marble formed a colonnade along the eastern side of the room, while pilasters of marble decorated the circular wall. Marble busts of former Chief Justices were arranged around the walls. From above the seat of the Chief Justice looked down the gilded eagle which had previously sat above the presiding officer of the Senate, while over the door facing the Justices was a white marble clock. Soft brown carpet deadened the footfalls of persons coming and going and con-

---

[10] For a number of years this library was at Morrison's, at 23 4½ Street.
[11] Thomas U. Walter to W. T. Carroll, May 17, 1860, Clerk's Files.
[12] 12 Stat. 104, 110.
[13] J. Catron to William Thomas Carroll, Sept. 29, 1860, Clerk's Files.

tributed to the hushed atmosphere, as did the red velvet cushioning of the benches which were available to the public and which faced the enclosure for members of the bar just in front of the bench.[14] At each end of the bench were desks for Court officials.

Having a robing room on the west side of the corridor from which they could proceed eastward across the hall to a side entrance to the Court chamber, the Justices began their sessions much more formally than they had in earlier years in the basement chamber when they donned their robes from pegs on the wall in the presence of the audience. It was said that at eleven o'clock the small north door of the columned passage opened and the Marshal of the court (or his deputy) entered, for the most part moving backward the length of the room with his eyes fixed on the door. He then, in a tremulous voice unlike the trained voices of later criers, intoned, "The Honorable, the Judges of the Supreme Court of the United States." The people in the courtroom arose, including the lawyers, "and if any have their hats on off they instantly come." The Justices moved in one after the other in their loose-flowing black silk gowns and ranged themselves before their chairs. At this point the crier intoned:

> O Yea! O Yea! All persons having business before the Honorable, the
> Judges of the Supreme Court of the United States, are admonished
> to draw near and give their attendance, for the Court is now in session.
> God save the United States, and this Honorable Court.

At this point, it was said, the judges "looked relieved," and took their seats, and the Court was opened.[15] At this time the Court seems to have sat from eleven o'clock until three, when the Justices withdrew in a similarly dignified procession.

When Abraham Lincoln was inaugurated as President on March 4, 1861, the Supreme Court had received only one new member since the appointment of Justice Campbell in 1853: Nathan Clifford, who was appointed in 1858 to replace Justice Curtis. It was on the whole an aged Court; one member had already died, leaving an unfilled position, another was within a month of his death, and others showed various degrees of decrepitude. The age and health problems of the Justices in this period play an important part in the history of the Court.

---

[14] See S. D. Wyeth, *The Federal City*, 92–93. There are other descriptions in books about Washington or the Capitol. See for example Glenn Brown, *History of the U.S. Capitol*. The room itself is preserved as it was left when the Supreme Court moved to its new building in 1935.

[15] Wyeth, *The Federal City*, 94–95. See also George G. Evans, *Visitors' Companion at Our National Capital: A Complete Guide for Washington and Its Environs*, 56–58.

XXIX: *The Court on the Eve of the War*

For Chief Justice Taney the middle and late 1850s constituted a difficult period. Until that time his life had been arranged in a delicate balance of work and recreation so that he was able to handle his Supreme Court and circuit duties with only occasional absences. For many years he had spent part of each summer resting and rebuilding his health at some popular resort. In recent years he had gone with his family to Old Point Comfort, where he did his writing on the history of the bank war. In 1855 his son-in-law, J. Mason Campbell, a Baltimore attorney, planned to take his own family northward for a vacation at Newport, Rhode Island, and raised the question of taking with them Alice Taney, the youngest daughter of the Chief Justice. Although Newport was virtually a Southern colony, Taney gave his consent only with reservations and expressions of disapproval, saying that he had "not the slightest confidence in superior health of Newport over Old Point, and look upon it as nothing more than that unfortunate feeling of inferiority in the South, which believes every thing in the North to be superior to what we have."[16] So it was that the Taney family, including Alice, went back to Old Point.

In late August of that summer Taney was writing of the ravages of yellow fever in Norfolk and Portsmouth but giving assurance that it had not come near Old Point. Yet Mrs. Taney and the girls were worried about the reports of illness and death, and Taney was sufficiently saddened and depressed that he was doing only such work as was necessary.[17] He admitted that "The terrible pestilence near us has made the present month a sad one, and if we could have forseen it, some other place would undoubtedly have been more desirable for the summer." He spoke of "boats passing several times every day within two hundred yards of my cottage door filled with men and women and children flying from their homes, and the chief topic of conversation with every one you meet being the ravages of the pestilence and the sickness or death of friends."[18]

Two weeks later Taney wrote that the pestilence showed no signs of abatement but added that "We do not think there is the least danger that the infected atmosphere can extend to this place."[19] In late September, however, he was writing frantically to urge Dr. Thomas Buckler to come to Old Point because of the serious illness of his wife.[20] The letter was followed by a telegram saying that Mrs. Taney was dying

---

[16] R. B. Taney to J. Mason Campbell, June 26, 1855, Campbell Papers. On Newport as a resort for Southerners see Ward McAllister, *Society as I Have Found It*, 7.

[17] R. B. Taney to J. Mason Campbell (at Newport, Rhode Island), Aug.

31, 1855, Campbell Papers.

[18] R. B. Taney to D. M. Perine, Aug. 30, 1855, Perine Papers.

[19] R. B. Taney to J. Mason Campbell, Sept. 15, 1855, Campbell Papers.

[20] R. B. Taney to J. Mason Campbell, Sept. 26, 1855, Campbell Papers.

and asking that a boat be chartered to bring the family back to Baltimore. No boat was available for charter, so they had to rely on public transportation.[21] Mrs. Taney's illness was at first attributed to the condition which had already impaired her memory and speech, but it was said that soon after her death the signs of yellow fever appeared. Immediately after Alice fell ill, unmistakably with yellow fever, and died quickly. Because of the danger from the disease public authorities refused to permit transportation of the bodies, so they had to be buried there.[22]

He had never witnessed a scene of greater distress, wrote Charles Howard, a relative by marriage, at Taney's arrival at the wharf in Baltimore:

> The Old Chief is literally the strong man bowed down. The scenes he has gone through have completely prostrated him; and God knows they have been enough to do so. I could not have conceived that any circumstances whatsoever could have completely broken down all his self control, and marked self reliance. He says he shall not live, that he can never take his seat on the bench again and that he is, to use his own expression to me, "completely unmanned and broken down." He has been in tears like an infant, and he has given way to the most bitter self reproaches, for keeping his family at the Point in reliance on his own judgment that they were there free from danger, though in this opinion he was supported by that of all intelligent physicians.[23]

Taney recovered gradually and in some degree, but with inevitable effects on a constitution always frail and now seventy-eight years of age. In three weeks he was writing to a cousin that the support of God had enabled him to see that it was his duty to submit to this chastisement with calmness and resignation, and he had no doubt that, severe as was the trial for those who survived, it was in the mysterious ways of Providence introduced in mercy to the living and the dead.[24] In another letter he expressed his abiding religious faith, saying, "Most thankful I am, that the reading, reflection, studies, and experience of a long life have strengthened and confirmed my faith in the Catholic Church, which has never ceased to teach her children how they should live and how they should die." [25] In early November he replied to an expres-

---

21 Charles Howard to B. C. Howard, Sept. 30, 1855, Howard Papers.

22 *Baltimore Sun*, Oct. 4, 1855.

23 Charles Howard to B. C. Howard, Oct. 2, 1855, Howard Papers.

24 R. B. Taney to Ethelbert Taney, Oct. 22, 1855, Samuel Tyler, *Memoir*

of Roger Brooke Taney, LL.D, 473–74.

25 *Ibid.*, 475. As between religious denominations, issues even at this time were deeply imbedded in local politics. A Baltimore newspaper reported Bishop McGill of Richmond as saying that the pestilence of yellow fever was an infliction from the Al-

sion of sympathy from Justice Curtis by saying that he had resigned himself to God's will and was again attempting to fulfill his worldly duties. He expected to sit in the Circuit Court in Baltimore the following week, and to meet with the Supreme Court in December.[26]

Taney disposed of his family residence in Baltimore, evidently planning to stay at the home of his daughter and his son-in-law when returning to Baltimore to hold Circuit Court, and arranged to make Washington his home.[27] Thus in all probability he was the first member of the Supreme Court to make his primary residence in the capital city. He took rooms in a group of houses known as Blagden's Row, his own location being at 23 Indiana Avenue.[28] He was to live there with his unmarried daughter Ellen, and also for at least part of the time with his daughter Sophia, who was separated from her husband.

Illness delayed his move to Washington and the beginning of his Supreme Court work after arrival there. Although the *New York Tribune* was later to flay the Chief Justice for his performance in the Dred Scott case, which was first argued at this term, the case had not yet become highly controversial, and James E. Harvey, one of its prominent reporters, wrote of Taney in high praise and remarked that his loss at this time would be a public calamity. Taney exercised a moral balance of power on the Court, he explained, which served as an effective check on the latitudinarian dogmas of some of his colleagues.[29] In mid-January, 1856, Taney wrote from Washington that he was recovering and might be able to take his seat on the Court the following week.[30] Two weeks later he wrote that he was taking his full share of the business of the Court except that he did not write so many opinions and did not write any that were necessarily of great length.[31] On March

---

mighty for the sin of Know-Nothingism—a sentiment which the Chief Justice might well have shared. The paper, evidently of the Know-Nothing stamp, replied with an attack on the bishop for his condemnation of Protestants as heretics and threatened that the so-called heretics would "take care that the Popish priests who are sent here to regulate not only the concerns of the Roman Church, but the affairs of the country, shall be kept within their proper sphere of action, and that they shall have nothing to do with the regulation of our public schools, or our secular concerns." *Baltimore Clipper*, Sept. 29, 1855.
[26] R. B. Taney to B. R. Curtis,

Nov. 3, 1855, Tyler, *Memoir of Roger Brooke Taney*, 327–28.
[27] *Baltimore Republican*, Dec. 7, 1855.
[28] See Douglas Zevely, "Old Residences and Family History in the City Hall Neighborhood," *Records of the Columbia Historical Society*, 6:104, 112, 1903; Joseph T. Kelly, "Memories of a Lifetime in Washington," *Records of the Columbia Historical Society*, 31:117, 118, 1930.
[29] *New York Tribune*, Dec. 18, 1855.
[30] R. B. Taney to J. Mason Campbell, Jan. 16, 1856, Boston Public Library.
[31] R. B. Taney to D. M. Perine, Jan. 26, 1856, Perine Papers.

2 he expressed relief that the Court's adjournment for a month gave him time to rest and take exercise in the open air. Although he had taken his place on the Court on February 4, and had missed only one day when the weather was bad, he had had to abstain from writing opinions:

> This I was obliged to do, because my eyes are not yet well, and inflame again, if I read or write by candlelight. Indeed I do not know that I could have written an opinion, upon any question of interest, even if my eyes were free from disease. For a day in Court and a night in conference, fatigued me greatly, and I was glad to lie down and rest myself as soon as I reached my own room. Yet with this daily sense of pain and fatigue, my strength has improved, and for the last fortnight of the Court I walked to and from the Capitol every day when the weather permitted. But my mind and heart is not in the business of the Court, and I go into it unwillingly and sluggishly, and force myself to attend to it.[32]

When in April the Court resumed its work—at the time when the reargument of the Dred Scott case was decided upon—the Chief Justice returned to his place and continued until the end of the term. In mid-July he remarked that his health had continued to improve and throughout the spring he enjoyed walking in the public grounds around the Capitol and in the vicinity of the President's house.[33]

For his summer vacation in 1856 Taney went not to Old Point, the place of grim memories, but to Fauquier White Sulphur Springs in Virginia, where he discussed the fate of the country with Franklin Pierce and other men with Southern sympathies. He returned to Washington just after the election of President Buchanan for the beginning term of the Court at which the Dred Scott case was to be decided. His letters reflect preoccupation with tensions of many kinds. It is possible that the death of his wife and daughter and the breaking up of his home deprived him of the emotional reserves necessary to preserve the judicial balance for which he had hitherto received credit and led to the taking of more and more extreme positions.

Money problems pressed in upon him. He had sent to his family physician, Dr. Thomas Buckler, a check for five hundred dollars when the latter refrained from sending a bill. For a long time the doctor left the check uncashed, leading the Chief Justice to believe that it would never be presented. After Taney had moved his account to another

---

[32] R. B. Taney to D. M. Perine, Mar. 2, 1856, Perine Papers.

[33] R. B. Taney to D. M. Perine, July 18, 1856, Perine Papers.

bank, the doctor demanded payment of the amount of his check, creating embarrassment and hurt feelings.[34]

Having sold his house in Baltimore, and concerned about finances not only for himself but also for his two dependent daughters, Taney gave much thought to investments. Because of the conflict between the North and the South public affairs were much unsettled, and he doubted that banks would be able to survive. Riots in Cincinnati and elsewhere caused by the Know-Nothings threatened the stability of municipal governments and the value of their securities. He knew not into what hands municipal powers might fall or to what excesses they might run. He found the greatest promise of stability in the state governments, and among the states he relied a good deal upon the stability of Virginia "and upon her high sense of honor and self respect."[35] He therefore asked his business friend and adviser, David M. Perine of Baltimore, to make a purchase of Virginia bonds to the amount of thirty-five hundred dollars, and authorized additional purchases thereafter.[36] In a few years he was to find his finances tied up in a state with which the United States was at war.

In perennial search for aids to his health, he continued to visit mineral springs and to buy mineral waters with supposed curative powers.[37] He did not like Rockford Baths in Virginia, but he was grateful to the railroad executive who provided a special car to bring him back to Washington, with a mattress on which he could lie when he desired. He ought not to have gone to a watering place so distant, he admitted, and whatever benefit he had received was counteracted by the length and the fatigue of the journey.[38]

Although in view of his advanced age and his periodic illnesses a somewhat ghoulish interest in his health on the part of newspapers and the general public was not surprising, he was provoked by reports which might lead his friends to think that he was at death's door. At the end of April, 1860, when he had returned to his work after an attack of pneumonia, much was made of a fall which he had suffered on the unpolished marble pavement at the entrance to the Capitol as he stepped from a carriage, which led to additional days of absence from Court. "I see by the Baltimore Sun of yesterday that I am again

---

[34] See R. B. Taney to D. M. Perine, Sept. 23, 1856, Perine Papers. See also letters of Oct. 5, 1856, Feb. 1, 3, and 8, 1860, and (copy) R. B. Taney to Dr. Thomas H. Buckler, Perine Papers.

[35] R. B. Taney to D. M. Perine, Dec. 3, 1856, Perine Papers.

[36] See R. B. Taney to D. M. Perine, Dec. 24, 1856, Jan. 9, Jan. 23, Apr. 5, 1857, Apr. 19, 1858, Perine Papers.

[37] See for example R. B. Taney to John Rutherford, July 1, 1859, Rutherford Papers.

[38] R. B. Taney to David M. Perine, Sept. 23, 1859, Perine Papers.

put to death, with a short reprieve," he wrote to Perine, "and I am sure you will be anxious to know something about it. I cannot understand why the Baltimore press should choose to copy such accounts from papers known to be hostile to me, when I have family connections and friends in Baltimore from whom they could readily learn the truth if they desire to publish it. I am fully sensible that in the course of nature, it cannot be long before my last hour may come, but it would seem that there are some political writers of letters, and some newspapers who think that the event has been delayed too long, and mean to kill me at least in public opinion, by the influence of the press."[39]

When in the summer of 1860 United States District Judge A. G. Miller of Wisconsin—of *Booth Cases* fame—visited Washington, he expressed to William Thomas Carroll, Clerk of the Supreme Court, the hope that Taney would resign, particularly if there was a prospect of the election of Abraham Lincoln, in order to permit Buchanan to appoint his successor. Carroll intimated that Taney needed the salary for himself and his dependents. Miller asked whether he would accept a gift from the American bar in lieu of salary if handled in the proper manner. Carroll seemed to indicate approval of the idea but cagily said that it would be better for someone other than himself to broach the subject.[40]

Although shortly after the election it was rumored that the Chief Justice had resigned,[41] the rumor was false, and there is no record that any person had the temerity to recommend to him that he do so. Indeed, for all his physical frailty and apart from his financial need, he kept an active interest in public affairs. He lauded his son-in-law for taking an active part in local politics, saying that the time had come when it was the duty of every man to render what service he could in preserving the institutions of the country. If the upright and intelligent did not put themselves forward and exert their natural influence, the government would fall into the hands of the corrupt or selfishly ambitious, and everything worth preserving would soon be destroyed.[42]

He harshly judged men with whom he disagreed. In the Presidential race his sympathies, like those of most of his pro-Southern Baltimore friends, were with John C. Breckenridge, the candidate of the extreme proslavery wing of the Democratic Party. In reply to a comment on a speech by Edward Everett of Massachusetts, Vice Presidential candidate with John Bell of Tennessee for another splinter party, he said that he had seen the speech but had not read it. He had read

[39] R. B. Taney to David M. Perine, May 9, 1860, Perine Papers.
[40] A. G. Miller to J. S. Black, Sept. 13, 1860, Black Papers.
[41] *New York World*, Nov. 27, 1860.

See the denial in *New York Tribune*, Nov. 29, 1860.
[42] R. B. Taney to J. Mason Campbell, July 11, 1860, Howard Papers.

none of Everett's speeches for some years, never having seen in him anything like genius of heart or courage to maintain the right. He regarded Everett as "a cold heartless rhetorician always getting himself before the public, upon every occasion that may add to his own popularity or consequence in the public esteem."[43]

He was pleased with the outcome of an October election in Baltimore but pessimistic about the national election to occur in November. He despaired particularly because of the divisions among the Southern leaders. The evidence of faltering and division there had utterly destroyed the influence of Breckenridge in the free states, where he might otherwise have expected extensive support. "But how could they be expected to quarrel with their neighbors for southern rights, while the South was everywhere quarreling among themselves, engaged in petty disputes and personal rivalships, at a moment when the knife of the assassin is at their throats?"[44]

As for the outbreak of violence forecast in the event of Lincoln's election, which Taney evidently thought of in terms of an uprising of slaves, he predicted it would not wait for Lincoln's inauguration but would "burst out in the first flush of victory and excitement upon the news of his election." Yet as far as he could see, not the slightest preparation was being made in any state to guard against it. Nothing was heard except talk about a fusion of Bell, Douglas, and Breckenridge, the friends of each seeking to promote this fusion by abusing one another. He himself was old enough to remember the horrors of St. Domingo, and he prayed that a repetition might be averted in the United States. As for secession, the divisions of the Southerners made such a project absurd and impractical.[45]

The election of Lincoln brought not the outbreak of violence among slaves but the beginnings of secession. It also brought new fictitious reports of the resignation of the Chief Justice to enable Buchanan to fill the position. Taney's friend, Judge Ellis Lewis, now retired from

---

[43] *Ibid.*

[44] R. B. Taney to J. Mason Campbell, Oct. 19, 1860, Howard Papers.

[45] *Ibid.* Taney's position here resembles that taken in 1856 when he predicted that the South was doomed to sink to a position of inferiority like that of Ireland in relation to England or Poland in relation to Russia, because Southern people were too divided among themselves to do effective battle for their rights. R. B. Taney to J. Mason Campbell, Oct. 2, 1856, Campbell Papers.

About Taney's attitude toward Lincoln as influenced by Lincoln's criticism of the Dred Scott decision it is possible only to speculate. The following newspaper comment about Lincoln is at least suggestive: "Is this the man, we ask Americans, who defies the highest Court in the Government, and who *hates* an institution which is the life-blood of fifteen States, a fit man to preside over the destinies of the whole people and Government?" *The Express*, quoted in the *Constitution* (Washington, D.C.), Aug. 15, 1860.

the chief justiceship of Pennsylvania, expressed pleasure that Taney was retaining his position: "It is very clear to my mind that your retirement, at this time, would be dangerous, and might furnish grounds for comments which your friends might not desire to hear."[46] Taney replied that the rumor of his resignation had been a pure invention from some unknown source. He agreed that public affairs were full of gloom and believed the country would pass through a season of great suffering and danger: "You are right in supposing that at such a time I should not think of resigning my place on the Bench of the Supreme Court. I am sensible that it would at this moment be highly injurious to the public, and subject me to the suspicion of acting from unworthy motives."[47]

Of the Associate Justices of the Supreme Court as the war period approached, the senior member from the time of the death of Justice Story in 1845 was Justice McLean, who had served since his appointment by President Jackson in 1829. Because of the frequent absences of Chief Justice Taney stemming from ill health, Justice McLean had a great deal of experience as the presiding officer of the Court. McLean worked hard throughout his career, and in spite of probable bias in his favor the *New York Tribune* may well have been accurate with respect to one such period in 1860 when it said that "During the illness of Judge Taney, he dispatched more business than was almost ever known before by the profession."[48] He was similarly efficient on circuit, leading United States District Judge Elisha M. Huntington of Indiana to urge, "Take the world a little easier—don't work so hard—you set us a bad example."[49]

Down to and including 1860 when Lincoln was nominated and elected, McLean continued to be an aspirant for the Presidency. In his later years he showed great bitterness and despondency about political matters. Hoping in 1856 for the first Republican nomination, McLean poured out in confidence his low opinion of the other candidates. He thought Frémont an energetic and enterprising young man who lacked the experience needed for the Presidency and under whose rule the Union would be dissolved. He thought Fillmore selfish and timid, and saw Buchanan also as weak and likely to fall under the influence of the proslavery men of the South. Altogether, he was deeply despondent about the future of the country.[50] Distrusting the extreme

---

[46] Copy, Ellis Lewis to R. B. Taney, Dec. 8, 1860, Lewis Papers.

[47] R. B. Taney to Ellis Lewis, Dec. 24, 1860, Lewis Papers.

[48] *New York Tribune*, Apr. 14, 1860.

[49] E. M. Huntington to John McLean, May 22, 1858, McLean Papers.

[50] See *Diary of Orville Hickman Browning*, Theodore C. Pease and James G. Randall, eds., I, 244–46.

antislavery positions of Horace Greeley and of his Ohio rival, Salmon P. Chase, he characterized them both as dishonest and unsafe.[51] His enmity to Chase continued through the 1860 Republican national convention, when they both went down in defeat.[52]

The beginnings of secession deepened his gloom but left him with the determination to do all he could to preserve the Union. He and Mrs. McLean dined with President Buchanan while the latter was vacillating over the question of what to do about Fort Sumter, and while he was considering removal of Major Robert Anderson, who showed more vigor in maintaining the fort than Buchanan thought expedient. When Justice McLean asked the President about the matter he replied that Anderson had exceeded his instructions and must be recalled. Mrs. McLean recorded in a letter that "The Judge raised his hand with vehemence, almost in the President's face, and asserted with emphasis: 'You dare not do it, sire, you dare not do it.' And he did not."[53]

Shortly after the Lincoln inauguration it was reported that Justice McLean was ill. He died on April 4, 1861, at the age of seventy-six. Cincinnati newspapers said of his funeral that "the obsequies were distinguished by an attendance seldom witnessed upon a similar occasion in and about this city."[54] In the United States Circuit Court for the First Circuit former Justice Curtis, closely linked with Justice McLean in the Dred Scott case, submitted a eulogy and a lament— "Would that there were many such men left us, in this dark hour of our country's peril."[55] In presenting resolutions before the Supreme Court at the opening of the term the following December, Attorney General Edward Bates characterized him as "a ripe scholar; an able lawyer . . . ; a bland and amiable gentleman; a strict moralist; a virtuous man; and, above all, a modest and unobtrusive Christian philosopher."[56] Chief Justice Taney, always restrained and dignified

---

[51] *Ibid.*, 294–95. "In respect to Chase, he is the most unprincipled man, politically, that I have ever known. He is selfish, beyond that of any other man. And I know, from the bargain he has made, in being elected to the Senate, he is ready to make any bargain to promote his interest. He married a niece of my wife's and I know him well. I speak positively, because I know what I say." John McLean to John Teesdale, Sept. 3, 1859, McLean Papers (O.H.S.).

[52] See Earl W. Wiley, "Behind Lincoln's Visit to Ohio in 1859," *Ohio State Archaeological and Historical Quarterly*, 60:28, 1951; Earl W. Wiley, " 'Governor' John Greiner and Chase's Bid for the Presidency in 1860," *Ohio State Archaeological and Historical Quarterly*, 58:245, 1949; "Thomas Corwin and the Republican Reaction, 1858–1861," *Ohio State Archaeological and Historical Quarterly*, 57:1, 1948.

[53] Quoted in Horace White, *The Life of Lyman Trumbull*, 122.

[54] Quoted in *Cincinnati Enquirer*, Apr. 7, 1861.

[55] Filed among miscellaneous manuscripts at the American Antiquarian Society.

[56] Death of Judge McLean, 1 Black 8, 11 (1861).

in the performance of such a duty, stated that McLean's best eulogy was to be found in the reports of the decisions of the Court, and added that words of eulogy were hardly needed in memory of one so widely known and respected.[57]

Justice Wayne, next in line in terms of seniority, was less involved in controversy than the Chief Justice or Justice McLean. Although regarded as a skilled politician on the Supreme Court itself, and suspected of being involved in Georgia politics behind the scenes, he did not while a member of the Court seek political office or speak as a leader on behalf of any political position. On the Court he managed to operate as a nationalist in constitutional law without incurring broad enmity in his native state. He was able to adhere to his broad conception of the federal commerce power while still supporting the power of the slave states to restrict the movement of free Negroes. He took his firm negative stand where the slave trade was involved, as in the instance of his grand jury charge delivered in the light of the landing of a cargo of slaves from the *Wanderer*. He was a handsome man, graceful in social life, and much in society. During the late 1850s Mrs. Wayne was often with him in Washington to share in the social life. The Civil War posed for him a choice between remaining with Georgia in the Confederacy or moving to Washington. He chose Washington. With the death of Justice McLean, Wayne became the senior Associate Justice, with responsibility for presiding over the Court during the frequent absences of the Chief Justice.

Next in seniority was Justice Daniel, ardently agrarian, ardently pro–states' rights, and ardently Virginian. Quite as much as the "proper Bostonians" far to the North, he took pride in old families and family lineage. Justice Catron, by contrast quite plebeian in ancestry, was much amused when visiting Richmond in 1850 at Daniel's knowledge of and pride in the history of Richmond families, and also at evidence of the dilution of those families by nonaristocratic blood. He wrote to James Buchanan of a tour on which Daniel had taken him, displaying the opulent mansions of the aristocracy, some of them well maintained and others subject to neglect and now owned by people who neither rode Medley horses nor had servants in scarlet liverys. In the recounting of pedigrees Catron noticed that it was usually the wife who had claims to high ancestry and that the husband appeared to have formed the alliance with mixed motives—much to Daniel's dis-

---

[57] *Ibid.*, 12.

approval. Out of his own earthy knowledge of livestock, Catron ruminated on the effect on aristocracy of "downward breeding."[58]

When the reallocation of judicial circuits took him away from Virginia for circuit work in faraway Mississippi and Arkansas, Justice Daniel felt like an exile. In 1853, at the age of sixty-nine, having lost by death his first wife who was a daughter of Edmund Randolph, he married a woman in her early thirties to whom two children were born. During the late 1850s the Daniel family, like Chief Justice Taney, made Washington their home and for a time lived in the same row of houses. Daniel, like Taney, suffered a major tragedy—in 1857 he lost his wife, who died when her dress caught fire from a candle.[59] Depressed thereafter and in poor health, though writing vigorous opinions in the Dred Scott case and in a few other cases, Daniel played only a limited part in the work of the Supreme Court. In November, 1859, a Washington dispatch stated that he was so dangerously ill that Chief Justice Taney could not be admitted to see him, and it was thought that he would not recover.[60] He recovered only enough to be moved back to Richmond.[61] He died May 31, 1860,[62] like Justice McLean at the age of seventy-six.

On December 4, 1860, the first day of the ensuing term of the Supreme Court and the first day of its meeting in its new quarters, Attorney General Black submitted resolutions in honor of the deceased member. He stressed the fervor of Justice Daniel's devotion to his native state, his pride in ancestry, his commitment to the constitutional system as he understood it, his memory, his literary capacity, his integrity, and his love of justice. Chief Justice Taney responded, noting the nineteen years of joint service and saying that "some of us have been accustomed for that long period of time to meet him on the bench and at private consultations and conferences among the members of the court; and we all feel that he well deserves to be remembered for the many high and excellent qualities which he constantly displayed both as a man and a judicial officer." Members of the bar who had argued before him could bear witness to his urbanity, and "members of the court who so often met him and heard him when assembled in their private conferences well know the patient and earnest industry with which he investigated and considered every case before he formed his judgment upon it." His opinions showed his learning and careful research

---

[58] John Catron to James Buchanan, Mar. 24, 1850, Buchanan Papers.

[59] *New York Tribune*, Jan. 5, 13, 1857; *Washington National Intelligencer*, Jan. 6, 1857.

[60] *New York Tribune*, Nov. 24, 1859.

[61] *Southern Literary Messenger*, 31: 72, 1860.

[62] *New York Tribune*, June 1, 1860.

and his firmness and independence. "His death has made our first meeting in this new hall a sad and painful one."[63]

Justice Catron, next in seniority, seems to have exercised in the Buchanan Administration his deep-seated penchant for political activities—as illustrated by his correspondence with Buchanan about the Dred Scott case. With the close of that Administration his political entree was to be terminated. He continued to hold Circuit Court throughout Kentucky, Tennessee, and Missouri, although when in 1857 Missouri was divided into an eastern and western district with the designation of an eastern and western district judge, he felt less obligation to attend there. He could hardly be expected to be in St. Louis for the October term, he wrote to Judge Samuel Treat, who was assigned to the eastern district, but would come if the importance of the cases required it. The statute provided that the Circuit Court for Missouri should consist of the assigned Justice of the Supreme Court and the two district judges but might be held by any one or more of them.[64] He remarked that "the *two* Judges there are so little in need of my aid, that I can safely stay away. At the April Term I shall be there of course, if able to come."[65]

Justice Catron continued to be actively interested in the affairs of his own state. Without design he gave his name to an important decision of the Tennessee Supreme Court on the power of a married woman to make contracts and the liability of her husband for their fulfillment. At some time, from a source not explained, Justice Catron had settled a separate estate upon Mrs. Catron. She was a highly independent person. During the winter of 1853, one of the seasons when she did not go to Washington for the term of the Supreme Court, from the Catron home in Nashville she bought with funds from her estate a lot in the village of Tullahoma and made contracts for the construction of a summer home, which was built and which she and her husband occupied in succeeding summers. Mrs. Catron made her plans without her husband's knowledge, and although he later had additional rooms added with his own funds, she was exclusively responsible for the original contracts. Apparently some of the charges were excessive and she refused to pay the bills. Justice Catron himself carried on informal negotiations about the bills, saying that they ought to have been settled long ago, but the contractors refused to reduce their claims and he refused to pay.

The contractors brought suit against Justice Catron in the Circuit

---

[63] Proceedings in Relation to the Death of the Late Justice Daniel, 24 How. iii–vi (1860).

[64] 11 Stat. 197–98.

[65] J. Catron to Samuel Treat, May 9, 1858, Treat Papers.

Court for Davidson County and won a verdict from the jury. He appealed to the Tennessee Supreme Court, which reversed the decision. In a case much discussed thereafter both because of its holding and because it involved the Catrons, the court held that in general, and in this case, a married woman had no power to enter into a contract so as to incur any legal liability, and that her husband was not responsible for any contract she might have made independently of him unless by a positive act of his own he assumed the debt.[66] The record does not show whether the Catrons eventually liquidated the debt at some compromise figure.

More important than his involvement in private litigation was Justice Catron's concern about the race problems that were dividing the country. His public letter criticizing the bill in the legislature which proposed to enslave free black people in Tennessee gained widespread attention,[67] and presumably made enemies among the more extreme proslavery people. Like Justice Wayne, he would soon have to make a choice between the state of his residence and the nation he was serving.

About Justice Nelson, next in seniority, little is to be said beyond reference to the part which he played early in 1861 along with Justice Campbell in attempting to mediate between the North and the South, a matter which is discussed subsequently. It has already been noted that he played little part in the statement of broad principles of constitutional law and that his major contribution to the work of the Supreme Court was in matters of common law and admiralty. By contrast with most of his brethren, few of his letters are to be found in the papers of the statesmen of his time, and of these not many are particularly revealing. Although he was in some degree a "northern man with southern principles," he was in no sense a crusader for the Southern cause like President Buchanan. He was primarily a technical performer in the law.

Of Justice Grier it was said in 1849 that he represented "with more power than polish the talent and learning of Pennsylvania in the great Federal Court at Washington."[68] Both his vigor and his roughness showed themselves to fullest effect in cases involving the return of fugitive slaves, though his colorful personality expressed itself in other connections as well. He was something of a sportsman and was particularly interested in fishing, going off each summer with Benjamin Patton, the former Pittsburgh judge who had played a prominent part in his appointment to the Supreme Court and whom he appointed in 1858

---

[66] Catron v. Warren, 41 Tenn. (1 Coldwell) 358 (1860).

[67] For an approving comment about the letter see the *Washington National Intelligencer*, Jan. 21, 1860.

[68] *Am. L.J.*, 8:335, 1849.

clerk of the Circuit Court in Philadelphia.[69] Although he was interested in politics his interest seems to have been primarily in local people. The fact that as late as 1858 he could not be sure of the first name of Salmon P. Chase,[70] a former United States Senator who was then governor of Ohio, an ardent abolitionist who had appeared before the Supreme Court in important slavery cases, and who in six years would replace Chief Justice Taney, indicates that he was not widely familiar with the group of men who, as Republicans, would soon take over the leadership of the nation. He continued loyal to Buchanan throughout his Administration and congratulated Attorney General Black on his demolition of the popular sovereignty argument of Stephen A. Douglas.[71]

Justice Campbell found the deepening conflict putting him in an even more difficult position than that of Justices Wayne and Catron. He was substantially younger, with more opportunities for choice of vocation and service. He had never been as fully committed to American nationalism as had the two Jackson appointees. He had tried hard to enforce laws against the slave trade and against filibustering, and he was to attempt to negotiate to save the Union at the last moment, but his conduct on and off the Bench reflected the permeation of states' rights doctrines and probably an acceptance of secession as constitutional. A rumor had been spread that in the struggle for the nomination of a Presidential candidate at the Democratic national convention, to be held in Charleston in 1860, he might be settled upon as a compromise candidate.[72] He sharply disapproved of the action of the extreme proslavery wing of the party when it seceded from the convention after failing to secure adoption of a platform plank rejecting the doctrine of territorial sovereignty, evidently believing that all members should have remained and made their settlement in terms of a compromise candidate. To Lucius Q. C. Lamar, one of the seceders, he wrote that if he had the powers of a Turkish cadi he would condemn some of the Southern actors to wear veils for four years. Their faces should not be seen among Democrats. He was not sure that he would not prescribe bastinadoes as well, in which case Lamar and some of his friends would have sore feet for a long time.[73] With the election of Lincoln and

---

[69] J. W. F. White, "The Judiciary of Allegheny County," *Pennsylvania Magazine of History and Biography*, 7:143, 168, 1883. Newspapers had said that Justice Grier had removed George Plitt from the clerkship in order to give it to an unnamed son-in-law. *New York Tribune*, Nov. 12, 1857, Jan. 30, 1858. The appointment went to his friend Patton.

[70] See R. C. Grier to James M. Bell, Sept 7, 13, 1858, Bell Papers.
[71] R. C. Grier to J. S. Black, Sept. 15, 1859, Black Papers.
[72] *New York Tribune*, Jan. 26, 1860.
[73] Edward Mayes, *Lucius Q. C. Lamar: His Life, Times, and Speeches*, 84.

the secession of the states composing his circuit, Justice Campbell was faced with a decision about his judicial position. This he postponed to ascertain whether mediation between the seceding states and the Union would be possible.

Justice Clifford, the newest member of the Court and an appointee of President Buchanan in 1858, continued to express full orthodoxy in terms of Buchanan's views and to take an active part in Democratic politics in behalf of the Administration. As he put it, "my views are fully expressed in the opinion of the Supreme Court in the case of Dred Scott, and I most fully approve the principles of your administration."[74] With the approach of the Civil War it was clear that this latest appointment of a Northern Democrat would do nothing toward promoting adjustment to the new order.

In 1860 and early 1861 there was widespread speculation over the vacancy created by the death of Justice Daniel and the sucessor to Chief Justice Taney if he resigned. Republicans and abolitionists were eager to gain representation on the Court. Charles O'Conor and Benjamin F. Butler were mentioned, but with little hope as far as a Buchanan appointment was concerned. The *New York Tribune* thought a more probable selection was Reverdy Johnson of Maryland, whose volunteered argument had been the source of the Dred Scott decision.[75] Johnson was a Whig, however, and though an admirer and personal friend of Chief Justice Taney was no admirer of Buchanan, and his appointment was therefore improbable.

At the death of Justice Daniel, in the summer of 1860, leading Virginians rushed to propose candidates from their own state, even though Justice Daniel's circuit had not for many years included Virginia but only Mississippi and Arkansas. Francis Minor wrote from Charlottesville that "The appointment of a successor to Judge Daniel is of very little less importance to the South than the election of the next president. One is for life, the other for but four years." He was concerned about a rumor that Buchanan favored James Lyons. He and his friends believed that the man for the place was William J. Robertson of the Virginia Court of Appeals, a man of firmness and fidelity and great learning.[76] John Randolph Tucker of Richmond reported that Senator James M. Mason preferred Judge Lee, presumably George H.

[74] Nathan Clifford to James Buchanan, July 19, 1859, Buchanan Papers.

[75] *New York Tribune*, Feb. 16, 1860. For a variety of speculation see Charles Warren, *The Supreme Court in United States History*, II, 358–67.

[76] Franklin Minor to R. M. T. Hunter, June 5, 1860, *Annual Report of the American Historical Association for the Year 1916*, II, 332–33.

Lee of the same court. Judge Lee, said Tucker, was a good lawyer and a clear-headed judge with studious habits. He would hate to lose for Virginia the services of either of these men.[77]

States farther south also had candidates. Alabama talked of William L. Yancey, firebrand secessionist leader. Mississippi, which was in the vacated circuit, proposed a number of names. One was Alexander H. Handy, then on the state's high court of errors and appeals. Another was A. M. Clayton, who had served on that court for nine years, ending in 1851 in a political readjustment. He was praised by Judge James F. Trotter in the statement that "for thorough and profound learning as a lawyer, coupled with a rare capacity for close research and close, clear and analytical reasoning he has no superior in this country."[78]

Another Mississippian was Samuel S. Boyd, who, having been a classmate of Franklin Pierce at Bowdoin College, was praised to Pierce as worthy of "a seat in that great tribunal where a Marshall has presided and which a Taney still adorns."[79] Boyd wrote to Pierce that he wanted the position "mainly and before all other considerations, that I may share with other devoted friends of the Constitutional Union, in all the responsibility of indicating the great principles so dear to the State Rights Democracy, without which the Constitution becomes a bond of subjection and a badge of inferiority, inequality and disgrace."[80] If Pierce interceded for his classmate, however, his intercession was without avail.

Another name prominently mentioned was that of Caleb Cushing of Massachusetts,[81] who had been Pierce's Attorney General and who, through the power of his mind and diligence and determination, had made more of the attorney generalship than had any of his predecessors.[82] Like his friend Pierce, Cushing was proslavery and pro-Southern in his leanings, but he had the fine art of making enemies rather than friends[83] even while he won admiration for his professional capacity, and the nomination was never made.[84]

---

[77] John Randolph Tucker to R. M. T. Hunter, June 12, 1860, *ibid.*, 335.

[78] James F. Trotter to Joseph Holt, Nov. 13, 1860, Miscellaneous File, Duke University.

[79] S. Malin Davis to Franklin Pierce, Aug. 8, 1860, Pierce Papers.

[80] Samuel S. Boyd to Franklin Pierce, Aug. 18, 1860, Pierce Papers.

[81] *New York Tribune*, June 15, 28, July 2, 1860; *New York World*, Dec. 17, 1860; *New York Evening Post*, Dec. 20, 1860; *New York Herald*, Feb. 6, 1861.

[82] See Homer Cummings and Carl McFarland, *Federal Justice*, 142–60.

[83] Claude M. Fuess, *The Life of Caleb Cushing*, 122–23; Sister M. Michael Catherine Hodgson, *Caleb Cushing: Attorney General of the United States*, 220–21.

[84] Immediately after Justice Daniel's death, Cushing wrote to Attorney General Black that his name had been submitted for the vacancy without his knowledge, and that he wished to speak to Black on behalf of another person. Caleb Cushing to J. S. Black, June 5, 1860, Black Papers.

XXIX: *The Court on the Eve of the War*

From the time of Justice Daniel's death until the end of the Buchanan Administration the man most discussed for a Supreme Court appointment was Attorney General Black. Among those who wrote to Buchanan in Black's behalf, a friend from Iowa quoted United States District Judge James M. Love, then of Iowa but formerly a Virginian, as saying that even Maryland and Virginia would support the appointment of an additional Pennsylvanian to the Supreme Court. There was no Virginian now competent to fill the position, and Reverdy Johnson, the only man competent in Maryland, was in the wrong party.[85] The *New York Tribune* remarked that Black's friends were exerting every influence to secure his appointment in spite of his nonresidence in the circuit involved,[86] a factor which might prove an obstacle similar to that which had confronted George E. Badger during the Fillmore Administration.[87] William B. Reed, a prominent lawyer and one of Black's friends in Philadelphia, warned that if Black was to be nominated the step should be taken early, lest he suffer the fate of J. M. Read when the Senate failed to confirm his nomination by President Tyler: "The Senate may be very insecure next fall. I want you to be Judge for your own sake and the public's."[88]

Whether because of his general indecisiveness or because of his need for Black in his Cabinet, Buchanan permitted the Senate to adjourn in the summer of 1860 without submitting a nomination. In November occurred the election of Lincoln, followed immediately by the beginnings of secession. In reply to a question from Buchanan as to what he could do to enforce the laws in the seceding states, Black submitted an official opinion that although the President had no power to recognize the independence of a seceding state, he likewise had no power to make war to punish the people of a state for the misdeeds of their state governments or to prevent the violation of the Constitution or to enforce the supreme authority of the United States.[89] This position became the official position of the Buchanan Administration.

Judge George W. Woodward of Pennsylvania, who wanted Black to become Chief Justice partly because he himself wanted to be the Reporter of the Court,[90] and who accepted as true the most recent rumor that Taney had resigned, assured Black that Buchanan had taken exactly the right position. "Though I would have him dissuade from secession as long as moral suasion can avail, but if it can't avail, coercion

---

[85] Richard McAllister to J. S. Black, June 2, 1860, Black Papers.
[86] *New York Tribune*, June 15, 1860.
[87] *New York Tribune*, June 18, 1860.

[88] William B. Reed to J. S. Black, June 25, 1860, Black Papers.
[89] 9 Op. Att'y Gen. 516 (1860).
[90] G. W. Woodward to J. S. Black, Nov. 28, 1860, Black Papers.

735

is not to be thought of as a preventive."[91] Black read Woodward's letter to Buchanan and other like-minded persons and pronounced it "admirable."[92]

In mid-December the secessionist proclivities of some members of his Cabinet had become pronounced. Perhaps partly for that reason and partly for other reasons Buchanan had to undertake a wholesale reorganization. Black was deemed so valuable to the Administration that he was shifted to the position of Secretary of State, and although the Supreme Court was now in session no attempt was made to fill the vacancy. As more and more states prepared to secede, Democratic Senators friendly to the Buchanan Administration said their farewells and departed, reducing the number of votes to be counted on for confirmation of a Buchanan appointee. Early in February it was reported that Republican Senators were being canvassed to find out whether they would cast votes to confirm Black, and that little such support could be found.[93]

The nomination was officially submitted on February 5, by which time twelve Southern Senators had taken their leave. Among the remaining Democrats little enthusiasm was shown on the part of the Douglas group, who resented Black's attack on Douglas and his theory of popular sovereignty. The Republican press poured out scathing attacks on the nominee, with the *New York Tribune* taking the lead.[94] On February 21, at a turbulent executive session, the Senate voted against taking up the nomination, thus rejecting it without directly acting upon it.[95] Buchanan then considered a last-minute appointment of either John M. Reed of Philadelphia, or Joseph Holt of Kentucky, who was currently Secretary of War, but apparently realized the futility of such a step and refrained from taking it.[96]

On February 25 occurred a seemingly routine event with a portent for the future of the Supreme Court. Abraham Lincoln, whom Black had characterized a month earlier in private correspondence as "very small potatoes and few in a hill," who made "loose stump speeches consisting mainly in making comical faces and telling smutty anecdotes,"[97] came with William H. Seward to pay his respects to the Justices in their consultation room, and then visited each of the two

[91] G. W. Woodward to J. S. Black, Nov. 18, 1860, Black Papers.

[92] Draft, J. S. Black to G. W. Woodward, Nov. 24, 1860, Black Papers.

[93] *New York Tribune*, Feb. 4, 1861.

[94] *New York Tribune*, Feb. 7, 1861; *New York Herald*, Feb. 6, 7, 1861.

[95] William N. Brigance, *Jeremiah Sullivan Black*, 114–16.

[96] Warren, *The Supreme Court in United States History*, II, 364–65.

[97] J. C. Black to Charles R. Buckalew, Jan. 28, 1861, Black Papers.

houses of Congress.[98] There was a suggestion that when further appointments were made to the Supreme Court they would bring a fresh outlook to that tribunal.

Both individually and collectively, the members of the Court at the December term of 1860 were kept aware of disturbing national events. Concluding an argument before the Court on December 13, Reverdy Johnson predicted solemnly that "This may be the last time that the Court will sit in a peaceful judgment on a Constitution acknowledged and obeyed by all." He followed with a lament over all that might be lost and asked that Heaven might forbid the threatened disaster.[99] Later in the month George W. Paschal, concluding his argument in a case which he had brought up from Texas, predicted that before the mandate of the Supreme Court could go down in the case Texans would have decreed that the Court no longer had the jurisdiction to enforce the Constitution and laws under which the case was tried.[100]

The situation was particularly disturbing to the members of the Court who came from states that were preparing to secede or were likely to do so—Justices Wayne, Catron, and Campbell, and of these particularly the last, who was the youngest and the least committed to a nationalist position. Campbell was by no means a secessionist at the beginning of the secession movement, and he was among the last to admit that nothing could be done to prevent it. On December 19 he wrote to Franklin Pierce that he had urged Buchanan to send commissioners to a convention of the states to see whether sectional differences might be resolved. There was a wild and somewhat hysterical excitement in all the Southern states, he said, and particularly in the tier of states from South Carolina west. This excitement had greatly increased with Lincoln's election, even though the result had been anticipated. It had "produced all the effect of a sudden and direct attack upon the rights of the people." He believed that a final settlement of the slavery question must be made or that disunion would follow. "I think that a constitutional settlement, at all events, is better—far better—than a sudden and violent disruption."[101]

Ten days later Campbell wrote to Pierce again to say that he did not believe the President had given any further thought to sending commissioners to the forthcoming convention in Alabama. "In truth, his mind has lost its power of comprehending a complicated situation.

---

[98] *New York World, New York Tribune, New York Herald*, Feb. 26, 1861.

[99] *New York Evening Post*, Dec. 17, 1860; *Washington National Intelligen-* cer, Dec. 15, 1861.

[100] *Washington National Intelligen-* cer, Dec. 29, 1860.

[101] J. A. Campbell to Franklin Pierce, Dec. 19, 1860, Pierce Papers.

He is nervous and hysterical and I think completely unmanned." Some of his advisers seemed disposed to add to that confusion.[102]

Unable to get action through direct communication with the President, Campbell next tried to operate through Black, now Secretary of State. He went to see Black and then followed his oral recommendations with a letter. The President, he said, was the only person who could speak with the certainty of having an audience in all sections of the Union. Because of his position, every word said by him had vast importance. It was because he had not hitherto spoken to meet the demands of the public mind that there was so much anarchy in public opinion. He proposed that the President make a forthright statement of the issues on which there were major differences between the North and the South, and recommend constitutional amendments to resolve them. The President should take into account the many past legislative declarations on these critical topics, and also proposals for compromise being made by William H. Seward, John J. Crittenden, and Stephen A. Douglas. Of the proposals being made to guarantee the security of Southern institutions, the Crittenden Compromise would be most acceptable to the South. The Fugitive Slave Act would require amendment, and perhaps some indemnity would be required for past inefficiency of enforcement: "I would place all the amendments to the Constitution beyond the reach of future amendment, except at the instance of the State directly concerned." He would feel he had done his duty if he could obtain from the executive department a full, clear, and statesmanlike presentation of the whole matter.[103]

Justice Campbell had been writing long letters to political leaders in Alabama attempting to persuade them that the election of Lincoln was not a sufficient ground for secession, that Seward's reference to an "irrepressible conflict" was not to be taken as the inflammatory remark it was believed to be in the South, and that the Southern states should await further attempts at the compromise of differences. Perhaps in order to maximize his influence in Alabama by showing his basic loyalty to the state, he remarked that he had retained his position thus far rather in deference to others and upon public considerations than from any personal desire to hold it. Although his commission would not be affected by the action of his state, he had long since determined that in the event of secession it would be his obligation to follow the fortunes of the people of Alabama: "I shall terminate my connection with the Government, as a consequence of her acts."[104]

---

[102] J. A. Campbell to Franklin Pierce, Dec. 29, 1860, Pierce Papers.
[103] J. A. Campbell to J. S. Black, Jan. 4, 1861, Black Papers.

[104] John A. Campbell to Daniel Chandler, Nov. 26, 1860, originally published in the *Mobile Daily Mercury,* May 17, 1861. Reprinted,

In spite of his efforts, on January 11, 1861, Alabama adopted an ordinance of secession. In terms of his announced purpose, Campbell was expected to resign. The Buchanan Administration gave him no grounds for remaining in office by taking his advice and seeking an overall settlement of differences between the North and the South, and it appeared Justice Campbell might therefore have been expected to resign immediately. Yet whether from a belief that a compromise might yet be reached, or from a hope that he might be able to help preserve peace between the Union and the new Confederacy, for a time he retained his office. On January 23 he sent an inquiry to Secretary of State Black as a spokesman for the Administration, himself acting on behalf of businessmen in his own state. He reported that in Mobile the collector of the port and his staff of officers and the United States District Judge and the United States Attorney had resigned and that the authority of the United States had been superseded, or at all events was not represented. How would all this affect the daily business of dispatching ships? He wished all the information he could properly obtain in order to be able to give authoritative answers to interested parties.[105]

Black replied that the United States government could not officially recognize clearances of ships made by state officers as fulfilling financial and other obligations to the United States. But he would give it as his private opinion that the United States had no right to punish a person for doing what the local authorities in command of the custom house compelled him to do.[106] Campbell presumably sent this information to the inquiring parties.

For a time it was not known whether the real leader of the incoming Republican Administration would be the rail-splitter from Illinois or Senator William H. Seward of New York, whom many regarded as the head of the party. Justice Campbell seems to have been among those who made that mistake. At a dinner given in February for the French foreign minister he was much impressed by a toast given by Seward: "Away with all parties, all platforms, all previous committals, and whatever else will stand in the way of restoration of the American Union." After the dinner John J. Crittenden called Seward into a conversation at which Campbell was saying that slavery ought not to cause the dissolution of the Union, since it had been receding with increasing rapidity since the adoption of the Constitution, and for all the furor over slavery in the territories it was not actually being

George W. Duncan, "John Archibald Campbell," *Transactions of the Alabama Historical Society*, 5:147–51, 1905.

[105] J. A. Campbell to J. S. Black, Jan. 23, 1861, Black Papers.

[106] Draft, J. S. Black to J. A. Campbell, Jan. 1861, filed in Vol. 35 of the Black Papers, between folios 56132 and 56133.

established there. Justice Campbell implied agreement among a number of leaders, but Seward, telling of a telegram that indicated Salmon P. Chase was to be Secretary of the Treasury and saying his own position in the new Cabinet was not yet assured, asked rhetorically, "What can I do?"[107]

In February Texas joined the ranks of the seceding states, making a total of seven. Many of the states lying north of the seceding tier were torn with differences about their policies. On February 4 a so-called Peace Conference, called by a resolution of the Virginia legislature and consisting of representatives of Northern and middle states, met in Washington to try to work out a compromise for saving the Union.[108] The conference labored until February 27 under the presidency of John Tyler, but achieved no major result. It divided ten to nine on its major proposal,[109] and achieved neither for itself nor for its recommendation enough prestige to make it important. An ironic item in the proceedings of the conference was the quotation—evidently much to the exasperation of Reverdy Johnson—from a speech of Roger B. Taney before a local court in 1819 in which he had characterized slavery as a blot on the national character and said that every real lover of freedom looked to its eventual gradual obliteration: "And until it shall be accomplished, until the time shall come when we can point, without a blush, to the language of the Declaration of Independence, every part of humanity will seek to lighten the galling chain of slavery, and better, to the utmost of his power, the wretched condition of the slave."[110]

The futile conference came to an end, and five days later, on March 4, 1861, came the inauguration of the new President. According to custom the Vice President was sworn in first, in the Senate chamber—the first time the new chamber was so used. Present along with other dignitaries were the members of the Supreme Court, led by Chief Justice Taney. Then the procession moved to the platform in front of the Capitol, where the principal dignitaries sat beneath a canopy in red plush armchairs from the Senate chamber.[111] There, in the presence

---

[107] Henry G. Connor, *John Archibald Campbell*, 116–18.

[108] See L. E. Chittenden, *A Report of the Debates and Proceedings in the Secret Sessions of the Conference Convention for Proposing Amendments to the Constitution of the United States.*

[109] Robert R. Howison, "History of the War," *Southern Literary Messenger*, 34–36:337–44, 1862.

[110] Chittenden, *A Report of the Debates and Proceedings . . . for Proposing Amendments to the Constitution*, 236. For the full account of the incident see David Martin, *Trial of the Rev. Jacob Gruber, Minister in the Methodist Episcopal Church, at the March Term, 1819, in the Frederick County Court, for a Misdemeanor.*

[111] *New York World*, Mar. 5, 1861.

of his weary and troubled predecessor, the tall, homely man from Illinois arose to make his appeal for the preservation of the Union. He made it clear that he was not committed to the destruction of slavery but only to the upholding of the Constitution. The only true sovereign was a majority of the people, held in check by constitutional limitations. He admitted that constitutional questions were to be decided by the Supreme Court and that each decision was binding upon the parties. It was also entitled to high respect in all parallel cases and by all departments of the government. But, he continued:

> At the same time, the candid citizen must confess that if the policy of the Government upon vital questions affecting the whole people is to be irrevocably fixed by the decisions of the Supreme Court, the instant they are made in ordinary litigation between parties in personal actions the people will have ceased to be their own rulers, having to that extent practically resigned their Government into the hands of that eminent tribunal. Nor is there in this view any assault upon the court or the judges. It is a duty from which they may not shrink to decide cases properly brought before them, and it is no fault of theirs if others seek to turn their decisions to political purposes.[112]

After Lincoln's closing appeal for unity—"We are not enemies but friends. We must not be enemies"—Chief Justice Taney stepped forward and administered the oath of office, a task which he had first performed at the inauguration of Martin Van Buren in 1837. Thereafter, it was said, "Chief Justice Taney took the hand of Mr. Lincoln, and shaking it warmly expressed his pleasure at the effort."[113] Yet it was also said that "The Chief Justice seemed very much agitated, and his hand shook very perceptibly with emotion."[114]

While men of moderate sentiments regarded the address as conciliatory, the Southern extremists called it "a declaration of war, and it is said that Judge Campbell of the Supreme Court holds to that opinion, and, moreover, declares his intention to resign his position upon the bench."[115] The *Baltimore Sun* selected the passage about the Supreme Court for particular denunciation. "It is a deliberate attempt to put number above right—to put opinion above law—to subordinate the Supreme Court to the policy of the government in its exaction of assumed and illegitimate powers to the same extent that the court is subordinated to the policy of the government when it exercises legitimate and constitutional powers." With such a creed, concluded the *Sun*,

---

[112] J. D. Richardson, *A Compilation of the Messages and Papers of the Presidents*, VI, 9–10.

[113] *New York Herald*, Mar. 6, 1861.

[114] *Baltimore Daily Exchange*, Mar. 5, 1861. See also *New York Herald*, Mar. 5, 1861.

[115] *New York Evening Post*, Mar. 5, 1861.

secession was not the essence of anarchy, as Lincoln claimed, but the only measure of escaping from the despotism of the majority.[116]

The Supreme Court completed the work of the term on March 14. Although Georgia was among the seceding states, and of his circuit only North Carolina still recognized the jurisdiction of the federal government, Justice Wayne showed no disposition to resign from the Court. In spite of repeated rumors no resignation from Justice Campbell was forthcoming, and he lingered on in Washington instead of taking his immediate departure. Records later showed that he and Justice Nelson, with whom he was much in consultation about the powers of the federal government with respect to the seceding states, were acting as intermediaries between three emissaries sent to Washington by the Confederate government and the Lincoln Administration, with Seward as Secretary of State taking a leading part in the negotiations.

According to Justice Campbell's account, Justice Nelson had been for some time engaged in a study of the constitutional powers of the executive, and, discussing the matter with Chief Justice Taney, had reached the conclusion that coercion could not be used against the seceding states—the position hitherto taken by Buchanan and Black. He seems to have linked his constitutional theory to expediency, arguing that a policy of moderation and peace would inevitably lead to the restoration of the Union. On April 15 Justice Nelson visited three members of Lincoln's Cabinet, Seward, Chase, and Bates, to state his convictions.[117] On Pennsylvania Avenue he met Justice Campbell, and the two of them began a discussion which was continued at length in Justice Nelson's hotel room. Eventually the two Justices returned to Seward's office to urge upon him the belief that the three commissioners of the Confederate government, Martin J. Crawford, A. B. Roman, and John Forsyth, ought to be received informally without, of course, a recognition of the legitimacy of the Confederate government.

A compromise arrangement was worked out whereby Justice Campbell himself would see the commissioners and talk with them only about the matter of Fort Sumter, off the coast of South Carolina, which was still held by the federal government but was in need of reinforcement. Summaries of the story of these negotiations have been presented many times, utilizing primarily Justice Campbell's own account.[118] Campbell believed that he had from Seward ample assurances that Sumter would be evacuated. Yet the evacuation did not take place, and

---

[116] *Baltimore Sun*, Mar. 9, 1861.
[117] Samuel W. Crawford, *The Genesis of the Civil War*, 325–27.

[118] Connor, *John Archibald Campbell*, 122–48; Crawford, *The Genesis of the Civil War*, 324–45.

he was left in an embarrassing position with the commissioners, and with Southern leaders to whom they were reporting. Inquiries as to why the assurances given were not supported by action brought no replies.

Justice Nelson had been posted on happenings until his departure from Washington on March 23. On April 15 Campbell wrote to Nelson bringing him up to date and asking him for the sake of history to record the events they knew in common, including the interview of March 15 with Seward and the fact that the papers which Campbell delivered to the commissioners had been submitted in advance to Nelson. He did not wish to expose Seward, he said, "because I think he meant well but has succumbed to the superior energies of old Frank Blair who is understood to preside over the 'Cabinet improper.' We were not far wrong in saying that he was the most dangerous man, to the real welfare of the country in it." But he condemned Seward's pusillanimous conduct in exciting hopes and feeding expectations that could not be realized when the Cabinet to which he belonged was engaged in their frustration.[119]

On the day Campbell was writing, President Lincoln called for seventy-five thousand militia to enforce obedience to federal laws.[120] "I trust there will be expressions from the North to stop the madness of this administration," Campbell wrote further to Nelson. "How every day has increased the dangers of the country since they have come in."

Justice Campbell failed for some time to realize that it was not Seward, nor Frank Blair, nor the Cabinet, but rather President Lincoln who was giving direction to the Administration. Lincoln tried at first by reassurance to call the Southern states back to their allegiance. Then he began the building up of military forces to preserve the Union, keeping in mind always the need to retain as many of the border states as possible. Virginia and North Carolina left the Union as the lines of control drew tighter. During the period of Campbell's imprisonment after the close of the war and after the assassination of Lincoln, he wrote in his diary that the counsel he had given Lincoln, and which Lincoln was ready to adopt, would have composed the country. That counsel, he indicated, involved calling together the leading men of the country to work out a peace program, which would have included adequate provision for betterment of the position of the black race.[121] It is hard to tell whether he had in mind a program similar to that which

---

[119] J. A. Campbell to Samuel Nelson, Apr. 15, 1861, N.Y. State Historical Association.
[120] Richardson, *A Compilation of* the *Messages and Papers of the Presidents*, VI, 13.
[121] John A. Campbell, Manuscript Diary, item for June 20, 1865, No. 43, Groner Papers.

he had proposed to Black for submission to Buchanan, or whether, indeed, he may inadvertently have substituted in his postwar diary the name of the deceased President for that of his predecessor.

On April 18, in a letter to Justice Clifford, Campbell traced the course of negotiations as they involved Nelson and himself, and predicted that "the great excitement that rages at the North will soon subside and then sober counsels will resume their sway."[122] But after the clash of arms at Fort Sumter President Lincoln, on April 19, 1861, proclaimed the blockade of Southern ports, beginning the program of coercion which Justice Campbell had believed inexpedient and unconstitutional. Although in some degree discredited among his Confederate friends because of his lingering in the North and also because of his failure in the negotiations, Campbell on April 25 sent the President a one-sentence letter of resignation as Associate Justice of the Supreme Court.[123] Four days later he sent a farewell letter to Chief Justice Taney, saying:

> I shall never forget the uprightness, fidelity, learning, thought and labor, that have been brought by you to the consideration of the judgments of the court, or the urbanity, gentleness, kindness and tolerance that have distinguished your intercourse with the members of the court and bar. From your hands I have received all that I could have desired and in leaving the court, I carry with me feelings of mingled reverence, affection and gratitude.[124]

To Justice Clifford, who had evidently urged Campbell not to leave the Court, Campbell replied that he regretted to differ with him, adding that his deference to the wishes of others had almost consigned him to disgrace among his own people. The Administration seemed to him determined to have a sectional war. The extremists in the North were countered by an equally desperate party in the South: "Oh for peace, peace."[125] Soon afterward, leaving his household possessions in Washington where they became the object of haggling between United States Marshals and the military, he departed for the South, where he served in undistinguished fashion in the office of Assistant Secretary of War in the Confederate government.

So it was that on the eve of the war the Supreme Court found itself with only seven members, some of whom were hostile to the

---

[122] J. A. Campbell to Nathan Clifford, Apr. 18, 1861, Clifford Papers.
[123] J. A. Campbell to the President, Apr. 25, 1861, Attorney General's Papers.

[124] "J. A. Campbell to R. B. Taney, Apr. 29, 1861," *Maryland Historical Magazine*, 5:35, 1910.
[125] J. A. Campbell to Nathan Clifford, Apr. 29, 1861, Clifford Papers.

Administration and to the war program. One of these, Justice Wayne, was completely deprived of his circuit by the secession of the states which composed it. Part of the circuit of Justice Catron was lost for a considerable period. Chief Justice Taney's circuit was the scene of intense border strife. The outlook for effective action on the part of the Supreme Court during the years immediately ahead was grim indeed.

CHAPTER XXX

Property in Land

WHILE THE NATION WAS ENGAGED in the Civil War, and Congress and the executive were giving most of their attention to the war, the Supreme Court, though it decided some war cases, was giving much of its time to controversies over land titles in faraway California. Those controversies, it is true, were in some degree related to the war. They dealt with titles not only to potentially valuable agricultural and residential areas but also to fantastic richness in minerals useful in connection with war financing, and the quasi-loyalty to the Union of some powerful men on the West Coast seems to have been conditioned in part by what the government did with respect to their claims to mineral lands. The federal judicial system was affected in that the need for courts adequate to deal with land claims produced an experiment with an independent circuit judge for this region, a device that might be used throughout the country, and resulted also for a brief period in provision for a tenth Justice of the Supreme Court, to operate in connection with a Far Western circuit.

The story of California land litigation, in turn, relates back to earlier litigation with respect to the scope and validity of English land grants made in the colonies, concerning which most of the governing rules were worked out during the Marshall period, and litigation concerning tracts in the huge Louisiana Purchase and in Florida (acquired in 1803 and 1819, respectively) which gave rise to voluminous litigation during the Taney period. Some of the cases dealt with issues so technical as to be incomprehensible to all except specialists in land law,[1]

---

[1] While to the law student making his first investigations into the law of real property the intricacies may have seemed appalling, Justice Grier remarked in 1852 that "The very arti-ficial and complicate[d] system of conveyancing in England, has never been adopted and is little known in the United States." R. C. Grier to T. and J. W. Johnson, Feb. 21, 1852,

746

some nevertheless attracted wide attention because of the immense wealth at stake, and some, as in the instance of the famous "Gaines Case," evoked so much drama and so much scandal as to become the subject of nationwide interest and partisanship. The importance of the story of land litigation is highlighted by the fact that down to the war period, for all the growth of industry and steady accumulation of capital in other forms, land was the principal form and source of wealth in the country—providing, indeed, even the basic materials for speculation, by contrast with the stock market and other areas of investment in later decades. The American people were still committed to a belief in the sanctity of private property, and they thought of property largely in terms of real estate and its appurtenances. Nothing was more important for good government and a prosperous country than the clarification and protection of titles to land.

Despite the fact that many of the hard-fought land cases belong exclusively to the period in which they were decided and are never cited as precedents in modern litigation, it is of interest that controversies over land titles in the Louisiana Purchase gave rise to some fifty major cases in the Supreme Court, affecting titles to immense tracts. One case had to do with claims to more than five million acres and another to more than half a million, and other areas in dispute were of only lesser dimensions.[2] The largest of these claims was defeated on the ground that a certificate of survey was forged.[3] Other cases turned on the question of whether grantees had fulfilled conditions of the grants, such as colonization or development within a specified time.[4] From Florida the Supreme Court also decided some fifty cases, affecting claims to some fifteen million acres. Of this amount twelve million acres were included in one claim or aggregation of claims, covering

---

Carson Collection. The comment was made on receiving from the publisher a copy of William H. Rawle's *A Practical Treatise on the Law of Covenants* (1852).

Among general works dealing with United States land policy during the Taney period and going far beyond the scope of this chapter, which is concerned only with outstanding cases in the Supreme Court, see Benjamin H. Hibbard, *A History of the Public Land Policies*; Roy M. Robbins, *Our Landed Heritage: The Public Domain, 1776–1936*; George M. Stephenson, *The Political History of the Public Lands from 1840 to 1862.* Among the many treatments of land problems in the Louisiana Purchase see Harry L.

Coles, Jr., "Applicability of the Public Land System to Louisiana," *Mississippi Valley Historical Review*, 43:39, 1956; Harry L. Coles, Jr., "Confirmation of Foreign Land Titles in Louisiana," *Louisiana Historical Quarterly*, 38:1, 1955; Francis P. Burns, "The Spanish Land Laws of Louisiana," *Louisiana Historical Quarterly*, Vol. II:557, 1928.

[2] See Homer Cummings and Carl McFarland, *Federal Justice*, 124.

[3] See United States v. King, 3 How. 773 (1845), 7 How. 833 (1849); United States v. Turner, 11 How. 662 (1851); United States v. Coxe, 17 How. 41 (1855).

[4] See for example Glenn v. United States, 13 How. 250 (1852).

about one-third of the state. The grant had supposedly been abrogated by the terms of the treaty of cession of Florida to the United States, but the grantee contended that the King of Spain had no power thus to nullify his own grant. The Supreme Court held that under the treaty of cession the tract came to the United States as part of the public domain, and that the question of the power of the King was a political question into which the Court could not inquire.[5]

Little in the way of clear lines of principle is to be discovered in these Louisiana and Florida land cases. Many were decided unanimously. In a considerable number, however, the Justices tended to fall into two groups. One group put emphasis on the sanctity of alleged grants, and the other on the right of settlers to acquire possession by entering upon unoccupied lands under the preemption laws of the federal government. As in the instance of the largest of the Louisiana claims, the group leaning toward the rights of settlers included Chief Justice Taney and Justices Catron, Daniel, Nelson, and Woodbury, while the group more preoccupied with the rights of claimants under alleged grants included Justices McLean, Wayne, McKinley, and Grier. While alignments inevitably changed somewhat with changes in Court membership, divisions in these cases forecast those later to appear in the California cases, save for the fact that there Chief Justice Taney shifted his position in terms of certain differences which he saw in the character of grants in the respective areas.[6] The divisions, although of course involving points of law, reflected views of public policy regarding the nation's land heritage.

Legal battles were fought not merely over lands in rural interiors but also over acreages in thriving cities such as Mobile, St. Louis, Chicago, and New Orleans. It was cases coming from such regions and other cases raising questions of riparian rights along the Atlantic Ocean and the Gulf of Mexico that gave rise to precedents of abiding influence. A troublesome problem was that riparian and seaward rights were affected by the shifting of boundaries where the ocean beat upon the shore and by changes in river courses, and more important, by the deposit of alluvial soil in seawater and the creation of new expanses of exposed land at the mouths of rivers. Important also were the rights to fisheries and oyster beds near river mouths and in relatively shallow saltwater bays jutting toward the interiors of a number of states. Cases involving underwater tracts and newly created land were before the

---

[5] Doe *ex dem.* Clark v. Braden, 16 How. 635 (1854), Cummings and McFarland, *Federal Justice*, 127–28.

[6] See Frémont v. United States, 17 How. 542 (1855).

Supreme Court at or near the same time, and judicial thinking cut across lines between the two areas.

In *Martin v. Waddell*[7] the Supreme Court in 1842 decided one of the seminal cases affecting riparian rights, dealing with confusing and conflicting theories of sovereign jurisdiction and title to ownership, and leaving those theories in about the same state of confusion and conflict as it found them. Yet it did settle some questions as to right of possession. The case arose in the form of a dispute between competing claimants to oyster beds in bays and river mouths along the coast of New Jersey. Some claimants asserted succession from the Duke of York, who in the seventeenth century had received from his brother, Charles II, a grant which included both sovereign rights over the territory and rights of property. Political rights had been ceded back to the English sovereign and property rights retained, without definition of the line between the two such as would determine rights to the fisheries in question.

The opposing group of claimants relied on a New Jersey statute of 1824 which provided for leasing the oyster beds as a source of revenue to the state. The rival oystermen clashed in the United States Circuit Court in New Jersey, which upheld the claims based on the original grant. The claimants under the state of New Jersey appealed to the Supreme Court. The case was argued in 1841 in the absence of certain of the Justices, and carried over for reargument before a full Court when the importance and difficulty of the questions had been made clear.[8] Chief Justice Taney, who wrote the opinion of the Court in 1842, knew of the difficulties first hand, having argued a similar case twenty years earlier, in the Maryland Court of Appeals, with respect to Maryland's vast oyster beds in the Chesapeake Bay.[9] He knew full well why eminent counsel had been employed on both sides—Garrett D. Wall the leader on one side and David B. Ogden on the other—and why Governor William Pennington of New Jersey appeared in Washington to watch over the interests of the state.[10]

Dividing eight to two, with Justices Thompson and Baldwin dissenting, the Supreme Court upheld the claims based on the state statute. Chief Justice Taney portrayed the rights to submerged lands as rights of sovereignty rather than merely rights of property. At the time of the Revolution, he contended, New Jersey had succeeded to the sovereign rights of the Crown, and the people thereafter held "the absolute right to all their navigable waters and the soil under them for their own

---

[7] 16 Pet. 367.
[8] *Ibid.*, 406–07.

[9] Browne v. Kennedy, 5 Har. & J. (Md.) 195 (1821).
[10] *Baltimore Sun*, Jan. 12, 1842.

common use, subject only to the rights since surrendered by the Constitution to the general government."[11] The applicable principles of law were those which prevailed with respect to the same subject matter in England.[12]

The jurisdiction of the state over the submerged lands was thereby preserved.[13] A reporter for a Charleston newspaper commented that the decision was in accordance with the public good as well as with law and substantial justice, and predicted that it would "increase the general confidence in the uprightness and legal capacity of this truly august tribunal."[14] There is no reason to believe that either this reporter or the public sensed the intricacy of the legal questions.

Both before and after its decision in *Martin v. Waddell* the Supreme Court in a number of cases was inquiring into the ownership of newly made land to seaward from the city of Mobile.[15] The surface was washed up in the form of sand and silt at the mouth of the Mobile River. On the underwater base, which according to the decision in the New Jersey case the state government held in trust for the people, gathered an accumulation which was exposed above the water at low tide. With the growth of the city and the need for expansion of commercial facilities it proved expedient to add land fill to this accumulation to make permanently exposed land, affording transit to newly made wharves in the Gulf of Mexico.

The underwater accumulation, once something of a nuisance since it interfered with shipping, was thus transformed into valuable property and claimed in fee simple by private owners.

Questions of ownership were rendered the more difficult by confusion over boundaries eastward and westward. At the time of the purchase of Louisiana in 1803 the United States regarded the eastern boundary of that territory as the Perdido River—the present boundary between Florida and Alabama—far to the east of Mobile, so that Mobile and its vicinity were acquired as part of the United States. Spain, however, which held Florida until 1819, claimed the Mobile area as part of West Florida, and was permitted by the United States to govern Mobile for a number of years, during which Spanish authorities proceeded to make grants of land.

Since Congress accepted the Perdido as the true boundary between the two territories the Supreme Court refused to inquire into the

---

[11] 16 Pet. 410.
[12] *Ibid.*, 413–14.
[13] For analysis of the decision see "The Right of Sovereignty in the Shore of the Sea," *Am. L. Mag.*, 1: 76, 1843.

[14] *Charleston Courier*, Feb. 18, 1842.
[15] See for example Foster and Elam v. Neilson, 2 Pet. 253 (1829); Garcia v. Lee, 12 Pet. 511 (1838).

matter, regarding it as a political question on which the courts must defer to the political branches of the government. Spanish grants in the Mobile area made after 1803 would therefore have had no validity but for the fact that in certain instances Congress had found it expedient to convey to recipients of grants from Spain, or from the Spanish governor of Florida, such rights to the granted property as inhered in the United States. In 1824 Congress granted to the city of Mobile all the rights of the United States to a tract within the limits of the city.[16] Beyond that, in language far from clear when read in relation to the changing seaward terrain, Congress granted certain other tracts fronting on the Mobile River, to be effective unless the Spanish government had disposed of the same land "during the time at which they had the power to grant the same."

Such a confusing statutory provision was a teasing invitation to litigation. In 1809 the governor of Florida had granted to William Pollard a lot near the waterfront on which to deposit lumber for his sawmill. Much of the litigation which was to result in the statement of important legal principles arose from disputes over ownership of this lot, with much of the language of the opinions dealing with the particular terrain and with the phraseology of particular statutes.[17] In 1840, through an opinion by Justice Thompson, with Justices Barbour and Catron dissenting, the Supreme Court upheld the Spanish grant as allegedly confirmed by Act of Congress.[18] Still other cases reached the Supreme Court partly as a result of the holding of the Supreme Court of Alabama, in which Mobile was now included, that Congress had no power to make land grants along the shore of navigable waters in the state.[19]

The Supreme Court for a time decided interstitial questions without reaching the question of constitutional power.[20] It reached that question, finally, in 1845, in *Pollard v. Hagan*.[21] That question, already vigorously dealt with in the Alabama Supreme Court, was whether the partly inundated lands on the shore of the Gulf of New Mexico fell within the jurisdiction of the federal government or of the state. The Mobile area both resembled and differed from the New Jersey area

---

[16] 4 Stat. 66.

[17] One of the items in the confusion was an Act of Congress of 1836 which purported to confirm in the heirs of William Pollard the ownership of the lot but which ended with the proviso "That this act shall only operate as a relinquishment, on the part of the United States, of all their right and claim to the above described lot of ground, and shall not interfere with or affect the claim of third persons." 6 Stat. 680.

[18] Pollard v. Kibbe, 14 Pet. 353 (1840).

[19] Pollard v. Files, 3 Ala. 47 (1841).

[20] Mobile v. Enslava, 16 Pet. 234 (1842); Mobile v. Hallet, 16 Pet. 261 (1842); Mobile v. Emmanuel, 1 How. 95 (1843); Pollard v. Files, 2 How. 591 (1844).

[21] 3 How. 212.

dealt with in *Martin v. Waddell*. It had at one time been completely submerged, as were the New Jersey oyster beds; then it had built up to such a level that it was submerged only at high tide; and finally, probably as a result of building up by interested individuals, it stood completely above the water level even at high tide. The factors determining property rights were claimed to differ, furthermore, in that while New Jersey had acquired sovereignty and property rights stemming from sovereignty over submerged lands by virtue of the transfer of sovereignty from England, the Mobile terrain was acquired by the United States before the existence of the state of Alabama. When in 1819 Congress authorized the steps that would lead to Alabama statehood, it provided that when admitted the new state should be "upon the same footing with the original states, in all respects whatever," but it also provided that "the waste and unappropriated lands lying within the said territory" should "remain at the sole and entire disposition of the United States."[22] Alabama was admitted to the Union under the conditions of this act.

In this case, as in a number of other cases in the same area, the distinguished opposing counsel were John Sergeant and Richard S. Coxe. Sergeant, defending the rights of claimants under the state, noted that in earlier cases only Justice Catron had asserted the right of the United States to grant tidelands, the other Justices refraining from dealing with the question.[23] Since under the Constitution Alabama had been admitted into the Union on an equal footing with other states, it had the same rights as New Jersey under *Martin v. Waddell*. This fact the Supreme Court could not change. "This court, although inexpressibly valuable to the country, is yet a court of limited jurisdiction."[24] Coxe, on the other hand, contended that the lands in question were part of the public domain of which the United States had the unquestioned power to dispose, and that a decision to the contrary would unsettle title to millions of acres of reclaimed lands in some ten states.[25]

The Sergeant argument convinced or coincided with the beliefs of all members of the Supreme Court, and Justice McKinley, who had been appointed from Alabama, here wrote one of his few important opinions for the Court. Relying on *Martin v. Waddell* and on the "equal footing" requirement as to admission of new states, he held that "to Alabama belong the navigable waters, and soils under them, in controversy in this case, subject to the rights surrendered by the Constitution of the United States; and no compact that might be made between her and the United States could diminish or enlarge these rights."[26]

---

[22] 3 Stat. 489, 490, 492.
[23] 3 How. 215.
[24] *Ibid.*, 216.

[25] *Ibid.*, 218–19.
[26] *Ibid.*, 229.

Only Justice Catron dissented and suggested the position to be taken by the Supreme Court a century later when the Court held that the United States and not the states, had dominion over rich oil lands completely submerged within the three-mile limit of the marginal sea, by virtue of national sovereignty and the position of the nation within the family of nations.[27] Catron contended that the decision would further unsettle title to land essential to the prosperity of Mobile. Alabama had disclaimed title as a condition of admission, and therefore could not make grants. If the seaward lands were held not as property but as an attribute of sovereignty, and if, as claimed, the United States could not give title to them, then neither could Alabama dissipate her sovereignty to the extent of giving title, even apart from the disclaimer. He saw power of disposition in the United States and not in the state.[28]

In spite of Justice Catron's dissent and some criticism of the decision,[29] it long remained in good standing despite the difficulty and confusion of doctrine demonstrated on both sides. As to merely partly submerged lands, tidelands in the strict sense, it was not to be displaced.[30] With respect to the shaping of the federal system, it represented the moderate drift in the direction of states' rights that might have been expected of the Taney Court. Even though the rights of the states were grounded in their sovereignty rather than in the position of proprietors, the Court recognized the validity of titles to ownership given by the states. In New Jersey, giving rise to a later case, land was reclaimed from water coverage to compose part of Jersey City. Instead of deciding that the previously submerged area had been held by the state in perpetuity for the benefit of its citizens, the Supreme Court upheld its right to give title. Looking back to *Martin v. Waddell,* Chief Justice Taney found that in that case the action had not been merely one for disturbing a right of fishery under lease from the state but an action for possession of the soil itself. Under that decision the state therefore had the power to dispose of the land.[31] Within the realm of state custodianship, on the other hand, the Court recognized the right of Maryland to govern the taking of oysters in the vast permanently inundated inland area of the Chesapeake Bay, a right which extended even to confiscating a vessel licensed by the United States when it violated Maryland law.[32]

---

[27] See United States v. California, 332 U.S. 19 (1947), and subsequent decisions dealing with the same question. For discussion see Ernest R. Bartley, *The Tidelands Oil Controversy.*

[28] 3 How. 233.

[29] See "Power of Congress Over Shores of Rivers," *West. L.J.,* 8:346, 1851.

[30] See Kennedy's Executors v. Beebe, 13 How. 25 (1852); Pollard's Heirs v. Kibbe, 9 How. 471 (1850).

[31] Russell v. Jersey Co., 15 How. 426 (1854).

[32] Smith v. Maryland, 18 How. 71 (1855).

Many land cases of the period derived from faulty records of grants, most of which were made by Spanish or French officials. Descriptions were apt to be inadequate. Many grants were conditioned upon the making of improvements, whose adequacy was in dispute. Congress enacted statutes to clarify the law with respect to the grants of earlier sovereigns, but these statutes too had to be interpreted.[33] The Court tended to allocate to Justice Wayne the writing of opinions in cases from Florida, which adjoined his circuit. Justice Catron wrote many opinions in cases from the Louisiana Purchase, with Justice McLean handling a minor allotment of them. When in 1862 judicial circuits were being rearranged, with the result that Justice Catron was no longer to serve Missouri, a long-time member of the Missouri bar deplored the necessity, "for the reason that Justice Catron has by long experience become familiar with our extremely complicated system of law and land titles, derived from old French and Spanish claims and a long list of confirming Acts of Congress running through a period of more than fifty years."[34]

Many of the Western cases had to do with land titles in or near St. Louis, which had not even been incorporated when Louisiana was bought but was a thriving commercial metropolis long before the Civil War. Here, as elsewhere, were problems of indefinite grants, incomplete claims, and land thrown up by the flow of the Mississippi River.[35] In dispute in one case was new land in the form of a sandbar in the river which, like new land adjacent to Mobile, was to become valuable. A holder of shore land under a grant from St. Louis claimed title extending to the middle of the river, including the new land. His opponent contended that on a huge navigable stream like the Mississippi the borders of a grant extended only to the water's edge, and that this grant therefore did not include the new land, which had not built to the surface at the time when the grant was made. Before the Supreme Court Montgomery Blair and P. B. Garesche argued for the latter position, while the former was advocated by Thomas T. Gantt and Thomas C. Reynolds. Justice Catron presumably knew nothing of the fact that in private correspondence Gantt had characterized him as a

---

[33] For discussion of the extent and complexity of the litigation see Paul Wallace Gates, "Private Land Claims in the South," *Journal of Southern History*, 22:183, 1956.

[34] Charles C. Whittlesey to A. Lincoln, Feb. 6, 1862, Lincoln Papers. For certain of Justice McLean's opinions see Strother v. Lucas, 12 Pet.

410 (1838); Mills v. Stoddard, 8 How. 345 (1850).

[35] In addition to *Strother v. Lucas* and *Mills v. Stoddard* see Bagnell v. Broderick, 13 Pet. 436 (1839); Barry v. Gamble, 3 How. 32 (1845); Mackay v. Dillon, 4 How. 421 (1846); Les Bois v. Bramell, 4 How. 449 (1846); Kissell v. St. Louis Public Schools, 18 How. 19 (1856).

"monstrous old humbug."[36] At any rate, Catron wrote the opinion of a unanimous Court to the effect that where property was bounded by a navigable stream the right of the owner extended to the middle of the stream, even when the body of water was as large as the Mississippi. The size of the river did not alter the rule, and the doctrine with respect to tidewater rivers that ownership extended only to the ordinary high-water mark was here inapplicable.[37]

Disputes arose in connection with land carved from the public domain, either under preemption laws, or through grants made to squatters, or otherwise. Here again, boundaries were often poorly defined. In some instances the government created confusion by failing to distinguish clearly between land held for ultimate distribution and tracts held for military fortresses or other national purposes. A series of legal battles was fought over a seventy-five–acre tract in the heart of Chicago, which had been designated for military purposes but was so used only in part; land-hungry opportunists wished to get rid of the military establishment altogether and turn the land to private advantage. In the one-time Indian trading post now turned Western metropolis there developed the astonishing situation where private parties claiming under preemption laws were selling off part of the government land while another part was occupied by the federal military, and the suit brought in a state court against the commander himself to oust him from the premises was decided for the claimants.[38]

In the Supreme Court on writ of error the case was argued for the commander by Attorney General Felix Grundy and by his predecessor in office, Benjamin F. Butler. For the private claimants it was argued by Francis Scott Key and Daniel Webster. The Court, speaking unanimously through Justice Barbour, came to the defense of the

---

[36] Thomas T. Gantt to Mrs. Lisinka Brown, June 29, 1855, Brown-Ewell Papers.

[37] Jones v. Soulard, 24 How. 41 (1860).

By the common law of Massachusetts the grantee of land bordering on navigable tidewater acquired ownership of the soil between high- and low-water mark. When after nonuse of land owned by it for many years and the building up of adjacent private facilities the city of Boston created private obstructions by erection of sewer structures on its tidewater property, the Supreme Court held that although the public had a right of navigation over such property the city had not lost any rights in its property by delay in development. Said Justice Grier for the Court, "A man cannot lose the title to his lands by leaving them in their natural state without improvement, or forfeit them by non use." Boston v. Lecraw, 17 How. 426, 436 (1855). See also Richardson v. Boston, 19 How. 263 (1857).

[38] See Bessie Louise Pierce, *A History of Chicago*, I, 44, 65; John Wentworth, *Early Chicago*, 39–40; McConnell v. Wilcox, 2 Ill. (1 Scam.) 344 (1837).

military against the land-hungry privateers by holding that existing statutes did not give preemption rights on the military reservation.[39] Later, pursuant to another statute, federal officials sold for more than one hundred thousand dollars the part of the reservation not being used by the military,[40] retaining as much of it as was still needed.

The city continued to grow. By 1845 it had a population of more than twelve thousand.[41] The northward extension of Michigan Avenue was blocked by the military holding. The city council directed the street commissioner to open the street and remove obstructions. The United States sought in the federal Circuit Court an injunction to prevent the city and its officers from entering upon government property. District Judge Nathaniel Pope issued a temporary restraining order. The question of making the order permanent was argued before Judge Pope and Justice McLean sitting together in the Circuit Court. Whether because of a real difference of opinion or from a desire to have the Supreme Court determine the competing rights of the city and the federal government, the two judges certified to that Court a difference of opinion.

The case, for some reason delayed in the Supreme Court for three years, was presented for the United States in December, 1848, by Attorney General Isaac Toucey. For Chicago it was not argued at all. The Court held that the city had no power to encroach upon land held by the United States for military purposes, with disagreement only from Justice Catron on the ground that the certification of difference had been but a subterfuge to get a decision from the Supreme Court, to which there was no other procedure for appeal.[42] The time quickly came, of course, when the United States found it inexpedient to maintain a fortress in the heart of the growing city, and the remainder of the reservation was allowed to pass into private ownership.

The most famous set of land cases and the most prolonged stretch of land litigation—running for more than fifty years—had to do with titles to areas in the heart of New Orleans. Usually referred to as the "Gaines Case," the multiple legal battles, while illuminating but little the development of the law itself, reveal much of the drama of litigation when great wealth was at stake. The series of legal battles, beginning in the 1830s, was fought over titles to property as affected by marriages or romantic adventures dating from around the beginning

---

[39] Wilcox v. Jackson *ex dem.* McConnell, 13 Pet. 498 (1839).

[40] Wentworth, *Early Chicago*, 39–40.

[41] Pierce, *A History of Chicago*, 44.

[42] United States v. Chicago, 7 How. 185 (1849).

of the nineteenth century. They continued until a final Supreme Court decision in 1891.[43]

The coveted real estate had been owned by Daniel Clark, a wealthy merchant and influential statesman who died in 1813. The court battles had to do with whether a girl raised by a family of his friends, and who retroactively called herself Myra Clark, was in fact his legitimate daughter and heir entitled to inherit his property; and whether, apart from her legitimacy, she was entitled to his property by virtue of a will allegedly made in her behalf shortly before his death but which disappeared, if indeed it had been made at all, possibly leaving in effect an earlier will.

The story has all the incredible drama of bad romantic fiction. Myra's mother was a luscious and flamboyant young resident of the Creole city, who before her marriage was known as Zulime Carrière. Zulime first married a roving Frenchman named Geronimo Des Grange, who for some years disappeared from New Orleans and whose behavior was such as to cast doubt on the validity of this marriage. During his absence Zulime became enamored of Daniel Clark and, with or without benefit of a marriage said to have taken place secretly in Philadelphia where she had followed him, she became the mother of his daughter. Clark had the daughter, Myra, brought up as a member of the family of Samuel B. Davis but paid visits to her from time to time. Clark never declared Zulime his wife, and she, bigamously or not, eventually married still another man.

With the Davis family Myra moved to the vicinity of Wilmington, Delaware, where she grew up unaware of her true parentage. She eloped with and married William Wallace Whitney, of a good New York family, and at the time of this marriage learned the truth—or some of the truth—of her origin. She and her husband set out for New Orleans, gathering information on the way about the Clark estate, which had not yet been settled. They arrived in 1835. Whitney began to make charges that Richard Relf and Beverley Chew, Clark's former partners and the administrators of his estate under a will of 1811, had suppressed a will made in 1813 in Myra's behalf. Relf countered with a charge of libel and had Whitney imprisoned, with bail set by a local court at the high figure of twenty-five thousand dollars with an additional impo-

---

[43] For the background and for the story of the litigation see Nolan B. Harmon, Jr., *The Famous Case of Myra Clark Gaines*; Anna Clyde Plunkett, *Corridors by Candlelight*; Perry Scott Rader, "The Romance of American Courts: Gaines v. New Orleans," *Louisiana Historical Quarterly*, 27:5, 1944; John S. Kendall, "The Strange Case of Myra Clark Gaines," *Louisiana Historical Quarterly*, 20:5, 1937.

sition of ten thousand dollars by the sheriff for "security of the person."[44]

Whitney was able to get out of jail only by effecting removal of the case to the federal court in New Orleans, where his bail was reduced to five thousand dollars. At the trial his defense was the truth of his accusation. Disclosures made there publicized the Whitney claims but also produced a great deal of information derogatory to the reputation of Myra's parents and injurious to her claims. Relf won his suit for libel but Whitney had to pay only nominal damages.[45] In the meantime the Whitneys brought suit in the same federal court to compel Relf and Chew to render an account of their trust in holding the property for more than twenty years and to restore to Myra her rightful inheritance from her father. The federal court informed the Whitneys, however, that matters of probate were not within its jurisdiction and that if Myra had rights under the later will she must have that will probated.[46] The Whitneys headed homeward, planning to return to New Orleans at a later date for further litigation.

In 1837 the Whitneys were back in New Orleans pursuing their claims, to the discomfort of Relf and Chew and those who had purchased Clark real estate from them. Perhaps deeming their cause hopeless in the Louisiana courts, they again sought help from the federal judiciary—in the year in which the federal circuit system was extended to Louisiana, with Philip K. Lawrence as district judge and Justice McKinley the Supreme Court Justice assigned to that circuit. The Whitneys met obstructions of many kinds, one of them being opposition to the use of equity powers by the federal courts in Louisiana, a code state which gave no recognition to equity procedures. Sitting in the Circuit Court before the arrival of Justice McKinley, Judge Lawrence adopted as the rules of the court the code of practice of Louisiana and ignored the equity rules prescribed for the federal courts by the Supreme Court in 1822. During his four years on the District Court Judge Lawrence adhered to his determination not to permit invasion on the part of equity.

While the Whitneys were pursuing their claims in New Orleans Myra's husband died in one of the periodic epidemics that swept the city, but the widow fought on alone. In 1839 her case was back before the Supreme Court in the form of a petition for a writ of mandamus directing the federal Circuit Court in Louisiana to observe the equity rules prescribed for it. Her case was presented by Walter Jones, one of the leading practitioners in Washington. Jones seems to have im-

---

[44] Harmon, *The Famous Case of Myra Clark Gaines*, 186.

[45] *Ibid.*, 189–92.
[46] *Ibid.*, 188–89.

pressed well upon the minds of the Justices the erroneous conduct of the Circuit Court. Justice Story, as spokesman for the Court, held that there could be no doubt of the obligation of the Circuit Court to follow the prescribed equity rules. Nevertheless the writ of mandamus was not an available remedy for enforcing that duty. The appropriate redress, if any, was to be obtained through an appeal to the Supreme Court after a final decree was had in the case.[47]

Had McKinley been able to attend the Circuit Court regularly, and had he been respected for professional learning and strength of personality, he might have been able to compel proper use of the equity rules. He was able to participate only infrequently, however, and Judge Lawrence seems to have been the stronger man of the two. Lawrence, furthermore, had the backing of powerful opponents of the Whitney claims and of the sentiments of a civil law community. When the Circuit Court next met with the two judges present they agreed to certify certain questions to the Supreme Court, of which the major one was that on which the Supreme Court had already spoken with respect to the applicability of the equity rules. Resort to this unnecessary step brought two additional years of delay.

Litigation was costly but by 1841 Myra had married General Edmund P. Gaines, possessed of considerable resources of his own, and she was back before the Supreme Court with her case registered in a new name, which it was to carry through the next half-century. This time she was represented by Walter Jones and Francis Scott Key, while Relf and others were represented by Richard S. Coxe. In a stern opinion by Justice Thompson the Court restated earlier decisions directing observance of equity rules and remarked that it was a "matter of extreme regret that it appears to be the settled determination of the district judge not to suffer chancery practice to prevail in the Circuit Court in Louisiana, in equity causes; in total disregard of the repeated decisions of this court and the rules of practice established by the Supreme Court to be observed in chancery cases."[48] Repeating that the Supreme Court could not compel the Circuit Court to proceed according to the established rules, Justice Thompson remarked that "all we can do is to prevent proceedings otherwise, by reversing them when brought here on appeal."[49]

Myra and her husband returned to New Orleans once more to press their case in the Circuit Court, finding themselves harassed by a suit against them in a local court charging Myra with having illegally

---

[47] *Ex parte* Whitney, 13 Pet. 404 (1839).

[48] Gaines v. Relf, 15 Pet. 9, 17 (1841).
[49] *Ibid.*, 17.

taken possession of some of the Clark property. Her defense was successful in the trial court but the Louisiana Supreme Court reversed the judgment and held that the property in question belonged to the claimants under Clark's 1811 will.[50] In the Circuit Court, although Judge Lawrence had been replaced by Judge Theodore H. McCaleb, differences cropped up on still other questions to be certified to the Supreme Court.

In the Supreme Court Myra was again represented by Walter Jones and by Reverdy Johnson as replacement for the recently deceased Francis Scott Key. Richard S. Coxe again represented the opposing parties, with Seth Barton of Louisiana, and one Henderson.[51] The Supreme Court decided the questions in favor of Myra to the extent that the defendants were required to submit to suit in the Circuit Court. In writing the opinion of the Court Justice McLean again asserted in the face of Louisiana sentiment the power and the duty of the Circuit Court to exercise equity jurisdiction in spite of the fact that equity had no place in the Louisiana courts, and denied the charge that "the federal court has imposed a foreign law upon Louisiana."[52] Although the decision was unanimous there was for Myra an ominous note in the concurring opinion of Justice Catron, who warned that the will of 1813 could not be set up without destruction of the will of 1811, which had been duly proved in a local court. This will could not be set aside by the federal court but only by a probate court of the state.

In the middle 1840s the Mexican War took much of the time of General Gaines and probably delayed somewhat the course of litigation. It was not until 1848, four years after the preceding decision, that the Supreme Court again dealt with Myra's claims. This case involved only a small portion of the Clark property, which had been purchased by Charles Patterson. Patterson had responded to an appeal published by General Gaines in 1840 that some purchaser of Clark property permit the question of title to be dealt with on its merits in a chancery trial, so that the merits with respect to ownership of the entire estate might be determined on appeal to the Supreme Court of the United States— in recognition of the possible bias of the Louisiana Supreme Court, some of whose members were themselves purchasers of Clark property. Should the cooperating litigant lose his case, General Gaines promised him financial concessions.[53] According to Patterson, General and Mrs.

---

[50] Barnes v. Gaines, 5 Robinson (La.) 314 (1843). See Harmon, *The Famous Case of Myra Clark Gaines*, 225, 232–38.

[51] Presumably John Henderson, United States Senator from Mississippi, who had New Orleans connec-

tions.

[52] Gaines v. Chew, 2 How. 619, 650 (1844).

[53] Letter of General Gaines, Apr. 14, 1840, reprinted in Alexander Walker, *A Full Report of the Great Gaines Case*, 32–33.

Gaines agreed to pay the cost of the necessary litigation and agreed also not to take from him his house and lot.[54]

Although Patterson, thus protected, professed to have put forth every effort to win the case, he lost in the Circuit Court and appealed to the Supreme Court. He established no contact with Relf and Chew and other claimants under Clark's 1811 will, and before the Supreme Court he was represented by different counsel.[55] The Gaines interests were again represented by Walter Jones and Reverdy Johnson, in this, the fourth time the case had been before the Court within a decade. Because of the interests involved and the scandal affecting people in high places, it had now become notorious. This presentation was made under handicap in that only five Justices were sitting. Justice McKinley was absent the entire term because of illness. Justice Catron was ill at the time of this argument. Chief Justice Taney withdrew because a "near family relative" was "interested in the event."[56] Whatever the degree of collusion between the litigants, possibly involving counsel in the Circuit Court, Brent and May, representing Patterson, seem to have done their best to disprove Myra's claims to legitimacy and to the estate of her father. While expressing sympathy for Mrs. Gaines they denounced the scandalous conduct of both her parents, presumably amid rapt attention from the audience packing the courtroom.[57]

When on January 13, 1848, the five Justices met to hand down their decision they found the courtroom crowded to overflowing with what a reporter called "the wit, beauty, and fashion of the city." Henry Clay and Daniel Webster sat among the lawyers. It was said that as

---

[54] Walker, *A Full Report of the Great Gaines Case*, 21, 33.

[55] The Supreme Court Reporter listed his counsel as "Mr. Brent and Mr. May." In 1850 Patterson stated that William Leigh Brent, "the old gentleman formerly a member of Congress from Louisiana, was employed to defend my interests before the Supreme Court in Washington. On the first trial Mr. Brent was paid for his services. Mr. Brent's son appeared upon the second trial and he and Mr. May were paid by draft, for $100 each, on me, through Mr. May's brother, in this city. The amount has been reimbursed to me by General Gaines." *Ibid.*, 22. Harmon, *The Famous Case of Myra Clark Gaines*, 310, refers to the latter counsel as Henry May. He says nothing of the son of William Leigh Brent.

[56] Reporter's footnote, Patterson v. Gaines, 6 How. 550 (1848). Harmon, *The Famous Case of Myra Clark Gaines*, 310, suggests that the relative may have been the now deceased Francis Scott Key, brother-in-law of the Chief Justice, whose estate might be affected by the ultimate outcome of the litigation. But the record in the case (p. 229), also shows that a Louis Taney, who may have been a relative of the Chief Justice, was one of the witnesses to the transfer of some of the property involved.

[57] 6 How. 581–82. It was characteristic of Benjamin C. Howard's performances as Reporter that he added, "The Reporter is compelled to omit the arguments of Mr. Johnson and Mr. Jones, the counsel for Gaines and wife, as their insertion would make the report of this case too long." *Ibid.*, 582.

Justice Wayne began reading the opinion of the Court the audience became breathless and silent as death:

> The form of the lovely and accomplished Mrs. Gaines was bent forward, catching every sound as it fell; while every eye was riveted upon her, and every heart throbbed in unison with her own. As the Judge proceeded, it became manifest that there was an earthly tribunal before which the rights of the child, the mother, and the wife could be protected, and *every heart* was moved, and every eye was lighted up with gladness and delight.[58]

The Court found that Myra was the lawful child of a lawful marriage and the heir to four-fifths of the property of her father, which under Louisiana law could not by will be passed to illegitimate descendants.

The decision seemed to imply Myra's rightful ownership of property estimated at fifteen million dollars, out of what was "probably the largest individual estate in this country."[59] For all the implications to be drawn from the decision, however, this particular suit had to do with only the house and lot claimed by Charles Patterson, which General and Mrs. Gaines had promised not to take from him. While a statement of principle had been gotten from the Supreme Court at the expense of the cost of litigation on both sides, no property was transferred as a result of it.

Indeed, Relf and Chew and many other claimants in New Orleans, convinced that the decision was the product of collusion and concerned lest they lose their property through the sharp practice of an illegitimate contender, rushed to the task of gathering additional evidence about the relationship between Myra's parents, matrimonial or adulterous as the case might be. Interested parties proclaimed their rage and mobs threatened her life.[60] Another cholera epidemic in New Orleans brought the death of General Gaines, Myra's second husband to succumb amid her search for justice, but the widow fought on, seeking on her own part additional evidence for use in further litigation.

In January, 1863, the case was again in the Circuit Court before Justice McKinley and Judge McCaleb. Both sides presented huge quantities of additional evidence, much of it conflicting and some of it highly scandalous, and all of it in some degree envenomed by the prolonged conflict over possession of the Clark estate. Each side was represented by three lawyers, the outstanding counsel for Mrs. Gaines being John A. Campbell, who in three years would be appointed to the Supreme Court. Apart from the additional evidence, Mrs. Gaines

---

[58] *Washington National Intelligencer*, Feb. 1, 1848.
[59] *Niles' National Register*, 73:322, 1848.
[60] Harmon, *The Famous Case of Myra Clark Gaines*, 318.

relied on the favorable decision in the Patterson case, which her opponents challenged as the product of conniving between the then opposing parties.

From the beginning Justice McKinley and Judge McCaleb disagreed over the status of the Patterson decision. In the midst of the argument McKinley announced that he would not consent to review and reverse in the Circuit Court a decision of the Supreme Court. McCaleb spoke up to say that he would deem it his duty to examine the decision in the Patterson case to see whether it did not "conflict with our own jurisprudence, by which the decision in this case ought to be controlled." McKinley repeated that he could not reverse a decision of the Supreme Court. That tribunal did not seem to be held in much respect in New Orleans, and he repelled the charge that adherence here to the Supreme Court decision would be a mark of corruption on his part.[61]

Yet when the time came for decision, Justice McKinley again weakened in the face of pressure. On February 21, 1850, he announced to a crowded courtroom that since he and Judge McCaleb differed as to the force of the Patterson decision, he had decided to retire and let the district judge decide the case. He was induced to do so because as a member of the Supreme Court he would have to sit in the case on appeal and because, not knowing of a case in which even the Supreme Court itself had overruled one of its own decisions, he would consider it disrespectful to that Court for him, sitting in Circuit Court, to review and reverse one of its judgments. Furthermore, he thought it better that the decision be rendered by Judge McCaleb, who was better acquainted than he was with the laws of Louisiana, so the case could go to the Supreme Court with an opinion written by a judge familiar with the peculiar jurisprudence of the state.[62] In writing the Circuit Court opinion Judge McCaleb examined the accumulated evidence at great length and decided that Myra's birth was illegitimate, with the result that she was not entitled to inherit her father's property.[63] He disposed of the problem of the Supreme Court's decision in the Patterson case by making no mention of it!

Once more the famous controversy returned to the Supreme Court. This time Reverdy Johnson, again representing Mrs. Gaines, was joined by John A. Campbell, who had had experience in the case from the lower court.[64] The opposing interests were represented by counsel

---

[61] Walker, *A Full Report of the Great Gaines Case*, 58.

[62] *Ibid.*, 73. See also a statement reprinted from the *New Orleans Delta*, "The Gaines Case," *West. L.J.*, 7:434, 1850.

[63] *Ibid.*, 73–83.

[64] With Johnson and Campbell, says the Supreme Court Reporter, was also a Mr. Lawrence. Gaines v. Relf, 12 How. 472, 486 (1852).

new in the Supreme Court phase, including Greer B. Duncan, who had argued the case in the Circuit Court, and the now elderly Daniel Webster, currently Secretary of State in the Fillmore Administration. Argument took place in early February, 1852. Ominous was the appearance of attorneys for Patterson in the preceding case to apologize for their connection with it, and to assert that they had had no knowledge of any collusive agreement between Patterson and General and Mrs. Gaines.[65] Once more, to the delectation of an avid audience, counsel combed and sorted and assessed evidence of cohabitation and bigamy and adultery. Public sentiment, it was said, was that the case would go against Mrs. Gaines.[66] Apart from the matter of atmosphere, the personality and power of mind of Daniel Webster also weighed against Daniel Clark's persistent daughter. "It was a powerful speech, impressively delivered," wrote a nephew of Justice Daniel, Moncure Daniel Conway, though he also noted "several passages meant for the fashionable audience with which the room was crowded." Conway thought Webster's metaphor infelicitous when in condemning Mrs. Gaines, "who was pleading for her legitimacy as well as property," he described Relf as "persistently besieged by litigation as a rock beaten by ocean waves."[67]

At the argument only six Justices were present. Chief Justice Taney and Justice McLean had again withdrawn, and Justice McKinley was reported absent because of indisposition.[68] Although the decision was not announced until March 1, 1852, rumors spread widely as to the outcome. A newspaper dispatch of February 22 reported that Mrs. Gaines had lost the suit, and that, having been given false hopes by her counsel, Reverdy Johnson, and by others, she was deeply depressed over the result.[69] On February 26 Daniel Webster sent to a friend information given to him as "strictly confidential" to the effect that the decision would be handed down the following Monday, with the opinion of the Court by Justice Catron and a "long argumentative opinion adverse to the majority" by Justice Wayne.[70]

The opinions were written as predicted, with further reworking of the malodorous materials in the search for the legal merits. For the Court Justice Catron stressed the fact that the mere admission on the part of Des Grange that his marriage to Zulime was bigamous was not sufficient to obliterate his marriage to her to the extent of freeing her to marry Clark.

---

[65] Harmon, *The Famous Case of Myra Clark Gaines*, 354.
[66] *New York Times*, Feb. 5, 1852.
[67] Moncure Daniel Conway, *Autobiography*, I, 99.
[68] *New York Times*, Feb. 5, 1852;

Baltimore American, Feb. 6, 1852.
[69] *New York Times*, Feb. 25, 1852.
[70] Daniel Webster to Franklin Haven, Feb. 26, 1852, *Writings and Speeches of Daniel Webster*, J. W. McIntyre, ed., XVI, 641.

> The great basis of human society throughout the civilized world is founded on marriages and legitimate offspring; and to hold that either of the parties could, by a mere declaration, establish the fact that a marriage was void, would be an alarming doctrine.[71]

On the various other grounds he likewise found unjustified the claims advanced by Mrs. Gaines. As for the Patterson case, that it had been "amicable, and that no earnest litigation was had is too manifest for controversy."[72] It could therefore not stand as a precedent in this case.

With the concurrence only of Justice Daniel, Justice Wayne wrote a dissenting opinion of some fifty-eight pages, setting forth at great length the conflicts in testimony about the marital status of Myra's parents. All who had participated in the decision would pass away, he wrote emotionally in a peroration seemingly written for the edification of the avid courtroom audience, but the case would live. Years hence the profession would look to it for the rulings on its merits and for the kind of testimony leading to the decision. It showed the hollowness of friendships based on the greed for gain. It showed how carelessness in business could impoverish the holders of capital. It showed "how a mistaken confidence given to others by a man who dies rich, may be the cause of diverting his estate into an imputed insolvency, depriving every member of his family of any part of their inheritance." He did not know of his own reasoning that the sins of parents were visited upon children, but he was able to quote Scripture to that effect: "If it be, let the victim submissively recognize him who inflicts the chastisement, and it may be the beginning of a communion with our Maker, to raise the hope of a richer inheritance than this world can give or take away."[73]

In closing the opinion of the Court, Justice Catron had expressed regret that the harshness of judicial duty had made necessary the exposures involved in the case.[74] In a letter to his bachelor friend, James Buchanan, however, he dealt with the case in quite another vein:

> The ladies have been edified by hearing Mrs. Gaines' suit—and on Monday they heard the opinion in such like phrases as these: that the plan of driving off Des Grange, (Mrs. G.'s mother's first husband) so as to enjoy the society of Clark unencumbered, and without restraint, originated beyond question in profligacy highly criminal; that of committing adultery in the absence of Des Grange to France, and being delivered of a child in his absence, for more than a year; and of hiding that child in a foreign country so as to delude Society & her

---

[71] Gaines v. Relf, 12 How. 472, 534 (1852).
[72] *Ibid.*, 538.

[73] *Ibid.*, 597.
[74] *Ibid.*, 539.

husband: and then, returning from Philadelphia where the child was secreted, to New Orleans, & presenting herself to society, and to her husband as an innocent woman; and immediately causing her husband to be tried for bigamy, committed against her; because he had a previous wife, as she alleged, when she married him. As Byron said to Murray, when he sent from Italy Don Juan to be published—"it is full of passion & profligacy, & will be read by half the men, & *all* the women. They are albut [*sic*] dead to see it in print. Of course the little woman makes the smoke rise off the writer—your humble servant.[75]

An able commentator on the 1852 decision of the Supreme Court wrote:

It is one that has attracted a larger share of public attention and inspired a stronger feeling of interest, than any other in all the records of the American courts; and this interest is one of a sort permanently to affect society, particularly in a country where law is too little settled, and where society itself is but too liable to be swayed, to and fro, from the anchorages of fast principles, by every gust of passion, and every wind of doctrine, no matter from what quarter it blows.[76]

Although only four Justices supported the majority position, with two in the minority, it seems clear that the Supreme Court, the general public, most of the litigants, and perhaps for a time even the persistent Mrs. Gaines, thought this case would mark the end of the litigation. People in New Orleans who for forty years had seen a cloud on the title to a vast amount of property in the heart of the city could now buy and sell with confidence. A building boom took place. Vacant lots were built up, old buildings gave way to new ones, additional streets were cut through, and the city itself became the owner of some of the land hitherto in controversy.[77]

But Mrs. Gaines, who had become a nationally known figure through the litigation, with hosts of loyal fans, and whose claims to millions attracted adventuresome lawyers, was soon again on the legal warpath. Having been declared a bastard with no right to inherit as the daughter of her father, she turned again to the story of the last will, allegedly made in her favor in 1813 shortly before her father's death. With the testimony of such living witnesses as she could find, she reconstructed a draft of the will and presented it for probate before Judge J. N. Lea in a local court in New Orleans. Parties with opposing

---

[75] J. Catron to James Buchanan, Mar. 3, 1852, Buchanan Papers.
[76] "The Gaines Case," *Southern*
Quarterly Rev., 18:274, 1854.
[77] Harmon, *The Famous Case of Myra Clark Gaines*, 365–66.

interests, including the city of New Orleans itself, intervened to prevent the probate, and the battle was on once more.

Judge Lea decided against Mrs. Gaines, and she appealed to the state supreme court. At this stage Louisiana was in process of electing a new chief justice. The Gaines Case became involved in the election, and Mrs. Gaines went into politics to fight for the election of Edwin T. Merrick, the candidate of Whigs and anti-Catholic Know-Nothings. Merrick won, and the case came before him as chief justice.[78] One judge withdrew because of previous involvement in the case. Judge Lea, who was also a member of the supreme court, remained to fight for the position he had taken in the lower court, but the supreme court, speaking through Chief Justice Merrick, held that under the law of Louisiana it was possible to prove the existence and bring to probate the lost will of 1813, though without prejudice to the rights of possible contestants.[79] Thus while Mrs. Gaines had succeeded in probating her father's will forty-three years after her father's death, about the only thing of which she stood assured was the prospect of further litigation.

In both state[80] and federal courts[81] the stream of litigation was soon flowing. At the term of the Supreme Court beginning in December, 1860, nine years after the decision which had presumably settled the Gaines controversy for all time, a case appealed from the United States Circuit Court in New Orleans awaited the attention of the high tribunal. It was appealed by Mrs. Gaines, who, as usual, had lost before Judge McCaleb when she had sought to recover from Douglas U. Hennen a portion of the Clark estate.[82] Although the scope of the Hennen tract was limited, a newspaper noted that the case involved "about two-thirds of the city of New Orleans."[83]

The case came up for argument in mid-February, 1861, when the country was watching plans for a change of Administration from James Buchanan to Abraham Lincoln and when Southern states one by one were adopting ordinances of secession. Hennen appeared before the Supreme Court to defend his own interests and another New Orleans attorney, Louis Janin, appeared to protect the interests of the city.

---

[78] *Ibid.*, 378–79.

[79] Succession of Clark, 11 *La. Ann.* 124, 131, (1856).

[80] For cases reaching the Louisiana Supreme Court see Heirs of Clark v. Gaines, 13 *La. Ann.* 138 (1858); De La Croix v. Gaines, 13 *La. Ann.* 177, 1858; Van Wych v. Gaines, 13 *La. Ann.* 235 (1858).

[81] For discussion of litigation in the United States Circuit Court in New Orleans see Harmon, *The Famous Case of Myra Clark Gaines*, 382–86.

[82] This was presumably the same Douglas U. Hennen who, some two decades earlier, had been before the Supreme Court in a controversy over his right to the position of clerk of the United States Circuit Court, from which Judge Lawrence had removed him.

[83] *Nashville Republican Banner,* Dec. 28, 1860.

Caleb Cushing was the leading spokesman for Mrs. Gaines. This time seven members of the Court were sitting. Chief Justice Taney and Justice McLean apparently no longer felt an obligation to withdraw. The position left vacant by the death of Justice Daniel had not yet been filled, and Justice Campbell withdrew because he had been of counsel. Justice Wayne's biographer suggests that the presence of the Gaines Case on the docket, a case in which he "tenaciously espoused a litigant's cause,"[84] may have been a factor in his decision to remain a member of the Court in spite of the secession of the state from which he came, he having noted that "To break up the Court would be to the injury of many private rights, involving much money, before it."[85]

At the argument of the case Cushing was described as a man of good appearance, with a large head and penetrating eyes. A newspaper reporter quoted by Cushing's biographer said that "In his summing up of the case I have rarely heard anything that surpassed it. His voice was not loud, but deep and firm, and every word carried a singular power. In gesture he was very sparing, using his left hand mostly, and closed, with the exception of the third finger, which was thrust straight out. . . . At the close of Mr. Cushing's remarks, he closed his books as coolly as if in his own library, stepped across the room to the right, and shook hands with some ladies who had been listening."[86]

Prominent among other spokesmen for the Gaines cause was Franklin Perin of Louisiana, who had represented Mrs. Gaines in Louisiana and had advanced money to enable her to keep the litigation going. Perin entered the chamber of the Supreme Court and began his argument in a state of illness and exhaustion. In the midst of his presentation he crumpled to the floor. It is said that Justice Wayne, presiding in the absence of Chief Justice Taney, announced that he might proceed with his argument from his chair, so that "for the first time in the history of the Supreme Court a lawyer was allowed to address that august body while seated."[87]

This sixth appearance of the Gaines Case in the Supreme Court brought seemingly ever greater complications. Instead of summarizing the facts and the arguments of counsel the Reporter despairingly noted that the record consisted of a thousand printed pages and had added to it the records in the preceding cases. He was "saved from the almost hopeless task of following the counsel through this wide range of inquiry by the minute examination of the points of the case contained"[88] in the majority and minority opinions. The case remained in the hands

---

[84] Alexander A. Lawrence, *James Moore Wayne, Southern Unionist,* 127.

[85] *Ibid.,* 170.

[86] Claude M. Fuess, *The Life of Caleb Cushing,* II, 295.

[87] Plunkett, *Corridors by Candlelight,* 91–92.

[88] Gaines v. Hennen, 24 How. 553, 555 (1861).

of the Court for a calendar month, during which the change of Administration was effected. The decision was scheduled for March 14, the last day of the term, on which *Kentucky v. Dennison* was also decided.[89] The *Baltimore American* reported that "The Supreme Court room presented a scene of more than ordinary interest today. It was crowded with lawyers, politicians and distinguished strangers, including a number of ladies. It was known that the Court would adjourn today, and that many interesting cases remained to be disposed of, the leading one of which was the celebrated Gaines Case."[90]

This time, as far as relations to the majority and minority were concerned, Justices Wayne and Catron reversed their positions of 1852. Justice Wayne now spoke for the majority of four and Justice Catron dissented along with Chief Justice Taney and Justice Grier. The presentation, as the Reporter indicated, had been immensely complicated, and the opinions revealed the same complications. Mrs. Gaines, who had been found to be the legitimate daughter of Daniel Clark in the Patterson case but illegitimate in the decision of 1852, was this time pressing her rights under the reconstructed will of 1813. But since it had been found that under the Louisiana code an illegitimate person could not inherit from a parent even by will, it had been necessary in pressing the will to introduce still further evidence on the matter of legitimacy. In order to consider this an open question the Supreme Court found it expedient to deal again with the Patterson case and the alleged collusion between the parties and to state more precisely than the Court had hitherto done the rights at stake in the 1852 decision.

Justice Wayne, who had written the opinion in the Patterson case, reexamined the charges of collusion and found that, although objectionable, the collaboration between the parties had not been such as to prevent a fair determination of the points decided: "It was an indiscreet arrangement between General Gaines and Mr. Patterson, not to be tolerated in a court of justice, but not one of intentional deception in contemplation of any undue advantage."[91] As for the 1852 decision, it and the current case were dissimilar as to the parties and the things sued for and as to the object of the judgment.[92] Although it was stated

---

[89] For discussion see Chapter XXVII, "Fugitives from Justice."

[90] *Baltimore American*, Mar. 15, 1861.

[91] 24 How. 576.

[92] In the 1852 case as interpreted by Justice Wayne Mrs. Gaines' demand had been "for one half and four fifths of another half of the property owned by her father when he died. She then claimed as the donee of her mother to the one half, and as *forced heir of her father* to four fifths of another half of his estate. Now she claims as universal legatee and legitimate child of her father, under his will of 13th July, 1813, which has been admitted to probate by the supreme court of Louisiana, and ordered to be executed as such." *Ibid.*, 578–79.

in the Louisiana code that "natural fathers and mothers can in no case dispose of property in favor of their adulterine and incestuous children, unless to the mere amount of what is necessary to their sustenance, or to procure them an occupation or possession by which to support themselves,"[93] Justice Wayne found this restriction did not apply to Mrs. Gaines for if either of the parents contracted the marriage in good faith, the status of the child would not be that of adulterous bastardy. Since of the two parents Clark, at least, had been in position to marry, the status of Myra was legitimate for the purpose of inheritance even apart from the Supreme Court's decision to that effect in the Patterson case.

Thus on the eve of the Civil War the Supreme Court saved the estate for Mrs. Gaines. Justice Wayne optimistically remarked that after litigation of thirty years the principles applicable to her rights were finally settled, and added that when some retired lawyer wrote the history of his country's jurisprudence he would find this case to be the most remarkable in the records of the courts.[94]

In dissent Justice Catron deplored particularly the disturbance of rights of property consequent on failure to take the 1852 decision as a precedent.[95] A city had been built on the property. Its value had increased probably five hundred fold. He thought the increased value ought not to go to the heirs of Daniel Clark, whose property had been sold to pay his debts, and whose estate, he said, was "wholly insolvent." He thought the respondents had already been sufficiently harassed by litigation, which had included the "fictitious" Patterson case; "for us now to declare that so gross a contempt to this court, and the practice of a fraud so disgraceful to the administration of justice, established any matter of fact or any binding principle of law, would be to sanction and uphold that proceeding, and to invite its repetition."[96]

Chief Justice Taney dissented without comment. Justice Grier, who had participated in the two preceding Gaines decisions but had not expressed himself in writing, wrote a single and acrid dissenting paragraph, bursting into Latin at its close:

> I wholly dissent from the opinion of the majority of the court in this case, both as to the law and the facts. But I do not think it necessary to vindicate my opinion by again presenting to the public view a history of the scandalous gossip which has been buried under the dust of half a century, and which a proper feeling of delicacy should have suffered to remain so; I, therefore, dismiss the case, as I hope, for the last time, with the single remark, that if it be the law of Louisiana that

---

[93] *Ibid.*, 593.　　[94] *Ibid.*, 614–15.　　[95] *Ibid.*, 622.　　[96] *Ibid.*, 628.

a will can be established by the dim recollections, imaginations, or inventions of anile gossips, after forty-five years, to disturb the titles, and possessions of bona fide purchasers, without notice, of an apparently indefeasible legal title, *"Haud equidem invideo, miror magis."*[97]

Impoverished by the expenses of litigation to the point that a hotel manager had seized her trunks to insure payment of her hotel bill,[98] Mrs. Gaines now found herself with credit restored and surrounded by hosts of congratulatory admirers.[99] The principal cloud on her horizon lay in the fact that Louisiana had adopted an ordinance of secession. Although the ordinance contained a provision that it was not to affect rights of parties involved in suits in the United States courts, the outbreak of war made it improbable that the rights of Mrs. Gaines could be enforced in New Orleans. For a time she remained in Washington, enjoying her triumph and the congratulations of her friends, attending, among other gatherings, a levee given by President Lincoln.[100] Eventually she went to Richmond, the Confederate capital, to see what could be done to advance her cause, but she found the Confederate government too preoccupied with the war to give attention to private disputes, even over such enormous amounts of property as were here involved. She traveled back northward, to Brooklyn, to await the end of the war, when she would try to secure the fruits of the Supreme Court decision of 1861.

In the postwar and post–Taney Court period the already fantastic life of the Gaines Case was further prolonged by an additional series of cases, until the Supreme Court finally saw an end of it in 1891.[101] By the final decision the city of New Orleans as owner of part of the property in dispute was ordered to pay well over half a million dollars to the estate of the now deceased Mrs. Gaines. Other amounts flowed from private sources, much of which was eaten up by counsel fees and other costs of litigation.[102] In the meantime, more than a third of a

---

[97] *Ibid.*, 631.
[98] Harmon, *The Famous Case of Myra Clark Gaines*, 393–94.
[99] For newspaper comments on the decision see *New York Tribune*, Mar. 15, 1861; *New York Times*, Mar. 16, 1861; *New York Herald*, Mar. 16, 20, 1861; *Baltimore Sun*, Mar. 15, 1861; *Baltimore American*, Mar. 15, 1861.
[100] *New York World*, Apr. 5, 1861.
[101] For later Supreme Court decisions in the Gaines Case see Gaines v. New Orleans, 6 Wall. 642 (1868); Gaines v. De La Croix, 6 Wall. 719 (1868); Gaines v. Lizardi, 18 L. ed. 967 (1868); New Orleans v. Gaines, 15 Wall. 624 (1873); Gaines v. Fuentes, 92 U.S. 10 (1876); Smith v. Gaines, 93 U.S. 341 (1876); Davis v. Gaines, 104 U.S. 386 (1881); New Orleans v. Christmas, 131 U.S. 191 (1889); New Orleans v. Whitney, 138 U.S. 595 (1891).
[102] For the story of the outcome of the litigation see Harmon, *The Famous Case of Myra Clark Gaines*, 432–56.

century before the end of the Gaines Case, the Supreme Court was facing a growing burden of land cases from newly acquired California, which in difficulty and diversity of legal questions and the extent of property involved rivaled the cases already discussed.

CHAPTER XXXI

The Wealth of El Dorado

C ALIFORNIA, the American El Dorado, became a prized possession of the United States in 1848 with ratification of the Treaty of Guadalupe Hidalgo, which ended the Mexican War. The treaty assured protection to land titles in California as they had existed under the Mexican government. Unfortunately in California, as earlier in Louisiana and Florida, the validity of many claims to land was hard to determine. Some grants made by Mexico had not conformed strictly to Mexican law. The conditions included in some of them had not been fulfilled, whether without excuse or because of interference by war or by hostile Indians. Some of the grants, characterized as "floating," were made with only the most general reference to region and without prescription of boundaries, so that rival claimants to grants in the same regions each tried to select boundaries that would incorporate newly discovered mineral areas. Finally, as government investigation of titles got under way it was discovered that many land claims were based entirely on fraud.[1]

Following upon the discovery of gold in 1849 and the beginning of the "gold rush," federal agents began inquiry into the validity of California land titles even before that state was admitted to the Union

---

[1] Almost all histories of California deal in one way or another with this subject. Among others see the relevant chapters in Hubert Howe Bancroft's *History of California*, Volumes VI (1888) and VII (1890), which constitute Volumes XXIII and XXIV of *The Works of Hubert Howe Bancroft*; Theodore H. Hittell, *History of California*; John Walton Caughey, *California*, especially Chapter 20; Joseph Ellison, *California and the Nation, 1850–1869*; Paul W. Gates, "Adjudication of Spanish-Mexican Land Claims in California," *Huntington Library Quarterly*, 3:213, 1958. Additional sources will appear in subsequent footnotes.

as part of the Compromise of 1850.[2] With respect to confirmation of titles, two opposing bodies of opinion quickly developed. One advocated speedy confirmation of all plausible claims so that property rights throughout the state could be treated as settled. The other advocated a jaundiced scrutiny of all claims for the purpose of transfer to the public domain of all land not clearly shown to be privately held, in order to make it available for settlement under the preemption laws. Both points of view had staunch protagonists in Congress.

By an act of March 3, 1851, Congress threw its weight on the side of land- and mineral-hungry "squatters." It required "each and every person claiming lands in California by virtue of any right or title derived from the Spanish or Mexican government" to present his claim and evidence in its support to a land commission of three members to be appointed by the President. Claims which were not established were to be taken as public lands.[3] Under this statute even bona fide owners of long standing were compelled to prove their claims and were deprived of their property if they failed to do so, however great might be the task of locating old and poorly preserved records. True, a right of appeal was provided from the land commissioners to the regional federal District Court, and further right of appeal to the Supreme Court. But litigation was slow and expensive. Men rich in acreage might not have the money to press their claims in courts. While it was often possible to borrow on the property claimed, interest rates, frequently running to several percent a month, were apt to be ruinous.

The board of commissioners, a political body appointed pursuant to the statute, did not get under way with its assignment until early in 1852. Its work was disrupted in 1853 when a new Administration in Washington chose new personnel. Meanwhile hordes of migrants were moving into California and settling on unoccupied land or mining for gold without reference to ownership or filing claims under preemption laws, on the assumption that the land was public domain. Board decisions began to come thick and fast, with a growing stream of appeals inundating the two federal District Courts. The larger percentage of cases were in the northern district, presided over by Judge Ogden Hoffman, a New Yorker educated at Columbia with legal training at Harvard. Judge Hoffman was an able judge but the burden of cases from his own district was heavy and his task was made all the more difficult when cases from the southern district were also assigned to him. He was the victim of a political deadlock in Washington. There the Presi-

---

[2] See House Exec. Doc. No. 17, 31st Cong., 1st Sess. (1850); Senate Exec. Doc. No. 18, 31st Cong., 1st Sess. (1850). For discussion see Ellison, *California and the Nation*, 9–15.

[3] 9 Stat. 631.

dent and the Senate, being of different political parties, proved unable to agree upon a replacement for a deceased judge in the southern district.[4] The Democratic Congress, hoping that in the ensuing election President Fillmore would be replaced by a Democrat, who might be expected to favor Democrats in making judicial appointments, added for the time being the work of the southern district to the duties of Judge Hoffman.[5]

Democratic hopes were realized. Early in the Pierce Administration Attorney General Caleb Cushing drafted a bill providing for appointment of a judge to the southern district and authorizing each judge to hold court in the district of the other in the event of need.[6] The California delegation was reported as saying that the burden of work for the entire state was impossibly heavy for one judge, especially because of the mass of land cases.[7] Congress passed the bill.[8] To the position was appointed Isaac S. K. Ogier, a man of no great repute who had been born in Charleston and studied and practiced law in New Orleans.

The pressure of land cases gave rise also to a movement for creation of a circuit judgeship to serve the California area. By the middle 1850s, as prior to 1837 when the number of circuits had been increased from seven to nine, there was a fringe of new states or parts of states in which Supreme Court Justices did not ride circuit and where circuit duties were conferred on district judges. It was contended that the heavily burdened California district judges, however, should not have this added responsibility, and also that it was not feasible for a Supreme Court Justice to travel so far from Washington. In 1854 the situation became worse when Judge Hoffman was ill for a number of months, and cases piled up on the docket in the northern district. Senator William M. Gwin of California, who had sought allocation of a Supreme Court Justice to California in spite of the travel difficulties, stressed the need for relief because of the confusion in land titles. It would have been better, he contended, if when California was acquired Congress had either confiscated all land claims or indiscriminately confirmed all claims, valid and fraudulent, rather than subject the people to a period of

---

[4] *Cong. Globe*, 31 Cong., 1st Sess. 171 (1854). When in 1850 Congress had provided for the two judicial positions, Daniel Webster, as Secretary of State, had complained to President Fillmore of the difficulty of filling them because of the low salaries. An offer had been made to his friend John P. Healy of Massachusetts, but it would probably be declined. Daniel Webster to Millard Fillmore, Oct. 19, 1850, *Writings and Speeches of Daniel Webster*, J. W. McIntyre, ed., XVI, 571.

[5] 10 Stat. 84.

[6] *Cong Globe*, 31st Cong., 1st Sess. 51 (1854).

[7] *Ibid.*, 171.

[8] 10 Stat. 265.

ruinous unsettlement. As of February, 1855, California had been in our possession for seven years, without as yet a Supreme Court decision disclosing the policy to be followed.[9]

The debate led once more to the question of relieving the Supreme Court Justices from circuit duties to enable them better to perform their duties in Washington, with circuit duties to be allocated to newly appointed circuit judges. Some legislators favored reform, others preferred to retain the familiar system. Some opposed creating an anomaly in the form of a circuit judgeship for only one circuit, while others thought that the special circumstances justified this exception in a system which otherwise ought not to be changed.[10]

Interested in the proposed circuit judgeship was Matthew Hall McAllister, a prominent Georgia lawyer and social figure who had been for a time mayor of Savannah. Drawn by the lure of quick wealth, McAllister in 1850 followed his son Hall McAllister to San Francisco where within two years he made a comfortable fortune.[11] Having lost most of his wealth in speculation while on a European trip, he is reported to have boasted to one of his sons that he would get the Democratic Congress to create the position and would himself return to California as its circuit judge. He preferred a modest competence in the form of a salary to the larger income as a practicing lawyer which was apt to turn to ashes at the touch.[12]

Be that as it may, the position was created and he was appointed to it. The court was given the usual pattern of circuit duties, the judge being authorized to sit also as a district judge in land cases. The District Courts were limited as were other District Courts in areas served by Supreme Court Justices, save for the special jurisdiction conferred on them in land cases. In these cases the right of appeal was to operate directly from District Courts to the Supreme Court.[13] In this fashion the United States began its experiment with an independent circuit judge, an experiment eventually extended in 1891 to a slate of judges for the entire country.

When in 1852 and 1853 cases began to flow from the board of land commissioners to the two District Courts, for decision by Judge Hoffman whatever the district, the task could hardly have been more confusing. Even the line of division between the two districts was poorly defined—so that it was hard to determine in which of the two courts the judge should be sitting when he dealt with land cases from the

[9] *Cong. Globe*, 33rd Cong., 2nd Sess. 605 (1855).
[10] For discussion see *ibid.*, 581–83, 604–09.

[11] Ward McAllister, *Society as I Have Found It*, 21.
[12] *Ibid.*, 21–22.
[13] 10 Stat. 631.

vicinity of that line. While obligated to decide cases involving property of immense value, he lacked guidance as to the law. The Supreme Court had not yet interpreted the treaty and the relevant statutes. Although some land cases were already being decided in the California courts, those courts were under similar pressures, and it was rumored that the corruption pervading the new state government extended to its judiciary, so that, even if relevant, decisions there could not be confidently followed. The board of land commissioners, from which the federal cases were appealed, consisted of political appointees who gradually learned much about the intricacies of land problems but were not learned in the law.

When Judge Hoffman, sitting as judge of the northern district, decided the first of many cases, he deplored the statutory requirement that he do more than decide the case pro forma to speed it on its way to the Supreme Court and the necessity of acting on the conviction that in this case the board of commissioners was wrong.[14] The claimant, Cruz Cervantez, appealed to the Supreme Court.

Aware of difficult tasks ahead, the Supreme Court required that land cases be handled to minimize the difficulties. In December, 1851, in immediate connection with Louisiana cases but presumably with prospective California litigation also in mind, it adopted its Rule 60 requiring translation of foreign-language documents included in the record of any case and directing that untranslated documents be returned to the inferior court for translation.[15] Although the Cervantez case was argued relatively promptly, it was said that the Court had refused to proceed until a collection of Spanish and Mexican law books could be acquired, translated, and studied. When a clerk from the Attorney General's office was sent to Mexico City to make the necessary acquisitions, he had only limited success.[16] The Court further delayed passing on the merits of the Cervantez case by sending it back for clarification, since it had been decided by Judge Hoffman without a showing that the land in question lay within that district. The Justices had seen a recently published map which led them to believe that the land lay within the southern district.[17] Consequently this case fell behind others in the Supreme Court and became one of little importance as far as statement of principle was concerned.[18]

It was not until March, 1855, after millions of dollars in mineral wealth had been garnered, that the Supreme Court decided the first of

---

[14] United States v. Cervantez, 25 Fed. Cas. 367 (No. 14768) (D.C.N.D. Cal. 1853).

[15] 12 How. xi (1851).

[16] Homer Cummings and Carl Mc-Farland, *Federal Justice*, 129–30; *New York Times*, Jan. 9, 10, 1854.

[17] Cervantez v. United States, 16 How. 619 (1854).

[18] See United States v. Cervantez, 18 How. 553 (1856).

the major land cases. At stake was the claim of John Charles Frémont to a tract of ten square leagues (some seventy square miles or about forty-three thousand acres). The tract consisted of land granted in 1844 by Governor Manuel Micheltorena to Colonel Juan B. Alvarado as a reward for patriotic services to his country. Like other grants, this one was subject to approval by the Mexican Departmental Assembly, and the recipient was required to build and occupy a house on it within a year.

Because of the conflict then pending with the United States the period of the middle 1840s was one of great unsettlement in Mexican-owned territory. In a note written for inclusion in a volume of reports of decisions of his court, Judge Hoffman remarked that the Mexican governor seemed to have "distributed grants with a lavishness that would justify the suspicion that he hoped to assure to his countrymen, by the pen, the lands he foresaw they were about to be deprived of by the sword."[19] The chaos which resulted from the war sometimes prevented completion of grants by action of the Departmental Assembly and fulfillment of requirements as to settlement and occupancy.

Frémont, the colorful and controversial explorer and soldier, helped to wrest California from Mexican hands. Upon heading eastward, under arrest in connection with a military controversy, he left with Thomas Larkin three thousand dollars to buy land in the hills back of San Francisco. For some reason Larkin used the money to buy not the land designated but the Alvarado grant, known as the Mariposa tract, back against the Sierras and far from any settlement.[20] The grant to Alvarado had not been confirmed by the Departmental Assembly. Because of the hostility of Indians it had not been possible to occupy any portion of the property, and no survey had been made. Frémont, disgruntled at the purchase of seemingly worthless land, nevertheless tried to occupy it through an agent, but was at first prevented by Indians. No portion of the property was settled until Frémont's return in 1849, the year of the discovery of gold. Mines were opened on land which Frémont claimed as part of his tract and were worked by laborers for part of the yield. It seemed that Frémont was on the way to a position of great wealth.

The Frémont claim of course had to be submitted for the approval of the board of land commissioners. The board confirmed the claim in spite of lack of action by the Departmental Assembly and lack of settlement within the prescribed time. The federal government, contending that title had never passed to Alvarado and that the land should be

---

[19] Note appended to United States v. Cambuston, 25 Fed. Cas. 266, 274 (No. 14713) (D.C.D. Cal. 1859).

[20] Allen Nevins, Frémont, Pathmarker of the West, 371.

transferred to the public domain, appealed to Judge Hoffman's court. Finding that the conditions of the grant had not been met, that court reversed the decision of the board,[21] and Frémont appealed to the Supreme Court.

In the Supreme Court Frémont's interest amounted not to the original investment of three thousand dollars but, in view of the discovery of gold, to millions of dollars. For protection of that interest he chose an imposing array of counsel, including William Carey Jones, John J. Crittenden, and George M. Bibb. Jones was Frémont's brother-in-law, the two having married daughters of Thomas Hart Benton. Benton, with this family interest in California land, had fought in the Senate for validation of Mexican claims without extensive investigation. Frémont himself had done likewise during a brief period as a member of the Senate. Jones had investigated for the government the problem of land claims and had likewise recommended validation of most of the claims, in some of which he had acquired an interest.[22] Thus the Benton relatives presented a solid front against fulfillment of the purpose of the statute of 1851, which was to challenge all Mexican claims and permit recognition only of those clearly invulnerable to attack. The battle lost in Congress was now transferred to the courts. In the handling of the case Jones was evidently the major strategist.

The argument for Frémont, which took place February 19–22, 1855, was opened by Jones. He was followed by Bibb, who had held judicial offices in Kentucky and had been a United States Senator and Secretary of the Treasury. More important was the fact that he had recently been chief clerk in the office of the Attorney General, where he had become familiar with the materials and the strategy of the office in dealing with California land cases. A few days before the argument he had opposed the Attorney General in another such case, in which he was to be the victor.[23] He was a gentleman of the old school, never having abandoned the garb of knee breeches in court appearances, but he was shrewd withal, "crowding the merits of the case into the brief space of half an hour."[24]

Bibb was followed by Attorney General Caleb Cushing for the United States, who was no mean opponent for all the fact that he stood as one man against three. It was said that he "charmed a large and brilliant audience, during two hours on Tuesday and two hours on

---

[21] United States v. Frémont, 25 Fed. Cas. 1214 (No. 15164) (D.C.N.D. Cal. 1853).

[22] See Ellison, *California and the Nation*, 12, Gates, "Adjudication of Spanish-Mexican Land Claims in California," *Huntington Library*

Quarterly, 3:221, 1958; Hittell, *History of California*, II, 743–44.

[23] United States v. Ritchie, 17 How. 525 (1855).

[24] *Washington National Intelligencer*, Feb. 26, 1855.

Wednesday morning, by a discourse of unusual interest and strength; a good portion of it historical and having the attractiveness of romance, and all of it such as to engross the attention of the court, the bar, and all hearers."[25] Then for Frémont, Senator Crittenden likewise won paeans of praise for his eloquence and graphic descriptions, as he portrayed the chaos of universal litigation over land titles for which the federal government was responsible.[26]

Dividing six to two with Justice Daniel not sitting, the Supreme Court upheld Frémont's claim. Voting with the majority and writing the opinion of the Court was Chief Justice Taney, who in connection with claims in Louisiana and Florida had shown no leniency as to claims not fully established.[27] Many of those grants, he contended, had been made primarily to encourage settlement and improvement, and were not complete as grants until the conditions of occupation and improvement were fulfilled. Many of the California grants, on the other hand, as in the instance of the grant to Alvarado, were made primarily as awards to and for the benefit of the recipients. The conditions attached to them were merely conditions subsequent, and their fulfillment was not necessary to establish the validity of the grants. In the instance of the Alvarado grant, purchased by Frémont, the intervention of war and Indian hostility that delayed settlement and the establishment of boundaries did not vitiate the grant itself.[28]

The decision in the Frémont case was a boon not only to Frémont himself but to other original grantees and purchasers from them whose claims were similarly based. On the other hand, it dashed the hopes of many who had settled on undeveloped land assuming it to be part of the public domain and now found themselves disestablished through the medium of Mexican grants. On the Supreme Court the latter found a spokesman in Justice Catron, who in dissenting contended that the Frémont claim had no standing and deplored the effect of the decision on the rights of settlers under preemption laws enacted by Congress: "The country in California is filled up with inhabitants cultivating the valleys and best lands, and where they rely almost as confidently on their government titles, founded on Acts of Congress, as if they had a patent for the land. No other American title is known in the State of California, except such as are founded on the pre-emption laws." He regarded these agricultural people virtually as contractors with the government in fulfillment of its policy to populate the country, and

---

[25] *Ibid.* See also Cummings and McFarland, *Federal Justice*, 131.

[26] *Ibid.*

[27] See United States v. Boisdoré, 11 How. 63 (1851); Glenn v. United States, 13 How. 250 (1852); Vilemont's Heirs v. United States, 13 How. 261 (1852).

[28] Frémont v. United States, 17 How. 542 (1855).

contended that they had equitable rights that ought not to be nullified by recognition of floating concessions such as that made to Alvarado.[29]

Although in later cases Justice Daniel rejoined his brethren to dissent with Justices Catron and Campbell against the position taken by the majority in the Frémont case,[30] the majority position remained unchanged until the government shifted its strategy after the accumulation of evidence of fraud in connection with many alleged grants. To reduce the burdens of litigation on all parties, Attorney General Cushing sifted the records of grants approved by the board of commissioners and dropped about four-fifths of them without appealing them to the District Courts.[31] Of those that were appealed, many were decided against the government on the basis of the Frémont decision. Included in the government's protection were grants that were floating as to location as well as those seemingly incompletely made or having unfulfilled conditions, often to the great injury of other claimants to particular lands. Henry George, who developed his single-tax theories while observing the warfare over land titles in California, noted that Frémont's Mariposa claim, "after two or three locations in the valley, was finally carried up into the mountains, where it had as much business as it would have had in Massachusetts or Ohio, and stretched out into the shape of a boot, to cover a rich mining district. Among the property given to John Charles Frémont and his partners, by this location, was the Ophir mine and mill, upon which an English company had spent over $100,000, after assurances from the Mariposa people that the mine was outside their claim."[32] The pulling and tugging to draw various other floating grants over rich mining areas had its counterpart with respect to rich agricultural lands.[33]

If the Supreme Court seemed inclined to be generous in approval of Mexican grants incompletely made or inadequately located, it could

---

[29] *Ibid.*, 572–73.

[30] See his dissenting opinion in Arguello v. United States, 18 How. 539, 553 (1856), where he said, "Upon such a foundation, such a pretense, or rather such a defiance of authority, I will not, by an abuse of language, call it even a pretense of right, I cannot consent to impair or destroy the sovereign rights and the financial interests of the United States in the public domain. I can perceive no merit, no claim whatsoever, to favor, on the part of the grasping and unscrupulous speculator and monopolist; no propriety in retarding, for his advantage or profit, the settlement and population of new states, by excluding therefrom the honest citizen of small means, by whose presence and industry the improvement and wealth, and social and moral health, and the advancement of the country are always sure to be promoted."

[31] Cummings and McFarland, *Federal Justice*, 133.

[32] Henry George, *Our Land and Land Policy*, 15.

[33] *Ibid.*, 14–15. For discussion of the location of the Frémont tract and of litigation in the California courts to determine the ownership of minerals see "Mines—Mariposa Grant," *Am. L. Reg.*, 10:462, 1862.

not be expected to condone fraud. When in 1857 Jeremiah S. Black became Attorney General he found evidence of fraud rapidly accumulating. Particularly malodorous were the claims of a Frenchman, José Y. Limantour, to land in San Francisco and islands in the bay area involving private property worth some thirty-six million dollars and United States fortifications and other property worth some twelve million dollars.[34] For a fee of twenty-five thousand dollars and traveling expenses, Black sent Edwin M. Stanton to California to study land records in this and other cases and work with the district attorney in protecting the interests of the government.[35] By collecting records hitherto unassembled and comparing them with Limantour's documents and by transporting to California from the East a disaffected participant in forgery, Stanton was able to expose a gigantic fraud and win the case for the government.[36]

The government was put to great expense in winning the case, and some property owners were injured by the threat. To punish Limantour and provide an example for others likeminded, a criminal suit was instituted against him for fraud, forgery, and perjury. He posted bond, fled to Mexico, and complained to the French government that the suit had been instituted to prevent his appealing the land case to the Supreme Court. Black assured the French minister that such was not the case. There had been no "menace" of a prosecution to prevent his appealing to the Supreme Court. Limantour had been so completely exposed that he was not likely to exercise the right of appeal. He had fled the country to escape an entirely proper criminal prosecution.[37]

The case was never appealed to the Supreme Court but the Justices were kept informed about it. Black donated to the Court a book of photographs and documents used in the case, and received from Chief Justice Taney an expression of appreciation and a promise that the book would be placed in the Supreme Court library.[38] The Court was being educated.

With growing awareness of fraudulent practices, the drift of Supreme Court decisions began to go against the sponsors of doubtful claims. Black defeated the claim of Henry Cambuston for land on the Sacramento River, opposing Volney E. Howard and E. L. Goold of

---

[34] Cummings and McFarland, *Federal Justice*, 134.

[35] See the correspondence and other documents included in Expenditures on Account of Private Land Claims in California, H.R. Exec. Doc. No. 84, 36th Cong., 1st Sess.

[36] Cummings and McFarland, *Federal Justice*, 135–38; United States v. Limantour, 26 Fed. Cas. 947 (No. 15601) (D.C.N.D. Cal. 1858).

[37] J. S. Black to The Count de Sartiges, Feb. 14, 1859, Attorney General's Letter Book A–3, 357.

[38] R. B. Taney to J. S. Black, Feb. 14, 1859, Black Papers.

California, and J. Mason Campbell, Chief Justice Taney's son-in-law.[39] The relationship of son-in-law to the Chief Justice seems not to have caused criticism in this or other cases; in any event, in this case the son-in-law was defeated. "I really did think I would carry Cambuston," Campbell wrote to Black. "It was my unlucky destiny to meet the keenest of weapons just when it was keenest and before it had cut down anything else or had its edge turned." He had evidently served for a contingent fee, with ownership of some California land in prospect. "Can't you send me on a foreign mission," he continued wryly, "or get me a few square leagues somewhere (I will take them in Pennsylvania) to replace what I have lost, or have an act of Congress passed putting me at the head of the California division of the Attorney General's office with a special eye to missing petitions?"[40]

Opposing Montgomery Blair, now of Maryland, and Calhoun Benham of California, Black defeated a claim to a huge tract of mission land in the vicinity of San Jose.[41] More important as far as the value of the property was concerned, with the aid of William B. Reed he won the Bolton case, again involving San Francisco property, against Robert J. Walker, J. Mason Campbell, St. George T. Campbell, and John W. Dwinelle.[42] The victory was perhaps particularly pleasing because a report had circulated in San Francisco that Black and Stanton had each received a third of a one hundred thousand dollar fund as the price of dismissing the appeal to the Supreme Court.[43] Black had replied that the author of the rumor was "a cold blooded and deliberate liar" and that the report was "a sheer fabrication from the whole cloth."[44] A group of San Franciscans who wrote to urge Black to fight against the Bolton claim told of a letter attacking him by a presumably fictitious R. L. Roman in connection with the claim.[45] Chief Justice Taney sent Black a copy of a letter with the Roman signature and told him that Justice Daniel had likewise received a copy. Everyone would see, said the Chief Justice, "that such a letter written to Judges before whom the case was to be tried could not have been intended for any honest purpose, but was designed to prejudice their minds in advance of the time and to prevent a fair and impartial hearing of the case."[46]

---

[39] United States v. Cambuston, 20 How. 59 (1858).

[40] J. M. Campbell to J. S. Black, Jan. 26, 1858, Black Papers. In his argument of the case Black had made much of the absence of a petition alleged to be essential to the validity of the grant.

[41] Fuentes v. United States, 22 How. 443 (1860).

[42] United States v. Bolton, 23 How.

341 (1860).

[43] Isaac N. Thorne to J. S. Black, June 19, 1858, Black Papers.

[44] Copy, J. S. Black to Isaac N. Thorne, July 17, 1858, Black Papers.

[45] Robert C. Page, et. al., to John Nugent, Sept. 6, 1858, Black Papers.

[46] R. B. Taney to J. S. Black, Sept. 10, 1858, Black Papers. A document was printed in San Francisco over the printed signature of W. Z. Wash-

If the accusations were intended to stir Black's zeal for winning the Bolton case, they may well have had the desired effect. He asked the United States Attorney in San Francisco to render him extensive services in preparation for argument of the case. He asked for a comparison of the list of witnesses in the Bolton case with the list in the Limantour case, to see how many of them were "professional witnesses," used by claimants over and over to prove the validity of Mexican grants. He asked for maps and information about streets and buildings in the area involved. The grant had allegedly been made to a secular priest, José Prudencia Santillan. Black was convinced that it was forgery and he was eager to have someone go to Mazatlan to get a sworn statement from Santillan. He would send "the President's pardon of Santillan as a pledge that he shall be pardoned upon good behavior in future. If we use him in this way, it is right he should be freed from the fear of swearing himself into the Penitentiary."[47]

There is no evidence that Black received or was able to use before the Supreme Court all the materials he sought, but he did win his case. Justice Catron, speaking for a unanimous Court, was unable to find evidence of a good title in "the grant made to this necessitous Padre."[48]

Opposing Judah P. Benjamin of New Orleans and E. L. Goold, Black won another case involving the interests of Joseph C. Palmer, who was prominent in political and banking affairs and in land speculation in California. Palmer had originally been interested in the Frémont estate and had allegedly skirted the edge of the law in advancing his interests. Montgomery Blair had reported litigation gossip to his father in 1854 when in California attending to the estate of his deceased brother. Palmer had consulted directly with Judge Hoffman in an at-

---

ington and dated January, 1860, saying that Black was engaged in speculation in California land and title forging. A copy is filed in the papers of Justice McLean, Vol. 19, initial page 4485.

[47] J. S. Black to Peter Della Torre, June 2, 1859, Attorney General's Letter Book B-3, at 27, 30.

[48] How. 351. For day-to-day comments on the argument of the case see *New York Tribune*, Apr. 3, 4, 5, 6, 1860. Justices McLean and Daniel were absent and Chief Justice Taney fell ill during the argument. The Bolton interests were now held by the San Francisco Land Association, of which most of the stock was owned in Philadelphia. *Washington National Intelligencer*, May 7, 1860. After the

argument the rumor was spread that Chief Justice Taney was to write the opinion of the Court upholding the validity of the grant, with the result that the stock was selling at three hundred dollars a share. William B. Reed pleaded with Black for a telegram saying whether the report was true. W. B. Reed to J. S. Black, Apr. 10, 1860, Black Papers. Reed was delighted at the report of the actual decision. He wished that the opinion might immediately be made available. He was coming to Washington soon, but "I take for granted Mr. Carroll's red tapism will prevent our seeing the opinion." W. B. Reed to J. S. Black, May 8, 1860, Black Papers.

tempt to influence his decision, but without avail. He had then promised a fee of ten thousand dollars to Hall McAllister, the son of Judge McAllister, for a "right" decision from Judge Hoffman. McAllister and Judge Hoffman, who were courting two sisters, belles from New Orleans, saw a great deal of each other and "talked love to the sisters and talked law to each other." McAllister, who according to Blair was much the better lawyer, gave Hoffman a great deal of advice "amicus curiae." The strategy failed, however, for Judge Hoffman decided in favor of Frémont and against the interest of Palmer. Palmer then proposed to have a California Senator put pressure on the Supreme Court, but Blair warned him not to attempt it: "The Supreme Court was an unimpeachable body. Its purity was beyond question. Its ability might be questioned possibly but there were several of the judges whose ability was of the highest order."[49] When Blair prepared to leave California he hoped to get Palmer to manage his property and collect rents, saying that "whilst he is charged with buying legislators and judges &c nobody suspects him of bad faith to friends or want of heart."[50]

The land claim which Palmer pressed in the Supreme Court involved a tract in the vicinity of San Francisco said to have been granted originally by Governor Pio Pico to one Benito Diaz, after which it had passed through various hands to Palmer and his associates. The claim had been rejected by the board of land commissioners and by Judge Hoffman's court. By this time Black's subordinates had acquired a great deal of skill in detecting evidence of fabrication. In this instance the document was given as made out and signed in Los Angeles, whereas the government had proof that on the date of the document Governor Pico was in Santa Barbara, some seventy miles away. Justice Grier wrote a unanimous opinion rejecting the claim.[51]

---

[49] Montgomery Blair to F. P. Blair, Apr. 9, 1854, Blair-Lee Papers. See also letter of June 1, 1854.

[50] Montgomery Blair to Mrs. Montgomery Blair, July 9, 1854, Blair-Lee Papers.

[51] Palmer v. United States, 24 How. 125 (1861).
Black had been very sure of his case, writing shortly before the argument that "I shall beat them handsomely with the materials already on hand." J. S. Black to James F. Shunk, Dec. 11, 1860, Attorney General's Letter Book B–3, at 504. Palmer's counsel seems to have been hesitant about coping with the government's attack upon the claim. E. L. Goold discussed with Black the proposal that Congress enact a statute whereby Palmer would give up all claim on such portion of the alleged grant as was occupied by government fortifications and other buildings, and the government would in turn surrender claim to the portion of the grant privately occupied. Black made it clear that he would oppose any measure curbing in any way the right of occupants to defend their rights against the claims advanced by Palmer. No such statute was enacted and the case was permitted to go to trial. See J. S. Black to E. L. Goold, May 24, June 25, 1859, and to J. P. Benjamin, Dec. 22, 1859, Attorney General's Letter Book B–3, 23, 49, 189.

So great were the interests involved in these and other land claims, so great the pressure, and so ruthless the competitors, that corruption in public life was taken almost as a matter of course. In referring to one case decided when he was a member of the California Supreme Court, Justice Stephen J. Field recorded, "Attacks full of venom were made upon Judge Baldwin and myself, who had agreed to the decision. No epithets were too vile to be applied to us; no imputations were too gross to be cast at us. The Press poured out curses upon our heads. Anonymous circulars filled with falsehoods, which malignity alone could invent, were spread broadcast throughout the city, and letters threatening assassination in the streets or by-ways were sent to us through the mail."[52] In faraway Washington, however, the Supreme Court of the United States seems to have escaped most of the imputations of criminality.

Perhaps the most outstanding of the legal struggles over land claims were those over the New Almaden quicksilver mines, located some twelve or fifteen miles from San Jose. By the middle 1850s the mines were yielding around a million dollars' worth of mercury a year, a yield all the more important because of the use of the product in the production of gold and silver. Such a stream of wealth naturally attracted groups of competing claimants.[53] The group operating the mine, consisting of persons largely of British and Mexican extraction, did so by virtue of a grant alleged to have been made to Don Andres Castillero, who in 1845 had been sent into California to buy a fort constructed by Captain John Sutter for protection against the Indians, and who came upon the quicksilver mining area and realized its enormous value even before the discovery of gold. The laws with respect to mineral grants were different from those with respect to agricultural grants, but the records were as poorly kept, and charges of forgery and fraud were as rife in one area as in the other.

The mining area was claimed also by the successors to two agri-

---

[52] Stephen J. Field, *Personal Reminiscences of Early Days in California*, 159–60. Among the items still preserved see "The Gold Key Court or the Corruptions of a Majority of It," allegedly written by an "Ex-Supreme Court Broker," of which a copy is preserved at the Henry E. Huntington Library. For discussion of the problems of the California courts in connection with land litigation see Carl B. Swisher, *Stephen J. Field: Craftsman of the Law*, 82–101.

[53] Among the sources on this topic see "Down in the Cinnebar Mines, A Visit to New Almaden in 1865," *Harper's*, 21:555, 1865; Edgar H. Bailey, "The New Almaden Quicksilver Mines," *California Natural Resources Bulletin, Geologic Guidebook of the San Francisco Bay Counties*, 154:263, 1951; Henry Winfrid Splitter, "Quicksilver at New Almaden," *Pacific Historical Review*, 26:33, 1957. See also the cases hereafter cited.

cultural grants, both of which were found to be valid but with boundaries undetermined. One of the grants, made in the name of Justo Lorios, was carried in the name of Charles Fossat during the period of litigation. By virtue of rights derived from it, the Quicksilver Mining Company, organized by Eastern capitalists, claimed the right to the New Almaden mines, but pending litigation ousting the company operating the mines it had no mines to operate in. An adjacent tract, originally granted to José R. Berreyesa, likewise said to cover the mining area, was apparently eventually acquired by the group claiming originally under Castillero in order to protect their alleged rights. The United States government challenged the claims of all private parties and contended that the flow of quicksilver was part of the public heritage.

Without attempting to determine boundaries, which it had no right to do, the board of land commissioners upheld all the private claims. In the name of the United States, though at times with rival private litigants providing much of the impetus, the claims of all the private litigants were challenged in the lower federal courts in California, the District Court being called upon to determine the validity of claims and the Circuit Court in one instance using its injunctive power to prevent the wasting of mineral resources pending the determination of ownership.[54]

When Jeremiah S. Black became Attorney General in 1857 he found the contending parties always eager to advance their own interests by any use they could make of the federal government. United States Senator James A. Bayard of Delaware, counsel for the Fossat interests, complained about the harassment of his client involved in appealing to the District Court the decision of the board of land commissioners.[55] John A. Rockwell, whose real client was not the United States but the Castillero interests, urged that the appeal be carried through,[56] offering as inducement the statement that:

> if the claims of the parties whom I represent are at last decided against them and the appeal in the case of Fossatt[57] is dismissed and the tract is confirmed and patented as claimed by him, the United States are forever deprived of property of immense value embracing perhaps the most valuable quick silver mines in the world.[58]

---

[54] See United States v. Parrott, 27 Fed. Cas. 416 (No. 15998) (C.C.N.D. Cal. 1858). For failure of earlier attempts to get such protection see Tobin v. Walkinshaw, 23 Fed. Cas. 1331 (No. 14068) (C.C.N.D. Cal. 1855), and in later suits between the same parties at 1338, 1346.

[55] James A. Bayard to J. S. Black, Mar. 30, 1857, Black Papers.

[56] John A. Rockwell to J. S. Black, Mar. 30, 1857, Black Papers.

[57] The name was spelled variously "Fossat" and "Fossatt."

[58] John A. Rockwell to J. S. Black, Apr. 4, 1857, Black Papers.

When Black refused to dismiss the appeal, the Fossat interests turned to Buchanan, who referred the matter back to Black. The appeal having been taken by his predecessor, Black contended, he had no power to dismiss it, nor any inclination in the light of the national interests involved. He noted that "A party may have one counsel at San Francisco to try his cause before the Judge who has charge of it, and another at Washington to convince the Attorney General that the appeal ought to be dismissed. He is safe if he succeeds on either side of the continent, though he fail at the other. No such anomalous power has been given me by the law, and I will not take it without law."[59] When Fossat won his case in the District Court,[60] similar efforts were made to prevent an appeal to the Supreme Court,[61] but without avail.

In deciding the case on April 30, 1858, the Supreme Court upheld the validity of Fossat's claim and sent the case back for determination of the exact location of the grant. Reverdy Johnson and J. A. Rockwell gave aid in presenting the government's cause, even though their interest was not in helping the United States but in protecting the Castillero claim. In writing the unanimous opinion, Justice Campbell criticized the government's reliance on private counsel for presentation of its cases. He noted that in preparation of the case on appeal from the board of land commissioners to the District Court, the law officers of the government seemed to have committed the preparation to the counsel for private interests, "who were allowed to maintain, in the name of the United States, the alternative of the issue tendered by the claimant." He asserted it as "the opinion of the court that the intervention of adversary claimants in the suit of a petitioner" was "a practice not to be encouraged."[62]

The United States Attorney in San Francisco chose to interpret the comment as rebuking merely "the entire surrender of those cases to third parties whose rights conflict as among themselves, without involving any right of the United States." He thought the government should be free to avail itself of information from any source, including private parties contending with each other. Furthermore, in view of the many duties of his office he was often needed in two places at once, and had to resort to the employment of assistant counsel, with resulting difficulties from sparseness of Congressional appropriations. He did not say whether private counsel at times received government employment to give them government status with only nominal compensation.[63] In

---

[59] Attorney General's Letter Book A–3, June 1, 1857, 7, 11.

[60] United States v. Fossat, 25 Fed. Cas. 1157 (No. 15137) (D.C.N.D. Cal. 1857).

[61] See J. A. Bayard to J. S. Black, Nov. 23, 1857, Black Papers.

[62] United States v. Fossat, 20 How. 413, 424–25 (1858).

[63] P. Della Torre to J. S. Black, July 19, 1858, Attorney General Papers.

the light of what the Supreme Court had said, Attorney General Black wrote to Edwin M. Stanton, then special counsel in land cases in California, that "no person ought to be recognized as speaking for the United States in any case of that kind, unless specially employed and paid for that purpose."[64]

The District Court determined three of the boundaries of the Fossat tract and left the other to be determined by a survey. Without waiting for the survey the United States, following the practice of appealing all cases, again appealed to the Supreme Court. When Black was urged to dismiss the appeal, presumably on the ground that it was premature, Reverdy Johnson, counsel for the Castillero interests, urged that he could not do so without affecting seriously the rights of the United States.[65] On a Fossat motion to dismiss the appeal on the ground that the decree of the District Court was not final, Johnson joined Black in opposing the motion, but the Court nevertheless granted it.[66] In the considerable time that passed before the case again returned to the Supreme Court, emphasis shifted to its rival, the Castillero case.

Because the Castillero interests were already working the mine, they were in no hurry to bring to completion litigation by which they might lose possession. To prevent this depletion of the ore, the United States sought and got from the Circuit Court, consisting of Judges McAllister and Hoffman, an injunction which closed the mine.[67] Thereafter, without trying to speed the litigation to a conclusion, the Castillero interests attempted in many ways to inveigle the government into commitments helpful to them and damaging to the government.[68] In spite of the fact that the use of depositions was limited by the Act of 1851 to those taken in the district with notice to the district attorney, the Castillero people asked permission to take depositions in Mexico, where, it was known, these people would have a decided advantage over the government. The Circuit Court denied permission.[69] The attempt was then made to take testimony in Mexico with cooperation of the United States legation there. The Attorney General objected and the Secretary of State refused to cooperate.[70] Castillero's counsel invoked

---

[64] J. S. Black to E. M. Stanton, Aug. 4, 1858, Attorney General Letter Book A–3, 275.

[65] Reverdy Johnson to J. S. Black, Nov. 20, 1858, Black Papers.

[66] United States v. Fossat, 21 How. 446 (1859).

[67] United States v. Parrott, 27 Fed. Cas. 416 (No. 15998) (C.C.N.D. Cal. 1858).

[68] For summary see the argument

of the then former Attorney General Black, United States v. Castillero, 2 Black 17, 102–04 (1863).

[69] United States v. Parrott, 27 Fed. Cas. 444 (No. 15999) (C.C.N.D. Cal. 1859).

[70] See J. S. Black to Lewis Cass, Apr. 22, 1859, Attorney General's Letter Book A–3, 415; Same to Same, Oct. 11, 15, 1859, Attorney General's Letter Book B–3, 215, 145.

the intervention of President Buchanan to force acceptance in evidence of documents believed to be forged and otherwise to give them aid. Buchanan referred the petition to Black, who in an official opinion explained the situation and advised against intervention.[71] Black complained to the Secretary of State that "The counsel of the claimants have had the freest access to all the papers of this office; and were furnished with every facility for making out their case that could be afforded consistently with what I supposed to be law and justice. I did for them works of supererogation, and conceded privileges which they were not entitled to. They were indeed denied no favor which they could decently ask."[72] Nevertheless Johnson and Rockwell again appealed to the President for favors which Black refused to grant. Buchanan merely forwarded the petition to Black, who restated his position.[73] Castillero counsel in California asked Judge McAllister to dissolve the injunction, but he refused.[74]

Government counsel in California reported to Black that the Almaden Mine party, despairing of obtaining through the courts the control of the mine, was now seeking to accomplish its ends through the machinery of politics. Its principal counsel, Archibald S. Peachy, had gotten himself elected to the California legislature to work for his client's cause. The death of United States Senator David C. Broderick in a duel with Judge David S. Terry of the California Supreme Court had worked to the advantage of the company, in that it was able to influence the election of its friend Milton S. Latham to the Senate. The press of San Francisco had been subsidized and the opinion of Judge McAllister had been denounced in leading editorials: "In a word, the New Almaden Co. is fast getting to be to California what the old U.S. Bank was to the Union!"[75]

Friends of the company secured adoption by the California legislature of a resolution asking California Senators and Representatives in Congress to work for dissolution of the injunction, saying that stoppage of work at the mine had been injurious to the people and dangerous to the mining interests of the state. Buchanan received a copy of the resolution and sent it to Black. Black replied that an injunction could be decreed only by a court and that to dissolve it was no less a judicial

---

[71] The Castillero Claim, 9 Op. Att'y Gen. 320 (1859).

[72] J. S. Black to Lewis Cass, Oct. 11, 1859, Attorney General's Letter Book B–3, 215.

[73] J. S. Black to James Buchanan, Dec. 1, 1859, Attorney General's Letter Book B–3, 178.

[74] Tully R. Wise to J. S. Black, Jan. 23, 1860, Attorney General Papers.

[75] John B. Williams to J. S. Black, Jan. 23, 1860, Attorney General Papers.

function.[76] He therefore urged that the application be refused and the matter left in the hands of the judiciary.[77]

A change took place in the office of United States Attorney during the year 1860—the departing occupant evidently leaving to engage in more lucrative private practice—and Black found himself inadequately informed about the status of the mass of the California land cases. In September he sent his son-in-law, James F. Shunk, to California with a summary account of each of the cases and with instructions to look into the business and make himself useful where he could. He warned Shunk that "It is not improbable that attempts will be made to annoy you by false and slanderous assaults through the newspapers. The New Almaden Mining Company alone keeps a score of hireling defamers in their constant pay. Do not be tempted to go out of your way for the purpose of repelling these missiles whether they be discharged at the Government, at me, or at yourself."[78] He reported to Shunk that Reverdy Johnson and Judah P. Benjamin had gone to California to handle the Castillero case in the District Court. For the United States the case would be handled by the United States Attorney, Calhoun Benham, and special counsel, Edmund M. Randolph. Shunk was to inform himself about the case but take no part in the argument.[79]

By the time the case was ready for argument later in the year, it had a record of such dimensions that the printing cost was nearly five thousand dollars,[80] and the total costs fifteen thousand dollars.[81] The Castellero interests, unable to get usable affidavits from people in Mexico, were said to have chartered a steamship to bring a load of them to California where the testimony could be taken under the watchful eye and counterquestioning of the United States Attorney. The trial covered

---

[76] J. S. Black to James Buchanan, July 12, 1860, Attorney General's Letter Book B-3, 369, 371-72. Black said of the Circuit Court that its ability and impartiality were unquestioned by either party or by anybody else. *Ibid.*, 380.

[77] As evidence of the concern of the California delegation about the matter see the letter of Senator William M. Gwin of June 28, 1860, to President Buchanan, asking for a copy of Black's written report, in the Attorney General Papers. Since this letter antedates the report, it may be that the report was written primarily to serve the needs of the Administra-

tion in Congress rather than merely to inform the President.

[78] J. S. Black to James F. Shunk, Sept. 5, 1860, Attorney General's Letter Book B-3, 424, 442.

[79] *Ibid.*, 426. As evidence of Randolph's concern lest the management of the case be taken from his hands see J. S. Black to E. M. Randolph, Sept. 29, 1860, Attorney General's Letter Book B-3, 459.

[80] The exact figure was $4,874.42. See Edwin M. Stanton to Valentine & Co., Mar. 4, 1861, Attorney General's Letter Book B-4, 29.

[81] Edward Bates to L. Trumbull, July 29, 1861, Attorney General's Letter Book B-5, 98.

791

a period of weeks and delved into innumerable intricate problems of law and conflicting statements of facts, with accusations of forgery and fraud. In San Francisco the case attracted attention comparable to major cases before the Supreme Court in Washington: "Day after day the court room was thronged with the beauty, wealth, and fashion of San Francisco. For the first time in the history of its judicial proceedings places were assigned to the gentler sex. The forensic discussion was worthy the cause and the scene. The fame of the speakers, the novelty of the questions, the magnitude of the prize at stake, rendered the occasion one of surpassing interest."[82]

When the case was decided on January 18, 1861, the Castillero interests won their claim to the immediate vicinity of the mine although not to the larger surrounding area,[83] and both parties appealed to the Supreme Court. When the new Administration came into power it found that, in spite of the fact that the dispute was still pending in the courts, the injunction had been dissolved with the consent of the outgoing district attorney and the company was back in possession of the mine. The Assistant Attorney General advised the new district attorney, "He had no authority to give any such consent, and should not have given it."[84]

Taking up the case where the Buchanan Administration had left off, Attorney General Edward Bates found himself hampered by difficulties similar to those which had hampered his predecessors. According to his letter to Lyman Trumbull, chairman of the Senate Judiciary Committee, the claimants had filed in the Supreme Court a transcript of the record of the case in the District Court consisting of several large printed volumes, but they refused to aid the government by permitting the record to be used in both appeals (the case being one of cross appeals). Since the record had been printed it would seem that the government should be able to get a copy at small cost, but the clerk of the District Court refused to certify a copy unless paid a total of thirty-four hundred dollars in advance. Since the clerk held his appointment from the court and not from the Administration, the government was in danger of having to meet his terms or see the time elapse during which the appeal could be taken. Bates therefore sent to Congress for enactment a bill providing that where both parties appealed, a record filed by either party was to be sufficient for both. It provided further that where a certified copy of a record was required, the district attorney might hire clerks to make the copy, and the clerk of the District Court,

---

[82] "Down in the Cinnebar Mines," *Harper's*, 31:545, 548, 1865.
[83] The opinion of Judge Hoffman is printed as part of the dissenting opinion of Justice Wayne in Castil-

lero v. United States, 2 Black 17, 214 (1863).
[84] T. J. Coffey to William H. Sharp, July 12, 1861, Attorney General's Letter Book B-4, 84.

under penalty of five thousand dollars for each refusal, was required to surrender records for the use of district attorneys.[85] The measure was enacted.[86]

For a time the government was unable to procure a copy of the record. A request to the district attorney at first brought no reply, creating anxiety lest accident or maneuvering on the West Coast prevent the government's appeal,[87] but the copy eventually appeared.[88]

Correspondence about the case reflected the complexity of interests among the parties and their counsel. One of them wrote grimly about corruption on the part of Judge Hoffman.[89] The president of the Quicksilver Mining Company, waiting to take over the mine if the old company lost, in irritation at the slowness of the government in preparing to argue the case spoke contemptuously of "Old father procrastination Bates."[90] The argument did not take place until the latter part of January, 1863. The geographical range of the interests involved is suggested by the fact that the claimants were represented by Archibald C. Peachy of California, Charles O'Conor of New York, and Reverdy Johnson of Maryland. Former Supreme Court Justice Benjamin R. Curtis appeared for the United States, and, of equal interest, former Attorney General Black appeared with Curtis, but for some of the private interests opposing the current operators of the mine. In his combined position as counsel and as Reporter for the Court, Black was able to highlight his own

---

[85] Edward Bates to L. Trumbull, July 29, 1861, Attorney General's Letter Book B–5, 98.

[86] 12 Stat. 319.

[87] T. J. Coffey to William H. Sharp, Oct. 5, 1861, Attorney General's Letter Book B–4, 159.

[88] The Washington correspondent of the *New York Tribune* noted that the record covered thirty-five hundred pages. "The decision will be one of the most important, involving as it does such immense interests, ever made by our Supreme Court." Reprinted in *Maryland News Sheet*, Jan. 2, 1862.

[89] "I am afraid that the Supreme Court will send us back for either Hoffman's action or a new survey, and Hoffman has been paid for intervening delays; and a rebuke from the Supreme Court would be what Hoffman would most pray for, as he thinks it would secure to him some of the ill gotten gains of the Almaden Company who have promised the protection and reward he covets more

than place and power—Money to live in Europe in elegance—this is his day dream and his nightly prayer.

"It is the machinery of the Court which gives me so much alarm in all this. They may presume the lower court to err in judgment but not in integrity; however much the Supreme Court may think Hoffman to be a scamp, but they will hardly say as much even by implication. If they could or would draw us away from Hoffman, all would be well, but it is a thankless gratuity for the Supreme Court to assume that a court below is dishonest; therefore before they will say so, they will push us back into the grasp of this corrupt tribunal, to be put off again and again and procrastinates till life is worn out and [we] have another case of 'Jarndyce vs. Jarndyce.'" James Eldredge to J. S. Black, Apr. 29, 1862, Black Papers.

[90] Samuel F. Butterworth to J. S. Black, June 9, 1862, Black Papers.

argument in the published volume. He began by saying that in terms of the bulk of the record and the magnitude of the interests at stake, this was probably the "heaviest" case ever heard before a judicial tribunal. Firmly believing the claim to be illegal and fraudulent, the United States had always met it with uncompromising hostility: "From first to last they have shown it nothing but the edge of the naked knife."[91] He told of the pressure put by the Castillero interests on the government, boldly proposing even *to take the counsel for both sides under their own pay.*" This proposal had been scornfully and indignantly rejected, and "the claimants were notified that from that time forth they must keep their distance."[92]

Once again the complicated story of the mine and the complex pattern of law and facts were presented. The docket of the Supreme Court shows that the case was before the Court January 21–22 and 26–30, 1863, for what was obviously prolonged and detailed discussion.

Some four weeks after the argument but before the decision was announced, Justice Swayne gave Attorney General Bates a hint of what the decision was likely to be. He intimated that steps should be taken to secure the interests of the government against the rush of squatters should the land turn out to belong to the government.[93] In a dispatch of March 9, the day before the decision was to be announced, the *New York Times* confidently stated what the decision would be, and got the facts completely reversed.[94] On March 10 Justice Clifford occupied three hours[95] reading the opinion of five members of the Court rejecting the claim of the Castillero interests and leaving the property in the hands either of the United States or of Fossat or other private groups. Justice Catron, dissenting with Justice Grier, deferred to Judge Hoffman's astuteness and knowledge of the facts,[96] and Justice Wayne adopted Judge Hoffman's fifty-eight–page opinion as his own.[97] The minutes of the Court for the date of the decision carry the statement that "Mr. Ch. Jus. Taney who was prevented by indisposition from attending, authorized Judge Clifford to say that he concurred in the opinion of the Court."[98]

One of the unique features of this case was the fact that former Attorney General Black, whose financial future had for a time looked so dark that he had had to accept a position as Reporter for the Supreme

---

[91] United States v. Castillero, 2 Black 17, 102 (1863).

[92] *Ibid.*, 103.

[93] "The Diary of Edward Bates," Howard K. Beale, ed., *Annual Report of the American Historical Association for the Year 1930*, 4:282, 1933.

[94] *New York Times*, Mar. 10, 1863.

[95] *Ibid.*, Mar. 11, 1863.

[96] 2 Black 211.

[97] *Ibid.*, 214.

[98] See also Castillero v. United States, 17 L. Ed. 360, 448 (1863).

Court, received a fee of one hundred and eighty thousand dollars, the largest paid in any of the California land cases.[99] Records of the fees of other counsel are not available. Benjamin R. Curtis received a mere three thousand dollars from the United States,[100] but the records do not show what, if anything, he may have received from private litigants.

While the Supreme Court decision determined that title to the New Almaden Mine could not be based on the Castillero claim, it did not settle the question as to who did own the property. Claims were asserted by the United States and by the Quicksilver Mining Company, and apparently by some other interests as well. The *New York Times*, again in error, asserted that the decision not only annihilated the title of the old company but also "makes that of the new company absolute and perfect." Indicative of the complications of ownership, it quoted Robert J. Walker as saying "with his habitual quiet, that his interest in the winning issue of the Almaden case was half a million dollars."[101]

Other individuals made profits out of the decision, under such circumstances as to raise the question whether the erroneous report about the decision might have been deliberately circulated. Leonard Swett of Bloomington, Illinois, a friend of President Lincoln and even more a friend of Justice Davis, thought he had a clue regarding the decision that was coming, and went to New York where he invested more than a hundred thousand dollars in the stock of the Quicksilver Mining Company, and thereafter made still further investments, which went up in value when the title of the Castillero interests was declared bad.[102] Soon afterward the President and his advisers decided to offer the Quicksilver Mining Company a contract whereby it would take over the mine and operate it pending litigation between that company and the United States to determine ownership. Leonard Swett was made the agent of the United States to negotiate with the company.[103] Swett prepared to go to California with a guaranteed fee of ten thousand dollars from the company, with still more if the company was satisfied with the results achieved.[104] President Lincoln made out to United States Marshal Charles W. Rand an order directing him in the light of

---

[99] William N. Brigance, *Jeremiah Sullivan Black*, 143.

[100] Notation of Feb. 14, 1863, in the Attorney General Papers.

[101] *New York Times*, Mar. 12, 1863.

[102] Leonard Swett to Mrs. Leonard Swett, Mar. 11, 1863, Davis Papers.

[103] Copy, J. P. Usher to S. F. Butterworth, May 6, 1863; Copy, J.

P. Usher to Leonard Swett, May 18, 1863, Lincoln Papers. See also Edward Bates to W. T. Otto, Mar. 21, 1863, Attorney General's Letter Book B–5, 410.

[104] Typewritten copy, Leonard Swett to William W. Orme, May 23, 1863, Davis Papers.

the Supreme Court decision to take possession of the property at the mine and turn it over to Swett.[105]

The old company and its friends determined not to surrender willingly. Letters began to pour in upon the President and his Cabinet. Former Senator Milton S. Latham assured Montgomery Blair that seizure of the mine would be regarded as a precedent, and all capital being timid, it would thereafter be hard to obtain capital to work rich mines conceded to be on "Uncle Sam's" domain.[106] Others apparently gave similar advice. Swett nevertheless went to California, accompanied by Samuel F. Butterworth, president of the Quicksilver Mining Company, and with the United States Marshal approached the mine to take possession. When they were met by a group of miners, armed and determined, they withdrew to get the help of United States troops.[107]

Pursuant to the authorization in the President's order, the marshal called for the aid of troops.[108] Frederick F. Low, then United States collector in San Francisco and later governor of California, along with other leading people, urged General George Wright not to use troops until orders could be checked in Washington, and proceeded to bombard various officials in Washington with protests against seizure of the mine. General Wright wired General-in-Chief Henry W. Halleck to urge that in the critical state of affairs on the Pacific Coast the President's order to take possession of the Almaden Mine should be deferred.[109] The President wired Swett and Low that they should consult together and avoid a riot or great difficulty in getting possession.[110]

Because of the number of departments involved, there was confusion of command in Washington. General Halleck wired General Wright that Secretary of War Stanton knew nothing of an order allowing the use of troops, and that if there was one it had been obtained surreptitiously. General Wright was to obey no order that did not come through proper channels.[111] Halleck wired John Parrott, one of the New

---

[105] Abraham Lincoln, *Collected Works*, VI, 205–06.

Judge Hoffman wrote to Justice Wayne a long letter criticizing the opinion of the Supreme Court written by Justice Clifford and saying, "The Agent of the Quicksilver Co. wielded all the powers of the Government. His threat of military dispossession, obliged the Almaden Co. to come to terms. The Agent of the Government here is a party to the negotiation, and of course the moment that the possession is transferred to the Quicksilver Mining Co. in which Mr. Swett is said to have a large interest, we shall hear no more

of Government interference to expel the possessors." David Hoffman to James M. Wayne, Sept. 3, 1863, Wayne Papers.

[106] Milton S. Latham to Montgomery Blair, May 4, 1863, Attorney General Papers.

[107] Edgar H. Bailey, "The New Almaden Quicksilver Mines," *California Natural Resources Bulletin, Geologic Guidebook of the San Francisco Bay Counties*, 154:264, 1951.

[108] *Ibid.*, 264.

[109] 50 O.R. (1st) Pt. 2, 515.

[110] *Ibid.*, 515.

[111] *Ibid.*, 518.

Almaden people, that there had been no military order to interfere with the New Almaden Mine.[112] One Frederick Billings nevertheless wired Halleck that troops had gotten as far as San Jose. There was great excitement, he reported, and unless the mandate was revoked California was in danger of being lost to the Union. Indeed, the people would not stand for it even if the mine were taken without the use of force.[113] Swett wired to General Wright that he had come to California to take possession of the mine and asked about a report that the writ had been countermanded.[114] Halleck wired Billings that the order was "surreptitiously obtained" and was suspended by direction of the Secretary of War.[115] Attorney General Bates was enraged at what he called Halleck's "*false* telegram," read it to the President and denounced it at a meeting of the Cabinet.[116] Presumably he knew that Halleck had earlier been an attorney for the company involved and had served it in an executive capacity,[117] and suspected him of continuing to serve it from his high military position.

Swett notified the President that lack of decisive action was working to the disadvantage of the government. He could have had possession of the mine had delay not been ordered. He could still get it. If the order was not to be executed, he should be authorized to apply for an injunction against operation of the mine and for appointment of a receiver.[118] Lincoln replied that many persons were telegraphing him from California begging him, for the peace of the state, to suspend military enforcement of the writ for the possession of the mine. Swett was the only one who urged to the contrary: "You know I would like to oblige you, but it seems to me my duty in this case is the other way."[119] It was undoubtedly true, as stated by General Wright, that although

---

[112] *Ibid.*, 518.

[113] *Ibid.*, 519–19.

[114] *Ibid.*, 519.

[115] *Ibid.*, 522.

[116] "The Diary of Edward Bates," Howard K. Beale, ed., *Annual Report of the American Historical Association for the Year 1930*, 4: 303–04, 1933.

[117] *Ibid.*, 303, n. 80. President Lincoln wrote to Frederick F. Low that there had been misunderstanding of the government's movement to take possession of the mine. The mine was peculiar in that while it was claimed on the basis of a Mexican grant, the Supreme Court had found the claim of the occupants to be utterly fraudulent. The government had therefore felt obligated to take possession, the Attorney General had made out the writ, and the President had signed it. It was not obtained surreptitiously, although General Halleck had presumably assumed it to have been so taken because he thought possession was to be taken by military order and he knew that he as general-in-chief had made no such order. The writ had been suspended on urgent representations from California, "simply to keep the peace." It had had no connection with any mine, place or person except the New Almaden mine and the persons connected with it. Lincoln, *Collected Works*, VI, 393–94.

[118] 50 O.R. (1st) Pt. 2, 523.

[119] *Ibid.*, 524.

the government disavowed intention to interfere with mining operations other than in connection with the New Almaden Mine, designing politicians inimical to the government would use the seizure to create the impression that the tenure of all mining interests was at the mercy of the government.[120]

After weeks of wrangling, Swett notified the President that, subject to approval and with the advice of the governor and other leading men, the case had been compromised in such a way as to respect the rights of the government. The President replied that he would be satisfied if the rights of the government were reserved.[121] It is said that immediately thereafter the Quicksilver Mining Company took possession of the mine on payment of $1,750,000 to the company operating the mine, through the arbitration of King William I of Prussia.[122] It seems to have been agreed that the company working the mine would give the United States a third of the proceeds pending final determination of title, and in the event of a decision in favor of the government would give peaceable possession.[123] Attorney General Bates noted in his diary the report that Swett and Ward H. Lamon, marshal of the District of Columbia and hence of the Supreme Court and also one of Lincoln's and Justice Davis' friends from Bloomington, Illinois, made a great deal of money in the New Almaden stock after Swett's return from California, and that Swett's arrangement for the possession of the mine had been made expressly to that end.[124]

It will be recalled that while in 1863 the Supreme Court found wholly invalid the Castillero claim on which the operators of the New Almaden Mine had been relying, the Court many years earlier had found the Fossat claim to be valid but had sent it back to the District Court for determination of its boundaries. The particular concern, of course, was whether the grant included the mining ridge in which this and other mines were located. Proceedings in the Fossat case were delayed as a result of an Act of Congress in 1860 authorizing intervention of third parties in connection with government surveys.[125] The case was argued in the Supreme Court over a period of several days in late February and early March, 1864. Chief Justice Taney, who had been absent during the argument of the Castillero case, was absent at this argument as well. At one stage proceedings had to be suspended for a

---

[120] Ibid., 524.
[121] Ibid., 596.
[122] Bailey, "The New Almaden Quicksilver Mines," California National Resources Bulletin, Geologic Guidebook of the San Francisco Bay Counties, 154:264, 1951.

[123] New York Times, Feb. 13, 1864.
[124] "The Diary of Edward Bates," Howard K. Beale, ed., Annual Report of the American Historical Association for the Year 1930, 4:338, 1933.
[125] 12 Stat. 33.

few days because Justice Grier was incapacitated by a fall.[126] The array of counsel, for the government and for Fossat (or the Quicksilver Mining Company) and intervenors, included Attorney General Bates, J. A. Wills, Jeremiah S. Black, Caleb Cushing, J. M. Carlisle, John B. Williams, and Reverdy Johnson. Bates, who made here one of his few presentations in Court, recorded that the government had against it three former Attorneys General in Johnson, Cushing, and Black. For two of them he seems to have had appropriate deference. About Cushing he had only unkind remarks, characterizing him as a man of very little knowledge though a good deal of learning, and "destitute of morals."[127] He thought Cushing had excited the "implacable disgust" of the Court by his manner of handling the case, but was nevertheless offended by Justice Grier's loud whisper to him about Cushing: "Ef you speak, give that damned Yankee hell." Justice Grier, he said, was a natural-born vulgarian, and, by long habit, coarse and harsh.[128]

On some days of the argument the courtroom was crowded with spectators, among them speculators in mining stock. Bates noted that Swett, "who made the shameful arrangement about the mine last year," became frightened at the power of the government's argument and sold his stock at a loss of thirty thousand dollars.[129] The *New York Times* reported that the argument "caused quite a fluttering among the Quick Silver speculators."[130] So intricate were the questions of geography, of surveys, of descriptions in the Spanish language, of jurisdiction of both the District Court and the Supreme Court, and of procedure generally that the prolonged arguments ended with a highly confused picture as to what the Court was likely to do. It was said from time to time between the close of the argument and the decision that the judges were "unusually reticent" about the decision,[131] and that they had "on all occasions, repelled every attempt to sound them."[132]

The decision of the Court, announced April 4 by Justice Nelson with only Justice Clifford dissenting, adhered to the earlier decision that the Fossat claim was valid, and accepted the determination of boundaries as worked out by the District Court and the Surveyor General. It therefore found the mine included within the Fossat tract, hence in the possession of the Quicksilver Mining Company, and the United States was denied the right of possession. It appears from the argument and from the opinion of the Court that the office of the Attorney General, in its preoccupation with the Castillero case, may have neglected to give

---

[126] "The Diary of Edward Bates," Howard K. Beale, ed., *Annual Report of the American Historical Association for the Year 1930*, 4:341, 1933.
[127] *Ibid.*, 339.
[128] *Ibid.*, 340.

[129] *Ibid.*, 342.
[130] *New York Times*, Feb. 26, 1864. See also the *Times* of the preceding day.
[131] *Ibid.*, Mar. 30, 1864.
[132] *Ibid.*, Apr. 2, 1864.

adequate protection to the rights of the United States in the Fossat case. Justice Clifford, speaking only for himself, declared that for his part he was not willing to cast upon the office of the Attorney General responsibility for depriving the government of twenty million dollars in property or to base such a decision on a mere technicality: "Patient and thorough investigation has convinced me that the title to the quicksilver mine is in the United States, and it shall never pass into other hands by my vote while that conviction remains, although I may stand alone."[133] Attorney General Bates, in the discomfort of defeat, predicted that the judgment would cost the Court a great deal of mortification and that it would be many years before the Court could retrace its steps back to good doctrine.[134]

These cases exemplify the variety and dimensions of the California land claims which provided grist for the Supreme Court. As for total figures, Attorney General Black estimated in 1860 that the value of lands claimed under grants ascertained to be forged was probably not less than one hundred fifty million dollars. He wrote to President Buchanan:

A very large portion of the best mineral and agricultural region in California, the ports, commercial points, sites for fortifications, light houses and other national purposes, were covered by Mexican grants, real or fabricated. In all the territory conquered or purchased from Mexico, there seemed to be not an island or place for a fort, a custom house, hospital or post office, but must be purchased upon his own terms, from some private claimant under a pretended title from Alvarado, Micheltorena, or Pio Pico. It was incredible that such grants could have been made in good faith by any government.[135]

The task of handling the complex problems of litigation on the far side of a country not yet spanned by railroads, and during much of the period not even spanned by telegraph, was enormously difficult. Government compensation for legal services was low in comparison with that provided by the more opulent of the land and mineral monopolists, and success in government employment was apt to lead to private employment that was more lucrative. The men appointed as United States Attorneys, or district attorneys as they were still called much of the time, were apt to be more highly skilled as politicians than as lawyers. As for Calhoun Benham, the last of the United States Attorneys appointed

---

[133] Fossat v. United States, 2 Wall. 649, 727–28 (1864).

[134] "The Diary of Edward Bates," Howard K. Beale, ed., *Annual Report of the American Historical Association for the Year 1930*, 4:354, 1933.

[135] J. S. Black to James Buchanan, May 22, 1860, Attorney General's Letter Book B–3, 316.

for California by President Buchanan, Black's nephew found him a superficial and effective politician but not much concerned about his legal duties, remarking as to certain cases that "Benham knows little and *cares* less about these claims."[136] Black, however, to keep Benham in office or to promote his diligence, encouraged him to accept fees from private parties when doing so was not inconsistent with his duties to the United States.[137] Government efforts had been greatly boosted by sending Stanton to California in 1858, and presumably Black hoped for similar results from sending Shunk there in 1860, although he may also have had in mind the possibility that Shunk would do for him what he did do, namely, line up profitable business for Black and himself after Black was out of office. Shunk brought into employment as special counsel John B. Williams, who had formerly worked in the United States Attorney's office and who continued to serve the government under the Lincoln Administration, but Williams also worked for private clients and aided in securing retainers for Black in Washington.

When no longer Attorney General, Black saw no reason why he should not receive compensation from the government and from private clients in the same cases. In one case Attorney General Bates agreed to let Black participate in an argument along with government counsel but refused to retain him in view of the fact that he was also to be employed by California settlers.[138] In a later case the Assistant Attorney General declined to pay Black a fee of five hundred dollars, saying, "You know that we have adopted the policy of paying but nominal fees in cases where counsel are employed by the settlers. The Galbraith case[139] is one of this kind and in handing you the record we not only took into account your preeminent and conceded legal knowledge and your commanding and recognized intellectual power, to say nothing of your sentient and moral faculties, but also the fact that you were already counsel for the squatters and would be well paid by them, and we considered it immensely proper that they should pay you for doing work in which they have so much more interest than the United States."[140]

The Attorney General's office began to find it irksome, indeed, that the government should have to conduct boundary litigation in its name and at its expense when the real parties in interest were claimants from Mexican grants on the one hand and settlers on the other. There was discussion of a possible statute under which the litigation would be

---

[136] James F. Shunk to J. S. Black, Nov. 23, 1860, Black Papers.

[137] J. S. Black to Calhoun Benham, Sept. 29, 1860, Attorney General's Letter Book B-3, 456.

[138] T. J. Coffey to J. S. Black, Sept. 19, 1861, Black Papers.

[139] United States v. Galbraith, 2 Black 394 (1863).

[140] T. J. Coffey to J. S. Black, Sept. 11, 1862, Black Papers.

conducted by the real parties.[141] The settlers were quite willing and eager to have the government serve as their litigating agent, and no such legislation was enacted within this period.

Attorney General Bates continued Black's practice of automatically appealing to the Supreme Court all cases lost in the District Court, as a means of seeing that no important government interest was neglected. When Vice President Hannibal Hamlin urged him to drop an appeal in a case involving a friend, Bates declined to interfere with the normal course of events, even though he admitted that it would be possible for him to do so were it not for the pressure of work in his office. But he also declined to take a different kind of responsibility in California when asked to do so by the attorney general of that state. As a result of a decision against them it was reported that a band of a thousand settlers had armed and entrenched themselves to resist a court decree which would oust them from land on which they had settled. Bates turned down a plea by saying that he had no power or right to interfere with the judgment as it stood or with its execution.[142]

One other set of cases, too intricate and prolonged for presentation in detail, warrants brief mention. Title to another quicksilver mine was the prize to be won. The story seems more fiction than fact, and indeed was used by Bret Harte as the basis for his novel *The Story of a Mine*. The tract claimed was Panoche Grande, and the mine, the New Idria, was some one hundred miles to the southeast of the New Almaden Mine.

The tract was claimed by Vincente Gomez, who tried to prove a grant by parol evidence, alleging that the original papers had been destroyed. Before the board of land commissioners, which rejected his claim, and before the United States District Court for the Southern District of California, Gomez was greatly aided by his attorney, Pacificus Ord, who while serving in that capacity got himself appointed United States Attorney for the district and received from Gomez title to half his claim. Without disclosing his own involvement, Ord persuaded another attorney to present the Gomez claim before Judge Isaac Ogier as one to which the government had no objection, whereupon the judge, in spite of its rejection by the board of land commissioners, confirmed it without looking further into the matter.

Without allowance of an appeal to the Supreme Court by Judge Ogier, Ord then sought to eliminate the possibility of reversal of the decision by the Supreme Court by sending up a copy of the record as

---

[141] T. J. Coffey to John B. Williams, Mar. 4, 1862, Attorney General's Letter Book B–5, 25, 27.

[142] Edward Bates to F. M. Pixley, Sept. 10, 1862, Attorney General's Letter Book B–5, 192.

if the appeal had been allowed; thereafter, when the United States, as the supposedly appealing party, failed to proceed with the appeal within the time limit prescribed, the Court granted the request that the appeal be docketed and dismissed. Discovering that the government had been tricked in the matter, Attorney General Black asked the Court to vacate its order so that an appeal might be prosecuted. Some suggestion of the dimensions of the interests at stake is found in the fact that as opposing counsel he faced Reverdy Johnson and R. H. Gillet, men who did not touch such litigation unless there was prospect of high returns. Recounting the unsavory history of the case and speaking for a unanimous Court, Justice Wayne granted the motion of the Attorney General.[143]

Upon the disclosure of operations of which he had evidently been unaware, Judge Ogier vacated the decree and reopened the case. He died before further action could be taken, however, and was replaced by Judge Fletcher M. Haight, who was described by a touring geologist as a wealthy San Francisco gentleman who had a fine ranch near Monterey and spent part of each year there.[144] Judge Haight set aside the order reopening the case on the ground that the judge issuing it could not reopen it after the close of the term at which it was issued, but remarked that the parties were not without remedy by appeal or otherwise.[145] Attorney General Bates then directed United States Attorney B. C. Whiting to take an appeal and have a copy of the record transmitted to the Clerk of the Supreme Court. Judge Haight, however, directed the clerk of the District Court not to provide transcripts in cases in which no appeal was taken, and took the position that there could be no appeal in this case because the time limit of five years had been passed. For many months no reason for the clerk's refusal was given, and the Attorney General continued to press him and the United States Attorney and special counsel for a certified copy of the record.

Finally the Attorney General wrote a scathing letter to Judge Haight himself. He had not seen the record, said Bates, "because the clerk of your court flatly refuses to let me have a transcript." He could not have the record "without the good will and pleasure of your clerk who seems to regard himself as vested with plenary powers over the records of your court." If Haight himself had any influence with the clerk, "I beg you to exert it in my behalf." Bates proceeded to quote from documents in further proceedings in Judge Haight's court in which

---

[143] United States v. Gomez, 23 How. 326 (1860).

[144] William H. Brewer, *Up and Down California in 1860–1864*, 106.

[145] Edward Bates to John P. Usher, May 23, 1863, Attorney General's Letter Book C, 159, 161.

Judge Haight had allegedly said that procuring copies of records on behalf of the United States where no appeal was pending was "a fraud upon the government and not to be tolerated," adding that in this case the government had no interests and he would not certify an account for copies at the expense of the United States. Bates pretended to believe that the document was not authentic, noting that certifying expenses was not the responsibility of the judge. The letter was in effect a blistering attack on the conduct of the judge.[146]

Copies of the Bates letter to Judge Haight were circulated among the people involved. E. L. Goold, who was at once special counsel for the United States and counsel for the New Idria interests—the private interests opposed to the Gomez claimants—wrote to J. S. Black that the Bates letter to Haight was a "scorcher," and that Haight had said there were portions of it that his self-respect forbade him to answer. He reported Judge Hoffman as saying that in the light of his conduct in this case it should be agreed in San Francisco that no gentlemen would recognize Haight.[147]

Judge Haight did, however, attempt a plausible explanation to Bates, giving it as his opinion that in the light of the principle that court decrees should be regarded as stable, Judge Ogier's decree could not be vacated even though fraud had been involved; that there could be no appeal to the Supreme Court because more than five years had passed since the Ogier decision in 1857; and that no certified transcript need be submitted where no appeal was possible.[148]

Judge Haight did send copies of the relevant papers in the case, but, significantly, he did not have them certified as the record, and it was increasingly apparent that he was determined to prevent an appeal. "As to Panoche Grande," he wrote in his letter of enclosure, "you are undoubtedly aware that the parties in possession claim under school land warrants and the other side under grant and confirmation. In this as in other cases, private interests stimulate prejudices, and it is quite probable as in the New Almaden case the government will shake the bush and others catch the bird."[149]

Bates was determined to "shake the bush" no matter who caught the bird, and not to be prevented by judges or their clerks. He continued to press for a certified copy of the record. The United States Attorney was not inclined to fight the local judge, particularly since he was not being paid for his work in the case, while Goold, special

---

[146] Edward Bates to Fletcher M. Haight, June 1, 1863, Attorney General's Letter Book C, 171.

[147] E. L. Goold to J. S. Black, Aug. 28, 1863, Black Papers.

[148] F. M. Haight to Edward Bates, July 4, 1863, Attorney General Papers.

[149] F. M. Haight to Edward Bates, July 25, 1863, Attorney General Papers.

counsel, was being paid by both the United States and the New Idria Mining Company.[150]

It was Isaac Hartman, the other special counsel in the case, who devised the scheme whereby the Attorney General was to outwit the judge and the clerk and get a certified transcript. The documents which Haight had sent to Bates were to be sent to Hartman in San Francisco— so that mail or express would not come under the eyes of the clerk as they might if sent to the office of the United States Attorney in Monterey. Hartman would then take them to Whiting. Whiting, who had the power to do so under the 1861 statute, would then certify them as the official record and send them back to Washington.[151] This arrangement was carried out.[152]

The case came before the Supreme Court in April, 1864, by motion on the part of Gomez to dismiss the appeal, on the ground, among others, that the five-year period for appeal had passed and that there was not a properly certified record. Taking advantage of what may have been negligence on the part of Judge Ogier, in that though the case had been decided in 1857 the decree had not been entered until 1858, the Supreme Court held that the appeal had been taken in time. As for the transcript, if the Justices knew of the struggle that had been going on, they kept the fact officially concealed. They found that the certificate had been made by an officer authorized by law to make it, and they were unable to "perceive that it is fatally defective." To grant the motion "would be to leave the decree below in full force and unreversed, which is a result that at present we are not prepared to sanction."[153] The Court therefore left itself in position to hear the case on the merits.

At this point the case disappears into the post-Taney period, with further litigation to come.[154] In a volume of his history published in 1888, Hubert Howe Bancroft said that the case bade fair never to end, the parties being indefatigable in seeking relief from the courts and from Congress.[155] Judge Haight seems to have predicted correctly that if birds were caught when the government shook the tree the catchers would be private parties and not the government itself.

Soon after Lincoln took office members of that Adminstration began reconsideration of the arrangement whereby an independent circuit

---

[150] B. C. Whiting to Edward Bates, Aug. 17, 1863, Attorney General Papers. See also B. C. Whiting to E. L. Goold, Aug. 2, 1863, Black Papers.

[151] Isaac Hartman to T. J. Coffey, Aug. 17, 1863, Attorney General Papers.

[152] Isaac Hartman to T. J. Coffey, Oct. 21, 1863, Attorney General's Letter Book C, 293.

[153] United States v. Gomez, 1 Wall. 690, 702 (1864).

[154] See United States v. Gomez, 3 Wall. 752 (1866); Cox *ex rel.* McGarrahan, 9 Wall. 298 (1870).

[155] Bancroft, *The Works of H. H. Bancroft*, VI, 553.

judgeship had been established uniquely in California. From the single published volume of Judge McAllister's decisions, from the year 1855 to 1859, it is clear that his presence as circuit judge relieved the district judges, or at any rate Judge Hoffman of the northern district, of a great deal of circuit work that had to be done in some court. Judge McAllister seems during these years to have been a man of considerable professional ability. In January, 1862, however, the United States Marshal for the northern district wrote to President Lincoln that Judge McAllister's health was such that he was not capable of discharging the ordinary duties of his office. He would either be compelled to resign or he would have to be ousted by reorganization of the judiciary.[156] One of the subordinates of Secretary of the Treasury Salmon P. Chase made a similar report, and expressed the belief that Judge Hoffman, for all his high reputation as a jurist, should not be promoted to the position of circuit judge because he was needed in the District Court for the special work in connection with land cases with which he was familiar.[157]

Attorney General Bates, troubled about the matter, wrote to the United States Attorney in San Francisco that at the request of the Senators from California he had granted McAllister a six-month leave of absence. He thought the California circuit an anomaly and he had never seen need of it. He would be pleased if Congress decided to abandon the circuit, creating as many District Courts as might be needed.[158] Members of Congress began to express concern about the matter,[159] and the President sent Bates a resolution from the House of Representatives asking whether Judge McAllister had left California, and if so for what reason and for what length of time, and by what authority of law he had absented himself from his official duties. Bates was able to give little information beyond the fact that a leave had been granted and that such leaves seemed to be granted as a matter of course.[160]

In January, 1863, writing from New York where one of his sons lived, Judge McAllister resigned.[161] On March 3 the President signed a bill creating a tenth judicial circuit on the Pacific Coast,[162] and on March 10 the Senate confirmed the President's nomination of Stephen J. Field, chief justice of the Supreme Court of California, for the new circuit and the new position on the Supreme Court.

---

[156] William Rabe to A. Lincoln, Jan. 8, 1862, Attorney General Papers.

[157] D. N. Cheesman to S. P. Chase, Apr. 19, 1862, Chase Papers.

[158] Edward Bates to W. H. Sharp, Apr. 26, 1862, Attorney General's Letter Book B–5, 75.

[159] For Bates' refusal to give members of Congress copies of corres-

pondence in his files about Judge McAllister, see Bates to T. G. Phelps, Apr. 30, 1862, Attorney General's Letter Book B–5, 80.

[160] Edward Bates to A. Lincoln, June 12, 1862, *ibid.*, 127.

[161] M. Hall McAllister to Abraham Lincoln, Jan. 12, 1863, Attorney General Papers.

[162] 12 Stat. 794.

While there is no doubt that the importance of the California land cases and Field's familiarity with the land problems led to the establishment of the new position and his appointment, it is hard to appraise the scope of his contribution, which of course was made for the most part after the end of the Taney period. During the term of the Supreme Court beginning in December, 1863, he wrote the opinion of the Court in six of the ten California land cases. Yet he did not speak for the Court or otherwise express himself in the important Fossat case, discussed above.

During his first term, indeed, his most important contribution in the California land area may have been in the legislative rather than the judicial province. According to John B. Williams, an attorney active in California land cases, Field worked with Senator John Conness of California in an attempt to combine the clerkship of the Circuit and District courts in San Francisco, thereby giving Field the appointment of the clerk for both courts. More important, he tried to consolidate once more the northern and southern districts, thereby vacating both positions, and secure appointment of a devoted friend to the new position.[163]

If Field made such attempts, and it seems probable that he did so at least in part, his efforts failed; but, as demonstrated by his own record, he succeeded with respect to land legislation in another area. Land titles in San Francisco had been insecure, not merely because of alleged grants claimed by Limantour and others but because of the right of the city itself to the four square leagues granted under Mexican law to each pueblo. The board of land commissioners had confirmed to the city part but not all of that area. The United States had appealed as to the tract that was confirmed and the city had appealed as to the portion not confirmed. The United States had dropped its appeal but with no final settlement in the matter. The city's appeal had never been heard in the District Court, perhaps because of Judge Hoffman's personal interest in the property, which had become immensely valuable, with vast confusion as to titles resulting from failure to determine the validity of the original grant.

If Justice Field and Senator Conness failed with respect to part of their legislative strategy, they also succeeded in part through the enactment of a statute of which Field drafted major sections.[164] One section of the statute surrendered to the city of San Francisco so much of the four square leagues of land as lay within the incorporating boundaries of the city. Another was calculated to have the title of the

---

[163] John B. Williams to Ogden Hoffman, May, 12, 1864, Huntington Library.

[164] For Field's account of his participation in the legislation see his *Personal Reminiscences of Early Days in California*, 160–61, 241–42.

remainder of the four square leagues judicially determined by transferring the dormant case from the District Court to the Circuit Court where it would be heard by Justice Field. It provided that whenever the district judge of any District Court in California was interested in any claim on appeal from the board of commissioners the case should be transferred to the Circuit Court.[165]

As a result of this transfer the case was heard by Justice Field and decided on October 31, 1864. He upheld the claim of the city to the entire tract, except for the areas of some installations of the United States.[166] The decision redounded to the benefit not so much of the city as of persons who had long held property under grants from the city. It dashed the hopes of persons who claimed under the preemption laws of the United States.

Field had no more than departed for Washington when John B. Williams, counsel for the unsuccessful parties and evidently still in some matters special counsel for the United States, filed a motion for a rehearing, in which the United States Attorney joined on instructions from the Attorney General. Williams alleged that the case had been decided under a misapprehension in that the clerk of the Circuit Court had suppressed his brief as special counsel of the United States.[167] Judge Hoffman, watching the case from the sidelines, was said to have expressed the opinion that the clerk had no right to withhold the brief from Judge Field.[168] Williams apparently did not dare directly challenge the integrity of Justice Field, but he tried at first to bring the rehearing before Judge Hoffman alone. According to Justice Field, the district attorney refused to participate in such an arrangement, which, in light of the fact that Hoffman had not sat in the case, would have been "to ask him to do an act of judicial discourtesy."[169] Williams then tried to arrange that the hearing would be before "a full bench," which would have meant that Judge Hoffman would sit with Justice Field, but he failed here also.[170]

When Justice Field returned to California the following summer he sat alone in the Circuit Court, heard the motion for a rehearing, took upon himself responsibility for the handling of Williams' brief as in reality counsel for outside parties, scolded him soundly for his conduct,

---

[165] 13 Stat. 332, 333.
[166] San Francisco v. United States, 21 Fed. Cas. 365 (No. 12316) (C.C.-N.D. Cal. 1864).
[167] Ibid., 371. See also John B. Williams to Edward Bates, Nov. 12, 1864, and to J. Hubley Ashton, Dec. 2, 1864, Attorney General Papers.

[168] San Francisco Evening Bulletin, Nov. 25, 1864, from a clipping filed with John B. Williams to J. Hubley Ashton, Dec. 2, 1864, Attorney General Papers.
[169] 21 Fed. Cas. 371.
[170] John B. Williams to J. Hubley Ashton, Dec. 28, 1864, Ashton Papers.

and denied the motion.[171] Because of dissatisfaction with different parts of the decree, both the United States and San Francisco appealed. Justice Field maintained that in a case transferred from the District Court to the Circuit Court there was no right of appeal. The Supreme Court, with Field and two other Justices dissenting, decided this question against him.[172] Before the case could be argued on its merits in the Supreme Court, Justice Field drafted a bill to confirm the title of the city to the lands in dispute. It was introduced in Congress by members of the California delegation and passed.[173] As a result the appeals in the Supreme Court were dismissed.[174]

As already suggested, members of the Supreme Court (with the exception of Justice Field) seem to have preserved with respect to the dramatic and highly controversial and sometimes malodorous land claims from California an aloofness comparable to their geographical distance from that area. If they were sometimes confused, both as to law and facts, they shared their confusion with almost everybody else involved. Justice Field brought close knowledge of the subject to the Court, but he also brought criticism, of which one of the milder statements is that of Bancroft: "It might reasonably be questioned whether a judge should be allowed so far to interfere with matters originating in another court as to procure an act of Congress transferring it to his own court."[175] It remained true throughout the litigation that the participation of the United States was usually but a cover for the interests of some private party. Whatever the outcome of particular cases, the United States seldom stood to gain a great deal. In the exceptional case, that of the New Almaden Mine, expediency in terms of saving the Union jeopardized its chances of victory, and the case was ultimately lost anyway. From the point of view of hindsight it now seems clear that much confusion with respect to land ownership could have been prevented had Congress, immediately after the acquisition of California, established a clear policy with adequate administrative machinery. But Congress was then concerned primarily with the issues of the Compromise of 1850 and the threat of civil war. The discovery of gold had taken place, the westward stream of population was flowing, and the transformation of seemingly worthless land into a rich heritage was under way before policy had

---

[171] 21 Fed. Cas. 371.

[172] United States *ex rel.* Attorney General v. Judges of Circuit Court, 3 Wall. 673 (1866).

[173] Bancroft, *The Works of H. H. Bancroft*, VI, 232.

[174] See Townsend v. Greeley, 5 Wall. 326 (1867).

[175] Bancroft, *The Works of H. H. Bancroft*, VI, 231. It also brought an attack on his life. For discussion see Field's *Personal Reminiscences*, 164–69.

been established. The courts had to work in the context of social and economic as well as legal confusion. In any event, the California land cases gave the Supreme Court large responsibilities at a time when war was keeping the judiciary in the background.

CHAPTER XXXII

Lincoln's Appointments to the Court

T HE SUMMARY STORY of President Lincoln's appointments to the Supreme Court prior to the death of Chief Justice Taney in October, 1864, is that he added four members to that tribunal. The four, with the dates of their nominations, were: Noah H. Swayne of Ohio, January 21, 1862; Samuel F. Miller of Iowa, July 16, 1862; David Davis of Illinois, October 17, 1862; and Stephen J. Field of California, March 6, 1863. Yet Lincoln's preoccupation with Supreme Court personnel goes far beyond this summary statement. Consideration of those proposed for appointment got entangled with the issues of the sectional conflict, with problems of keeping particular states in the Union, with obligations of the President to friends who had served him before and after the election, and with problems of the rearrangement of judicial circuits to include states not yet incorporated into them.

Early on the morning of March 5, 1861, before Edward Bates of Missouri had qualified as Lincoln's Attorney General, Secretary of State William H. Seward entered upon his duties and, with a characteristic assumption of authority, asked Edwin M. Stanton, the outgoing Attorney General, to draw up a nomination of John J. Crittenden for membership on the Supreme Court in the position vacated by Justice Daniel.[1] Crittenden, born in Kentucky and now nearly seventy-four years of age, had served prominently in each of the two houses of Congress, had been Attorney General in each of two Whig Administrations, and was a distinguished member of the bar who had appeared many times before the Supreme Court. His appeal at this time, however, lay primarily in the fact that, coming from Kentucky, he represented a border state which had not yet committed itself with respect to seces-

---

[1] Edwin M. Stanton to James Buchanan, Mar. 10, 1861, *Works of James Buchanan*, John Cassett Moore, ed., XI, 163.

sion and which the Lincoln Administration would willingly pay a high price to keep in the Union. Lincoln was reported to have said, indeed, that he hoped to have God on his side, but he *must* have Kentucky.[2] During the final Congress of the Buchanan Administration, Crittenden had achieved unusual prominence through his sponsorship of the so-called Crittenden Compromise, designed to save the Union by writing into the Constitution in unamendable form a commitment to the earlier Missouri Compromise, which Congress under proslavery pressure had abandoned by enactment of the Kansas-Nebraska Act of 1854, and a guarantee against interference with slavery in the slave states even by constitutional amendment. But the rift between the North and the South was already too great to permit majority support of the Crittenden Compromise from either side. On the Northern side, for example, Gideon Welles, soon to be Lincoln's Secretary of the Navy, characterized Crittenden as an old Whig compromiser who was restating the Breckenridge platform and wanted the Republicans to adopt it as a compromise.[3]

Newspapers picked up the report that Crittenden was to be nominated for the Supreme Court and confirmed if possible at the continued session of the Senate which was to act on Cabinet and other nominations.[4] It began to appear, however, that like the compromise bearing his name, his nomination would be opposed from both extremes in the Senate, and that it might share the fate of that of Jeremiah S. Black. So it seems that the Crittenden nomination, if indeed he had ever been the choice of President Lincoln, was never submitted.

While the possibility of Crittenden's nomination was being discussed, the name of Joseph Holt, likewise from Kentucky, was also prominently mentioned.[5] Stanton predicted to Buchanan that Holt would be nominated, saying that he now appeared to be the favorite of the Republicans. He predicted that Holt, most recently Buchanan's Secretary of War, who had remained in office a few days under Lincoln, would "receive the nomination of Supreme Judge as a reward for what he terms his efforts to arrest the downward course of public affairs at the time he became Secretary of War."[6]

Holt, born in 1807, had achieved early prominence, particularly

---

[2] E. Merton Coulter, *The Civil War and Readjustment in Kentucky*, 53.
[3] Gideon Welles to Edgar T. Welles, Feb. 1, 1861, Welles Papers.
[4] See *Baltimore American*, Mar. 7, 8, 9, 14, 1861; *Baltimore Sun*, Mar. 8, 9, 11, 13, 1861; *New York World*, Mar. 7, 9, 1861; *New York Times*,

Mar. 15, 1861; *New York Herald*, Mar. 20, 1861. See also materials presented in Charles Warren, *The Supreme Court in United States History*, II, 365–66.
[5] *New York Evening Post*, Mar. 8, 1861.
[6] Buchanan, *Works*, XI, 163–64.

as a prosecutor. Eager to establish a fortune, he had gone to Mississippi in the 1830s, reaped substantial fees from the prosperity of the period and then from the results of the panic of 1837, and as a result of shrewd investments was able to retire from practice and return to Louisville as a man of substance. In 1850 his second marriage had allied him with the socially and politically prominent Wickliffe family. He supported Buchanan for the Presidency in 1856, and as a reward was appointed Commissioner of Patents in 1857, and established his home in Washington. Moving speedily up the political ladder, he was made Postmaster General in 1859. In that position he defended slavery interests by supporting a local rule in Virginia for excluding abolitionist materials from the mails, and he denounced as unconstitutional the personal liberty laws of the North. He was no friend of secession, however, or of the secession leader, Jefferson Davis, and when the secessionist John B. Floyd resigned as Buchanan's Secretary of War, Holt replaced him and joined with Stanton and Black in avoiding a pro-secessionist position.[7]

Although it was probably War Department business that brought Holt into contact with Lincoln, the association was noted by political observers and conclusions were drawn. Charles Eames, a lawyer who was later to appear prominently in connection with Civil War litigation, wrote to him confidently as "the future Justice of the Supreme Court," and invited him to tea at his home with Attorney General Bates.[8] Although no nomination at all was made at this time, and Holt was never nominated to the Supreme Court, he developed an increasingly close relationship with the Administration, his name was mentioned from time to time as a possibility, and he may well have been seriously considered on a number of occasions and his availability may have played a part in the controversy over rearrangement of the circuits, discussed below. It was the impression of Rose O'Neal Greenhow, notorious woman spy for the Confederacy, that both Crittenden and Holt, subject to the conflicting pressures prevalent in the border states, had been won over to a degree of commitment to the Union, "bribed with the same bait—a seat on the Supreme Court bench." In any event, whereas Crittenden returned to Kentucky and successfully sought election to the House of Representatives as an advocate of the state's neu-

---

[7] For an account of Holt's life and his service to the Lincoln Administration see Mary Bernard Allen, *Joseph Holt, Judge Advocate General (1862–1865), A Study in the Treatment of Political Prisoners by* *the United States Government During the Civil War.*

[8] Charles Eames to Joseph Holt, Mar. 8, 1861, Holt Papers. For the Greenhow comment see Ishbel Ross, *Rebel Rose: Life of Rose O'Neal Greenhow, Confederate Spy,* 96.

trality (leading a friend of Holt's to predict that his course would "precipitate Kentucky into disunion"[9]) Holt announced himself as a staunch defender of the Union. He wrote to Buchanan that now that the South had begun an unprovoked and malignant war upon the United States, he was for prosecuting the war at whatever cost.[10] He made speeches and wrote letters which were circulated far and wide for the purpose of keeping Kentucky in the Union and aiding the Union cause generally.[11] He aided the Administration in correcting financial mismanagement in military affairs and made himself generally useful.[12]

It was not until September, 1862, that Lincoln found a permanent position for Holt. He was made Judge Advocate General in the War Department under Stanton, who by that time held the top post, and was given the assignment of reviewing military trials. It was expected that as a Kentuckian he would be much more acceptable to the country than an abolitionist from the North. As holder of the office he became a staunch defender of the exercise of power by military tribunals, to such an extent that after the war he broke with his friend David Davis, who spoke for the Supreme Court in the *Milligan* case, which limited the scope of the authority of military tribunals.[13] In 1864 some mention was made of the possibility of his nomination to succeed Chief Justice Taney, but the nomination was never submitted. He was offered instead the Attorney Generalship which Edward Bates had resigned after the election of 1864. The President particularly wanted him for this position because he needed a Southern man to help counterbalance the Northern representation in the Cabinet, but Holt declined the offer, saying that he could better serve Lincoln where he was.[14] His reason was said to lie in an unwillingness to undertake the task of representing the government before the Supreme Court,[15] perhaps because of the fact that the Court would be called upon to assess the legality of the program of military trials for which he was in part responsible.[16]

---

[9] Lewis N. Dembitz to Joseph Holt, June 14, 1861, Holt Papers. Dembitz was an uncle of Louis D. Brandeis.

[10] Joseph Holt to James Buchanan, May 24, 1861, Buchanan, *Works*, XI, 195.

[11] Coulter, *The Civil War and Readjustment in Kentucky*, 93–97.

[12] While Holt was aiding David Davis in investigating military mismanagement in St. Louis, as referred to below, Lincoln told J. F. Speed of Kentucky that he expected to reward Holt in some form commensurate with the services rendered.

[13] *Ex parte* Milligan, 4 Wall. 2 (1866).

[14] Joseph Holt to A. Lincoln, Nov. 30, 1864, Holt Papers.

[15] See Holt's obituary notice in *Philadelphia Public Ledger*, Aug. 2, 1894. For a contemporary expression of puzzlement at his unwillingness to take the office see Mary Cash (unsigned) to Joseph Holt, Dec. 18, 1864 (misfiled with 1862), Vol. 36, folio 4722, Holt Papers.

[16] Holt was in many respects a highly complex person. The zeal which he had displayed in his youth as a prosecutor in civil courts (see obituary notice, *Louisville Courier-Journal*, Aug. 8, 1894) may have reexpressed itself in his defense of the

With the position left vacant at the death of Justice Daniel still unfilled, the death of Justice McLean occurred on April 4, 1861, precipitating large numbers of recommendations and applications for the position. Acting with maximum promptness, Noah H. Swayne of Columbus, Ohio, wrote on the day of McLean's death to Secretary of the Treasury Salmon P. Chase, likewise from Ohio:

> Intelligence of the death of Judge McLean reached here this morning. My friends will name me to the President as one of those from whom a selection is to be made to fill the vacancy upon the Bench of the Supreme Court, thus created. If you can deem it proper to give me your friendly support you will lay me under a lasting obligation.[17]

For Chase, with perennial aspirations to the Presidency, it was eminently desirable to have "under lasting obligation" to him a man with the prestige and influence of Swayne.

Swayne was born in Frederick County, Virginia, in 1804. Of Quaker heritage, at the age of thirteen he began two years of study at a Quaker academy at Waterford. He then studied medicine for two years in the office of a physician, but on the death of his teacher he began the study of law in the office of John Scott and Francis Brooks at Warrenton. After his admission to the bar in 1823 he moved to Zanesville, Ohio, where he practiced law and worked his way into politics, serving for a time in the legislature. In 1830 Andrew Jackson appointed him United States Attorney for Ohio, a position which he held for nine years. Thereafter he maintained a lucrative practice in Columbus while continuing to serve his state in various capacities and making himself an expert particularly in the field of banking.[18] He became active in the Republican Party from its organization, attending the national convention in Philadelphia in 1856[19] and vigorously sup-

---

exercise of military power when he became judge advocate general. After the war he lost much of his popular support in connection with his prosecution of Mary Surratt as one of the murderers of President Lincoln. Intense and determined in the professional positions he took, he was also deeply emotional in personal relationships—as is illustrated by his correspondence with each of his two wives and members of their families and with other friends. Bits of evidence about a romance carried on during the Civil War period with a cousin of his second wife, a woman much younger than himself, further illuminate his character. "You dear old sinner, you have had a mighty good time in your life," she wrote to him on one occasion. Vol. 41, folio 5487, Holt Papers.

[17] N. H. Swayne to S. P. Chase, Apr. 4, 1861, Chase Papers.

[18] See Emilius O. Randall and Daniel J. Ryan, *History of Ohio*, III, 352; Tod B. Galloway, "The Ohio-Michigan Boundary Line Dispute," *Ohio Archaeological and Historical Society Publications*, 4:199, 221–23, 1909.

[19] See Charles A. Jones, "Ohio in the Republican National Conventions," *Ohio Archaeological and Historical Quarterly*, 38:1, 10, 1929.

porting Lincoln for the Presidency in 1860.[20] He was a friend of Justice McLean[21] and was said to have been McLean's choice for his own succession.

Governor William Dennison of Ohio, who was prominent among the Republican leadership, urged Swayne's appointment both by letter and in a personal interview with the President,[22] and other Ohio leaders likewise gave support. Aaron F. Perry, a prominent Cincinnati lawyer, wrote to say that he would welcome Chase as a member of the Court, but if Chase were not to be appointed he would prefer Swayne. Chase himself apparently hoped for the appointment of a Justice who might find the Fugitive Slave Law unconstitutional. Perry told him the time was past when that issue should play an important part, expressing the hope that "slavery will be so shaken by the war as to render this class of questions less likely to be important."[23] Perry thought Swayne's antislavery opinions at least as pronounced as those of Justice McLean, and judged this fact important in a member of a Virginia family, "keeping along as Judge McLean did, within speaking distance of public opinion." William B. Ogden, a prominent railroad executive in Chicago, wrote to Lincoln in warm support of Swayne, saying that he had no superior in the West and adding what might be an important point for those times of inflation: "he has means to live handsomely independent of his salary."[24]

Although for the nomination Swayne faced competition from other persons in his own state,[25] the major rivals resided elsewhere in the

[20] See Earl W. Wiley, "Behind Lincoln's Visit to Ohio in 1859," *Ohio State Archaeological Quarterly*, 60: 28, 33, 37 (1951); Earl W. Wiley, " 'Governor' John Greiner and Chase's Bid for the Presidency in 1860," *Ohio State Archaeological Quarterly*, 58:245, 254, 271–72, 1949.

[21] See John McLean to J. S. Black, Dec. 15, 1859, where the former speaks of "my friend Col. Swayne," and says that "Col. Swayne is a man of high respectability."

[22] W. Dennison to A. Lincoln, July 11, 1861, Attorney General Papers.

[23] Aaron F. Perry to S. P. Chase, Dec. 2, 1861, Chase Papers.

[24] W. B. Ogden to A. Lincoln, May 25, 1861, Attorney General Papers.

[25] Among Swayne's Ohio rivals was the state's attorney general, C. P.

Walcott, whose appointment, it was said, would infuse new life into the Supreme Court and give great satisfaction to the Northwest. *New York Evening Post*, Apr. 10, 1861. Another was William Y. Gholson, a member of the Ohio Supreme Court, of whom it was said that he would be backed by the entire bar and by Senators Lyman Trumbull, John P. Fessenden, and John J. Crittenden. *New York Times*, Apr. 9, 1861. T. G. Mitchell of Cincinnati wrote to Chase recommending a Judge Gholson and suggesting that he should have one of the Supreme Court positions even though Walcott was appointed to the other. T. G. Mitchell to S. P. Chase, Apr. 5, 1861, Attorney General Papers. The author has been unable to verify the statement that at some time during 1861 President Lincoln offered a Supreme Court appointment to

Seventh Circuit. Three prominent ones lived in Illinois. They were David Davis of Bloomington, Orville H. Browning of Quincy, and United States District Judge Thomas Drummond of Chicago.[26] Although after division of the circuit an appointment went to Davis, the other two were such serious competitors that they require discussion along with Davis.

David Davis was born in Cecil County, Maryland, in 1815. He graduated from Kenyon College in Ohio, and studied law in the office of Judge Henry W. Bishop of Lenox, Massachusetts, and for less than a year at the New Haven Law School. He moved to Illinois in 1835 to begin practice and in 1836 established his permanent home in Bloomington. He worked his way into politics as a Whig, and served in the state legislature and in the constitutional convention of 1847. For many years he served as judge of the eighth circuit of Illinois, having before him as counsel many times the outstanding lawyers of the state, among them Abraham Lincoln, whom he aided as campaign manager to win the Presidency. Like Swayne, Davis was a man of considerable wealth. But while Swayne had become wealthy in part through his law practice, Davis had done so largely through buying for small sums land sold for taxes during the depression years of the 1840s.[27] Although he may at times have been pressed for ready cash,[28] he was always a man of substantial property and not concerned about the level of his judicial salary, either on the Illinois circuit or on the Supreme Court.

Davis worked hard and effectively to secure Lincoln's nomination and election, inducing another judge to take over part of his court work to free himself for the campaign.[29] Immediately after the election he joined in the competition to determine appointments to the Cabinet and to other positions. He worked so effectively that even Mrs. Lincoln sought him out to urge the exercise of his influence with her husband, in one instance against a proposed Cabinet appointment and in another in favor of an appointment for her brother-in-law.[30] When during the second week in February, 1861, the Lincoln party set out for a zigzag speaking tour of cities in Indiana, Ohio, Pennsylvania, and New York, the huge and rotund figure of Judge Davis was conspicuous among them. It was a killing trip, he wrote to his wife from Buffalo. He was never able to retire before twelve o'clock at night, and had to be up at

---

Aaron F. Perry of Cincinnati, and that Perry declined it. See *Biographical Directory of the American Congress, 1774–1927*, H.R. Doc. No. 783, 69th Cong., 2nd Sess. 1403 (1928).

[26] Less prominent among the Illinois candidates was Stephen T. Logan, who may have been considered partly because he had been Lincoln's law partner. *New York Evening Post*, Apr. 10, 1861.

[27] See Willard L. King, *Lincoln's Manager, David Davis*, 51–52.

[28] See D. Davis to George P. Davis, Dec. 9, 1861, Davis Papers.

[29] King, *Lincoln's Manager, David Davis*, 156.

[30] *Ibid.*, 172, 184.

half past five to prepare for the next day,[31] but he enjoyed the excitement. He thought the enthusiastic reception of the President-elect due not so much his person or character as to the state of the country.[32] When at the end of the trip Lincoln, on the advice of detectives, slipped quietly through Baltimore by night instead of visiting and speaking there as in other cities along the way, Davis, with Mrs. Lincoln and the rest of the party, made an uneventful trip on the day when Lincoln had been expected to go through the city with its turbulent enthusiasm for the Southern cause.[33]

Davis shared in the excitement of the launching of the new Administration, and was instrumental, according to his biographer, in the appointment of two Cabinet members, two territorial judges, a Commissioner of Indian affairs, and the Marshal of the District of Columbia.[34] Then, two weeks after the inauguration, he arrived dejectedly back in his home town of Bloomington, having achieved much for others but nothing for himself. There is little reason for believing Davis had been much concerned initially about his own advancement. With great enthusiasm he had promoted the Presidential candidate of his party and had urged the appointment of loyal friends. But when leading friends were themselves appointed to federal offices, Davis found himself less influential with them than he had hoped to be in the placement of still other office seekers, and he sensed that the stream of events was leaving him behind. He knew nothing to do except hold court, he wrote despondently to Ward Hill Lamon, Lincoln's swashbuckling former law partner who was now Marshal of the District of Columbia and hence also of the Supreme Court.[35] Yet after so much political excitement during the past year, and so much notoriety, it looked like small and insignificant business to go on holding court for a thousand dollars a year. He admitted that he was hurt at leaving Washington empty-handed, and he felt it all the more deeply as his Illinois friends were commenting on his being left without an office.[36]

Two days after the inauguration and before Davis had left Washington, his cousin Henry Winter Davis of Maryland, now a prominent Republican, wrote to the President urging the appointment of Judge Davis to the position on the Supreme Court vacated at the death of Justice Daniel. He thought Davis peculiarly fitted for the position in experience, learning, judicial habits, and cast of mind. The appointment, he urged, should not go to a slave state, the slave states already having sufficient representation. In any event, Judge Davis was a native Mary-

[31] D. Davis to Mrs. Davis, Feb. 17, 1861, Davis Papers.

[32] King, *Lincoln's Manager, David Davis*, 176.

[33] *Ibid.*, 178.

[34] *Ibid.*, 181.

[35] D. Davis to Ward Hill Lamon, Mar. 24, 1861, Davis Papers.

[36] D. Davis to Ward Hill Lamon, Mar. 30, 1861, Davis Papers.

lander, and was a large landholder in that state. His appointment would lead to a long term of service, so essential to the stability of the administration of justice.[37]

The recommendation brought no action, but when a month later Justice McLean died, Davis and various friends quickly got into communication about this vacancy, for a circuit in which the state of Illinois was then included. On April 14, the day on which he learned of the attack on Fort Sumter—"God only knows what will become of our beloved country"—Davis wrote to Lamon that he had no hope or expectation that Lincoln would appoint him to the Supreme Court. Lyman Trumbull, Senator from Illinois and influential with the President, was reputed to desire the position, and Salmon P. Chase would never permit the appointment of Davis. If the appointment should go to Judge Thomas Drummond of the United States District Court in Chicago, Davis would like to have the district judgeship. He urged Lamon to find out what he could about the prospect.[38]

Lamon, who lived at the White House to guard the President and was busy with Washington intrigue, seems to have answered little of his correspondence. William W. Orme, another of Davis' Bloomington friends, wrote from Washington that he could get little news. Chase was a candidate, and he had learned in Springfield that Judge Stephen T. Logan was also a candidate. Simon Cameron of Pennsylvania, who headed the War Department, was in favor of making the appointments from Northern states, and would support Davis.[39] Unfortunately for Davis, the master politician from Pennsylvania was soon to give forth a bad odor in the allotment of war contracts, and quickly lost influence with the President.

Davis replied to Orme, "If Chase wants the appointment of Supreme Judge, I would bet my farm he will get it." He proceeded to discuss federal judgeships in the South and the problems of reorganizing the federal judicial system. He did not see how the government could fill the district judgeships in the South already vacated by men going over to the Confederacy, and he thought public sentiment would force the resignation of the remaining Southern judges. Furthermore, he thought this the time for reorganization of the Supreme Court. There ought to be a Court of five judges, limited to duty in Washington. There should be a system of Circuit Courts held not by Supreme Court judges but by independent circuit judges sitting along with district judges. He urged Orme to discuss the matter with Lincoln, reminding

---

[37] H. Winter Davis to A. Lincoln, Mar. 6, 1861, Lincoln Papers.
[38] David Davis to Ward Hill Lamon, Apr. 14, 1861, Lamon Papers.

See also King, *Lincoln's Manager, David Davis*, 191.
[39] W. W. Orme to David Davis, May 11, 1861, Davis Papers.

him that there was already a precedent for independent circuit judges in the operation of the California circuit. In any event, Judge McLean's circuit was already much too large to be served by one judge, and it was bordered on the north and west by new states as much entitled to circuit service as the older states.[40]

Orme, having exhausted the President's patience by urging some kind of appointment for Leonard Swett of Bloomington, was unable to do anything for Davis. Davis wrote again to Lamon of the report that the Chicago bar was supporting Judge Drummond and repeated that he would like to have Judge Drummond's place: "I would like a judicial position, in preference to anything else, and would like something higher than I now hold."[41] Would Lamon find out how he stood with Lincoln? Some time later Lamon wrote to Orme that the choice lay between Davis and Browning and he believed that it would go to Davis,[42] but the year passed with no appointment being made.

Although he had been a friend of Lincoln's since the 1830s, Orville H. Browning, Davis' leading Illinois rival for the Supreme Court position, had not supported Lincoln for the Presidency until it was clear that his own candidate, Edward Bates of Missouri, would not be nominated. Thereafter he had tried to unify the Bates-Lincoln factions. While Davis accompanied the President-elect all the way to Washington, Browning, although also invited, went only as far as Indianapolis and then returned to his practice of law. Yet five days after the death of Justice McLean, Browning was writing confidentially to the President to say that he would like to have the position, noting that for more than twenty years he had been fighting the battles of his party and his country without expectation of reward. He had refused to permit petitions to be drawn up in support of his nomination, however, and he had written to no other person on the subject, "not even Mr. Bates."[43] Two months later Mrs. Browning, likewise well known to Lincoln, in her husband's absence wrote a letter in his support. She knew him to be one of the wisest and best men in the nation, an unselfish patriot, and not a miserable office seeker. She could write volumes enumerating the sacrifices Browning had made for his country. She told Lincoln in confidence that two or three years earlier, while making laborious political speeches in the open air, Browning had suffered a rupture of the bowels that threatened to disable him for active practice, with the result that his income might be cut off. She knew the position was desired by Judge

---

[40] David Davis to W. W. Orme, May 17, 1861, Lamon Papers.

[41] David Davis to Ward Hill Lamon, May 31, 1861, Lamon Papers.

[42] Typewritten copy, Ward H. Lamon to W. W. Orme, July 25, 1861, Davis Papers.

[43] O. H. Browning to A. Lincoln, Apr. 9, 1861, Lincoln Papers.

Davis and by men in Indiana and Ohio, but she thought that Browning had the stronger claim.[44]

Stephen A. Douglas died on June 3, 1861, and Governor Richard Yates appointed Browning to fill out Douglas' unexpired term in the Senate. Friends of Judge Thomas Drummond of Chicago were concerned rather than relieved by the appointment, for Browning was reported as saying, as Mrs. Browning had reported confidentially to Lincoln, that he had only a temporary interest in the Senatorial position and that his real goal was a position on the Supreme Court.[45] In Washington during the five-week special session of Congress which began on July 4, 1861, Browning was much in conference with the President and other officers of the government, but he left without the coveted appointment.

In September, after his return to Illinois, Browning made the political mistake of challenging Lincoln's modification of a proclamation of General Charles A. Frémont, in command of troops in Missouri, which disregarded a recently enacted statute concerning the confiscation of enemy property. The statute provided for confiscation through federal courts of enemy property used in aid of the rebellion. It gave freedom to those slaves used specifically in the same fashion.[46] Frémont's proclamation provided for large-scale military confiscation and for outright liberation of the slaves of Southern sympathizers. In strange language for a man seeking a position on the highest Court in the land, Browning wrote to Lincoln that while it was true that there was no express authorization in law for the Frémont proclamation, "war is never carried on, and can never be, in strict accordance with previously adjusted constitutional and legal provisions. Have traitors who are warring upon the Constitution and laws, and rejecting all their restraints, any right to invoke their protection? . . . Is a traitor's negro more sacred than his life? and is it true that the power which may dispose absolutely of the latter is impotent to touch the former? . . . There has been too much tenderness toward traitors and rebels. We must strike them terrible blows, and strike them hard and quick, or the government will go hopelessly to pieces."[47]

Lincoln replied sternly that the part of the proclamation in question was strictly illegal, that it was outright "dictatorship." It went beyond the range of military law or necessity to the making of policy, which was the province of Congress. As for saving the government, this measure was in itself a surrender of the government: "What I object to,

---

[44] E. H. Browning to A. Lincoln, June 8, 1861, Lincoln Papers.

[45] William A. Bradley to E. B. Washburne, July 10, 1861, Washburne Papers.

[46] 12 Stat. 319.

[47] O. H. Browning to A. Lincoln, Sept. 17, 1861, Lincoln Papers.

is, that I as President, shall expressly or impliedly seize and exercise the permanent legislative functions of the government." As for the policy of the matter as distinguished from the law, he was concerned with keeping loyal to the Union the border states of Missouri, Kentucky, and Maryland. Particularly in Kentucky, he had ample evidence of the disastrous effects of the proclamation.[48] Browning found his way back into Lincoln's good graces but his aspirations were not helped by his position on the Frémont proclamation.

Judge Thomas Drummond was less active in politics and less well known generally than his rivals for the Supreme Court position. He was born in Maine in 1809, graduated from Bowdoin College in 1830, studied law in Philadelphia, and was admitted to the bar there in 1833. He had moved to Galena, Illinois, in 1835, had practiced law and served in the legislature, and had been appointed United States District Judge in 1850. When in 1855 the state was divided into two districts he was assigned the northern district, with his court in Chicago.[49] One of Drummond's leading sponsors was Elihu B. Washburne, a member of Congress from Illinois who was close to the President. Prominent among those urging Washburne to advance Drummond's cause were William A. Bradley, clerk of the federal courts in Chicago who was concerned about his position, and Joseph R. Jones, United States Marshal there. Bradley thought the President would like to give the position to Drummond but feared that Browning would worry it out of him.[50] Judge Drummond pressed his own cause with obvious reluctance but admitted that he needed the income the position would bring.[51] "I feel very anxious to know the result of your next interview with Lincoln in regard to Judge D.," Jones wrote to Washburne. "Does he know that Drummond is poor as d—n and has a house full of children, while Browning is rich and has not a chick or child in the world, and that Davis is very rich. Or does he care for such considerations." He urged that if the President must do something for Davis or Browning he could give one of them Judge Drummond's place.[52]

It became evident that the demands of the war and the need for Congressional action on judicial districts were forcing delay in the

---

[48] A. Lincoln to O. H. Browning, Sept. 22, 1861, Lincoln, *Collected Works,* IV, 531–33. For Browning's reply see his letter of September 30, Lincoln Papers.

[49] "Letter of E. B. Washburne to John Dixon," *Journal of the Illinois Historical Society,* 6:214, 1913.

[50] William A. Bradley to E. B. Washburne, July 10, 1861, Washburne Papers.

[51] David M. Silver, *Lincoln's Supreme Court,* 73.

[52] Joseph R. Jones to E. B. Washburne, June 18, 1862, Washburne Papers.

making of any Supreme Court appointments. The special session of Congress in the summer of 1861 took no action except to adopt a House resolution requesting the Secretary of the Interior to assemble before the next December information about the amount of business transacted on the several circuits during the preceding decade.[53] In his message to Congress on December 3, 1861, the President explained why he had refrained from filling the three positions on the Supreme Court. Two of the outgoing judges had resided in states now overrun by revolt. Successors could not now serve circuits in the same areas, and many of the most competent men there probably would not take the personal hazard of accepting Supreme Court appointments. He had been unwilling to throw all the appointments northward, although some regional readjustment would not be unjust. Justice McLean's circuit had grown into an empire, and was too large for one judge to give more than nominal attendance.

The President suggested, furthermore, that the country had outgrown the present judicial system. If Circuit Court services were to be provided for some of the states they should be provided for all. Yet to provide enough Supreme Court appointees to serve all the states on circuit would make the Court too large. He suggested any of three modifications. The Supreme Court might be kept at a convenient size, and independent circuit judges appointed to serve those circuits not reached by Supreme Court Justices; or the Supreme Court might be relieved of circuit duties and independent circuit judges appointed for all circuits; or Circuit Courts might be dispensed with, leaving all judicial functions in the hands of District Courts and the Supreme Court.[54]

Congressional discussion of the Supreme Court began in a mood much less thoughtful than that suggested by the President. On December 4, 1861, Senator John P. Hale of New Hampshire submitted a resolution proposing an inquiry into the expediency of abolishing the existing Supreme Court and establishing another. The present Court, he contended, was bankrupt as to every purpose it was intended to serve; it had lost public confidence and it did not have and ought not to have public respect. The present judges had been appointed as politicians. The Supreme Court had been a part of the machinery of the Democratic Party. The judge serving his circuit (Justice Clifford) had been appointed against the all but unanimous voice of the people, because of his approval of the Dred Scott decision. Now that a different party was in power, there ought to be a different Court. As Senator Hale saw it,

---

[53] *Cong. Globe*, 37th Cong., 1st Sess. 131 (1861).
[54] J. D. Richardson, *A Compilation* *of the Messages and Papers of the Presidents*, VI, 49.

823

the Constitution required that judicial power be vested in "one Supreme Court," but it did not require that the vestment be in *this* Supreme Court.[55]

For all the flamboyance of Senator Hale's performance, it won a measure of support both in and out of Congress. One expression of general agreement came from John Jay, grandson of the first Chief Justice and himself a prominent lawyer. In a letter to Hale, while admitting with President Lincoln that it might be well to postpone complete reorganization of the Court until the rebellion was crushed, he agreed with Hale that a considerable amount of reorganization was needed immediately. It was necessary that the government be assured of the complete loyalty of a majority of the Court. This, as Jay saw it, meant not merely acquiescence in measures of government but "earnest devotion to republican principles of freedom, which must exist to make the Court what Washington declared it ought to be, the sheet anchor of our liberties."[56]

Jay asked rhetorically whether the Court as presently constituted could sustain this confidence: "Can we rely upon the Court to overrule the views of Chief Justice Taney on the Habeas Corpus question? and to sustain the Acts which Congress may pass for the conduct of the war and the Emancipation of slaves and Confiscation of the property of rebels?" There were thousands of Democrats in the North, he asserted, who cared more for party than for country and who were anxiously awaiting some misstep on the part of the government to array themselves against it: "If they can assume this position with the sanction of the Supreme Court, and under the cry of law and order, and stand by the Judiciary! our troubles will be greatly complicated, and the North be hopelessly divided."[57]

Although some legislators sympathized with Senator Hale's position, there was support also for the position of Senator Lafayette S. Foster of Connecticut, that one branch of the government ought not thus to attack another, and that if there was a lack of public confidence in the Supreme Court, the lack ought not to be intensified by attacks such as this: "Suppose the people adopt the opinion, and it is very widespread over the land, that the judiciary is wholly unworthy of public confidence—what is the result? . . . We shall have anarchy; chaos will have come again; and that, I apprehend, is not a desirable condition of things."[58]

Other Republican Senators were likewise critical. Jacob Collamer

---

[55] *Cong. Globe*, 37th Cong., 2nd Sess. 27–28 (1861).

[56] John Jay to John P. Hale, Dec. 13, 1861, Hale Papers.

[57] *Ibid*.

[58] *Cong. Globe*, 37th Cong., 2nd Sess. 27 (1861).

of Vermont contended that Congress had no power to abolish the Supreme Court.[59] O. H. Browning of Illinois took the same position, adding that "If you repeal the Supreme Court out of existence to-day for the purpose of getting rid of obnoxious judges, and reorganize it, and have new judges appointed, the very moment there is a change in the political complexion of Congress the same 'town-meeting proceeding' recurs and the court is again abolished, and it will be abolished as often as the political complexion of Congress changes."[60]

Senator Hale's resolution was amended out of existence and members of Congress, as far as war problems permitted, turned to the reorganization of the judicial circuits. On December 9 Senator John Sherman of Ohio introduced a bill merging into one circuit the two hitherto served by Justices Daniel and Campbell, and adding thereto Texas, not previously included in any circuit. The bill added to Justice Wayne's circuit the state of Florida, which had not been included in any circuit before. It then limited to Ohio, Indiana, and Michigan what had been Justice McLean's Seventh Circuit, and included in a new Ninth Circuit Illinois, Wisconsin, Minnesota, Iowa, and Kansas.[61]

In the Senate Judiciary Committee, from which it was reported out on December 18, the bill had run into difficulties with those who preferred different combinations of states in the different circuits. The same difficulties were met on the floor. The Sherman bill made the minimum number of changes necessary to get the additional states included within nine circuits. As reported by the committee, a number of changes had been made to promote equality as to population and amounts of business in the respective circuits.[62]

The legislators moved so slowly that before the Senate had passed its own bill, and before the House of Representatives had acted on its parallel bill, the weakness of the Supreme Court with only six members, some of them chronically ill, made it necessary to add a new member in advance of circuit rearrangement. Noah H. Swayne of Ohio was nominated on January 21 and confirmed on January 24, 1862. The appointment left undetermined the question whether Ohio would thereafter be linked northward with Michigan, westward with Indiana, or southward with Kentucky. As the bill passed the Senate on the day of Swayne's confirmation, Ohio was linked with Kentucky to make up the Seventh Circuit, but the House of Representatives was yet to be heard from.

In the House a hard fight was made to secure the linkage of Ohio with some other state than Kentucky to compose the Seventh Circuit.

---

[59] *Ibid.*, 27.
[60] *Ibid.*, 28.
[61] S. 89, 37th Cong., 2nd Sess.

[62] *Cong. Globe*, 37th Cong., 2nd Sess. 187–88 (1862).

The House amendment linked Ohio with Michigan. Back in the Senate, Senator Joseph A. Wright of Indiana presented a petition from members of the bar of every county of his state asking that Indiana be included in the circuit served by Justice Swayne. During its forty years as a state, he said, Indiana had been linked with Ohio, and its bar and its people wanted to remain so. That arrangement would leave a federal judge within three or four hours' distance of the great cities of Chicago, Cleveland, Cincinnati, and Indianapolis: "Questions frequently arise there growing out of this war; and how important it is to have a gentleman of the character of Judge Swayne, who can be called for at any time to grant an injunction or anything of that sort."[63]

Legislators from Iowa were particularly interested in linkage in a north-south tier of states rather than in an east-west tier combining Iowa with Illinois. Senator James W. Grimes gave as one of his reasons the fact that Missouri, Iowa, Kansas, and Minnesota had "adopted a different system of pleading from the other States, with which it has been proposed to unite them."[64] Congressman James F. Wilson made the same point and added that the four states were more or less affected by laws related to Spanish and French land grants, they had close commercial relations in connection with business on the Mississippi and Missouri rivers, and they bordered on the area where still other new states would soon be added. As a further item of relevance he added a reference to the outstanding bravery of Iowa soldiers on the battlefield.[65]

But the real concern of the Iowa Representatives in keeping Iowa separate from Illinois was their desire to have one of their own people, Samuel F. Miller, appointed to the Supreme Court. If Iowa were linked with Illinois, Davis and Browning and perhaps others would outshine Miller, whereas he was the outstanding man in the north-south tier of states. An Illinois Congressman made reference to this kind of interest, in this and other proposals for changes in circuit arrangements, by remarking, "I fear that too many mantles for Supreme Court judges have already been cut out, and made up."[66]

So disruptive were the various pressures connected with circuit reorganization that the measure was not enacted until July 15, 1862.[67] In its final form Ohio was linked with Indiana in the Seventh Circuit,[68] and the Western tier was included in the Ninth Circuit, paving the way for the appointment of Miller.

The appointment of Justice Swayne took care of one of the three

---

[63] *Ibid.*, 3090.
[64] *Ibid.*, 469.
[65] *Ibid.*, 2562.
[66] *Ibid.*, 2564.
[67] 12 Stat. 576.

[68] Though note that on Jan. 28, 1863, Ohio was linked with Michigan and Indiana with Illinois and Wisconsin. 12 Stat. 637.

vacancies. As indicated above, he was obviously a popular choice in the Middle West. Judge Davis characterized him as an able man and the best appointment the Administration had made except Edwin M. Stanton, who had replaced Cameron as Secretary of War. Davis thought, however, that from a political point of view Joseph Holt, of the border state of Kentucky, ought to have been appointed.[69] On appointment from the President, Davis had recently served with Holt and Hugh Campbell of Missouri on a commission in St. Louis to examine gross financial mismanagement and frauds in John C. Frémont's military command.[70] The task may have created political enemies for the members of the commission. Campbell wrote to Davis that abolitionists were savage about the report because it spoke rather freely of their idol, Frémont.[71]

Davis continued to aspire to the Supreme Court position while professing little faith that he would get it. Leonard Swett, he said, was writing everywhere in the state to get up pressure.[72] Many letters produced by Swett's industry are to be found in the Davis papers and in those of Lincoln. He reached outside the state to urge United States District Judge Samuel Treat of St. Louis to work for Davis, saying that the choice lay between Davis and Browning.[73] He wrote to John F. Henry of Burlington, Iowa, with a like end in view.[74] Davis heard that if Illinois was linked in the same circuit with Indiana, Caleb B. Smith of the latter state, now Secretary of the Interior, would be an additional rival.[75] Certainly Smith had judicial aspirations, as indicated by the fact that in December, 1862, after the Supreme Court positions had been filled, he accepted appointment as United States District Judge for Indiana. Davis heard rumor of a plan to give Supreme Court positions to both Smith and Browning, and make Davis Secretary of the Interior. A "precious piece of planning," he called it.[76] An attempt was made to get Davis out of the way by having him appointed to the Court of Claims, but he refused to cooperate.[77]

---

[69] Typewritten copy, D. Davis to W. W. Orme, Jan. 27, 1862, Davis Papers.

[70] War Claims at St. Louis, H.R. Exec. Doc. No. 94, 37th Cong., 2nd Sess.

[71] Hugh Campbell to David Davis, Apr. 28, 1862, Davis Papers.

[72] D. Davis to W. W. Orme, Jan. 27, 1862, Davis Papers.

[73] Leonard Swett to Samuel Treat, Jan. 31, 1862, Treat Papers.

[74] Leonard Swett to John F. Henry, Feb. 6, 1862, Davis Papers.

[75] D. Davis to Leonard Swett, Feb.

16, 1862, Davis Papers. It is possible, although the possibility is not here verified, that one reason why some residents of Indiana desired circuit connections with Ohio, from which Justice Swayne had been appointed, was factional opposition to Caleb B. Smith in his own state.

[76] D. Davis to Leonard Swett, Feb. 23, 1862, Davis Papers. Typewritten copy, David Davis to W. W. Orme, Feb. 23, 1862, Davis Papers.

[77] King, *Lincoln's Manager, David Davis*, 194–95.

President Lincoln continued to delay appointing a Justice from the Eighth Circuit, in which Illinois was included, even after the enactment of the statute of July 15, 1862, in spite of the obvious need for circuit service. He moved promptly, however, with respect to the Ninth Circuit, where Samuel F. Miller of Iowa was the outstanding candidate. Miller was born in Richmond, Kentucky, in 1816. After study of medicine at Transylvania University he practiced as a physician for twelve years, became a justice of the peace and involved in politics, studied law privately, and was admitted to the bar in 1847. In 1850 he moved to Keokuk, Iowa, to practice law. In Iowa's courts and in the United States District Court he moved to a position of leadership at the bar. He became a leader also of the newly organized Republican Party, and aided in the election of Lincoln.

While working for the arrangement of judicial circuits to make Miller's appointment feasible, the Iowa delegation took care that a stream of letters of recommendation flowed to the President and that personal representations were made. On July 16, 1862, the day after the enactment of the circuit statute, the President sent Miller's nomination to the Senate, where it was immediately confirmed.[78] Miller was not well known beyond the borders of his circuit—was hardly known at all in the East—but for the power of his mind, the firmness of his convictions, and his stocky and well-rounded figure he was to become known as an outstanding member of the Supreme Court.

After Miller's appointment to the position on the Ninth Circuit, that on the Eighth Circuit remained to be filled. Friends of Browning and Davis continued to press their claims. Leonard Swett, still working for Davis by letter and through face-to-face persuasion, called on Mrs. Lincoln, who told him that she had been fighting Davis' battles and was glad that at the close of the session of Congress Browning had gone home; for he had "become distressingly loving before he left."[79] Lincoln waited until August 27, some six weeks after the adjournment of Congress and nearly seventeen months after the area was deprived of circuit services by the death of Justice McLean, and then wrote to Davis saying, "My mind is made up to appoint you Supreme Judge." Even then the political character of his thinking was such that he attempted to pacify the friends of Judge Drummond by adding in the same sentence, "but I am so anxious that Mr. Bradley, present clerk at Chicago, shall be retained, that I think it no dishonor for me to ask, and for you to tell me, that you will not remove him. Please answer."[80] Davis

---

[78] For biographical presentation see Charles Fairman, *Mr. Justice Miller and the Supreme Court, 1862–1890*.

[79] Leonard Swett to Mrs. Laura Swett, Aug. 10, 1862, Davis Papers.

For summary of evidence see King, *Lincoln's Manager, David Davis*, 195.

[80] A. Lincoln to David Davis, Aug. 27, 1862, Davis Papers.

accepted gratefully, saying that he would not in any event think of displacing Bradley, whose fitness for the position he knew, but especially in view of Lincoln's request he would take pleasure in retaining him.[81]

Having at last decided to appoint Davis, Lincoln asked Attorney General Bates whether he could do so in advance of the next meeting of the Senate. Bates recited his power to make recess appointments.[82] On October 19 Lincoln wrote to Davis enclosing his commission, saying that "After the fall election in Illinois shall be past" he would be glad to see him.[83] On November 15 Davis sent Lincoln a telegram from New York saying that he would be in Washington the following day.[84] When the Senate assembled at the beginning of December the nomination was presented and confirmed without incident.

In debates in Congress over the reorganization of judicial circuits east of the Rocky Mountains it was for the most part assumed that circuit service for California and Oregon would have to be provided separately, as it was in California at the time by the independent appointment of Matthew Ward McAllister as a circuit judge. Then questions began to be raised about the failure of Judge McAllister to perform the duties of his office and about the need for his replacement, with the possibility of elevating the position to the rank of the circuits served by Supreme Court Justices. For the Western states a matter of prestige was involved in having the services of a member of the Supreme Court, and also the matter of having on the Court a man who knew the land and mining problems of the area which gave rise to much litigation. For the country as a whole there was the need to have on the Supreme Court a sufficient number of Justices strictly loyal to the Union to protect the national interest, a problem highlighted by the presence on the docket of the Court of the critical *Prize Cases*.[85]

Judge McAllister submitted his resignation January 12, 1863.[86] Six days previously the chairman of the House Judiciary Committee had reported a bill to abolish the existing California circuit and create a new one consisting of California and Oregon, which was to be served by a member of the Supreme Court. The membership of that Court was to be increased to ten.[87] No action was taken on the House bill, but a similar one, introduced six weeks later in the Senate by Milton S.

---

[81] King, *Lincoln's Manager, David Davis*, 196.

[82] Edward Bates to A. Lincoln, Oct. 15, 1861, Lincoln Papers.

[83] A. Lincoln to David Davis, Oct. 19, 1862, Davis Papers.

[84] David Davis to A. Lincoln, Nov. 15, 1862, Lincoln Papers.

[85] 2 Black 635 (1863).

[86] M. Hall McAllister to A. Lincoln, Jan. 12, 1863, Attorney General Papers.

[87] *Cong. Globe*, 37th Cong., 3rd Sess. 210 (1863). A copy of the bill H.R. 652, is preserved in the papers of the House of Representatives.

Latham of California [88] was passed by both houses and became a law on March 3, 1863.[89]

It seems probable that from the very beginning Stephen J. Field, chief justice of the Supreme Court of California, had been regarded as the most desirable appointee to the new position. Field was born in Haddam, Connecticut, in 1816, a member of a large and distinguished family which included among his brothers David Dudley Field, the great advocate of codification of the law, and Cyrus W. Field, of Atlantic cable fame. Stephen Field had graduated from Williams College and studied law in the office of his brother David, and was admitted to the bar in 1841. He went to California in 1849, at the time of the gold rush, and began immediately to play an important part in the affairs of the state. As a member of the legislature he drafted the codes of civil and criminal practice, making use of the work of his elder brother, and worked for other important measures as well. As a member of the California Supreme Court he displayed a decisive capacity for molding the law and stating it clearly, with no compunctions about the vigorous assertion of his own convictions as determining the ingredients of the law. Although a Democrat, he was an ardent defender of the Union, and was therefore to be trusted on critical issues.[90]

David Dudley Field was a prominent consultant of the Lincoln Administration, and incidently also was involved in the New Almaden quicksilver mine litigation.[91] According to the record of the Field family, John A. C. Gray, a New York friend of the President, went to him while the bill was approaching enactment to ask the appointment of Stephen Field to the new position. The President had no question on the ground of fitness, but asked, "Does David want his brother to have it?" Receiving an affirmative answer, Lincoln said at once, "Then he shall have it."[92] The bill was passed on March 3 and the nomination was submitted and confirmed immediately thereafter, as the Thirty-Seventh Congress came to an end.

The four Lincoln appointees to the Taney Court, Swayne, Miller, Davis, and Field, all seem to have been selected primarily for their loyalty to the Union, to the Administration in power, and to Lincoln and his more influential advisers. Merit and leadership at the bar were

---

[88] *Ibid.*, 1121.

[89] 12 Stat. 794.

[90] For more elaborate discussion see Carl B. Swisher, *Stephen J. Field: Craftsman of the Law.*

[91] See D. D. Field to Edward Bates, July 2, 1863, Attorney General Papers.

[92] Henry M. Field, *The Life of David Dudley Field*, 196, n. According to Field's own account, immediately after Judge McAllister's

often mentioned, but recommendations seldom dwelt on expertness in any field of law, or power of mind, or experience and skill in judicial performance. Swayne had had no judicial experience. Miller's judicial experience had been limited to that of a justice of the peace. Davis' many years of experience on circuit in Illinois involved professional activities very different from those required on the Supreme Court. His correspondence before his appointment shows a continuing doubt as to his competence to serve on the high tribunal, and he may have correctly estimated his abilities as at the level of a United States District Court. Field had had more nearly corresponding judicial experience, and he displayed no doubt whatever of his ability to perform duties on the Supreme Court.

Of the three Justices who occupied portions of what had been Justice McLean's Seventh Circuit, none followed the McLean example of editing and publishing Circuit Court opinions. Swayne, and perhaps the others as well, seems to have preferred to present his circuit opinions orally and to leave no record. Although he had high standing with the bar of his region, with few exceptions during the Taney period[93] or thereafter did he make important contributions to the opinions of the Supreme Court. The Davis contribution was similarly not extensive, though with important exceptions after the end of the Taney period, as in the famous *Milligan* case.[94] Miller and Field, on the other hand, both of whom remained on the Court longer than the other two, had a great impact on the work of the Court because of the quality of their performance as well as the length of their terms.

Justice Swayne took his place as a member of the Supreme Court in Washington in late January, 1862, shortly after his appointment. Justices Miller and Davis joined the Court at the beginning of the term in December, 1862, and Justice Field a year later. The Court had been under attack ever since the Dred Scott decision. Chief Justice

---

resignation the California Senators in Washington telegraphed Field that they had recommended him to replace McAllister as circuit judge. Field replied that he preferred his present position of chief justice of the California Supreme Court to that of judge of an inferior federal court, but would be interested if the federal position were given Supreme Court status. His appointment was nevertheless urged for the inferior position, with the thought that its status would be raised at a later date, and the nomination was made by the President, but it was not acted upon in the light of the progress of the bill to change the status of the court. See Stephen J. Field, *Personal Reminiscences of Early Days in California*, 130–31. See also George C. Gorham, *Biographical Notice of Stephen J. Field*, 40.

[93] As one exception see Gelpcke v. Dubuque, 1 Wall. 175 (1864).

[94] *Ex parte* Milligan, 4 Wall. 2 (1866).

Taney stirred new hostility in May, 1861, by his decision in the *Merryman* case.[95] In connection with the filling of vacancies President Lincoln was reminded of his own earlier generalization that "in all history, the most efficient instruments of tyranny have been judges."[96] Yet if the Republican Administration distrusted the Supreme Court, the members of the Court probably also distrusted the Administration. It is also true that although in the courtroom the Justices were accustomed to hear perorations lauding their high tribunal and their individual merits, they were likewise accustomed to reading denunciations of their opinions and of their performances generally. They were not easily disturbed by temporary reactions.

Whatever their feelings about the new President, members of the Court attended the inauguration and Chief Justice Taney administered the oath of office. Whatever the feelings stirred by the *Merryman* case, the Chief Justice accompanied his brethren when they made their formal call on the President at the beginning of the term in December, 1861.[97] Taney, it is true, kept such relations on a strictly formal basis. When he was asked whether he would join the rest of the Court in calling on the President on New Year's Day, he replied that since there was no established etiquette which required such a visit "as a matter of official courtesy," and as he expected a visit from some friends, he would ask his brethren to excuse him.[98] The other Justices, however, seem to have made their rounds not only of the White House but of the homes of Cabinet members and other dignitaries as well.[99] Justices other than Chief Justice Taney, who was absent because of illness, intermingled with the throng of legislators, military men, and foreign ministers who on February 22, 1862, met in the hall of the House of Representatives to celebrate the birthday of George Washington.[100]

A number of the Justices had important personal contacts which maintained their sense of belonging in Washington, in spite of attitudes of the new Administration. Justice Wayne, who had taken up residence in Washington for the period of the war, and who was noted for his prominence in social life, was quite at home both with the new people and the older and Southern-sympathizing Washingtonians. At the beginning of the Lincoln Administration Justice Grier was invited to the War Department to administer the oath of office as Secretary of War

---

[95] *Ex parte* Merryman, 17 Fed. Cas. 144 (No. 9487) (C.C.D. Md. 1861).

[96] H. A. Nelson to A. Lincoln, Dec. 28, 1861, Lincoln Papers.

[97] *Washington National Intelligencer*, Dec. 2, 1861.

[98] "R. B. Taney to James M. Wayne, Dec. 31, 1861," *Maryland Historical Magazine*, 13:167, 1918.

[99] "The Diary of Edward Bates," Howard K. Beale, ed., *Annual Report of the American Historical Association for the Year 1930*, 4:221, 1933.

[100] *Ibid.*, 235–36. See also James M. Wayne, speaking for the Supreme Court, to Hannibal Hamlin, Feb. 20, 1862, Clerk's Files.

to Simon Cameron of Pennsylvania, whom he had known since boyhood.[101] When President Lincoln found it expedient to get rid of Cameron and to appoint in his place Edwin M. Stanton, who was likewise from Pennsylvania and who had served in President Buchanan's Cabinet, Grier wrote urging him to accept and to give and ask no pledges. In this conviction he was supported by Justices Nelson, Clifford, and Catron, with whom he had talked. Stanton would have the backing of the great Democratic Party of the North and of conservative Whigs. Stanton could "gain great glory if there be success to our arms, and can only sink in the common ruin in case of defeat."[102] Jeremiah S. Black, who after serving as Buchanan's Attorney General and then Secretary of State was made Reporter of the Supreme Court, maintained close connections with the office of the Attorney General and provided some interknitting between the Court and the Administration.[103]

The inevitable concern of members of the Court about the filling of vacancies among them is for the most part not recorded. During the summer of 1862 Chief Justice Taney, who was introduced to Justice Miller by Attorney General Bates, and who administered to Miller the oath of office, wrote to Justice Clifford that Bates and Miller had told him that the appointment of Browning was probable but not certain. The Chief Justice had heard that Judge Drummond was a competitor but he could not remember the name of the other competitor, David Davis who had been the manager of Lincoln's campaign.[104] Earlier, Justice Swayne had reported to Bates that there was an attempt to gerrymander the circuits in such a way as to make a place for Caleb B. Smith.[105] Swayne himself, along with his friend Governor William Dennison of Ohio, was going beyond his judicial duties to make recommendations about military policies in the Ohio Valley.[106]

Fragmentary pictures of the activities of the Justices while in Washington are to be found in the voluminous correspondence of Justice Davis.[107] Davis, huge in physical dimensions like Justices Clifford and Miller, and persistent and indefatigable in pressing the political claims of his friends, because of his lack of self-confidence was dependent on his wife and friends for reassurance. He was for a time

---

[101] *Baltimore Sun*, Mar. 15, 1861.

[102] R. C. Grier to Edwin M. Stanton, Jan. 13, 1862, Stanton Papers.

[103] See for example Bates, *Diary*, 252–53.

[104] Silver, *Lincoln's Supreme Court*, 72. R. B. Taney to Nathan Clifford, Aug. 2, 1862, Clifford Papers.

[105] "The Diary of Edward Bates,"

Howard K. Beale, ed., *Annual Report of the American Historical Association for the Year 1930*, 4:244, 1933.

[106] See *Diary of Gideon Welles*, Howard K. Beale, ed., 90.

[107] For summary see King, *Lincoln's Manager, David Davis*, 200–08.

most unhappy in Washington, wished he had not taken the position, and talked from the beginning about resigning, as he was ultimately to do though not until many years had passed. "Men don't breathe free here,"[108] he lamented in a letter to Leonard Swett. "The yearning for *you* has been like the yearning of a child for its mother,"[109] he wrote to his wife.

One of Davis' early difficulties lay in the fact that he had made a bad selection of rooms for himself. During the war the pressure for space was even greater than in earlier times. Rooms were expensive and hard to find. Once they were leased, it was hard to recover the money involved if they were surrendered. Davis, knowing little about Washington, had made his selection on the advice of one Albert Jones and Justice Wayne. He had hardly arrived before he was complaining to Mrs. Davis of the isolation of his quarters, the quality of the people with whom he had to dine, and the lack of comfort. He had more space than he needed, unless Mrs. Davis joined him, and he knew she would not be pleased with the rooms. The bed was hard as a brickbat. There was no man servant about the house, though there was a good Irish girl whom he liked very much. Because the rental season was under way, he could not give up his quarters without the loss of five hundred dollars invested or committed. Justices Nelson and Swayne had told him that he ought to have gone to Morrison's, at 23 4½ Street, a three-story building in which a number of the Justices lived and took their meals at a table set apart for them, and where the downtown library of the Justices was located. He needed convenient access to the library for study.[110]

Mrs. Davis by letter advised him to move to comfortable quarters even at the loss of the money involved, and he did so and was happier with the new arrangement. "I feel that I made a wise change," he wrote to Mrs. Davis. "The society of the Judges is a good deal, and the Library is every thing."[111] The stairs were pretty steep for the climb to his third-floor quarters, and the walls were thin, but on the whole he was much happier.[112] He found his brethren pleasant and agreeable: "Some of them are learned men, others not. I feel my want of learning lamentably but I will try to get along by study."[113] "Judge Swayne is a great man," he wrote. "I feel my littleness by the side of him, although

---

[108] D. Davis to Leonard Swett, Dec. 16, 1862, Davis Papers.

[109] D. Davis to Mrs. Davis, Dec. 7, 1862, Davis Papers.

[110] *Ibid.*, and D. Davis to Julius Rockwell, Dec. 22, 1862, Davis Papers.

[111] D. Davis to Mrs. Davis, Dec. 16, 1862, Davis Papers.

[112] D. Davis to Mrs. Davis, Dec. 12, 1862, Davis Papers.

[113] D. Davis to Mrs. Davis, Dec. 14, 1862, Davis Papers.

we are on the same bench."[114] About Justice Miller, the other Lincoln appointee, who lived with his wife at the National Hotel, Davis had little to say: "I will reserve my comments about Judge Miller until I see you."[115]

Davis was fascinated by the social life of Washington and described in detail a dinner given on December 31 by the Justices residing at Morrison's, at which all the Justices were present except Chief Justice Taney, who never went out, and Justice Nelson, who was absent because of the death of a daughter. It was an elegant dinner, wrote Davis, and would probably cost twenty dollars a plate. It had been gotten up by Justice Clifford, who had once been minister to Mexico, and who took pride in these matters. Describing the seven courses, which kept the diners at the table from five o'clock until nine, Davis assured Mrs. Davis that he had sipped only a little of the wine, keeping his promise to her. Present in addition to members of the Supreme Court were former Justice Curtis, William H. Seward, Reverdy Johnson, Orville H. Browning, Jeremiah S. Black, Ward H. Lamon, Caleb Cushing, Edward Bates, and others. It was not often, wrote Davis, that as many distinguished men were assembled.[116]

On New Year's Day, 1862, Marshal Lamon sent a carriage, "free," to take the Justices to the White House to be received by the President. Present also were the foreign corps, all properly bedecked, and "enough military floating around here, to take Charleston." They also called on Chief Justice Taney, Justice Wayne, and many others, ending up at Hill Lamon's—"a few oysters and drank a little egg nogg." There was not much social life in Washington that winter, for which Davis was glad, but on that day the whole city seemed to be out.[117]

Davis wrote that he dined at the White House from time to time, as did also Justice Swayne, and he visited and dined with various members of the Cabinet, concluding, incidentally, that he did not much like Secretary of the Treasury Chase.[118] At Seward's home Davis and four other Justices attended a dinner which Justice Clifford thought nearly equal to that given by the Court, and Davis characterized it as "the most elegant dinner I ever sat down to." He was particularly interested in the social skills of Justice Catron, who accompanied Justice Grier's daughter to the dinner: "Judge Catron is a polished gentleman.

---

[114] D. Davis to Mrs. Davis, Dec. 7, 1862, Davis Papers.

[115] D. Davis to Mrs. Davis, Feb. 12, 1863, Davis Papers.

[116] D. Davis to Mrs. Davis, Jan. 1, 1863, Davis Papers. See also *Diary of Orville Hickman Browning,* Theodore Calvin Pease and James G. Randall, eds., I, 606.

[117] D. Davis to Mrs. Davis, Jan. 1, 1863, Davis Papers.

[118] D. Davis to Mrs. Davis, Feb. 22, 1863, Davis Papers.

He seemed to be in his element waiting on a young lady, who was very showy, dressed in figured silk." Although six or eight different kinds of wine were served, Davis assured his wife that he tasted only one, a glass of champagne.[119] Davis and other Justices attended also a dinner at the home of Jeremiah S. Black, the Court Reporter, which Davis hoped would end the "dissipation" for the term,[120] but there were still other dinners at the homes of Secretary Chase and Joseph Holt.[121]

Justice Miller, who took seriously his duties as a member of the Court but who professed no "morbid self-distrust,"[122] presented his first opinion for the Court on December 15, 1862,[123] the first day on which opinions were announced. Justice Davis took a draft of his own first opinion to Baltimore where he spent Christmas with his cousin, Henry Winter Davis, who read it and corrected the phraseology of a few sentences.[124] He presented the opinion on January 5, 1863.[125] He continued to have doubts about his ability. One opinion kept him busy at revision until midnight after a dinner at William H. Seward's.[126] He began to feel more assurance when it was accepted by the Court without alteration.[127] He was much relieved when Justice Catron told him that the judges liked the style of his opinions very much and that he expressed himself better than anyone else on the bench.[128]

Yet Davis, so self-doubting in the area of judicial performance, was persistent and tireless in the area of politics. He was constantly urging appointments upon the President and his subordinates and giving advice on matters of public policy. During his first term in Washington he in some way persuaded Congress to enact two statutes changing the boundaries of his circuit, the Eighth, which originally consisted of Illinois, Michigan, and Wisconsin. Before he had been a month on the Supreme Court he was writing to his wife that he was hoping to get Michigan transferred into Justice Swayne's circuit and Indiana transferred into his: "In Indiana, three weeks court will suffice. In Michigan, at least 5 or 6 weeks, and Detroit is two days ride from home, while Indianapolis is but one. If I could swap Wisconsin for Missouri, I should be pretty well fixed, for I should then be but a day's

---

[119] D. Davis to Mrs. Davis, Feb. 6, 1863, Davis Papers.
[120] D. Davis to Mrs. Davis, Feb. 12, 16, 1863, Davis Papers.
[121] D. Davis to Mrs. Davis, Feb. 22, 1863, Davis Papers.
[122] Charles Fairman, *Mr. Justice Miller and the Supreme Court*, 58.
[123] Russell v. Ely, 2 Black 575 (1862).
[124] D. Davis to Mrs. Davis, Dec. 25, 1862, Davis Papers.
[125] Randall v. Howard, 2 Black 585 (1863).
[126] D. Davis to Mrs. Davis, Feb. 6, 1863, Davis Papers.
[127] D. Davis to Mrs. Davis, Feb. 7, 1863, Davis Papers; Koehler v. Black River Falls Iron Co., 2 Black 715 (1863).
[128] D. Davis to Mrs. Davis, Feb. 12, 16, 1863, Davis Papers.

ride from St. Louis, Chicago, or Indianapolis."[129] Congress eventually made the exchange of Indiana for Michigan,[130] and then, without transferring Missouri to the Eighth Circuit, shifted Wisconsin over to Justice Miller on the Ninth Circuit, so that the Eighth Circuit consisted only of Illinois and Indiana.[131] Justice Davis thereafter had only closely circumscribed circuit responsibilities, principally at Springfield, Chicago, and Indianapolis, whereas Justice Miller had Missouri, Iowa, Kansas, Minnesota, and Wisconsin. When for the first time he held Circuit Court in Indianapolis, Justice Davis wrote that he did so with distrust because Judge Swayne had held the previous terms, but he thought that he got along very well.[132]

For those who had to secure temporary accommodations in Washington during the war period the task grew more difficult year by year. In early September, 1863, Justice Grier, who had been one of the first Justices to take rooms at Morrison's, learned that space had not been reserved for him by the landlady for the forthcoming term of the Court. He wrote to D. W. Middleton, assistant clerk of the Court— William Thomas Carroll having recently died—that he had not expected to be turned out first, "to accommodate a speculating greedy Yankee woman." He asked Middleton to do the best he could for him. As he was very weak in the legs, he preferred not to have to climb to a third story. He preferred not to inhabit a cellar or a garret or to camp out. "I have very little notion of paying the Yankee woman *three* dollars a day for 'feeding' me (dear as *old butter* may be) besides one dollar a day for a garret."[133]

Justice Grier's continued extensive correspondence with Middleton about the housing situation contained further aspersions about the rapacious conduct of Northern people. He continued to get letters, he said, pestering him with recommendations for the office of Clerk of the Court to replace Carroll: "There will be a great effort with politicians around the president with the *new judges* to have some abolitionist from the *north*, their argument being that the *south* has had the office too long. But the old judges *are still the majority* of *ten* and will not be moved by such arguments." How was the health of the Chief Justice, he asked. "I hope he will continue to live if for no other reason than to *spite* the reptiles who so anxiously desire his *death*."[134] Mid-

---

[129] D. Davis to Mrs. Davis, Dec. 28, 1862, Davis Papers. See also letters of Jan. 1, Jan. 28, Feb. 6, 1863.

[130] 12 Stat. 637.

[131] 12 Stat. 648.

[132] Typewritten copy, David Davis to W. W. Orme, May 30, 1863, Davis Papers.

[133] R. C. Grier to D. W. Middleton, Sept. 8, 1863, Clerk's Files.

[134] R. C. Grier to D. W. Middleton, Oct. 19, 1863, Clerk's Files.

dleton replied that the Chief Justice was in his normal health and he hoped he might continue for many years.[135]

Justice Grier's housing problems were complicated in that he expected to have with him in Washington his daughter, Mrs. Sarah G. Beck. Middleton continued the search on his behalf and also for Justice Clifford, who vacillated between rooms in a private boarding house at high prices and at the National Hotel where prices were similarly high, being concerned about space, board, wood for fire, and closeness to the rooms of his brethren. He was unused to chaffering about the price of board, he said, and he found it unpleasant, but the change of matters at Morrison's left him no alternative.[136] There had never been such an opportunity for hotel and boardinghouse keepers to charge high prices, Middleton replied, and they all seemed disposed to take advantage of it.[137] He had at last been able to secure rooms for Justice Grier and his daughter at Mrs. Taylor's, at the corner of C and Third streets. It was "a very nice house and kept by very gentle people." Judge Grier was to have three rooms with board and pay one-hundred and eighty dollars per month for himself and his daughter. They were anxious to have Justice Clifford there also, where he could have two rooms on the second floor for ninety dollars a month. They would have few boarders, and the judges could probably have a private table if desired.[138] This arrangement was worked out.[139]

At this term Justices Catron, Swayne, and Davis again returned to Morrison's. Mrs. Davis spent most of the term with her husband and engaged somewhat reluctantly in the formal life of the capital,[140] apparently having a reassuring effect on her husband. "The ladies in this boarding house are very pleasant and kind," Davis wrote. "I get along in the Court better than last winter. *Great* men, when in daily intercourse with them, do not come up to original ideas. There is a good deal of hard work. But for a man who has a family and pleasant home, and who is not over ambitious, the office is undesirable."[141]

Justice Miller resided at 27 4½ Street, adjacent or almost adjacent to Morrison's. The new Justice, Field, lived at 390 Fourth Street. Justice Nelson went to Willard's Hotel. Chief Justice Taney and Justice

[135] D. W. Middleton to R. C. Grier, Oct. 22, 1863, Clerk's Files.

[136] Nathan Clifford to D. W. Middleton, Oct. 7, 1863, Clerk's Files.

[137] D. W. Middleton to Nathan Clifford, Oct. 20, 1863, Clerk's Files.

[138] D. W. Middleton to Nathan Clifford, Oct. 16, 1863, Clerk's Files.

[139] Nathan Clifford to D. W. Middleton, Oct. 22, 1863, Clerk's Files.

[140] See Sarah W. Davis to George Perrin Davis, Jan. 15, 1864, Davis Papers.

[141] Typewritten copy, D. Davis to Julius Rockwell, Jan. 24, 1864, Davis Papers.

Wayne remained at their permanent residences, at 23 Indiana Avenue and 2 Franklin Place.[142]

The Court assembled on December 7, 1863. This was one of the few occasions on which all of the ten Justices were present, for Chief Justice Taney was absent during much of the term because of illness, and other absences kept attendance reduced until the number of Justices was officially curtailed. In spite of the foreboding of Justice Grier, there seems to have been no effort on the part of Northern Justices to enforce the selection of an abolitionist as a Clerk, that position being conferred on Middleton, long employed by the Court as Carroll's deputy.[143]

There was more difficulty during that term over the selection of a new Reporter, to replace Jeremiah S. Black, who was now garnering wealth handling California land cases. A long roster of members of the bar of the District of Columbia recommended Philip Richard Fendall. Chief Justice Taney, having seen the petition of the local bar and knowing Fendall personally, sent word to Justice Wayne that his vote was to be cast for Fendall, with a Mr. Law of New York as his second choice.[144] Attorney General Bates also supported Fendall.[145] The Court decided, however, upon John William Wallace of Pennsylvania, then reporter of the decisions of the Third Circuit, apparently without important reference to regional affiliations.

The personnel situation on the Court itself was still regarded as unsatisfactory by members of Congress, even though there were four Lincoln appointees who were relatively young and vigorous. The almost continuous absence of Chief Justice Taney meant that there were really only nine Justices rather than ten, and his comparable absence from his circuit meant that little circuit work got done. Other members were likewise of advanced age and in varying degrees of physical decrepitude. It was recognized that Chief Justice Taney and perhaps others as well remained on the Court primarily because they had no other income and no adequate reserves to pay their living expenses. It was assumed that some of them might resign if arrangement were made to give them an adequate retirement income. In December, 1863, Senator James Harlan of Iowa introduced a bill for the retirement of physically infirm Justices at or above the age of seventy, with schedules of income varying with the number of years served.[146] The bill was

---

[142] The residences are listed in the *Washington National Intelligencer,* Dec. 17, 1863.

[143] *New York Times,* Dec. 8, 1863.

[144] Letter from Ellen M. Stevenson, Chief Justice Taney's daughter, to James M. Wayne, Feb. 19, 1864, Clerk's Files.

[145] Edward Bates to R. B. Taney, Feb. 26, 1864, Clerk's Files.

[146] *Cong. Globe,* 38th Cong., 1st Sess. 42.

referred to the Judiciary Committee but for some reason was reported adversely,[147] with the result that no action was taken.[148] The personnel of the Supreme Court therefore remained unchanged until the death of Chief Justice Taney the following October.

---

[147] *Ibid.*, 319.

[148] During the same session of Congress the *New York Tribune* discussed in an ably written editorial the growing burden of circuit work on the Supreme Court and the increasing mass of litigation resulting from the war. It proposed the subdivision of the circuits to make way for a Supreme Court of thirteen members, of whom seven would constitute a quorum. Congress, however, seems not to have given serious attention to the proposal. *New York Tribune*, Dec. 31, 1863.

CHAPTER XXXIII

The War and the Federal Judges

ALTHOUGH DURING THE CIVIL WAR, as in most major wars, the judiciary was for the most part outside the mainstream of events, the early months engaged most of the members of the depleted Supreme Court and many of the federal district judges. Among their concerns were the suspension of the privilege of the writ of habeas corpus, the definition of treason, and prize law. The Lincoln Administration first considered suspending habeas corpus after the turbulent events in Baltimore in April, 1861. In that period Marylanders were deeply divided and confused as to their loyalties. Although many quickly committed themselves to the Union cause, various government officials, editors, and leading businessmen and politicians sympathized with the South or were at least more hostile to the Yankees of the North than they were loyal to the Union.

Some Marylanders, furthermore, recognized that their state's interests were not identical with those of either adjacent region. Eager to prevent Maryland from becoming a battleground between the North and the South, they talked of establishing a middle-states republic, free from military commitments, presumably with the dream of profitable trade in both directions. In December, 1860, soon after he had given up his position as Supreme Court Reporter, Benjamin C. Howard had discussed the possibility that "our country is destined to be cut up into parallel slices as you would slice a piece of bread."[1] Thomas H. Hicks, Know-Nothing governor of Maryland in this critical period who is given much credit for keeping Maryland from joining the seceding states, himself wavered before taking a stand. For a time he seems to have taken much the same position as Howard, proposing to Governor William Burton of Delaware that the two states unite in a central con-

---

[1] B. C. Howard to John P. Kennedy, Dec. 26, 1860, Kennedy Papers.

federacy opposed to both the North and the South. Governor Burton, however, insisted that Delaware must remain with the Union.[2]

With the outbreak of hostilities people who had speculatively shifted their positions were driven toward some kind of commitment. Governor Hicks moved slowly toward support of the Union. He was in Baltimore on April 19, 1861, when Baltimore lived up to its reputation as "Mob City" by producing a riot when at the call of the President a Massachusetts regiment marched through the city from one railroad station to another, causing bloodshed on both sides.[3] That night Governor Hicks, who was at the home of Mayor George William Brown, was awakened to hear from Marshal George P. Kane of the Baltimore police and Mayor Brown an appeal that he as governor authorize the destruction of the railroad bridges to the east of the city to prevent the entrance of more Northern troops. According to an unsympathetic account by William Watkins Glenn, editor of the pro-Southern *Baltimore Exchange*, Hicks was most reluctant to give his assent. He was said to have twisted the sheet over his head, rolled and groaned, and finally moaned, "Oh! Yes. Go ahead and do it." Early next morning, however, according to Glenn's report, Hicks "sneaked out of the house" and headed for Annapolis so that it proved impossible to get from him a written order for the burning of bridges.[4] The destruction of the bridges nevertheless proceeded, to the disruption of Union military transport.

Volunteer troops continued to move southward from the Northern states, with concentrations building up at Philadelphia and Harrisburg and other points so that it would soon be possible to occupy the city. Although part of the story is lost in the record of the confusion, it is clear that someone somewhere feared that dissident Marylanders might seek to use the federal courts to defeat Union strategy. In any event, without giving it publicity, President Lincoln on April 27, 1861, issued an order to Commanding General Winfield Scott to enable him to cope with judicial interference, a document which began: "You are engaged

---

[2] T. H. Hicks to William Burton, Jan. 2, 1861, and Burton to Hicks, Jan. 8, 1861, as excerpts were quoted in an advertisement in the catalog of the American Art Association, May, 1923; Carl B. Swisher, *Roger B. Taney*, 540.

[3] For an account of these events see George William Brown, *Baltimore and the Nineteenth of April, 1861*; George L. P. Radcliffe, *Governor Thomas H. Hicks of Maryland and*

the Civil War; Edward G. Everett, "The Baltimore Riots, April, 1861," Pennsylvana History, 24:331, 1957; Charles B. Clark, *Politics in Maryland During the Civil War* (1952) (reprinting articles appearing under the same title, in *American Historical Magazine*, 38–41.

[4] Manuscript Diary of William Watkins Glenn, entry of Apr. 19, 1861, Glenn Papers.

in repressing an insurrection against the laws of the United States." If at any point between Philadelphia and Washington the general found resistance such that it was necessary to suspend the writ of habeas corpus for the public safety, the general himself or the local commanding officer was authorized to suspend the writ.[5]

On May 2, 1861, Major W. W. Morris, claiming to act exclusively on his own initiative, administered to a federal court the first military rebuff. On that day Judge William F. Giles issued a writ of habeas corpus, not for an offender in connection with military obstruction, but for the release of a minor who had enlisted in local Union forces without the consent of his parents. A deputy marshal presented the writ to Major Morris, commander at Fort McHenry. Morris read the document and handed it back with the remark that he would see the court and the marshal damned before he would surrender one of his men.[6]

Judge Giles immediately issued an order directing Morris to appear in court on May 8 to show why an attachment should not be issued against him for his refusal to obey the writ. He drafted the order in the form of a denunciation of military disobedience to the writ and gave it to the press for publication even before its delivery at the fort. This was the first time in his thirty-three years at the bar and bench, he wrote, that the writ had failed in Maryland to procure obedience. He sincerely hoped that in this crisis wiser counsels might prevail at the post, "and that no unnecessary conflict of authority may be brought in, between those owing allegiance to the same government and bound by the same laws."[7]

In his order Judge Giles stated that there had been no suspension of habeas corpus by competent authority. Major Morris, reading the Giles order in a newspaper, replied to it in a formal letter, not indicating any knowledge of the Presidential order and saying that his action was taken "entirely on my own responsibility without instructions from, or consultation with any person whatever." There might have been a question whether the Presidential authorization extended to the status of an illegally enlisted minor, since it was couched in terms of resistance to military forces along the line from Philadelphia to Washington.

---

[5] The order appears in somewhat varying phraseology in John J. Nicolay and John Hay, *Abraham Lincoln: A History*, IV, 169, and Abraham Lincoln, *Collected Works*, Roy P. Basler, ed., IV, 347.

[6] Affidavit of James Gettings, May 2, 1861, Attorney General Papers.

[7] In the matter of the petition of John G. Muller before Judge Giles, in the District Court of the United States for the State of Maryland. A clipping from the *Baltimore Exchange*, May 4, 1861, Attorney General Papers.

In justifying his action, Morris scathingly denounced the violence of Baltimore people against the Union forces. He argued that the writ of habeas corpus in the hands of an unfriendly power might depopulate the fortification and place it at the mercy of a "Baltimore Mob" in much less time than it could be done by all the appliances of modern warfare. Furthermore, in view of the ferocious attitude of the community against the military, he would be averse to appearing publicly and unprotected on the streets of Baltimore. In these circumstances, he said to Judge Giles, "I think it your duty to sustain the federal military and to strengthen their hands instead of endeavoring to strike them down."[8]

Judge Giles replied by saying that the statement in the newspapers represented what he had said in court and that he had given it to the press to prevent unintentional misrepresentation. He refrained from further discussing the issues beyond saying that the power to suspend the writ of habeas corpus was "a power which in my opinion belongs to Congress alone,"[9] thereby getting into the record one of the major points made later in criticism of suspension by the President. When a marshal was sent to serve on Major Morris the order of the court he refused to receive it, remarking that he would not obey any order or permit service of a writ of any kind issued by this or any other court.[10] Judge Giles, unable to act further, sent copies of the correspondence to the district attorney, William Meade Addison, with the suggestion that they be sent to Washington. Addison forwarded them to Attorney General Bates[11] and, according to Morris, the matter became an issue in the Cabinet the next day, even as the minor was quietly released.[12]

The signal for the next judicial attempt at restraint of the military came when at 2:00 A.M. on the morning of May 25, 1861, troops under the command of Captain Samuel Yohe charged with protection of the railroad between Baltimore and Harrisburg, under the overall direction of Major General William H. Keim, entered the home of John Merryman near Cockeysville, some miles north of Baltimore, and arrested him for participation in the destruction of railroad bridges after the Baltimore riot of April 19. Merryman was imprisoned in Fort McHenry.[13] The records do not reveal the urgency that led to the arrest at this time

---

[8] W. W. Morris to William F. Giles, May 6, 1861, Attorney General Papers. See also *New York Evening Post*, May 14, 1861.

[9] William F. Giles to W. W. Morris, May 7, 1861, Attorney General Papers.

[10] John W. Watkins to William F. Giles, May 8, 1861, Attorney General Papers.

[11] William Meade Addison to Edward Bates, May 8, 1861, Attorney General Papers.

[12] Manuscript diary of William Watkins Glenn, entry of June 2, 1861, Glenn Papers.

[13] For the records and papers in the case, from which primarily the materials presented hereafter are taken, see 1 O.R. (2d) 574–85.

of night but they do show that about this time Captain Yohe found it expedient to make in the heart of the secessionist area in Baltimore an ostentatious display of Union military strength.[14]

Southern sympathizers used the arrest as the occasion for pouring out their indignation at what they regarded as the unspeakable arrogance of the military and of the government in Washington. Merryman was a prominent farmer, politician, and member of the state legislature as well as of a state company of cavalry. His father and Chief Justice Taney had attended Dickinson College in the same period.

Merryman was given immediate access to counsel, who drafted a petition for a writ of habeas corpus. Since Judge Giles had already failed to procure obedience from Major Morris at Fort McHenry, Merryman's counsel decided to go directly to the Chief Justice, not as circuit judge but as the head of the Supreme Court. The writ was addressed not to Major Morris but to General George Cadwalader,[15] commander of the military district in which Fort McHenry was included, who was himself a lawyer and the brother of Judge John Cadwalader, federal district judge in Philadelphia.[16]

On Sunday, May 26, the petition was presented for Taney's signature in Baltimore. When Taney at the appointed time took his place on the bench in the Masonic Hall where he was accustomed to hold Circuit Court, General Cadwalader did not appear. Instead, arriving some twenty minutes late, an aide-de-camp, a Colonel Lee, decked out in full uniform and wearing a red sash and a sword, appeared to convey the general's regrets and say that engagements at the fort had prevented his coming. Lee presented a statement in which Cadwalader said that Merryman was "charged with various acts of treason, and with being publicly associated with, and holding a commission as lieutenant in a company having possession of arms belonging to the United States, and avowing his purpose of armed hostility against the Government." The general's statement officially brought into the open the Presidential suspension of the privilege of the writ of habeas corpus—or suspension of the writ, as loosely expressed in most of the official documents of the time. "He has further to inform you that he is duly authorized by the President of the United States, in such cases to suspend the writ of *Habeas Corpus*, for the public safety. This is a high and delicate trust, and it has been enjoined upon him that it should be executed with

---

[14] See *Baltimore South*, May 27, 1861.

[15] This is the spelling currently used. At that time it was frequently spelled "Cadwallader."

[16] See *Baltimore South*, May 27,

1861; *Baltimore American*, May 28, 1861. The proceedings are detailed at length in the several local newspapers and in the Tyler and Steiner and Swisher biographies of the Chief Justice.

judgment and discretion—but he is nevertheless instructed that in times of civil strife, errors, if any, should be on the side of safety to the country."

Finally, the general administered a politely phrased rebuke to the court for its interference: "He most respectfully submits for your consideration, that those who should co-operate in the present trying and painful position in which our country is placed, should not, by reason of any unnecessary want of confidence in each other, increase our embarrassments." He therefore requested postponement of any action by the court until he could receive instructions from the President.

The Chief Justice refused to debate with the general, or with his aide, either the matter of public policy or the law of the suspension of the writ. Counsel for Merryman asked formally whether Colonel Lee had produced the body of Merryman, according to the order of the court. Colonel Lee replied that he had not. Chief Justice Taney thereupon issued the following stern pronouncement:

> General Cadwalader was commanded to produce the body of Mr. Merryman before me this morning, that the case might be heard, and the petitioner be either remanded to custody, or set at liberty, if held on insufficient grounds; but he has acted in disobedience to the writ, and I therefore direct that an attachment be at once issued against him, returnable before me here, at twelve o'clock tomorrow.

In great excitement the people of Baltimore waited to see the outcome of this contest between the Chief Justice and the general, who in this affair represented the military authority of the President. On May 28, well before the appointed hour, the courtroom was tightly packed and a crowd of some two thousand people were assembled in the street outside. Among the lawyers crowding into the area reserved for the bar was Benjamin C. Howard, who was given a place at the clerk's desk.[17] Leaving for the court from the home of his son-in-law, J. Mason Campbell, in the company of his grandson, Taney remarked that he himself might be imprisoned in Fort McHenry before nightfall but he was determined to do his duty.

At the session of the court held on the preceding day Judge Giles had sat with Chief Justice Taney, but he was absent at the second session, avowedly because of some church duty scheduled for that time. Actually his absence on this occasion may have been for the purpose of enabling the Chief Justice to highlight the fact that this was not a session of the Circuit Court but was a session at chambers by the Chief

---

[17] *Baltimore Patriot*, May 28, 1861.

Justice of the Supreme Court, and Taney so announced, though at that time and for many years thereafter opinions written at chambers were not usually printed in official reports.

Taking his seat on the bench the Chief Justice asked, "Marshal, have you your return, sir?" Marshal Washington Bonifant handed him a folded paper which was in turn handed to the clerk to be read aloud. It stated that the marshal had gone to the fort pursuant to the writ of attachment and had sent in his name from the outer gate, but had been told that there was no answer, so that he had been unable to serve the writ. After further colloquy the Chief Justice read the following statement:

> I ordered the attachment yesterday, because upon the face of the return the detention of the prisoner was unlawful upon two grounds.
>
> 1. The President, under the Constitution and laws of the United States, cannot suspend the privilege of the writ of *habeas corpus,* nor authorize any military officer to do so.
>
> 2. A military officer has no right to arrest and detain a person, not subject to the rules and articles of war, for an offence against the laws of the United States, except in and of the judicial authority and subject to its control—and if the party is arrested by the military, it is the duty of the officer to deliver him over immediately to the civil authority, to be dealt with according to law.
>
> I forbore yesterday to state orally the provisions of the Constitution of the United States, which make these principles the fundamental law of the Union, because an oral statement might be misunderstood in some portions of it, and I shall therefore put my opinion in writing and file it in the office of the Clerk of the Circuit Court, in the course of this week.[18]

Having eschewed oral statement the Chief Justice nevertheless proceeded to make one, as if carried on by the weight of his emotions. The marshal, he said, had the legal power to summon a posse and bring the general into court, but since the marshal would undoubtedly be met by superior force, such action could not be taken. If the general were before the Court, it would inflict such punishment as lay within its power, of fine and imprisonment. Under the circumstances he would write out the conclusions on which the opinion was based and would "report them with these proceedings to the President of the United States, and call upon him to perform his constitutional duty to enforce the laws. In other words, to enforce the process of this Court." At this point the reporter noted the word "Sensation," to describe the reaction of the

---

[18] *Baltimore American,* May 29, 1861.

audience. With this statement the proceedings ended, but it was said that for hours thereafter a large crowd remained assembled in the street outside.[19]

After the Court had adjourned, George William Brown, mayor of Baltimore, went up to congratulate Chief Justice Taney on preserving the integrity of the writ of habeas corpus. The latter replied, "Mr. Brown, I am an old man, a very old man, but perhaps I was preserved for this occasion." "Sir, I thank God that you were," replied the mayor. Taney added that he knew that his own imprisonment had been considered but that the danger had now passed. The time of the mayor, he prophesied, was yet to come.[20]

News of the Merryman case and of Chief Justice Taney's action spread over the country even before his opinion was made public a few days later. The *New York Tribune* gloated over General Cadwalader's "rebuke of the hoary apologist for crime" and asserted that Merryman was undoubtedly a traitor of the deepest dye.[21] A reporter for the *New York Times* asserted that Taney's purpose was to bring on a collision between the judicial and the military branches of the government; Taney himself was at heart a rebel, who was reported to have expressed the hope that in the war in Virginia the Virginians would wade to their waists in Northern blood; his going to Baltimore to hear the case disclosed the alacrity with which he was willing to serve the Southern cause.[22] Less inclined to condemn, the *New York Herald* voiced the belief that Taney had unknowingly made himself the tool of Maryland secession.[23] The *New York Evening Post* remarked that while newly selected servants of the nation were being required to take an oath of loyalty it might be well to tender the same oath to the Chief Justice.[24]

Taney plunged immediately into the composition of his opinion in the Merryman case, writing and correcting as was his custom to secure the most effective statement possible, labeling it "Before the Chief Justice of the Supreme Court of the United States at Chambers."[25] It was drafted as a challenge to the power of the President to suspend the writ of habeas corpus and to delegate that power to a military officer. No official notice, he said, had been given to the courts of justice or to the public, by proclamation or otherwise, that the President claimed this power. He had listened with surprise to General Cadwalader's

---

[19] *Ibid.*

[20] George William Brown, *Baltimore and the Nineteenth of April, 1861*, 90.

[21] *New York Tribune*, May 29, 30, 1861.

[22] *New York Times*, May 29, 1861.

[23] *New York Herald*, May 30, 1861.

[24] *New York Evening Post*, May 29, 1861.

[25] An early and much corrected draft of the opinion in Taney's longhand is preserved in the Howard Papers.

statement of the President's claim, "for I had assumed it to be one of those points of constitutional law upon which there was no difference of opinion, and that it was admitted on all hands, that the privilege of the writ could not be suspended, except by act of Congress."[26] Alluding to President Jefferson's treatment of the writ as capable of suspension only by Congress, Taney stated that had the refusal to obey the writ been voiced by the military commander on his own responsibility he would merely have referred to the Constitution and its unanimous interpretation on this point. But since the official claimed to act under the authority of the President, and since he believed the President to have exercised a power which he did not possess, he deemed it expedient to examine the whole subject.

The constitutional provision stated that "The privilege of the writ of habeas corpus shall not be suspended, unless when in cases of rebellion or invasion the public safety may require it." Taney emphasized the fact that the provision was included in section 9 of Article I, a section which followed an enumeration of the powers of Congress and "has not the slightest reference to the executive department." It consisted, as he read it, only of prohibitions upon Congress. Therefore the statement of exceptional circumstances under which the writ might be suspended seemed to him to apply only to Congress. The writ, or its privilege, could be suspended only by Congress, and Congress, not the President, was the judge of what the public safety might require. He stressed the brevity of the Presidential term—ignoring the fact that members of the House of Representatives were chosen for only half the length of that term—and dwelt upon the limitations on the Presidential office. In contrast to the delight Taney had once taken at the vigorous exercise of Presidential power by Andrew Jackson, he now saw the President as little more than a ministerial officer doing the will of Congress and necessarily leaving a great deal even of administrative responsibility to other officers of the government.

The Chief Justice delved into Blackstone's *Commentaries* and Hallam's *Constitutional History* to show that in England restriction on the privilege of the writ had been a legislative and not an executive power. He turned to Story's *Commentaries* to show that the same was true in the United States, and to an opinion by Chief Justice Marshall with an incidental comment to the same effect.[27] He contended, furthermore, that even if the privilege of the writ were suspended by Act of

---

[26] *Ex parte* Merryman, 17 Fed. Cas. 144, 148 (No. 9487) (C.C.D. Md. 1861). This citation of the case as in the Circuit Court for the district of Maryland is not to be taken as an admission on the part of the Chief Justice that the case was disposed of in that court. He continued to treat it as a decision by the Chief Justice at chambers.

[27] *Ex parte* Bollman and Swartwout, 4 Cranch 75, 101 (1807).

Congress, persons not subject to the rules and articles of war could not be detained by the military or tried before a military tribunal. In a concluding paragraph he stated that he would file the opinion with the clerk of the Circuit Court and direct him to transmit a copy, under seal, to the President. "It will then remain for that high officer, in fulfillment of his constitutional obligation to 'take care that the laws be faithfully executed,' to determine what measures he will take to cause the civil process of the United States to be respected and enforced."[28]

By contrast with his Dred Scott opinion, which he had worked on for weeks after delivery before giving it to the public, Taney made his Merryman opinion available within a week. It was published in newspapers and journals all over the country, as well as in pamphlets distributed by or for the Chief Justice himself.[29] He did some additional writing in the case as comments came in, appending a paragraph to a copy given to his grandson, R. B. Taney Campbell, and wished that the added material had been incorporated in the original opinion,[30] but the addendum has apparently not been preserved.

The opinion had the impact of a military victory for the South and was hailed with delight by enemies of the Administration. To a Maryland friend who had written to him in praise of it, Taney replied that he had no desire for conflict with the executive branch of the government, and would prefer to spend the rest of his life in peace, yet "I trust I shall always be found ready to meet any responsibility or any consequence that my official duty may require me to encounter."[31] In reply to an approving letter from Franklin Pierce, Taney said that in the present state of the public mind, inflamed with passion and seeking to accomplish its object by force of arms, he sensed his grave responsibility in the Merryman case. Public sentiment was almost at the stage of delirium. His hope was that the North as well as the South would soon see that a peaceful separation with free institutions in each section was better than union under a military government based on civil war and a reign of terror ruinous to the victors as well as the vanquished.[32] He did not say how he reconciled his retention of his position as Chief Justice with his conviction that the Union should be dissolved.

The *Baltimore Sun* provided an example of the reaction of pro-Southern newspapers:

---

[28] 17 Fed. Cas. 153.

[29] See R. B. Taney to J. Mason Campbell, June 13, 1861, Howard Papers.

[30] R. B. Taney to J. Mason Campbell, Mar. 15, 1862, Howard Papers.

[31] R. B. Taney to George W. Hughes, June 6, 1861, Samuel Tyler, *Memoir of Roger Brooke Taney*, 430–31.

[32] "R. B. Taney to Franklin Pierce, June 12, 1861," *American Historical Review*, 10:368, 1905.

It is not possible to read the opinion of Chief Justice Taney, in the Merryman case, without an impressive sense of the power of truth, and the convincing logic of the constitution and the laws. The paper is unanswerable. Like a stream first issuing as a spring clear and pellucid, it moves forward gathering breadth and strength, majesty and power, till in the accumulating volume of unvarying truth and right principle, it sweeps away all corruption and pours its tribute abundantly into the popular mind. . . .

Long after this terrible conflict shall have been brought to an end; when the fanaticism and commercial aggrandizement it is waged to serve shall have subsided; when the peace of desolation or of prosperity shall brood over the land, the grand, true, cogent, resistless influence of this document from the mind of Roger B. Taney will live, at once a vindication of the principles of the republic, and of the fundamental rights of the people, and an overwhelming protest against the action of those who have so rudely assailed them. It will take its place among the historic records of the period, as a precedent in all the future commotion and collision which may disturb the nation; or, as a monumental scroll, over-written with the words, "In memoriam," mark the era at which the nation ceased to exist, and the liberties of the people were immolated upon the altar of political and commercial ambition.[33]

Northern attitudes toward Taney's opinion were comparable to that expressed by the *New York Tribune* with respect to his original performance in court—"No Judge whose heart was loyal to the Constitution would have given such aid and comfort to public enemies." The editor renounced fear of a military despotism, which so disturbed the Chief Justice, and warned that "Of all the tyrannies that afflict mankind, that of the judiciary is the most insidious, the most intolerable, the most dangerous."[34] Taney's critics called attention to alleged inconsistencies between his challenge to the President and to the military in the *Merryman* case and his opinion in *Luther v. Borden* where no North-South issue was directly involved.[35] In the earlier case the Chief Justice had asked rhetorically whether a federal court could inquire into the correctness of the decision of the President to call out the militia. If it could, and if it differed with the President, it would be the duty of the court "to discharge those who were arrested or detained by the troops in the service of the United States or the government, which the President was endeavoring to maintain. If the judicial power extends so far, the guarantee contained in the Constitution of the United States is a guaran-

---

[33] *Baltimore Sun*, June 4, 1861.
[34] *New York Tribune*, May 30, 1861.

[35] See for example the *New York Herald*, June 9, 1861.

tee of anarchy and not of order."[36] By contrast with his disparaging comments in the *Merryman* case on the scope of Presidential power, and stress on the safeguards erected against Presidential tyranny, Taney had said in the *Luther* case, "It is said that this power in the President is dangerous to liberty, and may be abused. All power may be abused if placed in unworthy hands. But it would be difficult, we think, to point out any other hands in which this power would be more safe and at the same time equally effectual."[37] While the situations were not identical, the Chief Justice in the two cases dealt so differently with similar constitutional issues as further to convince Northern critics that in the Merryman case he was using constitutional principles to aid the secessionist cause.

Most immediate reactions to the Merryman case, whether approving or hostile, reflected primarily political considerations, with critical legal analysis to come later. When read without reference to the sectional controversy, the Taney opinion contains little to which critics can object and much to be applauded. It rings clear for all who fear the unnecessary expansion of executive power or irresponsible military behavior. That the danger to liberty was very real is shown by the tyrannical conduct during the war period on the part of various military leaders, including many who had not been brought up in a military tradition but who seem to have used their novel positions for behaving ruthlessly in the Union cause.

On the other hand the arrest of Merryman was not an instance of persecution of a harmless civilian. He was a lieutenant in the Maryland militia. The governor, because of the Southern sympathies of many of his people, had not responded to the President's act in calling the militia into the federal service. While the burning of bridges of which Merryman was accused had not been done pursuant to a written order from the governor, Mayor Brown, who had heard Governor Hicks' reluctant oral agreement, spread that information abroad,[38] even though Hicks made no public admission.

Thus the question of Merryman's military responsibility for his acts was anything but clear. It could have been argued, though subject to criticism from many angles, that a state militiaman in committing an offense against the military forces of the Union when a federal call had been issued for such militia was subject to the laws of war. It is also probably true, however, that Merryman was arrested not for offenses already committed, but rather to prevent the commission of others.

---

[36] Luther v. Borden, 7 How. 1, 43 (1849).

[37] *Ibid.*, 44.

[38] Brown, *Baltimore and the Nineteenth of April, 1861*, 73–74.

Punishment of Merryman by court-martial or military commission seems not to have been seriously considered, but the reasons were probably more political than legal. The President was far more concerned about keeping Maryland and other border states in the Union than about having punishment properly meted out in all cases. Indeed, the arrest of Merryman and the subsequent handling of the case did the Union cause far more harm than he could have done if left at large. There is some indication, indeed, that his release was about to be ordered from Washington when the embroilment of Chief Justice Taney in the case made his release inexpedient from a propaganda point of view.[39] That clash having taken place, Merryman continued to be held at Fort McHenry, in spite of the crowded condition of the place and the need for all the space and facilities for military purposes, and he was permitted to see callers from his family and numerous friends in Baltimore.[40] They in turn continued to make propaganda out of his detention; a report of a committee of the legislature pictured him as "the victim of military lawlessness and arbitrary power—the great remedial writ of *habeas corpus*, and all the guaranties of freedom which it embodies, having been stricken down, at one blow, for his oppression."[41]

The Administration got Merryman off its hands by the expedient of having him indicted in a civil court and transferred to civil jurisdiction where he was granted bail. The grand jury, wrote a reporter, were "all unconditional Union men."[42] Merryman was indicted for treason or for conspiracy to commit treason, the indictment charging that he had conspired with five hundred persons for armed resistance to the government and had participated in the destruction of the bridges to prevent the passage of troops, along with other illegal acts.[43] The Secretary of War thereupon authorized the transfer of Merryman to civil jurisdiction, and the Attorney General authorized his admission to bail.[44] He was released on bail fixed at forty thousand dollars.[45] He then became one of that considerable number of Marylanders under indictment whose prosecution was considered from time to time throughout the war but was prevented either because of the strategy of Chief Justice Taney,

---

[39] See Bernard C. Steiner, "James Alfred Pearce," *Maryland Historical Magazine*, 19:25, 1924.

[40] *Baltimore Sun*, quoted in *New York Evening Post*, June 3, 1861.

[41] *New York Evening Post*, June 17, 1861. The report was said to have been made by the Committee on Federal Relations of the Maryland legislature.

[42] *New York Herald*, June 22, 1861.

[43] *New York Evening Post*, July 12, 1861.

[44] Edward Bates to William Meade Addison, July 12, 1861, Attorney General's Letter Book B-4, 85.

[45] *New York Herald*, July 14, 1861.

as discussed hereafter, or because the Administration feared that more would be lost than gained through such prosecutions.

While Judge Giles and Chief Justice Taney were clashing with the military in Maryland, United States District Judge Samuel Treat was having similar difficulties in St. Louis. Missouri, like Maryland, was a border state, with a powerful secessionist faction which included the governor and other officers. Militia stationed at Camp Jackson, near St. Louis, were said to be receiving Confederate supplies and to constitute a threat to the United States arsenal in the city. On May 10, 1861, Captain Nathaniel Lyon moved against Camp Jackson with United States troops and forced its surrender. It was said that many of the prisoners moved through the streets hurrahing for Jeff Davis, and that writs of habeas corpus would be applied for by many of them but would be ignored by Captain Lyon.[46] All the enlisted men took an oath not to fight against the United States, and all but one of the fifty captured officers gave their parole to the same effect, with the appended sentence that "While we sign this parole with a full intention of observing it, we nevertheless protest against the justice of its exactions."[47] Captain Emmet McDonald, the officer who refused to give his parole, applied to Judge Treat for a writ of habeas corpus. On May 13, the day before the writ was served, and probably with the knowledge that service was planned, Captain McDonald was sent across the Mississippi River and some ten miles into Illinois, where he would be out of the jurisdiction of Judge Treat's court.[48]

When the writ was served on Brigadier General William S. Harney, he replied that McDonald was not imprisoned by him and had not been held by him since the issuing of the writ. Furthermore, the events at Camp Jackson had taken place before his arrival there. But he was unwilling to say anything to cast doubt on the validity of those proceedings, and was willing to take responsibility for them.[49]

Thereupon, Judge Treat, like Chief Justice Taney, proceeded to write an opinion on the scope of the power of the federal courts with respect to the writ of habeas corpus. General Harney had said nothing about the suspension of the writ by the President but had merely said that he would not obey it by releasing or subjecting to release a man in McDonald's position. Judge Treat argued elaborately from the Constitution and federal statutes and cases that the federal courts had the power in question, and thought it all the more important that the

---

[46] J. B. Eads to Simon Cameron, May 11, 1861, 1 O.R. (2d) 107.

[47] N. Lyon to S. Williams, May 17, 186, ibid., 112.

[48] William S. Harney to E. D. Townsend, May 18, 1861, ibid., 114–15.

[49] W. S. Harney to Samuel Treat, May 15, 1861, ibid., 115–16.

lodgment of the power be found there in view of the fact that the state courts did not have the power to take a prisoner from federal jurisdiction.[50]

It was reported that an application for a writ of habeas corpus for McDonald was filed in a federal District Court in Springfield, Illinois, before another judge of almost identical name, Samuel H. Treat, but the military apparently kept McDonald out of judicial reach. To Southern sympathizers, General Harney's defiance of Judge Treat was "equalled only by that of General Cadwallader in refusing to obey a similar writ issued by Judge Taney."[51] On the other hand, a newspaper with Northern sympathies was quoted as condemning the two judges for their meddling and traitorous efforts to thwart the government in its hour of peril, and suggested that suspension of the writ might well be followed by "suspension" (that is, hanging) of the two judges.[52]

Chief Justice Taney and Judge Treat exchanged copies of their opinions, the former calling it an alarming state of the public mind when the question of jurisdiction could be held in doubt. No one, he wrote somberly, could foresee the disastrous results to which inflamed passions might lead. It was gratifying to see the judiciary firmly performing its duty "and resisting all attempts to substitute military power in the place of the judicial authorities."[53]

In spite of the military frustration of Judge Treat's court, Captain McDonald, whether by exchange of prisoners or otherwise, eventually found his way into the Confederate forces, where he served well the cause of the South until he was killed, sometime in 1864. Judge Treat, on the other hand, having incurred the enmity of Francis P. Blair, Jr., commonly known as Frank Blair, who was elected to the House of Representatives from St. Louis, came close to losing his judicial position. Born in New Hampshire and educated at Harvard, Treat had moved to St. Louis in 1841 and had become a local leader of the Democratic Party. Although never a secessionist or a particular friend of slavery, he had displayed early his dislike of Frank Blair, who in 1856 was reported to be in Washington "*lionizing* amid the 'negro worshippers.' "[54] In March, 1857, at the very end of the Pierce Administration and just before the beginning of the Administration of James Buchanan (whom Treat disparaged for his lack of boldness), Congress divided into two judicial districts the one district in Missouri then served by Judge Robert W. Wells. The asserted ground was the need for a

---

[50] *In re* McDonald, 16 Fed. Cas. 17, 33 (No. 8751) (D.C.E.D. Mo. 1861). See *Cong. Globe*, 37th Cong., 1st Sess. 66 (1861).

[51] *Nashville Union and American*, June 6, 1861.

[52] *Ibid.*

[53] R. B. Taney to Samuel Treat, June 5, 1861, Treat Papers.

[54] Samuel Treat to Thomas G. Reynolds, Aug. 26, 1856, *ibid.*

federal judge continuously residing in St. Louis because of the growing admiralty business in that area. Blair insisted later, however, that the enactment was "an amendment that was slipped onto a bill at the tail end of a session of Congress, at midnight, to provide for a couple of politicians in that State."[55] After his appointment to the bench Judge Treat continued to serve his party, among other things preparing a statement for the Baltimore convention of 1860 denouncing the "dangerous sectional organization" which was the new Republican Party, calling for equal rights in the territories, and insisting that there was no "irrepressible conflict" between the North and the South.[56]

In spite of his concern about military encroachment on civil rights, Judge Treat, soon after he wrote his habeas corpus opinion, was working with Justice Catron and Judge Wells in the attempt to keep Missouri in the Union.[57] At the special session of Congress which began July 4, 1861, Frank Blair took advantage of Judge Treat's unpopularity resulting from the McDonald opinion to introduce in the House of Representatives a bill to repeal the act creating his judicial position and attach eastern Missouri to the western district which was served by Judge Wells.[58]

Blair's bill was not reported out of committee, but he succeeded in having it adopted as an amendment to another bill to increase the number of judicial districts in Kentucky from one to two, for the purpose of abolishing the present single district and thereby getting rid of Judge Thomas B. Monroe, a man of pronounced secessionist sympathies. The bill was passed by the House, in spite of the great improbability that Kentucky needed two judicial districts or that Missouri could be adequately served by only one district judge,[59] but the Senate delayed action until the ensuing regular session. Meanwhile Judge Treat got in touch with Attorney General Bates, also from St. Louis, and with other friends to urge them to fight the bill in the Senate, explaining the background of the controversy and the need for having a federal judge permanently in St. Louis. Bates talked with Justice Catron, who insisted that passage of the bill would be a public misfortune and agreed if necessary to appear before the Senate committee in opposition to the bill.[60] The Senate killed the bill by first sending it back to committee and

---

[55] *Cong. Globe*, 37th Cong., 1st Sess. 229 (1861).

[56] A draft of the statement is in the Thomas C. Reynolds Papers, Missouri Historical Society.

[57] See "The Late Mr. Justice Catron," *Legal Intelligencer*, 23:132, 1866.

[58] H.R. 60, 37th Cong., 1st Sess. (1861).

[59] For discussion see *Cong. Globe*, 37th Cong., 1st Sess. 228–29, 421–26 (1861).

[60] Edward Bates to Samuel Treat, Dec. 7, 1861, Treat Papers. Judge Treat noted on the letter: "This letter refers to Blair's effort to abolish the U.S. District Court here, in order to gratify his personal hatred of the Judge who had defeated his many

then discharging the committee from further consideration of it. Judge Treat in the meantime established himself firmly in the good graces of David Davis, who used Treat's courtroom to investigate military expenditures in the area, and of President Lincoln and other prominent Republicans,[61] so that his position became secure.

In Kentucky the fiery Judge Monroe acted very differently. On September 8, 1861, he sent to President Lincoln a cryptic note saying, "I have determined to emigrate and hereby resign the office I have held of district judge of the United States in and for the District of Kentucky."[62] Thereupon he headed for Nashville, where on October 6 he took an oath of allegiance to the Confederacy before West H. Humphreys, formerly a district judge of the United States, who had abandoned that office without taking the trouble to submit a resignation to the President, and was now serving the Confederacy in the same capacity.[63]

In Tennessee Judge Humphreys had done all he could to push his state into the ranks of the Confederacy. Beginning in December, 1860, he made speeches in support of secession and published newspaper articles to the same effect.[64] Immediately after the outbreak of war he delivered in court a speech in the form of a charge to a grand jury in which he called unconstitutional the President's request for military aid and urged the governor of Tennessee to disregard it. He maintained that in the conflict there was no such thing as treason against the United States on the part of enemies of the Union, and that persons captured

---

partisan intrigues, and his brother's candidacy for Judge of the Common Pleas in St. Louis." Judge Treat also wrote to John J. Crittenden, who in turn consulted Justice Catron and worked with other legislators for defeat of the bill. J. J. Crittenden to Samuel Treat, Apr. 20, 1861, Treat Papers.

[61] See H.R. Exec. Doc. No. 94, 37th Cong., 2nd Sess. 1 (1862); David Davis to Samuel Treat, Dec. 7, 1862, Davis Papers; Samuel Treat to David Davis, Nov. 20, 21, 1862, Lincoln Papers; Samuel Treat to A. Lincoln, Sept. 29, 1863, July 4, 1864, Lincoln Papers.

[62] Thomas B. Monroe to A. Lincoln, Sept. 28, 1861, Attorney General Papers.

In the House of Representatives, on Dec. 4, 1861, Charles A. Wickliffe of Kentucky, who had been elected on a Union Whig ticket, referred as follows to Judge Monroe and other Southern sympathizers who had left

the state: "Sir, I have been very much amused, and at the same time distressed, at finding men, when this invasion had taken place, running from their homes for fear of being seized and imprisoned. I have lately seen it stated that a judge of the Federal court in that State had fled from oppression. Why, sir, there was no more intention of imprisoning that man than there was of a woman in labor in Kentucky. There was some intention of asking the Senate to dispose of him this session for incompetency or malfeasance in office, but none of imprisoning him." *Cong. Rec.*, 37th Cong., 2nd Sess. 8 (1861).

[63] See Lewis Collins, *History of Kentucky*, I, 409. For discussion of plans advocated by Justice Catron for the federal courts in Kentucky see *Cong. Globe*, 37th Cong., 2nd Sess. 2055–56 (1862).

[64] See Impeachment of West H. Humphreys, H.R. Rep. No. 44, 37th Cong., 2nd Sess. 1, 7 (1862).

on each side should be treated as prisoners of war and not as traitors.[65] In so doing he advanced a position which the Administration in Washington was by no means ready to take.

Tennessee leaders were concerned about what attitudes would be taken by both federal judges in the area, Judge Humphreys and Justice Catron. In May, 1861, S. R. Cockrill, a Confederate agent in Nashville, wrote to the Confederate Secretary of War that "The position of Judge Humphreys is right and his conduct highly praiseworthy. He richly merits his place on the bench when the court is organized in the Confederacy." As for Justice Catron, he continued, "My old friend, Judge Catron, has not returned to Tennessee yet since the adjournment of the Supreme Court. I do not know his opinion of the Washington rulers."[66]

To some friends of the Union on his circuit, Justice Catron had made known in the late months of 1860 his own opposition to the secessionist movement. At the close of the ensuing term of the Supreme Court he set out for his circuit to exert such influence as he could, observing, in the language of Judge Treat, that "a tempest of passion and folly and crime was sweeping over this circuit."[67] Justice Catron held Circuit Court at one of his posts in Kentucky, which was tottering on the edge of secession, and then, Mrs. Catron being in poor health, hurried on to his home in Nashville in spite of the fact that by this time it was in effect behind enemy lines. Meanwhile, in Missouri, Judges Treat and Wells became deeply concerned about the apparent plans of Governor Claiborne F. Jackson and other leaders to take Missouri out of the Union. They deemed it important to hold in St. Louis a session of the Circuit Court to take a stand on the definition of treason and related topics and to have the prestige of a full court, deeming the presence of Justice Catron particularly important. Word was sent to him and he replied that he would be present if he could get through enemy lines. A legal journal stated:

> Not knowing whether either he or Judge Wells would be able to reach the place in time, the necessary charge to the Grand Jury was prepared by Justice Treat in advance, and met, on their arrival, their cordial approbation. Its delivery to the grand jury and immediate publication, as well as the finding of indictments, showed that there was no difference of opinion on the Bench here, while the opinions delivered on kindred subjects at that term manifested that there would be no judicial hesitancy in upholding the Constitution and laws.[68]

---

[65] *Nashville Union and American,* Apr. 17, 1861.

[66] S. R. Cockrill to L. P. Walker, May 14, 1861, 52 O.R. (1st) Pt. 2, 99.

[67] Quoted in "The Late Mr. Justice Catron," *Legal Intelligencer,* 23:132, 1866.

[68] *Ibid.*

Having arrived safely in St. Louis, Justice Catron sat with the two district judges and delivered the grand jury charge which Judge Treat had prepared. It went before the public in Catron's name, shocking many of his Southern friends and giving pleasure throughout the North. The charge proclaimed that giving aid to the rebellion constituted treason and was punishable as such, and it detailed other offenses among which was that of obstructing any United States court in the performance of its duties. The *New York Tribune* headlined the charge as "Light out of Darkness," and "An Upright Judge Among Rebels."[69]

Among Missouri officials the secessionist lieutenant governor, Thomas C. Reynolds, read the charge while out of the state, evidently on a tour on behalf of the Confederacy. He wrote Justice Catron an open letter warning him against attempting to punish rebels as traitors.[70] Although he closed his letter with the statement that this was merely an official notice to the court and was not intended to interrupt the friendly relations he had long enjoyed with Justice Catron, it stood as a grim warning of what the court might expect if the secessionist faction remained dominant in Missouri. The most difficult position of all was that of Judge Treat, who stood between two fires, that of the secessionists and that of the Republican opposition led by Frank Blair in the House of Representatives in Washington. On the whole it was probably his good fortune and that of the court that after delivery of the grand jury charge and the handling of some other business there was not time at that term of court to proceed with the trial of persons charged with treason.

In Tennessee the report of Justice Catron's grand jury charge in St. Louis and the publication of the Reynolds letter brought a series of attacks upon him and the demand that, as a loyal son of Tennessee, he resign and give his support to the Confederacy.[71] From St. Louis he returned to Nashville, where he had left Mrs. Catron, who was still in poor health. Because of threats of violence against him, a friend, V. K. Stevenson, published a notice that he had returned only because of the ill health of a friend and that he had no intention of holding court in Tennessee.[72] The notice, however, was not enough to curb the rising tide of hostility. A vigilance committee waited on him and demanded that he leave Nashville within twenty-four hours.[73] He set out for Louisville, expecting at leisure to find a house there and to send for his wife

[69] *New York Tribune*, July 14, 1861.

[70] Thomas C. Reynolds to John Catron, July 25, 1861; *Nashville Union and American*, July 27, 1861.

[71] See *Nashville Union and American*, Aug. 1, 1861.

[72] See *Baltimore American*, Aug. 1, 1861; *New York Times*, Aug. 15, 1861.

[73] *New York Times*, Aug. 14, 1861; *New York Herald*, Aug. 14, 1861; *New York Tribune*, Aug. 20, 1861.

and their household possessions. About a week later, however, Mrs. Catron too was expelled from Nashville, and she and some companions departed for Louisville having left behind all their possessions except their clothing.[74]

Although in some parts of Kentucky secessionist sentiment was as strong as in Tennessee, Justice Catron proceeded to hold court in Louisville. To the Clerk of the Supreme Court he reported that "Indictments for treason are rife, which I will have to return from Washington to try next January unless there is a District Judge appointed in Judge Monroe's place."[75] In Kentucky, as in Maryland and Missouri, many were taken into custody merely on suspicion, oftentimes not of things already done but of intention to commit disloyal acts in the future. Some sought writs of habeas corpus from a federal court—which at this time, in view of the resignation of Judge Monroe, meant that they had to be sought from Justice Catron. One of the more distinguished persons arrested was Charles S. Morehead, governor of Kentucky, who was charged with treason on the oath of the United States Marshal for the state, A. H. Sneed. At the approximate time when Justice Catron issued the writ for Governor Morehead, the marshal followed the strategy used by the military in Missouri with respect to Captain McDonald and transferred him to Indianapolis, "for the safety of his person," so that the return on the writ showed him to be outside the jurisdiction of the court. He was transferred from point to point until January 6, 1862, when he was released on his parole not to enter Kentucky or any insurrectionary state or otherwise to aid the rebellion—although he refused to take an oath of allegiance to the United States.[76]

Apparently other prisoners were rushed out of the jurisdiction of the court to prevent their possible release. In one instance Secretary Seward, "By direction of the President," gave an order to "disregard the habeas corpus and send the prisoners under guard tonight to Indiana and forward them direct to Fort Lafayette,"[77] unless otherwise advised by certain local people. The attitude of Justice Catron, however, bore no resemblance to the concern of Chief Justice Taney and Judge Giles for keeping prisoners out of the hands of the military. In this instance, after consultation with Justice Catron himself, certain prisoners were kept within the jurisdiction of the court because their testimony was needed to establish the guilt of still another important prisoner.[78] Justice Catron cooperated with the military, both in seeking to prevent

[74] J. Catron to William Thomas Carroll, Oct. 9, 1861, Lincoln Papers.
[75] Ibid.
[76] 2 O.R. (2d) 805, 814–15.
[77] William H. Seward to Robert Anderson, Sept. 28, 1861, 2 O.R. (2d) 885.
[78] Robert Anderson to W. H. Seward, Sept. 29, 1861, 2 O.R. (2d) 885. But see R. T. Durrett to W. H. Seward, Dec. 2, 1861, ibid., 820–22.

irresponsible arrests and in facilitating those that ought to be made. At the request of General William T. Sherman he appointed a number of commissioners in Kentucky who were to serve as committing magistrates. So many improper arrests were being made by self-constituted authorities that it was physically impossible to keep those arrested in custody: "To inflict any cruelty on them would not be tolerated by the laws of war or peace, and the consequence is many dangerous men are set free. Judge Catron says the commissioners can put them under bond, and the bond will be good against their property or the property of their sureties."[79]

In December, 1861, Justice Catron returned to Washington for the term of the Supreme Court, leaving a newly appointed district judge, Bland Ballard, in charge of the work of the federal courts in Kentucky. In Tennessee Judge West H. Humphreys refrained from resigning his federal commission, but when appointed district judge for the Confederacy merely converted the three District Courts in the state into Confederate courts. In that capacity he officiated in proceedings at which United States Senator Andrew Johnson, a resident of eastern Tennessee and the future Vice President and President of the United States, was declared an alien enemy and his property confiscated to the Confederacy.[80] Many others were banished from the state and their property confiscated. It was believed for a time that the property of Justice Catron had not merely been taken over and occupied but that it had been officially confiscated as well.[81]

By the spring of 1862 enough of middle Tennessee was back in Union hands to permit Justice Catron to return to Nashville and recover possession of his real estate and such other property as was left, and to give advice on the appointment of new officers to the District Court there.[82] Eastern Tennessee, on the other hand, where the larger percentage of people loyal to the Union resided, remained in the hands of the Confederacy. Many of the people suffered banishment, imprisonment, confiscation of property or other mistreatment. Like some judges in the North, Judge Humphreys seems to have ameliorated somewhat the harshness of treatment of prisoners,[83] but he was nevertheless very much a thorn in the side of all Union people. Furthermore, his failure to

---

[79] W. T. Sherman to W. T. Ward, Nov. 2, 1861, 2 O.R. (2d) 125–26.

[80] Jesse S. Jones, *Life of Andrew Johnson*, 79–80.

[81] See the statement attributed to Justice Nelson, estimating the value of the property at $90,000, in *New York Times*, Dec. 10, 1861, and *Baltimore American*, Dec. 11, 1861.

[82] See Edward Bates to John Catron (addressed to him at Nashville), Apr. 9, 1862, Attorney General's Letter Book B–5, 62.

[83] See for example Robertson Topp to Robert Josselyn, Oct. 26, 1861, 1 O.R. (2d) 834, and William H. Carroll to J. P. Benjamin, Nov. 29, 1861, 1 O.R. (2d) 850.

resign as a federal judge left a barrier in the way of his replacement in the federal judiciary. In consequence Judge Humphreys provided the one and only instance during the Civil War of the removal of a federal judge by process of impeachment.[84] To the vacancy thus created President Lincoln appointed Connally F. Trigg, who had been one of the leading witnesses against Judge Humphreys. With Judge Trigg in office, and with Justice Catron in the Circuit Court charging grand juries to "ferret out and indict all persons guilty of aiding and abetting the marauding parties who infested the State,"[85] the federal courts in Tennessee were once again functioning in support of the Union.

While Chief Justice Taney and Justice Catron were left with continuing circuit duties in such portions of their circuits as remained within Union lines, Justice Wayne took up permanent residence in Washington in the knowledge that his entire circuit was under the control of the Confederacy. Even so, he found himself under pressure during the summer of 1861 to declare himself officially on important questions involving national policy. His difficulties arose at the hands of Richard S. Coxe, a prominent Washington lawyer who had been a college classmate at Princeton and a personal and family friend in Washington for a quarter of a century. When defeated Union troops retreated into the capital city after the disastrous defeat at Bull Run, Coxe had opened his home to the sick and wounded, among them men from the first Minnesota regiment. One of these, Edward A. Stevens, complained to Coxe that he was illegally held in the service, since he had enlisted as a volunteer for only three months, whereas the army was claiming him as re-enlisted for the period of three years pursuant to the President's later call. As an attorney, Coxe agreed to look into the matter. He went first to the office of General Winfield Scott, but was told that he should take the matter to the adjutant general, Lorenzo Thomas. He sent a letter stating his case, but the letter was ignored.

At this point Coxe decided to seek a judicial determination of the power of the military to hold the soldier who claimed that his enlistment period had expired. It is quite possible that, out of a lifetime of experience at the bar, Coxe thought of the proceeding as strictly legal in character and not at all in terms of what might happen if federal judges, on one ground or another, began to release from badly harassed armed forces young men who had had their fill of fighting. According to his

---

[84] See Impeachment of West H. Humphreys, H.R. Rep. No. 44, 37th Cong., 2nd Sess. (1862). For action of the Senate see *Cong. Globe*, 37th Cong., 2nd Sess. 2943–53.

[85] *Appleton's American Cyclopaedia, 1862*, 765.

statement he "prepared the proper petition and presented it to Judge Wayne of the Supreme Court."[86] Justice Wayne stated that "the said writ of habeas corpus was issued by Mr. Thos. Carroll, Clerk of the Supreme Court of the United States, with the direction that it should be served by the Marshal of the District of Columbia, or by one of the legally authorized deputies."[87] Records do not show whether Chief Justice Taney, likewise residing in Washington, was consulted in the matter, or whether application to him rather than to Justice Wayne was considered. If it was considered, it may have been agreed that Taney had already incurred sufficient ill will from the Administration by his *Merryman* decision, and that responsibility in the Stevens case should be allocated to another member of the Court.

The War Department recognized that the case might call into question the power of the President to increase the size of the armed forces without previous authorization from Congress, the power of Congress to ratify retroactively the steps the President had taken before Congress met, and the scope and character of the war powers generally. It therefore employed Edwin M. Stanton to defend the interests of the United States—and thereby perhaps inadvertently paved the way for his appointment as Secretary of War. From the materials included in the opinion it appears that, as may happen in any national crisis, the military had not taken all the steps prescribed by law for the enlistment of new personnel. A judge inclined to be meticulous in such matters might well have ordered the release of Stevens and cast doubt on the validity of the enlistment of many others. Justice Wayne, however, chose to overlook such irregularities as may have existed, and to find that the enlistment proceedings were ratified by a blanket Act of Congress of August 6, 1861.[88] Concerning the power of retroactive ratification he said—no doubt greatly to the relief of the Administration:

> It is my opinion that Congress has constitutional power to legalize and confirm Executive acts, proclamations, and orders done for the public good, although they were not, when done, authorized by any existing laws. That such legislation by Congress may be made to operate retroactively to confirm what may have been done under such proclamations and orders, so as to be binding upon the Government in regard to contracts made, and the persons with whom they were made.[89]

---

[86] Richard S. Coxe to S. P. Chase, Mar. 24, 1863, Chase Papers.

[87] "*Ex parte* Stevens," *Washington National Intelligencer*, Sept. 10, 1861.

[88] 12 Stat. 326.

[89] "*Ex parte* Stevens," *Washington National Intelligencer*, Sept. 10, 1861. The opinion was printed in *Law Rep.*, 24:205, 1861, but, presumably because the proceedings took place "at chambers" rather than in court, it was not printed in *Federal Cases*.

The decision marked a victory for the Administration and was widely hailed as such.[90] Coxe, however, incurred the lasting enmity of some members of the Administration for his temerity in bringing up the case. Two years later he found his appointment to an important position blocked because of his "unfortunate action in the habeas corpus case," in connection with which it was said that "The court before which it was brought or proposed to be brought was very unfriendly to the government." These comments, in a letter by Secretary Chase, led Coxe to write a long letter defending his own patriotism and that of Justice Wayne.[91]

The recollection of Secretary Chase two years later that the court before which the Stevens case was proposed to be brought was "very unfriendly to the government" suggests the possibility that bringing the case before the Circuit Court of the District of Columbia rather than before any member of the Supreme Court at chambers had been considered. At least one of the judges of that court, William M. Merrick, who came from one of Maryland's old families, had been suspected of disloyalty even before the outbreak of military hostilities. He was said to have predicted, indeed, that by the time set for the inauguration of Abraham Lincoln, Washington would be in the hands of secessionists.[92] Judge Merrick's clash with the Administration came in connection with one of the many attempts of fathers to secure the release of sons from military service on the ground that they were underage.[93] In October, 1861, Judge Merrick issued a writ of habeas corpus to bring before him one James Murphy, who was held by General Andrew Porter, provost marshal of the District of Columbia. When for some reason no deputy marshal was available or willing to serve the writ, it was delivered by D. D. Foley, counsel for Murphy's father, who found himself under arrest for thus seeking to interfere with the jurisdiction of the military.[94] At the same time, William H. Seward directed General Porter

[90] See Alexander A. Lawrence, *James Moore Wayne, Southern Unionist*, 186–87.

[91] Richard S. Coxe to S. P. Chase, Mar. 24, 1863, Chase Papers.

[92] See unsigned letter to General Winfield Scott, 2 O.R. (2d) 1021. Counter evidence with respect to Judge Merrick's loyalty exists in the form of a statement of his brother, Richard T. Merrick, dated Apr. 15, 1885, that when after the Battle of Bull Run Washington was thought to be threatened by Confederate troops, Judge Merrick said that in

the event of such an attack he would leave the bench and go into the trenches to defend the capital. The statement is filed with appointment papers in Judge Merrick's name in the Department of Justice files, under the date of Oct. 22, 1861.

[93] For summary statement see W. B. Bryan, *History of the National Capital*, II, 487.

[94] For an extended account of the many maneuvers in the case see United States *ex rel.* Murphy v. Porter, 27 Fed. Cas. 599 (No. 16074a) (C.C.D.C. 1861).

to establish a strict military guard over Judge Merrick's residence.[95] When asked by General Porter whether Judge Merrick was to be confined to his house, Seward replied in the negative, saying, "Indeed it may be sufficient to make him understand that at a juncture like this when the public enemy is as it were at the gates of the capital the public safety is deemed to require that his correspondence and proceedings should be observed."[96]

In the meantime, the court not being in session, Judge Merrick had gone to Georgetown to consult with his fellow judges. When he returned to his home that evening he found it surrounded by a military guard. His brethren ordered a rule to be served on General Porter directing him to appear before the court and show cause why he should not be held in contempt for his interference with judicial proceedings. If martial law was to be the guide to action, said Judge James S. Morsell, it was up to the President to proclaim martial law. The deputy marshal who was directed to serve the rule reported that he had not done so because he had been ordered by the President not to and because he had been directed to report to the court that on the order of the President the privilege of the writ of habeas corpus had been suspended for the present. On October 30, in the face of a combination of power with which it could not cope, Judge James Dunlop announced the acquiescence of the court, noting the oddity of the suspension of a writ without public notification. In any event, however, "The issue ought to be and is with the president, and we have no physical power to enforce the lawful process of this court on his military subordinates against the President's prohibition."[97]

In addition to intimidating Judge Merrick with a military guard, the Administration harassed him for a time by an order that his salary should not be paid.[98] If Judge Merrick should persist in embarrassing the government, said the *New York Evening Post*, "he will be visited with punishment. The course he has already taken has fanned anew the secession flames in Washington."[99]

In the face of the Administration's apparent lack of concern for

---

[95] William H. Seward to Andrew Porter, Oct. 21, 1861, 2 O.R. (2d) 1021.

[96] William H. Seward to Andrew Porter, Oct. 21, 1861, *ibid.*, 1022.

[97] 27 Fed. Cas. 602.

[98] William H. Seward to Elisha Whittlesey, Oct. 21, 1861, 2 O.R. (2d) 1022.

[99] *New York Evening Post*, Oct. 25, 1861. There were, it is true, thoughtful friends of the Administration who feared the government was going too far in its ruthless treatment of the judge. For example, Charles Eames wrote to the Secretary of the Navy as follows: "It is said that Judge Merrick of Washington has been placed under *surveillance* and deprived of salary (!) for his *judicial* action in granting a writ of habeas corpus. If so, is it not a very grave and impolitic proceeding?" Charles Eames to Gideon Welles, Oct. 22, 1861, Welles Papers.

the maintenance of judicial prerogatives during the military emergency, Judge Merrick was left for a time merely to fume behind the doors of his home, which was stigmatized for the loyal members of the community by the presence of a military sentry. His wife vented her own hostility by ostracizing her formerly popular brother-in-law, Joseph Holt,[100] who was serving as a strong-arm of the Administration.

Intimidation of a judge, however, provided an unsatisfactory method of dealing with a refractory court—if, indeed, the court could be correctly described as refractory. The somewhat unsatisfactory organization of the courts of the District of Columbia provided a new approach. A bill was submitted to merge into a supreme court the Circuit and District courts and the Criminal Court, with the appointment of new judges instead of the transfer of the old ones. While some legislators denied that elimination of the sitting judges was the purpose of the bill, the presence of that motive was indicated by some of the debates and by the contrast between this bill and one lately enacted which reorganized the Court of Claims and added new members without dropping the old ones.[101] A Massachusetts Senator, more outspoken than his colleagues, said bluntly, "As to one of their Judges, I mean Judge Merrick, I believe his heart is sweltering with treason. He has been under arrest since this rebellion broke out. I believe that during this session of Congress his home has been the resort where sympathizers with disloyal men have held councils, and I have good reason to believe this to be true."[102]

During the debates much was said about whether the courts of the District of Columbia were established under Article III of the Constitution and therefore subject to the life tenure provision for judges, or whether they were "legislative" courts with tenure at the will of Congress.[103] No clear answer was provided but Congress nevertheless enacted the measure, and Judge Merrick and his colleagues of the Circuit Court gave way to new personnel in new tribunals.

In connection with their Circuit Court responsibilities Chief Justice Taney and Justices Wayne and Catron operated virtually on the firing line of the sectional conflict. Of the other three judges on the

---

[100] See Mary Cash to Joseph Holt, Nov. 25, 1862, June 20, 1863, Holt Papers.

[101] For debates in the Senate see *Cong. Globe*, 27th Cong., 3rd Sess. 1049–52, 1128–30, 1135–40 (1863).

[102] Senator Henry Wilson, *ibid.*, 1139.

[103] *Ibid.*, 1136–37. For discussion of the establishment of the Supreme Court of the District of Columbia see Job Barnard, "Early Days of the Supreme Court of the District of Columbia," *Records of the Columbia Historical Society*, 22:1, 1919. Not until 1933 was it settled that the federal courts in the District of Columbia are Article III courts. O'Donoghue v. United States, 289 U.S. 516.

Supreme Court during the early months of the war, Justices Grier and Nelson were hardly less involved, since considerable numbers of Confederate privateers were taken into their courts for trial, along with persons accused of treason in cases of corresponding difficulty. It was contended that since the Confederate government was not a lawful government it had no power to commission privateers and render their destructive acts lawful under international law, and that since their depredations on the seas were unlawful they constituted piracy when committed by Southerners who were citizens of the United States and subject to American statutes on the subject. Piracy by Americans committed against American shipping was regarded as the equivalent of treason.[104]

Justice Nelson's first important privateering case involved men who had operated the *Savannah*, a privateer commissioned by Jefferson Davis which, after some initial success against Northern merchant vessels, had been captured by an armed vessel of the Union. President Lincoln had declared Union policy in such matters in his proclamation of April 19, 1861, closing the Southern ports by blockade. Concerning the Confederate threat to issue letters of marque, whereby privateering was to be authorized, he proclaimed that any person so commissioned who molested any vessel of the United States should be held amenable to laws for the prevention and punishment of piracy.[105]

Pirates, as the term was commonly used, were sea robbers. They were deemed enemies of mankind, warring against the human race. They operated on the ocean, which was the common highway of nations, over which every government had criminal jurisdiction. In the language of Judge Peleg Sprague, "Pirates are highwaymen of the sea, and all civilized nations have a common interest, and are under a moral obligation, to arrest and suppress them."[106] The Constitution authorized Congress to define and punish felonies committed on the high seas,[107] and Congress had done so.[108] Although the statutes did not define all privateering as piracy, a statute enacted by the first congress did define as piracy the act of any American citizen so directed against the United States who operated under a commission from any foreign prince or state, "or on pretence of authority from any person."[109] Assuming Southerners to

---

[104] See Judge Peleg Sprague, Charge to Grand Jury—Treason and Piracy, 30 Fed. Cas. 1049 (No. 18277) (C.C.-D. Mass. 1861).

[105] 12 Stat. 1258.

[106] 30 Fed. Cas. 1049.

[107] Art. I, Sec. 8.

[108] 1 Stat. 113, 114; 3 Stat. 600; 9 Stat. 73.

[109] 1 Stat. 114. Although the letters

of marque issued to Confederate privateers were issued in the name of the Confederate States of America, and not in the names of individual states or of states of the Union, it is to be remembered that the Constitution forbade states to issue letters of marque—Art. I, Sec. 10. Since the United States recognized no such entity as the Confederacy, and since

be citizens of the United States acting under privateering instructions from Jefferson Davis, they seemed clearly subject to the provisions of the statute and liable to the death penalty on conviction.

To return to the story of the Confederate privateer *Savannah*, it had captured the United States brig *Joseph*, laden with Cuban sugar, and sent it into Charleston as prize. But it had then had the bad fortune to run afoul of the brig-of-war *Perry*, which in turn took the *Savannah* as prize and put the crew aboard the steam frigate *Minnesota* to be sent to New York to be tried for piracy. On the way northward an embarrassing jurisdictional problem was inadvertently created when it was found expedient to enter the harbor at Hampton Roads, Virginia, and transfer the prisoners to the steam cutter *Harriet Lane* for completion of the journey. The prisoners were nevertheless eventually delivered in New York, where an excited populace watched the marching of the manacled "pirates" to prison.

Elaborate arrangements were made for the trial. The United States was represented by the district attorney, E. Delafield Smith, the eminent lawyer William M. Evarts, and Samuel Blatchford, a future member of the Supreme Court. The prisoners were represented by Daniel Lord, James T. Brady, Jeremiah Laroque, Algernon S. Sullivan, Joseph H. Dukes, Isaac Davega, and Maurice Mayer. Following the indictment, the prosecution sought a speedy trial before Judge William D. Shipman of Rhode Island, who was helping with Circuit Court work in New York. Counsel for the prisoners sought delay while they secured evidence from Charleston and other places and because of a desire to have two judges sit in the case. Justice Nelson had recently been thrown from his carriage by a runaway horse and severely injured. Defense counsel had heard that he thought it his duty to sit in the case, and they were desirous of having him do so, especially since a writ of error was not allowed in criminal cases: "The prisoner has the right to a review of any decision that might be made in this Court, [only] in case a difference of opinion should arise between the Judges who preside."[110] Judge Shipman found that Justice Nelson would be unable to sit in August because of his injury and in September because of engagements elsewhere, and therefore postponed the trial until the third Monday in October.[111] The prosecution was seeking an early trial in the hope of making an example of the privateers for others who were roaming the Atlantic and preying upon United States shipping.

---

the Constitution debarred the states from commissioning privateers, the so-called privateers of the Confederacy could have in the eyes of the United States the status only of pirates.

[110] *Trial of the Officers and Crew of the Privateer Savannah on the Charge of Piracy in the United States Circuit Court for the Southern District of New York*, xv.

[111] *Ibid.*, xxii.

Immediately upon the capture of the officers and crew of the *Savannah*, Jefferson Davis proposed their exchange for prisoners of corresponding rank held by the Confederacy, but he was told by the captain in charge of the blockading squadron that they were not in his custody. Later, hearing that they were being treated as ordinary pirates and were about to be tried for piracy, he wrote to President Lincoln announcing his determination to give to Union prisoners the same harsh treatment as that which might be given to the men from the *Savannah*.[112] The United States nevertheless proceeded with plans for the trial.

The preparatory strategy of counsel for the prisoners included attempts to demonstrate the legitimacy of the prisoners as privateers under authorization of an established government. The United States, because of its desire to prevent recognition of the Confederacy by foreign governments, tried to avoid all recognition of the claimed legitimacy. Daniel Lord and other counsel wrote to the district attorney seeking his aid in getting from the South authenticated documents demonstrating the secession of the Southern States, the establishment of the Confederate government, and the authorization of privateering. The district attorney refused to be used in this fashion, and proposed that if more was needed than the process of the court eminent counsel might apply directly to those in charge of the government, which had cut off intercourse with the South. He then sent copies of the correspondence to Attorney General Bates.[113]

After considerable delay the Attorney General wrote to Lord that because the heads of government were engaged with matters of "paramount importance and extreme pressure," he had been unable to get an official reply as to whether aid would be provided in procuring evidence for the defendants. He suggested, however, that the claim of the accused was "new and strange," and that there was no ground for a demand for aid from the government. As for the documents enumerated, "The purpose for which they are wanted is not disclosed, and I am left to conjecture that they are intended to be used as proof of the existence of the nation called Confederate States of America, and of its national action." He argued that national existence was not provable by documentary evidence, "but by open and notorious facts, of which the world must, at its peril, take notice." National existence was a political question determinable by the political branches of the government and not properly cognizable collaterally in a judicial court. "And in this instance

---

[112] Jefferson Davis to A. Lincoln, July 6, 1861, Lincoln Papers.

[113] E. Delafield Smith to Edward Bates, Oct. 14, 1861, enclosing copies of Daniel Lord *et al.* to E. Delafield Smith, Sept. 7, 1861, and E. Delafield Smith to Daniel Lord *et al.*, Sept. 20, 1861, Attorney General Papers.

the Political Government—both Congress and the President—have determined against the nationality of the C.S.A."[114] Later, after consulting the President, he wrote that "Considering the character of the testimony which you seek and the probable object (you have not disclosed the object, and I only conjecture it) the only answer I can give is, that the Government declines to take any active part, in aid of the accused from the procurement of such testimony."[115]

The government brought twelve of the thirteen prisoners to trial before Justice Nelson and Judge Shipman, using the remaining prisoner as one of its few witnesses. The greater portion of the time devoted to the trial was used in arguments of counsel. Counsel for the prisoners contended, and counsel for the government denied, that the Circuit Court in New York lacked jurisdiction, since under the statute prescribing jurisdiction the trial was to be held in the first judicial district into which persons committing crimes on the high seas were brought.

More important than the jurisdictional question—which was decided against the defendants—was the substantive question whether the Confederate government had a status which enabled it to issue letters of marque, and whether oceangoing personnel serving pursuant to such letters were therefore entitled to be treated as prisoners of war and not as ordinary criminals. Daniel Lord, citing cases decided by Judges Dunlop, Cadwalader, and Betts, contended that the military struggle was a civil war, and the military opponent must have a status as a belligerent which would enable it to assert rights under international law.[116] He stressed again his contention that the Confederate government was at least a de facto government, with rights of a belligerent which included the right to issue letters of marque and have its captured personnel on the sea treated as prisoners of war: "The Confederation you may call illegal and improper, but it is a Confederation *de facto*; its right may be questioned, but it is a *de facto* Government, with this gentleman presiding over it, and performing the duties which, as the Ruler of a great nation, devolve upon him—bringing out armies by hundreds of thousands, bringing out treasures by the million,—and yet you are to say it has no color of authority."[117]

Counsel for the United States contended that whether or not a state of war existed, a federal court could not recognize in the opposing party the rights of a nation unless the government had granted recognition. Said William M. Evarts, "No judicial tribunal has a right to recognize a nation, of its own motion. No judicial tribunal has authority

---

[114] Edward Bates to Daniel Lord, Oct. 8, 1861, Attorney General's Letter Book B–4, 162.
[115] Edward Bates to Daniel Lord

et al., Oct. 12, 1861, Attorney General's Letter Book B–4, 167.
[116] *Trial of the Officers and Crew of the Privateer Savannah*, 124–25.
[117] *Ibid.*, 132.

to recognize a Government which the Government from which it derives its authority does not recognize."[118] Therefore, "What our Government has said shall remain in the quality of criminality, must so remain, notwithstanding this proclamation of Jefferson Davis, or any commission that may issue in pursuance of it."[119]

Justice Nelson's charge to the jury had a particularly ominous sound with respect to the four of the defendants who were citizens of the United States. He stressed the fact that the Act of 1790 applied to citizens and that it forbade their serving as privateers or engaging in piracy or robbery against American vessels under commission of any foreign power or "on pretense of authority from any person." Eight of the defendants, however, were not American citizens. If the Confederacy had the status of a foreign power, as their counsel contended, there was question whether in view of existing international law the United States could punish duly commissioned privateers as mere criminals. Here Justice Nelson followed Attorney General Bates and government counsel in holding that in the matter of recognition of the new government the courts must follow the lead of the political branches of the government: "Until this recognition of the new government, the courts are obliged to regard the ancient state of things as remaining unchanged."[120]

On the surface it would appear that Justice Nelson's charge was all that government counsel might desire. Yet having said that the courts must look to the acts of the legislative and executive branches of the government to determine whether the Confederacy had been recognized as a belligerent power, he nowhere stated specifically that such recognition had not taken place. It was obvious that the government made no admission of such recognition, yet the question remained whether in its method of conducting the war as a war, by taking prisoners of war as against capturing criminals, by its land operations, by the blockade of Southern ports, and by other acts, the government had not in effect given the necessary recognition. The question troubled at least one member of the jury, and he put it to the court. After consultation with Judge Shipman, Justice Nelson rephrased his statement, but he did little to clarify it.[121] The jury was not told whether the United States was

---

[118] *Ibid.*, 193.

[119] *Ibid.*, 196. On Evarts' performance see Brainerd Dyer, *Public Career of William M. Evarts*, 53–60; Chester L. Barrows, *William M. Evarts*, 103–06.

[120] United States v. Baker, 24 Fed. Cas. 962, 966 (No. 14501) (C.C.S.D. N.Y. 1861).

[121] "As it respects the first inquiry of the juror—whether the government has recognized a state of civil war between the Confederate states and itself—the instruction which the court gave the jury was, that this court could not recognize a state of civil war, or a government of the Confederate States, unless the legislative and executive departments of the government had recognized such a

waging civil war against a power possessing belligerent rights or what were the implications of the existence of a civil war.

Justice Nelson's lack of explicitness on this point may well have been responsible for the fact that the jury disagreed and had to be discharged without reaching a verdict. One of the jurors gave it as his belief that the failure to agree resulted from the fact that other jurors did not understand the charge, though he did not specify the area of disagreement.[122] Already, in retaliation for the treatment of the privateers as ordinary criminals, the Confederacy had selected from among United States prisoners of war in Southern custody an equal number of men of comparable rank for incarceration as criminals.[123] The failure to convict in the Circuit Court in New York forestalled the execution of the privateers and the retaliatory execution of the hostages in the South.

Upon discharge of the divided jury, the district attorney moved for an immediate new trial. Justice Nelson replied that he could remain in New York only until November 20, and that during that time he would be busy with other causes. A second trial must await another term of the court.[124] Attention with respect to the punishment of Confederate privateers shifted to Philadelphia where other trials had already been held or were in prospect.

While the trial of the *Savannah* privateers was in progress in New York, counsel on both sides indicated deep interest in a similar trial in the United States Circuit Court in Philadelphia before Justice Grier and Judge Cadwalader.[125] The defendant there was William Smith, who had been part of the crew of the *Jefferson Davis*, or the *Jeff. Davis*, as it was commonly called (it was the slaver *Echo* renamed and refitted), which had a much longer and more successful career of depredations against United States shipping than had the *Savannah*.[126] Smith was put aboard the *Enchantress*, one of the merchant victims of the *Jefferson Davis*, in command of a prize crew. A Negro cook was carried on the *Enchantress* for his services and also for sale when the vessel was delivered as prize. When the *Enchantress* attracted the suspicious attention of the U.S.S. *Albatross*, the cook leaped overboard and disclosed the captivity of the *Enchantress*, whereupon it and the prize crew were

state of things, or the president had, or both; and that the act of recognition was a national act, and that we must look to the acts of these departments of the government as the evidence and for the evidence of the recognition of this state of things, and the only evidence." *Ibid.*, 966.

[122] *Trial of the Officers and Crew of the Privateer Savannah*, 375.
[123] William Morrison Robinson, Jr., *The Confederate Privateers*, 148–49.
[124] *Trial of the Officers and Crew of the Privateer Savannah*, 376.
[125] *Ibid.*, 67, 143–44, 163.
[126] See Robinson, *The Confederate Privateers*, 61–88.

taken into the port of Philadelphia and Smith was brought to trial for piracy.[127]

The United States Attorney in Philadelphia, George A. Coffey, impressed with the task of trying privateers from the *Jefferson Davis* and other vessels who had been brought into the port of Philadelphia, wrote to Attorney General Bates that it would be proper to try them for "treason or piracy," and got permission to employ as his assistant George H. Earle, whom he characterized as "one of the ablest, most learned, skilled, and successful lawyers of the bar of Philadelphia."[128] Coffey himself having fallen ill, William D. Kelley was added to the staff of the prosecution.[129] Evidence was presented at greater length than in the case of the *Savannah* privateers. Arguments of counsel were less extended,[130] but covered much the same ground as those in New York.

Judge Cadwalader had already committed himself in a prize case to the supremacy of the Union and against the alleged right of secession,[131] and during the course of the argument Justice Grier, for all his reservation about "Yankees," revealed a similar attitude.[132] When Smith's counsel contended that Smith had been coerced by the laws of his state into serving the Confederacy, either in its armed forces or as a privateer, and ought not therefore to be held responsible for his acts, Justice Grier replied, "You might, more justifiably, I think, plead the total insanity of the people in the South altogether. The question was once asked whether a nation could be insane, as well as an individual. I have no doubt that it can. You might as well set up national insanity."[133] When one of Smith's counsel relied on Calhoun to support the doctrine of nullification, Justice Grier replied, "Mr. Calhoun denied the right of secession as absolutely as any man in the North."[134] In interchange with

---

[127] For account of the capture see *The Jeff Davis Piracy Case: Full Report of the Trial of William Smith for Piracy as one of the Crew of Confederate Privateer Jeff Davis.* The story of the capture is summarized in Robinson, *The Confederate Privateers,* 79–84.

[128] George A. Coffey to Edward Bates, Aug. 19, 1861, Attorney General Papers.

[129] William D. Kelley, *Speech . . . United States v. William Smith, Piracy,* 1.

[130] Robinson, *The Confederate Privateers,* 147.

[131] *The Parkhill,* 18 Fed. Cas. 1187 (No. 10755a) (D.C.E.D. Pa. 1861).

[132] See Kelley, *Speech . . . United States v. William Smith, Piracy,* 10.

[133] *Full Report of the Trial of William Smith for Piracy,* 46.

[134] *Ibid.,* 63. There may be differences of opinion concerning Justice Grier's statement about Calhoun's position with respect to secession. Strictly speaking, he may have been correct. Calhoun sought to preserve the Union for limited purposes not inconsistent with the interests of the South. His doctrines of the "concurrent majority" and of the right of nullification were evolved for the purpose of preserving the Union as he envisaged it, rather than for the purpose of destroying it. Yet it is also true that nullification, pushed to the limit of its logic, would have destroyed the Union, with secession as one of the means of its expression. Presumably he hoped that the limit of

counsel he continued to stress the fact that the conflict was a rebellion and the rebellious faction was not a power that could issue letters of marque as a member of the family of nations.[135]

Both Justice Grier and Judge Cadwalader charged the jury, the former generally and the latter more specifically. Justice Grier stressed the fact that though the insurrection was of the dimensions of a civil war this did not mean that the Confederacy was entitled to be considered a state. The very fact that the United States was waging war to suppress the rebellion showed the refusal of the government of the United States to recognize such status. Therefore the court could recognize the insurgents only as traitors and those who plundered the property of American citizens on the high seas as pirates and robbers. He did not think it necessary to "refute the sophisms and platitudes put forth by speculating theorists or political demagogues on the constitutional right of any portion of this one nation, or of any of the States composing it, to destroy the Constitution and Union because they are displeased at the result of an election. The right to secede is not to be found in the Constitution, either in its letter or its spirit. . . . Judge the tree by its fruits, and we see the results of this miserable heresy in the present situation of our country, . . . with more than half a million of men in arms drenching our fields in blood."[136]

On October 26, 1861, J. Hubley Ashton, Assistant United States Attorney at Philadelphia, reported to Attorney General Bates that the government had secured a conviction and that both judges had delivered charges strongly in favor of the government: "The case presented for the first time in our history, the question of the Constitutional power of States to secede from the Union, and whether the revolutionary action of a State could in law have the effect of impairing the allegiance of its citizens to the United States. Both questions were promptly and unequivocally determined in favor of the Government. The political importance of these opinions of the Judges of the Circuit Court may be easily understood."[137]

The trial and conviction of three of Smith's confederates followed quickly, and the trial and exoneration of another who claimed to have given aid in the recapture of the *Enchantress*.[138] With the zest of victory, government prosecutors wished to proceed with other privateer cases. Justice Grier, however, and Judge Cadwalader only less outspokenly so,

---

that logic would never have to be reached.

[135] *Ibid.*, 92.

[136] *Ibid.*, 96. See also *Philadelphia Ledger and Transcript*, Oct. 26, 1861. For a milder statement of Justice Grier's charge see United States v.

Smith, 27 Fed. Cas. 1134 (No. 16318) (C.C.E.D. Pa. 1861).

[137] J. Hubley Ashton to Edward Bates, Oct. 26, 1861, Attorney General Papers.

[138] Robinson, *The Confederate Privateers*, 147–48.

thought it better to suspend further prosecutions now that an example had been made. Justice Grier, indeed, announced openly in court that he did not intend to try any more such cases. He would leave them to Judge Cadwalader. He had other business to attend to, and did not mean to be delayed in Philadelphia trying charges against a few unfortunate men out of the half million who were in arms against the government: "Why should this difference be made between men captured on land and on the Sea?"

To George H. Earle's reply that these men were privateers, Justice Grier rejoined:

> But why make a difference between those taken on land and on Water? Why not try all those on land and hang them? That might do with a mere insurrection; but when it comes to civil war, the laws of War must be observed, or you will lay it open to the most horrid reactions that can possibly be thought of: hundreds of thousands of men will be sacrificed upon mere brutal rage. If this were once (and God grant it soon may be) suppressed and when we have the right to treat it as an insurrection, then bring them forward and I will try them. If I should be called a Jeffry[139] or a Scroggs,[140] I care not, provided you bring one of the leaders before me. But I must say I see no use of this course, and I do not approve of it. I suppose the government does not care whether I do or not; but I will not sit in another case. I have seventy cases to try at Pittsburg, and I promised today to hear a case on the civil list here. I am not going to have the whole civil business of the Court and private suitors set aside for useless trifling.[141]

---

[139] George Jeffreys, a seventeenth-century English judge noted for the harshness of his courtroom performances.

[140] Sir William Scroggs, a lord chief justice of the seventeenth century, likewise noted for his harshness.

[141] A transcript of this interchange is filed with J. Hubley Ashton to Edward Bates, Nov. 4, 1861, Attorney General Papers. See J. G. Randall, *Constitutional Problems under Lincoln*, 92–93. This quotation, like others reproduced herein, illustrates the roughness with which Justice Grier was accustomed to express himself, whether orally or in writing. The following letter to the Attorney General, written in approximately the same period, provides another illustration:

"In March last a certificate of division was ordered to be certified, in the case of a man (Jackalow) convicted of Robbery and Murder on *high seas.*

"The man lies in prison, and would I presume like to know whether he is to be hanged or not. I do not find the case on our *list.* Has the record been *sent to your office* and *been forgotten* or has the drunken worthless clerk of the court neglected to send up a record:

The latter I presume to be the case. Please let me know." R. C. Grier to Edward Bates, Jan. 24, 1862, Carson Collection. The record in the case in question was presumably found, for it was argued in the Supreme Court soon afterward and was sent back to the United States Circuit Court in New Jersey for a new trial to determine whether the place where the offense was committed was such that the Circuit Court had jurisdiction. United States v. Jackalow, 1 Black 484 (1862).

Justice Grier set out for Pittsburgh, and Judge Cadwalader granted a continuance in the case of other privateers on the ground of the absence of an important witness. Ashton wrote to the Attorney General in protest against the making of policy as to prosecution by the court instead of by the government. Bates, however, advised prudent delay, reminding Ashton that the Confederate government had "avowed the purpose to take an atrocious vengeance, for any punishment which we may inflict upon these convicts." He therefore advised that, with a minimum of explanation, the prosecution abstain from urging the cases to final judgment.[142]

In the light of these grim considerations some of the privateers were never brought to trial. Eventually those convicted and those not tried at all and those tried without the reaching of a verdict were transferred from civil to military jurisdiction and were held as prisoners of war rather than as criminals.[143]

Thus during the early months of the war, long before any case involving war issues was decided by the Supreme Court, the Justices were deeply involved on circuit along with the district judges with whom they sat. For considerable time vast confusion prevailed as to the scope of the habeas corpus power, the reach of the law of treason, and the status of Confederate privateers. A measure of clarification was to come, part of it through the courts and part through action of Congress and the executive branch.

---

[142] Edward Bates to J. Hubley Ashton, Nov. 20, 1861, Attorney General's Letter Book B–4, 218–19.

[143] See "The Diary of Edward Bates," Howard K. Beale, ed., *Annual Report of the American Historical Association for the Year 1930*, 4: 237–38, 1933, and Edward Bates to J. Hubley Ashton, Feb. 14, 1862, Attorney General's Letter Book B–5, 10. For an account of the habeas corpus proceedings by which William Smith and those tried with him were transferred from civil to military custody see United States v. William Smith, 1 Cadwalader 516, 525 (D.C.E.D. Pa. 1861).

CHAPTER XXXIV

The Blockade and the Laws of War

FROM THE PROCLAMATIONS of the blockade of Southern ports on April 19 and 27, 1861,[1] controversy raged over the nature and scope of the power of the federal government to close the ports and to invoke international law as a means of taking ships as prize. The immediate purpose of the blockade was to cripple the Confederacy at a point where it was peculiarly vulnerable, since it needed foreign markets for its crops and manufactured goods and required food supplies that the South did not produce in sufficient quantities. "We cannot eat cotton, nor dine off tobacco and sugar," a Southern writer grimly warned.[2] To survive at all the Confederacy would have to maintain its foreign commerce or completely transform its economy. Since its economy was geared to a slave system which the South was determined to maintain, such a transformation would be difficult or impossible.

Because the United States never admitted that the Southern ports were anything other than ports of the United States, it would have been legally possible to close them, or at any rate to proclaim them as closed, without resort to international law as a source of power —subject of course to the limiting provision in the Constitution that "No preference shall be given by any regulation of commerce or revenue to the ports of one state over those of another."[3] Indeed, one of the first measures enacted by Congress when it assembled in July, 1861, was an authorization to close ports where federal collection of revenue was impeded.[4] The Secretary of the Navy believed that the Administration should resort to this measure as a primary means of dealing with

---

[1] 12 Stat. 1258, 1259.
[2] C. C. H., "The Resources of the South," *Southern Literary Messenger*, 34–36:189, 1862.

[3] Constitution, Art. I, Sec. 9, Clause 6.

[4] 12 Stat. 255, 256.

the Southern ports and thereby avoid the difficult questions involved in blockading them pursuant to international law.[5]

But serious difficulties stood in the way of relying exclusively on municipal law. Had the United States controlled the land on which the ports were located or by which they were surrounded, then it could have closed them against all but an overwhelmingly powerful invading force. The difficulty lay in the fact that this land was in the control of the enemy. While the United States had a substantial navy for that time, and at the beginning of the war the Confederacy had almost none, the navy could not be used against neutral shipping seeking to enter and leave Southern ports without resort to international law, to the law of blockade. The Administration did use the blockade, but in doing so it faced difficulties in the propaganda war as well as the shooting war in which it was engaged.

Few Americans were deeply learned in international law, and members of the Administration were not much concerned about it save as it could be used to promote and protect our national interests. They were concerned with cutting off the maximum amount of trade from Southern territory. They were determined to exclude foreign shipping, and to do so in part by taking as prize the carriers of goods to and from the South, whoever might be the owners and operators. They insisted on the exercise of all the rights that one belligerent might exercise against another. Yet throughout the war they also insisted that Southern territory was territory of the United States and denied that any element of sovereignty belonged to the enemy. Regarding the recognition of belligerency as a step in the direction of recognition of sovereignty, they resented recognition of belligerency on the part of Great Britain and other countries. They were aware that the blockade deprived Great Britain and others of raw cotton for their mills and of profitable foreign trade and resulted in serious unemployment, but in this time of crisis they could not concern themselves overmuch about the welfare of neutrals. Judge Peleg Sprague outlined the United States attitude toward the conduct of Great Britain by saying:

> Believing ourselves to be fighting the battle of human liberty and free institutions, and having heretofore cherished strong sympathy for others, the attitude assumed by Great Britain was not regarded as one merely of chilling indifference, but rather as an indication of unfriendly, if not hostile, feelings, exciting emotions of surprise and resentment.[6]

---

[5] Gideon Welles to A. Lincoln, Aug. 5, 1861, Lincoln Papers.
[6] Charge to Grand Jury—Treason and Piracy, 30 Fed. Cas. 1049, 1050 (No. 18277) (C.C.D. Mass. 1861).

XXXIV: *The Blockade and the Laws of War*

International law at this time did not make adequately clear the distinctions between a war between hostile sovereign nations and a civil war of major proportions. In seeking to protect the United States at all points, its leaders seemed at times to take the position that while the United States was engaged in a lawful war, the Confederacy was engaged merely in a lawless insurrection with none of the rights of a belligerent party such as the United States possessed. Political strategy here was concerned not merely with relations between the United States and foreign powers but also with the assertion of full municipal rights in Southern territory, rights which would be exercised as soon as the insurrection was suppressed. Into discussions of this subject from the very beginning entered questions of dealing with the inhabitants of the Southern states once full control of the territory had been regained: how the revolting leaders were to be punished and whether the offending states were to be permitted to return to their former status in the Union or were to be treated more or less as conquered territory. Every pronouncement of the government bearing on the war needs to be read in the light of these often confused considerations.

Cases involving the blockade were quickly brought into a number of federal courts. The first of them was decided in the Circuit Court of the District of Columbia, some three weeks before Congress assembled to give legislative support to the war measures of the Administration. It involved the capture of the English schooner *The Tropic Wind*. Taking advantage of the strategy of the Administration in attempting to deny to the enemy the status of a belligerent power, James M. Carlisle argued for the owners that the capture was illegal because the conflict did not have the status of war, which was essential to exercise of the right of blockade: "The Southern Confederacy is not recognized as a government de facto, those in arms under that supposed authority are merely rebels and traitors on lands and pirates on the seas."[7]

For the court, however, Judge James Dunlop held that it was for the President to determine whether the insurrection had culminated in a civil war. He found that the facts as set forth by the President amounted to a declaration that a state of civil war existed. Blockade was a right incident to a state of war, and in this respect he could find no difference between a foreign war and a civil war. The Administration won its case, and it had no cause for regret save for the implication that the opposing power, the Confederate government, might likewise have belligerent rights.

---

[7] United States v. *The Tropic Wind*, 28 Fed. Cas. 218 (No. 16541a) (C.C.-D.C. 1861).

In the United States District Court in Philadelphia, Judge John Cadwalader likewise upheld the blockade and the taking of prize, while skirting the politically sensitive question of belligerency. The vessel involved, *The Parkhill*, was owned in the South and was captured near Charleston when returning from a voyage to Liverpool. Judge Cadwalader held that in a civil war a nation seeking to restore its authority might prosecute hostilities by modes lawful in foreign wars against public enemies. He held, furthermore, that the claimants had no right to advance their claims in a court of the United States, saying that "Neither the power nor the right of revolt against a government can be asserted in its own courts."[8]

In Baltimore, a few weeks after Congress had adjourned, Judge Giles likewise upheld the establishment of the blockade, but he did so in such a way as to suggest embarrassment for the government. He quoted from Chief Justice Taney's opinion in *Luther v. Borden* to show that the military might be used to put down an insurrection that could not be controlled by the civil government. He referred to the scope of an insurrection, which determined when it became a civil war. He delicately alluded to, without setting forth at length, the opinion of Justice Samuel Chase in 1796 in *Ware v. Hylton* stating that by its act of adopting a new constitution Virginia had established independence which did not really require a declaration, whereupon "all dependence on, and connection with Great Britain absolutely and forever ceased," and that thereafter the war became a civil war and a public war "between independent governments."[9] The allusion, not fully drawn out, established the right to resort to blockade under the laws of war, but it carried implications with respect to the status of the Confederacy that were distasteful to the North. Here Judge Giles was most careful. He merely said:

> In the discussion of this question I have said nothing in reference to sovereign rights of the government; whether it may not at the same time exercise both sovereign and belligerent rights. Such a question does not arise in the case. I have confined myself to the examination of the existence or not of belligerent rights by the government in reference to the present unfortunate state of the country.[10]

A Baltimore writer for the *New York Tribune* commented: "The whole animus of this opinion is in sympathy with secession, and the Baltimore bar almost unanimously approves of it, because it takes this

---

[8] *The Parkhill*, 18 Fed. Cas. 1187, 1189 (No. 10775a) (D.C.E.D. 1861).
[9] Ware v. Hylton, 3 Dall. 199, 223, 224 (1796).
[10] The case, that of United States

v. The Schooner *W. F. Johnson*, was not officially reported but the opinion was printed in the *Baltimore Sun*, Sept. 23, 1861.

secessional ground, for you must know that eight out of ten of the lawyers of our city are devotees of secession. The Unionists here think that the Judge has rendered himself liable to the necessity of a visit to Fort Lafayette."[11]

These three decisions by Judges Dunlop, Cadwalader, and Giles were followed by another in New York by Judge Betts, which was to be selected as a test case to be taken to the Supreme Court. Actually involved were a large number of cases, argued over a period of fifteen days, with opinions linked together under the names of *The Hiawatha* and *The Crenshaw*. Outstanding among the many counsel were the district attorney, E. Delafield Smith, and William M. Evarts on behalf of the libellants, and Charles Edwards, Benjamin D. Silliman, and Daniel Lord on the part of the claimants. In these arguments almost every conceivable legal question was raised about the status of the war, the applicability of international law, and the impact on the situation of newly enacted Acts of Congress. The value of the property immediately involved in these several cases was enormous, and the decision would probably affect rights in other vast amounts of property.

Judge Betts held that a blockade was a legitimate means of conducting a civil war as well as a war between sovereign powers, and he so phrased his opinion as to avoid any suggestion that the Confederacy was entitled to recognition as a sovereign power by virtue of the employment of the blockade against it. He asserted the right of the United States to take as prize any property belonging to American citizens in the revolting states without proof of individual misconduct on the part of owners. The situs of the property alone gave it the status of enemy property.[12]

The leading cases were speedily appealed to the United States Circuit Court, where hearings before Justice Nelson occupied nearly a week.[13] Justice Nelson confirmed the decrees, but made it clear that he did so not necessarily because of agreement on the merits but to facilitate a hearing before the Supreme Court.[14] He was said to have given the impression that the case could be advanced on the calendar and heard early in the term beginning in December, 1861.[15] Counsel for the owners were eager for a hearing as quickly as possible, but counsel for the government objected to haste in the matter. In late December Evarts wrote to Attorney General Bates that he could not prepare for the argument before the middle of February, adding that

---

[11] *New York Tribune*, Sept. 30, Oct. 1, 1861.

[12] *The Hiawatha*, 12 Fed. Cas. 95 (No. 6451) (D.C.S.D. N.Y.).

[13] William M. Evarts to Edward Bates, Nov. 23, 1861, Attorney General Papers.

[14] *The Hiawatha*, 12 Fed. Cas. 94 (No. 6450) (C.C.S.D. N.Y.).

[15] Charles Edwards to Edward Bates, Dec. 13, 1861, Attorney General Papers.

the government should not call for argument of the cases, involving as they did such important political and constitutional questions, until the vacancies on the Court were filled.[16] A month later it was reported that argument of the cases was being delayed to promote the convenience of counsel. It was said that the fullest preparation was deemed desirable because of the importance of the questions and that the responsibility of the present judges would be all the heavier since there were three vacancies.[17]

With the passing weeks counsel for the owners continued to press for an early hearing.[18] On March 11 the Attorney General told Evarts that the cases could be reached at that term only if advanced on the calendar at the request of the government. He had evidence that some of the Justices would prefer to have the arguments postponed until the following term. If they were advanced and argued immediately it was nevertheless probable that the decision would go over. Since the courts thus far had sustained the government with respect to the leading principles involved in the prize cases, and since he felt confident they would finally be sustained in the Supreme Court, he thought he had no right to ask for advancement of the cases on the ground of public necessity.[19] Unstated was the consideration that delay might be desirable until new Justices were appointed to fill the three vacancies on the Court.

The 1861–1862 term of the Supreme Court came to an end without action in the prize cases. Prizes continued to be taken and were supported in the lower federal courts, but in spite of the confidence expressed by the Attorney General some uneasiness prevailed as to what the Supreme Court might do when test cases were reached. An encouraging omen was provided when in the United States Circuit Court in Philadelphia on July 1, 1862, Justice Grier upheld on appeal a prize decision of the District Court.[20] "Judge Grier's opinion is the more important," said the *Philadalphia Public Ledger* in a statement reprinted in the *New York Times*, "from the fact that it is the first given by a member of the Supreme Court."[21] It was remembered that in the case of the *Hiawatha* Justice Nelson had been careful not to express an opinion on the merits of the case, but had only affirmed the District

---

[16] William M. Evarts to Edward Bates, Dec. 27, 1861, *ibid*.

[17] *New York Times*, Jan. 21, 1862.

[18] See Charles Edward to Edward Bates, Jan. 31, 1862, Daniel Lord to Edward Bates, Jan. 31, 1862, Attorney General Papers.

[19] Edward Bates to William M. Evarts, Mar. 11, 1862, Attorney General's Letter Book B–5, 33.

[20] United States v. The Cargo of the *Prize Barque Meaco*. Unreported. For reference see *Philadelphia Public Ledger*, July 1, 1862; *Philadelphia Inquirer*, July 2, 1862; H.R. Exec. Doc. No. 73, 37th Cong., 3rd Sess. 76 (1863).

[21] *New York Times*, July 2, 1862.

Court decision for the purpose of speeding the case on its way to the Supreme Court.

Among the pending prize cases was that of the *Amy Warwick*, in Boston, which was to be linked with others in a series of test case arguments before the Supreme Court. In the District Court it was decided by Judge Peleg Sprague in such a way as to give full support to the position of the government. "I am satisfied," said Judge Sprague on an important aspect of the controversy, "that the United States, as a nation, has full and complete belligerent rights, which are in no degree impaired by the fact that its enemies owe allegiance, and have superadded the guilt of treason to that of unjust war."[22] In a later opinion in the same prize case Judge Sprague took into account current debates over the implications of prize cases for the treatment of the Southern states when the war would come to an end:

> It has been supposed that, if the government have the rights of a belligerent, then, after the rebellion is suppressed, it will have the rights of conquest; that a state and its inhabitants may be permanently divested of all political privileges, and treated as foreign territory acquired by arms. This is an error,—a grave and dangerous error. The rights of war exist only while the war continues. Thus, if peace be concluded, a capture made immediately afterwards on the ocean, even where the peace could not have been known, is unauthorized, and property so taken is not prize of war, and must be restored.[23]

No belligerent rights would continue, and the sovereign rights of the United States in the South would be merely those which had existed before the war.

From Judge Sprague's decision in the *Amy Warwick* an appeal was taken to the Circuit Court where it was argued before Justice Clifford, who disposed of the case with obvious discomfort. He tried to steer a course between full affirmation of Judge Sprague's decision and strictly pro forma affirmation as resorted to by Justice Nelson in *The Hiawatha*:

> It is desirable that this cause should be decided at this term of the Court, in order that it may be taken at once, such being the wish of the parties, to the Supreme Court. I have given the cause such an

---

[22] *The Amy Warwick*, 1 Fed. Cas. 799, 803 (No. 341) (D.C.D. Mass. 1862).

Horace Binney said of the Sprague opinion, "It has great excellence in its style, which is indeed a characteristic of Judge Sprague; and it has the impregnable strength of legal rea-

son. Nothing could be better. It will be a light house to all who shall hereafter come upon that coast of the law." Horace Binney to R. H. Dana, Feb. 27, 1862, Dana Papers.

[23] *The Amy Warwick*, 1 Fed Cas. 808, 810 (No. 342) (D.C.D. Mass. 1862).

examination as enables me to reach a satisfactory solution, but not so thorough and complete an examination as, under the circumstances, I should desire. Still, I have arrived at such a conviction as makes it proper for me to enter a decree. It is not a decree *pro forma*, but a decree founded on the best opinion I am able to form. But my mind is open to conviction on this great question, if it shall come before me, as one of the judges of the Supreme Court, in any of the appealed cases.[24]

Richard H. Dana, Jr., the United States Attorney who won the decision in the *Amy Warwick* in the two federal courts in Boston, joined William M. Evarts, Charles Eames, and others as counsel for the government in a group of prize cases before the Supreme Court.[25]

Even at the 1862–1863 term of the Supreme Court, when there were again nine members, further delay was threatened. Dana reported to the Attorney General that counsel for the claimants in the *Amy Warwick* case had written to the Chief Justice asking for a delay. The reason given revealed that in spite of the position earlier taken by Judge Cadwalader in *The Parkhill* that rebels could not sue in the courts of the United States for the recovery of their property captured in the course of the war, there was at least mixed rebel ownership of the cargo of the *Amy Warwick*. The statement was that the agent for the rebel owners was not willing to pay Mr. Bartlett all he required for an argument in Washington.[26] Argument in the group of cases was

---

[24] Not officially reported. Printed in *Boston Daily Advertiser*, Nov. 15, 1862. For references see H.R. Exec. Doc. No. 73, 37th Cong., 3rd Sess. 10 (1863); T. J. Coffey to R. H. Dana, Jr., Nov. 22, 1862, Attorney General's Letter Book B–5, 254.

[25] See R. H. Dana, Jr., to T. J. Coffey, Nov. 24, 28, 1862, Attorney General Papers; T. J. Coffey to R. H. Dana, Jr., Nov. 26, 1862, Attorney General's Letter Book B–5, at 256.

[26] R. H. Dana, Jr., to Edward Bates, Feb. 5, 1863, Attorney General Papers. The reference is to Sidney Bartlett, an eminent Boston lawyer in whose office Justice Holmes began the practive of law. He did not appear in the case but left the presentation to Edward Bangs.

The question of the right of persons resident in the seceded states to sue in the federal courts added complications to the much debated question of the relation of these persons to the Union while the rebellion was in progress. In a case decided in the United States District Court in Pittsburgh in October, 1862, Judge Wilson McCandless decided that he could not hear a part owner who was a resident of one of the states in rebellion: "This point has been decided by my Brother Cadwalader at Philadelphia, and the decision affirmed by Judge Grier." United States v. Hammett, 26 Fed. Cas. 547 (No. 15446) (D.C.-W.D. Pa. 1862). Yet, as indicated by the District Court decision in the case of the *Amy Warwick* and the later Supreme Court decision in the group of cases known as the *Prize Cases*, discussed hereafter, Southern owners seem to have made direct or indirect arrangements for representation by counsel in cases where non-Southern owners were also involved, and by this means the questions in which they were interested were determined, though in these cases adversely to their interests.

begun, however, on February 10, 1863, the case of *The Brilliante*,[27] from the southern district of Florida, having been added to the list. The presentation continued over twelve days, ending on February 25.

From the point of view of public understanding the cases were well explained by a Washington newspaper, which said in part:

> The parties before the Court are: First, the United States government; second, the captors; and third, the claimants, who were owners of the vessels and cargoes. There are some half dozen cases which have been brought, on appeal, from the District Courts, where they were originally tried, and though each case has its own peculiar circumstances, yet, in all of them, two great questions are raised, which are of general interest: First, is our Government engaged in a war in the sense in which that term is understood, so as to bring it within the principles and regulations which affect foreign and commercial nations in their commercial dealings on the seas? and, second, whether, if so, the blockade declared to exist of the rebel ports has been established in such a manner as to make the vessels captured lawful prizes, subject to condemnation in our Admiralty Courts?
>
> The property seized is mostly owned by British subjects, and they urge that, under our Constitution and laws, no war has been declared; and that, according to the laws of nations, war does not now exist; that the present state of things is nothing but an internal civil rebellion, which gives no right to our Government to declare a blockade of a portion of our own territory, so as to affect the rights of citizens of other nations, who are carrying on commerce with our own citizens. How deeply these questions touch the powers of our Government, at this interesting period, can at once be seen; and the decision of the Supreme Court upon them cannot fail to be one of the most grave duties of their session.[28]

Counsel for the appellants, the owners of the vessels at the time of their capture, included James M. Carlisle, Daniel Lord, Charles Edwards, and Edward Bangs. Counsel representing either or jointly the government and the claimants of prize benefits included Charles Eames, William M. Evarts, Richard H. Dana, Jr., and C. B. Sedgwick. For the owners of the Schooner *Brilliante*, and indirectly for all the owners, James M. Carlisle, a prominent Washington lawyer, struck heavy blows at the claims of the United States. He cited Seward's diplomatic correspondence to show denial of belligerent rights to the South, and refusal to recognize the existence of anything but a municipal question, in the light of which, he contended, there could be no blockade

---

[27] The case was unreported in the lower court. See H.R. Exec. Doc. No. 73, 37th Cong., 3rd Sess. 115 (1863).

[28] *Washington Republican*, Feb. 12, 1863, quoted in *New York Times*, Feb. 15, 1863.

in the international sense and hence no capture pursuant to the laws of war. The seizure had been made prior to any authorization by Congress, and he denied that subsequent ratification had reached the prior operations of the blockade. Without a lawful blockade there could be no lawful capture.

The matter came back necessarily, Carlisle contended, to the question of the power of the President under the Constitution. The argument for the government, he said, made the President some sort of impersonation of the country and invoked for him the power and right to use all the force at his command to save the life of the nation. It was assumed that the Constitution authorized the President to operate as a dictator whenever he thought the life of the nation in danger. It came to a plea of "necessity," a word not known to the Constitution. War, in the sense of the condition under which rights under international law could be enforced by blockade, was a matter of law as well as of fact. In law there could be a state of war only when it was declared by Congress. In law there was no war when this vessel was taken into custody.[29]

Three Justices, and perhaps a fourth as well, were delighted with the Carlisle argument. Justice Catron wrote to Carlisle to say that he and Justices Nelson and Clifford were eager to have it printed in the forthcoming volume of Black's *Reports*, and would see that it was inserted verbatim if it was written out. Catron added:

> It is idle to disguise the fact that the claim set up to forfeit these ships & cargoes, *by the force of a proclimation* [sic], is not founded on constitutional power, but on a power claimed to be *created* by Military necessity. *Necessity* is an old plea—old as the reign of Tiberias; its limits should be looked for in Tacitus. It is the commander's will. The End, we are told is to crush out the Rebellion; that the whole means are at the Presdt's discretion and that he is the sole Judge in the Selection of the means to accomplish the End. That is a rejection of the Constitution with its limitations.[30]

Government counsel confidently asserted the power to use international law as an instrument for subduing an internal enemy. At one point in the argument, however, the government was seriously embarrassed by the reaction of the Supreme Court to one of its spokesmen. Attorney General Bates, deciding not to participate in the argument himself, had given the management of the case for the government to Charles Eames, a native of Massachusetts and a graduate of Harvard.

---

[29] For the text of Carlisle's speech as subsequently written out, see Prize Cases, 2 Black 635, 639–650 (1863).

[30] "J. Catron to James M. Carlisle, Feb. 26, 1863," *Legal Historian*, 1: 51–52, 1958.

Eames had varied experience as an attorney, as a government employee in subordinate positions, and as a newspaper editor. He had an extensive law practice during the Civil War period, much of it with the Navy Department. At the time of his death in 1867, Gideon Welles, Secretary of the Navy, called him "the most correct admiralty lawyer in the country," and "the best authority on questions of maritime law."[31] In December, 1862, and January, 1863, he, along with Reverdy Johnson, was counsel at the court-martial of Fitz-John Porter, who as a result of the trial was dismissed from the army for failing to obey orders from his commanding officer and thereby helping to bring about the defeat of Union troops at the second Battle of Bull Run.[32] The trial engendered much controversial public discussion and was still in the minds of lawyers and judges.

After Eames' argument in the *Prize Cases*, Justice Swayne called on Attorney General Bates, for himself and Justice Davis and perhaps other Justices, to voice concern about the effect of the argument. As Bates interpreted the intervention, Eames had made himself obnoxious to the Court, delivering a speech which critics on the Court said was no argument at all, "did no good, but harm, to the cause, acting like a harlequin, and turning a solemn trial into a farce." Chief Justice Taney was reported as saying that he no longer wondered at General Porter's conclusion that "he deserved to be convicted for trusting his case to such a counsel." Bates remarked in his diary that this showing of passion and prejudice was not very creditable to the Court, but he feared that it might endanger the *Prize Cases*.[33]

Apparently much more effective was the argument of Evarts. In *Currie v. United States*, the case of the *Crenshaw*, Evarts contended that the war was a civil war between a national sovereignty and a rebellious population, and that "the complex frame of State and Federal power, enabled the revolted population to give to the hostilities, on their part, the shape of *public*, as distinguished from *private*, war, and presents to foreign nations a close resemblance, and to ourselves an indisputable analogy, to *public war*, to which both parties are political communities."[34] The state of civil war carried to the sovereign the rights of war as toward neutrals, "without depriving him of the full dominion, as sovereign over his rebellious subjects."[35] A state of war was a question of actualities and not of law, and did not depend on a declaration by Congress. The *fact* of war introduced the law of war,[36] and with it the right to maintain the blockade under international law. The owner-

---

[31] *Diary of Gideon Wells*, Howard K. Beale, ed., III, 67.
[32] See 12 O.R. (1st) Part II, Supp.
[33] "The Diary of Edward Bates," Howard K. Beale, ed., *Annual Report of the American Historical Assocation for the Year 1930*, 4:281, 1933.
[34] Evarts brief, 25.
[35] *Ibid.*, 26.
[36] *Ibid.*, 30.

ship of some of the vessels by American citizens residing in the South did not protect the property against taking as prize. The status of the property depended on its situs, and not on the loyalty or disloyalty of the owners.[37]

Perhaps more spectacular was the presentation of Richard H. Dana, Jr., who covered approximately the same points made by Evarts but emphasized the meaning of "enemy property" as far as the capture of prize was concerned. A day before the Supreme Court argument began, Dana had written to Charles Francis Adams about the startling fact that, after the war had been under way for twenty-three months, the Supreme Court was to decide whether the government had the legal capacity to exert the war powers. He spoke of the horrible possibility that the Court might decide that the blockade was illegal, after we had created for two years a cotton famine in foreign countries with consequent domestic dangers and distress. It would end the war, he predicted, and leave us in a fearful position with neutrals. He did not think such an outcome probable but there had been danger of it before the three new judges had been appointed.[38]

It was said of Dana's argument that "Dry legal questions were lifted into the higher region of international discussion, and the philosophy of the barbaric right of capture of private property at sea was for the first time in the hearing of most of the judges then on the bench applied to the pending situation with a power of reasoning and a wealth of illustration and a grace and felicity of style that swept all before them." After Dana's argument Justice Grier, meeting a friend in the corridor, said with a burst of unjudicial enthusiasm, "Well, your little 'Two Years before the Mast' has settled that question; there is nothing more to be said about it!"[39]

Dana found the compliments of judges and audience and counsel too flattering to put on paper. People seemed to think that the philosophy of the law of prize had been developed for the first time in its bearing on the Civil War situation. In a letter of February 23 he reported that "I have won Judge Grier's heart. He pats me on the shoulder and says I have cleared up all his doubts, and that it is the best argument he has heard for five years."[40] The Attorney General, if

---

[37] *Ibid.*, 35–37. For the story of Evarts' participation in the case see Chester L. Barrows, *William M. Evarts*, 110–12.

[38] Charles Francis Adams, *Richard Henry Dana: A Biography*, II, 266–77.

[39] *Ibid.*, 269. See Dana's widely read *Two Years Before the Mast* (1840).

[40] *Ibid.*, 270. On reading Dana's brief, Charles Francis Adams wrote from London, "Nothing shows so conclusively how disjointed the machinery of government has become in America. Considering the composition of the Supreme Court, I think we may count the effect upon it of secession, to vacate some of the seats, as a piece of good fortune. I know not how

disappointed in the impression made by Eames, was enthusiastic about that made by Dana. Seward, whose policy and tactics were under close scrutiny, was flattering along with others.

During the argument Justice Swayne had evidently made clear to the Attorney General the support of the three new Justices—himself, Miller, and Davis. Justice Grier, here as so often in other cases, was outspoken in court. Indeed, for all his lack of enthusiasm for the Administration and for particular war methods and for Yankees generally, he had from the beginning been vigorously loyal to the Union. As early as the summer of 1861 he had written to Justice Clifford about a visit to the home of his son-in-law, Thomas B. Monroe, Jr., in Kentucky, where he had found Monroe "a secessionist, as insane as the others." In view of the outcome of the Battle of Bull Run he foresaw a long war, but he contended that "We must conquer this rebellion or declare our republican government a failure."[41] Justice Nelson, on the other hand, early involved with Justice Campbell in abortive peace negotiations between the North and the South, had shared the sentiments of Chief Justice Taney in his belief that "Necessity will compel a peaceful separation."[42] A year and a half later he wrote somberly of the Emancipation Proclamation and the growth of executive and military power, "The darkness deepens."[43] The letter of Justice Catron to James M. Carlisle, discussed above, disclosed the fact that Justices Catron, Grier, and Clifford stood together in opposition to Lincoln's exercise of executive power in advance of authorization from Congress, and, in view of his *Merryman* opinion and expressions of sentiment to Franklin Pierce and other friends, it would have been astonishing had Chief Justice Taney taken a different position. As for Justice Wayne, residing in Washington and deprived by the war of his circuit, not much is said about his position in connection with the *Prize Cases*. On the record, however, was his tradition of nationalism and his recent decision at chambers in the *Stevens* habeas corpus case. There was reason to hope for his support of the Union cause.

The decision in the *Prize Cases* was handed down on March 10, 1863, sharing space in public announcements with the case involving

---

good the subsequent appointments may have been, but I trust they will at least avail so far as to save the very cornerstone of the edifice. The prejudices of thirty years work strongly in me to wish that this presidential term should not be permitted to pass away without a change of the Chief on that Bench. And yet I do not know how sure we may be of a suitable successor." C. F. Adams to R. H. Dana, Jr., Apr. 8, 1863, Dana Papers.

[41] R. C. Grier to Nathan Clifford, July 24, 1861, Clifford Papers.

[42] Charles Fairman, *Mr. Justice Miller and the Supreme Court*, 81.

[43] Samuel Nelson to Nathan Clifford, Sept. 25, 1862, Clifford Papers.

ownership of the New Almaden Mine in California. Justice Grier wrote the opinion of the Court, in language suggesting the vigor with which he was accustomed to express himself but attempting, nevertheless, a highly disciplined presentation. He found the decision dependent, first of all, on answers to two questions—whether the President had the power to establish the blockade pursuant to international law, and whether the property of persons domiciled in the Confederate states was a proper subject of capture on the high seas as "enemies' property," quite apart from the matter of the loyalty or disloyalty of the particular owners. It will be recalled that Evarts had stressed one of these questions in the argument and Dana the other. Of the two, the first was the more critical, in that on the answer to it depended the question of the legal status of the war during the months of hostilities before Congress had ratified the measures already instituted by the President.

As for the existence of a war, Justice Grier took the position previously taken by Evarts, that it was a question of fact rather than of law. A civil war was never publicly proclaimed. This civil war was a fact of domestic history which the Court was bound to notice and to know. While Congress alone could declare a foreign war, no clause in the Constitution authorized it to declare war on a state. On the other hand, the President, obligated to see that the laws were faithfully executed and in command of the armed forces, had to accept the challenge of war if war occurred, without waiting for special legislative authority: "The President was bound to meet it in the shape it presented itself, without waiting for Congress to baptize it with a name; and no name given to it by him or them could change the fact."[44]

Justice Grier made much of the fact that on May 13, 1861, before Congress had met to enact measures with respect to the war, the Queen of England had issued her proclamation of neutrality, a proclamation which was followed by similar declarations or by the acquiescence of other nations. After such a proclamation no citizen of a proclaiming country could deny the existence of a war with all its consequences as to neutrals. He could not ask a court to affect a technical ignorance of that which all the world acknowledged to be the greatest civil war known to history. As for the status of individual enemies, international law gave no support to the doctrine that a civil war was not a war because they were traitors as well as military enemies.

Summarizing his statement of the scope of Presidential power in the absence of supporting statutes, Justice Grier said:

Whether the President in fulfilling his duties, as Commander-in-Chief, in suppressing an insurrection, has met with such armed hostile re-

---

[44] Prize Cases, 2 Black 635, 669 (1863).

sistance, and a civil war of such alarming proportions as will compel him to accord to them the character of belligerents, is a question to be decided by him, and this court must be governed by the decisions and acts of the Political Department of the government to which this power was intrusted. "He must determine what degree of force the crisis demands." The proclamation of blockade is, itself, official and conclusive evidence to the court that a state of war existed which demanded and authorized a recourse to such a measure, under the circumstances peculiar to the case.[45]

Having said as much, Justice Grier faced also the question of the technical legality of the war had it required legislative sanction—an assumption which he did not admit. If such sanction had been required, it had been provided by the several acts of the ensuing Congress which had been passed to enable the government to prosecute the war. He denied the contention that such retroactive ratification was unconstitutional because ex post facto. Such an objection might have some weight on the trial of an indictment in a criminal court, but not in a tribunal administering public and international law.

Dealing thus with the power of the President to invoke the war powers and assert the rights of the United States under international law, Justice Grier gave the Lincoln Administration all the support it could possibly expect from a judicial tribunal. He likewise gave all the Administration could ask in his discussion of "enemies' property," following here the argument made by Dana. This term, he explained, was a technical phrase peculiar to prize courts, and depended on principles of public policy as distinguished from common law. Residents of the Confederate states having property on the high seas were not entitled to special immunities derived from municipal laws in the United States merely because they were also citizens of the United States:

All persons residing within this territory whose property may be used to increase the revenues of the hostile power are, in this contest, liable to be treated as enemies, though not foreigners. They have cast off their allegiance and made war on their government, and are none the less enemies because they are traitors.[46]

The opinion of the Court was skillfully drafted to avoid any implication that recognition of the status of belligerency carried with it the assumption that both belligerents were necessarily independent sovereign powers and that the Confederacy was entitled to recognition as a sovereign as well as a belligerent. Participants in the Confederate

---

[45] *Ibid.*, 670.   [46] *Ibid.*, 674.

action were repeatedly referred to as rebels or traitors. They were "enemies, though not foreigners." The Court thus attempted to minimize any propaganda value which the Confederacy or foreign and domestic critics of the United States could derive from the decision.

Following the delivery of the opinion of the Court Justice Nelson announced a dissenting opinion. He by no means matched the ringing criticism of executive usurpation which Carlisle had delivered or which Justice Catron had characterized in his letter to Carlisle. Yet he did take the position that the conflict, however violent, did not become a war until it was declared by Congress, and that a lawful blockade could not be maintained until a lawful war existed. The power to declare war, he insisted, "cannot be delegated or surrendered to the Executive. Congress alone can determine whether war exists or should be declared."[47] The so-called war carried on by the President against the insurrectionary districts of the Southern states was therefore from necessity "a personal war, until Congress assembled and acted upon this state of things."[48]

Had the Nelson dissent been delivered as the opinion of the Court, it would have invalidated enforcement of the blockade prior to the time when Congress met and took action. Nelson admitted that the Act of Congress of July 13, 1861, authorizing the closing of the ports in the areas of rebellion amounted to a recognition of a state of civil war,[49] but denied that Congress could give such recognition a retroactive effect, even though it had phrased the statute in an attempt to do so.[50]

When Justice Nelson concluded the reading of his opinion he announced that Chief Justice Taney and Justice Catron concurred with him. Justice Clifford, while concurring privately in the Catron letter to Carlisle, had been embarrassed to join in an opinion contrary to that which he had delivered in the Circuit Court in the case of the *Amy Warwick*, for all the lack of confidence that he had shown at that time. Now, however, when Justice Nelson had concluded, he announced for himself that he joined in the dissent.[51] The decision was therefore arrived at by a vote of five to four. Since the minority opinion admitted that the war had lawful status after the enactment of the statute of July 13, 1861, it would not, had it been made the opinion of the Court, have done as much damage as had been feared by those who thought the Court of the Dred Scott decision might deny altogether the right to maintain a blockade in waging a civil war. Although all the cases involved in this decision were the result of the blockade maintained

---

47 *Ibid.*, 693.
48 *Ibid.*, 695.
49 12 Stat. 255.
50 12 Stat. 326.
51 *New York Tribune*, Mar. 11, 1863.

before Congress met, most of the prize vessels had been captured after Congress took action, and as to them the Court was unanimous in upholding enforcement of the blockade.

The annual term of the Supreme Court came to an end on March 10, 1863, the day on which the *Prize Cases* were decided, and Justice Grier took the opinion of the Court with him to Philadelphia for final revision. At the same time Jeremiah S. Black, as Reporter of the Court, prepared for inclusion of the opinion in what was to be his final volume of reports. He asked Dana to write a statement of his argument for use in presenting the case, saying that he already had one from Carlisle, and that the two of them, Dana and Carlisle, had given "at once the fullest, clearest and strongest expositions of the several doctrines you contended for. I am sure that such is the sentiment of the Judges. They as well as I are anxious that some memory of both should be preserved." The case, Black remarked, had a historical as well as a professional interest and it was a great case in both respects and would be cited in all civilized countries. Dana should therefore be willing to do justice to himself and his opinions by preparing the statement. "Besides, it is due to a majority of the Court whose judgment being that of a bare majority may need whatever support it can get."[52]

Dana prepared the coveted draft. In introducing the case in his volume, Black stated that only one argument on each side could be given. The arguments of Dana and Carlisle had been selected "because they came to his hands in a form which relieved him of the labor which the others would have cost to re-write and condense them."[53] When the volume appeared, Evarts wrote to Dana, "I see Black has left Lord, and Eames, and me out entirely because we did not make his report for him. He is a sad reporter. I hear the Court wish to get rid of him."[54]

When Justice Grier completed revision of the opinion of the Court, he submitted it to the *American Law Register* for publication, in advance of publication in the official reports.[55] J. Hubley Ashton, United States Attorney in Philadelphia, sent a copy of the journal to Attorney General Bates, reporting Justice Grier as saying that this was the form in which the opinion would make its official appearance. Said Ashton, "He has added to the original draft one or two strong and pregnant sentences, which you will discover as you run your eye over it."[56] The

---

[52] J. S. Black to R. H. Dana, Jr., Aug. 17, 1863, Dana Papers.

[53] Prize Cases, 2 Black 635, 639 (1863).

[54] William M. Evarts to R. H. Dana, Jr., Dec. 28, 1863, Dana Papers.

[55] "Schooner *Brilliante* v. United States," *Am. L. Reg.*, 11:334, 1863.

[56] J. Hubley Ashton to Edward Bates, Apr. 8, 1863, Attorney General Papers.

opinion as printed or summarized in newspapers at the time of delivery had already been used to support the Union cause.[57] The *New York Times* boasted that the hope of the Copperheads "to cast a vast burden upon the Treasury by annulling the blockade" had been dashed by the decision. The Copperhead contention that the Union had no right to coerce the citizens of the seceding states had been answered by the assertion that citizens owed allegiance both to the Union and to the states. "This principle of concurrent allegiance crushes at once the so-called right of secession. It is the cornerstone of loyalty, and we are glad to see it again solemnly authenticated."[58]

The argument over the right of the Union to coerce the seceding states continued, both in the United States and in England, with important propaganda goals at stake in both countries. Francis Lieber, one of the few recognized American authorities on international law and political theory and deeply loyal to the Union, published a letter answering the argument that the South had the same right to secede from the Union that the colonies had had to secede from the British Empire. The colonies had been mere dependencies of the Empire, he said, and as such had been deprived of many of their rights. The Southern states, on the other hand, had never been dependent. They had been an integral, even a dominant portion of the Union. Secession was therefore ruthless destruction, and not a struggle for independence.[59]

In the same period the *Law Magazine*, then the most prominent law journal in London, published with qualified approval an anonymous article calculated to show that secession was not rebellion and that the Union ought not to coerce the seceding states into obedience. The author scoffed at the political party in America which had long maintained the dogma of an American nationality, "*one and indivisible*, springing from the whole people of the Union, in opposition to those who assert that the nationality is a *composite* nationality, springing from a federation of sovereign states."[60] Since the Union was a federation of states founded on compact, a state was bound to continue a member of the federation only so long as it pleased. He concluded that in any event the North should admit the principle of secession and let the South go, since it was much better to reconcile an enemy than to conquer him.

The article brought reactions from Americans concerned both about strained relations with Great Britain[61] and about the impact of

---

[57] See Charles Warren, *The Supreme Court in United States History*, II, 384–85.

[58] *New York Times*, Mar. 13, 1863.

[59] "Francis Lieber to H. Smith *et al.*, Sept. 29, 1863," *New York Times*, Oct. 2, 1863.

[60] "On American Secession and State Rights," *L. Mag. & L. Rev.*, 15: 318–20, 1863.

[61] Among the many discussions of such subjects as British building and equipment of ships intended for use by the Confederacy in preying on

constitutional theory on the treatment of the South after the war had been won. The leading reply[62] was made by Judge Isaac F. Redfield, an author on many legal subjects who by 1860 had been for twenty-five years a member of the Supreme Court of New Hampshire and for the last eight years of the period had been chief justice. Judge Redfield was a Democrat who classified himself as a states' rights advocate. He had no use for what seemed to him the nullifying and secessionist theories of John C. Calhoun as embodied in the original article. Redfield regarded the Constitution as a compact among the states which could not be dissolved and which preserved inviolate certain rights of the states. As for the so-called dogma of American nationality, it was not a dogma but a doctrine generally held by all groups and sections except one, the section now in rebellion.

But while concerned about the indissolubility of the Union, Judge Redfield was also concerned with preserving the integrity of the states, whatever their misbehavior in attempted secession—a topic much belabored among English friends of the Confederacy and American friends as well. As he saw it:

> if the States have forfeited all their rights, and may be held as conquered provinces of the empire, and all their laws and even property rights disregarded without reference to the guarantees contained in the national constitution, we do not perceive why this will not practically result in the establishment of a military despotism, wholly irresponsible to all law over the entire territory of these States now in rebellion. And after this *fait accompli* he must be a sanguine and hopeful man, who expects the prevalence of the same free principles in any portion of the empire, which have thus far obtained to a certain extent, at least, in the remaining portions of the Republic which have never swerved from their allegiance.[63]

He believed the preservation of freedom required the preservation of both the Union and the states.

While this discussion was under way, the same London journal published another article disparaging the conduct of foreign affairs by the Lincoln Administration and interpreting the Supreme Court deci-

---

American shipping see Charles G. Loring, *Neutral Relations of England and the United States* (pamphlet, 1863), written originally as a series of articles for publication in the *Boston Daily Advertiser*. For comment see *The New York Times*, Nov. 10, 1863, and *New York Tribune*, Dec. 5, 1863.

[62] For another, published under the original title, see an article by G. S. H., "Boston, U.S.A., October, 1863," *L. Mag. & L. Rev.*, 16: 212, 1864. For a reply by the original contributor see *ibid.*, 240.

[63] Isaac F. Redfield, "On American Secession and State Rights," *L. Mag. & L. Rev.*, 16:81, 99, 1864.

sion in the *Prize Cases* in such a way as to suggest that it was a political decision arrived at for the purpose of circumscribing and curtailing the rights of Southerners, whether derived from municipal or international law. The article appeared in the form of a letter from William Beach Lawrence, a man of repute in international law who earlier in 1863 had published his second edition of *Elements of International Law*, originally written by Henry Wheaton, the former Reporter of the Supreme Court. Although he resided in the North and wrote from Newport, Rhode Island, Lawrence's statement of facts and his discussion of them revealed an obviously pro-Southern bias. He called attention to the protest of the Secretary of State at European recognition of the belligerent rights of the South, and the subsequent contrasting decision of the Supreme Court in the *Prize Cases* finding that a state of war had existed since the proclamation of the blockade in April, 1861. Lawrence either misunderstood the decision or deliberately misinterpreted it by saying:

[It] recognized the war as made by the States in their political capacities, and, as a corollary therefrom, it declared all the inhabitants of the Seceded States, on account of their residence, and without regard to their individual locality, alien enemies. Indeed, among the first condemnations of the prize courts, were cases where the sole inquiry was the place of residence of the claimants.[64]

From this interpretation he inferred the suspension of most civil rights in the South, and as a horrible example pointed to the Proclamation of Emancipation and to other provisions for the confiscation of property, the latter in disregard of "the time-honoured principle, as well as of our common law, derived from our English ancestors, as of international law, that protection and allegiance are reciprocal."[65]

The Lawrence letter served the purposes not only of those who wished to put the United States in a bad light abroad but also those who wished to claim Supreme Court sanction for ruthless measures of reconstruction when the war was over. It needed to be answered. Richard Henry Dana, who had a clarity of thought and utterance not possessed by Lawrence, took the task upon himself and published in the *Boston Daily Advertiser* an article entitled "What the Supreme Court Decided in the Prize Causes."[66] Dana quoted the Lawrence statement on the *Prize Cases* and asserted flatly that "The Supreme Court decided nothing

---

[64] "Letter from the Hon. William Beach Lawrence," *L. Mag. & L. Rev.*, 16: 138, 139–40, 1863.

[65] *Ibid.*, 140.

[66] *Boston Daily Advertiser*, Dec. 18, 1863. It was reprinted in part in *L. Rep.*, 25:737, 1863.

of the kind." He explained the classification of enemy property as any property captured at sea which was owned by any person residing in the rebellious territory, whatever might be their personal relations to the Union. He then listed with sharp clarity the points that had not been decided and the points that in fact had been decided by the Court. Points not decided:

1. The court did not decide that the passing of the ordinances of secession made the territory of the insurgent States enemy's territory, or its inhabitants alien enemies.
2. The court did not decide that the passing of the secession ordinances terminated, or in any way impaired, the legal relations of the insurgent States, as bodies politic, with the general government, or the political relations of their inhabitants with the general government or with their respective States.
3. The court decided absolutely nothing as to the effect of the passing of the secession ordinances on the civil or political relations of the inhabitants of the insurgent States with the general government or with their respective States, or on the relations of the insurgent States, as bodies politic, with the general government.
4. The court did not decide that the inhabitants of the seceding States are alien enemies, at all, or that the territory of those States is enemy's territory.

What the Court did decide:

1. That in case of domestic war, the Government of the United States may, at its option, use the powers and rights, known to the international laws of war as blockade, and capture of enemy's property at sea.
2. That to determine whether property found at sea is "enemy's property," within the meaning of the law of Prize, the same tests may be applied in domestic as in international wars.
3. One of these tests is that the owner of the property so found has his domicil and residence in a place of which the enemy (whether rebel or foreign enemy) has a certain kind and degree of possession, with the exercise of a *de facto* jurisdiction.
4. Richmond, Virginia, was, at the time of the capture and condemnation of those vessels, under such possession and control of the enemy as to render it indisputably "enemy's territory" within the strictest definitions known to the laws of war.

Not content with mere newspaper publication, Dana circulated copies far and wide, in the United States and in Great Britain, to members of the Supreme Court and to other prominent persons. Justice Grier thanked Dana for what he called certainly "a correct statement of our decision in the Prize Cases." The Court, he said, had decided the questions before it and nothing more. He had thought the opinion so plain that it could not be misapprehended. Since he deemed Lawrence incapable of perverting the opinion, he wondered at his failure to understand it correctly.[67] Two weeks later, as if forgetting that he had written his first letter, Grier wrote again, saying of the Court opinion that "with your commentary no one can be so stupid as to misunderstand it, however willing he may be to *pervert* it."[68]

Justice Davis thought Dana's article well conceived and unanswerable. He had always thought the decision so plain that it could not be either misunderstood or perverted.[69] Justice Swayne wrote, "You have vindicated the truth and rendered a public service."[70] Attorney General Bates had already read Dana's article, which except for introductory paragraphs had been immediately reprinted and made the basis of an approving editorial in the *National Intelligencer*.[71] He could account for Lawrence's deliberate misrepresentations of the *Prize Cases* only in terms of Dana's phrase, evidently included in his covering letter, that he did it "in his effort to sustain the right of secession."[72] Assistant Attorney General Coffey thought the article should be reprinted in the more ardent Union papers such as the *Times*, the *Tribune*, and the *Washington Chronicle*.[73]

It was George S. Boutwell, a member of Congress from Massachusetts, who in correspondence with Dana showed mixed feelings about the interpretation of the *Prize Cases*. He thought Dana's statement correct as far as it went, but he thought it a legitimate inference that the government might use powers and rights known to international law in its capacity as conqueror when the rebel territory should be regained. Among those rights was that of changing the institutions of the conquered enemy—presumably in this instance the institution of slavery. Furthermore, apart from the opinion of the Court, he found ample authority for refusing to "allow the rebellious states to reappear in this Union upon their own motion and without the consent of Congress."[74] Boutwell was here dealing with the currently critical issue which Dana's other correspondents for the most part refrained from discussing.

Dana sent copies of his article to Charles Francis Adams, Ameri-

[67] R. C. Grier to R. H. Dana, Dec. 24, 1863, Dana Papers.

[68] R. C. Grier to R. H. Dana, Jan. 15, 1864, *ibid.*

[69] David Davis to R. H. Dana, Dec. 26, 1863, *ibid.*

[70] N. H. Swayne to R. H. Dana, Dec. 24, 1863, *ibid.*

[71] *Washington National Intelligencer*, Dec. 23, 1863.

[72] Edward Bates to R. H. Dana, Dec. 28, 1863, Dana Papers.

[73] T. J. Coffey to R. H. Dana, Dec. 24, 1863, *ibid.*

[74] George S. Boutwell to R. H. Dana, Dec. 26, 1863, *ibid.*

can minister in London, for distribution to influential people and for possible republication. Adams did not think Lawrence would get far, and he wondered what heinous offense Henry Wheaton had committed that his name should go down to posterity saddled with the weight of the name of Lawrence as editor of his treatise on international law.[75] Adams was doubtful about getting republication of Dana's article in London, saying that it was hard to get things reprinted there. In a compressed form and with the blunt treatment of Lawrence eliminated, the Dana article was reprinted, however, in the *Law Magazine*, the editor saying briefly that Dana, as counsel in the cases, might "be supposed to know the views which he presented to the court, and which the court adopted in rendering their judgment."[76]

Throughout the period from 1861 to 1864 when the *Prize Cases* were being argued and decided and discussed, the United States was winning acceptance at home and abroad of its claims under international law concerning maintenance of the blockade and the taking of prize. As for the Supreme Court decision, Jeremiah S. Black was right in his prediction that it would be cited in all civilized countries.[77] It became a landmark in the history of the Court and of the country. The implications of the decision for the process of restoring the rebel states to the Union were no doubt restricted by the wide circulation of Dana's careful analysis.[78]

A postscript carries somewhat further the story of the controversy between Dana and Lawrence. Lawrence angrily contended that Dana's article was written for the purpose of having him incarcerated with other suspects in Fort Warren.[79] Lawrence was further disturbed when Dana made an arrangement with the Wheaton family to edit and publish an edition of the Wheaton treatise, which would sell in competition with the Lawrence edition of 1863. When in 1866 the Dana edition made its appearance, using the original Wheaton text but allegedly with only new notes by Dana, Lawrence sought in the United States Circuit Court in Boston an injunction against its distribution, being represented by former Justice Benjamin R. Curtis. Justice Clifford, reading most meticulously the law of copyright, decided in favor of Lawrence.[80] In some

---

[75] C. F. Adams to R. H. Dana, Jan. 27, 1864, *ibid.*

[76] "Enemy Territory," *L. Mag. & L. Rev.*, 16:350, 351, 1864.

[77] J. S. Black to R. H. Dana, Aug. 17, 1863, Dana Papers.

[78] For an attempt by radical reconstructionists to escape the implica-

tions of the decision see John C. Hurd, "Theories of Reconstruction," *Am. L. Rev.*, 1:238, 252–53, 1867.

[79] Adams, *Richard Henry Dana*, II, 289–90.

[80] Lawrence v. Dana, 15 Fed. Cas. 26 (No. 8136) (C.C.D. Mass. 1869).

degree the decision marked a projection of personal and doctrinal bitterness into the postwar period. Dana wrote to Judge John Lowell that Justice Clifford hated him because of his success in the *Prize Cases*, and because he had never flattered the Justice as did most of the bar, who knew that the interests of themselves and their clients required it.[81]

---

[81] Adams, *Richard Henry Dana*, II, 326, n. 1.

CHAPTER XXXV

Wartime Curtailment of Civil Rights

BECAUSE THE WAR WAS A CIVIL WAR, adherence to the Constitution and loyalty to the Union were much less universal, even in non-seceding states, than during the foreign wars in which the United States has been engaged. In official and private circles our national title, The United States of America, was still referred to in the plural—"they," rather than "it." For many citizens, loyalty to their state came first; loyalty to the United States was derivative from state loyalty. While it was not generally argued that the Constitution gave the right to secede, friends of the South denied that the Constitution created an obligation not to secede. They had no feeling of guilt in urging that the seceding states be permitted to leave the Union without interference, or even in joining Southern forces to fight for the "right" of Southern states to attain their own independence. To the extent that constitutional convictions and sentiments of loyalty to the Union were absent, the ingredients essential to law enforcement were lacking.

It is therefore not surprising that the federal government yielded to necessity and resorted at times to ruthless repression. Under the suspension of the privilege of the writ of habeas corpus, men deemed dangerous to the Union cause were summarily arrested and, without necessarily being charged with any offense and without a trial, were held in military prisons. Newspapers sympathetic to the Southern cause were suppressed, briefly or for the period of the war. Ministers found themselves in trouble with the government if they expressed Southern sympathies or even if they refused to pray publicly for the Union cause.

While this story belongs to the history of the Supreme Court only to a limited extent, at points it touches the federal judiciary. The very fact of judicial noninvolvement suggests the degree to which the courts were unable to afford customary protections. Petitioners applied to the President and to military leaders rather than to the courts. So great indeed was the scope of executive power, and so limited the power of the courts, that by the end of the war much of the deference ordinarily accorded to the judiciary was accorded elsewhere—not, it is true, to executive and military subordinates but to the looming figure of the President, Abraham Lincoln.

This story in any event can be told only in part, and only through selected illustrations. It can well begin, therefore, with military arrests in Maryland, which were virtually of a piece with the facts of the *Merryman* case and were affected by Chief Justice Taney's *Merryman* decision.

Until mid-February of 1862, when it was given to the Secretary of War, the power to direct military arrests was in the hands of the Secretary of State, William H. Seward. Simon Cameron, Lincoln's first Secretary of War, was not a strong and effective leader. The Department of Justice had not yet been established. Although the office of the Attorney General had been expanding with the handling of the California land cases, it was not until the Act of August 6, 1861, that the Attorney General was given superintendence of the work of United States Attorneys and Marshals.[1] Attorney General Bates, although in many respects able, was a mild-mannered and conservative politician from a badly divided border state. While he fought back when Seward issued instructions to the United States Marshals and Attorneys,[2] it is not surprising that he made no attempt to acquire military jurisdiction or that he constantly resisted military encroachment on civil jurisdiction. Seward, on the other hand, was self-confident and inclined to reach out for power. His attitude was reflected in a boastful statement, said to have been made to Lord Lyons in negotiations with the British government:

> My lord, I can touch a bell on my right hand and order the imprisonment of a citizen of Ohio; I can touch a bell again and order the imprisonment of a citizen of New York; and no power on earth, except that of the President, can release them. Can the Queen of England do so much?[3]

---

[1] 12 Stat. 285.

[2] See Edward Bates to William H. Seward, Sept. 23, 1861, Frederic Bancroft, *The Life of William H. Seward*, II, 355.

[3] George William Brown, *Baltimore and the Nineteenth of April, 1861*, 91. In his biography of Seward, Frederic Bancroft says that if Seward made this statement it is a matter of no special importance: "It is a fact that he was almost as free from restraint as a dictator or a sultan, and he was charged with acting accordingly." Bancroft thought the surprising fact to be that the power was so little abused. Bancroft, *The Life of William Seward*, 280.

XXXV: *Wartime Curtailment of Civil Rights*

From the time of the Baltimore riot of April 19, 1861, and the burning of railroad bridges on lines leading into the city over which troops and supplies might be brought from the North, it was obvious to Union leaders that the protection of Washington and the containment of the Confederacy required the establishment of effective Union control in Baltimore and throughout Maryland. Many of the people were loyal—a great majority of them as was later proved—but most of the aristocratic families and those looked to for leadership were at best lukewarm in their loyalty to the Union and outspoken in their sympathy for the South. The following quotation from a Baltimore correspondent of the *New York Tribune* probably misinterprets Chief Justice Taney's conception of his own authority but it probably also has in it ingredients of truth:

There is no doubt that Judge Taney has laid his traps for the arrest of Gen. Cadwalader, should he make his appearance outside the Fort. The instruments to be used will, of course, not be the United States Marshal or his deputies, but the Secession Police authority of the city. The Chief Justice is not a man to stop at trifles in the attainment of his purposes, as you may readily suppose. To bring about a hostile collision between the Judiciary and the Executive is the darling object of his heart at the present juncture. But Gen. Cadwalader will not give him the opportunity.[4]

To General Nathaniel P. Banks, who replaced General Cadwalader, Attorney General Bates wrote on June 16 that "Among the malcontents in Baltimore there are some men of position and influence, who are now so far perverted and so deeply committed that it is a waste of reason to argue with them. To keep them quiet we must make them conscious that they stand in the presence of a coercive power."[5] On June 27 General Banks directed the arrest of George P. Kane, marshal of the police, who was believed to have connection with unlawful combinations collecting arms and preparing to aid the enemy. He placed a provost marshal in charge of the police, and when the board of police commissioners protested, they were themselves taken into military custody.[6] The president of the board was Charles Howard, a close friend and a relative by marriage of Chief Justice Taney. Reverdy Johnson and other loyal Marylanders urged President Lincoln and Secretary Seward to have Howard released. In reply to a letter of inquiry from Seward General Banks, a Massachusetts Yankee, replied

---

[4] *New York Tribune*, June 11, 1861.
[5] Edward Bates to N. P. Banks, June 16, 1861, Attorney General's

Letter Book B-4, 75.
[6] J. Thomas Scharf, *History of Maryland*, III, 432-39.

903

that Howard, while perhaps not a bad man at heart, was one of the worst influences in Baltimore. Furthermore, he had three sons in the Confederate army, and a fourth, Frank Key Howard, was an editor of the *Baltimore Exchange*, which did not hesitate to recommend assassination to secessionists. To release the head of such a family would alarm the friends of the government for their safety.

With men like Howard, General Banks continued, "the wrong he commits is prospective, and the safety of the government requires his detention for the present." Beyond that, "I think the government must make these men feel its power, just as a matter of argument. They read nothing but their own papers. They talk only with each other. They live and move in small coteries into which no ideas can penetrate except their own. The President's Message or Secretary's Proclamations or State papers only reach them through their own distorted medium. They have as little idea of a national sentiment or power, as a man corked up in a phial would have of a natural atmosphere. And thus though they are pestilent traitors, they are innocent as babes. If the government makes them feel its power they will immediately understand the condition of things and think and talk and act as the rest of the world does."[7]

While General Banks proved unduly optimistic about the ease with which leading Baltimoreans in sympathy with secession could be educated, the arrest and incarceration of some of them in Fort McHenry, and their later transfer to other Northern forts as prisoners, did eliminate their inflaming presence while the federal government was strengthening its position in Maryland. A group of dissident members of the state legislature were also taken into custody, usually by night when the arrests would not attract the attention of potential mobs. Among those arrested was George William Brown, the mayor of Baltimore, whom Chief Justice Taney had warned that his time was yet to come. It was rumored that among those to be arrested was Benjamin C. Howard, former Reporter of the Supreme Court, but the rumor proved to be in error.[8] Also arrested were Frank Key Howard and William Watkins Glenn, editor and publisher of the *Baltimore Exchange*.[9] In most instances no attempt was made to secure indictment and trial. The prisoners were incarcerated and neutralized until Union control was so well established that they need no longer be feared.

---

[7] N. P. Banks to William H. Seward, July 9, 1861, Lincoln Papers.

[8] *Baltimore American*, Sept. 14, 1861.

[9] *Baltimore American*, Sept. 16, 19, 1861; *Maryland Times*, Sept. 19, 1861; *New York Tribune*, Sept. 23, 28, 1861; John A. Dix to S. Cameron, Sept. 13, 1861, Lincoln Papers; Scharf, *History of Maryland*, III, 439–42. See also Frank Key Howard's eighty-nine–page pamphlet, *Fourteen Months in American Bastilles*

One of the stormiest controversies arose over the arrest of Judge Richard B. Carmichael, a state circuit judge on the Eastern Shore of Maryland, in May, 1862, while he was holding court in Easton. Judge Carmichael was himself a friend of Chief Justice Taney, and was the son of William Carmichael, who had been an intimate friend of Taney during his early years. Judge Carmichael was a leader of a group of ardent supporters of the Confederacy on the Eastern Shore. According to General John A. Dix, who succeeded General Banks in command in Maryland, he was the author of "a treasonable memorial to the legislature, published and circulated under his own signature while holding a place on the bench."[10] As early as October 3, 1861, Seward forwarded to General Dix information about Judge Carmichael, and said that "It seems to me that that functionary should be arrested even in his court if need be and sent to Fort Lafayette. You may proceed accordingly."[11]

On the advice of Union leaders on the Eastern Shore General Dix postponed action. Meanwhile, Judge Carmichael delivered charges to grand juries in which he denounced recent military arrests as "without warrant of law." He included in his charges the text of the first ten Amendments to the Constitution, declaring that there was no power to suspend any of these, "as in regard to the Habeas Corpus." He charged juries to find indictments against persons making such arrests and against local citizens who had given information leading to them, saying that "it is hardly to be supposed that the strangers amongst you, would wantonly and without suggestions by mischievous persons, molest and harass your people."[12]

For the most part the military arresting officers were able to elude Judge Carmichael's court, but some of those who had given information about local secessionists were not so fortunate. In May, 1862, information reached General Dix that an indictment was being sought against Henry H. Goldsborough, president of the Maryland Senate. He wrote to Goldsborough that he was sending four officers who were summoned as witnesses and also Deputy Provost-Marshal J. L. McPhail and three policemen, "well armed." He thought it best that the bill of indictment be ignored or that trial take place immediately. While deferring to Goldsborough's judgment, he proposed that "if you have unquestionable proof that Judge Carmichael has uttered treasonable language in his charge to the grand jury and that the officers of the court have been so biased and are so controlled by the disloyalty of the judge as to

---

[10] John A. Dix to Augustus W. Bradford, Feb. 10, 1862, 2 O.R. (2d) 213.

[11] William H. Seward to John A. Dix, Oct. 3, 1861, *ibid.*, 85.

[12] A printed copy of one of the charges is filed with a manuscript letter, Richard B. Carmichael to A. Lincoln, July 22, 1862, Lincoln Papers.

render a fair trial hopeless, then the deputy provost-marshal, Mr. McPhail, is authorized on consultation with you to arrest him and bring him to Fort McHenry."[13]

Marshal McPhail went to Easton, talked with Senator Goldsborough and others, and decided to arrest Judge Carmichael and the state's attorney, I. C. W. Powell, before the Goldsborough trial could take place. According to General Dix, "It was, on full consideration, deemed expedient that the arrest should be made in court in order that the proceeding might be more marked."[14] Accordingly, in the midst of a trial, the marshal and his men entered the courtroom, advanced to the bench, and informed Judge Carmichael that he was under arrest.

From this stage the tale depends on the teller. Friends of the judge reported that when he asked for the warrant for his arrest, he was told that the authority was that of the United States government and that there was no warrant. The nature of the charge would be made known at Fort McHenry. The judge protested that the marshal had no right so to arrest him or to interfere with the proceedings of his court. The marshal thereupon proclaimed the court adjourned. A deputy seized the judge by the throat but the judge pushed him off. He was then beaten over the head with a gun and dragged, bruised and bleeding, from the courtroom, put aboard a boat, and taken to Fort McHenry. While secessionists made the most of the military invasion of judicial proceedings, General Dix played down the story of violence. According to him, the marshal and his men ascended the bench and "respectfully" told the judge of his arrest, whereupon he denied the authority of the government and "unluckily received a superficial wound on the head before he ceased to resist." The general argued that "The prostitution of his judicial authority to the persecution of loyal men and of public officers, who had only performed their duty, is considered as fully justifying the manner in which it was decided to make the arrest."[15]

Protests at this military invasion of the courtroom poured in on the President and other officers of the government. To one of the petitioners the President replied that he had read Judge Carmichael's grand jury charge, and remarked, "I was not very favorably impressed towards the Judge." He saw the object of the charge as that of prosecuting and

[13] John A. Dix to H. H. Goldsborough, May 23, 1862, 3 O.R. (2d) 576–77.

[14] John A. Dix to Edwin M. Stanton, June 25, 1862, Lincoln Papers. For an account of the arrest as printed in the *Baltimore Sun* see Frederic Emory, *Queen Anne's County, Maryland: Its Early History and Development*, 505–06. See also

Charles B. Clark, "Suppression and Control of Maryland, 1861–1865," *Maryland Historical Magazine*, 54: 241, 254–57, 1959.

[15] John A. Dix to Edwin M. Stanton, June 25, 1862, Lincoln Papers. Reprinted in 4 O.R. (2d) 63–64. See also John A. Dix to Lorenzo Thomas, June 19, 1862, *ibid.*, 29–40.

punishing men for arresting or doing violence to some secessionists. That is, said the President:

> the Judge was trying to help a little, by giving the protection of law to those who were endeavoring to overthrow the Supreme law—trying if he could to find a safe place for certain men to stand on the constitution, whilst they should stab it in another place.[16]

The President and the Secretary of War, who in February, 1862, had been made responsible for the military arrest of civilians, agreed that Judge Carmichael might be released if he would take the oath of allegiance. Apparently, however, the judge, like many other Marylanders, refused. He wrote to the President from Fort Lafayette, saying that he was a citizen who was without redress except in the exercise of executive authority. He had never been charged with any offense but had read in the *Baltimore Sun* that his arrest and imprisonment were for "treason committed in the discharge of official duty." By way of answer he sent a copy of his grand jury charge—apparently not knowing that the President had already read it with disfavor—saying that the extent of his offending was the attempt to maintain the Constitution as the supreme law: "If in *this* there be any treason, then indeed I cannot claim to be released. But if the law be as declared in that paper, then is it too much to ask in the *name* of the law, that I be discharged from these bonds?"[17]

The President evidently made no reply, and there was no action except to transfer the judge from Fort Lafayette to Fort Delaware. In October his release was ordered but the order was countermanded by the Secretary of War.[18] Finally, in December, after most of the other prominent Maryland prisoners had been released, Judge Carmichael's release was ordered[19] and carried out. He returned home and resumed his duties on the bench.

In the border areas where the civilian populations were sharply divided over secession, provost marshals, basically military police for preservation of order among military personnel,[20] expanded their func-

---

[16] A. Lincoln to John W. Crisfield, June 26, 1862, Abraham Lincoln, *Collected Works*, Roy P. Basler, ed., V, 285.

[17] Richard B. Carmichael to A. Lincoln, July 22, 1862, Lincoln Papers.

[18] Edwin M. Stanton to Commanding Officer, Fort Delaware, Oct. 29, 1862, 4 O.R. (2d) 662.

[19] E. D. Townsend to Commanding Officer, Fort Delaware, Dec. 2, 1862, 5 O.R. (2d) 9.

[20] Stanley Matthews, a future member of the Supreme Court, described as follows his duties as provost marshal in Nashville, Tennessee: "My business is, to keep the streets clear of straggling soldiers, wandering about without leave, and to preserve the

tions to cover the behavior of civilians where war issues were concerned, even where the normal civil machinery was in operation. The arrest of Judge Carmichael in Maryland provided but one of many examples in that area. For what was called the "Department of the Missouri," with headquarters in St. Louis, the office of provost marshal general was created, without statutory authorization,[21] with authority over provost marshals in the several counties of the district. Divisions of sentiment in Missouri were sharp and bitter. The provost marshals lent themselves vigorously to the enforcement of loyalty.

Evidently knowing that protests against his military zeal were going to Washington, Frederick A. Dick, signing himself as lieutenant colonel and provost marshal general, explained his activities in a letter to the President and said that "I have instructed provost marshals in the interior to select out the leading dangerous men and banish them from the State during the war." He urged the President not to require relaxation of efforts to fight the enemy in the most effective manner.[22] To Postmaster General Montgomery Blair, an ex-Missourian with continuing Missouri ties, Dick wrote on the same day to ask for support in his efforts to banish fashionable women spies and disloyal preachers, who kept the fire burning briskly in Missouri and cost the government much money and many lives. Dick added that he had issued an order banishing the Reverend Samuel McPheeters and his wife—who in other letters was said to be a more ardent or at any rate a more open secessionist than her husband—and had ordered the minister to turn his church over to the Union men of his congregation.[23]

The order brought from Hugh Campbell, a loyal and prominent citizen of St. Louis, a letter of protest to Justice Davis, with the obvious intention that it be passed along to the President. McPheeters had been

---

peace, quiet and good order of the City and protect the citizens and their property from insult and depredation, and to grant passes to all persons leaving the City. It is a very delicate position, full of labor and responsibility and my assignment to it was very complimentary to me." Stanley Matthews to Mrs. Matthews, typewritten copy, Matthews Papers. For the duties of provost marshals as formally prescribed after enactment of the Armed Forces Act of March 3, 1863, see Regulations for the Government of the Bureau of the Provost-Marshal-General of the United States, 3 O.R. (3d) 125, 127–32.

[21] See Hugh Campbell to David Davis, Dec. 20, 1862, Lincoln Papers.

The office was similarly established in other military departments. By Act of March 3, 1863, Congress established the office of Provost-Marshal-General as a bureau in the War Department. The primary duty of the office and of provost marshals was to be that of arresting deserters and apprehending spies. 12 Stat. 731, 732.

[22] F. A. Dick to A. Lincoln, Dec. 19, 1862, Lincoln Papers.

[23] F. A. Dick to M. Blair, Dec. 19, 1862. See the attached printed defense of his conduct by Samuel B. McPheeters, Pastor of the Pine Street Church, and the order of banishment, Special Order No. 152 of the Provost Marshal General, Dec. 19, 1862, Lincoln Papers.

banished, said Campbell, "without a trial, or even a hearing!" He thought this a startling proceeding, especially as McPheeters had neither in nor out of the pulpit said one disloyal word or committed a disloyal act. He had been the victim of an overzealous minority of his own congregation and a fanatical and vindictive provost marshal general who was in every respect unfit for the discharge of the duties of his office. The President ought to be informed without delay.[24]

Governor Archibald Gamble of Missouri wrote to Attorney General Bates, another Missourian, in defense of McPheeters,[25] and McPheeters wrote to Bates a long letter in his own behalf, explaining his desire to preach only religion and leave politics out of his performance.[26]

The President directed Major General Samuel R. Curtis, commander of the Department of the Missouri, to suspend the order of banishment.[27] Curtis in the meantime wrote to the President in defense of Dick's order. Curtis had apparently understood that McPheeters had refused to pray for the Union cause and that the Union men in his congregation were antagonized by the refusal: "Rebel priests are dangerous and diabolical in society."[28] He expressed surprise at suspension of the order, and announced that a committee unconnected with the church would visit the President.[29]

Bombardment from both sides continued. McPheeters himself went to Washington and was taken by Attorney General Bates to see the President. He showed the President a copy of an oath of loyalty he had taken, which the President found "very strong and specific." He asserted that he had prayed in church for the President and the government, as he had done before the war. The President believed that he did sympathize with the enemy, but in view of his oath and his good moral character he did not see how the man could be exiled upon mere suspicion as to his sympathies. He left the matter, however, in the hands of Curtis, who was on the ground, with a broad reservation:

I must add that the U.S. government must not, as by this order, undertake to run the churches. When an individual, in a church or out of it, becomes dangerous to the public interest, he must be checked; but let

---

[24] Hugh Campbell to David Davis, Dec. 20, 1862, Lincoln Papers.

[25] Archibald Gamble to Edward Bates, Dec. 22, 1862, Lincoln Papers.

[26] Samuel B. McPheeters to Edward Bates, Dec. 23, 1862, Lincoln Papers.

[27] A. Lincoln to S. R. Curtis, Dec. 27, 1862, Lincoln, *Collected Works*, VI, 20.

[28] S. R. Curtis to A. Lincoln, Dec. 28, 1862, Lincoln Papers. For the arrest in Alexandria, Virginia, of Episcopal Clergyman J. R. Stewart for refusal to pray publicly for the President see 2 O.R. (2d) 212–13, 217–19, 348.

[29] S. R. Curtis to A. Lincoln, Dec. 29, 1862; see also Curtis' letter of Dec. 30, 1862, introducing the members of the committee, Lincoln Papers.

the churches, as such take care of themselves. It will not do for the U.S. to appoint Trustees, Supervisors, or other agents for the churches.[30]

As a result of the President's intervention, McPheeters was permitted to remain in St. Louis but not to preach. When petitioned to relax this restriction, General Curtis catechized McPheeters about his loyalty but the minister refused to answer his questions. In exasperation Curtis refused to modify the order and reported the facts to the President.[31] In December, 1863, the President received a petition from residents of St. Louis requesting the removal of McPheeters' disability.[32] At the same time, Attorney General Bates passed along to him a letter marveling "that the question of who shall be allowed to preach in a church in St. Louis shall be decided by the *President of the United States*. It seems to me, that if I were in his stead I should be a strict constructionist, and states rights man, if for nothing else, to get rid of such questions."[33]

The President called attention to his letter to General Curtis and insisted that he had never interfered or thought of interfering in the question of who should preach in any church, or authorized anyone else to do so. He would not oust any minister or aid in restoring McPheeters to his pulpit over the protest of a majority of his congregation.[34]

Early in 1864 the President, in seeming exasperation, wrote to the Secretary of War quoting his language in opposition to interference with preaching in churches and calling attention to an order of the War Department giving control over groups of Methodist churches to a certain bishop. The order having already been issued, he asked Stanton what could be done about it.[35] The order seems to have been modified so as to exclude Missouri from the territory affected and leave it applicable only to secessionist areas.[36]

---

[30] A. Lincoln to S. R. Curtis, Jan. 2, 1863, Lincoln, *Collected Works*, VII, 34.

[31] S. R. Curtis to A. Lincoln, Apr. 3, 1863, Lincoln Papers.

[32] John Whitehill *et al.* to A. Lincoln [Dec. 1863], folio 29083, Lincoln Papers.

[33] John D. Coalter to Edward Bates, Dec. 13, 1863, Lincoln Papers.

[34] A. Lincoln to O. D. Filley, Dec. 22, 1863, Lincoln, *Collected Works*, VI, 86. See also his endorsement on the petition mentioned above, *ibid.*, 86. That this highly complicated mat-

ter may have involved also a disagreement between Attorney General Bates and Postmaster General Blair is suggested by a telegram from Blair's wife at St. Louis, to her husband saying, "Implore President not to revoke the order banishing Dr. McPheeters until you hear further." Appoline Blair to Montgomery Blair, Dec. 29, 1863, Lincoln Papers.

[35] A. Lincoln to Edwin M. Stanton, Feb. 11, 1864, Lincoln, *Collected Works*, VII, 178–79.

[36] A. Lincoln to John Hogan, Feb. 13, 1864, *ibid.*, 182–83.

Interference with churches continued along other lines. J. P. Sanderson, as provost marshal general under General William S. Rosecrans, issued a harsh military order directing provost marshals to attend all church conferences, break up any attended by persons who had not taken a special oath of allegiance, and subject such persons to military penalties. A Missouri minister, A. P. Forman, wrote to Attorney General Bates that though from the outset of the war he had earnestly desired the preservation of the Union he could not take the oath. He could not permit any earthly power to prescribe his qualifications as a minister: "This can be done only by Christ speaking in his word."[37]

Bates noted in his diary that he had written to Forman expressing the hope that the "judicatories" of the church would not degrade themselves by sitting under a provost marshal. He inserted a newspaper clipping announcing a meeting of the St. Louis Presbytery, at which an officer would be present to administer the prescribed oath. He added that at his instance the President had written to General Rosecrans to stop this "useless and wanton interference with the churches."[38]

The Lincoln letter to which Bates referred was anything but a peremptory order. It was sent as "more social than official, containing suggestions rather than orders." The President said that he somewhat dreaded the effect of Special Order No. 61:

> I have found that men who have not even been suspected of disloyalty, are very averse to taking an oath of any sort as a condition, to exercising an ordinary right of citizenship. The point will probably be made, that while men may without an oath, assemble in a noisy political meeting, they must take the oath, to assemble in a religious meeting.

Instead of clinching the matter he turned to other topics, and ended with congratulations that Rosecrans had done better in the Department of the Missouri than he had dared hope.[39]

In short, while the President sat as a kind of court of appeals for the protection of civil rights, he was restrained from acting firmly by his lack of assured knowledge of particular situations in the field and by his need to support the morale of his leaders on the ground. Yet in innumerable situations such as those recounted here, the military ruled

---

[37] A. P. Forman to Edward Bates, Mar. 15, 1864. A printed copy of General Order No. 61, dated Mar. 7, 1864, is attached thereto. Lincoln Papers.

[38] "The Diary of Edward Bates," Howard K. Beale, ed., *Annual Report of the American Historical Association for the Year 1930*, 4:357, 1933.

[39] A. Lincoln to William S. Rosecrans, Apr. 4, 1864, Lincoln, *Collected Works*, VII, 283–84.

and adjudicated, without interference from the President or the federal courts, even though those courts were nominally in full operation.

Newspapers were suppressed or kept from operating. In Baltimore the publication of seven papers was prevented by the arrest of editors. One of the more widely controversial suppressions was that of the *Baltimore Exchange*, which was brought about by the military arrest and detention of Frank Key Howard, the editor, and William Wilkins Glenn, the proprietor. "The Daily Exchange has been stopped by force," wrote Glenn, with obvious resentment but in necessary surrender. "Though disputing the right to commit the act I still submit to the superior power of the Government. I shall not edit the Exchange nor republish it nor contribute to any paper so long as the censorship of the press is exercised in Baltimore."[40] The *South*, which had been "openly and zealously advocating the cause of the insurrection and largely contributing to unsettle and excite the public mind,"[41] was dealt with in similar fashion.

Other Maryland newspapers suffered a similar fate, to the deep resentment of Southern sympathizers. It was said of one of the military men responsible that he received a letter saying in part:

> I see you have suppressed several newspapers. Let me tell you that you are a d——d old ass and I hope Lee will take you to the Libby prison at Richmond. You merit the utter contempt of every gentleman, and if I had you by the gallows I would pull a rope d——d quick on you.[42]

In Pennsylvania federal civil officers displayed similar repressive zeal. In Philadelphia the *Christian Observer* was suppressed, evidently for too much plain talk about the way the Administration was conducting itself. The editor, in a letter to the President, professed complete loyalty to the Union.[43] Whether or not this protest got through to the President, the Attorney General directed discontinuance of the proceedings against the *Christian Observer* in the United States Circuit Court in Philadelphia.[44]

Also seized by federal deputy marshals was the *Jeffersonian*, at West Chester, Pennsylvania, an opinionated and colorful newspaper edited by John Hodgson, who seemed to thrive on opposition. Hodgson had definite Copperhead leanings. When he protested to the United

---

[40] W. W. Glenn to John A. Dix, Oct. 3, 1861, 2 O.R. (2d) 781.
[41] 2 O.R. (2d) 787.
[42] Fred B. Joyner, "Robert Cumming Schenck, First Citizen and Statesman of the Ohio Valley," *Ohio State Archaeological and Historical Quarterly*, 58:286, 293–94, 1949.
[43] Amasa Converse to A. Lincoln, Aug. 28, 1861, Lincoln Papers.
[44] T. J. Coffey to George A. Coffey, Oct. 12, 1861, Attorney General's Letter Book B–4, 170.

States Attorney the suppression of his paper and demanded its return, George A. Coffey asked him to sign a pledge stating the belief that "the only way to put down the rebellion and restore the Union is by war." Hodgson replied that he would rather die than give any such pledge. When the case came up for a hearing, eminent defense counsel were able to plead lack of specific charge that the paper had been used "to aid and abet the insurrection." While the case was being delayed for amendment of the charge, Coffey received a direction from the Attorney General to drop the case.[45]

Not content with this victory, Hodgson brought suit for trespass in a state court against the marshal and his deputies. The presiding judge was Chief Justice Walter H. Lowrie, a man with secessionist sympathies. Hodgson won a verdict of $512.[46] Recovery was delayed, however, by a statute of March 3, 1863, which provided for transfer to United States Circuit Courts of suits against federal officers for acts committed during the rebellion under the direction of the President or Congress.[47] This case was therefore transferred for retrial before Justice Grier.[48] In charging the jury Justice Grier was reported as saying that there was "no evidence of malice but some evidence that the district attorney did this to satisfy some people out of doors"—that is, he had made himself the instrument of a rival paper. The federal jury likewise awarded damages, giving Hodgson the amount of $504.33.[49] In this probably rare instance, therefore, it had paid to fight against governmental zeal.

Military leaders in the Middle West threatened to deal harshly with all newspapers which encouraged resistance to conscription or any other war measure.[50] Newspapers in various parts of the country denounced this attempt at censorship. General Milo S. Hascall, writing from Indianapolis, demanded of the *New York Express*, published outside his district, whether reports of criticism were true. The *Express*, feeling safe under the circumstances, admitted the charge in what the general called a "scurrilous reply." The general then lashed back in a letter to the editors, saying, "It is fortunate for you that your paper is

---

[45] *Ibid.* For details of the case see Ray H. Abrams, "The Jeffersonian Copperhead Newspaper," *Pennsylvania Magazine of History and Biography*, 57:260, 1933.

[46] Abrams, "The Jeffersonian Copperhead Newspaper," *Pennsylvania Magazine of History and Biography*, 57:276, 1933. Hodgson v. Millward, 3 Grant (Pa.) 405 (1863).

[47] 12 Stat. 756.

[48] Hodgson v. Millward, 3 Grant (Pa.) 411 (1863); 3 Grant (Pa.) 418 (1863); Hodgson v. Millward, 12 Fed. Cas. 285 (No. 6568) (C.C.E.D. Pa. 1863).

[49] Abrams, "The Jeffersonian Copperhead Newspaper," *Pennsylvania Magazine of History and Biography*, 57:276–77, 1933.

[50] See General Order No. 9, issued at Indianapolis, Apr. 15, 1863, over the signature of Edward R. Kerstetter, 5 O.R. (2d) 485.

not published in my district."[51] To papers within his district he issued harsh warnings of suppression if they violated the order.[52]

A painful thorn in the side of the Administration was the *Chicago Times*. At the time of the arrest of Vallandigham in 1863, the *Times* poured out venomous denunciation, as did also the *New York World*. On June 1, 1863, a military order was issued at Cincinnati suppressing the *Times*, "on account of the repeated expression of disloyal and incendiary sentiments." The same order forbade distribution of the *New York World* in that military district, because of the tendency of its opinions and articles to "cast reproach upon the Government, and to weaken its efforts to suppress the rebellion, by creating distrust in its war policy," with a tendency to "exert a pernicious and treasonable influence."[53] General Burnside took full responsibility for the suppression of the *Times*, giving direction that, if necessary, military possession of the newspaper office be taken.[54]

Justice Davis, holding Circuit Court at Indianapolis and Springfield, had already become much disturbed by the repressive tactics of the military, and had recommended to Stanton the removal of General Hascall.[55] Dining with Orville Browning and others at the home of Judge Samuel J. Treat in Springfield, he said that if an application for an injunction against the suppression of the *Times* were made to him, as it had been made to Judge Drummond, he would not hesitate to grant it. He had received a telegraphed request to go to Chicago, and would go immediately.[56]

As protests against the suppression began to pour in, the President directed Stanton to tell Burnside that in his judgment the order should be revoked immediately because of the public irritation it had produced.[57] The order was revoked on June 4,[58] before a decision was reached in the injunction suit before Justice Davis and Judge Drum-

[51] "Milo S. Hascall to Editors of the *New York Express*," May 5, 1863, *ibid.*, 725.

[52] *Ibid.*, 725–26.

[53] See General Order No. 84, issued at Cincinnati June 1, 1863, over the signature of Assistant Adjutant-General Lewis Richmond, 23 O.R. (1st) Part II, 381.

[54] A. E. Burnside to Jacob Ammen, June 1, 1863, 5 O.R. (2d) 726.

[55] David Davis to E. M. Stanton, May 27, 1863, 23 O.R. (1st) Part II, 369.

[56] Orville Browning, *Diary* I, 632. See Willard L. King, *Lincoln's Manager, David Davis*. For Judge Drummond's statement of concern about the repressive tactics of the government and other relevant items, see Horace White, *The Life of Lyman Trumbull*, 206–09.

[57] Edwin M. Stanton to A. E. Burnside, June 1, 1863, 5 O.R. (2d) 724. See also A. Lincoln to Edwin M. Stanton, June 4, 1863, Lincoln, *Collected Works*, VI, 248.

[58] See General Order No. 91, issued at Cincinnati June 4, 1863, over the signature of Assistant Adjutant-General W. P. Anderson, 5 O.R. (2d) 741. See the same order issued at the same place on the same date over the signature of Assistant Adjutant-General N. H. McLean, 23 O.R. (1st), Part II, 386.

mond. The same revocation applied also to the order forbidding distribution of the *New York World.* By prompt retreat on the part of the military a clash with the civil courts was avoided.

Many other newspapers were suppressed, either permanently or for a time. On May 18, 1864, Stanton suppressed the *New York Journal of Commerce* and the *New York World* and ordered the arrest of editors, managers, owners, and others connected with the two papers. The occasion was the publication of what proved to be a spurious proclamation of President Lincoln naming a day of fasting, humiliation, and prayer in view of the expiration of the terms of service of large numbers of troops, and calling for the draft of four hundred thousand men. The falsified proclamation, calculated to embarrass the government, was sent to all New York newspapers. Some of them detected the fraud, but the *World* and the *Journal,* receiving the document just as they went to press, did not.[59]

The perpetrator of the fraud, one Joseph Howard, was captured and imprisoned in Fort Lafayette. According to Stanton, the President said that while ignorance or want of criminal intent did not excuse the people in charge of the two papers, he was not disposed to be vindictive and authorized the restoration of the papers. They quickly resumed publication.[60]

Among the multiple instances of the wartime repression of civil rights, that bringing most controversy was the suspension by the President, or by military commanders at their discretion on his authorization, of the privilege of the writ of habeas corpus. In his *Merryman* opinion Chief Justice Taney had thrown down the gauntlet to the President, maintaining that the power of suspension existed only in Congress. While Northern opinion had no difficulty in finding evidence of gross bias in this latest pronouncement by the author of the so-called opinion of the Court in the Dred Scott case, it must have been manifest, on the one hand, that the contention had to be answered, and on the other, that the President could not at this critical juncture afford to engage in a public controversy with the Chief Justice.

The obvious place for an answer was the message to Congress delivered at its assembly on July 4, 1861. There the President did tell of the suspension and the arrest and detention of persons "without resort to the ordinary processes and forms of law," but he stressed the fact that the authority had been exercised very sparingly. Nevertheless

---

[59] For the various documents see 4 O.R. (3d) 387–95. For general summary see John B. McMaster, *History of the People of the United States*

During Lincoln's Administration, 432–34.

[60] Frank A. Flower, *Edwin McMasters Stanton,* 212–13.

the legality and propriety of the action had been questioned, and the attention of the country called to the proposition that one sworn to take care that the laws be faithfully executed should not himself violate them.[61] While he questioned whether it would not be better to violate one law than to permit the government itself to go to pieces, he did not believe that any such choice had to be made. The Constitution did not say who might exercise the power of suspension. He did not believe that the executive was bound to forego action in a dangerous emergency until Congress had assembled and conferred the power.

The major treatment of the habeas corpus question, however, was left to Attorney General Bates, who issued an official opinion the following day.[62] Bates dealt but little with the exact placement of the suspension clause in the Constitution, of which Chief Justice Taney had made so much. He stressed the fact that while other officers of the government were required to take an oath to *support* the Constitution, the President must swear to "*preserve, protect,* and *defend*" it. He contended that in fulfilling his oath in an instance of insurrection or rebellion the President had the power to arrest and imprison dangerous persons, and that he had the auxiliary power to prevent interference by a court or a judge.

It was inevitable that the issue should be debated in Congress. There were repeated attacks on the arrest of the Baltimore commissioners of police, and sharp criticism of a resolution to legalize the acts of the President done before Congress assembled.[63] Many legislators who were willing to legalize the building up of the army and navy, the blockade, and other measures were unwilling to do the same with respect to suspension of the writ. Friends of the South remaining in Congress hailed the *Merryman* opinion. "We have only to look at that case, as it is stated by the Chief Justice in delivering his opinion," said Senator Trusten Polk of Missouri, "to see that this guarantee of the right of the security of the person of that man was trodden down without any authority of law."[64] "The newspapers of the country, and men excited by the violent passions which mark the times," said Senator John C. Breckenridge of Kentucky, "have denounced the Chief Justice, but they have not answered his opinion. . . . The abuse of the press, the refusal

---

[61] That the reference was to the Taney opinion was even more clearly indicated by the first draft of the passage, in which the President said, "I have been reminded from a high quarter that one who is sworn to 'take care that the laws be faithfully executed should not himself be one

to violate them.'" Lincoln, *Collected Works*, IV, 429, n. 50.

[62] 10 Op. Att'ys Gen. 74 (1861).

[63] For the text of the proposed Senate Joint Resolution No. 1, see *Cong. Globe*, 37th Cong., 1st Sess. 393 (1861).

[64] *Cong. Globe*, 37th Cong., 1st Sess. 49 (1861).

to respect just authority, the attempt to make that eminent judicial officer odious, will yet recoil upon those who attempt it."[65]

The special session of Congress came to an end without action in support of the President's acts with respect to habeas corpus. The measure adopted gave Congressional support only in matters "respecting the army and navy of the United States, and calling out or relating to the militia or volunteers from the States."[66] If the President had had the power of suspension, he still had it without the sanction of Congress. If his suspension had been illegal, it was to be allowed to remain so for the time being.

The Northern attitude toward the military arrest and detention of rebels was well expressed by the *New York Tribune*: "To talk of arresting and taking them before Judges who were their fellow-traitors is preposterous. To indict them and send them for trial before such judges with juries of whom a good part would inevitably be hale fellows, is to trifle with a very grave subject. There was no practicable course open but to arrest the ringleaders and put them where they could be found when wanted—where they would be certain to stay *until* wanted."[67] The suspension of the privilege of the writ of habeas corpus was authorized piecemeal, but by the end of November it covered all the states in the Union as far as military affairs were concerned.[68]

Debate continued, however, on the issue of constitutional power. Joel Parker, professor at the Harvard Law School, writing anonymously as was the custom at the time but indirectly letting his authorship be known, reviewed critically Chief Justice Taney's opinion in the *Merryman* case. As he saw it, the precedents and authorities cited by the Chief Justice had largely to do with habeas corpus privileges in times of peace, whereas war brought with it its own rules as to military commanders and their relation to persons within the military jurisdiction.[69] Parker regarded it as sheer nonsense to talk of a duty to suspend military operations to accede to the rituals and demands of the civil courts, and he saw the Taney position as close to absurd. As for the implication of the clause in the Constitution limiting the suspension of the writ, it conferred no power of suspension on either Congress or the President. The power to suspend existed not because it was anywhere specified but because it was to be inferred from other powers expressly granted, including the war powers of the President.

Horace Binney of Philadelphia contributed to the controversy a

---

[65] *Ibid.*, 139.
[66] 12 Stat. 326.
[67] *New York Tribune*, Sept. 13, 1861.

[68] *The New York Times*, Nov. 27, 1861.
[69] [Joel Parker], "Habeas Corpus and Martial Law," *North American Review*, 93:471, 480, 1861.

pamphlet justifying arrest and detention of persons in certain circumstances on the basis of constitutional language and the nature of the executive office. Taney's opinion, he contended, was not an authority, or in the full sense even an argument.[70] The Binney pamphlet was widely circulated and much discussed in Congress. Justice Grier read a copy and was much pleased with it. His copy was so much loaned that it was eventually lost, and he wrote to Judge Cadwalader in Philadelphia to inquire whether additional copies were available, saying that Justices Catron and Wayne wanted to see it. He asked that the clerk of the federal court in Philadelphia, Benjamin Patton, send him a dozen copies if they were available.[71]

Former Justice Benjamin R. Curtis, by contrast with Parker and Binney, aided the opposition by publishing a tract on "Executive Power" in which he deplored the Presidential assertion of authority in the several proclamations. Into one long sentence he packed the essentials of his protest:

> I do not yet perceive how it is that my neighbors and myself, residing remote from armies and their operations, and where all the laws of the land may be enforced by constitutional means, should be subjected to the possibility of military arrest and imprisonment, and trial before a military commission, and punishment at its discretion for offences unknown to the law; a possibility to be converted into a fact at the mere will of the President, or of some subordinate officer, clothed by him with this power.[72]

There is, unfortunately, no record of the pleasure Chief Justice Taney must have felt at this outburst from the man with whom he had been so severely at odds after the Dred Scott decision. The Curtis thesis, like that of Binney, found its way repeatedly into Congressional debates.

Congress renewed discussion of the habeas corpus question in December, 1861, when the House Committee on the Judiciary asked to be discharged from further consideration of a memorial about the Baltimore police commissioners. A minority insisted that the President lacked the power exercised, but the majority, saying that the argument had been answered by the Attorney General, tabled a motion on the subject.[73] The matter was taken up repeatedly in connection with resolutions of inquiry into the holding of prisoners. Congressmen showed little conception of the scope and limits of the war powers of the President; their views

---

[70] Horace Binney, *The Privilege of the Writ of Habeas Corpus Under the Constitution*, 32.

[71] R. C. Grier to John Cadwalader, Dec. 16, 1861, Cadwalader Papers.

[72] Executive Power, in B. R. Curtis, II, 306, 313.

[73] *Cong. Globe*, 37th Cong., 2nd Sess. 40–45 (1861).

ranged all the way from merely the execution of statutes to the doing of anything necessary for saving the Union. The subject was debated again and again without producing any consensus.

Clement L. Vallandigham of Ohio, always a thorn in the side of the Administration, provoked in the House of Representatives a thorough discussion of the subject of habeas corpus by one of his Ohio colleagues, Samuel Shellabarger, by denouncing the President as a tyrant and a despot and offering a bill to imprison the President for not more than two years if, in effect, he should repeat the conduct of which he had been guilty in connection with the imprisonment of Merryman.[74] Shellabarger quoted from Binney's pamphlet to show that the *Merryman* decision was not really justified by the dicta quoted from Chief Justice Marshall or the commentaries of Justice Story, and proceeded with his own analysis to challenge that opinion. He denied that the ninth section of Article I of the Constitution related only to Congress, and quoted Chief Justice Taney's opinion in *Luther v. Borden* on nonjusticiable questions in refutation of his opinion in the *Merryman* case.[75]

At this session of Congress—1861–1862—the House of Representatives passed a bill "to provide for the discharge of State prisoners and others, and to authorize the judges of the United States courts to take bail or recognizances to secure the trial of the same."[76] The bill required the Secretaries of State and War to furnish lists of political prisoners to circuit and district judges. All prisoners held beyond termination of the session of a grand jury without indictment were to be released. Those indicted and held for trial were to be released on bail. In addition, however, the bill authorized the President to suspend the privilege of the writ of habeas corpus, thereby regularizing proceedings in the matter if regularization was required, though without a statement sanctioning past executive action.

The bill went to the Senate for action at the ensuing session. In the meantime, in states where it could safely be done, federal officials were being haled into state courts to answer for allegedly unlawful arrests.[77] When Congress reassembled in December, the House of Representatives quickly passed a bill "to indemnify the President and other persons for suspending the privilege of the writ of habeas corpus, and acts done in

---

[74] H.R. No. 170. A bill to regulate and enforce the writ of habeas corpus and for the better securing the liberty of the citizen. *House Journal* 112, 37th Cong., 2nd Sess. (1862).

[75] *Cong. Globe*, 37th Cong., 2nd Sess. 2069–74 (1862).

[76] H.R. No. 362. For the first two sections of the bill as presented see

Cong. Globe, 37th Cong., 2nd Sess. 3359 (1862). For the bill as passed by the House of Representatives see *ibid.*, 3184.

[77] For discussion of this subject and of the Congressional effort to deal therewith see James G. Randall, *Constitutional Problems Under Lincoln*, 186–214.

pursuance thereof."[78] The bill, commonly known as the indemnity bill, noted the fact that there was "not entire unanimity of opinion as to which branch of the government possesses the constitutional power to declare such suspension." It confirmed past acts under the suspension and authorized suspension for the future, and ordered the discharge of all government agents held for things done pursuant to past orders.

The Senate Judiciary Committee rewrote the bill, providing, among other things, for the removal to federal courts of suits brought in state courts against federal officers. There was obvious overlapping between this so-called indemnity bill and the bill for the discharge of state prisoners, now likewise pending in the Senate. After bitter and prolonged debate the two bills were rewritten into one[79] and passed at the very end of the Thirty-seventh Congress, as an act "relating to habeas corpus, and regulating judicial proceedings in certain cases."[80] The statute stated that the President "is authorized to suspend the privilege of the writ of habeas corpus," avoiding by this language the question of whether the President had the authorization from the Constitution, with the statute as merely declaratory, or whether he derived the power from the statute.

While Congress was debating the subject, applications continued to be made to federal judges for writs of habeas corpus. On August 8, 1862, Stanton issued an order whereby United States Marshals and local police were directed to arrest and imprison any person discouraging volunteer enlistments "or in any way giving aid and comfort to the enemy." Judson D. Benedict, a Campbellite minister, preached in New York a sermon based on the "Sermon on the Mount," in which he characterized war as un-Christian.[81] Arrested for violating Stanton's order, he applied for a writ of habeas corpus to Nathan K. Hall, United States District Judge for the Northern District of New York. The writ was issued, but before it could be served on the marshal the prisoner had been transferred out of the district, on his way to imprisonment in Washington. Judge Hall wrote and published as a pamphlet a long opinion in which he agreed with Chief Justice Taney that the President had no power to suspend the privilege of the writ, and stated, furthermore, that although the order was issued in the name of the President he doubted that the President had authorized so palpable a violation of the Constitution as that here involved.[82]

[78] H.R. No. 591. See *Cong. Globe*, 37th Cong., 3rd Sess. 20–21 (1862).

[79] See the conference committee report, To Indemnify the President, H.R. Rep. No. 45, 37th Cong., 3rd Sess. (1863).

[80] 12 Stat. 755.

[81] For a perhaps biased account but one replete with official documents, see John A. Marshall, *American Bastille*, 183–205.

[82] *Ex parte* Benedict, 3 Fed. Cas. 159 (No. 1292) (D.C.N.D. N.Y. 1862). See *New York World*, Oct. 30, 1862. For discussion of military arrests from Stanton's point of view, see

XXXV: *Wartime Curtailment of Civil Rights*

William H. Winder, a resident of Philadelphia and a member of a prominent Baltimore family, a man with Southern sympathies, was held at Fort Lafayette and Fort Warren from September, 1861, until November, 1862.[83] Through counsel, Winder applied to Justice Clifford, in the United States Circuit Court in Boston, for a writ of habeas corpus. Justice Clifford issued the writ, remarking that this step was not intended to prejudice any question that might thereafter arise on the return to the writ.[84] Another clash between a member of the Supreme Court and the government, similar to that in the *Merryman* case, was here anticipated. As was expected, the marshal was denied admission to Fort Warren to serve the writ.[85] Instead of promising an indignant opinion such as that written by Chief Justice Taney, Justice Clifford ordered the papers filed, saying that the court had no power to enforce the writ,[86] and leaving no written record of his own opinion in the matter. Unlike Chief Justice Taney, he had no inclination to martyrdom.

In Wisconsin the suspension of the writ was challenged by the same state supreme court which a few years earlier had challenged federal enforcement of the Fugitive Slave Law. Facing in many parts of the country difficulty in enforcing the Conscription Act, the War Department on September 25, 1862, published the President's proclamation of the preceding day providing that persons interfering with volunteer enlistments or with militia drafts should be subject to martial law and to trial by courts-marshal or military commissions, and suspending the writ of habeas corpus as to persons so arrested.[87] Wisconsin sentiment about the war was sharply divided, and much the same opposition to federal coercion existed as had prevailed at the time of the trial of the *Booth Cases*. As a result of draft riots which took place at Port Washington in November, 1862, Governor Edward Salomon brought about the arrest of some one hundred fifty rioters and their delivery to the federal army for trial by court-martial.[88]

Flower, *Edwin McMaster Stanton*, 133–37. Note especially on p. 135: "There never has been any assistance rendered by the civil [judicial] officers to the Government in this war where they could get a colorable pretext for withholding it."

[83] For correspondence see 2 O.R. (2d) 721–47.

[84] *New York Herald*, Oct. 29, 1862; *New York World*, Oct. 29, 1862.

[85] *New York World*, Oct. 30, 1862.

[86] *New York World*, Oct. 31, 1862. See also Marshall, *American Bastille*, 283.

[87] For the text of the proclamation see Lincoln, *Collected Works*, V, 436–37.

[88] For accounts see Alfons J. Beitzinger, *Edward G. Ryan: Lion of the Law*, 72–74; Wood Gray, *The Hidden Civil War*, 111–12; Alfons J. Beitzinger, "The Father of Copperheadism in Wisconsin," *Wisconsin Magazine of History*, 39:17, 1955; Frank Klement, "Copperheads and Copperheadism in Wisconsin," *Wisconsin Magazine of History*, 42:182, 1959. See also Lynn I. Schoonover, *A History of the Civil War Draft in*

It was one thing to arrest and hold rioters under the threat of military trial and quite another thing to seek convictions of civilians with the harshness of military justice. Two weeks after the arrests had taken place the governor wrote to Secretary Stanton urging that the prisoners be tried rather than released on parole,[89] as seems to have been contemplated, but the Administration continued to wait. At about the same time the Wisconsin Supreme Court issued a writ of habeas corpus directing General W. L. Elliott to bring before it certain of the prisoners so that the lawfulness of their detention might be determined. General Elliott filed a return explaining the detention but refused to have anything further to do with the proceeding. The case was therefore argued without representation of the federal government, with two counsel appearing for the prisoners, one of them being Edward G. Ryan, who had played a prominent part in the *Booth Cases*, and who here contended, with Chief Justice Taney, that the President had no power to suspend the writ of habeas corpus.

Deploring the failure of the government to produce Nicholas Kemp, the prisoner in whose name the case was presented, and the absence of government counsel, the three judges in seriatim opinions denied that the President had the power to suspend the writ. The judges wrote in obvious discomfort at challenging the power of the federal government in the midst of the war crisis, and noted the fact that their decision was merely preliminary to a decision by the Supreme Court in Washington.[90] In discussing the case they made use of the Taney opinion in the *Merryman* case, the review of that opinion by Joel Parker, the Curtis exposition, and the opinion by Judge Nathan K. Hall in the *Benedict* case,[91] rejecting the Parker argument and deferring to the others. Yet in spite of the unanimity of the three judges, they deemed it expedient to avoid a collision with the military by refraining from issuing an attachment against General Elliott, apparently assuming that the case would be immediately appealed to Washington.[92]

In the light of the decision Governor Salomon wrote to Stanton urging that the prisoners be discharged, "to avoid a conflict between the civil and military authorities."[93] Disturbed by this judicial defeat, the War Department sent to Madison Timothy O. Howe, United States Senator from Wisconsin, to survey the situation and, reportedly, to

---

Wisconsin, unpublished Ph.D. thesis, University of Wisconsin, dated 1915, as cited in Bayrd Still, *Milwaukee: The History of a City*, 159, n. 108.

[89] E. Salomon to E. M. Stanton, Dec. 4, 1862, 5 O.R. (2d) 24.

[90] *In re* Kemp, 16 Wis. 359, 366 (1863).

[91] *Ex parte* Benedict, 3 Fed. Cas. 159 (No. 1292) (D.C.N.D. N.Y. 1862).

[92] See W. L. Elliott to E. M. Stanton, Jan. 13, 1863, 3 O.R. (3d) 15.

[93] Edward Salomon to E. M. Stanton, Jan. 13, 1863, 5 O.R. (2d) 174.

facilitate an appeal to the Supreme Court.[94] At the same time Stanton wrote to General Elliott that the President had referred the matter to the Attorney General "with a view to procuring the judgment of the Supreme Court of the United States," and that in the meantime the prisoners were to remain in custody.[95]

Senator Howe prepared to argue the motion for a writ of error and recommended that in the meantime the prisoners should be paroled,[96] whereupon Stanton gave instructions that Howe's advice be followed.[97]

In a letter of Attorney General Bates written to Stanton on January 31, 1863, it appears that it was only on the preceding day, fifteen days after Stanton had said that the matter had been referred to the Attorney General, that Bates heard of the controversy, or at any rate of the plan to take the case to the Supreme Court. At this time William Whiting, solicitor for the War Department, called on Bates to discuss the matter. In short, it appears that Stanton had taken upon himself the responsibility for deciding questions which belonged in the province of the Attorney General, while creating the impression that the Attorney General was the source of decision.

Writing confidentially to Stanton, Bates insisted emphatically that the Administration itself should not take responsibility for bringing the constitutional question before the Supreme Court as it was then constituted, lest it inflict upon itself a serious injury. If the action of the executive in this kind of cases needed to be vindicated by the Supreme Court, it was all-important that the Court be applied to only with the knowledge that vindication would be received. He anticipated no such result. The adverse opinion of the Chief Justice and, he thought, of Justice Clifford, had already been announced judicially, and "it is no imputation on the loyalty of the majority of the Court to presume that on this point they agree with their political school."[98]

Bates did not mean that the Administration should not meet in the Supreme Court any person who there asked for relief from military arrest by habeas corpus. He was contending, rather, that the executive should not take the initiative in the matter. But if the President through his subordinates initiated judicial review and lost the case, could he then disregard the decision he had himself invoked?[99]

At a time when the calendar of the Court was loaded with other important cases such as the *Prize Cases* and California land litigation, action was delayed until Congress passed the Act of March 3, 1863,

---

[94] Beitzinger, *Edward G. Ryan*, 73.
[95] E. M. Stanton to W. L. Elliott, Jan. 15, 1863, 5 O.R. (2d) 179.
[96] T. O. Howe to E. M. Stanton, Jan. 19, 1863, *ibid.*, 190.
[97] E. M. Stanton to T. O. Howe and to W. L. Elliott, Jan. 18, 1863, *ibid.*, 190.
[98] Edward Bates to E. M. Stanton, Jan. 31, 1863, Stanton Papers.
[99] *Ibid.*

mentioned above, authorizing the President to suspend the privilege of the writ of habeas corpus. In the Wisconsin Supreme Court some opposition continued, on the ground that the act constituted an unconstitutional delegation of legislative power to the President, but the court refused so to hold,[100] even as it admitted that the subject was one of great difficulty.

It was taken pretty much as one of the hazards of the war that judges appointed before the Lincoln Presidency might display Southern sympathies and render decisions embarrassing to the war effort. It was a matter of great concern, however, that cases should not be lost before Lincoln's own appointees. An early habeas corpus case in Justice Swayne's circuit, at Cincinnati, was that of Bethuel Rupert. Rupert was arrested by a United States Marshal and confined first in a county jail and then at Camp Chase under charges that he was a proselyting member of the Knights of the Golden Circle, a Copperhead organization, and that he had used his influence to discourage enlistments. In the Circuit Court, where both Justice Swayne and Judge Leavitt were sitting, he applied for a writ of habeas corpus to challenge the legality of his detention.

The affidavits on the basis of which Rupert had been arrested display a wide range of activities, from initiating new members into the secret order to persuading drafted soldiers not to fire at the enemy. The situation with respect to his status as a prisoner changed rapidly; he was moved from civil custody in jail to military custody at Camp Chase when a motion for the writ was filed. He was transferred on instructions from Washington, and the marshal was told that he should resist all attempts to take the prisoner, either by habeas corpus or otherwise.

The case marks one of the misfortunes of history—of the recording of history—that Justice Swayne did not, like his predecessor, Justice McLean, write out his Circuit Court opinions. About the case we have only the newspaper statement:

> Judge Swayne yesterday delivered his decision in the case. In his usual able manner, he dwelt upon the merits of the question and the issues at stake, and concluded by saying that he should "deny the application, without prejudice to any future application of a similar nature."[101]

Rupert was an unknown person. His arrest attracted little attention and stirred no public interest. The situation was vastly different in

---

[100] *In re* Oliver, 17 Wis. 681 (1864).

[101] *Cincinnati Gazette*, Nov. 7, 1862. The affidavits on the basis of which the arrest was made are likewise presented here. No record of the case has been found in such records of the court as have been preserved.

the case of Clement L. Vallandigham, handsome United States Senator and popular Ohio orator, who in Congress and at home denounced the war and the Lincoln Administration and demanded a negotiated peace. Early in 1863 Stanley Matthews of Ohio, a future member of the Supreme Court, expressed to Secretary Chase his amazement at the boldness of Vallandigham and other dissidents in their attacks on the government in its efforts to suppress the rebellion.[102] Defeated for re-election to Congress, Vallandigham increased the boldness of his utterances in the hope of winning the office of governor of Ohio.[103]

While Vallandigham was capturing public attention by his close to treasonable speeches, General Burnside was also capturing it with drastic restrictive orders. His famous General Order No. 38, issued April 13, 1863, declared that all persons who committed acts for the benefit of the enemy would be tried as spies or traitors, and if convicted would suffer death. Listing a series of specific offenses, he added generally that "The habit of declaring sympathies for the enemy will not be allowed in this department," and "It must be distinctly understood that treason expressed or implied will not be tolerated in this department."[104] To show that he was completely in earnest, he set up a military commission to try offenders.[105]

Delivering a May Day address to the Democratic Party, Vallandigham accepted Burnside's challenge. With all his scathing eloquence he denounced General Order No. 38 as a base usurpation of arbitrary power. He urged resistance to it, saying that "the sooner the people inform the minions of usurped power that they will not submit to such restrictions upon their liberties, the better."[106] Military men in the audience wearing civilian clothes reported the speech. On May 4 Vallandigham's arrest was ordered, and on the following morning soldiers broke into his home and took him into military custody.[107]

As Vallandigham intended and as General Burnside was too unfamiliar with politics and propaganda to foresee, the arrest set the country ablaze with excitement and made Vallandigham a martyr even with people who otherwise would have had little use for him. The excitement grew as Vallandigham was tried before a military commission for violation of General Order No. 38 and found guilty. Fortunately Burnside or his advisers had the good sense to give a sentence of im-

---

[102] Stanley Matthews to S. P. Chase, Feb. 10, 1863, Chase Papers.

[103] Eugene H. Roseboom, *The Civil War Era, 1850–1873*, 411.

[104] 5 O.R. (2d) 480.

[105] See General Order No. 114, May 4, 1863, referring to Special Order No. 135, Apr. 21, 1863, *ibid.*, 556.

[106] For further quotations see *Ex parte* Vallandigham, 28 Fed. Cas. 874 (No. 16816) (C.C.S.D. Ohio 1863).

[107] See Daniel J. Ryan, *History of Ohio*, IV, 216–17.

prisonment rather than death. The President, with contrastingly superb political judgment, stood by his general but, perhaps with a touch of humor, commuted the sentence to exile beyond the enemy lines.

In the meantime, however, Vallandigham applied to the United States Circuit Court at Cincinnati for a writ of habeas corpus. Stanton feared that the court might issue the writ in spite of a general order of suspension and advocated a special order of suspension in this case. Lincoln consulted Seward and Chase and decided against such a step. Chase knew about the *Rupert* case, thought that the court would be likely to follow it, and was convinced that in no event would Justice Swayne commit an imprudence.[108]

Making his application to "the honorable the Judges of the Circuit Court of the United States,"[109] Vallandigham evidently assumed, as did the authorities in Washington, that Justice Swayne would sit with Judge Leavitt in the case. Judge Leavitt, who for many years had been inclined to rely on Justice McLean, and who sought no position of leadership, presumably hoped for companionship in this delicate case. For some reason, however, Justice Swayne did not appear, and Judge Leavitt had to handle the case alone.

Vallandigham was represented by George E. Pugh, from 1855 to 1861 a Democratic member of the Senate from Ohio and an enthusiastic supporter of Vallandigham's dissident position.[110] General Burnside was represented by Aaron F. Perry, a distinguished member of the Cincinnati bar, and by the United States Attorney there, Flamen Ball. Pugh contended that Vallandigham was entitled to the writ of habeas corpus and to release because he was a civilian improperly held by military authority for an offense not known to the laws of the United States. Government counsel contended that General Burnside operated within the range of his military authority and that "A habeas corpus does not meddle with arrests legally made."[111]

---

[108] A. Lincoln to E. M. Stanton, May 13, 1863, Lincoln, *Collected Works*, VI, 215. Evidently discussing the possibility of bringing Vallandigham to trial in a civil court, Chase wrote that "If Vallandigham violated any law he should have been arrested, tried and convicted. To arrest, try and convict him now seems very much like a confession that the Burnside Court had no jurisdiction—if the charges be based on the acts which were proved before the Court." Chase admitted that he was not much afraid of men like Vallandigham and was no great admirer of Order No.

38. He thought that prosecutions should be reserved for cases that were very clear. S. P. Chase to Col. R. C. Parsons, June 15, 1863, Chase Papers (H.S.Pa.). He said later that he was pretty sure that arresting Vallandigham and sending him to "Dixie" was a mistake. S. P. Chase to Hiram Barney, June 17, 1863, Chase Papers (H.S.Pa.).

[109] 5 O.R. (2d) 573.

[110] See Roseboom, *The Civil War Era, 1850–1873*, 408.

[111] *Ex parte* Vallandigham, 28 Fed. Cas. 874 (No. 16816) (C.C.S.D. Ohio 1863).

Judge Leavitt denied the writ, basing his decision first of all on the unreported *Rupert* case, and discussing in connection therewith his conception of the relation between the district judge and the member of the Supreme Court constituting a Circuit Court of the United States. Stating that the *Rupert* case was substantially the same as that of Vallandigham, he said that "On full reflection, I do not see how it is possible for me, sitting alone, in the circuit court, to ignore the decision, made upon full consideration by Justice Swayne, with the concurrence of myself, and which, as referable to all cases involving the same principle, must be regarded as the law of this court until reversed by a higher court." For the district judge sitting alone to reverse a decision of the Circuit Court would violate all settled rules of judicial practice and courtesy: "It is well known that the district judge, though authorized to sit with the circuit judge in the circuit court, does not occupy the same official position, and that the latter judge, when present, is, ex officio, the presiding judge."[112]

Having thus taken shelter behind his absent colleague, Judge Leavitt nevertheless proceeded to discuss the case on its merits. He held that the writ of habeas corpus was not grantable as a matter of course but would issue only if the court thought the petitioner entitled to a discharge upon a hearing after its return. He further held that although the President was not above the Constitution, but derived his power from it, military commanders acting under him might detain civilians, as in this instance, if necessity required it—and he seemed to leave the judgment of necessity wholly to the executive. The civil courts had no power to inquire into the matter. He denied the application without discussing the power to suspend the writ, a question rendered largely moot by the Act of Congress of March 3, 1863, and without discussing the validity of Valandigham's trial before a military commission. He concluded his opinion in elaboration of the remark that "there is too much of the pestilential leaven of disloyalty in the community."[113]

Sent into enemy country by the President's order, Vallandigham found his way to the East Coast and sailed for Canada, where, just across the line from Ohio, he kept up contact with his friends, managed his campaign for the governorship of Ohio,[114] and presumably planned

---

[112] *Ibid.*, 920.

[113] *Ibid.*, 923. Flamen Ball wrote to Secretary Chase, "I trust you are satisfied with my services in the Vallandigham case. I succeeded in impressing on the mind of the Judge the necessity of the coordinate branches of the Government, at this crisis at least, acting in perfect harmony: albeit, when peace shall return a case like this should be left to the civil courts." Flamen Ball to S. P. Chase, May 20, 1863, Chase Papers.

[114] For a naturally somewhat biased account of the whole story see J. L. Vallandigham, *A Life of Clement L. Vallandigham*.

his appeal to the Supreme Court at the following term. The President was showered with petitions to cancel the order of banishment and with requests to stand firm. He told General Burnside that all members of the Cabinet had regretted the necessity of the arrest, and some had perhaps doubted that there was a real necessity for it, but "being done, all were for seeing you through with it."[115] He had to draw the line, as has been noted, when Burnside suppressed the *Chicago Times* and stopped circulation of the *New York World* because of criticism of his treatment of Vallandigham.

The case pointed up a swelling mass of criticism of the suppression of civil liberties and became an issue of national politics. The President was compelled to discuss it at length. The arrest was made, he contended, not merely because of criticism of the Administration. It was because Vallandigham was having an effect in preventing the raising of troops and in encouraging desertions. He was damaging the army, upon the vigor of which the life of the nation depended. He asked, "Must I shoot a simple-minded soldier boy who deserts, while I must not touch a hair of a wiley agitator who induces him to desert?"[116] He was not able to appreciate the apprehended danger that by means of military arrests during the rebellion the people would lose for all time the right of public discussion, the liberty of speech and press, the law of evidence, the right to trial by jury, and the writ of habeas corpus, "any more than I am able to believe that a man could contract so strong an appetite for emetics during temporary illness, as to persist in feeding upon them during the remainder of his healthful life."[117] While it may have been true even at this time that Lincoln, as later stated by Justice Davis, was opposed to the use of military commissions in the free states where the courts were open,[118] he could not then too fully disclose his hand in political argument. He did insist on the power to detain dangerous persons, and Vallandigham, banished from the country, was not treated more harshly than persons detained.

While Vallandigham fought his political battles from Canadian soil, and won a substantial block of votes but not the governorship of Ohio, his counsel prepared to carry the legal controversy to the Supreme Court. Since there had only been one judge on the case in the Circuit Court—not two, who might have contrived a division of opinion and certified the case to the Supreme Court as other judges were later to

---

[115] A. Lincoln to A. E. Burnside, May 29, 1863, Lincoln, *Collected Works*, VI, 237.

[116] A. Lincoln to Erastus Corning et al., June 12, 1863, *ibid.*, 260, 266.

[117] *Ibid.*, 267. See also A. Lincoln to Matthew Birchard et al., June 29, 1863, *ibid.*, 300–06.

[118] Willard L. King, *Lincoln's Manager, David Davis*, 254.

do in the *Milligan* case[119]—there was apparently no way of getting Judge Leavitt's decision reviewed by the Supreme Court. In any event, Vallandigham hoped to challenge not merely military detention but also his trial by military commission, a matter specifically not passed upon by Judge Leavitt. It was therefore decided to apply to the Supreme Court for a writ of certiorari to review directly the proceedings of the commission.

Senator Pugh remained with Vallandigham and argued the case before the Supreme Court on January 22, 1864, this time opposing Joseph Holt, who as Judge Advocate General was now the custodian of the records of the trial before the military commission. Pugh characterized a military commission as a court, evidently for the purpose of establishing the right of the Supreme Court to review the scope of its exercise of power, but characterized it as one limited to cases in the land or naval forces or the militia. He saw the writ of certiorari as the proper device for determining the validity of the proceeding. Holt, on the other hand, contended that the Supreme Court had no jurisdiction to review the proceedings of a military commission, either by writ of error or habeas corpus.[120] Courts-martial and military commissions exercised their power from sources under the Constitution other than the judicial power,[121] and direct review would therefore be an exercise of the Court's original, not appellate, jurisdiction, beyond the authority conferred by Article Three. As others were doing, and no doubt to the discomfort of the Chief Justice, he quoted from *Luther v. Borden* to justify broad exercise of military power.[122]

The Supreme Court, deciding the case on February 15, 1864, dealt cautiously with the critical issues. Speaking through Justice Wayne it agreed with Holt that military commissions were not the kind of tribunals whose decisions the Supreme Court had been given power to review directly, either by certiorari or by writ of habeas corpus *ad subjiciendum*, and denied the writ. The Court said nothing to throw light on Vallandigham's guilt or innocence. The Administration could draw comfort only from the reminder, apparently in answer to Pugh's contention that Vallandigham had committed no offense known to the law, that not all military power came from statutes. Some of it derived from "the common law of war."[123] But the Administration was not looking to the Court for comfort. It sought only to be let alone, while it went its

---

[119] *Ex parte* Milligan, 4 Wall. 2 (1876). See King, *Lincoln's Manager, David Davis*, 250.

[120] He relied heavily on quotations from opinions in the habeas corpus case of *In re* Kaine, 14 How. 103 (1853).

[121] See Dynes v. Hoover, 20 How. 65 (1858).

[122] For Holt's brief see 6 O.R. (2d) 620–24.

[123] *Ex parte* Vallandigham, 1 Wall. 243, 249 (1864).

way winning the war.[124] True, an assumption of some Presidential interest is justified by the presence in the Lincoln papers of a printed copy of the opinion, with a covering letter from the Clerk of the Court.[125] But a Supreme Court decision on the constitutionality of military trials was to be postponed until the *Milligan* decision, after the war had come to an end.

---

[124] There was no dissenting opinion. The minutes of the Court show that of the ten Justices, Miller was absent at the time of the decision and took no part in it. A manuscript copy and a printed copy of the opinion in the files of the Court show the statement by Justice Nelson that "I concur in the result of this opinion," which appears at the end of the opinion as reported in 17 L. Ed. 594. At the end of the opinion as printed in 1 Wall. 254 it is stated that Justices Grier and Field also concurred only in the result.

[125] D. W. Middleton to A. Lincoln, Mar. 1, 1864, Lincoln Papers.

CHAPTER XXXVI

Other Problems from the War

O THER PROBLEMS ARISING FROM THE WAR involved constitutional issues but touched the Supreme Court only sporadically or peripherally during the period of the war and the concluding years of the Taney regime: the confiscation of enemy property, emancipation, the raising of revenue to support the war, the issuing of emergency currency necessitated by the war, the conscription of military personnel, and the disposition of accusations of treason against the United States. Although they involved the work of the Court but little during the war, they were to give rise to extensive litigation in the postwar period.

Confiscation of enemy property took various forms. As already discussed, ships unsuccessfully attempting to run the blockade were captured, taken into port, and condemned in federal courts pursuant to international law. In connection with the waging of war on land it was assumed that the armed forces operating on enemy territory might lawfully seize whatever enemy property they could use or destroy what might be of use to the enemy. But on the part of both the North and the South, more in the way of confiscation was demanded. In the North there was clamor for confiscation not only of Southern property used specifically for war purposes but also of property of any kind owned by participants in or sympathizers with the rebellion. Closely linked was the controversy over the proposed destruction of Southern property rights through the emancipation of slaves.

The special session of Congress which met in the summer of 1861 provided for the confiscation only of property used in aiding the insurrection, which was to be condemned in United States District or Circuit courts. Action was to be initiated at the behest of the Attorney General, or any district attorney, or on information from a private informer, who was to receive half the proceeds of the property seized.

931

Furthermore, rights to persons "held to labor or service" were to be forfeited if the labor of such persons was used in immediate aid of the armed services of the enemy.[1]

But confiscation merely of property used in direct aid of the enemy did not satisfy people filled with growing zeal for prosecuting the war and with growing hatred for the enemy. At the session of Congress beginning in December, 1861, various measures were debated for attacking the enemy wherever his property could be found, both to cripple and to punish him. Such proposals were resisted by those of more moderate sentiments, often but not always Democrats or residents of border states with somewhat divided loyalties. Opposition was based on belief that vindictive confiscation would make all the more difficult the restoration of the Union and was usually phrased in constitutional terms.[2]

The act passed in July, 1862, was much less drastic than the proposal to confiscate all property of all rebels or of all persons living in rebel territory. Linked with provisions dealing with the punishment of treason, it was in considerable part punitive in concept. It applied to the property of all civil and military officers serving under the Confederacy; to the property of any person residing in the North who should assist and give aid and comfort to the rebellion; and to the property of persons "in any state" who, being engaged in the rebellion, did not reestablish their allegiance to the United States within sixty days after a proclamation of warning by the President.[3] Slaves were to be liberated in areas occupied by the armed forces, and the return of fugitive slaves to rebel owners was forbidden. The condemnation and sale of property to be confiscated was to be processed in the District Courts of the United States.

Although the armed forces had the power of seizure of enemy property needed for their own use,[4] the two confiscation acts placed administration in the hands of civil officers and civil courts. So lacking in uniformity were the proceedings in the several judicial districts, and so vigorous the competition of the military for jurisdiction, that the President found it expedient to lodge supervision in the hands of the Attorney General.[5] It will be recalled that shortly after enactment of

---

[1] 12 Stat. 319.
[2] E.g., *Cong. Globe*, 37th Cong., 3rd Sess. 1157 (1862).
[3] 12 Stat. 589, 590–91, to be read in the light of 12 Stat. 627. For President Lincoln's discussion of the constitutionality of certain provisions of the statute and the veto message which he would have used but for the enactment of a limiting resolution,

see Abraham Lincoln, *Collected Works*, Roy P. Basler, ed., V, 328.
[4] *Ibid.*, 337, n. 2.
[5] See order of Nov. 13, 1862, *ibid.*, 496, and order of Jan. 8, 1863, Lincoln, *Collected Works*, VI, 45. For discussion of both the policy and the program of confiscation see James G. Randall, *Constitutional Problems Under Lincoln*, 275–341.

the first confiscation statute the President had found it necessary to bring about revocation of a proclamation of General John Charles Frémont by which rebel property generally was to be confiscated under military authority, in violation of the existing statute.[6]

Civil officers ran into competition with military officers resorting to provost courts, especially in areas where control by the enemy had been exercised or was threatened. A provost court was used in Alexandria, Virginia, in the peripheral area of eastern Virginia of which Union forces retained control, in spite of protests of property owners and civil officers. Brigadier General William R. Montgomery defended use of the court, and sent the provost judge, Adjutant General Jacob R. Freese, to Washington to explain the situation. The court and its authority, General Montgomery contended, were necessary incidents to the abrogation of civil authority: "Otherwise an interregnum in all civil matters would ensue, and civil rights be resolved back into elemental principles, productive of discord and misrule destructive of all rights and best interest of society."[7]

The President referred to Attorney General Bates a memorial from the Chamber of Commerce of New York urging that the action of the Alexandria provost court be sanctioned and that similar courts be established "wherever the federal army establishes its authority, in a rebellious city or district." Bates, concerned about the encroachment of military jurisdiction in his own state of Missouri as well as elsewhere, warned the President against the proposal. Of necessity, he argued, the President had already been compelled to assume immense power over persons and property. But he did not see how the proposed further assumption of power properly belonging to the judicial courts could be justified.[8]

Bates proposed leaving the matter to Congress. Postmaster General Blair objected. The government had so often exercised civil and judicial functions through military officers in places held by military force, with the sanction of the Supreme Court, that the right to do so was not open to question.[9] The President nevertheless did mention the matter to Congress in a general way in his ensuing annual message. He observed that in Southern areas overrun by the armed forces of the Union there were no courts or officers to whom citizens of other states might apply for enforcement of lawful claims—which was probably the source of the interest of the New York Chamber of Commerce in the establishment

---

[6] A. Lincoln to John C. Frémont, Sept. 2, 11, 1861, Lincoln, *Collected Works*, IV, 506, 517–18. See Joseph Holt to A. Lincoln, Sept. 12, 1861, Lincoln Papers.

[7] W. R. Montgomery to A. Lincoln,

Nov. 8, 1861, Lincoln Papers.

[8] Edward Bates to A. Lincoln, Nov. 21, 1861, *ibid.* Copy, Attorney General's Letter Book B-4, 223.

[9] M. Blair to A. Lincoln, Nov. 27, 1861, Lincoln Papers.

of provost courts in such areas. Claims estimated as high as two hundred million dollars were involved. He had been urged to establish military tribunals to do summary justice but had thus far declined to do so, preferring to leave to Congress the establishment of adequate machinery.[10]

Congress proved unready to set up machinery for the government of recaptured territory. The House of Representatives took one step in that direction by passing a resolution authorizing the provost court at Alexandria to retain property taken from persons engaged in aiding the rebellion,[11] but the Senate failed to act. In March, 1862, writing to a United States Attorney who was confused by conflicting views of civil and military authorities with respect to confiscation, Attorney General Bates said, "I had some trouble to stop in the beginning, the establishment of *Provost Courts*, so called, of which precedents were set, both in Alexandria, Va., and St. Louis, Mo. It was done however, by a general order from the President, and in time to prevent any serious conflict."[12]

If he prevented the building up of provost courts in the border areas, as distinguished from secession territory where they were extensively employed, the Attorney General could not for some time resolve the conflict between military and civil officers over the seizure of enemy property. An example of the conflict was provided by the seizure of the furniture left in Washington by Justice Campbell when he resigned from the Supreme Court and departed for the South, where he became Assistant Secretary of War in the Cabinet of the Confederacy. In addition to its civil government the District of Columbia had for the period of the war a military governor, with his coterie of subordinates. The lines of jurisdiction between the civil and military governments were naturally poorly defined. In 1862 General James S. Wadsworth, who was then military governor of the District, directed the seizure of considerable amounts of property of Southern sympathizers, including a number of residences. The statutes did not authorize such military seizures, and clearly they were not the sort which the military might lawfully make in connection with a military advance into enemy territory. The owners of the houses were generally men who had gone into

---

[10] Annual Message of Dec. 3, 1861, Lincoln, *Collected Works*, V, 43; J. D. Richardson, *A Compilation of the Messages and Papers of the Presidents*, VI, 50–51.

[11] *Cong. Globe*, 37th Cong., 2nd Sess. 115 (1861).

[12] Edward Bates to Benjamin H. Smith, Mar. 5, 1862, Attorney General's Letter Book B–5, 28. For a brief discussion of the establishment of provost courts during the Civil War, for which there was apparently no firm statutory base, and for their continued and expanded use during the period of Reconstruction, see William W. Winthrop, *Military Law*, II, 24–27.

the service of the Confederacy and were not in a position to defend their rights, if rights they had. The seizure not of a house[13] but of the furniture of Justice Campbell, however, which was located at 339 I Street, stirred rivalry between the civil and military governments.

On October 29, 1862, by order of General Wadsworth, the military took possession of the furniture but left it in the house. On December 18 Ward H. Lamon, Marshal of the District of Columbia and of the Supreme Court, sent civil deputies to remove the furniture pursuant to a writ of replevin. The landlady sent word to an assistant adjutant general that carts were at the door to take the furniture and asked him to "send someone directly." Six men and a commissioned officer were sent with orders to hold the furniture "against all comers." The deputies sent by the Marshal had to leave empty-handed.

Attorney General Bates wrote an indignant letter to Brigadier General Martindale, who had replaced General Wadsworth as military governor, saying that he had laid the matter before the President and advised him to direct that "prompt measures be taken to suppress such dangerous irregularity," and that the President wanted to see the general about the matter. As a result of this intervention by the President at the request of the Attorney General, the dispute was resolved and property seized by the military, including houses as well as the furniture of the late Justice, was turned over to the civil government for proceedings under the confiscation acts.[14]

The Attorney General continued to have trouble, however, both with members of Congress and with the military. A resolution of the House of Representatives dated January 8, 1863, asked him to report whether the law for confiscation of the property of rebels had been enforced in the District of Columbia, and, if not, the reason for the delay. Bates had to admit that though property had been seized by the military, no confiscation proceedings had been completed in the civil courts. In explanation he referred to the recent placement of responsibility in his hands and the necessity of proceeding strictly according to law rather than on newspaper statements and public rumors. Arrangements had now been made, however, for the district attorney to proceed

---

[13] Concerning the sale of Justice Campbell's house see the following in the diary of the wife of a Confederate officer: "Gloom and unspoken despondency hangs like a pall everywhere. Today I saw an account of the sale of Judge Campbell's, Dr. Garnett's and Colonel Ives's houses in Washington. Patriotism is a pretty heavy load to carry some times." Entry of Dec. 7, 1863, Mary Boykin Chesnut, *A Diary from Dixie*, Ben Ames Williams, ed., 331.

[14] For the correspondence see Rebel Property Seized in Washington City, H.R. Exec. Doc. No. 44, 37th Cong., 3rd Sess. (1863).

against the property in court as soon as he could obtain the requisite testimony.[15]

In assuming control of confiscation proceedings, Bates found it necessary to write to Secretary of War Stanton of his instructions and to ask for his cooperation. He stated his belief that in many parts of the country the military authorities had seized and still held the property of supposed traitors and rebels. He asked Stanton to instruct the military to surrender such property to civil authorities for processing in the civil courts.[16] In many areas, however, the military continued to take matters into their own hands, and the jurisdictional conflict was not completely resolved until the end of the war.

The confiscation story is important primarily as illustrating the temporary subordination of civil government during the military crisis. The litigation in the federal courts over the confiscation acts started in the lower courts before the end of the war, but the major issues did not reach the Supreme Court for many years.[17] The actual amount of property confiscated had no such dimension as the tumultuous public discussion would seem to assume.[18] There was a time, however, when the inability of the judiciary to do adequate justice to the parties and interests involved was glaringly apparent.

Though issues of slavery had produced strife in the Supreme Court for decades, the struggle over emancipation proposals during the war involved the Court hardly at all, either then or later. Congress debated the subject from all angles. Some of the military sought to speed emancipation and others sought to maintain the status quo. The President looked at the issue from the point of view of winning the war. He held back when it was necessary to do so in his attempts to keep border states in the Union, to the resentment of impatient abolitionists. He made moderate proposals for compensated emancipation, for which he was unable to gain acceptance. When from the point of view of internal strength and prestige abroad it seemed best to commit himself and the country to emancipation, he did so in spite of an enormous amount of continuing opposition.

With respect to slavery, Congress never forgot that the Supreme

---

[15] For the Attorney General's reply, dated Jan. 14, 1863, see Confiscation Law in the District of Columbia, H.R. Exec. Doc. No. 32 (1863).

[16] Edward Bates to E. M. Stanton, Jan. 21, 1863, Attorney General's Letter Book B–5, 337.

[17] See for example Miller v. United States, 11 Wall. 268 (1871); Tyler v. Defrees, 11 Wall. 331 (1871); Confiscation Cases, 20 Wall. 92 (1874); Windson v. McVeigh, 93 U.S. 274 (1876); United States v. Lee, 106 U.S. 196 (1882).

[18] See Randall, *Constitutional Problems Under Lincoln*, 288–93.

Court was the tribunal responsible for the Dred Scott decision, and estimated its future conduct accordingly. "I am not willing to trust the court in relation to this question of slavery," said Congressman W. McKee Dunn of Indiana, "because very much of the trouble in which we are now involved may be attributed to the fact that we had a pro-slavery judiciary."[19] When the President issued his preliminary proclamation of September 22, 1862,[20] it was vigorously attacked on grounds of constitutionality by former Justice Benjamin R. Curtis, even though he had been in the minority in the Dred Scott case.[21] He demonstrated with irresistible force of logic, said the *New York World*, that both the emancipation and martial law proclamations were in violation of the Constitution.[22] When on January 1, 1863, the official proclamation was issued,[23] the *New York Times* was glad the President had based it on military necessity, and wished on constitutional grounds that it had been drafted strictly as a military order.[24] The *Times* added, "We think every dispassionate person must feel some doubt whether the Supreme Court will decide that the President has power to *repeal State laws on the subject of slavery*, or to continue those laws in force according to his judgment of the military necessities of the moment."[25]

Justice Davis, thinking politically as he tended to do, was for a time hopeful about the effects of the Proclamation, then disappointed, and then convinced that it would have to be abandoned.[26] He tried to persuade the President to change his strategy, but to no avail.[27] Neither his sentiments nor those of any of the other Justices were made public, but this fact did not prevent predictions as to what the Court might do or continued criticisms of the Court from the abolitionists. Outstanding among the critics was Wendell Phillips of Massachusetts, who, like William Lloyd Garrison, had condemned the Constitution itself for its protection of slavery. Phillips had long been a disunionist with the goal of expelling slavery from such portion of the United States as could be cleansed, with the recalcitrant states permitted to go their own way. He heartily approved the Proclamation of Emancipation but had little hope for its survival at the hands of the Supreme Court, which in the Dred Scott decision had said that the black man had no rights which the white man was bound to respect. The Proclamation was "to be filtered through the Secession heart of a man whose body is in Baltimore,

[19] *Cong. Globe*, 37th Cong., 2nd Sess. 1792 (1862).

[20] Lincoln, *Collected Works*, V, 433.

[21] See George T. Curtis, *Memoir of Benjamin Robbins Curtis*, II, 306 (1879).

[22] *New York World*, Oct. 22, 1862.

[23] Lincoln, *Collected Works*, VI, 28.

[24] *New York Times*, Jan. 3, 1863.

[25] *New York Times*, Jan. 6, 1863.

[26] Willard L. King, *Lincoln's Manager, David Davis*, 204, 207–08.

[27] Orville Browning, *Diary*, I, 616.

but whose soul, if he has got one, is in Richmond. . . . God help the negro if he hangs on Roger B. Taney for his liberty."[28]

Phillips sought a constitutional amendment which the Supreme Court could not touch. The Court, he maintained, was the point where our democratic system reached nearest to despotism. He wanted something more than the judges would be likely to give.[29] "We want a platform which the Supreme Court cannot touch. As the *quid pro quo* for this war, I want something of which I know the value today without consulting Judge Wayne, Judge Grier, Judge Taney, Judge Clifford, or Judge Catron, Secessionists from the tops of their heads to the soles of their feet."[30]

So extreme was Phillips' denunciation of the Supreme Court at Cooper Institute in New York that Horace Greeley, editor of the *New York Tribune* and himself a bitter critic of the Dred Scott decision, rose to make an extemporaneous defense of the Court and followed his speech with editorial comments. Justices Catron and Wayne, he reminded the audience, had broken with the predominant force in Tennessee and Georgia, respectively, leaving their homes and property at the mercy of the merciless, thereby giving the strongest evidence that they were not secessionists. He professed fullest confidence in the Supreme Court and willingness to abide by its judgments.[31] The *Tribune* further reminded its readers that Justices Wayne and Grier had been in the majority of the Court in the *Prize Cases*, recognizing the belligerent right of the government to maintain the blockade of Southern ports, and published the report that in the recent election in Pennsylvania Justice Grier, always hitherto a Democrat, had voted the Union ticket.[32]

Speculation over what the Court might do about the Proclamation proved futile. By its terms it liberated slaves only in the rebel states, and could be made effective only upon the success of the Union arms. Thereafter, citizens of those states claiming violation of their civil rights and rights of property were for a considerable period in no position to seek redress at the hands of the Supreme Court. Meanwhile, in 1865, the Thirteenth Amendment was adopted, outlawing slavery and in-

---

[28] *New York Tribune*, Dec. 23, 1863.

[29] *New York Times*, Dec. 23, 1863.

[30] *New York Tribune*, Dec. 23, 1863. The address seems to have been delivered extemporaneously, so that the record remains in the varied notes taken by reporters. See also *Washington National Intelligencer*, Dec. 29, 1863. The *New York Express*, pro-Southern in sympathy, was said to rely mainly on the Supreme Court to defeat the purpose of the Proclamation. Lorenzo Sherwood to S. P. Chase, Jan. 6, 1864, Chase Papers.

[31] *New York Tribune*, Dec. 24, 1863. For criticism of Phillips and his own disunionist record see *New York Times*, Dec. 25, 1863.

[32] *New York Tribune*, Dec. 25, 1863.

voluntary servitude except in the instance, here irrelevant, of punishment for crime. The constitutionality of the Proclamation was never tested.

Some of the problems of the Supreme Court, or of its members, arose from steps taken for the financing of the war. The gold and silver available was insufficient to provide a circulatory medium for the crisis. Most of the paper currency in circulation was issued by state banks, which likewise proved inadequate to the crisis and had to suspend specie payments with resulting depreciation in the value of their notes. The federal government found it necessary to do the same thing in order to protect its limited supply of specie. Taxes had to be increased and new sources of revenue had to be found. In any event, it was impossible to conduct the war on a pay-as-you-go basis and extensive borrowing was necessary. The power to borrow was hampered by doubts as to the soundness of government credit at a time when the very survival of the Union was threatened.

The Supreme Court came into focus in connection with a movement, begun in New York before the war, to find ways whereby the states might derive revenue from capital invested in government securities in spite of the unconstitutionality of state taxes levied directly upon federal instrumentalities.[33] In 1859 the City and County of New York levied a tax on the capital stock of local banks. From the taxable base it allowed deduction of so much of the stock as was represented by holdings of real estate, which were already taxable as real estate rather than as capital stock, but it required collection of the tax on stock the value of which was held in the form of federal securities (then commonly called stocks), which were themselves constitutionally exempt from state taxation. The following year a local supreme court—a court of original jurisdiction—held that this tax could be differentiated from a tax directly upon holdings of federal securities and could be constitutionally collected.[34] The case was taken to the court of appeals, where in 1861 the judgment was affirmed.[35] The decision, coming at this critical time, stood as a threat to the borrowing power of the United States, in that it was hoped that banks would be primary investors in federal securities, partly because of their tax-exempt status. As a result of this decision, Congress attempted to protect its borrowing power by including in a statute of February 25, 1862, a provision that "all stocks,

---

[33] See McCulloch v. Maryland, 4 Wheat. 316 (1819); Weston v. City of Charleston, 2 Pet. 449 (1829).

[34] People *ex rel.* Bank of the Commonwealth v. Commissioners of Assessment, 32 Barbour (N.Y.) 509 (1860).

[35] People *ex rel.* Bank of the Commonwealth v. Commissioner of Taxes, 23 N.Y. 192 (1861).

bonds, and other securities of the United States held by individuals, corporations, or associations, within the United States, shall be exempt from taxation by or under State authority."[36]

The City and County of New York attempted to collect the taxes in spite of the federal statute. The local supreme court held that as an incident of promoting the borrowing power of the United States Congress might confer exemption from taxation as to securities thereafter issued, but that since a tax on federal securities previously marketed by the government could have no effect on the power to borrow, revenue could be collected from prior issues.[37]

While New York was thus resisting curtailment of its taxing powers, the New Jersey Supreme Court of Judicature stopped a similar movement by relying on both the Constitution and the federal statute, "passed since the decision of the New York Court of Appeals, and probably in view of it, to correct the evils flowing from it."[38]

Two New York cases were taken to the Supreme Court of the United States on writ of error, and were argued February 27, 1863, and decided March 10, 1863 (which, incidentally, was the date of the decision in the *Prize Cases*, previously discussed). In the case in which the major issues were settled, Silliman and Lord appeared for the plaintiffs in error and John E. Devlin and James T. Brady for defendants in error. The latter argued to no avail for restriction of the rights and exemptions of the United States. Justice Nelson wrote for a unanimous Court a strong opinion upholding the exemption of federal securities, not on the basis of the statute of 1862 but on the basis of the Constitution as interpreted in basic decisions by the Marshall Court. The power to borrow money, he wrote, was one of the most important and even vital functions of the government. Its exercise was a means of supplying the necessary resources to meet exigencies in times of peace or war. Like Chief Justice Marshall, he held that if the power to tax were recognized at all, it would exist without limit. The tax therefore could not be upheld. The immunity extended even though the tax was levied on the aggregate of the capital stock of the bank and the federal securities were nowhere mentioned by name.[39]

---

[36] 12 Stat. 346. For this explanation of the enactment of the statutory provision see the brief of Benjamin D. Silliman and Daniel Lord, 6, for the Relators in Commissioner of Taxes v. People *ex rel.* Bank of Commerce, 2 Black 620 (1863).

[37] The case was unreported. For the opinions in People *ex rel.* Hanover Bank v. Commissioner of Taxes, see Record at 12–25 in People *ex rel.*

Bank of Commerce v. Commissioner of Taxes, 2 Black 620 (1863).

[38] Newark City Bank v. Assessor, 30 N.J.L. 13, 19 (1862).

[39] People *ex rel.* Bank of Commerce v. Commissioner of Taxes, 2 Black 620 (1863). For a summary of the briefs and for a short statement of the Court in the companion case of People *ex rel.* Bank of the Commonwealth v. Commissioner of Taxes see

As far as members of the Supreme Court were concerned there was a close relation between the 3 percent income tax which was levied on their salaries along with the incomes of others[40] and the legal tender acts which required acceptance of newly issued paper money in fulfillment of contracts,[41] paper money which depreciated well below the value of specie. In both instances the purchasing power of judicial salaries, along of course with the salaries of other persons, was reduced. The Constitution provided that the compensation of federal judges should not be diminished during their continuance in office.[42]

The constitutional status of the salaries of federal judges was discussed in Congress early in 1862 in connection with a bill intended to save money for the government by making a widespread reduction in government salaries. An amendment was proposed to the bill to exempt salaries of the President, federal judges, and certain other officials.[43] Senator John P. Hale, usually a sharp critic of the Supreme Court, urged that the exemptions be eliminated on the ground that the President and the judges should not be denied the privilege of sharing in the national burden. "I have not the shadow of a doubt," he said, "that if the President and the judges could be heard, they would, with one voice, beseech you not to make them such an odious and invidious example as holding them up as the few individuals in the land that were denied the privilege of bearing their part of the burdens of this war."[44] Others emphasized the fact, however, that the exception needed to be made to meet constitutional objections.[45]

When the government deducted from the salaries of the Justices the 3 percent income tax, the Justices revealed either a desire to preserve the Constitution inviolate or a notable lack of concern about sharing the burdens of the nation. Asserting that there was no mode of getting the question settled by a judicial proceeding, Chief Justice Taney wrote Secretary of the Treasury Chase a stern letter condemning the statute as unconstitutional as applied to judicial salaries. He was not willing to leave it to be inferred from his silence that he admitted the right of Congress to diminish in this or any other mode the compensation of judges when once fixed by law.[46]

Taney requested that Chase place his letter in the public files of the Treasury Department as evidence that he had done everything in his

---

17 L. ed. 456 (1863). In this case counsel for plaintiffs in error included Alexander W. Bradford and Irving Paris in addition to those appearing in the other case, and John E. Devlin in addition to the others representing defendants in error.

40 12 Stat. 473.

41 12 Stat. 345, 710.

42 Constitution, Art. III, Sec. 1.

43 *Cong. Globe*, 37th Cong., 2nd Sess. 1181 (1862).

44 *Ibid.*, 1185.

45 *Ibid.*, 676.

46 R. B. Taney to S. P. Chase, Feb. 16, 1863, Samuel Tyler, *Memoir of Roger Brooke Taney*, 432-34.

power to preserve the judicial department in the status prescribed by the Constitution. Chase, admitting no right of the Chief Justice to prescribe performance within the Treasury Department, sent the letter to Attorney General Bates with the remark that a number of the judges of the Supreme Court and other federal courts had challenged the constitutionality of the tax. Bates endorsed the letter, "No reply to be given," and tucked it away in his own official files.[47]

One of the protests received by Chase had come from Justice Grier. It seems that for a time Chase, or his subordinates, unable to determine whether the tax could rightfully be levied on judicial salaries, had postponed making any salary payments at all. Grier complained at the withholding of 97 percent of his salary while a decision was being reached about the remaining 3 percent. For want of the payment, his drafts on Philadelphia for family expenses were about to be protested.[48]

Because of the same delay in payment, Taney had to borrow to pay his life insurance. He had secured a temporary loan from his Baltimore friend, David M. Perine, who frequently aided him with loans and financial advice. Revealing the bitterness of his feelings about being compelled to accept depreciated United States notes, commonly called "greenbacks," when the salary was finally paid, he remarked that payment would be "in that miserable trash which soon will be utterly worthless, and which I certainly would not hand to you in payment of my debt. I must ask you to wait until I can get something more like money to pay you."[49]

Taney doubted whether the question of constitutionality was really the basis for the delay in paying any judicial salaries. He believed that Chase had no money with which to pay, "even in the trash he daily issues to pay contractors and soldiers' arrears."[50] In advance of sending his protest to Chase, while the latter was pretending to weigh the constitutional question, he had written out his protest, and he enclosed a copy which, in confidence, Perine might show to such of their friends as he thought proper.

Continuing to feel the grinding pressure of wartime finances, Taney later sent money to Perine, presumably in the hated greenbacks, and deplored his inability to fulfill all his obligations. All his life, he wrote, he had felt the obligation to pay his debts as part of his religion, and his inability to do so at this time was mortifying. But his rent had been raised from five hundred to eight hundred sixty dollars; the health

---

[47] S. P. Chase to Edward Bates, Mar. 26, 1863, Attorney General Papers.
[48] R. C. Grier to S. P. Chase, Jan. 30, 1863, Chase Papers.
[49] R. B. Taney to D. M. Perine, Feb. 1, 1863, Perine Papers.
[50] Ibid.

of his daughter, Ellen, who lived with him, was such that he could not move, and in any event it would be impossible to find a house fit to live in at a lesser cost. He added, "I sent in the protest of which I enclosed you a copy, and have by permission of all the Judges placed it on the records of the Supreme Court. But the tax is still deducted."[51] There was ultimate consolation for the friends and family of the Chief Justice in the fact that in 1872 another Secretary of the Treasury came to agree with him that the government had had no power to collect income taxes on the salaries of federal judges.[52]

For the government, the question of the constitutionality of an income tax on the salaries of federal judges was much less serious than the validity of the law requiring that the depreciated United States notes, or greenbacks (which Taney called the "paper trash of the government"), be accepted on their face value in payment of debts. Presumably the attitude of some of the Justices was known, or at least suspected. A holding that the legal tender provision was unconstitutional could have a disastrous effect on the financing of the war, or at any rate it was so believed.[53] In March, 1863, the *New York Tribune* announced the sensational rumor that a judge of the local supreme court was about to hold the legal tender provision unconstitutional. The *New York Times* advised caution in accepting such a rumor, saying that although in those days of Copperheadism a partisan judiciary might well give such a decision, it would certainly be reversed by a higher court.[54]

In the following June, speaking through Judge Daniel P. Ingraham, a local supreme court did hand down such a decision.[55] In the following September the New York Court of Appeals, speaking through a series of

---

[51] R. B. Taney to D. M. Perine, Apr. 4, 1863, Perine Papers.

[52] Tyler, *Memoir of Roger Brooke Taney*, 435. Many years later, in connection with other income tax statutes, the Supreme Court took the same position, in Evans v. Gore, 253 U.S. 245 (1920), and Miles v. Graham, 268 U.S. 501 (1925). In O'Malley v. Woodrough, 307 U.S. 277 (1939), however, the Court reversed its position, and held that an income tax of general application did not constitute a diminution of judicial salaries within the meaning of the constitutional provision.

[53] Secretary of the Treasury Chase, however, believed that such an effect would be limited: "No doubt a decision of a State Court, against the constitutionality of the legal-tender clauses of the Acts of Congress would have a prejudicial effect on the circulation of the United States Notes, but I do not apprehend very serious consequences from it. The interests concerned in the circulation are too great to allow such a decision to have very wide spread influence. Still, in my judgment, there ought to be some provision of the law by which cases of this character can be removed to the Federal Courts without reference to the amount involved." S. P. Chase to Hiram Barney, Feb. 10, 1863, Chase papers (H.S.Pa.).

[54] *New York Times*, Mar. 12, 1863.

[55] *Meyer v. Roosevelt*. The case was not officially reported. For the opinion see *Pittsburgh L. J.*, 10:401–04, 409–11, 416–18, 1863.

individual opinions and with two judges dissenting, reversed the decision, relying heavily on the broad doctrine of federal power asserted in *McCulloch v. Maryland* and in the recent decision of the United States Supreme Court denying to the states the power to tax federal securities. The case was decided along with another, in which the lower court had affirmed the power of the federal government.[56]

The case which had originally been decided against the government, but on appeal decided for it, was taken speedily to the Supreme Court on writ of error. There James J. Roosevelt contended that, in being compelled to accept from Lewis H. Meyer in full payment of a debt notes having a lower market value than the face value of the debt, he was denied constitutional rights. The act constituted a deprivation "without due process of good constitutional law."[57] From the sparseness of the briefs and the speed with which the case was disposed of, it would appear that the merits were never presented. The Supreme Court dealt only with the question of its jurisdiction on appeal. With only Justice Nelson dissenting—without full opinion—Justice Wayne stated the facts and then added briefly:

> I have been instructed by the court to announce it to be our conclusion, upon examination of the record, that, as the validity of the Act of the 25th of February, 1862, was drawn in question, and the decision was in favor of it and of the right set up by the defendant, this court has no jurisdiction to revise that judgment.[58]

More than eight years later, but with a considerable number of overlapping personnel, the Court held that by resort to another provision in the 25th section of the Judiciary Act the Court might have taken jurisdiction in the *Roosevelt* case.[59] Since the brief of the plaintiff in error plainly referred to the provision which Justice Wayne neglected, the reader is left to speculate on the possible eagerness of a majority of the Court to avoid coping with the constitutional question during the war. At any rate, it refrained from doing so until well after the war had come to an end.[60]

Whatever the other Justices may have thought of the constitu-

---

[56] Metropolitan Bank v. Van Dyck, Roosevelt v. Meyer, 27 N.Y. 400 (1863).

[57] Brief of plaintiff in error, at 4, Roosevelt v. Meyer, 1 Wall. 512 (1863).

[58] Roosevelt v. Meyer, 1 Wall. 512, 517 (1863).

[59] Trebilcock v. Wilson, 12 Wall. 687, 692–93 (1872). That is, the case had a double aspect. The state court decision, in upholding a federal statute, was not reviewable. But in rejecting the plaintiff's claim of deprivation of property without due process of law the decision was subject to review.

[60] See Hepburn v. Griswold, 8 Wall. 603 (1870); Legal Tender Cases, 12 Wall. 457 (1871).

tionality of the legal tender requirement, Chief Justice Taney had no doubts. Deprived of the opportunity to express his convictions in an official opinion, he composed a draft of an opinion as a reflection of his own thinking. The Constitution, he wrote, gave Congress no power over private contracts, except on the subject of bankruptcy, which was not here involved. The prohibition against the states' making anything but gold and silver legal tender carried no implication that the federal government did have that power. The power to coin money and regulate its value applied only to metallic currency and not to bills of credit. The power authorized in the statute virtually enabled the federal government to make forced loans whenever it might be in need of money. The power to borrow money could not be tortured into such a construction.[61]

Until the end of his life the Chief Justice continued to believe that the paper money structure was scheduled for early collapse—whether from its own lack of specie support or from defeat of the armed forces of the Union he did not say. Two months before his death he predicted that the paper would be worthless before the end of another year, and deplored the fact that he was nevertheless compelled to use it.[62] He wrote a few days later:

> My salary is withheld to the amount of $500, by the Executive Department and I have no means of redress. My fuel from Oct. 1863 to Oct. 1864, cost me upwards of $600, and a few days ago, I paid $16 a ton for range coal that in ordinary times cost me $8 or less, and paid 62¢ for coffee, which formerly cost me 20 cents a pound. With such prices which appear to be daily increasing, from the depreciated currency, and the increasing want of confidence in the ability of the government to meet its engagements, the paper money payed me by the government, will not, with the strictest economy on my part, support me more than six months.
>
> I little expected to be placed in this situation in my old age. It is trying enough. But I do not despond and think it must end in some way or other before the end of another year.[63]

The strain continued for the other Justices who did not have independent means, as indicated by their concern over the cost of living

---

[61] The document here summarized was copied for George Bancroft by M. L. York from an undated manuscript in Taney's hand. The draft here relied on is the typewritten manuscript, Taney's longhand manuscript not having been found. Longhand copies of this document and of Taney's legal tender opinion, discussed below, in the hand of a copyist, are included in a bound volume in the Perine Papers.

[62] R. B. Taney to D. M. Perine, Aug. 10, 1864, Perine Papers.

[63] R. B. Taney to D. M. Perine, Aug. 21, 1864, Perine Papers.

quarters while in Washington and about any delays in the payment of their salaries. Three days after the death of Chief Justice Taney, Justice Grier wrote to the Clerk of the Supreme Court, making no mention of the loss of his Chief but complaining about the failure of the Treasury Department to send a warrant for the quarter's salary due two weeks earlier. In expectation of prompt payment, he had overdrawn his account. Though his salary had been reduced one half in value, he could not live without it.[64]

With the highly controversial subject of the conscription of military manpower the Supreme Court was also only peripherally involved, but for a time there was a possibility that the constitutional question might have to be decided. To a limited extent the government resorted to conscription pursuant to an Act of July 17, 1862, which improved machinery for calling out the militia.[65] In the United States District Court in Philadelphia Judge John Cadwalader upheld the exercise of power under this act,[66] although not until Congress had enacted a more detailed and specific measure of March 3, 1863.[67]

In debating the latter measure Congress dealt with its implications in terms of the expansion of executive power and possible invasion of the prerogatives of the states through the conscription of state officials. The proposed measure carried from the beginning provisions to exempt the Vice President—there was no point in exempting the President since he was already Commander-in-Chief of the army and navy—and federal judges, the heads of executive departments, and the governors of the several states. Exemption of members of Congress and of the state legislatures was also discussed, but was not provided for.[68] The statute, covering ages from twenty to forty-five, provided for additional exemptions on the basis of dependents and on other grounds. Although the measure was set up to conscript the number of recruits the government might call for, it was in a sense an indirect stimulus to volunteering, in that a person drafted might secure exemption by sending in place of himself a nonconscripted person or, in lieu of a substitute, by paying to the government such an amount up to three hundred dollars as the Secretary of War might designate.[69]

---

[64] R. C. Grier to D. W. Middleton, Oct. 15, 1864, Clerk's Files.

[65] 12 Stat. 597. For discussion see Randall, *Constitutional Problems Under Lincoln*, 244–47, 252–56.

[66] McCall's Case, 15 Fed. Cas. 1225 (No. 8669) (D.C.E.D. Pa. 1863).

[67] 12 Stat. 731. See also 13 Stat. 6, 13 Stat. 379.

[68] See *Cong Globe*, 37th Cong., 3rd Sess. 976–87, 987–1002, 1260–75 (1863).

[69] This provision was repealed a year later. 13 Stat. 379. In the state of Maine various towns began voting in public meetings to raise the necessary sums to give immunity to drafted citizens. The Supreme Judicial Court of that state being empowered to give advisory opinions to the executive,

XXXVI: *Other Problems from the War*

Although doubtless necessary to the winning of the war, resort to conscription was unpopular for a variety of reasons. Throughout the North there were many who either sympathized with the South or at any rate felt no obligation to risk their lives and devote their energies to saving the Union. Conscription, furthermore, ran counter to prevailing beliefs in American liberty, and, beyond that, carried a stigma in that for many it implied a lack of courage and willingness to fight which were essential to effectiveness in battle. In the minds of legalistically trained persons, these objections were rationalized into constitutional or other legal objections. It was contended that the power to raise and support armies extended only to raising armies of volunteers and calling into federal service the militia of the several states. Coercion of state citizens was said to invade the militia rights of the states and the liberties of their citizens. In addition, since the Conscription Act carried various provisions as to means of conscription and exemptions, counsel for resisting conscripts found a variety of arguments for urging exemption of particular clients.

Given the varied grounds of objection to conscription, it is not surprising that there was widespread resistance. In New York City, and to a lesser extent elsewhere, draft riots brought temporary chaos and in some instances required for their suppression troops that ought to have been used for waging the war.[70] Many persons fled to escape detection, going abroad or to other parts of the country. Furthermore, since there was for some months no suspension of the privilege of the writ of habeas corpus applicable to drafted persons pursuant to the Habeas Corpus Act bearing the same date as the Conscription Act, federal and state judges, themselves sometimes hostile to the war and in any event living in communities or functioning as parts of governments that were hostile, heard many petitions for release.

On September 14, 1863, the President called a Cabinet meeting to discuss the advisability of suspending the privilege of the writ of habeas corpus with respect to persons seeking release from military service. The discussions were summarized in the diaries of two of the department heads present, Chase and Welles. With respect to action in the state courts, the Cabinet weighed the question whether it was better formally to suspend the writ or merely to direct military authorities to ignore it on the ground that the state courts had no jurisdiction in such matters. The President expressed determination to enforce the law in spite of anything the state courts might do. With respect to Chief

---

the governor asked for an official opinion whether a city or town had the power to pledge credit or raise money for such a purpose. The court replied that there was no power to use resources in this fashion. Opinion of the Justices of the Supreme Judicial Court, 52 Maine 596 (1863).

[70] Randall, *Constitutional Problems Under Lincoln*, 250–52.

Justice Lowrie of the Pennsylvania Supreme Court, who was one of the principal state court offenders, Lincoln remarked that if he and others continued to interfere he would send them after Vallandigham.[71] In the course of the discussion it was said that the two federal district judges in Pennsylvania, Cadwalader at Philadelphia and McCandless at Pittsburgh, had released persons far in excess of all the state courts put together.[72] When the Cabinet met again on the following day, Stanton, as described by Chase, "made a statement showing the great number of persons discharged by Habeas Corpus principally by the two Federal Judges Cadwalader and McCandless, and stated some very gross proceedings under color of judicial authority, manifestly intended to interfere with the recruiting and maintenance of the Army."[73]

The complaint of the military went not merely to actual instances of release but also to the right of a court to inquire at all into the validity of decisions of boards of enrollment. Although in an opinion handed down on September 9, 1863, Judge Cadwalader had upheld the constitutionality of the Conscription Act, he also held that board decisions as to exemption rights were reviewable by the courts in spite of a provision which was thought by some, and probably had been intended by Congress, to prevent frustration of recruitment by appeals to the courts.[74] The provost marshal general wrote to Stanton that "The necessity for having no appeal from the decision of the Board of Enrollment in questions of exemption is of the first importance to the military service and the word final used by the lawmakers in this instance seems to me to have been expressly intended to prevent the mischief arising from such appeal."[75] It was reported concerning Judge Cadwalader's court that habeas corpus cases of this kind were multiplying rapidly and bade fair to occupy much of the time of the court.[76] Presumably it was as a result of this situation that on September 15, 1863, the President did suspend the privilege of the writ of habeas corpus in this class of cases, among others.[77] In addition to issuing the proclamation the President seems to have sent General George Cadwalader to Philadelphia to talk with his brother, Judge John Cadwalader, about his damaging activities. The general thereafter wrote to the President that his brother would give him no further trouble.[78]

Supreme Court Justices on circuit appear to have been little in-

---

[71] *Diary of Gideon Welles*, Howard K. Beale, ed., I, 432.

[72] *Inside Lincoln's Cabinet: The Civil War Diaries of Salmon P. Chase*, David Donald, ed., 194.

[73] *Ibid.*, 195.

[74] Antrim's Case, 1 Fed. Cas. 1062 (No. 495) (D.C.E.D. Pa. 1863).

[75] James B. Fry to E. M. Stanton, 3 O.R. (3d) 794.

[76] Newspaper comment, reprinted in 3 O.R. (3d) 794.

[77] Lincoln, *Collected Works*, VI, 451–52.

[78] George Cadwalader to A. Lincoln, Sept. 17, 1863, 3 O.R. (3d) 919.

volved in conscription cases. The day after the President's proclamation of suspension was issued, and perhaps before it was generally circulated, Justice Nelson, at chambers in his home community at Cooperstown, New York, held in a habeas corpus case that a man who had been conscripted and then released because of his responsibility for dependents could not again be taken into custody if his draft board changed its mind about his rightful status.[79] Perhaps to give his opinion wider circulation, Justice Nelson later rewrote it and published it as an opinion of the Circuit Court for the Northern District of New York.[80]

In a case decided September 21, 1863, Judge McCandless, at Pittsburgh, gained the concurrence of Justice Grier. One Joseph Will had been indicted for obstructing an enrolling officer in the enforcement of the Conscription Act. The judge held that the statute provided no penalties for such obstruction, and even though the defendant had, as alleged, assaulted the enrollment officer, he was not guilty of an offense for which he could be prosecuted in that court. If a penalty clause was needed it would have to be supplied by Congress, and not by the court.[81]

Whatever their feelings about conscription, none of the federal judges seems to have cast doubt on the constitutionality of the statute. Indeed, it was said that, in one of the cases decided in Pennsylvania, Justice Grier had specifically affirmed it.[82] The Supreme Court of Pennsylvania, however, proceeded by a vote of three to two to declare the statute unconstitutional. The origin of the state case was in the application of three conscripted men to Justice George W. Woodward, a states' rights Democrat recently defeated for the governorship of the state, for injunctions against draft boards to prevent enforcement of the act. The application may have been filed before the date of the President's proclamation of suspension. Perhaps to protect himself politically and to get added weight for the decision, Justice Woodward asked his brethren to sit with him at the hearing, which was set for September 23, 1863. The United States Attorney was notified but he decided to ignore the hearing, presumably on the theory that, especially since the date of the proclamation of suspension, the state court had no jurisdiction in a habeas corpus case with respect to federal armed forces. The court proceeded with the case in the absence of government counsel.

The majority and minority opinions in the case were apparently given to the press early in October,[83] and then officially issued November 9, 1863. Chief Justice Lowrie, at that time running for reelection to the Pennsylvania Supreme Court, contended that conscription by the

---

[79] "*Ex Relatione* Daniel Irons," *New York Times*, Sept. 21, 1863.

[80] *In re* Irons, 13 Fed. Cas. 98 (No. 7076) (C.C.N.D. N.Y. 1863).

[81] United States v. Will, 28 Fed. Cas. 607 (No. 16697) (D.C.W.D. Pa. 1863).

[82] *New York Times*, Nov. 13, 1863.

[83] See *Pittsburgh L. J.*, 11:89–91, 97–99, 105–07, 113–15, 129–31, 1863.

federal government was inconsistent with the militia powers of the states, and unconstitutional. The act incorporated into the federal system every state civil officer except the governor. "Nothing is left that has any constitutional right to stand before the will of the federal government."[84] Justice Woodward found the great vice of the statute to be "an assumption that Congress may take away, not the state rights of the citizen, but the security and foundation of his state rights. And how long is civil liberty expected to last, after the securities of civil liberty are destroyed?"[85]

Justice James Thompson was part of the majority of three, and Justices William Strong and John M. Read, the former eventually to sit on the Supreme Court of the United States and the latter long ago an ignored nominee, dissented. The dissenters found in the war powers of the federal government sufficient authority to raise armies by conscription. As for the argument based on civil liberty, said Justice Strong:

> The argument was urged in a strange forgetfulness of what civil liberty is. In every free government the citizen or subject surrenders a portion of his absolute rights in order that the remainder may be protected and preserved. There can be no government at all where the subject retains unrestrained liberty to act as he pleases, and is under no obligation to the state. That is undoubtedly the best government which imposes the fewest restraints, while it secures ample protection to all under it. But no government has ever existed, none can exist, without a right to the personal military service of all its able-bodied men. The right to civil liberty in this country never included a right to exemption from such service.[86]

The New York Times was no doubt accurate in saying that the federal government would not recognize the jurisdiction of the state court in the case, that the decision had not the weight of straw. Its principal effect was to show that opposition to national authority reached even the highest and most sacred positions.[87] Even here the result was highly temporary. Chief Justice Lowrie was defeated in his campaign for reelection and was replaced by Daniel Agnew, who was more sympathetic to the war program. The new justice joined the two who had dissented, voting to dissolve the temporary injunctions that had been issued, with Justice Strong writing the opinion of the court.[88]

Although the constitutionality of the Conscription Act was not

---

[84] Kneedler v. Lane, 45 Pa. 238, 246 (1863).
[85] Ibid., 259.
[86] Ibid., 280.

[87] The New York Times, Nov. 13, 1863.
[88] 45 Pa. 295.

challenged before the Supreme Court during the Civil War, Chief Justice Taney, much of the time at his home because too ill or infirm to attend Court, could not help brooding about it. In the summer of 1863 he complained that "The supremacy of the military power over the civil, seems to be established; and the public mind has acquiesced in it and sanctioned it."[89] At some time during this period he undertook the writing of a draft opinion on the subject, as he had done with respect to the legal tender issue. Like the original majority in the Pennsylvania Supreme Court, he contended that the power of conscription by the federal government could destroy the power of the states with respect to their militia and disorganize the state governments by taking their civil officers, and was therefore unconstitutional. What was to become of the people of a state if their executive officers and judges were taken away and their courts of justice closed? While it was true that the power of the federal government pervaded the entire Union, it was to be remembered that state sovereignty also pervaded every part of the Union. The powers of the states were no less important to the happiness of the people than those exercised by the general government. Under the Constitution the people could not be presumed to have to choose between the anarchy produced by state paralysis on the one hand or an unlimited military despotism on the other.[90]

Always under consideration throughout the period of the war was the question of the most appropriate method of punishing persons disloyal to the Union. As already related, many whose guilt was primarily prospective were taken into military custody without formal charge and held in military prison. Again, some of those convicted of the crime of piracy were transferred from civil to military custody rather than formally punished, partly as a matter of preventing reprisals by the Confederacy. Beyond that, in many states large numbers of persons were indicted for treason, with resulting problems as to what to do about prosecutions, and district attorneys solicited from the Attorney General advice about seeking other indictments, or preventing them when grand juries were too rampant in their activities.[91]

In some areas the process of indictment for treason was turned into

---

[89] R. B. Taney to D. M. Perine, Aug. 6, 1863, Perine Papers.

[90] Philip G. Auchampaugh, ed., "A Great Justice on State and Federal Power. Being the Thoughts of Chief Justice Taney on the Federal Conscription Act," *Tyler's Historical and Genealogical Magazine*, 18:72, 1936. The Supreme Court did not deal with the constitutional question until the period of World War I, when it upheld the power of Congress in Selective Draft Law Cases, 245 U.S. 366 (1918).

[91] For summary discussion see Randall, *Constitutional Problems Under Lincoln*, 74–95.

a veritable crusade. In November, 1861, for example, the United States Marshal at Wheeling (in what was then still Virginia) made mention of about eight hundred indictments.[92] Hundreds who were rebels at heart, he contended, but who had committed no overt act, had been reclaimed by the awe-producing vigor displayed by the representatives of the government.[93] So great was the zeal for indictment on the part of grand juries that the district attorney for the western district of Virginia had to restrain them, and in some instances to refuse to permit them to assemble.[94]

As to prosecution of the persons indicted, the Attorney General was careful about giving advice, and he advised caution when he advised at all. In the autumn of 1861 he answered an inquiry from the district attorney in Baltimore by saying that personally he had no preference on the subject and had intended to leave it to the local officer. But since Reverdy Johnson, counsel for some of the accused, had asked that the cases might lie over, he would consent that the cases be continued.[95] A few months later he advised the district attorney in St. Louis not to try many treason cases and to try only those in which there was great probability of success. It was better to drop cases than to be beaten.[96] The same advice was repeated on other occasions.[97] He warned against making convicts into martyrs in the eyes of their partisans, and added shrewdly, "It is far better policy, I think, when you have the option to prosecute offenders for vulgar felonies and misdemeanors, than for *romantic* and *genteel* treason. The penitentiary will be far more effectual than the gallows."[98]

The federal statute on the subject of treason called for the death penalty. Prosecution was therefore an extremely serious matter. Because of Southern sympathy in the North, prosecutions were likely to be impeded by such sympathy among jurors, judges, or prosecutors. An unexpected difficulty developed, furthermore, with respect to indictments. The statute prescribed the penalty for any persons owing allegiance to the United States who "shall levy war against them, or shall adhere to their enemies, giving them aid and comfort within the United States or elsewhere."[99] Since many of the persons indicted took no direct part

---

[92] E. M. Norton to Edward Bates, Nov. 20, 1861, Attorney General Papers.

[93] E. M. Norton to Edward Bates, Nov. 30, 1861, Attorney General Papers.

[94] B. H. Smith to Edward Bates, May 16, 1862, Attorney General Papers.

[95] Edward Bates to William Meade Addison, Oct. 28, 1861, Attorney General's Letter Book B–4, 189.

[96] Edward Bates to James O. Broadhead, Apr. 10, 15, 16, 1862, Attorney General's Letter Book B–5, 62, 68–69, 70–71.

[97] See Edward Bates to Benjamin H. Smith, May 7, 1862, *ibid.*, 86.

[98] Edward Bates to R. J. Lackey, Jan. 19, 1863, *ibid.*, 331.

[99] I Stat. 112.

in military action against the United States but merely aided others who did so, the lawyers who drew indictments phrased them merely in terms of giving aid and comfort to the enemies of the United States. In an unreported decision handed down at Cincinnati in the spring of 1862, Justice Swayne held that domestic rebels were not "enemies" within the meaning of the Constitution and the statute.

The defendant, James W. Chenoweth, had purchased and delivered military supplies to the Confederacy. The indictment accused him of having purchased the supplies "with intent traitorously to deliver to the persons styling themselves as aforesaid said supplies and munitions of war." It stated that "in further prosecution of his traitorous adhering," he actually made the delivery. Former United States Senator George E. Pugh of Ohio, who was later to lead the defense in the *Vallandigham* case, here filed before Justice Swayne and Judge Leavitt a motion to quash the indictment on the ground that the meaning of terms in the treason statute was to be sought in the interpretation of the corresponding English statute on which it was based, and that in English law the enemies to which adherence was forbidden included only foreign enemies and not domestic persons engaged in insurrection or rebellion against their own government.

Although he gave indirect counsel to the prosecution by showing that the facts which constituted giving aid and comfort could as well be used in an indictment for levying war, Justice Swayne did hold that this particular indictment had to be quashed. The treason statute did not extend to giving aid and comfort to merely domestic enemies:

> We sit here to administer the law, not to make it. With the excitements of the hour, we, as Judges, have nothing to do. They cannot change the law nor affect our duty. Causeless and wicked as is this rebellion, and fearful as has been its cost already in blood and treasure, it is not the less our duty to hold the scales of justice, in all cases, with a firm and steady hand.[100]

Soon after Swayne's decision was handed down it played an extensive part in Congressional debate on a bill drafted to give the courts discretion to reduce the penalty for treason to fine and imprisonment.[101] The bill was calculated to promote convictions. Beyond that, it was calculated to get convictions of some offenders against whom it was not possible to fulfill the constitutional requirement of two witnesses to the

---

[100] United States v. Chenowith. Printed in *Washington National Intelligencer*, May 13, 1862. See *The New York Times*, May 16, 1862. See reference also to Justice Swayne's charge to a Detroit grand jury, *The New York Times*, June 28, 1862.

[101] *Cong. Globe*, 37th Cong., 2nd Sess. 2166–69, 3100, 3230 (1862).

same overt act: it prescribed fine and imprisonment for aiding the rebellion without labeling the offense as treason. As stated by Senator Daniel Clark of New Hampshire, "There may be cases where you cannot find more than one witness to the same overt act, where the man was clearly engaged in rebellion. You may convict him of the offense under the second section when you could not convict him of treason."[102]

Senator Lyman Trumbull of Illinois criticized the first section of the bill as "a provision simply to make treason easy."[103] He objected to giving judges power to reduce the sentence for treason, looking forward to the time when federal courts in Southern states would try Confederate leaders. The pardoning power of the President, he contended, provided all that might be needed in the way of clemency.[104] The statute was nevertheless enacted.[105]

With respect to the treason indictments found in Baltimore in 1861, the United States Attorney, William Meade Addison, contended that he had avoided the defect discovered in others in Ohio by Justice Swayne, and that the government could safely go to trial.[106] Nearly a year after the Attorney General had consented to their postponement, however, the cases were still pending. A newly appointed United States Attorney, William Price, wrote to the Attorney General that "You are aware that from the constitution of the Court, if the Chief Justice should be on the bench, the treason cases will have to be made very plain and conclusive if we expect a conviction."[107]

For some time thereafter, the sequence of events was determined by Chief Justice Taney's ill health, by his desire to prevent the trial of those indicted for treason in the prevailing atmosphere, and by his seeming determination to prevent their trial in a court on which he did not sit. On October 7, 1862, he wrote to the United States District Judge in Baltimore, William F. Giles, that his health would prevent his being present at the November term of the Circuit Court. Although each Circuit Court consisted of the Supreme Court Justice assigned to the circuit and the local district judge, it was specifically provided by statute that if the district judge should be absent, "such circuit court may consist of the said judge of the supreme court alone."[108] The statute did not say whether the Circuit Court might be held by the district judge sitting alone. Such a provision was thereafter made with respect to certain circuits, not including that of Maryland.[109] Then, in 1844, Congress sought to lighten the travel burden of Supreme Court Justices by limiting

---

102 *Ibid.*, 2169.
103 *Ibid.*, 2165.
104 *Ibid.*, 2172.
105 12 Stat. 589.
106 William Meade Addison to Edward Bates, June 5, 1862, Attorney

General Papers.
107 William Price to Edward Bates, Sept. 1, 1862, Attorney General Papers.
108 1 Stat. 334.
109 3 Stat. 554.

required attendance on circuit to once a year,[110] seeming clearly to imply that the district judge sitting alone could hold other terms of the Circuit Court. District judges did very extensively hold Circuit Courts sitting alone, and in 1858 Judge Giles had sat alone in a murder case in the Circuit Court for Maryland.[111]

In his letter to Judge Giles, however, Chief Justice Taney implied that the district judge sitting alone had no authority to try the treason cases, inferring that "the law intended to give the party standing on trial for his life the right to be heard before a Judge of the Supreme Court." He found further reason for this construction:

> If both Judges are present, any question that arises may be certified to the Supreme Court, and the party have the benefit of the judgment of the highest judicial tribunal in the United States. If the question should be a new one in criminal law and at all doubtful, no doubt the Circuit Court both Judges being present, could certify it to the Supreme Court. In a trial before the District Judge alone, the party has not the benefit of the judgment of any Judge of the Supreme Court, and cannot have his case certified to the Supreme Court. His fate must depend upon the District Judge, without appeal and without remission. I cannot think a just interpretation of the Act of Congress will author-ize the exercise of such a power by the District Judge.[112]

Judge Giles refrained from asserting his authority in the cases, probably holding much the same sympathies as the Chief Justice, and the cases were again postponed. Early in January, 1863, United States Attorney Price asked the Attorney General what to do about George P. Kane, former head of the Baltimore police, who in addition to under-going long detention by the military had been indicted for treason during the regime of Price's predecessor.[113] Bates replied, "Serious doubts are entertained here whether you could, at this time, safely go to trial in any treason case, in Baltimore, by reason of the supposed popular feeling and judicial bias."[114] Bates promised, however, to do all he could to shield Price against unjust assaults on account of the discharge of his judicial duties.

Price then wrote to Bates that he had been equipping himself to try the treason cases and had hoped to do so in part by using the notes

[110] 5 Stat. 676.
[111] W. Calvin Chesnut, *Some Ad-dresses . . . the By-Product of a Federal Judge*, 32–33.
[112] R. B. Taney to W. F. Giles, Oct. 7, 1861, Chase Papers, H.S.P. The letter is reproduced by Judge Ches-nut, in *Some Addresses . . . the By-Product of a Federal Judge*, 31–32.

See also William Price to Edward Bates, Oct. 15, 1862, Attorney Gen-eral Papers.
[113] William Price to Edward Bates, Jan. 5, 1863, Attorney General Papers.
[114] Edward Bates to William Price, Jan. 6, 1863, Attorney General's Letter Book B–5, 308.

taken by one of the grand jurors at the time of the indictment. The grand juror had seemed willing to provide the notes, but having some doubts about his duty had consulted Judge Giles, who told him he had no right to give to the district attorney information which he as a grand juror had sworn to keep secret.[115] It sounded strange to him as an old prosecutor, Bates replied, that it was improper for a grand juror to communicate to the prosecuting attorney the testimony on which an indictment was found. Still, since the law did not require the grand juror to keep notes, he did not know that the man was required by law to deliver notes he had kept for his own better information. Nevertheless he thought the refusal a "very suspicious fact."[116] He did not add that if it was suspicious with respect to the grand juror, the advice of Judge Giles was even more suspicious with respect to the bias of the court.

In March, 1863, Price wrote to Chief Justice Taney suggesting that because of the mass of business accumulating in the Circuit Court he designate some other member of the Supreme Court to take his place in the court in Baltimore. Such a designation could easily have been made, for Justice Wayne, deprived of access to his circuit during the war, was apparently without judicial responsibilities during many months of each year. Taney replied, however, that he hoped to perform the duties himself. He asked Judge Giles to adjourn the court until the following May, when the weather would be more favorable for traveling to Baltimore.[117]

Taney did take his place on the Circuit Court for the spring term, and aided in the disposal of a considerable amount of business. His work included an important decision reversing a decision of the District Court with respect to the confiscation of goods allegedly involved in trading with the enemy. To secure evidence for legal action, government agents had resorted to offensive techniques of entrapment, of a sort highly obnoxious to a Southern gentleman of Taney's character. He could see no possible benefit accruing to the government from such a seizure that would compare with the evil of countenancing in a court of justice the use of such procedures.[118] At the same term he held void a Treasury Department regulation resorted to in Maryland for the confiscation of goods involved in trading with the enemy.[119] But the court adjourned without trial of any of the treason cases.

Futile efforts continued to have the cases tried. Simon Cameron,

---

[115] William Price to Edward Bates, Jan. 16, 1863, Attorney General Papers.

[116] Edward Bates to William Price, Jan. 21, 1863, Attorney General's Letter Book B–5, 333.

[117] For an account of this correspondence see R. B. Taney to J. Mason Campbell, Mar. 18, 1863, Howard Papers.

[118] Claimants of . . . Merchandise v. United States, Tyler, Memoir of Roger Brooke Taney, 436–43.

[119] Carpenter v. United States, Baltimore Sun, June 20, 1863. Not officially reported.

Lincoln's first Secretary of War, became involved in that he seems to have been sued in a local Baltimore court for illegal imprisonment which took place under his orders. The case was transferred to the United States Circuit Court pursuant to the Act of March 3, 1863.[120] The Administration seems to have considered having members of the Baltimore police court arrested for treason as a countermeasure. Cameron advised against such a step but suggested that the treason cases already pending be brought to trial.[121] Attorney General Bates wrote to Price for a list of those indicted for treason in Baltimore, indicating particular interest in whether the persons suing Cameron were among them. Price's assistant sent a list of fifteen persons indicted, and replied that none of the persons suing Cameron was among them. He added, however, that the Chief Justice had asked his son-in-law to state that for reasons of health he would be unable to be present at the ensuing term of the Circuit Court: "In that event, from what he has previously announced in regard to the necessity of there being a full bench in the trial of treason cases, I suppose, although we are ready in most of them, they could not be tried at this term."[122]

Again in May, 1864, five months before his death, the Baltimore treason cases cropped up in the correspondence of the Chief Justice. In a letter to Justice Nelson he said that he did not know whether he would be able to go to Baltimore, but in any event he was determined not to allow the cases to be brought to trial at this time. The community was dominated by the military, and unexplained military arrests were being made almost every day. Maryland was in effect under martial law, and the civil authority was powerless. In view of the fear that witnesses, counsel, and jurors would have of military authority, the court could not assure a fair and impartial trial, or protect a defendant if he should be found not guilty. If acquitted, the defendant might be arrested by the military, even in the sight of the court, without the giving of a reason, and the court could not protect him or punish the offenders: "I will not place the judicial power in this humiliating position, nor consent thus to degrade and disgrace it, and if the District Attorney presses the prosecutions I shall refuse to take them up. I shall order the cases to be continued, and shall in a written opinion place my decision upon the ground above stated."[123]

Taney's son-in-law, J. Mason Campbell, reported to him a comment by Judge Giles that the district attorney might force the cases to trial. Taney replied to Campbell that he did not understand what Judge

---

[120] 12 Stat. 756.

[121] Simon Cameron to A. Lincoln, Nov. 2, 1863, Lincoln Papers.

[122] N. J. Thayer to Edward Bates, Nov. 3, 1863, Attorney General Papers.

[123] R. B. Taney to Samuel Nelson, May 8, 1864, from a typewritten copy provided by Judge Edward S. Delaplaine of Frederick, Maryland.

Giles meant. The treason cases could not be prosecuted because it was not now in the power of the court to protect the constitutional rights of the parties: "The treason cases cannot therefore be tried under present circumstances and I shall so write to my Brother Giles."[124]

The turmoil either in Baltimore or in the mind of the Chief Justice, or both, was alluded to in the last paragraph of his letter, where he expressed doubt that the bar would be in a proper state of mind to try the cases even if the opportunity were given. The draft had just taken place and the resulting militia were about to be called out. The attention of the whole community must be engrossed by these matters, and the bar be "but little fitted for a calm and full discussion of their cases. I think therefore I shall not come."[125]

In this way the Baltimore treason cases were postponed until after the death of the Chief Justice. By the time a new Chief Justice was appointed and assigned to the Fourth Circuit the end of the war was in sight, and continuance of the cases was permitted into a new era, when these, like most treason cases elsewhere, were dropped. Although there was not in all places the same judicial bias as that displayed by Taney, the great mass of cases elsewhere were likewise postponed from term to term and eventually dropped. One of the exceptions occurred in California, where trial was held before Justice Field and Judge Hoffman, even before the former had taken his seat on the Supreme Court. A group of men, headed by one Ridgely Greathouse and including Alfred Rubery, a young man who was a British subject, fitted out at San Francisco a vessel, the *J. B. Chapman*, to engage in privateering for the Confederacy. The vessel was stopped by federal officers as it got under way and its personnel charged with treason under the statute of July 17, 1862. Their position differed from that of the privateers on the East Coast, who were captured and tried for piracy but eventually transferred to military custody with the status of prisoners of war; the latter had committed their offenses on the high seas, while the members of the California expedition had been caught while engaged in a conspiracy within the borders of a loyal state.[126]

The case was tried at the October term, 1863. The trial lasted several weeks, and was carried on with the aid of testimony of two members of the party who were exempted from prosecution. The demonstration of guilt was obvious. In charging the jury, Justice Field took the same position as that earlier taken by Justice Swayne, that the enemies to whom the giving of aid and comfort was forbidden under the Treason

---

124 R. B. Taney to J. Mason Campbell, May 14, 1864, Howard Papers.
125 *Ibid.*
126 For a discussion of the geographical scope of the plot see Benjamin Alvord to Assistant Adjutant-General, May 28, 1863, 1 O.R. (1st) 462.

Clause of the Constitution were only foreign enemies, and did not include rebels within the country. But he held that giving aid and comfort to the rebellion constituted the offense of levying war, so that the defendants were subject both to this clause of the treason provision and to the later section of the same statute which forbade aiding the rebellion but did not classify the offense as treason.[127]

The defendants were found guilty and were sentenced to fine and imprisonment. When they began service of their sentences, efforts were already under way to secure their release. Even before the trial a War Department inquiry was made about the status of Rubery, evidently as a result of the intervention of friends in England. The general of whom the inquiry was made replied that Rubery was confined on Alcatraz Island, that the case was in the hands of the United States Attorney, and that no facts had been elicited showing Rubery to be an object of executive clemency. Furthermore, "The feeling here is strong against all such actions."[128]

When Justice Field arrived in Washington to take his position on the Supreme Court, Senator Charles Sumner called on him to say that John Bright, a warm friend of the United States and a member of Parliament whose constituency included the Rubery family, was seeking a pardon for the prisoner. The Senator asked how a pardon would be received in California. Justice Field replied that if given without explanation it would cause much irritation and anger, but that little complaint would be voiced if the pardon were based on fulfillment of an obligation to Bright as a friend of the United States.[129] The President therefore issued the pardon "especially as a public mark of the esteem held by the United States of America for the high character and steady friendship of the said John Bright."[130]

In the meantime, on December 8, 1863, the President had issued a proclamation of amnesty and pardon to rebels who would take a prescribed oath of allegiance.[131] The proclamation listed many exceptions, such as civil or diplomatic officers of the Confederacy, military and naval officers above a specified rank, and judicial and legislative officers of the United States who had left their positions to participate in the rebellion. In all probability the President did not intend the proclamation to extend to persons convicted of crime in the civil courts. But Senator John Conness of California immediately called on him to warn that the proclamation would be used as a basis for seeking release

---

[127] United States v. Greathouse, 26 Fed. Cas. 18 (No. 15254) (C.C.N.D. Calif. 1863).

[128] G. Wright to E. M. Stanton, June 1, 1863, 5 O.R. (2d) 726.

[129] George C. Gorham, *Biographical Notice of Stephen J. Field*, 44–45.

[130] Pardon of John Rubery, Dec. 16, 1863, Lincoln, *Collected Works*, VII, 71.

[131] *Ibid.*, 53.

of the criminals.[132] So also did Justice Field. It was said that the President promised to issue a supplemental proclamation to prevent release of prisoners in this and similar cases,[133] but before he could do so they had applied for a writ of habeas corpus to Judge Hoffman, sitting alone in the Circuit Court.

Judge Hoffman found that the prisoners came within the group of persons included in the proclamation and were not excluded by the exceptions. He relied on a relatively recent decision of the Supreme Court for the position that the President, who had the power to pardon outright, had also the power to issue conditional pardons,[134] as in this instance. He admitted that if the President had had the circumstances of this case in mind when he issued the proclamation he might have phrased it differently, but held that as the proclamation was phrased, the prisoners were entitled to release.[135] It was said that the facts concerning the release of the "pirates" were submitted to the Justices of the Supreme Court and to the War Department, but by that time it was too late to do anything about it.[136]

So it was that in many instances the Supreme Court and the lower federal courts dealt during the war haltingly and incompletely with problems growing out of the war. The hampering effect of the conflict upon effective judicial action was always apparent. Some of the problems were to linger with the courts for years to come in the form of seemingly endless litigation, helping to mold the postwar history of the Supreme Court.

---

[132] John Conness to A. Lincoln, Feb. 17, 1864, Lincoln Papers.
[133] New York Times, Feb. 18, 1864.
[134] Ex parte Wells, 18 How. 307 (1856).

[135] In re Greathouse, 10 Fed. Cas. 1057 (No. 5741) (C.C.N.D. Calif. 1864).
[136] New York Times, Mar. 21, 1864.

CHAPTER XXXVII

The End of the Taney Regime

THE TANEY PERIOD in the history of the Supreme Court could be said to end on the day of his death, October 12, 1864. Yet in a sense that period showed signs of approaching its close some years before. On the other hand, through the lives and sentiments of a minority of brethren who had long served with him, the period continued in part for some years after his death.

In terms of national politics, the transition away from the Taney Court began with the election of Abraham Lincoln, nearly four years before the Chief Justiceship was vacated. On the Court itself the transition came with the deaths of Justices Daniel and McLean and the resignation of Justice Campbell, and their replacement by Republicans with at least moderately abolitionist sympathies. The transition period saw the resignation of Benjamin C. Howard as Reporter and the breaking of this Baltimore connection with the Court, his brief replacement by Jeremiah S. Black, an ex-administrator from the Buchanan regime, and then a further shift to John William Wallace of Pennsylvania, who had little connection with the old order. It saw the death of William Thomas Carroll of the Maryland Carroll family, who had been Clerk of the Court since 1827, and his replacement by Daniel W. Middleton, a subordinate in his office.

From 1861 to 1864 Taney spent most of his time at his rented home at 23 Indiana Avenue in Washington, making occasional trips to Baltimore to hold Circuit Court or to visit his relatives there. As his feebleness increased he drew closer to members of his family and a few intimate friends, and saw less and less of the general public. He employed as his clerk at his home his grandson, R. B. Taney Campbell, the son of his eldest daughter and J. Mason Campbell. He made the arrangement partly for the benefit of the young man, and partly for his own. "I should even feel that his presence would be of real service to me," he wrote, "for I often copy a good deal of my own rough writings, and would be glad to have Taney here to do it for me, and to read to me some times by gaslight, as my own eyes are not as good as they once were."[1]

In 1864 R. B. Taney Campbell was admitted to the bar and prepared to go into practice with his father in Baltimore. His grandfather wrote him a congratulatory letter with some professional advice:

I congratulate you upon your admission to the Bar of the Superior Court. But you will not I am sure consider your labors as a student ended with your admission. You have a new field of labor to begin. So far you have seen the decisions of the court upon a certain state of facts. But in the cases that will come before you in practice, you will hardly find any case in the books exactly like it. And it must now be your study, to find the principle upon which the case in the books was decided and see how far the different circumstances in the case before you will affect the principle, decided in the books—and this is not always an easy matter to a young practitioner. . . . You must study your case yourself and be self reliant, but when you have formed an opinion consult your father, and conference will show you whether you have fallen into errors.[2]

Divorcement from war issues proved impossible. In addition to the involvements already discussed there were many others. Major Richard T. Allison, one of his sons-in-law, served in the Confederate army. When a grandson of General Charles Eager Howard, of Revolutionary War fame, said goodbye to him at leaving for the same army, Taney replied that the circumstances under which he was going were not unlike those under which his grandfather had gone into the Revolution.[3]

He read widely and tried to keep posted on governmental and scientific activities at home and abroad. He read a number of literary

---

[1] R. B. Taney to J. Mason Campbell, May 23, 1861, Howard Papers. In the same papers is a certificate signed by the Chief Justice Sept. 9, 1862, that R. B. T. Campbell was his clerk, living with him, and that he had been appointed to that position in May, 1861. A letter of Sept. 10, 1862, deals with this certificate. It may or may not have had something to do with the young man's draft status.

A printed page descriptive of a J. H. Benton sale of the American Art Association in 1920, on file in the manuscript division of the New York Public Library, refers to a portrait of the Chief Justice inscribed to his grandson. A note says that he has received photographs of his daughter Maria and her husband and hung them in his bedroom: "Ask your father and dear mother to send me theirs, as I wish to place them together and by the side of Mr. Allison and Maria."

[2] R. B. Taney to R. B. Taney Campbell, June 4, 1864, Howard Papers.

[3] Bernard C. Steiner, *Life of Roger Brooke Taney*, 503.

reviews from England and Scotland, the *London Times*, New York papers, Washington papers,[4] one or more Catholic journals, and apparently such Baltimore papers as could be delivered to him. Writing to J. Mason Campbell he expressed bitter resentment at the suppression of newspapers and inspection of the mails:

> I am thankful that my taste for reading, and a cheerful temper remain unabated. My newspaper reading is indeed a good deal curtailed, for although it may be difficult to say what are the boundaries of the President's power at this day, or whether it has any boundaries, I am not willing to admit that he has a *right* to prescribe what newspapers I shall read, although I know from experience that he has the *power* to prescribe what I shall not read.
>
> I fear the detectives will think themselves hardly paid for their trouble by its contents when they have opened and read and resealed this letter.[5]

He was angry when his name was dropped from the list of subscribers of certain Baltimore newspapers. They might restore his name or not, as they pleased, he wrote to his grandson, with instructions to show his letter to the publishers. He would not subscribe again, either now or hereafter.[6]

Taney was deeply offended by the military occupation of Baltimore. When there in the spring of 1863 to hold Circuit Court, he forbore for a time to write to his friend David M. Perine, who lived in the Homeland area which was then far beyond the suburbs. "I did not write to you while the streets of Baltimore were barricaded," he wrote during the summer of the Confederate invasion of Pennsylvania, "for I was not sure that you would be able to come into town to receive your letters and attend to your business as usual. But as the alarm has blown over, I suppose things are restored to their former condition, and my letters reach you as usual."[7]

An inveterate smoker of long, black cigars even when reading in bed, he was concerned lest the war cut off his supply, and wrote repeatedly to relatives and friends in Baltimore to secure replenishment of his stock. He could get along very well without the news of which he was deprived, he wrote, "but to deprive me of cigars is quite another matter, and my reviews and magazines would be hardly readable without the help of a pleasant cigar. You know I can smoke none but Shumacher's Principes, and my stock is getting low, and will hardly

---

[4] John B. Ellis, *Sights and Secrets of the National Capital*, 267.

[5] R. B. Taney to J. Mason Campbell, Sept. 13, 1861, Howard Papers.

[6] R. B. Taney to R. B. Taney Campbell, Oct. 29, 1861, Howard Papers.

[7] R. B. Taney to D. M. Perine, July 9, 1863, Perine Papers.

last the week."[8] He hoped the detectives who read and resealed his letter would not suppose his cigars contraband because, although manufactured in Cuba, they might be made of Virginia tobacco.[9]

His last box of cigars was getting low, he wrote to J. Mason Campbell a month before his death. He asked Campbell to see whether his old cigar merchant had any smokeable cigars at a reasonable price and asked for samples of smoking tobacco and a pipe, fearing that the effort to quit smoking at his time of life would be too much for him.[10] But five days later he wrote that he had given up the notion of pipe smoking, "not from the fear of injuring the few stumps I have left, but because it has occurred to me since I wrote my former letter that all the pipe tobacco will now be of northern growth, and very unpalatable to one who is accustomed to Spanish cigars."[11]

His physician advised him to drink "every day at dinner two or three glasses of pure old sherry wine." He asked his friend Perine to give advice as to brands and send some by express.[12] Perine sent a case, and then sent more. Out of one case of a dozen bottles, half were broken. Taney was angered, suspecting that the breakage had been deliberate.[13] Although embarrassed at his complaints when he discovered that the wine was a gift and not a purchase, he explained, "I confess I was greatly provoked, for the breakage was evidently wanton and wilful, and I imputed it to that feeling of some agent of the Express which in these evil times overpowers all sense of right and sense of duty."[14]

Taney's financial problems were intensified when, early in the war period, the legislature of Virginia forbade payment of interest on its securities to holders in the nonseceding states. When friends in Richmond proposed to make an exception in the case of the Chief Justice, all of whose capital was invested there, he declined to be the recipient of special favors. While it was true that the money was owed to him, his friends had overlooked the interpretation which baser minds might put on the offer.[15] It was this freezing of his capital, as well as wartime inflation and depreciation of the newly issued paper currency, that kept him in financial difficulties.

During his final years as during his earlier ones, health was a major subject of his correspondence. He had to have a truss made in

---

[8] R. B. Taney to J. Mason Campbell, Sept. 18, 1861, Howard Papers.

[9] R. B. Taney to J. Mason Campbell, Sept. 13, 1861, Howard Papers.

[10] R. B. Taney to J. Mason Campbell, Sept. 8, 1864, Howard Papers.

[11] R. B. Taney to J. Mason Campbell, Sept. 13, 1864, Howard Papers.

[12] R. B. Taney to D. M. Perine, Aug. 12, 1863, Perine Papers.

[13] R. B. Taney to D. M. Perine, Aug. 20, 25, Sept. 6, 18, 24, 29, Oct. 3, 1863, Perine Papers.

[14] R. B. Taney to D. M. Perine, Oct. 6, 1863, Perine Papers.

[15] R. B. Taney to D. M. Perine, July 18, 1861, Samuel Tyler, *Memoir of Roger Brooke Taney*, 481–82.

Baltimore and sent to him.[16] He had taken a warm bath in salted water, he wrote in the summer of 1861, and "All the organs of life became over excited," so that he was unable to sleep.[17] Illness after illness found its way into the records, indicating how rarely and for what brief periods he was able to attend Court. Even if it had been possible to go to some Virginia watering place for summer recuperation as he had done before the war, he was too feeble to do so. He could rarely make even personal visits. Both he and his daughter Ellen, he wrote to Perine in the summer of 1863, were such invalids that they were "fit for no place but home and feel that we ought not to sadden the homes of our friends by bringing to them our daily aches and pains."[18]

In appearance his frame, always flat-chested, was stooped and warped. His hair was allowed to grow long and shaggy and his face was deeply lined. Yet his eyes were always bright and alert, and he dressed becomingly and with dignity.[19] For all his want of energy, his courtesy and friendliness in the treatment of people with whom he came into direct contact bridged many barriers. Attorney General Bates, for example, despite his part in legal activities repugnant to the Chief Justice, came to feel deep friendship and respect for him.[20] Of the new Justices, Miller, at least, could say that before their first term of association had passed, "I more than liked him; I loved him."[21] To his older associates on the Court, who sympathized with his position, Taney confided his conviction of the impossibility of doing justice in treason trials in the Baltimore atmosphere of the war period. He confined to very close personal friends his lament that the Court would never again be the Court as he had known it—that he saw no ground for hope that it would ever be restored to the authority and rank which the Constitution intended to confer upon it.[22]

In April, 1864, Attorney General Bates noted the absence on account of illness of Taney, Wayne, Grier, and Catron, and predicted that the first three would never sit again.[23] On October 12, 1864, at the age of eighty-seven years and some months, death came to the Chief

---

[16] R. B. Taney to J. Mason Campbell, Sept. 10, 1860, Howard Papers.

[17] R. B. Taney to D. M. Perine, July 11, 1861, Perine Papers.

[18] R. B. Taney to D. M. Perine, July 9, 1863, Perine Papers.

[19] See John B. Ellis, *Sights and Secrets of the National Capital*, 266; Mrs. J. A. Logan, *Thirty Years in Washington*, 413.

[20] "The Diary of Edward Bates," Howard K. Beale, ed., *Annual Report of the American Historical Association for the Year 1930*, 4:204–05, 243, 354–55, 358, 400, 418–19, 1933.

[21] Charles Fairman, *Mr. Justice Miller and the Supreme Court*, 52.

[22] R. B. Taney to D. M. Perine, Aug. 6, 1863, Perine Papers.

[23] "The Diary of Edward Bates," Howard K. Beale, ed., *Annual Report of the American Historical Association for the Year 1930*, 4:354–55, 1933.

Justice, of the intestinal ailment that had long plagued him.[24] "His mind was always so clear and strong," wrote his eldest daughter to a friend, "that I think it made us lose sight of his great age, and he had recovered from so many attacks of the same kind, that we hoped to the very last."[25] Far and wide, newspapers announced the death of the once admittedly great man who in the press of wartime events and because of the obscurity of his way of life was tending already to be forgotten.

At a meeting held on October 14 the President's Cabinet discussed what they ought to do about attending the funeral. Seward thought it his duty to attend the service in Baltimore but not the burial at Frederick, where Taney was to be interred in a Catholic cemetery beside his mother and not far from the Protestant cemetery where his wife and daughter had been buried. Bates announced that he would go to Frederick as well, while Welles, who had had no association with the Chief Justice, felt no obligation to participate in the funeral of the man responsible for the Dred Scott decision.[26]

Taney had asked that his funeral ceremony be conducted quietly and with a minimum of display. Soon after six o'clock on the morning of October 15, friends, relatives, dignitaries, and onlookers began to assemble at his home on Indiana Avenue. "The corpse was encased in a handsome mahogany coffin, covered with black cloth and silver mounted, bearing on the breast a silver plate, with the inscription of the name and age of the deceased."[27] As Taney had submerged personal feelings to call on the President, so here was the President at this ceremony, along with Seward, Bates, and William Dennison who had supplanted Montgomery Blair as Postmaster General. After the mourners had filed by for a last look at the deceased the coffin was closed and a procession formed for the short trip to the railroad station, the whole proceeding organized by the always managerial Marshal Ward Hill Lamon. From reports it would seem that only Lamon and the Clerk, D. W. Middleton, were there to represent the Court on which Taney had served for more than twenty-eight years. His brethren were presumably riding circuit in distant parts of the country except for Justice Wayne, whose absence—if indeed he was absent—was unexplained.

---

[24] *New York Tribune*, Oct. 15, 1864.

[25] Anne Arnold Campbell to Margaret Birnie, Oct. 31, 1864, Taney House, Frederick, Maryland.

[26] *Diary of Gideon Welles*, Howard K. Beale, ed., 176–77. Welles' opinion of the Chief Justice seems to have improved when he heard the report that Taney had spoken highly of his administration of the Navy Department: "This was high praise from a quarter that makes it appreciated. The Chief Justice could, as well as any man, form a correct opinion, and in giving it he must have been disinterested." *Ibid.*, 184.

[27] *Frederick Examiner*, quoted in *Baltimore American*, Oct. 20, 1864.

The President and Seward and Dennison went with the procession to the station and remained until the departure of the train, and Bates accompanied the group to Frederick, where the funeral was held in the little Catholic church which Taney had helped to build, and which was now draped in mourning. There gathered many friends and descendants of friends who had known the deceased during the years he lived in Frederick and established his reputation at the bar. A requiem mass was sung, a funeral sermon was preached, and the final journey to the cemetery was made[28]—and a life and an era had come to an end.

The net estate of the Chief Justice, who had given his entire adult life to the practice of law and service on the bench, was appraised at less than nineteen thousand dollars. Within this estimate the value of twelve thousand five hundred dollars in Virginia securities was put at a little more than three thousand dollars.[29] The estate would not have been large, therefore, even had these securities been redeemable at their face value. Pursuant to his will, dated April 28, 1859, the estate, apart from a few specified gifts, was put in trust for his heirs,[30] among whom at least two of his daughters were almost completely dependent on his support.

The amount of the estate was obviously inadequate to serve its purpose. On February 11, 1871, a meeting of the bar of the Supreme Court was held in the Supreme Court room to provide for the raising of additional funds. Present were Montgomery Blair, William M. Evarts, J. M. Carlisle, Matthew H. Carpenter, and others. An unrecorded amount was raised.[31] It was said that David Dudley Field contributed five hundred dollars each year for a number of years, up to a total of nine thousand dollars.[32] Solicitation was evidently not extended as far as was originally intended. In 1883 Justice Horace Gray, successor to Justice Clifford, lamented the fact that the movement of the bar had not enabled judges and lawyers throughout the country "to testify their respect for his memory and eminent public services by making a suitable provision for his family."[33]

---

[28] *Ibid.* See also *Washington National Intelligencer*, Oct. 17, 1864. and other papers of the time. For obituarial bibliography and summary thereof see Charles Warren, *The Supreme Court in United States History*, II, 388–98.

[29] Baltimore Administrative Accounts, Folio 372, Book 77.

[30] Baltimore Wills, Folio 126, Book 32.

[31] *The Taney Fund, Proceedings of the Meeting of the Bar of the Supreme Court of the United States*, (1871).

[32] See "An Anecdote of David Dudley Field," *Am. L. Rev.*, 28:584, 1894.

[33] Horace Gray to Frank M. Etting, Jan. 7, 1883, Etting Collection.

In Washington, Baltimore, and many other cities members of the bar met to adopt resolutions in honor of the memory of the deceased Chief Justice. In the Supreme Court itself Justice Wayne spoke for the surviving brethren, doing so, it was said, "in a low tremulous voice."[34] In addition to the conventional though deeply felt words about learning, professional skill, and kindliness, Wayne noted the fact that both Marshall and Taney had come to the Chief Justiceship from high political office and were leaders in support of Administration politics. Both had been assailed as a result of party resentments, but both had received generous recantations from men who came to respect their judicial performances. It was a happy occurrence that the two of them had headed the Supreme Court for a total of sixty-three years.[35]

Of the others who eulogized the late Chief Justice on such occasions, former Justice Curtis, speaking in Boston, spoke most revealingly. Taney's power of subtle analysis, he said, exceeded that of any man he ever knew. It was a power not without its dangers, but in this instance it was balanced by common sense and great experience in practical business. The great qualities of his mind and character had been most fully displayed in the conference room, where "his dignity, his love of order, his gentleness, his caution, his accuracy, his discrimination, were of incalculable importance."[36]

Judge Curtis remarked that while in the time of Taney's predecessor the practice of the Court was understood to have been somewhat loosely administered, the crowding of the docket in the Taney period and Taney's natural aptitude in such matters had led to the reform of the system. He had made himself an authority on the jurisdiction of the Court, which was a matter exceedingly involved. In that connection it was to be remembered that, as between the United States and the several states, "questions of jurisdiction were questions of power."[37]

Although it was partly because of conditions of health that Chief Justice Taney had written a lesser proportion of the opinions of the Court on substantive issues than his predecessor, Curtis thought there was another reason: "He was as absolutely free from the slightest trace of vanity and self-conceit as any man I ever knew. He was aware that many of his associates were ambitious of doing this conspicuous part of their joint labor. The preservation of the harmony of the members of the Court, and of their good-will to himself, was always in his mind. And I have not the least doubt that these considerations often influenced

---

[34] Alexander A. Lawrence, *James Moore Wayne*, 192.
[35] 2 Wall. xii (1864).

[36] Quoted in Tyler, *Memoir of Roger Brooke Taney*, 512.
[37] *Ibid.*, 514.

him to request others to prepare opinions, which he could and otherwise would have written."[38]

Attorney General Bates said of Taney that "He was a man of great and varied talents; a model of a presiding officer; and the last specimen within my knowledge, of a graceful and polished old fashioned gentleman." Although Bates deplored the Dred Scott decision and its effect in dimming the luster of Taney's fame as a lawyer and judge, he thought that it would not and should not long tarnish his otherwise well-earned fame.[39]

Within the secession area, an editor commented that Taney had watched at the cradle of the Constitution and also followed its hearse.[40] Of Northern papers with definitely Northern sympathies, but nevertheless with some sense of responsibility to Taney's work as a whole, *The New York Times* provided a fairly typical example. It remarked that the disturbance of old associations at this time was all the greater because it happened at the very height of the conflict with which was linked the most important act of Taney's judicial life. It said of him that he was "a man of pure moral character, and of great legal learning and acumen. But for the Dred Scott decision, he would have been said to have nobly sustained his high office." The long editorial rethreshed the issues of that case and condemned judicial intervention in the solution of political issues. It noted that Taney's removal by death would mark the end of an epoch in the history of the Court, and it predicted approvingly that the place would be filled with someone in perfect accord with Union principles.[41]

The comments of hostile critics were sometimes cruel. "You have observed that Archbishop Hughes is gone to heaven," had written Francis Lieber, eminent authority on international and military law and onetime friend of Justice Story. "If he had only taken Chief Justice Taney along with him."[42] Did Lieber know, replied Henry W. Halleck, of Benjamin F. Wade's joke about the Chief Justice? Wade, the most profane man in Congress, said he used to pray for Taney every night during the Buchanan Administration that he might live until his successor could be appointed not by Buchanan but by the next President. But he had overdone the praying, and now he feared that his prayers

---

[38] *Ibid.*, 515. This document is preserved also as "Character and Public Services of Chief Justice Taney," in George T. Curtis, *A Memoir of Benjamin Robbins Curtis*, II, 336.

[39] "The Diary of Edward Bates," Howard K. Beale, ed., *Annual Report of the American Historical Association for the Year 1930*, 4:418, 1933.

[40] *Richmond Examiner*, Oct. 19, 1864.

[41] *New York Times*, Oct. 14, 1864.

[42] Francis Lieber to Henry W. Halleck, Jan. 6, 1864, Lieber Papers.

might carry Taney through Lincoln's Administration as well. If the Lord would forgive him, he would never pray for a Chief Justice again![43]

"This moment I learn that Taney is dead," wrote Lieber to Charles Sumner on October 13. "I suppose you will start at once for Washington to prevent wrong directions." He thought gratitude should be shown practically for God's having removed this fearful incubus.[44] "The Hon. old Roger B. Taney has earned the gratitude of his country by dying at last," George Templeton Strong wrote in his diary. "Better late than never. . . . Even should Lincoln be defeated, he will have time to appoint a new Chief Justice, and he cannot appoint anybody worse than Taney."[45]

"So old Taney is at last dead," mused Charles Francis Adams, Jr. With this victory in the realm of the judiciary, whereby Taney would be replaced by some such Administration man as Chase, and with legislative and executive departments won through elections, he saw the whole government coming within the control of forces that would work together in harmony. In any event the "darling wish of Taney's last days" would be unrealized, in that he would be unable to put the veto on the law of the Proclamation of Emancipation.[46]

In 1860, writing to Martin Van Buren about the struggle with the Bank of the United States in earlier years but thinking, no doubt, about the current sectional crisis, Taney had included the phrase, "a multitude of such evil spirits will be sure to gather about your grave and mine."[47] Although the evil spirits tended to leave Van Buren to oblivion, they did indeed hover a long time over the grave of Taney, and indeed have not even yet completely departed. In connection with a meeting of the bar in Philadelphia to do honor to the departed Chief Justice, John William Wallace, the recently appointed Reporter of the Supreme Court, wrote to the Clerk that it had been disappointing:

> We had a meeting of the bar here about him. The thing had a party complexion however; as every thing up here, now has unfortunately: and it came to less than one could have desired in regard to the memory of a Chief Justice of the United States.[48]

---

[43] H. W. Halleck to Francis Lieber, Jan. 11, 1864, Lieber Papers. See also *Complete Works of Abraham Lincoln*, John G. Nicolay and John Hay, eds., IX, 386.

[44] Francis Lieber to Charles Sumner, Oct. 13, 1864, Lieber Papers.

[45] *Diary of George Templeton Strong: The Civil War*, Allan Nevins, ed., III, 500.

[46] *A Cycle of Adams Letters*, Worthington Chauncey Ford, ed., II, 205–06.

[47] R. B. Taney to Martin Van Buren, May 8, 1860, Van Buren Papers.

[48] John William Wallace to D. W. Middleton, Oct. 27, 1864, Clerk's Files.

The same "evil spirits" revealed themselves in the Senate early in 1865 when the Judiciary Committee reported a bill, already passed by the House of Representatives without discussion, to appropriate money for a bust of the late Chief Justice to be placed in the Supreme Court room. Charles Sumner, grown more bitter and vindictive with the passing years, objected "that now an emancipated country should make a bust to the author of the Dred Scott decision." Lyman Trumbull of Illinois, who had reported the bill, himself no friend of slavery or the Chief Justice, replied hotly that a man who had presided over the Supreme Court for more than a quarter of a century and added reputation to the character of the judiciary of the United States throughout the world, was not to be hooted down by an exclamation that the country was to be emancipated. No man was infallible, and Taney was a great and learned and able man.[49]

Sumner, a master of vituperative utterance, leaped to the challenge: "Let me tell the Senator that the name of Taney is to be hooted down the page of history. Judgment is beginning now; and an emancipated country will fasten upon him the stigma which he deserves. The Senator says that he for twenty-five years administered justice. He administered justice at last wickedly, and degraded the judiciary of the country, and degraded the age."[50]

Reverdy Johnson, a lifelong friend of Taney who as a volunteer had argued in the Dred Scott case, leaped to the defense of the mind and character of a great man, and reminded the Senate that Taney had been but one of the majority in the Dred Scott case. James A. McDougall of California protested at Sumner's rude remarks and asserted that Sumner had not been worthy to stand at the door of Taney's chamber. Sumner stormed back that Jeffreys, Chief Justice and Chancellor of England, famous for his talents as for his crimes, had not found a niche in Westminster Hall. He had been left to the judgment of history. "I insist that Taney shall be left in sympathetic companionship."[51]

John P. Hale, always an outspoken and undisciplined critic of the Supreme Court, alluded to Taney's appointment as a result of the struggle with the Bank of the United States. He had hoped that Taney would have done something to redeem his memory, but throughout the ages Taney and the Dred Scott decision would be linked: "The name of Dred Scott will bring up Roger B. Taney, and the name of Roger B. Taney will bring up Dred Scott." He was unwilling to see the name of Taney honored along with the names of former Chief Justices, Jay and

---

[49] *Cong. Globe*, 38th Cong., 2nd Sess. 1012 (1865).

[50] *Ibid.*

[51] *Ibid.*, 1012–13.

Marshall, who had been truly worthy.[52] Benjamin F. Wade, who had deplored the effectiveness of his prayers for Taney's survival, joined in the fray. To him, everything said in behalf of Taney's legal ability only heightened his guilt for his one outstanding decision: "I am not here to criticise the general course of his decisions; I know nothing about them; I care nothing about them, because this one decision was so palpably wrong in point of law, and so contrary to the common sense, the common judgment, and the common propriety of mankind, that it has met with universal condemnation; and no attempt of the Senate to prop it up ... will have any other effect than to make the infamy of the decision more lasting and conspicuous."[53]

Throughout the remainder of his own life Sumner was able to prevent the appropriation of money for a bust of Taney, which to him suggested representing him as a saint—if, indeed, any further attempt was made to that end. At the death of Salmon P. Chase, Taney's successor, an appropriation was made for busts of the two men without controversy. Other busts and statues and honors were arranged for from time to time, but the controversy continued over the man's place in history. Taney's friend Samuel Tyler wrote an authorized biography which displayed an obvious bias in behalf of its subject. Most of the history involving the sectional struggle, however, was written in the North, from Northern sources, with Northern bias. A leading example was John W. Burgess who, writing at Columbia University in 1897, took it as a matter of course that history must be written by Northern men because the North was in the main right. No concessions should be made to the Southern position: "The time has come when the men of the South should acknowledge that they were in error in their attempt to destroy the Union, and it is unmanly in them not to do so."[54] And again, "The South must acknowledge its error as well as its defeat in regard to these things, and that, too, not with lip service, but from the brain and the heart and the manly will, before any real concord in thought and feeling, any real national brotherhood, can be established."[55]

It is not surprising that disinterested appraisal of the work of the Supreme Court and of its members during the Taney period was slow in coming. It was not until well into the twentieth century that constitutional histories, histories of the Supreme Court, biographies, and other studies attempted more objective valuation. The change in mood and attitude was illustrated in a speech delivered by Chief Justice Charles Evans Hughes. The occasion was that of the unveiling of a

---

[52] *Ibid.*, 1013–15.
[53] *Ibid.*, 1016.

[54] John W. Burgess, *The Middle Period, 1817–1858*, x.
[55] *Ibid.*, xi.

bust of Chief Justice Taney at Frederick, Maryland, where his home is maintained as a national shrine. Chief Justice Hughes summarized the Taney contribution through decisions in the fields of contracts, commerce, admiralty, taxation, federal-state relations, war powers in relation to civil liberties, and other areas. He concluded:

> With the passing of the years, and the softening of old asperities, the arduous service nobly rendered by Roger Brooke Taney has received its fitting recognition. He bore his wounds with the fortitude of an invincible spirit. He was a great Chief Justice.[56]

The contribution of the Taney Court, in the fields discussed by Chief Justice Hughes, is to be found deeply embedded in the day-to-day work of the Court, work which took place at what Justice Holmes later called "the quiet of the storm centre."[57] By contrast with the work of the same tribunal in various other periods, the essence of its contribution was seldom focused in eloquent philosophical statement from the Bench. The Taney Court was peculiarly unphilosophical. Theoretical assumptions lay always in the background for the determination of specifics, but the generalizations which illuminate assumptions and specifics were for the most part highly constricted. This sparseness of the kind of philosophical richness found in other periods in the opinions of Justices such as Marshall, Field, Holmes, Brandeis, Black, Frankfurter, and others was attributable to many factors. As exemplified by Taney's abandonment of the custom of delivering broadly educational charges to grand juries, it tended to be assumed that the federal constitutional system was now generally understood so that the earlier forms of judicial explanation were unnecessary. The government was now no longer experimental but was a going concern. It so happened, furthermore, that the men appointed to the Taney Court, like many of those appointed in other periods, were little given to generalization beyond the needs of particular cases, and that the increasing pressures of day-to-day activities tended to discourage philosophical expansiveness. Finally, philosophic caution may have been dictated in part by the steady drift of the nation toward the "irrepressible conflict," which few judges desired and none of reputation dared publicly to advocate but which imported questions that any profoundly philosophical treatment of critical constitutional issues would have had to take into account.

True, the Court dealt with the issues of American federalism, the respective dimensions of state and federal powers, the rights of property,

---

[56] Charles Evans Hughes, "Roger Brooke Taney," *A.B.A.J.*, 17:785, 790, 1931.

[57] Oliver Wendell Holmes, Jr., *Collected Legal Papers*, 292.

and the limits of governmental control. But it would be only after the war that specific issues could be confidently linked back to the natural-law principles of the Declaration of Independence and their implementation or their modified or more muted phrasing in the Constitution. Only then could the Court develop, as through the device of substantive due process, a body of theory of "oughtness" which related back to the broad generalizations of the Marshall period.

The predicament of the Taney Court is illuminated by the shifts in its relative prestige in comparison with the other two branches of the federal government and by the strategy and circumstances whereby in the postwar period its prestige was restored. When Taney was appointed to the Court the prestige of the tribunal was largely the product of its performance under Marshall's leadership. It was Marshall and his brethren who had given the Court high stature among the three branches, a stature only slightly diminished during the later Marshall years by signs of thinking geared too much to an irrevocable past, with growing restlessness not only on the part of the Jackson Administration but also of members of the Court itself. Throughout most of the Taney period, distortion of the Constitution as interpreted by Marshall was being proclaimed or predicted by Whig critics, yet the worst never seemed to happen. The Taney Court and the Marshall Court, for all the seeming difference in emphasis, proved to be very much the same.

The Taney Court fell upon evil times not because of Jacksonianism or even because of lack of ability on the part of its members, but because it was caught in the grinding pressures of sectional conflict. A Court committed to application of the law was bound to crash into difficulties when the nation itself divided over whether there was indeed a surviving body of constitutional law binding on all the states and all the people.

In any event, in this time of civil war the strident and clamorous voice of Mars too often drowned out the voice of the law, with its stress upon reason and rightness rather than upon ruthless power, and little deference was accorded to judicial spokesmen. To a considerable degree the executive won dominance in matters which in other times would have been left to the courts, and even Congress had to accept a measure of subordination not known in its tradition. The postwar years would see a swift restoration of Congressional authority through political rebellion against an unready Vice President suddenly elevated to Presidential office and through the device of trial on impeachment. The restoration of the judiciary came more slowly. In terms of prestige the Supreme Court had sunk lower than Congress, not merely because it had handed down the Dred Scott decision but because the rule of law as interpreted by the judiciary had given way to a rage for unrestricted exercise of power—which seemed to flare with even greater violence once the battlefields were stilled. There could be a restoration of the prestige of the judiciary only with restoration of respect for the rule of law.

That loss of prestige which the Taney Court witnessed but for which it was only to a very limited extent responsible was to be remedied only with the passing of years. In some instances the Supreme Court's survival through the turbulence of Reconstruction derived from the fine art of avoiding dangerous constitutional questions on jurisdictional grounds. In the interpretation of the postwar constitutional amendments it consciously or unconsciously handled race problems in terms of the drift of the sentiments of the changing times. It chose a middle path, and sought to restore a kind of balanced federalism with the judiciary as the delimiting agent, as it had been before the war. It seized upon "due process of law" in one of the new Amendments to reemphasize the sanctity of property under our constitutional system, with the judiciary as its prime guardian. By these and other means it brought itself gradually back to a position of prestige comparable to that of the legislative and executive branches, no longer beset by the ills which had afflicted the Court of Chief Justice Taney. While during the last third of the nineteenth century the Supreme Court, and the federal judiciary as a whole, reassumed their rightful position as a coordinate branch of the government, the historical refurbishing of the reputation of the Supreme Court, damaged during the later years of the Taney period, was left for completion during the twentieth century, and the task was by no means ended even at the centennial of the death of the man who had given the Taney period its name.

Bibliography

Throughout the text frequent citations are made to compilations of cases in federal and state courts, *e.g.*, 8 *Howard* or 2 *New York*. These sources are not listed in the bibliography.

BOOKS, PAMPHLETS, AND PERIODICALS

Abrams, Ray H. "The Jeffersonian, Copperhead Newspaper." *Pennsylvania Magazine of History and Biography*, 57, 1933.

Adams, Charles F. *Richard Henry Dana: A Biography*, Boston and New York: Houghton Mifflin and Co., 1890.

————, ed. *Memoirs of John Quincy Adams*. Philadelphia: J. B. Lippincott and Co., 1874–1877.

Adams, John Quincy. "John Quincy Adams to Alexander H. Everett, Dec. 1, 1835." *American Historical Review*, 9, 1906.

"Admiralty Jurisdiction Over Our Lakes and Rivers." *Western Law Journal*, 1, 1844.

Agnew, Daniel. "Address to the Allegheny County Bar Association." *Pennsylvania Magazine of History and Biography*, 13, 1888.

Allen, Mary B. *Joseph Holt, Judge Advocate General . . . A Study in the Treatment of Political Prisoners by the United States Government During the Civil War*. Ph.D. dissertation, University of Chicago, 1927.

American Anti-Slavery Society, *Annual Report . . . 1859*. 12 vols. New York: American Anti-Slavery Society, 1834–1861.

"The American Bar." *United States Magazine and Democratic Review*, 28, 1851.

"An Anecdote of David Dudley Field." *American Law Review*, 28, 1894.

"The Appointment of Mr. Curtis." *The Law Reporter*, 14, 1851.

"The Attack on the Judiciary of Massachusetts." *The Law Reporter*, 6, 1843.

Auchampaugh, Philip G., ed. "A Great Justice on State and Federal Power, Being the Thoughts of Chief Justice Taney on the Federal Conscription Act." *Tyler's Historical and Genealogical Magazine*, 18, 1936.

Bibliography

————. "James Buchanan, the Court and the Dred Scott Case." *Tennessee Historical Magazine*, 9, 1956.

Bailey, Edgar H. "The New Almaden Quicksilver Mines." *California National Resources Bulletin; Geologic Guidebook of the San Francisco Bay Counties*, 154, 1951.

Baldwin, Henry. *A General View of the Origin and Nature of the Constitution and Government of the United States*. Philadelphia: J. C. Clark, 1837.

Baldwin, Joseph G. *The Flush Times of Alabama and Mississippi*. New York: D. Appleton and Co., 1853; Americus, Ga.: Americus Book Co., 1908.

Bancroft, Frederic. *The Life of William H. Seward*. New York and London: Harper and Brothers, 1900.

————. *Slave Trading in the Old South*. Baltimore: J. H. Furst Co., 1931.

Bancroft, Hubert H. *The Works of H. H. Bancroft* . . . 39 vols. San Francisco: A. L. Bancroft and Co., 1882–1890,

"Bankruptcy." *Law Reporter*, 7, 1845.

Barnard, Job. "Early Days of the Supreme Court of the District of Columbia." *Records of the Columbia Historical Society*, 22, 1919.

Barrows, Chester L. *William M. Evarts*. Chapel Hill, N.C.: The University of North Carolina Press, 1941.

Bartley, Ernest R. *The Tidelands Oil Controversy*. Austin, Tex.: University of Texas Press, 1953.

Beale, Howard K., ed. "The Diary of Edward Bates." *Annual Report of the American Historical Association for the Year 1930*, 4, 1933.

————, ed. *Diary of Gideon Welles*. New York: W. W. Norton Co., 1960.

Beitzinger, Alfons J. "Chief Justice Taney and the Republication of Court Opinions." *Catholic University Law Review*, 7, 1958.

————. *Edward G. Ryan, Lion of the Law*. Madison, Wis.: State Historical Society of Wisconsin, 1960.

————. "The Father of Copperheadism in Wisconsin." *Wisconsin Magazine of History*, 39, 1955.

————. "Federal Law Enforcement and the Booth Cases." *Marquette Law Review*, 41, 1957.

Benton, Thomas Hart. *Historical and Legal Examination of* . . . *the Dred Scott Decision*. New York: D. Appleton and Co., 1857.

————. *Thirty Years View*. New York: Appleton, 1854–1856.

Beveridge, Albert J. *Abraham Lincoln, 1809–1858*. 4 vols. Boston and New York, Houghton Mifflin Co., 1928.

————. *The Life of John Marshall*. Boston and New York: Houghton Mifflin Co., 1916–1919.

Bicknell, George A., Jr. *A Commentary on the Bankrupt Law of 1841, Showing Its Operation and Effect*. New York: Gould, Banks and Co., 1842.

Binney, Charles C. *The Life of Horace Binney with Selections from his Letters*. Philadelphia and London: J. B. Lippincott Co., 1903.

Binney, Hiram and Charles Chauncey. *Opinion* . . . *on the Subject of the Acts of the Legislature of the State of New-Jersey, relative to the Dela-*

ware and Raritan Canal, and Camden and Amboy Railroad Companies, Oct. 24, 1833. Trenton, N.J.: G. Sherman, 1834.

Binney, Horace. *The Privilege of the Writ of Habeas Corpus Under the Constitution.* Philadelphia: T. B. Pugh, 1862.

Biographical Encyclopedia of Kentucky . . . Cincinnati: J. M. Armstrong and Co., 1878.

Blaine, James G. *Twenty Years of Congress.* 2 vols. Norwich, Conn.: The Henry Bill Publishing Co., 1884–1886.

Blandi, Joseph G. *The Maryland Corporation.* Baltimore: The Johns Hopkins Press, 1934.

Bogart, Ernest L. "Financial History of Ohio." *University of Illinois Studies in the Social Sciences,* 1912.

Boucher, Chauncey S. and Robert P. Brooks, eds. "Correspondence Addressed to John C. Calhoun 1837–1849." *Annual Report of the American Historical Association for the Year 1929.* 1930.

Brewer, William H. and Francis P. Farquhar, eds. *Up and Down California in 1860–1864.* New Haven, Conn.: Yale University Press; London: H. Milford, Oxford University Press, 1930.

Brigance, William N. *Jeremiah Sullivan Black.* Philadelphia: University of Pennsylvania Press; London: H. Milford, Oxford University Press, 1934.

Brown, David P. *The Forum; or Forty Years Full Practice at the Philadelphia Bar.* 2 vols. Philadelphia: R. H. Small Co., 1856.

Brown, George W. *Baltimore and the Nineteenth of April, 1861.* Baltimore: N. Murray, 1887.

Brown, Glenn. *History of the United States Capitol.* Washington, D.C.: Government Printing Office, 1902.

Brown, Timothy. "The Wisconsin Supreme Court." *Wisconsin Magazine of History,* 36, 1952.

Browning, Orville Hickman. *See* Pease, Theodore Calvin.

Bruchey, Stuart, ed. "Roger Brooke Taney's Account of His Relations with Thomas Ellicott in the Bank War." *Maryland Historical Magazine,* 53, 1958.

Bryan, Wilhelmus B. *A History of the National Capital.* 2 vols. New York: The Macmillan Co., 1914–1916.

Buchanan, James. *Works of James Buchanan* . . . *1908–1911.* John Bassett Moore, ed. Philadelphia and London: J. B. Lippincott Co., 1910.

Burgess, John W. *The Middle Period, 1817–1858.* New York: The American History Series, C. Scribner's Sons, 1897.

Burnette, Lawrence, Jr. "Peter V. Daniel: Agrarian Justice." *Virginia Magazine of History and Biography,* 62, 1954.

Burns, Francis P. "The Spanish Land Laws of Louisiana." *Louisiana Historical Quarterly,* 9, 1928.

Busey, Samuel C. *Pictures of the City of Washington in the Past.* Washington, D.C.: Ballantyne and Sons, 1898.

Butler, Frances Anne, see: Kemble Frances Anne. *Journal* [*Aug. 1, 1832 to July 17, 1833*]. 2 vols. Philadelphia: Carey Lea and Blanchard, 1835.

Butler, Pierce. *Judah P. Benjamin.* Philadelphia: G. W. Jacobs Co., 1907.

Bibliography

Butler, William A. *A Retrospect of Forty Years, 1825–1865*. Harriet Allen Butler, ed. New York: Scribner's Sons. 1911.

Cadman, John W., Jr. *The Corporation in New Jersey; Business and Politics, 1781–1875*. Cambridge, Mass.: Harvard University Press, 1949.

Caldwell, Robert G. *The Lopez Expeditions to Cuba, 1848–1851*. Ph.D. dissertation, Princeton, N.J.: Princeton University Press, 1915.

Calhoun, John C. "Correspondence of John C. Calhoun." J. Franklin Jameson, ed. *Annual Report of the American Historical Association for the Year 1899*, 2, 1900.

Callahan, James M. "The Pittsburgh-Wheeling Rivalry for Commercial Headship on the Ohio." *Ohio Archaeological and Historical Quarterly*, 57, 1913.

[Campbell, John A.] "Slavery in the United States." *Southern Quarterly Review*, 12, 1847.

Cardozo, Benjamin N. *Law and Literature . . . and Addresses*. New York: Harcourt, Brace and Co., 1931.

Carter, George W. "The Booth War in Ripon." *Proceedings of the State Historical Society of Wisconsin . . . 1902*. 1903.

"The Case of Anthony Burns." *The Law Reporter*, 17, 1854.

"The Case of Dred Scott." *The Law Reporter*, 20, 1857.

"The Case of Thomas Sims." *The Law Reporter*, 14, 1851.

Casson, Herbert N. *Cyrus Hall McCormick, His Life and Work*. Chicago: A. C. McClurg and Co., 1909.

Catron, John. "Biographical Letter from Judge Catron." *United States Monthly Law Magazine*, 5, 1845.

Catterall, R. C. H. *The Second Bank of the United States*. Chicago: The University of Chicago Press, 1903.

Caughey, John W. *California*. New York: Prentice-Hall, 1940.

Chandler, William. *The Centenary of Associate Justice John Catron of the United States Supreme Court, . . . June 11, 1937*. Washington D.C.: Government Printing Office, 1937.

Chase, Salmon P. *Reclamation of Fugitives from Service. An Argument for the Defendant, Submitted to the Supreme Court of the United States, at the December Term, 1846, in the case of Wharton Jones v. John Van-Zandt*. Cincinnati: R. P. Donogh and Co., 1847.

———. *The Electric Telegraph, Summary of . . . Argument . . . Before the Supreme Court of the United States . . . O'Reilly v. Morse*. New York: Baker, Godwin, 1853.

Chestnut, Mary Boykin. *A Diary from Dixie*. Ben Ames Williams, ed. Boston: Houghton Mifflin, 1949.

Chestnut, W. Calvin, "Chicago Convention." *United States Magazine and Democratic Review*, 21, 1850.

Chittenden, L. E. *A Report of the Debates and Proceedings in the Secret Sessions of the Conference Convention for Proposing Amendments to the Constitution of the United States*. New York: D. Appleton and Co., 1864.

Clark, Charles B. *Politics in Maryland During the Civil War*. Chestertown, Md., 1952.

979

————. "Suppression and Control of Maryland, 1861–1865." *Maryland Historical Magazine*, 54, 1959.

Clay, Henry. *Works of Henry Clay*. 7 vols. Calvin Colton, ed. New York: Henry Clay Publishing Co., 1897.

Clifford, Philip G. *Nathan Clifford, Democrat, 1803–1881*. New York and London: G. P. Putnam's Sons, 1922.

Coleman, Mrs. Chapman, ed. *The Life of John J. Crittenden*. Philadelphia: J. B. Lippincott and Co., 1871.

Coles, Harry L., Jr. "Applicability of the Public Land System to Louisiana." *Mississippi Valley Historical Review*, 43, 1956.

————. "Confirmation of Foreign Land Titles in Louisiana." *Louisiana Historical Quarterly*, 9, 1928.

Collins, Lewis. *History of Kentucky*. Richard H. Merton, rev. by Richard H. Collins, Louisville, Ky.: J. P. Morton and Co., 1924.

"Competency of Witnesses." *American Law Register* (N.S.), 1, 1862.

Conkling, Alfred. *The Admiralty Jurisdiction, Law and Practice of the Courts of the United States*. 2 vols. Albany, N.Y.: W. C. Little and Co., 1857.

————. *The Jurisdiction Law and Practice of the Courts of the United States in Admiralty and Maritime Causes, Including Those of Quasi Admiralty Jurisdiction Arising Under the Act of February 26, 1845*. 2 vols. Albany and Boston: W. C. Little and Co.; C. C. Little and J. Brown, 1848.

Connor, Henry G. *John Archibald Campbell . . . U.S. Supreme Court, 1853–1861*. Boston and New York: Houghton Mifflin Co., 1920.

"Contempt of Court, Habeas Corpus." *Livingston's Monthly Law Magazine*, 3, 1855.

"Contests for the Trade of the Mississippi Valley." *De Bow's Commercial Review*, 3, 1847.

Conway, Moncure D. *Autobiography . . . of Moncure Daniel Conway with Two Portraits*. London, Paris, New York and Melbourne: Cassell and Co., Ltd., 1904.

Corwin, Edward S. "The Doctrine of Due Process of Law Before the Civil War." *Harvard Law Review*, 24, 1911.

————. *The Doctrine of Judicial Review . . . and Other Essays*. Princeton, N.J.: Princeton University Press, 1914.

Coulson, Thomas. *Joseph Henry, His Life and Work*. Princeton, N.J.: Princeton University Press, 1950.

Coulter, E. Merton. *The Civil War and Readjustment in Kentucky*. Chapel Hill, N.C.: The University of North Carolina Press, 1926.

"Courts of the United States," in *Encyclopedia Americana*, III. Philadelphia: Thomas Cowperwait, 1835.

Crawford, Samuel W. *The Genesis of the Civil War . . . Sumter, 1860–1861*. New York: C. L. Webster and Co., 1887.

"Cuban Expedition." *Western Law Journal*, 7, 1850.

"Cuban Expedition." *Western Law Journal*, 9, 1852.

Cummings, Homer and Carl McFarland. *Federal Justice; Chapters . . . and the Federal Executive*. New York: The Macmillan Co., 1937.

Bibliography

Curtis, Benjamin R. "Debts of the States." *North American Review*, 53, 1844.

———. *Jurisdiction, Practice, and Peculiar Jurisdiction of the Courts of the United States*. Boston: Little, Brown and Co., 1896.

Curtis, Benjamin R. II, ed. *Life and Writings of Benjamin R. Curtis*. Boston: Little, Brown and Co., 1879.

Curtis, George T. *A Digest of Cases Adjudicated in the Courts of Admiralty and in the High Court of Admiralty in England*. Boston: C. C. Little and J. Brown Co., 1839.

———. *A Memoir of Benjamin Robbins Curtis . . .* 2 vols. Benjamin R. Curtis, ed. Boston: Little, Brown and Co., 1879.

———. *Argument . . . in the Case of Dred Scott, Plaintiff in Error, v. John F. Sanford*. Boston: Little, Brown and Co., 1856.

———. "Enlargement of the Admiralty Jurisdiction in England." *American Jurist*, 24, 1841.

———. *Life of Daniel Webster*. 2 vols. New York: D. Appleton and Co., 1870.

Cushing, Luther S. "The Greatest-Happiness Principle." *American Jurist*, 20, 1839.

———. "Livingston's Penal Codes." *American Jurist*, 22, 1840.

———. "Reform in Remedial Law." *American Jurist*, 17, 1837.

Cushman, Robert C. "Smith Thompson." *Dictionary of American Biography*, 18: 471–72, 1936.

"Codification and Reform of the Law." *American Jurist*, 21, 1839.

"Codification and Reform of the Law." *American Jurist*, 22, 1840.

Dana, Richard H. *Two Years Before the Mast; A Personal . . . Narrative*. Boston and New York: Houghton Mifflin Co., 1911.

———. "History of Admiralty Jurisdiction in the Supreme Court of the United States." *American Law Review*, 5, 1871.

"Daniel Webster." *Southern Literary Messenger*, 3, 1837.

Davies, Charles S. "Constitutional Law," *North American Review*, 46, 1838.

"Death of Judge Woodbury." *Western Law Journal*, 9, 1851.

"Death of Mr. Justice Story." *The Law Reporter*, 8, 1845.

"Decision in the Wheeling Bridge Case." *Pittsburgh Legal Journal*, 4, 1856.

"Disfederation of the States." *Southern Literary Messenger*, 32, 1861.

"The Doctrine of the 'Higher Law,' Mr. Seward's Speech." *Southern Literary Messenger*, 17, 1851.

Dodd, Edwin M. *American Business Corporations until 1860, with Special Reference to Massachusetts*. Cambridge, Mass.: Harvard University Press, 1954.

Donald, David, ed. *Inside Lincoln's Cabinet: The Civil War Diaries of Salmon P. Chase*. New York: Longmans, Green, 1954.

"Down in the Cinnebar Mines: A Visit to New Almaden in 1865." *Harper's*, 21, 1865.

DuBois, William E. B. *The Suppression of the African Slave-Trade . . .* New York, London [etc.]: Longmans Green and Co., 1904.

Duncan, George W. "John Archibald Campbell," *Transactions of the Alabama Historical Society, 1904*, 5, 1906.

Dunn, James T., ed. *James Wickes Taylor: "A Choice Nook of Memory."* *The Diary of a Cincinnati Law Clerk, 1842–1844*. Columbus, Ohio: Ohio State Archaeological and Historical Society, 1950.

Dunne, Gerald T. *Justice Joseph Story and the Rise of the Supreme Court*. New York: Simon and Schuster, 1970.

"Duty of Grand Jurors." *The Law Reporter*, 14, 1852.

Dyer, Brainerd. *Public Career of William M. Evarts*. Berkeley, Calif.: University of California Press, 1933.

Edmonds, John W. "An Address on the Constitution and Code of Procedure," *The Law Reporter*, 11, 1848.

"Edward Livingston and His Code." *United States Magazine and Democratic Review*, 3, 1841.

"Election of Judges." *American Law Journal*, 8, 1849.

"The Election of Judges." *Western Law Journal*, 8, 1851.

"An Elective Judiciary." *United States Magazine and Democratic Review*, 22, 1848.

"An Elective Judiciary." *The Law Reporter*, 23, 1860.

"The Elective Principle as Applied to the Judiciary." *Western Law Journal*, 5, 1847.

Ellis, John B. *The Sights and Secrets of the National Capital*. New York: United States Publishing Co., 1869.

Ellison, Joseph. *California and the Nation, 1850–1869, . . . Government*. Berkeley, Calif.: University of California Press, 1927.

Emory, Frederic. *Queen Anne's County, Maryland: Its Early History and Development*. Baltimore, Maryland Historical Society, 1950.

Evans, George G. *Visitors' Companion at Our National Capital: A Complete Guide for Washington and Its Environs . . .* Philadelphia: G. G. Evans, 1892.

Evans, George H. *Business Incorporations in the United States, 1800–1943*. New York: National Bureau of Economic Research, 1948.

Everett, C. W. "Bentham in the United States," in George W. Keeton and George Schwartzenberger, *Jeremy Bentham and the Law*. London: Stevens, 1948.

Everett, Edward G. "The Baltimore Riots." *Pennsylvania History*, 24, 1957.

"Ex Parte Stevens." *The Law Reporter*, 24, 1861.

"Extension of Federal Jurisdiction over State Canals." *American Law Review*, 37, 1903.

"Extradition, Case of Metzger, Under the Treaty with France." *Western Law Journal*, 5, 1847.

"The Extradition of Fugitives." *Pennsylvania Law Journal*, 6, 1847.

Fairman, Charles. *Mr. Justice Miller and the Supreme Court*. Cambridge, Mass.: Harvard University Press, 1939.

———. *Reconstruction and Reunion, 1864–1888, Part I. Oliver Wendell Holmes Devise History of the Supreme Court*. Vol. VI. New York: The Macmillan Company, 1971.

982

Bibliography

————. "The Retirement of Federal Judges." *Harvard Law Review*, 51, 1938.

[Farrar, Timothy]. "The Dred Scott Case." *North American Review*, 85, 1857.

Field, David D. "Chicago Convention." *United States Magazine and Democratic Review*, 21, 1847.

————. *Speeches, Arguments and Miscellaneous Papers of* . . . 3 vols. A. P. Sprague, ed. New York: D. Appleton and Co., 1884–1890.

Field, Henry M. *The Life of David Dudley Field.* New York: C. Scribner's Sons, 1898.

Field, Stephen J. *Personal Reminiscences of Early Days in California* . . . *Sketches.* [San Francisco?]: Printed for a few friends, n. p. [1880?]

Fisher, Sydney G. "Diaries." *Pennsylvania Magazine of History and Biography*, 76, 1952.

Flanders, Henry. *A Treatise on Maritime Law.* Boston: Little, Brown and Co., 1852.

Flower, Frank A. *Edwin McMasters Stanton . . . and Reconstruction.* New York and Akron, Ohio [etc.]: The Saalfield Publishing Co., 1905.

Ford, Worthington C., ed. *A Cycle of Adams Letters.* Boston and New York: Houghton Mifflin Co., 1920.

Frank, John P., *Justice Daniel Dissenting.* Cambridge, Mass.: Harvard University Press, 1964.

Frankfurter, Felix. *The Commerce Clause under Marshall, Taney and Waite.* Chapel Hill, N.C.: The University of North Carolina Press, 1937.

"From Judicial Grant to Legislative Power: The Admiralty Clause in the Nineteenth Century." *Harvard Law Review*, 67, 1954.

Fuess, Claude M. *The Life of Caleb Cushing.* New York: Harcourt, Brace and Co., 1923.

"Fugitive Slave Case." *Western Law Journal*, 8, 1850.

"Fugitive Slaves." *United States Magazine and Democratic Review*, 13, 1850.

"The Gaines Case." *Southern Quarterly Review*, 18, 1854.

"The Gaines Case." *Western Law Journal*, 7, 1850.

Gallagher, Thomas J. "Judicial Salaries." *Western Law Journal*, 3, 1846.

Galloway, Tod B. "The Ohio-Michigan Boundary Line Dispute." *Ohio Archaeological and Historical Society Publications*, 4, 1909.

Gates, Paul W. "Adjudication of Spanish-Mexican Land Claims in California." *Huntington Library Quarterly*, 3, 1958.

————. "Private Land Claims in the South." *Journal of Southern History*, 22, 1956.

George, Henry. *Our Land and Land Policy.* San Francisco: White and Brewer [etc.], 1871.

Georgia. *Governor's Letter Book, January 1, 1841–May 31, 1843.*

Gifford, George. *Argument of George Gifford, Esq., of New York . . . O'Reilly v. Morse.* New York: William C. Bryant and Co., 1853.

Goebel, Julius, Jr. "The Common Law and the Constitution," in W. Melville

Jones, ed., *Chief Justice John Marshall, A Reappraisal*. Ithaca, N.Y.: Cornell University Press, 1956.

Gorham, George C. *Biographical Notice of Stephen J. Field*. Washington, D.C.: Printed only for use of the family, n. p. [1892?].

———. *Life and Public Services of Edwin M. Stanton*. Boston and New York: Houghton Mifflin and Co., 1899.

Gorrell, Donald G. "Presbyterians in the Ohio Temperance Movement of the 1850's." *Ohio State Archaeological and Historical Quarterly*, 60, 1951.

Govan, Thomas P. *Nicholas Biddle, Nationalist and Public Banker, 1786–1844*. Chicago: University of Chicago Press, 1959.

Graves, W. Brooke. *American State Government*. Boston: D. C. Heath and Co., 1946.

Gray, Horace and John Lowell. *A Legal Review of the Case of Dred Scott*. Boston: Crosby, Nichols and Co., 1857.

Gray, John C. *The Nature and Sources of the Law*. New York: The Macmillan Co., 1921.

Gray, Wood. *The Hidden Civil War*. New York: The Viking Press, 1942.

Gregory, Stephen S. "A Historic Judicial Controversy and Some Reflections Suggested by It." *Michigan Law Review*, 11, 1913.

Grimke, Archibald H. *William Lloyd Garrison, the Abolitionist*. New York [etc.]: Funk and Wagnalls, 1891.

Guild, Josephus C. *Old Times in Tennessee*. Nashville, Tenn.: Travel, Eastman and Howell, 1878.

Haines, Charles G. and Foster H. Sherwood. *The Role of the Supreme Court in American Government and Politics, 1835–1864*. 2 vols. Berkeley, Calif.: University of California Press, 1944–1957.

Hamer, Philip M. "Great Britain, the United States, and the Negro Seamen Acts, 1822–1860." *Journal of Southern History*, 1, 1935.

Hamilton, Holman. "Democratic Leadership and the Compromise of 1850." *Mississippi Valley Historical Review*, 41, 1954.

Hamilton, J. G. D. "William Smith," in *Dictionary of American Biography*, XVII, 1935.

Hammond, Bray. *Banks and Politics in America from the Revolution to the Civil War*. Princeton, N.J.: Princeton University Press, 1957.

Handlin, Oscar and Mary F. Handlin. *Commonwealth; A Study of the Role of Government in the American Economy: Massachusetts, 1774–1861*. New York: New York University Press, 1947.

Harmon, Nolan B., Jr. *The Famous Case of Myra Clark Gaines*. Baton Rouge, La.: Louisiana State University Press, 1946.

Harrison, Joseph H., Jr. "Martin Van Buren and His Southern Supporters." *Journal of Southern History*, 22, 1956.

Hartz, Louis. *Economic Policy and Democratic Thought, 1776–1860*. Cambridge, Mass.: Harvard University Press, 1948.

Hatcher, William S. *Edward Livingston . . . Democrat*. Louisiana: Louisiana State University Press, 1940.

Hayes, Rutherford B. *Diary and Letters of Rutherford B. Hayes*. 5 vols.

Bibliography

Columbus, Ohio: The Ohio State Archaeological and Historical Society, 1922–1926.

Heaney, Howell J., ed. "The Letters of Joseph Story." *American Journal of Legal History*, 2, 1958.

Hellerich, Mahlon H. "The Luther Cases in the Lower Courts." *Rhode Island History*, 2, 1952.

Henderson, Gerard C. *The Position of Foreign Corporations in American Constitutional Law.* Cambridge, Mass.: Harvard University Press, 1918.

Hensel, William U. "The Christiana Riot and the Treason Trial of 1841." *Lancaster County Historical Society—Historical Papers and Addresses*, 15, 1911.

———. "Thaddeus Stevens as a Country Lawyer." *Lancaster County Historical Society—Historical Papers and Addresses*, 10, 1906.

Hepburn, Charles M. *The Historical Development of Code Pleading in America and England.* Cincinnati: W. H. Anderson and Co., 1897.

Hibbard, Benjamin H. *A History of the Public Land Policies.* New York: The Macmillan Co., 1924.

"The Higher Law." *United States Magazine and Democratic Review*, 27, 1850.

Hillard, G. S., ed. *Memoir and Correspondence of Jeremiah Mason.* Cambridge, Mass.: Riverside Press, 1873.

Hinchcliff, Emerson. "Lincoln and the 'Reaper Case.'" *Illinois State Historical Society Journal*, 33, 1940.

"History of Admiralty Jurisdiction in the Supreme Court of the United States." *American Law Review*, 5, 1871.

Hittel, Theodore H. *History of California.* 4 vols. San Francisco: Pacific Press Publishing House, Occidental Publishing Co., N. J. Stone and Co., 1885–1897.

Hoar, George F. *Autobiography of Seventy Years.* 2 vols. New York: C. Scribner's Sons, 1903.

Hodder Frank H. "The Authorship of the Compromise of 1850." *Mississippi Valley Historical Review*, 22, 1936.

———. "Some Phases of the Dred Scott Case." *Mississippi Valley Historical Review*, 16, 1929.

Hodgson, Sister M. Michael Catherine. *Caleb Cushing, Attorney General of the United States.* Washington, D. C.: Catholic University of America Press, 1955.

Hogan, John C. "Joseph Story's Anonymous Law Articles." *Michigan Law Review*, 52, 1954.

———. "The Role of Chief Justice Taney in the Decision of the Dred Scott Case." *Case and Comment*, 58, 1953.

Holdsworth, Sir William. "Bentham's Place in English Legal History." *California Law Review*, 28, 1940.

Holmes, Oliver W. "Stage Coach Days in the District of Columbia." *Records of the Columbia Historical Society*, 50, 1952.

Holmes, Oliver Wendell, Jr. *Collected Legal Papers.* New York: Harcourt, Brace and Howe, 1920.

985

Holt, Edgar A. "Party Politics in Ohio, 1840–1850." *Ohio Archaeological and Historical Quarterly*, 37, 1928.

Hopkins, Vincent C., S.J. *Dred Scott's Case*. New York: Fordham University Press, D. X. McMullen Co., Distributors, 1951.

Howard, Frank K. *Fourteen Months in American Bastilles*. Baltimore: Kelly, Hedian & Piet, 1863.

Howe, Mark D., ed., *Holmes-Laski Letters*. 2 vols. Cambridge, Mass.: Harvard University Press, 1953.

Howison, Robert R. "History of the War." *Southern Literary Messenger*, 34–36, 1862.

Hoyt, William D., Jr., ed. "Benjamin C. Howard and the 'Toledo War.' Some Letters of a Federal Commissioner." *Ohio State Archaeological and Historical Quarterly*, 60, 1951.

———. "Justice Daniel in Arkansas," *Arkansas Historical Quarterly*, 1, 1942.

———. "Travel to Cincinnati in 1853." *Ohio Archaeological and Historical Quarterly*, 51, 1942.

Hudon, Edward G. "The Library Facilities of the Supreme Court of the United States: A Historical Study." *University of Detroit Law Journal*, 34, 1965.

Hughes, Charles Evans. "Roger Brooke Taney." *American Bar Association Journal*, 17, 1931.

———. *The Supreme Court of the United States . . . An Interpretation*. New York: Columbia University Press, 1926.

Hulbert, Archer B. *The Cumberland Road*. Cleveland: The A. H. Clark Co., 1904.

Hunt, Charles H. *Life of Edward Livingston*. New York: D. Appleton and Co., 1864.

Hunter, Louis C. *Steamboats on the Western Rivers*. Cambridge, Mass.: Harvard University Press, 1949.

Hutchinson, William T. *Cyrus Hall McCormick*. 2 vols., Vol. I, *Seed-Time, 1809–1856*. New York and London: The Century Company, 1930–1935.

"The Independence of the Judiciary." *North American Review*, 57, 1843.

"The Independence of the Judiciary." *United States Magazine and Democratic Review*, 23, 1848.

Ingersoll, Charles J. "Speech in the Convention of Pennsylvania, on Legislative and Judicial Control over Charters of Incorporation." *Democratic Review*, 5, 1839.

Inlow, E. Burke. *The Patent Grant*. Baltimore: Johns Hopkins Press, 1950.

"The Insolvent Law of Massachusetts." *The Law Reporter*, 10, 1848.

Jackson, Andrew. *Correspondence of Andrew Jackson*. 7 vols. John S. Bassett, ed. Washington, D. C.: Carnegie Institution of Washington, 1926–1935.

Jackson, Robert H. "The Rise and Fall of *Swift v. Tyson*." *American Bar Association Journal*, 24, 1938.

Jaffa, Harry V. *Crisis of the House Divided . . . Lincoln-Douglas Debates*. Garden City, N.Y.: Doubleday, 1959.

986

Bibliography

Jameson, J. Franklin, *see*: Calhoun, John C.

Johns, Arthur J. "On the Legal Arguments Urged in England for a Continuation of the Separation of the Law and Equity Jurisdictions." *American Jurist*, 20, 1838.

Johnston, Elizabeth B. "The Seal of the Columbia Historical Society." *Records of the Columbia Historical Society*, 6, 1903.

Johnston, Richard M. and William H. Browne. *Life of Alexander H. Stephens*. Philadelphia: J. B. Lippincott and Co., 1883.

Jones, Charles A. "Ohio in the Republican National Conventions." *Ohio Archaeological and Historical Quarterly*, 38, 1929.

Jones, Jesse S. *Life of Andrew Johnson*. Greenville, Tenn.: East Tennessee Publishing Co., [1901].

Jones, Wilbur. "The Influence of Slavery on the Webster-Ashburton Negotiations." *Journal of Southern History*, 22, 1956.

Joyner, Fred B. "Robert Cumming Schenck, First Citizen and Statesman of the Ohio Valley." *Ohio State Archaeological and Historical Quarterly*, 58, 1949.

"Judges—Interesting Statistics." *Western Law Journal*, 7, 1850.

"Judicial Encroachment." *United States Magazine and Democratic Review*, 26, 1850.

"Judiciary System of New York." *American Jurist*, 26, 1841.

"Jurisdiction of the Courts of Admiralty in Cases of Collision on a Tide-Waters Within the Body of a Country. The Case of Luda and De Sota, on the Mississippi." *De Bow's Commercial Review*, 2, 1846.

"Mr. Justice Woodbury." *The Law Reporter*, 14, 1852.

Kelley, William D. *Speech . . . United States v. William Smith, Piracy*. Philadelphia: 1861.

Kelly, Joseph T. "Memories of a Lifetime in Washington." *Records of the Columbian Historical Society*, 31, 1930.

Kempin, Frederick G., Jr. "Precedent and Stare Decisis: The Critical Years, 1800 to 1850." *American Journal of Legal History*, 3, 1959.

Kendall, Amos. *Autobiography of Amos Kendall*. William Stickney, ed. Boston: Lee and Shepard; New York: Lee, Shepard, and Dillingham, 1872.

Kendall, John S. "The Strange Case of Myra Clark Gaines." *Louisiana Historical Quarterly*, 20, 1937.

Kent, James. *Commentaries on American Law*. 4 vols. New York: Published by the author, 1840.

———. "The Law of Corporations." *The Law Reporter*, 1838.

———. "Review of Joseph Story: 'Commentaries on the Law of Partnership.'" *American Jurist*, 26, 1842.

[———.] "Supreme Court of the United States." *New York Review*, 2, 1838.

Kilbourn, William. *The Firebrand: William Lyon Mackenzie and the Rebellion in Upper Canada*. Toronto: Clarke, Irwin Co., 1956.

King, Willard L. *Lincoln's Manager, David Davis*. Cambridge, Mass.: Harvard University Press, 1960.

Klement, Frank. "Copperheads and Copperheadism in Wisconsin." *Wisconsin Magazine of History*, 42, 1959.

Koren, John. *Economic Aspects of the Liquor Problem*. Boston and New York: Houghton, Mifflin and Co., 1899.

Krout, John A. *The Origins of Prohibition*. New York: A. A. Knopf, 1925.

"The Late Bankrupt Law of the United States." *Pennsylvania Law Journal*, 3, 1844.

"The Late Cuba State Trials." *United States Magazine and Democratic Review*, 30, 1852.

"The Late Mr. Justice Baldwin." *Pennsylvania Law Journal*, 6, 1846.

"The Late Mr. Justice Catron." *Legal Intelligencer*, 23, 1866.

"Law Legislation Codes," in *Encyclopaedia Americana*, VII, 1835.

"The Law of Corporations." *The Law Reporter*, 1838.

"The Law of Real Property as Affected by the Revised Statutes of the State of New York." *American Law Magazine*, 4, 1845.

"Law Reform." *United States Magazine and Democratic Review*, 21, 1847.

Lawrence, Alexander A. *James Moore Wayne, Southern Unionist*. Chapel Hill, N.C.: The University of North Carolina Press, 1943.

Lawson, John D., ed. *American State Trials*. 17 vols. St. Louis: F. H. Thomas Law Book Co., 1914–1936.

Leach, Richard H. "Benjamin Robbins Curtis: Judicial Misfit." *New England Quarterly*, 25, 1952.

———. "Justice Curtis and the Dred Scott Case." *Essex Institute Historical Collections*, 94, 1958.

"Legislation in Massachusetts." *The Law Reporter*, 6, 1844.

"Legislative and Judicial Power." *Western Law Journal*, 4, 1847.

"Letters of John McLean to John Teesdale." *Bibliotheca Sacra*, 56, 1899.

Levy, Leonard W. *The Law of the Commonwealth and Chief Justice Shaw*. Cambridge, Mass.: Harvard University Press, 1957.

"The Library: The Mystery of the Dallas Papers." *Pennsylvania Magazine of History and Biography*, 73, 1949.

"License Laws." *Western Law Journal*, 4, 1847.

"The Limitation of the Liability of Ship-Owners by Statute. *American Law Review*, 1, 1867.

Lincoln, Abraham. *Collected Works of Abraham Lincoln*. Roy P. Basler, ed. New Brunswick, N.J.: Rutgers University Press, 1953.

———. *Complete Works of Abraham Lincoln*. 10 vols. John G. Nicolay and John Hay, eds. New York: Francis D. Tandy Co., 1905.

Logan, Mary Simmerson (Mrs. John A.). *Thirty Years in Washington*. Hartford, Conn.: A. D. Worthington and Co., 1901.

Loring, Charles G. *Neutral Relations of England and the United States*. Boston: W. V. Spencer, 1863.

Lowrie, Samuel H. *Culture Conflict in Texas, 1821–1835*. New York: Ph.D. dissertation, Columbia University, 1932.

Malone, Dumas. "Philip H. Barbour," in *Dictionary of American Biography*,

Mangum, Willie Person. *Papers of Willie Person Mangum*. 4 vols. Henry T. I, 1936.

Bibliography

Shanks, ed. Raleigh, N.C.: State Department of Archives and History, 1950–1956.

Manning, William R. *Diplomatic Correspondence of the United States, Canadian Relations, 1784–1860.* 4 vols. Washington, D.C.: Carnegie Endowment for International Peace, 1940–1945.

Marshall, John A. *American Bastille.* Philadelphia: Evans, Stoddart and Co., 1870.

Martin, David. *Trial of the Rev. Jacob Gruber, Minister in the Methodist Episcopal Church, at the March Term, 1819, in the Frederick County Court, for a Misdemeanor.* Fredericktown, Md.: David Martin and Geo. Kolb, Printers, 1819.

Martineau, Harriet. *Retrospect of Western Travel.* 2 vols. New York: Harpers and Brothers; London: Saunders and Otley, 1838.

————. *Society in America.* 3 vols. London: Saunders and Otley, 1837.

Maryland. *Debates and Proceedings of the Maryland Reform Convention to Revise the State Constitution.* 2 vols. Annapolis: W. M'Neir, Printer, 1851.

————. *Executive Proceedings, 1834–1839.*

————. *Governor's Letter Book, 1845–1854.*

————. *Journal of the Proceedings of the House of Delegates. December Session, 1834.* Annapolis: Jeremiah Hughes, Printer, 1834.

Mason, Jeremiah. *Memoir and Correspondence of Jeremiah Mason.* Cambridge, Mass.: privately printed, 1873.

Mason, Vroman. "The Fugitive Slave Law in Wisconsin, with Reference to Nullification Sentiment." *Proceedings of the State Historical Society of Wisconsin . . . 1895,* 1896.

Matthews, Sidney T. "Control of the Baltimore Press During the Civil War." *Maryland Historical Magazine,* 36, 1942.

Mayes, Edward. *Lucius Q. C. Lamar: His Life, Times, and Speeches.* Nashville, Tenn.: Publishing House of the Methodist Episcopal Church, South, 1896.

McAllister, Ward. *Society As I Have Found It.* New York: Cassell Publishing Co., 1890.

McCormick, Cyrus. *The Century of the Reaper.* Boston and New York: Houghton Mifflin Co., 1931.

McGrane, Reginald C., ed. *The Correspondence of Nicholas Biddle Dealing with National Affairs, 1807–1844.* Boston and New York: Houghton Mifflin Co., 1919.

McKnight, Joseph W. "The Spanish Legacy to Texas Law," *American Journal of Legal History,* 3, 1959.

McMaster, John B. *History of the People of the United States During Lincoln's Administration.* New York and London: D. Appleton and Co., 1927.

Mearns, David C. "The Story Up to Now." *Annual Report of the Librarian of Congress for the Fiscal Year Ending June 30, 1946,* 1947.

Meigs, William M. *The Life of Charles Jared Ingersoll.* Philadelphia: J. B. Lippincott Co., 1897.

Mendelson, Wallace. "Dred Scott's Case—Reconsidered." *Minnesota Law Review*, 38, 1953.

Millar, Robert W. *Civil Procedure of the Trial Court in Historical Perspective*. New York: Law Center of New York University for the National Conference of Judicial Councils, 1952.

Miller, Perry. "The Common Law and Codification in Jacksonian America." *Proceedings of the American Philosophical Society*, 103, 1959.

———. *The Life of the Mind in America from the Revolution to the Civil War*. New York: Harcourt, Brace and World, 1965.

"Mines . . . Mariposa Grant." *American Law Register*, 10, 1862.

Mood, Fulmer and Cranville Ricks. "Letters to Dr. Channing on Slavery and the Annexation of Texas, 1837." *New England Quarterly*, 5, 1932.

Morgan, Donald G. *Justice William Johnson, The First Dissenter*. Columbia, S.C.: University of South Carolina Press, 1954.

Morpeth, Lord. *Travels in America*. New York: G. P. Putnam Co., 1851.

Morse, Edward L., ed. *Samuel F. B. Morse, His Letters and Journals*. Boston and New York: Houghton Mifflin Co., 1914.

Mowry, Arthur M. *The Dorr War, or the Constitutional Struggle in Rhode Island*. Providence: Preston and Rounds Co., 1901.

———. "Tammany Hall and the Dorr Rebellion." *American Historical Review*, 3, 1898.

———. "Nathan Clifford." *United States Magazine and Democratic Review*, 20, 1847.

Murphy, D. F. *The Jeff Davis Piracy Case: Full Report of the Trial of William Smith for Piracy as one of the men of Confederate Privateer Jeff Davis*. Philadelphia: King and Baird Printers, 1861.

Nettels, Curtis. "The Mississippi Valley and the Federal Judiciary, 1807–1837." *Mississippi Valley Historical Review*, 12, 1925.

"The Neutrality Law: What Does It Mean, What Prohibit and What Permit?" *United States Magazine and Democratic Review*, 30, 1847.

Nevins, Allan, ed. *The Diary of George Templeton Strong: The Civil War*. New York: Macmillan and Co., 1952.

———, ed. *The Diary of Philip Hone, 1828–1851*. 2 vols. New York: Dodd, Mead and Co., 1927.

———. *The Emergence of Lincoln*. New York: Scribner, 1950.

———. *Frémont, Pathmarker of the West*. New York and London: D. Appleton Century Co., 1939.

"The New Constitution of Kentucky." *Western Law Journal*, 7, 1850.

"The New York Code of Procedure." *American Law Journal*, 8, 1848.

"The New York Code of Procedure." *The Law Reporter*, 11, 1848.

Newberry, Farrar. "The Nashville Convention and Southern Sentiment of 1850." *South Atlantic Quarterly*, 11, 1912.

New Jersey. *Votes and Proceedings of the Sixty-Fifth General Assembly of the State of New Jersey*. Trenton, N.J.: Phillips and Boswell, 1841.

Nicolay, John G. and John Hay. *Abraham Lincoln: A History*. 10 vols. New York: The Century Company, 1890.

990

Bibliography

Norwood, John N. *The Schism in the Methodist Church, 1844; a Study . . . Ecclesiastical Politics.* Alfred, N.Y.: Alfred University Press, 1923.

Nye, Russel B. *Fettered Freedom: Civil Liberties and the Slavery Controversy, 1830–1860.* East Lansing, Mich.: State College Press, 1949.

"The Obligation of a Contract—What Is It?" *Western Law Journal,* 4–5, 1847, 1848.

Official Records of the Union and Confederate Armies, The War of the Rebellion. 70 vols. Washington, D.C. Government Printing Office, 1880–1901.

O'Neall, John B. *Biographical Sketches of the Bench and Bar of South Carolina.* Charleston, S.C.: S. G. Courtenay, 1859.

Owen, Samuel. *A Treatise on the Law and Practice of Bankruptcy, with Reference to the General Bankrupt Act.* New York: J. S. Voorhies, 1842.

[Parker, Joel]. "Habeas Corpus and the Martial Law." *North American Review,* 93, 1861.

Parsons, Theophilus. *A Treatise on Maritime Law.* 2 vols. Boston: Little, Brown and Co., 1859.

Pease, Theodore Calvin and James G. Randall, eds. *The Diary of Orville Hickman Browning.* Springfield, Ill.: The Trustees of the Illinois State Historical Library, 1925–1933.

"Pennsylvania Judiciary." *American Law Journal,* 10, 1851.

Phillips, Ulrich B., ed. "The Correspondence of Robert Toombs, Alexander H. Stephens and Howell Cobb." *Annual Report of the American Historical Association for the Year 1911,* 2, 1913.

————. *A History of Transportation in the Eastern Cotton Belt to 1860.* New York: Columbia University Press, 1908.

Pierce, Bessie L. *A History of Chicago.* New York and London: A. A. Knopf, 1937.

Pierce, Edward L. *Memoir and Letters of Charles Sumner.* 4 vols. Boston: Roberts Brothers, 1877–1893.

Pleasants, Hugh R. "Sketches of the Virginia Convention of 1829–30." *Southern Literary Messenger,* 17, 1851.

Plunkett, Anna C. *Corridors by Candlelight.* San Antonio, Texas.: Naylor Company, 1949.

"Political Portraits with Pen and Pencil: Ellis Lewis." *United States Magazine and Democratic Review,* 20, 1847.

"Political Portraits with Pen and Pencil: Robert Rantoul, Jr., of Massachusetts." *United States Magazine and Democratic Review,* 27, 1850.

Post, Charles G., Jr. *The Supreme Court and Political Questions.* Baltimore: Ph.D. dissertation, The Johns Hopkins Press, 1936.

Pound, Roscoe. "The Place of Judge Story in the Making of American Law." *American Law Review,* 44, 1914.

————. "Organization of Courts." *Journal of American Judicature Society,* 11, 1927.

"Power of Congress Over Shores and Rivers." *Western Law Journal,* 8, 1851.

"The Power of the Legislature to Create and Abolish Courts of Justice. *The Law Reporter,* 21, 1858.

991

"Practice in Bankruptcy." *Pennsylvania Law Journal*, 1, 1842.

Prager, Frank D. "The Changing Views of Justice Story on the Construction of Patents." *American Journal of Legal History*, 4, 1960.

"Preliminary Report of the Criminal Law Commissioners of Massachusetts." *American Jurist*, 21, 1839.

Prime, Samuel I. *Life of Samuel F. B. Morse*. New York: D. Appleton and Co., 1875.

Primm, James N. *Economic Policy in the Development of a Western State—Missouri, 1820–1860*. Cambridge, Mass.: Harvard University Press, 1954.

"Prospects of the Legal Profession in America." *United States Magazine and Democratic Review*, 18, 1846.

Quaife, Milo, ed. *The Diary of James K. Polk*. 4 vols. Chicago: Published for the Chicago Historical Society, 1910.

Quitman, John A. *Speech . . . on the Subject of the Neutrality Laws: Delivered in Committee of the Whole House on the State of the Union, April 29, 1856*. Washington, D.C.: Printed at the Union Office, 1856.

Radcliffe, George L. P. *Governor Thomas H. Hicks of Maryland and the Civil War*. Baltimore: The Johns Hopkins Press, 1901.

Rader, Perry S. "The Romance of American Courts, Gaines v. New Orleans." *Louisiana Historical Quarterly*, 27, 1944.

Randall, Emilius O. and Daniel J. Ryan. *History of Ohio . . . of an American State*. 5 vols. New York: The Century History Co., 1912.

Randall, James G. *Constitutional Problems Under Lincoln*. Urbana, Ill.: University of Illinois Press, 1951.

Rantoul, Robert, Jr. "Memoirs, Writings and Speeches," in Mark D. Howe, ed., *Readings in Legal History*. Cambridge, Mass.: Harvard University Press, 1949.

Rayback, Joseph G., ed. "Martin Van Buren's Desire for Revenge in the Campaign of 1848." *Mississippi Valley Historical Review*, 40, 1954.

———. "The Presidential Ambitions of John C. Calhoun, 1844–1848." *Journal of Southern History*, 14, 1948.

[Raymond, Daniel] "Constitutional Law." *United States Magazine and Democratic Review*, 23, 1848. Republished, *Western Law Journal*, 6, 1848.

———. "Law Reform in Regard to Real Estate." *Western Law Journal*, 3, 1846.

———. "Remarks on the Case of Jones v. Van Zandt," *Western Law Journal*, 2, 1845.

Raymond, Henry. "The Late Bankrupt Law." *Pennsylvania Law Journal*, 3, 1844.

Redfield, Isaac F. *Judge Redfield's Letter to Senator Foot Upon the Status of the States Attempting Secession*, New York: Hurd and Houghton, 1865.

Redlich, Fritz. *The Molding of American Banking, Men and Ideas*. 2 vols. New York: Hafner Publishing Co., 1947.

"Reform in Pleading . . . Massachusetts." *The Law Reporter*, 13, 1851.

"Report of the Judicial Department." *Western Law Journal*, 8, 1851.

Bibliography

Reppy, Alison, ed. *David Dudley Field, Centenary Essays . . . of Legal Reform*. New York: University of New York School of Law, 1949.

"Representative Men: Andrew Jackson and Henry Clay." *Southern Literary Messenger*, 19, 1853.

"The Resignation of the Judges." *The Law Reporter*, 7, 1844.

"The Resources of the South." *Southern Literary Messenger*, 1862.

Ribble, Frederick D. G. *State and National Power over Commerce*. New York: Columbia University Press, 1937.

Richardson, J. D. *A Compilation of the Messages and Papers of the Presidents*. 20 vols. New York: Bureau of National Literature [1917?].

"The Right of Sovereignty in the Shore of the Sea." *American Law Magazine*, 1, 1843.

"River and Harbor Improvements." *DeBow's Commercial Review*, 4, 1841.

Robbins, Roy M. *Our Landed Heritage: The Public Domain, 1776–1936*. Princeton, N.J.: Princeton University Press, 1942.

"Robert J. Walker." *United States Magazine and Democratic Review*, 16, 1845.

Robinson, William M., Jr. *The Confederate Privateers*. New Haven, Conn.: Yale University Press; London: H. Milford, Oxford University Press, 1928.

Robinton, Madeline R. *An Introduction to the Papers of the New York Prize Court, 1861–1865*. New York: Columbia University Press, 1945.

"Roger Brooke Taney." *Southern Literary Messenger*, 4, 1838.

Roseboom, Eugene H. *The Civil War Era, 1850–1873* in *The History of Ohio*, 6 vols., Carl Wittke, ed. Columbus, Ohio: Ohio State Archaeological and Historical Society, 1944.

Ross, Ishbel. *Rebel Rose: Life of Rose O'Neal Greenhow, Confederate Spy*. New York: Harpers, 1954.

Ruffin, Thomas D. *The Papers of Thomas Ruffin*. 4 vols. J. G. D. Hamilton, ed. Raleigh, N.C.: Edwards and Broughton Printing Co., 1918–1920.

Ruffner, Ernest H. *Practice of Improvement of the Non-Tidal Rivers of the United States*. New York: J. Wiley and Sons, 1885.

Russell, Robert R. "What Was the Compromise of 1850?" *Journal of Southern History*, 22, 1956.

Ryan, Daniel J. *History of Ohio . . . of an American State*. 5 vols. New York: The Century History Co., 1912.

Sanborn, John B. "The Supreme Court of Wisconsin in the Eighties." *Wisconsin Magazine of History*, 15, 1931.

Scharf, J. Thomas. *History of Maryland . . . to the Present Day . . .* Baltimore: J. B. Piet, 1879.

Schlesinger, Arthur M., Jr. *The Age of Jackson*. Boston: Little, Brown and Co., 1945.

Schmidhauser, John R. "Jeremy Bentham, the Contract Clause and Justice John Archibald Campbell." *Vanderbilt Law Review*, 11, 1958.

Schoonover, Lynn I. *A History of the Civil War Draft in Wisconsin*. Unpublished thesis, University of Wisconsin, 1915.

Schuckers, J. W. *The Life and Public Services of Salmon Portland Chase*. New York: D. Appleton and Co., 1874.

Schurz, Carl. *Reminscences of Carl Schurz.* 3 vols. New York: The McClure Co., 1907.

Scroggs, William O. *Filibusters and Financiers: The Story of William Walker and His Associates.* New York: The Macmillan Co., 1916.

Sedgwick, Theodore. "Law Reform." *Western Law Journal,* 3, 1846.

Sellers, Charles. *James K. Polk, Jacksonian, 1795–1843.* Princeton, N.J.: Princeton University Press, 1957.

Sellers, James L. "Republicanism and State Rights in Wisconsin." *Mississippi Valley Historical Review,* 17, 1930.

Semmes, John E. *John H. B. Latrobe and His Times.* Baltimore: The Norman Remington Co., 1917.

Seward, William H. *Works of William H. Seward.* 5 vols. George E. Baker, ed. New York: Redfield, 1853.

Shanks, Henry T., ed. *The Papers of Willie Person Mangum.* Raleigh, N.C.: State Department of Archives and History, 1950–1956.

Shapiro, Samuel. *Richard Henry Dana, Jr., 1815–1882.* East Lansing, Mich.: State University Press, 1961.

Shipman, Benjamin J. *Handbook of Common-Law Pleading.* Henry Winthrop Ballantine, ed. St. Paul, Minn.: West Publishing Co., 1923.

Silver, David M. *Lincoln's Supreme Court.* Urbana, Ill.: University of Illinois Press, 1956. [Series: Illinois University, Ill. Studies in the Social Sciences, vol. 38].

Sioussat, St. George L. "Some Phases of Tennessee Politics in the Jackson Period." *American Historical Review,* 14, 1908.

————. "Tennessee, The Compromise of 1850, and the Nashville Convention." *Mississippi Valley Historical Review,* 2, 1915.

"Slavery in Louisiana." *The Law Reporter,* 16, 1853.

"A Slave-Trader's Letter Book." *North American Review,* 143, 1886.

"The Slavery Question." *American Law Journal,* 9, 1850.

"Some of the Provisions of the Original and Recent Constitutions of the Several States Relating to the Judiciary." *The Law Reporter,* 14, 1852.

Smith, Charles W. Jr. *Roger B. Taney: Jacksonian Jurist.* Chapel Hill, N.C.: The University of North Carolina Press, 1936.

Smith, William E. *The Francis Preston Blair Family in Politics.* 2 vols. New York: The Macmillan Co., 1933.

Spears, John R. *The American Slave-Trade . . . and Suppression.* New York: C. Scribner's Sons, 1907.

Splitter, Henry W. "Quicksilver at New Almaden." *Pacific Historical Review,* 26, 1957.

Sprague, A. P., ed. *Speeches, Arguments, and Miscellaneous Papers of David Dudley Field.* New York: D. Appleton and Co., 1884–1890.

Sprague, George C. "The Extension of Admiralty Jurisdiction and the Growth of the Substantive Maritime Law in the United States Since 1835." *Law: A Century of Progress,* 3, 1937.

"State Credit." *United States Magazine and Democratic Review,* 10, 1842.

"State Debts." *North American Review,* 51, 1840.

994

Bibliography

"The State Debts." *United States Magazine and Democratic Review*, 14, 1844.

Steiner, Bernard C. "James Alfred Pearce." *Maryland Historical Magazine*, 19, 1924.

———. *Life of Reverdy Johnson*. Baltimore: The Norman Remington Co., 1914.

———. *Life of Roger Brooke Taney*. Baltimore: Williams & Wilkins Co., 1922.

Stephenson, George M. *The Political History of the Public Lands from 1840 to 1862*. Boston: R. G. Badger, 1917.

Stevenson, Charles E. "Influence of Bentham and Humphreys on the New York Property Legislation of 1828." *American Journal of Legal History*, 1, 1957.

Still, Bayrd. *Milwaukee: The History of a City*. Madison, Wis.: State Historical Society of Wisconsin, 1948.

Story, Joseph. "Codification of the Common Law," in *Miscellaneous Writings*. W. W. Story, ed. 8 vols. Boston: Little, Brown, 1852.

———. *Commentaries on the Constitution of the United States*. 3 vols. Boston: Hilliard, Gray and Co.; Cambridge, Mass.: Brown, Shattuck and Co., 1833.

———. *Commentaries on the Law of Bills of Exchange*. Boston: Little and J. Brown Co., 1843.

———. "Progress of Jurisprudence," in *Miscellaneous Writings*. W. W. Story, ed. 8 vols. Boston: Little, Brown, 1852.

Story, William W., ed. *Life and Letters of Joseph Story*. Boston: C. C. Little and J. Brown Co., 1851.

"The Study and Practice of Law." *United States Magazine and Democratic Review*, 14, 1844.

"The Supreme Court of New York and Mr. Webster, on the M'Leod Question." *United States Magazine and Democratic Review*, 10, 1842.

"Supreme Court of the United States." *The Law Reporter*, 6, 1844.

"The Supreme Court of the United States." *United States Magazine and Democraic Review*, 7, 1840.

"The Supreme Court of the United States, Its Judges and Jurisdiction." *United States Magazine and Democratic Review*, 1, 1838.

Swisher, Carl B. *Roger B. Taney*. New York: The Macmillan Co., 1935.

———. "Roger B. Taney's Bank War Manuscript." *Maryland Historical Magazine*, 53, 1958.

———. *Stephen J. Field: Craftsman of the Law*. Washington, D.C.: The Brookings Institution, 1930.

"The Taney Fund." *Proceedings of the Meeting of the Bar of the Supreme Court of the United States*, 1871.

"The Telegraph." *De Bow's Review*, 16, 1854.

"The Telegraph Case." *Western Law Journal*, 7, 1849.

Telkampf, J. Louis. "On Codification or the Systematizing of the Law." *American Jurist*, 26, 1841.

"Territorial Government." *United States Magazine and Democratic Review*, 23, 1848.

Thayer, James B. *Cases on Constitutional Law*. Cambridge, Mass.: C. W. Sever Co., 1895.

"The Thirty-First Congress." *United States Magazine and Democratic Review*, 28, 1851.

Thompson, Robert L. *Wiring a Continent: The History of the Telegraph Industry in the United States*. Princeton, N.J.: Princeton University Press. 1947.

Tiffany, Orrin. "The Relation of the United States to the Canadian Rebellion of 1837–1838." *Publications of the Buffalo Historical Society*, 8, 1905.

Tyler, Lyon G. *Letters and Times of the Tylers*. 3 vols. Richmond Va.: Whittel and Shepperson, 1884–1896.

Tyler, Samuel. *Memoir of Roger Brooke Taney, LL.D*. Baltimore: J. Murphy and Co., 1872.

United States House of Representatives.

Executive Documents:

No. 185, 26th Congress, 1st Session
No. 223, 29th Congress, 1st Session
No. 99, 29th Congress, 2nd Session
No. 61, 30th Congress, 2nd Session
No. 17, 31st Congress, 1st Session
No. 105, 34th Congress, 1st Session
No. 24, 35th Congress, 1st Session
No. 25, 35th Congress, 2nd Session
No. 90, 35th Congress, 2nd Session
No. 84, 36th Congress, 1st Session
No. 7, 36th Congress, 2nd Session
No. 94, 37th Congress, 2nd Session
No. 32, 37th Congress, 3rd Session
No. 44, 37th Congress, 3rd Session
No. 73, 37th Congress, 3rd Session
No. 783, 69th Congress, 2nd Session

Miscellaneous Documents:

No. 31, 35th Congress, 1st Session
No. 135, 35th Congress, 1st Session

Reports:

No. 80, 27th Congress, 3rd Session
No. 546, 28th Congress, 1st Session
No. 581, 28th Congress, 1st Session
No. 113, 29th Congress, 1st Session
No. 530, 29th Congress, 1st Session
No. 72, 31st Congress, 1st Session
No. 14, 37th Congress, 2nd Session
No. 44, 37th Congress, 2nd Session

Bibliography

No. 45, 37th Congress, 3rd Session
No. 646, 58th Congress, 2nd Session
United States Senate
Executive Documents:
No. 155, 23rd Congress, 1st Session
No. 80, 25th Congress, 2nd Session
No. 432, 25th Congress, 2nd Session
No. 273, 26th Congress, 1st Session
No. 99, 27th Congress, 2nd Session
No. 19, 27th Congress, 3rd Session
No. 91, 29th Congress, 1st Session
No. 18, 31st Congress, 1st Session
No. 11, 35th Congress, 1st Session
No. 63, 35th Congress, 1st Session
No. 40, 37th Congress, 2nd Session
Miscellaneous Documents:
No. 60, 30th Congress, 2nd Session
No. 4, 31st Congress, 1st Session
No. 231, 35th Congress, 1st Session
Reports:
No. 338, 24th Congress, 1st Session
No. 50, 25th Congress, 3rd Session
No. 127, 26th Congress, 2nd Session
No. 121, 27th Congress, 3rd Session
No. 48, 31st Congress, 1st Session
No. 15, 33rd Congress, 1st Session

Vail, Alfred. *Description of the American Electro-Magnetic Telegraph Now in Operation Between the Cities of Washington and Baltimore.* Washington, D.C.: J. and G. S. Gideon Co., 1847.

Vallandigham, J. L. *A Life of Clement L. Vallandigham.* Baltimore: Turnbull Brothers, 1872.

Van Buren, Martin. "The Autobiography of Martin Van Buren." John C. Fitzpatrick, ed. *Annual Report of the American Historical Association for the Year 1918*, 2, 1920.

————. *Inquiry into the Origin and Course of Political Parties in the United States.* Edited by his son. New York: Hurd and Houghton, 1867.

Van Tyne, Claude H., ed. *The Letters of Daniel Webster.* New York: McClure, Phillips and Co., 1902.

"Vermont 'Democratic' State Convention, Speech of Mr. Van Buren." *United States Magazine and Democratic Review*, 29, 1851.

[Walker, Timothy.] "Death of Judge Story." *Western Law Journal*, 3, 1845.

————. "Law Reform in Missouri." *Western Law Journal*, 6, 1849.

————. "The Project of Extending Admiralty Jurisdiction over the Lakes and Rivers of the United States." *Western Law Journal*, 2, 1845.

Wallace, John W. *The Want of Uniformity in the Commercial Law Between the Different States of Our Union.* Philadelphia: L. R. Bailey, Printer, 1851.

997

Warden, Robert B. *An Account of the Life and Public Services of Salmon Portland Chase*. Cincinnati: Wilstoch, Baldwin and Co., 1874.

Warren, Charles. *Bankruptcy in United States History*. Cambridge, Mass.: Harvard University Press, 1935.

———. *A History of the American Bar*. Boston: Little, Brown and Co., 1911.

———. *History of the Harvard Law School*. 3 vols. New York: Lewis Publishing Co., 1908.

———. "New Light on the History of the Federal Judiciary Act of 1789." *Harvard Law Review*, 37, 1927.

———. *The Supreme Court in United States History*. 2 vols. Boston: Little, Brown and Co., 1926.

Watt, Alastair. "The Case of Alexander McLeod." *Canadian Historical Review*, 12, 1931.

Webster, Daniel. *Writings and Speeches of Daniel Webster*. J. W. McIntyre, ed. Boston: Little, Brown and Co., 1903.

Weisenberger, Francis P. *The Life of John McLean*. Columbus, Ohio: The Ohio State University Press, 1937.

———. *The Passing of the Frontier, 1825–1850*. 6 vols. Carl Wittke, ed. Columbus, Ohio: Ohio State Archaeological and Historical Society, 1941–1944.

Wells, R. T. "Law of the State of Missouri, Regulating Practice in the Courts of Justice." *Western Law Journal*, 6, 1849.

Wentworth, John. *Early Chicago*. Chicago: Fergus Printing Co., 1881.

"The Wheeling Bridge Case." *Western Law Journal*, 9, 1852.

White, Horace. *The Life of Lyman Trumbull*. Boston and New York: Houghton Mifflin Co., 1913.

White, J. F. W. "The Judiciary of Allegheny County." *Pennsylvania Magazine of History and Biography*, 7, 1883.

White, Leonard D. *The Jacksonians: A Study in . . . History, 1829–1861*. New York: The Macmillan Co., 1954.

Whitson, Thomas. "The Hero of the Christiana Riot." *Lancaster County Historical Society—Historical Papers and Addresses*, 1, 1896.

Wiley, Earl W. "Behind Lincoln's Visit to Ohio in 1859." *Ohio State Archaeological and Historical Quarterly*, 60, 1951.

———. " 'Governor' John Greiner and Chase's Bid for the Presidency in 1860." *Ohio State Archaeological and Historical Quarterly*, 58, 1942.

———. "Thomas Corwin and the Republican Reaction." *Ohio State Archaeological and Historical Quarterly*, 37, 1948.

"The Wilkesbarre Slave Case." *The Law Reporter*, 16, 1853.

Wilson, Rufus R. *Washington: The Capital City*. Philadelphia and London: J. B. Lippincott Co., 1901.

Winthrop, William W. *Military Law*. 2 vols. Washington, D.C.: W. H. Morrison, 1886.

Wise, Henry A. *Seven Decades of the Union*. Philadelphia: J. B. Lippincott and Co., 1872.

Bibliography

Wyeth, S. D. *The Federal City . . . of Washington.* Washington, D.C.: Gibson Brothers, 1865.

Zevely, Douglas. "Old Residences and Family History in the City Hall Neighborhood." *Records of the Columbian Historical Society,* 6, 1903.

MANUSCRIPT SOURCES

Allen, William. Papers, Library of Congress, Washington, D.C. (This repository is hereafter listed as DLC.)

Ashton, J. Hubley. Papers, Historical Society of Pennsylvania, Philadelphia.

Bayard, Richard H. Maryland Historical Society, Baltimore.

Bell, James M. Papers, Duke University, Durham, North Carolina.

Biddle, Nicholas. Papers, DLC.

Bigelow, John. Diary, New York Public Library.

Black, Jeremiah S. Papers, DLC.

Blair-Lee. Papers, Princeton University, Princeton, New Jersey.

Brown-Ewell. Papers, Tennessee State Library and Archives, Nashville, Tennessee.

Buchanan, James. Papers. The corpus of Buchanan's Papers is in the Historical Society of Pennsylvania, Philadelphia. A small collection is in DLC.

Cabell, William H. Papers, Virginia State Library, Richmond.

Cadwalader, John. Papers, Historical Society of Pennsylvania.

Campbell, J. Mason. Papers, Maryland Historical Society, Baltimore.

Campbell, John A. Diary, Groner Papers, University of Virginia, Charlottesville.

Carson, Hampton L. Collection, Free Library of Philadelphia.

Chase, Salmon P. Papers, DLC and Historical Society of Pennsylvania, Philadelphia.

Clay, Henry. Papers, DLC.

Clifford, Nathan B. Papers, Maine Historical Society, Portland.

Conarroe Collection. Historical Society of Pennsylvania, Philadelphia.

Crittenden, John J. Papers, DLC.

Curtis, Benjamin R. Papers, DLC.

Dana, Richard H. Papers, Massachusetts Historical Society, Boston.

Davis, David. Papers, Chicago Historical Society.

Dreer Collection. Historical Society of Pennsylvania, Philadelphia.

Etting Collection. Historical Society of Pennsylvania, Philadelphia.

Everett, Edward, Papers, Massachusetts Historical Society.

Gist-Blair Papers, DLC.

Glenn, William W. Papers, Maryland Historical Society, Baltimore.

Gratz Collection, Historical Society of Pennsylvania, Philadelphia.

Greenleaf, Simon. Papers, Harvard University Law School, Cambridge, Massachusetts.

Groner, Duncan L. Papers, University of Virginia Library, Charlottesville.

Hale, John P. Papers, DLC, New Hampshire Historical Society, Concord.

Holt, Joseph. Papers, DLC.

Howard, Benjamin C. Papers, Maryland Historical Society, Baltimore.

Jackson, Andrew. Papers, DLC.

Kennedy, John P. Papers, Peabody Institute Library, Baltimore.

Kent, James. Papers, DLC.

Lamon, Ward H. Papers, Henry E. Huntington Library, San Marino, California.

Lewis, Ellis. Papers, Historical Society of Pennsylvania, Philadelphia.

Lieber, Francis. Papers, Henry E. Huntington Library, San Marino, California.

Lincoln, Abraham. Papers, DLC.

Livingston, Edward. Papers, DLC.

Manuscript Wills, Baltimore.

Matthews, Stanley. Papers, Rutherford B. Hayes Memorial Library, Fremont, Ohio.

McLean, John. Papers, DLC, Ohio Historical Society, Columbus.

Mitchell, William D. Papers, Minnesota Historical Society.

Morse, Samuel F. B. Papers, DLC.

National Archives, Washington, D.C.
    RG 46, Records of the United States Senate.
    RG 59, Records of the Department of State.
    RG 60, Records of the Department of Justice.
    RG 223, Records of the United States House of Representatives.
    RG 267, Records of the Supreme Court of the United States.

O'Reilly, Henry. Papers, New York Historical Society.

Perine, David M. Papers, Maryland Historical Society, Baltimore.

Peters, Richard. Papers, Historical Society of Pennsylvania, Philadelphia.

Pierce, Franklin. Papers, DLC and New Hampshire Historical Society, Concord.

Polk, James K. Papers, DLC.

Reynolds, Thomas C. Papers, Missouri Historical Society, St. Louis.

Rutherford, John. Papers, Duke University Library, Durham, North Carolina.

Stanton, Edwin M. Papers, DLC.

Story, Joseph. Papers, DLC, Massachusetts Historical Society, Boston, and the University of Texas Library, Austin.

Sumner, Charles. Papers, Houghton Library, Harvard University, Cambridge, Massachusetts.

Treat, Samuel. Papers, Missouri Historical Society, St. Louis.

Trumbull, Lyman. Papers, DLC.

Van Buren, Martin. Papers, DLC and Georgia Historical Society, Savannah, Georgia.

Washburne, Elihu B. Papers, DLC.

Wayne, James M. Papers, Georgia Department of Archives and History, Atlanta.

Webster, Daniel. Papers, Dartmouth University Library, Hanover, New Hampshire, and New Hampshire Historical Society, Concord.

Bibliography

Welles, Gideon. Papers, DLC.
Winthrop, Robert C. Papers, Massachusetts Historical Society, Boston.

NEWSPAPER SOURCES

Baltimore *American*
Baltimore *Clipper*
Baltimore *Daily Exchange*
Baltimore *Patriot*
Baltimore *Republican*
Baltimore *South*
Baltimore *Sun*
Boston *Columbian Sentinel*
Boston *Daily Advertiser*
Boston *Daily Atlas*
Boston *Post*
Boston *Statesman*
Charleston *Courier*
Charleston *Mercury*
Chicago *Daily Democratic Press*
Cincinnati *Daily Enquirer*
Cincinnati *Gazette*
Cincinnati *Philanthropist*
Congressional Globe
Frederick *Examiner* (Maryland)
Harrisburg *Pennsylvania Reporter*
The Liberator (Boston)
Louisville *Courier*
Madison *Angus and Democrat* (Wisconsin)
Maryland *News Sheet* (Baltimore)
Maryland *Times* (Baltimore)
Milwaukee *Daily Wisconsin*
Mobile *Daily Mercury*
Nashville *Daily Union & American*
Nashville *Republican Banner*
Nashville *Union*
New Orleans *Delta*
New York *Commercial Advertiser*
New York *Courier and Enquirer*
New York *Daily Tribune*
New York *Evening Post*
New York *Express*
New York *Herald*
New York *Journal of Commerce*
New York *Times*
New York *World*
Newark *Daily Advertiser*
Niles' *National Register*
Northampton *Courier* (Massachusetts)
Philadelphia *Inquirer*
Philadelphia *Ledger and Transcript*
Philadelphia *Public Ledger*
Portland Maine *Eastern Angus*
Portsmouth *Journal*
Richmond *Enquirer*
Richmond *Examiner*
St. Louis *Commercial Bulletin*
San Francisco *Evening Bulletin*
Salem *Essex Register* (Massachusetts)
Salem *Register*
Savannah *Republican*
Springfield, *Sangamo Journal* (Illinois)
Washington *Evening Star*
Washington *Globe*
Washington *National Intelligencer*
Washington *Union*
Wilmington *Delaware State Journal*
Worcester *Massachusetts Spy*
Worcester *Republican*

Table of Cases

Index

A NOTE ON THE BOOK

This book is set in Linotype Times Roman. Composition
by Maryland Linotype Composition Company, Baltimore,
Maryland. Printed and bound by The Kingsport Press,
Kingsport, Tennessee. Paper is Carfax Eggshell, manu-
factured by Oxford Paper Company, Rumford, Maine.
Woodcut of seal of the Supreme Court by Fritz Kredel.

Typography and binding design by
WARREN CHAPPELL